Principles of Microeconomics

Principles of Microeconomics

Dirk Mateer
University of Kentucky

Lee Coppock
University of Virginia

W. W. Norton & Company has been independent since its founding in 1923, when William Warder Norton and Mary D. Herter Norton first published lectures delivered at the People's Institute, the adult education division of New York City's Cooper Union. The firm soon expanded its program beyond the Institute, publishing books by celebrated academics from America and abroad. By midcentury, the two major pillars of Norton's publishing program—trade books and college texts—were firmly established. In the 1950s, the Norton family transferred control of the company to its employees, and today—with a staff of four hundred and a comparable number of trade, college, and professional titles published each year—W. W. Norton & Company stands as the largest and oldest publishing house owned wholly by its employees.

Printed in the United States of America.

Editor: Jack Repcheck

Developmental Editor: Rebecca Kohn

Manuscript Editor: Alice Vigliani

Project Editor: Jack Borrebach

Media Editor: Cassie del Pilar

Associate Media Editors: Nicole Sawa, Carson Russell

Assistant Editor: Hannah Bachman

Marketing Manager, Economics: John Kresse

Production Manager: Eric Pier-Hocking

Photo Editor: Nelson Colón

Photo Researcher: Dena Digilio Betz

Permissions Manager: Megan Jackson

Text Design: Lisa Buckley

Art Director: Rubina Yeh

Cover Design and "Snapshot" Infographics: Kiss Me I'm Polish

Composition: Jouve

Manufacturing: Courier Kendallville

A catalogue record for the full edition is available from the Library of Congress.
This edition: ISBN 978-0-393-93576-9 (pbk.)

W. W. Norton & Company, Inc., 500 Fifth Avenue, New York, NY 10110-0017
wwnorton.com

W. W. Norton & Company Ltd., Castle House, 75/76 Wells Street, London W1T 3QT
1 2 3 4 5 6 7 8 9 0

To my father, who gave up a successful career in business and found his passion teaching finance. Thanks for encouraging me to become a teacher as well.

D.M.

To Krista: Many women do noble things, but you surpass them all.—Proverbs 31:29

L.C.

BRIEF CONTENTS

PART I Introduction

1 The Five Foundations of Economics 4

2 Model Building and Gains from Trade 24

PART II The Role of Markets

3 The Market at Work: Supply and Demand 68

4 Elasticity 108

5 Price Controls 146

6 The Efficiency of Markets and the Costs of Taxation 176

7 Market Inefficiencies: Externalities and Public Goods 210

PART III The Theory of the Firm

8 Business Costs and Production 240

9 Firms in a Competitive Market 270

10 Understanding Monopoly 302

11 Price Discrimination 332

12 Monopolistic Competition and Advertising 354

13 Oligopoly and Strategic Behavior 382

PART IV Labor Markets and Earnings

14 The Demand and Supply of Resources 420

15 Income, Inequality, and Poverty 456

PART V Special Topics in Microeconomics

16 Consumer Choice 492

17 Behavioral Economics and Risk Taking 526

18 Health Insurance and Health Care 548

CONTENTS

Preface xxiii
Acknowledgments xxxvii
About the Authors xli

PART I Introduction

1 The Five Foundations of Economics 4

Big Questions 6

What Is Economics? 6
Microeconomics and Macroeconomics 7

What Are the Five Foundations of Economics? 7
Incentives 7
Economics in the Real World: How Incentives Create Unintended Consequences 10
Economics in the Media: Incentives: *Ferris Bueller's Day Off* 12
Trade-offs 12
Opportunity Cost 13
Practice What You Know: The Opportunity Cost of Attending College 14
Economics in the Real World: Breaking the Curse of the Bambino: How Opportunity Cost Causes a Drop in Hospital Visits While the Red Sox Play 15
Marginal Thinking 15
Economics in the Real World: Why Buying and Selling Your Textbooks Benefits You at the Margin 16
Trade 17

Conclusion 18
SNAPSHOT: The Foundations of Economics 19
ECONOMICS FOR LIFE: Midcareer Earnings by Selected Majors 20
Answering the Big Questions 21

Concepts You Should Know 22
Questions for Review 22
Study Problems 22
Solved Problems 23

2 Model Building and Gains from Trade 24

Big Questions 26

How Do Economists Study the Economy? 26

The Scientific Method in Economics 26

Positive and Normative Analysis 27

Economic Models 28

Practice What You Know: Positive versus Normative Statements 30

What Is a Production Possibilities Frontier? 31

The Production Possibilities Frontier and Opportunity Cost 32

The Production Possibilities Frontier and Economic Growth 34

Practice What You Know: The Production Possibilities Frontier: Bicycles and Cars 36

What Are the Benefits of Specialization and Trade? 37

Gains from Trade 37

Comparative Advantage 40

Finding the Right Price to Facilitate Trade 41

Economics in the Real World: Why Shaquille O'Neal Has Someone Else Help Him Move 42

SNAPSHOT: Shaq and Comparative Demand 43

Practice What You Know: Opportunity Cost 44

Economics in the Media: Opportunity Cost: *Saving Private Ryan* 45

What Is the Trade-off between Having More Now and Having More Later? 45

Consumer Goods, Capital Goods, and Investment 46

Economics in the Media: The Trade-off between the Present and the Future: *A Knight's Tale* 48

Practice What You Know: Trade-offs 49

Conclusion 49

ECONOMICS FOR LIFE: Failing to Account for Exogenous Factors When Making Predictions 50

Answering the Big Questions 51

Concepts You Should Know 52

Questions for Review 52

Study Problems 52

Solved Problems 54

Appendix 2A: Graphs in Economics 55

Graphs That Consist of One Variable 55

Time-Series Graphs 57

Graphs That Consist of Two Variables 57

The Slope of a Curve 59

Formulas for the Area of a Rectangle and a Triangle 62

Cautions in Interpreting Numerical Graphs 63

Concepts You Should Know 65

Study Problems 65

Solved Problems 65

PART II The Role of Markets

3 The Market at Work: Supply and Demand 68

Big Questions 70

What Are the Fundamentals of Markets? 70
Competitive Markets 71
Imperfect Markets 72

What Determines Demand? 72
SNAPSHOT: The Invisible Hand 73
Practice What You Know: Markets and the Nature of Competition 74
The Demand Curve 75
Market Demand 75
Shifts in the Demand Curve 76
Practice What You Know: Shift or Slide? 81
Economics in the Media: Shifting the Demand Curve: *The Hudsucker Proxy* 83

What Determines Supply? 84
The Supply Curve 84
Market Supply 86
Shifts in the Supply Curve 87
Economics in the Real World: Why Do the Prices of New Electronics Always Drop? 91
Practice What You Know: The Supply and Demand of Ice Cream 92

How Do Supply and Demand Shifts Affect a Market? 93
Supply, Demand, and Equilibrium 93
ECONOMICS FOR LIFE: Bringing Supply and Demand Together: Advice for Buying Your First Place 97

Conclusion 98
Answering the Big Questions 98

Concepts You Should Know 100
Questions For Review 100
Study Problems 100
Solved Problems 102

Appendix 3A: Changes in Both Demand and Supply 103
Practice What You Know: When Supply and Demand Both Change: Hybrid Cars 106
Questions for Review 107
Study Problem 107

4 Elasticity 108

Big Questions 110

What Is the Price Elasticity of Demand, and What Are Its Determinants? 110
Determinants of the Price Elasticity of Demand 110
Computing the Price Elasticity of Demand 113
Economics in the Media: Price Elasticity of Demand: *Jingle All the Way* 115
Graphing the Price Elasticity of Demand 117
Price Elasticity of Demand and Total Revenue 123
Economics in the Media: Elasticity and Total Revenue: D'oh! The Simpsons and Total Revenue 126

How Do Changes in Income and the Prices of Other Goods Affect Elasticity? 127
Income Elasticity 127
Practice What You Know: The Price Elasticity of Demand 128

Cross-Price Elasticity 130

Economics in the Real World: The Wii Rollout and Changes in the Video Game Industry 132

SNAPSHOT: Elasticity and Demand 133

Practice What You Know: Income Elasticity 134

What Is the Price Elasticity of Supply? 134

Determinants of the Price Elasticity of Supply 135

Practice What You Know: The Price Elasticity of Supply 138

How Do the Price Elasticity of Demand and Supply Relate to Each Other? 138

Practice What You Know: Elasticity: Trick or Treat Edition 140

Conclusion 140

ECONOMICS FOR LIFE: Price Elasticity of Supply and Demand: Buying Your First Car 141

Answering the Big Questions 142

Concepts You Should Know 143

Questions for Review 143

Study Problems 143

Solved Problems 145

5 Price Controls 146

Big Questions 148

When Do Price Ceilings Matter? 148

Understanding Price Ceilings 148

The Effect of Price Ceilings 150

Price Ceilings in the Long Run 152

Economics in the Media: Price Ceilings: *Moscow on the Hudson* 153

Practice What You Know: Price Ceilings: Concert Tickets 154

What Effects Do Price Ceilings Have on Economic Activity? 154

Rent Control 154

Price Gouging 155

Practice What You Know: Price Ceilings: Student Rental Apartments 158

When Do Price Floors Matter? 158

Understanding Price Floors 159

The Effect of Price Floors 159

Price Floors in the Long Run 162

Practice What You Know: Price Floors: Fair-Trade Coffee 163

What Effects Do Price Floors Have on Economic Activity? 164

The Minimum Wage 164

Economics in the Real World: Wage Laws Squeeze South Africa's Poor 165

The Minimum Wage Is Often Nonbinding 166

Economics in the Real World: A Sweet Deal, If You Can Get It 167

Economics in the Media: The Minimum Wage: *30 Days* 168

SNAPSHOT: Minimum Wage: Always the Same? 169

Practice What You Know: Price Ceilings and Price Floors: Would a Price Control on Internet Access Be Effective? 170

Conclusion 171

Answering the Big Questions 172

ECONOMICS FOR LIFE: Price Gouging: Disaster Preparedness 173

Concepts You Should Know 174

Questions for Review 174

Study Problems 174

Solved Problems 175

6 The Efficiency of Markets and the Costs of Taxation 176

Big Questions 178

What Are Consumer Surplus and Producer Surplus? 178

Consumer Surplus 178

Using Demand Curves to Illustrate Consumer Surplus 179

Producer Surplus 181

Using Supply Curves to Illustrate Producer Surplus 181

Practice What You Know: Consumer and Producer Surplus: Trendy Fashion 183

When Is a Market Efficient? 184

The Efficiency-Equity Debate 185

Economics in the Media: Efficiency: *Old School* 186

Practice What You Know: Total Surplus: How Would Lower Income Affect Urban Outfitters? 187

Why Do Taxes Create Deadweight Loss? 188

Tax Incidence 188

Deadweight Loss 191

Economics in the Media: Taxing Inelastic Goods: "Taxman" by the Beatles 192

Economics in the Real World: The Short-Lived Luxury Tax 198

Balancing Deadweight Loss and Tax Revenues 199

SNAPSHOT: Bizarre Taxes 201

Practice What You Know: Deadweight Loss of Taxation: The Politics of Tax Rates 202

Conclusion 202

Answering the Big Questions 203

ECONOMICS FOR LIFE: Excise Taxes Are Almost Impossible to Avoid 204

Concepts You Should Know 205

Questions for Review 205

Study Problems 205

Solved Problems 209

7 Market Inefficiencies: Externalities and Public Goods 210

Big Questions 212

What Are Externalities, and How Do They Affect Markets? 212

The Third-Party Problem 212

Economics in the Real World: Congestion Charges 216

Practice What You Know: Externalities: A New Theater Is Proposed 219

What Are Private Goods and Public Goods? 219

Private Property 220

Private and Public Goods 222

SNAPSHOT: The Case Behind the Coase Theorem 223

Practice What You Know: Public Goods: Are Parks Public Goods? 226

What Are the Challenges of Providing Nonexcludable Goods? 227

Cost-Benefit Analysis 227

Economics in the Real World: Internet Piracy 228

Common Resources and the Tragedy of the Commons 228

Solutions to the Tragedy of the Commons 230

Economics in the Real World: Deforestation in Haiti 231

Practice What You Know: Common Resources: President Obama's Inauguration 232

Economics in the Media: Tragedy of the Commons: *South Park* and Water Parks 232

ECONOMICS FOR LIFE: Buying Used Is Good for Your Wallet and for the Environment 233

Conclusion 233

Answering the Big Questions 234

Concepts You Should Know 235

Questions for Review 235

Study Problems 235

Solved Problems 237

PART III The Theory of the Firm

8 Business Costs and Production 240

Big Questions 242

How Are Profits and Losses Calculated? 242

Calculating Profit and Loss 242

Explicit Costs and Implicit Costs 243

Accounting Profit versus Economic Profit 244

Practice What You Know: Accounting Profit versus Economic Profit: Calculating Summer Job Profits 246

How Much Should a Firm Produce? 247

The Production Function 247

Diminishing Marginal Product 249

What Costs Do Firms Consider in the Short Run and the Long Run? 250

Practice What You Know: Diminishing Returns: Snow Cone Production 251

Costs in the Short Run 252

Economics in the Media: Costs in the Short Run: *The Office* 257

Costs in the Long Run 257

SNAPSHOT: Bigger Is Not Always Better 261

Economics in the Media: Economies of Scale: *Modern Times* 262

Practice What You Know: Marginal Cost: The True Cost of Admission to Universal Studios 263

Conclusion 263

Answering the Big Questions 264

ECONOMICS FOR LIFE: How Much Does It Cost to Raise a Child? 265

Concepts You Should Know 266

Questions for Review 266

Study Problems 266

Solved Problems 269

9 Firms in a Competitive Market 270

Big Questions 272

How Do Competitive Markets Work? 272

Economics in the Real World: Aalsmeer Flower Auction 274

How Do Firms Maximize Profits? 274

Practice What You Know: Price Takers: Mall Food Courts 275

The Profit-Maximizing Rule 275

Economics in the Media: Competitive Markets: *The Simpsons* 277

Deciding How Much to Produce in a Competitive Market 278

The Firm in the Short Run 279

The Firm's Short-Run Supply Curve 282

The Firm's Long-Run Supply Curve 283

Economics in the Real World: Blockbuster and the Dynamic Nature of Change 284

Practice What You Know: The Profit-Maximizing Rule: Show Me the Money! 285

Sunk Costs 286

What Does the Supply Curve Look Like in Perfectly Competitive Markets? 286

SNAPSHOT: Sunk Costs: If You Build It, They Will Come 287

The Short-Run Market Supply Curve 288

The Long-Run Market Supply Curve 288

How the Market Adjusts in the Long Run: An Example 291

Economics in the Media: Entry and Exit: *I Love Lucy* 293

Practice What You Know: Long-Run Profits: How Much Can a Firm Expect to Make? 295

Conclusion 296

Answering the Big Questions 297

ECONOMICS FOR LIFE: Tips for Starting Your Own Business 298

Concepts You Should Know 299

Questions for Review 299

Study Problems 299

Solved Problems 301

10 Understanding Monopoly 302

Big Questions 304

How Are Monopolies Created? 304

Natural Barriers 304

Government-Created Barriers 305

Economics in the Real World: Merck's Zocor 306

Practice What You Know: Monopoly: Can You Spot the Monopolist? 307

Economics in the Media: Barriers to Entry: *Forrest Gump* 308

How Much Do Monopolies Charge, and How Much Do They Produce? 309

The Profit-Maximizing Rule for the Monopolist 310

Economics in the Real World: The Broadband Monopoly 314

Practice What You Know: Monopoly Profits: How Much Do Monopolists Make? 315

What Are the Problems with, and Solutions for, Monopoly? 315

The Problems with Monopoly 316

Practice What You Know: Problems with Monopoly: Coffee Consolidation 319

Economics in the Real World: New York City Taxis 320

Economics in the Media: The Problems of Monopoly: *One-Man Band* 321

Solutions to the Problems of Monopoly 321

SNAPSHOT: The Demise of a Monopoly 323

Conclusion 325

Answering the Big Questions 326

ECONOMICS FOR LIFE: Playing Monopoly Like an Economist 327

Concepts You Should Know 328

Questions for Review 328

Study Problems 328

Solved Problems 331

11 Price Discrimination 332

Big Questions 334

What Is Price Discrimination? 334

Conditions for Price Discrimination 334

One Price versus Price Discrimination 335

The Welfare Effects of Price Discrimination 338

Economics in the Media: Perfect Price Discrimination: *Legally Blonde* 340

Economics in the Real World: Outlet Malls—If You Build It, They Will Come 341

Practice What You Know: Price Discrimination: Taking Economics to New Heights 342

How Is Price Discrimination Practiced? 344

Price Discrimination at the Movies 344

Price Discrimination on Campus 345

SNAPSHOT: Now Playing: Economics! 347

Practice What You Know: Price Discrimination in Practice: Everyday Examples 348

Economics in the Media: Price Discrimination: *Extreme Couponing* 349

Economics in the Real World: Groupon 349

Conclusion 350

Answering the Big Questions 350

ECONOMICS FOR LIFE: Outsmarting Grocery Store Tactics 351

Concepts You Should Know 352

Questions for Review 352

Study Problems 352

Solved Problems 353

---

12 Monopolistic Competition and Advertising 354

Big Questions 356

What Is Monopolistic Competition? 356

Product Differentiation 357

Practice What You Know: Product Differentiation: Would You Recognize a Monopolistic Competitor? 358

What Are the Differences among Monopolistic Competition, Competitive Markets, and Monopoly? 358

Monopolistic Competition in the Short Run and the Long Run 359

Monopolistic Competition and Competitive Markets 361

Monopolistic Competition, Inefficiency, and Social Welfare 363

Practice What You Know: Markup: Punch Pizza versus Pizza Hut 366

Why Is Advertising Prevalent in Monopolistic Competition? 366

Economics in the Media: Advertising: Super Bowl Commercials 367

Why Firms Advertise 367

Advertising in Different Markets 369

Economics in the Media: Advertising: *E.T.: The Extra-Terrestrial* 370

SNAPSHOT: Advertising and the Super Bowl 371

The Negative Effects of Advertising 372

Practice What You Know: Advertising: Brands versus Generics 374

Economics in the Real World: The Federal Trade Commission versus Kevin Trudeau 376

ECONOMICS FOR LIFE: Product Differentiation: Would You Buy a Franchise? 377

Conclusion 377

Answering the Big Questions 378

Concepts You Should Know 379

Questions for Review 379

Study Problems 379

Solved Problems 381

13 Oligopoly and Strategic Behavior 382

Big Questions 384

What Is Oligopoly? 384

Measuring the Concentration of Industries 384

Collusion and Cartels in a Simple Duopoly Example 386

Economics in the Real World: OPEC: An International Cartel 389

Economics in the Media: Nash Equilibrium: *A Brilliant Madness* 390

Oligopoly with More Than Two Firms 391

Practice What You Know: Oligopoly: Can You Recognize the Oligopolist? 391

How Does Game Theory Explain Strategic Behavior? 392

Strategic Behavior and the Dominant Strategy 392

Duopoly and the Prisoner's Dilemma 394

Economics in the Media: Prisoner's Dilemma: *Murder by Numbers* 395

Advertising and Game Theory 396

SNAPSHOT: Airlines in the Prisoner's Dilemma 397

Economics in the Real World: The Cold War 398

Escaping the Prisoner's Dilemma in the Long Run 398

Economics in the Media: Prisoner's Dilemma: *The Dark Knight* 399

A Caution about Game Theory 401

How Do Government Policies Affect Oligopoly Behavior? 402

Antitrust Policy 402

Practice What You Know: Dominant Strategy: To Advertise or Not—That Is the Question! 403

Predatory Pricing 405

What Are Network Externalities? 405

Practice What You Know: Predatory Pricing: Price Wars 406

ECONOMICS FOR LIFE: Why Waiting Is Generally a Good Idea 408

Practice What You Know: Examples of Network Externalities 409

Conclusion 409

Answering the Big Questions 410

Concepts You Should Know 411

Questions for Review 411

Study Problems 411

Solved Problems 414

Appendix 13A: Two Alternative Theories of Pricing Behavior 415

The Kinked Demand Curve 415

Price Leadership 415

Concepts You Should Know 417

Study Problems 417

PART IV Labor Markets and Earnings

14 The Demand and Supply of Resources 420

Big Questions 422

What Are the Factors of Production? 422

Practice What You Know: Derived Demand: Tip Income 423

Where Does the Demand for Labor Come From? 423

The Marginal Product of Labor 424

Changes in the Demand for Labor 426

Practice What You Know: Value of the Marginal Product of Labor: Flower Barrettes 428

Where Does the Supply of Labor Come From? 428

The Labor-Leisure Trade-off 428

Changes in the Supply of Labor 429

Economics in the Media: Immigration: *A Day without a Mexican* 432

Practice What You Know: The Labor Supply Curve: What Would You Do with a Big Raise? 433

What Are the Determinants of Demand and Supply in the Labor Market? 434

How Does the Market for Labor Reach Equilibrium? 434

Economics in the Real World: Where Are the Nurses? 435

Change and Equilibrium in the Labor Market 436

Outsourcing 436

Economics in the Real World: Pregnancy Becomes the Latest Job to Be Outsourced to India 438

Economics in the Media: Outsourcing: *Outsourced* 441

Monopsony 441

Economics in the Real World: Pay and Performance in Major League Baseball 442

Practice What You Know: Labor Supply: Changes in Labor Supply 443

Economics in the Media: Value of the Marginal Product of Labor: *Moneyball* 444

What Role Do Land and Capital Play in Production? 444

The Market for Land 445

SNAPSHOT: Outsourcing 447

The Market for Capital 448

When to Use More Labor, Land, or Capital 448

Economics in the Real World: The Impact of the 2008 Financial Crisis on Labor, Land, and Capital 449

Practice What You Know: Bang for the Buck: When to Use More Capital or More Labor 450

Conclusion 450

Answering the Big Questions 451

ECONOMICS FOR LIFE: Will Your Future Job Be Outsourced? 452

Concepts You Should Know 453

Questions for Review 453

Study Problems 453

Solved Problems 455

PREFACE

Preface to the First Edition

We are teachers of principles of economics. That is what we do. We each teach principles of microeconomics and macroeconomics to over a thousand students a semester, every single semester, at the University of Kentucky and the University of Virginia.

We decided to write our own text for one big reason. We simply were not satisfied with the available texts and felt strongly that we could write an innovative book to which dedicated instructors like us would respond. It's not that the already available texts are bad or inaccurate—it's that they lack an understanding of what we, as teachers, have learned through fielding the thousands of questions that our students have asked us over the years. We do not advise policy makers, but we do advise students, and we know how their minds work.

For instance, there really is no text that shows an understanding for where students consistently trip up (for example, cost curves) and therefore provides an additional example, or better yet, a worked exercise. There really is no text that is careful to reinforce new terminology and difficult sticking points with explanations in everyday language. There really is no text that leverages the fact that today's students are key participants in the twenty-first-century economy, and that uses examples and cases from markets in which they interact all the time (for example, the markets for cell phones, social networking sites, computing devices, online book sellers, etc.).

What our years in the classroom have brought home to us is the importance of meeting students where they are. This means knowing their cultural touchstones and trying to tell the story of economics with those touchstones in mind. In our text we meet students where they are through resonance and reinforcement. In fact, these two words are our mantra—we strive to make each topic resonate and then make it stick through reinforcement.

Whenever possible, we use student-centered examples that resonate with students. For instance, many of our examples refer to jobs that students often hold and businesses that often employ them. If the examples resonate, students are much more likely to dig into the material wholeheartedly and internalize key concepts.

When we teach, we try to create a rhythm of reinforcement in our lectures that begins with the presentation of new material, followed by a concrete example, followed by a reinforcing device, and then closes with a "make it stick" moment. We do this over and over again. We have tried to bring that rhythm to the book. We believe strongly that this commitment to reinforcement works. To give just one example, in our chapter "Oligopoly and Strategic Behavior," while presenting the crucial-yet-difficult subject of game theory, we work through the concept of the prisoner's dilemma at least six different ways.

No educator is happy with the challenge we all face to motivate our students to read the assigned text. No matter how effective our lectures are, if our students are not reinforcing those lectures by reading the assigned text chapters, they are only partially absorbing the key takeaways that properly trained citizens need to thrive in today's world. A second key motivation for us to undertake this ambitious project was the desire to create a text that students would read, week in and week out, for the entire course. By following our commitment to resonance and reinforcement, we are confident that we have written a text that's a good read for today's students. So good, in fact, that we believe students will read entire chapters and actually enjoy them. Certainly the reports from our dozens of class testers indicate that this is the case.

What do we all want? We want our students to leave our courses having internalized fundamentals that they will remember for life. The fundamentals (understanding incentives, opportunity cost, thinking at the margin, etc.) will allow them to make better choices in the workplace, their personal investments, their long-term planning, their voting, and all their critical choices. The bottom line is that they will live more fulfilled and satisfying lives if we succeed. The purpose of this text is to help you succeed in your quest.

What does this classroom-inspired, student-centered text look like?

A Simple Narrative

First and foremost, we keep the narrative simple. We always bear in mind all those office-hour conversations with students where we searched for some way to make sense of this foreign language—for them—that is economics. It is incredibly satisfying when you find the right expression, explanation, or example that creates the "Oh, now I get it . . ." moment with your student. We have filled the narrative with those successful "now I get it" passages.

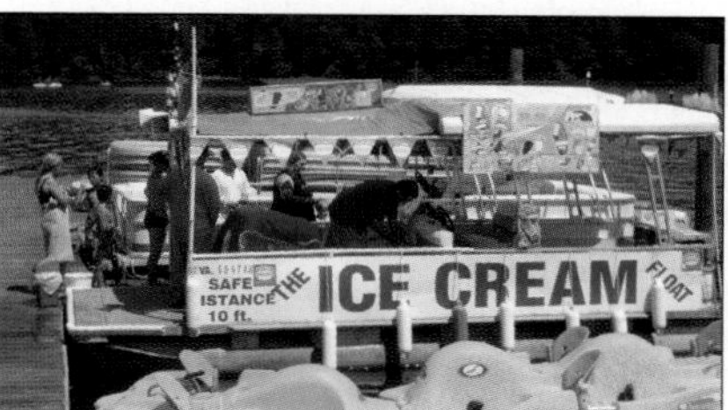

The Ice Cream Float, a cool idea on a hot day at the lake.

stores often close by 9 p.m. because operating overnight would not generate enough revenue to cover the costs of remaining open. Or consider the Ice Cream Float, which crisscrosses Smith Mountain Lake in Virginia during the summer months. You can hear the music announcing its arrival at the public beach from over a mile away. By the time the float arrives, there is usually a long line of eager customers waiting for the float to dock. This is a very profitable business on hot and sunny summer days. However, during the late spring and early fall the float operates on weekends only. Eventually, colder weather forces the business to shut down until the crowds return the following season. This shutdown decision is a short-run calculation. If the float were to operate during the winter, it would need to pay for employees and fuel. Incurring these variable costs when there are so few customers would result in greater total costs than simply dry-docking the boat. When the float is dry-docked over the winter, only the fixed cost of storing the boat remains.

Fortunately, a firm can use a simple, intuitive rule to decide whether to operate or shut down in the short run: if the firm would lose less by shutting down than by staying open, it should shut down. Recall that costs are broken into two parts—fixed and variable. Fixed costs must be paid whether the business is open or not. Since variable costs are only incurred when the business is op

employee

will choo

Incentives

Large generator: $900 after Hurricane Wilma hit.

Prices act to ration scarce resources. When the demand for generators or other necessities is high, the price rises to ensure that the available units are distributed to those who value them the most. More important, the ability to charge a higher price provides sellers with an incentive to make more units available. If there is limited ability for the price to change when demand increases, there will be a shortage. Therefore, price gouging legislation means that devastated communities must rely exclusively on the goodwill of others and the slow-moving machinery of government relief efforts. This closes off a third avenue, entrepreneurial activity, as a means to alleviate poor conditions.

Figure 5.5 shows how price gouging laws work and the shortage they create. If the demand for gas generators increases immediately after a disaster (D_{after}), the market price rises from $530 to $900. But since $900 is considered excessive, sales at that price are illegal. This creates a binding price ceiling for as long as a state of emergency is in effect. Whenever a price ceiling is binding, it creates a shortage. You can see this in Figure 5.5 in the difference between quantity demanded and quantity supplied at the price ceiling level mandated by the law. In this case, the normal ability of supply and demand to ration the available generators is short-circuited. Since more people demand generators after the disaster than before it, those who do not get to the store soon enough are out of luck. When the emergency is lifted and the market returns to normal, the temporary shortage created by legislation against price gouging is eliminated.

Examples and Cases That Resonate and Therefore Stick

Nothing makes this material stick for students like good examples and cases that they relate to, and we have peppered our book with them. They are not in boxed inserts. They are part of the narrative, set off with an Economics in the Real World heading.

ECONOMICS IN THE REAL WORLD

The Wii Rollout and Changes in the Video Game Industry

The Wii rollout generated long waiting lines.

When Nintendo launched the Wii console in late 2006, it fundamentally changed the gaming industry. The Wii uses motion-sensing technology. Despite relatively poor graphics, it provided a completely different gaming experience from its competitors, Playstation 3 (PS3) and the Xbox 360. Yet the PS3 and Xbox 360 had larger storage capacities and better graphics, in theory making them more attractive to gamers than the Wii.

During the 2006 holiday shopping season, the three systems had three distinct price points:

Wii = $249
Xbox = $399

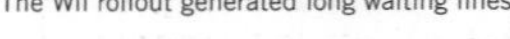

Wii and X
ply in stor
had hope
360 outso
ing, a mo
the deteri

ECONOMICS IN THE REAL WORLD

Blockbuster and the Dynamic Nature of Change

What happens if your customers do not return? What if you simply had a bad idea to begin with, and the customers never arrived in the first place?

When the long-run profit outlook is bleak, the firm is better off shutting down. This is a normal part of the ebb and flow of business. For example, once there were thousands of buggy whip companies. Today, as technology has improved and we no longer rely on horse-drawn carriages, few buggy whip makers remain. However, many companies now manufacture automobile parts.

Similarly, a succession of technological advances has transformed the music industry. Records were replaced by 8-track tapes, and then by cassettes. Already, the CD is on its way to being replaced by better technology as iPods, iPhones, and MP3 players make music more portable and as web sites such as Pandora and Spotify allow live streaming of almost any selection a listener wants to hear. However, there was a time when innovation meant playing music on the original Sony Walkman. What was cool in the early 1980s is antiquated today. Any business engaged in distributing music has had to adapt or close.

Similar changes are taking place in the video rental industry. Blockbuster was founded in 1982 and experienced explosive growth, becoming the nation's largest video store chain by 1988. The chain's growth was fueled by its large selection and use of a computerized tracking system that made the checkout process faster than the one at competing video stores. However, by the early 2000s Blockbuster faced stiff competition from online providers like Netflix and in-store dispensers like Redbox. Today, the chain has one-quarter the number of employees it once had and its future is very uncertain.

In addition to changes in technology, other factors such as downturns in the economy, changes in tastes, demographic factors, and migration can all force businesses to close. These examples remind us that the long-run decision to go out of business has nothing to do with the short-term profit outlook. ✳

Blockbuster's best days are long gone.

So far, we have examined the firm's decision-making process in the short run in the context of revenues versus costs. This has enabled us to determine the profits each firm makes. But now we pause to consider *sunk costs*, a special type of cost that all firms, in every industry, must consider when making decisions.

Reinforcers

Practice What You Know boxes are in-chapter exercises that allow students to self-assess while reading and provide a bit more hand-holding than usual. While other books have in-chapter questions, no other book consistently frames these exercises within real-world situations that students relate to.

PRACTICE WHAT YOU KNOW

Income Elasticity

Question: A college student eats ramen noodles twice a week and earns \$300/week working part-time. After graduating, the student earns \$1,000/week and eats ramen noodles every other week. What is the student's income elasticity?

Yummy, or all you can afford?

Answer: The income elasticity of demand using the midpoint method is

$$\frac{Q_2 - Q_1) \div [(Q_1 + Q_2) \div 2]}{(I_2 - I_1) \div [(I_1 + I_2) \div 2]}$$

$$\frac{5 - 2.0) \div [(2.0 + 0.5) \div 2]}{- \$300) \div [(\$300 + \$1000) \div 2]}$$

$$E_I = \frac{-1.5 \div 1.25}{\$700 \div \$650}$$

emand is positive for normal goods and negative
he negative coefficient indicates that ramen noo-
the range of income—in this example, between
should confirm your intuition. The higher post-
student to substitute away from ramen noodles
rovide more nourishment and enjoyment.

PRACTICE WHAT YOU KNOW

Shift or Slide?

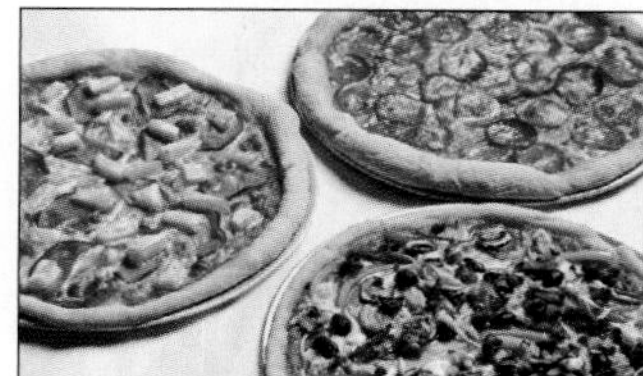

Cheap pizza or . . .

. . . cheap drinks?

Suppose that a local pizza place likes to run a "late-night special" after 11 p.m. The owners have contacted you for some advice. One of the owners tells you, "We want to increase the demand for our pizza." He proposes two marketing ideas to accomplish this:

1. Reduce the price of large pizzas.
2. Reduce the price of a complementary good—for example, offer two half-priced bottles or cans of soda with every large pizza ordered.

Question: What will you recommend?

Answer: First, consider why "late-night specials" exist in the first place. Since most people prefer to eat dinner early in the evening, the store has to encourage late-night patrons to buy pizzas by stimulating demand. "Specials" of all sorts are used during periods of low demand when regular prices would leave the establishment largely empty.

Next, look at what the question asks. The owners want to know which option would "increase demand" more. The question is very specific; it is looking for something that will increase (or shift) demand.

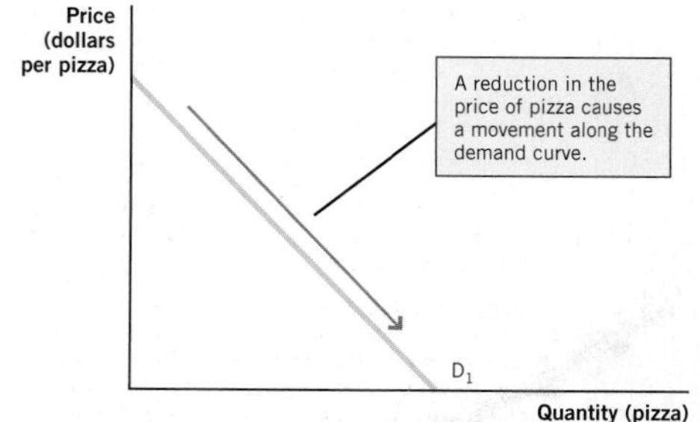

(CONTINUED)

Additional Reinforcers

Another notable reinforcement device is the Snapshot that appears in each chapter. We have used the innovation of modern infographics to create a memorable story that reinforces a particularly important topic.

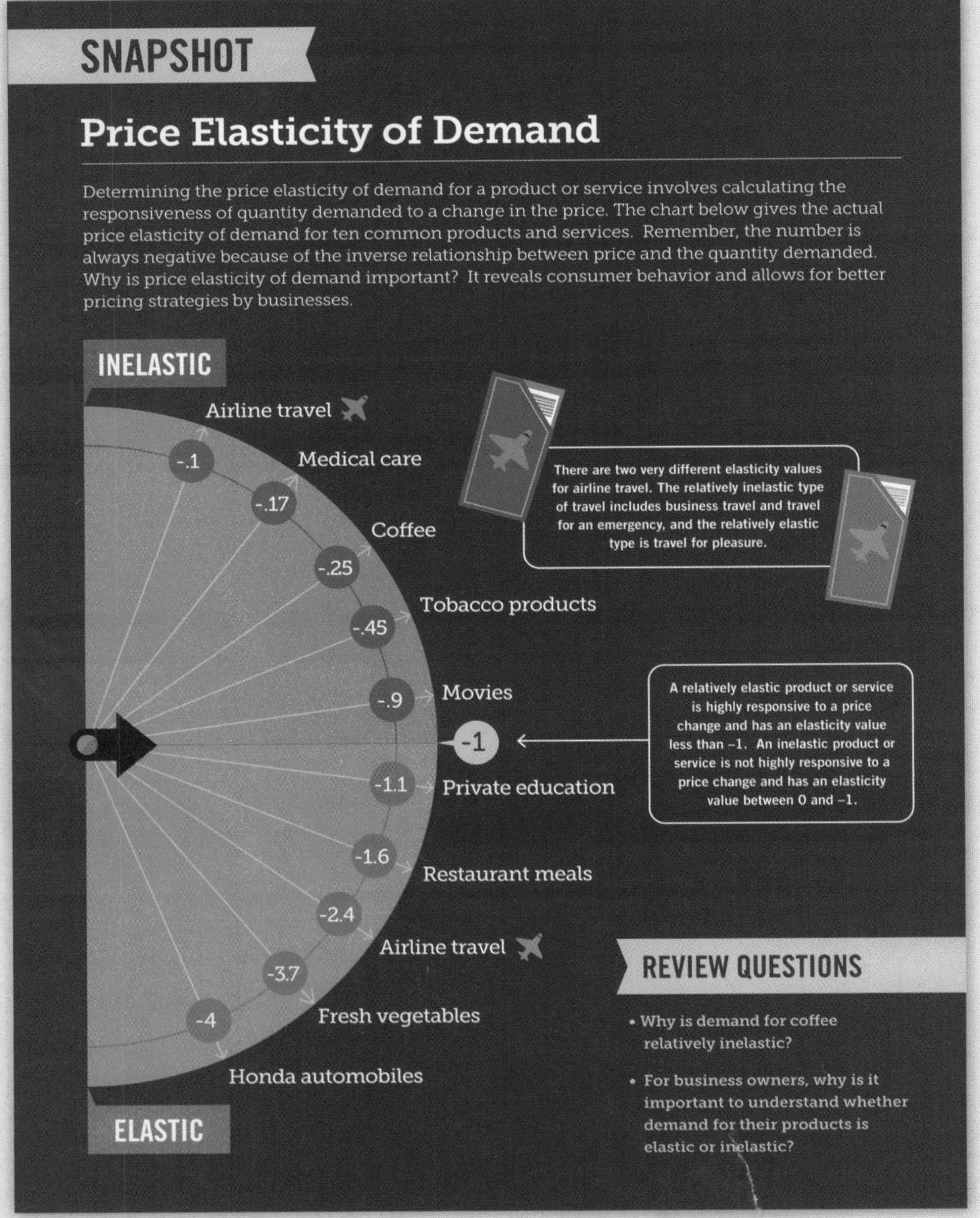

SNAPSHOT
Price Elasticity of Demand
Determining the price elasticity of demand for a product or service involves calculating the responsiveness of quantity demanded to a change in the price. The chart below gives the actual price elasticity of demand for ten common products and services. Remember, the number is always negative because of the inverse relationship between price and the quantity demanded. Why is price elasticity of demand important? It reveals consumer behavior and allows for better pricing strategies by businesses.
INELASTIC
Airline travel
-.1
Medical care
-.17
Coffee
-.25
Tobacco products
-.45
Movies
-.9
-1
-1.1
Private education
-1.6
Restaurant meals
-2.4
Airline travel
-3.7
Fresh vegetables
-4
Honda automobiles
ELASTIC
There are two very different elasticity values for airline travel. The relatively inelastic type of travel includes business travel and travel for an emergency, and the relatively elastic type is travel for pleasure.
A relatively elastic product or service is highly responsive to a price change and has an elasticity value less than −1. An inelastic product or service is not highly responsive to a price change and has an elasticity value between 0 and −1.
REVIEW QUESTIONS
• Why is demand for coffee relatively inelastic?
• For business owners, why is it important to understand whether demand for their products is elastic or inelastic?

We have two additional elements that may seem trivial to you as a fellow instructor, but we are confident that they will help to reinforce the material with your students. The first appears near the end of each chapter, and is called Economics for Life. The goal of this insert is to apply economic reasoning to important decisions that your students will face early in their post-student lives, such as buying or leasing a car. And the second is Economics in the Media. These boxes refer to classic scenes from movies and TV shows that deal directly with economics. One of us has written the book (literally!) on economics in the movies, and and we have used these clips year after year to make economics stick with students.

Costs in the Short Run

The Office

The popular TV series *The Office* had an amusing episode devoted to the discussion of costs. The character Michael Scott establishes his own paper company to compete with both Staples and his former company, Dunder Mifflin. He then outcompetes his rivals by keeping his fixed and variable costs low.

In one inspired scene, we see the Michael Scott Paper Company operating out of a single room and using an old church van to deliver paper. This means the company has very low *fixed costs*, which enables it to charge unusually low prices. In addition, Michael Scott keeps *variable costs* to a minimum by hiring only essential employees and not paying any benefits, such as health insurance. But this is a problem, since Michael Scott does not fully accou for the cost of the paper he is selling. In fact, he selling below unit cost!

As we will discover in upcoming chapters, firn with lower costs have many advantages in the mar Such firms can keep their prices lower to attract additional customers. Cost matters because price matters.

Price Elasticity of Supply and Demand: Buying Your First Car

ECONOMICS FOR LIFE

When you buy a car, your knowledge of price elasticity can help you negotiate the best possible deal.

Recall that the three determinants of price elasticity of demand are (1) the share of the budget, (2) the number of available substitutes, and (3) the time you have to make a decision.

Let's start with your budget. You should have one in mind, but don't tell the salesperson what you are willing to spend; that is a vital piece of personal information you want to keep to yourself. If the salesperson suggests that you look at a model that is too expensive, just say that you are not interested. You might reply, "Buying a car is a stretch for me; I've got to stay within my budget." If the salesperson asks indirectly about your budget by inquiring whether you have a particular monthly payment in mind, reply that you want to negotiate over the invoice price once you decide on a vehicle. Never negotiate on the sticker price, which is the price you see in the car window, because it includes thousands of dollars in markup. You want to make it clear to the salesperson that the price you pay matters to you—that is, your demand is elastic.

Next, make it clear that you are gathering information and visiting other dealers. That is, reinforce that you have many available substitutes. Even if you really want a Honda, do not voice that desire to the Honda salesperson. Perhaps mention that you are also visiting the Toyota, Hyundai, and Ford showrooms. Compare what you've seen on one lot versus another. Each salesperson you meet should hear that you are seriously considering other options. This indicates to each dealership that your demand is elastic and that getting your business will require that they offer you a better price.

Taking your time to decide is also important. Never buy a car the first time you walk onto a lot. If you convey the message that you want a car immediately, you are saying that your demand is inelastic. If the dealership thinks that you have no flexibility, the staff will not give you their best offer. Instead, tell the salesperson that you appreciate their help and that you will be deciding over the next few weeks. A good salesperson will know you are serious and will ask for your phone number or email address and contact you. The salesperson will sweeten the deal if you indicate you are narrowing down your choices and they are in the running. You wait. You win.

Also know that salespeople and dealerships have times when they want to move inventory. August is an especially good month to purchase. In other words, the price elasticity of supply is at work here as well. A good time to buy is when the dealer is trying to move inventory to make room for new models, because prices fall for end-of-the-model-year closeouts. Likewise, many sales promotions and sales bonuses are tied to the end of the month, so salespeople will be more eager to sell at that time.

Watch out for shady negotiation practices!

Big-Picture Pedagogy

Chapter-Opening Misconceptions

When we first started teaching we assumed that most of our students were taking economics for the first time and were therefore blank slates that we could draw on. Boy, were we wrong. We now realize that students come to our classes with a number of strongly held misconceptions about economics and the economy, so we begin each chapter recognizing that fact and then establishing what we will do to clarify that subject area.

CHAPTER 12 **Monopolistic Competition and Advertising**

Advertising increases the price of products without adding value for the consumer.

MISCONCEPTION

If you drive down a busy street, you will find many competing businesses, often right next to one another. For example, in most places a consumer in search of a quick bite has many choices, and more fast-food restaurants appear all the time. These competing firms advertise heavily. The temptation is to see advertising as driving up the price of a product, without any benefit to the consumer. However, this misconception doesn't account for why firms advertise. In markets where competitors sell slightly differentiated products, advertising enables firms to inform their customers about new products and services; yes, costs rise, but consumers also gain information to help make purchase decisions.

In this chapter, we look at *monopolistic competition*, a widespread market structure that has features of both competitive markets and monopoly. We also explore the benefits and disadvantages of advertising, which is prevalent in markets with monopolistic competition.

Big Questions

After the opening misconception, we present the learning goals for the chapter in the form of Big Questions. We come back to the Big Questions in the conclusion to the chapter with Answering the Big Questions.

BIG QUESTIONS

* **What is monopolistic competition?**
* **What are the differences among monopolistic competition, compe and monopoly?**
* **Why is advertising prevalent in monopolistic competition?**

ANSWERING THE BIG QUESTIONS

What is monopolistic competition?

* Monopolistic competition is a market characterized by free entry and many firms selling differentiated products.
* Differentiation of products takes three forms: differentiation by style or type, location, and quality.

What are the differences among monopolistic competition, competitive markets, and monopoly?

* Monopolistic competitors, like monopolists, are price makers who have downward-sloping demand curves. Whenever the demand curve is downward sloping, the firm is able to mark up the price above marginal cost. This leads to excess capacity and an inefficient level of output.
* In the long run, barriers to entry enable a monopoly to earn an economic profit. This is not the case for monopolistic competition or competitive markets.

Why is advertising prevalent in monopolistic competition?

* Advertising performs useful functions under monopolistic competition: it conveys information about the price of the goods offered for sale, the location of products, and new products. It also signals differences in quality. However, advertising also encourages brand loyalty, which makes it harder for other businesses to successfully enter the market. Advertising can be manipulative and misleading.

Solved Problems

Last but certainly not least, we conclude each chapter with two fully solved problems that appear in the end-of-chapter material.

102 / **CHAPTER 3** The Market at Work

SOLVED PROBLEMS

5.

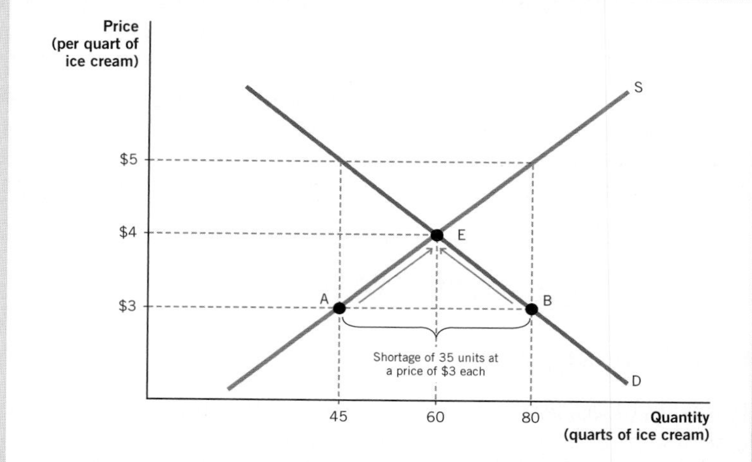

a. The equilibrium price is $4 and quantity is 60 units (quarts). The next step is to graph the curves. This is done above.

b. A shortage of 35 units of ice cream exists at $3; therefore, there is excess demand. Ice cream sellers will raise their price as long as excess demand exists. That is, as long as the price is below $4. It is not until $4 that the equilibrium point is reached and the shortage is resolved.

8. a. The first step is to set $Q_D = Q_S$. Doing so gives us $90 - 2P = P$. Solving for price, we find that $90 = 3P$, or $P = 30$. Once we know that $P = 30$, we can plug this value back into either of the original equations, $Q_D = 90 - 2P$ or $Q_S = P$. Beginning with Q_D, we get $90 - (30) = 90 - 60 = 30$, or we can plug it into $Q_S = P$, so $Q_S = 30$. Since we get a quantity of 30 for both Q_D and Q_S, we know that the price of $30 is correct.

b. In this part, we plug $20 into Q_D. This yields $90 - 2(20) = 50$. Now we plug $20 into Q_S. This yields 20.

c. Since $Q_D = 50$ and $Q_S = 20$, there is a shortage of 30 units.

d. Whenever there is a shortage of a good, the price will rise in order to find the equilibrium point.

Specifics about *Principles of Microeconomics*

Principles of Microeconomics follows the traditional structure found in most texts. Why? Because it works! One difference is the separate chapter on price discrimination. We have done this because the digital economy has made price discrimination much more common than it ever was before, so what was once a fun but somewhat marginal topic is no longer marginal. Plus, students really relate to it because they are subject to it in many of the markets in which they participate—for example, college sporting events.

The consumer theory chapter has been placed toward the end of the volume, but that does not mean that we consider it an optional chapter. We have learned that there is tremendous variation among instructors for when to present this material in the course, and we wanted to allow for maximum flexibility.

Though every chapter is critical, in our opinion, supply and demand, elasticity, and production costs are the *most* fundamental, since so many other insights and takeaways build off of them. We tried triply hard to reinforce these chapters with extra examples and opportunities for self-assessment.

Supplements and Media

Norton Coursepack

Bring tutorial videos, assessment, and other online teaching resources directly into your new or existing online course with the Norton Coursepack. It's easily customizable and available for all major learning management systems including Blackboard, Desire2Learn, Angel, Moodle, and Canvas.

The Norton Coursepack for *Principles of Economics* includes:

- Concept Check quizzes
- A limited set of adapted Norton SmartWork questions
- Infographic quizzes
- Office Hours video tutorials
- Flashcards
- Links to the e-book
- Test bank

The Ultimate Guide to Teaching Economics

The Ultimate Guide to Teaching Economics isn't just a guide to using *Principles of Economics,* it's a guide to becoming a better teacher. Combining more than 50 years of teaching experience, authors Dirk Mateer, Lee Coppock, Wayne Geerling (Penn State University), and Kim Holder (University of West Georgia) have compiled hundreds of teaching tips into one essential teaching resource. The *Ultimate Guide* is thoughtfully designed, making it easy for new instructors to incorporate best teaching practices into their courses and for veteran teachers to find new inspiration to enliven their lectures.

The hundreds of tips in *The Ultimate Guide to Teaching Microeconomics* and *The Ultimate Guide to Teaching Macroeconomics* include:

- Think-pair-share activities to promote small-group discussion and active learning
- "Recipes" for in-class activities and demonstrations that include descriptions of the activity, required materials, estimated length of time, estimated difficulty, recommended class size, and instructions. Ready-to-use worksheets are also available for select activities.
- Descriptions of movie clips, TV shows, commercials, and other videos that can be used in class to illustrate economic concepts
- Clicker questions
- Ideas for music examples that can be used as lecture starters
- Suggestions for additional real-world examples to engage students

DEMONSTRATION

TIP #11 Rent Seeking and the Inefficiency of Non-Market Allocations

Teams of students will compete for "prizes," under a variety of situations.

Materials

- ☐ four teams of students
- ☐ a deck of cards
- ☐ Files for instructor: Get additional materials for this demonstration in the interactive instructor's guide

Class Time: 20 minutes

Class Size: Any

Difficulty: Difficult

Procedure

1. Treatment 1
   Four teams of investors compete for each prize or FCC "license."
   Each team is given 13 cards of the same suit and an initial capital account of $100,000.
   Each team can play any of their 13 cards by placing them in an envelope, so that no one else sees how many cards they played.
   Each card should be thought of as a lottery ticket in a drawing for a license that is initially worth $16,000.
   Each lottery ticket costs the team $3,000. (Think of this as the cost of preparing and filing the paperwork for the license.)
   The number of cards each team plays determines the chance that each team wins a random drawing based on the total number of cards entered.
   Record your teams results for round 1.
   The cards are returned to each team without revealing how many cards were played.
   We will repeat this process two times.
2. Treatment 2
   Now we change the earnings structure for the license, by decreasing the cost associated with filing the lottery application from $3,000 to $1,000.
   You can think of this as an efficiency move by the FCC that lowers the amount of paperwork and documentation required for the application.

In addition to the teaching tips, each chapter begins with an introduction by Dirk Mateer, highlighting important concepts to teach in the chapter and pointing out his favorite tips. Each chapter ends with solutions to the unsolved end-of-chapter problems in the textbook.

Interactive Instructor's Guide

The Interactive Instructor's Guide brings all the great content from *The Ultimate Guide to Teaching Economics* into a searchable online database that can be filtered by topic and resource type. Subscribing instructors will be alerted by email as new resources are made available.

In order to make it quick and easy for instructors to incorporate the tips from *The Ultimate Guide to Teaching Economics,* the IIG will include:

- Links for video tips when an online video is available
- Links to news articles for real-world examples when an article is available
- Downloadable versions of student worksheets for activities and demonstrations
- Downloadable PowerPoint slides for clicker questions
- Additional teaching resources from dirkmateer.com and leecoppock.com

Office Hours Video Tutorials

This collection of more than 45 videos brings the office-hour experience online. Each video explains a fundamental concept and was conceived by and filmed with authors Dirk Mateer and Lee Coppock.

Perfect for online courses, each Office Hours video tutorial is succinct (90 seconds to two minutes in length) and mimics the office-hour experience. The videos focus on topics that are typically difficult to explain just in writing (or over email), such as shifting supply and demand curves.

The Office Hours videos have been incorporated throughout the Norton SmartWork online homework system as video feedback for questions, integrated into the e-book, included in the Norton Coursepack, and available in the instructor resource folder.

Test Bank

Every question in the *Principles of Economics* test bank has been author reviewed and approved. Each chapter (except Chapter 1) includes between 100 and 150 questions and incorporates graphs and images where appropriate.

The test bank has been developed using the Norton Assessment Guidelines. Each chapter of the test bank consists of three question types classified according to Bloom's taxonomy of knowledge types (Remembering, Understanding Applying, Analyzing Evaluating, and Creating). Questions are further classified by section and difficulty, making it easy to construct tests and quizzes that are meaningful and diagnostic.

Presentation Tools

Norton offers a variety of presentation tools so new instructors and veteran instructors alike can find the resources that are best suited for their teaching style.

Enhanced Lecture Powerpoint Slides

These comprehensive, "lecture-ready" slides are perfect for new instructors and instructors who have limited time to prepare for lecture. In addition to lecture slides, the slides also include images from the book, stepped-out versions of in-text graphs, additional examples not included in the chapter, and clicker questions.

Art Slides and Art JPEGs

For instructors who simply want to incorporate in-text art into their existing slides, all art from the book (tables, graphs, photos, and Snapshot infographics) will be available in both PowerPoint and .jpeg formats. Stepped-out versions of in-text graphs and Snapshot infographics will also be provided and will be optimized for screen projection.

Instructor Resource Folder

The Instructor Resource Folder includes the following resources in an all-in-one folder:

- The test bank in ExamView format on a CD
- Instructor's Resource Disc: PDFs of *The Ultimate Guide to Teaching Economics,* PowerPoints (enhanced lecture slides, active teaching slides, Snapshot slides, art slides, art .jpegs)
- Office Hours video tutorial DVD

dirkmateer.com

Visit dirkmateer.com to find a library of over 100 recommended movie and TV clips, and links to online video sources to use in class.

Coming for Fall 2014: Norton SmartWork for *Principles of Economics*

Norton SmartWork is a complete learning environment and online homework course designed to (1) support and encourage the development of problem-solving skills, and (2) deliver a suite of innovative tutorials, learning tools, and assessment woven together in a pedagogically effective way. Highlights include:

- Pre-created assignments to help instructors get started quickly and easily
- Guided learning tutorials to help students review each chapter objective
- Answer-specific feedback for every question to help students become better problem solvers
- An intuitive, easy-to-use graphing tool consistent with the coloration and notation of in-text graphs and art

ACKNOWLEDGMENTS

We would like to thank the literally hundreds of fellow instructors who have helped us refine both our vision and the actual words on the page for this text. Without your help, we would never have gotten to the finish line. We hope that the result is the economics teacher's text that we set out to write.

Our class testers:

Jennifer Bailly, California State University, Long Beach
Mihajlo Balic, Harrisburg Community College
Erol Balkan, Hamilton College
Susan Bell, Seminole State College
Scott Benson, Idaho State University
Joe DaBoll-Lavoie, Nazareth College
Michael Dowell, California State University, Sacramento
Abdelaziz Farah, State University of New York, Orange
J. Brian O'Roark, Robert Morris University
Shelby Frost, Georgia State University
Karl Geisler, University of Nevada, Reno
Nancy Griffin, Tyler Junior College
Lauren Heller, Berry College
John Hilston, Brevard Community College
Kim Holder, University of West Georgia
Todd Knoop, Cornell College
Katharine W. Kontak, Bowling Green State University
Daniel Kuester, Kansas State University
Herman Li, University of Nevada, Las Vegas
Gary Lyn, University of Massachusetts, Lowell
Kyle Mangum, Georgia State University
Shah Mehrabi, Montgomery College
Sean Mulholland, Stonehill College
Vincent Odock, State University of New York, Orange
Michael Price, Georgia State University
Matthew Rousu, Susquehanna University
Tom Scales, Southside Virginia Community College
Tom Scheiding, University of Wisconsin, Stout
Clair Smith, St. John Fisher College
Tesa Stegner, Idaho State University
James Tierney, State University of New York, Plattsburgh
Nora Underwood, University of Central Florida
Michael Urbancic, University of Oregon
Marlon Williams, Lock Haven University

Our reviewers and advisors from focus groups:

Mark Abajian, California State University, San Marcos
Teshome Abebe, Eastern Illinois University
Rebecca Achee Thornton, University of Houston
Mehdi Afiat, College of Southern Nevada
Seemi Ahmad, State University of New York, Dutchess
Abdullah Al-Bahrani, Bloomsburg University
Frank Albritton, Seminole State College
Rashid Al-Hmoud, Texas Tech University
Tom Andrews, West Chester University
Becca Arnold, San Diego Mesa College
Lisa Augustyniak, Lake Michigan College
Dennis Avola, Bentley University
Roberto Ayala, California State University, Fullerton
Ron Baker, Millersville University
Kuntal Banerjee, Florida Atlantic University
Jude Bayham, Washington State University
Mary Beal-Hodges, University of North Florida
Stacie Beck, University of Delaware
Jodi Beggs, Northeastern University

Richard Beil, Auburn University
Doris Bennett, Jacksonville State University
Karen Bernhardt-Walther, The Ohio State University
Prasun Bhattacharjee, East Tennessee State University
Richard Bilas, College of Charleston
Kelly Blanchard, Purdue University
Inácio Bo, Boston College
Michael Bognanno, Temple University
Donald Boudreaux, George Mason University
Austin Boyle, Penn State
Elissa Braunstein, Colorado State University
Kristie Briggs, Creighton University
Stacey Brook, University of Iowa
Bruce Brown, California State Polytechnic University, Pomona
John Brown, Clark University
Vera Brusentsev, Swarthmore College
Laura Maria Bucila, Texas Christian University
Richard Burkhauser, Cornell University
W. Jennings Byrd, Troy University
Joseph Calhoun, Florida State University
Charles Callahan, State University of New York, Brockport
Douglas Campbell, University of Memphis
Giorgio Canarella, University of Nevada, Las Vegas
Semih Cekin, Texas Tech University
Sanjukta Chaudhuri, University of Wisconsin, Eau Claire
Shuo Chen, State University of New York, Geneseo
Monica Cherry, State University of New York, Buffalo
Larry Chisesi, University of San Diego
Steve Cobb, University of North Texas
Rhonda Collier, Portland Community College
Glynice Crow, Wallace State Community College
Chad D. Cotti, University of Wisconsin, Oshkosh
Damian Damianov, University of Texas, Pan American
Ribhi Daoud, Sinclair Community College
Kacey Douglas, Mississippi State University
William Dupor, The Ohio State University
Harold W. Elder, University of Alabama
Diantha Ellis, Abraham Baldwin Agricultural College
Tisha Emerson, Baylor University
Lucas Englehardt, Kent State University
Erwin Erhardt, University of Cincinnati
Molly Espey, Clemson University
Patricia Euzent, University of Central Florida
Brent Evans, Mississippi State University
Carolyn Fabian Stumph, Indiana University–Purdue University, Fort Wayne
Leila Farivar, The Ohio State University
Roger Frantz, San Diego State University
Gnel Gabrielyan, Washington State University
Craig Gallet, California State University, Sacramento
Wayne Geerling, Pennsylvania State University
Elisabetta Gentile, University of Houston
Menelik Geremew, Texas Tech University
Dipak Ghosh, Emporia State University
J. Robert Gillette, University of Kentucky
Rajeev Goel, Illinois State University
Bill Goffe, State University of New York, Oswego
Michael Gootzeit, University of Memphis
Paul Graf, Indiana University, Bloomington
Jeremy Groves, Northern Illinois University
Dan Hamermesh, University of Texas, Austin
Mehdi Haririan, Bloomsburg University
Oskar Harmon, University of Connecticut
David Harrington, The Ohio State University
Darcy Hartman, The Ohio State University
John Hayfron, Western Washington University
Jill Hayter, East Tennessee State University
Marc Hellman, Oregon State University
Wayne Hickenbottom, University of Texas, Austin
Mike Hilmer, San Diego State University
Lora Holcombe, Florida State University
Charles Holt, University of Virginia
James Hornsten, Northwestern University
Yu-Mong Hsiao, Campbell University
Alice Hsiaw, College of the Holy Cross
Yu Hsing, Southeastern Louisiana University
Paul Johnson, University of Alaska, Anchorage
David Kalist, Shippensburg University of Pennsylvania
Ara Khanjian, Ventura College
Frank Kim, University of San Diego
Colin Knapp, University of Florida
Mary Knudson, University of Iowa
Ermelinda Laho, LaGuardia Community College
Carsten Lange, California State Polytechnic University, Pomona
Tony Laramie, Merrimack College
Paul Larson, University of Delaware

Teresa Laughlin, Palomar College
Eric Levy, Florida Atlantic University
Charles Link, University of Delaware
Delores Linton, Tarrant County College
Xuepeng Liu, Kennesaw State University
Monika Lopez-Anuarbe, Connecticut College
Bruce Madariaga, Montgomery College
Brinda Mahalingam, University of California, Riverside
Chowdhury Mahmoud, Concordia University
Mark Maier, Glendale Community College
Daniel Marburger, Arkansas State University
Cara McDaniel, Arizona State University
Scott McGann, Grossmont College
Christopher McIntosh, University of Minnesota, Duluth
Evelina Mengova, California State University, Fullerton
William G. Mertens, University of Colorado, Boulder
Ida Mirzaie, The Ohio State University
Michael A. Mogavero, University of Notre Dame
Moon Moon Haque, University of Memphis
Mike Nelson, Oregon State University
Boris Nikolaev, University of South Florida
Caroline Noblet, University of Maine
Fola Odebunmi, Cypress College
Paul Okello, Tarrant County College
Stephanie Owings, Fort Lewis College
Caroline Padgett, Francis Marion University
Kerry Pannell, DePauw University
R. Scott Pearson, Charleston Southern University
Andrew Perumal, University of Massachusetts, Boston
Rinaldo Pietrantonio, West Virginia University
Irina Pritchett, North Carolina State University
Sarah Quintanar, University of Arkansas at Little Rock
Ranajoy Ray-Chaudhuri, The Ohio State University
Mitchell Redlo, Monroe Community College
Debasis Rooj, Northern Illinois University
Jason Rudbeck, University of Georgia
Naveen Sarna, Northern Virginia Community College
Noriaki Sasaki, McHenry County College
Jessica Schuring, Central College
Robert Schwab, University of Maryland
James Self, Indiana University, Bloomington
Gina Shamshak, Goucher College
Neil Sheflin, Rutgers University
Brandon Sheridan, North Central College
Joe Silverman, Mira Costa College
Brian Sloboda, University of Phoenix
Todd Sorensen, University of California, Riverside
Liliana Stern, Auburn University
Joshua Stillwagon, University of New Hampshire
Burak Sungu, Miami University
Vera Tabakova, East Carolina University
Yuan Emily Tang, University of California, San Diego
Anna Terzyan, Loyola Marymount University
Henry Thompson, Auburn University
Mehmet Tosun, University of Nevada, Reno
Robert Van Horn, University of Rhode Island
Adel Varghese, Texas A&M University
Marieta Velikova, Belmont University
Will Walsh, Samford University
Ken Woodward, Saddleback College
Jadrian Wooten, Washington State University
Anne York, Meredith College
Arindra Zainal, Oregon State University
Erik Zemljic, Kent State University
Kent Zirlott, University of Alabama

All of the individuals listed above helped us to improve the text and ancillaries, but a smaller group of them offered us extraordinary insight and support. They went above and beyond, and we would like them to know just how much we appreciate it. In particular, we want to recognize Alicia Baik (University of Virginia), Jodi Beggs (Northeastern University), Dave Brown (Penn State University), Jennings Byrd (Troy University), Douglas Campbell (University of Memphis), Shelby Frost (Georgia State University), Wayne Geerling (Penn State University), Paul Graf (Indiana University), Oskar Harmon (University of Connecticut), Jill Hayter (East Tennessee State University), John Hilston (Brevard Community College), Kim Holder (University of West Georgia), Todd Knoop (Cornell College), Katie Kontak (Bowling Green State

University), Brendan LaCerda (University of Virginia), Paul Larson (University of Delaware), Ida Mirzaie (Ohio State University), Charles Newton (Houston Community College), Boris Nikolaev (University of South Florida), J. Brian O'Roark (Robert Morris University), Andrew Perumal (University of Massachusetts, Boston), Irina Pritchett (North Carolina State University), Matt Rousu (Susquehanna College), Tom Scheiding (Cardinal Stritch University), Brandon Sheridan (North Central College), Clair Smith (Saint John Fisher College), James Tierney (SUNY Plattsburgh), Nora Underwood (University of Central Florida), Joseph Whitman (University of Florida), Erik Zemljic (Kent State University), and Zhou Zhang (University of Virginia).

We would also like to thank our partners at W. W. Norton & Company, who have been as committed to this text as we've been. They have been a pleasure to work with and we hope that we get to work together for many years. We like to call them Team Econ: Hannah Bachman, Jack Borrebach, Cassie del Pilar, Dan Jost, Lorraine Klimowich, John Kresse, Pete Lesser, Sasha Levitt, Jack Repcheck, Spencer Richardson-Jones, Carson Russell, and Nicole Sawa. Our development editor, Becky Kohn, was a big help, as was our copy editor, Alice Vigliani. The visual appeal of the book is the result of our photo researchers, Dena Digilio Betz and Nelson Colón, and the team at Kiss Me I'm Polish who created the front cover and the Snapshot infographics: Agnieszka Gasparska, Andrew Janik, and Annie Song. Thanks to all—it's been a wonderful adventure.

Finally, from Dirk: I'd like to thank my colleagues at Penn State—especially Dave Brown and Wayne Geerling—for their hard work on the supplements, my friends from around the country for the encouragement to write a textbook, and my family for their patience as the process unfolded. In addition, I want to thank the thousands of former students who provided comments, suggestions, and other insights that helped shape the book.

Finally, from Lee: First, I'd like to acknowledge Krista, my excellent wife, who consistently sacrificed to enable me to write this book. I'd also like to thank Jack Repcheck, who had the vision and the will to make this project a reality; we can't thank him enough. Finally, I'd also like to acknowledge Ken Elzinga, Charlie Holt, and Mike Shaub: three great professors who are my role models in the academy and beyond.

ABOUT THE AUTHORS

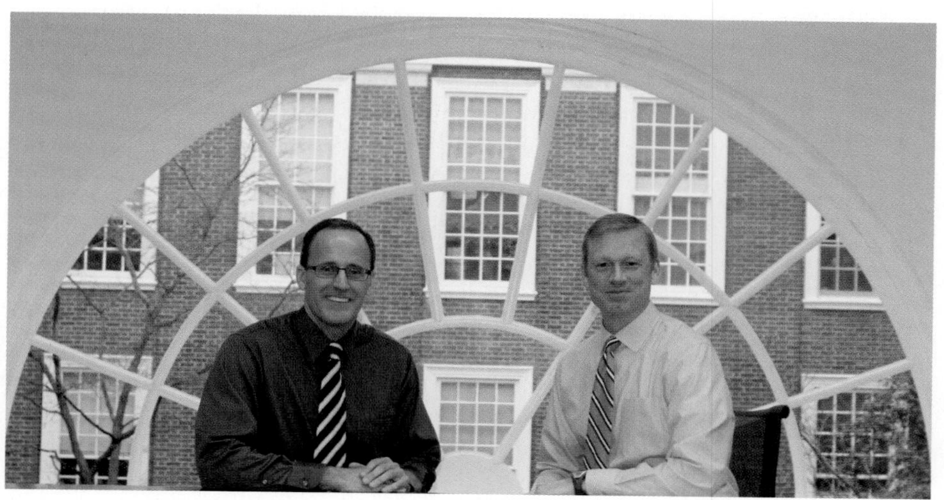

Dirk Mateer

is Senior Lecturer at the University of Kentucky. He is the author of *Economics in the Movies*. He is also nationally recognized for his teaching. While at Penn State, he received the George W. Atherton Award, the university's highest teaching award (2011), and was voted the best overall teacher in the Smeal College of Business by the readers of *Critique* magazine (2010). He was profiled in the "Great Teachers in Economics" series of the Gus A. Stavros Center for the Advancement of Free Enterprise and Economic Education at Florida State University.

Lee Coppock

is Associate Professor in the Economics Department at the University of Virginia. He has been teaching principles of economics for over twenty years, specializing in principles of macroeconomics. Before moving to UVA, he spent 9 years at Hillsdale College, where he learned how to reach college students. At UVA, Lee teaches two large sections (500+) of macro principles each spring. He has received teaching awards at both Hillsdale College and UVA. Lee lives in Charlottesville with his wife Krista and their four children: Bethany, Lee III, Kara, and Jackson.

Principles of Microeconomics

INTRODUCTION

CHAPTER 1

The Five Foundations of Economics

MISCONCEPTION

Economics is the dismal science.

Perhaps you have heard of the "dismal science"? This derogatory term was first used by historian and essayist Thomas Carlyle in the nineteenth century. He called economics the dismal science after he read a prediction from economist Thomas Malthus stating that because our planet had limited resources, continued population growth would ultimately lead to widespread starvation.

Malthus was a respected thinker, but he was unduly pessimistic. The world population was one billion in 1800, and it is seven billion today. One of the things that Malthus did not take into account was increases in technology and productivity. Today, the efficiency of agricultural production enables seven billion people to live on this planet. Far from being the dismal science, economics in the twenty-first century is a vital social science that helps world leaders improve the lives of their citizens.

This textbook will provide the tools you need to be able to make your own assessments about the economy. What other discipline helps you discover how the world works, how to be an informed citizen, and how to live your life to the fullest? Economics can improve your understanding of the stock market and help you make better personal finance decisions. If you are concerned about Social Security, this textbook explains how it works. If you are interested in learning more about health care, the answers are here. Economics provides answers to all of these questions and much more.

In this chapter, you will learn about the five foundations of economics—incentives, trade-offs, opportunity cost, marginal thinking, and the principle that trade creates value. You will find that many of the more complex problems presented later in the text are derived from one of

Predicting the future is a tough business.

these foundations. Once you have mastered these five concepts, even the most complex processes can be reduced to combinations of these foundations. Think of this chapter as a road map that provides a broad overview of your journey into economics. Let's get started!

BIG QUESTIONS

- **What is economics?**
- **What are the five foundations of economics?**

What Is Economics?

Economists study how decisions are made. Examples of economic decisions include whether or not you should buy or lease a car, sublet your apartment, and buy that Gibson guitar you've been eyeing. And, just as individuals must choose what to buy within the limits of the income they possess, society as a whole must determine what to produce from its limited set of resources.

Scarcity
refers to the limited nature of society's resources, given society's unlimited wants and needs.

Economics
is the study of how people allocate their limited resources to satisfy their nearly unlimited wants.

Of course, life would be a lot easier if we could have whatever we wanted whenever we wanted it. Unfortunately, life does not work that way. Our wants and needs are nearly unlimited, but the resources available to satisfy these wants and needs are always limited. The term used to describe the limited nature of society's resources is **scarcity**. Even the most abundant resources, like the water we drink and the air we breathe, are not always abundant enough everywhere to meet the wants and needs of every person. So, how do individuals and societies make decisions about scarce resources? This is the basic question economists seek to answer. **Economics** is the study of how people allocate their limited resources to satisfy their nearly unlimited wants.

Water is scarce . . .

. . . and so are diamonds!

Microeconomics and Macroeconomics

The study of economics is divided into two subfields: *microeconomics* and *macroeconomics*. **Microeconomics** is the study of the individual units that make up the economy. **Macroeconomics** is the study of the overall aspects and workings of an economy, such as inflation, growth, employment, interest rates, and the productivity of the economy as a whole. To see if you understand the difference, consider a worker who gets laid off and becomes unemployed. Is this an issue that would be addressed in microeconomics or macroeconomics? The question seems to fit parts of both definitions. The worker is an individual, which is micro, but employment is one of the broad areas of concern for economists, which is macro. Don't let this confuse you. Since only one worker is laid off, this is a micro issue. If many workers had been laid off and this led to a higher unemployment rate across the entire economy, it would be an issue broad enough to be studied by macroeconomists.

Microeconomics
is the study of the individual units that make up the economy.

Macroeconomics
is the study of the overall aspects and workings of an economy.

What Are the Five Foundations of Economics?

The study of economics can be complicated, but we can make it very accessible by breaking down the specific economic process that you are exploring into a set of component parts. The five foundations that are presented here are the key component parts of economics. They are a bit like the natural laws of physics or chemistry. Almost every economic subject can be analyzed through the prism of one of these foundations. By mastering the five foundations, you will be on your way to succeeding in this course and thinking like an economist.

The five foundations of economics are: incentives; trade-offs; opportunity cost; marginal thinking; and the principle that trade creates value. Each of the five foundation concepts developed in this chapter will reappear throughout the book and enable you to solve complex problems.

Every time we encounter one of the five concepts, you will see an icon of a house to remind you of what you have learned. As you become more adept at economic analysis, it will not be uncommon to use two or more of these foundational ideas to explain the economic world around us.

Incentives
Trade-offs
Opportunity cost
Marginal thinking
Trade creates value

Incentives

Incentives

When you are faced with making a decision, you usually make the choice that you think will most improve your situation. In making your decision, you respond to **incentives**—factors that motivate you to act or to exert effort. For example, the choice to study for an exam you have tomorrow instead of spending the evening with your friends is based on the belief that doing well on the exam will provide a greater benefit. You are incentivized to study because you know that an A in the course will raise your grade-point average and make you a more attractive candidate on the job market when you are finished with school. We can further divide incentives into two paired categories: *positive and negative*, and *direct and indirect*.

Incentives
are factors that motivate a person to act or exert effort.

Positive and Negative Incentives

Positive incentives are those that encourage action. For example, end-of-the-year bonuses motivate employees to work hard throughout the year, higher oil prices cause suppliers to extract more oil, and tax rebates encourage citizens to spend more money. Negative incentives also encourage action. For instance, the fear of receiving a speeding ticket keeps motorists from driving too fast, and the dread of a trip to the dentist motivates people to brush their teeth regularly. In each case, a potential negative consequence spurs individuals to action.

PRACTICE WHAT YOU KNOW

This mosaic of the flag illustrates the difference between micro and macro.

Microeconomics and Macroeconomics: The Big Picture

Identify whether each of the following statements identifies a microeconomic or a macroeconomic issue.

The national savings rate is less than 2% of disposable income.

Answer: The national savings rate is a statistic based on the average amount each household saves as a percentage of income. As such, this is a broad measure of savings and something that describes a macroeconomic issue.

Jim was laid off from his last job and is currently unemployed.

Answer: Jim's personal financial circumstances constitute a microeconomic issue.

Apple decides to open up 100 new stores.

Answer: Even though Apple is a very large corporation and 100 new stores will create many new jobs, Apple's decision is a microeconomic issue because the basis for its decision is best understood as part of the firm's competitive strategy.

The government passes a jobs bill designed to stabilize the economy during a recession.

Answer: You might be tempted to ask how many jobs are created before deciding, but that is not relevant to this question. The key part of the statement refers to "stabiliz[ing] the economy during a recession." This is an example of a *fiscal policy*, in which the government takes an active role in managing the economy. Therefore, it is a macroeconomic issue.

Conventional wisdom tells us that "learning is its own reward," but try telling that to most students. Teachers are aware that incentives, both positive and negative, create additional interest among their students to learn the course material. Positive incentives include bonus points, gold stars, public praise, and extra credit. Many students respond to these encouragements by studying more. However, positive incentives are not enough. Suppose that your instructor never gave any grade lower than an A. Your incentive to participate actively in the course, do assignments, or earn bonus points would be small. For positive incentives to work, they generally need to be coupled with negative incentives. This is why instructors require students to complete assignments, take exams, and write papers. Students know that if they do not complete these requirements they will get a lower grade, perhaps even fail the class.

Direct and Indirect Incentives

In addition to being positive and negative, incentives can also be direct and indirect. For instance, if one gas station lowers its prices, it most likely will get business from customers who would not usually stop there. This is a direct incentive. Lower gasoline prices also work as an indirect incentive, since lower prices might encourage consumers to use more gas.

Direct incentives are easy to recognize. "Cut my grass and I'll pay you $30" is an example of a direct incentive. Indirect incentives are much harder to recognize. But learning to recognize them is one of the keys to mastering economics. For instance, consider the indirect incentives at work in welfare programs. Almost everyone agrees that societies should provide a safety net for those without employment or whose income isn't enough to meet basic needs. Thus, a society has a direct incentive to alleviate suffering caused by poverty. But how does a society provide this safety net without taking away the incentive to work? In other words, if the amount of welfare a person receives is higher than the amount that person can hope to make from a job, the welfare recipient might decide to stay on welfare rather than go to work. The indirect incentive to stay on welfare creates an *unintended consequence*—people who were supposed to use government assistance as a safety net until they can find a job use it instead as a permanent source of income.

Policymakers have the tough task of deciding how to balance such conflicting incentives. To decrease the likelihood that a person will stay on welfare, policymakers could cut benefits. But this might leave some people without enough to live on. For this reason, many government programs specify limits on the amount of time people can receive benefits. Ideally, this allows the welfare programs to continue to meet basic needs while creating incentives that encourage recipients to search for jobs and acquire skills that will enable them to do better in the workforce. We'll learn more about the issues of welfare in Chapter 15.

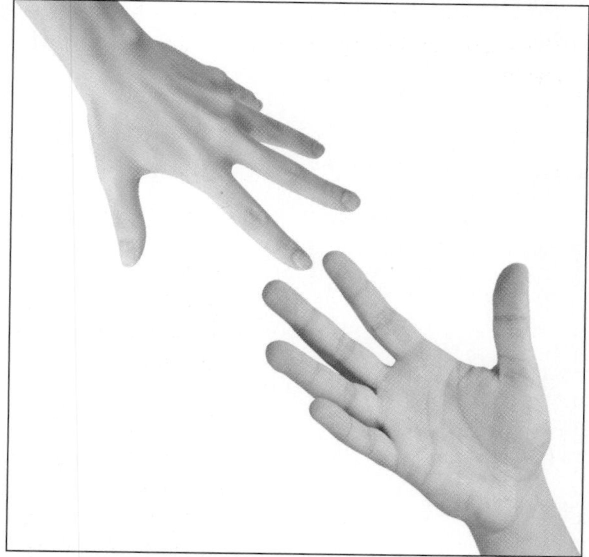

Public assistance: a hand in time of need or an incentive not to work?

ECONOMICS IN THE REAL WORLD

How Incentives Create Unintended Consequences

Let's look at an example of how incentives operate in the real world and how they can lead to consequences no one envisioned when implementing them. Two Australian researchers noted a large spike in births on July 1, 2004, shown in Figure 1.1. The sudden spike was not an accident. Australia, like many other developed countries, has seen the fertility rate fall below replacement levels, which is the birthrate necessary to keep the population from declining. In response to falling birthrates, the Australian government decided to enact a "baby bonus" of $3,000 for all babies born on or after July 1, 2004. (One Australian dollar equals roughly one U.S. dollar.)

The policy was designed to provide a direct incentive for couples to have children and, in part, to compensate them for lost pay and the added costs of raising a newborn. However, this direct incentive had an indirect incentive attached to it, too—the couples found a way to delay the birth of their children until after July 1, perhaps jeopardizing the health of both the infants and the mothers. This was clearly an unintended consequence. Despite reassurances from the government that would-be parents would not put financial gain over the welfare of their newborns, over 1,000 births were switched from late June to early July through a combination of additional bed rest and push-

FIGURE 1.1

Australian Births by Week in 2004

The plunge and spike in births are evidence of an unintended consequence.

Source: See Joshua S. Gans and Andrew Leigh, "Born on the First of July: An (un)natural experiment in birth timing," *Journal of Public Economics* 93 (2009): 246–263.

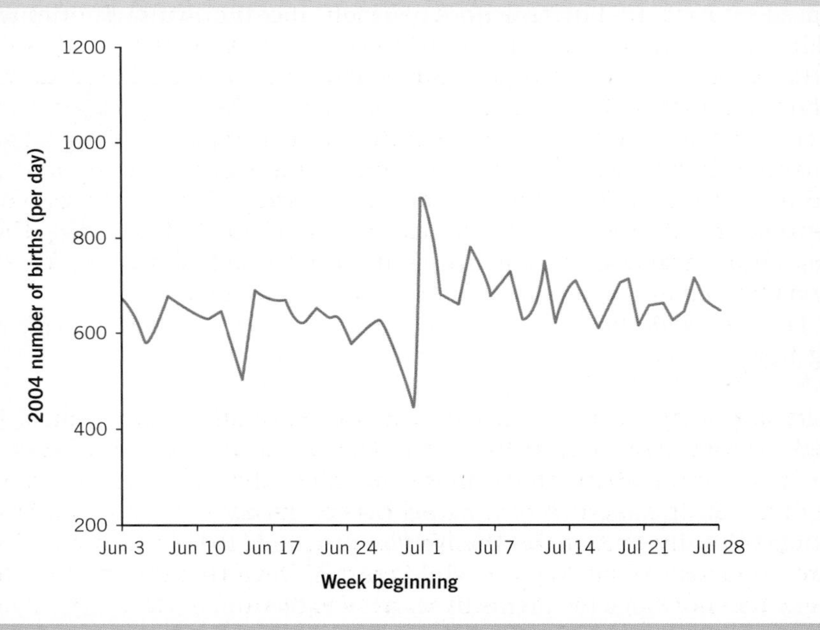

ing scheduled caesarian sections back a few days. This behavior is testament to the power of incentives.

On a much smaller scale, the same dynamic exists in the United States around January 1 each year. Parents can claim a tax credit for the entire year, whether the child is born in January or in December. This gives parents an incentive to ask for labor to be induced or for a caesarian section to be performed late in December so they can have their child before January 1 and thereby capitalize on the tax advantages. Ironically, hospitals and newspapers often celebrate the arrival of the first baby of the new year even though his or her parents might actually be financially worse off because of the infant's January 1 birthday. ✳

Incentives and Innovation

Incentives also play a vital role in innovation, the engine of economic growth. There is no better example than Steve Jobs and Apple: between them, he and the company he founded held over 300 patents at the time of his death in 2011.

In the United States, the patent system and copyright laws guarantee inventors a specific period of time in which they can exclusively sell their work. This system encourages innovation by creating a powerful financial reward for creativity. Without patents and copyright laws, inventors would bear all the costs, and almost none of the rewards, for their efforts. Why would firms invest in research and development or artists create new music if others could immediately copy and sell their work? To reward the perspiration and inspiration required for innovation, society needs patents and copyrights to create the right incentives for economic growth.

In recent years, new forms of technology have made the illegal sharing of copyrighted material quite easy. As a result, illegal downloads of music and movies are widespread. When musicians, actors, and studios cannot effectively protect what they have created, they earn less. So illegal downloads reduce the incentive to produce new content. Will the next John Lennon or Jay-Z work so hard? Will the next Dan Brown or J. K. Rowling hone their writing craft so diligently if there is so much less financial reward for success? Is the "I want it for free" culture causing the truly gifted to be less committed to their craft, thus depriving society of excellence? Maintaining the right rewards, or incentives, for hard work and innovation is essential for advancing our society.

Incentives Are Everywhere

There are many sides to incentives. However, financial gain almost always plays a prominent role. In the film *All the President's Men*, the story of the Watergate scandal that led to the unraveling of the Nixon administration in the early 1970s, a secret source called "Deep Throat" tells Bob Woodward, an investigative reporter at the *Washington Post*, to "follow the money." Woodward responds, "What do you mean? Where?" Deep Throat responds, "Just . . . follow the money." That is exactly what Woodward did. He eventually pieced everything together and followed the "money" trail all the way to President Nixon.

ECONOMICS IN THE MEDIA

Incentives

Ferris Bueller's Day Off

Many people believe that the study of economics is boring. In *Ferris Bueller's Day Off* (1986), Ben Stein plays a high school economics teacher who sedates his class with a monotone voice while referring to many abstract economic theories and uttering the unforgettable "Anyone, anyone?" while trying to engage his students. The scene is iconic because it is a boring economics lecture that inspires Ferris and his friends to skip school, which leads to his wild adventures. In fact, the movie is really about incentives and trade-offs.

Was this your first impression of economics?

Understanding the incentives that caused the participants in the Watergate scandal to do what they did led Bob Woodward to the truth. Economists use the same process to explain how people make decisions, how firms operate, and how the economy functions. In fact, understanding incentives, from positive to negative and direct to indirect, is the key to understanding economics. If you remember only one concept from this course, it should be that incentives matter!

Trade-offs

Trade-offs

In a world of scarcity, each and every decision incurs a cost. Even time is a scarce resource; after all, there are only 24 hours in a day. So deciding to read one of the Harry Potter books now means that you won't be able to read one of the Twilight books until later. More generally, doing one thing often means that you will not have the time, resources, or energy to do something else. Similarly, paying for a college education can require spending tens of thousands of dollars that might be used elsewhere instead.

Trade-offs are an important part of policy decisions. For instance, one decision that some governments face is the trade-off between a clean environment and a higher level of income for its citizens. Transportation and industry cause air pollution. Developed nations can afford expensive technology that reduces pollution-causing emissions. But developing nations, like China, generally have to focus their resources elsewhere. In the months leading up to the 2008 Olympics, China temporarily shut down many factories and discouraged the use of automobiles in order to reduce smog in Beijing. The air improved, and the Olympics showcased China's remarkable growth into a global economic powerhouse. However, the cost of keeping the air clean—shutting down factories and restricting transportation—was not a trade-off China is willing to make for longer than a few weeks. The Chinese people, like the rest of us, want clean air *and* a high standard of living, but for the time being most Chinese seem willing to accept increased pollution if it means the potential for a higher level of income. In more developed countries, higher standards of living already exist, and the cost of pollution control will not cause the economy's growth to slow down to unacceptable levels. People in these countries are much less likely to accept more pollution in order to raise the level of income even further.

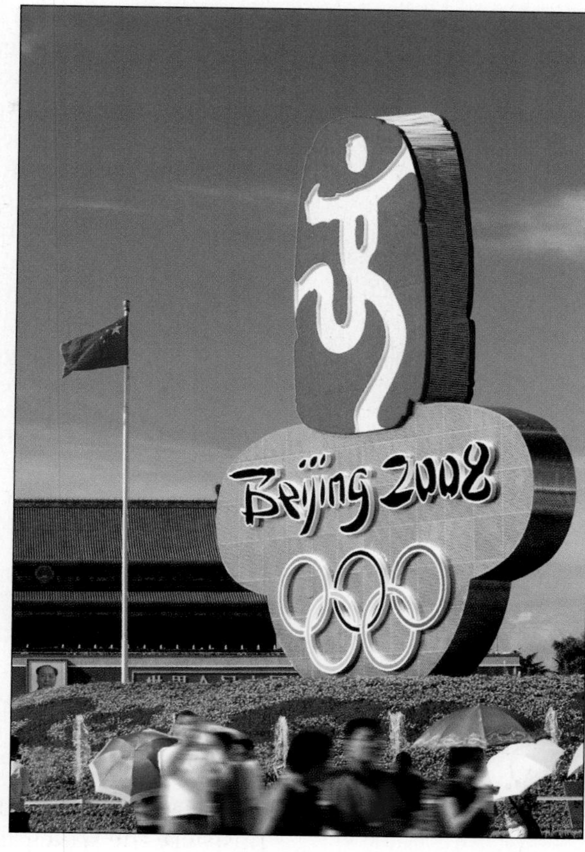

Would you choose clean air or economic prosperity?

Opportunity Cost

The existence of trade-offs requires making hard decisions. Choosing one thing means giving up something else. Suppose that you receive two invitations—the first to spend the day hiking, and the second to go to a concert—and both events occur at the same time. No matter which event you choose, you will have to sacrifice the other option. In this example, you can think of the cost of going to the concert as the lost opportunity to be on the hike. Likewise, the cost of going hiking is the lost opportunity to go to the concert. No matter what choice you make, there is an *opportunity cost*, or next-best alternative, that must be sacrificed. **Opportunity cost** is the highest-valued alternative that must be sacrificed in order to get something else.

Opportunity cost

Opportunity cost is the highest-valued alternative that must be sacrificed in order to get something else.

Every time we make a choice, we experience an opportunity cost. The key to making the best possible decision is to minimize your opportunity cost by selecting the option that gives you the largest benefit. If you prefer going to a concert, you should go to the concert. What you give up, the hike, has less value to you than the concert; so it has a lower opportunity cost.

The hiking/concert choice is a simple and clear example of opportunity cost. Usually, it takes deliberate effort to see the world through the opportunity-cost prism. But it is a worthwhile practice because it will help you make better decisions. For example, imagine you are a small-business owner. Your financial officer informs you that you have had a successful year and made a sizable profit. So everything is good, right? Not so fast. An economist will tell you to ask yourself, "Could I have made *more* profit doing something differently?" Good economic thinkers ask this question of themselves all the time. "Could I be using my time, talents, or energy on another activity that would be even more profitable for me?"

Do you have the moves like Jagger?

Profits on an income statement are only part of the story, because they only measure how well a business does relative to the bottom line. Accountants cannot measure what *might* have been better. For example, suppose that your business had decided against an opportunity to open a new store. A few months later, a rival opened a very successful store in the same location you had considered. Your profits were good for the year, but if you had made the investment in the new store, your profits could have been even better. So when economists mention opportunity cost, they are assessing whether the alternatives are better than what you are currently doing, which considers a larger set of possible outcomes.

Mick Jagger did just that. Before joining the Rolling Stones, he had been attending the London School of Economics. For Mick, the opportunity cost of becoming a musician was forgoing a degree in economics. Given the success of the Rolling Stones, it is hard to fault his decision!

PRACTICE WHAT YOU KNOW

The Opportunity Cost of Attending College

Question: What is the opportunity cost of attending college?

Answer: When people think about the cost of attending college, they usually think of tuition, room and board, textbooks, and travel-related expenses. While those expenses are indeed a part of going to college, they are not its full opportunity cost. The opportunity cost is the next-best alternative that is sacrificed. This means that the opportunity cost—or what you potentially could have done if you were not in college—includes the lost income you could have earned working a full-time job. If you take the cost of attending college plus the forgone income lost while in college, it is a very expensive proposition. Setting aside the question of how much more you might have to pay for room and board at college rather than elsewhere, consider the costs of tuition and books. Those fees can be $40,000 or more at many of the nation's most expensive colleges. Add those out-of-pocket expenses to the forgone income from a full-time job that might pay $40,000, and your four years in college can easily cost over a quarter of a million dollars.

Spending thousands on college expenses? You could be working instead!

ECONOMICS IN THE REAL WORLD

Breaking the Curse of the Bambino: How Opportunity Cost Causes a Drop in Hospital Visits While the Red Sox Play

If you are injured or severely ill, you head straight to the emergency room, right? Not so fast! A 2005 study published in the *Annals of Emergency Medicine* found that visits to the ER in the Boston area fell by as much as 15% when the Red Sox were playing games in the 2004 playoffs. Part of the decline is attributable to more people sitting inside at home—presumably watching the ballgame—instead of engaging in activities that might get them hurt. But the study was able to determine that this did not explain the entire decline in emergency room visits. It turns out that a surprising number of people are willing to put off seeking medical attention for a few hours. Apparently, for some people the opportunity cost of seeking medical attention is high enough to postpone care until after the Red Sox game. ✳

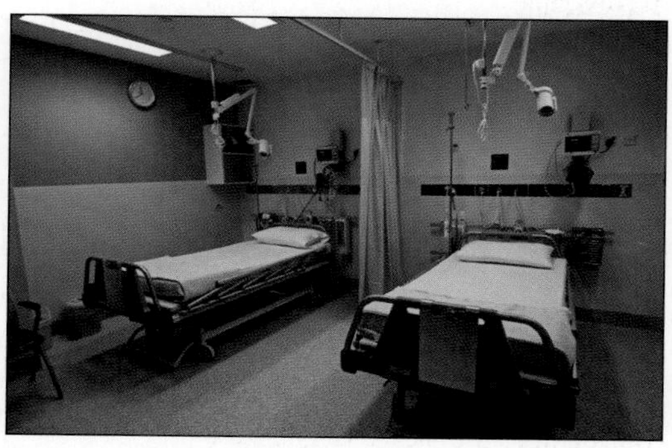

Emergency room beds are empty. Are the Sox playing?

Marginal Thinking

Marginal thinking

The process of systematically evaluating a course of action is referred to as *economic thinking*. **Economic thinking** involves a purposeful evaluation of the available opportunities to make the best decision possible. In this context, economic thinkers use a process called *marginal analysis* to break down decisions into smaller parts. Often, the choice is not between doing and not doing something, but between doing more or less of something. For instance, if you take on a part-time job while in school, you probably wrestle with the question of how many hours to work. If you work a little more, you can earn additional income. If you work a little less, you have more time to study. Working more has a tangible benefit (more money) and a tangible cost (poor grades). All of this should sound familiar from our earlier discussion about trade-offs. The work-study trade-off affects how much money you have and what kind of grades you make.

Economic thinking requires a purposeful evaluation of the available opportunities to make the best decision possible.

An economist would say that your decision—weighing how much money you want against the grades you want—is a decision at the *margin*. What exactly does the word "margin" mean? There are many different definitions. To a reader, the margin is the blank space bordering a page. A "margin" can also be thought of as the size of a victory. In economics, **marginal thinking** requires decision-makers to evaluate whether the benefit of one more unit of something is greater than its cost. This can be quite challenging, but understanding how to analyze decisions at the margin is essential to becoming a good economist.

Marginal thinking requires decision-makers to evaluate whether the benefit of one more unit of something is greater than its cost.

For example, have you ever wondered why people straighten their places, vacuum, dust, scrub the bathrooms, clean out their garages, and wash their windows, but leave the dust bunnies under the refrigerator? The answer lies in thinking at the margin. Moving the refrigerator out from the wall to clean requires a significant effort for a small benefit. Guests who enter the kitchen can't see under the refrigerator. So most of us ignore the dust bunnies and just clean the visible areas of our homes. In other words, when economists say that you should think at the margin, what they really mean is that people weigh the costs and benefits of their actions and choose to do the things with the greatest payoff. For most of us, that means being willing to live with dust bunnies. The *marginal cost* of cleaning under the refrigerator (or on top of the cabinets, or even behind the sofa cushions) is too high and the added value of making the effort, or the *marginal benefit,* is too low to justify the additional cleaning.

ECONOMICS IN THE REAL WORLD

Why Buying and Selling Your Textbooks Benefits You at the Margin

New textbooks are expensive. The typical textbook purchasing pattern works as follows: you buy a textbook at the start of the term, often at full price, and sell it back at the end of the term for half the price you paid. Ouch. Nobody likes to make a bad investment, and textbooks depreciate the moment that students buy them. Even non-economists know not to buy high and sell low—but that is the textbook cycle for most students.

One solution would be to avoid buying textbooks in the first place. But that is not practical, nor is it a good decision. To understand why, let's use marginal analysis to break the decision into two separate components: the decision to buy and the decision to resell.

Let's start with the decision to buy. A rational buyer will only purchase a textbook if the expected value of the information included in the book is greater than the cost. For instance, say the book contains mandatory assignments or information that is useful for your major and you decide that it is worth \$200 to you. If you are able to purchase the book for \$100, the gain from buying the textbook would be \$100. But what if the book is supplemental reading and you think it is worth only \$50? If you value the book at \$50 and it costs \$100, purchasing the book would entail a \$50 loss. If students only buy the books from which they receive gains, every textbook bought will increase the welfare of someone.

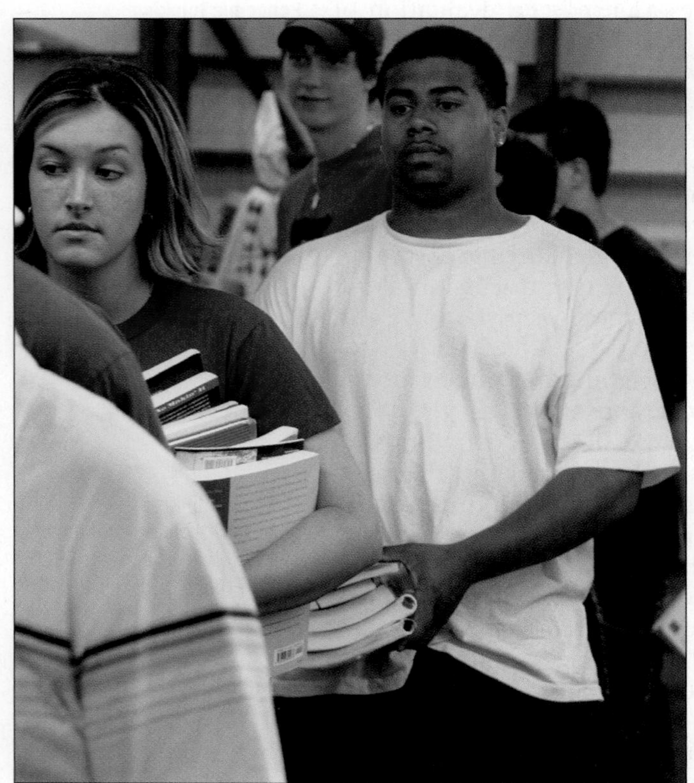

Why do students buy and sell textbooks?

A similar logic applies to the resale of textbooks. At the end of the course, once you have learned the information inside the book, the value of hanging on to it is low. You might think it is worth \$20 to keep the textbook for future reference, but if you can sell it for \$50, the difference represents a gain of \$30. In this case, you would decide to sell.

We have seen that buying and selling are two separate decisions made at the margin. If you combine these two decisions and argue that the purchase price (\$100) and resale price (\$50) are related, as most students typically think they are, you will arrive at a faulty conclusion that you have made a poor decision. That is simply not true.

Textbooks may not be cheap, but they create value twice—once when bought and again when sold. This is a win-win outcome. Since we assume that decision-makers will not make choices that leave them worse off, the only way to explain why students buy textbooks and sell them again later is because the students benefit at the margin from both sides of the transaction. ✷

Trade

Trade creates value

Imagine trying to find food in a world without grocery stores. The task of getting what you need to eat each day would require visiting many separate locations. Traditionally, this need to bring buyers and sellers together was met by weekly markets, or bazaars, in central locations like town squares. **Markets** bring buyers and sellers together to exchange goods and services. As commerce spread throughout the ancient world, trade routes developed. Markets grew from infrequent gatherings, where exchange involved trading goods and services for other goods and services, into more sophisticated systems that use cash, credit, and other financial instruments. Today, when we think of markets we often think of eBay or Craigslist, where goods can be transferred from one person to another with the click of a mouse. For instance, if you want to find a rare DVD of season 1 of *Entourage*, there is no better place to look than eBay, which allows users to search for just about any product, bid on it, and then have it sent directly to their homes.

Markets
bring buyers and sellers together to exchange goods and services.

Trade is the voluntary exchange of goods and services between two or more parties. Voluntary trade among rational individuals creates value for everyone involved. Imagine you are on your way home from class and you want to pick up a gallon of milk. You know that milk will be more expensive at a convenience store than it will be at the grocery store five miles away, but you are in a hurry to study for your economics exam and are willing to pay up to $5.00 for the convenience of getting it quickly. At the store, you find that the price is $4.00 and you happily purchase the milk. This ability to buy for less than the price you are willing to pay provides a positive incentive to make the purchase. But what about the seller? If the store owner paid $3.00 to buy the milk from a supplier, and you are willing to pay the $4.00 price that he has set in order to make a profit, the store owner has an incentive to sell. This simple voluntary transaction has made both sides better off.

Trade
is the voluntary exchange of goods and services between two or more parties.

By fostering the exchange of goods, trade helps to create additional growth through specialization. **Comparative advantage** refers to the situation in which an individual, business, or country can produce at a lower opportunity cost than a competitor can. Comparative advantage harnesses the power of specialization. As a result, it is possible to be a physician, teacher, or plumber and not worry about how to do everything yourself. The physician becomes proficient at dispensing medical advice, the teacher at helping students, and the plumber at fixing leaks. The physician and the teacher call the plumber when they need work on their plumbing. The teacher and the plumber see the doctor when they are sick. The physician and the plumber send their children to school to learn from the teacher. On a broader scale, this type of trading of services increases the welfare of everyone in society. Trade creates gains for everyone involved.

Comparative advantage
refers to the situation where an individual, business, or country can produce at a lower opportunity cost than a competitor can.

Our economy depends on specialization.

The same process is at work among businesses. For instance, Starbucks specializes in making coffee and Honda makes automobiles. You would not want to get your morning cup of joe at Honda any more than you would want to buy a car from Starbucks!

Specialization exists at the country level as well. Some countries have highly developed workforces capable of managing and solving complex processes. Other countries have large pools of relatively unskilled labor. As a result, businesses that need skilled labor gravitate to countries where they can easily find the workers they need. Likewise, firms with production processes that rely on unskilled labor look for employees in less-developed countries. By harnessing the power of increased specialization, global companies and economies create value through increased production and growth.

However, globalized trade is not without controversy. When goods and jobs are free to move across borders, not everyone benefits equally. Consider the case of an American worker who loses her job when her position is outsourced to a call center in India. The jobless worker now has to find new employment—a process that will require significant time and energy. In contrast, the new position in the call center in India provides a job and an income that improve the life of another worker. Also, the American firm enjoys the advantage of being able to hire lower-cost labor elsewhere. The firm's lower costs often translate into lower prices for domestic consumers. None of those advantages make the outsourcing of jobs any less painful for affected workers, but it is an important component of economic growth in the long run.

Conclusion

Is economics the dismal science?

We began this chapter by discussing this misconception. Now that you have begun your exploration of economics, you know that this is not true. Economists ask, and answer, big questions about life. This is what makes the study of economics so fascinating. Understanding how an entire economy operates and functions may seem like a daunting task, but it is not nearly as hard as it sounds. If you remember the first time you drove a car, the process is similar. When you are learning to drive, everything seems difficult and unfamiliar. Learning economics is the same way. However, once you learn a few key principles, and practice them, you can become a good driver quite quickly. In the next chapter, we will use the ideas developed here to explore the issue of trade in greater depth.

SNAPSHOT

The Foundations of Economics

There are five foundations of economics—incentives, trade-offs, opportunity cost, marginal thinking, and the principle that trade creates value. Once you have mastered these five concepts, even complex economic processes can be reduced to smaller, more easily understood parts. If you keep these foundations in mind, you'll find that understanding economics is rewarding and fun.

OPPORTUNITY COST

INCENTIVES

In making a decision, you respond to incentives—factors that motivate you to act or to exert effort. Incentives also play a vital role in innovation, the engine of economic growth.

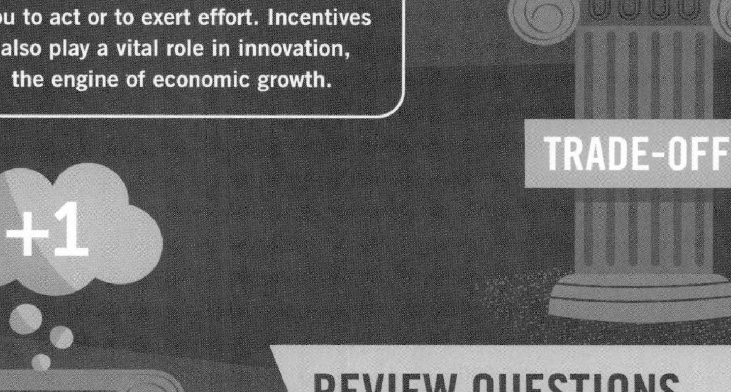

TRADE-OFFS

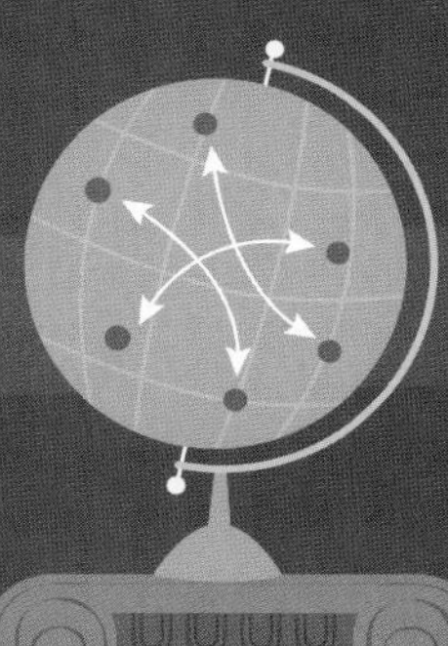

TRADE CREATES VALUE

MARGINAL THINKING

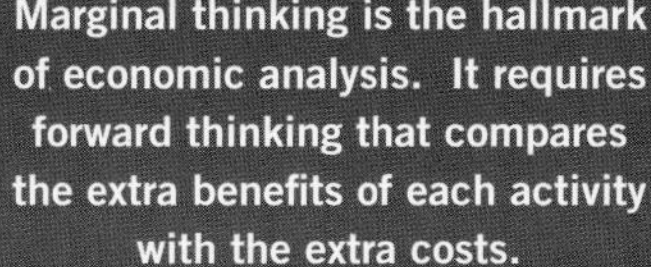

Marginal thinking is the hallmark of economic analysis. It requires forward thinking that compares the extra benefits of each activity with the extra costs.

REVIEW QUESTIONS

- Which of the five foundations explains what you give up when you choose to buy a new pair of shoes instead of attending a concert?
- What are four types of incentives discussed in the chapter? Why do incentives sometimes create unintended consequences?

ECONOMICS FOR LIFE

Midcareer Earnings by Selected Majors

A 2012 study by PayScale surveyed full-time employees across the United States who possessed a bachelor's degree but no advanced degree. Twenty popular subjects are listed in the graph below.

Not all majors are created equal. However, the majors that produce more income initially do not necessarily keep their advantage a decade or two later. That means that today's newly minted economics majors, with a median starting salary of $48,500, will likely surpass those who majored in civil engineering in earnings by the time they reach midcareer. The same holds true for political science majors, who have a lower starting salary than business majors but eventually surpass them. In the long run, pay growth matters to income level as much as, if not more than, starting salary. In terms of salary, any decision about what to major in that only looks at starting pay is misleading. How much you make over your whole career is what matters!

Will you make more by majoring in economics or finance?

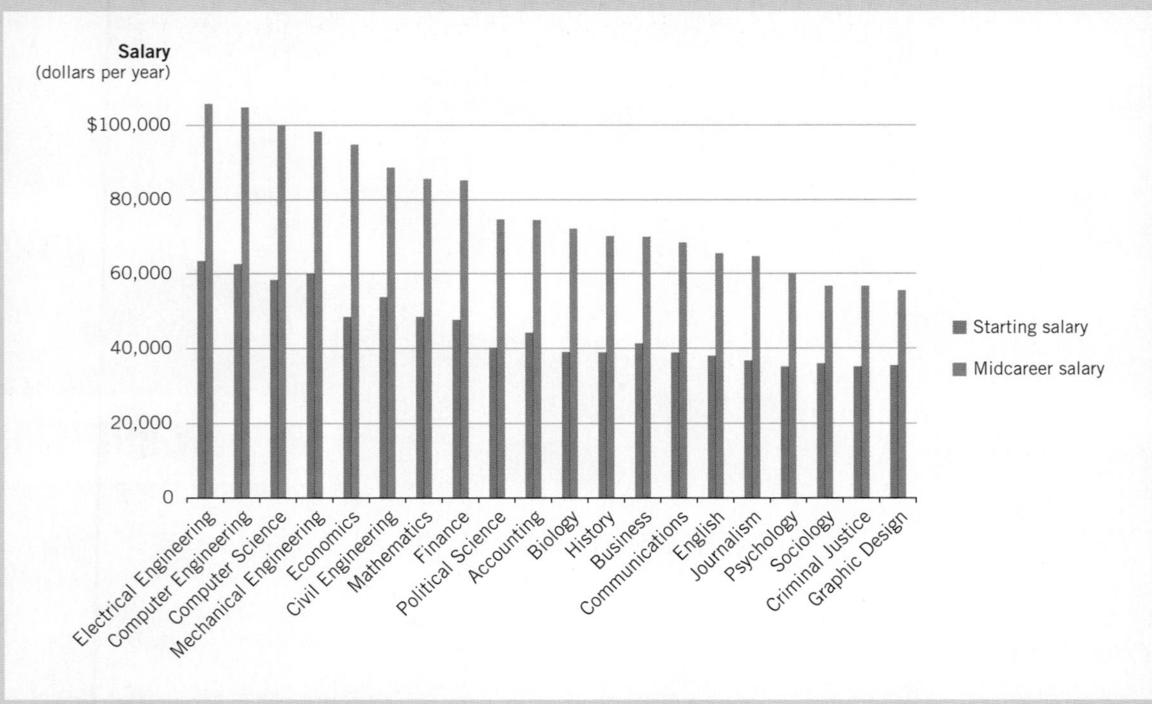

ANSWERING THE BIG QUESTIONS

What is economics?

* Economics is the study of how people allocate their limited resources to satisfy their nearly unlimited wants. Because of the limited nature of society's resources, even the most abundant resources are not always plentiful enough everywhere to meet the wants and needs of every person. So how do individuals and societies make decisions about how to use the scarce resources at our disposal? This is the basic question economists seek to answer.

What are the five foundations of economics?

The five foundations of economics are: incentives; trade-offs; opportunity cost; marginal thinking; and the principle that trade creates value.

* Incentives matter because they help economists explain how decisions are made.
* Trade-offs exist when a decision-maker has to choose a course of action.
* Each time we make a choice, we experience an opportunity cost, or a lost chance to do something else.
* Marginal thinking requires a decision-maker to weigh the extra benefits against the extra costs.
* Trade creates value because participants in markets are able to specialize in the production of goods and services that they have a comparative advantage in making.

CONCEPTS YOU SHOULD KNOW

comparative advantage (p. 17)
economics (p. 6)
economic thinking (p. 15)
incentives (p. 7)
macroeconomics (p. 7)
marginal thinking (p. 15)
markets (p. 17)
microeconomics (p. 7)
opportunity cost (p. 13)
scarcity (p. 6)
trade (p. 17)

QUESTIONS FOR REVIEW

1. How would you respond if your instructor gave daily quizzes on the course readings? Is this a positive or a negative incentive?
2. Explain why many seniors often earn lower grades in their last semester before graduation. Hint: this is an incentive problem.
3. What is the opportunity cost of reading this textbook?
4. Evaluate the following statement: "Trade is like football: one team wins and the other loses."
5. Give a personal example of how pursuing your self-interest has made society better off.

STUDY PROBLEMS (✱ *solved at the end of the section*)

✱ 1. What role do incentives play in each of the following situations?
   a. You learn that you can resell a ticket to next week's homecoming game for twice what you paid.
   b. A state government announces a "sales tax holiday" for back-to-school shopping during one week each August.

2. Compare your standard of living with that of your parents when they were the same age as you are now. Ask them or somebody you know around their age to recall where they were living and what they owned. What has happened to the average standard of living over the last 25 years? Explain your answer.

3. By referencing events in the news or something from your personal experiences, describe one example of each of the five foundations of economics.

✱ 4. Suppose that Colombia is good at growing coffee but not very good at making computer software, and that Canada is good at making computer software but not very good at growing coffee. If Colombia decided to grow only coffee and Canada only made computer software, would both countries be better or worse off? Can you think of a similar example from your life?

5. After some consideration, you decide to hire someone to help you move. Wouldn't it be cheaper to move yourself? Do you think this is a rational choice? Explain your response.

✱ 6. The website ultrinsic.com has developed an "***ult***erior motive that causes the person to have an int***rinsic*** love of knowledge." At Ultrinsic, students pay a small entry fee to compete in grades-based contests for cash prizes. Suppose that 20 students from your economics class each pay $20 to enter a grades-based contest. This would create a $400 prize pool. An equal share of the $400 pot is awarded at the end of the term to each contestant who earns an A in the course. If four students earn A's, they each receive $100. If only one student earns an A, that person gets the entire $400 pot. What economic concept is Ultrinsic harnessing in order to encourage participants to learn more?

SOLVED PROBLEMS

1.a. Since your tickets are worth more than you paid for them, you have a direct positive incentive to resell them.

b. The "sales tax holiday" is a direct positive incentive to buy more clothes during the back-to-school period. An unintended consequence of this policy is that fewer purchases are likely to be made both before and after the tax holiday.

4. If Colombia decided to specialize in the production of coffee, it could trade coffee to Canada in exchange for computer software. This process illustrates gains from specialization and trade. Both countries have a comparative advantage in producing one particular good. Colombia has ideal coffee-growing conditions, and Canada has a workforce that is more adept at writing software. Since each country specializes in what it does best, they are able to produce more value than what they could produce by trying to make both products on their own.

6. Ultrinsic is using the power of incentives to motivate learning. Earning a letter grade is a positive motivation to do well, or a penalty—or negative incentive—when you do poorly. Ultrinsic takes this one step further, as the student who earns an A also receives a small cash payment—a positive incentive. This provides extra motivation to study hard and achieve an A, since it pays, as opposed to earning a B or lower.

CHAPTER

2

Model Building and Gains from Trade

MISCONCEPTION

Trade always results in winners and losers.

When most people think of trade, they think of it as a zero-sum game. For instance, suppose that you and your friends are playing Magic. Players collect cards with special powers in order to assemble decks to play the game. Magic players love to trade their cards, and it is often the case that novice players do not know which cards are the most powerful or rare. When someone swaps one of the desirable cards, the other player is probably getting a much better deal. In other words, there is a winner and a loser. Now think of international trade. Many people believe that rich countries exploit the natural resources of poor countries and even steal their most talented workers. In this view, the rich countries are winners and the poor countries are losers. Still others think of trade as the redistribution of goods. If you trade your kayak for a friend's bicycle, no new goods are created; so how can this possibly create value? After all, someone must have come out ahead in the trade.

In this chapter, we will see that trade is not an imbalanced equation of winners and losers. To help us understand trade, the discussion will make a number of simplifying assumptions. We will also consider how economists use the scientific method to help explain the world we live in. These foundations will serve as the tools we need to explore the more nuanced reasons why trade creates value.

Jace, Memory Adept
3
Planeswalker — Jace
+1: Draw a card. Target player puts the top card of his or her library into his or her graveyard.
0: Target player puts the top ten cards of his or her library into his or her graveyard.
-7: Any number of target players each draw twenty cards.
4
D. Alexander Gregory
™ & © 1993–2012 Wizards of the Coast LLC 56/249
Chandra, the Firebrand
3
Planeswalker — Chandra
+1: Chandra, the Firebrand deals 1 damage to target creature or player.
-2: When you cast your next instant or sorcery spell this turn, copy that spell. You may choose new targets for the copy.
-6: Chandra, the Firebrand deals 6 damage to each of up to six target creatures and/or players.
3
D. Alexander Gregory
™ & © 1993–2012 Wizards of the Coast LLC 123/249
Garruk, Primal Hunter
2
Planeswalker — Garruk
+1: Put a 3/3 green Beast creature token onto the battlefield.
-3: Draw cards equal to the greatest power among creatures you control.
-6: Put a 6/6 green Wurm creature token onto the battlefield for each land you control.
3
D. Alexander Gregory
™ & © 1993–2012 Wizards of the Coast LLC 174/249
Ajani, Caller of the Pride
1
Planeswalker — Ajani
+1: Put a +1/+1 counter on up to one target creature.
-3: Target creature gains flying and double strike until end of turn.
-8: Put X 2/2 white Cat creature tokens onto the battlefield, where X is your life total.
4
D. Alexander Gregory
™ & © 1993–2012 Wizards of the Coast LLC 1/249

Trade is vital to Magic players, and vital to the economy.

BIG QUESTIONS

* How do economists study the economy?
* What is a production possibilities frontier?
* What are the benefits of specialization and trade?
* What is the trade-off between having more now and having more later?

How Do Economists Study the Economy?

Economics is a social science that uses the scientific method. This is accomplished by the use of economic models that focus on specific relationships in the economy. In order to create these models, economists make many simplifying assumptions. This approach helps identify the key relationships that drive the economic decisions that we are interested in exploring. In this section, you will begin to learn about how economists approach their discipline and the tools they use.

The Scientific Method in Economics

On the television show *MythBusters*, popular myths are put to the test by Jamie Hyneman and Adam Savage. In Savage's words, "We replicate the circumstances, then duplicate the results." The entire show is dedicated to scientifically testing the myths. At the end of each episode, the myth is confirmed, labeled plausible, or busted. For instance, during a memorable episode Hyneman and Savage explored the reasons behind the *Hindenburg* disaster. The *Hindenburg* was a German passenger airship, or zeppelin, that caught fire and was destroyed as it attempted to dock in New Jersey on May 6, 1937. Thirty-six people died during the disaster.

Some people have hypothesized that the painted fabric used to wrap the zeppelin sparked the fire. Others have claimed that the hydrogen used to give the airship lift was the primary cause of the disaster. To test the hypothesis that the potentially incendiary paint used on the fabric was to blame, Hyneman and Savage built two small-scale models. The first model was filled with hydrogen and had a nonflammable skin; the second model used a replica of the original fabric for the skin but did not contain any hydrogen. Hyneman and Savage then compared the burn times of their models with the original footage of the disaster.

After examining the results, they determined that the myth of the incendiary paint was "busted"; the model containing the hydrogen burned twice as fast as the one with just the painted fabric skin.

Economists work in much the same way: they use the scientific method to answer questions about observable phenomena and to explain how the world works. The scientific method consists of several steps. First, researchers observe a phenomenon that interests them. Based on these observations, they develop a hypothesis, which is an explanation for the phenomenon. Then, they construct a model to test the hypothesis. Finally, they design experiments to test how well the model (which is based on the hypothesis) works. After collecting the data from the experiments, they can verify, revise, or refute the hypothesis. After many tests, they may agree that the hypothesis is well supported enough to qualify as a theory. Or, they may determine that it is not supported by the evidence and that they must continue searching for a theory to explain the phenomenon.

The scientific method was used to discover why the *Hindenburg* caught fire.

The economist's laboratory is the world around us, and it ranges from the economy as a whole to the decisions made by firms and individuals. As a result, economists cannot always design experiments to test their hypotheses. Often, they must gather historical data or wait for real-world events to take place—for example, the Great Recession of 2008–2009—in order to better understand the economy.

Positive and Normative Analysis

As scientists, economists strive to approach their subject with objectivity. This means that they rigorously avoid letting personal beliefs and values influence the outcome of their analysis. In order to be as objective as possible, economists deploy positive analysis. A **positive statement** can be tested and validated. Each positive statement can be thought of as a description of "what is." For instance, the statement "the unemployment rate is 7.0%" is a positive statement because it can be tested by gathering data. In contrast, a **normative statement** cannot be tested or validated; it is about "what ought to be." For instance, the statement "an unemployed worker should receive financial assistance to help make ends meet" is a matter of opinion. One can reasonably argue that financial assistance to the unemployed is beneficial for society as a whole because it helps eliminate poverty. However, many would argue that financial assistance to the unemployed provides the wrong incentives. If the financial assistance provides enough to meet basic needs, workers may end up spending more time remaining unemployed than they otherwise would. Neither opinion is right or wrong; they are differing viewpoints based on values, beliefs, and opinions.

A **positive statement** can be tested and validated; it describes "what is."

A **normative statement** is an opinion that cannot be tested or validated; it describes "what ought to be."

Economists are concerned with positive analysis. In contrast, normative statements are the realm of policy-makers, voters, and philosophers. For example, if the unemployment rate rises, economists try to understand the conditions that created the situation. Economics does not attempt to determine who should receive unemployment assistance, which involves normative analysis. Economics, done properly, is confined to positive analysis.

Economic Models

Thinking like an economist means learning how to analyze complex issues and problems. Many economic topics, such as international trade, Social Security, job loss, and inflation, are complicated. To analyze these phenomena and to determine the effect of various policy options related to them, economists use models, or simplified versions of reality. Models help us analyze the component parts of the economy.

The Wright brothers' wind tunnel

A good model should be simple to understand, flexible in design, and able to make powerful predictions. Let's consider one of the most famous models in history, designed by Wilbur and Orville Wright. Before the Wright brothers made their famous first flight in 1903, they built a small wind tunnel out of a six-foot-long wooden box. Inside the box they placed an aerodynamic measuring device, and at one end they attached a small fan to supply the wind. The brothers then tested over 200 different wing configurations to determine the lifting properties of each design. Using the data on aerodynamics they collected, the Wright brothers were able to determine the best type of wing to use on their aircraft.

Similarly, economic models provide frameworks that enable us to predict the effect that changes in prices, production processes, and government policies have on real-life behavior.

Ceteris Paribus

Using a controlled setting that held many other variables constant enabled the Wright brothers to experiment with different wing designs. By altering only a single element—for example, the angle of the wing—they could test whether the change in design was advantageous. The process of examining a change in one variable while holding everything else constant involves a concept known as ***ceteris paribus***, from the Latin meaning "other things being equal." This idea is central to model building. If the Wright brothers had changed many variables simultaneously and found that the wing worked better, they would have had no way of knowing which change was responsible for the improved performance. For this reason, engineers generally modify only one element at a time and test only that one element before moving on to test additional elements.

Ceteris paribus is the concept under which economists examine a change in one variable while holding everything else constant.

Like the Wright brothers, economists start with a simplified version of reality. Economists build models, change one variable at a time, and ask whether the change in the variable had a positive or negative impact on performance. Perhaps the best-known economic model is supply and demand, which economists use to explain how markets function. We'll get to supply and demand in Chapter 3.

Endogenous versus Exogenous Factors

Models must account for factors that we can control and factors that we can't. The Wright brothers' wind tunnel was critical to their success because it enabled them to control for as many *endogenous factors* as possible before attempting to fly. Factors that we know about and can control are **endogenous factors**. For example, the wind tunnel enabled the Wright brothers to see how well each wing design—an important part of the model—performed under controlled conditions.

Endogenous factors are the variables that can be controlled for in a model.

Once the Wright brothers had determined the best wing design, they built the full-scale airplane that took flight at Kitty Hawk, North Carolina. At that point the plane, known as the "Flyer," was no longer in a controlled environment. It was subject to the gusting wind and other *exogenous factors* that made the first flight so challenging. Factors beyond our control—outside the model—are known as **exogenous factors**.

Exogenous factors are the variables that cannot be controlled for in a model.

Building an economic model is very similar to the process Wilbur and Orville used. We need to be mindful of three factors: (1) what we include in the model, (2) the assumptions we make when choosing what to include in the model, and (3) the outside conditions that can affect our model's performance. In the case of the first airplane, the design was an endogenous factor because it was within the Wright brothers' control. In contrast, the weather (wind, air pressure, and other atmospheric conditions) was an exogenous factor because it was something that the Wright brothers could not control. Because the world is a complex place, an airplane model that flies perfectly in a wind tunnel may not fly reliably once it is exposed to the elements. Therefore, if we add more exogenous variables, or factors we cannot control—for example, wind and rain—to test our model's performance, the test becomes more realistic.

The Danger of Faulty Assumptions

In every model, we make certain choices about which variables to include and how to model them. Ideally, we would like to include all the important variables inside the model and exclude all the variables that should be ignored.

However, no matter what we include, using a model that contains faulty assumptions can lead to spectacular policy failures. There is no better example than the financial crisis and Great Recession that began in December 2007.

In the years leading up to the crisis, banks sold and repackaged mortgage-backed securities under the faulty assumption that real estate prices would always rise. (Mortgage-backed securities are investments that are backed by the underlying value of a bundle of mortgages.) In fact, the computer models used by many of the banks did not even have a variable for declining real estate prices. Investors around the globe bought these securities because they thought they were safe. This sounded perfectly reasonable in a world where real estate prices were rising on an annual basis. Unfortunately, that assumption turned out to be false. From 2006 to 2008, real estate prices fell. Because of one faulty assumption, the entire financial market teetered on the edge of collapse. This vividly illustrates the danger of poor modeling.

In the late 1990s and early 2000s, some investors believed that real estate prices could only rise.

Models can be useful, but as the financial crisis shows, they are also potentially dangerous. Because a model is always a simplification, decision-makers must be careful about assuming that a model can present a solution for complex problems.

PRACTICE WHAT YOU KNOW

Positive versus Normative Statements

Question: Which of the following statements are positive and which ones are normative?

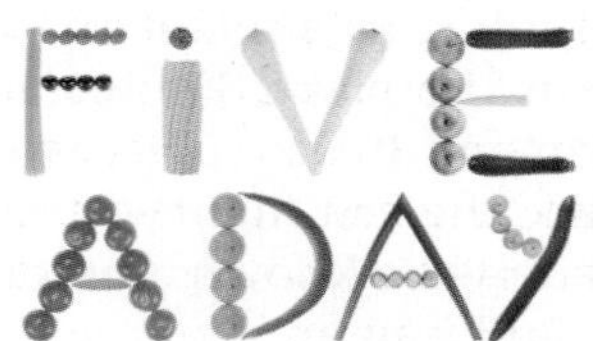

You should eat five servings of fruit or vegetables each day. Is that a positive or a normative statement?

1. Winters in Arkansas are too cold.
2. Everyone should work at a bank to see the true value of money.
3. The current exchange rate is 0.7 British pounds per U.S. dollar.
4. On average, people save 15% when they switch to Geico.
5. Everyone ought to have a life insurance policy.
6. University of Virginia graduates earn more than Duke University graduates.
7. Harvard University is the top education institution in the country.
8. The average temperature in Fargo, North Dakota, in January is 56 degrees Fahrenheit.

Answers

1. The word "too" is a matter of opinion. This is a normative statement.
2. While working at a bank might give someone an appreciation for the value of money, the word "should" is an opinion. This is a normative statement.
3. You can look up the current exchange rate and verify if this statement is true or false. This is a positive statement.
4. This was a claim made by the insurance company Geico in one of its commercials. Don't let that fool you. It is still a testable claim. If you had the data from Geico, you could see if the statement is correct or not. This is a positive statement.
5. It sounds like a true statement, or at least a very sensible one. However, the word "ought" makes it an opinion. This is a normative statement.
6. You can look up the data and see which university's graduates earn more. This is a positive statement.
7. Many national rankings indicate that this is true, but others do not. Since different rankings are based on different assumptions, it is not possible to identify a definitive "top" school. This is a normative statement.
8. The statement is wrong. North Dakota is much colder than that in January. However, the statement can be verified by looking at climatological data. This is a positive statement.

What Is a Production Possibilities Frontier?

Now it's time for our first economic model. However, before you go on, you might want to review the appendix on graphing at the end of this chapter. It covers graph-reading skills that are used in this section. Graphs are one of the key tools in economics because they provide a visual display of the relationship between two variables over time. Your ability to read a graph and understand the model it represents is crucial to learning economics.

In Chapter 1, we learned that economics is about the trade-offs individuals and societies face every day. For instance, you may frequently have to decide between spending more time studying to get better grades or going to a party with your friends. The more time you study, the less time you have for your friends. Similarly, a society has to determine how to allocate its resources. The decision to build new roads will mean there is less money available for new schools, and vice versa.

Trade-offs

A **production possibilities frontier** is a model that illustrates the combinations of outputs that a society can produce if all of its resources are being used efficiently. In order to preserve *ceteris paribus*, we assume that the technology available for production and the quantity of resources remain constant. These assumptions allow us to model trade-offs more clearly.

A **production possibilities frontier** is a model that illustrates the combinations of outputs that a society can produce if all of its resources are being used efficiently.

Let's begin by imagining a society that produces only two goods—pizzas and chicken wings. This may not seem very realistic, since a real economy comprises millions of different goods and services, but the benefit of this approach is that it enables us to understand the trade-offs in the production process without making the analysis too complicated.

Figure 2.1 shows the production possibilities frontier for our two-product society. Remember that the number of people and the total resources in this two-product society are fixed. Later, we will relax these assumptions and make our model more realistic. If the economy uses all of its resources to produce pizzas, it can produce 100 pizzas and 0 wings. If it uses all of its resources to produce wings, it can make 300 wings and 0 pizzas. These outcomes are represented by points A and B on the production possibilities frontier. It is unlikely that the society will choose either of these extreme outcomes because it is human nature to enjoy variety.

If our theoretical society decides to spend some of its resources producing pizzas and some of its resources making wings, its economy will end up with a combination of pizzas and wings that can be placed somewhere along the production possibilities frontier (PPF) between points A and B. At point C, for example, the society would deploy its resources to produce 70 pizzas and 90 wings. At point D, the combination would be 50 pizzas and 150 wings. Each point along the production possibilities frontier represents a possible set of outcomes that the society can choose if it uses all of its resources efficiently.

Notice that some combinations of pizza and wings cannot be produced. This is because resources within the society are scarce. Our theoretical society would enjoy point E, but given the available resources, it cannot produce at that output level. Points beyond the production possibilities frontier are desirable but not feasible, given the resources and technology that the society has available.

FIGURE 2.1

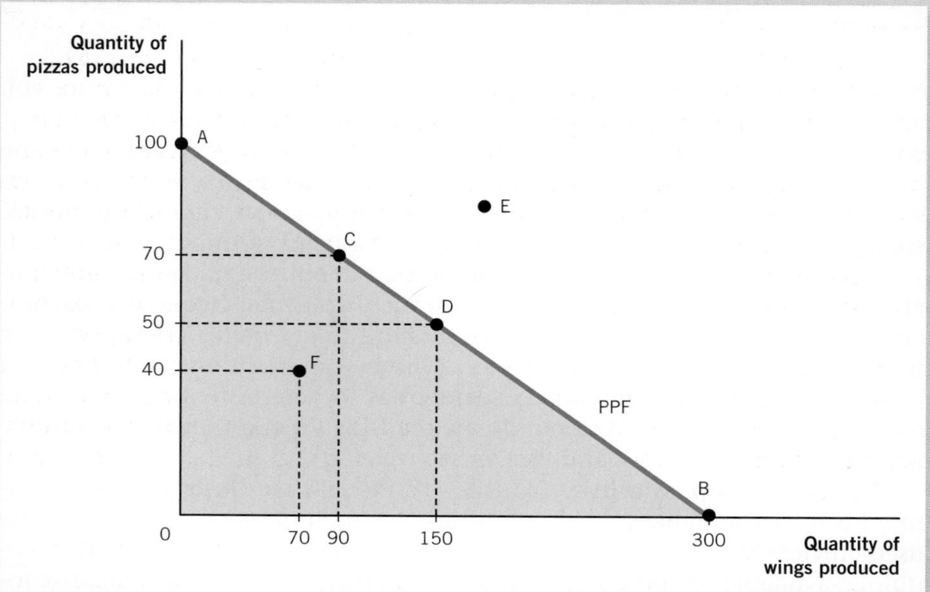

The Production Possibilities Frontier for Pizza and Wings
The production possibilities frontier shows the trade-off between producing pizzas and producing wings. Any combination of pizzas and wings is possible along, or inside, the line. Combinations of pizza and wings beyond the production possibilities frontier—for example, at point E—are not possible with the current set of resources. Point F and any other points located in the shaded region are inefficient.

At any combination of wings and pizzas along the production possibilities frontier, the society is using all of its resources in the most productive way possible. But what about point F and any other points that might be located in the shaded region? These points represent outcomes inside the production possibilities frontier, which indicate an inefficient use of the society's resources. Consider, for example, the resource of labor. If employees spend many hours at work surfing the Web instead of doing their jobs, the output of pizzas and wings will drop and will no longer be efficient. As long as the workers use all of their time efficiently, they will produce the maximum amount of pizza and wings.

Whenever society is producing on the production possibilities frontier, the only way to get more of one good is to accept less of another. Since an economy operating along the frontier will be efficient at any point, economists do not favor one point over another. But a society may favor one particular point over another because it prefers that combination of goods. For example, in our theoretical two-good society, if wings suddenly become more popular, the movement from point C to point D will represent a desirable trade-off. The society will have 20 fewer pizzas (from 70 to 50) but 60 additional wings (from 90 to 150).

The Production Possibilities Frontier and Opportunity Cost

Trade-offs

Since our two-good society produces only pizzas and wings, the trade-offs that occur along the production possibilities frontier represent the opportunity cost of producing one good instead of the other. As we noted in Chapter 1, an opportunity cost is the highest-valued alternative given up to pursue another course of action. As Figure 2.1 shows, when society moves from point C to point D, it gives up 20 pizzas; this is the opportunity cost of producing more wings. The movement from D to C has an opportunity cost of 60 wings.

Until now, we have assumed that there would be a constant trade-off between the number of pizzas and the number of wings produced. However, that is not typically the case. Not all resources in our theoretical society are perfectly adaptable for use in making pizzas and wings. Some workers are good at making pizzas, and others are not so good. When the society tries to make as many pizzas as possible, it will be using both types of workers. That is, to get more pizzas, the society will have to use workers who are increasingly less skilled at making them. This means that pizza production will not expand at a constant rate. You can see this in the new production possibilities frontier in Figure 2.2; it is bowed outward rather than a straight line.

Since resources are not perfectly adaptable, production does not expand at a constant rate. For example, in order to produce 20 extra pizzas, the society can move from point D (30 pizzas) to point C (50 pizzas). But moving from

FIGURE 2.2

The Law of Increasing Relative Cost

To make more pizzas, the society will have to use workers who are increasingly less skilled at making them. As a result, as we move up along the PPF, the opportunity cost of producing an extra 20 pizzas rises from 30 wings between points D and C to 80 wings between points B and A.

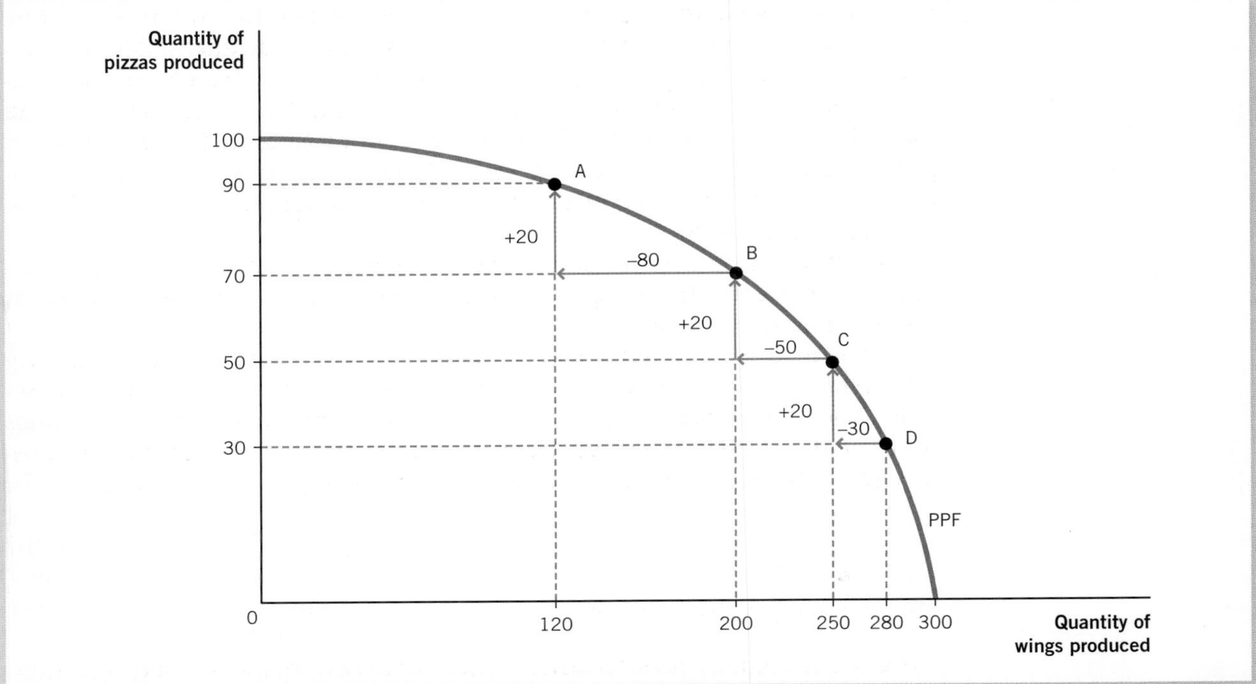

point D (280 wings) to point C (250 wings) means giving up 30 wings. So moving from D to C has an opportunity cost of 30 wings. Suppose that the society decides it wants even more pizza and moves from point C (50 pizzas) to point B (70 pizzas). Now the opportunity cost of more pizza is 50 wings, since wing production declines from 250 to 200. If the society decides that 70 pizzas are not enough, it can expand pizza production from point B (70 pizzas) to point A (90 pizzas). Now the society gives up 80 wings. Notice that as we move up along the PPF, the opportunity cost of producing an extra 20 pizzas rises from 30 wings to 80 wings. This reflects the increased trade-off necessary to produce more pizzas.

The **law of increasing relative cost** states that the opportunity cost of producing a good rises as a society produces more of it.

A bowed-out production possibilities frontier reflects the increasing opportunity cost of production. This is described by the **law of increasing relative cost**, which states that the opportunity cost of producing a good rises as a society produces more of it. Changes in relative cost mean that a society faces a significant trade-off if it tries to produce an extremely large amount of a single good.

The Production Possibilities Frontier and Economic Growth

So far, we have modeled the location of the production possibilities frontier as a function of the resources available to society at a particular moment in time. However, most societies hope to create economic growth. Economic growth is the process that enables a society to produce more output in the future.

We can use the production possibilities frontier to explore economic growth. For example, we can ask what would happen to the PPF if our two-good society developed a new technology that increases efficiency and, therefore, productivity. Suppose that a new pizza assembly line improves the pizza production process and that the development of the new assembly line does not require the use of more of the society's resources—it is simply a redeployment of the resources that already exist. This development would allow the society to make more pizza with the same number of workers. Or it would allow the same amount of pizza to be made with fewer workers than previously. Either way, the society has expanded its resource base. The change is shown in Figure 2.3.

With the new technology, it becomes possible to produce 120 pizzas using the same number of workers and in the same amount of time that it previously took to produce 100 pizzas. Although the ability to produce wings has not changed, the new pizza-making technology causes the production possibilities frontier to expand outward from PPF_1 to PPF_2. It is now possible for the society to move from point A to point B, where it can produce more of both (80 pizzas and 220 wings). Why can the society produce more of both? Because the improvement in pizza-making technology—the assembly line—allows a redeployment of the labor force that also increases the production of wings. Improvements in technology make point B possible.

The production possibilities frontier will also expand if the population grows. A larger population means more workers to help make pizza and wings. Figure 2.4 illustrates what happens when the society adds a worker to help

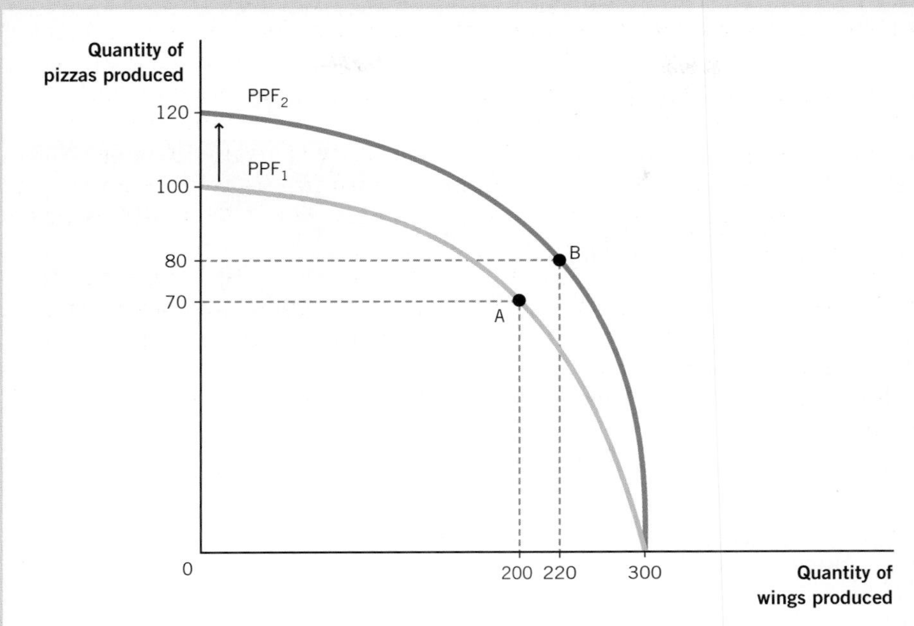

FIGURE 2.3

A Shift in the Production Possibilities Frontier

A new pizza assembly line that improves the productive capacity of pizza-makers shifts the PPF upward from PPF_1 to PPF_2. Not surprisingly, more pizzas can be produced. Comparing points A and B, you can see that the enhanced pizza-making capacity also makes it possible to produce more wings at the same time.

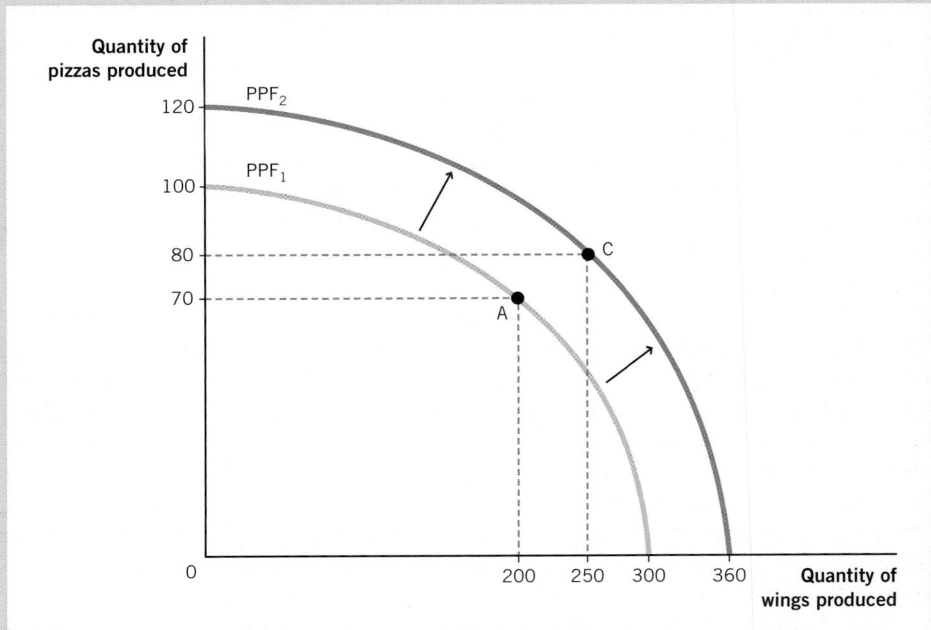

FIGURE 2.4

More Resources and the Production Possibilities Frontier

When more resources are available for the production of either pizza or wings, the entire PPF shifts upward and outward. This makes a point like C, along PPF_2, possible.

PRACTICE WHAT YOU KNOW

The Production Possibilities Frontier: Bicycles and Cars

Question: Are the following statements true or false? Base your answers on the PPF shown below.

There is a trade-off between making bicycles and cars.

1. Point A represents a possible amount of cars and bicycles that can be sold.
2. The movement along the curve from point A to point B shows the opportunity cost of producing more bicycles.
3. If we have high unemployment, the PPF shifts inward.
4. If an improved process for manufacturing cars is introduced, the *entire* PPF will shift outward.

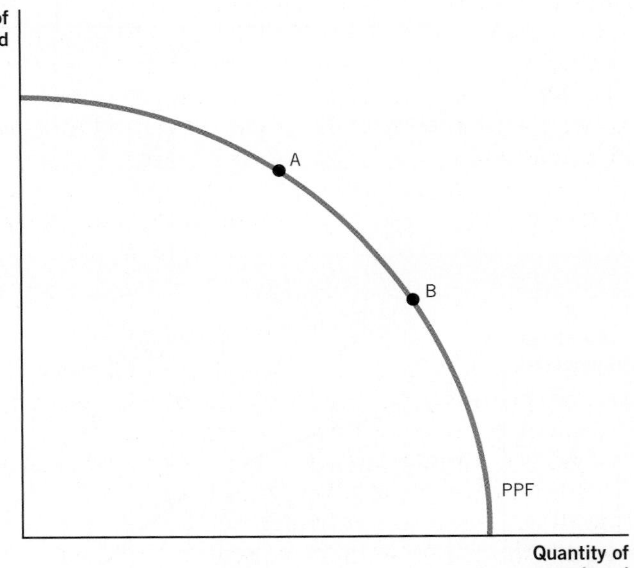

Answers

1. False. Point A represents a number of cars and bicycles that can be *produced*, not sold.
2. False. Moving from point A to point B shows the opportunity cost of producing more cars, not more bicycles.
3. False. Unemployment does not shift the curve inward, since the PPF is the maximum that can be produced when all resources are being used. More unemployment would locate society at a point inside the PPF, since some people who could help produce more cars or bicycles would not be working.
4. False. The PPF will shift outward along the car axis, but it will not shift upward along the bicycle axis.

produce pizza and wings. With more workers, the society is able to produce more pizzas and wings than before. This causes the curve to shift from PPF_1 to PPF_2, expanding up along the *y* axis and out along the *x* axis. Like improvements in technology, additional resources expand the frontier and enable the society to reach a point—in this case, C—that was not possible before. The extra workers have pushed the entire frontier out, not just one end, as the pizza assembly line did.

What Are the Benefits of Specialization and Trade?

We have seen that improving technology and adding resources make an economy more productive. A third way to create gains for society is through specialization and trade. Determining what to specialize in is an important part of this process. Every worker, business, or country is relatively good at producing certain products or services. Suppose that you decide to learn about information technology. You earn a certificate or degree and find an employer who hires you for your specialized skills. Your information technology skills determine your salary. As a result, you can use your salary to purchase other goods and services that you desire and that you are not so skilled at making yourself.

In the next section, we will explore why specializing and exchanging your skilled expertise with others makes gains from trade possible.

Gains from Trade

Let's return to our two-good economy. Now we'll make the further assumption that this economy has only two people. One person is better at making pizzas, and the other is better at making wings. When this is the case, the potential gains from trade are clear. Each person will specialize in what he or she is better at producing and then will trade in order to acquire some of the good that the other person produces.

Trade creates value

Figure 2.5 shows the production potential of the two people in our economy, Debra Winger and Mike Piazza. From the table, we see that if Debra Winger devotes all of her work time to making pizzas, she can produce 60 pizzas. If she does not spend any time on pizzas, she can make 120 wings. In contrast, Mike Piazza can spend all his time on pizzas and produce 24 pizzas, or all his time on wings and produce 72 wings.

The graphs show an illustration of the amount of pizza and wings that each person produces daily. Wing production is plotted on the *x* axis, and pizza production is on the *y* axis. Each of the production possibilities frontiers is drawn from data in the table at the top of the figure.

Debra and Mike each face a constant trade-off between producing pizza and producing wings. Debra produces 60 pizzas for every 120 wings; this means her trade-off between producing pizza and wings is fixed at 1:2. Mike produces 24 pizzas for every 72 wings. His trade-off between producing pizzas and wings is fixed at 1:3. Since Debra and Mike can choose to produce at

FIGURE 2.5

The Production Possibilities Frontier with No Trade

Debra Winger (a) can produce more pizza and more wings than Mike Piazza (b). Since Debra is more productive in general, she produces more of each food. If Debra and Mike each want to produce an equal number of pizzas and wings on their own, Debra makes 40 units of each and Mike makes 18 units of each.

	Daily production	
Person	Pizzas	Wings
Debra Winger	60	120
Mike Piazza	24	72

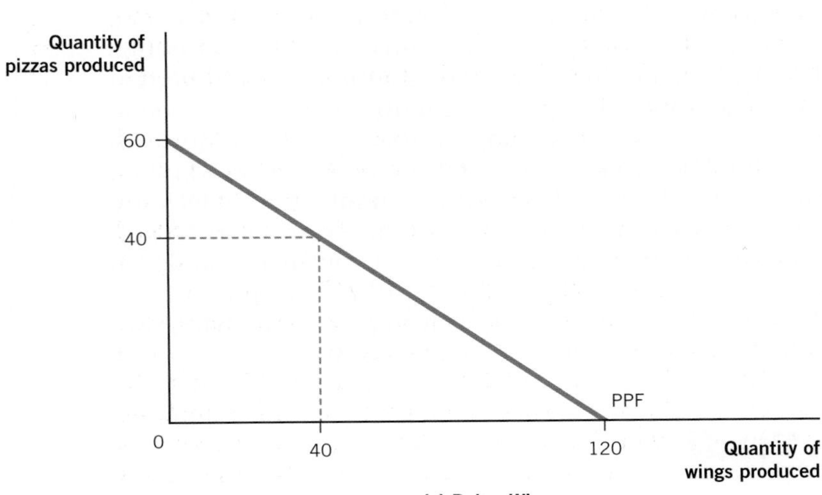

(a) Debra Winger

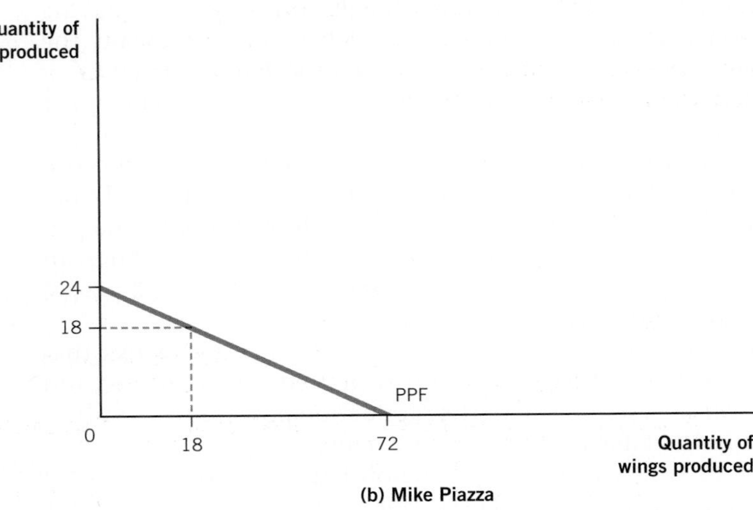

(b) Mike Piazza

any point along their production possibilities frontiers, let's assume that they each want to produce an equal number of pizzas and wings. When this is the case, Debra produces 40 pizzas and 40 wings, while Mike produces 18 pizzas and 18 wings. Since Debra is more productive in general, she produces more of each food. We say that Debra has an **absolute advantage**, meaning that she has the ability to produce more with the same quantity of resources than Mike can produce.

Absolute advantage refers to the ability of one producer to make more than another producer with the same quantity of resources.

At first glance, it would appear that Debra should continue to work alone. But consider what happens if they each specialize and then trade. Table 2.1 compares production with and without specialization and trade. Without trade, Debra and Mike have a combined production of 58 units of pizza and wings (Debra's 40 + Mike's 18). But when Debra specializes and produces only pizza, her production is 60 units. In this case, her individual pizza output is greater than the combined output of 58 pizzas (Debra's 40 + Mike's 18). Similarly, if Mike specializes in wings, he is able to make 72 units. His individual wing output is greater than their combined output of 58 wings (Debra's 40 + Mike's 18). Specialization has resulted in the production of 2 additional pizzas and 14 additional wings.

Trade creates value

Specialization leads to greater productivity. But Debra and Mike would like to eat both pizza and wings. So if they specialize and then trade with each other, they will benefit. If Debra gives Mike 19 pizzas in exchange for 47 wings, they are each better off by 1 pizza and 7 wings. This result is evident in the final column of Table 2.1 and in Figure 2.6.

In Figure 2.6a, we see that at point A Debra produces 60 pizzas and 0 wings. If she does not specialize, she produces 40 pizzas and 40 wings, represented at B. If she specializes and then trades with Mike, she can have 41 pizzas and 47 wings, shown at C. Her value gained from trade is 1 pizza and 7 wings. In Figure 2.6b, we see a similar benefit for Mike. If he produces only wings, he will have 72 wings, shown at A. If he does not specialize, he produces 18 pizzas and 18 wings. If he specializes and trades with Debra, he can have 19 pizzas and 25 wings, shown at C. His value gained from trade is 1 pizza and 7 wings. In spite of Debra's absolute advantage in making both pizzas and wings, she is still better off trading with Mike. This amazing result occurs because of specialization. When they spend their time on what they do best, they are able to produce more collectively and then divide the gain.

TABLE 2.1

The Gains from Trade

		Without trade		With specialization and trade		
Person	**Good**	**Production**	**Consumption**	**Production**	**Consumption**	**Gains from trade**
Debra	Pizza	40	40	60	41 (keeps)	+ 1
	Wings	40	40	0	47 (from Mike)	+ 7
Mike	Pizza	18	18	0	19 (from Debra)	+ 1
	Wings	18	18	72	25 (keeps)	+ 7

FIGURE 2.6

The Production Possibilities Frontier with Trade

(a) If Debra produces only pizza, she will have 60 pizzas, shown at point A. If she does not specialize, she will produce 40 pizzas and 40 wings (B). If she specializes and trades with Mike, she will have 41 pizzas and 47 wings (C).

(b) If Mike produces only wings, he will have 72 wings (A). If he does not specialize, he will produce 18 pizzas and 18 wings (B). If he specializes and trades with Debra, he can have 19 pizzas and 25 wings (C).

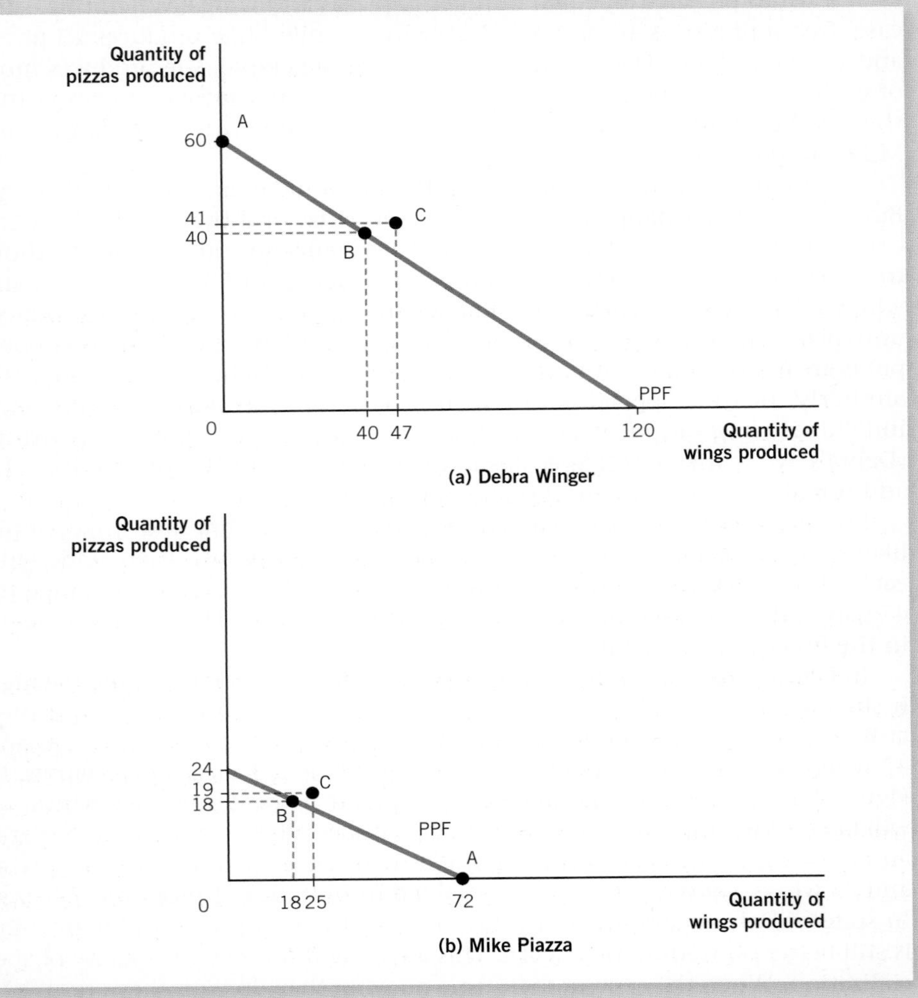

Comparative Advantage

We have seen that specialization enables workers to enjoy gains from trade. The concept of opportunity cost provides us with a second way of validating the principle that trade creates value. Recall that opportunity cost is the highest-valued alternative that is sacrificed to pursue something else. Looking at Table 2.2, you can see that in order to produce 1 more pizza Debra must give up producing 2 wings. We can say that the opportunity cost of 1 pizza is 2 wings. We can also reverse the observation and say that the opportunity cost of one wing is $\frac{1}{2}$ pizza. In Mike's case, each pizza he produces means giving up the production of 3 wings. In other words, the opportunity cost for him to produce 1 pizza is 3 wings. In reverse, we can say that when he produces 1 wing, he gives up $\frac{1}{3}$ pizza.

Recall from Chapter 1 that comparative advantage is the ability to make a good at a lower cost than another producer. Looking at Table 2.2, you can see

TABLE 2.2

The Opportunity Cost of Pizza and Wings

Person	Opportunity cost	
	1 Pizza	**1 Wing**
Debra Winger	2 wings	$\frac{1}{2}$ pizza
Mike Piazza	3 wings	$\frac{1}{3}$ pizza

that Debra has a lower opportunity cost of producing pizzas than Mike—she gives up 2 wings for each pizza she produces, while he gives up 3 wings for each pizza he produces. In other words, Debra has a comparative advantage in producing pizzas. However, Debra does not have a comparative advantage in producing wings. For Debra to produce 1 wing, she would have to give up production of $\frac{1}{2}$ pizza. Mike, in contrast, gives up $\frac{1}{3}$ pizza each time he produces 1 wing. So Debra's opportunity cost for producing wings is higher than Mike's. Because Mike is the low-opportunity-cost producer of wings, he has a comparative advantage in producing them. Recall that Debra has an absolute advantage in the production of both pizzas and wings; she is better at making both. However, from this example we see that she cannot have a comparative advantage in making both goods.

Opportunity cost

Applying the concept of opportunity cost helps us to see why specialization enables people to produce more. Debra's opportunity cost of producing pizzas (she gives up making 2 wings for every pizza) is less than Mike's opportunity cost of producing pizzas (he gives up 3 wings for every pizza). Therefore, Debra should specialize in producing pizzas. If you want to double-check this result, consider who should produce wings. Debra's opportunity cost of producing wings (she gives up $\frac{1}{2}$ pizza for every wing she makes) is more than Mike's opportunity cost of producing wings (he gives up $\frac{1}{3}$ pizza for every wing he makes). Therefore, Mike should specialize in producing wings. When Debra produces only pizzas and Mike produces only wings, their combined output is 60 pizzas and 72 wings.

Finding the Right Price to Facilitate Trade

We have seen that Debra and Mike will do better if they specialize and then trade. But how many wings should it cost to buy a pizza? How many pizzas for a wing? In other words, what trading price will benefit both parties? To answer this question, we need to return to opportunity cost. This process is similar to the trading of lunch food that you might recall from grade school. Perhaps you wanted a friend's apple and he wanted a few of your Oreos. If you agreed to trade three Oreos for the apple, the exchange benefited both parties because you valued your three cookies less than your friend's apple and your friend valued your three cookies more than his apple.

In our example, Debra and Mike will benefit from exchanging a good at a price that is lower than the opportunity cost of producing it. Recall that Debra's opportunity cost is 1 pizza per 2 wings. We can express this as a ratio of 1:2. This means that any exchange with a value lower than 1:2 (0.50) will be beneficial to her since she ends up with more pizza and wings than she

Opportunity cost

TABLE 2.3

Gaining from Trade

Person	Opportunity cost	Ratio
Debra Winger	1 pizza equals 2 wings	1:2 = 0.50
Terms of trade	19 pizzas for 47 wings	19:47 = 0.40
Mike Piazza	1 pizza equals 3 wings	1:3 = 0.33

had without trade. Mike's opportunity cost is 1 pizza per 3 wings, or a ratio of 1:3 (0.33). For trade to be mutually beneficial, the ratio of the amount exchanged must fall between the ratio of Debra's opportunity cost of 1:2 and the ratio of Mike's opportunity cost of 1:3. If the ratio falls outside of that range, Debra and Mike will be better off without trade, since the price of trading, which is the ratio in this case, will not be attractive to both parties. In the example shown in Table 2.3, Debra trades 19 pizzas for 47 wings. The ratio of 19:47 (0.40) falls between Debra's and Mike's opportunity costs.

Trade creates value

As long as the terms of trade fall between the opportunity costs of the trading partners, the trade benefits both sides. But if Mike insists on a trading ratio of 1 wing for 1 pizza, which would be a good deal for him, Debra will refuse to trade because she will be better off producing both goods on her own. Likewise, if Debra insists on receiving 4 wings for every pizza she gives to Mike, he will refuse to trade with her because he will be better off producing both goods on his own.

ECONOMICS IN THE REAL WORLD

Why Shaquille O'Neal Has Someone Else Help Him Move

Shaquille O'Neal is a mountain of a man—7′1″ tall and over 300 pounds. At times during his Hall of Fame basketball career, he was traded from one team to another. Whenever he was traded, he had to relocate to a new city. Given his size and strength, you might think that Shaquille would have moved his household himself. But despite the fact that he could replace two or more ordinary movers, he kept playing basketball and hired movers. Let's examine the situation to see if this was a wise decision.

During his career, Shaquille had an absolute advantage in both playing basketball and moving furniture. But, as we have seen, an absolute advantage doesn't mean that Shaquille should do both tasks himself. When he was traded to a new team, he could have asked for a few days to pack up and move, but each day spent moving would have been one less day he was able to work with his new team. When you are paid millions of dollars to play a game, the time spent moving is time lost practicing or playing basketball, which incurs a substantial opportunity cost. The movers, with a much lower opportunity cost of their time, have a comparative advantage in moving—so Shaq made a smart decision to hire them!

However, since Shaquille is now retired, the value of his time is lower. If the opportunity cost of his time becomes low enough, it is conceivable that next time he will move himself rather than pay movers. ✳

SNAPSHOT

Shaq and Comparative Advantage

If you ever saw Shaquille O'Neal use his size and strength on the basketball court, you might wonder how someone could have any kind of advantage over him. But when it comes to comparative advantage, opportunity costs tell the tale. Let's take a look at the numbers.

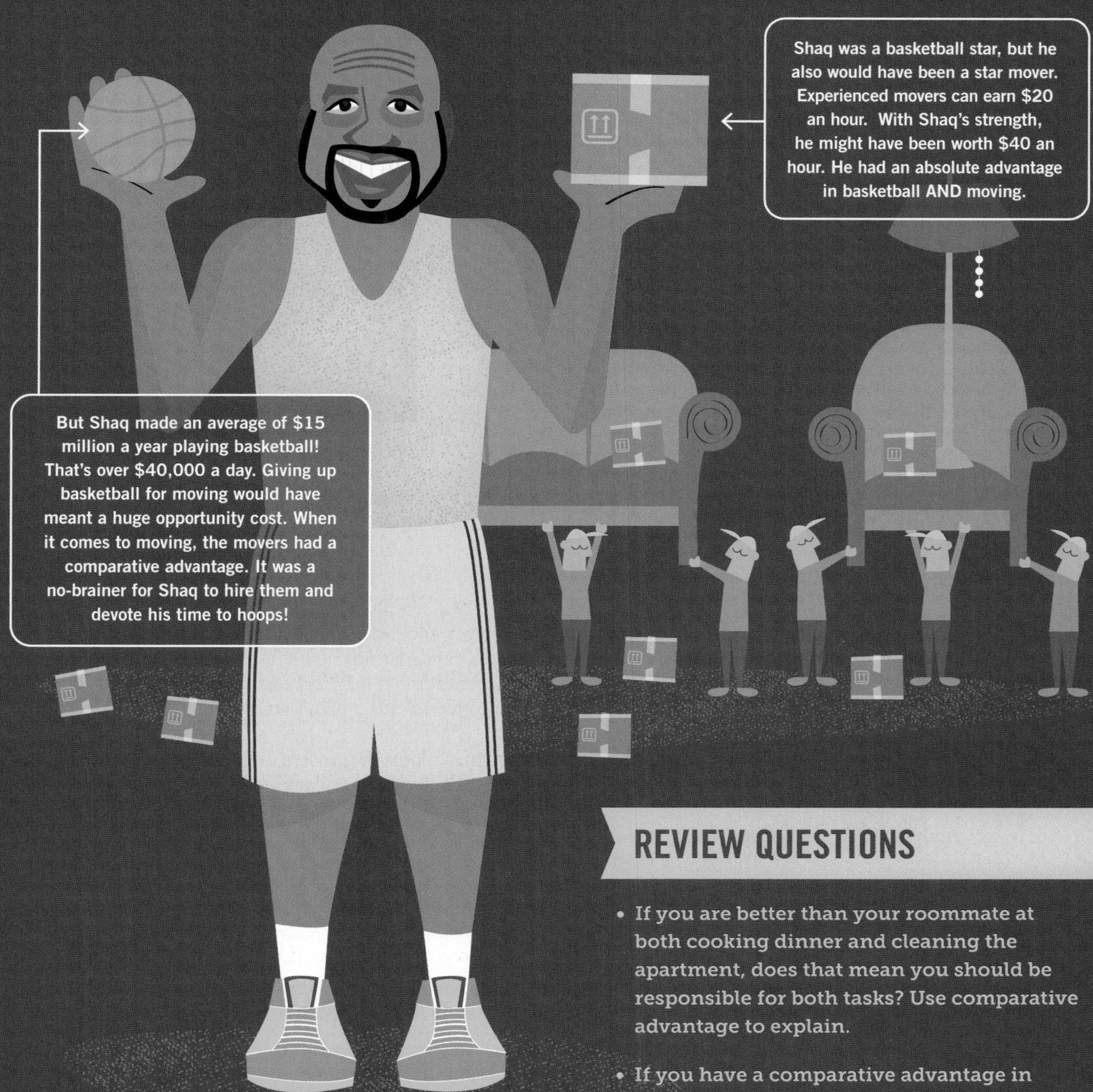

Shaq was a basketball star, but he also would have been a star mover. Experienced movers can earn $20 an hour. With Shaq's strength, he might have been worth $40 an hour. He had an absolute advantage in basketball AND moving.
But Shaq made an average of $15 million a year playing basketball! That's over $40,000 a day. Giving up basketball for moving would have meant a huge opportunity cost. When it comes to moving, the movers had a comparative advantage. It was a no-brainer for Shaq to hire them and devote his time to hoops!

REVIEW QUESTIONS

- If you are better than your roommate at both cooking dinner and cleaning the apartment, does that mean you should be responsible for both tasks? Use comparative advantage to explain.
- If you have a comparative advantage in doing something, do you experience a high or low opportunity cost?

PRACTICE WHAT YOU KNOW

Opportunity Cost

Question: Imagine that you are traveling to visit your family in Chicago. You can take a train or a plane. The plane ticket costs $300, and it takes 2 hours each way. The train ticket costs $200, and it takes 12 hours each way. Which form of transportation should you choose?

Will you travel by plane or train?

Answer: The key to answering the question is learning to value time. The simplest way to do this is to calculate the financial cost savings of taking the train and compare that to the value of the time you would save if you took the plane.

Cost savings with train	Round-trip time saved with plane
\$300 − \$200 = \$100	24 hours − 4 hours = 20 hours
(plane) − (train)	(train) − (plane)

A person who takes the train can save \$100, but it will cost 20 hours to do so. At an hourly rate, the savings would be \$100/20 hours = \$5/hour. If you value your time at exactly \$5 an hour, you will be indifferent between plane and train travel. If your time is worth more than \$5 an hour, you should take the plane, and if your time is worth less than \$5 an hour, you should take the train.

Opportunity cost

It is important to note that this approach gives us a more realistic answer than simply observing ticket prices. The train has a lower ticket price, but very few people ride the train instead of flying because the opportunity cost of their time is worth more to them than the difference in the ticket prices. This is why most business travelers fly—it saves valuable time. Good economists learn to examine the full opportunity cost of their decisions, which must include both the financials and the cost of time.

We have examined this question by holding everything else constant, or applying the principle of *ceteris paribus*. In other words, at no point did we discuss possible side issues such as the fear of flying, sleeping arrangements on the train, or anything else that might be relevant to someone making the decision.

Opportunity Cost

ECONOMICS IN THE MEDIA

Saving Private Ryan

In most war movies, the calculus of battle is quite apparent. One side wins if it loses fewer airplanes, tanks, or soldiers during the course of the conflict or attains a strategic objective worth the cost. These casualties of war are the trade-off that is necessary to achieve victory. The movie *Saving Private Ryan* (1998) is different because in its plot the calculus of war does not add up: the mission is to save a single man. Private Ryan is one of four brothers who are all fighting on D-Day—June 6, 1944—the day the Allies landed in Normandy, France, to liberate Europe from Nazi occupation. In a twist of fate, all three of Ryan's brothers are killed. As a result, the general in charge believes that the family has sacrificed enough and sends orders to find Ryan and return him home.

The catch is that in order to save Private Ryan the army needs to send a small group of soldiers to find him. A patrol led by Captain Miller loses many good men in the process, and those who remain begin to doubt the mission. Captain Miller says to the sergeant, "This Ryan better be worth it. He better go home and cure a disease, or invent a longer-lasting light bulb." Captain Miller hopes that saving Private Ryan will be worth the sacrifices they are making. That is how he rationalizes the decision to try to save him.

Saving one life means sacrificing another.

The opportunity cost of saving Private Ryan ends up being the lives that the patrol loses—lives that otherwise could have been pursuing a strategic military objective. In that sense, the entire film is about opportunity cost.

What Is the Trade-off between Having More Now and Having More Later?

So far, we have examined short-run trade-offs. In looking at our wings-pizza trade-off, we were essentially living in the moment. But both individuals and society as a whole must weigh the benefits available today with those available tomorrow.

Many of life's important decisions are about the long run. We must decide where to live, whether and whom to marry, whether and where to go to college, and what type of career to pursue. Getting these decisions right is far more important than simply deciding how many wings and pizzas to produce. For instance, the decision to save money requires giving up something you want to buy today for the benefit of having more money available in the future. Similarly, if you decide to go to a party tonight, you benefit today, while staying home to study creates a larger benefit at exam time. We are constantly making decisions that reflect this tension between today and

Study now . . .

. . . enjoy life later.

Trade-offs

tomorrow—eating a large piece of cake or a healthy snack, taking a nap or exercising at the gym, buying a jet ski or investing in the stock market. Each of these decisions is a trade-off between the present and the future.

Consumer Goods, Capital Goods, and Investment

Consumer goods are produced for present consumption.

Capital goods help produce other valuable goods and services in the future.

Investment is the process of using resources to create or buy new capital.

We have seen that the trade-off between the present and the future is evident in the tension between what we consume now and what we plan to consume later. Any good that is produced for present consumption is a **consumer good**. These goods help to satisfy our wants now. Food, entertainment, and clothing are all examples of consumer goods. **Capital goods** help in the production of other valuable goods and services in the future. Capital goods are everywhere. Roads, factories, trucks, and computers are all capital goods.

For households, education is also a form of capital. The time you spend earning a college degree makes you more attractive to future employers. Even though education is not a durable good, like a house, it can be utilized in the future to earn more income. When you decide to go to college instead of working, you are making an *investment* in your human capital. **Investment** is the process of using resources to create or buy new capital.

Opportunity cost

Since we live in a world with scarce resources, every investment in capital goods has an opportunity cost of forgone consumer goods. For example, if you decide to buy a new laptop to take notes in class, you cannot use the money you spent to travel over spring break. Similarly, a firm that decides to invest in a new factory to expand future production is unable to use that money to hire more workers now.

The decision between whether to consume or to invest has a significant impact on economic growth in the future, or the long run. What happens when society makes a choice to produce many more consumer goods than capital goods? Figure 2.7a shows the result. When relatively few resources

FIGURE 2.7

Investing in Capital Goods and Promoting Growth

(a) When a society chooses point A in the short run, very few capital goods are created. Since capital goods are needed to enhance future growth, the long-run PPF_2 expands, but only slightly.

(b) When a society chooses point B in the short run, many capital goods are created, and the long-run PPF_2 expands significantly.

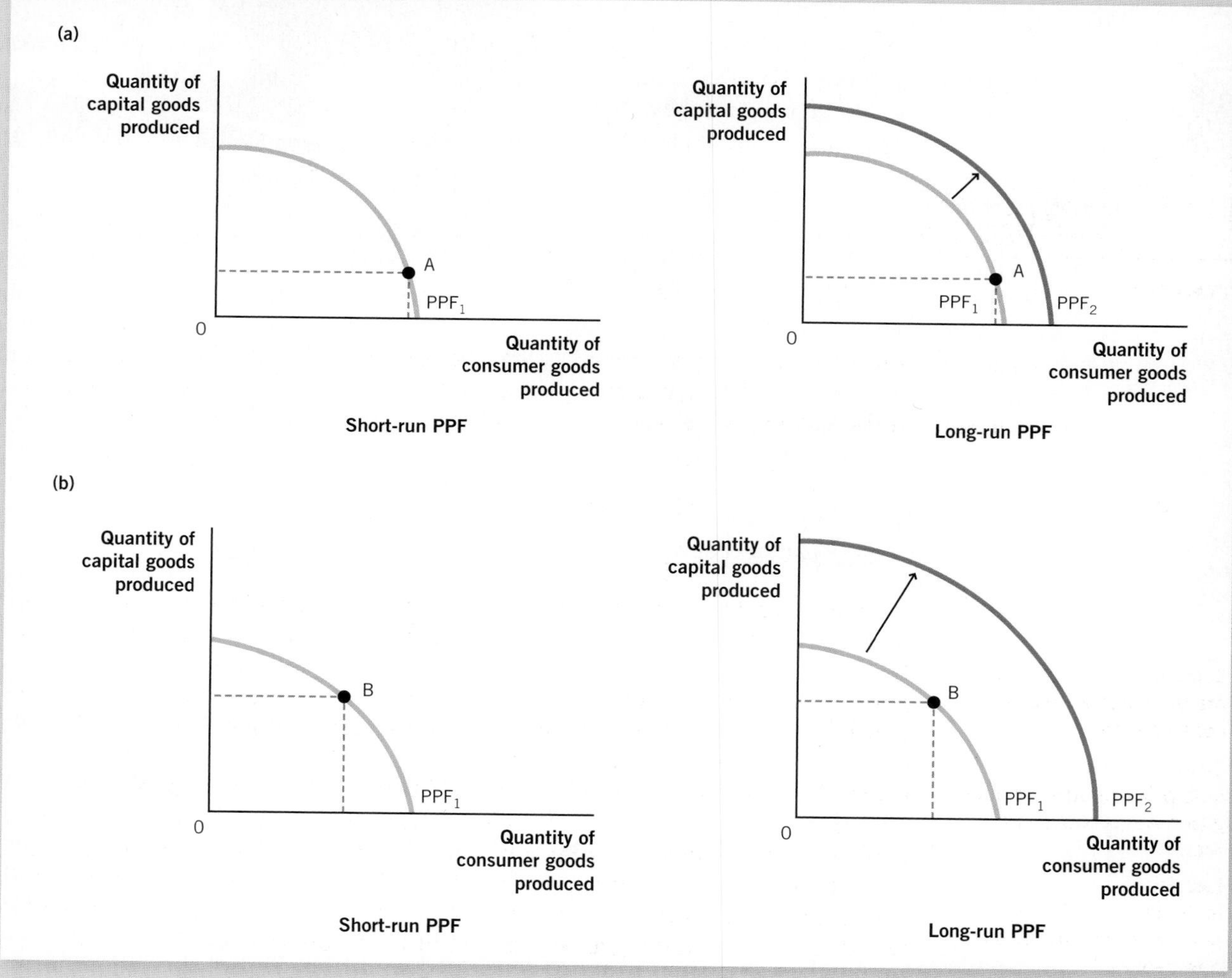

are invested in producing capital goods in the short run, not very much new capital is created. Since new capital is a necessary ingredient for economic growth in the future, the long-run production possibilities curve only expands a small amount.

What happens when society makes a choice to plan for the future by producing more capital goods than consumer goods? Figure 2.7b shows the

ECONOMICS IN THE MEDIA

The Trade-off between the Present and the Future

A Knight's Tale

Before the late Heath Ledger starred in *Brokeback Mountain*, or played the Joker in *The Dark Knight*, he played an entrepreneurial peasant in *A Knight's Tale* (2001).

In the movie, three peasants unexpectedly win a jousting tournament and earn 15 silver coins. Then they face a choice about what to do next. Two of the three want to return to England and live the high life for a while, but the third (played by Ledger) suggests that they take 13 of the coins and reinvest them in training for the next tournament. He offers to put in all 5 of his coins and asks the other two for 4 coins each. His partners are skeptical about the plan because Ledger's character is good with the sword and not very good with the lance. For them to win additional tournaments, they will have to invest considerable resources in training and preparation.

The movie illustrates the trade-off between enjoying consumer goods in the short run and investing in capital goods in the long run. The peasants' choice to forgo spending their winnings to enjoy themselves now in order to prepare for the next tournament is not easy. None of the three has ever had any money. Five silver coins represent an opportunity, at least for a few days, to live the good life. However, the plan will elevate the three out of poverty in the long term if they can learn to compete at the highest level. Therefore, investing the 13 coins is like choosing point B in Figure 2.8b. Investing now will allow their production possibilities frontier to grow over time, affording each of them a better life in the long run.

Learning to joust is a long-term skill.

result. With investment in new capital, the long-run production possibilities curve expands outward much more.

All societies face the trade-off between spending today and investing for tomorrow. Emerging global economic powers like China and India are good examples of the benefit of investing in the future. Over the last 20 years, the citizens of these countries have invested significantly more on the formation of capital goods than have the citizens in wealthier nations in North America and Europe. Not surprisingly, economic growth rates in China and India are much higher than in more developed countries. Part of the difference in these investment rates can be explained by the fact that the United States and Europe already have larger capital stocks per capita and have less to gain than developing countries from operating at point B in Figure 2.7b. China clearly prefers point B at this stage of its economic development, but point B is not necessarily better than point A. Developing nations, like China, are sacrificing the present for a better future, while many developed countries, like the United States, take a more balanced approach to weighing current needs against future growth. For Chinese workers, this trade-off typically means longer work hours and higher savings rates than their American counterparts

Trade-offs

PRACTICE WHAT YOU KNOW

Trade-offs

Question: Your friend is fond of saying he will study later. He eventually does study, but he often doesn't get quite the grades he had hoped for because he doesn't study enough. Every time this happens, he says, "It's only one exam." What advice would you give?

No pain, no gain.

Answer: Your friend doesn't understand long-term trade-offs. You could start by reminding him that each decision has a consequence at the margin and also later in life. The marginal cost of not studying enough is a lower exam grade. To some extent, your friend's reasoning is correct. How well he does on one exam over four years of college is almost irrelevant. The problem is that many poor exam scores have a cumulative effect over the semesters. If your friend graduates with a 2.5 GPA instead of a 3.5 GPA because he did not study enough, his employment prospects will be significantly diminished.

Marginal thinking

can claim, despite far lower average salaries. In contrast, American workers have much more leisure time and more disposable income, a combination that leads to far greater rates of consumption.

Conclusion

Does trade create winners and losers? After reading this chapter, you should know the answer: trade creates value. We have dispelled the misconception that many first-time learners of economics begin with—that every trade results in a winner and a loser. The simple, yet powerful, idea that trade creates value has far-reaching consequences for how we should organize our society. Voluntary trades will maximize society's wealth by redistributing goods and services to people who value them the most.

Trade creates value

We have also developed our first model, the production possibilities frontier. This model illustrates the benefits of trade and also enables us to describe ways to grow the economy. Trade and growth rest on a more fundamental idea—specialization. When producers specialize, they focus their efforts on those goods and services for which they have the lowest opportunity cost and trade with others who are good at making something else. In order to have something valuable to trade, each producer, in effect, must find its comparative advantage. As a result, trade creates value and contributes to an improved standard of living in society.

In the next chapter, we examine the supply-and-demand model to illustrate how markets work. While the model is different, the fundamental result we learned here—that trade creates value—still holds.

ECONOMICS FOR LIFE

Failing to Account for Exogenous Factors When Making Predictions

Predictions are often based on past experiences and current observations. Many of the least accurate predictions fail to take into account how much technological change influences the economy. Here, we repeat a few predictions as a cautionary reminder that technology doesn't remain constant.

PREDICTION: "There is no reason anyone would want a computer in their home." Said in 1977 by Ken Olson, founder of Digital Equipment Corp. (DEC), a maker of mainframe computers.

FAIL: Over 80% of all American households have a computer today.

PREDICTION: "There will never be a bigger plane built." Said in 1933 by a Boeing engineer referring to the 247, a twin-engine plane that holds 10 people.

FAIL: Today, the Airbus A380 can hold more than 800 people.

PREDICTION: "The wireless music box has no imaginable commercial value. Who would pay for a message sent to no one in particular?" Said by people in the communications industry when David Sarnoff (founder of NBC) wanted to invest in the radio.

FAIL: Radio programs quickly captured the public's imagination.

PREDICTION: "The world potential market for copying machines is five thousand at most." Said in 1959 by executives of IBM to the people who founded Xerox.

FAIL: Today, a combination printer, fax machine, and copier costs less than $100. There are tens of millions of copiers in use throughout the United States.

PREDICTION: "The Americans have need of the telephone, but we do not. We have plenty of messenger boys." Said in 1878 by Sir William Preece, chief engineer, British Post Office.

FAIL: Today, almost everyone in Britain has a telephone.

These predictions may seem funny to us today, but note the common feature: they did not account for how the new technology would affect consumer demand and behavior. Nor do these predictions anticipate how improvements in technology through time make future versions of new products substantially better. The lesson: don't count on the status quo. Adapt with the times to take advantage of opportunities.

Source: Listverse.com, "Top 30 Failed Technology Predictions"

Epic fail: planes have continued to get larger despite predictions to the contrary.

ANSWERING THE BIG QUESTIONS

How do economists study the economy?

* Economists design theories and then test them by collecting real data. The economist's laboratory is the world around us; it ranges from the economy as a whole to the decisions that firms and individuals make. A good model should be simple to understand, flexible in design, and able to make powerful predictions. A model is both more realistic and harder to understand when it involves many variables. Maintaining a positive framework is crucial for economic analysis because it allows decision-makers to observe the facts objectively.

What is a production possibilities frontier?

* A production possibilities frontier is a model that illustrates the combinations of outputs that a society can produce if all of its resources are being used efficiently. Economists use this model to illustrate trade-offs and to explain opportunity costs and the role of additional resources and technology in creating economic growth.

What are the benefits of specialization and trade?

* Society is better off if individuals and firms specialize and trade on the basis of the principle of comparative advantage.
* Parties that are better at producing goods and services than their potential trading partners, or hold an absolute advantage, still benefit from trade because this allows them to specialize and trade what they produce for other goods and services that they are not as skilled at making.
* As long as the terms of trade fall between the opportunity costs of the trading partners, the trade benefits both sides.

What is the trade-off between having more now and having more later?

* All societies face a crucial trade-off between consumption in the short run and greater productivity in the long run. Investments in capital goods today help to spur economic growth in the future. However, since capital goods are not consumed in the short run, this means that society must be willing to sacrifice how well it lives today in order to have more later.

CONCEPTS YOU SHOULD KNOW

absolute advantage (p. 39)
capital goods (p. 46)
ceteris paribus (p. 28)
consumer goods (p. 46)
endogenous factors (p. 29)
exogenous factors (p. 29)
investment (p. 46)
law of increasing relative cost (p. 34)
normative statement (p. 27)
positive statement (p. 27)
production possibilities frontier (p. 31)

QUESTIONS FOR REVIEW

1. What is a positive economic statement? What is a normative economic statement? Provide an example of each.
2. Is it important to build completely realistic economic models? Explain your response.
3. Draw a production possibilities frontier curve. Illustrate the set of points that is feasible, the set of points that is efficient, and the set of points that is infeasible.
4. Why does the production possibilities frontier bow out? Give an example of two goods for which this would be the case.
5. Does having an absolute advantage mean that you should undertake everything on your own? Why or why not?
6. What criteria would you use to determine which of two workers has a comparative advantage in performing a task?
7. Why does comparative advantage matter more than absolute advantage for trade?
8. What factors are most important for economic growth?

STUDY PROBLEMS (*✳ solved at the end of the section*)

✳ 1. Michael and Angelo live in a small town in Italy. They work as artists. Michael is the more productive artist. He can produce 10 small sculptures each day but only 5 paintings. Angelo can produce 6 sculptures each day but only 2 paintings.

	Output per day	
	Sculptures	**Paintings**
Michael	10	5
Angelo	6	2

a. What is the opportunity cost of a painting for each artist?
b. Based on your answer in part a, who has a comparative advantage in producing paintings?
c. If the two men decide to specialize, who should produce the sculptures and who should produce the paintings?

✳ 2. The following table shows scores that a student can earn on two upcoming exams according to the amount of time devoted to study:

Hours spent studying for economics	Economics score	Hours spent studying for history	History score
10	100	0	40
8	96	2	60
6	88	4	76
4	76	6	88
2	60	8	96
0	40	10	100

a. Plot the production possibilities frontier.
b. Does the production possibilities frontier exhibit the law of increasing relative cost?
c. If the student wishes to move from a grade of 60 to a grade of 88 in economics, what is the opportunity cost?

3. Think about comparative advantage when answering this question: Should your professor, who has highly specialized training in economics, take time out of his teaching schedule to mow his lawn? Defend your answer.

* 4. Are the following statements positive or normative?
   a. My dog weighs 75 pounds.
   b. Dogs are required by law to have rabies shots.
   c. You should take your dog to the veterinarian once a year for a check-up.
   d. Chihuahuas are cuter than bulldogs.
   e. Leash laws for dogs are a good idea because they reduce injuries.

5. How does your decision to invest in a college degree add to your capital stock? Show this on your projected production possibilities frontier for 10 years from now compared to your production possibilities frontier without a degree.

* 6. Suppose that an amazing new fertilizer doubles the production of potatoes. How would this discovery affect the production possibilities frontier between potatoes and carrots? Would it now be possible to produce more potatoes *and* more carrots, or only more potatoes?

7. Suppose that a politician tells you about a plan to create two expensive but necessary programs to build more production facilities for solar power and wind power. At the same time, the politician is unwilling to cut any other programs. Use the production possibilities frontier graph below to explain if this is possible.

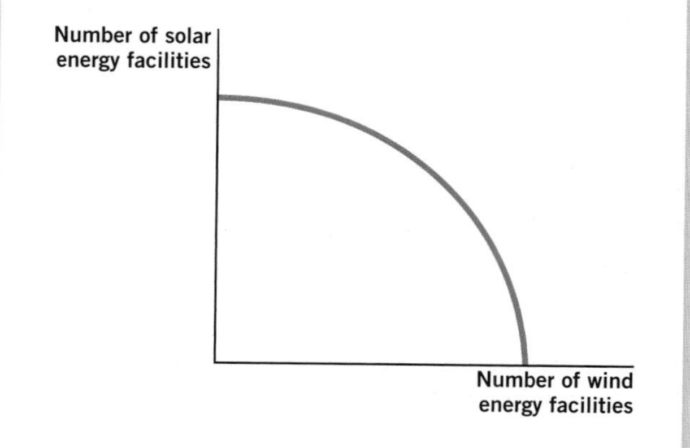

* 8. Two friends, Rachel and Joey, enjoy baking bread and making apple pies. Rachel takes 2 hours to bake a loaf of bread and 1 hour to make a pie. Joey takes 4 hours to bake a loaf and 4 hours to make a pie.
   a. What are Joey's and Rachel's opportunity costs of baking bread?
   b. Who has the absolute advantage in making bread?
   c. Who has a comparative advantage in making bread?
   d. If Joey and Rachel each decides to specialize in order to increase their joint production, what should Joey produce? What should Rachel produce?
   e. The price of a loaf of bread can be expressed in terms of an apple pie. If Joey and Rachel are specializing in production and decide to trade with each other, what range of ratios of bread and apple pie would allow both parties to benefit from trade?

9. Where would you plot unemployment on a production possibilities frontier? Where would you plot full employment on a production possibilities frontier? Now suppose that in a time of crisis everyone pitches in and works much harder than usual. What happens to the production possibilities frontier?

SOLVED PROBLEMS

1.a. Michael's opportunity cost is 2 sculptures for each painting he produces. How do we know this? If he devotes all of his time to sculptures, he can produce 10. If he devotes all of his time to paintings, he can produce 5. The ratio 10:5 is the same as 2:1. Michael is therefore twice as fast at producing sculptures as he is at producing paintings. Angelo's opportunity cost is 3 sculptures for each painting he produces. If he devotes all of his time to sculptures, he can produce 6. If he devotes all of his time to paintings, he can produce 2. The ratio 6:2 is the same as 3:1.

b. For this question, we need to compare Michael's and Angelo's relative strengths. Michael produces 2 sculptures for every painting, and Angelo produces 3 sculptures for every painting. Since Michael is only twice as good at producing sculptures, his opportunity cost of producing each painting is 2 sculptures instead 3. Therefore, Michael is the low-opportunity-cost producer of paintings.

c. If they specialize, Michael should paint and Angelo should do the sculptures. You might be tempted to argue that Michael should just work alone, but if Angelo does the sculptures, it frees up Michael to concentrate on the paintings. This is what comparative advantage is all about.

2.a.

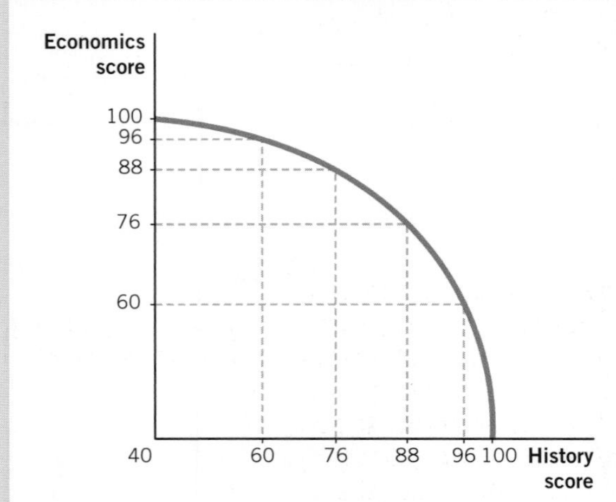

b. Yes, since it is not a straight line.

c. The opportunity cost is that the student's grade falls from 96 to 76 in history.

4.a. Positive.

b. Positive.

c. Normative.

d. Normative.

e. Normative.

6. A new fertilizer that doubles potato production will shift the entire PPF out along the potato axis but not along the carrot axis. Nevertheless, the added ability to produce more potatoes means that less acreage will have to be planted in potatoes and more land can be used to produce carrots. This makes it possible to produce more potatoes and carrots at many points along the production possibilities frontier. Figure 2.3 has a nice illustration if you are unsure how this works.

8.a. Rachel gives up 2 pies for every loaf she makes. Joey gives up 1 pie for every loaf he makes.

b. Rachel.

c. Joey.

d. Joey should make the bread and Rachel the pies.

e. Rachel makes 2 pies per loaf and Joey makes 1 pie per loaf. So any trade between 2:1 and 1:1 would benefit them both.

APPENDIX

2A Graphs in Economics

Many beginning students try to understand economics without taking the time to learn the meaning and importance of graphs. This is shortsighted. You can "think" your way to a correct answer in a few cases, but the models we build and illustrate with graphs are designed to help analyze the tough questions, where your intuition can lead you astray.

Economics is fundamentally a quantitative science. That is, in many cases economists solve problems by finding a numerical answer. For instance, economists determine the unemployment rate, the rate of inflation, the growth rate of the economy, prices, costs, and much more. Economists also like to compare present-day numbers to numbers from the immediate past and historical data. Throughout your study of economics, you will find that many data-driven topics—for example, financial trends, transactions, the stock market, and other business-related variables—naturally lend themselves to graphic display. You will also find that many theoretical concepts are easier to understand when depicted visually in graphs and charts.

Economists also find that graphing can be a powerful tool when attempting to find relationships between different sets of observations. For example, the production possibilities frontier model we presented earlier in this chapter involved the relationship between the production of pizzas and wings. The graphical presentations made this relationship, the trade-off between pizzas and wings, much more vivid.

In this appendix, we begin with simple graphs, or visuals, involving a single variable and then move to graphs that consist of two variables. Taking a few moments to read this material will help you learn economics with less effort and with greater understanding.

Graphs That Consist of One Variable

There are two common ways to display data with one variable: bar graphs and pie charts. A **variable** is a quantity that can take on more than one value. Let's look at the market share of the largest carbonated beverage companies. Figure 2A.1 shows the data in a bar graph. On the vertical axis is the market share held by each firm. On the horizontal axis are the three largest firms (Coca-Cola, Pepsi, and Dr. Pepper Snapple) and the separate category for the remaining firms, called "Others." Coca-Cola Co. has the largest market share at 42%, followed by PepsiCo Inc. at 30% and Dr. Pepper Snapple at 16%. The height of each firm's bar represents its market share percentage. The combined market share of the other firms in the market is 12%.

A **variable** is a quantity that can take on more than one value.

We illustrate the same data from the beverage industry on a pie chart in Figure 2A.2. Now the market share is expressed as the size of the pie slice for each firm.

The information in a bar graph and a pie chart is the same, so does it matter which visualization you use? Bar graphs are particularly good for comparing sizes or quantities, while pie charts are generally better for illustrating proportions. But it doesn't really matter which visualization you use; what matters is how the audience sees your graph or chart.

FIGURE 2A.1

Bar Graphs

Each firm's market share in the beverage industry is represented by the height of the bar.

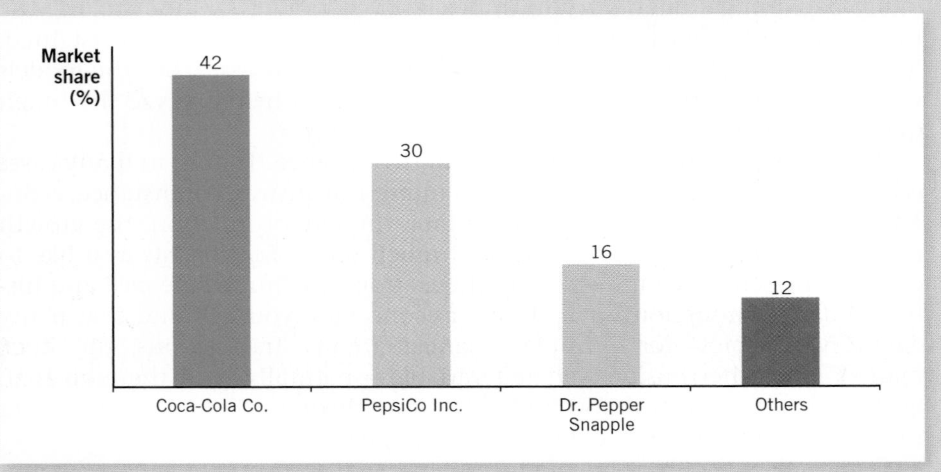

FIGURE 2A.2

Pie Chart

Each firm's market share in the beverage industry is represented by the size of the pie slice.

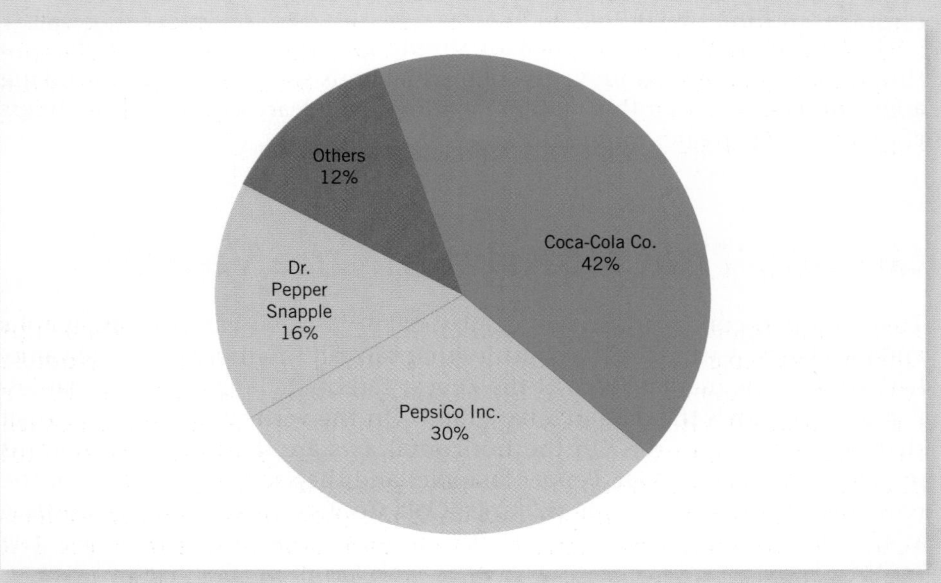

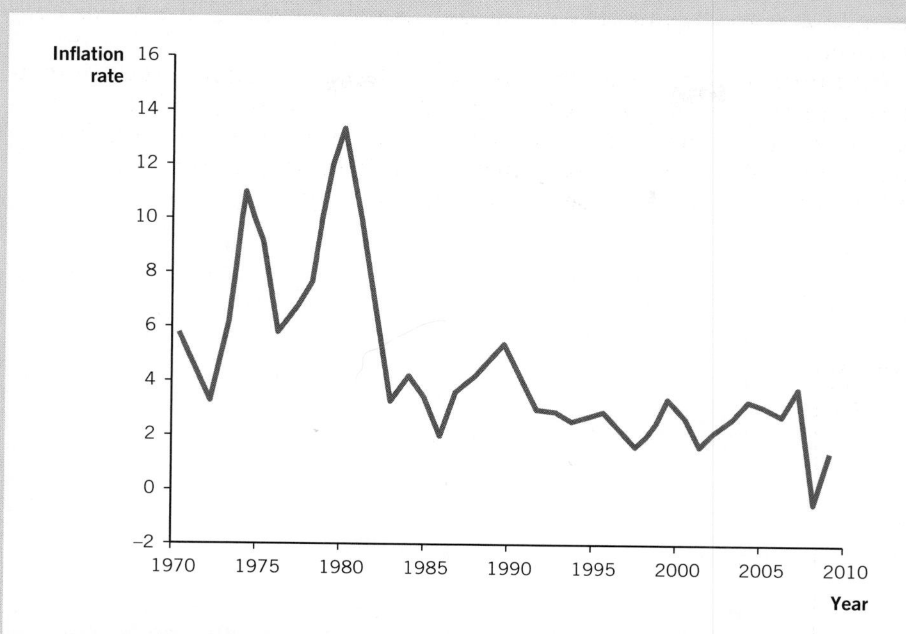

FIGURE 2A.3

Time-Series Graph
In a time-series graph, you immediately get a sense of when the inflation rate was highest and lowest, the trend through time, and the amount of volatility in the data.

Time-Series Graphs

A time-series graph displays information about a single variable across time. For instance, if you want to show how the rate of inflation has varied over a certain period of time, you could list the annual inflation rates in a lengthy table, or you could illustrate each point as part of a time series in a graph. Graphing the points makes it possible to quickly determine when inflation was at its highest and lowest without having to scan through the entire table. Figure 2A.3 illustrates this point.

Graphs That Consist of Two Variables

Sometimes, understanding graphs requires you to visualize relationships between two economic variables. Each variable is plotted on a coordinate system, or two-dimensional grid. The coordinate system allows us to map a series of ordered pairs that show how the two variables relate to each other. For instance, suppose that we examine the relationship between the amount of lemonade sold and the air temperature, as shown in Figure 2A.4.

The air temperature is graphed on the x axis (horizontal) and cups of lemonade sold on the y axis (vertical). Within each ordered pair (x,y), the first value, x, represents the value along the x axis and the second value, y, represents the value along the y axis. For example, at point A, the value of x, or the

FIGURE 2A.4

Plotting Points in a Coordinate System

Within each ordered pair (x,y), the first value, x, represents the value along the x axis and the second value, y, represents the value along the y axis. The combination of all the (x,y) pairs is known as a scatterplot.

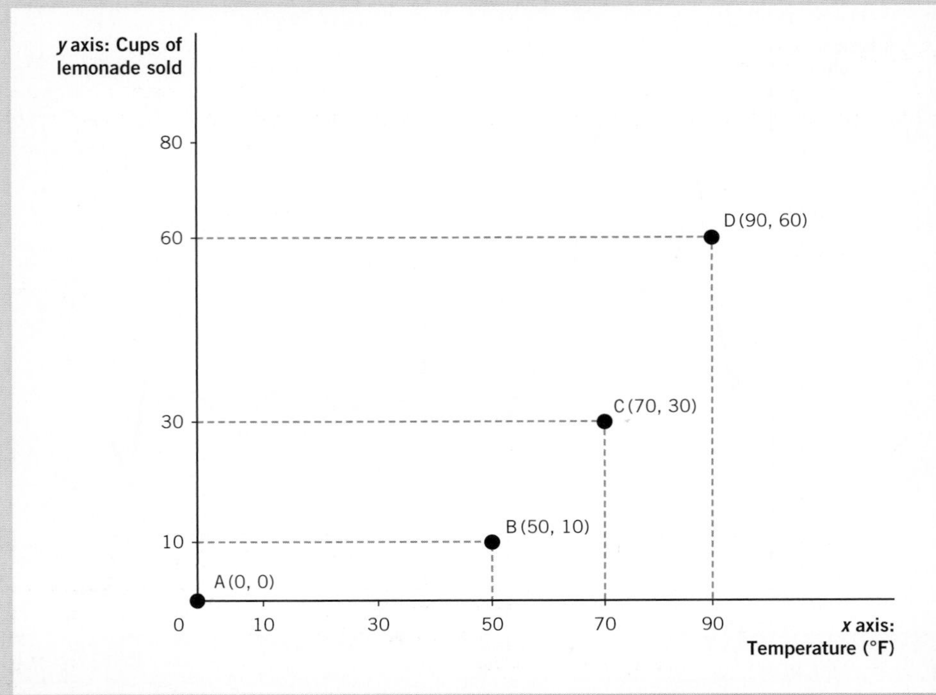

temperature, is 0 and the value of y, or the amount of lemonade sold, is also 0. No one would want to buy lemonade when the temperature is that low. At point B, the value of x, the air temperature, is 50 degrees and y, the number of cups of lemonade sold, is 10. By the time we reach point C, the temperature is 70 degrees and the amount of lemonade sold is 30 cups. Finally, at point D, the temperature has reached 90 degrees and 60 cups of lemonade are sold.

A **scatterplot** is a graph that shows individual (x,y) points.

The type of graph you see in Figure 2A.4 is known as a **scatterplot**; it shows the individual (x,y) points in a coordinate system. Note that in this example the amount of lemonade sold rises as the temperature increases. When the two variables move together in the same direction, we say that there is a **positive correlation** between them. Conversely, if we graph the relationship between hot chocolate sales and temperature, we find that they move in opposite directions; as the temperature rises, hot chocolate consumption goes down (see Figure 2A.5). This data reveals a **negative correlation**; it occurs when two variables, such as hot chocolate and temperature, move in opposite directions. Since economists are ultimately interested in using models and graphs to make predictions and test theories, the coordinate system makes both positive and negative correlations easy to observe.

Positive correlation occurs when two variables move in the same direction.

Negative correlation occurs when two variables move in the opposite direction.

Figure 2A.5 illustrates the difference between a positive correlation and a negative correlation. Figure 2A.5a uses the same information as Figure 2A.4. When the temperature increases, the quantity of lemonade sold increases as well. However, in 2A.5b we have a very different set of ordered pairs. Now, as the temperature increases, the quantity of hot chocolate sold falls. This

FIGURE 2A.5

Positive and Negative Correlations

Panel (a) displays the positive relationship, or correlation, between lemonade consumption and higher temperatures. Panel (b) displays the negative relationship, or correlation, between hot chocolate consumption and higher temperatures.

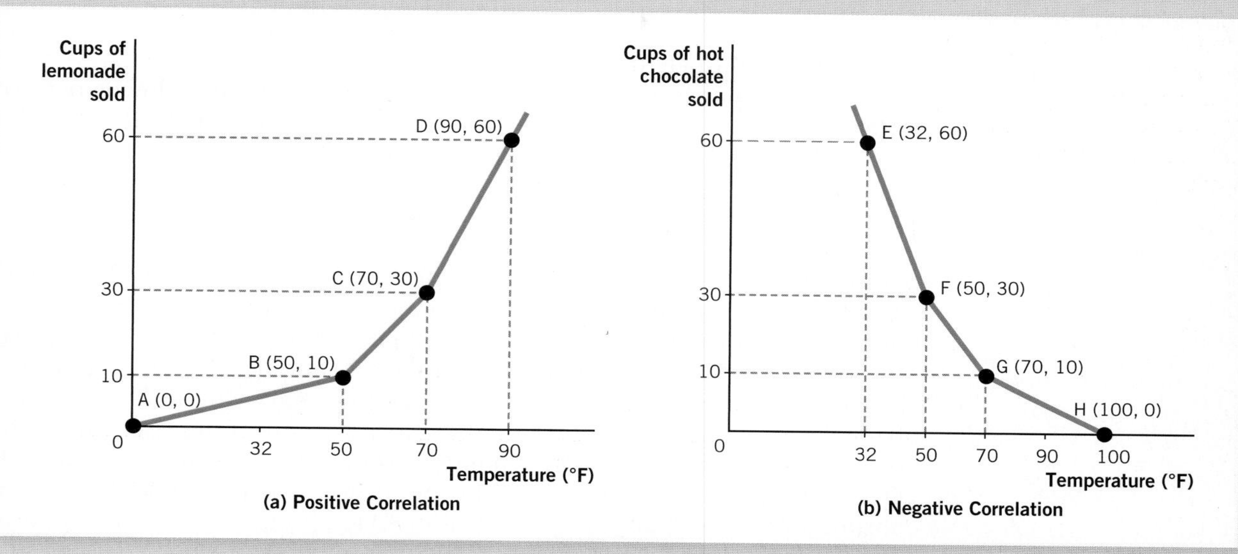

can be seen by starting with point E, where the temperature is 32 degrees and hot chocolate consumption is 60 cups. At point F, the temperature rises to 50 degrees, but hot chocolate consumption falls to 30 cups. Finally, at point G the temperature is 70 degrees and hot chocolate consumption is down to 10 cups. The green line connecting points E–G illustrates the negative correlation between hot chocolate consumption and temperature, since the line is downward sloping. This contrasts with the positive correlation in Figure 2A.5a, where lemonade consumption rises from point B to point D and the line is upward sloping.

The Slope of a Curve

A key element in any graph is the **slope**, or the rise along the y axis (vertical) divided by the run along the x axis (horizontal). The *rise* is the amount that the vertical distance changes. The *run* is the amount that the horizontal distance changes.

Slope
refers to the change in the rise along the y axis (vertical) divided by the change in the run along the x axis (horizontal).

$$\text{slope} = \frac{\text{change in } y}{\text{change in } x}$$

A slope can take on a positive, negative, or zero value. A slope of zero—a straight horizontal line—indicates that there is no change in y for a given change in x. However, that result is not very interesting. The slope can be positive, as it is in Figure 2A.5a, or negative, as it is in 2A.5b. Figure 2A.6 highlights the changes in x and y between the points on Figure 2A.5. (The change in a variable is often notated with a Greek delta symbol, Δ.)

In Figure 2A.6a, the slope from point B to point C is

$$\text{slope} = \frac{\text{change in } y}{\text{change in } x} = \frac{(30 - 10) \text{ or } 20}{(70 - 50) \text{ or } 20} = 1$$

All of the slopes in Figure 2A.6 are tabulated in Table 2A.1.

Each of the slopes in Figure 2A.6a is positive, and the values slowly increase from 0.2 to 1.5 as you move along the curve from point A to point D. However, in Figure 2A.6b, the slopes are negative as you move along the curve from E to H. An upward, or positive, slope indicates a positive correlation, while a downward, or negative, slope indicates a negative correlation.

Notice that in both panels of Figure 2A.6 the slope changes values from point to point. Because of this, we say that the relationships are *nonlinear*. The slope tells us something about how responsive consumers are to changes in temperature. Consider the movement from point A to point B in Figure 2A.6a. The change in y is 10, while the change in x is 50 and the slope (10/50) is 0.2. Since zero indicates no change and 0.2 is close to zero, we can say that lemonade customers are not very responsive as the temperature rises from 0 to 50 degrees. However, they are much more responsive from point C to point D, when the temperature rises from 70 to 90 degrees. At this point, lemonade consumption—the change in y—rises from 30 to 60 cups and the slope is now 1.5. The strength of the positive relationship is much stronger, and as a result the curve is much steeper, or more vertical. This contrasts with the movement from point A to point B, where the curve is flatter, or more horizontal.

The same analysis can be applied to Figure 2A.6b. Consider the movement from point E to point F. The change in y is -30, the change in x is 18, and the slope is -1.7. This value represents a strong negative relationship, so we would say that hot chocolate customers were quite responsive; as the temperature rose from 32 to 50 degrees, they cut their consumption of hot chocolate by 30 cups. However, hot chocolate customers are not very responsive from point G to point H, where the temperature rises from 70 to 100 degrees. In this case, consumption falls from 10 to 0 cups and the slope is -0.3. The strength of the negative relationship is much weaker (closer to zero) and, as a result, the line is much flatter, or more horizontal. This contrasts with the movement from point E to point F, where the curve was steeper, or more vertical.

TABLE 2A.1

Positive and Negative Slopes

(a)		(b)	
Points	**Slope**	**Points**	**Slope**
A to B	0.2	E to F	−1.7
B to C	1.0	F to G	−1.0
C to D	1.5	G to H	−0.3

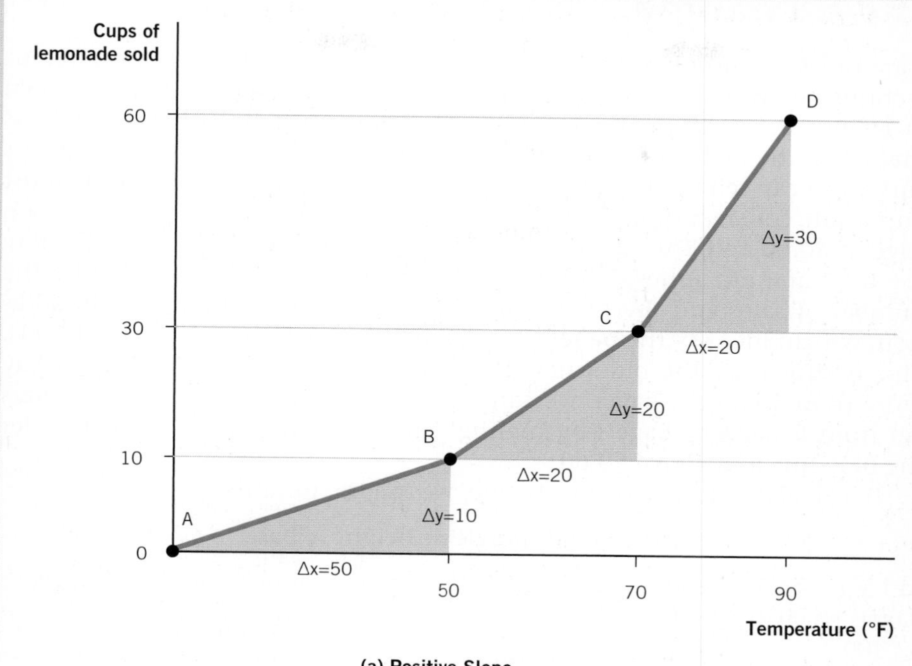

(a) Positive Slope

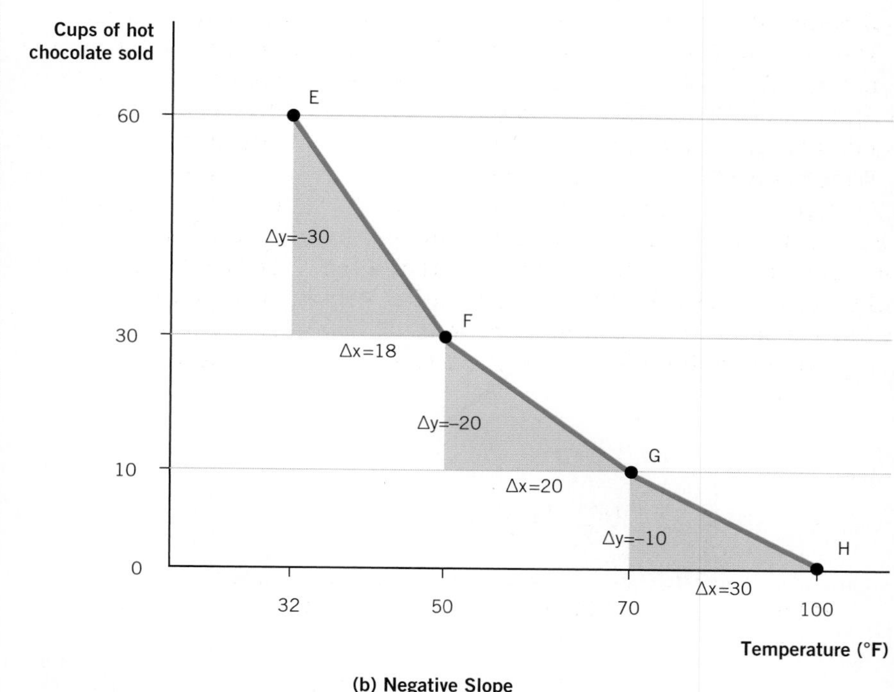

(b) Negative Slope

FIGURE 2A.6

Positive and Negative Slopes

Notice that in both panels the slope changes value from point to point. Because of this we say that the relationships are nonlinear. In (a), as you move along the curve from point A to point D, the slopes are positive. However, in (b) the slopes are negative as you move along the curve from E to H. An upward, or positive, slope indicates a positive correlation, while a negative slope indicates a negative correlation.

Formulas for the Area of a Rectangle and a Triangle

Sometimes, economists interpret graphs by examining the area of different sections below a curve. Consider the demand for Bruegger's bagels shown in Figure 2A.7. The demand curve has a downward slope, which tells us that when the price of bagels falls, consumers will buy more bagels. But this curve also can tell us about the revenue the seller receives—one of the most important considerations for the firm. In this case, the sale price of each bagel is $0.60 and Bruegger's sells 4,000 bagels each week. We can illustrate the total amount Bruegger's takes in by shading the area bounded by the number of sales and the price—the green rectangle in the figure. In addition, we can identify the benefit consumers receive from purchasing bagels. This is shown by the blue triangle. Since many buyers are willing to pay more than $0.60 per bagel, we can visualize the "surplus" that consumers get from Bruegger's Bagels by highlighting the blue triangular area under the blue line and above $0.60.

To calculate the area of a rectangle, we use the formula:

$$\text{Area of a rectangle} = \text{height} \times \text{base}$$

In Figure 2A.7, the green rectangle is the amount of revenue that Bruegger's Bagels receives when it charges $0.60. The total revenue is $0.60 × 4,000, or $2,400.

To calculate the area of a triangle, we use the formula:

$$\text{Area of a triangle} = \frac{1}{2} \times \text{height} \times \text{base}$$

FIGURE 2A.7

Working with Rectangles and Triangles

We can determine the area of the green rectangle by multiplying the height by the base. This gives us $0.60 × 4,000, or $2,400 for the total revenue earned by Bruegger's Bagels. We can determine the area of a triangle by using the formula $\frac{1}{2}$ × height × base. This gives us $\frac{1}{2}$ × $0.60 × 4,000, or $1,200 for the area of consumer surplus.

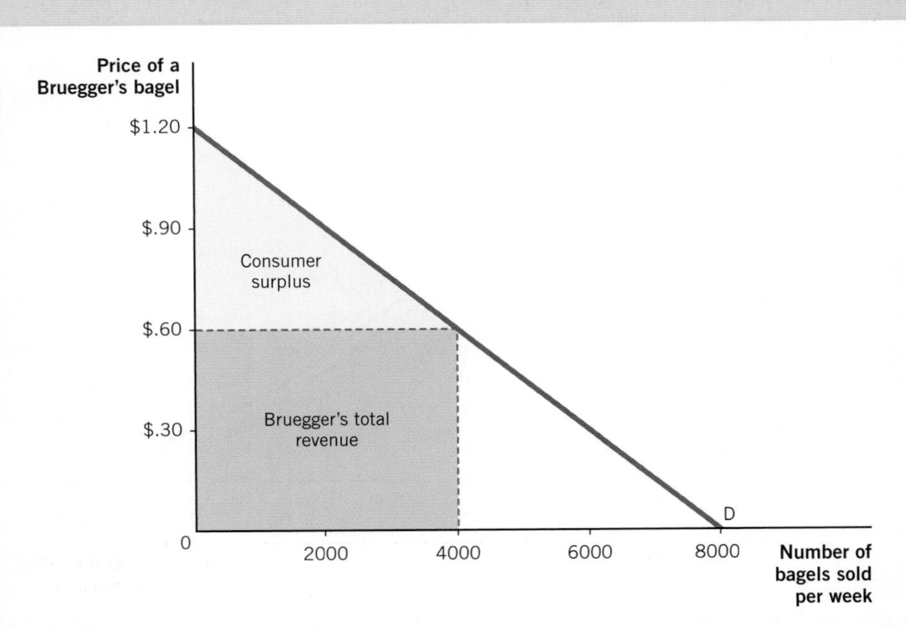

In Figure 2A.7, the blue triangle represents the amount of surplus consumers get from buying bagels. The amount of consumer surplus is $\frac{1}{2} \times \$0.60 \times \$4{,}000$, or $1,200.

Cautions in Interpreting Numerical Graphs

In Chapter 2, we utilized *ceteris paribus*, or the condition of holding everything else around us constant while analyzing a specific relationship. Suppose that you omitted an important part of the relationship. What effect would this have on your ability to use graphs as an illustrative tool? Consider the relationship between lemonade consumption and bottles of suntan lotion. The graph of the two variables would look something like Figure 2A.8.

Looking at Figure 2A.8, you would not necessarily know that something is misleading. However, when you stop to think about the relationship, you quickly recognize that the result is deceptive. Since the slope is positive, the graph indicates that there is a positive correlation between the number of bottles of suntan lotion used and the amount of lemonade people drink. At first glance this seems reasonable, since we associate suntan lotion and lemonade with summer activities. But the association is not **causal**, occurring when one variable influences the other. Using more suntan lotion does not cause people to drink more lemonade. It just so happens that when it is hot outside, more suntan lotion is used and more lemonade is consumed. In

Causality occurs when one variable influences the other.

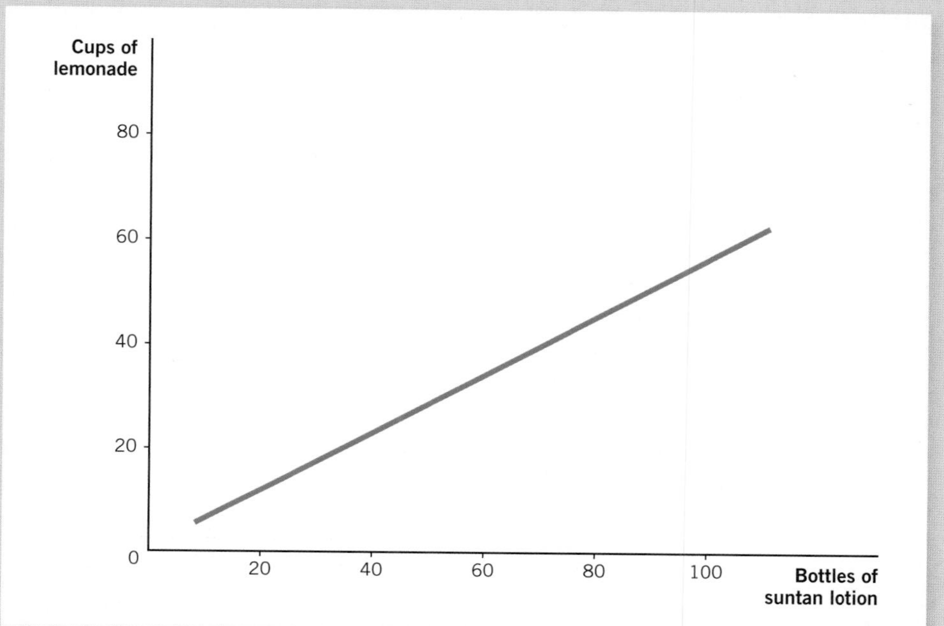

FIGURE 2A.8

Graph with an Omitted Variable

What looks like a strongly positive correlation is misleading. The demand for both lemonade and suntan lotion rises because the temperature rises, so the correlation between lemonade and suntan lotion use is deceptive, not informative.

this case, the causal factor is heat! The graph makes it look like the number of people using suntan lotion affects the amount of lemonade being consumed, when in fact they are not directly related.

Reverse causation occurs when causation is incorrectly assigned among associated events.

Another possible mistake is known as **reverse causation,** which occurs when causation is incorrectly assigned among associated events. Suppose that in an effort to fight the AIDS epidemic in Africa, a research organization notes the correlation shown in Figure 2A.9.

After looking at the data, it is clear that as the number of doctors per 1,000 people goes up, so do rates of death from AIDS. The research organization puts out a press release claiming that doctors are responsible for increasing AIDS deaths, and the media hypes the discovery. But hold on! Maybe there happen to be more doctors in areas with high incidences of AIDS because that's where they are most needed. Coming to the correct conclusion about the data requires that we do more than simply look at the correlation.

FIGURE 2A.9

Reverse Causation and an Omitted Variable

At a quick glance, this figure should strike you as odd. AIDS deaths are associated with having more doctors in the area. But the doctors are there to help and treat people, not harm them. This is an example of reverse causation.

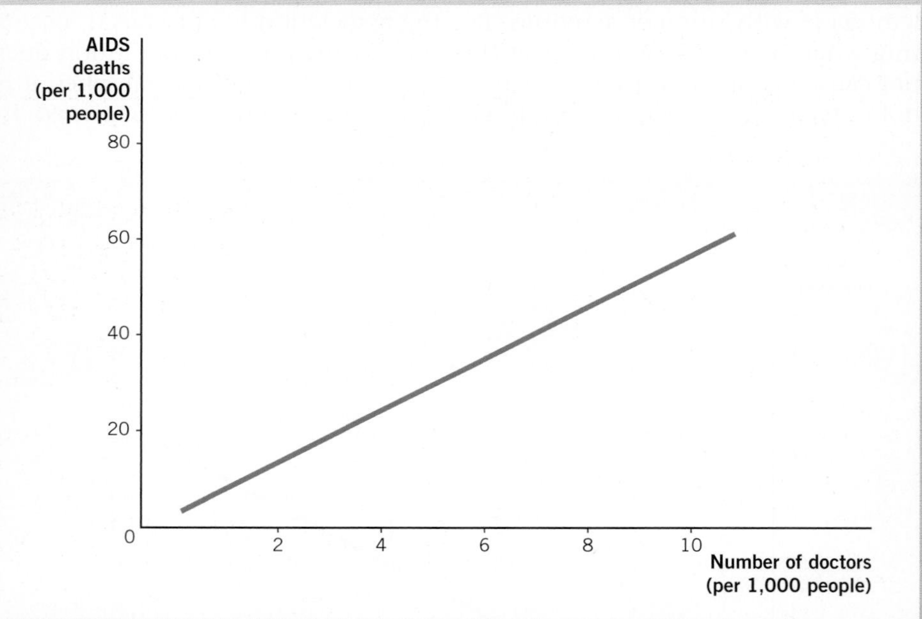

CONCEPTS YOU SHOULD KNOW

causality (p. 63)
negative correlation (p. 58)
positive correlation (p. 58)
reverse causation (p. 64)
scatterplot (p. 58)
slope (p. 59)
variable (p. 55)

STUDY PROBLEMS

1. The following table provides the price and the quantity demanded of apples (per week).

Price per Apple	Quantity Demanded
$0.25	10
$0.50	7
$0.75	4
$1.00	2
$1.25	1
$1.50	0

   a. Plot the data provided in the table into a graph.
   b. Is the relationship between the price of apples and the quantity demanded negative or positive?

* 2. In the following graph, calculate the value of the slope if the price rises from $20 to $40.

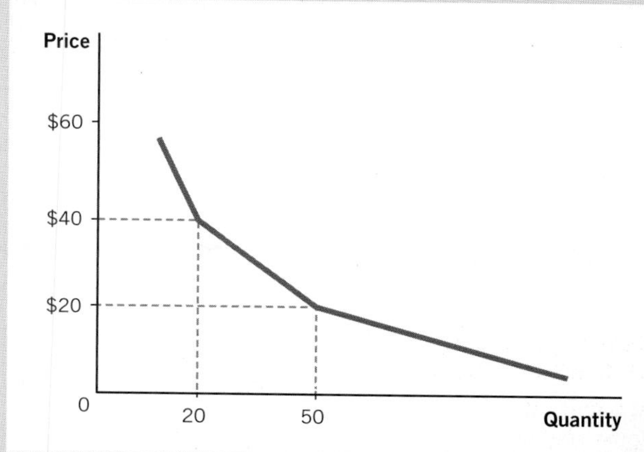

3. Explain the logical error in the following sentence: "As ice cream sales increase, the number of people who drown increases sharply. Therefore, ice cream causes drowning."

SOLVED PROBLEMS

2. The slope is calculated by using the formula:

$$\text{slope} = \frac{\text{change in } y}{\text{change in } x} = \frac{\$40 - \$20}{20 - 50} = \frac{\$20}{-30} = -0.6667$$

MARKET

PART

2

The Role of MARKETS

CHAPTER 3

The Market at Work

Supply and Demand

MISCONCEPTION

Demand matters more than supply.

What do Starbucks, Nordstrom, and Microsoft have in common? If you guessed that they all have headquarters in Seattle, that's true. But even more interesting is that each company supplies a product much in demand by consumers. Starbucks supplies coffee from coast to coast and seems to be everywhere someone wants a cup of coffee. Nordstrom, a giant retailer with hundreds of department stores, supplies fashion apparel to meet a broad spectrum of individual demand, from the basics to designer collections. Microsoft supplies software for customers all over the world. Demand for Microsoft products has made large fortunes for founder Bill Gates and the other investors in the company.

Notice the two recurring words in the previous paragraph: "supply" and "demand." These words are consistently used by economists when describing how an economy functions. Many people think that demand matters more than supply. This occurs because most people have much more experience as buyers than as sellers. Often our first instinct is to wonder how much something costs to buy rather than how much it costs to produce. This one-sided impression of the market undermines our ability to fully appreciate how prices are determined. To help correct this misconception, this chapter describes how markets work and the nature of competition. To shed light on the process, we will introduce the formal model of demand and supply. We will begin by looking at demand and supply separately. Then we will combine them to see how they interact to establish the market price and determine how much is produced.

Black Friday crush at Target.

BIG QUESTIONS

- What are the fundamentals of markets?
- What determines demand?
- What determines supply?
- How do supply and demand shifts affect a market?

What Are the Fundamentals of Markets?

In a **market economy**, resources are allocated among households and firms with little or no government interference.

Markets bring trading partners together to create order out of chaos. Companies supply goods and services, and customers want to obtain the goods and services that companies supply. In a **market economy**, resources are allocated among households and firms with little or no government interference. Adam Smith, the founder of modern economics, described the dynamic best: "It is not from the benevolence of the butcher, the brewer, or the baker, that we expect our dinner, but from their regard to their own interest." In other words, producers earn a living by selling the products that consumers want. Consumers are also motivated by self-interest; they must decide how to use their money to select the goods that they need or want the most. This process, which Adam Smith called the *invisible hand*, guides resources to their highest-valued use.

The exchange of goods and services in a market economy happens through prices that are established in markets. Those prices change according to the level of demand for a product and how much is supplied. For instance, hotel rates near Disney World are reduced in the fall when demand is low, and they peak in March near the week of Easter when spring break occurs. If spring break takes you to a ski resort instead, you will find lots of company and high prices. But if you are looking for an outdoor adventure during the summer, ski resorts have plenty of lodging available at great rates.

Peak season is expensive . . .

Similarly, many parents know how hard it is to find a reasonably priced hotel room in a college town on graduation weekend. Likewise, a pipeline break or unsettled political conditions in the Middle East can disrupt the supply of oil and cause the price of gasoline to spike overnight. When higher gas prices continue over a period of time, consumers respond by changing their driving habits or buying more fuel-efficient cars.

Why does all of this happen? Supply and demand tell the story. We will begin our exploration of supply and demand by looking at where they interact—in markets. The degree of control over the market price is the distinguishing feature between *competitive markets* and *imperfect markets*.

. . . but off-season is a bargain.

Competitive Markets

Buyers and sellers of a specific good or service come together to form a market. Formally, a market is a collection of buyers and sellers of a particular product or service. The buyers create the demand for the product, while the sellers produce the supply. It is the interaction of the buyers and sellers in a market that establishes the price and the quantity produced of a particular good or the amount of a service offered.

Markets exist whenever goods and services are exchanged. Some markets are online, and others operate in traditional "brick and mortar" stores. Pike Place Market in Seattle is a collection of markets spread across nine acres. For over a hundred years, it has brought together buyers and sellers of fresh, organic, and specialty foods. Since there are a number of buyers and sellers for each type of product, we say that the markets at Pike Place are *competitive*. A **competitive market** is one in which there are so many buyers and sellers that each has only a small impact on the market price and output. In fact, the impact is so small that it is negligible.

A **competitive market** exists when there are so many buyers and sellers that each has only a small impact on the market price and output.

At Pike Place Market, like other local produce markets, the goods sold are similar from vendor to vendor. Because each buyer and seller is small relative to the whole market, no single buyer or seller has any influence over the market price. These two characteristics—similar goods and many participants—create a highly competitive market in which the price and quantity sold are determined by the market rather than by any one person or business.

To understand how this works, let's take a look at sales of salmon at Pike Place Market. On any given day, dozens of vendors sell salmon at this market. So, if a single vendor is absent or runs out of salmon, the quantity supplied that day will not be significantly altered—the remaining sellers will have no trouble filling the void. The same is true for those buying salmon—customers will have no trouble finding

One of many vendors at Pike Place Market

salmon at the remaining vendors. Whether a particular salmon buyer decides to show up on a given day makes little difference when hundreds of buyers visit the market each day. No single buyer or seller has any appreciable influence over the price that prevails in the salmon market. As a result, the market for salmon at Pike Place Market is a competitive one.

An **imperfect market** is one in which either the buyer or the seller has an influence on the market price.

A **monopoly** exists when a single company supplies the entire market for a particular good or service.

The **quantity demanded** is the amount of a good or service that buyers are willing and able to purchase at the current price.

Imperfect Markets

Markets are not always competitive, though. An **imperfect market** is one in which either the buyer or the seller has an influence on the market price. For example, the Empire State Building affords a unique view of Manhattan. Not surprisingly, the cost of taking the elevator to the top of the building is not cheap. But many customers buy the tickets anyway because they have decided that the view is worth the price. The managers of the Empire State Building can set a high price for tickets because there is no other place in New York City with such a great view. From this, we see that when sellers produce goods and services that are different from their competitors', they gain some control, or leverage, over the price that they charge. The more unusual the product being sold, the more control the seller has over the price. When a seller has some control over the price, we say that the market is imperfect. Specialized products, such as popular video games, front-row concert tickets, or dinner reservations at a trendy restaurant, give the seller substantial pricing power.

The Empire State Building has the best view in New York City.

In between the highly competitive environment at the Pike Place Market and markets characterized by a lack of competition, such as the Empire State Building with its iconic view, there are many other varieties of markets. Some, like the market for fast-food restaurants, are highly competitive but sell products that are not identical. Other businesses—for example, Comcast cable—function like *monopolies*. A **monopoly** exists when a single company supplies the entire market for a particular good or service. We'll talk a lot more about different market structures such as monopoly in later chapters. But even in imperfect markets, the forces of supply and demand have a significant influence on producer and consumer behavior. For the time being, we'll keep our analysis focused on supply and demand in competitive markets.

What Determines Demand?

Demand exists when an individual or a group wants something badly enough to pay or trade for it. How much an individual or a group actually buys will depend on the price. In economics, the amount of a good or service purchased at the current price is known as the **quantity demanded**.

SNAPSHOT

The Invisible Hand

Why is the fish you want for dinner available in the store? It is because at each point in the economy's supply chain, the participants are concerned with their own profit. The process starts with the boat that catches the fish, then moves to the processing facility, to the truck, and finally to the store where the clerk sells the fish to you and me. At each step, the participant works to deliver the fish because they are acting in their own self-interest—matching supply to demand as if guided by an invisible hand.

1. CAUGHT

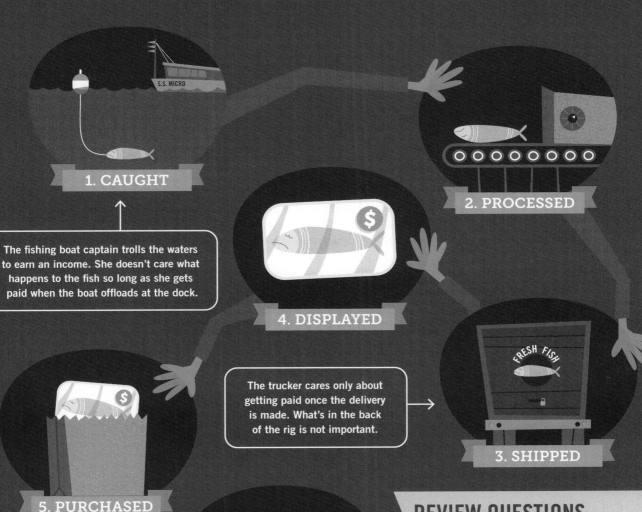

The fishing boat captain trolls the waters to earn an income. She doesn't care what happens to the fish so long as she gets paid when the boat offloads at the dock.

2. PROCESSED

3. SHIPPED

The trucker cares only about getting paid once the delivery is made. What's in the back of the rig is not important.

4. DISPLAYED

5. PURCHASED

The consumers care about freshness and price. They don't care to know the name of the fishing captain or trucker that brought the fish to the store for them to enjoy.

6. EATEN

REVIEW QUESTIONS

- What if someone in the supply chain is not allowed to earn a profit? How will this affect their actions and the supply chain as a whole?
- If fewer Alaskan salmon are caught, what will happen the price of salmon?

PRACTICE WHAT YOU KNOW

Markets and the Nature of Competition

Question: Which of the following are competitive markets?

1. Gas stations at a busy interstate exit
2. A furniture store in an isolated small town
3. A fresh produce stand at a farmer's market

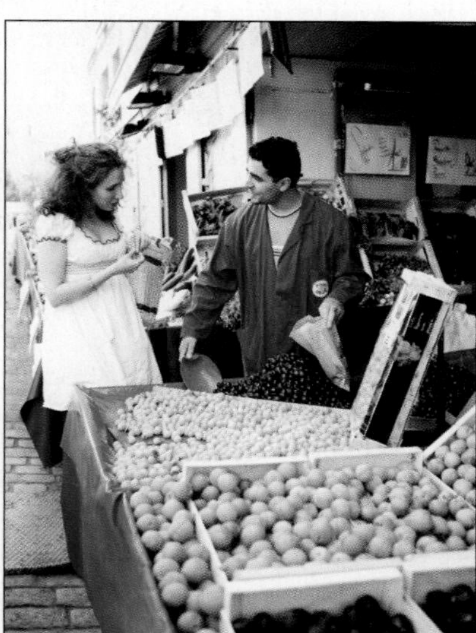

Is this a competitive market?

Answers

1. Because each gas station sells the same product and competes for the same customers, they often charge the same price. This is a competitive market. However, gas stations also differentiate themselves by offering many conveniences such as fast food, clean restrooms, ATM machines, and so forth. The result is that individual stations have some market power.
2. Residents would have to travel a significant distance to find another store. This allows the small-town store to charge more than other furniture stores. The furniture store has some monopoly power. This is not a competitive market.
3. Since consumers can buy fresh produce in season from many stands at a farmer's market, individual vendors have very little market pricing power. They must charge the same price as other vendors in order to attract customers. This is a competitive market.

When the price of a good increases, consumers often respond by purchasing less of the good or buying something else. For instance, many consumers who would buy salmon at $5.00 per pound would likely buy something else if the price rose to $20.00 per pound. Therefore, as price goes up, quantity demanded goes down. Similarly, as price goes down, quantity demanded goes up. This inverse relationship between the price and the quantity demanded is referred to as the *law of demand*. The **law of demand** states that, all other things being equal, the quantity demanded falls when the price rises, and the quantity demanded rises when the price falls. This holds true over a wide range of goods and settings.

The **law of demand** states that, all other things being equal, quantity demanded falls when prices rise, and rises when prices fall.

The Demand Curve

A table that shows the relationship between the price of a good and the quantity demanded is known as a **demand schedule**. Table 3.1 shows Meredith Grey's hypothetical demand schedule for salmon. When the price is $20.00 or more per pound, Meredith will not purchase any salmon. However, below $20.00 the amount that Meredith purchases is inversely related to the price. For instance, at a price of $10.00, Meredith's quantity demanded is 4 pounds per month. If the price rises to $12.50 per pound, she demands 3 pounds. Every time the price increases, Meredith buys less salmon. In contrast, every time the price falls, she buys more. If the price falls to zero, Meredith would demand 8 pounds. That is, even if the salmon is free, there is a limit to her demand because she would grow tired of eating the same thing.

A **demand schedule** is a table that shows the relationship between the price of a good and the quantity demanded.

The numbers in Meredith's demand schedule from Table 3.1 are plotted on a graph in Figure 3.1, known as a *demand curve*. A **demand curve** is a graph of the relationship between the prices in the demand schedule and the quantity demanded at those prices. For simplicity, the demand "curve" is often drawn as a straight line. Economists always place the independent variable, which is the price, on the *y* axis, and the dependent variable, which is the quantity demanded, on the *x* axis. The relationship between the price and the quantity demanded produces a downward-sloping curve. In Figure 3.1, we see that as the price rises from $0.00 to $20.00 along the *y* axis, the quantity demanded decreases from 8 to 0 pounds along the *x* axis.

A **demand curve** is a graph of the relationship between the prices in the demand schedule and the quantity demanded at those prices.

Market Demand

So far, we have studied individual demand, but markets comprise many different buyers. In this section, we will examine the collective demand of all of the buyers in a given market.

TABLE 3.1

Meredith's Demand Schedule for Salmon

Price of salmon (per pound)	Pounds of salmon demanded (per month)
$20.00	0
$17.50	1
$15.00	2
$12.50	3
$10.00	4
$ 7.50	5
$ 5.00	6
$ 2.50	7
$ 0.00	8

FIGURE 3.1

Meredith's Demand Curve for Salmon

Meredith's demand curve for salmon plots the data from Table 3.1. When the price of salmon is $10.00 per pound, she buys 4 pounds. If the price rises to $12.50 per pound, Meredith reduces the quantity that she buys to 3 pounds. The figure illustrates the law of demand by showing a negative relationship between price and the quantity demanded.

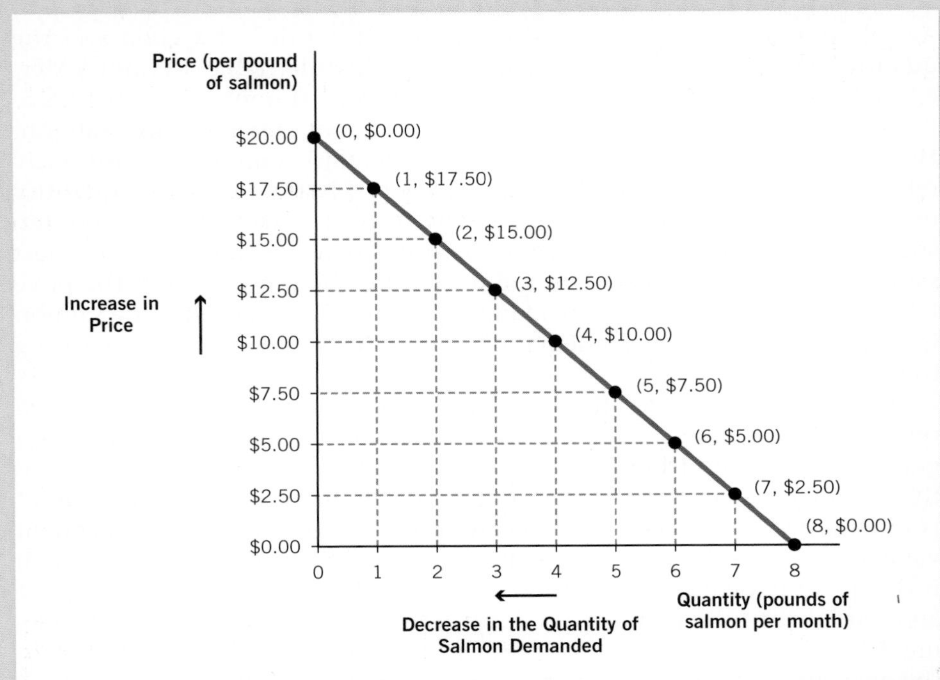

Market demand is the sum of all the individual quantities demanded by each buyer in the market at each price.

The **market demand** is the sum of all the individual quantities demanded by each buyer in a market at each price. During a typical day at Pike Place Market, over 100 individuals buy salmon. However, to make our analysis simpler, let's assume that our market consists of only two buyers, Derek and Meredith, each of whom enjoys eating salmon. Figure 3.2 shows individual demand schedules for the two people in this market, a combined market demand schedule, and the corresponding graphs. At a price of $10.00 per pound, Derek buys 2 pounds a month, while Meredith buys 4 pounds. To determine the market demand curve, we add Derek's 2 pounds to Meredith's 4 for a total of 6. As you can see in the table within Figure 3.2, by adding Derek and Meredith's demand we arrive at the total (that is, combined) market demand. The law of demand is shown on any demand curve with movements up or down the curve that reflect the effect of a change in price on the quantity demanded for the good or service. Only a change in price can cause a movement along a demand curve.

Shifts in the Demand Curve

We have examined the relationship between price and quantity demanded. This relationship, described by the law of demand, shows us that when price changes, consumers respond by altering the amount they purchase. But in addition to price, many other variables influence how much of a good or service is purchased. For instance, news about the possible risks or benefits associated with the consumption of a good or service can change overall demand.

FIGURE 3.2

Calculating Market Demand

To calculate the market demand for salmon, we add Derek's demand and Meredith's demand.

Price of salmon (per pound)	Derek's demand (per month)	Meredith's demand (per month)	Combined market demand
$20.00	0	0	0
$17.50	0	1	1
$15.00	1	2	3
$12.50	1	3	4
$10.00	2	4	6
$ 7.50	2	5	7
$ 5.00	3	6	9
$ 2.50	3	7	10
$ 0.00	4	8	12

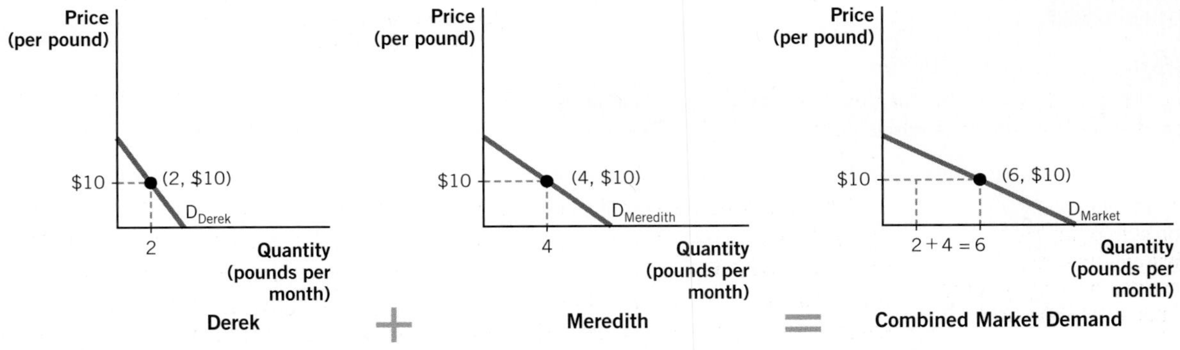

Suppose that the government issues a nationwide safety warning that cautions against eating cantaloupe because of a recent discovery of the *Listeria* bacteria in some melons. The government warning would cause consumers to buy fewer cantaloupes at any given price, and overall demand would decline. Looking at Figure 3.3, we see that an overall decline in demand will cause the entire demand curve to shift to the left of the original curve (which represents 6 cantaloupes), from D_1 to D_2. Note that though the price remains at $5 per cantaloupe, demand has moved from 6 melons to 3. Figure 3.3 also shows what does *not* cause a shift in demand curve: the price. The orange arrow along D_1 indicates that the quantity demanded will rise or fall in response to a price change. *A price change causes a movement along a given demand curve, but it cannot cause a shift in the demand curve.*

A decrease in overall demand causes the demand curve to shift to the left. What about when a variable causes overall demand to increase? Suppose that the press has just announced the results of a medical study indicating that cantaloupe contains a natural substance that lowers cholesterol. Because of the newly discovered health benefits of cantaloupe, overall demand for it would increase. This increase in demand would shift the demand curve to the right, from D_1 to D_3, as Figure 3.3 shows.

If a new medical study indicates that eating more cantaloupe lowers cholesterol, would this finding cause a shift in demand or a slide along the demand curve?

In the example above, we saw that demand shifted because of changes in consumers' tastes and preferences. However, there are many different variables that can shift demand. These include changes in buyers' income, the price of related goods, changes in buyers' taste and preferences, expectations regarding the future price, and the number of buyers.

Figure 3.4 provides an overview of the variables or factors that can shift demand. The easiest way to keep all of these elements straight is to ask yourself a simple question: *Would this change cause me to buy more or less of the good?* If the change lowers your demand for the good, you shift the demand curve to the left. If the change increases your demand for the good, you shift the curve to the right.

FIGURE 3.3

A Shift in the Demand Curve

When the price changes, the quantity demanded changes along the existing demand curve in the direction of the orange arrow. A shift in the demand curve, indicated by the black arrows, occurs when something other than price changes.

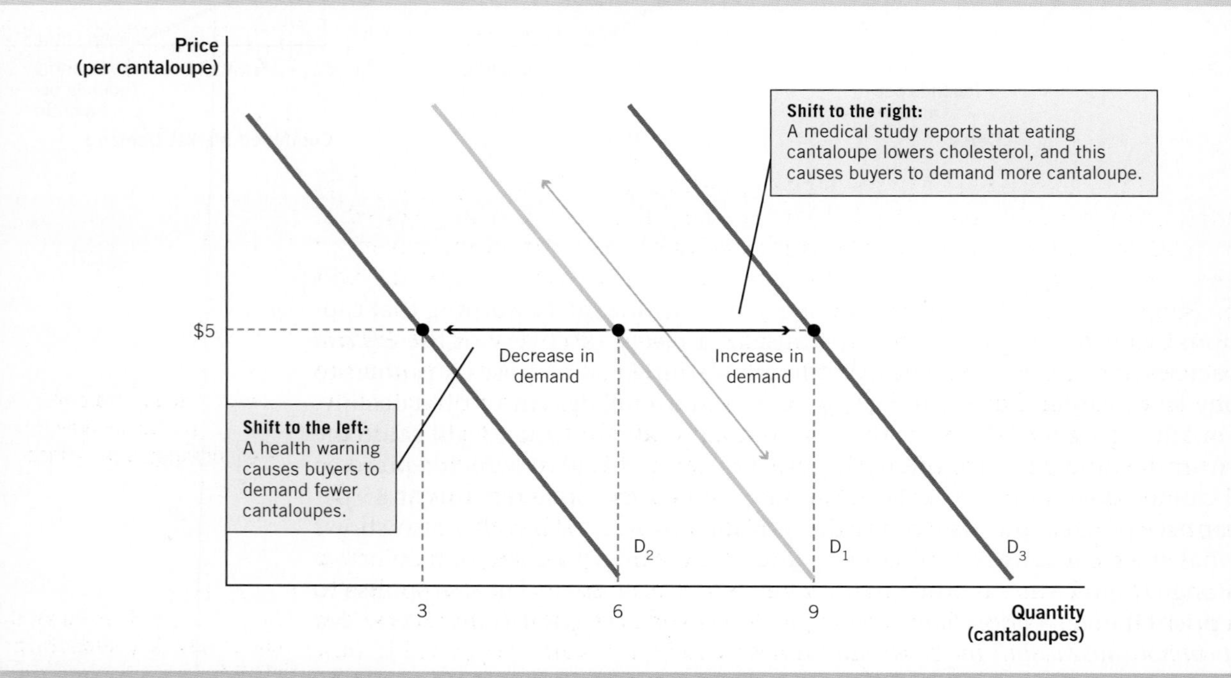

FIGURE 3.4

Factors That Shift the Demand Curve

The demand curve shifts to the left when a factor adversely affects—decreases—demand. The demand curve shifts to the right when a factor positively affects—increases—demand. (*Note*: a change in price does not cause a shift. Price changes cause slides along the demand curve.)

Factors That Shift Demand to the Left (Decrease Demand)

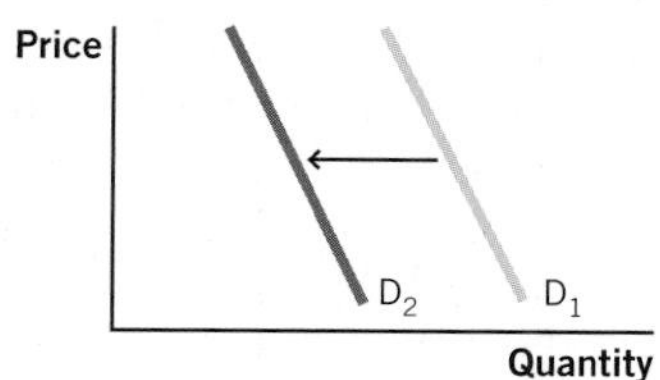

- Income falls (demand for a normal good).
- Income rises (demand for an inferior good).
- The price of a substitute good falls.
- The price of a complementary good rises.
- The good falls out of style.
- There is a belief that the future price of the good will decline.
- The number of buyers in the market falls.

Factors That Shift Demand to the Right (Increase Demand)

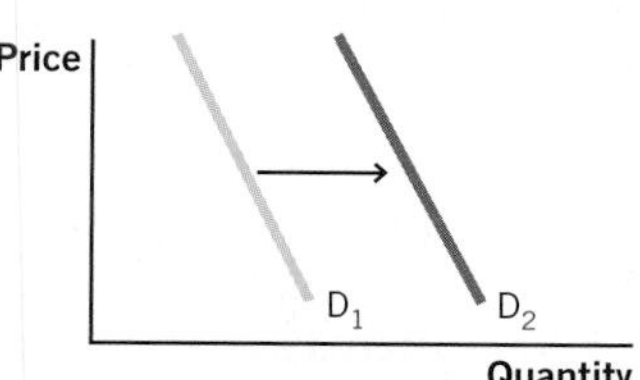

- Income rises (demand for a normal good).
- Income falls (demand for an inferior good).
- The price of a substitute good rises.
- The price of a complementary good falls.
- The good is currently in style.
- There is a belief that the future price of the good will rise.
- The number of buyers in the market increases.

Changes in Income

When your income goes up, you have more to spend. Assuming that prices don't change, individuals with higher incomes are able to buy more of what they want. Similarly, when your income declines, your purchasing power, or how much you can afford, falls. In either case, the amount of income you make affects your overall demand.

When economists look at how consumers spend, they often differentiate between two types of goods: *normal* and *inferior*. A consumer will buy more of a **normal good** as his or her income goes up (assuming all other factors remain constant). An example of a normal good is a meal at a restaurant. When income goes up, the demand for restaurant meals increases and the demand curve shifts to the right. Similarly, if income falls and the demand for restaurant meals goes down, the demand curve shifts to the left.

Consumers buy more of a **normal good** as income rises, holding other things constant.

While a consumer with an increase in income may purchase more of some things, the additional purchasing power will mean that he or she purchases less of other things, such as *inferior goods*. An **inferior good** is purchased out of necessity rather than choice. Examples include used cars as opposed to new cars, rooms in boarding houses as opposed to one's own apartment or house, and hamburger as opposed to filet mignon. As income goes up, consumers

An **inferior good** is purchased out of necessity rather than choice.

buy less of an inferior good because they can afford something better. Within a specific product market, you can often find examples of inferior and normal goods in the form of different brands.

The Price of Related Goods

Complements
are two goods that are used together. When the price of a complementary good rises, the demand for the related good goes down.

Substitutes
are two goods that are used in place of each other. When the price of a substitute good rises, the quantity demanded falls and the demand for the related good goes up.

Another factor that can shift the demand curve is the price of related goods. Certain goods directly influence the demand for other goods. These goods are known as *complements* and *substitutes*. **Complements** are two goods that are used together. **Substitutes** are two goods that are used in place of each other.

Consider this pair of complements: color ink cartridges and photo paper. You need both to print a photo in color. What happens when the price of one—say, color ink cartridges—rises? As you would expect, the quantity demanded of ink cartridges goes down. But demand for its complement, photo paper, also goes down. This is because people are not likely to use one without the other.

Substitute goods work the opposite way. When the price of a substitute good increases, the quantity demanded declines and the demand for the alternative good increases. For example, if the price of the Nintendo Wii goes up and the price of Microsoft's Xbox remains unchanged, the demand for Xbox will increase while the quantity demanded of the Wii will decline.

Changes in Tastes and Preferences

In fashion, types of apparel go in and out of style quickly. Walk into Nordstrom or another clothing retailer, and you will see that fashion changes from season to season and year to year. For instance, what do you think of Madras shorts? They were popular 20 years ago and they may be popular again now, but it is safe to assume that in a few years Madras shorts will once again go out of style. While something is popular, demand increases. As soon as it falls out of favor, you can expect demand for it to return to its former level. Tastes and preferences can change quickly, and this fluctuation alters the demand for a particular good.

Though changes in fashion trends are usually purely subjective, other changes in preferences are often the result of new information about the goods and services that we buy. Recall our example of shifting demand for cantaloupe as the result of either the *Listeria* infection or new positive medical findings. This is one example of how information can influence consumers' preferences. Contamination would cause a decrease in demand because people would no longer care to eat cantaloupe. In contrast, if people learn that eating cantaloupe lowers cholesterol, their demand for the melon will go up.

Fashion faux pas, or *c'est magnifique*?

Expectations Regarding the Future Price

Have you ever waited to purchase a sweater because warm weather was right around the corner and you expected the price to come down? Conversely, have you ever purchased an airline ticket well in advance because you figured that the price would rise as the flight filled up? In both cases, expectations about the future influenced your current demand. If we expect a price to be higher tomorrow, we are likely to buy more today to beat the price increase. This leads to an increase in current demand. Likewise, if you expect a price to decline soon, you might delay your purchases to try to capitalize on a lower price in the future. An expectation of a lower price in the future will therefore decrease current demand.

PRACTICE WHAT YOU KNOW

Shift or Slide?

Cheap pizza or . . .

. . . cheap drinks?

Suppose that a local pizza place likes to run a "late-night special" after 11 p.m. The owners have contacted you for some advice. One of the owners tells you, "We want to increase the demand for our pizza." He proposes two marketing ideas to accomplish this:

1. Reduce the price of large pizzas.
2. Reduce the price of a complementary good—for example, offer two half-priced bottles or cans of soda with every large pizza ordered.

Question: What will you recommend?

Answer: First, consider why "late-night specials" exist in the first place. Since most people prefer to eat dinner early in the evening, the store has to encourage late-night patrons to buy pizzas by stimulating demand. "Specials" of all sorts are used during periods of low demand when regular prices would leave the establishment largely empty.

Next, look at what the question asks. The owners want to know which option would "increase demand" more. The question is very specific; it is looking for something that will increase (or shift) demand.

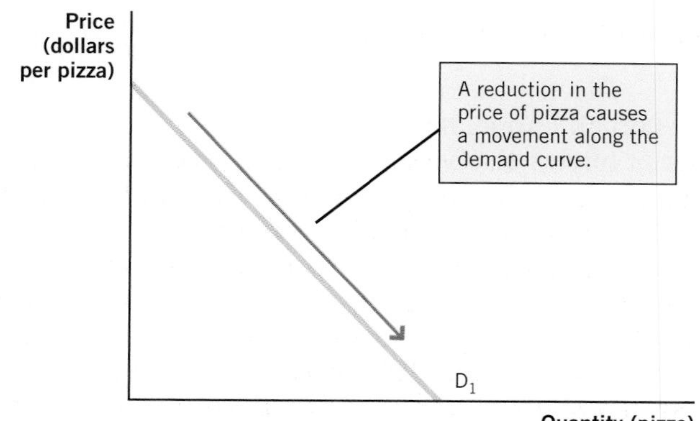

(CONTINUED)

(CONTINUED)

Consider the first option, a reduction in the price of pizzas. Let's look at this graphically (see above). A reduction in the price of a large pizza causes a movement along the demand curve, or a change in the quantity demanded.

Now consider the second option, a reduction in the price of a complementary good. Let's look at this graphically (see below). A reduction in the price of a complementary good (like soda) causes the entire demand curve to shift. This is the correct answer, since the question asks which marketing idea would increase (or shift) demand more.

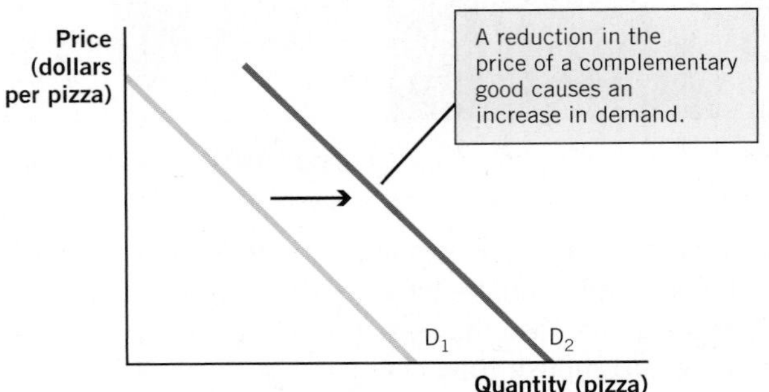

Recall that a reduction in the price of a complementary good shifts the demand curve to the right. This is the correct answer by definition! The other answer, cutting the price of pizzas, will cause an increase in the quantity demanded, or a movement along the existing demand curve.

If you move along a curve instead of shifting it, you will analyze the problem incorrectly.

The Number of Buyers

Recall that the market demand curve is the sum of all individual demand curves. Therefore, another way for the market demand to increase is for more individual buyers to enter the market. In the United States, we add 3 million people each year to our population through immigration and births. All those new people have needs and wants like the 300 million of us who are already here. Collectively, they add about 1% to the overall size of many existing markets on an annual basis.

The number of buyers also varies by age. Consider two markets—one for baby equipment, such as diapers, high chairs, and strollers, and the other for health care, including medicine, cancer treatments, hip replacement surgery, and nursing facilities. In countries with aging populations—for example, in Italy, where the birthrate has plummeted over several generations—the demand for baby equipment will decline and the demand for health care will expand. Therefore, demographic changes in society are another source of shifts in demand. In many markets, ranging from movie theater attendance to home ownership, population trends play an important role in determining whether the market is expanding or contracting.

Shifting the Demand Curve

ECONOMICS IN THE MEDIA

The Hudsucker Proxy

This 1994 film chronicles the introduction of the hula hoop, a toy that set off one of the greatest fads in U.S. history. According to Wham-O, the manufacturer of the hoop, when the toy was first introduced in the late 1950s over 25 million were sold in four months.

One scene from the movie clearly illustrates the difference between movements along the demand curve and a shift of the entire demand curve.

The Hudsucker Corporation has decided to sell the hula hoop for $1.79. We see the toy-store owner leaning next to the front door waiting for customers to enter. But business is slow. The movie cuts to the president of the company, played by Tim Robbins, sitting behind a big desk waiting to hear about sales of the new toy. It is not doing well. So the store lowers the price, first to $1.59, then to $1.49, and so on, until finally the hula hoop is "free with any purchase." But even this is not enough to attract consumers, so the toy-store owner throws the unwanted hula hoops into the alley behind the store.

One of the unwanted toys rolls across the street and around the block before landing at the foot of a boy who is skipping school. He picks up the hula hoop and tries it out. He is a natural. When school lets out, a throng of students rounds the corner and sees him playing with the hula hoop. Suddenly, everyone wants a hula hoop and there is a run on the toy store. Now preferences have changed, and the overall demand has increased. The hula hoop craze is born. In economic terms, we can say that the increased demand has shifted the entire demand curve to the right. The toy store responds by ordering new hula hoops and raising the price to $3.99—the new market price after the increase, or shift, in demand.

This scene reminds us that changes in price cannot shift the demand curve. Shifts in demand can only happen when an outside event influences human behavior. The graph below uses demand curves to show us the effect.

How did the hula hoop craze start?

First part of the scene: The price drops from $1.79 to "free with any purchase." Demand does not change—we only slide downward along the demand curve (D_1), resulting in a negligible increase in the quantity demanded.

Second part of the scene: The hula hoop craze begins and kids run to the toy store. The sudden change in behavior is evidence of a change in tastes, which shifts the demand curve to the right (D_2).

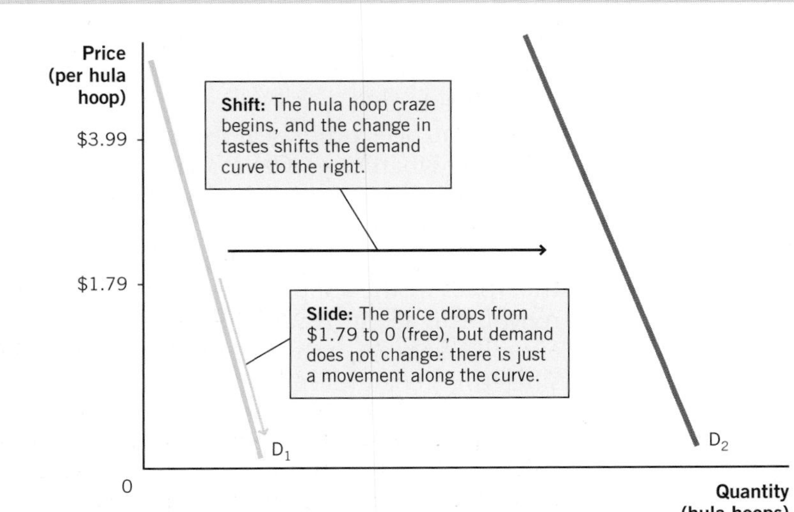

What Determines Supply?

Even though we have learned a great deal about demand, our understanding of markets is incomplete without also analyzing supply. Let's start by focusing on the behavior of producers interested in selling fresh salmon at Pike Place Market.

We have seen that with demand, price and output are negatively related. With supply, however, the price level and quantity supplied are positively related. For instance, few producers would sell salmon if the market price was \$2.50 per pound, but many would sell it if the price was \$20.00. (At \$20.00, producers earn more profit than when the price they receive is \$2.50.) The **quantity supplied** is the amount of a good or service that producers are willing and able to sell at the current price. Higher prices cause the quantity supplied to increase. Conversely, lower prices cause the quantity supplied to decrease.

The **quantity supplied** is the amount of a good or service that producers are willing and able to sell at the current price.

When price increases, producers often respond by offering more for sale. As price goes down, quantity supplied also goes down. This direct relationship between price and quantity supplied is referred to as the *law of supply*. The **law of supply** states that, all other things being equal, the quantity supplied increases when the price rises, and the quantity supplied falls when the price falls. This law holds true over a wide range of goods and settings.

The **law of supply** states that, all other things being equal, the quantity supplied of a good rises when the price of the good rises, and falls when the price of the good falls.

The Supply Curve

A **supply schedule** is a table that shows the relationship between the price of a good and the quantity supplied.

A **supply schedule** is a table that shows the relationship between the price of a good and the quantity supplied. The supply schedule for salmon in Table 3.2 shows how many pounds of salmon Sol Amon, owner of Pure Food Fish, would sell each month at different prices (Pure Food Fish is a fish stand that sells all kinds of freshly caught seafood). When the market price is \$20.00 per pound, Sol is willing to sell 800 pounds. At \$12.50, Sol's quantity offered is 500 pounds. If the price falls to \$10.00, he offers 100 fewer pounds, or 400. Every time the price falls, Sol offers less salmon. This means he is constantly adjusting the amount he offers. As the price of salmon falls, so does Sol's profit from selling it. Since Sol's livelihood depends on selling seafood, he has to find a way to compensate for the lost income. So he might offer more cod instead.

Sol and the other seafood vendors must respond to price changes by adjusting what they offer for sale in the market. This is why Sol offers more salmon when the price rises, and less salmon when the price declines.

When we plot the supply schedule in Table 3.2, we get the *supply curve* shown in Figure 3.5. A **supply curve** is a graph of the relationship between the prices in the supply schedule and the quantity supplied at those prices. As you can see in Figure 3.5, this relationship produces an upward-sloping curve. Sellers are more willing to supply the market when prices are high, since this generates more profits for the business. The upward-sloping curve means that the slope of the supply curve is positive, which illustrates a direct relationship between the price and the quantity offered for sale. For instance, when the price of salmon increases from \$10.00 to \$12.50 per pound, Pure Food Fish will increase the quantity it supplies to the market from 400 to 500 pounds.

A **supply curve** is a graph of the relationship between the prices in the supply schedule and the quantity supplied at those prices.

TABLE 3.2

Pure Food Fish's Supply Schedule for Salmon

Price of salmon (per pound)	Pounds of salmon supplied (per month)
$20.00	800
$17.50	700
$15.00	600
$12.50	500
$10.00	400
$ 7.50	300
$ 5.00	200
$ 2.50	100
$ 0.00	0

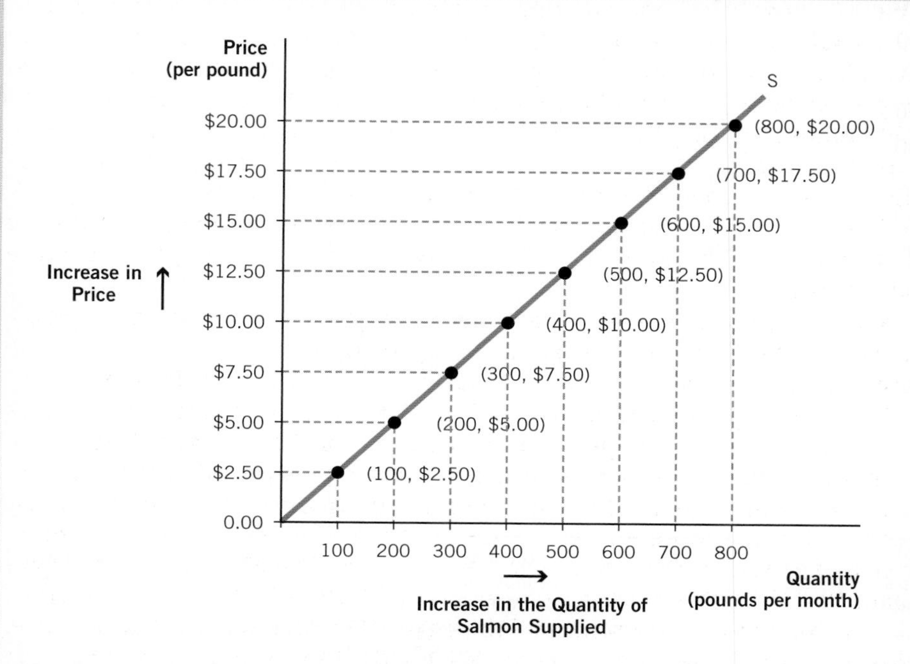

FIGURE 3.5

Pure Food Fish's Supply Curve for Salmon

Pure Food Fish's supply curve for salmon plots the data from Table 3.2. When the price of salmon is $10.00 per pound, Pure Food Fish supplies 400 pounds. If the price rises to $12.50 per pound, Pure Food Fish increases the quantity that it supplies to 500 pounds. The figure illustrates the law of supply by showing a positive relationship between price and the quantity supplied.

Market Supply

Market supply
is the sum of the quantities supplied by each seller in the market at each price.

Sol Amon is not the only vendor selling fish at the Pike Place Market. The **market supply** is the sum of the quantities supplied by each seller in the market at each price. However, to make our analysis simpler, let's assume that our market consists of just two sellers, City Fish and Pure Food Fish, each of which sells salmon. Figure 3.6 shows supply schedules for those two fish sellers and the combined, total-market supply schedule and the corresponding graphs.

Looking at the supply schedule (the table within the figure), you can see that at a price of $10.00 per pound, City Fish supplies 100 pounds of salmon, while Pure Food Fish supplies 400. To determine the total market supply, we add City Fish's 100 pounds to Pure Food Fish's 400 for a total market supply of 500.

FIGURE 3.6

Calculating Market Supply

Market supply is calculated by adding together the amount supplied by individual vendors. Each vendor's supply, listed in the second and third columns of the table, is illustrated graphically below. The total supply, shown in the last column of the table, is illustrated in the Combined Market Supply graph below.

Price of salmon (per pound)	City Fish's supply (per month)	Pure Food Fish's supply (per month)	Combined Market supply (pounds of salmon)
$20.00	200	800	1000
$17.50	175	700	875
$15.00	150	600	750
$12.50	125	500	625
$10.00	100	400	500
$ 7.50	75	300	375
$ 5.00	50	200	250
$ 2.50	25	100	125
$ 0.00	0	0	0

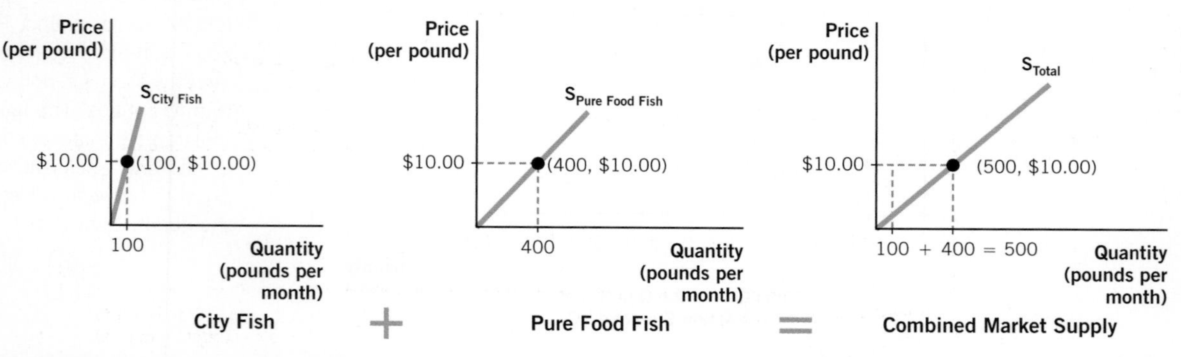

Shifts in the Supply Curve

When a variable other than the price changes, the entire supply curve shifts. For instance, suppose that beverage scientists at Starbucks discover a new way to brew a richer coffee at half the cost. The new process would increase the company's profits because its costs of supplying a cup of coffee would go down. The increased profits as a result of lower costs motivate Starbucks to sell more coffee and open new stores. Therefore, overall supply increases. Looking at Figure 3.7, we see that the supply curve shifts to the right of the original curve, from S_1 to S_2. Note that the retail price of coffee ($3 per cup) has not changed. When we shift the curve, we assume that price is constant and that something else has changed. In this case, the new brewing process, which has reduced the cost of producing coffee, has stimulated additional supply.

The first Starbucks opened in 1971 in Pike Place Market.

FIGURE 3.7

A Shift in the Supply Curve

When price changes, the quantity supplied changes along the existing supply curve, illustrated here by the orange arrow. A shift in supply occurs when something other than price changes, illustrated by the black arrows.

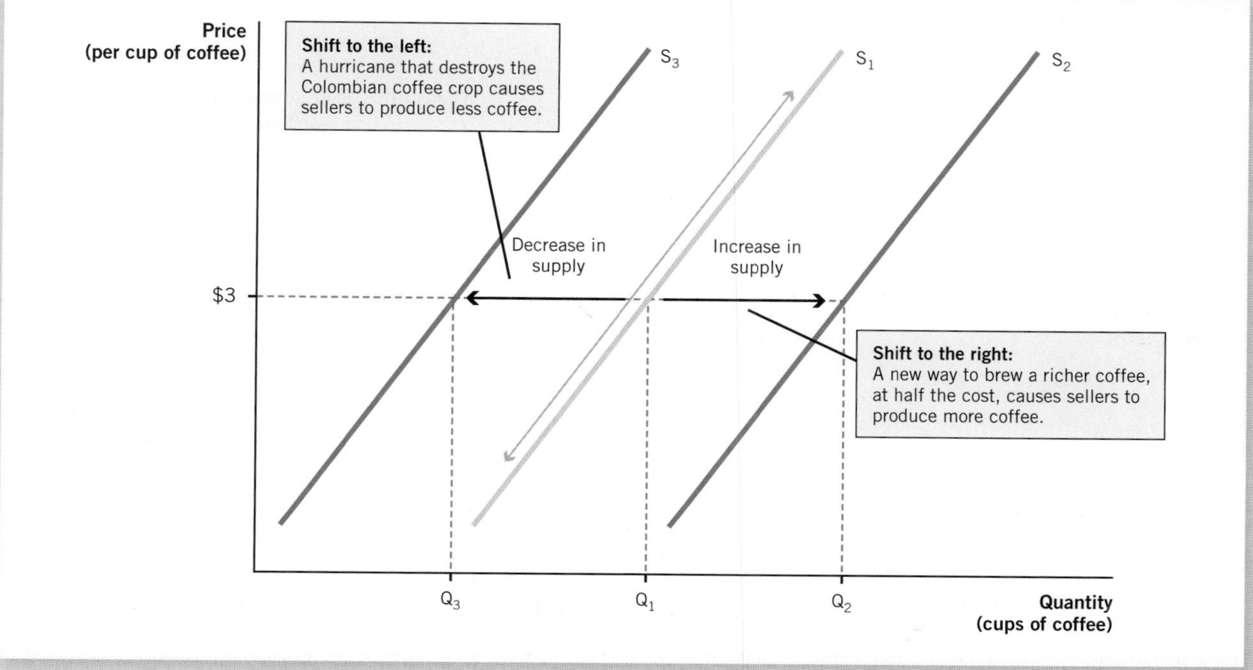

We have just seen that an increase in supply causes the supply curve to shift to the right. But what happens when a variable causes supply to decrease? Suppose that a hurricane devastates the coffee crop in Colombia and reduces world supply by 10% for that year. There is no way to make up for the destroyed coffee crop, and for the rest of the year at least, the quantity of coffee supplied will be less than the previous year. This decrease in supply shifts the supply curve in Figure 3.7 to the left, from S_1 to S_3.

Many variables can shift supply, but Figure 3.7 also reminds us of what does *not* cause a shift in supply: the price. Recall that price is the variable that causes the supply curve to slope upward. The orange arrow along S_1 indicates that the quantity supplied will rise or fall in response to a price change. *A price change causes a movement along the supply curve, not a shift in the curve.*

Factors that shift the supply curve include the cost of inputs, changes in technology and the production process, taxes and subsidies, the number of firms in the industry, and price expectations. Figure 3.8 provides an overview of these variables that shift the supply curve. The easiest way to keep them all straight is to ask yourself a simple question: *Would the change cause a*

FIGURE 3.8

Factors That Shift the Supply Curve

The supply curve shifts to the left when a factor negatively affects—decreases—supply. The supply curve shifts to the right when a factor positively affects—increases—supply. (*Note*: a change in price does not cause a shift. Price changes cause slides along the supply curve.)

Factors That Shift Supply to the Left (Decrease Supply)

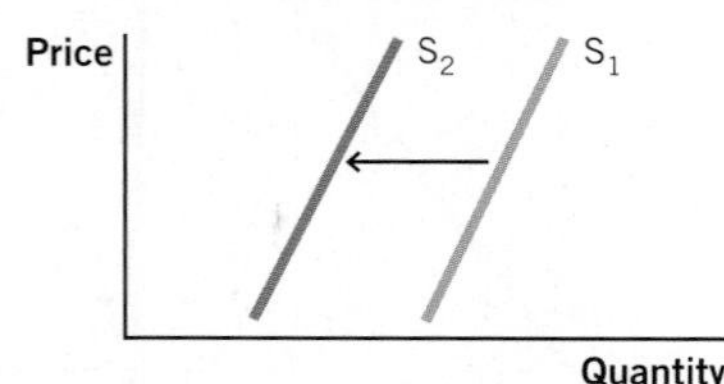

- The cost of an input rises.
- Business taxes increase or subsidies decrease.
- The number of sellers decreases.
- The price of the product is anticipated to rise in the future.

Factors That Shift Supply to the Right (Increase Supply)

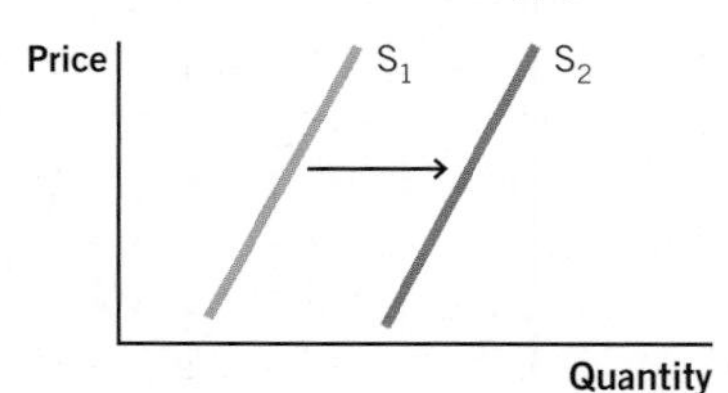

- The cost of an input falls.
- Business taxes decrease or subsidies increase.
- The number of sellers increases.
- The price of the product is expected to fall in the future.
- The business deploys more efficient technology.

business to produce more or less of the good? If the change would lower the business's willingness to supply the good or service, the supply curve shifts to the left. If the change would increase the business's willingness to supply the good or service, the supply curve shifts to the right.

The Cost of Inputs

Inputs are resources used in the production process. Inputs can take a number of forms and may include workers, equipment, raw materials, buildings, and capital. Each of these resources is critical to the production process. When the prices of inputs change, so does the seller's profit margin. If the cost of inputs declines, profit margins improve. Improved profit margins make the firm more willing to supply the good. So, for example, if Starbucks is able to purchase coffee beans at a significantly reduced price, it will want to supply more coffee. Conversely, higher input costs reduce profits. For instance, at Starbucks, the salaries of store employees, or baristas as they are commonly called, are a large part of the production cost. An increase in the minimum wage would require Starbucks to pay its workers more. This would raise the cost of making coffee, cut into Starbucks' profits, and make Starbucks less willing to supply coffee at the same price.

Inputs
are resources used in the production process.

Baristas' wages make up a large share of the cost of selling coffee.

Changes in Technology or the Production Process

Technology encompasses knowledge that producers use to make their products. An improvement in technology enables a producer to increase output with the same resources or to produce a given level of output with fewer resources. For example, if a new espresso machine works twice as fast as the old technology, Starbucks could serve its customers more quickly, reduce long lines, and increase the number of sales it makes. As a result, Starbucks would be willing to produce and sell more espressos at each price in its established menu. In other words, if the producers of a good discover a new and improved technology or a better production process, there will be an increase in supply; the supply curve for the good will shift to the right.

Taxes and Subsidies

Taxes placed on suppliers are an added cost of doing business. For example, if property taxes are increased, this raises the cost of doing business. A firm may attempt to pass along the tax to consumers through higher prices, but this will discourage sales. In other cases, the firm will simply have to accept the taxes as an added cost of doing business. Either way, a tax makes the firm less profitable. Lower profits make the firm less willing to supply the product and, thus, shift the supply curve to the left. As a result, the overall supply declines.

The reverse is true for a subsidy, which is a payment made by the government to encourage the consumption or production of a good or service. Consider a hypothetical example where the government wants to promote flu shots for high-risk cohorts like the young and elderly. One approach would be to offer large subsidies to producers such as clinics and hospitals, offsetting the production costs of immunizing the targeted groups. The supply curve of immunizations greatly shifts to the right under the subsidy, so the price falls. As a result, vaccination rates increase over what they would be in a market where the price was determined solely by the intersection of the market demand and supply curves.

The Number of Firms in the Industry

We saw that when there were more total buyers, the demand curve shifted to the right. A similar dynamic happens with an increase in the number of sellers in an industry. Each additional firm that enters the market increases the available supply of a good. In graphic form, the supply curve shifts to the right to reflect the increased production. By the same reasoning, if the number of firms in the industry decreases, the supply curve will shift to the left.

Changes in the number of firms in a market are a regular part of business. For example, if a new pizza joint opens up nearby, more pizzas can be produced and supply expands. Conversely, if a pizza shop closes, the number of pizzas produced falls and supply contracts.

Price Expectations

A seller who expects a higher price for a product in the future may wish to delay sales until a time when it will bring a higher price. For instance, florists know that the demand for roses spikes on Valentine's Day and Mother's Day. Because of higher demand, they can charge higher prices. In order to be able to sell more flowers during the times of peak demand, many florists work longer hours and hire temporary employees. This allows them to make more deliveries and therefore increase their ability to supply flowers while the price is high.

Likewise, the expectation of lower prices in the future will cause sellers to offer more while prices are still relatively high. This is particularly noticeable in the electronics sector where newer—and much better—products are constantly being developed and released. Sellers know that their current offerings will soon be replaced by something better and that consumer demand for the existing technology will then plummet. This means that prices typically fall when a product has been on the market for a time. Since producers know that the price will fall, they supply as many of the new models as possible before the next wave of innovation cuts the price that they can charge.

ECONOMICS IN THE REAL WORLD

Why Do the Prices of New Electronics Always Drop?

The first personal computers released in the 1980s cost as much as $10,000. Today, a laptop computer can be purchased for less than $500. When a new technology emerges, prices are initially very high and then tend to fall rapidly. The first PCs created a profound change in the way people could work with information. Prior to the advent of the PC, complex programming could be done only on large mainframe computers that often took up as much space as a whole room. But at first only a few people could afford a PC. What makes emerging technology so expensive when it is first introduced and so inexpensive later in its life cycle? Supply and demand tell the story.

In the case of PCs and other recent technologies, both demand and supply increase through time. Demand increases as consumers find more uses for the new technology. An increase in demand, by itself, would ordinarily drive the price up. However, producers are eager to supply this new market and ramp up production quickly. Since the supply expands more rapidly than the demand, there is both an increase in the quantity sold and a lower price.

Differences in expectations account for some of the difference between the increase in supply and demand. Both parties expect the price to fall, and they react accordingly. Suppliers try to get their new products to market as quickly as possible—before the price starts to fall appreciably. Therefore, the willingness to supply the product expands quickly. Consumer demand is slower to pick up because consumers expect the price to fall. This expectation tempers their desire to buy the new technology immediately. The longer they wait, the lower the price will be. Therefore, demand does not increase as fast as the supply. ✳

Why did consumers pay $5,000 for this?

PRACTICE WHAT YOU KNOW

The Supply and Demand of Ice Cream

Question: Which of the following will increase the demand for ice cream?

a. A decrease in the price of the butterfat used to make ice cream
b. A decrease in the price of ice cream
c. An increase in the price of the milk used to make ice cream
d. An increase in the price of frozen yogurt, a substitute for ice cream

I scream, you scream, we all scream for ice cream.

Answer: If you answered b, you made a common mistake. A change in the price of a good cannot change overall market demand; it can only cause a movement along an existing curve. So, as important as price changes are, they are not the right answer. First, you need to look for an event that shifts the entire curve.

Answers a and c refer to the prices of butterfat and milk. Since these are the inputs of production for ice cream, a change in prices will shift the supply curve. That leaves answer d as the only possibility. Answer d is correct since the increase in the price of frozen yogurt will cause the consumer to look elsewhere. Consumers will substitute away from frozen yogurt and toward ice cream. This shift in consumer behavior will result in an increase in the demand for ice cream even though its price remains the same.

Question: Which of the following will decrease the supply of chocolate ice cream?

a. A medical report finding that consuming chocolate prevents cancer
b. A decrease in the price of chocolate ice cream
c. An increase in the price of chocolate, an ingredient used to make ice cream
d. An increase in the price of whipped cream, a complementary good

Answer: We have already seen that b cannot be the answer because a change in the price of the good cannot change supply; it can only cause a movement along an existing curve. Answers a and d would both cause a change in demand without affecting the supply curve. That leaves answer c as the only possibility. Chocolate is a necessary ingredient used in the production process. Whenever the price of an input rises, it squeezes profit margins, and this results in a decrease in supply at the existing price.

How Do Supply and Demand Shifts Affect a Market?

We have examined supply and demand separately. Now it is time to see how the two interact. The real power and potential of supply and demand analysis is in how well it predicts prices and output in the entire market.

Supply, Demand, and Equilibrium

Let's consider the market for salmon again. This example meets the conditions for a competitive market because the salmon sold by one vendor is essentially the same as the salmon sold by another, and there are many individual buyers.

In Figure 3.9, we see that when the price of salmon fillets is $10 per pound, consumers demand 500 pounds and producers supply 500. This is represented graphically at point E, known as the point of **equilibrium**, where the demand curve and the supply curve intersect. At this point, the two opposing forces of supply and demand are perfectly balanced.

Equilibrium
occurs at the point where the demand curve and the supply curve intersect.

Notice that at $10.00 per fillet, the quantity demanded equals the quantity supplied. At this price, and only this price, the entire supply of salmon in the market is sold. Moreover, every buyer who wants salmon is able to find some and every producer is able to sell his or her entire stock. We say that $10.00 is the **equilibrium price** because the quantity supplied equals the quantity demanded. The equilibrium price is also called the *market-clearing*

The **equilibrium price** is the price at which the quantity supplied is equal to the quantity demanded. This is also known as the *market-clearing price.*

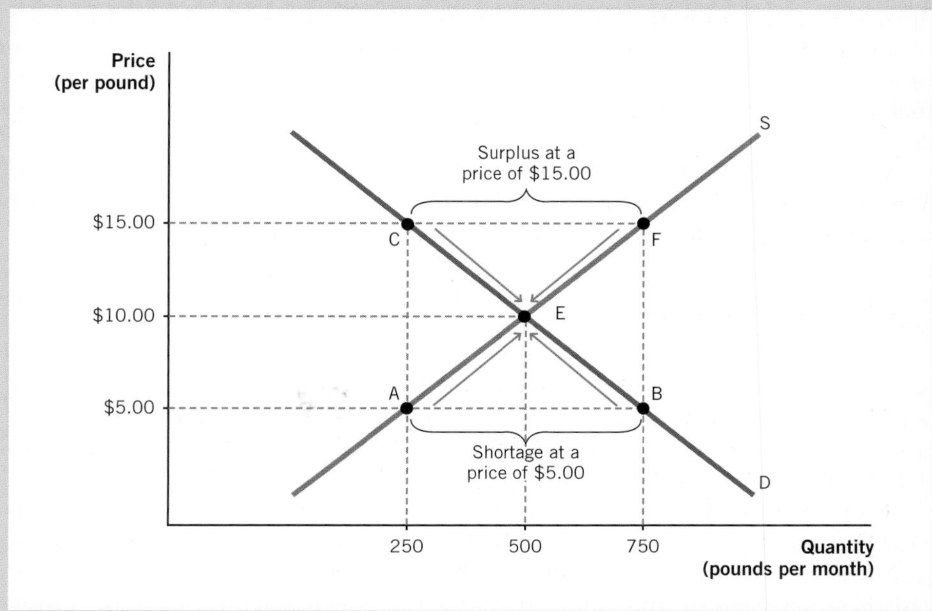

FIGURE 3.9

The Salmon Market

At the equilibrium point, E, supply and demand are perfectly balanced. At prices above the equilibrium price, a surplus of goods exists, while at prices below the equilibrium price, a shortage of goods exists.

The **equilibrium quantity** is the amount at which the quantity supplied is equal to the quantity demanded.

The **law of supply and demand** states that the market price of any good will adjust to bring the quantity supplied and the quantity demanded into balance.

price, since this is the only price at which no surplus or shortage of the good exists. Similarly, there is also an **equilibrium quantity**, of 500 pounds, at which the quantity supplied equals the quantity demanded. When the market is in equilibrium, we sometimes say that *the market clears* or that *the price clears the market.* The equilibrium point has a special place in economics because movements away from that point throw the market out of balance. The equilibrium process is so powerful that it is often referred to as the *law of supply and demand.* According to the **law of supply and demand**, market prices adjust to bring the quantity supplied and the quantity demanded into balance.

Shortages and Surpluses

How does the market respond when it is not in equilibrium? Let's look at two other prices for salmon shown on the *y* axis in Figure 3.9: $5.00 and $15.00 per pound.

At a price of $5.00 per pound, salmon is quite attractive to buyers but not very profitable to sellers—the quantity demanded is 750 pounds, represented by point B on the demand curve (D). However, the quantity supplied, which is represented by point A on the supply curve (S), is only 250. So at $5.00 per pound there is an excess quantity of 500 pounds demanded. This excess demand creates disequilibrium in the market.

A **shortage** occurs whenever the quantity supplied is less than the quantity demanded.

When there is more demand for a product than sellers are willing or able to supply, we say there is a *shortage*. A **shortage** occurs whenever the quantity supplied is less than the quantity demanded. In our case, at a price of $5.00 there are three buyers for each pound of salmon. New shipments of salmon fly out the door. This is a strong signal for sellers to raise the price. As the market price increases in response to the shortage, sellers continue to increase the quantity that they offer. You can see this on the graph in Figure 3.9 by following the upward-sloping arrow from point A to point E. At the same time, as the price rises, buyers will demand an increasingly smaller quantity, represented by the upward-sloping arrow from point B to point E along the demand curve. Eventually, when the price reaches $10.00, the quantity supplied and the quantity demanded will be equal. The market will be in equilibrium.

What happens when the price is set above the equilibrium point—say, at $15.00 per pound? At this price, salmon is quite profitable for sellers but not very attractive to buyers. The quantity demanded, represented by point C on the demand curve, is 250 pounds. However, the quantity supplied, represented by point F on the supply curve, is 750. In other words, sellers provide 500 pounds more than buyers wish to purchase. This excess supply creates disequilibrium in the market. Any buyer who is willing to pay $15.00 for a pound of salmon can find some since there are three pounds available for every customer. This situation is known as a *surplus*. A **surplus**, or excess supply, occurs whenever the quantity supplied is greater than the quantity demanded.

A **surplus** occurs whenever the quantity supplied is greater than the quantity demanded.

When there is a surplus, sellers realize that salmon has been oversupplied. This is a strong signal to lower the price. As the market price decreases in response to the surplus, more buyers enter the market and purchase salmon. This is represented on the graph in Figure 3.9 by the downward-sloping arrow moving from point C to point E along the demand curve. At the same time, sellers reduce output, represented by the downward-sloping arrow moving

from point F to point E on the supply curve. As long as the surplus persists, the price will continue to fall. Eventually, the price will reach $10.00 per pound. At this point, the quantity supplied and the quantity demanded will be equal and the market will be in equilibrium again.

In competitive markets, surpluses and shortages are resolved through the process of price adjustment. Buyers who are unable to find enough salmon at $5.00 per pound compete to find the available stocks; this drives the price up. Likewise, businesses that cannot sell their product at $15.00 per pound must lower their prices to reduce inventories; this drives the price down.

Every seller and buyer has a vital role to play in the market. Venues like the Pike Place Market bring buyers and sellers together. Amazingly, all of this happens spontaneously, without the need for government planning to ensure an adequate supply of the goods that consumers need. You might think that a decentralized system would create chaos, but nothing could be further from the truth. Markets work because buyers and sellers can rapidly adjust to changes in prices. These adjustments bring balance. When markets were suppressed in communist command economies during the twentieth century, shortages were commonplace, in part because there was no market price system to signal that additional production was needed. (A command economy is one in which supply and price are regulated by the government rather than by market forces.) This led to the creation of many black markets (see Chapter 5).

How do markets respond to additional demand? In the case of the bowling cartoon shown above, the increase in demand comes from an unseen customer who wants to use a bowling lane already favored by another patron. An increase in the number of buyers causes an increase in demand. The lane is valued by two buyers, instead of just one, so the owner is contemplating a price increase! This is how markets work. Price is a mechanism to determine which buyer wants the good or service the most.

In summary, Figure 3.10 provides four examples of what happens when either the supply or the demand curve shifts. As you study these, you should develop a sense for how price and quantity are affected by changes in supply and demand. When one curve shifts, we can make a definitive statement about how price and quantity will change. In the chapter appendix that follows, we consider what happens when supply and demand change at the same time. There you will discover the challenges in simultaneously determining price and quantity when more than one variable changes.

FIGURE 3.10

Price and Quantity When Either Supply or Demand Changes

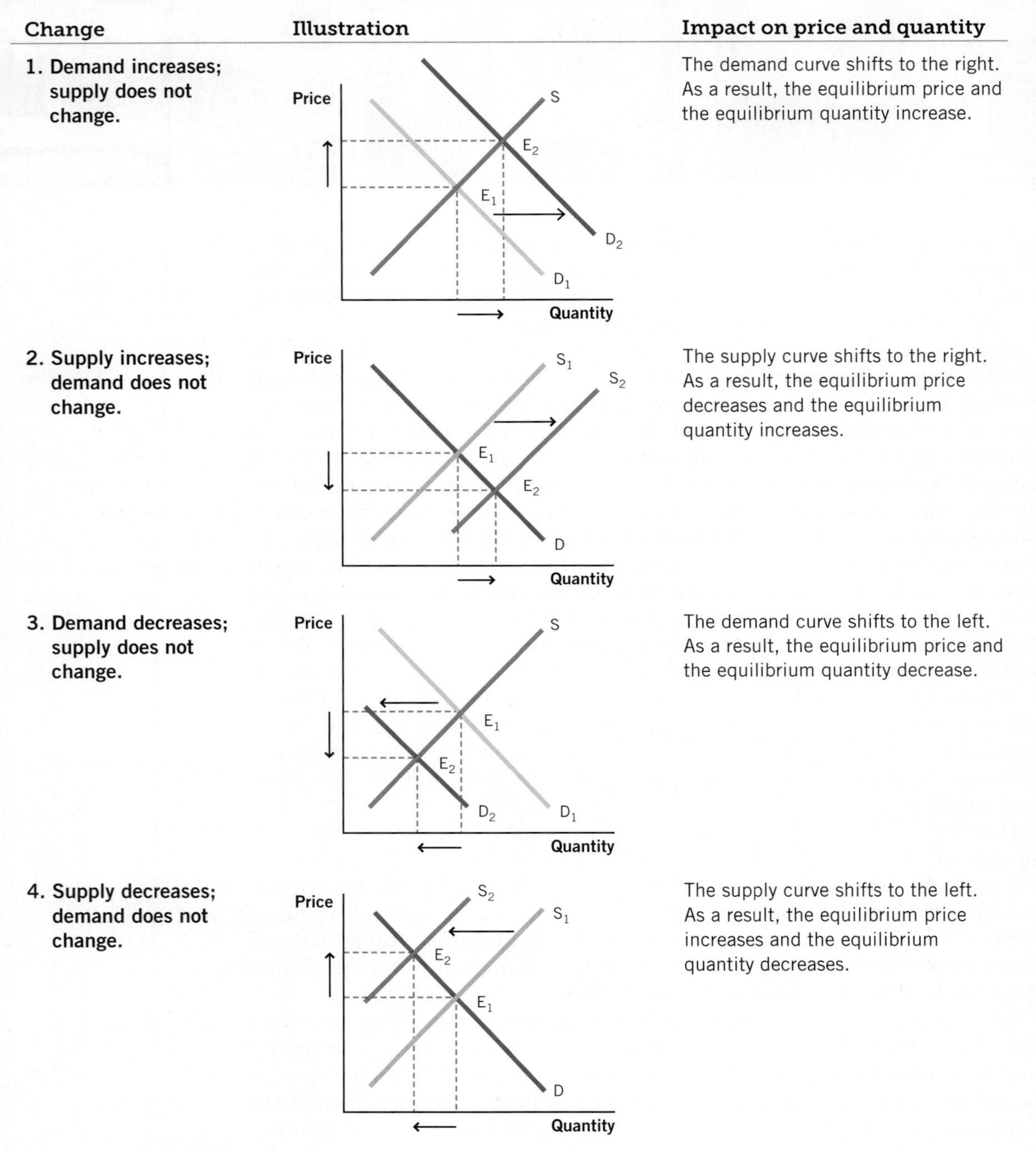

Change	Impact on price and quantity
1. Demand increases; supply does not change.	The demand curve shifts to the right. As a result, the equilibrium price and the equilibrium quantity increase.
2. Supply increases; demand does not change.	The supply curve shifts to the right. As a result, the equilibrium price decreases and the equilibrium quantity increases.
3. Demand decreases; supply does not change.	The demand curve shifts to the left. As a result, the equilibrium price and the equilibrium quantity decrease.
4. Supply decreases; demand does not change.	The supply curve shifts to the left. As a result, the equilibrium price increases and the equilibrium quantity decreases.

ECONOMICS FOR LIFE

Bringing Supply and Demand Together: Advice for Buying Your First Place

There is an old adage in real estate, "location, location, location." Why does location matter so much? Simple. Supply and demand. There are only so many places to live in any given location—that is the supply. The most desirable locations have many buyers who'd like to purchase in that area—that is the demand.

Consider for a moment all of the variables that can influence where you want to live. As you're shopping for your new home, you may want to consider proximity to where you work, your favorite restaurants, public transportation, and the best schools. You'll also want to pay attention to the crime rate, differences in local tax rates, traffic concerns, noise issues, and nearby zoning restrictions. In addition, many communities have restrictive covenants that limit how owners can use their property. Smart buyers determine how the covenants work and whether they would be happy to give up some freedom in order to maintain an attractive neighborhood. Finally, it is always a good idea to visit the neighborhood in the evening or on the weekend to meet your future neighbors before you buy. All of these variables determine the demand for any given property.

Once you've done your homework and settled on a neighborhood, you will find that property values can vary tremendously across very short distances. A home along a busy street may sell for half the price of a similar property that backs up to a quiet park a few blocks away. Properties near a subway line command a premium, as do properties with views or close access to major employers and amenities (such as parks, shopping centers, and places to eat). Here is the main point to remember, even if some of these things aren't important to you: when it comes time to sell, the location of the home will always matter. The number of potential buyers depends on the characteristics of your neighborhood and the size and condition of your property. If you want to be able to sell your place easily, you'll have to consider not only where you want to live now but who might want to live there later.

All of this discussion brings us back to supply and demand. The best locations are in short supply and high demand. The combination of low supply and high demand causes property values in those areas to rise. Likewise, less desirable locations have lower property values because demand is relatively low and the supply is relatively high. Since first-time buyers often have wish lists that far exceed their budgets, considering the costs and benefits will help you find the best available property.

There is a popular HGTV show called *Property Virgins* that follows first-time buyers through the process of buying their first home. If you have never seen the show, watching an episode is one of the best lessons in economics you'll ever get. Check it out, and remember that even though you may be new to buying property, you still can get a good deal if you use some basic economics to guide your decision.

Where you buy is more important than *what* you buy.

Conclusion

Does demand matter more than supply? As you have learned in this chapter, the answer is no. Demand and supply contribute equally to the functioning of markets. Five years from now, if someone asks you what you remember about your first course in economics, you will probably respond with two words, "supply" and "demand." These two opposing forces enable economists to model market behavior through prices. Prices help establish the market equilibrium, or the price at which supply and demand are in balance. At the equilibrium point, every good and service produced has a corresponding buyer who wants to purchase it. When the market is out of equilibrium, it causes a shortage or surplus. These conditions persist until buyers and sellers have a chance to adjust the quantity they demand and the quantity they supply, respectively. This refutes the misconception we noted at the beginning of the chapter.

In the next chapter, we will extend our understanding of supply and demand by examining how sensitive, or responsive, consumers and producers are to price changes. This will allow us to determine whether price changes have a big effect on behavior or not.

ANSWERING THE BIG QUESTIONS

What are the fundamentals of markets?

- A market consists of a group of buyers and sellers for a particular product or service.
- When competition is present, markets produce low prices.
- Not all markets are competitive. When suppliers have market power, markets are imperfect and prices are higher.

What determines demand?

- The law of demand states that there is an inverse relationship between the price and the amount that the consumer wishes to purchase.
- As a result of the law of demand, the demand curve is downward sloping.
- A price change causes a movement along the demand curve, not a shift in the curve.
- Changes in something other than price cause the demand curve to shift.

What determines supply?

* The law of supply states that there is a direct relationship between the price and the amount that is offered for sale.
* The supply curve is upward sloping.
* A price change causes a movement along the supply curve, not a shift in the curve.
* Changes in the prices of inputs, new technologies, taxes, subsidies, the number of sellers, and expectations about the future price all influence the location of the new supply curve and cause the original supply curve to shift.

How do supply and demand shifts affect a market?

* Supply and demand interact through the process of market coordination.
* Together, supply and demand create a process that leads to equilibrium, the balancing point between the two opposing forces. The market-clearing price and output are determined at the equilibrium point.
* When the price is above the equilibrium point, a surplus exists and inventories build up. This will cause suppliers to lower their price in an effort to sell the unwanted goods. The process continues until the equilibrium price is reached.
* When the price is below the equilibrium point, a shortage exists and inventories are depleted. This will cause suppliers to raise their price in order to ration the good. The price rises until the equilibrium point is reached.

CONCEPTS YOU SHOULD KNOW

competitive market (p. 71)
complements (p. 80)
demand curve (p. 75)
demand schedule (p. 75)
equilibrium (p. 93)
equilibrium price (p. 93)
equilibrium quantity (p. 94)
imperfect market (p. 72)
inferior good (p. 79)
inputs (p. 89)
law of demand (p. 74)
law of supply (p. 84)
law of supply and demand (p. 94)
market demand (p. 76)
market economy (p. 70)
market supply (p. 86)
monopoly (p. 72)
normal good (p. 79)
quantity demanded (p. 72)
quantity supplied (p. 84)
shortage (p. 94)
substitutes (p. 80)
supply curve (p. 84)
supply schedule (p. 84)
surplus (p. 94)

QUESTIONS FOR REVIEW

1. What is a competitive market, and how does it depend on the existence of many buyers and sellers?
2. Why does the demand curve slope downward?
3. Does a price change cause a movement along a demand curve or a shift of the entire curve? What factors cause the entire demand curve to shift?
4. Describe the difference between inferior and normal goods.
5. Why does the supply curve slope upward?
6. Does a price change cause a movement along a supply curve or a shift of the entire curve? What factors cause the entire supply curve to shift?
7. Describe the process that leads the market toward equilibrium.
8. What happens in a competitive market when the price is above or below the equilibrium price?
9. What roles do shortages and surpluses play in the market?

STUDY PROBLEMS (* *solved at the end of the section*)

1. In the song "Money, Money, Money" by ABBA, the lead singer, Anni-Frid Lyngstad, is tired of the hard work life requires and plans to marry a wealthy man. If she is successful, how would this marriage change the artist's demand for goods? How would it change her supply of labor? Illustrate both changes with supply and demand curves. Be sure to explain what is happening in the diagrams. (Note: the full lyrics for the song can be found by Googling the song title and ABBA. For inspiration, try listening to the song while you solve the problem!)

2. For each of the following scenarios, determine if there is an increase or a decrease in demand for the good in *italics*.

   a. The price of *oranges* increases.
   b. The cost of producing *tires* increases.
   c. Samantha Brown, who is crazy about *air travel*, gets fired from her job.
   d. A local community has an unusually wet spring and a subsequent problem with mosquitos, which can be deterred with *citronella*.
   e. Many motorcycle enthusiasts enjoy riding without *helmets* (in states where this is permitted by law). The price of new motorcycles rises.

3. For each of the following scenarios, determine if there is an increase or a decrease in supply for the good in *italics*.

   a. The price of *silver* increases.
   b. Growers of *tomatoes* experience an unusually good growing season.

c. New medical evidence reports that consumption of *organic products* reduces the incidence of cancer.
d. The wages of low-skill workers, a resource used to help produce *clothing*, increase.
e. The price of movie tickets, a substitute for *video rentals*, goes up.

4. Are laser pointers and cats complements or substitutes? (Not sure? Search for videos of cats and laser pointers online.) Discuss.

* 5. The market for ice cream has the following demand and supply schedules:

Price (per quart)	Quantity demanded (quarts)	Quantity supplied (quarts)
\$2	100	30
\$3	80	45
\$4	60	60
\$5	40	75
\$6	20	90

a. What are the equilibrium price and equilibrium quantity in the ice cream market? Confirm your answer by graphing the demand and supply curves.
b. If the actual price was \$3 per quart, what would drive the market toward equilibrium?

6. Starbucks Entertainment announced in a 2007 news release that Dave Matthews Band's *Live Trax* CD was available only at the company's coffee shops in the United States and Canada. The compilation features recordings of the band's performances dating back to 1995. Why would Starbucks and Dave Matthews have agreed to partner in this way? To come up with an answer, think about the nature of complementary goods and how both sides can benefit from this arrangement.

7. The Seattle Mariners wish to determine the equilibrium price for seats for each of the next two seasons. The supply of seats at the ballpark is fixed at 45,000.

Price (per seat)	Quantity demanded in year 1	Quantity demanded in year 2	Quantity supplied
\$25	75,000	60,000	45,000
\$30	60,000	55,000	45,000
\$35	45,000	50,000	45,000
\$40	30,000	45,000	45,000
\$45	15,000	40,000	45,000

Draw the supply curve and each of the demand curves for years 1 and 2.

* 8. Demand and supply curves can also be represented with equations. Suppose that the quantity demanded, Q_D, is represented by the following equation:

$$Q_D = 90 - 2P$$

The quantity supplied, Q_S, is represented by the equation:

$$Q_S = P$$

a. Find the equilibrium price and quantity. **Hint:** Set $Q_D = Q_S$ and solve for the price, P, and then plug your result back into either of the original equations to find Q.
b. Suppose that the price is \$20. Determine Q_D and Q_S.
c. At a price of \$20, is there a surplus or a shortage in the market?
d. Given your answer in part c, will the price rise or fall in order to find the equilibrium point?

SOLVED PROBLEMS

5.

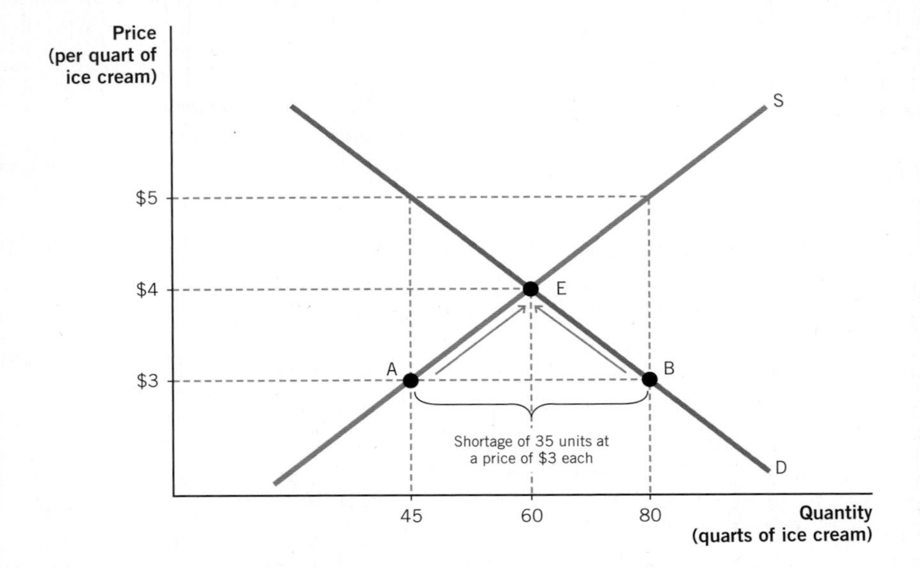

a. The equilibrium price is $4 and quantity is 60 units (quarts). The next step is to graph the curves. This is done above.

b. A shortage of 35 units of ice cream exists at $3; therefore, there is excess demand. Ice cream sellers will raise their price as long as excess demand exists. That is, as long as the price is below $4. It is not until $4 that the equilibrium point is reached and the shortage is resolved.

8. a. The first step is to set $Q_D = Q_S$. Doing so gives us $90 - 2P = P$. Solving for price, we find that $90 = 3P$, or $P = 30$. Once we know that $P = 30$, we can plug this value back into either of the original equations, $Q_D = 90 - 2P$ or $Q_S = P$. Beginning with Q_D, we get $90 - (30) = 90 - 60 = 30$, or we can plug it into $Q_S = P$, so $Q_S = 30$. Since we get a quantity of 30 for both Q_D and Q_S, we know that the price of $30 is correct.

b. In this part, we plug $20 into Q_D. This yields $90 - 2(20) = 50$. Now we plug $20 into Q_S. This yields 20.

c. Since $Q_D = 50$ and $Q_S = 20$, there is a shortage of 30 units.

d. Whenever there is a shortage of a good, the price will rise in order to find the equilibrium point.

Changes in Both Demand and Supply

APPENDIX

3A

We have considered what would happen if supply *or* demand changed. But life is often more complex than that. To provide a more realistic analysis, we need to examine what happens when supply and demand both shift at the same time. Doing this adds considerable uncertainty to the analysis.

Suppose that a major drought hits the northwest United States. The water shortage reduces both the amount of farmed salmon and the ability of wild salmon to spawn in streams and rivers. Figure 3A.1a shows the ensuing decline in the salmon supply, from point S progressively leftward, represented by the dotted supply curves. At the same time, a medical journal reports that people who consume at least four pounds of salmon a month live five years longer than those who consume an equal amount of cod. Figure 3A.1b shows the ensuing rise in the demand for salmon, from point D progressively rightward, represented by the dotted demand curves. This scenario leads to a twofold change. Because of the water shortage, the supply of salmon shrinks. At the same time, new information about the health benefits of eating salmon causes demand for salmon to increase.

It is impossible to predict exactly what happens to the equilibrium point when both supply and demand are shifting. We can, however, determine a region where the resulting equilibrium point must reside.

In this situation, we have a simultaneous decrease in supply and increase in demand. Since we do not know the magnitude of the supply reduction or the demand increase, the overall effect on the equilibrium quantity cannot be determined. This result is evident in Figure 3A.1c, as illustrated by the purple region. The points where supply and demand cross within this area represent the set of possible new market equilibriums. Since each of the possible points of intersection in the purple region occurs at prices greater than $10.00 per pound, we know that the price must rise. However, the left half of the purple region produces equilibrium quantities less than 500 pounds of salmon, while the right half of the purple region results in equilibrium quantities greater than 500. Therefore, the equilibrium quantity may rise or fall.

The world we live in is complex, and often more than one variable will change simultaneously. When this occurs, it is not possible to be as definitive as when only one variable—supply or demand—changes. You should think of the new equilibrium, E_2, not as a single point but as a range of outcomes represented by the shaded purple area in Figure 3A.1c. Therefore, we cannot be exactly sure at what point the new price *and* quantity will settle. For a closer look at four possibilities, see Figure 3A.2.

FIGURE 3A.1

A Shift in Supply and Demand

When supply and demand both shift, the resulting equilibrium can no longer be identified as an exact point. This is seen in (c), which combines the supply shift in (a) with the demand shift in (b). When supply decreases and demand increases, the result is that the price must rise, but the equilibrium quantity can either rise or fall.

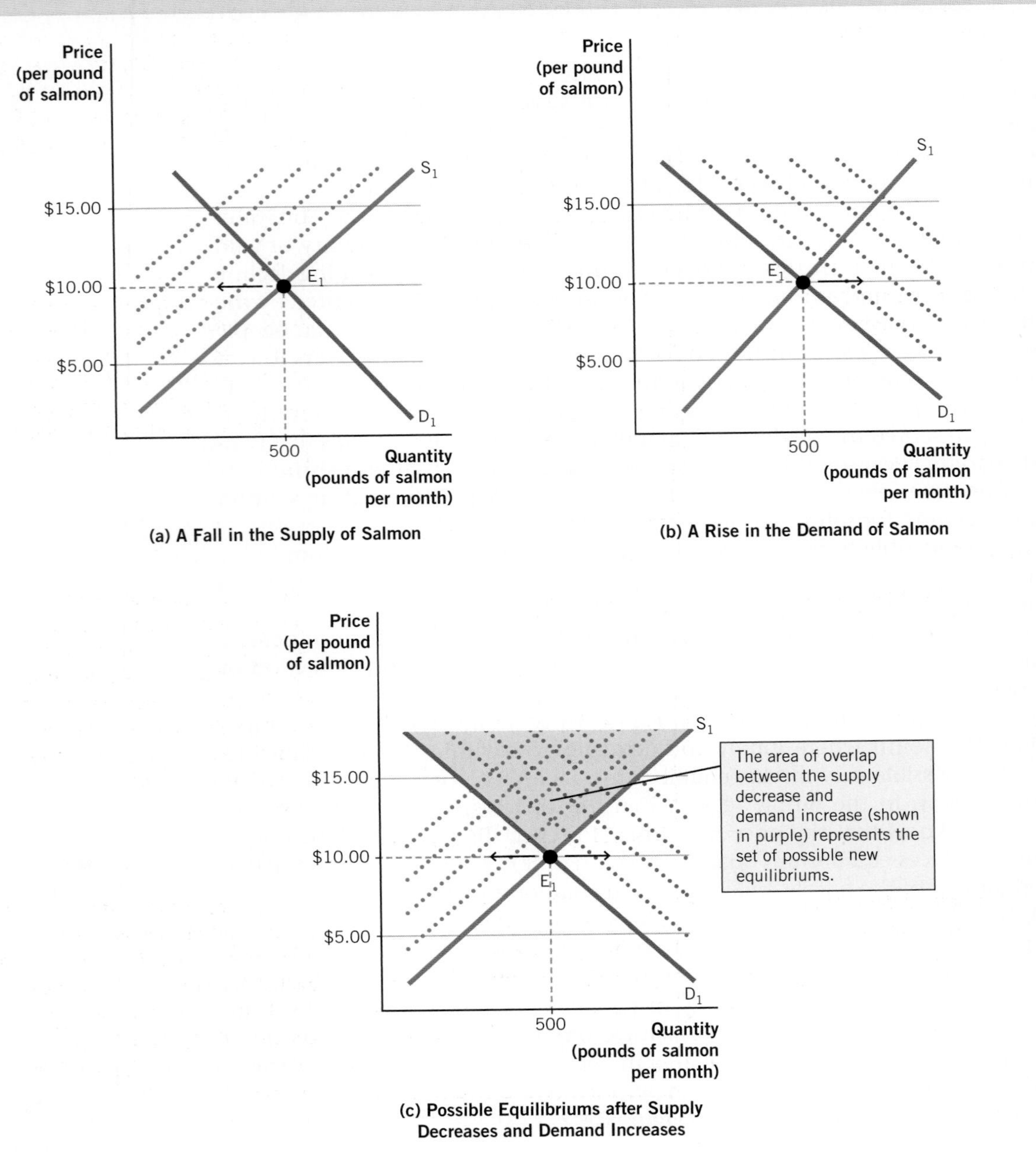

(a) A Fall in the Supply of Salmon

(b) A Rise in the Demand of Salmon

(c) Possible Equilibriums after Supply Decreases and Demand Increases

FIGURE 3A.2

Price and Quantity When Demand and Supply Both Change

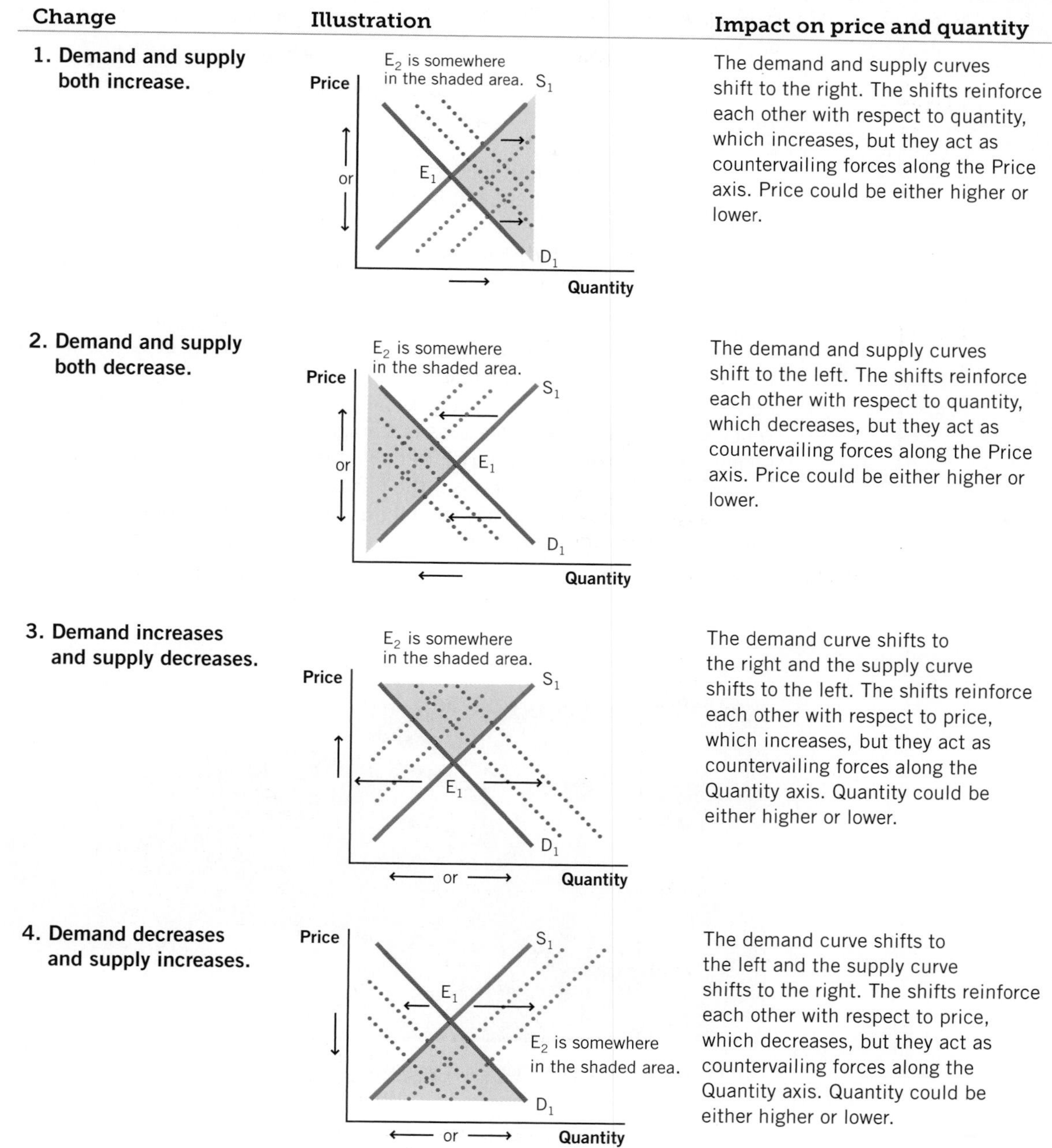

Change	Illustration	Impact on price and quantity
1. Demand and supply both increase.	E₂ is somewhere in the shaded area.	The demand and supply curves shift to the right. The shifts reinforce each other with respect to quantity, which increases, but they act as countervailing forces along the Price axis. Price could be either higher or lower.
2. Demand and supply both decrease.	E₂ is somewhere in the shaded area.	The demand and supply curves shift to the left. The shifts reinforce each other with respect to quantity, which decreases, but they act as countervailing forces along the Price axis. Price could be either higher or lower.
3. Demand increases and supply decreases.	E₂ is somewhere in the shaded area.	The demand curve shifts to the right and the supply curve shifts to the left. The shifts reinforce each other with respect to price, which increases, but they act as countervailing forces along the Quantity axis. Quantity could be either higher or lower.
4. Demand decreases and supply increases.	E₂ is somewhere in the shaded area.	The demand curve shifts to the left and the supply curve shifts to the right. The shifts reinforce each other with respect to price, which decreases, but they act as countervailing forces along the Quantity axis. Quantity could be either higher or lower.

PRACTICE WHAT YOU KNOW

When Supply and Demand Both Change: Hybrid Cars

Question: At lunch, two friends are engaged in a heated argument. Their exchange goes like this:

The first friend begins, "The supply of hybrid cars and the demand for hybrid cars will both increase, I'm sure of it. I'm also sure the price of hybrids will go down."

The second friend interrupts, "I agree with the first part of your statement, but I'm not sure about the price. In fact, I'm pretty sure that hybrid prices will rise."

They go back and forth endlessly, each unable to convince the other, so they turn to you for advice. What do you say to them?

Answer: Either of your friends could be correct. In this case, supply and demand both shift out to the right, so we know the quantity bought and sold will increase. However, an increase in supply would normally lower the price and an increase in demand would typically raise the price. Without knowing which of these two effects on price is stronger, you can't predict how it will change. The overall price will rise if the increase in demand is larger than the increase in supply. However, if the increase in supply is larger than the increase in demand, prices will fall. But your two friends don't know which condition will be true—so they're locked in an argument that no one can win!

Hybrid cars are becoming increasingly common.

QUESTIONS FOR REVIEW

1. What happens to price and quantity when supply and demand change at the same time?
2. Is there more than one potential equilibrium point when supply and demand change at the same time?

STUDY PROBLEM

1. Check out the short video at forbes.com called "Behind Rising Oil Prices," from 2008. (Search online for "behind rising oil prices forbes video.") Using your understanding of the market forces of supply and demand, explain how the market works. In your explanation, be sure to illustrate how increasing global demand for oil has impacted the equilibrium price.

CHAPTER

4 Elasticity

Sellers charge the highest price possible.

MISCONCEPTION

Many students believe that sellers charge the highest price possible for their product or service—that if they can get one more penny from a customer, they will, even if it makes the customer angry. It turns out that this belief is wrong. What *is* accurate is that producers charge the highest price they can while maintaining the goodwill of most of their customers.

In the previous chapter, we learned that demand and supply help regulate economic activity by balancing the interests of buyers and sellers. We also observed how that balance is achieved through prices. Higher prices cause the quantity supplied to rise and the quantity demanded to fall. In contrast, lower prices cause the quantity supplied to fall and the quantity demanded to rise. In this chapter, we will examine how decision-makers respond to differences in price and also to changes in income.

The concept of *elasticity*, or responsiveness to a change in market conditions, is a tool that we need to master in order to fully understand supply and demand. By utilizing elasticity in our analysis, our understanding will become much more precise. This will enable us to determine the impact of policy measures on the economy, to vote more intelligently, and even to make wiser day-to-day decisions, like whether or not to eat out. Elasticity will also help us to understand the faulty logic behind the common misconception that sellers charge the highest possible price.

How much do high prices affect the quantity demanded?

BIG QUESTIONS

* What is the price elasticity of demand, and what are its determinants?
* How do changes in income and the prices of other goods affect elasticity?
* What is the price elasticity of supply?
* How do the price elasticity of demand and supply relate to one another?

What Is the Price Elasticity of Demand, and What Are Its Determinants?

Trade-offs

Many things in life are replaceable, or have substitutes: boyfriends come and go, people rent DVDs instead of going out to a movie, and students ride their bikes to class instead of taking the bus. Pasta fans may prefer linguini to spaghetti or angel hair, but all three taste about the same and can be substituted for one another in a pinch. In cases such as pasta, where consumers can easily purchase a substitute, we think of demand as being *responsive*. That is, a small change in price will likely cause many people to switch from one good to another.

In contrast, many things in life are irreplaceable or have few good substitutes. Examples include electricity, a hospital emergency room visit, or water for a shower. A significant rise in price for any of these items would probably not cause you to consume a smaller quantity. If the price of electricity goes up, you might try to cut your usage somewhat, but you would probably not start generating your own power. Likewise, you could try to treat a serious medical crisis without a visit to the ER—but the consequences of making a mistake would be enormous. Even something as simple as taking a shower has few good alternatives. In cases such as these, we say that consumers are *unresponsive*, or unwilling to change their behavior, even when the price of the good or service changes.

Your "average"-looking boyfriend is replaceable.

The responsiveness of buyers and sellers to changes in price or income is known as **elasticity**. Elasticity is a useful concept because it allows us to measure how much consumers and producers change their behavior when prices or income changes. In the next section, we look at the factors that determine the elasticity of demand.

Determinants of the Price Elasticity of Demand

Elasticity is a measure of the responsiveness of buyers and sellers to changes in price or income.

The law of demand tells us that as price goes up, quantity demanded goes down, and as price goes down, quantity demanded goes up. In other words, there is an inverse relationship between the price of a good and the quantity demanded. Elasticity allows us to measure how much the quantity demanded changes in response to a change in price. If the quantity demanded changes significantly as a result of a price change, then demand is *elastic*. If the quantity demanded changes a small amount as a result of a price change, then demand is *inelastic*. For instance, if the price of a sweatshirt with a college logo rises by $10 and the quantity demanded falls by half, we'd say that the price elasticity of demand for those sweatshirts is elastic. But if the $10 rise in price results in very little or no change in the quantity demanded, the price elasticity of demand for the sweatshirts is inelastic. The **price elasticity of demand** measures the responsiveness of quantity demanded to a change in price.

The **price elasticity of demand** is a measure of the responsiveness of quantity demanded to a change in price.

Four determinants play a crucial role in influencing whether demand will be elastic or inelastic. These are the existence of substitutes, the share of the budget spent on a good, whether the good is a necessity or a luxury good, and time.

The Existence of Substitutes

The most important determinant of price elasticity is the number of substitutes available. When substitutes are plentiful, market forces tilt in favor of the consumer. For example, imagine that an unexpected freeze in Florida reduces the supply of oranges. As a result, the supply of orange juice shifts to the left (picture the supply curves we discussed in Chapter 3), and since demand remains unchanged, the price of orange juice rises. However, the consumer of orange juice can find many good substitutes. Since cranberries, grapes, and apple crops are unaffected by the Florida freeze, prices for juices made with those fruits remain constant. This leads to a choice: a consumer could continue to buy orange juice at a higher price or choose to pay a lower price for a fruit juice that may not be his first choice but is nonetheless acceptable. Faced with higher orange juice prices, some consumers will switch. How quickly this switch takes place, and to what extent consumers are willing to replace one product with another, determines whether demand is elastic or inelastic. Since many substitutes for orange juice exist, the price elasticity of demand for orange juice is elastic, or responsive to price changes.

Beyoncé is irreplaceable.

What if there are no good substitutes? Let's return to the Empire State Building example from the previous chapter. Where else in New York City can you get such an amazing view? Nowhere! Since the view is unbeatable, the number of close substitutes is small; this makes demand more inelastic, or less responsive to price changes.

To some degree, the price elasticity of demand depends on consumer preferences. For instance, sports fans are often willing to shell out big bucks to follow their passions. Amateur golfers can play the same courses that professional golfers do. But the opportunity to golf where the professionals play does not come cheaply. A round of golf at the Tournament Players Club at Sawgrass, a famous course in Florida, costs close to $300. Why are some golfers willing to pay that much? For an avid golfer with the financial means, the experience of living out the same shots seen on television tournaments is worth $300. In this case, demand is inelastic—the avid golfer does not view

Saving 10% on this purchase amounts to a few pennies.

other golf courses as good substitutes. However, a less enthusiastic golfer, or one without the financial resources, is happy to golf on a less expensive course even if the pros don't play it on TV. When less expensive courses serve as good substitutes, the price tag makes demand elastic. Ultimately, whether demand is inelastic or elastic depends on the buyer's preferences and resources.

The Share of the Budget Spent on the Good

Despite the example above of an avid and affluent golfer willing to pay a premium fee to play at a famous golf course, in most cases fee is a critical element in determining what we can afford and what we will choose to buy. If you plan to purchase a 70-inch-screen TV, which can cost as much as $3,000, you will probably be willing to take the time to find the best deal. Because of the high cost, even a small-percentage discount in the price can cause a relatively large change in consumer demand. A "10% off sale" may not sound like much, but when purchasing a big-ticket item like a TV, it can mean hundreds of dollars in savings. In this case, the willingness to shop for the best deal indicates that the price matters, so demand is elastic.

Incentives

The price elasticity of demand is much more inelastic for inexpensive items on sale. For example, if a candy bar is discounted 10%, the price falls by pennies. The savings from switching candy bars is not enough to make a difference in what you can afford elsewhere. Therefore, the incentive to switch is small. Most consumers still buy their favorite candy since the price difference is so insignificant. In this case, demand is inelastic because the savings gained by purchasing a less desirable candy bar are small in comparison to the consumer's budget.

Necessities versus Luxury Goods

A big-screen TV and a candy bar are both luxury goods. You don't need to have either one. But some goods are necessities. For example, you have to pay your rent and water bill, purchase gasoline for your car, and eat. When a consumer purchases a necessity, he or she is generally thinking about the need, not the price. When the need trumps the price, we expect demand to be relatively inelastic. Therefore, the demand for things like soap, toothpaste, and heating oil all tend to have inelastic demand.

Saving 10% on this purchase adds up to hundreds of dollars.

Time and the Adjustment Process

When the market price changes, consumers and sellers respond. But that response does not remain the same over time. As time passes, both consumers and sellers are able to find substitutes. To understand these different market responses, economists consider time in three distinct periods: the *immediate run*, the *short run*, and the *long run*.

In the **immediate run**, there is no time for consumers to adjust their behavior. Consider the demand for gasoline. When the gas tank is empty, you have to stop at the nearest gas station and pay the posted price. Filling up as soon as possible is more important than driving around searching for the lowest price. Inelastic demand exists whenever price is secondary to the desire to attain a certain amount of the good. So in the case of an empty tank, the demand for gasoline is inelastic.

This is *not* the time to try and find cheap gas.

But what if your tank is not empty? The **short run** is a period of time when consumers can partially adjust their behavior (and, in this case, can search for a good deal on gas). When consumers have some time to make a purchase, they gain flexibility. This allows them to shop for lower prices at the pump, carpool to save gas, or even change how often they drive. In the short run, flexibility reduces the demand for expensive gasoline and makes consumer demand more elastic.

Finally, if we relax the time constraint completely, it is possible to use even less gasoline. The **long run** is a period of time when consumers have time to fully adjust to market conditions. If gasoline prices are high in the long run, consumers can relocate closer to work and purchase fuel-efficient cars. These changes further reduce the demand for gasoline. As a result of the flexibility that additional time gives the consumer, the demand for gasoline becomes more elastic.

In the **immediate run**, there is no time for consumers to adjust their behavior.

The **short run** is a period of time when consumers can partially adjust their behavior.

The **long run** is a period of time when consumers have time to fully adjust to market conditions.

We have looked at four determinants of elasticity—substitutes, the share of the budget spent on the good, necessities versus luxury goods, and time. Each is significant, but the number of substitutes tends to be the most influential factor and dominates the others. Table 4.1 will help you develop your intuition about how different market situations influence the overall elasticity of demand.

Computing the Price Elasticity of Demand

Until this point, our discussion of elasticity has been descriptive. However, to apply the concept of elasticity in decision-making, we need to be able to view it in a more quantitative way. For example, if the owner of a business is trying to decide whether to put a good on sale, he or she needs to be able to estimate how many new customers would purchase it at the sale price. Or if a government is considering a new tax, it needs to know how much revenue that tax would generate. These are questions about elasticity that we can evaluate by using a mathematical formula.

The Price Elasticity of Demand Formula

Let's begin with an example of a pizza shop. Consider an owner who is trying to attract more customers. For one month, he lowers the price by 10% and is pleased to find that sales jump by 30%.

Here is the formula for the price elasticity of demand (E_D):

$$\text{Price Elasticity of Demand} = E_D = \frac{\text{percentage change in the quantity demanded}}{\text{percentage change in price}} \quad \text{(Equation 4.1)}$$

TABLE 4.1

Developing Intuition for the Price Elasticity of Demand

Example	Discussion	Overall elasticity
Football tickets for a true fan	Being able to watch a game live and go to pre- and post-game tailgates is a unique experience. For many fans, the experience of going to the game has few close substitutes; therefore, the demand is relatively inelastic.	Tends to be relatively inelastic
Assigned textbooks for a class	The information inside a textbook is valuable. Substitutes such as older editions and free online resources are not exactly the same. As a result, most students buy the required course materials. Acquiring the textbook is more important than the price paid; therefore, the demand is inelastic. The fact that a textbook is needed in the short run (for a few months while taking a class) also tends to make the demand inelastic.	Tends to be inelastic
A slice of pizza from Domino's	In most locations, many pizza competitors exist, so there are many close substitutes. This tends to make the demand for a particular brand of pizza elastic.	Tends to be elastic
A Silver Ford Escape	There are many styles, makes, and colors of cars to choose from. With large purchases, consumers are sensitive to smaller percentages of savings. Moreover, people typically plan their car purchases many months or years in advance. The combination of all these factors makes the demand for any particular model and color relatively elastic.	Tends to be relatively elastic

Using the data from the example, we can calculate the price elasticity of demand as follows:

$$\text{Price Elasticity of Demand} = E_D = \frac{30\%}{-10\%} = -3$$

What does that mean? The price elasticity of demand, −3 in this case, is expressed as a coefficient (3) with a specific sign (it has a minus in front of it). The coefficient, 3, tells us how much the quantity demanded changed (30%) compared to the price change (10%). In this case, the percentage change in the quantity demanded is three times the percentage change in the price. Whenever the percentage change in the quantity demanded is larger than the percentage change in price, we say that demand was elastic. In other words, the price drop made a big difference in how much pizza consumers purchased from the pizza shop. If the opposite occurs and a price drop makes a small difference in the quantity that consumers purchase, we say that demand was inelastic.

The negative (minus) sign in front of the coefficient is equally important. Recall that the law of demand describes an inverse relationship between the

ECONOMICS IN THE MEDIA

Price Elasticity of Demand

Jingle All the Way

This amusing comedy from 1996 features two fathers who procrastinate until Christmas Eve to try to buy a Turbo Man action figure for their children for Christmas morning. It's the only present that their kids truly want from Santa. The problem is that almost every child in America feels the same way—demand has been so unexpectedly strong that the stock of toys has almost completely sold out, creating a short-term shortage. However, related items, like Turbo Man's pet, Booster, are readily available.

The two dads wind up at the Mall of America, where a toy store has received a last-minute shipment of Turbo Man, attracting a crowd of desperate shoppers. The store manager announces that the list price has doubled and institutes a lottery system to determine which customers will be able to buy the toy. The bedlam that this creates is evidence that the higher price did not decrease the demand for Turbo Man.

Based on this description, what can we say about the price elasticity of demand for Turbo Man and Booster?

Turbo Man: The toy is needed immediately, and because kids are clamoring for it specifically, no good substitutes exist. Also, because the cost of the toy is relatively small (as a share of a shopper's budget), people are not as concerned about getting a good deal. Demand is, therefore, relatively inelastic.

Is the demand for Turbo Man elastic or inelastic?

Booster: Without Turbo Man, Booster is just another toy. Therefore, the demand for Booster is much more elastic than for Turbo Man, since there are many good substitutes. We see this in the movie when the toy store manager informs the crowd that the store has plenty of Boosters available, and the throng yells back, "We don't want it!"

price of a good and the quantity demanded; when prices rise, the quantity demanded falls. The E_D coefficient reflects this inverse relationship with a negative sign. In other words, the pizza shop drops its price and consumers buy more pizza. Since pizza prices and consumer purchases of pizza generally move in opposite directions, the sign of the price elasticity of demand is almost always negative.

The Midpoint Method

The calculation above was simple because we looked at the change in price and the change in the quantity demanded from only one direction—that is, from a high price to a lower price. However, the complete—and proper—way to calculate elasticity is from both directions. Consider the following demand schedule (it doesn't matter what the product is):

Price	Quantity demanded
\$12	20
\$ 6	30

Let's calculate the elasticity of demand. If the price drops from \$12 to \$6—a drop of 50%—the quantity demanded increases from 20 to 30—a rise of 50%. Plugging the percentage changes into E_D yields

$$\text{Price Elasticity of Demand} = E_D = \frac{50\%}{-50\%} = -1.0$$

But if the price rises from \$6 to \$12—an increase of 100%—the quantity demanded falls from 30 to 20, or decreases by 33%. Plugging the percentage changes into E_D yields

$$\text{Price Elasticity of Demand} = E_D = \frac{-33\%}{100\%} = -0.33$$

This result occurs because percentage changes are usually calculated by using the initial value as the base, or reference point. In this example, we worked the problem two ways: by using \$12 as the starting point and dropping the price to \$6, and by using \$6 as the starting point and increasing the price to \$12. Even though we are measuring elasticity over the same range of values, the percentage changes are different.

To avoid this problem, economists use the *midpoint method*, which gives the same answer for the elasticity no matter what point you begin with. Equation 4.2 uses the midpoint method to express the price elasticity of demand. While this equation looks more complicated than Equation 4.1, it is not. The midpoint method merely specifies how to plug in the initial and ending values for price and the quantity to determine the percentage changes. Q_1 and P_1 are the initial values, and Q_2 and P_2 are the ending values.

(Equation 4.2)

$$E_D = \frac{\text{change in Q} \div \text{average value of Q}}{\text{change in P} \div \text{average value of P}}$$

$$= \frac{(Q_2 - Q_1) \div [(Q_1 + Q_2) \div 2]}{(P_2 - P_1) \div [(P_1 + P_2) \div 2]}$$

The change in the quantity demanded, $(Q_2 - Q_1)$, and the change in price, $(P_2 - P_1)$, are each divided by the average of the initial and ending values, or $[(Q_1 + Q_2) \div 2]$ and $[(P_1 + P_2) \div 2]$, to provide a way of calculating elasticity.

The midpoint method is the preferred method for solving elasticity problems. To see why this is the case, let's return to our pizza demand example.

If the price rises from \$6 to \$12, the quantity demanded falls from 30 to 20. Here the initial values are $P_1 = \$6$ and $Q_1 = 30$. The ending values are $P_2 = \$12$ and $Q_2 = 20$. Using the midpoint method:

$$E_D = \frac{(20 - 30) \div [(30 + 20) \div 2]}{(\$12 - \$6) \div [(\$12 + \$6) \div 2]} = \frac{-10 \div 25}{\$6 \div \$9} = -0.58$$

If the price falls from \$12 to \$6, quantity rises from 20 to 30. This time, the initial values are $P_1 = \$12$ and $Q_1 = 20$. The ending values are $P_2 = \$6$ and $Q_2 = 30$. Using the midpoint method:

$$E_D = \frac{(30 - 20) \div [(20 + 30) \div 2]}{(\$6 - \$12) \div [(\$6 + \$12) \div 2]} = \frac{10 \div 25}{-\$6 \div \$9} = -0.58$$

When we calculated the price elasticity of demand from \$6 to \$12 using \$6 as the initial point, $E_D = -0.33$. Moving in the opposite direction, from \$12 to \$6, made \$12 the initial reference point and $E_D = -1.0$. The midpoint method shown above splits the difference and uses \$9 and 25 pizzas as the midpoints. This approach makes the calculation of the elasticity coefficient the same, −0.58, no matter what direction the price moves. Therefore, economists use the midpoint method to standardize the results. So, using the midpoint method, we arrived at an elasticity coefficient of −0.58, which is between 0 and −1. What does that mean? In this case, the percentage change in the quantity demanded is less than the percentage change in the price. Whenever the percentage change in the quantity demanded is smaller than the percentage change in price, we say that demand is inelastic. In other words, the price drop does not make a big difference in how much pizza consumers purchased from the pizza shop. When the elasticity coefficient is less than −1, the opposite is true, and we say that demand is elastic.

Graphing the Price Elasticity of Demand

Visualizing elasticity graphically helps us understand the relationship between elastic and inelastic demand. Figure 4.1 shows elasticity graphically. As demand becomes increasingly elastic, or responsive to price changes, the demand curve flattens.

Figure 4.1a depicts the price elasticity for pet care. Many pet owners report that they would pay any amount of money to help their sick or injured pet get better. (Of course, pet care is not perfectly inelastic, because there is certainly a price beyond which some pet owners would not or could not pay; but for illustrative purposes, let's say that pet care *is* perfectly elastic.) For these pet owners, the demand curve is a vertical line. If you look along the Quantity axis, you will see that the quantity of pet care demanded (Q_D) remains constant no matter what it costs. At

For many pet owners, the demand for veterinary care is perfectly inelastic.

FIGURE 4.1

Elasticity and the Demand Curve

For any given price change across two demand curves, demand will be more elastic on the flatter demand curve than on the steeper demand curve. In (a), the demand is perfectly inelastic, so the price does not matter. In (b), the demand is relatively inelastic, so the price is less important than the quantity purchased. In (c), the demand is relatively elastic, so the price matters more than quantity. In (d), the demand is perfectly elastic, so price is all that matters.

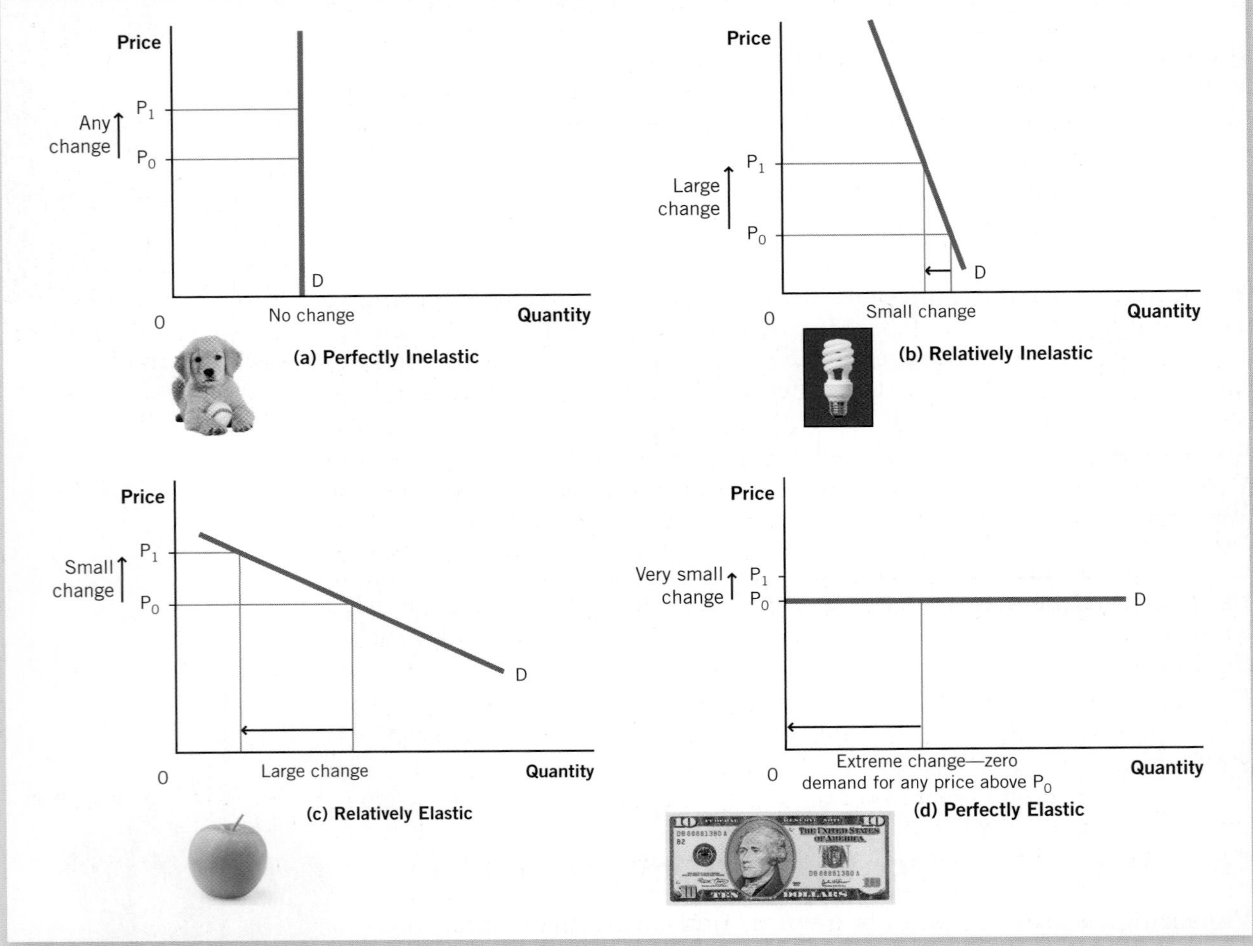

the same time, the price increases from P_0 to P_1. We can calculate the price elasticity coefficient as follows:

$$E_{\text{pet care}} = \frac{\text{percentage change in } Q_D}{\text{percentage change in P}} = \frac{0}{\text{percentage change in P}} = 0$$

When zero is in the numerator, we know that the answer will be zero no matter what we find in the denominator. This makes sense. Many pet owners will try to help their pet feel better no matter what the cost, so we can say that their demand is *perfectly inelastic*. This means that value of E_D will always be zero.

Moving on to Figure 4.1b, we consider the demand for electricity. Whereas many pet owners will not change their consumption of health care for their pet no matter what the cost, consumers of electricity will modify their use of electricity in response to price changes. When the price of electricity goes up, they will use less, and when it goes down, they will use more. But since living without electricity is not practical, using less is a matter of making relatively small lifestyle adjustments—buying energy-efficient light bulbs or turning down the thermostat a few degrees. As a result, the demand curve in 4.1b is relatively steep, but not completely vertical as it was in 4.1a.

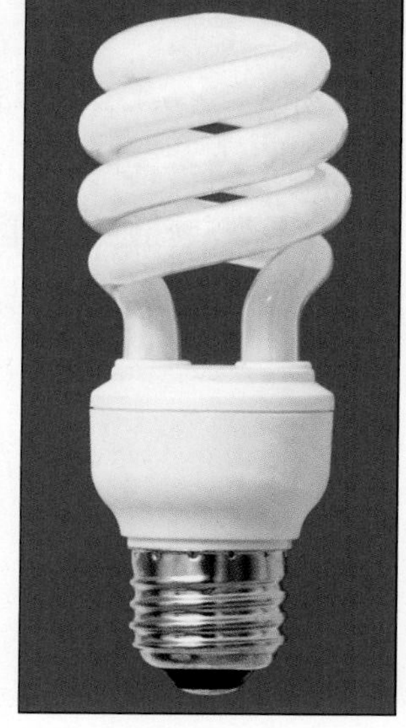

The demand for electricity is relatively inelastic.

When the variation on the Quantity axis is small compared to the variation on the Price axis, the price elasticity is *relatively inelastic*. Plugging these changes into the elasticity formula, we get

$$E_{electricity} = \frac{\text{percentage change in } Q_D}{\text{percentage change in P}} = \frac{\text{small change}}{\text{large change}}$$

Recall that the law of demand describes an inverse relationship between price and output. Therefore, the changes along the Price and Quantity axes will always be in the opposite direction. A price elasticity of zero tells us there is no change in the quantity demanded when price changes. So when demand is relatively inelastic, the price elasticity of demand must be relatively close to zero. The easiest way to think about this is to consider how a 10% increase in electric rates works for most households. How much less electricity would you use? The answer for most people would be a little less, but not 10% less. You can adjust your thermostat, but you still need electricity to run your appliances and lights. When the price changes more than quantity changes, there is a larger change in the denominator. Therefore, the price elasticity of demand is between 0 and −1 when demand is relatively inelastic.

In Figure 4.1c, we consider an apple. Since there are many good substitutes for an apple, the demand for an apple is *relatively elastic*. The flexibility of consumer demand for apples is illustrated by the degree of responsiveness we see along the Quantity axis relative to the change exhibited along the Price axis. We can observe this by noting that a relatively elastic demand curve is flatter than an inelastic demand curve. So, whereas perfectly inelastic demand shows no change in demand with an increase in price, and relatively inelastic demand shows a small change in demand with an increase in price, relatively elastic demand shows a large change. Placing this information into the elasticity formula gives us

The demand for an apple is relatively elastic.

$$E_{apples} = \frac{\text{percentage change in } Q_D}{\text{percentage change in P}} = \frac{\text{large change}}{\text{small change}}$$

Now the numerator—the percentage change in Q_D—is large, and the denominator—the percentage change in P—is small. E_D is less than −1. Recall that the sign must be negative, since there is an inverse relationship between price and the quantity demanded. As the price elasticity of demand moves farther away from zero, the consumer becomes more responsive to price change. Since many other

The demand for a $10 bill is perfectly elastic.

fruits are good substitutes for apples, a small change in the price of apples will have a large change in the quantity demanded.

Figure 4.1d provides an interesting example: the demand for a $10 bill. Would you pay $11.00 to get a $10 bill? No. Would you pay $10.01 for a $10 bill? Still no. However, when the price drops to $10.00, you will probably become indifferent. Most of us would exchange a $10 bill for two $5 bills. The real magic here occurs when the price drops to $9.99. How many $10 bills would you buy if you could buy them for $9.99 or less? The answer: as many as possible! This is exactly what happens in currency markets, where small differences among currency prices around the globe motivate traders to buy and sell large quantities of currency and clear a small profit on the difference in exchange rates. This extreme form of price sensitivity is illustrated by a perfectly horizontal demand curve, which means that demand is *perfectly elastic*. Solving for the elasticity yields

$$E_{\$10\text{ bill}} = \frac{\text{percentage change in } Q_D}{\text{percentage change in P}} = \frac{\text{nearly infinite change}}{\text{very small (\$0.01) change}}$$

We can think of this very small price change, from $10.00 to $9.99, as having essentially an unlimited effect on the quantity of $10 bills demanded. Traders go from being uninterested in trading at $10.00 to seeking to buy as many $10 bills as possible when the price drops to $9.99. As a result, the price elasticity of demand approaches negative infinity ($-\infty$).

There is a fifth type of elasticity, not depicted in Figure 4.1. *Unitary elasticity* is the special name that describes the situation in which elasticity is neither elastic nor inelastic. This occurs when the E_D is exactly -1, and it happens when the percentage change in price is exactly equal to the percentage change in quantity demanded. This characteristic of unitary elasticity will be important when we discuss the connection between elasticity and total revenue later in this chapter. You're probably wondering what an example of a unitary good would be. Relax. It is impossible to find a good that has a price elasticity of exactly -1 at all price points. It is enough to know that unitary demand represents the crossover from elastic to inelastic demand.

Now that you have had a chance to look at all four panels in Figure 4.1, here is a handy mnemonic that you can use to keep the difference between inelastic and elastic demand straight.

I = inelastic and **E** = elastic

The "I" in the word "inelastic" is vertical, just like the inelastic relationships we examined in Figure 4.1. Likewise, the letter "E" has three horizontal lines to remind us that elastic demand is flat.

Finally, it is possible to pair the elasticity coefficients with an interpretation of how much price matters. You can see this in Table 4.2. When price does not matter, demand is perfectly inelastic (denoted by the coefficient of zero). Conversely, when price is the only thing that matters, demand becomes

TABLE 4.2

The Relationship between Price Elasticity of Demand and Price

Elasticity	E_D coefficient	Interpretation	Example in Figure 4.1
Perfectly inelastic	$E_D = 0$	Price does not matter.	Saving your pet
Relatively inelastic	$0 > E_D > -1$	Price is less important than the quantity purchased.	Electricity
Unitary	$E_D = -1$	Price and quantity are equally important.	
Relatively elastic	$-1 > E_D > -\infty$	Price is more important than the quantity purchased.	An apple
Perfectly elastic	$E_D \rightarrow -\infty$	Price is everything.	A $10 bill

perfectly elastic (denoted by $-\infty$). In between these two extremes, the extent to which price matters determines whether demand is relatively inelastic, unitary, or relatively elastic.

Time, Elasticity, and the Demand Curve

We have already seen that increased time makes demand more elastic. Figure 4.2 shows this graphically. When the price rises from P_1 to P_2, consumers cannot immediately avoid the price increase. For example, if your gas tank is almost empty, you must purchase gas at the new price. Over a slightly longer time horizon—the short run—consumers are more flexible and are able to drive less in order to avoid higher-priced gasoline. This means that in the short run, consumption declines to Q_2. In the long run, when consumers have time to purchase a more fuel-efficient vehicle or move closer to work, purchases fall even further. As a result, the demand curve continues to flatten and the quantity demanded falls to Q_3.

Slope and Elasticity

In this section, we pause to make sure that you understand what you are observing in the figures. The demand curves shown in Figures 4.1 and 4.2 are straight lines, and therefore they have a constant slope, or steepness. (A refresher on slope is part of the appendix to Chapter 2.) So, looking at

Figures 4.1 and 4.2, you might think that slope is the same as the price elasticity. But slope does not equal elasticity.

Consider, for example, a trip to Starbucks. Would you buy a tall skinny latte if it cost $10? How about $7? What about $5? Say you decide to buy the skinny latte because the price drops from $5 to $4. In this case, a small price change, a drop from $5 to $4, causes you to make the purchase. You can say the demand for skinny lattes is relatively elastic. Now look at Figure 4.3, which shows a demand curve for skinny lattes. At $5 the consumer purchases 0 lattes, at $4 she purchases 1 latte, at $3 she purchases 2, and she continues to buy one additional latte with each $1 drop in price. As you progress downward along the demand curve, price becomes less of an inhibiting factor and, as a result, the price elasticity of demand slowly becomes more inelastic. Notice that the slope of a linear demand curve is constant. However, when we calculate the price elasticity of demand between the various points in Figure 4.3, it becomes clear that demand is increasingly inelastic as we move down the demand curve. You can see this in the change in E_D from −9.1 to −0.1.

FIGURE 4.2

Elasticity and the Demand Curve over Time

Increased time acts to make demand more elastic. When the price rises from P_1 to P_2, consumers are unable to avoid the price increase in the immediate run (D_1). In the short run (D_2), consumers become more flexible and consumption declines to Q_2. Eventually, in the long run (D_3), there is time to make lifestyle changes that further reduce consumption. As a result, the demand curve continues to flatten and the quantity demanded falls to Q_3 in response to higher prices.

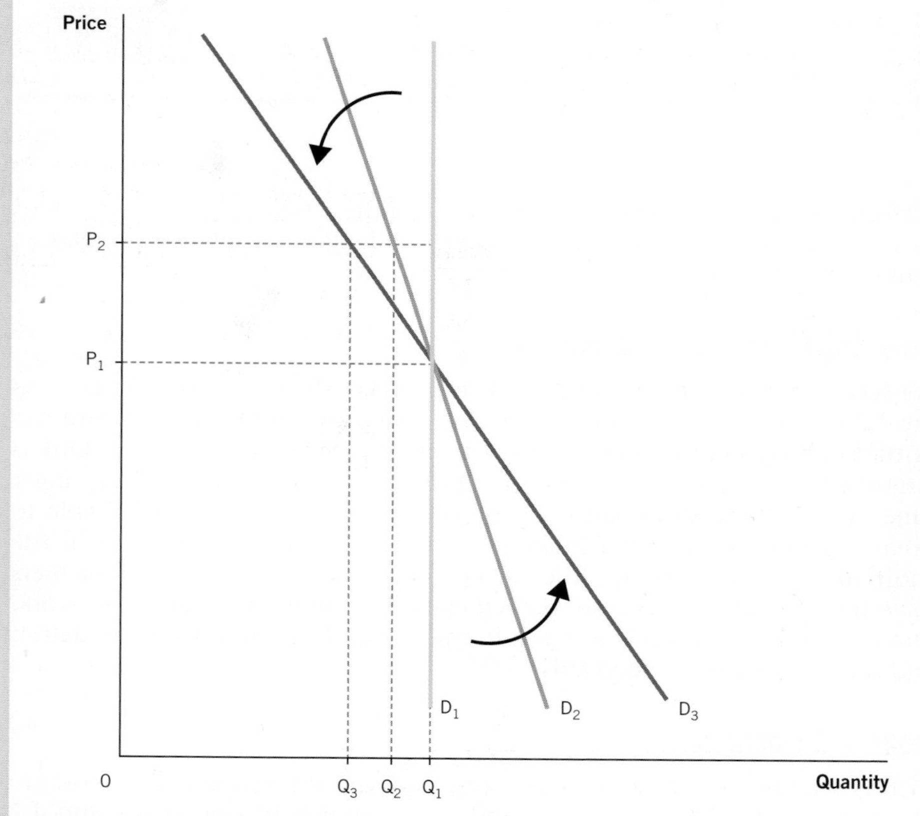

Perfectly inelastic demand would exist if the elasticity coefficient reached zero. Recall that a value of zero means that there is no change in the quantity demanded as a result of a price change. Therefore, values close to zero reflect inelastic demand, while those farther away reflect more elastic demand.

Price Elasticity of Demand and Total Revenue

Understanding the price elasticity of demand for the product you sell is important when running a business. The responsiveness of consumers to price changes determines whether a firm would be better off raising or lowering its price for a given product. In this section, we explore the relationship between the price elasticity of demand and a firm's total revenue.

But first we need to understand the concept of *total revenue*. **Total revenue** is the amount that consumers pay and sellers receive for a good. It is calculated by multiplying the price of the good by the quantity of the good that

Total revenue is the amount that consumers pay and sellers receive for a good.

FIGURE 4.3

The Difference between Slope and Elasticity

Along any straight demand curve, the price elasticity of demand (E_D) is not constant. You can see this by noting how the price elasticity of demand changes from highly elastic near the top of the demand curve to highly inelastic near the bottom of the curve.

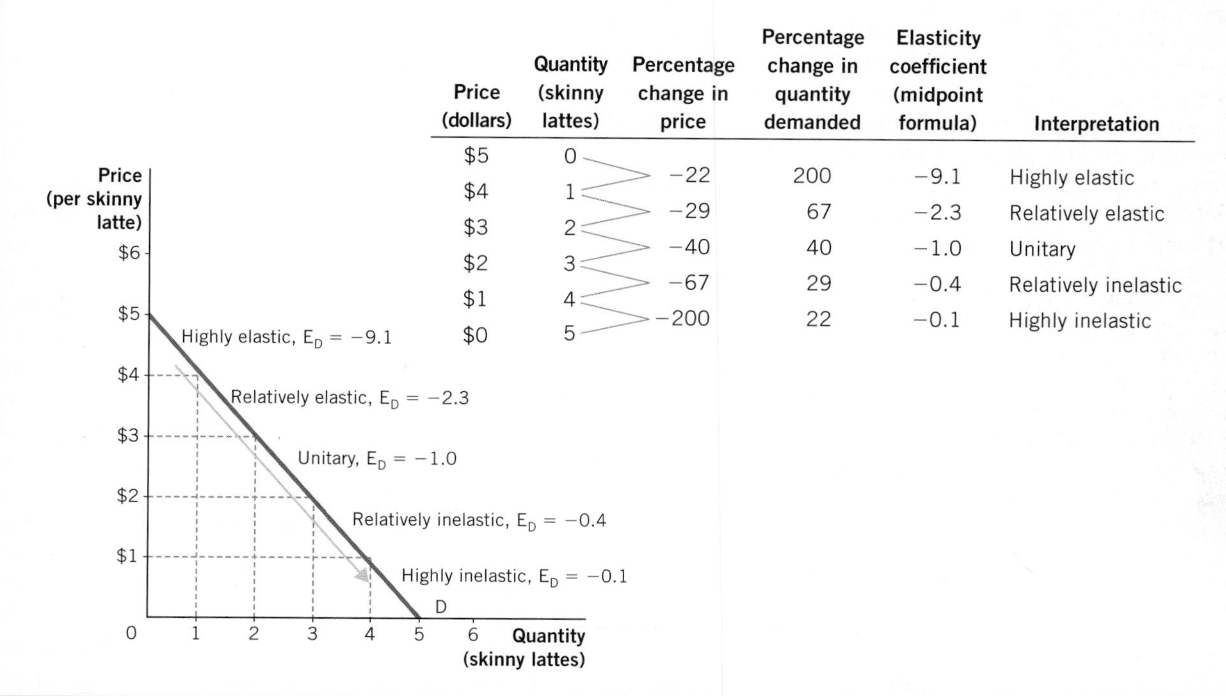

Price (dollars)	Quantity (skinny lattes)	Percentage change in price	Percentage change in quantity demanded	Elasticity coefficient (midpoint formula)	Interpretation
$5	0				
		−22	200	−9.1	Highly elastic
$4	1				
		−29	67	−2.3	Relatively elastic
$3	2				
		−40	40	−1.0	Unitary
$2	3				
		−67	29	−0.4	Relatively inelastic
$1	4				
		−200	22	−0.1	Highly inelastic
$0	5				

TABLE 4.3

The Price Elasticity of Demand and Total Revenue

Price (P) (per skinny latte)	Quantity (Q) (skinny lattes)	Total revenue P × Q	Percentage change in price	Percentage change in quantity	Elasticity coefficient	Interpretation
$5	0	$0	−22	200	−9.1	Highly elastic
$4	1	$4	−29	67	−2.3	Relatively elastic
$3	2	$6	−40	40	−1.0	Unitary
$2	3	$6	−67	29	−0.4	Relatively inelastic
$1	4	$4	−200	22	−0.1	Highly inelastic
$0	5	$0				

is sold. Table 4.3 reproduces the table from Figure 4.3 and adds a column for the total revenue. We find the total revenue by multiplying the price of a tall skinny latte by the quantity purchased.

After calculating total revenue at each price, we can look at the column of elasticity coefficients for a possible relationship. When we link revenues with the price elasticity of demand, a trade-off emerges. (This occurs because total revenue and elasticity relate to price differently. Total revenue involves multiplying the price times the quantity, while elasticity involves dividing the change in quantity demanded by the price.) Total revenue is zero when the price is too high ($5 or more) and when the price is $0. Between these two extremes, prices from $1 to $4 generate positive total revenue. Consider what happens when the price drops from $5 to $4. At $4, the first latte is purchased. Total revenue is $4 × 1 = $4. This is also the range at which the price elasticity of demand is highly elastic. As a result, lowering the price increases revenue. This continues when the price drops from $4 to $3. Now two lattes are sold, so the total revenue continues to rise to $3 × 2 = $6. At the same time, the price elasticity of demand remains elastic. From this we conclude that when the price elasticity of demand is elastic, lowering the price will increase total revenue. This relationship is shown in Figure 4.4a. By lowering the price from $4 to $3, the business has generated $2 more in revenue. But to generate this extra revenue, the business has lowered the price from $4 to $3 and therefore has given up $1 for each unit it sells. This is represented by the red-shaded area under the demand curve in Figure 4.4a.

When the price drops from $3 to $2, the total revenue stays at $6. This result occurs because demand is unitary, as shown in Figure 4.4b. This special condition exists when the percentage price change is exactly offset by an equal percentage change in the quantity demanded. In this situation, revenue remains constant. At $2, three lattes are purchased, so the total revenue is $2 × 3, which is the same as it was when $3 was the purchase price. As a result, we can see that total revenues have reached a maximum. Between $3 and $2, the price elasticity of demand is unitary. This finding does not necessarily mean that the firm will operate at the unitary point. Maximizing profit, not revenue, is the ultimate goal of a business, and we have not yet accounted for costs in our calculation of profits.

Once we reach a price below unitary demand, we move into the realm of inelastic demand, shown in Figure 4.4c. When the price falls to $1, total

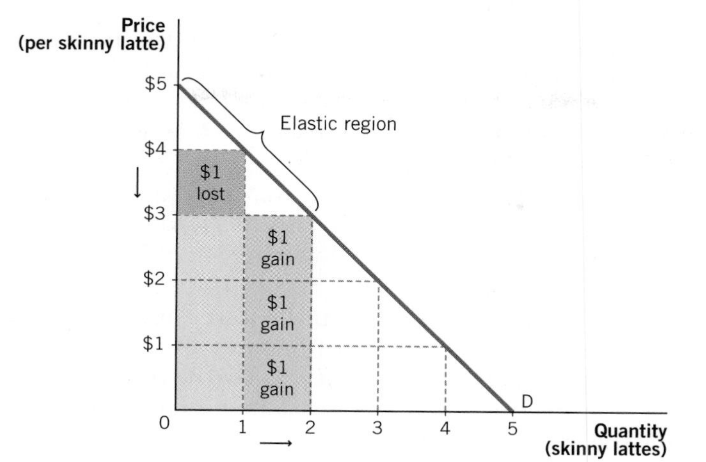

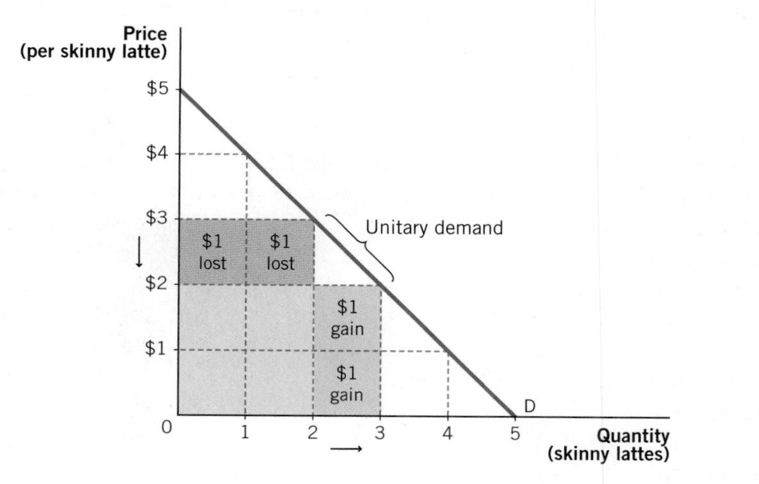

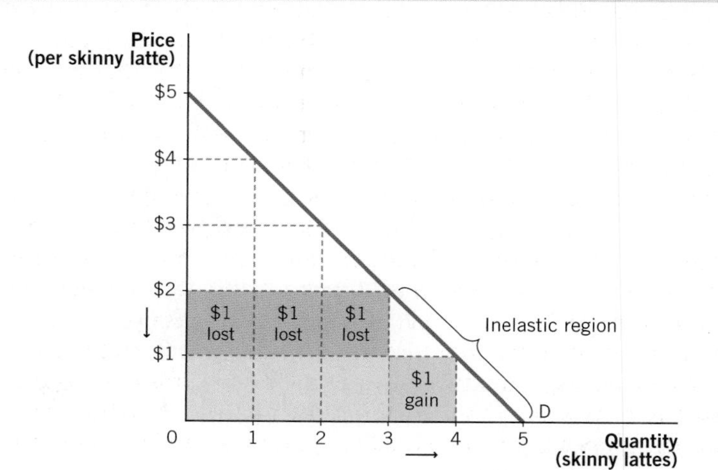

FIGURE 4.4

(a) The Total Revenue Trade-off When Demand Is Elastic

In the elastic region of the demand curve, lowering the price will increase total revenue. The gains from increased purchases, shown in the blue-shaded area, are greater than the losses from a lower purchase price, shown in the red-shaded area.

(b) . . . When Demand Is Unitary

When demand is unitary, lowering the price will no longer increase total revenue. The gains from increased purchases, shown in the blue-shaded area, are equal to the losses from a lower purchase price, shown in the red-shaded area.

(c) . . . When Demand Is Inelastic

In the inelastic region of the demand curve, lowering the price will decrease total revenue. The gains from increased purchases, shown in the blue-shaded area, are smaller than the losses from a lower purchase price, shown in the red-shaded area.

revenue declines to $4. This result occurs because the price elasticity of demand is now relatively inelastic, or price insensitive. In other words, latte consumers adding a fourth drink will not gain as much benefit as they did when they purchased the first. Even though the price is declining by $1, price is increasingly unimportant; as you can see by the blue square, it does not spur a large increase in consumption.

As we see in Figure 4.4c, at a price of $2, three units are sold and total revenue is $\$2 \times 3 = \$6$. When the price falls to $1, four units are sold, so the total revenue is now $\$4 \times 1 = \$4$. By lowering the price from $2 to $1, the business has lost $2 in extra revenue. This occurs because the business does not generate enough extra revenue from the lower price. Lowering the price from $2 to $1 causes a loss of $3 in existing sales revenue (the red boxes). At the same time, it generates only $1 in new sales (the blue box).

In this analysis, we see that once the demand curve enters the inelastic area, lowering the price decreases total revenue. This is an unambiguously bad

ECONOMICS IN THE MEDIA

Elasticity and Total Revenue

D'oh! The Simpsons and Total Revenue

In the episode "Bart Gets an Elephant," the Simpsons find that their pet elephant, Stampy, is eating them out of house and home. So Bart devises a plan to charge admission for people to see the elephant. He begins by charging $1. However, the revenue collected is not enough to cover Stampy's food bill. When Homer discovers that they are not covering their costs, he raises the cost to see the elephant to $100. However, Homer is not the smartest businessman in the world, and all of the customers who would have paid Bart's $1 admission stay away. We can use our understanding of elasticity to explain why Homer's plan backfires.

Homer's plan is to increase the price. This would work if the demand to see the elephant were inelastic, but it is not. For $100 you could see a concert, attend a major sporting event, or eat out at a very nice restaurant! You'd have to really want to see the elephant to be willing to pay $100. It doesn't help that you can also go to any of the best zoos in the country, and see hundreds of other animals as well, for much less money. Homer's plan is doomed to fail because no one is willing to pay $100. Remember that total revenue = price × quantity purchased. If the quantity demanded falls to zero, zero times anything is still zero. So Homer's plan does not generate any revenue.

The Simpsons cannot afford Stampy. What should they do?

In contrast, Bart's admission price of $1 brings in $58 in revenue. This is a good start, but not enough to cover Stampy's $300 food bill. Homer actually had the right idea here. Raising the price above $1 would generate more revenue up to a point. Would most of the customers pay $2 to see the elephant? Most likely. $5? Possibly. $10? Maybe. $100? Definitely not. Why not? There is a trade-off dictated by the law of demand. Higher prices will reduce the quantity demanded and vice versa. Therefore, the trick to maximizing total revenue is to balance increases in price against decreases in the quantity purchased.

outcome for a business. The lower price brings in less revenue and requires the business to produce more goods. Since making goods is costly, it does not make sense to lower prices into the region where revenues decline. We can be sure that no business will intentionally operate in the inelastic region of the demand curve.

How Do Changes in Income and the Prices of Other Goods Affect Elasticity?

We have seen how consumer demand responds to changes in the price of a single good. In this section, we will examine how responsive demand is to changes in income and to price changes in other goods.

Income Elasticity

Changes in personal income can have a large effect on consumer spending. After all, the money in your pocket influences not only how much you buy, but also the types of purchases you make. A consumer who is low on money may opt to buy a cheap generic product, while someone with a little extra cash can afford to upgrade. The grocery store aisle reflects this. Store brands and name products compete for shelf space. Lower-income shoppers can choose the store brand to save money, while more affluent shoppers can choose their favorite brand-name product without worrying about the purchase price. The **income elasticity of demand** (E_I) measures how a change in income affects spending. It is calculated by dividing the change in the quantity demanded by the change in personal income:

The **income elasticity of demand** measures how a change in income affects spending.

$$E_I = \frac{\text{percentage change in the quantity demanded}}{\text{percentage change in income}} \qquad \text{(Equation 4.3)}$$

Unlike the price elasticity of demand, which is negative, the income elasticity of demand can be either positive or negative. When higher levels of income enable the consumer to purchase more, the goods that are purchased are *normal goods*, a term we learned about in Chapter 3. Since the demand for normal goods goes up with income, they have a positive income elasticity—a rise in income will cause a rise in the quantity demanded. For instance, if you receive a 20% pay raise and you decide to pay an extra 10% on your cable TV bill to add HBO, the resulting income elasticity is positive, since 10% divided by 20% is 0.5. Whenever the good is normal, the result is a positive income elasticity of demand, and purchases of the good rise as income expands.

Clothing purchases expand with income.

Normal goods fall into two categories: *necessities* and *luxuries*. Goods that people consider to be necessities generally

PRACTICE WHAT YOU KNOW

The Price Elasticity of Demand

In this section, there are two questions to give you practice computing the price elasticity of demand. Before we do the math, ask yourself whether you think the price elasticity of demand for either subs or the antibiotic amoxicillin is elastic.

Is the demand for a sub elastic or inelastic?

Question: A store manager decides to lower the price of a featured sandwich from \$3 to \$2, and she finds that sales during the week increase from 240 to 480 sandwiches. Is demand elastic?

Answer: Consumers were flexible and bought significantly more sandwiches in response to the price drop. Let's calculate the price elasticity of demand (E_D) using Equation 4.2. Recall that

$$E_D = \frac{(Q_2 - Q_1) \div [(Q_1 + Q_2) \div 2]}{(P_2 - P_1) \div [(P_1 + P_2) \div 2]}$$

Plugging in the values from above yields

$$E_D = \frac{(480 - 240) \div [(240 + 480) \div 2]}{(\$2 - \$3) \div [(\$2 + \$3) \div 2]} = \frac{240 \div 360}{-\$1 \div \$2.50}$$

Therefore, $E_D = -1.67$.

Whenever the price elasticity of demand is less than −1, demand is considered elastic: the percentage change in the quantity demanded is greater than the percentage change in price. This outcome is exactly what the store manager expected. But subs are just one option for a meal; there are many other choices, such as salads, burgers, and chicken—all of which cost more than the now-reduced sandwich. Therefore, we should not be surprised that there is a relatively large percentage increase in sub purchases by price-conscious customers.

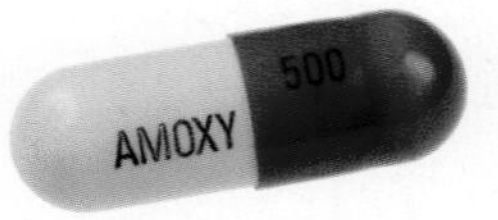

Is the demand for amoxicillin elastic or inelastic?

Question: A local pharmacy manager decides to raise the price of a 50-pill prescription of amoxicillin from \$8 to \$10. The pharmacy tracks the sales of amoxicillin over the next month and finds that sales decline from 1,500 to 1,480 boxes. Is the price elasticity of demand elastic?

Answer: First, let's consider the potential substitutes for amoxicillin. To be sure, it's possible to substitute other drugs, but they might not be as effective. Therefore, most patients prefer to use the drug prescribed by their doctor. Also, in this case the cost of the drug is relatively small. Finally, patients' need for amoxicillin is a short-run consideration. They want the medicine now so they will get better! All three factors would lead us to believe that the demand for amoxicillin is relatively inelastic. Let's find out if that intuition is confirmed in the data.

(CONTINUED)

(CONTINUED)

The price elasticity of demand using the midpoint method is

$$E_D = \frac{(Q_2 - Q_1) \div [(Q_1 + Q_2) \div 2]}{(P_2 - P_1) \div [(P_1 + P_2) \div 2]}$$

Plugging in the values from the example yields

$$E_D = \frac{(1480 - 1500) \div [(1480 + 1500) \div 2]}{(\$10 - \$8) \div [(\$8 + \$10) \div 2]}$$

Simplifying produces this:

$$E_D = \frac{-20 \div 1490}{\$2 \div \$9}$$

Therefore, $E_D = -0.06$. Recall that an E_D near zero indicates that the price elasticity of demand is highly inelastic, which is what we suspected. The price increase does not cause consumption to fall very much. If the store manager had been hoping to bring in a little extra revenue from the sales of amoxicillin, his plan was successful. Before the price increase, the business sold 1,500 units at $8, so revenues were $12,000. After the price increase, sales decreased to 1,480 units, but the new price is $10, so revenues now are $14,800. Raising the price of amoxicillin helped the pharmacy make an additional $2,800 in revenue.

have income elasticities between 0 and 1. For example, expenditures on items such as milk, clothing, electricity, and gasoline are unavoidable, and consumers at any income level must buy them no matter what. Although purchases of necessities will increase as income rises, they do not rise as fast as the increase in income does. Therefore, as income increases, spending on necessities will expand at a slower rate than the increase in income.

Air travel is a luxury good.

Rising income enables consumers to enjoy significantly more luxuries. This produces an income elasticity of demand greater than 1. For instance, a family of modest means may travel almost exclusively by car. However, as the family's income rises, they can afford air travel. A relatively small jump in income can cause the family to fly instead of drive.

In Chapter 3, we saw that *inferior goods* are those that people will choose not to purchase when their income goes up. Inferior goods have a negative income elasticity, because as income expands, the demand for the good declines. We see this in Table 4.4 with the example of macaroni and cheese, an inexpensive meal. As a household's income rises, it is able to afford healthier food and more variety in the meals it enjoys. Consequently, the number of times that mac and cheese is served declines. The decline in consumption indicates that mac and cheese is an inferior good, and this is reflected in the negative sign of the income elasticity.

TABLE 4.4

Income Elasticity

Type of good	Subcategory	E_I coefficient	Example
Inferior		$E_I < 0$	Macaroni and cheese
Normal	Necessity	$0 < E_I > 1$	Milk
Normal	Luxury	$E_I > 1$	Diamond ring

Cross-Price Elasticity

The **cross-price elasticity of demand** measures the responsiveness of the quantity demanded of one good to a change in the price of a related good.

Now we will look at how a price change in one good can affect the demand for a related good. For instance, if you enjoy pizza, the choice between ordering from Domino's or Pizza Hut is influenced by the price of both goods. The **cross-price elasticity of demand** (E_C) measures the responsiveness of the quantity demanded of one good to a change in the price of a related good.

(Equation 4.4)

$$E_C = \frac{\text{percentage change in the quantity demanded of one good}}{\text{percentage change in the price of a related good}}$$

Consider how two goods are related to each other. If the goods are substitutes, a price rise in one good will cause the quantity demanded of that good to decline. At the same time, since consumers can purchase the substitute good for the same price as before, demand for the substitute good will increase. When the price of Domino's pizza rises, consumers will buy more pizza from Pizza Hut.

The opposite is true if the goods are complements. When goods are related to each other, a price increase in one good will make the joint consumption of both goods more expensive. Therefore, the consumption of both goods will decline. For example, a price increase for turkeys will cause the quantity demanded of both turkey and gravy to decline. This means that the cross-price elasticity of demand is negative.

What if there is no relationship? For example, if the price of basketballs goes up, that probably will not affect the quantity demanded of bedroom slippers. In this case, the cross-price elasticity is neither positive nor negative; it is zero. Table 4.5 lists cross-price elasticity values according to type of good.

To learn how to calculate cross-price elasticity, let's consider an example from the skit "Lazy Sunday" on *Saturday Night Live*. The skit features Chris Parnell and Andy Samberg rapping about going to see *The Chronicles of Narnia* and eating cupcakes. In one inspired scene, they describe enjoying the soft drink Mr. Pibb with Red Vines candy and call the combination "crazy

TABLE 4.5

Cross-Price Elasticity

Type of good	E_I coefficient	Example
Substitutes	$E_C > 0$	Pizza Hut and Domino's
No relationship	$E_C = 0$	A basketball and bedroom slippers
Complements	$E_C < 0$	Turkey and gravy

delicious." From this, we can construct a cross-price elasticity example. Suppose that the price of a two-liter bottle of Mr. Pibb falls from \$1.49 to \$1.29. In the week immediately preceding the price drop, a local store sells 60 boxes of Red Vines. After the price drop, sales of Red Vines increase to 80 boxes. Let's calculate the cross-price elasticity of demand for Red Vines when the price of Mr. Pibb falls from \$1.49 to \$1.29.

Have you tried Mr. Pibb and Red Vines together?

The cross-price elasticity of demand using the midpoint method is

$$E_C = \frac{(Q_{RV2} - Q_{RV1}) \div [(Q_{RV1} + Q_{RV2}) \div 2]}{(P_{MP2} - P_{MP1}) \div [(P_{MP1} + P_{MP2}) \div 2]}$$

Notice that there are now additional subscripts to denote that we are measuring the percentage change in the quantity demanded of good RV (Red Vines) in response to the percentage change in the price of good MP (Mr. Pibb).

Plugging in the values from the example yields

$$E_C = \frac{(80 - 60) \div [(60 + 80) \div 2]}{(\$1.29 - \$1.49) \div [(\$1.49 + \$1.29) \div 2]}$$

Simplifying produces

$$E_C = \frac{20 \div 70}{-\$0.20 \div \$1.39}$$

Solving for E_C gives us a value of −1.01. Because the result is a negative value, this confirms our intuition that two goods that go well together ("crazy delicious") are complements, since the decrease in the price of Mr. Pibb causes consumers to buy more Red Vines.

ECONOMICS IN THE REAL WORLD

The Wii Rollout and Changes in the Video Game Industry

The Wii rollout generated long waiting lines.

When Nintendo launched the Wii console in late 2006, it fundamentally changed the gaming industry. The Wii uses motion-sensing technology. Despite relatively poor graphics, it provided a completely different gaming experience from its competitors, Playstation 3 (PS3) and the Xbox 360. Yet the PS3 and Xbox 360 had larger storage capacities and better graphics, in theory making them more attractive to gamers than the Wii.

During the 2006 holiday shopping season, the three systems had three distinct price points:

Wii = $249
Xbox = $399
Playstation 3 = $599

Wii and Xbox sales were very strong. As a result, both units were in short supply in stores. However, PS3 sales did not fare as well as its manufacturer, Sony, had hoped. The Wii outsold the PS3 by a more than 4:1 ratio, and the Xbox 360 outsold the PS3 by more than 2:1 during the first half of 2007. More telling, a monthly breakdown of sales figures across the three platforms shows the deterioration in the PS3 and Xbox 360 sales.

Console	Units sold, January 2007	Units sold, April 2007	Percentage change
Wii	460,000	360,000	−22%
Xbox 360	249,000	174,000	−30%
PS3	244,000	82,000	−66%

Faced with quickly falling sales, Sony lowered the price of the PS3 console. The company understood that consumer demand was quite elastic and that lowering the price was the only way to retain customers. Indeed, the lower price stimulated additional interest in the PS3 and helped to increase the number of units sold in the second half of the year. Without a firm grasp of the price elasticity of demand, Sony would not have made this move.

Meanwhile, interest in the Wii continued to be strong. For Nintendo, the market demand was relatively inelastic. Nintendo could have raised the price of its console but chose not to do so. One reason is that Nintendo also makes money by selling peripherals and games. These are strong complements to the console, and a higher console price would discourage customers from purchasing the Wii. Since the cross-price elasticity of demand for peripherals and games is highly negative, this strategy makes economic sense. Nintendo had chosen not to do this, in part, because the company wanted to maximize not only the console price, but also the prices of all of the related components. Nintendo's strategy worked. The four top-selling games during 2007 were all associated with the Wii rollout. ✱

SNAPSHOT

Price Elasticity of Demand

Determining the price elasticity of demand for a product or service involves calculating the responsiveness of quantity demanded to a change in the price. The chart below gives the actual price elasticity of demand for ten common products and services. Remember, the number is always negative because of the inverse relationship between price and the quantity demanded. Why is price elasticity of demand important? It reveals consumer behavior and allows for better pricing strategies by businesses.

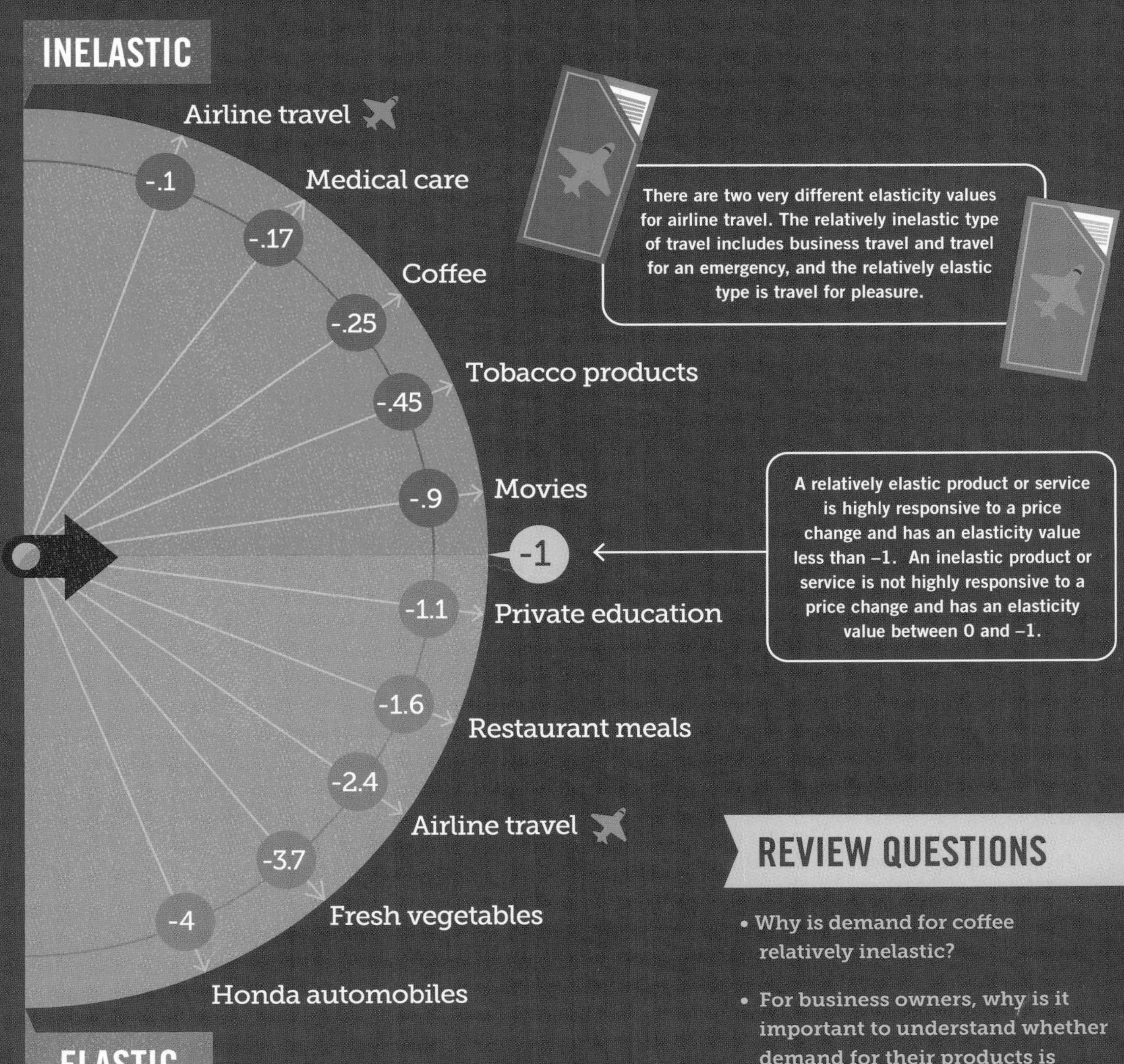

INELASTIC
Airline travel
-.1
Medical care
-.17
Coffee
-.25
Tobacco products
-.45
Movies
-.9
-1
Private education
-1.1
Restaurant meals
-1.6
Airline travel
-2.4
Fresh vegetables
-3.7
Honda automobiles
-4
ELASTIC
There are two very different elasticity values for airline travel. The relatively inelastic type of travel includes business travel and travel for an emergency, and the relatively elastic type is travel for pleasure.
A relatively elastic product or service is highly responsive to a price change and has an elasticity value less than –1. An inelastic product or service is not highly responsive to a price change and has an elasticity value between 0 and –1.

REVIEW QUESTIONS

- Why is demand for coffee relatively inelastic?
- For business owners, why is it important to understand whether demand for their products is elastic or inelastic?

PRACTICE WHAT YOU KNOW

Income Elasticity

Yummy, or all you can afford?

Question: A college student eats ramen noodles twice a week and earns $300/week working part-time. After graduating, the student earns $1,000/week and eats ramen noodles every other week. What is the student's income elasticity?

Answer: The income elasticity of demand using the midpoint method is

$$E_I = \frac{(Q_2 - Q_1) \div [(Q_1 + Q_2) \div 2]}{(I_2 - I_1) \div [(I_1 + I_2) \div 2]}$$

Plugging in yields

$$E_I = \frac{(0.5 - 2.0) \div [(2.0 + 0.5) \div 2]}{(\$1000 - \$300) \div [(\$300 + \$1000) \div 2]}$$

Simplifying yields

$$E_I = \frac{-1.5 \div 1.25}{\$700 \div \$650}$$

Therefore, $E_I = -1.1$.

The income elasticity of demand is positive for normal goods and negative for inferior goods. Therefore, the negative coefficient indicates that ramen noodles are an inferior good over the range of income—in this example, between $300 and $1,000. This result should confirm your intuition. The higher post-graduation income enables the student to substitute away from ramen noodles and toward other meals that provide more nourishment and enjoyment.

What Is the Price Elasticity of Supply?

The **price elasticity of supply** is a measure of the responsiveness of the quantity supplied to a change in price.

Sellers, like consumers, are sensitive to price changes. However, the determinants of the *price elasticity of supply* are substantially different from the determinants of the price elasticity of demand. The **price elasticity of supply** is a measure of the responsiveness of the quantity supplied to a change in price.

In this section, we examine how much sellers respond to price changes. For instance, if the market price of gasoline increases, how will oil companies respond? The answer depends on the elasticity of supply. Oil must be refined into gasoline. If it is difficult for oil companies to increase their output of gasoline significantly, even if the price increases a lot, the quantity of gasoline supplied will not increase much. In this case, we say that the price elasticity of supply is inelastic, or unresponsive. However, if the price increase is small and suppliers respond by offering significantly more gasoline for sale, the price elasticity of supply is elastic. We would expect to observe this outcome if it were easy to refine oil into gasoline.

What would it take to own a slice of paradise?

When supply is not able to respond to a change in price, we say it is inelastic. Think of an oceanfront property in Southern California. The amount of land next to the ocean is fixed. If the price of oceanfront property rises, the supply of land cannot adjust to the price increase. In this case, the supply is perfectly inelastic and the elasticity is zero. Recall that a price elasticity coefficient of zero means that supply does not change as price changes.

When the ability of the supplier to make quick adjustments is limited, the elasticity of supply is less than 1. For instance, when a cellular network becomes congested, it takes suppliers a long time to provide additional capacity. They have to build new cell towers, which requires the purchase of land and additional construction costs. In contrast, a local hot dog vendor can easily add another cart in relatively short order. As a result, for the hot dog vendor, supply elasticity is elastic with an elasticity coefficient that is greater than 1. Table 4.6 examines the price elasticity of supply. Recall that the law of supply states that there is a direct relationship between the price of a good and the quantity that a firm supplies. As a result, the percentage change in the quantity supplied and the percentage change in price move in the same direction. The E_S coefficient reflects this direct relationship with a positive sign.

Determinants of the Price Elasticity of Supply

When we examined the determinants of the price elasticity of demand, we saw that consumers had to consider the number of substitutes, how expensive the item was compared to their overall budget, and the amount of time they had to make a decision. Time and the adjustment process are also key elements in determining the price elasticity of supply. However, there is

TABLE 4.6

A Closer Look at the Price Elasticity of Supply

Elasticity	E_S coefficient	Example
Perfectly inelastic	$E_S = 0$	Oceanfront land
Relatively inelastic	$0 < E_S < 1$	Cellphone tower
Relatively elastic	$E_S > 1$	Hot dog vendor

a critical difference: the degree of flexibility that producers have in bringing their product to the market quickly.

The Flexibility of Producers

When a producer can quickly ramp up output, supply tends to be elastic. One way to maintain flexibility is to have spare production capacity. Extra capacity enables producers to quickly meet changing price conditions, so supply is more responsive, or elastic. The ability to store the good is another way to stay flexible. Producers who have stockpiles of their products can respond more quickly to changes in market conditions. For example, De Beers, the international diamond conglomerate, stores millions of uncut diamonds. As the price of diamonds fluctuates, De Beers can quickly change the supply of diamonds it offers to the market. Likewise, hot dog vendors can relocate quickly from one street corner to another or add carts if demand is strong. However, many businesses cannot adapt to changing market conditions quickly. For instance, a golf course cannot easily build nine new holes to meet additional demand. This limits the golf course owner's ability to adjust quickly and increase the supply of golfing opportunities as soon as the fee changes.

Time and the Adjustment Process

In the immediate run, businesses, just like consumers, are stuck with what they have on hand. For example, a pastry shop that runs out of chocolate glazed donuts cannot bake more instantly. As we move from the immediate run to the short run and a price change persists through time, supply—just like demand—becomes more elastic. For instance, a golf resort may be able to squeeze extra production out of its current facility by staying open longer hours or moving tee times closer together, but those short-run efforts will not match the production potential of adding another course in the long run.

Figure 4.5 shows how the two determinants of supply elasticity are mapped onto the supply curve. In the immediate run, the supply curve is vertical (S_1). A vertical curve tells us that there is no responsiveness when the price changes. As producers gain additional time to make adjustments, the supply curve rotates from S_1, the immediate run, to S_2, the short run, to S_3, the long run. Like the demand curve, the supply curve becomes flatter through time. The only difference is that the supply curve rotates clockwise, whereas, as we saw in Figure 4.2, the demand curve rotates counterclockwise. With both supply and demand, the most important thing to remember is that more time allows for greater adjustment, so the long run is always more elastic.

Calculating the Price Elasticity of Supply

Like the price elasticity of demand, we can calculate the price elasticity of supply. This is useful when a business owner must decide how much to produce at various prices. The elasticity of supply measures how quickly the producer is able to change production in response to changes in price. When the price elasticity of supply is elastic, producers are able to quickly adjust production. If the price elasticity of supply is inelastic, production tends to remain roughly constant, despite large swings in price.

Here is the formula for the price elasticity of supply (E_S):

(Equation 4.5)

$$E_S = \frac{\text{percentage change in the quantity supplied}}{\text{percentage change in the price}}$$

This equation is almost exactly the same as that of the price elasticity of demand. The only difference is that we are measuring the percentage change in the quantity supplied in the numerator.

Consider how the manufacturer of Solo cups might respond to an increase in demand that causes the cups' market price to rise. The company's ability to change the amount it produces depends on the flexibility of the manufacturing process and the length of time needed to ramp up production. Suppose that the price of the cups rises by 10%. The company can increase its production by 5% immediately, but it will take many months to expand production by 20%. What can we say about the price elasticity of supply in this case? Using Equation 4.5, we can take the percentage change in the quantity supplied immediately (5%) and divide that by the percentage change in price (10%). This gives us an $E_S = 0.5$, which signals that the elasticity of supply is relatively inelastic. However, with time the firm is able to increase the quantity supplied by 20%. If we divide 20% by the percentage change in the price (10%), we get $E_S = 2.0$, which indicates that the price elasticity of supply is relatively elastic in the long run.

Have you ever shopped for Solo cups?

FIGURE 4.5

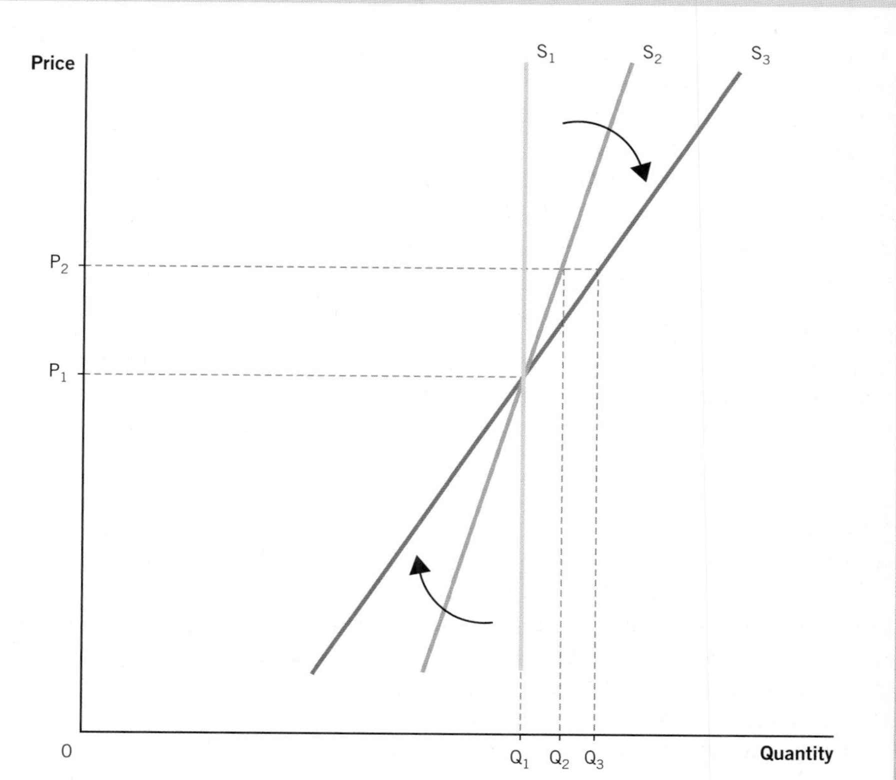

Elasticity and the Supply Curve

Increased flexibility and more time make supply more elastic. When price rises from P_1 to P_2, producers are unable to expand output immediately and the supply curve remains at Q_1. In the short run (S_2), the firm becomes more flexible and output expands to Q_2. Eventually, in the long run (S_3), the firm is able to produce even more, and it moves to Q_3 in response to higher prices.

PRACTICE WHAT YOU KNOW

The Price Elasticity of Supply

Oil companies have us over a barrel.

Question: Suppose that the price of a barrel of oil increases from $60 to $100. The new output is 2 million barrels a day, and the old output is 1.8 million barrels. What is the price elasticity of supply?

Answer: The price elasticity of supply using the midpoint method is

$$E_D = \frac{(Q_2 - Q_1) \div [(Q_1 + Q_2) \div 2]}{(P_2 - P_1) \div [(P_1 + P_2) \div 2]}$$

Plugging in the values from the example yields

$$E_S = \frac{(2.0M - 1.8M) \div [(1.8M + 2.0M) \div 2]}{(\$100 - \$60) \div [(\$60 + \$100) \div 2]}$$

Simplifying yields

$$E_S = \frac{0.2M \div 1.9M}{\$40 \div \$80}$$

Therefore, $E_S = 0.20$.

Recall from our discussion of the law of supply that there is a direct relationship between the price and the quantity supplied. Since E_S in this case is positive, we see that output rises as price rises. However, the magnitude of the output increase is quite small—this is reflected in the coefficient 0.20. Because oil companies cannot easily change their production process, they have a limited ability to respond quickly to rising prices. That inability is reflected in a coefficient that is relatively close to zero. A zero coefficient would mean that suppliers could not change their output at all. Here suppliers are able to respond, but only in a limited capacity.

How Do the Price Elasticity of Demand and Supply Relate to Each Other?

The interplay between the price elasticity of supply and the price elasticity of demand allows us to explain more fully how the economy operates. With an understanding of elasticity at our disposal, we can make a much richer and deeper analysis of the world around us. For instance, suppose that we are concerned about what will happen to the price of oil as economic development spurs additional demand in China and India. An examination of the determinants of the price elasticity of supply quickly confirms that oil producers have a limited ability to adjust production in response to rising prices. Oil wells can be uncapped to meet rising demand, but it takes years to bring the new capacity online. Moreover, storing oil reserves, while possible, is expensive. Therefore, the short-run supply of oil is quite inelastic. Figure 4.6 shows the combination of inelastic supply-side production constraints in the short run and the inelastic short-run demand for oil.

An increase in global demand from D_1 to D_2 will create significantly higher prices (from \$60 to \$90) in the short run. This occurs because increasing oil production is difficult in the short run. Therefore, the short-run supply curve (S_{SR}) is relatively inelastic. In the long run, though, oil producers are able to bring more oil to the market when prices are higher, so the supply curve rotates clockwise (S_{LR}), becoming more elastic, and the market price falls to \$80.

What does this example tell us? It reminds us that the interplay between the price elasticity of demand and the price elasticity of supply determines the magnitude of the resulting price change. We cannot observe demand in isolation without also considering how supply responds. Similarly, we cannot simply think about the short-run consequences of demand and supply shifts; we also must consider how prices and quantity will vary in the long run. Armed with this knowledge, you can begin to see the power of the supply and demand model to explain the world around us.

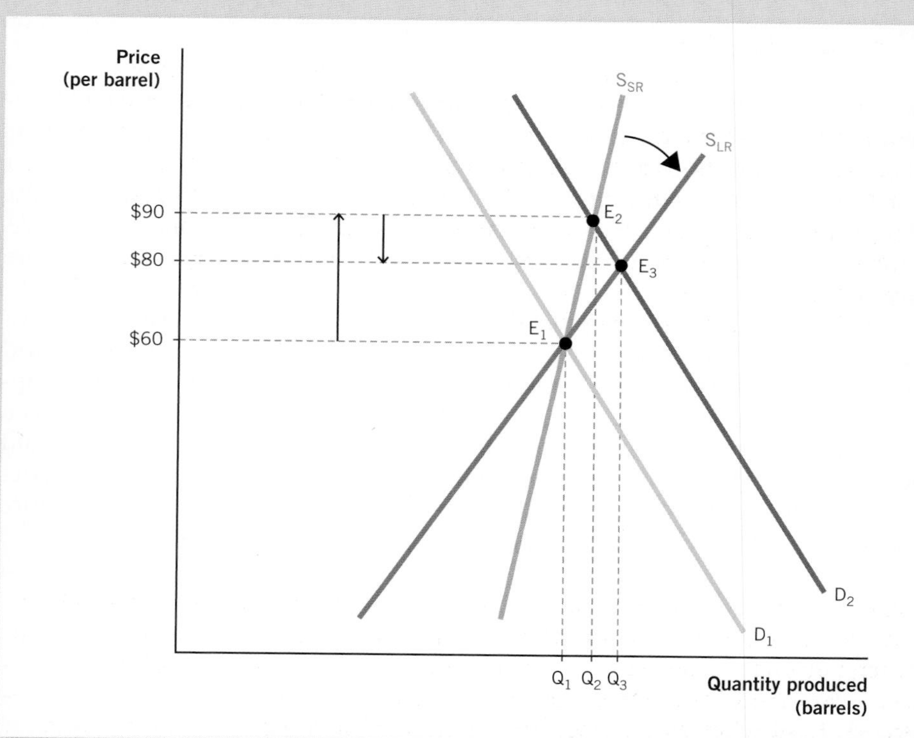

FIGURE 4.6

A Demand Shift and the Consequences for Short- and Long-Run Supply

When an increase in demand causes the price of oil to rise from \$60 to \$90 per barrel, initially producers are unable to expand output very much—production expands from Q_1 to Q_2. However, in the long run, as producers expand production, the price will fall back to \$80.

PRACTICE WHAT YOU KNOW

Elasticity: Trick or Treat Edition

How much would you spend on a Halloween pumpkin?

Question: An unusually bad growing season leads to a small pumpkin crop. What will happen to the price of pumpkins as Halloween approaches?

Answer: The demand for pumpkins peaks in October and rapidly falls after Halloween. Purchasing a pumpkin is a short-run decision to buy a unique product that takes up a relatively small share of the consumer's budget. As a result, the price elasticity of demand for pumpkins leading up to Halloween tends to be quite inelastic. At the same time, a small crop causes the entire supply curve to shift left. This causes the market price of pumpkins to rise. Since the demand is relatively inelastic in the short run and the supply of pumpkins is fixed, we expect the price to rise significantly. After Halloween, the price of any remaining pumpkins falls, since demand declines dramatically.

Conclusion

Do sellers charge the highest price possible? We can now answer this misconception definitively: no. Sellers like higher prices in the same way consumers like lower prices, but that does not mean that they will charge the highest price possible. At very high prices, we learned that consumer demand is quite elastic. Therefore, a seller who charges too high a price will not sell much. As a result, firms learn that they must lower their price in order to attract more customers.

The ability to determine whether demand and supply are elastic or inelastic also enables economists to calculate the effects of personal, business, and policy decisions. When you combine the concept of elasticity with the supply and demand model from Chapter 3, you get a very powerful tool. As a result, we can now say much more about how the world works than we could before. In subsequent chapters, we will employ the understanding of elasticity to refine our models of economic behavior and make our results more realistic.

Price Elasticity of Supply and Demand: Buying Your First Car

ECONOMICS FOR LIFE

When you buy a car, your knowledge of price elasticity can help you negotiate the best possible deal.

Recall that the three determinants of price elasticity of demand are (1) the share of the budget, (2) the number of available substitutes, and (3) the time you have to make a decision.

Let's start with your budget. You should have one in mind, but don't tell the salesperson what you are willing to spend; that is a vital piece of personal information you want to keep to yourself. If the salesperson suggests that you look at a model that is too expensive, just say that you are not interested. You might reply, "Buying a car is a stretch for me; I've got to stay within my budget." If the salesperson asks indirectly about your budget by inquiring whether you have a particular monthly payment in mind, reply that you want to negotiate over the invoice price once you decide on a vehicle. Never negotiate on the sticker price, which is the price you see in the car window, because it includes thousands of dollars in markup. You want to make it clear to the salesperson that the price you pay matters to you—that is, your demand is elastic.

Next, make it clear that you are gathering information and visiting other dealers. That is, reinforce that you have many available substitutes. Even if you really want a Honda, do not voice that desire to the Honda salesperson. Perhaps mention that you are also visiting the Toyota, Hyundai, and Ford showrooms. Compare what you've seen on one lot versus another. Each salesperson you meet should hear that you are seriously considering other options. This indicates to each dealership that your demand is elastic and that getting your business will require that they offer you a better price.

Taking your time to decide is also important. Never buy a car the first time you walk onto a lot. If you convey the message that you want a car immediately, you are saying that your demand is inelastic. If the dealership thinks that you have no flexibility, the staff will not give you their best offer. Instead, tell the salesperson that you appreciate their help and that you will be deciding over the next few weeks. A good salesperson will know you are serious and will ask for your phone number or email address and contact you. The salesperson will sweeten the deal if you indicate you are narrowing down your choices and they are in the running. You wait. You win.

Also know that salespeople and dealerships have times when they want to move inventory. August is an especially good month to purchase. In other words, the price elasticity of supply is at work here as well. A good time to buy is when the dealer is trying to move inventory to make room for new models, because prices fall for end-of-the-model-year closeouts. Likewise, many sales promotions and sales bonuses are tied to the end of the month, so salespeople will be more eager to sell at that time.

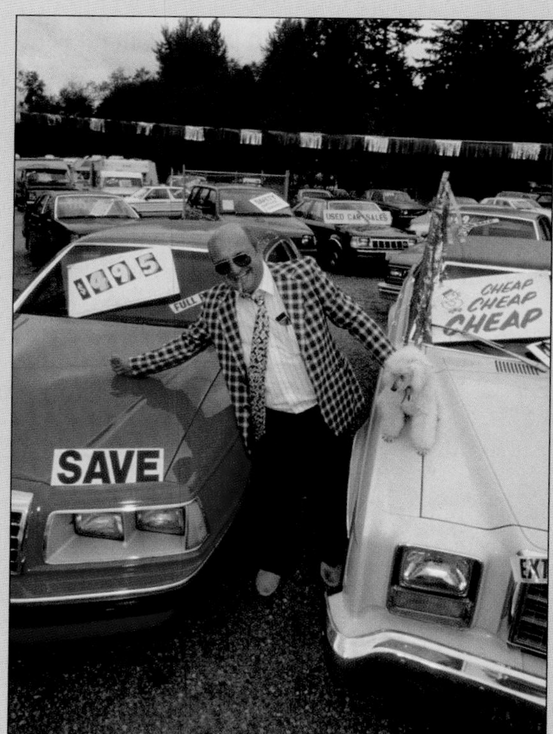

Watch out for shady negotiation practices!

ANSWERING THE BIG QUESTIONS

What is the price elasticity of demand, and what are its determinants?

* The price elasticity of demand is a measure of the responsiveness of quantity demanded to a change in price.
* Demand will generally be more elastic if there are many substitutes available, if the item accounts for a large share of the consumer's budget, if the item is a luxury good, or if the consumer has plenty of time to make a decision.
* Economists categorize time in three distinct periods: the immediate run, where there is no time for consumers to adjust their behavior; the short run, where consumers can adjust, but only partially; and the long run, where consumers have time to fully adjust to market conditions.
* The price elasticity of demand can be calculated by taking the percentage change in the quantity demanded and dividing it by the percentage change in price. A value of zero indicates that the quantity demanded does not respond to a price change; if the price elasticity is zero, demand is said to be perfectly inelastic. When the price elasticity of demand is between 0 and −1, demand is inelastic. If the price elasticity of demand is less than −1, demand is elastic.

How do changes in income and the prices of other goods affect elasticity?

* The income elasticity of demand measures how a change in income affects spending. Normal goods have a positive income elasticity. Inferior goods have a negative income elasticity.
* The cross-price elasticity of demand measures the responsiveness of the quantity demanded of one good to a change in the price of a related good. Positive values for the cross-price elasticity mean that the two goods are substitutes, while negative values indicate that the two goods are complements. If the cross-price elasticity is zero, then the two goods are not correlated with each other.

What is the price elasticity of supply?

* The price elasticity of supply is a measure of the responsiveness of the quantity supplied to a change in price. Supply will generally be more elastic if producers have flexibility in the production process and ample time to adjust production.
* The price elasticity of supply is calculated by dividing the percentage change in the quantity supplied by the percentage change in price. A value of zero indicates that the quantity supplied does not respond to a price change; if the price elasticity is zero, supply is said to be perfectly inelastic. When the price elasticity of supply is between 0 and 1, demand is relatively inelastic. If the price elasticity of supply is greater than 1, supply is elastic.

How do the price elasticity of demand and supply relate to each other?

* The interplay between the price elasticity of demand and the price elasticity of supply determines the magnitude of the resulting price change.

CONCEPTS YOU SHOULD KNOW

cross-price elasticity of demand (p. 130)
elasticity (p. 110)
immediate run (p. 113)
income elasticity of demand (p. 127)
long run (p. 113)
price elasticity of demand (p. 111)
price elasticity of supply (p. 134)
short run (p. 113)
total revenue (p. 123)

QUESTIONS FOR REVIEW

1. Define the price elasticity of demand.
2. What are the four determinants of the price elasticity of demand?
3. Give an example of a good that has elastic demand. What is the value of the price elasticity if demand is elastic? Give an example of a good that has inelastic demand. What is the value of the price elasticity if demand is inelastic?
4. What is the connection between total revenue and the price elasticity of demand? Illustrate this relationship along a demand curve.
5. Explain why slope is different from elasticity.
6. Define the price elasticity of supply.
7. What are the two determinants of the price elasticity of supply?
8. Give an example of a good that has elastic supply. What is the value of the price elasticity if supply is elastic? Give an example of a good that has an inelastic supply. What is the value of the price elasticity if supply is inelastic?
9. Give an example of a normal good. What is the income elasticity of a normal good? Give an example of a luxury good. What is the income elasticity of a luxury good? Give an example of a necessity. What is the income elasticity of a necessity? Give an example of an inferior good. What is the income elasticity of an inferior good?
10. Define the cross-price elasticity of demand. Give an example with negative cross-price elasticity, another with zero cross-price elasticity, and a third with positive cross-price elasticity.

STUDY PROBLEMS (** solved at the end of the section*)

* 1. If the government decided to impose a 50% tax on gray T-shirts, would this policy generate a large or small increase in revenues? Use elasticity to explain your answer.

2. College logo T-shirts priced at $15 sell at a rate of 25 per week, but when the bookstore marks them down to $10, it finds that it can sell 50 T-shirts per week. What is the price elasticity of demand for the logo T-shirts?

3. Search YouTube for the video titled "Black Friday 2006—Best Buy Line." Do the early shoppers appear to have elastic or inelastic demand on Black Friday? Explain your response.

4. If a 20% increase in price causes a 10% drop in the quantity demanded, is the price elasticity of demand for this good elastic, unitary, or inelastic?

5. Characterize each of the following goods as perfectly elastic, relatively elastic, relatively inelastic, or perfectly inelastic.
   a. a life-saving medication
   b. photocopies at a copy shop, when all competing shops charge 10 cents per copy
   c. a fast-food restaurant located in the food court of a shopping mall
   d. the water bill you pay

6. A local paintball business receives total revenue of $8,000 a month when it charges $10 per person, and $9,600 in total revenue when it charges $6 per person. Over that range of prices, does the business face elastic, unitary, or inelastic demand?

7. At a price of $200, a cellphone company manufactures 300,000 units. At a price of $150, the company produces 200,000 phones. What is the price elasticity of supply?

8. Do customers who visit convenience stores at 3 a.m. have a price elasticity of demand that is more or less elastic than those who visit at 3 p.m.?

* 9. A worker gets a 25% raise. As a result, he decides to eat out twice as much as before and cut back on the number of frozen lasagna dinners from once a week to once every other week. Determine the income elasticity of demand for eating out and for having frozen lasagna dinners.

10. The cross-price elasticity of demand between American Eagle and Hollister is 2.0. What does that tell us about the relationship between these two stores?

11. A local golf course is considering lowering its fees in order to increase the revenue coming in. Under what conditions is the fee reduction going to achieve its goal?

12. A private university notices that in-state and out-of-state students seem to respond differently to tuition changes.

Tuition	Quantity demanded (in-state applicants)	Quantity demanded (out-of-state applicants)
$10,000	6,000	12,000
$15,000	5,000	9,000
$20,000	4,000	6,000
$30,000	3,000	3,000

As the price of tuition rises from $15,000 to $20,000, what is the price elasticity of demand for in-state applicants and also for out-of-state applicants?

SOLVED PROBLEMS

1. To answer this question, we need to consider the price elasticity of demand. The tax is only on gray T-shirts. This means that T-shirt customers who buy other colors can avoid the tax entirely—which means that the demand for gray T-shirts is relatively elastic. Since not many gray T-shirts will be sold, the government will generate a small increase in revenues from the tax.

9. In this question a worker gets a 25% raise, so we can use this information in the denominator when determining the income elasticity of demand. We are not given the percentage change for the meals out, so we need to plug in how often the worker ate out before (once a week) and the amount he eats out after the raise (twice a week).

   Plugging into E_I gives us

$$E_I = \frac{(2 - 1) \div [(1 + 2) \div 2]}{0.25}$$

   Simplifying yields

$$E_I = \frac{1 \div 1.5}{0.25}$$

   Therefore, $E_I = 2.67$.

   The income elasticity of demand for eating out is positive for normal goods. Therefore, eating out is a normal good. This result should confirm your intuition.

   Let's see what happens with frozen lasagna once the worker gets the 25% raise. Now he cuts back on the number of lasagna dinners from once a week to once every other week.

   Plugging into E_I gives us

$$E_I = \frac{(0.5 - 1) \div [(1 + 0.5) \div 2]}{0.25}$$

   Simplifying yields

$$E_I = \frac{-0.5 \div 0.75}{0.25}$$

   Therefore, $E_I = -2.67$. The income elasticity of demand for having frozen lasagna is negative. Therefore, frozen lasagna is an inferior good. This result should confirm your intuition.

CHAPTER

5 Price Controls

MISCONCEPTION

The minimum wage helps everyone earn a living wage.

You are probably familiar with the minimum wage, which is an example of a *price control*. If you have ever worked for the minimum wage, you probably think that raising it sounds like a great idea. You may support minimum wage legislation because you believe it will help struggling workers to make ends meet. After all, it seems reasonable that firms should pay workers at least enough to cover the necessities of life, or what is referred to as a living wage.

Price controls are not a new idea. The first recorded attempt to control prices was four thousand years ago in ancient Babylon, when King Hammurabi decreed how much corn a farmer could pay for a cow. Similar attempts to control prices occurred in ancient Egypt, Greece, and Rome. Each attempt ended badly. In Egypt, farmers revolted against tight price controls and intrusive inspections, eventually causing the economy to collapse. In Greece, the Athenian government set the price of grain at a very low level. Predictably, the quantity of grain supplied dried up. In 301 CE, the Roman government under Emperor Diocletian prescribed the maximum price of beef, grains, clothing, and many other articles. Almost immediately, markets for these goods disappeared.

History has shown us that price controls generally do not work. Why? Because they disrupt the normal functioning of the market. By the end of this chapter, we hope that you will understand why price controls such as minimum wage laws are rarely the win-win propositions that legislators often claim. To help you understand why price controls lead to disequilibrium in markets, this chapter focuses on the two most common types of price controls: *price ceilings* and *price floors*.

The Code of Hammurabi established the first known price controls.

BIG QUESTIONS

* When do price ceilings matter?
* What effects do price ceilings have on economic activity?
* When do price floors matter?
* What effects do price floors have on economic activity?

When Do Price Ceilings Matter?

Price controls are an attempt to set prices through government involvement in the market. In most cases, and certainly in the United States, price controls are enacted to ease perceived burdens on society. A **price ceiling** creates a legally established maximum price for a good or service. In the next section, we will consider what happens when a price ceiling is in place. Price ceilings create many unintended effects that policymakers rarely acknowledge.

Price controls
are an attempt to set prices through government involvement in the market.

Price ceilings
are legally established maximum prices for goods or services.

Understanding Price Ceilings

To understand how price ceilings work, let's try a simple thought experiment. Suppose that prices are rising because of inflation. The government is concerned that people with low incomes will not be able to afford enough to eat. To help the disadvantaged, legislators pass a law stating that no one can charge more than $0.50 for a loaf of bread. (Note that this price ceiling is about one-third the typical price of generic white bread.) Does the new law accomplish its goal? What happens?

Empty shelves signal a shortage of products.

The law of supply and demand tells us that if the price drops, the quantity that consumers demand will increase. At the same time, the quantity supplied will fall because producers will be receiving lower profits for their efforts. This twin dynamic of increased quantity demanded and reduced quantity supplied will cause a shortage of bread.

On the demand side, consumers will want more bread than is available at the legal price. There will be long lines for bread, and many people will not be able to get the bread they want. On the supply side, producers will look for ways to maintain their profits. They can reduce the size of each loaf they produce. They can also use cheaper ingredients, thereby lowering the quality of their product, and they can stop making fancier varieties. In addition, *black markets* will develop to help supply meet demand.

Black markets are illegal markets that arise when price controls are in place. For instance, in the former Soviet Union price controls on bread and other essentials led to very long lines. In our bread example, many people who do not want to wait in line for bread, or who do not obtain it despite waiting in line, will resort to illegal means to obtain it. This means that sellers will go underground and charge higher prices to deliver customers the bread they want.

Black markets are illegal markets that arise when price controls are in place.

Incentives

Table 5.1 summarizes the likely outcome of price controls on bread.

TABLE 5.1

A Price Ceiling on Bread

Question	Answer / Explanation	Result	
Will there be more or less bread for sale?	Consumers will want to buy more since the price is lower (the law of demand), but producers will manufacture less (the law of supply). The net result will be a shortage of bread.		Empty shelves.
Will the size of a typical loaf change?	Since the price is capped at $0.50 per loaf, manufacturers will try to maintain profits by reducing the size of each loaf.		No more giant loaves.
Will the quality change?	Since the price is capped, producers will use cheaper ingredients, and many expensive brands and varieties will no longer be profitable to produce. Thus the quality of available bread will decline.		Focaccia bread will disappear.
Will the opportunity cost of finding bread change?	The opportunity cost of finding bread will rise. This means that consumers will spend significant resources going from store to store to see if a bread shipment has arrived and waiting in line for a chance to get some.		Bread lines will become the norm.
Will people have to break the law to buy bread?	Since bread will be hard to find and people will still need it, a black market will develop. Those selling and buying on the black market will be breaking the law.		Black-market bread dealers will help reduce the shortage.

If you can touch the ceiling, you can't go any higher. A binding price ceiling stops prices from rising.

The Effect of Price Ceilings

Now that we have some understanding of how a price ceiling works, we can transfer that knowledge into the supply and demand model for a deeper analysis of how price ceilings affect the market. To explain when price ceilings matter in the short run, we will examine the outcomes of two types of price ceilings: nonbinding and binding.

Nonbinding Price Ceilings

The effect of a price ceiling depends on the level at which it is set. When a price ceiling is above the equilibrium price, we say it is *nonbinding*. Figure 5.1 shows a price ceiling of \$2.00 per loaf in a market where \$2.00 is above the equilibrium price (P_E). All prices at or below \$2.00 (the green area) are legal. Prices above the price ceiling (the red area) are illegal. But since the market equilibrium (E) occurs in the green area, the price ceiling does not influence the market; it is nonbinding. As long as the equilibrium price remains below the price ceiling, price will continue to be regulated by supply and demand. Since there is rarely a compelling political reason to set a price ceiling above the equilibrium price, nonbinding price ceilings are unusual.

Binding Price Ceilings

When a price ceiling is below the market price, it creates a binding constraint that prevents supply and demand from clearing the market. In Figure 5.2,

FIGURE 5.1

A Nonbinding Price Ceiling

The price ceiling (\$2.00) is set above the equilibrium price (\$1.00). Since market prices are set by the intersection of supply (S) and demand (D), as long as the equilibrium price is below the price ceiling, the price ceiling is nonbinding and has no effect.

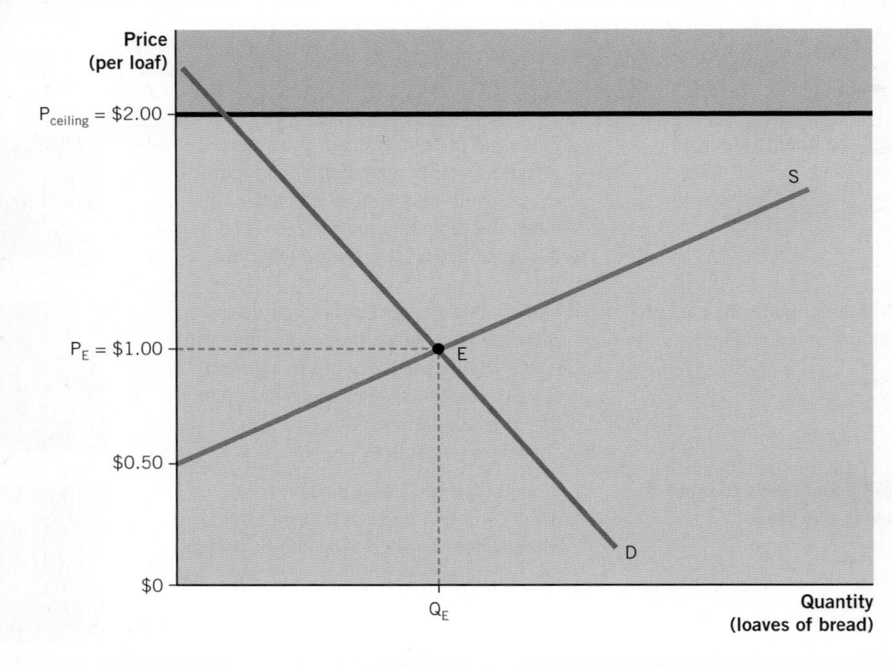

the price ceiling for bread is set at \$0.50 per loaf. Since \$0.50 is well below the equilibrium price of \$1.00, this creates a binding price ceiling. Notice that at a price of \$0.50, the quantity demanded (Q_D) is greater than the quantity supplied (Q_S)—in other words, a shortage exists. Shortages typically cause prices to rise, but the imposed price ceiling prevents that from happening. A price ceiling of \$0.50 allows only the prices in the green area. The market cannot reach the equilibrium point E at \$1.00 per loaf because it is located above the price ceiling, in the red area.

The black-market price is also set by supply and demand. Since prices above \$0.50 are illegal, sellers are unwilling to produce more than Q_S. Once the price ceiling is in place, sellers cannot legally charge prices above the ceiling, so the incentive to produce along the original supply curve vanishes. Since a shortage still exists, an illegal market will form to resolve the shortage. At that point, purchasers can illegally resell what they have just bought at \$0.50 for far more than what they just paid. Since the supply of legally produced bread is Q_S, the intersection of the vertical dashed line that reflects Q_S and the demand curve at point $E_{black\ market}$ establishes a black-market price $P_{black\ market}$, at \$2.00 per loaf for illegally sold bread. Since the black-market price is substantially more than the market equilibrium price (P_E) of \$1.00, illegal suppliers (underground bakers) will also enter the market in order to satisfy demand. As a result, the black-market price eliminates the shortage caused by the price ceiling. However, the price ceiling has created two unintended consequences: a smaller quantity of bread supplied (Q_S is less than Q_E), and a higher price for those who are forced to purchase it on the black market.

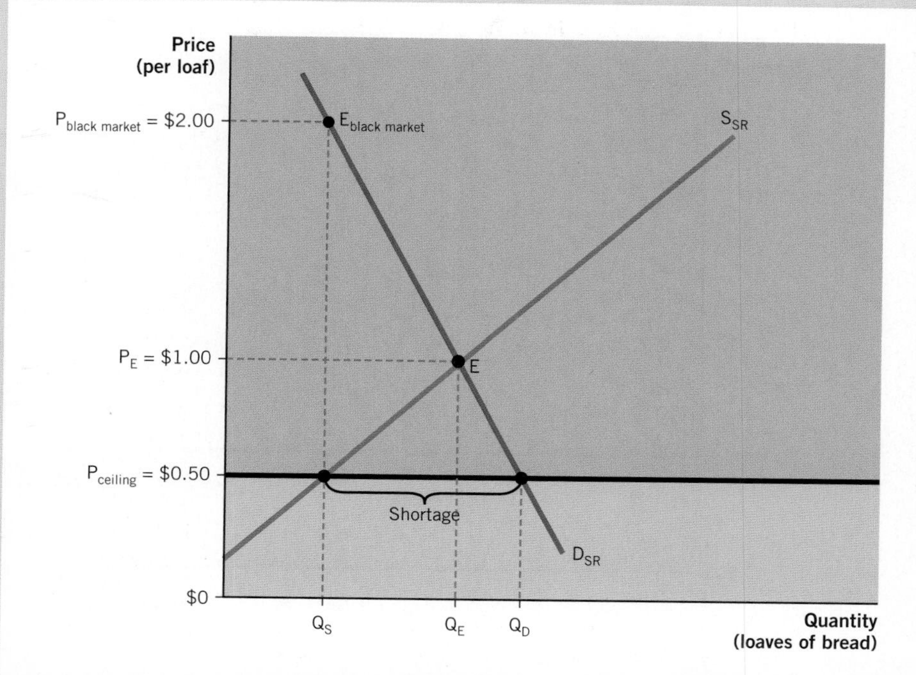

FIGURE 5.2

A Binding Price Ceiling

A binding price ceiling prevents sellers from increasing the price and causes them to reduce the quantity they offer for sale. As a consequence, prices no longer signal relative scarcity. Consumers desire to purchase the product at the price-ceiling level, and this creates a shortage in the short run; many will be unable to obtain the good. As a result, those who are shut out of the market will turn to other means to acquire the good. This establishes an illegal market for the good at the black market price.

Price Ceilings in the Long Run

In the long run, supply and demand become more elastic, or flatter. Recall from Chapter 4 that when consumers have additional time to make choices, they find more ways to avoid high-priced goods and more ways to take advantage of low prices. Additional time also gives producers the opportunity to produce more when prices are high and less when prices are low. In this section, we consider what will happen if a binding price ceiling on bread remains in effect for a long time. We have already observed that when binding price ceilings are in effect in the short run, shortages and black markets develop. Are the long-run implications of price ceilings more or less problematic than the short-run implications? Let's find out by looking at what happens to both supply and demand.

Figure 5.3 shows the result of a price ceiling that remains in place for a long time. Here the supply curve is more elastic than its short-run counterpart in Figure 5.2. The supply curve is flatter because in the long run producers respond by producing less bread and converting their facilities to make similar products that are not subject to price controls—for example, bagels and rolls—that will bring them a reasonable return on their investments. Therefore, in the long run the quantity supplied (Q_S) grows even smaller.

The demand curve is also more elastic in the long run. In the long run, more people will attempt to take advantage of the low price ceiling by changing their eating habits to consume more bread. Even though consumers will

FIGURE 5.3

The Effect of a Binding Price Ceiling in the Long Run

In the long run, increased elasticity on the part of both producers and consumers makes the shortage larger than it was in the short run. Consumers adjust their demand to the lower price and want more bread. Producers adjust their supply and make less of the unprofitable product. As a result, products become progressively harder to find.

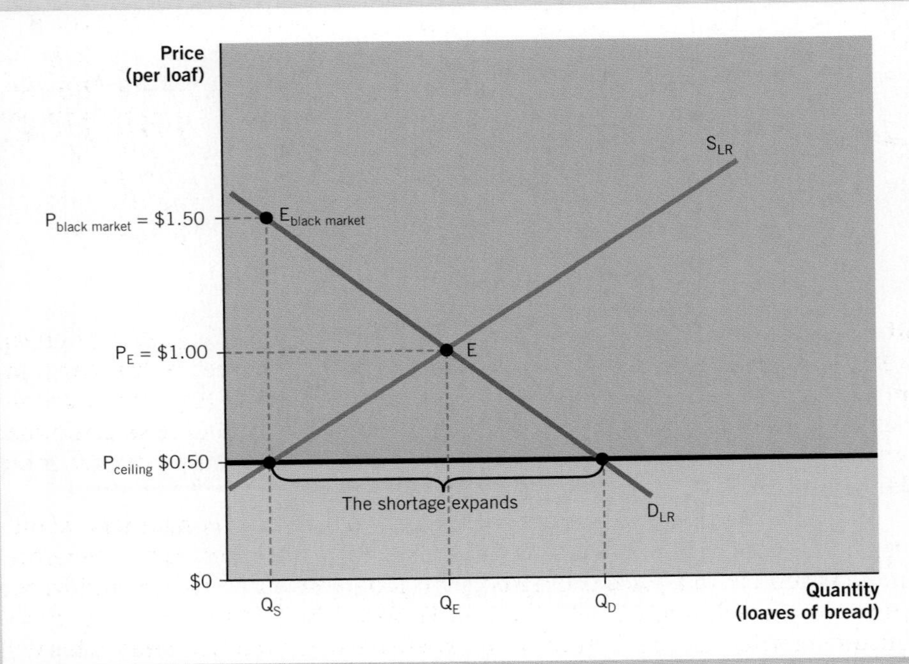

ECONOMICS IN THE MEDIA

Price Ceilings

Moscow on the Hudson

This 1984 film starring Robin Williams chronicles the differences between living in the United States and the former Soviet Union. In Moscow, we see hundreds of people waiting in line to receive essentials like bread, milk, and shoes. In the Soviet Union, production was controlled and prices were not allowed to equalize supply and demand. As a result, shortages were common. Waiting in line served as a rationing mechanism in the absence of price adjustments.

This film is memorable because of the reactions that Robin Williams's character has once he immigrates to the United States. In one inspired scene, he walks into a supermarket to buy coffee. He asks the manager where the coffee aisle is located, and when he sees that the aisle is not crowded, he asks the manager where the coffee line is located. The manager responds that there is no coffee line, so Williams walks down the coffee aisle slowly, naming each variety. We see his joy at being able to buy coffee without waiting and at having so many options to choose from. This scene nicely showcases the differences between the market system of the United States and the controlled economy of the former Soviet Union.

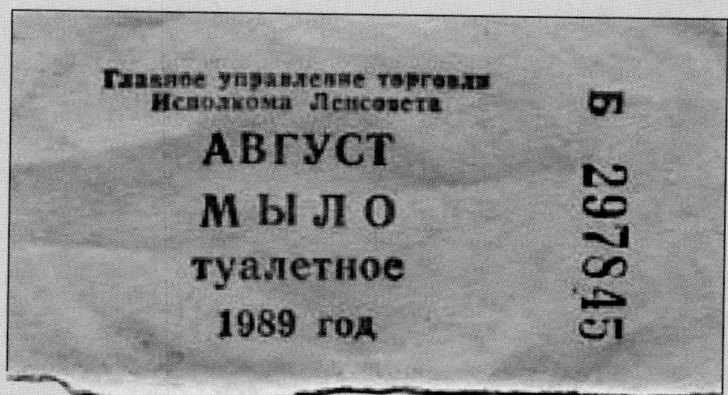

Soviet-era food-rationing coupon

Soviet-era bread line

often find empty shelves in the long run, the quantity demanded of cheap bread will increase. At this point, a flatter demand curve means that consumers are more flexible. As a result, the quantity demanded (Q_D) expands and bread is hard to find at $0.50 per loaf. The shortage will become so acute that consumers will turn to bread substitutes, like bagels and rolls, that are more plentiful because they are not price controlled.

Increased elasticity on the part of both producers and consumers magnifies the unintended consequences we observed in the short run. Therefore, products subject to a price ceiling become progressively harder to find in the long run. A black market will develop. However, in the long run our bread consumers will choose substitutes for expensive black-market bread. This will cause somewhat lower black-market prices in the long run.

PRACTICE WHAT YOU KNOW

Price Ceilings: Concert Tickets

Question: Suppose that fans of Avicii persuade Congress to impose a price ceiling of $25 for every Avicii concert ticket. Would this policy affect the number of people who attend his concerts?

You've got a good feeling about this concert.

Answer: The price ceiling prevents supply and demand from reaching the equilibrium price. As a result, at $25 there is a shortage of tickets. Since Avicii controls when and where he tours, he will choose to tour less in the United States and more in countries that do not regulate the ticket prices he can charge. This will make it more difficult for his U.S. fans to see him perform live, so the answer to the question is yes: the policy will influence the number of people who attend Avicii concerts (fewer in the United States, and more abroad).

What Effects Do Price Ceilings Have on Economic Activity?

We have seen the logical repercussions of a hypothetical price ceiling on bread and the incentives it creates. Now let's use supply and demand analysis to examine two real-world price ceilings: *rent control* and *price gouging laws*.

Rent Control

Rent control is a price ceiling that applies to the housing market.

Under **rent control**, a local government caps the price of apartment rentals to keep housing affordable. While this may be a laudable goal, rent control doesn't work. In fact, it doesn't help poor residents of a city to find affordable housing or gain access to housing at all. In addition, these policies contribute to dangerous living conditions.

Mumbai, India, provides a chilling example of what can happen when rent controls are applied over an extended period. In Mumbai, many rent-controlled buildings have become dilapidated. Every monsoon season, several of these buildings fall—often with tragic consequences. Since the rent that property owners are permitted to charge is so low, they have less income to use for maintenance. Therefore, they cannot afford to maintain the buildings properly and make a reasonable profit. As a result, rent-control policies have led to the decay of many apartment buildings. Similar controls have caused the same problem in cities worldwide.

To understand how a policy can backfire so greatly, let's look at the history of rent control in New York City. In 1943, in the midst of World War II, the federal government established the Emergency Price Control Act. The act was designed to keep inflation in check during the war, when many essential commodities were scarce. After the war, the federal government ended price controls, but the city of New York continued rent control. Today, there are approximately one million rent-controlled units in New York City. Rent controls limit the price a landlord can charge a tenant for rent. They also require that the landlord provide certain basic services; but not surprisingly, landlords keep maintenance to a minimum.

Many apartment buildings in Mumbai, India, are dilapidated as a result of rent-control laws.

Incentives

Does the presence of so many rent-controlled apartments mean that less affluent households can easily find a cheap place to rent? Hardly. When a rent-controlled unit is vacated, the property is generally no longer subject to rent control. Since most rent-controlled apartments are passed by tenants from generation to generation to remain in the program, rent control no longer even remotely serves its original purpose of helping low-income households. Clearly, the law was never intended to subsidize fancy vacation homes, but that's what it does! This has happened, in part, because some tenants who can afford to live elsewhere choose not to. Their subsidized rent enables them to save enough money to have a second or third home in places such as upstate New York, Florida, or Europe.

The attempt to make housing more affordable in New York City has, ironically, made housing harder to obtain. It has encouraged the building of upscale properties rather than low-income units, and it has created a set of behaviors among landlords that is inconsistent with the ideals of justice and affordability that rent control was designed to address. Figure 5.4 shows why rent control fails. As with any price ceiling, rent control causes a shortage since the quantity demanded in the short run (Q_{DSR}) is greater than the quantity supplied in the short run (Q_{SSR}). Because rent-controlled apartments are vacated slowly, the supply of rent-controlled units contracts in the long run, which causes the supply curve to become more elastic (S_{LR}). Demand also becomes more elastic in the long run (D_{LR}), which causes the quantity demanded for rent-controlled units to rise ($Q_{D_{LR}}$). The combination of fewer available units and more consumers looking for rent-controlled units leads to a larger shortage in the long run.

Price Gouging

Price gouging laws place a temporary ceiling on the prices that sellers can charge during times of emergency.

Another kind of price control, **price gouging laws**, places a temporary ceiling on the prices that sellers can charge during times of national emergency until markets function normally again. Over 30 states in the United States have laws against price gouging. Like all price controls, price gouging laws have unintended consequences. This became very apparent in the southern United States in 2005.

The hurricane season of 2005 was arguably the worst in U.S. history. Katrina and Rita plowed through the Gulf of Mexico with devastating effects, especially in Louisiana and Texas. Later that year, Wilma grew into the most powerful hurricane ever recorded in the Atlantic basin. When Wilma hit Fort Myers, Florida, in November, it ended a season for the record books. Florida has one of the strictest price gouging laws in the country. The statute makes it illegal to charge an "excessive" price immediately following a natural disaster. The law is designed to prevent the victims of natural disasters from being exploited in a time of need. But does it work?

Consider David Medina of Miami Beach. Immediately after Wilma hit, he drove to North Carolina, purchased 35 gas-powered generators, and returned to Florida, where he sold them from the back of his truck. He charged $900 for large generators, which he had purchased for $529.99, and $600 for small generators, which had cost him $279.99. After selling most of the units, Medina was arrested for price gouging. Under Florida law, his remaining generators were confiscated, and he was fined $1,000 for each sale. In addition, he was charged with selling without a business license. While there is no doubt that Medina intended to capitalize on the misfortune of others, it is hard to prove that he did any harm. The people who bought from him did so voluntarily, each believing that the value of the generator was greater than the price Medina was charging.

FIGURE 5.4

Rent Control in the Short Run and Long Run

Because rent-controlled apartments are vacated slowly, the supply of units contracts in the long run and the supply curve becomes more elastic. Demand also becomes more elastic in the long run, causing the quantity demanded to rise. The combination of fewer units available to rent and more consumers looking to find rent-controlled units leads to a larger shortage in the long run.

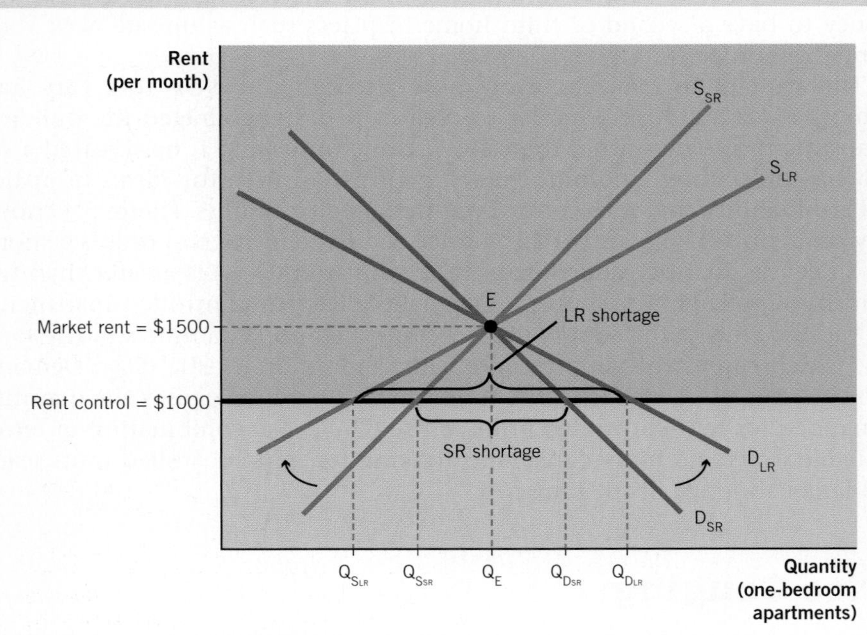

Prices act to ration scarce resources. When the demand for generators or other necessities is high, the price rises to ensure that the available units are distributed to those who value them the most. More important, the ability to charge a higher price provides sellers with an incentive to make more units available. If there is limited ability for the price to change when demand increases, there will be a shortage. Therefore, price gouging legislation means that devastated communities must rely exclusively on the goodwill of others and the slow-moving machinery of government relief efforts. This closes off a third avenue, entrepreneurial activity, as a means to alleviate poor conditions.

Incentives

Figure 5.5 shows how price gouging laws work and the shortage they create. If the demand for gas generators increases immediately after a disaster (D_{after}), the market price rises from $530 to $900. But since $900 is considered excessive, sales at that price are illegal. This creates a binding price ceiling for as long as a state of emergency is in effect. Whenever a price ceiling is binding, it creates a shortage. You can see this in Figure 5.5 in the difference between quantity demanded and quantity supplied at the price ceiling level mandated by the law. In this case, the normal ability of supply and demand to ration the available generators is short-circuited. Since more people demand generators after the disaster than before it, those who do not get to the store soon enough are out of luck. When the emergency is lifted and the market returns to normal, the temporary shortage created by legislation against price gouging is eliminated.

Large generator: $900 after Hurricane Wilma hit.

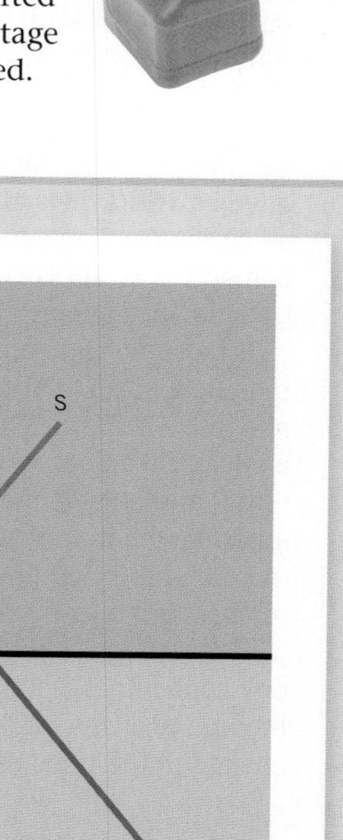

FIGURE 5.5

Price (per generator)
S
$P_{after\ the\ disaster}$ = $900
E_{after}
$P_{maximum\ under\ gouging\ law}$
Shortage
$P_{before\ the\ disaster}$ = $530
E_{before}
D_{before}
D_{after}
Q_{before}
Q_{after}
Quantity (gas generators)

Price Gouging

Price gouging laws serve as a nonbinding price ceiling during normal times. However, when a natural disaster strikes, price gouging laws go into effect. In our example, this shifts the demand curve for generators to the right and causes the new equilibrium price (E_{after}) to rise above the legal limit. This creates a shortage. When the emergency is lifted, the market demand returns to normal, and the temporary shortage created by price gouging legislation is eliminated.

PRACTICE WHAT YOU KNOW

Price Ceilings: Student Rental Apartments

Here is a question that often confuses students.

Question: Imagine that a city council decides that the market price for renting student apartments is too high and passes a law that establishes a rental price ceiling of $600 per month. The result of the price ceiling is a shortage. Which of the following caused the shortage of apartments?

a. **Both suppliers and demanders. Landlords will cut the supply of apartments, and the demand from renters will increase.**

b. **A spike in demand from many students who want to rent cheap apartments**

c. **The drop in supply caused by apartment owners pulling their units off the rental market and converting them into condos for sale**

d. **The price ceiling set by the city council**

Answer: Many students think that markets are to blame when shortages (or surpluses) exist. The first reaction is to find the culpable party—either the supplier or the demander, or both.

Answer (a) is a typical response. But be careful. Supply and demand have not changed—they are exactly the same as they were before the price ceiling was implemented. What *has* changed is the quantity of apartments supplied at $600. This change in quantity would be represented by a movement along the existing supply curve. The same is true for renters. The quantity demanded at $600 is much larger than it was when the price was not controlled. Once again, there will be a movement along the demand curve.

The same logic applies to answers (b) and (c). Answer (b) argues that there is a spike in student demand caused by the lower price. But price cannot cause a shift in the demand curve; it can only cause a movement along a curve. Likewise, (c) argues that apartment owners supply fewer units for rent. Landlords cannot charge more than $600 per unit, so they convert some apartments into private residences and offer them for sale in order to make more profit. Since fewer apartments are available at $600, this would be represented by a movement along the apartment supply curve.

This brings us to (d). There is only one change in market conditions: the city council passed a new price ceiling law. A binding price ceiling disrupts the ability of the market to reach equilibrium. Therefore, we can say that the change in the price as a result of the price ceiling caused the shortage.

When Do Price Floors Matter?

In this section, we examine price floors. Like price ceilings, price floors create many unintended effects that policymakers rarely acknowledge. However, unlike price ceilings, price floors result from the political pressure of suppliers to keep prices high. Most consumers prefer lower prices when they shop, so the idea of a law that keeps prices high may sound like a bad one to you. However, if you are selling a product or service, you might think that legislation to keep prices high is a very good idea. For instance, many states establish minimum prices for milk. As a result, milk prices are higher than they would be if supply and demand set the price. **Price floors** create legally established minimum prices for goods or services. The minimum wage law is another example of a price floor. In this section, we will follow the same progression that we did with price ceilings. We begin with a simple thought experiment. Once we understand how price floors work, we will use supply and demand analysis to examine the short- and long-term implications for economic activity.

If you're doing a handstand, you need the floor for support. A binding price floor keeps prices from falling.

Understanding Price Floors

To understand how price floors affect the market, let's try a thought experiment. Suppose that a politician suggests we should encourage dairy farmers to produce more milk so that supplies will be plentiful and everyone will get enough calcium. In order to accomplish this, a price floor of $6 per gallon—about twice the price of a typical gallon of fat-free milk—is enacted to make production more attractive to producers. What repercussions should we expect?

First, more milk will be available for sale. We know this because the higher price will cause dairies to increase the quantity that they supply. At the same time, because consumers must pay more, the quantity demanded will fall. The result will be a surplus of milk. Since every gallon of milk that is produced but not sold hurts the dairies' bottom line, sellers will want to lower their prices enough to get as many sales as possible before the milk goes bad. But the price floor will not allow the market to respond, and sellers will be stuck with milk that goes to waste. They will be tempted to offer illegal discounts in order to recoup some of their costs.

Price floors
are legally established minimum prices for goods or services.

What happens next? Since the surplus cannot be resolved through lower prices, the government will try to help equalize supply and demand through other means. This can be accomplished in one of two ways: by restricting the supply of the good or by stimulating additional demand. Both solutions are problematic. If production is restricted, dairy farmers will not be able to generate a profitable amount of milk. Likewise, stimulating additional demand is not as simple as it sounds. Let's consider how this works with other crops.

In many cases, the government purchases surplus agricultural production. This occurs most notably with corn, soybeans, cotton, and rice. Once the government buys the surplus production, it often sells the surplus below cost to developing countries to avoid having the crop go to waste. This strategy has the unintended consequence of making it cheaper for consumers in these developing nations to buy excess agricultural output from developed nations like the United States than to have local farmers grow the crop. International treaties ban the practice of dumping surplus production, but it continues under the guise of humanitarian aid. This practice makes little economic sense. Table 5.2 summarizes the result of our price-floor thought experiment using milk.

Got milk? Maybe not, if there's a price floor.

The Effect of Price Floors

We have seen that price floors create unintended consequences. Now we will use the supply and demand model to analyze how price floors affect the market. We'll take a look at the short run first.

TABLE 5.2

A Price Floor on Milk

Question	Answer / Explanation	Result
Will the quantity of milk for sale change?	Consumers will purchase less since the price is higher (the law of demand), but producers will manufacture more (the law of supply). The net result will be a surplus of milk.	There will be a surplus of milk.
Would producers sell below the price floor?	Yes. A surplus of milk would give sellers a strong incentive to undercut the price floor in order to avoid having to discard leftover milk.	Illegal discounts will help to reduce the milk surplus.
Will dairy farmers be better off?	Not if they have trouble selling what they produce.	There might be a lot of spoiled milk.

Nonbinding Price Floors

Like price ceilings, price floors can be binding or nonbinding. Figure 5.6 illustrates a nonbinding price floor of $2 per gallon on milk. As you can see, at $2 the price floor is below the equilibrium price (P_E), so the price floor is nonbinding. Since the actual market price is above the legally established minimum price (P_{floor}), the price floor does not prevent the market from reaching equilibrium at point E. Consequently, the price floor has no impact on the market. As long as the equilibrium price remains above the price floor, price is regulated by supply and demand.

Full shelves signal a market at equilibrium.

Binding Price Floors

For a price floor to have an impact on the market, it must be set above the market equilibrium price. In that case, it is known as a binding price floor. And with a binding price floor, the quantity supplied will exceed the quantity demanded. Figure 5.7 illustrates a binding price floor in the short run. Continuing our example of milk prices, at $6 per gallon the price floor is above the equilibrium price of $3. Market forces always attempt to restore the equilibrium between supply and demand at point E. So we know that there is downward pressure on the price. At a price floor

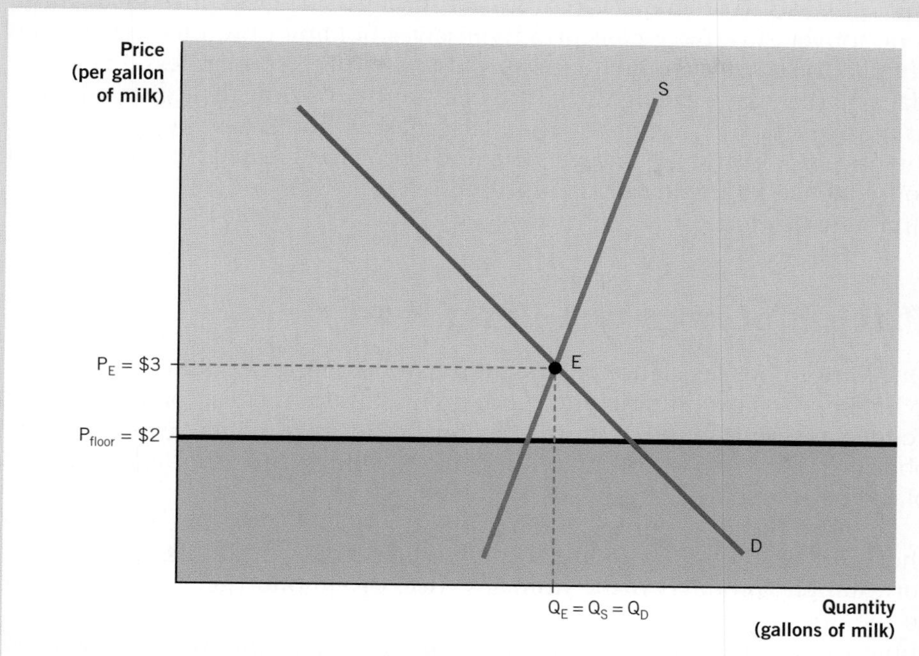

FIGURE 5.6

A Nonbinding Price Floor

Under a nonbinding price floor, price is regulated by supply and demand. Since the price floor ($2) is below the equilibrium price ($3), the market will voluntarily charge more than the legal minimum. Therefore, this price floor will have no effect on sales and purchases of milk.

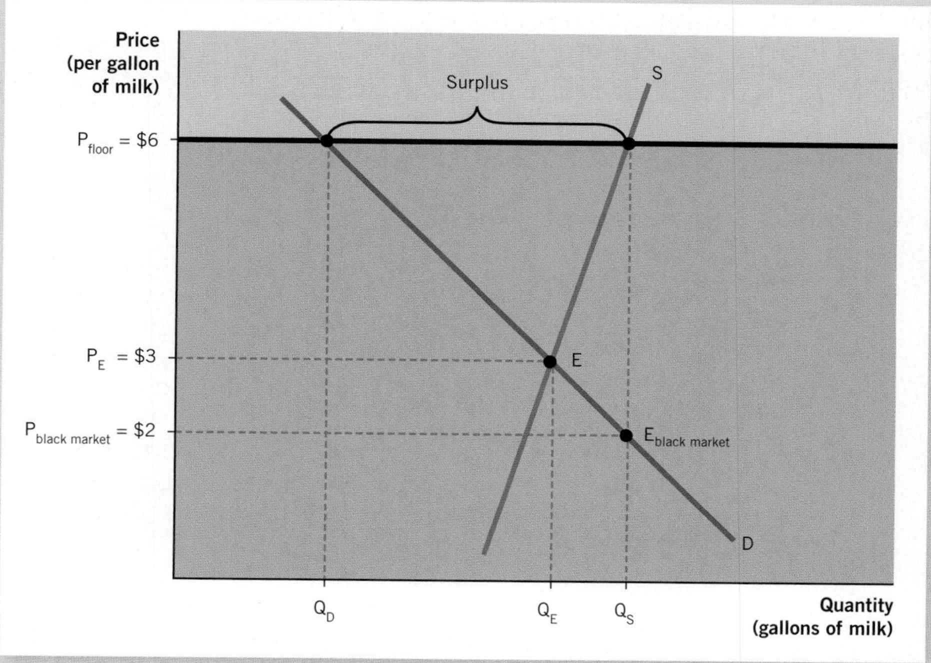

FIGURE 5.7

A Binding Price Floor in the Short Run

A binding price floor creates a surplus. This has two unintended consequences: a smaller demand than the equilibrium quantity ($Q_D < Q_E$), and a lower black-market price to eliminate the glut of the product.

of \$6, we see that $Q_S > Q_D$. The difference between the quantity supplied and the quantity demanded results in a surplus. Since the price mechanism is no longer effective, sellers find themselves holding unwanted inventories of milk. In order to eliminate the surplus, which will spoil unless it is sold, a black market may develop with prices substantially below the legislated price. At a price ($P_{black\ market}$) of \$1, the black market eliminates the surplus that the price floor caused. However, the price floor has created two unintended consequences: a smaller demand for milk ($Q_D < Q_E$), and a black market to eliminate the glut.

Incentives

Price Floors in the Long Run

Once price-floor legislation is passed, it can be politically difficult to repeal. What happens if a binding price floor on milk stays in effect for a long time? To help answer that question, we need to consider elasticity. We have already observed that in the short run binding price ceilings cause shortages and that black markets follow.

Figure 5.8 shows a price floor for milk that remains in place well past the short run. The long run gives consumers a chance to find milk substitutes—for example, products made from soy, rice, or almond that are not subject to the price floor—at lower prices. This added flexibility on the part of consumers makes the long-run demand for milk more elastic in an unregulated market. As a result, the demand curve depicted in Figure 5.8 is more elastic

FIGURE 5.8

The Effect of a Binding Price Floor in the Long Run

When a price floor is left in place over time, supply and demand each become more elastic. This leads to a larger surplus ($Q_S > Q_D$) in the long run. Since sellers are unable to sell all that they produce at \$6 per gallon, a black market develops in order to eliminate the glut of milk.

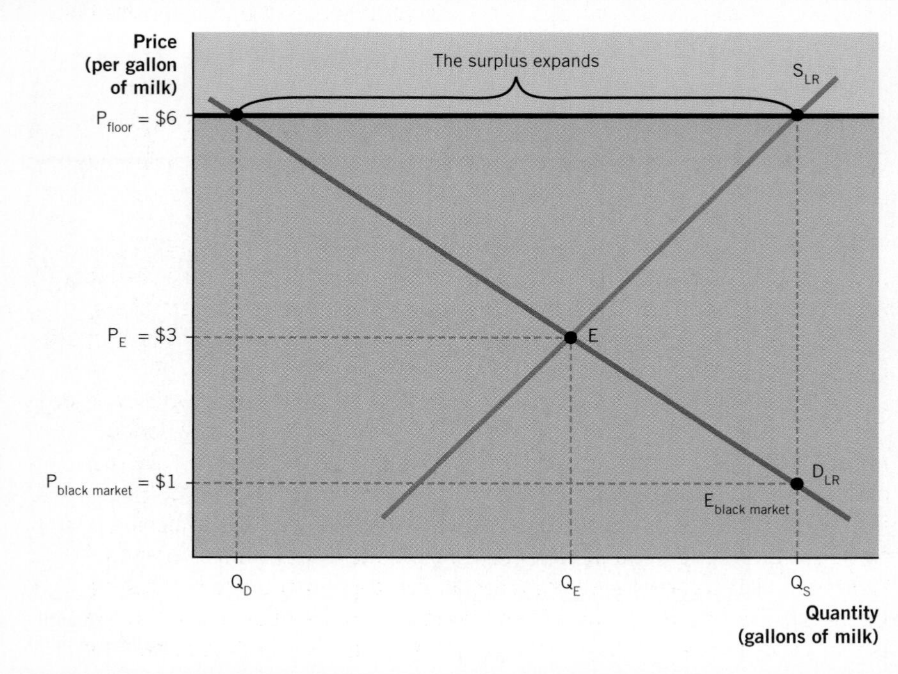

than its short-run counterpart in Figure 5.7. The supply curve also becomes flatter since firms (dairy farms) are able to produce more milk by acquiring additional land and production facilities. Therefore, a price floor ($6) that remains in place over time causes the supply and demand curves to become more elastic. This magnifies the shortage.

What happens to supply? In the long run, producers are more flexible and therefore supply is more elastic. The pool of potential milk producers rises as other closely related businesses retool their operations to supply more milk. The flatter supply curve in Figure 5.8 reflects this flexibility. As a result, Q_S expands and becomes much larger than it was in Figure 5.7. The increased elasticity on the part of both producers and consumers (1) makes the surplus larger in the long run and (2) magnifies the unintended consequences we observed in the short run.

PRACTICE WHAT YOU KNOW

Price Floors: Fair-Trade Coffee

Fair-trade coffee is sold through organizations that purchase directly from growers. The coffee is usually sold for a higher price than standard coffee. The goal is to promote more humane working conditions for the coffee pickers and growers. Fair-trade coffee has become more popular but still accounts for a small portion of all coffee sales, in large part because it is substantially more expensive to produce.

Would fair-trade coffee producers benefit from a price floor?

Question: Suppose that a one-pound bag of standard coffee costs $8 and that a one-pound bag of fair-trade coffee costs $12. Congress decides to impose a price floor of $10 per pound. Will this policy cause more or fewer people to buy fair-trade coffee?

Answer: Fair-trade producers typically sell their product at a higher price than mass-produced coffee brands. Therefore, a $10 price floor is binding for inexpensive brands like Folgers but nonbinding for premium coffees, which include fair-trade sellers. The price floor will reduce the price disparity between fair-trade coffee and mass-produced coffee.

To see how this works, consider a fair-trade coffee producer who charges $12 per pound and a mass-produced brand that sells for $8 per pound. A price floor of $10 reduces the difference between the price of fair-trade coffee and the inexpensive coffee brands, which now must sell for $10 instead of $8. This lowers the consumer's opportunity cost of choosing fair-trade coffee. Therefore, some consumers of the inexpensive brands will opt for fair-trade instead. As a result, fair-trade producers will benefit indirectly from the price floor. Thus the answer to the question at the top is that *more* people will buy fair-trade coffee as a result of this price-floor policy.

Opportunity cost

What Effects Do Price Floors Have on Economic Activity?

We have seen the logical repercussions of a hypothetical price floor on milk and the incentives it creates. Now let's use supply and demand analysis to examine two real-world price floors: *minimum wage laws* and *agricultural price supports*.

The Minimum Wage

The **minimum wage** is the lowest hourly wage rate that firms may legally pay their workers.

The **minimum wage** is the lowest hourly wage rate that firms may legally pay their workers. Minimum wage workers can be skilled or unskilled and experienced or inexperienced. The common thread is that these workers, for a variety of reasons, lack better prospects. A minimum wage functions as a price floor. Figure 5.9 shows the effect of a binding minimum wage. Note that the wage, or the cost of labor, on the *y* axis ($10 per hour) is the price that must be paid. However, the market equilibrium wage ($7), or W_E, is below the minimum wage. The minimum wage prevents the market from reaching W_E at E (the equilibrium point) because only the wages in the green shaded area are legal. Since the demand for labor depends on how much it costs, the minimum wage raises the cost of hiring workers. Therefore, a higher minimum wage will lower the quantity of labor demanded. However, since

FIGURE 5.9

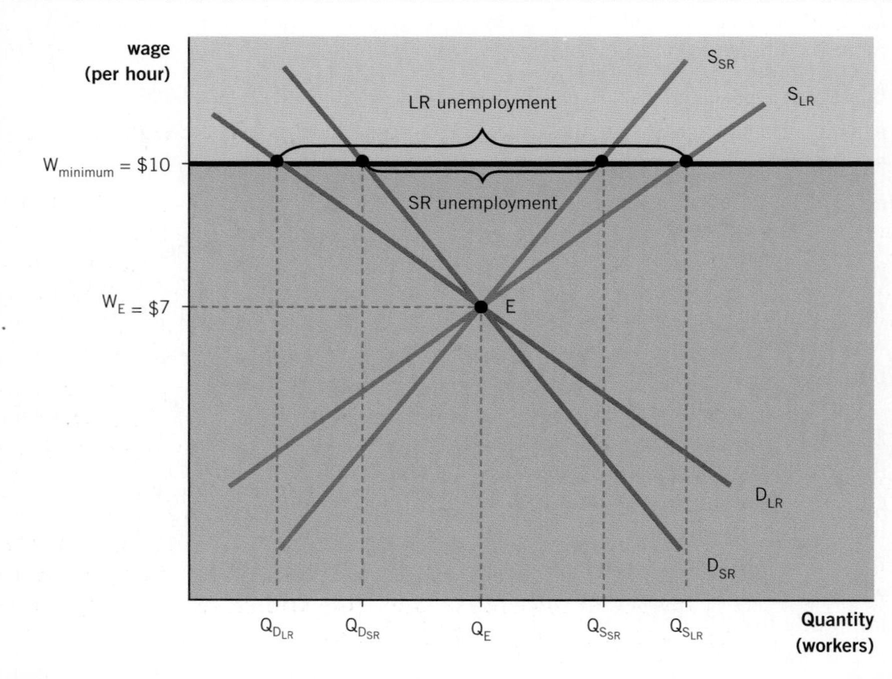

Price Floors and a Binding Minimum Wage Market in the Short and Long Run

A binding minimum wage is a price floor above the current equilibrium wage, W_E. At $10 per hour, the number of workers willing to supply their labor (S_{SR}) is greater than the demand for workers (D_{SR}). The result is a surplus of workers (which we recognize as unemployment). Since the supply of workers and demand for workers both become more elastic in the long run, unemployment expands ($S_{LR} > D_{LR}$).

businesses still need to serve their customers, this means that labor expenses for the firm ordinarily rise in the short run. At the same time, firms will look for ways to substitute additional capital for workers. As a result, a binding minimum wage results in unemployment in the short run since $Q_{SSR} > Q_{DSR}$.

Businesses generally want to keep costs down, so in the long run they will try to reduce the amount they spend on labor. They might replace workers with machinery, shorten work hours, offer reduced customer service, or even relocate to countries that do not have minimum wage laws. As we move past the short run, more people will attempt to take advantage of higher minimum wages. Like firms, workers will adjust to the higher minimum wage over time. Some workers who might have decided to go to school full-time or remain retired, or who simply want some extra income, will enter the labor market because the minimum wage is now higher. As a result, minimum wage jobs will become progressively harder to find and unemployment will be magnified. The irony is that in the long run the minimum wage, just like any other price floor, has created two unintended consequences: a smaller demand for workers by employers (Q_{DLR} is significantly less than Q_E), and a larger supply of workers (Q_{SLR}) looking for those previously existing jobs.

Proponents of minimum wage legislation are aware that it often creates unemployment. To address this problem, they support investment in training, education, and the creation of government jobs programs to provide more work opportunities. While jobs programs increase minimum wage jobs, training and additional education enable workers to acquire skills needed for jobs that pay more than the minimum wage. Economists generally believe that education and training programs have longer-lasting benefits to society as a whole since they enable workers to obtain better-paying jobs on a permanent basis.

ECONOMICS IN THE REAL WORLD

Wage Laws Squeeze South Africa's Poor

Consider this story that appeared in the *New York Times* in 2010.*

NEWCASTLE, South Africa—The sheriff arrived at the factory here to shut it down, part of a national enforcement drive against clothing manufacturers who violate the minimum wage. But women working on the factory floor—the supposed beneficiaries of the crackdown—clambered atop cutting tables and ironing boards to raise anguished cries against it. Thoko Zwane, 43, who has worked in factories since she was 15, lost her job in Newcastle when a Chinese-run factory closed in 2004. More than a third of South Africans are jobless. "Why? Why?" shouted Nokuthula Masango, 25, after the authorities carted away bolts of gaily colored fabric. She made just $36 a week, $21 less than the minimum wage, but needed the meager pay to help support a large extended family that includes her five unemployed siblings and their children.

The women's spontaneous protest is just one sign of how acute South Africa's long-running unemployment crisis has become. With their own economy saddled with very high unemployment rates, the women feared being out of work more than getting stuck in poorly paid jobs.

Trade-offs

---

*Celia W. Dugger, "Wage Laws Squeeze South Africa's Poor," *New York Times*, September 27, 2010.

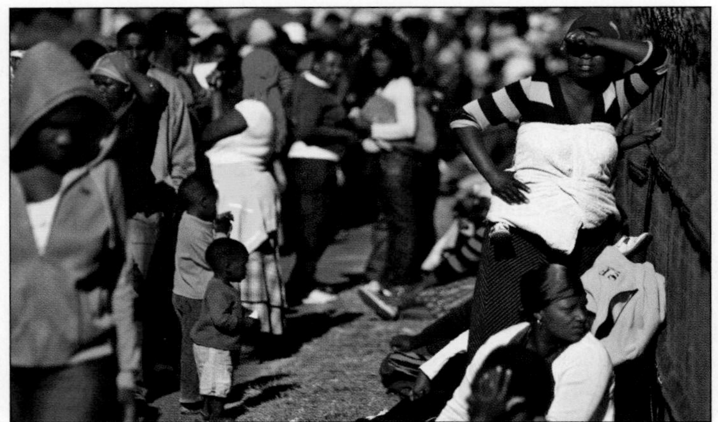

South Africans wait in line for unemployment benefits.

In the years since the end of apartheid, the South African economy has grown, but not nearly fast enough to end an intractable unemployment crisis. For over a decade, the jobless rate has been among the highest in the world, fueling crime, inequality, and social unrest in the continent's richest nation. The global economic downturn has made the problem much worse, wiping out more than a million jobs. Over a third of South Africa's workforce is now idle. And 16 years after Nelson Mandela led the country to black majority rule, more than half of blacks ages 15 to 34 are without work—triple the level for whites.

"The numbers are mind-boggling," said James Levinsohn, a Yale University economist. ✷

The Minimum Wage Is Often Nonbinding

Most people believe that raising the minimum wage is a simple step that the government can take to improve the standard of living of the working poor. However, in most places the minimum wage is often nonbinding and therefore has no impact on the market. Adjusting for inflation, the federal minimum wage was highest in 1968, so in real terms minimum wage workers are earning less today than they did almost half a century ago. Why would we have a minimum wage if it is largely nonbinding?

To help us answer this question, consider the two nonbinding minimum wage rates ($7 and $9) shown in Figure 5.10. A minimum wage of $7 per hour is far below the equilibrium wage of $10 ($W_E$), so at that point supply and demand push the equilibrium wage up to $10. Suppose that politicians decide to raise the minimum wage to $9. This new minimum wage of $9 would remain below the market wage, so there would be no impact on the labor market for workers who are willing to accept the minimum wage. Therefore, an increase in the minimum wage from $7 to $9 an hour will not create unemployment. Unemployment will occur only when the minimum wage rises above $10.

Politicians know that most voters have a poor understanding of basic economics. As a result, a politician can seek to raise the minimum wage with great fanfare. Voters would support the new rate because they do not know that it is likely to be nonbinding; they expect wages to rise. In reality, nothing will change, but the perception of a benevolent action will remain. In fact, since its inception in 1938, increases in the minimum wage in the United States have generally trailed the market wage and therefore have avoided creating unemployment. The minimum wage adjusts sporadically upward every few years but rarely rises enough to cause the market wage to fall below it. This creates the illusion that the minimum wage is lifting wages. However, it does not cause any of the adverse consequences of a binding minimum wage.

In an effort to raise the minimum wage beyond the national rate, a number of states have enacted higher minimum wage laws. Not surprisingly, some of the states with the highest minimum wage rates, like Washington, Oregon,

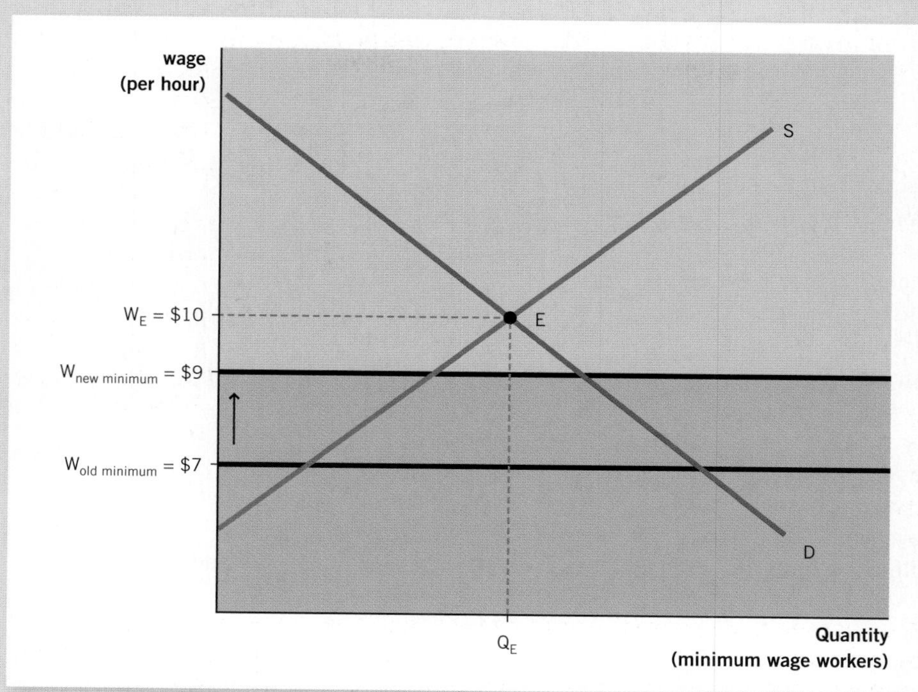

FIGURE 5.10

A Nonbinding Minimum Wage

An increase in the minimum wage from $7 to $9 remains nonbinding. Therefore, it will not change the demand for labor or the unemployment rate. If the minimum wage rises above the market wage, additional unemployment will occur.

and California, also have unemployment rates that are among the highest in the country—evidence that binding minimum wage rates can have serious consequences.

ECONOMICS IN THE REAL WORLD

A Sweet Deal, If You Can Get It

Sugar is one of life's small pleasures. It can be extracted and refined from sugar cane and sugar beets, two crops that can be grown in a variety of climates around the world. Sugar is both plentiful and cheap. As a result, Americans enjoy a lot of it—an average of over 60 pounds of refined sugar per person each year!

We would consume a lot more sugar if it was not subject to price controls. After the War of 1812, struggling sugar cane producers asked the government to pass a tariff that would protect domestic production. Over the years, price supports of all kinds have served to keep domestic sugar production high. The result is an industry that depends on a high price to survive. Under the current price-support system, the price of U.S.-produced sugar is roughly two to three times the world price. This has led to a bizarre set of incentives whereby U.S. farmers grow more sugar than they should and use land that is not well suited to the crop. For instance, sugar cane requires a subtropical climate, but most of the U.S. crop is grown in Louisiana, a region that is prone to hurricanes in the summer and killing freezes in the late fall. As a result, many sugar cane crops there are completely lost.

Incentives

ECONOMICS IN THE MEDIA

The Minimum Wage

30 Days

The (2005) pilot episode of this reality series focused on the minimum wage. Morgan Spurlock and his fiancée spend 30 days in a poor neighborhood of Columbus, Ohio. The couple attempt to survive by earning minimum wage (at that time, $5.15 an hour) in order to make ends meet. In addition, they are required to start off with only one week's minimum wage (about $300) in reserve. Also, they cannot use credit cards to pay their bills. They experience firsthand the struggles that many minimum wage households face when living paycheck to paycheck. *30 Days* makes it painfully clear how difficult it is for anyone to live on the minimum wage for a month, let alone for years.

A quote from Morgan Spurlock sums up what the episode tries to convey: "We don't see the people that surround us. We don't see the people who are struggling to get by that are right next to us. And I have seen how hard the struggle is. I have been here. And I only did it for a month, and there's people who do this their whole lives."

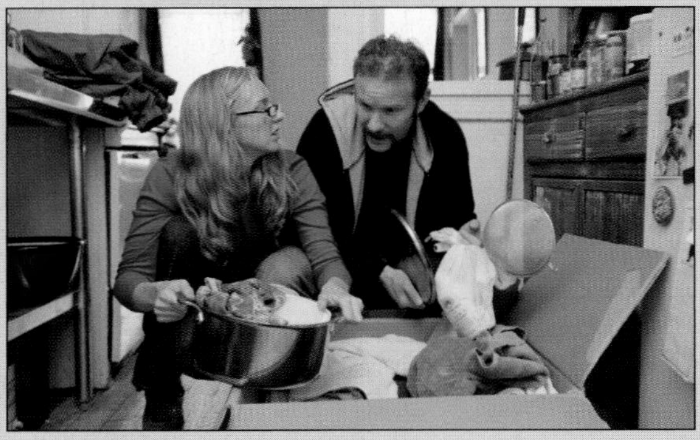

Could you make ends meet earning the minimum wage?

After watching this episode of *30 Days*, it is hard not to think that raising the minimum wage is a good idea. Unfortunately, the economic reality is that raising the minimum wage does not guarantee that minimum wage earners will make more and also be able keep their jobs.

Which of these is the *real* thing? The Coke on the right, with high-fructose corn syrup, was made in the United States; the other, with sugar, was made in Mexico.

Why do farmers persist in growing sugar cane in Louisiana? The answer lies in the political process: sugar growers have effectively lobbied to keep prices high through tariffs on foreign imports. Since lower prices would put many U.S. growers out of business and cause the loss of many jobs, politicians have given in to their demands.

Meanwhile, the typical sugar consumer is largely oblivious to the political process that sets the price floor. It has been estimated that the sugar subsidy program costs consumers over one billion dollars a year. To make matters worse, thanks to corn subsidies high-fructose corn syrup has become a cheap alternative to sugar and is often added to processed foods and soft drinks. In 1980, Coca-Cola replaced sugar with high-fructose corn extract in the United States in order to reduce production costs. However, Coca-Cola continues to use sugar cane in many Latin American countries because it is cheaper. New research shows that high-fructose corn syrup causes a metabolic reaction that makes people who ingest it more inclined to obesity. Ouch! This is an example of an unintended consequence that few policymakers could have imagined. There is no reason why the United States must produce its own sugar cane. Ironically, sugar is cheaper in Canada primarily because Canada has no sugar growers—and thus no trade restrictions or government support programs. ✷

SNAPSHOT

Minimum Wage: Always the Same?

A minimum wage is a price floor, a price control that doesn't allow prices—in this case the cost of labor—to fall below an assigned value. Although the media and politicians often discuss the minimum wage in America as if there is only one minimum wage, it turns out that there are numerous minimum wages in the USA. In states where the state minimum wage is not the same as the federal minimum wage, the higher of the two wage rates takes effect.

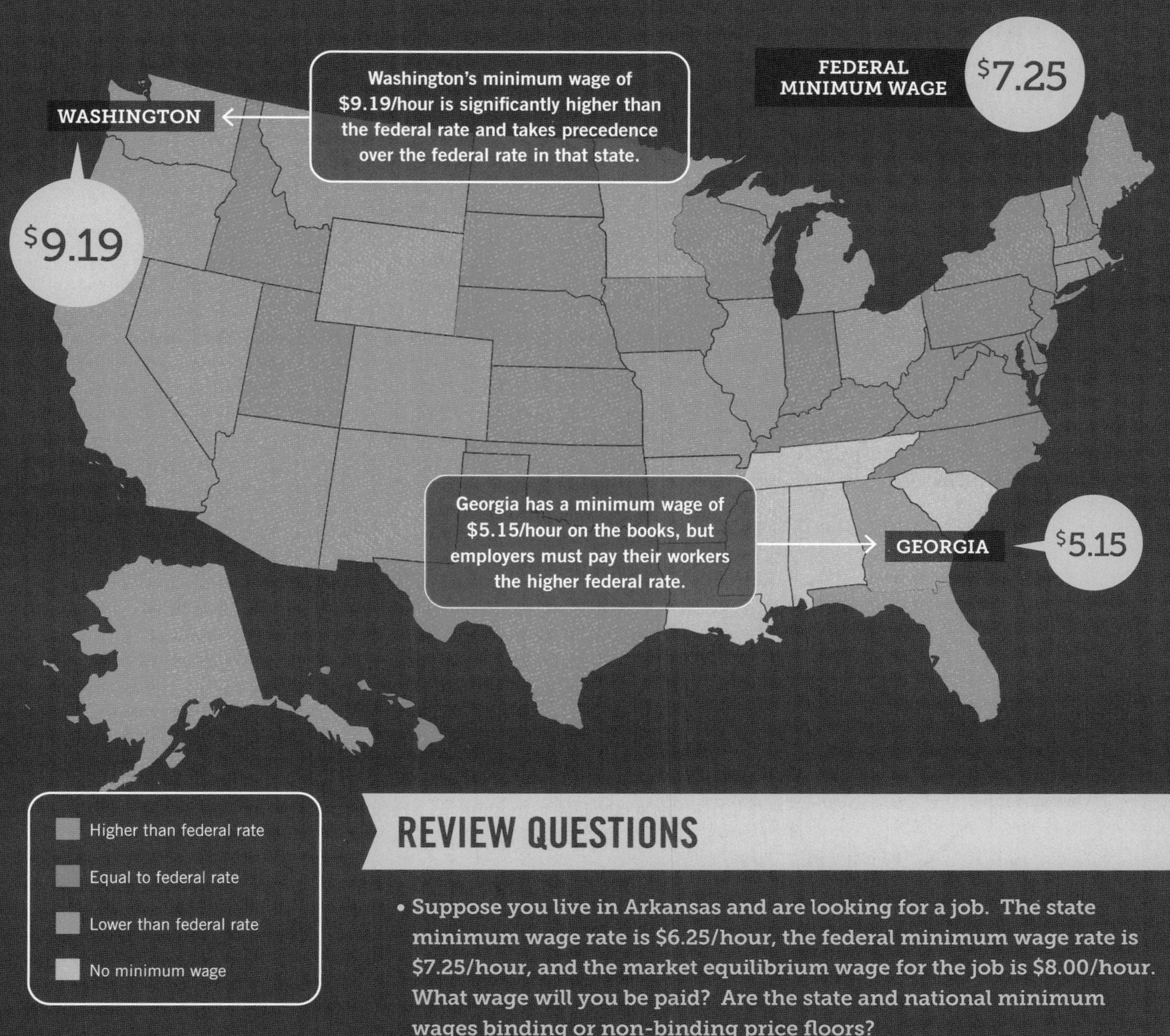
WASHINGTON
Washington's minimum wage of $9.19/hour is significantly higher than the federal rate and takes precedence over the federal rate in that state.
$9.19
FEDERAL MINIMUM WAGE
$7.25
Georgia has a minimum wage of $5.15/hour on the books, but employers must pay their workers the higher federal rate.
GEORGIA
$5.15
Higher than federal rate
Equal to federal rate
Lower than federal rate
No minimum wage

REVIEW QUESTIONS

- Suppose you live in Arkansas and are looking for a job. The state minimum wage rate is $6.25/hour, the federal minimum wage rate is $7.25/hour, and the market equilibrium wage for the job is $8.00/hour. What wage will you be paid? Are the state and national minimum wages binding or non-binding price floors?
- Suppose Wisconsin increases its minimum wage from $7.25/hour, which is below the market wage for low-skill labor, to $11.00/hour, which is above the market wage. Using supply and demand curves, show how this might affect the number of employed workers.

PRACTICE WHAT YOU KNOW

Price Ceilings and Price Floors: Would a Price Control on Internet Access Be Effective?

In today's Internet age, four degrees of separation are all that stand between you and the rest of the world.

A recent study found the following demand and supply schedule for high-speed Internet access:

Price of Internet	Connections demanded (millions of units)	Connections supplied (millions of units)
$60	10.0	62.5
$50	20.0	55.0
$40	30.0	47.5
$30	40.0	40.0
$20	50.0	32.5
$10	60.0	25.0

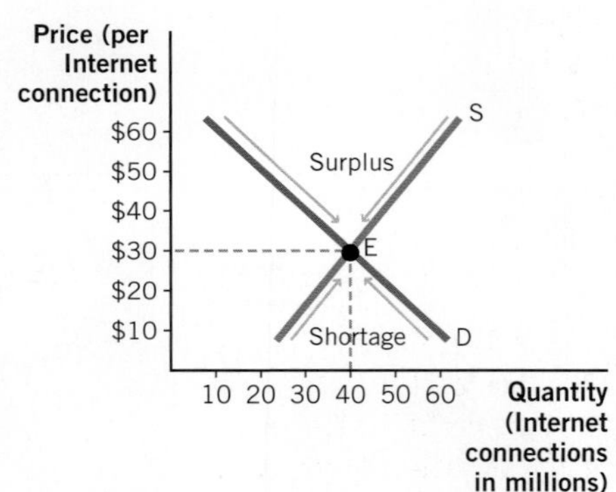

Question: What are the equilibrium price and equilibrium quantity of Internet service?

Answer: First, look at the table to see where supply and demand are equal. At a price of $30, consumers purchase 40 million units and producers supply 40 million units. Therefore, the equilibrium price is $30 and the equilibrium quantity is 40 million. At any price above $30, the quantity supplied exceeds the quantity demanded, so there is a surplus. The surplus gives sellers an incentive to cut the price until it reaches the equilibrium point, E. At any price below $30, the quantity demanded exceeds the quantity supplied, so there is a shortage. The shortage gives sellers an incentive to raise the price until it reaches the equilibrium point, E.

Price (per Internet connection)
$60
$50
P_{floor} = $40
$30
$20
$10
Surplus
S
E
D
30 40 47.5
Quantity (Internet connections in millions)

Question: Suppose that providers convince the government that maintaining high-speed access to the Internet is an important element of technology infrastructure. As a result, Congress approves a price floor at $10 above the equilibrium price to help companies provide Internet service. How many people are able to connect to the Internet?

Answer: Adding $10 to the market price of $30 gives us a price floor of $40. At $40, consumers demand 30 million connections. Producers provide 47.5 million connections. This is a surplus of 17.5 million units (shown). A price floor means that producers cannot cut the price below that point to increase the quantity that consumers demand. As a result, only 30 million units are sold. So only 30 million people connect to the Internet.

(CONTINUED)

(CONTINUED)

Question: When teachers realize that fewer people are purchasing Internet access, they demand that the price floor be repealed and a price ceiling be put in its place. Congress acts immediately to remedy the problem, and a new price ceiling is set at $10 below the market price. Now how many people are able to connect to the Internet?

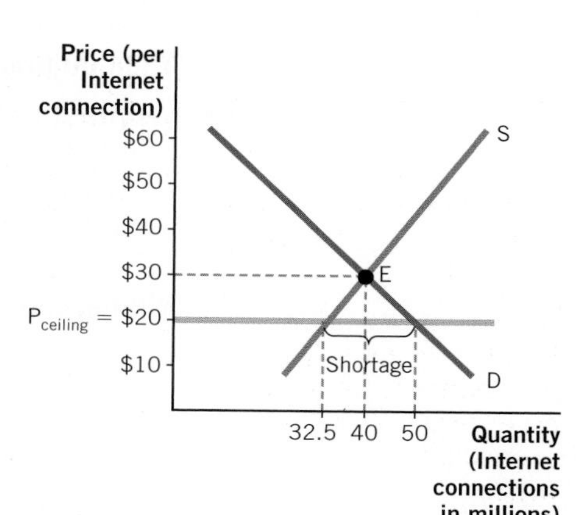

Answer: Subtracting $10 from the market price of $30 gives us a price ceiling of $20. At $20 per connection, consumers demand 50 million connections. However, producers provide only 32.5 million connections. This is a shortage of 17.5 million units (shown). A price ceiling means that producers cannot raise the price, which will cause an increase in the quantity supplied. As a result, only 32.5 million units are sold, so only 32.5 million people connect to the Internet.

Question: Which provides the greatest access to the Internet: free markets, price floors, or price ceilings?

Answer: With no government intervention, 40 million connections are sold. Once the price floor is established, there are 30 million connections. Under the price ceiling, 32.5 million connections exist. Despite legislative efforts to satisfy both producers and consumers of Internet service, the best solution is to allow free markets to regulate access to the good.

Conclusion

Trade-offs

Does the minimum wage help everyone earn a living wage? We learned that it is possible to set the minimum wage high enough to guarantee that each worker will earn a living wage. However, the trade-off in setting the minimum wage substantially higher is that it becomes binding and many workers will no longer have jobs. In other words, setting the minimum wage high enough to earn a living wage won't raise every worker out of poverty because many of those workers will no longer have jobs.

The policies presented in this chapter—rent control, price gouging laws, the minimum wage, and agricultural price controls—create unintended consequences. Attempts to control prices should be viewed cautiously. When the price signal is suppressed through a binding price floor or a binding price ceiling, the market's ability to maintain order is diminished, surpluses and shortages develop and expand through time, and obtaining goods and services becomes difficult.

The role of markets in society has many layers, and we've only just begun our analysis. In the next chapter, we will develop a technique to measure the gains that consumers and producers enjoy in unregulated markets, and we will consider the distortions created by tax policy. Then, in Chapter 7, we will consider two cases—externalities and public goods—in which the unregulated market produces an output that is not socially desirable.

ANSWERING THE BIG QUESTIONS

When do price ceilings matter?

* A price ceiling is a legally imposed maximum price. When the price is set below the equilibrium price, the quantity demanded will exceed the quantity supplied. This will result in a shortage. Price ceilings matter when they are set below the equilibrium price.

What effects do price ceilings have on economic activity?

* Price ceilings create two unintended consequences: a smaller supply of the good (Q_S) and a higher price for consumers who turn to the black market.

When do price floors matter?

* A price floor is a legally imposed minimum price. The minimum wage is an example of a price floor. If the minimum wage is set above the equilibrium wage, a surplus of labor will develop. However, if the minimum wage is nonbinding, it will have no effect on the market wage. Thus price floors matter when they are set above the equilibrium price.

What effects do price floors have on economic activity?

* Price floors lead to many unintended consequences, including surpluses, the creation of black markets, and artificial attempts to bring the market back into balance. For example, proponents of a higher minimum wage are concerned about finding ways to alleviate the resulting surplus of labor, or unemployment.

ECONOMICS FOR LIFE

Price Gouging: Disaster Preparedness

Disasters, whether natural or human-made, usually strike quickly and without warning. You and your family may have little or no time to decide what to do. That's why it is important to plan for the possibility of disaster and not wait until it happens. Failing to plan is planning to fail. In this box, we consider a few simple things you can do now to lessen the impact of a disaster on your personal and financial well-being.

During a disaster, shortages of essential goods and services become widespread. In the 30 states where price gouging laws are on the books, they prevent merchants from charging unusually high prices. If you live in one of these states, cash alone can't save you. You will have to survive on your own for a time before help arrives and communication channels are restored.

Taking measures to prepare for a disaster reduces the likelihood of injury, loss of life, and property damage far more than anything you can do after a disaster strikes. An essential part of disaster planning should include financial planning. Let's begin with the basics. Get adequate insurance to protect your family's health, lives, and property; plan for the possibility of job loss or disability by building a cash reserve; and safeguard your financial and legal records. It is also important to set aside extra money in a long-term emergency fund. Nearly all financial experts advise saving enough money to cover your expenses for six months. Most households never come close to reaching this goal, but don't let that stop you from trying.

Preparing a simple disaster supply kit is also a must. Keep enough water, nonperishable food, sanitation supplies, batteries, medications, and cash on hand for three days. Often, the power is out after a disaster, so you cannot count on ATMs or banks to be open. These measures will help you to weather the immediate impact of a disaster.

Finally, many documents are difficult to replace. Consider investing in a home safe or safe deposit box to ensure that your important records survive. Place your passports, Social Security cards, copies of drivers' licenses, mortgage and property deeds, car titles, wills, insurance records, and birth and marriage certificates out of harm's way.

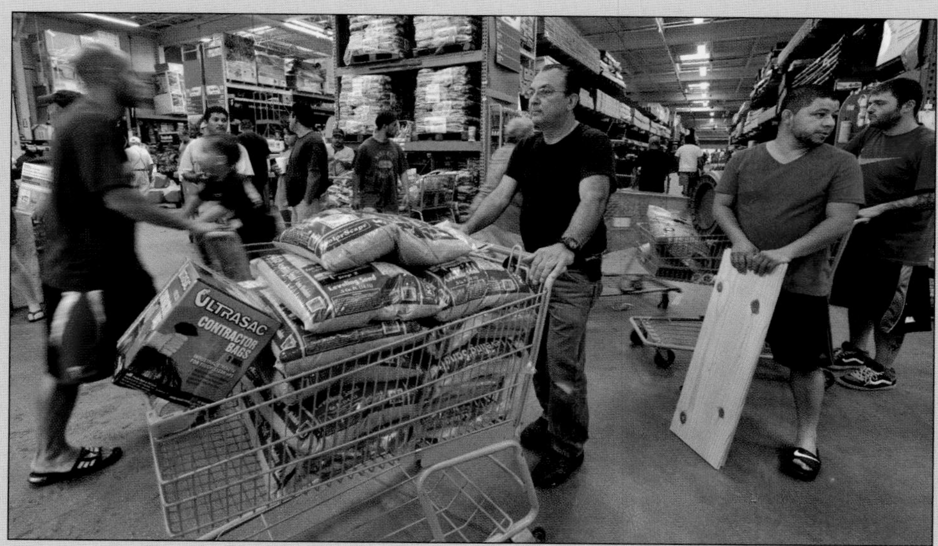

Will you be ready if disaster strikes?

CONCEPTS YOU SHOULD KNOW

black market (p. 149)
minimum wage (p. 164)
price ceiling (p. 148)
price control (p. 148)
price floor (p. 159)
price gouging laws (p. 155)
rent control (p. 154)

QUESTIONS FOR REVIEW

1. Does a binding price ceiling cause a shortage or a surplus? Provide an example to support your answer.
2. Does a nonbinding price floor cause a shortage or a surplus? Provide an example to support your answer.
3. Will a surplus or a shortage caused by a price control become smaller or larger over time?
4. Are price gouging laws an example of a price floor or a price ceiling?
5. What will happen to the market price when a price control is nonbinding?
6. Why do most economists oppose attempts to control prices? Why does the government attempt to control prices anyway, in a number of markets?

STUDY PROBLEMS (✻ *solved at the end of the section*)

1. In the song "Minimum Wage," the punk band Fenix TX comments on the inadequacy of the minimum wage to make ends meet. Using the poverty thresholds provided by the Census Bureau,* determine whether the federal minimum wage of $7.25 an hour provides enough income for a single full-time worker to escape poverty.

✻ 2. Imagine that the community you live in decides to enact a rent control of $700 per month on every one-bedroom apartment. Using the following table, determine the market price and equilibrium quantity without rent control. How many one-bedroom apartments will be rented after the rent-control law is passed?

Monthly rent	Quantity demanded	Quantity supplied
$600	700	240
$700	550	320
$800	400	400
$900	250	480
$1,000	100	560

3. Suppose that the federal government places a binding price floor on chocolate. To help support the price floor, the government purchases all of the leftover chocolate that consumers do not buy. If the price floor remains in place for a number of years, what do you expect to happen to each of the following?
   a. quantity of chocolate demanded by consumers
   b. quantity of chocolate supplied by producers
   c. quantity of chocolate purchased by the government
4. Suppose that a group of die-hard sports fans is upset about the high price of tickets to many games. As a result of their lobbying efforts, a new law caps the maximum ticket price to any sporting event at $50. Will more people be able to attend the games? Explain your answer. Will certain teams and events be affected more than others? Provide examples.
5. Many local governments use parking meters on crowded downtown streets. However, the parking spaces along the street are typically hard to find because the metered price is often set below the market price. Explain what happens when local governments set the meter price too low. Why do you think the price is set below the market-clearing price?

*See: www.census.gov/hhes/www/poverty/data/threshld/index.html

6. Imagine that local suburban leaders decide to enact a minimum wage. Will the community lose more jobs if the nearby city votes to increase the minimum wage to the same rate? Discuss your answer.

* 7. Examine the following graph, showing the market for low-skill laborers.

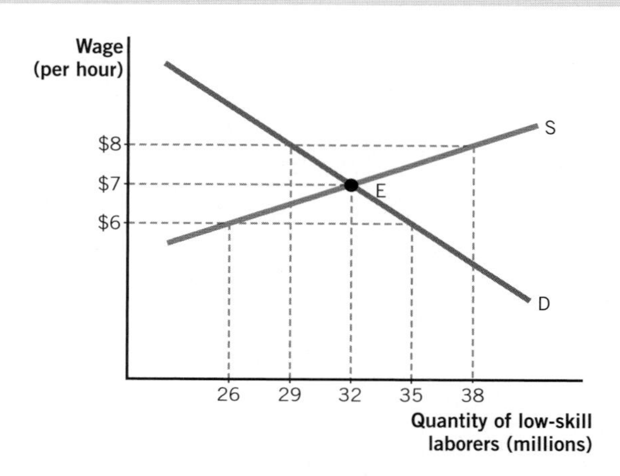

How many low-skill laborers will be unemployed when the minimum wage is $8 an hour? How many low-skill workers will be unemployed when the minimum wage is $6 an hour?

8. The demand and supply curves that we use can also be represented with equations. Suppose that the demand for low-skill labor, Q_D, is represented by the following equation, where W is the wage rate:

$$Q_D = 53{,}000{,}000 - 3{,}000{,}000W$$

The supply of low-skill labor, Q_S, is represented by the equation

$$Q_S = -10{,}000{,}000 + 6{,}000{,}000W$$

   a. Find the equilibrium wage. (**Hint**: Set $Q_D = Q_S$ and solve for the wage, W.)
   b. Find the equilibrium quantity of labor. (**Hint**: Now plug the value you got in part (a) back into Q_D or Q_S. You can double-check your answer by plugging the answer from part (a) into both Q_D and Q_S to see that you get the same result.)
   c. What happens if the minimum wage is $8? (**Hint**: Plug $W = 8$ into both Q_D and Q_S.) Does this cause a surplus or a shortage?
   d. What happens if the minimum wage is $6? (**Hint**: Plug $W = 6$ into both Q_D and Q_S.) Does this cause a surplus or a shortage?

SOLVED PROBLEMS

2. The equilibrium price occurs where the quantity demanded is equal to the quantity supplied. This occurs when $Q_D = Q_S = 800$. When the quantity is 800, the monthly rent is $800. Next, the question asks how many one-bedroom apartments will be rented after a rent-control law limits the rent to $700 a month. When the rent is $700, the quantity supplied is 320 apartments. It is also worth noting that the quantity demanded when the rent is $700 is 550 units, so there is a shortage of 550 − 320 = 230 apartments once the rent-control law goes into effect.

7. How many low-skill laborers will be unemployed when the minimum wage is $8 an hour? The quantity demanded is 29M, and the quantity supplied is 38M. This results in 38M − 29M = 9M unemployed low-skill workers.

   How many low-skill workers will be unemployed when the minimum wage is $6 an hour? Since $6 an hour is below the market-equilibrium wage of $7, it has no effect. In other words, a $6 minimum wage is nonbinding, and therefore no unemployment is caused.

CHAPTER 6

The Efficiency of Markets and the Costs of Taxation

MISCONCEPTION

Raising tax rates always generates more tax revenue.

Many people believe that if a government needs more revenue, all it needs to do is raise tax rates. If only it were that simple. Gasoline taxes demonstrate why this is a misconception.

Most people find it painful to pay more than $3 a gallon for gas. In many places, sales and excise taxes add a significant amount to the price. For example, the price of gasoline throughout Europe is often more than double that in the United States, largely because of much higher gasoline taxes. Other countries, like Venezuela, Saudi Arabia, and Mexico, subsidize gasoline so that their citizens pay less than the market price. In countries where gasoline is subsidized, consumers drive their cars everywhere, mass transportation is largely unavailable, and there is little concern for fuel efficiency. In contrast, as you might imagine, in countries with high gasoline taxes consumers drive less, use public transportation more, and tend to purchase fuel-efficient vehicles.

How high do gasoline taxes have to rise before large numbers of people significantly cut back on their gasoline consumption? The answer to that question will help us understand the misconception that raising tax rates always generates more tax revenue.

In the previous chapter, we learned about the market distortions caused by price controls. We observed that efforts to manipulate market prices not only cause surpluses and shortages, but also lead to black markets. In this chapter, we will quantify how markets enhance the welfare of society. We begin with consumer surplus and producer surplus, two concepts that illustrate how taxation, like price controls, creates distortions in economic behavior by altering the incentives that people face when consuming and producing goods that are taxed.

How much do taxes cost the economy?

BIG QUESTIONS

- What are consumer surplus and producer surplus?
- When is a market efficient?
- Why do taxes create deadweight loss?

What Are Consumer Surplus and Producer Surplus?

Welfare economics is the branch of economics that studies how the allocation of resources affects economic well-being.

Markets create value by bringing together buyers and sellers so that consumers and producers can mutually benefit from trade. **Welfare economics** is the branch of economics that studies how the allocation of resources affects economic well-being. In this section, we develop two concepts that will help us measure the value that markets create: *consumer surplus* and *producer surplus*. In competitive markets, the equilibrium price is simultaneously low enough to attract consumers and high enough to encourage producers. This balance between demand and supply enhances the welfare of society. That is not to say that society's welfare depends solely on markets. People also find satisfaction in many nonmarket settings, including spending time with their families and friends, and doing hobbies and charity work. We will incorporate aspects of personal happiness into our economic model in Chapter 16. For now, let's focus on how markets enhance human welfare.

Consumer Surplus

Willingness to pay is the maximum price a consumer will pay for a good.

Consider three students: Frank, Beanie, and Mitch. Like students everywhere, each one has a maximum price he is willing to pay for a new economics textbook. Beanie owns a successful business, so for him the cost of a new textbook does not present a financial hardship. Mitch is a business major who really wants to do well in economics. Frank is not serious about his studies. Table 6.1 shows the maximum value that each student places on the textbook. This value, called the **willingness to pay**, is the maximum price a consumer will pay for a good. The willingness to pay is also known as the reservation price. In an auction or a negotiation, the willingness to pay, or reservation price, is the price beyond which the consumer decides to walk away from the transaction.

How much will they pay for an economics textbook?

Consider what happens when the price of the book is $151. If Beanie purchases the book at $151, he pays $49 less than the $200

TABLE 6.1

Willingness to Pay for a New Economics Textbook

Buyer	Willingness to pay
Beanie	$200
Mitch	$150
Frank	$100

maximum he was willing to pay. He values the textbook at $49 more than the purchase price, so buying the book will make him better off.

Consumer surplus is the difference between the willingness to pay for a good and the price that is paid to get it. While Beanie gains $49 in consumer surplus, a price of $151 is more than either Mitch or Frank is willing to pay. Since Mitch is willing to pay only $150, if he purchases the book he will experience a consumer loss of $1. Frank's willingness to pay is $100, so if he buys the book for $151 he will experience a consumer loss of $51. Whenever the price is greater than the willingness to pay, a rational consumer will decide not to buy.

Consumer surplus is the difference between the willingness to pay for a good and the price that is paid to get it.

Using Demand Curves to Illustrate Consumer Surplus

In the previous section, we discussed consumer surplus as an amount. We can also illustrate it graphically with a demand curve. Figure 6.1 shows the demand curve drawn from the data in Table 6.1. Notice that the curve looks like a staircase with three steps—one for each additional textbook purchase. Each point on a market demand curve corresponds to one unit sold, so if we added more consumers into our example, the "steps" would become narrower and the demand curve would become smoother.

At any price above $200, none of the students wants to purchase a textbook. This relationship is evident on the *x* axis where the quantity demanded is 0. At any price between $150 and $200, Beanie is the only buyer, so the quantity demanded is 1. At prices between $100 and $150, Beanie and Mitch are each willing to buy the textbook, so the quantity demanded is 2. Finally, if the price is $100 or less, all three students are willing to buy the textbook, so the quantity demanded is 3. As the price falls, the quantity demanded increases.

We can measure the total extent of consumer surplus by examining the area under the demand curve for each of our three consumers, as shown in Figure 6.2. In Figure 6.2a the price is $175, and only Beanie decides to buy. Since his willingness to pay is $200, he is better off by $25; this is his consumer surplus. The green-shaded area under the demand curve and above the price represents the benefit Beanie receives from purchasing a textbook at a price of $175. When the price drops to $125, as shown in Figure 6.2b, Mitch also decides to buy a textbook. Now the total quantity demanded is 2 textbooks. Mitch's willingness to pay is $150, so his consumer surplus, represented by the red-shaded area, is $25. However, since Beanie's willingness to pay is $200, his consumer surplus rises from $25 to $75. So a textbook price of $125 raises the total consumer surplus to $100. In other words, lower prices create more consumer surplus in this market—and in any other.

FIGURE 6.1

Demand Curve for an Economics Textbook

The demand curve has a step for each additional textbook purchase. As the price goes down, more students buy the textbook.

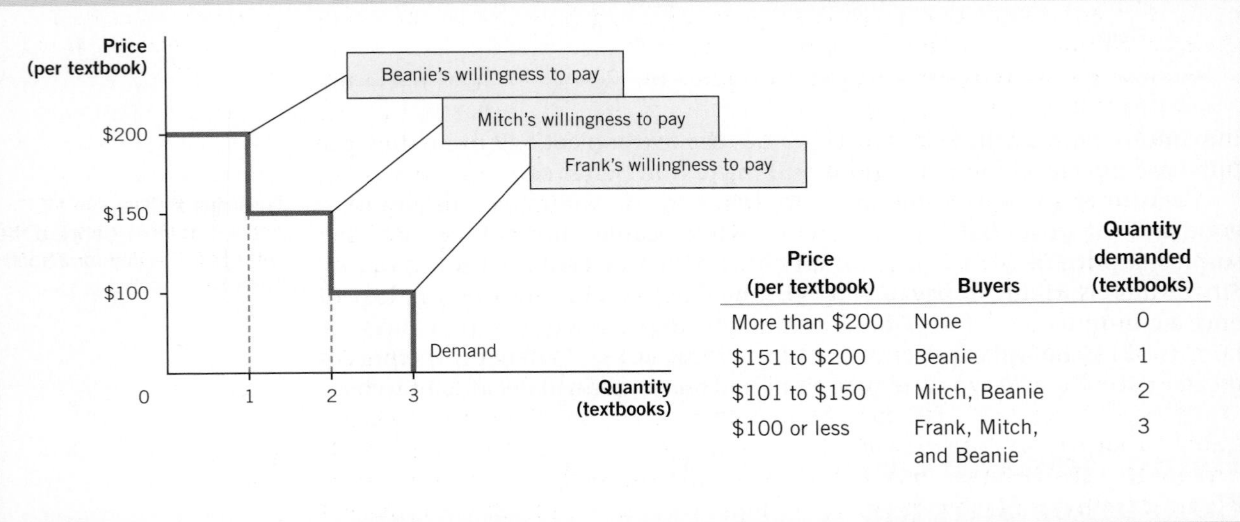

Price (per textbook)	Buyers	Quantity demanded (textbooks)
More than $200	None	0
$151 to $200	Beanie	1
$101 to $150	Mitch, Beanie	2
$100 or less	Frank, Mitch, and Beanie	3

FIGURE 6.2

Determining Consumer Surplus from a Demand Curve

(a) At a price of $175, Beanie is the only buyer, so the quantity demanded is 1. (b) At a price of $125, Beanie and Mitch are each willing to buy the textbook, so the quantity demanded is 2.

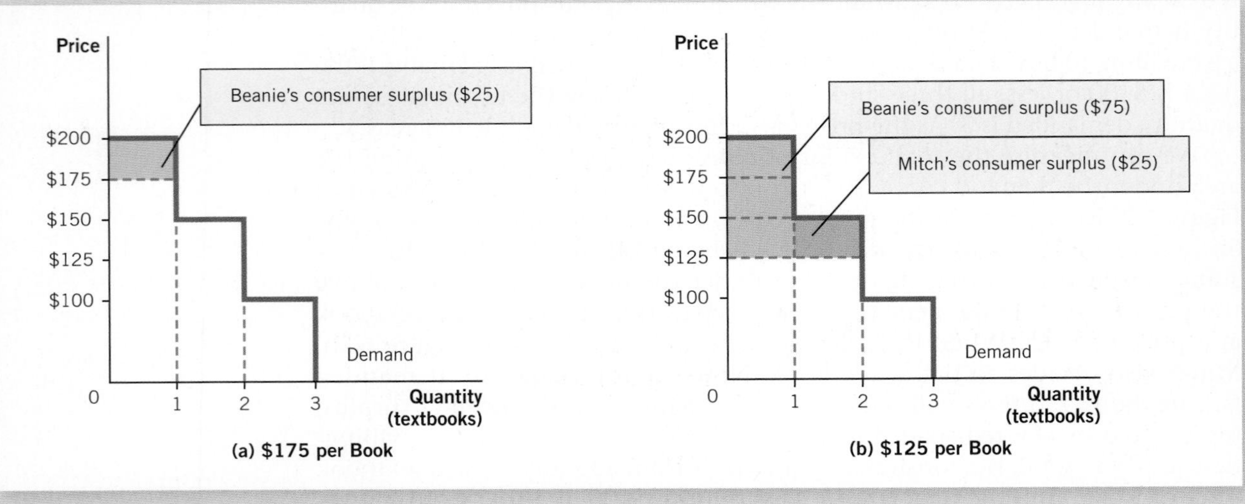

Producer Surplus

Sellers also benefit from market transactions. In this section, our three students discover that they are good at economics and decide to go into the tutoring business. They do not want to provide this service for free, but each has a different minimum price, or *willingness to sell*. The **willingness to sell** is the minimum price a seller will accept to sell a good or service. Table 6.2 shows each tutor's willingness to sell his services.

Willingness to sell is the minimum price a seller will accept to sell a good or service.

Consider what happens at a tutoring price of $25 per hour. Since Frank is willing to tutor for $10 per hour, every hour that he tutors at $25 per hour earns him $15 more than his willingness to sell. This extra $15 per hour is his *producer surplus*. **Producer surplus** is the difference between the willingness to sell a good and the price that the seller receives. Mitch is willing to tutor for $20 per hour and earns a $5 producer surplus for every hour he tutors. Finally, Beanie's willingness to tutor, at $30 per hour, is more than the market price of $25. If he tutors, he will have a producer loss of $5 per hour.

Producer surplus is the difference between the willingness to sell a good and the price that the seller receives.

How do producers determine their willingness to sell? They must consider two factors: the direct costs of producing the good and the indirect costs, or opportunity costs. Students who are new to economics often mistakenly assume that the cost of producing an item is the only cost to consider in making the decision to produce. But producers also have opportunity costs. Beanie, Mitch, and Frank each has a unique willingness to sell because each has a different opportunity cost. Beanie owns his own business, so for him the time spent tutoring is time that he could have spent making money elsewhere. Mitch is a business student who might otherwise be studying to get better grades. Frank is neither a businessman nor a serious student, so the $10 he can earn in an hour of tutoring is not taking the place of other earning opportunities or studying more to get better grades.

Opportunity cost

Using Supply Curves to Illustrate Producer Surplus

Continuing our example, the supply curve in Figure 6.3 shows the relationship between the price for an hour of tutoring and the quantity of tutors who are willing to work. As you can see on the supply schedule (the table within the figure), at any price less than $10 per hour no one wants to tutor. At prices between $10 and $19 per hour, Frank is the only tutor, so the

TABLE 6.2

Willingness to Sell Tutoring Services

Seller	Willingness to sell
Beanie	$30/hr
Mitch	$20/hr
Frank	$10/hr

FIGURE 6.3

Supply Curve for Economics Tutoring

The supply curve has three steps, one for each additional student who is willing to tutor. Progressively higher prices will induce more students to become tutors.

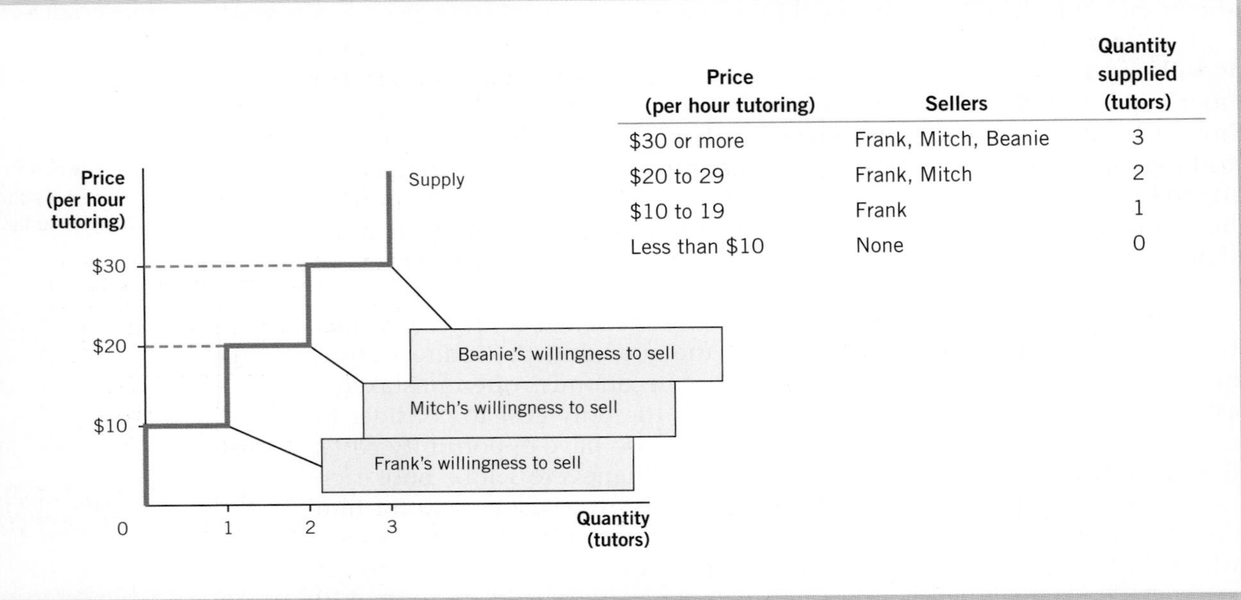

Price (per hour tutoring)	Sellers	Quantity supplied (tutors)
$30 or more	Frank, Mitch, Beanie	3
$20 to 29	Frank, Mitch	2
$10 to 19	Frank	1
Less than $10	None	0

quantity supplied is 1. Between $20 and $29 per hour, Frank and Mitch are willing to tutor, so the quantity supplied rises to 2. Finally, if the price is $30 or more, all three friends are willing to tutor, so the quantity supplied is 3. As the price they receive for tutoring rises, the number of tutors increases from 1 to 3.

What do these relationships between price and supply tell us about producer surplus? Let's turn to Figure 6.4. By examining the area above the supply curve, we can measure the extent of producer surplus. In Figure 6.4a, the price of an hour of tutoring is $15. At that price, only Frank decides to tutor. Since he would be willing to tutor even if the price were as low as $10 per hour, he is $5 better off tutoring. Frank's producer surplus is represented by the red-shaded area between the supply curve and the price of $15. Since Beanie and Mitch do not tutor when the price is $15, they do not receive any producer surplus. In Figure 6.4b, the price for tutoring is $25 per hour. At this price, Mitch also decides to tutor. His willingness to tutor is $20, so when the price is $25 per hour his producer surplus is $5, represented by the blue-shaded area. Since Frank's willingness to tutor is $10, at $25 per hour his producer surplus rises to $15. By looking at the shaded boxes in Figure 6.4b, we see that an increase in the rates for tutoring raises the combined producer surplus of Frank and Mitch to $20.

FIGURE 6.4

Determining Producer Surplus from a Supply Curve

(a) The price of an hour of tutoring is $15. At this price, only Frank decides to tutor. (b) The price for tutoring is $25 per hour. At this price, Mitch also decides to tutor.

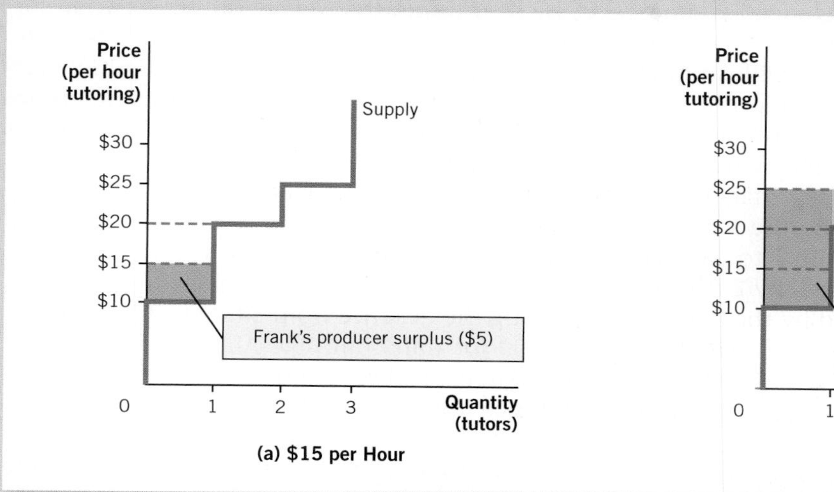

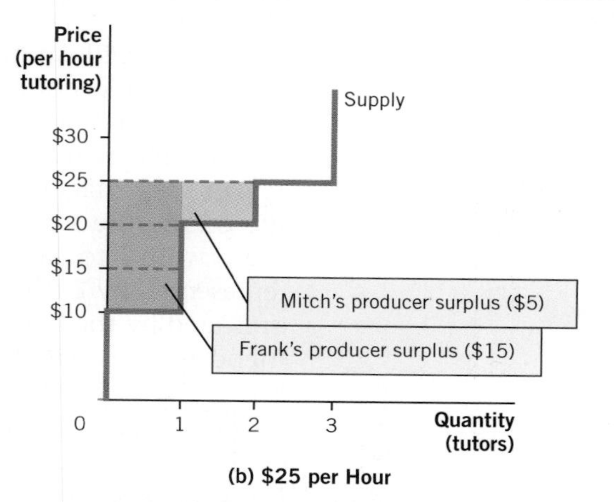

PRACTICE WHAT YOU KNOW

Consumer and Producer Surplus: Trendy Fashion

Leah decides to buy a new jacket from D&G for $80. She was willing to pay $100. When her friend Becky sees the jacket, she loves it and thinks it is worth $150. So she offers Leah $125 for the jacket, and Leah accepts. Leah and Becky are both thrilled with the exchange.

Rachel Bilson wearing a D&G jacket

Question: Determine the total surplus from the original purchase and the additional surplus generated by the resale of the jacket.

Answer: Leah was willing to pay $100 and the jacket cost $80, so she keeps the difference, or $20, as consumer surplus. When Leah resells the jacket to Becky for $125, she earns $25 in producer surplus. At the same time, Becky receives $25 in consumer surplus, since she was willing to pay Leah up to $150 for the jacket but Leah sells it to her for $125. The resale generates an additional $50 in surplus.

When Is a Market Efficient?

Total surplus, also known as **social welfare,** is the sum of consumer surplus and producer surplus.

We have seen how consumers benefit from lower prices and how producers benefit from higher prices. When we combine the concepts of consumer and producer surplus, we can build a complete picture of the welfare of buyers and sellers. Adding consumer and producer surplus gives us **total surplus**, also known as **social welfare**, because it measures the welfare of society. Total surplus is the best way economists have to measure the benefits that markets create.

Figure 6.5 illustrates the relationship between consumer and producer surplus for a gallon of milk. The demand curve shows that some customers are willing to pay more for a gallon of milk than others. Likewise, some sellers (producers) are willing to sell milk for less than others.

Trade creates value

Let's say that Alice is willing to pay \$7.00 per gallon for milk, but when she gets to the store she finds it for \$4.00. The difference between the price she is willing to pay, represented by point A, and the price she actually pays, represented by E (the equilibrium price), is \$3.00 in consumer surplus. This is indicated by the blue arrow showing the distance from \$4.00 to \$7.00. Alice's friend Betty is willing to pay \$5.00 for milk, but, like Alice, she finds it for \$4.00. Therefore, she receives \$1.00 in consumer surplus, indicated by the blue arrow at point B showing the distance from \$4.00 to \$5.00. In fact, all consumers who are willing to pay more than \$4.00 are better off when they purchase the milk at \$4.00. We can show this total area of consumer surplus on the graph as the blue-shaded triangle bordered by the demand curve, the *y* axis, and the equilibrium price (P_E). At every point in this area, the consumers who are willing to pay more than the equilibrium price for milk will be better off.

FIGURE 6.5

Consumer and Producer Surplus for a Gallon of Milk

Consumer surplus is the difference between the willingness to pay along the demand curve and the equilibrium price, P_E. It is illustrated by the blue-shaded triangle. Producer surplus is the difference between the willingness to produce along the supply curve and the equilibrium price. It is illustrated by the red-shaded triangle.

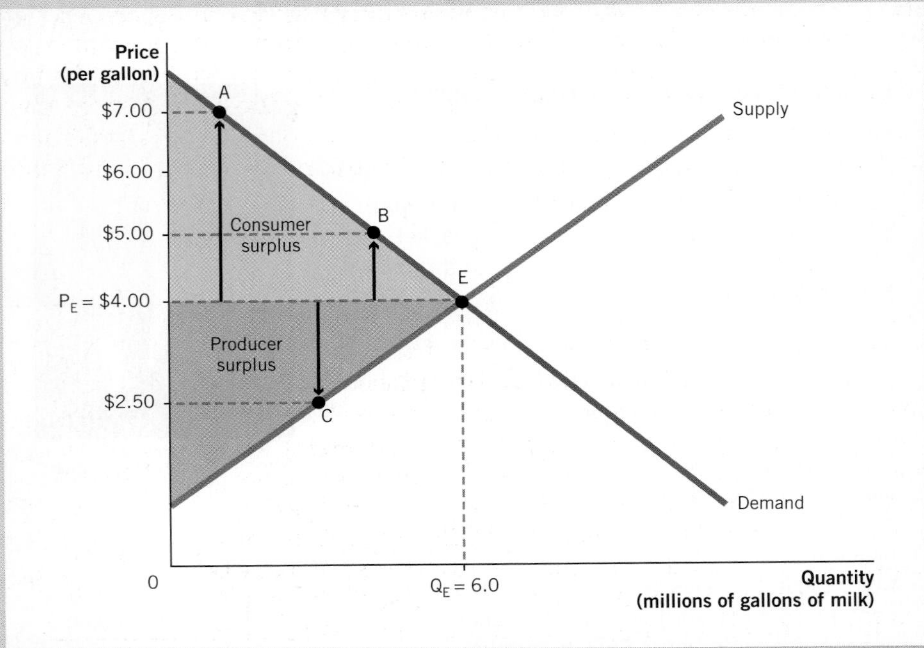

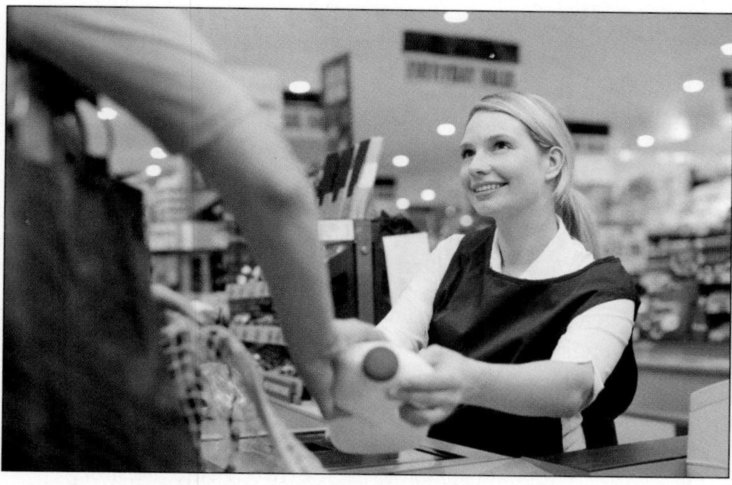
The buyer and seller each benefit from this exchange.

Continuing with Figure 6.5, producer surplus follows a similar process. Suppose that the Contented Cow dairy is willing to sell milk for $2.50 per gallon, represented by point C. Since the equilibrium price is $4.00, the business makes $1.50 in producer surplus. This is indicated by the red arrow at point C showing the distance from $4.00 to $2.50. If we think of the supply curve as representing the costs of many different sellers, we can calculate the total producer surplus as the red-shaded triangle bordered by the supply curve, the *y* axis, and the equilibrium price. The shaded blue triangle (consumer surplus) and the shaded red triangle (producer surplus) describe the increase in total surplus, or social welfare, created by the production and exchange of the good at the equilibrium price. At the equilibrium quantity of 6 million gallons of milk, output and consumption reach the largest possible combination of producer and consumer surplus. In the region of the graph beyond 6 million units, buyers and sellers will experience a loss.

When an allocation of resources maximizes total surplus, the result is said to be **efficient**. Efficiency occurs at point E when the market is in equilibrium. To think about why the market creates the largest possible total surplus, or social welfare, it is important to recall how the market allocates resources. Consumers who are willing to pay more than the equilibrium price will buy the good because they will enjoy the consumer surplus. Producers who are willing to sell the good for less than the market-equilibrium price will enjoy the producer surplus. In addition, consumers with a low willingness to buy (less than $4.00) and producers with a high willingness to sell (more than $4.00) do not participate in the market since they would be worse off. Therefore, the equilibrium output at point E maximizes the total surplus and is also an efficient allocation of resources.

An outcome is **efficient** when an allocation of resources maximizes total surplus.

The Efficiency-Equity Debate

When economists model behavior, we assume that participants in a market are rational decision-makers. We assume that producers will always operate in the region of the triangle that represents producer surplus and that consumers will always operate in the region of the triangle that represents consumer surplus. We do not, for example, expect Alice to pay more than $7.00 for a gallon of milk or the Contented Cow dairy to sell a gallon of milk for less than $2.50 per gallon. In other words, for the market to work efficiently, voluntary instances of consumer loss must be rare. We assume that self-interest helps to ensure that all participants will benefit from an exchange.

Efficiency only requires that the pie gets eaten. Equity is a question of who gets the biggest share.

ECONOMICS IN THE MEDIA

Efficiency

Old School

In the 2003 movie *Old School*, Frank tries to give away a bread maker he received as a wedding present. First he offers it to a friend as a housewarming gift, but it turns out that this is the friend who originally gave him the bread maker. Ouch! Later in the movie, we see Frank giving the bread maker to a small boy at a birthday party. Both efforts at re-gifting fail miserably.

From an economic perspective, giving the wrong gift makes society poorer. If you spend $50 on a gift and give it to someone who thinks it is only worth $30, you've lost $20 in value. Whenever you receive a shirt that is the wrong size or style, a fruitcake you won't eat, or something that is worth less to you than what the gift-giver spent on it, an economic inefficiency has occurred. Until now, we have thought of the market as enhancing efficiency by increasing the total surplus in society. But we can also think of the billions of dollars spent on mismatched gifts as a failure to maximize the total surplus involved in exchange. In other words, we can think of the efficiency of the gift-giving process as less than 100 percent.

Given what we have learned so far about economics, you might be tempted to argue that cash is the best gift you can give. When you give cash, it is never the wrong size or color, and the recipients can use it to buy whatever they want. However, very few people actually give cash (unless it is requested). Considering the advantages of cash, why don't more people give it instead of gifts? One reason is that cash seems impersonal. A second reason is that cash communicates exactly how much the giver spent. To avoid both problems, most people rarely give cash. Instead, they buy personalized gifts to communicate how much they care, while making it hard for the recipient to determine exactly how much they spent.

One way that society overcomes inefficiency in gifting is through the dissemination of information. For instance, wedding registries provide a convenient way for people who may not know the newlyweds very well to give them what they want. Similarly, prior to holidays many people tell each other what they would like to receive. By purchasing gifts that others want, givers can exactly match what the recipients would have purchased if they had received a cash transfer. This eliminates any potential inefficiency. At the same time, the giver conveys affection—an essential part of giving. To further reduce the potential inefficiencies associated with giving, many large families practice holiday gift exchanges. And another interesting mechanism for eliciting information involves Santa Claus. Children throughout the world send Santa Claus wish lists for Christmas, never realizing that the parents who help to write and send the lists are the primary beneficiaries.

Frank re-gifts a bread maker.

To the economist, the strategies of providing better information, having gift exchanges, and sending wish lists to Santa Claus are just a few examples of how society tries to get the most out of the giving process—and that is something to be joyful about!

PRACTICE WHAT YOU KNOW

Total Surplus: How Would Lower Income Affect Urban Outfitters?

Question: If a drop in consumer income occurs, what will happen to the consumer surplus that customers enjoy at Urban Outfitters? What will happen to the amount of producer surplus that Urban Outfitters receives? Illustrate your answer by shifting the demand curve appropriately and labeling the new and old areas of consumer and producer surplus.

Does less income affect total surplus?

Answer: Since the items sold at Urban Outfitters are normal goods, a drop in income causes the demand curve (D) to shift to the left. The black arrow shows the leftward shift in graph (b) below. When you compare the area of consumer surplus (in blue) before and after the drop in income—that is, graphs (a) and (b)—you can see that it shrinks. The same is true when comparing the area of producer surplus (in red) before and after.

Your intuition might already confirm what the graphs tell us. Since consumers have less income, they buy fewer clothes at Urban Outfitters—so consumer surplus falls. Likewise, since fewer customers buy the store's clothes, Urban Outfitters sells less—so producer surplus falls. This is also evident in graph (b), since $Q_2 < Q_1$.

However, the fact that both parties benefit from an exchange does not mean that each benefits equally. Economists are also interested in the distribution of the gains. **Equity** refers to the fairness of the distribution of benefits among the members of a society. In a world where no one cared about equity, only efficiency would matter and no particular division would be preferred. Another way of thinking about fairness versus efficiency is to consider a pie. If our only concern is efficiency, we will simply want to make sure that none of the pie goes to waste. However, if we care about equity, we will also want to make sure that the pie is divided equally among those present and that no one gets a larger piece than any other.

Equity
refers to the fairness of the distribution of benefits within the society.

In our first look at consumer and producer surplus, we have assumed that markets produce efficient outcomes. But in the real world, this is not always the case. Markets also fail; their efficiency can be compromised in a number of ways. We will discuss market failure in much greater detail in subsequent chapters. For now, all you need to know is that failure can occur.

Why Do Taxes Create Deadweight Loss?

Taxes provide many benefits. They also remind us that "there is no free lunch"; for example, we don't pay the police dispatcher before dialing 911, but society has to collect taxes in order for the emergency service to exist. Taxes help to pay for many of modern society's needs—public transportation, schools, police, the court system, and the military, to name just a few. Most of us take these services for granted, but without taxes it would be hard to pay for them. How much does all of this cost? When you add all the federal, state, and local government budgets in the United States, you get five trillion dollars a year!

Opportunity cost

These taxes incur opportunity costs, since the money could have been used in other ways. In this section, we will use the concepts of consumer and producer surplus to explain the effect of taxation on social welfare and market efficiency. Taxes come in many sizes and shapes. Considering there are taxes on personal income, payroll, property, corporate profits, sales, and inheritances, the complexity makes it difficult to analyze the broad impact of taxation on social welfare and market efficiency. Fortunately, we do not have to examine the entire tax code all at once. In this chapter, we will explore the impact of taxes on social welfare by looking at one of the simplest taxes, the *excise tax*.

Excise taxes
are taxes levied on a particular good or service.

Incidence
refers to the burden of taxation on the party who pays the tax through higher prices, regardless of whom the tax is actually levied on.

Tax Incidence

Economists want to know how taxes affect the choices that consumers and producers make. When a tax is imposed on an item, do buyers switch to alternative goods that are not taxed? How do producers respond when the products they sell are taxed? Since taxes cause prices to rise, they can affect how much of a good or service is bought and sold. This is especially evident with **excise taxes**, or taxes levied on one particular good or service. For example, all fifty states levy excise taxes on cigarettes, but the amount assessed varies tremendously. In New York, cigarette taxes are over $4.00 per pack, while in a handful of tobacco-producing states such as Virginia and North Carolina, the excise tax is less than $0.50. Overall, excise taxes, such as those on cigarettes, alcohol, and gasoline, account for less than 4% of all tax revenues. But because we can isolate changes in consumer behavior that result from taxes on one item, they help us understand the overall effect of a tax.

Why do we place excise taxes on cigarettes . . .

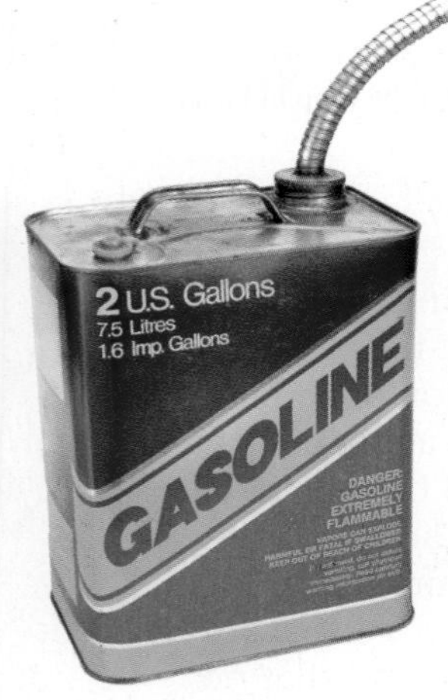

. . . and gasoline?

In looking at the effect of a tax, economists are also interested in the **incidence** of taxation, which refers to the burden of taxation on the party who pays the tax through higher prices. To understand this idea, consider a $1.00 tax on milk purchases. Each time a consumer buys a gallon of milk, the cash register adds $1.00 in tax. This means that to purchase the milk, the consumer's willingness to pay must be greater than the price of the milk plus the $1.00 tax.

The result of the $1.00 tax on milk is shown in Figure 6.6. Because of the tax, the price of milk goes up and the demand curve shifts down (from D_1 to D_2). Why does the demand curve shift? Since consumers must pay the purchase price as well as the tax, the extra cost makes them less likely to buy milk at every price, which causes the entire demand curve to shift down. The intersection of the new demand curve (D_2) with the existing supply curve (S) creates a new equilibrium price of $3.50 ($E_2$), which is $0.50 lower than the original price of $4.00. But even though the price is lower, consumers are still worse off. Since they must also pay part of the $1.00 tax, the total price to them rises to $4.50 per gallon.

At the same time, because the new equilibrium price after the tax is $0.50 lower than it was before the tax, the producer splits the tax incidence with the buyer. The producer receives $0.50 less, and the buyer pays $0.50 more.

The tax on milk purchases also affects the amount sold in the market, which we also see in Figure 6.6. Since the after-tax equilibrium price (E_2) is lower, producers of milk reduce the quantity they sell to 750 gallons. Therefore, the market for milk becomes smaller than it was before the good was taxed.

Excise taxes paid by consumers are relatively rare because they are highly visible. If every time you bought milk you were reminded that you had to pay a $1.00 tax, it would be hard to ignore. As a result, politicians often prefer

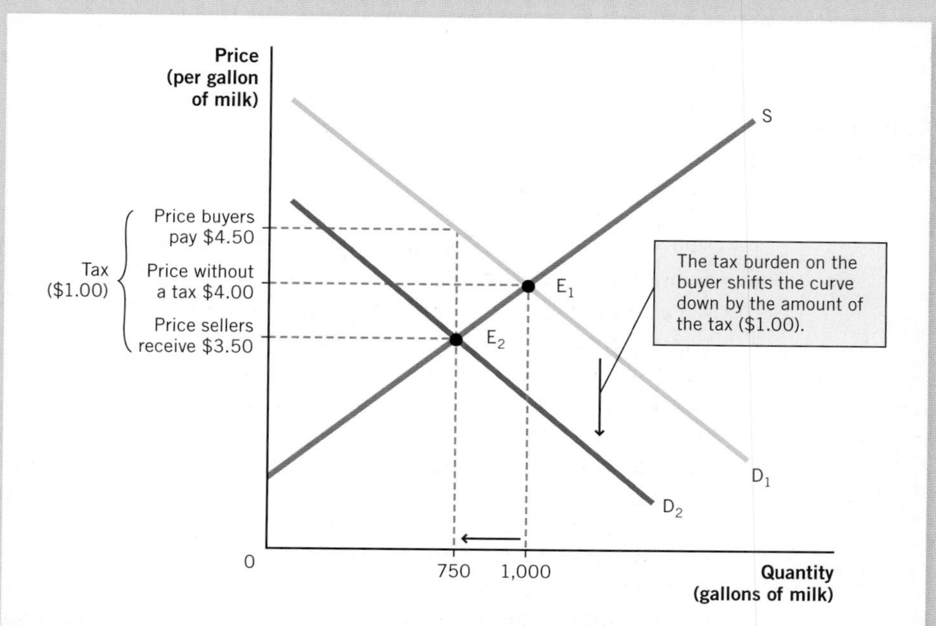

FIGURE 6.6

A Tax on Buyers

After the tax, the new equilibrium price (E_2) is $3.50, but the buyer must also pay $1.00 in tax. Therefore, despite the drop in price, the buyer still owes $4.50. A similar logic applies to the producer. Since the new equilibrium price after the tax is $0.50 lower, the producer shares the tax incidence equally with the seller in this example. The consumer pays $0.50 more, and the seller nets $0.50 less.

to place the tax on the seller. The seller will then include the tax in the sale price, and buyers will likely forget that the sale price is higher than it would be without the tax.

Let's return to the $1.00 tax on milk. This time, the tax is placed on the seller. Figure 6.7 shows the result. First, look at the shift in the supply curve. Why does it shift? The $1.00 per gallon tax on milk lowers the profits that milk producers expect to make, which causes them to produce less milk at every price level. As a result, the entire supply curve shifts to the left in response to the tax that milk producers owe the government. The intersection of the new supply curve (S_2) with the existing demand curve creates a new equilibrium price (E_2) of $4.50—which is $0.50 higher than the original equilibrium price of $4.00 ($E_1$). This occurs because the seller passes part of the tax increase along to the buyer in the form of a higher price. However, the seller is still worse off. After the tax, the new equilibrium price is $4.50, but $1.00 goes as tax to the government. Therefore, despite the rise in price, the seller nets only $3.50, which is $0.50 less than the original equilibrium price.

The tax also affects the amount of milk sold in the market. Since the new equilibrium price after the tax is higher, consumers reduce the quantity demanded from 1,000 gallons to 750 gallons.

It's important to notice that the result in Figure 6.7 looks much like that in Figure 6.6. This is because it does not matter whether a tax is levied on the buyer or the seller. The tax places a wedge of $1.00 between the price that buyers ultimately pay ($4.50) and the net price that sellers ultimately receive ($3.50), regardless of who is actually responsible for paying the tax.

FIGURE 6.7

A Tax on Sellers

After the tax, the new equilibrium price (E_2) is $4.50, but $1.00 must be paid in tax to the government. Therefore, despite the rise in price, the seller nets only $3.50. A similar logic applies to the consumer. Since the new equilibrium price after the tax is $0.50 higher, the consumer shares the $1.00/gallon tax incidence equally with the seller. The consumer pays $0.50 more, and the seller nets $0.50 less.

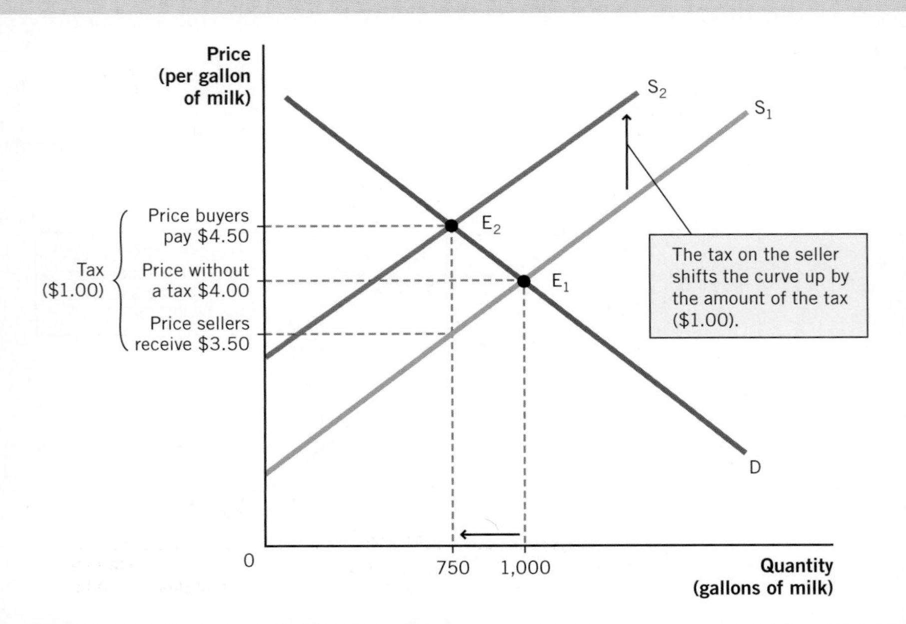

Continuing with our milk example, when the tax was levied on sellers, they were responsible for collecting the entire tax ($1.00 per gallon), but they transferred $0.50 of the tax to the consumer by raising the market price to $4.50. Similarly, when the tax was levied on consumers, they were responsible for paying the entire tax, but they essentially transferred $0.50 of it to the producer, since the market price fell to $3.50. Therefore, we can say that the incidence of a tax is independent of whether it is levied on the buyer or the seller. However, depending on the price elasticity of supply and demand, the tax incidence need not be shared equally, as we will see later. All of this means that the government doesn't get to determine whether consumers or producers bear the tax incidence—the market does!

Deadweight Loss

Recall that economists measure economic efficiency by looking at total consumer and producer surplus. We have seen that a tax raises the total price consumers pay and lowers the net price producers receive. For this reason, taxes reduce the amount of economic activity. The decrease in economic activity caused by market distortions, such as taxes, is known as **deadweight loss.**

Deadweight loss is the decrease in economic activity caused by market distortions.

In the previous section, we observed that the tax on milk caused the amount purchased to decline from 1,000 to 750 gallons—a reduction of 250 gallons sold in the market. In Figure 6.8, the yellow triangle represents the deadweight loss caused by the tax. When the price rises, consumers who

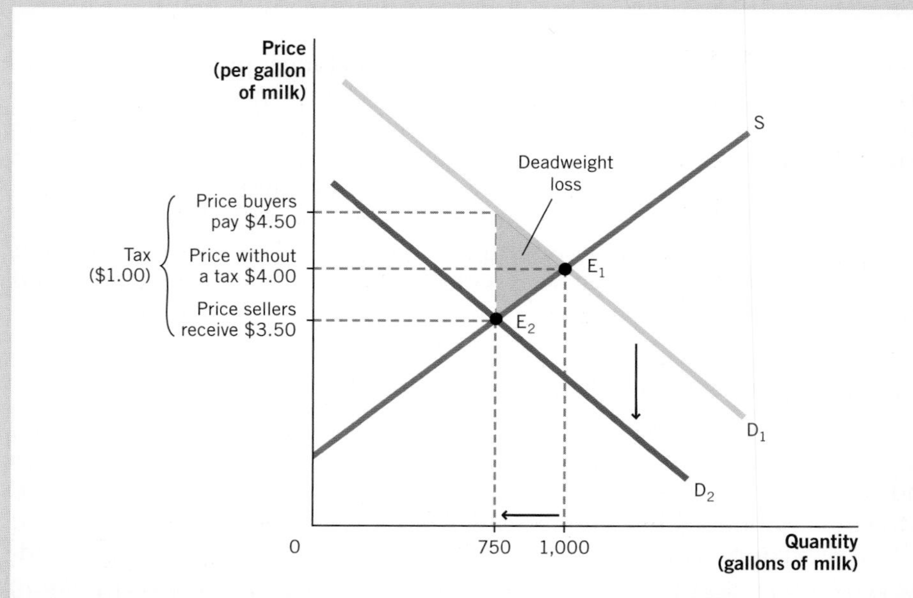

FIGURE 6.8

The Deadweight Loss from a Tax

The yellow triangle represents the deadweight loss caused by the tax. When the price rises, all consumers who would have paid between $4.00 and $4.49 no longer purchase milk. Likewise, the reduction in revenue the seller receives means that producers who were willing to sell a gallon of milk for between $3.51 and $4.00 will no longer do so.

ECONOMICS IN THE MEDIA

Taxing Inelastic Goods

"Taxman" by the Beatles

"Taxman" was inspired by the theme song from the popular 1960s television series *Batman*. The Beatles—especially George Harrison, who wrote the song—had grown quite bitter about how much they were paying in taxes. In the beginning of the song, Harrison sings, "Let me tell you how it will be. There's one for you, nineteen for me." This refers to the fact that the British government taxed high-wage earners £19 out of every £20 they earned. Since the Beatles' considerable earnings placed them in the top income tax bracket in the United Kingdom, a part of the group's earnings was subject to the 95% tax introduced by the government in 1965. As a consequence, the Beatles became tax exiles living in the United States and other parts of Europe, where tax rates were lower.

The Beatles avoided high taxes by living outside the United Kingdom.

The inevitability of paying taxes is a theme that runs throughout the song. The lyrics mention that when you drive a car, the government can tax the "street"; if you try to sit, the government can tax "your seat"; if you are cold, the government can tax "the heat"; and if you decide to take a walk, it can tax your "feet"! The only way to avoid doing and using these things is to leave the country—precisely what the Beatles did. All these examples (streets, seats, heat, and walking) are necessary activities, which makes demand highly inelastic. Anytime that is the case, the government can more easily collect the tax revenue it desires.

would have paid between $4.00 and $4.49 will no longer purchase milk. Likewise, the reduction in the price the seller can charge means that producers who were willing to sell a gallon of milk for between $3.51 and $4.00 will no longer do so. The combined reductions in consumer and producer surplus equal the deadweight loss produced by a $1.00 tax on milk.

In the next sections, we will examine how differences in the price elasticity of demand lead to varying amounts of deadweight loss. We will evaluate what happens when the demand curve is perfectly inelastic, somewhat elastic, and perfectly elastic.

Tax Revenue and Deadweight Loss When Demand Is Inelastic

In Chapter 4, we saw that necessary goods and services—for example, water, electricity, and phone service—have highly inelastic demand. These goods and services are often taxed. For example, consider all the taxes associated with your cell phone bill: sales tax, city tax, county tax, federal excise tax, and annual regulatory fees. In addition, many companies add surcharges, including activation fees, local number portability fees, telephone number pooling charges, emergency 911 service, directory assistance, telecommunications relay service surcharges, and cancellation fees. Of course, there is a way to avoid all these fees: don't use a cell phone! However, many people today feel that cell phones are a necessity. Cell phone providers and government agencies take advantage of the consumer's strongly inelastic demand by tacking on these extra charges.

Figure 6.9 shows the result of a tax on products with almost perfectly inelastic demand, such as phone service—something people feel they need to have no matter what the price. The demand for access to a phone (either a landline or a cell phone) is perfectly inelastic. Recall that whenever demand is perfectly inelastic, the demand curve is vertical. Figure 6.9a shows the market for phone service before the tax. The blue rectangle represents consumer surplus (C.S.), and the red triangle represents producer surplus (P.S.). Now imagine that a tax is levied on the seller, as shown in Figure 6.9b. The supply curve shifts from S_1 to S_2. The shift in supply causes the equilibrium point to move from E_1 to E_2 and the price to rise from P_1 to P_2, but the quantity supplied, Q_1, remains the same. We know that when demand is perfectly inelastic, a price increase does not alter how much consumers purchase. So the quantity demanded remains constant at Q_1 even after the government collects tax revenue equal to the green-shaded area.

There are two reasons why the government may favor excise taxes on goods with almost perfectly (or highly) inelastic demand. First, because these

How do phone companies get away with all the added fees per month? Answer: inelastic demand.

FIGURE 6.9

A Tax on Products with Almost Perfectly Inelastic Demand

(a) Before the tax, the consumer enjoys the consumer surplus (C.S.) noted in blue, and the producer enjoys the producer surplus (P.S.) noted in red. (b) After the tax, the incidence, or the burden of taxation, is borne entirely by the consumer. A tax on a good with almost perfectly inelastic demand, such as phone service, represents a transfer of welfare from consumers of the good to the government, reflected by the reduced size of the blue rectangle in (b) and the creation of the green tax-revenue rectangle between P_1 and P_2.

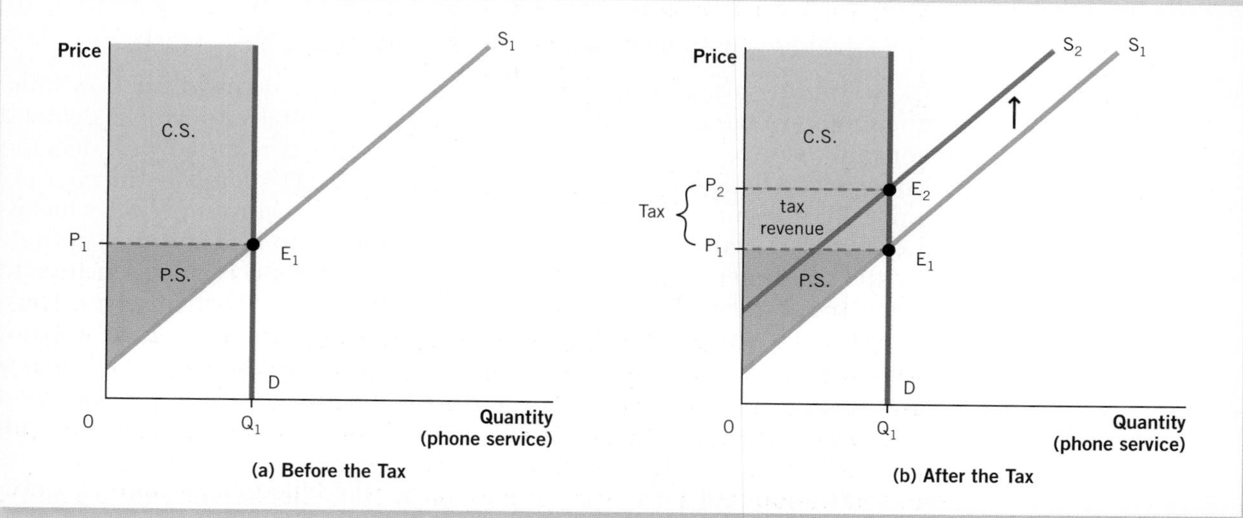

goods do not have substitutes, the tax will not cause consumers to buy less. Thus, the revenue from the tax will remain steady. Second, since the number of transactions, or quantity demanded (Q_1), remains constant, there will be no deadweight loss. As a result, the yellow triangle we observed in Figure 6.8 disappears in Figure 6.9 because the tax does not alter the efficiency of the market. Looking at Figure 6.9, you can see that the same number of transactions exist in (a) and (b). This means that the total surplus, or social welfare, is equal in both panels. You can also see this by comparing the shaded areas in both panels. The sum of the blue-shaded area of consumer surplus and the red-shaded area of producer surplus in (a) is equal to the sum of the consumer surplus, producer surplus, and tax revenue in (b). The green area is subtracted entirely from the blue rectangle, which indicates that the surplus is redistributed from consumers to the government. But society overall enjoys the same total surplus. Thus, we see that when demand is perfectly inelastic, the incidence, or the burden of taxation, is borne entirely by the consumer. A tax on a good with almost perfectly inelastic demand represents a transfer of welfare from consumers of the good to the government, reflected by the reduced size of the blue rectangle in (b).

Tax Revenue and Deadweight Loss When Demand Is More Elastic

Now consider a tax on a product with more elastic demand, such as milk, the subject of our earlier discussion on calculating total surplus. The demand for milk is price sensitive, but not overly so. This is reflected in a demand curve with a typical slope as shown in Figure 6.10. Let's compare the after-tax price, P_2, in Figures 6.9b and 6.10b. When demand is almost perfectly inelastic, as it is in Figure 6.9b, the price increase from P_1 to P_2 is absorbed entirely by the consumer. But in Figure 6.10b, because demand is more sensitive to price, suppliers must absorb part of the tax, from P_1 to P_3, themselves. Thus, they net P_3, which is less than what they received when the good was not taxed. In addition, the total tax revenue generated (the green-shaded area) is not as large in Figure 6.9b as in Figure 6.10b, because as the price of the good rises some consumers no longer buy it and the quantity demanded falls from Q_1 to Q_2.

Notice that both consumer surplus (C.S.), the blue triangle, and producer surplus (P.S.), the red triangle, are smaller after the tax. Since the price rises after the tax increase (from P_1 to P_2), those consumers with a relatively low

FIGURE 6.10

A Tax on Products with More Elastic Demand

(a) Before the tax, the consumer enjoys the consumer surplus (C.S.) noted in blue, and the producer enjoys the producer surplus (P.S.) noted in red. (b) A tax on a good for which demand and supply are each somewhat elastic will cause a transfer of welfare from consumers and producers to the government, the revenue shown as the green rectangle. It will also create deadweight loss (D.W.L.), shown in yellow, since the quantity bought and sold in the market declines (from Q_1 to Q_2).

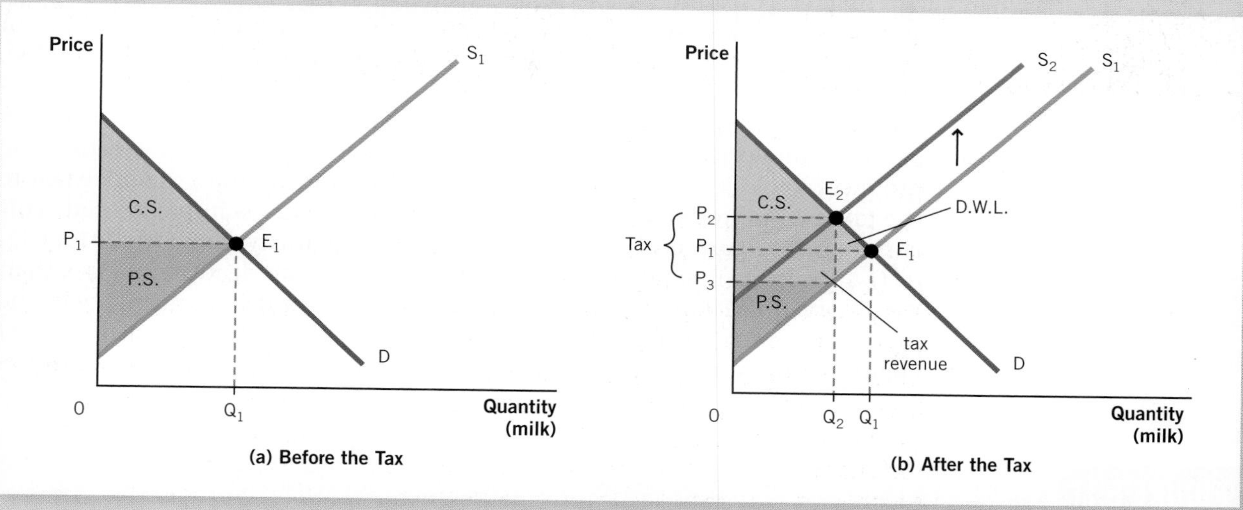

willingness to pay for the good are priced out of the market. Likewise, sellers with relatively high costs of production will stop producing the good, since the price they net after paying the tax drops to P_3. The total reduction in economic activity, the change from Q_1 to Q_2, is the deadweight loss (D.W.L.) indicated by the yellow triangle.

The incidence of the tax also changes from Figure 6.9 to Figure 6.10. A tax on a good for which demand and supply are each somewhat elastic will cause a transfer of welfare from consumers and producers of the good to the government. At the same time, since the quantity bought and sold in the market declines, it also creates deadweight loss. Another way of seeing this result is to compare the red- and blue-shaded areas in Figure 6.10a with the red- and blue-shaded areas in Figure 6.10b. The sum of the consumer surplus and producer surplus in (a) is greater than the sum of the consumer surplus, tax revenue, and producer surplus in (b). Therefore, the total surplus, or efficiency of the market, is smaller. The tax is no longer a pure transfer from consumers to the government, as was the case in Figure 6.9.

Tax Revenue and Deadweight Loss When Demand Is Highly Elastic

We have seen the effect of taxation when demand is inelastic and somewhat elastic. What about when demand is highly elastic? For example, a customer who wants to buy fresh lettuce at a produce market will find many local growers charging the same price and many varieties to choose from. If one of the vendors decides to charge $1 per pound above the market price, consumers will stop buying from that vendor. They will be unwilling to pay more when they can get the same product from another grower at a lower price; this is the essence of elastic demand.

Figure 6.11 shows the result of a tax on lettuce, a good with highly elastic demand. After all, when lettuce is taxed consumers can switch to other greens such as spinach, cabbage, or endive and completely avoid the tax. In this market, consumers are so price sensitive that they are unwilling to accept any price increase. And because sellers are unable to raise the equilibrium price, they bear the entire incidence of the tax. This has two effects. First, producers are less willing to sell the product at all prices. This shifts the supply curve from S_1 to S_2. Since consumer demand is highly elastic, consumers pay the same price as before ($P_1 = P_2$). However, the tax increase causes the producer to net less, or P_3. Since P_3 is substantially lower than the price before the tax, or P_2, producers offer less for sale after the tax is implemented. This is shown in Figure 6.11b in the movement of quantity demanded from Q_1 to Q_2. Since Q_2 is smaller than Q_1, there is also more deadweight loss than we observed in Figure 6.10b. Therefore, the total surplus, or efficiency of the market, is much smaller than before. Comparing the green-shaded areas of Figures 6.10b and 6.11b, you see that the size of the tax revenue continues

FIGURE 6.11

A Tax on Products with Highly Elastic Demand

(a) Before the tax, the producer enjoys the producer surplus (P.S.) noted in red. (b) When consumer demand is highly elastic, consumers pay the same price after the tax as before. But they are worse off because less is produced and sold; the quantity produced moves from Q_1 to Q_2. The result is deadweight loss (D.W.L.), as shown by the yellow triangle in (b). The total surplus, or efficiency of the market, is much smaller than before. The size of the tax revenue (in green) is also noticeably smaller in the market with highly elastic demand.

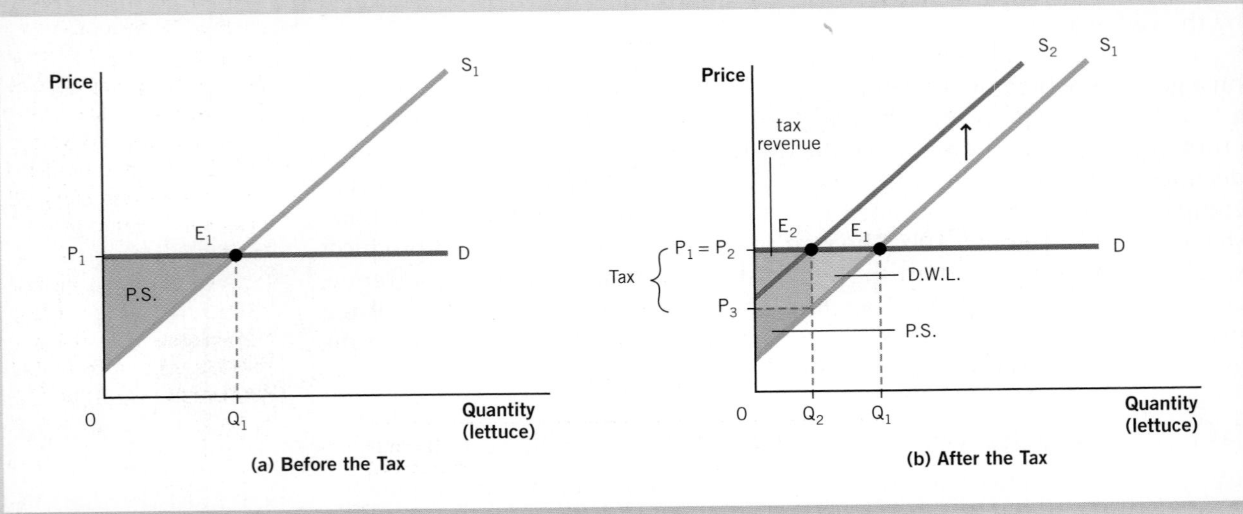

to shrink. There is an important lesson here for policymakers—they should tax goods with relatively inelastic demand. Not only will this lessen the deadweight loss of taxation, but it will also generate larger tax revenues for the government.

So far, we have varied the elasticity of the demand curve while holding the elasticity of the supply curve constant. What would happen if we did the reverse and varied the elasticity of the supply curve while keeping the elasticity of the demand curve constant? It turns out that there is a simple method for determining the incidence and deadweight loss in this case. The incidence of a tax is determined by the relative steepness of the demand curve compared to the supply curve. When the demand curve is steeper (more inelastic) than the supply curve, consumers bear more of the incidence of the tax. When the supply curve is steeper (more inelastic) than the demand curve, suppliers bear more of the incidence of the tax. Also, whenever the supply and/or demand curves are relatively steep, deadweight loss is minimized.

Let's explore an example in which we consider how the elasticity of demand and elasticity of supply interact. Suppose that a $3 per pound tax is placed on shiitake mushrooms, an elastic good. Given the information in Figure 6.12, we will compute the incidence, deadweight loss, and tax revenue from the tax.

Let's start with the incidence of the tax. After the tax is implemented, the market price rises from $7 to $8 per pound. But since sellers must pay $3 to the government, they keep only $5. Tax incidence measures the share of the tax paid by buyers and sellers, so we need to compare the incidence of the tax paid by each party. Since the market price rises by $1 (from $7 to $8), buyers are paying $1 of the $3 tax, or $\frac{1}{3}$. Since the amount the seller keeps falls

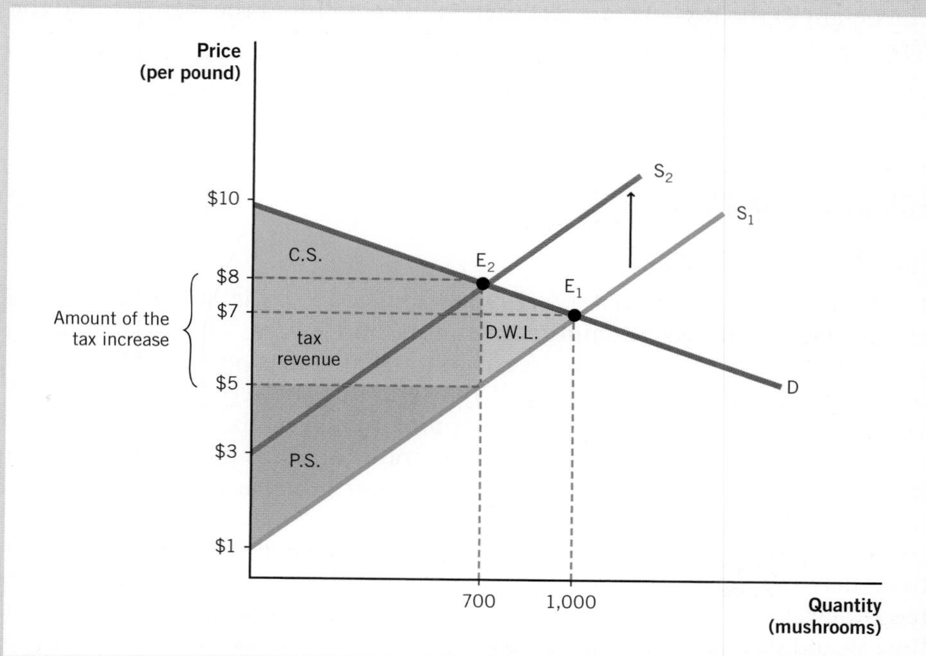

FIGURE 6.12

A Realistic Example
A $3 per pound tax is placed on mushroom suppliers. This drives the equilibrium price up from E_1 ($7) to E_2 ($8). Notice that the price only rises by $1. This means that the consumer picks up $1 of the $3 tax and the seller must pay the remaining $2. Therefore, most of the incidence is borne by the seller. Finally, neither the demand curve nor the supply curve is relatively inelastic, so the amount of deadweight loss (D.W.L.) is large.

How much would you pay per pound for these mushrooms?

by \$2 (from \$7 to \$5), sellers are paying \$2 of the \$3 tax, or $\frac{2}{3}$. Notice that the demand curve is more elastic (flatter) than the supply curve; therefore, sellers have a limited ability to raise price.

Now let's determine the deadweight loss caused by the tax—that is, the decrease in economic activity. This is represented by the decrease in the total surplus found in the yellow triangle in Figure 6.12. In order to compute the amount of the deadweight loss, we need to determine the area of the triangle:

$$\text{The area of a triangle} = \frac{1}{2} \times \text{base} \times \text{height}$$

The triangle in Figure 6.12 is sitting on its side, so its height is 1000 − 700 = 300, and its base is \$8 − \$5 = \$3.

$$\text{Deadweight loss} = \frac{1}{2} \times 300 \times \$3 = \$450$$

Finally, what is the tax revenue generated by the tax? In Figure 6.12, the tax revenue is represented by the green-shaded area, which is a rectangle. We can calculate the tax revenue by determining the area of the rectangle:

$$\text{The area of a rectangle} = \text{base} \times \text{height}$$

The height of the tax-revenue rectangle is the amount of the tax (\$3), and the number of units sold after the tax is 700.

$$\text{Tax revenue} = \$3 \times 700 = \$2{,}100.$$

ECONOMICS IN THE REAL WORLD

The Short-Lived Luxury Tax

The Budget Reconciliation Act of 1990 established a special luxury tax on the sale of new aircraft, yachts, automobiles, furs, and jewelry. The act established a 10% surcharge on new purchases as follows: aircraft over \$500,000; yachts over \$100,000; automobiles over \$25,000; and furs and jewelry over \$10,000. The taxes were expected to generate approximately \$2 billion a year. However, revenue fell far below expectations, and thousands of jobs were lost in each of the affected industries. Within three years, the tax was repealed. Why was the luxury tax such a failure?

When passing the Budget Reconciliation Act, lawmakers failed to consider basic demand elasticity. Because the purchase of a new aircraft, yacht, car, fur, or jewelry is highly discretionary, many wealthy consumers decided that they would buy substitute products that fell below the tax threshold or buy a used product and refurbish it. Therefore, the demand for these luxury goods turned out to be highly elastic. We have seen that when goods with elastic demand are taxed, the resulting tax revenues are small. Moreover, in this example the resulting decrease in purchases was significant. As a result, jobs were lost in the middle of an economic downturn. The combination of low revenues and crippling job losses in these industries was enough to convince Congress to repeal the tax in 1993.

The failed luxury tax is a reminder that the populist idea of taxing the rich is far more difficult to implement than it appears. In simple terms, it is nearly impossible to tax the toys that the rich enjoy because wealthy people can spend their money in so many different ways. In other words, they have options about whether to buy or lease, as well as many good substitutes to choose from. This means that they can, in many cases, avoid paying luxury taxes. ✳

If you were rich, would this be your luxury toy?

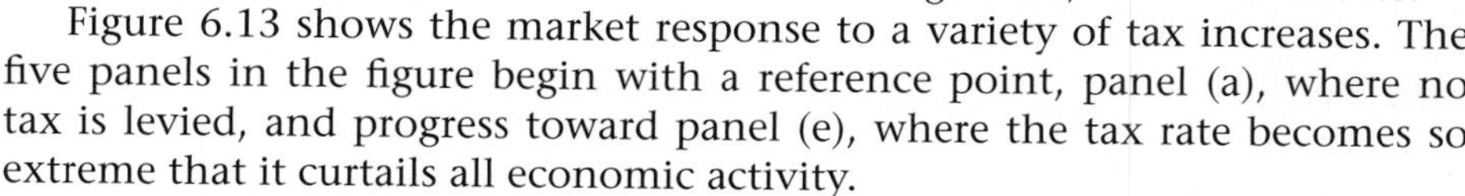

Balancing Deadweight Loss and Tax Revenues

Incentives

Up to this point, we have kept the size of the tax increase constant. This enabled us to examine the impact of the elasticity of demand and supply on deadweight loss and tax revenues. But what happens when a tax is high enough to significantly alter consumer or producer behavior? For instance, in 2002 the Republic of Ireland instituted a tax of 15 euro cents on each plastic bag in order to curb litter and encourage recycling. As a result, consumer use of plastic bags quickly fell by over 90%. Thus, the tax was a major success because the government achieved its goal of curbing litter. In this section, we will consider how consumers respond to taxes of different sizes, and we will determine the relationship among the size of a tax, the deadweight loss, and tax revenues.

Figure 6.13 shows the market response to a variety of tax increases. The five panels in the figure begin with a reference point, panel (a), where no tax is levied, and progress toward panel (e), where the tax rate becomes so extreme that it curtails all economic activity.

Trade-offs

As taxes rise, so do prices. You can trace this rise from (a), where there is no tax and the price is P_1, all the way to (e), where the extreme tax causes the price to rise to P_5. At the same time, deadweight loss (D.W.L.) also rises. You can see this by comparing the sizes of the yellow triangles. The trade-off is striking. Without any taxes, deadweight loss does not occur. But as soon as taxes are in place, the market-equilibrium quantity demanded begins to decline, moving from Q_1 to Q_5. As the number of transactions (quantity demanded) declines, the area of deadweight loss rapidly expands.

When taxes are small, as in Figure 6.13b, the tax revenue (green rectangle) is large relative to the deadweight loss (yellow triangle). However, as we progress through the panels, this relationship slowly reverses. In (c) the size of the tax revenue remains larger than the deadweight loss. However, in (d) the magnitude of the deadweight loss is far greater than the tax revenue. This means that the size of the tax in (d) is creating a significant cost in terms of economic efficiency. Finally, (e) shows an extreme case in which all market activity ceases as a result of the tax. Since nothing is produced and sold, there is no tax revenue.

FIGURE 6.13

Examining Deadweight Loss and Tax Revenues

The panels show that increased taxes result in higher prices. Progressively higher taxes also lead to more deadweight loss (D.W.L.), but higher taxes do not always generate more revenue, as evidenced by the reduction in revenue that occurs when tax rates become too large in panels (d) and (e).

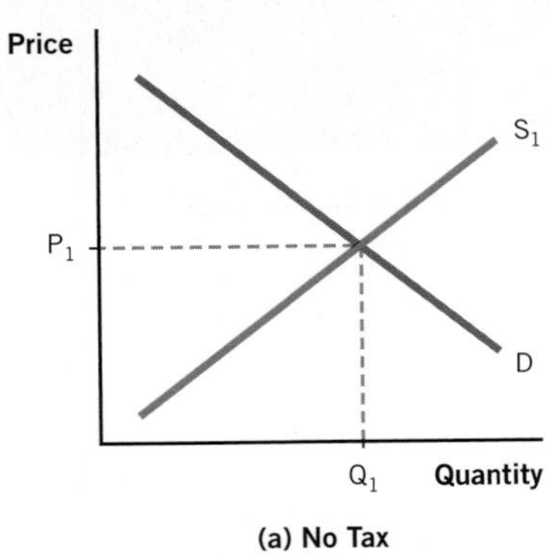

(a) No Tax

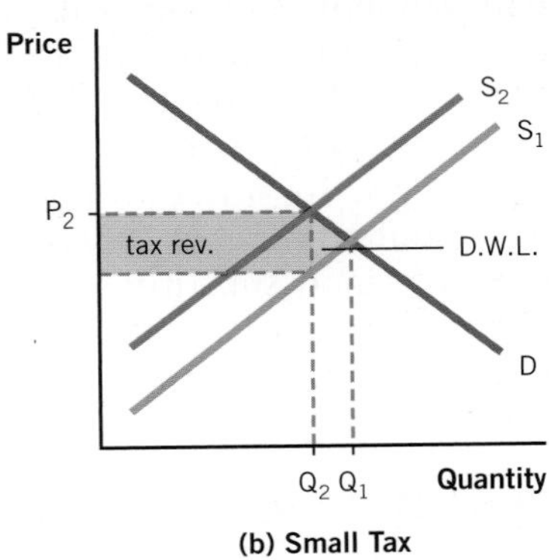

(b) Small Tax

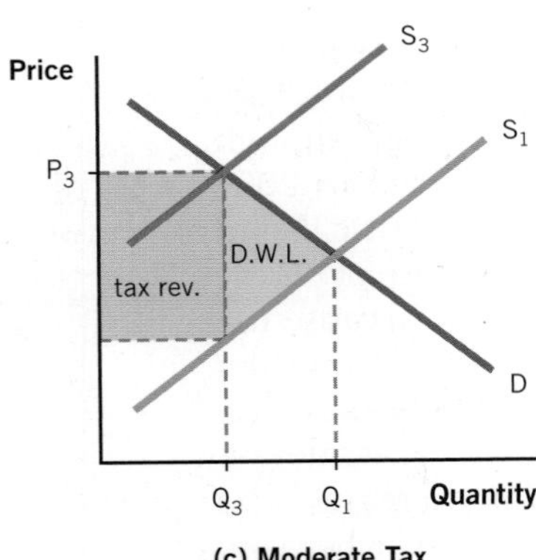

(c) Moderate Tax

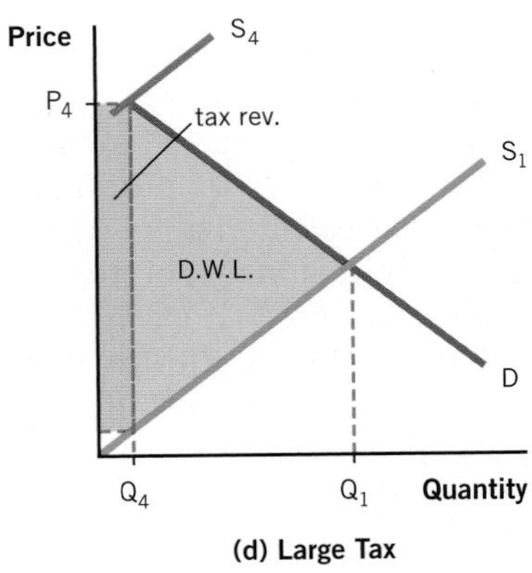

(d) Large Tax

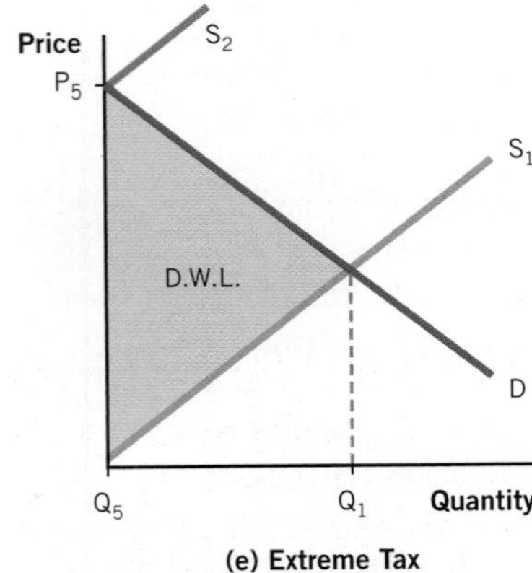

(e) Extreme Tax

SNAPSHOT

Bizarre Taxes

Governments tax their citizens for a variety of reasons. Often it's to raise revenue. Sometimes, taxes are levied to influence citizens' behavior. Occasionally, both of these reasons are in play. These two motivations have led to some very bizarre tax initiatives, as seen below. Though they all seem a bit unusual, these taxes get (or got) paid every single day.

Flush Tax

Maryland's "Flush Tax," a fee added to sewer bills, went up from $2.50 to $5.00 a month in 2012. The tax is paid only by residents who live in the Chesapeake Bay Watershed, and it generates revenue for reducing pollution in Chesapeake Bay.

Bagel Tax

New Yorkers love their bagels and cream cheese from delis. In the state, any bagel that has been sliced or has any form of spread on it (like cream cheese) is subject to a 9% sales tax on prepared food. Any bagel that is purchased "unaltered" is classified as unprepared and is not taxed.

Playing Card Tax

The state of Alabama really doesn't want you playing solitaire. Buyers of playing cards are taxed ten cents per deck, while sellers must pay a $2 annual licensing fee. How much revenue does just a ten-cent tax generate? In 2011, it was almost $90,000.

Tattoo Tax

Arkansas imposes a 6% tax on tattoos and body piercings to discourage this behavior, meaning that the people of Arkansas pay extra when getting inked or pierced.

Window Tax

England passed a tax in 1696 targeting wealthy citizens—the more windows in one's house, the higher the tax. Many homeowners simply bricked over their windows. But they could not seal all of them, and the government did indeed collect revenue.

Blueberry Tax

Maine levies a penny-and-a-half tax per pound on anyone growing, handling, processing, selling, or purchasing the state's delicious wild blueberries. The tax is an effort to make sure that the blueberries are not overharvested.

Maine produces 99% of the wild blueberries consumed in the USA, meaning that blueberry lovers have few substitutes available to avoid paying the tax and that demand is therefore inelastic.

Marylanders are being taxed on a negative externality, which we'll cover in the next chapter.

REVIEW QUESTIONS

- Suppose that because of Alabama's playing card tax, fewer consumers purchase cards and fewer store owners sell them. What is this loss of economic activity called?
- Do you think the New York bagel tax is an effective tool to raise government revenue? Think about how the tax may or may not affect the purchasing behavior of New Yorkers.

PRACTICE WHAT YOU KNOW

Deadweight Loss of Taxation: The Politics of Tax Rates

What is the optimal tax rate?

Imagine that you and two friends are discussing the politics of taxation. One friend, who is fiscally conservative, argues that tax rates are too high. The other friend, who is more progressive, argues that tax rates are too low.

Question: Is it possible that both friends could be right?

Answer: Surprisingly, the answer is yes. When tax rates become extraordinarily high, the amount of deadweight loss dwarfs the amount of tax revenue collected. We observed this in the discussion of the short-lived luxury tax above. Fiscal conservatives often note that taxes inhibit economic activity. They advocate lower tax rates and limited government involvement in the market, preferring to minimize the deadweight loss on economic activity—see panel (b) in Figure 6.13. However, progressives prefer somewhat higher tax rates than fiscal conservatives, since a moderate tax rate—see panel (c)—generates more tax revenue than a small tax does. The additional revenues that moderate tax rates generate can fund more government services. Therefore, a clear trade-off exists between the size of the public sector and market activity. Depending on how you view the value created by markets versus the value added through government provision, there is ample room for disagreement about the best tax policy.

Conclusion

Let's return to the misconception we started with: raising tax rates always generates more tax revenue. That's true up to a point. At low and moderate tax rates, increases do lead to additional tax revenue. However, when tax rates become too high, tax revenues decline as more consumers and producers find ways to avoid paying the tax.

In the first part of this chapter, we learned that society benefits from unregulated markets because they generate the largest possible total surplus. However, society also needs the government to provide an infrastructure for the economy. The tension between economic activity and the amount of government services needed is reflected in tax rates. The taxation of specific goods and services gives rise to a form of market failure called deadweight loss, which causes reduced economic activity. Thus, any intervention in the market requires a deep understanding of how society will respond to the incentives created by the legislation. In addition, unintended consequences can affect the most well-intentioned tax legislation and, if the process is not well thought through, can cause inefficiencies with far-reaching consequences. Of course, this does not mean that taxes are undesirable. Rather, society must balance (1) the need for tax revenues and the programs those revenues help fund, with (2) trade-offs in the market.

Incentives

Trade-offs

ANSWERING THE BIG QUESTIONS

What are consumer surplus and producer surplus?

* Consumer surplus is the difference between the willingness to pay for a good and the price that is paid to get it. Producer surplus is the difference between the willingness to sell a good and the price that the seller receives.
* Total surplus is the sum of consumer and producer surplus that exists in a market.

When is a market efficient?

* Markets maximize consumer and producer surplus, provide goods and services to buyers who value them most, and reward sellers who can produce goods and services at the lowest cost. As a result, markets create the largest amount of total surplus possible.
* Whenever an allocation of resources maximizes total surplus, the result is said to be efficient. However, economists are also interested in the distribution of the surplus. Equity refers to the fairness of the distribution of the benefits among the members of the society.

Why do taxes create deadweight loss?

* Deadweight loss occurs because taxes increase the purchase price, which causes consumers to buy less and producers to supply less. Deadweight loss can be minimized by placing a tax on a good or service that has inelastic demand or supply.
* Economists are also concerned about the incidence of taxation. Incidence refers to the burden of taxation on the party who pays the tax through higher prices, regardless of whom the tax is actually levied on. The incidence is determined by the balance between the elasticity of supply and the elasticity of demand.

ECONOMICS FOR LIFE

Excise Taxes Are Almost Impossible to Avoid

The federal government collected $75 billion in excise taxes in 2011. Excise taxes are placed on many different products, making them almost impossible to avoid. They also have the added advantages of being easy to collect, hard for consumers to detect, and easier to enact politically than other types of taxes. You'll find excise taxes on many everyday household expenses—what you drink, the gasoline you purchase, plane tickets, and much more. Let's add them up.

1. **Gasoline.** 18.3 cents per gallon. This generates $37 billion and helps finance the interstate highway system.
2. **Cigarettes and tobacco.** $1 per pack and up to 40 cents per cigar. This generates $18 billion for the general federal budget.
3. **Air travel.** 7.5% of the base price of the ticket plus $3 per flight segment. This generates $10 billion for the Transportation Security Administration and the Federal Aviation Administration.
4. **Alcohol.** 5 cents per can of beer, 21 cents per bottle of wine, and $2.14 for spirits. This generates $9 billion for the general federal budget.

These four categories account for $74 billion in excise taxes. You could still avoid the taxman with this simple prescription: don't drink, don't travel, and don't smoke. Where does that leave you? Way out in the country somewhere far from civilization. Since you won't be able to travel to a grocery store, you'll need to live off the land, grow your own crops, and hunt or fish.

But there is still one last federal excise tax to go.

5. **Hunting and fishing.** Taxes range from 3 cents for fishing tackle boxes to 11% for archery equipment. This generates $1 billion for fish and wildlife services.

Living off the land and avoiding taxes just got much harder, and that's the whole point. The government taxes products with relatively inelastic demand because most people will still purchase them after the tax is in place. As a result, avoiding excise taxes isn't practical. The best you can do is reduce your tax burden by altering your lifestyle or what you purchase.

Data from Jill Barshay, "The $240-a-Year Bill You Don't Know You're Paying," *Fiscal Times*, Sept. 7, 2011.

Excise taxes are everywhere.

CONCEPTS YOU SHOULD KNOW

consumer surplus (p. 179)
deadweight loss (p. 191)
efficient (p. 185)
equity (p. 187)
excise taxes (p. 188)
incidence (p. 188)
producer surplus (p. 181)
social welfare (p. 184)
total surplus (p. 184)
welfare economics (p. 178)
willingness to pay (p. 178)
willingness to sell (p. 181)

QUESTIONS FOR REVIEW

1. Explain how consumer surplus is derived from the difference between the willingness to pay and the market-equilibrium price.
2. Explain how producer surplus is derived from the difference between the willingness to sell and the market-equilibrium price.
3. Why do economists focus on consumer and producer surplus and not on the possibility of consumer and producer loss? Illustrate your answer on a supply and demand graph.
4. How do economists define efficiency?
5. What type of goods should be taxed in order to minimize deadweight loss?
6. Suppose that the government taxes a good that is very elastic. Illustrate what will happen to the consumer surplus, producer surplus, tax revenue, and deadweight loss on a supply and demand graph.
7. What happens to tax revenues as tax rates increase?

STUDY PROBLEMS (*✱ solved at the end of the section*)

1. A college student enjoys eating pizza. Her willingness to pay for each slice is shown in the following table:

Number of pizza slices	Willingness to pay (per slice)
1	\$6
2	\$5
3	\$4
4	\$3
5	\$2
6	\$1
7	\$0

   a. If pizza slices cost \$3 each, how many slices will she buy? How much consumer surplus will she enjoy?
   b. If the price of slices falls to \$2, how much consumer surplus will she enjoy?

2. A cash-starved town decides to impose a $6 excise tax on T-shirts sold. The following table shows the quantity demanded and the quantity supplied at various prices.

Price per T-shirt	Quantity demanded	Quantity supplied
$19	0	60
$16	10	50
$13	20	40
$10	30	30
$ 7	40	20
$ 4	50	10

   a. What are the equilibrium quantity demanded and the quantity supplied before the tax is implemented? Determine the consumer and producer surplus before the tax.
   b. What are the equilibrium quantity demanded and the quantity supplied after the tax is implemented? Determine the consumer and producer surplus after the tax.
   c. How much tax revenue does the town generate from the tax?

3. Andrew paid $30 to buy a potato cannon, a cylinder that shoots potatoes hundreds of feet. He was willing to pay $45. When Andrew's friend Nick learns that Andrew bought a potato cannon, he asks Andrew if he will sell it for $60, and Andrew agrees. Nick is thrilled, since he would have paid Andrew up to $80 for the cannon. Andrew is also delighted. Determine the consumer surplus from the original purchase and the additional surplus generated by the resale of the cannon.

4. If the government wants to raise tax revenue, which of the following items are good candidates for an excise tax? Why?
   a. granola bars
   b. cigarettes
   c. toilet paper
   d. automobile tires
   e. bird feeders

* 5. If the government wants to minimize the deadweight loss of taxation, which of the following items are good candidates for an excise tax? Why?
   a. bottled water
   b. prescription drugs
   c. oranges
   d. batteries
   e. luxury cars

6. A new medical study indicates that eating blueberries helps prevent cancer. If the demand for blueberries increases, what will happen to the size of the consumer and producer surplus? Illustrate your answer by shifting the demand curve appropriately and labeling the new and old areas of consumer and producer surplus.

7. Use the graph at the top of p. 207 to answer questions a–f.
   a. What area represents consumer surplus before the tax?
   b. What area represents producer surplus before the tax?
   c. What area represents consumer surplus after the tax?
   d. What area represents producer surplus after the tax?
   e. What area represents the tax revenue after the tax?
   f. What area represents the deadweight loss after the tax?

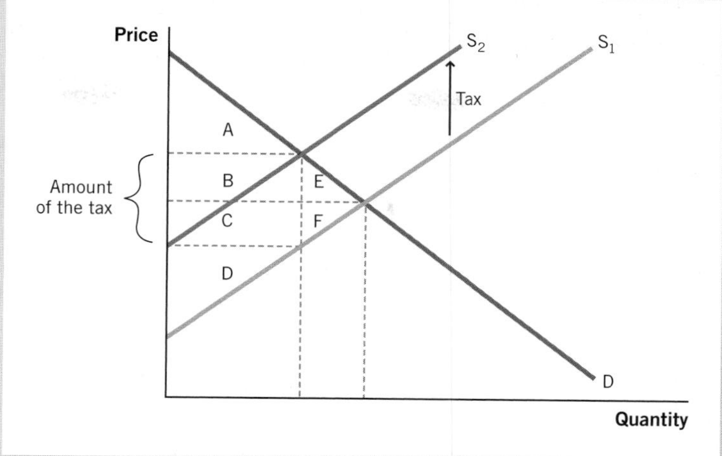

8. The cost of many electronic devices has fallen appreciably since they were first introduced. For instance, computers, cell phones, microwaves, and calculators not only provide more functions but do so at a lower cost. Illustrate the impact of lower production costs on the supply curve. What happens to the size of the consumer and producer surplus? If consumer demand for cell phones is relatively elastic, who is likely to benefit the most from the lower production costs?

9. Suppose that the demand for a concert, Q_D, is represented by the following equation, where P is the price of concert tickets and Q is the number of tickets sold:

$$Q_D = 2500 - 20P$$

The supply of tickets, Q_S, is represented by the equation:

$$Q_S = -500 + 80P$$

   a. Find the equilibrium price and quantity of tickets sold. (**Hint**: Set $Q_D = Q_S$ and solve for the price, P, and then plug the result back into either of the original equations to find Q_E.)
   b. Carefully graph your result in part a.
   c. Calculate the consumer surplus at the equilibrium price and quantity. (**Hint**: Since the area of consumer surplus is a triangle, you will need to use the formula for the area of a triangle [$\frac{1}{2} \times$ base $\times$ height] to solve the problem.)

10. In this chapter, we have focused on the effect of taxes on social welfare. However, governments also subsidize goods, or make them cheaper to buy or sell. How would a $2,000 subsidy on the purchase of a new hybrid vehicle impact the consumer surplus and producer surplus in the hybrid market? Use a supply and demand diagram to illustrate your answer. Does the subsidy create deadweight loss?

* 11. Suppose that a new $50 tax is placed on each cell phone. From the information in the graph below, compute the incidence, deadweight loss, and tax revenue of the tax.

a. What is the incidence of the tax?
b. What is the deadweight loss of the tax?
c. What is the amount of tax revenue generated?

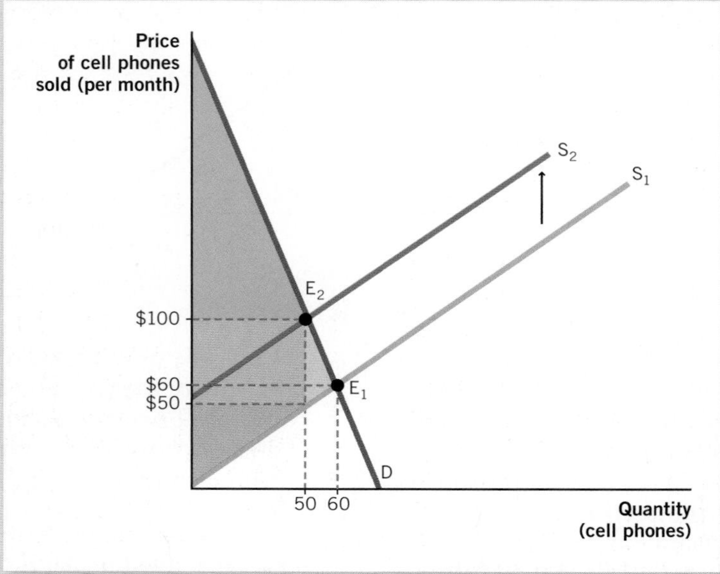

SOLVED PROBLEMS

5. a. Many good substitutes are available: consumers can drink tap water, filtered water, or other healthy beverages instead of bottled water. Therefore, bottled water is not a good candidate for an excise tax.
   b. Taxing prescription drugs will generate significant revenues without reducing sales much, if at all. There is almost no deadweight loss because consumers have few, if any, alternatives. Thus, prescription drugs are a good candidate for an excise tax.
   c. Consumers can select many other fruits to replace oranges. The deadweight loss will be quite large. Therefore, oranges are not a good candidate for an excise tax.
   d. Without batteries, many devices won't work. The lack of substitutes makes demand quite inelastic, so the deadweight loss will be small. Thus, batteries are an excellent candidate for an excise tax.
   e. Wealthy consumers can spend their income in many ways. They do not have to buy luxury cars. As a result, the tax will create a large amount of deadweight loss. Therefore, luxury cars are a poor candidate for an excise tax.

11. a. After the tax is implemented, the market price rises from \$60 to \$100; but since sellers must pay \$50 to the government, they net only \$50. Tax incidence measures the share of the tax paid by buyers and sellers. Since the market price rises by \$40 (from \$60 to \$100), buyers are paying \$40 of the \$50 tax, or $\frac{4}{5}$. Since the net price falls by \$10 (from \$60 to \$50), sellers are paying \$10 of the \$50 tax, or $\frac{1}{5}$.
   b. The deadweight loss is represented by the decrease in the total surplus found in the yellow triangle. In order to compute the amount of the deadweight loss, we need to determine the area inside the triangle. The area of a triangle is found by taking $\frac{1}{2}$ × base × height. The triangle is sitting on its side, so the height of the triangle is 10 (60 − 50) and the base is \$5 (\$10 − \$5). Hence the deadweight loss is $\frac{1}{2}$ × 10 × \$5 = \$25.
   c. The tax revenue is represented by the green-shaded area. You can calculate the tax revenue by multiplying the amount of the tax (\$50) by the number of units sold after the tax (50). This equals \$2,500.

CHAPTER 7

Market Inefficiencies

Externalities and Public Goods

MISCONCEPTION

Pollution should always be eliminated, no matter the cost.

We would all agree that it's important to protect the environment. So when we face pollution and other environmental degradation, should we eliminate it? If your first thought is "yes, always," you're not alone—after all, there's only one Earth, and we'd better get tough on environmental destruction wherever we find it, whatever it takes. Right?

It's tempting to think this way, but as a useful social policy, the prescription comes up short. No one wants to go back to the way it was when businesses were free to dump their waste anywhere, but it is also impractical to eliminate all pollution. Some amount of environmental damage is inevitable whenever we extract resources, manufacture goods, fertilize croplands, or power our electrical grid—all activities that are integral to modern society. But how do we figure out what the "right" level of pollution is, and how do we get there? The answer is to examine the tension between social costs and benefits, and to look carefully at markets to ensure that they are accounting for both.

In the preceding chapters, we have seen that markets provide many benefits and that they work because participants pursue their own self-interests. But sometimes markets need a helping hand. For example, some market exchanges harm innocent bystanders, and others are not efficient because the ownership of property is not clearly defined or actively enforced. To help explain why markets do not always operate efficiently, this chapter will explore two important concepts: *externalities* and the differences between *private* and *public goods.*

What is the most efficient way to deal with pollution?

BIG QUESTIONS

* What are externalities, and how do they affect markets?
* What are private goods and public goods?
* What are the challenges of providing nonexcludable goods?

What Are Externalities, and How Do They Affect Markets?

Externalities are the costs or benefits of a market activity that affect a third party.

We have seen that buyers and sellers benefit from trade. But what about the effects that trade might have on bystanders? **Externalities**, or the costs and benefits of a market activity that affect a third party, can often lead to undesirable consequences. For example, in April 2010, an offshore oil rig in the Gulf of Mexico operated by British Petroleum (BP) exploded, causing millions of barrels of oil to spill into the water. Even though both BP and its customers benefit from the production of oil, others along the Gulf coast had their lives severely disrupted. Industries dependent on high environmental quality, like tourism and fishing, were hit particularly hard by the costs of the spill.

Internal costs are the costs of a market activity paid by an individual participant.

External costs are the costs of a market activity paid by people who are not participants.

Social costs are the internal costs plus the external costs of a market activity.

For a market to work as efficiently as possible, two things must happen. First, each participant must be able to evaluate the **internal costs** of participation—the costs that only the individual participant pays. For example, when we choose to drive somewhere, we typically consider our personal costs—the time it will take to reach our destination, the amount we will pay for gasoline, and what we will pay for routine vehicle maintenance. Second, for a market to work efficiently, the *external costs* must also be paid. **External costs** are costs imposed on people who are not participants in that market. In the case of driving, the congestion and pollution that our cars create are external costs. Economists define **social costs** as a combination of the internal costs and the external costs of a market activity.

In this section, we will consider some of the mechanisms that encourage consumers and producers to account for the social costs of their actions.

The Third-Party Problem

A **third-party problem** occurs when those not directly involved in a market activity nevertheless experience negative or positive externalities.

An externality exists whenever a private cost (or benefit) diverges from a social cost (or benefit). For example, manufacturers who make vehicles and consumers who purchase them benefit from the transaction, but the making and using of those vehicles leads to externalities—including air pollution and traffic congestion—that adversely affect others. A **third-party problem** occurs when those not directly involved in a market activity experience negative or positive externalities.

If a third party is adversely affected, the externality is negative. This occurs when the volume of vehicles on the roads causes air pollution. Negative externalities present a challenge to society because it is difficult to make consumers and producers take responsibility for the full costs of their actions. For example, drivers typically consider only the internal costs (their own costs) of reaching their destination. Likewise, manufacturers would generally prefer to ignore the pollution they create, because addressing the problem would raise their costs without providing them with significant direct benefits.

Incentives

In general, society would benefit if all consumers and producers considered both the internal and external costs of their actions. Since this is not a reasonable expectation, governments design policies that create incentives for firms and people to limit the amount of pollution they emit.

An effort by the city government of Washington, D.C., shows the potential power of this approach. Like many communities throughout the United States, the city instituted a five-cent tax on every plastic bag a consumer picks up at a store. While five cents may not sound like much of a disincentive, shoppers have responded by switching to cloth bags or reusing plastic ones. In Washington, D.C., the city estimated that the number of plastic bags used every month fell from 22.5 million in 2009 to just 3 million in 2010, significantly reducing the amount of plastic waste entering landfills in the process.

Not all externalities are negative, however. Positive externalities also exist. For instance, education creates a large positive externality for society beyond the benefits to individual students, teachers, and support staff. For example, a more knowledgeable workforce benefits employers looking for qualified employees and is more efficient and productive than an uneducated workforce. And because local businesses experience a positive externality from a well-educated local community, they have a stake in the educational process. A good example of the synergy between local business and higher education is Silicon Valley in California, which is home to many high-tech companies and Stanford University. As early as the late nineteenth century, Stanford's leaders felt that the university's mission should include fostering the development of self-sufficient local industry. After World War II, Stanford encouraged faculty and graduates to start their own companies. This led to the creation of Hewlett-Packard, Varian Associates, Bell Labs, and Xerox. A generation later, this nexus of high-tech firms gave birth to leading software and Internet firms like 3Com, Adobe, and Facebook, and—more indirectly—Cisco, Apple, and Google.

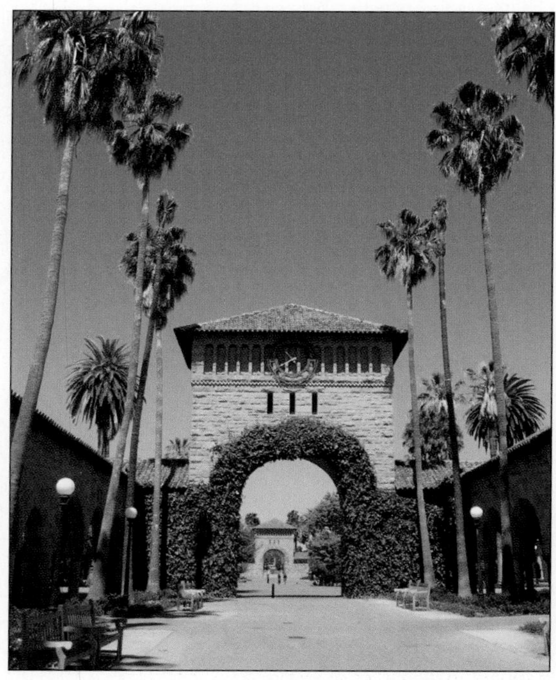
Many of the most successful businesses associated with Stanford have made large donations to the university.

Recognizing the benefits that they received, many of the most successful businesses associated with Stanford have donated large sums to the university. For

When oil refineries are permitted to pollute the environment without additional costs imposed, they are likely to overproduce.

instance, the Hewlett Foundation gave $400 million to Stanford's endowment for the humanities and sciences and for undergraduate education—an act of generosity that highlights the positive externality that Stanford University had on Hewlett-Packard.

Correcting for Negative Externalities

In this section, we explore ways to correct for negative externalities. To do this, we use supply and demand analysis to understand how they affect the market. Let's begin with supply and compare the difference between what market forces produce and what is best for society in the case of an oil refinery. A refinery converts crude oil into gasoline. This complex process generates many negative externalities, including the release of pollutants into the air and the dumping of waste by-products.

The **social optimum** is the price and quantity combination that would exist if there were no externalities.

Figure 7.1 illustrates the contrast between the market equilibrium and the *social optimum* in the case of an oil refinery. The **social optimum** is the price and quantity combination that would exist if there were no externalities. These costs are indicated on the graph by the supply curve $S_{internal}$, which

FIGURE 7.1

Negative Externalities and Social Optimum

When a firm is required to internalize the external costs of production, the supply curve shifts to the left, pollution is reduced, and output falls to the socially optimal level, Q_S. The deadweight loss that occurs from overproduction is eliminated.

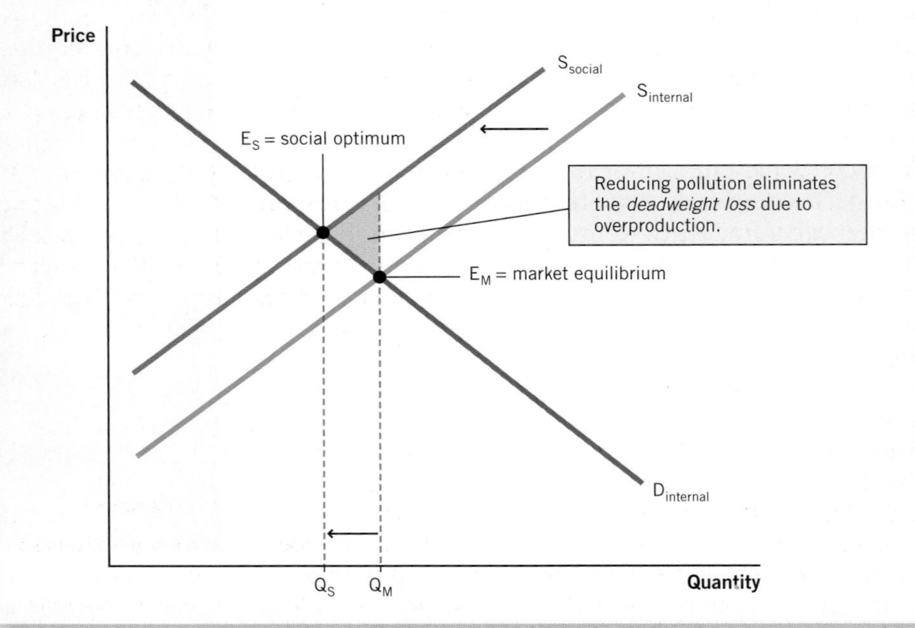

represents how much the oil refiner will produce if it does not have to pay for the negative consequences of its activity. In this situation, the market equilibrium, E_M, accounts only for the internal costs of production.

When a negative externality occurs, the government may be able to restore the social optimum by requiring externality-causing market participants to pay for the cost of their actions. In this case, there are three potential solutions. First, the refiner can be required to install pollution abatement equipment or to change production techniques to reduce emissions and waste by-products. Second, a tax can be levied as a disincentive to produce. Finally, the government can require the firm to pay for any environmental damage it causes. Each solution forces the firm to **internalize** the externality, meaning that the firm must take into account the external costs (or benefits) to society that occur as a result of its actions.

Incentives

An externality is **internalized** when a firm takes into account the external costs (or benefits) to society that occur as a result of its actions.

Having to pay the costs of imposing pollution on others reduces the amount of the pollution-causing activity. This result is evident in the shift of the supply curve to S_{social}. The new supply curve reflects a combination of the internal and external costs of producing the good. Since each corrective measure requires the refiner to spend money to correct the externality, the willingness to sell the good declines, or shifts to the left. The result is a social optimum at a lower quantity, Q_S, than at the market equilibrium quantity demanded, Q_M. The trade-off is clear. We can reduce negative externalities by requiring producers to internalize the externality. However, doing so does not occur without cost. Since the supply curve shifts to the left, the quantity produced will be lower. In the real world, there is always a cost.

Trade-offs

In addition, when an externality occurs, the market equilibrium creates deadweight loss, as shown by the yellow triangle in Figure 7.1. In Chapter 6, we considered deadweight loss in the context of governmental regulation or taxation. These measures, when imposed on efficient markets, created deadweight loss, or a less-than-desirable amount of economic activity. In the case of a negative externality, the market is not efficient because it is not fully capturing the cost of production. Once the government intervenes and requires the firm to internalize the external costs of its production, output falls to the socially optimal level, Q_S, and the deadweight loss from overproduction is eliminated.

Table 7.1 outlines the basic decision-making process that guides private and social decisions. Private decision-makers consider only their internal costs, but society as a whole experiences both internal and external costs. To align the incentives of private decision-makers with the interests of society, we must find mechanisms that encourage the internalization of externalities.

Private and Social Decision Making

Personal decision	Social optimum	The problem	The solution
Based on internal costs	Social costs = internal costs plus external costs	To get consumers and producers to take responsibility for the externalities they create	Encourage consumers and producers to *internalize* externalities.

ECONOMICS IN THE REAL WORLD

Congestion Charges

In 2003, London instituted a congestion charge. Motorists entering the charge zone must pay a flat rate of £10 (approximately $16) between 7 a.m. and 6 p.m. Monday through Friday. A computerized scanner automatically bills the driver, so there is no wait at a toll booth. When the charge was first enacted, it had an immediate effect: the number of vehicles entering the zone fell by a third, the number of riders on public transportation increased by 15%, and bicycle use rose by 30%.

Motorists must pay a flat-rate congestion charge to enter the central business area of London on weekdays.

Why impose a congestion charge? The major goal is to prevent traffic-related delays in densely populated areas. Time is valuable, and when you add up all the hours that people spend stuck in traffic, it's a major loss for the economy! Heavy traffic in cities also exposes lots of people to extra pollution, with costs to health and quality of life. The congestion charge puts a price on these negative externalities and helps to restore the socially optimal level of road usage.

In 2007, Stockholm established a congestion-charge system with a new wrinkle—dynamic pricing. The pricing changes between 6:30 a.m. and 6:30 p.m. During the peak morning and evening commutes, motorists are charged 20 Swedish krona (approximately $3). At other times, the price ratchets down to 15 or even 10 krona. This pricing scheme encourages motorists to enter the city at nonpeak times.

Marginal thinking

Because congestion charges become part of a motorist's internal costs, they cause motorists to weigh the costs and benefits of driving into congested areas. In other words, congestion charges internalize externalities. In London, a flat £10 fee encourages motorists to avoid the zone or find alternative transportation. But once motorists have paid the fee, they do not have an incentive to avoid peak flow times. The variable pricing in Stockholm causes motorists to make marginal adjustments in terms of the time when they drive. This spreads out the traffic flow, as drivers internalize the external costs even more precisely. ✳

Correcting for Positive Externalities

Positive externalities, such as vaccines, have benefits for third parties. As with negative externalities, economists use supply and demand analysis to compare the efficiency of the market with the social optimum. This time, we will focus on the demand curve. Consider a person who gets a flu shot. When the vaccine is administered, the recipient is immunized. This creates an internal benefit. But there is also an external benefit: because the recipient likely will not come down with the flu, fewer other people will catch the flu and become contagious, which helps to protect even those who do not get flu shots. Therefore, we can say that vaccines convey a positive externality to the rest of society.

Why do positive externalities exist in the market? Using our example of flu shots, there is an incentive for people in high-risk groups to get vaccinated for the sake of their own health. In Figure 7.2, we capture this internal benefit in the demand curve labeled $D_{internal}$. However, the market equilibrium, E_M, only accounts for the internal benefits of individuals deciding whether to get vaccinated. In order to maximize the health benefits for everyone, public health officials need to find a way to encourage people to consider the external benefit of their vaccination, too. One way is to issue school vaccination laws, which require that all children entering school provide proof of vaccination against a variety of diseases. The requirement creates a direct incentive for vaccination and produces positive benefits for all members of society by internalizing the externality. The overall effect is that more people get vaccinated early in life, helping to push the market toward the socially optimal number of vaccinations.

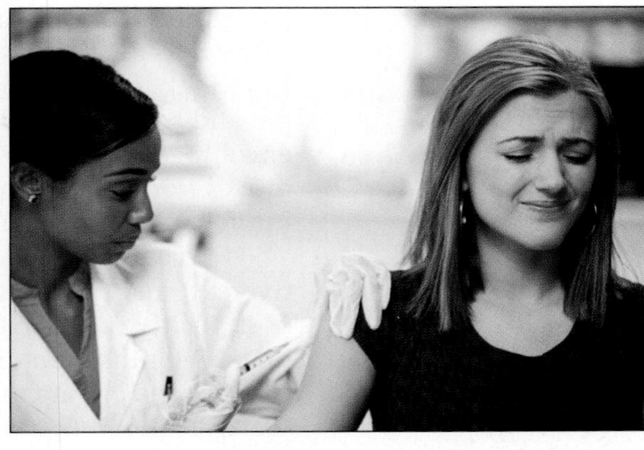

A vaccine offers both individual and social benefits.

Government can also promote the social optimum by encouraging economic activity that helps third parties. For example, it can offer a subsidy, or price break, to encourage more people to get vaccinated. The subsidy acts as a consumption incentive. In fact, governments routinely provide free or reduced-cost vaccines to those most at risk from flu and to their caregivers.

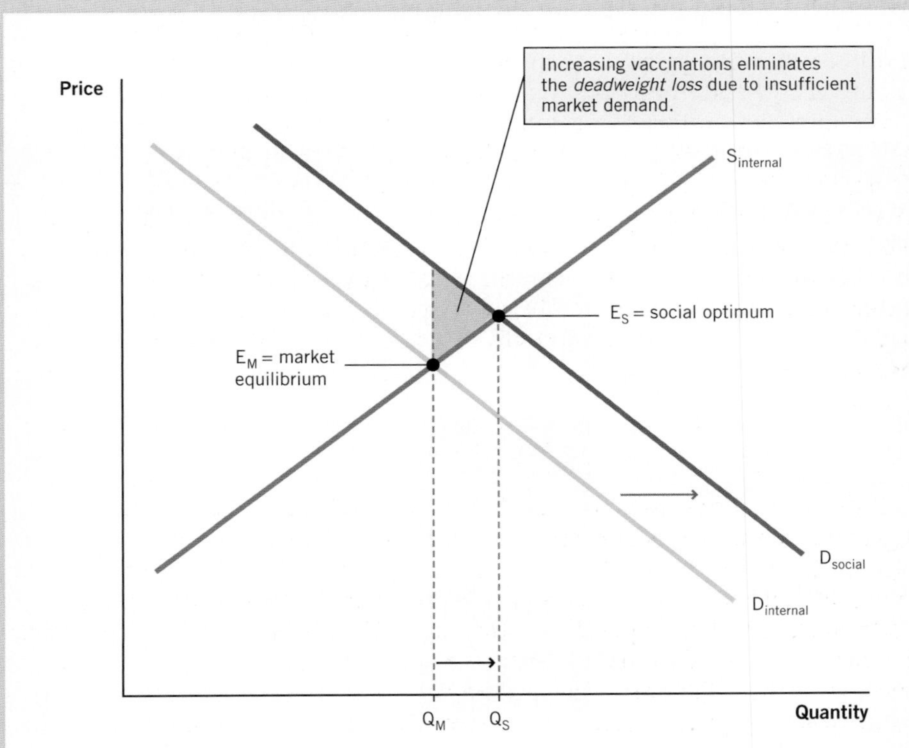

FIGURE 7.2

Positive Externalities and Social Optimum

The subsidy encourages consumers to internalize the externality. As a result, consumption moves from the market equilibrium, Q_M, to a social optimum at a higher quantity, Q_S, vaccinations increase, and the deadweight loss from insufficient market demand is eliminated.

Since the subsidy enables the consumer to spend less money, his or her willingness to get the vaccine increases, shifting the demand curve in Figure 7.2 from $D_{internal}$ to D_{social}. The social demand curve reflects the sum of the internal and social benefits of getting the vaccination. In other words, the subsidy encourages consumers to internalize the externality. As a result, the output moves from the market equilibrium quantity demanded, Q_M, to a social optimum at a higher quantity, Q_S.

We have seen that markets do not handle externalities well. With a negative externality, the market produces too much of a good. But in the case of a positive externality, the market produces too little. In both cases, the market equilibrium creates deadweight loss. When positive externalities are present, the private market is not efficient because it is not fully capturing the social benefits. In other words, the market equilibrium does not maximize the gains for society as a whole. When positive externalities are internalized, the demand curve shifts outward and output rises to the socially optimal level, Q_S. The deadweight loss that results from insufficient market demand, and therefore underproduction, is eliminated.

Table 7.2 summarizes the key characteristics of positive and negative externalities and presents additional examples of each type.

Before moving on, it is worth noting that not all externalities warrant corrective measures. There are times when the size of the externality is negligible and does not justify the cost of increased regulations, charges, taxes, or subsidies that might achieve the social optimum. Since corrective measures also have costs, the presence of externalities does not by itself imply that the government should intervene in the market.

TABLE 7.2

A Summary of Externalities

	Negative externalities	Positive externalities
Definition	Costs borne by third parties	Benefits received by third parties
Examples	Oil refining creates air pollution.	Flu shots prevent the spread of disease.
	Traffic congestion causes all motorists to spend more time on the road waiting.	Education creates a more productive workforce and enables citizens to make more informed decisions for the betterment of society.
	Airports create noise pollution.	Restored historic buildings enable people to enjoy beautiful architectural details.
Corrective measures	Taxes or charges	Subsidies or government provision

PRACTICE WHAT YOU KNOW

Externalities: A New Theater Is Proposed

How would a new theater affect your community?

Suppose that a developer wants to build a new movie theater in your community. It submits a development proposal to the city council.

Question: What negative externalities might the theater generate?

Answer: A successful new theater will likely create traffic congestion. As a result, planning commissions often insist that developers widen nearby streets, install traffic lights, and establish new turning lanes to help traffic flows. These are all negative externalities.

Question: What positive externalities might the theater generate?

Answer: Many local businesses will indirectly benefit from increased activity in the area of the movie theater. Nearby convenience stores, gas stations, restaurants, and shopping areas will all get a boost from the people who attend the movies. Since the demand for these local services will rise, businesses in the area will earn more profits and employ more workers. These are positive externalities.

What Are Private Goods and Public Goods?

The presence of externalities reflects a divide between the way markets operate and the social optimum. Why does this happen? The answer is often related to *property rights*. **Property rights** give the owner the ability to exercise control over a resource. When property rights are not clearly defined, resources can be mistreated. For instance, since no one owns the air, manufacturing firms often emit pollutants into it.

Property rights give the owner the ability to exercise control over a resource.

To understand why firms sometimes overlook their actions' effects on others, we need to examine the role of property rights in market efficiency. When property rights are poorly established or not enforced effectively, the wrong incentives come into play. The difference is apparent when we compare situations in which people do have property rights. Private owners have an incentive to keep their property in good repair because they bear the costs of fixing what they own when it breaks or no longer works properly. For instance, if you own a personal computer, you will probably protect your investment by treating it with care and dealing with any problems immediately. However, if you access a public computer terminal in a campus lab or library and find that it is not working properly, you will most likely ignore the problem and simply look for another computer that is working. The difference between solving the problem and ignoring it is crucial to understanding why property rights matter.

Incentives

Private Property

Private property provides an exclusive right of ownership that allows for the use, and especially the exchange, of property.

One way to minimize externalities is to establish well-defined *private property* rights. **Private property** provides an exclusive right of ownership that allows for the use, and especially the exchange, of property. This creates incentives to maintain, protect, and conserve property and to trade with others. Let's consider these four incentives in the context of automobile ownership.

Incentives

1. *The incentive to maintain property*. Car owners have an incentive to maintain their vehicles. After all, routine maintenance, replacement of worn parts, and repairs keep the vehicle safe and reliable. In addition, a well-maintained car can be sold for more than one in poor condition.
2. *The incentive to protect property*. Owners have an incentive to protect their vehicles from theft or damage. They do this by using alarm systems, locking the doors, and parking in well-lit areas.
3. *The incentive to conserve property*. Car owners also have an incentive to extend the usable life of their automobiles by limiting the number of miles they put on their cars each year.
4. *The incentive to trade with others*. Car owners have an incentive to trade with others because they may profit from the transaction. Suppose someone offers to buy your car for $5,000 and you think it is worth only $3,000. Because you own the car, you can do whatever you want with it. If you decline to sell, you will incur an opportunity cost: you will be giving up $5,000 to keep something you value at $3,000. There is no law requiring you to sell your vehicle, so you *could* keep the car—but you probably won't. Why? Because private property gives you as the owner an incentive to trade for something better in the market.

The incentives to maintain, protect, and conserve property help to ensure that owners keep their private property in good shape. The fourth incentive, to trade with others, helps to ensure that private property is held by the person with the greatest willingness to pay for it.

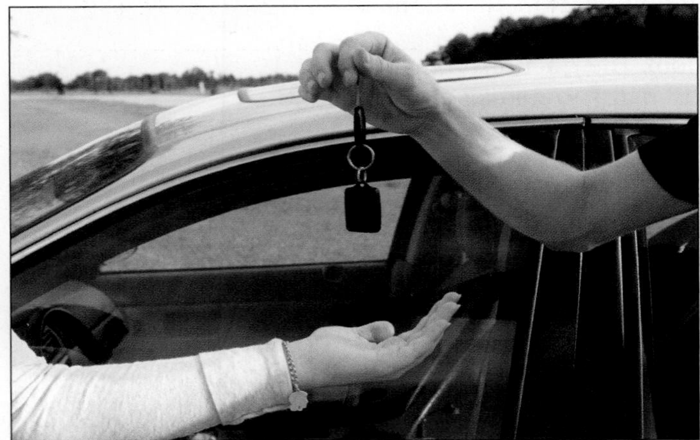
Selling a car benefits both the owner and the buyer.

The Coase Theorem

In 1960, economist Ronald Coase argued that establishing private property rights can close the gap between internal costs and social costs.

Consider an example involving two adjacent landowners, one who raises cattle and another who grows wheat. Because neither landowner has built a fence, the cattle wander onto the neighboring land to eat the wheat. Coase concluded that in this situation both parties are equally responsible for solving the problem. He arrived at that conclusion by considering two possible scenarios.

The first scenario supposes that the wheat farmer has the legal right to expect cattle-free

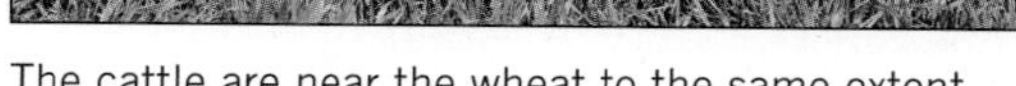

The cattle are near the wheat to the same extent . . .

. . . that the wheat is near the cattle.

fields. In this scenario, the cattle rancher is liable for the damage caused to the wheat farmer. If the damage is costly and the rancher is liable, the rancher will build a fence to keep the cattle in rather than pay for the damage they cause. The fence internalizes the negative externality and forces the rancher to bear the full cost of the damage. If the cost of the damage to the crop is much smaller than the cost of building a fence, then the rancher is more likely to compensate the wheat farmer for his losses rather than build the fence.

What if the wheat farmer does not have the legal right to expect cattle-free fields? In this scenario, the cattle rancher is not liable for any damages his cattle cause to the wheat farmer. If the damage to the nearby wheat field is large and the rancher is *not* liable, the wheat farmer will build a fence to keep the cattle out. The fence internalizes the negative externality and forces the wheat farmer to bear the full cost of the damage. If the amount of damage is smaller than the cost of a fence, the farmer may accept occasional damage as the lower-cost option.

The **Coase theorem** states that if there are no barriers to negotiations, and if property rights are fully specified, interested parties will bargain to correct any externalities that exist.

From comparing these two scenarios, Coase determined that whenever the externality is large enough to justify the expense, the externality gets internalized. As long as the property rights are fully specified (and there are no barriers to negotiations; see below), either the cattle rancher or the wheat farmer will build a fence. The fence will keep the cattle away from the wheat, remove the externality, and prevent the destruction of property.

With this in mind, we can now appreciate the **Coase theorem**, which states that if there are no barriers to negotiations, and if property rights are fully specified, interested parties will bargain privately to correct any externalities. As a result, the assignment of property rights, under the law, gives each party an incentive to internalize any externalities. If it is difficult to bargain, because the costs of reaching an agreement are too high, private parties will

A fence internalizes the externality.

be unable to internalize the externality between themselves. Therefore, the Coase theorem also suggests that private solutions to externality problems are not always possible. This implies a role for government in solving complex externality issues.

To think about the case for a government role, consider the difference between the example of a rancher and a farmer with adjacent land and the example of a community-wide problem such as pollution. With two landowners, a private solution should be possible because the parties can bargain with each other at a low cost. With pollution, though, so many individuals are impacted that the polluting company cannot afford to bargain with each one. Since bargaining costs are high in this case, an intermediary, like the government, may be necessary to ensure that externalities are internalized.

Private and Public Goods

Excludable goods are those that the consumer must purchase before being able to use them.

Rival goods are those that cannot be enjoyed by more than one person at a time.

Private goods have two characteristics: they are both excludable and rival in consumption.

Public goods can be jointly consumed by more than one person, and nonpayers are difficult to exclude.

When we think of private goods, most of us imagine something that we enjoy, like a slice of pizza or a favorite jacket. When we think of public goods, we think of goods provided by the government, like roads, the post office, and the military. The terms "private" and "public" typically imply ownership or production, but that is not how economists categorize private and public goods. To understand the difference between private and public goods, you need to know whether a good is *excludable*, *rival*, or both. An **excludable good** is one that the consumer is required to purchase before being able to use it. A **rival good** is one that cannot be enjoyed by more than one person at a time.

Private Goods

A **private good** is both excludable and rival in consumption. For instance, a slice of pizza is excludable because it must be purchased before you can eat it. Also, a slice of pizza is rival; only one person can eat it. These two characteristics, excludability and rivalry, allow the market to work efficiently in the absence of externalities. Consider a pizza business. The pizzeria bakes pizza pies because it knows it can sell them to consumers. Likewise, consumers are willing to buy pizza because it is a food they enjoy. Since the producer gets to charge a price and the consumer gets to acquire a rival good, the stage is set for mutual gains from trade.

Gains from trade

Public Goods

Markets have no difficulty producing purely private goods, like pizza, since in order to enjoy them you must first purchase them. But when was the last time you paid to see a fireworks display? Hundreds of thousands of people view many of the nation's best displays of fireworks, but only a small percentage of them pay admission to get a preferred seat. Fireworks displays are a **public good** because (1) they can be jointly consumed by more than one person, and (2) it is difficult to exclude nonpayers. Since consumers cannot be easily forced to pay to observe fireworks, they may desire more of the good than is typically supplied. This leads a market economy to underproduce fireworks displays and many other public goods.

Pizza is a private good.

SNAPSHOT

The Case behind the Coase Theorem

The scene is London in the 1870s. The properties of a doctor and candy maker sit next to each other. For years they coexist peacefully, but as both businesses expand, they start using rooms that are separated by only a common wall. The candy-making process in the candy maker's room makes so much noise that the doctor has trouble using his stethoscope. This difficult situation must be resolved. The doctor can file a civil complaint and sue the candy maker, or the two parties can arrive at a solution on their own.

In the Coase Theorem, the clear delineation of property rights is vital to the bargaining of private parties to correct externalities. If it's not clear whether the doctor has the legal right to expect a noise-free office, the case will likely be decided in court.

If the doctor has the right to a noise-free office, the candy maker must decide what's cheaper: build a soundproof wall, or move?

But if the doctor does not have the legal right to expect a noise-free office, then it's his choice to make: build the soundproof wall, or move?

This was an actual case! Want to find out what happened? Search online for "Sturges v. Bridgman."

REVIEW QUESTIONS

- What is the negative externality involved in the case above?
- Suppose an agreement can't be reached and that the doctor files a civil complaint against the candy maker. What possible risks or losses does the doctor face when filing the complaint?

World-renowned violinist Joshua Bell performs incognito in the Washington, D.C., Metro.

Public goods are often underproduced because people can get them without paying for them. Consider Joshua Bell, one of the most famous violinists in the world. The day after giving a concert in Boston where patrons paid $100 a ticket, he decided to reprise the performance in a Washington, D.C., subway station and just ask for donations.* Any passer-by could listen to the music—it did not need to be purchased to be enjoyed. In other words, it was nonexcludable and nonrival in consumption. But because it is impossible for a street musician to force bystanders to pay, it is difficult for the musician—even one as good as Joshua Bell—to make a living. Suppose he draws a large crowd and the music creates $500 worth of enjoyment among the audience. At the end of the performance, he receives a loud round of applause and then motions to the donation basket. A number of people come up and donate, but when he counts up the contributions he finds only $30—the actual amount he earned while playing in the Metro.

A **free-rider problem** occurs whenever someone receives a benefit without having to pay for it.

Why did Joshua Bell receive $30, when he created many times that amount in value? This phenomenon, known as a **free-rider problem,** occurs whenever people receive a benefit they do not need to pay for. A street musician provides a public good and must rely on the generosity of the audience to contribute. If very few people contribute, many potential musicians will not find it worthwhile to perform. We tend to see very few street performances because free-riding lowers the returns. This means that the private equilibrium amount of street performances is undersupplied in comparison to the social optimum. When payment cannot be linked to use, the efficient quantity is not produced.

Street performances are just one example of a public good. National defense, lighthouses, streetlights, clean air, and open-source software such as Mozilla Firefox are other examples. Let's examine national defense since it is a particularly clear example of a public good that is subject to a free-rider problem. All citizens value security, but consider the difficulty of trying to organize and provide adequate national defense through private contributions alone. How could you voluntarily coordinate a missile defense system or get enough people to pay for an aircraft carrier and the personnel to operate it? Society would be underprotected because many people would not voluntarily contribute their fair share of the expense. For this reason, defense expenditures are normally provided by the government and funded by tax revenues. Since most people pay taxes, this almost eliminates the free-rider problem in the context of national defense.

Concerned about security? Only the government is capable of providing adequate national defense.

Most people would agree that government should provide certain public goods for society including, among others, national defense, the interstate high-

* This really happened! The *Washington Post* and Bell conducted an experiment to test the public's reaction to performances of "genius" in unexpected settings. Our discussion here places the event in a hypothetical context—for the real-life result, see Gene Weingarten, "Pearls before Breakfast," *Washington Post,* April 8, 2007.

way system, and medical and science-related research to fight pandemics. In each case, public-sector provision helps to eliminate the free-rider problem and restore the socially optimal level of activity.

"How much would it cost to see a sunset if God decided to charge for it?"

Club Goods and Common-Resource Goods

There are two additional goods that we have not yet introduced. Since *club* and *common-resource goods* have characteristics of both private and public goods, the line between private provision and public provision is often blurred.

Club goods are nonrival in consumption and excludable. Satellite television is an example; it is excludable because you must pay to receive the signal, yet because more than one customer can receive the signal at the same time, it is nonrival in consumption. Since customers who wish to enjoy club goods can be excluded, markets typically provide these goods. However, once a satellite television network is in place, the cost of adding customers is low. Firms are motivated to maximize profits, not the number of people they serve, so the market price is higher and the output is lower than what society desires.

Club goods have two characteristics: they are nonrival in consumption and excludable.

Common-resource goods have two characteristics: they are rival in consumption and nonexcludable.

Common-resource goods are rival in consumption but nonexcludable. King crab in the Bering Sea off Alaska is an example. Since any particular crab can be caught by only one boat crew, the crabs are a rival resource. At the same time, exclusion is not possible because any boat crew that wants to brave the elements can catch crab.

We have seen that the market generally works well for private goods. In the case of public goods, however, the market generally needs a hand. In between, club and common-resource goods illustrate the tension between the private and public provision of many goods and services. Table 7.3 highlights each of the four types of goods we have discussed.

Satellite television is a club good.

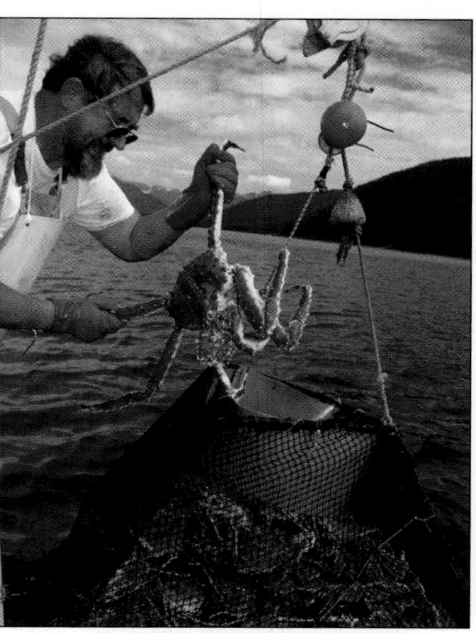

Alaskan king crab is a common-resource good.

TABLE 7.3

The Four Types of Goods

		Consumption	
		Rival	**Nonrival**
Excludable?	**Yes**	*Private goods* are rival and excludable: pizza, watches, automobiles.	*Club goods* are nonrival and excludable: satellite television, education, country clubs.
	No	*Common-resource goods* are rival and not excludable: Alaskan king crab, a large shared popcorn at the movies, congested roads.	*Public goods* are nonrival and not excludable: street performers, defense, tsunami warning systems.

PRACTICE WHAT YOU KNOW

Public Goods: Are Parks Public Goods?

Many goods have the characteristics of a public good, but few goods meet the exact definition.

Question: Are parks public goods?

Answer: We tend to think of public parks as meeting the necessary requirements to be a public good. But not so fast. Have you been to any of America's top national parks on a peak summer weekend? Parks are subject to congestion, which makes them rival. In addition, most national and state parks require an admission fee—translation: they are excludable. Therefore, public parks do not meet the exact definition of a public good.

Not surprisingly, there are many good examples of private parks that maintain, protect, and conserve the environment alongside their public counterparts. For instance, Natural Bridge is a privately owned and operated park in Virginia that preserves a rare natural arch over a small stream. The East Coast is dotted with private parks that predate the establishment of the national park system. Like their public counterparts, private parks are also not public goods.

Natural Bridge in Virginia

What Are the Challenges of Providing Nonexcludable Goods?

Understanding the four types of goods provides a solid foundation for understanding the role of markets and the government in society. Next, we consider some of the special challenges that arise in providing nonexcludable goods.

Cost-Benefit Analysis

To help make decisions about providing public goods, economists turn to **cost-benefit analysis,** a process used to determine whether the benefits of providing a public good outweigh the costs. It is relatively easy to measure the cost of supplying a public good. For instance, if a community puts on a Fourth of July celebration, it will have to pay for the fireworks and labor involved in setting up the event. The costs are a known quantity. But benefits are difficult to quantify. Since people do not need to pay to see the fireworks, it is hard to determine how much benefit the community receives. If asked, people might misrepresent the social benefit in two ways. First, some residents who value the celebration highly might claim that the fireworks bring more benefit than they actually do, because they want the community fireworks to continue. Second, those residents who dislike the crowds and noise might understate the benefit they receive. Since there is no way to know how truthful respondents are when responding to a questionnaire, the actual social benefit of a fireworks show is hard to measure. As a result, there is no way to know the exact amount of consumer and producer surplus generated by a public good like fireworks.

Cost-benefit analysis is a process that economists use to determine whether the benefits of providing a public good outweigh the costs.

Since people do not pay to enjoy public goods, and since the government provides them without charging a direct fee, determining the socially optimal amount typically takes place through the political system. Generally speaking, elected officials do not get reelected if the populace believes that they have not done a good job with their cost-benefit analyses.

Figuring out the social benefit of a fireworks display is quite difficult.

ECONOMICS IN THE REAL WORLD

Internet Piracy

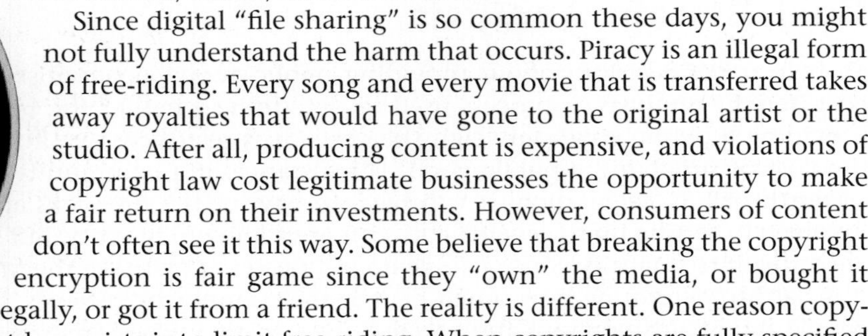

The digitization of media, and the speed with which it can be transferred across the Internet, has made the protection of property rights very difficult. Many countries either do not have strict copyright standards or fail to enforce them. The result is a black market filled with bootlegged copies of movies, music, and other media.

This Boy Scout merit badge signifies a commitment to honoring copyright.

Since digital "file sharing" is so common these days, you might not fully understand the harm that occurs. Piracy is an illegal form of free-riding. Every song and every movie that is transferred takes away royalties that would have gone to the original artist or the studio. After all, producing content is expensive, and violations of copyright law cost legitimate businesses the opportunity to make a fair return on their investments. However, consumers of content don't often see it this way. Some believe that breaking the copyright encryption is fair game since they "own" the media, or bought it legally, or got it from a friend. The reality is different. One reason copyright law exists is to limit free-riding. When copyrights are fully specified and enforced across international boundaries, content creators receive compensation for their efforts. But if copyrights are routinely violated, revenues to private businesses will decline and the amount of music and movies produced will decrease. In the long run, artists will produce less and society will suffer. (For other benefits of copyright law, see Chapter 10.)

Incentives

Think about the relationship between artists and the public as reciprocal: each side needs the other. In that sense, the music you buy or the movie you watch is not a true public good, but more of a club good. Copyright laws make the good excludable but nonrival. This means that some people will always have an incentive to violate copyright law, that artists and studios will insist on ever more complicated encryption methods to protect their interests, and that, for the betterment of society as a whole, the government will have to enforce copyright law to prevent widespread free-riding. ✱

Common Resources and the Tragedy of the Commons

Tragedy of the commons occurs when a good that is rival in consumption but nonexcludable becomes depleted.

Incentives

Common resources often give rise to the **tragedy of the commons**, a situation that occurs when a good that is rival in consumption but nonexcludable becomes depleted. The term "tragedy of the commons" refers to a phenomenon that the ecologist Garrett Hardin wrote about in the magazine *Science* in 1968. Hardin described the hypothetical use of a common pasture shared by local herders in pastoral communities. Herders know that intensively grazed land will be depleted and that this is very likely to happen to common land. Knowing that the pasture will be depleted creates a strong incentive for individual herders to bring their animals to the pasture as much as possible while it is still green, since every other herder will be doing the same thing. Each herder has the same incentive to overgraze, which quickly makes the pasture unusable. The overgrazing is a negative externality brought about by poorly designed incentives and the absence of clearly defined private property rights.

Even though the concept of common ownership sounds ideal, it can be a recipe for resource depletion and economic disaster. Common ownership, unlike public ownership (like national parks) and private ownership, leads to overuse. With a system of private property rights, an owner can seek damages in the court system if his property is damaged or destroyed. But the same cannot be said for common property, since joint ownership allows any party to use the resource as he or she sees fit. This creates incentives to use the resource now rather than later and to neglect it. In short, common property leads to abuse and depletion of the resource.

As already mentioned, the tragedy of the commons also gives rise to negative externalities. Consider global warming. Evidence points to a connection between the amount of CO_2 being emitted into the atmosphere and the Earth's recent warming. This is a negative externality caused by some but borne jointly by everyone. Since large CO_2 emitters consider only the internal costs of their actions and ignore the social costs, the amount of CO_2 released, and the corresponding increase in global warming, is larger than optimal. The air, a common resource, is being "overused" and degraded.

Private property rights give owners an incentive to maintain, protect, and conserve their property and to transfer it if someone else values it more than the current owner does. How are those incentives different under a system of common ownership? Let's examine a real-world example of the tragedy of the commons: the collapse of cod populations off Newfoundland, Canada, in the 1990s. Over the course of three years, cod hauls fell from over 200,000 tons annually to close to zero. Why did the fishing community allow this to happen? The answer: incentives. Let's consider the incentives associated with common property in the context of the cod industry.

Incentives

1. *The incentive to neglect.* No one owns the ocean. As a result, fishing grounds in international waters cannot be protected. Even fishing grounds within territorial waters are problematic since fish do not adhere to political borders. Moreover, the fishing grounds in the North Atlantic cannot be maintained in the same way that one can, say, check the oil in an automobile. The grounds are too large, and population of cod depends on variations in seawater temperature, salinity, and availability of algae and other smaller fish to eat. The idea that individuals or communities could "maintain" a population of cod in this wild environment is highly impractical.
2. *The incentive to overuse.* Each fishing-boat crew would like to maintain a sustainable population of cod to ensure future harvests. However, conservation on the part of one boat is irrelevant since other boats would catch whatever it leaves behind. Since cod are a rival and finite resource, boats have an incentive to harvest as much as they can before another vessel does. With common resources, no one has the authority to define how much of a resource can be used. Maintaining economic activity at a socially optimal level would require the coordination of thousands of vested interests, each of whom could gain by free-riding. For instance, if a socially responsible boat crew (or country) limits its catch in order to protect the species from depletion, this action does not guarantee that rivals will follow suit. Instead, rivals who disregard the socially optimal behavior stand to benefit by overfishing what remains.

Common resources, such as cod, encourage overuse (in this case, overfishing).

Since cod are a common resource, the incentives we discussed under a system of private ownership do not apply. With common property, resources are neglected and overused.

Solutions to the Tragedy of the Commons

Preventing the tragedy of the commons requires planning and coordination. Unfortunately, in our cod example, officials were slow to recognize that there was a problem with Atlantic cod until it was too late to prevent the collapse. Ironically, just as they placed a moratorium on catching northern cod, the collapse of the fish population became an unprecedented disaster for all of Atlantic Canada's fisheries. Cod populations dropped to 1 percent of their former sizes. The collapse of this and many other species led to the loss of 40,000 jobs and over $300 million in income annually. Because the communities in the affected region relied almost exclusively on fishing, this outcome crippled their economies.

The lesson of the northern cod is a powerful reminder that efforts to avoid the tragedy of the commons must begin before a problem develops. For example, king crab populations off the coast of Alaska have fared much better than cod thanks to proactive management. To prevent the collapse of the king crab population, the state and federal governments enforce several regulations. First, the length of the fishing season is limited so that populations have time to recover. Second, there are regulations that limit how much fishing boats can catch. Third, to promote sustainable populations, only adult males are harvested. It is illegal to harvest females and young crabs, since these are necessary for repopulation. It is important to note that without government enforcement of these regulations, the tragedy of the commons would result.

Trade-offs

Cap and trade
is an approach used to curb pollution by creating a system of pollution permits that are traded in an open market.

Can the misuse of a common resource be foreseen and prevented? If predictions of rapid global warming are correct, our analysis points to a number of solutions to minimize the tragedy of commons. Businesses and individuals can be discouraged from producing emissions through carbon taxes. This policy encourages parties to internalize the negative externality, since the tax acts as an internal cost that must be considered before creating carbon pollution.

Another solution, known as *cap and trade*, is an approach to emissions reduction that has received much attention lately. The theory behind **cap and trade** policy is to create the conditions for carbon producers to internalize the externality by establishing markets for tradable emission permits. Under cap and trade, the government sets a *cap*, or limit, on the amount of CO_2 that can be emitted. Businesses and individuals are then issued permits to emit a certain amount of carbon each year. Also, permit owners may *trade* permits. In other words, companies that produce fewer carbon emissions can sell the permits they do not use. By establishing property rights that control emissions permits, cap and trade causes firms to internalize externalities and to seek out methods that lower emissions.

What is the best way to curb global warming?

Global warming is an incredibly complex process, but this is one tangible step that minimizes free-riding, creates the incentives for action, and promotes a socially efficient outcome.

Cap and trade is a good idea in theory. However, there are negative consequences as well. For example, cap and trade presumes that nations can agree on and enforce emissions limits, but such agreements have proven difficult to negotiate. Without an international consensus, nations that adopt cap and trade policies will experience higher production costs, while nations that ignore them—and free-ride in the process—will benefit. Also, since cap and trade ultimately aims to encourage firms to switch sources of energy, the buying and selling of carbon permits can be seen to act as a kind of tax on businesses that produce carbon emissions. As an indicator of what cap and trade is likely to cost U.S. consumers, consider what other countries are already experiencing. Britain's Treasury, for example, estimates that the average family will pay roughly £25 a year in higher electric bills for carbon-cutting programs. As this example shows, with any policy there are always trade-offs to consider.

Trade-offs

ECONOMICS IN THE REAL WORLD

Deforestation in Haiti

Nothing symbolizes the vicious cycle of poverty in Haiti more than the process of deforestation. Haiti was once a lush tropical island covered with pines and broad-leaf trees. Today, only about 3% of the country has tree cover. A number of factors have contributed to this environmental catastrophe: shortsighted logging and agricultural practices, demand for charcoal, rapid population growth, and increased competition for land. Widespread deforestation caused soil erosion, which in turn caused the fertile topsoil layer to wash away. As a result, land that was once lush and productive became desert-like. Eventually, nearly all remaining trees were cut down. Not enough food could be produced on this impoverished land, which contributed to widespread poverty.

Haiti is an extreme example of the tragedy of the commons. Its tragedy is especially striking because Haiti shares the island of Hispaniola with the Dominican Republic. The starkest difference between the two countries is the contrast between the lush tropical landscape of the Dominican Republic and the eroded, deforested Haitian land. In Haiti, the land was a semi-public resource that was overused and abused and therefore subject to the tragedy of the commons. In the Dominican Republic, property rights preserved the environment. What does this mean for Haiti? The nation would not be as poor today if it had relied more on private property rights. ✷

Haiti, seen on the left in this aerial photo, is deforested. The Dominican Republic, seen on the right, has maintained its environment.

PRACTICE WHAT YOU KNOW

Common Resources: President Obama's Inauguration

Approximately two million people filled the National Mall for President Obama's 2009 inauguration. After the celebration concluded, the Mall was strewn with litter and trash.

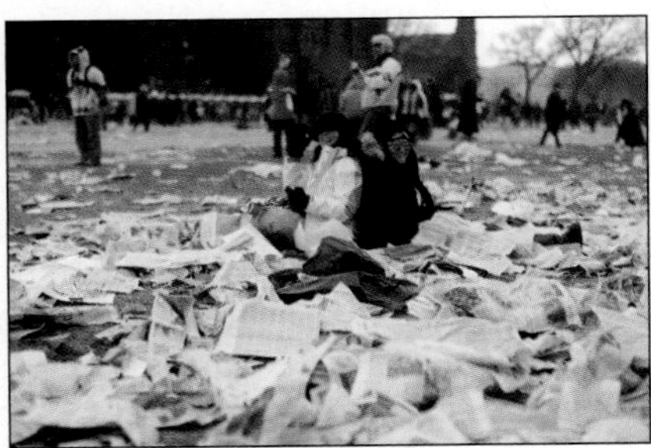

Inaugural trash

Question: What economic concept explains why the National Mall was trashed after the inauguration?

Answer: Attendees brought snacks to eat and newspapers to read during the long wait. They also bought commemorative programs. So a lot of trash was generated. Would you throw trash on your own lawn? Of course not. But otherwise conscientious individuals often don't demonstrate the same concern for public property. As a public space, the National Mall is subject to the *tragedy of the commons*. The grass is often trampled, and trash is very common on normal days. No one person can effectively keep the park green and clean so overuse and littering occurs. When two million people filled the space for Obama's inauguration, the result became much more apparent.

ECONOMICS IN THE MEDIA

Tragedy of the Commons

South Park and Water Parks

If you have ever been to a water park or community pool, you know that the staff checks the pH of the water regularly to make sure it is clean. However, in a 2009 episode of *South Park* everyone is peeing in Pi Pi's water park. The resulting pee concentration ends up being so high that it triggers a disaster-movie-style cataclysm, unleashing a flood of pee that destroys the place.

Why did this happen? Because each person looked at all the water and thought it wouldn't matter if *he* or *she* peed in it. But when *everyone* thought the same way, the water quality was affected. This led to the tragedy of the commons, in which the overall water quality became degraded. Pee-ew.

Thankfully, the real world is cleaner than South Park!

Buying Used Is Good for Your Wallet and for the Environment

ECONOMICS FOR LIFE

Many people waste their hard-earned money buying new. We could do our pocketbooks, and the environment, a favor by opting to buy used instead. Some customers are willing to pay a premium for that "new" feeling—but if you avoid that price markup, you'll save money *and* extend the usable life of a product. Here are a few ideas.

1. **Jewelry**. Would you buy something that immediately depreciates by 70%? When you buy at a retail store, you'll rarely get even a third of it back if you need to sell. If you are comfortable with the risk, search Craigslist or a local pawn shop instead—just be sure to get an appraisal before buying.
2. **Sports equipment**. Let the enthusiasts buy the latest equipment. When they tire of it and switch to the newest golf clubs or buy a new kayak, you can swoop in and make big savings.
3. **Video game consoles and games**. You can buy used and pay half price or less—the catch is you'll have to wait. But the good news is that you'll never find out that your expensive new system isn't as exciting as advertised. Waiting means better information *and* lower prices. That's how you find a good deal.
4. **Automobiles**. The average new car can lose as much as 20% of its value during the first year after purchase. For a $30,000 car, that means $6,000 in depreciation. Let someone else take that hit and buy a used vehicle instead.
5. **Tools and yard equipment**. Think twice before heading to the hardware store. Many tools like hammers and shovels are designed to last—they might not look shiny-new, but they work just as well.

Every time you buy used, you extend the usable life of a product, which helps maximize the value society gets from its resources. This also illustrates the benefit of private property: recall that owners have incentives to (1) maintain, (2) protect, and (3) conserve the products they own so that they can (4) maximize the value when they sell them.

Buying used can save you thousands.

Conclusion

Trade-offs

Although it's tempting to believe that the appropriate response to pollution is always to eliminate it, this is a misconception. As with all things, there are trade-offs. When pollution is taxed or regulated, business activity declines. It's possible to eliminate too much pollution, forcing businesses to shut down, creating undesirably high prices for anything from groceries to gasoline to electronics, and all in all creating an enormous deadweight loss to society. A truly "green" environment without any pollution would leave most people without enough "green" in their wallets. Therefore, the goal for pollution isn't zero—it's an amount that we need to determine through cost-benefit analysis and then attain by correcting market externalities.

In this chapter, we have considered two types of market failure: externalities and public goods. When externalities and public goods exist, the market does not provide the socially optimal amount of the good or service. One solution is to encourage businesses to internalize externalities. This can occur through taxes and regulations that force producers to account for the negative externalities that they create. Similarly, subsidies can spur the production of activities that generate positive externalities. However, not all externalities require active management from the government. Many are too small to matter and do not justify the costs associated with government regulation or taxation.

Likewise, public goods present a challenge for the market. Free-riding leads to the underproduction of goods that are nonrival and nonexcludable. Since not enough is produced privately, one solution is to eliminate free-riding by making involvement compulsory through taxation or regulation. A second problem occurs whenever goods are nonexcludable, as is the case with common-resource goods. This condition gives rise to the tragedy of the commons and can lead to the overuse of valuable resources.

ANSWERING THE BIG QUESTIONS

What are externalities, and how do they affect markets?

* Social costs include the internal costs and the external costs of an activity.
* An externality exists whenever an internal cost (or benefit) diverges from a social cost (or benefit). Third parties experience negative or positive externalities from a market activity.
* When a negative externality exists, government can restore the social optimum by discouraging economic activity that harms third parties. When a positive externality exists, government can restore the social optimum by encouraging economic activity that benefits third parties.
* An externality is internalized when decision-makers must pay for the externality created by their participation in the market.

What are private goods and public goods?

* Private goods, or property, ensures that owners have an incentive to maintain, protect, and conserve their property, and also to trade it to others.
* A public good has two characteristics: it is nonexcludable and nonrival in consumption. This gives rise to the free-rider problem and results in the underproduction of the good in the market.

What are the challenges of providing nonexcludable goods?

* Economists use cost-benefit analysis to determine whether the benefits of providing a type of good outweigh the costs, but benefits can be hard to determine.
* Under a system of common property, the incentive structure causes neglect and overuse.

CONCEPTS YOU SHOULD KNOW

cap and trade (p. 230)
club goods (p. 225)
Coase theorem (p. 221)
common-resource goods (p. 225)
cost-benefit analysis (p. 227)
excludable goods (p. 222)
external costs (p. 212)
externalities (p. 212)
free-rider problem (p. 224)
internal costs (p. 212)
internalize (p. 215)
private goods (p. 222)
private property (p. 220)
property rights (p. 219)
public goods (p. 222)
rival goods (p. 222)
social costs (p. 212)
social optimum (p. 214)
third-party problem (p. 212)
tragedy of the commons (p. 228)

QUESTIONS FOR REVIEW

1. Does the market overproduce or underproduce when third parties enjoy positive externalities? Show your answer on a supply and demand graph.
2. Is it possible to use bargaining to solve externality problems involving many parties? Explain your reasoning.
3. Describe all of the ways that externalities can be internalized.
4. Does cost-benefit analysis apply to public goods only? If yes, why? If not, name situations in which economists would use cost-benefit analysis.
5. What is the tragedy of the commons? Give an example that is not in the textbook.
6. What are the four incentives of private property? How do they differ from the incentives found in common property?
7. Give an example of a good that is nonrival in consumption and nonexcludable. What do economists call goods that share these characteristics?

STUDY PROBLEMS (** solved at the end of the section*)

1. Many cities have noise ordinances that impose especially harsh fines and penalties for early-morning and late-evening disturbances. Explain why this is the case.
2. Indicate whether the following activities create a positive or negative externality:
   a. Late-night road construction begins on a new bridge. As a consequence, traffic is rerouted past your house while the construction takes place.
   b. An excavating company pollutes a local stream with acid rock.
   c. A homeowner whose property backs up on a city park enjoys the sound of kids playing soccer.
   d. A student uses her cell phone discreetly during class.
   e. You and your friends volunteer to plant wildflowers along the local highway.
3. Indicate whether the following are private goods, club goods, common-resource goods, or public goods:
   a. a bacon double cheeseburger
   b. an NHL hockey game between the Detroit Red Wings and Boston Bruins
   c. a Fourth of July fireworks show
   d. a swimming pool
   e. a vaccination for the flu
   f. street lights
4. Can you think of a reason why making cars safer would create negative externalities? Explain.
5. Which of the following activities give rise to the free-rider problem?
   a. recycling programs
   b. biking
   c. studying for an exam
   d. riding a bus

* 6. The students at a crowded university have trouble waking up before 10 a.m., and most work jobs after 3 p.m. As a result, there is a great deal of demand for classes between 10 a.m. and 3 p.m., and classes before and after those hours are rarely full. To make matters worse, the university has a limited amount of classroom space and faculty. This means that not every student can take classes during the most desirable times. Building new classrooms and hiring more faculty are not options. The administration asks for your advice about the best way to solve the problem of demand during the peak class hours. What advice would you give?

7. Two roommates are opposites. One enjoys playing Modern Warfare with his friends all night. The other likes to get to bed early for a full eight hours of sleep. If Coase is right, the roommates have an incentive to solve the noise externality issue themselves. Name at least two solutions that will internalize, or eliminate, the externality.

* 8. Two companies, Toxic Waste Management and Sludge Industries, both pollute a nearby lake. Each firm dumps 1,000 gallons of goo into the lake every day. As a consequence, the lake has lost its clarity and the fish are dying. Local residents want to see the lake restored. But Toxic Waste's production process depends heavily on being able to dump the goo into the lake. It would cost Toxic Waste $10 per gallon to clean up the goo it generates. Sludge can clean up its goo at a cost of $2 per gallon.

   a. If the local government cuts the legal goo emissions in half for each firm, what are the costs to each firm to comply with the law? What is the total cost to both firms in meeting the goo-emissions standard?
   b. Another way of cutting goo emissions in half is to assign each firm tradable pollution permits that allow 500 gallons of goo to be dumped into the lake every day. Under this approach, will each firm still dump 500 gallons of goo? Why or why not?

9. A study finds that leaf blowers make too much noise, so the government imposes a $10 tax on the sale of every unit to correct for the social cost of the noise pollution. The tax completely internalizes the externality. Before the corrective tax, Blown Away Manufacturing regularly sold blowers for $100. After the tax is in place, the consumer price for leaf blowers rises to $105.

   a. Describe the impact of the tax on the number of leaf blowers sold.
   b. What is the socially optimal price to the consumer?
   c. What is the private market price?
   d. What net price is Blown Away receiving after it pays the tax?

10. In most areas, developers are required to submit environmental impact studies before work can begin on new construction projects. Suppose that a commercial developer wants to build a new shopping center on an environmentally protected piece of property that is home to a rare three-eyed toad. The shopping complex, if approved by the local planning commission, will cover ten acres. The planning commission wants the construction to go forward since that means additional jobs for the local community, but it also wants to be environmentally responsible. One member of the commission suggests that the developer relocate the toads. She describes the relocation process as follows: "The developer builds the shopping mall and agrees to create ten acres of artificial toad habitat elsewhere." Will this proposed solution make the builder internalize the externality? Explain.

SOLVED PROBLEMS

6. A flat-fee congestion charge is a good start, since this would reduce the quantity demanded between 10 a.m. and 3 p.m., but such a fee is a blunt instrument. Making the congestion charge dynamic (or varying the price by the hour) will encourage students to move outside the window with the most popular class times in order to pay less. For instance, classes between 11 a.m. and 2 p.m. could have the highest fee. Classes between 10 and 11 a.m. and between 2 and 3 p.m. would be slightly discounted. Classes between 9 and 10 a.m. and between 3 and 4 p.m. would be cheaper still, and those earlier than 9 a.m. and after 4 p.m. would be the cheapest. By altering the price of different class times, the university would be able to offer classes at less popular times and fill them up regularly, thus efficiently using its existing resources.

8\. a. If the local government cuts the legal goo emissions in half for each firm, Toxic Waste will cut its goo by 500 gallons at a cost of \$10 per gallon, for a total cost of \$5,000. Sludge Industries will cut its goo by 500 gallons; at \$2 per gallon, the cost is \$1,000. The total cost to both firms in meeting the goo-emissions standard is \$5,000 + \$1,000 = \$6,000.

b. It costs Toxic Waste \$10 per gallon to clean up its goo. It is therefore more efficient for Toxic to buy all 500 permits from Sludge—which enables Toxic to dump an additional 500 gallons in the lake and saves the company \$5,000. At the same time, Sludge could not dump any goo in the lake. Since it costs Sludge \$2 per gallon to clean up its goo, it will have to pay \$1,000. Since Toxic is saving more than it costs Sludge to clean up the goo, the two sides have an incentive to trade the permits.

LOSS
PROFIT

PART

3

The Theory of THE FIRM

CHAPTER

8 Business Costs and Production

MISCONCEPTION

Larger firms have lower costs than their smaller competitors do. Walmart, the nation's largest retailer, leverages its size to get price breaks on bulk purchases from its suppliers. People commonly believe that this kind of leverage enables larger firms to operate at lower costs than smaller firms do. This is often true; large firms also have broader distribution networks, and they benefit from more specialization and automation compared to their smaller competitors. However, not all industries enjoy lower costs with additional sales the way retailers do. And even Walmart, known for its very low prices, can be undercut by online outlets that have still lower costs and, therefore, better prices. This means that larger firms do not always have the lowest cost.

More generally, in any industry where transportation and advertising costs are high, smaller localized firms are not always at a disadvantage in terms of pricing. In fact, they often have the edge. For instance, in most college towns you will find many pizza shops—the national brands (Pizza Hut, Papa John's, Domino's) and the local shops. Often, the local shop is the one with the cheapest pizza special, while the name brands charge more. By the end of this chapter, you will be able to appreciate the importance of cost and understand why smaller and more nimble firms are sometimes able to undercut the prices of larger companies.

We begin the chapter with a rigorous examination of costs and how they relate to production. After we understand the basics, we will consider how firms can keep their costs low in the long run by choosing a scale of operation that best suits their needs.

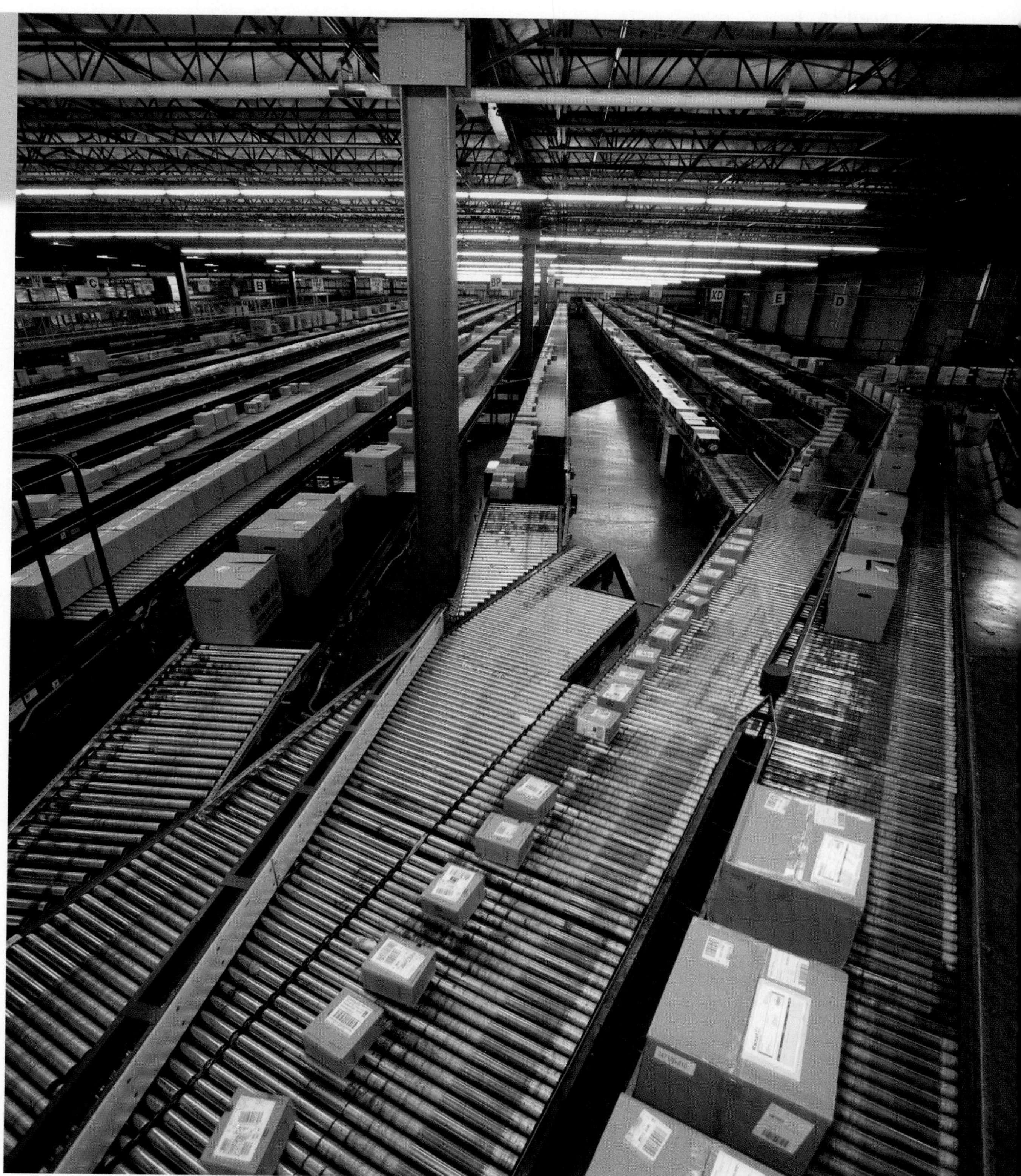

A Walmart distribution center speeds goods to its stores.

BIG QUESTIONS

- **How are profits and losses calculated?**
- **How much should a firm produce?**
- **What costs do firms consider in the short run and the long run?**

Profits and **losses** are determined by calculating the difference between expenses and revenues.

Total revenue is the amount a firm receives from the sale of the goods and services it produces.

Total cost is the amount a firm spends in order to produce the goods and services it produces.

How Are Profits and Losses Calculated?

To determine the potential profits of a business, the first step is to look at how much it will cost to run it. Consider a McDonald's restaurant. While you are probably familiar with the products McDonald's sells, you may not know how an individual franchise operates. For one thing, the manager at a McDonald's must decide how many workers to hire and how many to assign to each shift. Other managerial decisions involve the equipment needed and what supplies to have on hand each day—everything from hamburger patties to paper napkins. In fact, behind each purchase a consumer makes at McDonald's there is a complicated symphony of delivery trucks, workers, and managers.

For a company to be profitable, it is not enough to provide products that consumers want. It must simultaneously manage its costs. In this section, we will discuss how profits and costs are calculated.

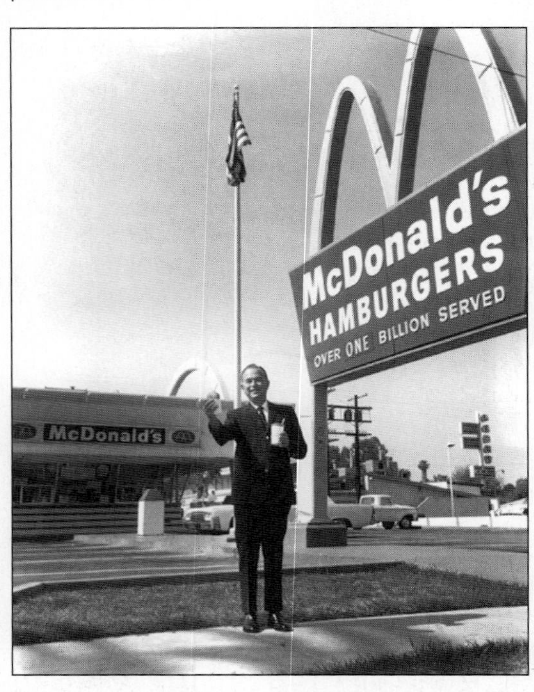

The first McDonald's—much like the one pictured here—opened in San Bernardino, California, in 1940.

Calculating Profit and Loss

The simplest way to determine **profit** or **loss** is to calculate the difference between expenses and revenues. Losses occur whenever total revenue is less than total cost. The **total revenue** of a business is the amount the firm receives from the sale of the goods and services it produces. In the case of McDonald's, the total revenue is determined on the basis of the number of items sold and their prices. **Total cost** is the amount that a firm spends in order to produce the goods and services it sells. This is determined by adding the individual costs of the resources used in producing the goods for sale. We can express this relationship as an equation:

(Equation 8.1) $$\text{Profit (or loss)} = \text{total revenue} - \text{total cost}$$

To calculate total revenue, we look at the dollar amount that the business earns over a specific period. For instance, suppose that in a given day McDonald's sells 1,000 hamburgers for $1.00 each, 500 orders of large fries for $2.00 each, and 100 shakes for $2.50 each. The total revenue is the sum of all of these values, or $2,250. The profit is therefore $2,250 (total revenue) minus the total cost.

Calculating costs, however, is a little more complicated than calculating revenue; we don't simply tally the cost of making each hamburger, order of large fries, and shake. Total cost has two parts—one that is visible and one that is largely invisible. In the next section, we will see that determining total costs is part art and part science.

Explicit Costs and Implicit Costs

Economists break costs into two components: *explicit costs* and *implicit costs*. **Explicit costs** are tangible out-of-pocket expenses. To calculate explicit costs, we add every expense incurred to run the business. For example, in the case of a McDonald's franchise, the weekly supply of hamburger patties is one explicit cost; the owner receives a bill from the meat supplier and has to pay it. **Implicit costs** are the opportunity costs of doing business.

Explicit costs are tangible out-of-pocket expenses.

Implicit costs are the opportunity costs of doing business.

Let's consider an example. Purchasing a McDonald's franchise costs about one million dollars; this is an explicit cost. However, there is also a high opportunity cost—the next-best possibility for investing a million dollars. That money could have earned interest in a bank, been used to open a different business, or been invested in the stock market. Each alternative is an implicit cost.

Implicit costs are hard to calculate and easy to miss. For example, it is difficult to determine how much an investor could have earned from an alternative activity. Is the opportunity cost the 3% interest he might have earned by placing the money in a bank, the 10% he might have hoped to earn in the stock market, or the 15% he might have gained by investing in a different business? We can be sure that there is an opportunity cost for owner-provided capital, but we can never know exactly how much that might be.

In addition to the opportunity cost of capital, implicit costs include the opportunity cost of the owner's labor. Often, business owners do not pay themselves a direct salary. However, since they could have been working somewhere else, it is reasonable to consider the fair value of the owner's time—income

TABLE 8.1

Examples of a Firm's Explicit and Implicit Costs

Explicit costs	Implicit costs
The electricity bill	The labor of an owner who works for the company but does not draw a salary
Advertising in the local newspaper	The capital invested in the business
Employee wages	The use of the owner's car, computer, or other personal equipment to conduct company business

the owner could have earned by working elsewhere—as part of the business's costs.

To fully account for all the costs of doing business, you must calculate the explicit costs, determine the implicit costs, and add them together:

(Equation 8.2)

$$\text{Total cost} = \text{explicit costs} + \text{implicit costs}$$

A simple way of thinking about the distinction between explicit costs and implicit costs is to consider someone who wants to build a bookcase. Suppose that John purchases $30 in materials and takes half a day off from work, where he normally earns $12 an hour. After four hours, he completes the bookcase. His explicit costs are $30, but his total cost is much higher because he also gave up four hours of work at $12 an hour. His implicit cost is therefore $48. When we add the explicit cost ($30) and the implicit cost ($48), we get John's total cost ($78).

Table 8.1 shows examples of a firm's implicit and explicit costs.

Accounting Profit versus Economic Profit

Accounting profit is calculated by subtracting the explicit costs from total revenue.

Now that you know about explicit and implicit costs, we can refine our definition of profit. In fact, there are two types of profit—*accounting profit* and *economic profit*.

A firm's **accounting profit** is calculated by subtracting only the explicit costs from total revenue. Accounting figures permeate company reports, quarterly and annual statements, and the media.

(Equation 8.3)

$$\textbf{Accounting profit} = \text{total revenues} - \text{explicit costs}$$

Economic profit is calculated by subtracting both the explicit and the implicit costs of business from total revenue.

As you can see, accounting profit does not take into account the implicit costs of doing business. To calculate the full cost of doing business, we need to consider both implicit and explicit costs. This will yield a firm's *economic profit*. **Economic profit** is calculated by subtracting both the explicit and the

TABLE 8.2

Historical Rates of Return in Stocks, Bonds, and Savings Accounts

Financial instrument	Historical average rate of return since 1928 (adjusted for inflation)
Stocks	6%
Bonds	3%
Savings account at a financial institution	2%

Source: Federal Reserve database in St. Louis (FRED) and author's adjustments. Data from 1928–2011.

implicit costs of business from total revenue. Economic profit gives a more complete assessment of how a firm is doing.

$$\textbf{Economic profit} = \text{total revenues} - (\text{explicit costs} + \text{implicit costs}) \qquad \text{(Equation 8.4)}$$

Simplifying the equation above gives us:

$$\textbf{Economic profit} = \text{accounting profit} - \text{implicit costs} \qquad \text{(Equation 8.5)}$$

Therefore, economic profit is always less than accounting profit.

The difference in accounting profits among various types of firms can be misleading. For instance, if a company with $1 billion in assets reports an annual profit of $10 million, we might think it is doing well. After all, wouldn't you be happy to make $10 million in a year? However, that $10 million is only 1% of the $1 billion the company holds in assets. As you can see in Table 8.2, a 1% return is far less than the typical return available in a number of other places, including the stock market, bonds, or a savings account at a financial institution.

If the return on $1 billion in assets is low compared to what an investor can expect to make elsewhere, the firm with the $10 million accounting profit actually has a negative economic profit. For instance, if the firm had invested the $1 billion in a savings account, according to Table 8.2 it would have earned 2% on $1 billion—that is, $20 million. That would have yielded an economic profit of:

$$\begin{aligned}\textbf{Economic profit} &= \text{accounting profit} - \text{implicit costs}\\ &= \$10 \text{ million} - \$20 \text{ million}\\ &= -\$10 \text{ million}\end{aligned}$$

As you can see, economic profit is never misleading. If a business has an economic profit, its revenues are larger than the combination of its explicit and implicit costs. The difficulty in determining economic profit lies in calculating the tangible value of implicit costs.

PRACTICE WHAT YOU KNOW

Accounting Profit versus Economic Profit: Calculating Summer Job Profits

How much economic profit do you make from painting?

Kyle is a college student who works during the summers to pay for tuition. Last summer he worked at a fast-food restaurant and earned $2,500. This summer he is working as a painter and will earn $4,000. To do the painting job, Kyle had to spend $200 on supplies.

Question: What is Kyle's accounting profit?

Answer: Accounting profit = total revenues − explicit cost
= $4,000 − $200 = $3,800

Question: If working at the fast-food restaurant was Kyle's next-best alternative, how much economic profit will Kyle earn from painting?

Answer: To calculate economic profit, we need to subtract the explicit and implicit costs from the total revenue. Kyle's total revenue from painting will be $4,000. His explicit costs are $200 for supplies, and his implicit cost is $2,500—the salary he would have earned in the fast-food restaurant. So:

Economic profit = total revenues − (explicit cost + implicit cost)
= $4,000 − ($200 + $2,500) = $1,300

Kyle's economic profit will be $1,300.

Question: Suppose that Kyle can get an internship at an investment banking firm. The internship provides a stipend of $3,000 and tangible work experience that will help him get a job after graduation. Should Kyle take the painting job or the internship?

Answer: The implicit costs have changed because Kyle now has to consider the $3,000 stipend and the increased chance of securing a job after graduation versus what he can make painting houses. Calculation of economic profit from painting is now:

Economic profit = $4,000 − ($200 + $3,000) = $800

But this number is incomplete. There is also the value of the internship experience, so at this point his economic profit from painting would be only $800. If Kyle wants to work in investment banking after graduation, then this is a no-brainer. He should take the internship—that is, unless some investment banks value painting houses more than work experience!

How Much Should a Firm Produce?

Every business must decide how much to produce. In this section, we describe the factors that determine output, and we explain how firms use inputs to maximize their production. Since it is possible for a firm to produce too little or too much, we must also consider when a firm should stop production.

The Production Function

For a firm to earn an economic profit, it must produce a product, known as its **output**, that consumers want. It must also control its costs. To accomplish this, the firm must use resources efficiently. There are three primary components of output, known as the **factors of production**: labor, land, and capital. Each factor of production is an input, or a resource used in the production process, to generate the firm's output. Labor consists of the workers, land consists of the geographic location used in production, and capital consists of all the resources that the workers use to create the final product. Consider McDonald's as an example. The labor input includes managers, cashiers, cooks, and janitorial staff. The land input includes the land on which the McDonald's building sits. And the capital input includes the building itself, the equipment used, the parking lot, the signs, and all the hamburger patties, buns, fries, ketchup, and other foodstuffs.

Output is the production the firm creates.

Factors of production are the inputs (labor, land, and capital) used in producing goods and services.

To keep costs down in the production process, a firm needs to find the right mix of these inputs. The **production function** describes the relationship between the inputs a firm uses and the output it creates. As we saw at the beginning of the chapter, the manager of a McDonald's must make many decisions about inputs. If she hires too little labor, some of the land and capital will be underutilized. Likewise, with too many workers and not enough land or capital, some workers will not have enough to do to stay busy. For example, suppose that only a single worker shows up at McDonald's one day. This employee will have to do all the cooking; bag up the meals; handle the register, the drive-thru, and the drinks; and clean the tables. This single worker, no matter how productive, will not be able to keep up with demand. Hungry customers will grow tired of waiting and take their business elsewhere—maybe for good!

The **production function** describes the relationship between inputs a firm uses and the output it creates.

When a second worker shows up, the two employees can begin to specialize at what they do well. Recall that specialization and comparative advantage lead to higher levels of output (see Chapter 2). Therefore, individual workers will be assigned to tasks that match their skills. For example, one worker can take the orders, fill the bags, and get the drinks. The other can work the grill area and drive-thru. When a third worker comes on, the specialization process can extend

McDonald's needs the correct amount of labor to maximize its output.

even further. This specialization and division of labor is key to the way McDonald's operates. Production per worker expands as long as additional workers become more specialized and there are enough capital resources to keep each worker occupied.

When only a few workers share capital resources, the resources that each worker needs are readily available. But what happens when the restaurant is very busy? The manager can hire more staff for the busiest shifts, but the amount of space for cooking and the number of cash registers, drink dispensers, and tables in the seating area are fixed. Because the added employees have less capital to work with, beyond a certain point the additional labor will not continue to increase the restaurant's productivity at the same rate as it did at first. You might recognize this situation if you have ever gone into a fast-food restaurant at lunchtime. Even though the space behind the counter bustles with busy employees, they can't keep up with the orders. Only so many meals can be produced in a short time and in a fixed space; some customers have to wait.

The restaurant must also maintain an adequate supply of materials. If a shipment is late and the restaurant runs out of hamburger patties, the shortage will impact sales. The manager must therefore be able to (1) decide how many workers to hire for each shift, and (2) manage the inventory of supplies to avoid shortages.

Marginal thinking

Marginal product is the change in output associated with one additional unit of an input.

Let's look more closely at the manager's decision about how many workers to hire. On the left side of Figure 8.1, we see what happens when workers are added, one by one. When the manager adds one worker, output goes from 0 meals to 5 meals. Going from one worker to two workers increases total output to 15 meals. This means that a second worker has increased the number of meals produced from 5 to 15, or an increase of 10 meals. This increase in output is the **marginal product**, which is the change in output associated with one additional unit of an input. In this case, the change in output (10 additional meals) divided by the increase in input (1 worker) gives us a marginal product of 10 ÷ 1, or 10. Since the table in Figure 8.1 adds one worker at a time, the marginal product is just the increase in output shown in the third column.

Looking down the three columns, we see that after the first three workers the rate of increase in the marginal product slows down. But the total output continues to expand, and it keeps growing through 8 workers. This occurs because the gains from specialization are slowly declining. By the ninth worker (going from 8 to 9), we see a negative marginal product. Once the cash registers, drive-thru, grill area, and other service stations are fully staffed, there is not much for an extra worker to do. Eventually, extra workers will get in the way or distract other workers from completing their tasks.

The graphs on the right side of Figure 8.1 show (a) total output and (b) marginal product of labor. The graph of total output in (a) uses data from the second column of the table. As the number of workers goes from 0 to 3 on the *x* axis, total output rises at an increasing rate from 0 to 30. The slope of the total output curve rises until it reaches 3 workers at the first dashed line. Between 3 workers and the second dashed line at 8 workers, the total output curve continues to rise, though at a slower rate; the slope of the curve is still positive but becomes progressively flatter. Finally, once we reach the ninth worker, total output begins to fall and the slope becomes negative. At this point, it is not productive to have so many workers.

FIGURE 8.1

The Production Function and Marginal Product

(a) Total output rises rapidly in the green-shaded zone from 0 to 3 workers, rises less rapidly in the yellow zone between 3 and 8 workers, and falls in the red zone after 8 workers. (b) The marginal product of labor rises in the green zone from 0 to 3 workers, falls in the yellow zone from 3 to 8 workers but remains positive, and becomes negative after 8 workers. Notice that the marginal product becomes negative after total output reaches its maximum at 8 workers. As long as marginal product is positive, total output rises. Once marginal product becomes negative, total output falls.

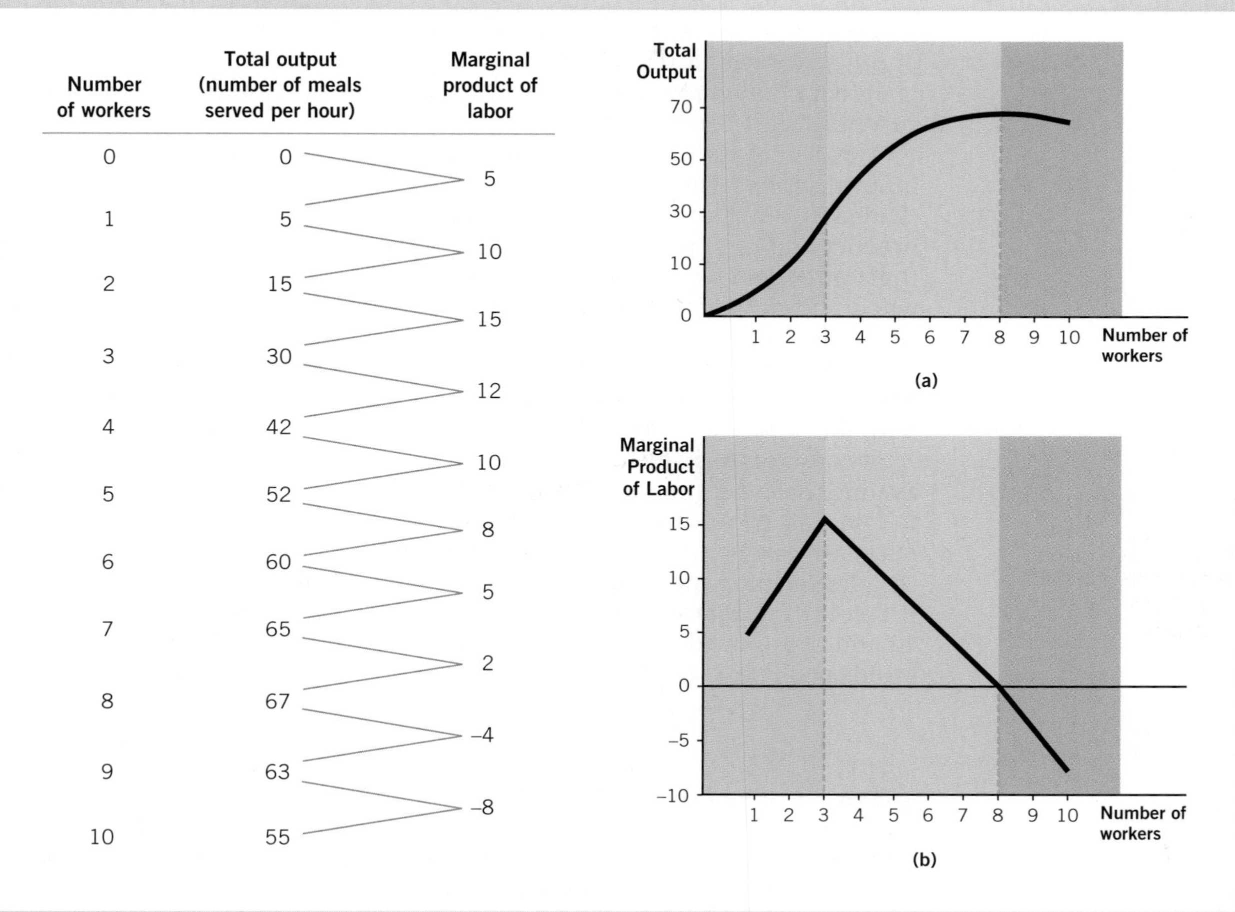

Number of workers	Total output (number of meals served per hour)	Marginal product of labor
0	0	
		5
1	5	
		10
2	15	
		15
3	30	
		12
4	42	
		10
5	52	
		8
6	60	
		5
7	65	
		2
8	67	
		−4
9	63	
		−8
10	55	

Diminishing Marginal Product

The marginal product curve in Figure 8.1b explains the shape of the total output curve above it. Consider that the marginal productivity of each worker either adds to or subtracts from the overall output of the firm. Marginal product increases from 5 meals served per hour with the first worker to 15 meals per hour with the third worker. From the first worker to the third, each additional worker leads to increased specialization and teamwork. This explains the rapid rise—from 0 to 30 meals—in the total output curve. By the fourth worker, marginal product begins to decline. Looking back to the table, you can see that the fourth worker produces 12 extra meals—3 fewer than the third worker. The point at which successive increases in inputs are associated with a slower rise in output is known as the point of **diminishing marginal product**.

Diminishing marginal product occurs when successive increases in inputs are associated with a slower rise in output.

Why does the rate of output slow? Recall that in our example the size of the McDonald's restaurant is fixed in the short run. Because the size of the building, the equipment, and other inputs do not increase, at a certain point additional workers have less to do or can even interfere with the productivity of other workers. After all inputs are fully utilized, additional workers cause marginal product to decline, which we see in the fall of the marginal product curve in Figure 8.1b.

What does diminishing marginal product tell us about the firm's labor input decision? Turning again to the two graphs, we see that in the green-shaded area as the number of workers increases from 0 to 3, the marginal product and total output also rise. But when we enter the yellow zone with the fourth worker, we reach the point of diminishing marginal product where the curve starts to decline. Total output continues to rise, though at a slower rate. Finally, in the red zone, which we enter with the ninth worker, total output declines and marginal product becomes negative. No rational manager would hire more than 8 workers in this scenario, since the total output drops.

Marginal thinking

A common mistake when considering diminishing marginal product is to assume that a firm should stop production as soon as marginal product starts to fall. This is not true. "Diminishing" does not mean "negative." There are many times when marginal product is declining but still high. In our example, diminishing marginal product begins with the fourth worker. However, that fourth worker still produces 12 extra meals. If McDonald's can sell those 12 additional meals for more than it pays the fourth worker, the company's profits will rise.

What Costs Do Firms Consider in the Short Run and the Long Run?

Production is one part of a firm's decision-making process. If you have run even a simple business—for example, cutting lawns—you know that it requires decision-making. How many lawns do you want to be responsible for? Should you work on different lawns at the same time or specialize by task, with one person doing all the mowing and another taking care of the trimming? These are the kinds of production-related questions every firm must address. The other major component of production is cost. Should you invest in a big industrial-size mower? How much gasoline will you need to run your mowers? What does it cost to hire someone to help get the work done? These are some of the types of cost-related concerns that firms face. Each one may seem like a small decision, but the discovery process that leads to the answers is crucial.

PRACTICE WHAT YOU KNOW

Diminishing Returns: Snow Cone Production

It's a hot day, and customers are lined up for snow cones at your small stand. The following table shows your firm's short-run production function for snow cones.

Number of workers	Total output of snow cones per hour
0	0
1	20
2	50
3	75
4	90
5	100
6	105
7	100
8	90

How many workers are too many?

Question: When does diminishing marginal product begin?

Answer: You have to be careful when calculating this answer. Total output is maximized when you have six workers, but diminishing marginal return begins before you hire that many workers. Look at the following table, which includes a third column showing marginal product.

Number of workers	Total output of snow cones per hour	Marginal product
0	0	0
1	20	20
2	50	30
3	75	25
4	90	15
5	100	10
6	105	5
7	100	−5
8	90	−10

The marginal product is highest when you hire the second worker. After that, each subsequent worker you hire has a lower marginal product. Therefore, the answer to the question is that diminishing marginal product begins after the second worker.

Every firm, whether just starting out or already well established and profitable, can benefit by assessing how much to produce and how to produce it more efficiently. In addition, production and cost consideration are different in the short run and in the long run. We begin with the short run because the majority of firms are most concerned with making the best short-run decisions, and then we extend our analysis to the long run, where planning ahead plays a central role.

Costs in the Short Run

All firms experience some costs that are unavoidable in the short run. These unavoidable costs—for example, a lease on space or a contract with a supplier—are a large part of short-run costs. In the short run, costs can be *variable* or *fixed*.

Variable costs
change with the rate of output.

Variable costs change with the rate of output. Let's see what this means for a McDonald's and further simplify our example by assuming that the McDonald's produces only Big Macs. In this case, the variable costs include the number of workers the firm hires; the electricity the firm uses; the all-beef patties, special sauce, lettuce, cheese, pickles, onions, and sesame-seed buns needed to create the Big Mac; and the packaging. These items are considered variable costs because the restaurant doesn't need them unless it has customers. The amount of these resources varies with the amount of output the restaurant produces.

Fixed costs
are unavoidable; they do not vary with output in the short run.

Fixed costs are unavoidable; they do not vary with output in the short run. For instance, no matter how many hamburgers the McDonald's sells, the costs associated with the building remain the same and the business must pay for them. These fixed costs—also known as overhead—include rent, insurance, property taxes, and so on.

Interpreting Tabular Data

Every business must be able to determine how much it costs to provide the products and services it sells. Table 8.3 lists many different ways to measure the costs associated with business decisions.

Let's begin with total variable cost (TVC) in column 2 and total fixed cost (TFC) in column 3. Notice that when output—the quantity (Q) of Big Macs produced per hour—is 0, total variable cost starts at $0 and rises with production at an uneven rate depending on the productivity of labor and the cost of the ingredients that go into each Big Mac. We attribute this to the simple fact that additional workers and other inputs are needed to generate additional output. In contrast, total fixed cost starts at $100, even when output is 0, and remains constant as output rises. As noted above, fixed costs include overhead expenses such as rent, insurance, and property taxes. For simplicity, we assume that this amount is $100 a day. When we add fixed cost and variable cost together, we get total cost, listed in column 4: TC = TVC + TFC.

Average variable cost (AVC)
is determined by dividing total variable costs by the output.

Column 5, *average variable cost*, and column 6, *average fixed cost*, enable us to determine the cost of producing a Big Mac by examining the average cost of production. **Average variable cost** (AVC) is the total variable cost

TABLE 8.3

Measuring Costs

(1)	(2)	(3)	(4)	(5)	(6)	(7)	(8)
Quantity (Q = Big Macs produced/hour)	Total Variable Cost	Total Fixed Cost	Total Cost	Average Variable Cost	Average Fixed Cost	Average Total Cost	Marginal Cost
Abbreviation:	TVC	TFC	TC	AVC	AFC	ATC	MC
Formula:			TVC + TFC	TVC ÷ Q	TFC ÷ Q	AVC + AFC	ΔTVC ÷ ΔQ
0	$0.00	$100.00	$100.00				
10	30.00	100.00	130.00	$3.00	$10.00	$13.00	$3.00
20	50.00	100.00	150.00	2.50	5.00	7.50	2.00
30	65.00	100.00	165.00	2.17	3.33	5.50	1.50
40	77.00	100.00	177.00	1.93	2.50	4.43	1.20
50	87.00	100.00	187.00	1.74	2.00	3.74	1.00
60	100.00	100.00	200.00	1.67	1.67	3.34	1.30
70	120.00	100.00	220.00	1.71	1.43	3.14	2.00
80	160.00	100.00	260.00	2.00	1.25	3.25	4.00
90	220.00	100.00	320.00	2.44	1.11	3.55	6.00
100	300.00	100.00	400.00	3.00	1.00	4.00	8.00

divided by the output produced: AVC = TVC ÷ Q. Notice that the average variable cost declines until 60 Big Macs are produced at an average cost of $1.67. This is the lowest average cost. Why should we care about AVC? Because it can be a useful signal. In this case, total variable costs in column 2 always rise, but the average variable cost falls until 60 Big Macs are produced. The decline in AVC is a powerful signal to the firm to increase its output up to a point.

Average fixed cost (**AFC**), listed in column 6, is calculated by dividing total fixed cost by the output: AFC = TFC ÷ Q. Since total fixed cost is constant, dividing these costs by the output means that as the output rises, the average fixed cost declines. In other words, higher output levels spread out the total fixed costs across more units. As Table 8.3 shows, average fixed costs are lowest at an output of 100 Big Macs, where:

Average fixed cost (AFC) is determined by dividing total fixed costs by the output.

AFC = TFC ÷ Q
AFC = $100 ÷ 100
AFC = $1

What does this example tell a business that wants to lower costs? Since overhead costs such as rent cannot be changed, the best way to lower fixed costs is to raise output.

Average total cost (ATC) is the sum of average variable cost and average fixed cost.

Average total cost (ATC), shown in column 7, is calculated by adding the AVC and AFC. Let's look at the numbers to get a better understanding of what average total cost tells us. Even though the average variable cost rises after 60 Big Macs are produced, from $1.67 to $1.71, the average fixed cost is still falling, from $1.67 to $1.43. The decline in average fixed cost is enough to pull the average total cost down to $3.14. Eventually, increases in variable cost overwhelm the cost savings achieved by spreading fixed cost across more production. We can see this if we compare the average total costs of making 70 Big Macs and 80 Big Macs.

For 70 Big Macs:

$$\text{ATC} = \text{AVC} + \text{AFC}$$
$$\text{ATC} = \$1.71 + \$1.43 = \$3.14$$

For 80 Big Macs:

$$\text{ATC} = \text{AVC} + \text{AFC}$$
$$\text{ATC} = \$2.00 + \$1.25 = \$3.25$$

At 80 Big Macs, the average variable cost rises from $1.71 to $2.00. And the average fixed cost falls from $1.43 to $1.25. Therefore, the rise in average variable cost—$0.29—is higher than the fall in average fixed cost—$0.18. This finding removes the benefit of higher output. Thus, the most efficient number of Big Macs to produce is between 70 and 80.

Interpreting Data Graphically

Now that we have walked through the numerical results in Table 8.3, it is time to visualize the cost relationships with graphs. Figure 8.2 shows a graph of total cost curves (a) and the relationship between the marginal cost curve and the average cost curves (b).

In panel (a) of Figure 8.2, we see that although the total cost curve continues to rise, the rate of increase in total cost is not constant. For the first 50 Big Macs, the total cost rises at a decreasing rate. This reflects the gains of specialization and comparative advantage that come from adding workers who concentrate on specific tasks. After 50 Big Macs, diminishing marginal product causes the total cost curve to rise at an increasing rate. Since a McDonald's restaurant has a fixed capacity, producing more than 50 Big Macs requires a significantly higher investment in labor, and those workers do not have any additional space to work in—a situation that makes the total cost curve rise more rapidly at high production levels. The total cost (TC) curve is equal to the sum of the fixed cost and variable cost curves, which are shown in panel (a). Total fixed costs (TFC) are constant, so it is the total variable costs (TVC) that give the TC curve its shape.

Marginal thinking

But that is not the most important part of the story. Any manager at McDonald's can examine total costs. Likewise, she can look at the average cost and compare that information to the average cost at other local businesses. But neither the total cost of labor nor the average cost will tell her anything about the cost of making additional units—that is, Big Macs.

Marginal cost (MC) is the increase in cost that occurs from producing additional output.

A manager can make even better decisions by looking at *marginal cost.* The **marginal cost** (MC) is the increase in extra cost that occurs from producing

FIGURE 8.2

The Cost Curves

(a) The total variable cost (TVC) dictates the shape of the total cost (TC) curve. After 50 Big Macs, diminishing marginal product causes the total cost curve to rise at an increasing rate. Notice that the total fixed cost curve (TFC) stays constant, or flat. (b) The marginal cost curve (MC) reaches its minimum before average variable cost (AVC) and average total cost (ATC). Marginals always lead the average either up or down. Average fixed cost (AFC), which has no variable component, continues to fall with increased quantity, since total fixed costs are spread across more units. The minimum point of the ATC curve is known as the efficient scale.

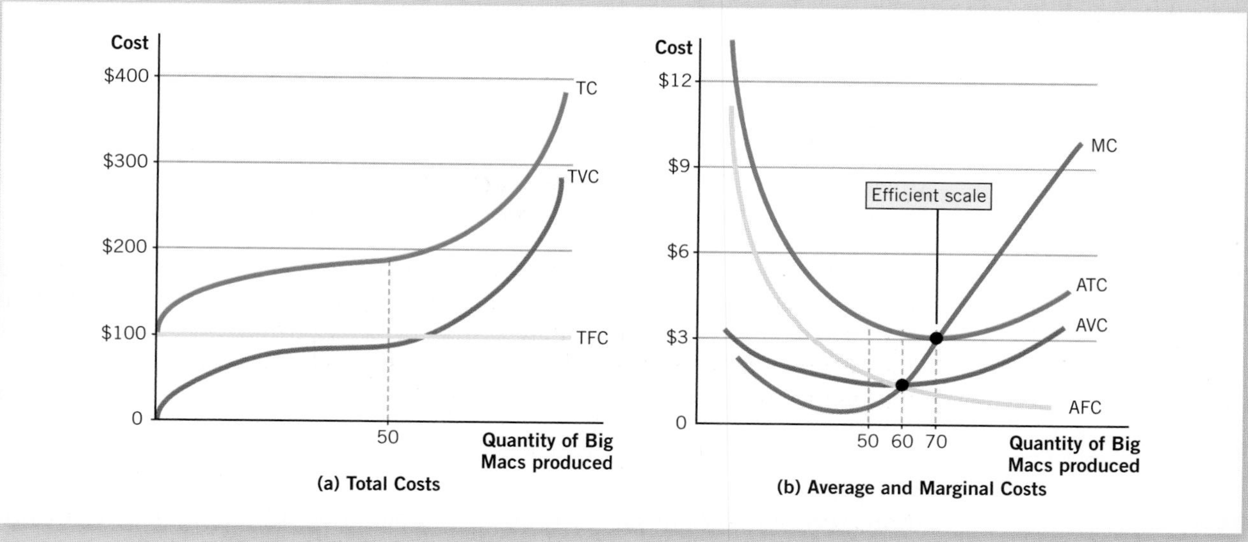

additional output. (In column 8 of Table 8.3, this relationship is shown as the change, or Δ, in TVC divided by the change, or Δ, in quantity produced.) For example, in planning the weekly work schedule the manager has to consider how many workers to hire for each shift. She wants to hire additional workers when the cost of doing so is less than the expected boost in profits. In this situation, it is essential to know the marginal cost, or extra cost, of hiring one more worker.

In Table 8.3, marginal cost (MC) falls to a minimum of $1.00 when between 40 and 50 Big Macs are produced. Notice that the minimum MC occurs at a lower output level than average variable cost (AVC) and average total cost (ATC) in panel (b) of Figure 8.2. When output is less than 50 Big Macs, marginal cost is falling because over this range of production the marginal product of labor is increasing on account of better teamwork and more specialization. After the fiftieth Big Mac, MC rises. This acts as an early warning indicator that average and total costs will soon follow suit. Why would a manager care about the last few units being produced more than the average cost of producing all the units? Because marginal cost tells the manager if making one more unit of output will increase profits or not!

Marginal thinking

The MC curve reaches its lowest point before the lowest point of the AVC and ATC curves. For this reason, a manager who is concerned about rising costs would look to the MC curve as a signal that average costs will eventually increase as well. Once marginal cost begins to increase, it continues to pull down average variable cost until sales reach 60 Big Macs. After that point, MC is above AVC and AVC begins to rise as well. However, ATC continues to fall until 70 Big Macs are sold.

Why does average total cost fall while MC and AVC are rising? The answer lies in the average fixed cost (AFC) curve shown in Figure 8.2. Since the ATC = AVC + AFC, and AFC always declines as output rises, ATC declines until 70 Big Macs are sold. This is a direct result of the decline in AFC overwhelming the increase in AVC between 60 and 70 Big Macs. Notice also that the AVC curve stops declining at 60 Big Macs. Variable costs should initially decline as a result of increased specialization and teamwork. However, at some point the advantages of continued specialization are overtaken by diminishing marginal product, and costs begin to rise. The transition from falling costs to rising costs is of particular interest because as long as costs are declining, the firm can lower its costs by increasing its output. Economists refer to the quantity of output that minimizes the average total cost as the **efficient scale**.

The **efficient scale** is the output level that minimizes the average total cost.

Once the marginal costs in Table 8.3 rise above the average total costs, the average total costs begin to rise as well. This is evident if we compare the average total cost of making 70 Big Macs ($3.14) and 80 Big Macs ($3.25) with the marginal cost ($4.00) of making those extra 10 Big Macs. Since the marginal cost ($4.00) of making Big Macs 71 through 80 is higher than the average total cost at 70 ($3.14), the average total cost of making 80 Big Macs goes up (to $3.25).

Marginal costs always lead (or pull) average costs along, no matter what we are considering. The MC eventually rises above the average total cost because of diminishing marginal product. In this case, since the firm has to pay a fixed wage, the cost to produce each hamburger increases as each worker decreases in productivity.

There is, however, one "average" curve that the marginal cost does not affect: average fixed costs. Notice that the AFC curve in panel (b) of Figure 8.2 continues to fall even though marginal costs eventually rise. The AFC curve declines with increased output. Since McDonald's has $100.00 in fixed costs each day, we can determine the average fixed costs by dividing the total fixed cost ($100.00) by the number of Big Macs sold. When 10 Big Macs are sold, the average fixed cost is $10.00 per Big Mac, but this value falls to $1.00 per Big

Costs in the Short Run

ECONOMICS IN THE MEDIA

The Office

The popular TV series *The Office* had an amusing episode devoted to the discussion of costs. The character Michael Scott establishes his own paper company to compete with both Staples and his former company, Dunder Mifflin. He then outcompetes his rivals by keeping his fixed and variable costs low.

In one inspired scene, we see the Michael Scott Paper Company operating out of a single room and using an old church van to deliver paper. This means the company has very low *fixed costs*, which enables it to charge unusually low prices. In addition, Michael Scott keeps *variable costs* to a minimum by hiring only essential employees and not paying any benefits, such as health insurance. But this is a problem, since Michael Scott does not fully account for the cost of the paper he is selling. In fact, he is selling below unit cost!

As we will discover in upcoming chapters, firms with lower costs have many advantages in the market. Such firms can keep their prices lower to attract additional customers. Cost matters because price matters.

Michael Scott doesn't understand the difference between fixed and variable costs.

Mac if 100 burgers are sold. Since McDonald's is a high-volume business that relies on low costs to compete, being able to produce enough Big Macs to spread out the firm's fixed costs is essential.

Costs in the Long Run

We have seen that in the short run, businesses have fixed costs and fixed capacities. In the long run, all costs are variable and can be renegotiated. Thus, firms have more control over their costs in the long run, which enables them to reach their desired level of production. One way that firms can adjust in the long run is by changing the **scale**, or size, of the production process. If the business is expected to grow, the firm can ramp up production. If the business is faltering, it can scale back its operations. This flexibility enables firms to avoid a situation of diminishing marginal product.

Scale refers to the size of the production process.

A long-run time horizon allows a business to choose a scale of operation that best suits its needs. For instance, if a local McDonald's is extremely popular, in the short run the manager can only hire more workers or expand the restaurant's hours to accommodate more customers. However, in the long run all costs are variable; the manager can add drive-thru lanes, increase the number of registers, expand the grill area, and so on.

The absence of fixed factors in the long-run production process means that we cannot explain total costs in the long run in the same way that we explained short-run costs. Short-run costs are a reflection of diminishing marginal product, whereas long-run costs are a reflection of scale and the cost of providing additional output. One might assume that since diminishing marginal product is no longer relevant in the long run, costs would fall as output expands. However, this is not the case. Depending on the industry and the prevailing economic conditions, long-run costs can rise, fall, or stay approximately the same.

Three Types of Scale

In this section, we describe three different scenarios for a firm in the long run. A firm may experience *economies of scale*, *diseconomies of scale*, or *constant returns to scale*. In the long run, whether costs fall, remain constant, or rise with increasing output will depend on *scale*, or the amount of output a firm desires to produce. Let's consider each of these in turn.

Economies of scale occur when costs decline as output expands in the long run.

If output expands and costs decline, businesses experience **economies of scale**. National homebuilders, like Toll Brothers, provide a good example of economies of scale. All builders, whether they are local or national, do the same thing—they build houses. Each builder needs lumber, concrete, excavators, electricians, plumbers, roofers, and many more specialized workers or subcontractors. A big company, such as Toll, is able to hire many specialists and also buy the equipment it needs in bulk. As a result, Toll can manufacture the same home as a local builder at a much lower cost than the local builder can.

Diseconomies of scale occur when costs rise as output expands in the long run.

But bigger isn't always better! Sometimes a company grows so large that coordination problems make costs rise. For example, as the scale of an enterprise expands, it might require more managers, highly specialized workers, and a coordination process to pull everything together. As the layers of management expand, the coordination process can break down. For this reason, a larger firm can become less effective at holding down costs and experience **diseconomies of scale**, or higher average total costs as output expands.

Building more than one house at a time would represent an economy of scale.

The problem of diseconomies of scale is especially relevant in the service sector of the economy. For example, large regional hospitals have many layers of bureaucracy. These added management costs and infrastructure expenses can make medical care more expensive beyond a certain point. If you are not convinced, ask yourself why large cities have many smaller competing hospitals rather than one centralized hospital. The answer becomes obvious: bigger doesn't always mean less expensive (or better)!

Finally, if the advantages of specialization, mass production, and bulk purchasing are approximately equal, then the long-run costs will remain constant as the firm expands its output. When costs remain constant even as output expands, we say that the firm has **constant returns to scale**. For example, large national restaurant chains like Olive Garden, which specializes in Italian cuisine, compete with local Italian restaurants. In each case, the local costs to hire workers and build the restaurant are the same. Olive Garden does have a few advantages; for example, it can afford to advertise on national television and buy food in bulk. But Olive Garden also has more overhead costs for its many layers of management. Constant returns to scale in the bigger chain mean that a small local Italian restaurant will have approximately the same menu prices as its bigger rivals.

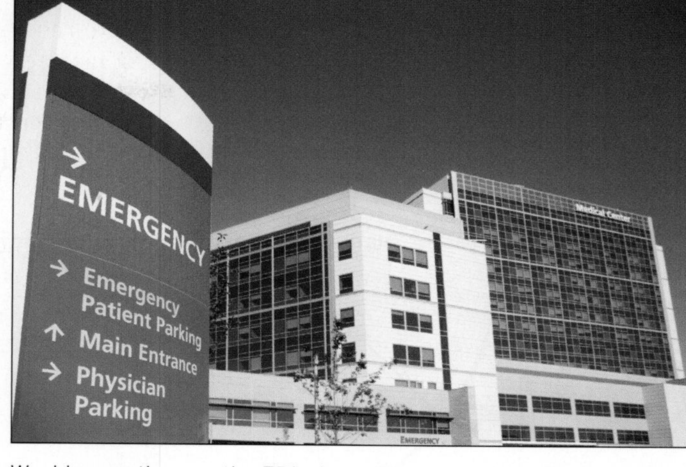

Would you rather see the ER's doctor du jour or your own physician?

Constant returns to scale occur when costs remain constant as output expands in the long run.

Long-Run Cost Curves

Now it is time to illustrate the long-run nature of cost curves. We have seen that increased output may not always lead to economies of scale. Costs can be constant or can even rise with output. Figure 8.3 illustrates each of the three possibilities graphically. The long-run average total cost curve (LRATC) is actually a composite of many short-run average total cost (SRATC) curves, which appear as the faint U-shaped dashed curves drawn in gray. By visualizing the short-run cost curves at any given output level, we can develop a composite of them to create the LRATC. From this, we see that the long-run average total cost curve comprises all the short-run cost curves that the firm may choose to deploy in the long run. In the long run, the firm is free to

Will you find lower prices at the Olive Garden or your local Italian restaurant?

FIGURE 8.3

Costs in the Long Run

In the long run, there are three distinct possibilities: the long-run average total cost curve (LRATC) can exhibit economies of scale (the green curve), constant returns to scale (the purple curve), or diseconomies of scale (the orange curve).

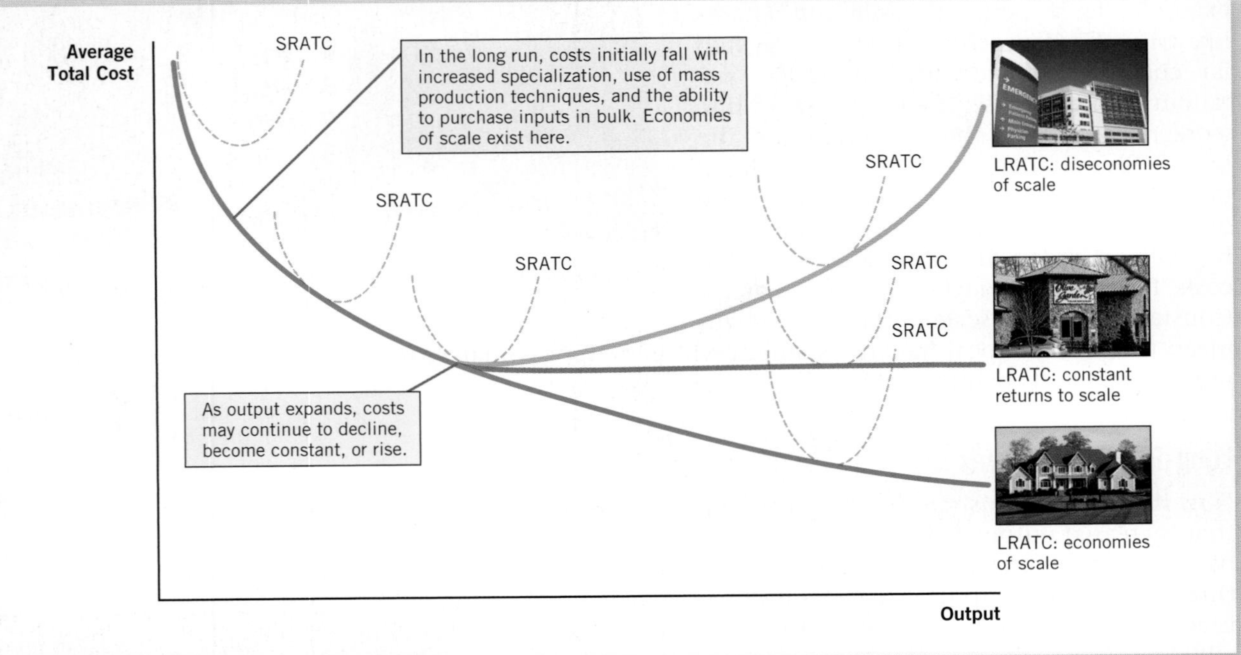
Average Total Cost
SRATC
In the long run, costs initially fall with increased specialization, use of mass production techniques, and the ability to purchase inputs in bulk. Economies of scale exist here.
SRATC
SRATC
SRATC
SRATC
SRATC
LRATC: diseconomies of scale
LRATC: constant returns to scale
LRATC: economies of scale
As output expands, costs may continue to decline, become constant, or rise.
Output

choose any of its short-run curves, so it always picks the output/cost combination that minimizes costs.

In the long run, there are three distinct possibilities: economies of scale, constant returns to scale, and diseconomies of scale. At first, each LRATC exhibits economies of scale as a result of increased specialization, the utilization of mass production techniques, bulk purchasing power, and increased automation. The main question in the long run is whether the cost curve will continue to decline, level off, or rise. In an industry with economies of scale at high output levels—for example, a homebuilder—the cost curve continues to decline, and the most efficient output level is always the largest output: the green curve in Figure 8.3. In this situation, we would expect only one large firm to dominate the industry because large firms have significant cost advantages. However, in an industry with constant returns to scale—for example, restaurants—the cost curve flattens out: the purple line. Once the curve becomes constant, firms of varying sizes can compete equally with one another because they have the same costs. Finally, in the case of diseconomies of scale—for example, big-city hospitals—bigger firms have higher costs: the orange curve.

SNAPSHOT

Bigger Is Not Always Better

Large firms take advantage of economies of scale in many ways, such as buying their inputs at discounted prices. But bigger is not always better. One major problem that confronts large firms is becoming "top-heavy"—that is, having a labor force that requires a large number of managers whose only job is to manage. This lowers the overall productivity of the labor force and increases costs.

Owner / Executive manager
Division manager
Line manager
Supervisor
Worker
Small Business
10% Reduced productivity
A typical small business might consist of 1 owner and 9 workers.
Mid-Sized Business
12.2% Reduced productivity
A typical mid-sized business might consist of 41 employees, including 1 executive manager and 4 supervisors who oversee 9 workers each.
Large Business
14.9% Reduced productivity
A typical large company might consist of 127 employees: 1 executive manager, 2 division managers, 4 line managers, 12 supervisors, and 108 workers.

REVIEW QUESTIONS

- Calculate the reduced productivity in a company of 1,000 employees when there are 2 executive managers, 6 line managers, and 12 supervisors for every 80 workers.
- Your friend owns a business and is looking to expand. Describe the risks and rewards of such a move using economies of scale and costs.

ECONOMICS IN THE MEDIA

Economies of Scale

Modern Times

The 1936 comedy *Modern Times* is regarded as one of the top 100 English-language films of all time. The movie features Charlie Chaplin in his final silent film role. Chaplin, who was a master of slapstick comedy, plays a tramp who finds work on an assembly line in a large factory. The company bosses are ruthless taskmasters. For the production process to remain in sync and maximum efficiency to occur, each assembly line worker must complete a small task and pass the product down the line.

As the movie progresses, the bosses introduce a novel product called the Billows Feeding Machine. The idea is simple: if the lunch break were shorter, the workers' downtime would be minimized and production increased. Here is the exact transcript from the film:

> May I take the pleasure of introducing Mr. J. Widdecombe Billows, the inventor of the Billows Feeding Machine, a practical device which automatically feeds your men while at work. Don't stop for lunch: be ahead of your competitor. The Billows Feeding Machine will eliminate the lunch hour, increase your production, and decrease your overhead. Allow us to point out some of the features of this wonderful machine: its beautiful, aerodynamic, streamlined body; its smoothness of action, made silent by our electro-porous metal ball bearings. Let us acquaint you with our automaton soup plate—its compressed-air blower, no breath necessary, no energy required to cool the soup. Notice the revolving plate with the automatic food pusher. Observe our counter-shaft, double-knee-action corn feeder, with its synchro-mesh transmission, which enables you to shift from high to low gear by the mere tip of the tongue. Then there is the hydro-compressed, sterilized mouth wiper: its factors of control insure against spots on the shirt front. These are but a few of the delightful features of the Billows Feeding Machine. Let us demonstrate with one of your workers, for actions speak louder than words. Remember, if you wish to keep ahead of your competitor, you cannot afford to ignore the importance of the Billows Feeding Machine.

Would a feeding machine for workers lower long-run costs?

The company bosses are eager to test the feeding machine, but things go terribly wrong—in a hilarious way—when they select Chaplin as the human guinea pig. Because the machine does not work as promised, the company decides that the feeding machine is not a practical idea.

Although no firm in the real world is likely to try something like the feeding machine, firms do constantly seek efficiency gains. Of course, not all ideas are practical, and sometimes there are insufficient economies of scale to implement an idea. For instance, the assembly line depicted in *Modern Times* is efficient, but it wouldn't make sense for a company to use this process unless it sells a large volume of bolts. This is analogous to production in the automobile industry. Large manufacturers like Toyota and Ford use assembly lines to create economies of scale, whereas a small specialty shop that produces only a handful of vehicles a year builds each car by hand and fails to enjoy the benefits of economies of scale.

PRACTICE WHAT YOU KNOW

Marginal Cost: The True Cost of Admission to Universal Studios

You and your family visit Orlando for a week. While there, you decide to go to Universal Studios. When you arrive, you notice that each family member can buy a day pass for $80 or a two-day pass for $90. Your parents are concerned about spending too much, so they decide to calculate the average cost of a two-day pass to see if it is a good value. The average cost is $90 ÷ 2, or $45 per day. The math is correct, but something you learned in economics tells you that they are not thinking about this in the correct way.

Is one day enough to do it all?

Question: What concept can you apply to make the decision more clear?

Answer: Tell them about *marginal cost*. The first day costs $80, but the marginal cost of going back to the park on the second day is only the extra cost per person, or $90 − $80, which equals $10. Your parents still might not want to spend the extra money, but only spending an extra $10 for the second day makes it an extraordinary value. Someone who does not appreciate economics might think the second day costs an extra $45 since that is the average cost. But the average cost is misleading. Looking at marginal cost is the best way to weigh these two options.

Conclusion

Do larger firms have lower costs? Not always. When diseconomies of scale occur, costs will rise with output. This result contradicts the common misconception that bigger firms have lower costs than their smaller competitors. Simply put, sometimes a leaner firm with less overhead can beat its larger rivals on cost.

Costs are defined in a number of ways, but marginal cost plays the most crucial role in a firm's cost structure. By observing what happens to marginal cost, you can understand changes in average cost and total cost. This is why economists place so much emphasis on marginal cost. Going forward, a solid grasp of marginal analysis will help you understand many of the most important concepts in microeconomics.

Marginal thinking

You now understand the cost, or supply side, of business decisions. However, to provide a complete picture of how firms operate, we still need to examine how markets work. Costs are only part of the story, and in the next chapter we will take a closer look at profits.

ANSWERING THE BIG QUESTIONS

How are profits and losses calculated?

* Profits and losses are determined by calculating the difference between expenses and revenue.
* There are two types of profit: economic profit and accounting profit. If a business has an economic profit, its revenues are larger than the combination of its explicit and implicit costs.
* Economists break cost into two components: explicit costs, which are easy to calculate, and implicit costs, which are hard to calculate. Since economic profit accounts for implicit costs, the economic profit is always less than the accounting profit.

How much should a firm produce?

* A firm should produce an output that is consistent with the largest possible economic profit.
* In order to maximize production, firms must effectively combine labor and capital in the right quantities.
* In any short-run production process, a point of diminishing marginal product will occur at which additional units of a variable input no longer generate as much output as before. This occurs because each firm has separate fixed and variable costs.
* The marginal cost (MC) curve is the key variable in determining a firm's cost structure. The MC curve always leads the average total cost (ATC) and average variable cost (AVC) curves up or down.

What costs do firms consider in the short run and the long run?

* Firms consider variable and fixed costs, as well as marginal costs. Firms also consider average variable cost (AVC), average fixed cost (AFC), and average total cost (ATC).
* With the exception of the average fixed cost (AFC) curve, which always declines, short-run cost curves are U-shaped. All variable costs initially decline due to increased specialization. At a certain point, the advantages of continued specialization give way to diminishing marginal product, and the MC, AVC, and ATC curves begin to rise.
* Long-run costs are a reflection of scale. They can experience diseconomies, economies, or constant returns to scale depending on the industry.

ECONOMICS FOR LIFE

How Much Does It Cost to Raise a Child?

Raising a child is one of life's most rewarding experiences, but it can be very expensive. According to the U.S. Department of Agriculture, the cost for a middle-income, two-parent family to raise a child from birth to age 18 is more than $250,000—and that does not include college. To determine this number, the government considers all related costs, such as food, clothing, medical care, and entertainment. In addition, the government apportions a share of the costs of the family home and vehicles to each child in the household. To put the cost of raising a child in perspective, the median home value in 2011 was $156,000. Talk about opportunity cost!

What if a family has more than one child? You wouldn't necessarily multiply the cost by two or three because there are economies of scale in raising more children. For example, some things can be shared: the children might share a bedroom and wear hand-me-downs. Also, the family can purchase food in bulk. As a result, families that have three or more children can manage to spend an average of 22% less on each child.

The cost of raising children also forces families to make trade-offs. In many households, both parents must work or work longer hours. When one parent steps out of the workforce, the household loses a paycheck. While this may save in expenses associated with working, including certain clothes, transportation, and childcare, there are also hidden costs. For example, the lack of workplace continuity lowers the stay-at-home parent's future earning power.

Raising a child is an expensive proposition in both the short run and the long run. But don't let this discourage you; it is also one of the most rewarding investments you will ever make.

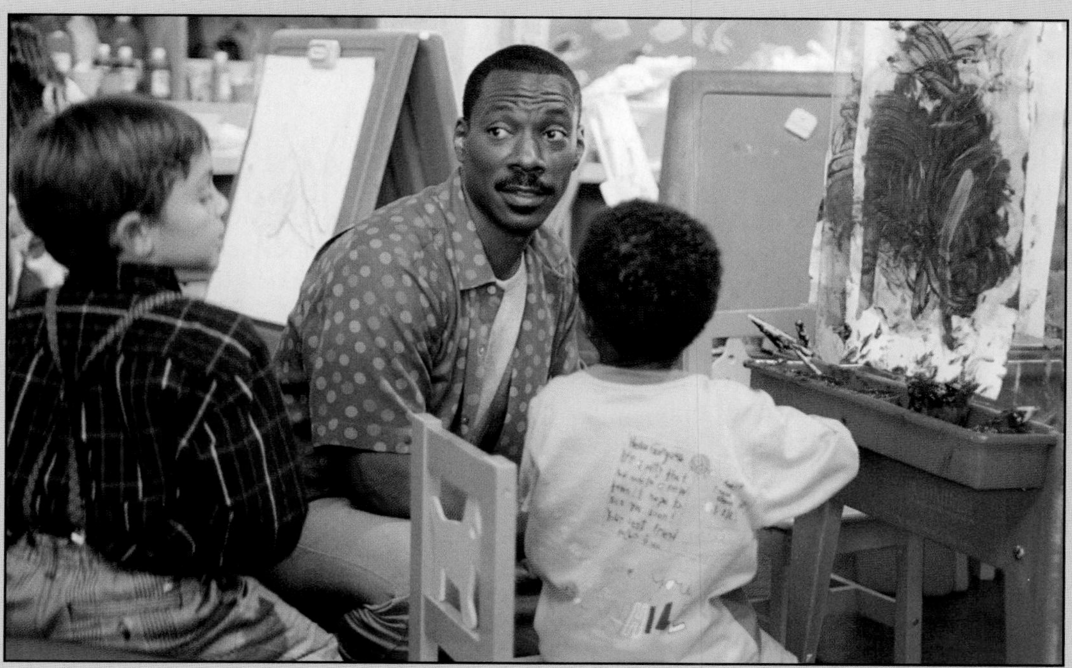

Daddy Day Care? Childcare expenses add up.

CONCEPTS YOU SHOULD KNOW

accounting profit (p. 244)
average fixed cost (AFC) (p. 253)
average total cost (ATC) (p. 254)
average variable cost (AVC) (p. 252)
constant returns to scale (p. 259)
diminishing marginal product (p. 250)
diseconomies of scale (p. 258)
economic profit (p. 244)
economies of scale (p. 258)
efficient scale (p. 256)
explicit costs (p. 243)
factors of production (p. 247)
fixed costs (p. 252)
implicit costs (p. 243)
losses (p. 242)
marginal cost (MC) (p. 254)
marginal product (p. 248)
output (p. 247)
production function (p. 247)
profits (p. 242)
scale (p. 257)
variable costs (p. 252)
total cost (p. 242)
total revenue (p. 242)

QUESTIONS FOR REVIEW

1. What is the equation for the profit (or loss) of a firm?
2. Why is economic profit a better measure of profitability than accounting profit? Give an example.
3. What role does diminishing marginal product play in determining the ideal mix of labor and capital a firm should use?
4. Describe what happens to the total product of a firm when marginal product is increasing, decreasing, and negative.
5. Explain why marginal cost is the glue that connects average variable cost and average total cost.
6. Compare the short-run and long-run cost curves. In a few sentences, explain their differences.
7. Name examples of industries that illustrate each of the following: economies of scale, constant returns to scale, and diseconomies of scale. Think creatively; do not use the textbook examples.

STUDY PROBLEMS (* *solved at the end of the section*)

1. Go to www.lemonadegame.com. This free online game places you in the role of a lemonade seller. Nothing could be simpler, right? Not so fast! You still need to control costs and ensure you have the right ingredients on hand to be able to sell. You will need to manage your supply of lemons, sugar, ice, and cups. You will also have to set a price and decide how many lemons and how much sugar and ice to put in each glass of lemonade you produce. This is not a trivial process, so play the game. Your challenge is to make $20 in profit over the first five days. (Your business starts with $20, so you need to have $40 in your account by the end of day 5 to meet the challenge. Are you up to it?)
2. The following table shows a short-run production function for laptop computers. Use the data to determine where diminishing product begins.

Number of workers	Total output of laptop computers
0	0
1	40
2	100
3	150
4	180
5	200
6	205
7	200
8	190

3. A pizza business has the cost structure described below. The firm's fixed costs are \$25 per day. Calculate the firm's average fixed costs, average variable costs, average total costs, and marginal costs.

Output (pizzas per day)	Total cost of output
0	\$25
10	75
20	115
30	150
40	175
50	190
60	205
70	225
80	250

* 4. A firm is considering changing its plant size, so it calculates the average cost of production for various plant sizes below. If the firm is currently using plant size C, is the firm experiencing economies of scale, diseconomies of scale, or constant returns to scale?

Plant size	Average total cost
A (smallest)	\$10,000
B	9,500
C	9,000
D	8,800
E	8,800
F (largest)	8,900

5. True or false?
   a. The AFC curve can never rise.
   b. Diminishing marginal product is a long-run constraint that prevents lower costs.
   c. The MC curve intersects the AVC and ATC curves at the minimum point along both curves.
   d. Accounting profit is smaller than economic profit.
   e. Total cost divided by output is equal to marginal cost.

6. Digital media distributed over the Internet often have marginal costs of zero. For instance, people can download music and movies instantly through many providers. Do these products exhibit economies, diseconomies, or constant returns to scale?

7. An airline has a marginal cost per passenger of \$30 on a route from Boston to Detroit. At the same time, the typical fare charged is \$300. The planes that fly the route are usually full, yet the airline claims that it loses money on the route. How is this possible?

8. Many amusement parks offer two-day passes at dramatically discounted prices. If a one-day pass costs \$40 but the two-day pass costs \$50, what is the average cost for the two-day pass? What is the marginal cost of the two-day pass?

* 9. Suppose that you own a yard care business. You have your own mower, flatbed truck, and other equipment. You are also the primary employee. Why might you have trouble calculating your profits? (**Hint:** think about the difference between accounting profits and economic profits.)

10. Use the information provided in the following table to fill in the blanks.

Output	Total fixed cost	Total variable cost	Total cost	Average fixed cost	Average variable cost	Average total cost	Marginal cost
0	$500	$0	$500	___	___	___	
1	$500	$200	___	___	___	___	___
2	___	___	$800	___	___	___	___
3	___	___	$875	___	___	___	___
4	___	___	$925	___	___	___	___
5	___	___	___	$100	___	___	$25
6	___	$450	___	___	___	___	___

SOLVED PROBLEMS

4. The key to solving this problem is recognizing the direction of change in the average total cost. If the firm were to switch to a smaller plant, like B, its average total cost would rise to $9,500. Since the smaller plant would cost more, plant C is currently enjoying economies of scale. When we compare the average total cost of C ($9,000) to D ($8,800), it continues to fall. Since the average total cost is falling from B to D, we again know that the firm is experiencing economies of scale.

9. When calculating your costs for the mower, truck, and other expenses, you are computing your explicit costs. Subtracting the explicit costs from your total revenue will yield the accounting profit you have earned. However, you still do not know your economic profit because you haven't determined your implicit costs. Because you are the primary employee, you also have to add in the opportunity cost of the time you invest in the business. You may not know exactly what you might have earned doing something else, but you can be sure it exists—this is your implicit cost. This is why you may have trouble computing your profits. You might show an accounting profit only to discover that what you thought you made was less than you could have made by doing something else. If that is the case, your true economic profit is actually negative.

CHAPTER 9

Firms in a Competitive Market

Firms control the prices they charge.

MISCONCEPTION

Many people believe that firms set the prices for their products with little concern for the consumer. However, this is incorrect. The misconception that firms control the prices they charge occurs because many people think that the firm is central to the functioning of the market. However, market forces are much stronger than individual firms. Under the right conditions, markets produce high-quality goods at remarkably low prices, to the benefit of both buyers and sellers. Competition drives prices down, which limits the firm's ability to charge as much as it would like.

In this chapter and the next four, we will look in more detail at how markets work, the profits firms earn, and how market forces determine the price that a firm can charge for its product or service. We begin our sequence on market structure, or how individual markets are interconnected, by examining the conditions necessary to create a competitive market. Although few real markets achieve the ideal market structure described in this chapter, this model provides a benchmark, or starting point, for understanding other market structures. In competitive markets, firms are completely at the mercy of market forces that set the price to be charged throughout the industry.

Our analysis of competitive markets will show that when competition is widespread firms have little or no control over the price they can charge and they make little or no economic profit. Let's find out why this is the case.

Individual vendors in flower markets face stiff competition.

BIG QUESTIONS

- How do competitive markets work?
- How do firms maximize profits?
- What does the supply curve look like in perfectly competitive markets?

How Do Competitive Markets Work?

Competitive markets exist when there are so many buyers and sellers that each one has only a small impact on the market price and output. Recall that in Chapter 3 we used the example of the Pike Place Market, where each fish vendor sells similar products. Because each fish vendor is small relative to the whole market, no single firm can influence the market price. It doesn't matter where you buy salmon because the price is the same or very similar at every fish stall. When buyers are willing to purchase a product anywhere, sellers have no control over the price they charge. These two characteristics—similar goods and many participants—create a highly competitive market where the price and quantity sold are determined by the market conditions rather than by any one firm.

In competitive markets, buyers can expect to find consistently low prices and a wide availability of the good that they want. Firms that produce goods in competitive markets are known as *price takers*. A **price taker** has no control over the price set by the market. It "takes"—that is, accepts—the price determined from the overall supply and demand conditions that regulate the market.

A **price taker** has no control over the price set by the market.

Competitive markets have another feature in common as well: new competitors can easily enter the market. If you want to open a copy shop, all you have to do is rent store space and several copy machines. There are no licensing or regulatory obstacles in your way. Likewise, there is very little to stop competitors from leaving the market. If you decide to close, you can lock the doors, return the equipment you rented, and move on to do something else. When barriers to entry into a marketplace are low, new firms are free to compete with existing businesses, which ensures the existence of competitive markets and low prices. Table 9.1 summarizes the characteristics of competitive firms.

TABLE 9.1

Characteristics of Competitive Firms

- Many sellers
- Similar products
- Free entry and exit
- Price taking

Real-life examples of competitive markets usually fall short of perfection. Examples that are almost perfectly competitive, shown in Table 9.2, include the stock market, farmers' markets, online ticket auctions, and currency trading. When markets are almost perfectly competitive, the benefit to society is still extremely large because markets create consumer and producer surplus (as we saw in Chapter 6).

TABLE 9.2

Almost Perfect Markets

Example	How it works	Reality check
Stock market 	Millions of shares of stocks are traded every day on various stock exchanges, and generally the buyers and sellers have access to real-time information about prices. Since most of the traders represent only a small share of the market, they have little ability to influence the market price.	Because of the volume of shares that they control, large institutional investors, like Pacific Investment Management Company (PIMCO), manage billions of dollars in funds. As a result, they are big enough to influence the market price.
Farmers' markets 	In farmers' markets, sellers are able to set up at little or no cost. Many buyers are also present. The gathering of numerous buyers and sellers of similar products causes the market price for similar products to converge toward a single price.	Many produce markets do not have enough sellers to achieve a perfectly competitive result. Without more vendors, individual sellers can often set their prices higher.
Online ticket auctions 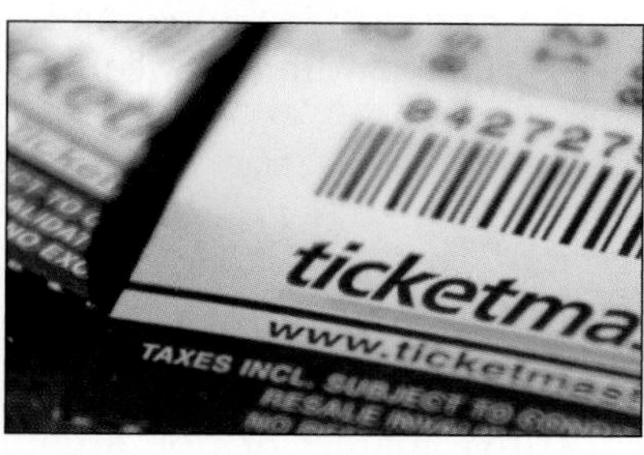	The resale market for tickets to major sporting events and concerts involves many buyers and sellers. The prices for seats in identical sections end up converging quickly toward a narrow range.	Some ticket companies and fans get special privileges that enable them to buy and sell blocks of tickets before others can enter the market.
Currency trading 	Hundreds of thousands of traders around the globe engage in currency buying and selling on any given day. Since all traders have very good real-time information, currency trades in different parts of the world converge toward the same price.	Currency markets are subject to intervention on the part of governments that might want to strategically alter the prevailing price of their currency.

ECONOMICS IN THE REAL WORLD

Aalsmeer Flower Auction

The world's largest flower auction takes place in Aalsmeer, a small town in the Netherlands. Each week, producers sell over 100 million flowers there. In fact, over one-third of all the flowers sold in the world pass through Aalsmeer. Since the Aalsmeer market serves thousands of buyers and sellers, it is one of the best examples of a competitive market you will ever find. The supply comes from approximately 6,000 growers worldwide. More than 2,000 buyers attend the auction to purchase flowers.

The Aalsmeer flower market is almost perfectly competitive.

Aalsmeer uses a method known as a Dutch auction to determine the price for each crate of flowers sold. Most people think of an auction as a situation in which two or more individuals try to outbid each other. However, in Aalsmeer that process is reversed. As each crate of flowers goes on sale, the price on a huge board starts at 100 euros and then goes down until the lot is sold. This special kind of auction was invented here, and it is a very efficient way of getting the highest price out of the buyer who wants the lot the most.

At Aalsmeer, individual buyers and sellers are small compared to the overall size of the market. In addition, the flowers offered by one seller are almost indistinguishable from those offered by the other sellers. As a result, individual buyers and sellers have no control over the price set by the market. ✷

In the next section, we will examine the profits that competitive firms make. After all, profits motivate firms to produce a product, so knowing how a business can make the most profit is central to understanding how competitive markets work.

How Do Firms Maximize Profits?

All firms, whether they are active in a competitive market or not, attempt to maximize profits. Making a profit requires that a firm have a thorough grasp of its costs and its revenues. In the previous chapter, we learned about the cost structure of the firm. In this section, we examine its revenues. Combining the firm's revenues with its costs enables us to determine how much profit the firm makes.

Profits are the goal of every firm, but they don't always materialize. Sometimes, firms experience losses instead of profits, so we also explore whether a firm should shut down or continue to operate in order to minimize its losses. Once we fully understand the firm's decision-making process, we will better

PRACTICE WHAT YOU KNOW

Price Takers: Mall Food Courts

Your instructor asks you to find an example of a competitive market nearby. Your friend suggests that you visit the food court at a nearby mall.

Question: Do the restaurants in a food court meet the definition of a price taker, thereby signaling a competitive market?

Answer: Most food courts contain a lot of competition. Customers can choose among burgers, sandwiches, salads, pizza, and much more. Everywhere you turn, there is another place to eat and the prices at each place are comparable. Is this enough to make each restaurant a price taker? Not quite, since each restaurant has some market power because it serves different food. This enables the more popular places to charge somewhat more.

Are the restaurants in a food court price takers?

While the restaurants in the court are not price takers, the drinks (both fountain drinks and bottled water) that they sell are essentially the same. Any customer who is only interested in getting something to drink has a highly competitive market to choose from.

comprehend how the entire market functions. To make this process easier, throughout this section we refer to Mr. Plow (from the *Simpsons* episode mentioned in the Economics in the Media box on p. 277) to examine the choices every business must make. We'll look at the price Mr. Plow charges and how many driveways he clears, and then we'll compare his revenues to his costs in order to determine whether he is maximizing his profit.

The Profit-Maximizing Rule

Let's imagine how much revenue Mr. Plow will make if he charges $10 for each driveway he clears. Table 9.3 shows how much profit he might make if he clears up to 10 driveways. As we learned in Chapter 8, total profits (column 4) are determined by taking the total revenue (column 2) and subtracting the total cost (column 3). Mr. Plow's profits start out at −$25 because even if he does not clear any driveways, he incurs a fixed cost of $50,000 to buy a snow plow before he can get started (this cost will enter into other calculations later in the chapter). In order to recover the fixed cost, he needs to generate revenue by clearing driveways. As Mr. Plow clears more driveways, the losses (the negative numbers) shown in column 4 gradually contract; he begins to earn a profit by the time he plows 6 driveways.

TABLE 9.3

Calculating Profit for Mr. Plow

(1)	(2)	(3)	(4)	(5)	(6)	(7)
Quantity (Q = driveways cleared)	**Total Revenue**	**Total Cost**	**Total Profit**	**Marginal Revenue**	**Marginal Cost**	**Change (Δ) in Profit**
Abbreviation:	**TR**	**TC**	**Π**	**MR**	**MC**	**ΔΠ**
Formula:			**TR − TC**	**ΔTR**	**ΔTC**	**MR − MC**
0	$0	$25	−$25			
1	10	34	−24	$10	$9	$1
2	20	41	−21	10	7	3
3	30	46	−16	10	5	5
4	40	49	−9	10	3	7
5	50	51	−1	10	2	8
6	60	54	6	10	3	7
7	70	60	10	10	6	4
8	80	70	10	**10** =	**10**	0
9	90	95	−5	10	25	−15
10	100	145	−45	10	50	−40

What does Table 9.3 tell us about Mr. Plow's business? Column 4 shows the company's profits at various output (Q) levels. Profits reach a maximum of $10 in a range of 7 to 8 driveways. From looking at this table, you might suppose that the firm can make a production decision based on the data in the profit column. However, firms don't work this way. The total profit (or loss) is typically determined after the fact. For example, Homer may have to fill up with gas at the end of the day, buy new tires for his plow, or purchase liability insurance. His accountant will take his receipts and deduct each expense to determine his profits. All of this takes time. An accurate understanding of Homer's profits may have to wait until the end of the quarter, or even the year, in order to fully account for all the irregular expenses associated with running a business. This means that the information found in the profit column is not available until long after the business decisions have been made. So, in day-to-day operations, the firm needs another way to make production decisions.

Marginal thinking

The key to determining Mr. Plow's profits comes from understanding the relationship between marginal revenue (column 5) and marginal cost (column 6). The marginal revenue is the change (Δ) in total revenue when the firm produces additional units. So, looking down column 5, we see that for every driveway Mr. Plow clears, he makes $10 in extra revenue. The marginal cost (column 6) is the change (Δ) in total cost when the firm produces additional units. Column 7 calculates the difference between the marginal revenue (column 5) and marginal cost (column 6).

Competitive Markets

ECONOMICS IN THE MEDIA

The Simpsons: Mr. Plow

In this episode, Homer buys a snow plow and goes into the snow removal business. After a few false starts, his business, Mr. Plow, becomes a huge success. Every snowy morning, he looks out the window and comments about "white gold."

The episode illustrates each of the factors that go into making a competitive market. Businesses providing snow removal all offer the *same* service. Since there are many buyers (homeowners) and many businesses (the "plow people"), the market is competitive.

However, Homer's joy, profits, and notoriety are short-lived. Soon his friend Barney buys a bigger plow and joins the ranks of the "plow people." Barney's *entry* into the business shows how easy it is for competitors to enter the market. Then Homer, who has begun to get lazy and rest on his success, wakes up late one snowy morning to find all the driveways in the neighborhood already plowed. A nasty battle over customers ensues.

Homer's great idea is about to melt away.

When firms can easily enter the market, any higher-than-usual profits that a firm enjoys in the short run will dissipate in the long run due to increased competition. As a result, we can say that this *Simpsons* episode shows an industry that is not just competitive; it is perfectly competitive.

In Chapter 8, we saw that to understand cost structure, a firm focuses on marginal cost. The same is true on the revenue side. To make a good decision on the level of investment, Mr. Plow must use marginal analysis. Looking at column 7, we see that where total profits equal \$10, the change in profits, MR − MC, is equal to \$0. (See the numbers in red in columns 4 and 7.) At output levels below 7, MR − MC is positive, as indicated by the numbers in green. Expanding output to 7 driveways adds to profits. But as Mr. Plow services more driveways, the marginal cost rises dramatically. For instance, Mr. Plow may have to seek driveways that are farther away and thus incur higher transportation costs for those additional customers. Whatever the cause, increased marginal costs (column 6) eventually overtake the constant marginal revenues (column 5).

Recall that we began our discussion by saying that a firm can't wait for the yearly, or even quarterly, profit statements to make production decisions. By examining the marginal impact, shown in column 7, a firm can make good day-to-day operational decisions. This means that Mr. Plow has to decide whether or not to clear more driveways. For instance, if he is plowing 4 driveways, he may decide to work a little harder the next time it snows and plow 1 more. At 5 driveways, his profits increase by \$8. Since he enjoys making this extra money, he could expand again from 5 to 6 driveways. This time, he makes an extra \$7. From 6 to 7 driveways, he earns \$4 more. However,

If you already own a truck and a plow, starting your own snow plow business is inexpensive.

when Mr. Plow expands from 7 to 8 driveways, he discovers that he does not earn any additional profits, and at 9 driveways he loses $15. This would cause him to scale back his efforts to a more profitable level of output.

The **profit-maximizing rule** states that profit maximization occurs when the firm chooses the quantity that causes marginal revenue to be equal to marginal cost, or MR = MC.

Marginal thinking helps Mr. Plow discover the production level at which his profits are maximized. The **profit-maximizing rule** states that profit maximization occurs when a firm expands output until marginal revenue is equal to marginal cost, MR = MC. (This is the point at which 10 = 10 in columns 5 and 6 of Table 9.3.) The profit-maximizing rule may seem counterintuitive, since at MR = MC (where marginal revenue is equal to the extra cost of production) there is no additional profit. However, according to the MR = MC rule, production should stop at the point at which profit opportunities no longer exist. Suppose that Mr. Plow chooses a point at which MR > MC. This means that the cost of producing additional units adds more to revenue than to costs, so production should continue. However, if MR < MC, the cost of producing additional units is more than the additional revenue those units bring in. At that point, production is not profitable. The point at which MR = MC is the exact level of production at which no further profitable opportunities exist and losses have not yet occurred. This is the optimal point at which to stop production. In the case of Mr. Plow, he should stop adding new driveways once he reaches 8.

Marginal thinking

Deciding How Much to Produce in a Competitive Market

We have observed that a firm in a highly competitive market is a price taker; it has no control over the price set by the market. Since snow removal companies provide the same service, they must charge the price that is determined from the overall supply and demand conditions that regulate that particular market.

To better understand these relationships, we can look at them visually. In Figure 9.1, we use the MR and MC data from Table 9.3 to illustrate the profit calculation. For reference, we also include the average cost curves such as the ones shown in Figure 8.2 on page 255 of Chapter 8. Recall that the marginal cost curve (shown in purple) always crosses the average total cost (ATC) curve and the average variable cost (AVC) curve at their lowest point. Figure 9.1 highlights the relationship between the marginal cost curve (MC) and the marginal revenue curve (MR). Since the price (P) Mr. Plow charges is constant at $10, marginal revenue is horizontal. Unlike MR, MC at first decreases and then rises due to diminishing marginal product. Therefore, the firm wants to expand production as long as MR is greater than MC, and it will stop production at the quantity where MR = MC = $10. When Q = 8, MR = MC and profits are maximized. At quantities beyond 8, the MC curve is above the MR curve; marginal cost is higher than marginal revenue, and the firm's profits will fall.

Note: we can use the profit-maximizing rule, MR = MC, to identify the most profitable output in a two-step process:

1. Locate the point at which the firm will maximize its profits: MR = MC. This is the point labeled A in Figure 9.1.
2. Look for the profit-maximizing output: move down the vertical dashed line to the *x* axis at point Q. Any quantity greater than, or less than, Q would result in lower profits.

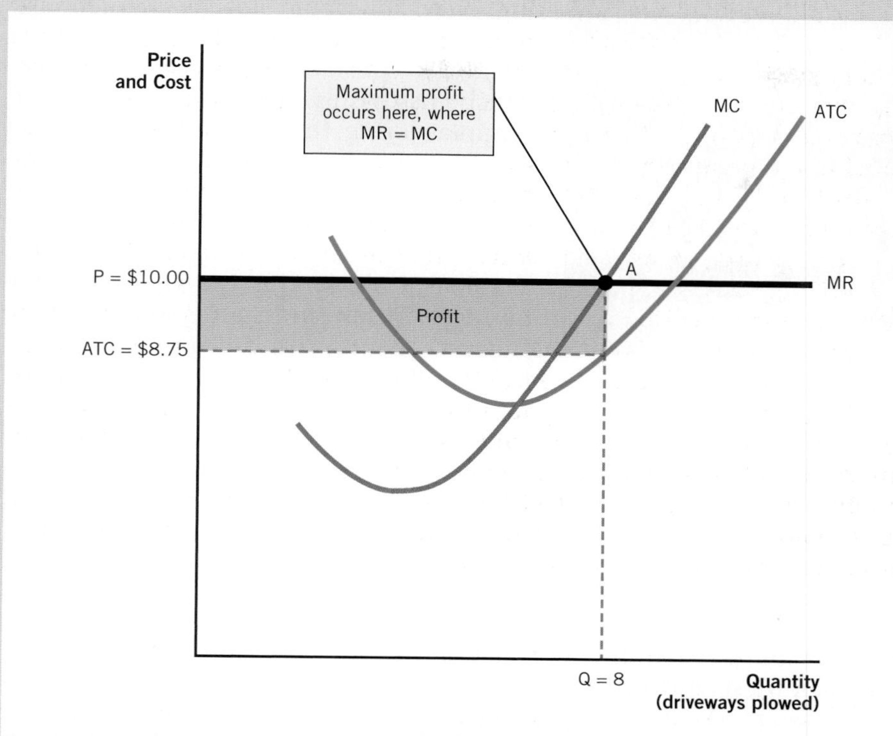

FIGURE 9.1

Profit Maximization

Mr. Plow uses the profit-maximizing rule to locate the point at which marginal revenue equals marginal cost, or MR = MC. This determines the ideal output level, Q. The firm takes the price from the market; this is shown as the horizontal MR curve where price = $10.00. Since the price charged is higher than the average total cost curve along the dashed line at quantity Q, the firm makes the economic profit shown in the green rectangle.

Once we know the profit-maximizing quantity, we can determine the average cost of producing Q units. From Q, we move up along the dashed line until it intersects with the ATC curve. From that point, we move horizontally until we come to the *y* axis. This tells us the average cost of making 8 units. Since the total cost in Table 9.3 is $70 when 8 driveways are plowed, dividing 70 by 8 gives us $8.75 for the average total cost. We can calculate Mr. Plow's profit rectangle from Figure 9.1 as follows:

$$\text{Profit} = (\text{Price} - \text{ATC [along the dashed line at quantity Q]}) \times \text{Q}$$

This gives us $(10-8.75) \times 8 = \$10$, which is the profit we see in Table 9.3, column 4, in red numbers. Since the MR is the price, and since the price is higher than the average total cost, the firm makes the profit visually represented in the green rectangle.

The Firm in the Short Run

Deciding how much to produce in order to maximize profits is the goal of every business. However, there are times when it is not possible to make a profit. When revenue is insufficient to cover cost, the firm suffers a loss—at which point it must decide whether to operate or temporarily shut down. Successful businesses make this decision all the time. For example, retail

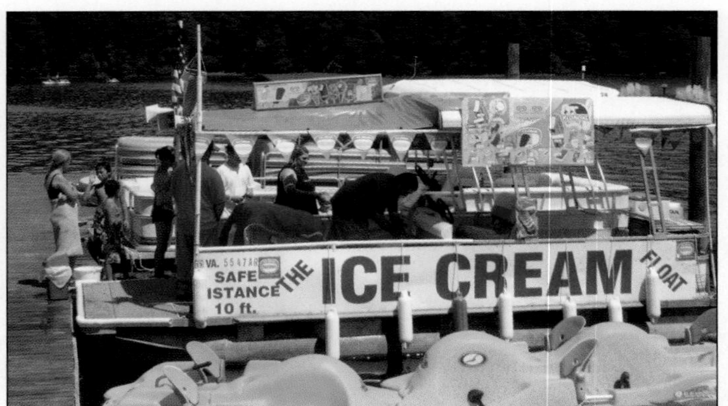

The Ice Cream Float, a cool idea on a hot day at the lake.

stores often close by 9 p.m. because operating overnight would not generate enough revenue to cover the costs of remaining open. Or consider the Ice Cream Float, which crisscrosses Smith Mountain Lake in Virginia during the summer months. You can hear the music announcing its arrival at the public beach from over a mile away. By the time the float arrives, there is usually a long line of eager customers waiting for the float to dock. This is a very profitable business on hot and sunny summer days. However, during the late spring and early fall the float operates on weekends only. Eventually, colder weather forces the business to shut down until the crowds return the following season. This shutdown decision is a short-run calculation. If the float were to operate during the winter, it would need to pay for employees and fuel. Incurring these variable costs when there are so few customers would result in greater total costs than simply dry-docking the boat. When the float is dry-docked over the winter, only the fixed cost of storing the boat remains.

Fortunately, a firm can use a simple, intuitive rule to decide whether to operate or shut down in the short run: if the firm would lose less by shutting down than by staying open, it should shut down. Recall that costs are broken into two parts—fixed and variable. Fixed costs must be paid whether the business is open or not. Since variable costs are only incurred when the business is open, if it can make enough to cover its variable costs—for example, employee wages and the cost of the electricity needed to run the lighting—it will choose to remain open. Once the variable costs are covered, any extra money goes toward paying the fixed costs.

A business should operate if it can cover its variable costs, and it should shut down if it cannot. Figure 9.2 illustrates the decision using cost curves. As long as the MR (marginal revenue) curve of the firm is greater than the minimum point on the AVC (average variable cost) curve—the green- and yellow-shaded areas—the firm will choose to operate. (Note that the MR curve is not shown in Figure 9.2. The colored areas in the figure denote the range of potential MR curves that are profitable or that cause a loss.) Recalling our example of the Ice Cream Float, you can think of the green-shaded area as the months during the year when the business makes a profit and the yellow-shaded area as the times during spring and fall when the float operates even though it is incurring a loss (because the loss is less than if the float were to shut down entirely). Finally, if the MR curve falls below the AVC curve—the red-shaded area—the firm should shut down. Table 9.4 summarizes these decisions.

To make the shut-down decision more concrete, imagine that the Ice Cream Float's minimum ATC (average total cost) is \$2.50 and its minimum AVC is \$2.00. During the summer, when many customers line up on the dock waiting for it to arrive, it can charge more than \$2.50 and earn a substantial profit. However, as the weather cools, fewer people want ice cream. The Ice Cream Float still has to crisscross the lake to make sales, burning expensive gasoline and paying employees to operate the vessel. If the Ice

FIGURE 9.2

When to Operate and When to Shut Down

If the MR (marginal revenue) curve is above the minimum point on the ATC (average total cost) curve, the Ice Cream Float will make a profit (shown in green). If the MR curve is below the minimum point on the ATC curve, $2.50, but above the minimum point on the AVC (average variable cost) curve, the float will operate at a loss (shown in yellow). If the MR curve is below the minimum point on the AVC curve, $2.00, the float will temporarily shut down (shown in red).

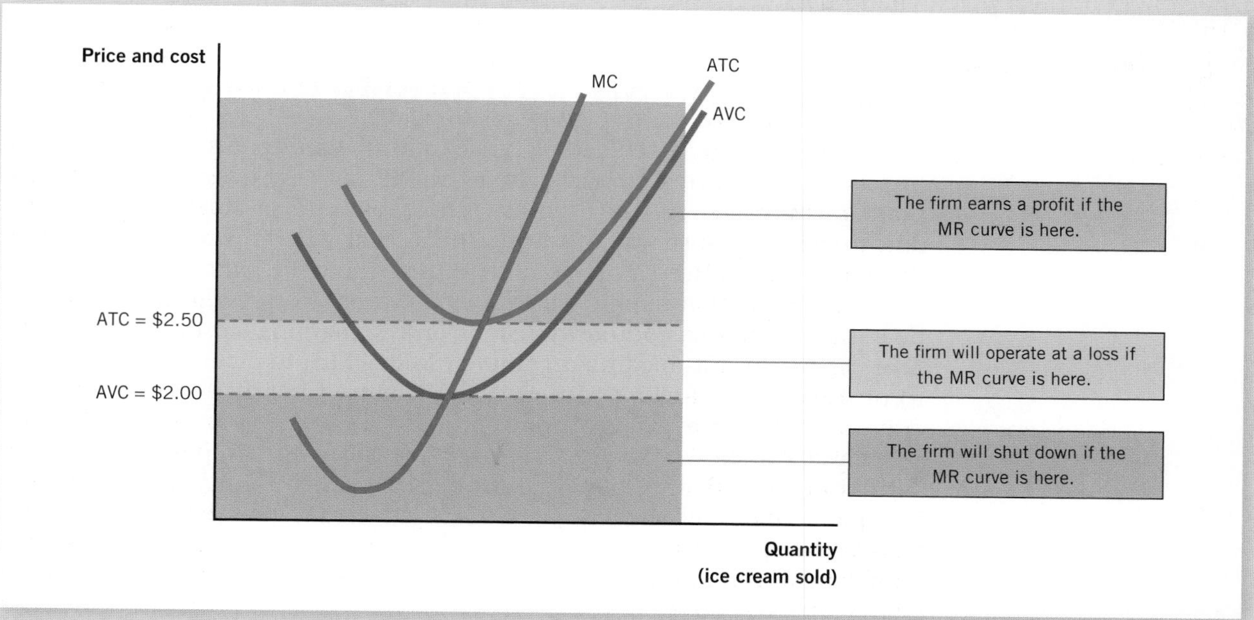

TABLE 9.4

Profit and Loss in the Short Run

Condition	In words	Outcome
P > ATC	The price is greater than the average total cost of production.	The firm makes a profit.
ATC > P > AVC	The average total cost of production is greater than the price the firm charges, but the price is greater than the average variable cost of production.	The firm will operate to minimize loss.
AVC > P	The price is less than the average variable cost of production.	The firm will temporarily shut down.

Cream Float is to keep its revenues high, it needs customers; but cooler weather suppresses demand. If the Ice Cream Float charges \$2.25 in the fall, it can make enough to cover its average variable costs of \$2.00, but not enough to cover its average total costs of \$2.50. Nevertheless, it will continue to operate because it makes enough in the yellow region to pay part of its fixed cost. Finally, it reaches a point at which the price drops below \$2.00. Now the business is no longer able to cover its average variable costs. At this point, it shuts down for the winter. It does this because operating when MR is very low causes the business to incur a larger loss.

The Firm's Short-Run Supply Curve

Cost curves provide a detailed picture of a firm's willingness to supply a good or service. We have seen that when the MR curve is below the minimum point on the AVC curve, the firm shuts down and production, or output, falls to zero. Another way of stating this is that when revenues are too low, no supply is produced. For example, during the winter the Ice Cream Float is dry-docked, so the supply curve does not exist. However, when the firm is operating, it bases its output decisions on the marginal cost. Recall that the firm uses the profit-maximizing rule, or MR = MC, to determine how much to produce. The marginal cost curve is therefore the firm's short-run supply curve as long as the firm is operating.

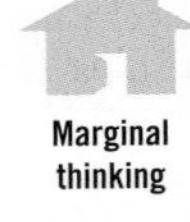

Marginal thinking

Figure 9.3 shows the Ice Cream Float's short-run supply curve. In the short run, diminishing marginal product causes the firm's costs to rise as the quantity produced increases. This is reflected in the shape of the firm's short-run supply curve, shown in red. The supply curve is upward sloping above the minimum point on the AVC curve. Below the minimum point on

FIGURE 9.3

The Firm's Short-Run Supply Curve

The supply curve (S_{SR}) and marginal cost curve (MC) are equivalent when the price is above the minimum point on the average variable cost curve (AVC). Below that point, the firm shuts down and no supply exists.

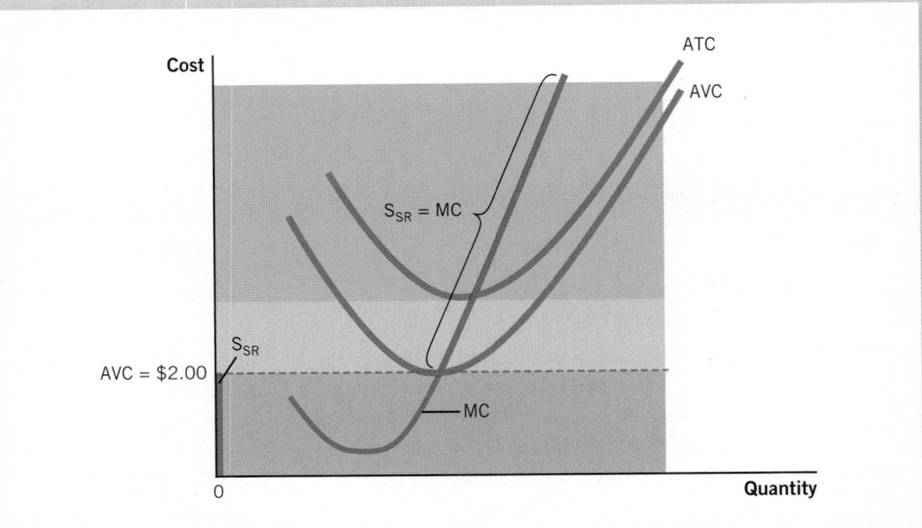

the AVC curve, the short-run supply curve becomes vertical at a quantity of zero, indicating that a willingness to supply the good does not exist below a price of $2.00. At prices above $2.00, the firm will offer more for sale as the price increases.

The Firm's Long-Run Supply Curve

In the long run, a firm's output decision is directly tied to profits. Since the firm is flexible in the long run, all costs are variable. As a result, the firm's long-run supply curve exists only when the firm expects to cover its total costs of production (because otherwise the firm would go out of business).

Returning to the Ice Cream Float example, recall that the boat shuts down over the winter instead of going out of business because demand is low but is expected to return. If for some reason the crowds do not come back, the float would go out of business. Turning to Figure 9.4, we see that at any point below the minimum point, $2.50 on the ATC curve, the float will experience a loss. Since, in the long run, firms are free to enter or exit the market, no firm will willingly produce in the market if the price is less than average total cost (P < ATC). As a result, no supply exists below $2.50. However, if price is greater than cost (P > ATC), the float expects to make a profit and thus will continue to produce.

The firm's long-run supply curve, shown in Figure 9.4 in red, is upward sloping above the minimum point on the ATC curve, which is denoted by ATC on the *y* axis. The supply curve becomes vertical at a quantity of zero, indicating that a willingness to supply the good does not exist below a price

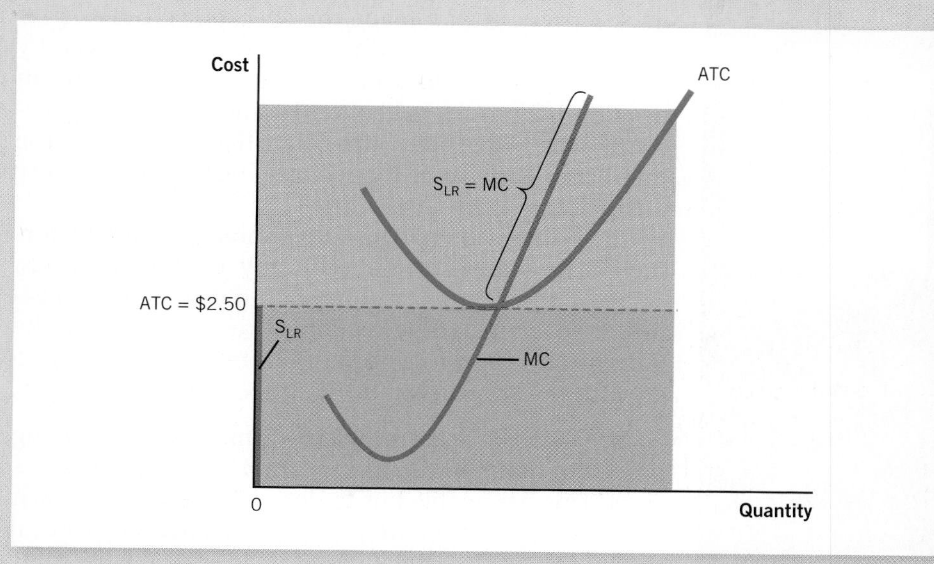

FIGURE 9.4

The Firm's Long-Run Supply Curve

The long-run supply curve (S_{LR}) and marginal cost curve (MC) are equivalent when the price is above the minimum point on the average total cost curve (ATC). Below that point, the firm shuts down and no supply exists.

of \$2.50. In the long run, a firm that expects price to exceed ATC will continue to operate, since the conditions for making a profit seem favorable. In contrast, a firm that does not expect price to exceed ATC should cut its losses and exit the industry. Table 9.5 outlines the long-run decision criteria.

ECONOMICS IN THE REAL WORLD

Blockbuster and the Dynamic Nature of Change

What happens if your customers do not return? What if you simply had a bad idea to begin with, and the customers never arrived in the first place?

When the long-run profit outlook is bleak, the firm is better off shutting down. This is a normal part of the ebb and flow of business. For example, once there were thousands of buggy whip companies. Today, as technology has improved and we no longer rely on horse-drawn carriages, few buggy whip makers remain. However, many companies now manufacture automobile parts.

Similarly, a succession of technological advances has transformed the music industry. Records were replaced by 8-track tapes, and then by cassettes. Already, the CD is on its way to being replaced by better technology as iPods, iPhones, and MP3 players make music more portable and as web sites such as Pandora and Spotify allow live streaming of almost any selection a listener wants to hear. However, there was a time when innovation meant playing music on the original Sony Walkman. What was cool in the early 1980s is antiquated today. Any business engaged in distributing music has had to adapt or close.

Blockbuster's best days are long gone.

Similar changes are taking place in the video rental industry. Blockbuster was founded in 1982 and experienced explosive growth, becoming the nation's largest video store chain by 1988. The chain's growth was fueled by its large selection and use of a computerized tracking system that made the checkout process faster than the one at competing video stores. However, by the early 2000s Blockbuster faced stiff competition from online providers like Netflix and in-store dispensers like Redbox. Today, the chain has one-quarter the number of employees it once had and its future is very uncertain.

In addition to changes in technology, other factors such as downturns in the economy, changes in tastes, demographic factors, and migration can all force businesses to close. These examples remind us that the long-run decision to go out of business has nothing to do with the short-term profit outlook. ✷

So far, we have examined the firm's decision-making process in the short run in the context of revenues versus costs. This has enabled us to determine the profits each firm makes. But now we pause to consider *sunk costs*, a special type of cost that all firms, in every industry, must consider when making decisions.

TABLE 9.5

The Long-Run Shut-Down Criteria

Condition	In words	Outcome
P > ATC	The price is greater than the average total cost of production.	The firm makes a profit.
P < ATC	The price is less than the average total cost of production.	The firm should shut down.

PRACTICE WHAT YOU KNOW

The Profit-Maximizing Rule: Show Me the Money!

Here is a question that often confuses students.

Question: At what point does a firm maximize profits?

a. where the profit per unit is greatest
b. where total revenue is maximized
c. where the total revenue is equal to the total cost
d. where marginal revenue equals marginal cost

What is the rule for making the most profit?

Answer: Each answer sounds plausible, so the key is to think about each one in a concrete way. To help do that, we will refer back to the Mr. Plow data in Table 9.3.

a. Incorrect. Making a large profit per unit sounds great. However, if the firm stops production when the profit per unit is the greatest—$8 in column 7—it will fail to realize the additional profits—$7 and $4 in column 7—that come from continuing to produce until MR = MC.

b. Incorrect. Recall that total revenue is only half of the profit function, Profit = TR − TC. No matter how much revenue a business brings in, if total costs are more, the firm will experience a loss. Therefore, the firm wishes to maximize profits, not revenue. For example, looking at column 2, we see that at 10 driveways Mr. Plow earns total revenues of $100. But column 3 tells us that the total cost of plowing 10 driveways is $145. With a total profit of −$45, this level of output would not be a good idea.

c. Incorrect. If total revenue and total cost are equal, the firm makes no profits.

d. Correct. Answers (a), (b), and (c) all sound plausible. But a firm maximizes profits where MR = MC, since at this point all profitable opportunities are exhausted. If Mr. Plow clears 7 or 8 driveways, his profit is $10. If he clears 9 driveways, his profits fall from $10 to −$5 since the marginal cost of clearing that ninth driveway, $25, is greater than the marginal revenue he earns of $10.

Sunk Costs

Costs that have been incurred as a result of past decisions are known as **sunk costs**. For example, the decision to build a new sports stadium is a good application of the principle of sunk costs. Many professional stadiums have been built in the past few years, even though the arenas they replaced were built to last much longer. For example, Three Rivers Stadium in Pittsburgh and Veterans Stadium in Philadelphia were built in the early 1970s as multi-use facilities for both football and baseball, each with an expected lifespan of 60 or more years. However, in the early 2000s both were replaced. Each city built two new stadiums with features such as luxury boxes and better seats that generate more revenue than Veterans and Three Rivers did. The additional revenue makes the new stadiums financially attractive even though the old stadiums were still structurally sound.

Stadium implosions are an example of marginal thinking.

Sunk costs are unrecoverable costs that have been incurred as a result of past decisions.

Demolishing a structure that is still in good working order may sound like a waste, but it can be good economics. When the extra benefit of a new stadium is large enough to pay for the cost of imploding the old stadium and constructing a new one, a city will do just that. In fact, since Pittsburgh and Philadelphia draw significantly more paying spectators with the new stadiums, the decision to replace the older stadiums has made the citizens in both cities better off. This occurs because new stadiums create increased ticket sales, higher tax revenues, and a more enjoyable experience for fans.

Opportunity cost

Continuing to use an out-of-date facility has an opportunity cost. Thinkers who do not understand sunk costs might point to the benefits of getting maximum use out of what already exists. But good economists learn to ignore sunk costs and focus on marginal value. They compare marginal benefits and marginal costs. If a new stadium, and the revenue it brings in, will create more value than the old stadium, the decision should be to tear the old one down.

What Does the Supply Curve Look Like in Perfectly Competitive Markets?

We have seen that a firm's willingness to supply a good depends on whether the firm is making a short-run or long-run decision. In the short run, a firm may choose to operate at a loss in order to recover a portion of its fixed costs. In the long run, there are no fixed costs, so a firm is willing to operate only if it expects the price it charges to cover total costs.

However, the supply curve for a single firm represents only a small part of the overall supply of a good provided in a competitive market. We will now turn to market supply and develop the short-run and long-run market supply curves.

SNAPSHOT

Sunk Costs: If You Build It, They Will Come

Replacing an old stadium with a new one is sometimes controversial. People often misunderstand sunk costs and argue for continuing with a stadium until it's completely worn down. But economics tells us not to focus on the sunk costs of the old stadium's construction. Instead, we should compare the marginal benefit of a new stadium to the marginal cost of demolition and new construction.

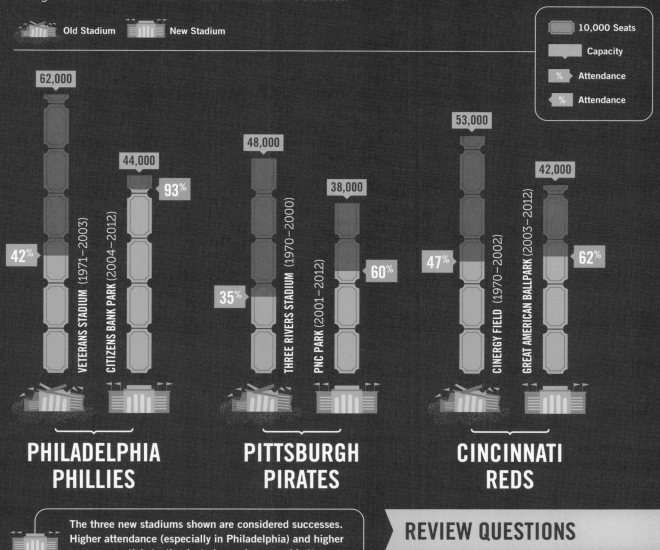

Old Stadium
New Stadium

10,000 Seats
Capacity
% Attendance
% Attendance

PHILADELPHIA PHILLIES

VETERANS STADIUM (1971–2003): 62,000; 42%
CITIZENS BANK PARK (2004–2012): 44,000; 93%

PITTSBURGH PIRATES

THREE RIVERS STADIUM (1970–2000): 48,000; 35%
PNC PARK (2001–2012): 38,000; 60%

CINCINNATI REDS

CINERGY FIELD (1970–2002): 53,000; 47%
GREAT AMERICAN BALLPARK (2003–2012): 42,000; 62%

The three new stadiums shown are considered successes. Higher attendance (especially in Philadelphia) and higher revenue per ticket—thanks to luxury boxes and better concessions—make the franchises happy.

An economist's analysis of the stadiums would go beyond attendance, however. The additional revenue generated by the new stadiums must be weighed against the costs of imploding the old stadiums and building new venues.

REVIEW QUESTIONS

- What do you think the smaller size of the new stadiums does to ticket prices, and why?
- Use the idea of sunk costs to analyze switching majors in college.

The Short-Run Market Supply Curve

A competitive market consists of a large number of identical sellers. Since an individual firm's supply curve is equal to its marginal cost curve, if we add together all the individual firm supply curves in a market, we arrive at the short-run market supply curve. Figure 9.5 shows the short-run market supply curve in a two-firm model consisting of Mr. Plow and the Plow King. At a price of $10, Mr. Plow is willing to clear 8 driveways (Q_A) and the Plow King is willing to clear 20 driveways (Q_B). When we horizontally sum the output of the two firms, we get a total market supply of 28 driveways (Q_{market}), seen in the third graph.

The Long-Run Market Supply Curve

Incentives

Recall that a competitive market is one in which a large number of buyers seek a product that many sellers offer. Competitive markets are also characterized by easy entry and exit. Existing firms and entrepreneurs decide whether to enter and exit a market based on incentives. When existing firms are enjoying profits, there is an incentive for them to produce more and also for entrepreneurs to enter the market. This leads to an increase in the quantity of the good supplied. Likewise, when existing firms are experiencing losses, there is an incentive for them to exit the market; then the quantity supplied decreases. Entry and exit have the combined effect of regulating the amount of profit a firm can hope to make in the long run. As long as profits exist, the quantity supplied will increase and the price will drop. When losses exist, the quantity supplied will decrease and the price will rise. So both profits and losses signal a need for an adjustment in market supply. Therefore, profits and losses act as

FIGURE 9.5

Short-Run Market Supply

The market supply is determined by summing the individual supply of each firm in the market. Although we have only shown this process for two firms, Mr. Plow and Plow King, the process extends to any number of firms in a market.

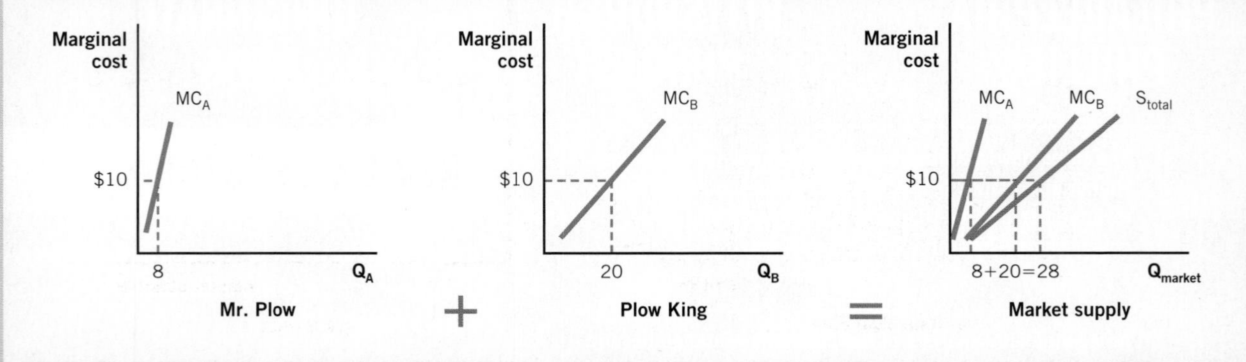

signals for resources to enter or leave an industry. **Signals** convey information about the profitability of various markets.

The **signals** of profits and losses convey information about the profitability of various markets.

The only time an adjustment does not take place is when participants in the market make zero economic profit—this is the long-run equilibrium. At that point, existing firms and entrepreneurs are not inclined to enter or exit the market; the adjustment process that occurs through price changes ends.

The benefit of a competitive market is that profits guide existing firms and entrepreneurs to produce more goods and services that society values. Losses serve the same valuable function by encouraging firms to exit and move elsewhere. Without profits and losses acting as signals for firms to enter or exit the market, resources will be misallocated and surpluses and shortages of goods will occur.

Figure 9.6 captures how entry and exit determine the market supply. The profit-maximizing point of the individual firm in panel (a), MR = MC, is located at the minimum point on the ATC curve. The price (P = min. ATC) that existing firms receive is just enough to cover costs, so profits are zero. As a result, new firms have no incentive to enter the market and existing firms have no reason to leave. At all prices above P = min. ATC, firms will earn a profit (the green-shaded area), and at all prices below P = min. ATC firms

Incentives

FIGURE 9.6

The Market Supply Curve and Entry and Exit

Entry into the market and exit from it force the long-run price to be equal to the minimum point on the average total cost curve (ATC). At all prices above P = min. ATC, firms will earn a profit (the green-shaded area), and at all prices below P = min. ATC, firms will experience a loss (the red-shaded area). This means the long-run supply curve (S_{LR}) must be horizontal at price P = min. ATC. If the price was any higher or lower, firms would enter or exit the market, and the market could not be in a long-run equilibrium.

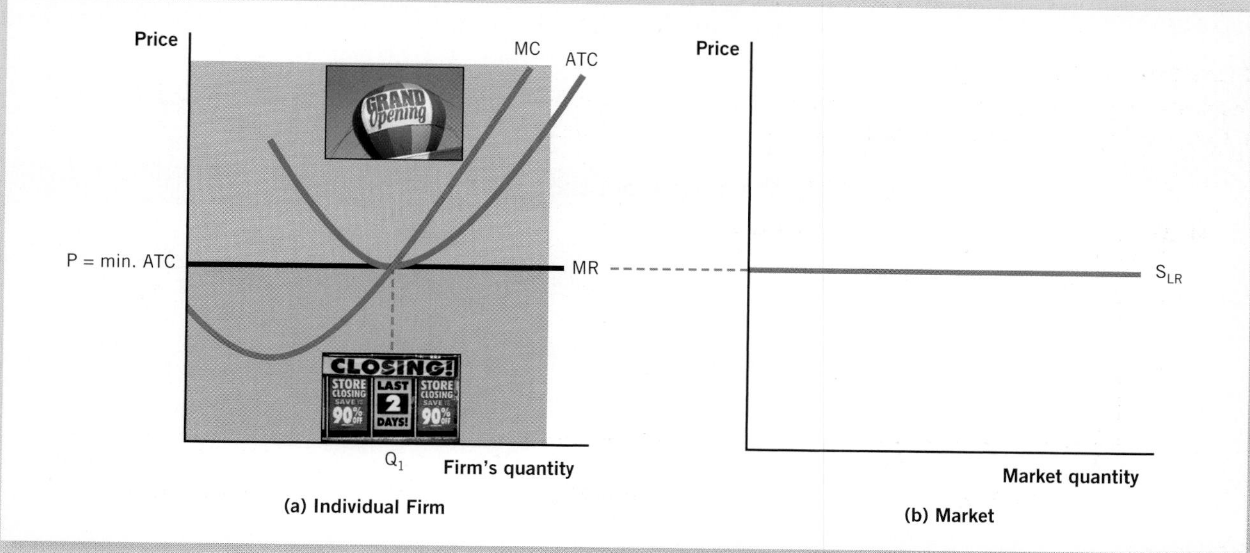

will experience a loss (the red-shaded area). This picture is consistent for all markets with free entry and exit; zero economic profit occurs at only one price, and that price is the lowest point of the ATC curve.

At this price, the supply curve in panel (b) must be a horizontal line at P = min. ATC. If the price was any higher, firms would enter, supply would increase, and this would force the price back down to P = min. ATC. If the price was any lower, firms would exit, supply would decrease, and this would force the price up to P = min. ATC. Since we know that these adjustments will have time to take place in the long run, the long-run supply curve must also be equal to P = min. ATC in order to satisfy the demand that exists at this price.

A Reminder about Economic Profit

Now that you have learned how perfect competition affects business profits in the long run, you may not think that it is a desirable environment for businesses seeking to earn profits. After all, if a firm cannot expect to make an economic profit in the long run, why bother? It's easy to forget the distinction between accounting profit and economic profit. Firms enter a market when they expect to be reasonably compensated for their investment. And they leave a market when the investment does not yield a satisfactory result. Economic profit is determined by deducting the explicit and implicit costs. Therefore, firms are willing to stay in perfectly competitive markets in the long run when they are breaking even because they are being reasonably compensated for the explicit expenses they have incurred and also for the implicit expenses—like the opportunity costs of other business ventures—that they would expect to make elsewhere.

Opportunity cost

For example, if Mr. Plow has the explicit and implicit costs shown in Table 9.6, we can see the distinction between accounting profit and economic profit more clearly. Mr. Plow has revenues of $25,000 during the year.

If Mr. Plow asks his accountant how much the business earned during the year, the accountant adds up all of Mr. Plow's explicit costs and subtracts them from his revenues. The accountant reports back that Mr. Plow earned

TABLE 9.6

Mr. Plow's Economic Profit and the Entry or Exit Decision

Explicit costs per year	
Payment on the loan on his snow plow	$7,000
Gasoline	2,000
Miscellaneous equipment (shovels, salt)	1,000
Implicit costs	
Forgone salary	$10,000
The forgone income that the $50,000 invested in the snow plow could have earned if invested elsewhere	5,000
Total cost	$25,000

\$25,000 − \$10,000, or \$15,000 in profit. Now \$15,000 in profit would sound good to a lot of firms, so we would expect many new entrants in the plowing business. But not so fast! We have not accounted for the implicit costs—the money Mr. Plow could have earned by working another job instead of plowing, and also the money he invested in the plow (\$50,000) that could have yielded a return (\$5,000) elsewhere. If we add in the explicit costs, we find the economic profit, \$25,000 − \$10,000 − \$15,000 = \$0. Zero profit sounds unappealing, but it is not. It means that Mr. Plow covered his forgone salary and also his next-best investment alternative. If you could not make any more money doing something else with your time or your investments, you might as well stay in the same place. So Mr. Plow is content to keep on plowing, while others, outside the industry, do not see any profit from entering the industry.

How the Market Adjusts in the Long Run: An Example

We have seen that profits and losses may exist in the short run; in the long run, the best the competitive firm can do is earn zero economic profit. This section looks in more detail at the adjustment process that leads to long-run equilibrium.

We begin with the market in long-run equilibrium, shown in Figure 9.7. Panel (a) represents an individual firm operating at the minimum point on

FIGURE 9.7

The Market in Equilibrium before a Decrease in Demand

When a market is in long-run equilibrium, the short-run supply curve (S_{SR}) and short-run demand curve (D_{SR}) intersect along the long-run supply curve (S_{LR}). When this occurs, the price that the firm charges is equal to the minimum point along the average total cost curve (ATC). This means that the existing firms in the market earn zero economic profit and there is no incentive for firms to enter or exit the market.

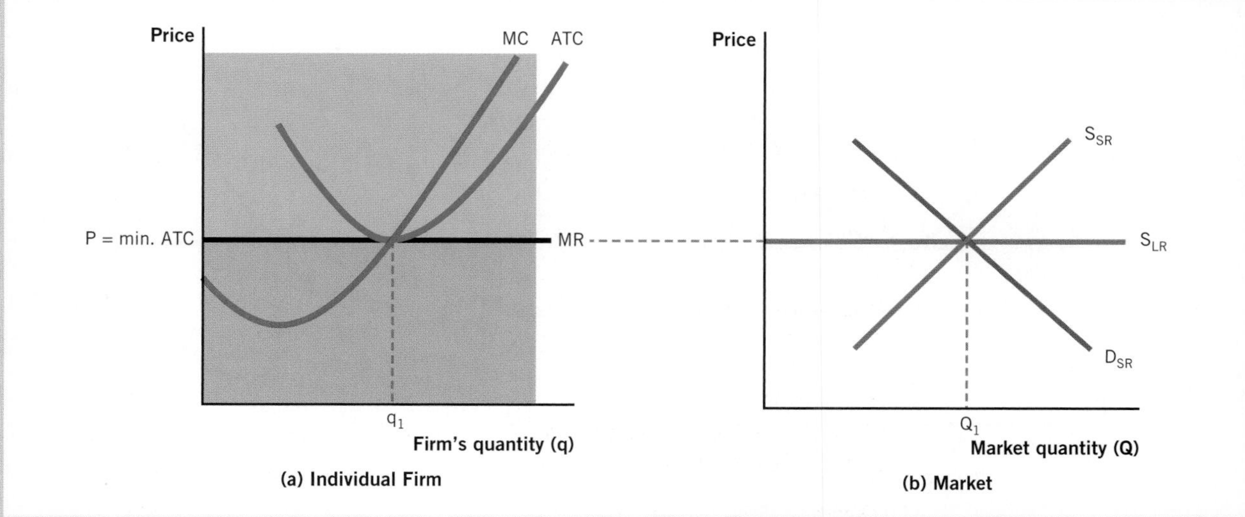

its ATC curve. In long-run equilibrium, all firms are operating as efficiently as possible. Since the price is equal to the average cost of production, economic profit for the firm is zero. In panel (b), the SR supply curve and the demand curve intersect along the LR supply curve, so the market is also in equilibrium. If, for instance, the SR supply curve and the demand curve happened to intersect above the LR supply curve, the price would be higher than the minimum point on the ATC curve. This would lead to short-run profits and indicate that the market was not in long-run equilibrium. The same would be true if the SR supply curve and the demand curve happened to intersect below the LR supply curve, since the price would be lower than the minimum point on the ATC curve. This would lead to short-run shortages, thus causing the price to rise, and then once again the market would be in long-run equilibrium.

Now suppose that demand declines, as shown in Figure 9.8. In panel (b), we see that the market demand curve shifts from D_1 to D_2. When demand falls, the equilibrium point moves from point A to point B. The price drops to P_2 and the market output drops to Q_2. The firms in this industry take their price from the market, so the new marginal revenue curve shifts down from MR_1 to MR_2 at P_2 in panel (a). Since the firm maximizes profits where $MR_2 = MC$, the firm will produce an output of q_2. When the output is q_2 the firm's costs, C_2, are higher than the price it charges, P_2, so it experiences a loss equal to the red-shaded area in panel (a). In addition, since the firm's output is lower, it is no longer producing at the minimum point on its ATC curve, so the firm is not as efficient as before.

FIGURE 9.8

The Short-Run Adjustment to a Decrease in Demand

A decrease in demand causes the price to fall in the market, as shown by the movement from D_1 to D_2 in panel (b). Since the firm is a price taker, the price it can charge falls to P_2. As we see in panel (a), the intersection of MR_2 and MC occurs at q_2. At this output level, the firm incurs the short-run loss shown in (a).

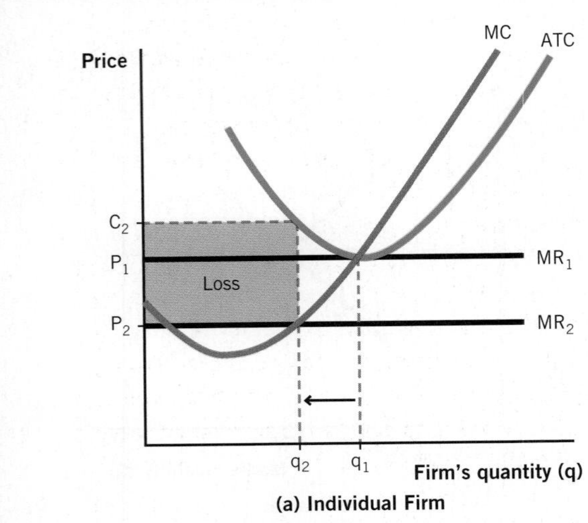

(a) Individual Firm

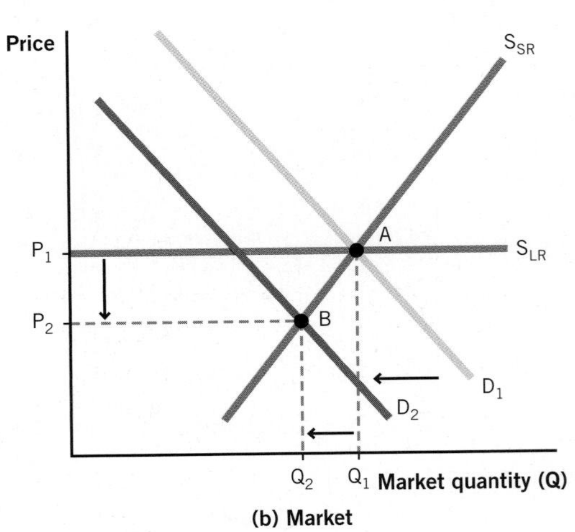

(b) Market

Entry and Exit

ECONOMICS IN THE MEDIA

I Love Lucy

I Love Lucy was the most watched television comedy of the 1950s. The show featured two couples who are best friends, the Ricardos and the Mertzes, who find themselves in the most unlikely situations.

One particular episode finds Ricky Ricardo disillusioned with show business. After some conversation, Ricky and Fred Mertz decide to go into business together and start a diner. Fred and Ethel Mertz have the experience to run the diner, and Ricky plans to use his name and star power to help get the word out about the restaurant, which they name A Little Bit of Cuba.

If you have seen any of the *I Love Lucy* series, you already know that the business venture is destined to fail. Sure enough, the Mertzes get tired of doing all of the hard work—cooking and serving the customers—while Ricky and Lucy Ricardo meet and greet the guests. Things quickly deteriorate, and the two couples decide to part ways. The only problem is that they are both part owners, and neither can afford to buy out the other. So they decide to split the diner in half right down the middle!

The result is absurd and hilarious. On one side, guests go to A Little Bit of Cuba. On the other side, the Mertzes set up Big Hunk of America. Since both restaurants use the same facilities and sell the same food, the only way they can differentiate themselves is by lowering their prices. This leads to a hamburger price war to attract customers:

Ethel: "Three!"
Lucy: "Two!"
Ethel: "One-cent hamburgers."
Fred: "Ethel, are you out of your mind?" *[Even in the 1950s, a penny was not enough to cover the marginal cost of making a hamburger.]*
Ethel: "Well, I thought this could get 'em."
Fred: "One-cent hamburgers?"

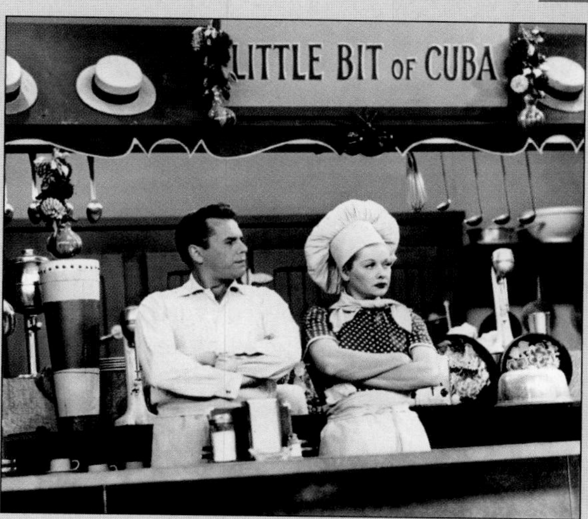

After the exchange, Lucy whispers in a customer's ear and gives him a dollar. He then proceeds to Big Hunk of America and says, "I'd like 100 hamburgers!"

Fred Mertz replies, "We're all out of hamburgers."

How do the falling prices described here affect the ability of the firms in this market to make a profit?

The exchange is a useful way of visualizing how perfectly competitive markets work. Competition forces the price down, but the process of entry and exit takes time and is messy. The Ricardos and Mertzes can't make a living selling one-cent hamburgers—one cent is below their marginal cost—so one of the couples will end up exiting. At that point, the remaining couple would be able to charge more. If they end up making a profit, that profit will encourage entrepreneurs to enter the business. As the supply of hamburgers expands, the price that can be charged will be driven back down. Since we live in an economically dynamic world, prices are always moving toward the long-run equilibrium.

What does it take to produce more mangoes?

Firms in a competitive market can exit the industry easily. Some will do so in order to avoid further losses. Figure 9.9 shows that as firms exit, the market supply contracts from S_{SR1} to S_{SR2} and the market equilibrium moves to point C. At point C, the price rises back to P_1. Market output then drops to Q_3 and the price returns to P_1. The firms that remain in the market no longer experience a short-run loss, since MR_2 returns to MR_1 and costs fall from C_2 to C_1. The end result is that the firm is once again efficient, and economic profit returns to zero.

For example, suppose there is a decline in demand for mangoes due to a false rumor that links the fruit to a salmonella outbreak. The decline in demand causes the price of mangoes to drop. As a consequence, mango producers experience negative economic profit—generating curves like the ones shown in Figure 9.8. In response to the negative profit, some mango growers will exit the industry, the mango trees will be sold for firewood, and the land will be converted to other uses. With fewer mangoes being produced, the supply will contract. Eventually, the smaller supply will cause the price of mangoes to rise until a new long-run equilibrium is reached at a much lower level of output, as shown in Figure 9.9.

FIGURE 9.9

The Long-Run Adjustment to a Decrease in Demand

Short-run losses cause some firms to exit the industry. Their exit shifts the market supply curve to the left in panel (b) until the price returns to long-run equilibrium at point C. This restores the price to P_1 and shifts the MR curve up in panel (a) to MR_1. At P_1 the firm is, once again, earning zero economic profit.

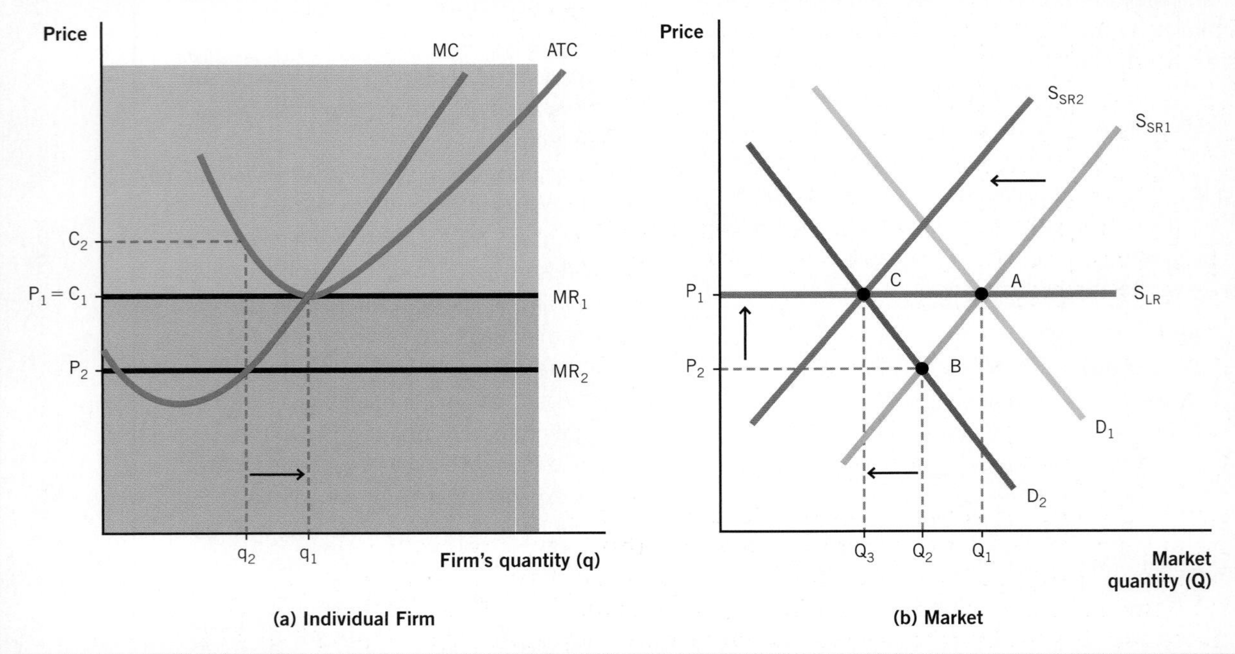

PRACTICE WHAT YOU KNOW

Long-Run Profits: How Much Can a Firm Expect to Make?

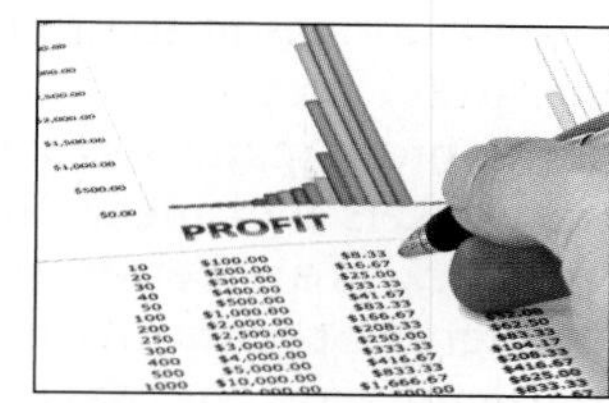

Calculating profits

Fill in the blank: In the long run, a firm in a perfectly competitive market earns __________________ profits.

(Caution: there may be more than one right answer!)

a. positive accounting
b. zero accounting
c. positive economic
d. zero economic

Answers:

a. **Correct**. Accounting profits only cover the explicit costs of doing business, so they are positive. But they do not include the implicit costs; once those costs are taken into account, the economic profit will be lower. If the implicit costs are exactly equal to the accounting profits, the firm will earn zero economic profit and the long-run equilibrium will be reached.
b. **Incorrect**. If a firm earns zero accounting profits, the implicit costs will make the economic profit negative. When economic profit is negative, firms will exit the market.
c. **Incorrect**. When a firm earns an economic profit, this sends a signal to firms outside the market to enter. The long-run equilibrium occurs when there is no incentive to enter or exit the market.
d. **Correct**. This answer only makes sense when you recall that *zero* does not mean *nothing*. Zero economic profit means that the firm can cover its explicit (accounting) and implicit (opportunity) costs. It also means that firms inside the market are content to stay and that firms outside the market do not see the value of entering. In the long run, the only condition that would not signal firms to enter or exit would be zero economic profit.

More on the Long-Run Supply Curve

To keep the previous example as simple as possible, we assumed that the long-run supply curve was horizontal. However, this is not always the case. There are two reasons why the long-run supply curve may slope upward. First, some resources needed to produce the product may only be available in limited supplies. As firms try to expand production, they must bid to acquire those resources—a move that causes the average total cost curve to rise. For instance, a mango grower who wants to plant more trees must acquire more suitable land. Since mangoes grow in tropical areas with warm, wet summers, not all land is perfectly adaptable for growing them. The limited supply of land will cause the price of producing mangoes to rise, which will cause the supply curve to be positively sloped.

Opportunity cost

A second reason the long-run supply curve may be upward sloping is the opportunity cost of the labor used in producing the good. If you want to produce more mangoes, you will need more workers to pick the fruit. Hiring extra workers will mean finding people who are both willing and capable. Some workers are better than others at picking mangoes, and some workers have higher opportunity costs. As your firm attempts to expand production, it must increase the wage it pays to attract additional help or accept new workers who are not quite as capable. Either way you slice it, this means higher costs, which would be reflected in a rising long-run supply curve.

This discussion simply means that higher prices are necessary to induce suppliers to offer more for sale. None of it changes the basic ideas we have discussed throughout this section. The entry and exit of firms ensures that the market supply curve is much more elastic in the long run than in the short run.

Conclusion

It is tempting to think that firms control the prices they charge. This is not true in competitive markets, where firms are at the mercy of market forces that set the price charged throughout the industry. Individual firms have no control over the price because they sell the same products as their competitors. In addition, profits and losses help regulate economic activity in competitive markets and also promote economic efficiency. Profits reward producers for producing a good that is valued more highly than the resources used to produce it. This encourages entry into those markets. Likewise, losses penalize producers who operate inefficiently or produce goods that consumers do not want. This encourages exit from the market. The process of entry and exit ensures that resources flow into markets that are undersupplied and away from markets where too many firms exist.

In this chapter, we have studied competitive markets to establish a benchmark that will help us understand how other market structures compare to this ideal. In the next few chapters, we will explore imperfect markets. These markets provide a significant contrast with the results we have just seen. The closer a market is to meeting the criteria of perfect competition, the better the result for consumers and society in general.

ANSWERING THE BIG QUESTIONS

How do competitive markets work?

* The firms in competitive markets sell similar products. Firms are also free to enter and exit the market whenever they wish.
* A price taker has no control over the price it receives in the market.
* In competitive markets, the price and quantity produced are determined by market forces instead of by the firm.

How do firms maximize profits?

* A firm can maximize profits by expanding output until marginal revenue is equal to marginal cost (MR = MC, or the profit-maximizing rule). The profit-maximizing rule is a condition for stopping production at the point where profit opportunities no longer exist.
* The firm should shut down if the price it receives does not cover its average variable costs. Since variable costs are only incurred when operating, if a firm can make enough to cover its variable costs in the short run, it will choose to continue to operate.

What does the supply curve look like in perfectly competitive markets?

* Profits and losses act as signals for firms to enter or leave an industry. As a result, perfectly competitive markets drive economic profit to zero in the long run.
* The entry and exit of firms ensure that the market supply curve in a competitive market is much more elastic in the long run than in the short run.

ECONOMICS FOR LIFE

Tips for Starting Your Own Business

Before you go into business for yourself, you need to devise a plan. Over 80% of all small businesses fail within five years because the businesses were ill conceived or counted on unrealistic sales projections. You don't need a hugely detailed plan as long as it covers these essential points:

Do a cost-benefit analysis, and determine how long it will take you to break even. If you don't do this, you could run out of money and have to close your doors before you start to make a profit. Reaching the break-even point is different from earning an economic profit. Breaking even requires that you cover your explicit expenses with your revenues, or have a positive cash flow. This is especially important if you enter a perfectly competitive market where long-run profits are not possible. You need to be lean and efficient just to survive.

Keep your start-up costs as low as possible. Consider investing as much of your own money as possible. It can be very tempting to take out loans to cover your start-up costs, but if you expect to start immediately paying back your loans with the profits from your new business, think again. It can take years to become profitable. To lessen this problem, you can invest more of your own capital into the business to ensure that loans don't sink you. Also, start small and grow your business slowly in order to avoid overreaching.

Protect yourself from risk. If you are a sole proprietor, you are liable for business debts and judgments, and your creditors can come after your personal assets—like your home and savings accounts. To protect against this possibility, you can incorporate into what is known as a limited liability corporation, which helps shield business owners from personal liability.

Make sure your plan covers the essential points.

Realize that you need a competitive advantage to attract customers. It could be price, better service, a better product—but it has to be something. Don't expect to be successful unless you can do something better than your rivals!

Hire the right people to help you. Remember what we learned about specialization: embrace it. You don't have to be an expert tax accountant, manager, and marketer. Offload some of these tasks on others who are better at them, and focus on doing what you do best. However, once you find the right people to help, treat them well and provide an environment in which they will thrive and give their all.

CONCEPTS YOU SHOULD KNOW

price taker (p. 272)
profit-maximizing rule (p. 278)
signals (p. 289)
sunk costs (p. 286)

QUESTIONS FOR REVIEW

1. What are the necessary conditions for a perfectly competitive market to exist?
2. Describe the two-step process used to identify the profit-maximizing level of output.
3. Under what circumstances will a firm have to decide whether to operate or to shut down?
4. What is the difference between the decision to go out of business and the decision to operate or to shut down?
5. How do profits and losses act as signals that guide producers to use resources to make what society wants most?
6. What are sunk costs? Give an example from your own experience.
7. Why do competitive firms earn zero economic profit in the long run?

STUDY PROBLEMS (** solved at the end of the section*)

1. Using the definition of a price taker as your guide, for the following industries explain why the outcome does not meet the definition.
   a. the pizza delivery business
   b. the home improvement business
   c. cell phone companies
   d. cereals

2. A local snow cone business sells snow cones in one size for $3 each. It has the following cost and output structure per hour:

Output (cones per hour)	Total cost (per hour)
0	$60
10	$90
20	$110
30	$120
40	$125
50	$135
60	$150
70	$175
80	$225

   a. Calculate the total revenue for the business at each rate of output.
   b. Calculate the total profit for the business at each rate of output.
   c. Is the business operating in the short run or the long run?
   d. Calculate the profit-maximizing rate of output using the MR = MC rule. (**Hint**: to do this, you should first compute the marginal revenue and marginal cost from the table.)

3. Determine whether the following statements are true or false. Explain your answers.
   a. A firm will make a profit when the price it charges exceeds the average variable cost of the chosen output level.
   b. In order to maximize profits in the short run, a firm must minimize its costs.
   c. If economic profit is positive, firms will exit the industry in the short run.
   d. A firm that receives a price greater than its average variable costs but less than its average total costs should shut down.

4. In the table at the top of p. 300, fill in the blanks. After you have completed the entire table, determine the profit-maximizing output.

Output	Price	Total revenue	Marginal revenue	Total cost	Marginal cost	Total profit
1	$20	___	___	$40	___	−$20
2	___	___	___	$50	___	___
3	___	___	___	$60	___	___
4	___	___	___	$65	5	___
5	___	___	___	$85	___	___
6	___	$120	___	$120	___	___

5. Use the graph to answer the questions that follow.

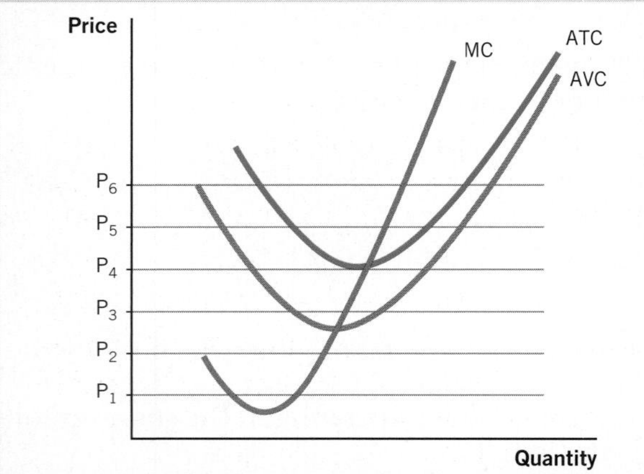

a. At what prices is the firm making an economic profit, breaking even, and experiencing an economic loss?
b. At what prices would the firm shut down?
c. At what prices does the firm's short-run supply curve exist? At what prices does the firm's long-run supply curve exist?

* 6. Identify as many errors as you can in the following graph.

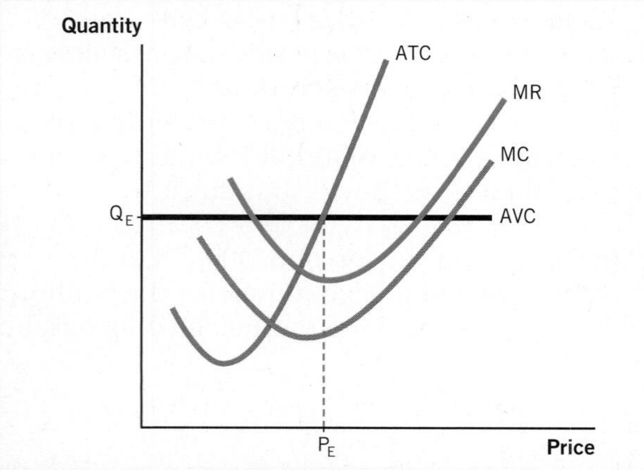

7. A firm is experiencing a loss of $5,000 per year. The firm has fixed costs of $8,000 per year.
   a. Should the firm operate in the short run or shut down?
   b. If the situation persists into the long run, should the firm stay in the industry or go out of business?
   c. Now suppose that the firm's fixed costs are $2,000. How would this change its short-run and long-run decisions?

8. Three students at the same school hear about the success of cookie delivery businesses on college campuses. Each student decides to open a local service. The individual supply schedules are shown below.

Delivery charge	Quantity supplied: Esra	Remzi	Camilo
$1	2	3	6
$2	4	6	7
$3	6	9	8
$4	8	12	9
$5	10	15	10
$6	12	18	11

   a. Draw the individual supply curves.
   b. Sum the individual supply schedules to compute the short-run industry supply schedule.
   c. Draw the industry supply curve.

9. Do you agree or disagree with the following statement? "A profit-maximizing, perfectly competitive firm should select the output level at which the difference between the marginal revenue and marginal cost is the greatest." Explain your answer.

10. Barney's snow removal service is a profit-maximizing, competitive firm. Barney clears driveways for $10 each. His total cost each day is $250, and half of his total costs are fixed. If Barney clears 20 driveways a day, should he continue to operate or shut down? If this situation persists, will Barney stay in the industry or exit?

* 11. Suppose you are the owner of a firm producing jelly beans. Your production costs are shown in the table. Initially, you produce 100 boxes of jelly beans per time period. Then a new customer calls and places an order for an additional box of jelly beans, requiring you to increase your output to 101 boxes. She offers you $1.50 for the additional box. Should you produce it? Why or why not?

Jelly Bean Production

Boxes	Average cost per box
100	$1.00
101	$1.01
102	$1.02
103	$1.03

SOLVED PROBLEMS

6. Here is the corrected graph with the errors struck out and some explanation below.

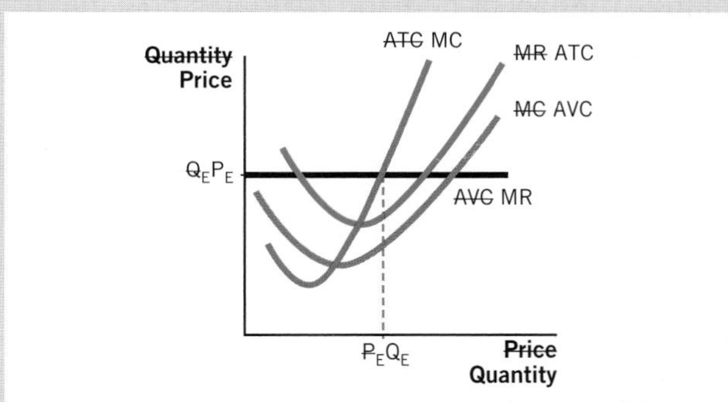

Also, the ATC and AVC curves did not intersect the MC curve at their minimum points. That is corrected here.

11. This problem requires marginal thinking. We know the profit-maximizing rule, or MR = MC. Here all we need to do is compare the additional costs, or MC, against the additional revenue, or MR, to see if the deal is a good idea. We know that MR = $1.50, because that is what the customer is offering to pay for another box of jelly beans. Now we need to calculate the marginal cost of producing the additional box.

Jelly Bean Production

Boxes	Average cost per box	Total cost	Marginal cost
100	$1.00	$100.00	—
101	$1.01	$102.01	$2.01
102	$1.02	$104.04	$2.03
103	$1.03	$106.09	$2.05

First we compute the total cost. To do this, we multiply the number of boxes, listed in the first column, by the average cost, shown in the second column. The results are shown in the total cost column.

Next we find the marginal cost. Recall that the marginal cost is the amount that it costs to produce one more unit. So we subtract the total cost of producing 101 boxes from the total cost of producing 100. For 101 boxes, MC = $102.01 − $100.00, or $2.01. Since MR − MC is $1.50 − $2.01, producing the 101st box would create a loss of $0.51. Therefore, at a price of $1.50, your firm should not produce the 101st box.

CHAPTER 10

Understanding Monopoly

MISCONCEPTION

Monopolists always make a profit.

In this chapter, we will explore another market structure: monopoly. Many people mistakenly believe that monopolists always make a profit. This is not true. Monopolists enjoy market power for their specific product, but they cannot force consumers to purchase what they are selling. The law of demand regulates how much a monopolist can charge. This means that when a monopolist charges more, people buy less. It also means that if demand is low, a monopolist may experience a loss instead of a profit.

While pure monopolies are unusual, this market structure is important to study because many markets exhibit some form of monopolistic behavior. Microsoft, the National Football League, the United States Postal Service (for first-class mail), and some small-town businesses are all examples of monopoly. In this chapter, we explore the conditions that give rise to monopolies and also the ways in which monopoly power can erode.

The typical result of monopoly is higher prices and less output than we find in a competitive market. Once we understand the market conditions that give rise to a monopoly, we will consider how governments seek to address the problems that monopolies present, and also how governments can be the cause of monopolies as well.

A small town's sole veterinarian functions as a monopolist.

BIG QUESTIONS

- **How are monopolies created?**
- **How much do monopolies charge, and how much do they produce?**
- **What are the problems with, and solutions for, monopoly?**

How Are Monopolies Created?

As we explained in Chapter 3, a monopoly is characterized by a single seller who produces a well-defined product for which there are no good substitutes. Two conditions enable a single seller to become a monopolist. First, the firm must have something unique to sell. Second, it must have a way to prevent potential competitors from entering the market.

Monopolies occur in many places and for several different reasons. For example, natural gas, water, and electricity are all examples of a monopoly that occurs naturally because of economies of scale. But monopolies can also occur when the government regulates the amount of competition. For example, trash pickup, street vending, taxicab rides, and ferry service are often licensed by local governments. This has the effect of limiting competition and creating **monopoly power**, which measures the ability of firms to set the price for a good.

Monopoly power measures the ability of firms to set the price for a good.

A monopoly operates in a market with high **barriers to entry**, which are restrictions that make it difficult for new firms to enter a market. As a result, monopolists have no competition nor any threat of competition. High barriers to entry insulate the monopolist from competition, which means that many monopolists enjoy long-run economic profits. There are two basic ways that this can happen: through natural barriers and through government-created barriers. Let's look at each.

Barriers to entry are restrictions that make it difficult for new firms to enter a market.

Natural Barriers

Some barriers exist naturally within the market. These include control of resources, problems in raising capital, and economies of scale.

Control of Resources

The best way to limit competition is to control a resource that is essential in the production process. This extremely effective barrier to entry is hard to accomplish. If you control a scarce resource, other competitors will not be able to find enough of it to compete. For example, in the early twentieth century the Aluminum Company of America (ALCOA) made a concerted effort to buy bauxite mines around the globe. Within a decade, the company owned 90% of the world's bauxite, an essential element in making aluminum. This effort enabled ALCOA to crowd out potential competitors and achieve dominance in the aluminum market.

Problems in Raising Capital

Monopolists are usually very big companies that have grown over an extended period. Even if you had a wonderful business plan, it is unlikely that a bank or a venture capital company would lend you enough money to start a business that could compete effectively with a well-established company. For example, if you wanted to design a new operating system to compete with Microsoft, you would need tens of millions of dollars to fund your start-up. Lenders provide capital for business projects when the chance of success is high, but the chance of a new company successfully competing against an entrenched monopoly is not high. Consequently, raising capital to compete against an entrenched monopolist is very difficult.

Economies of Scale

In Chapter 8, we saw that average costs fall as production expands. Low unit costs, and the low prices that follow, give larger firms the ability to drive out rivals. For example, imagine a market for electric power where companies compete to generate electricity and deliver it through their own grids. In such a market, it would be technically possible to run competing sets of wire to every home and business in the community, but the cost of installation and the maintenance of separate lines to deliver electricity would be both prohibitive and impractical. Even if a handful of smaller electric companies could produce electricity at the same cost, each would have to pay to deliver power through its own grid. This would be inefficient.

In an industry that enjoys large economies of scale, production costs per unit continue to fall as the firm expands. Smaller rivals then will have much higher average costs that prevent them from competing with the larger company. As a result, firms in the industry tend to combine over time. This leads to the creation of a **natural monopoly**, which occurs when a single large firm has lower costs than any potential smaller competitor.

A **natural monopoly** occurs when a single large firm has lower costs than any potential smaller competitor.

Government-Created Barriers

The creation of a monopoly can be either intentional or an unintended consequence of a government policy. Government-enforced statutes and regulations, such as laws and regulations covering licenses and patents, limit the scope of competition by creating barriers to entry.

Licensing

In many instances, it makes sense to give a single firm the exclusive right to sell a good or service. In order to minimize negative externalities, governments establish monopolies, or near monopolies, through licensing requirements. For example, in some communities trash collection is licensed to a single company. The rationale usually involves economies of scale, but there are also costs to consider. Since firms cannot collect trash without a government-issued operating license, opportunities to enter the business are limited, which leaves consumers with a one-size-fits-all level of service. This is the opposite of what we'd expect to see in a competitive market, where there would be many varieties of service at different price points.

Licensing also creates an opportunity for corruption. In fact, in many parts of the world bribery is such a common practice that it often determines which companies receive the licenses in the first place.

Patents and Copyright Law

Another area in which the government fosters monopoly is that of patents and copyrights. For example, when musicians create a new song and copyright their work, they earn royalties over the life of the copyright. The copyright is the government's assurance that no one else can play or sell the work without the artist's permission. Similarly, when a pharmaceutical company develops a new drug, the company receives a patent under which it has the exclusive right to market and sell the drug for as long as the patent is in force. By granting patents and copyrights to developers and inventors, the government creates monopolies. Patents and copyrights create stronger incentives to develop new drugs and produce new music than would exist if market competitors could immediately copy inventions. As a result, pharmaceutical companies invest heavily in developing new drugs and musicians devote their time to writing new music. At least in theory, these activities make our society a healthier and culturally richer place. After the patent or copyright expires, rivals can mimic the invention. This opens up the market and provides dual benefits: wider access to the innovation and more sellers—both of which are good for consumers in the long run.

Incentives

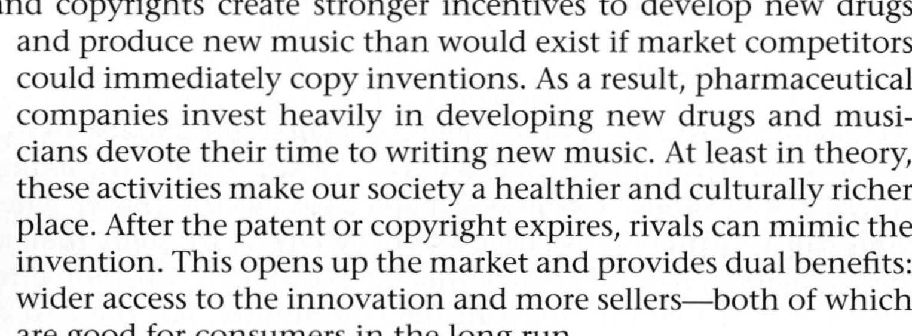

Does Justin Bieber need copyright protection to make money?

As appealing as the process described in the previous paragraph sounds, nothing works quite as well as advertised. Many economists wonder if patents and copyrights are necessary or have unintended consequences. For instance, illegal file sharing, downloads, and pirated DVDs are common in the music and movie business. At first glance, this appears to be a revenue loss for legitimate companies. But often the companies benefit from the exposure. For example, when a music video goes viral on YouTube, the exposure causes many people to buy the original artist's work. Consider Justin Bieber. He managed to leverage his YouTube fame into a successful album launch, concert tours, and appearance fees that might never have occurred if a music studio had tightly controlled his sound.

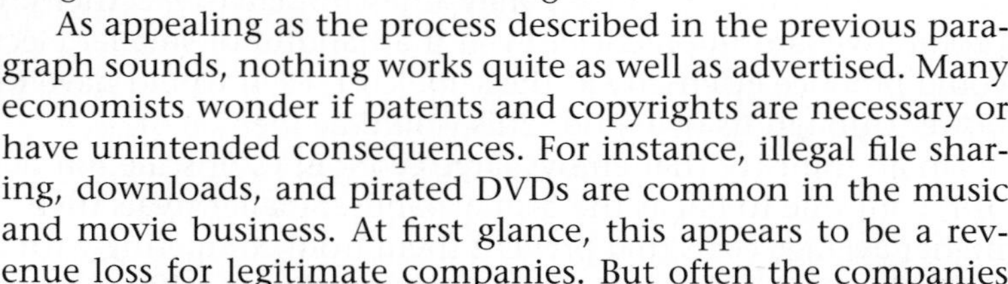

ECONOMICS IN THE REAL WORLD

Merck's Zocor

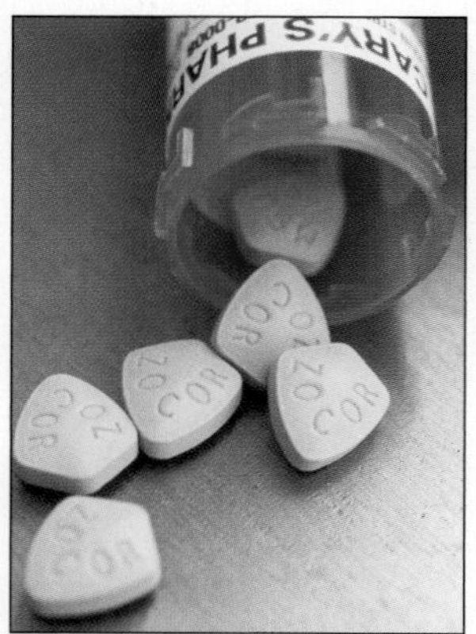

Do you want fries with that cholesterol medication?

In 1985, the pharmaceutical giant Merck released Zocor, the first statin drug for treating high cholesterol. The company spent millions of dollars developing the drug and bringing it to the market. Zocor is highly effective and has probably saved or extended millions of lives. It was also highly profitable for Merck, generating over $4 billion in annual revenues before the patent ran out in 2006. Zocor is now available in an inexpensive generic formulation at a price that is 80 to 90% lower than the original patent-protected price.

Would Zocor have been developed without patent protection? Probably not. Merck would have had little incentive to incur the cost of developing a cholesterol treatment if other companies could immediately copy the drug. In this case, society benefits because of the twofold nature of patents: they give firms the incentive to innovate, but they also limit the amount of time the patent is in place, thereby guaranteeing that competitive forces will govern long-run access to the product. ✷

TABLE 10.1

The Characteristics of Monopolies

- One seller
- A unique product without close substitutes
- High barriers to entry
- Price making

Though market-created and government-created barriers occur for different reasons, they have the same effect—they create monopolies. Table 10.1 summarizes the key characteristics of monopolies. In the next section, we will examine how the monopolist determines the price it charges and how much to produce.

PRACTICE WHAT YOU KNOW

Monopoly: Can You Spot the Monopolist?

Here are three questions to test your understanding of the conditions necessary for monopoly power to arise.

Question: Is Lebron James (an NBA superstar) a monopolist?

Answer: Lebron is a uniquely talented basketball player. Because of his physical gifts, he can do things that other players can't. But that does not mean there are no substitutes for him around the league. So no, Lebron is not a monopolist. Perhaps more important, his near-monopoly power is limited because new players are always entering the league and trying to establish themselves as the best.

Question: Is a sole small-town hairdresser a monopolist?

Answer: For all practical purposes, yes. He or she sells a unique service with inelastic demand. Because the nearest competitor is in the next town, the local hairdresser enjoys significant monopoly power. At the same time, the town's size limits potential competitors from entering the market, since the small community may not be able to support two hairdressers.

Question: Is Amazon a monopolist?

Answer: Amazon is the nation's largest bookseller, with sales that dwarf those of its nearest retail rival, Barnes & Noble. But Amazon's market share does not make it a monopolist. Amazon is a lot like Walmart: it relies on low prices to fend off its rivals.

Monopoly profits!

ECONOMICS IN THE MEDIA

Barriers to Entry

Forrest Gump

In this 1994 movie, Tom Hanks's character, Forrest Gump, keeps his promise to his deceased friend, Bubba, to go into the shrimping business after leaving the army. Forrest invests $25,000 in an old shrimp boat, but the going is tough—he only catches a handful of shrimp because of the competition for space in the shrimping waters. So Forrest tries naming his boat for good luck and brings on a first mate, Lieutenant Dan, who unfortunately is less knowledgeable and resourceful than Forrest. The fledgling enterprise continues to struggle, and eventually Forrest decides to pray for shrimp. Soon after, Forrest's boat, the *Jenny*, is caught out in the Gulf of Mexico during a hurricane. Miraculously, the *Jenny* makes it through the storm while the other shrimp boats, all anchored in the harbor, are destroyed.

Forrest recounts the events to some strangers while sitting on a park bench:

Forrest: After that, shrimping was easy. Since people still needed them shrimps for shrimp cocktails and barbecues and all, and we were the *only* boat left standing, Bubba-Gump shrimp's what they got. We got a whole bunch of boats. Twelve *Jennys*, big old warehouse. We even have hats that say "Bubba-Gump" on them. Bubba-Gump Shrimp. A household name.

Man on the bench: Hold on there, boy. Are you telling me you're the owner of the Bubba-Gump Shrimp Corporation?

Forrest: Yes. We got more money than Davy Crockett.

Man on the bench: Boy, I heard some whoppers in my time, but that tops them all. We were sitting next to a millionaire.

The film suggests that Forrest's good luck—being in the right place at the right time—explains how he became a millionaire. But is this realistic? Let's leave the movie's storyline for a moment and consider the situation in real-world economic terms.

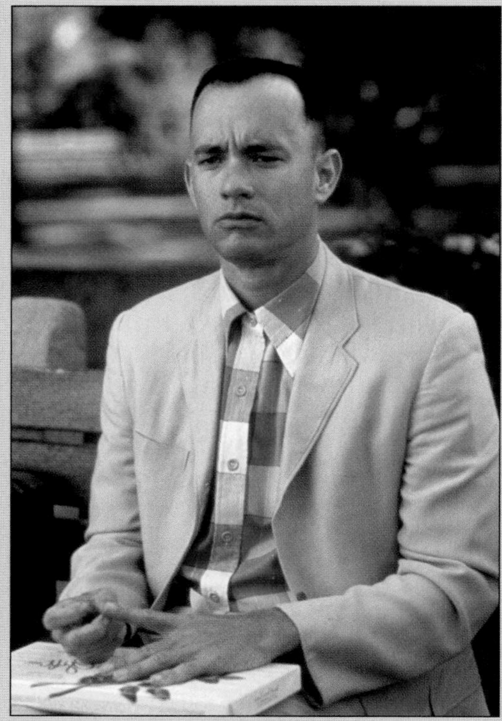

If shrimping were easy, everyone would do it.

Remember, Forrest was able to enter the business simply by purchasing a boat. To be sure, he would catch more shrimp in the short run, while the other boats were docked for repairs. However, once the competitors' boats return, they will catch shrimp and Forrest's short-run profits will disappear. The reason we can be so confident of this result is that shrimping, with low barriers to entry and undifferentiated product, is an industry that closely mirrors a perfectly competitive market. So when profits exist, new entrants will expand the supply produced and profits will return to the break-even level. Having Forrest become a "millionaire" makes for a good movie, but none of the elements are in place to suggest that he could attain a permanent monopoly. Forrest does not control an essential resource; the other shrimp captains will have little difficulty raising capital to repair their boats, and the economies of scale in this situation are small.

How Much Do Monopolies Charge, and How Much Do They Produce?

Both monopolists and firms in a competitive market seek to earn a profit. However, a monopolist is the sole provider of a product and holds market power. Thus, monopolists are *price makers*. A **price maker** has some control over the price it charges. As you learned in Chapter 9, a firm in a competitive market is a price taker.

A **price maker** has some control over the price it charges.

We can see the difference graphically in Figure 10.1. The demand curve for the product of a firm in a competitive market, shown here in panel (a), is horizontal. When individual firms are price takers, they have no control over what they charge. In other words, demand is perfectly elastic—or horizontal—because every firm sells the same product. Demand for an individual firm's product exists only at the price determined by the market, and each firm is such a small part of the market that it can sell its entire output without lowering the price. In contrast, because a monopolist is the only firm—the sole provider—in the industry, the demand curve for its product, shown in panel (b), constitutes the market demand curve. But the demand curve is downward sloping, which limits the monopolist's ability to make a profit. The monopolist would like to exploit its market power by charging a high price to many customers; however, the law of demand, which identifies an inverse relationship between price and

FIGURE 10.1

Comparing the Demand Curves of Perfectly Competitive Firms and Monopolists

(a) Firms in a competitive market have a horizontal demand curve. (b) Since the monopolist is the sole provider of the good or service, the demand for its product constitutes the industry—or market—demand curve, which is downward sloping. So while the perfectly competitive firm has no control over the price it charges, the monopolist gets to search for the profit-maximizing price and output.

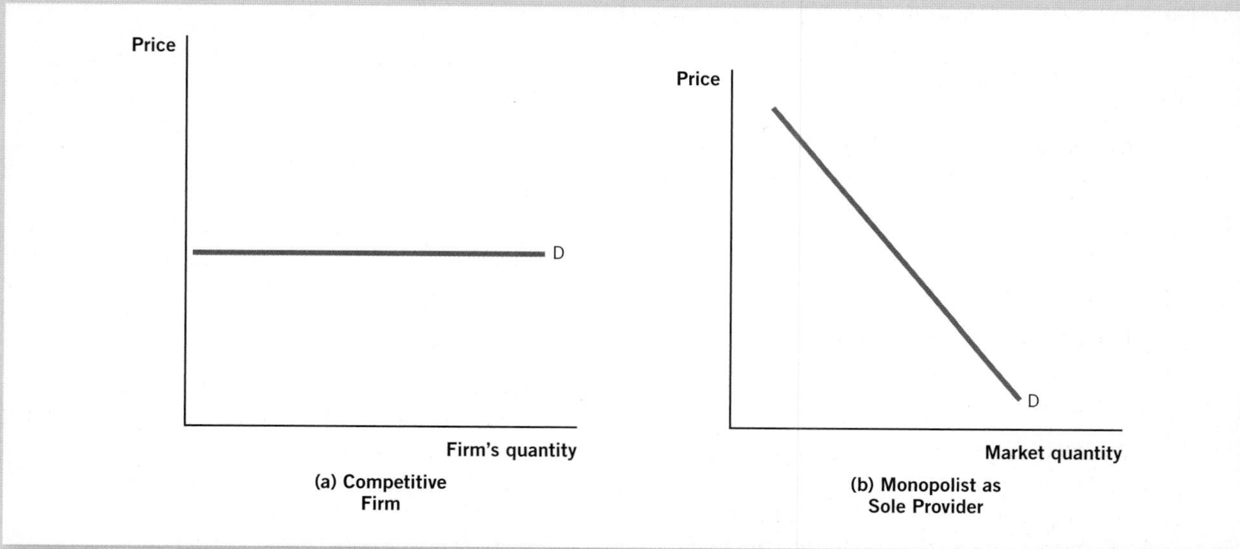

quantity demanded, dictates otherwise. Unlike the horizontal demand curve of a firm in a competitive market, the downward-sloping demand curve of the monopolist has many price-output combinations. If the monopolist charges a high price, only a few customers will buy the good. If it charges a low price, many customers will buy the good. As a result, monopolists get to search for the profit-maximizing price and output.

The Profit-Maximizing Rule for the Monopolist

Marginal thinking

A competitive firm can sell all it produces at the existing market price. But a monopolist, because of the downward-sloping demand curve, must search for the most profitable price. To maximize profits, a monopolist can use the profit-maximizing rule we introduced in Chapter 9: MR = MC. But the monopolist's marginal revenue is computed differently.

Table 10.2 shows the marginal revenue for a cable company that serves a small community. Notice the inverse relationship between output (quantity of customers) and price in columns 1 and 2: as the price goes down, the quantity of customers goes up. Total revenue is calculated by multiplying output by price (TR = Q × P). At first, total revenue rises as the price falls. Once the price becomes too low ($40), total revenue begins to fall. As a result, the total revenue function in column 3 initially rises to $250,000 before it falls off. The final column, marginal revenue, shows the change (Δ) in total revenue. Here we see positive (though falling) marginal revenue associated with prices above $50 (see the green dollar amounts in column 4). Below $50, marginal revenue becomes negative (see the red dollar amounts in column 4).

TABLE 10.2

Calculating the Monopolist's Marginal Revenue

(1) Quantity of customers (Q)	(2) Price of service (P)	(3) Total revenue (TR)	(4) Marginal revenue per 1,000 customers (MR)
Formula:		(Q) × (P)	Δ (TR)
0	$100	$0.00	
			$90,000
1,000	$90	90,000	
			70,000
2,000	$80	160,000	
			50,000
3,000	$70	210,000	
			30,000
4,000	$60	240,000	
			10,000
5,000	$50	250,000	
			−10,000
6,000	$40	240,000	
			−30,000
7,000	$30	210,000	
			−50,000
8,000	$20	160,000	
			−70,000
9,000	$10	90,000	
			−90,000
10,000	$0	0.00	

The change in total revenue reflects the trade-off that a monopolist encounters in trying to attract additional customers. To gain additional output, the firm must lower its price. But the lower price is available to both new and existing customers. The impact on total revenue therefore depends on how many new customers buy the good because of the lower price.

Figure 10.2 uses the linear demand schedule from Table 10.2 to illustrate the two separate effects that determine marginal revenue. First, there is a *price effect*, which reflects how the lower prices affect revenue. If the price of service drops from $70 to $60, each of the 3,000 existing customers will save $10. The firm would lose $10 × 3,000, or $30,000 in revenue, represented by the yellow-shaded area on the graph. But dropping the price also has an *output effect*, which reflects how the lower prices affect the number of customers. Since 1,000 new customers buy the product (that is, cable service) when the price drops to $60, revenue increases by $60 × 1,000, or $60,000, represented by the blue-shaded area. The output effect ($60,000) is greater than the price effect ($30,000). When we subtract the $30,000 in lost revenue (the yellow rectangle) from the $60,000 in revenue gained (the blue rectangle), this yields $30,000 in marginal revenue at an output level between 3,000 and 4,000 customers.

Lost revenues associated with the price effect are always subtracted from the revenue gains created by the output effect. Now let's think of this data at the individual level. Since the firm adds 1,000 new customers, the marginal revenue per customer—$30,000 ÷ 1,000 new customers—is $30. Notice that

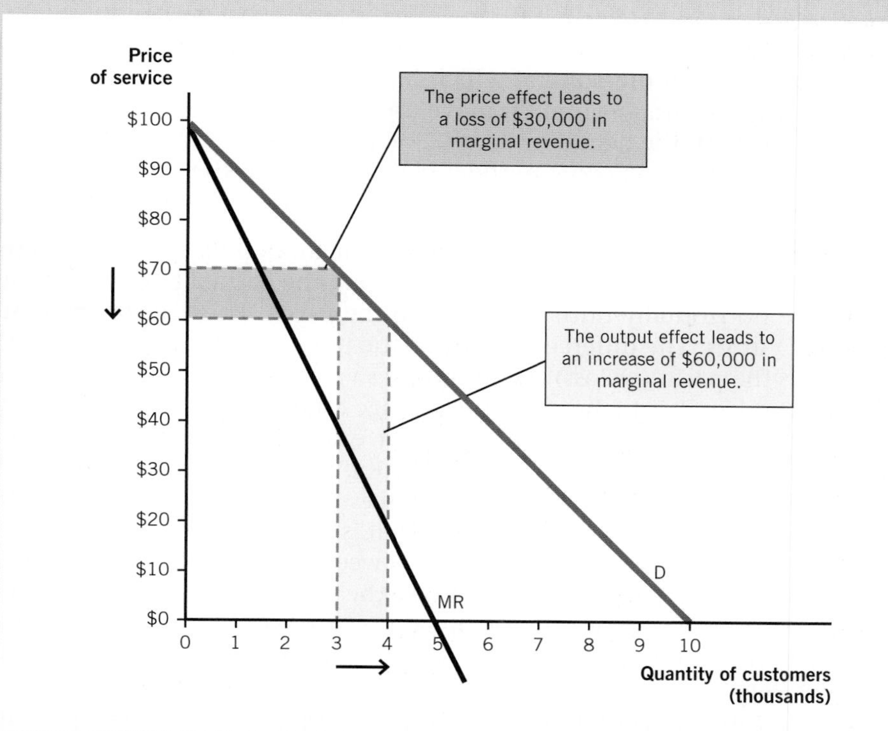

FIGURE 10.2

The Marginal Revenue Curve and the Demand Curve

A price drop has two effects. (1) Existing customers now pay less—this is the price effect. (2) New customers decide to purchase the good for the first time—this is the output effect. The relative size of the two effects, as shown by the yellow and blue rectangles, determines whether the firm is able to increase its revenue by lowering its price.

this is less than the price, \$60, that the firm charges. Since there is a price effect whenever the price drops, the marginal revenue curve lies below the demand curve. Therefore the *y* intercept is the same for the demand and marginal revenue curves and the *x* intercept of the MR curve is half of the demand curve's.

At high price levels—where demand is elastic—the price effect is small relative to the output effect. As the price drops, demand slowly becomes more inelastic. At this point, the output effect diminishes and the price effect increases. This means that as the price falls it becomes harder for the firm to acquire enough new customers to make up for the difference in lost revenue. Eventually, the price effect becomes larger than the output effect. When this happens, marginal revenue becomes negative and dips below the *x* axis, as shown by the MR curve in Figure 10.2. When the marginal revenue is negative, the firm cannot be profit-maximizing. This outcome puts an upper limit on the amount that the firm will produce. This is evident in Table 10.2: once the price becomes too low, the firm's marginal revenue is negative.

Marginal thinking

Deciding How Much to Produce

In Chapter 9, we explored the profit-maximizing rule for a firm in a competitive market. This rule also applies to a monopolist: marginal revenue should be equal to marginal cost. However, there is one big difference: a monopolist does not charge a price equal to marginal revenue.

Figure 10.3 illustrates the profit-maximizing decision-making process for a monopolist. We will use a two-step process to determine the monopolist's profit:

1. Locate the point at which the firm will maximize its profits: MR = MC.
2. Set the price. From the point at which MR = MC, determine the profit-maximizing output, Q. From Q, move up along the dashed line until it intersects with the demand curve (D). From that point, move horizontally until you come to the *y* axis. This tells us the price (P) the monopolist should charge.

Using this two-step process, we can determine the monopolist's profit. Locate the average total cost, C, of making Q units along the dashed line. From that point, move horizontally until you come to the *y* axis. This tells us the cost of making Q units. The difference between the price and the cost multiplied by Q tells us the profit (or loss) the firm makes.

Since the price (P) is higher than the average total cost (C), the firm makes the profit shown in the green rectangle. For example, if a small-town veterinarian charges \$50 for a routine examination and incurs a cost of \$35 for every exam, she earns \$15 every time she sees a pet. If she provides 1,000 examinations a year, her total economic profit is \$15 × 1,000, or \$15,000.

Table 10.3 summarizes the differences between a competitive market and a monopoly. The competitive firm must take the price established in the market. If it does not operate efficiently, it cannot survive. Nor can it make an economic profit in the long run. The monopolist operates very differently. Since high barriers to entry limit competition, the monopolist may be able to earn long-run profits by restricting output. It operates inefficiently from society's perspective, and it has significant market power.

FIGURE 10.3

The Monopolist's Profit Maximization

The firm uses the profit-maximizing rule to locate the point at which MR = MC. This determines the ideal output level, Q. Since the price (which is determined by the demand curve) is higher than the average total cost curve (ATC) along the dashed line at quantity Q, the firm makes the profit shown in the green-shaded area.

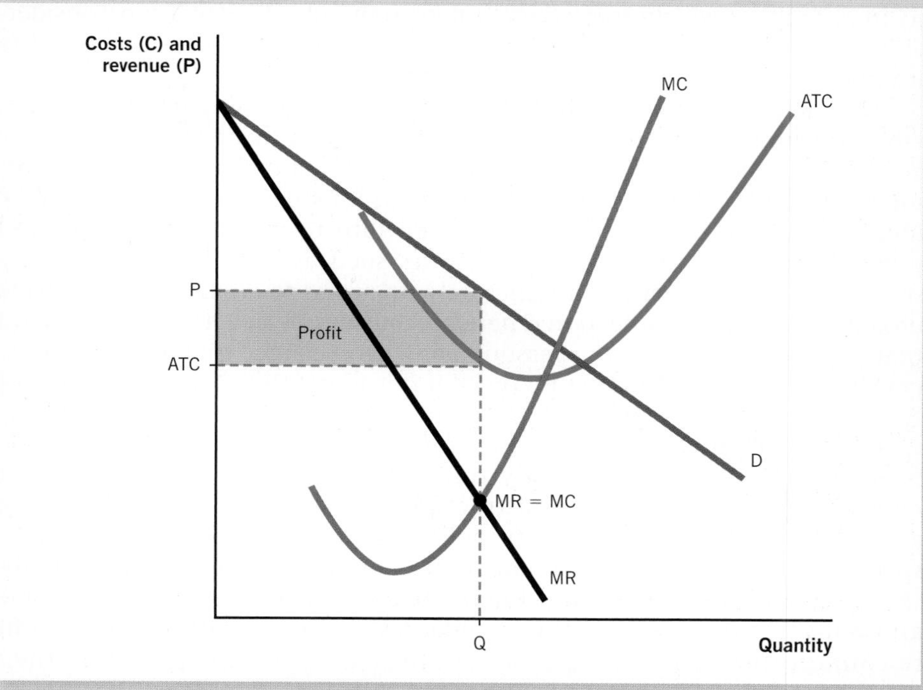

TABLE 10.3

The Major Differences between a Monopoly and a Competitive Market

Competitive market	Monopoly
Many firms	One firm
Produces an efficient level of output (since P = MC)	Produces less than the efficient level of output (since P > MC)
Cannot earn long-run economic profits	May earn long-run economic profits
Has no market power (is a price taker)	Has significant market power (is a price maker)

ECONOMICS IN THE REAL WORLD

The Broadband Monopoly

Many markets in the United States have only a single high-speed Internet provider. The technology race strongly favors cable over competing DSL. In fact, DSL is provided by telephone companies using aging copper wiring, whereas cable companies use the latest fiberoptic technology. When it comes to truly high-speed Internet access, cable companies benefit from considerable barriers to entry. In many places, Comcast effectively owns access to the Internet and can price its service accordingly.

The cable monopoly on high-speed Internet access resonates in two ways. First, consumers increasingly need more bandwidth to stream movies, view YouTube, and load media-rich web sites. A slow connection can make surfing the Internet a chore. In other words, consumer demand is high and very inelastic. Second, businesses rely on bandwidth to maintain web sites and provide services to customers. Companies such as Netflix, which delivers streaming content over the Internet, rely on access to a relatively affordable broadband Internet connection. Therefore, businesses also have high demand that is quite inelastic. For this reason, many people argue that relatively inexpensive access to the Internet is crucial if it is to continue to be an engine of economic growth. And without competition, access will remain expensive.

Our dependence on the Internet invites a larger question. Where the bandwidth is controlled by only one provider, should the government have a role in providing the infrastructure, or cables, in order to allow more access? This is a concern in metropolitan areas served by only one high-speed provider. Meanwhile, small rural communities may have no high-speed access at all. For example, Chireno, Texas, has a population of 413 people and remains off the grid. Cable companies wouldn't make enough profit to connect these low-density areas, but this makes it very difficult for their residents to participate in today's economy. ✷

Does Comcast own the Internet in your area?

PRACTICE WHAT YOU KNOW

Monopoly Profits: How Much Do Monopolists Make?

Question: A monopolist always earns _____ economic profit.

a. a positive

b. zero

c. a negative

d. We cannot be sure about the profit a monopolist makes.

Is there a key profit takeaway?

Answers:

a. Incorrect. A monopolist is a price maker with considerable market power. This usually, but not always, leads to a positive economic profit.

b. Incorrect. Zero economic profit exists in competitive markets in the long run. Since a monopolist, by definition, does not operate in competitive markets, it is protected from additional competition that would drive its profit to zero.

c. Incorrect. Whoa there! Negative profit? There is absolutely no reason to think that would happen. Monopolists sell a unique product without close substitutes in a market that is insulated from competitive pressures. Time to reread the first part of this chapter more carefully!

d. Correct. Since a monopolist benefits from barriers that limit the entry of competitors into the industry, we would expect an economic profit. However, this is not guaranteed. Monopolies do not control the demand for the product they sell. Consequently, in the short run the monopolist may experience either a profit (if demand is high) or a loss (if demand is low).

What Are the Problems with, and Solutions for, Monopoly?

Monopolies can adversely affect society by restricting output and charging higher prices than sellers in competitive markets do. This activity causes monopolies to operate inefficiently, provide less choice, promote an unhealthy form of competition known as *rent seeking* (see below), and make economic profits that fail to guide resources to their highest-valued use. The occurrence of an inefficient output is known as **market failure**. Once we have examined the problems with monopoly, we will turn to the potential solutions for it.

Market failure occurs when the output level of a good is inefficient.

The Problems with Monopoly

Monopolies result in an inefficient level of output, provide less choice to consumers, and encourage monopoly firms to lobby for government protection. Let's look at each of these concerns.

Inefficient Output and Price

From an efficiency standpoint, the monopolist charges too much and produces too little. This result is evident in Figure 10.4, which shows what happens when a competitive market (denoted by the subscript *c*) ends up being controlled by a monopoly (denoted by the subscript *m*).

First, imagine a competitive fishing industry in which each boat catches a small portion of the fish, as shown in panel (a). Each firm is a price taker that must charge the market price. In contrast, panel (b) depicts pricing and output decisions for a monopoly fishing industry when it confronts the same cost structure as presented in panel (a). When a single firm controls the entire fishing ground, it is the sole supplier; to set its price, it considers the downward-sloping demand and marginal revenue curves that serve the entire market. Therefore, it sets marginal revenue equal to marginal cost. This yields a smaller output ($Q_M < Q_C$) than the competitive industry and a higher price ($P_M > P_C$).

FIGURE 10.4

When a Competitive Industry Becomes a Monopoly

(a) In a competitive industry, the intersection of supply and demand determines the price (P_C) and quantity (Q_C). (b) When a monopoly controls an entire industry, the supply curve becomes the monopolist's marginal cost curve. The monopolist uses MR = MC to determine its price (P_M) and quantity (Q_M). This means that the monopolist charges a higher price and produces a smaller output than when an entire industry is populated with competitive firms.

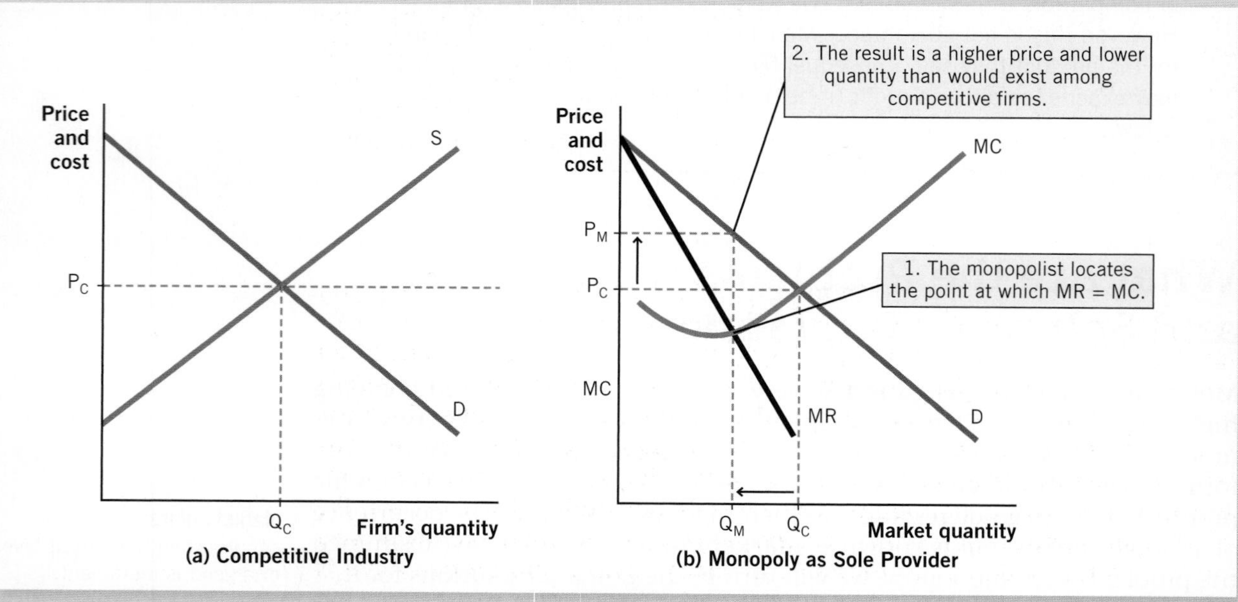

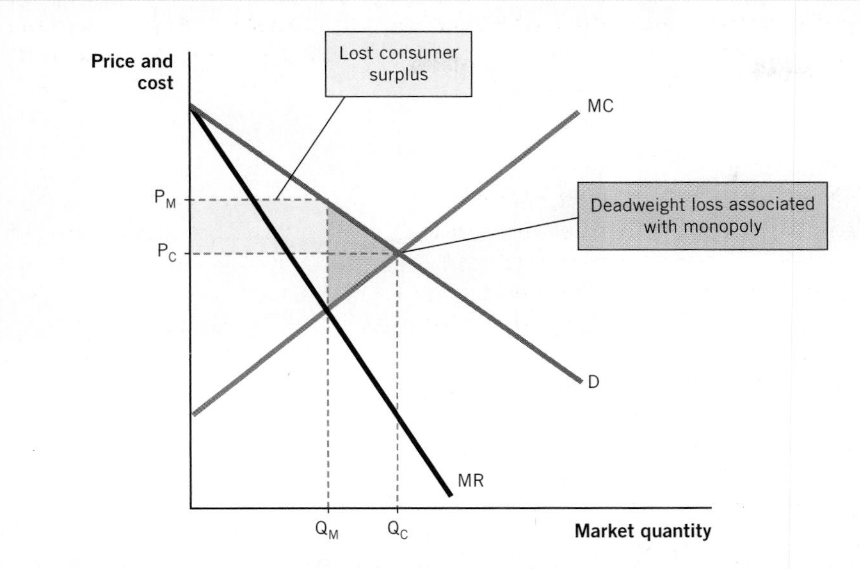

FIGURE 10.5

The Deadweight Loss of Monopoly

Since the profit-maximizing monopolist produces an output of Q_M, an amount that is less than Q_C, this results in the deadweight loss shown in the yellow triangle. The blue rectangle is the consumer surplus that is transferred to the monopolist.

The smaller output level is not efficient. In addition, the price the monopolist charges, P_M, is significantly above the marginal cost at the profit-maximizing level of output, which is higher than the price when there are many smaller competing firms.

Figure 10.5 captures the deadweight loss (see Chapter 6) of the monopoly. The monopolist charges too high a price and produces too little of the product, so some consumers who would benefit from a competitive market lose out. Since the demand curve, or the willingness to pay, is greater than the marginal cost between output levels Q_M and Q_C, society would be better off if output expanded to Q_C. But a profit-maximizing monopolist will limit output to Q_M. The result, a deadweight loss equal to the area of the yellow triangle, is inefficient for society. Consumer surplus is also transferred to the monopolist, as shown in the blue rectangle.

Few Choices for Consumers

Another problem associated with monopoly is the lack of choice. Have you ever wondered why cable companies offer their services in bundles? You can buy basic, digital, and premium packages, but the one thing you cannot do is buy just the cable channels you want. This is because cable companies function like monopolies, and monopolies limit consumer choice. Since the monopolist sells a good with few close substitutes, it can leverage its market power to offer product features that benefit itself at the expense of consumer choice. With a monopolist, there is only one outlet: if you do not like the design, features, price, or any other aspect of the good provided, you have few other options. For example, in many small communities there is only one cable television provider. In a hypothetical competitive market, we would expect each company to provide more options to satisfy consumer

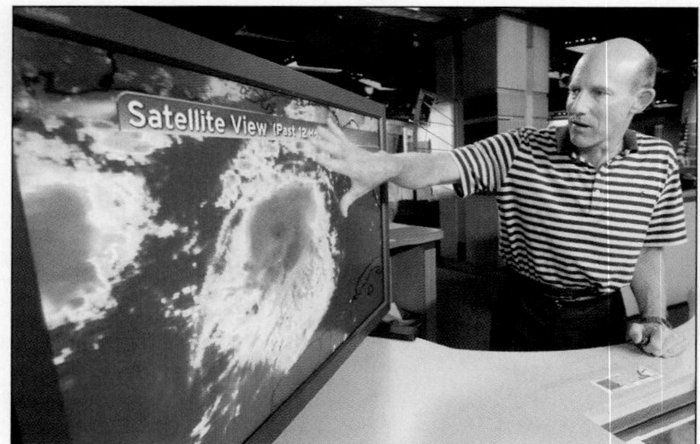

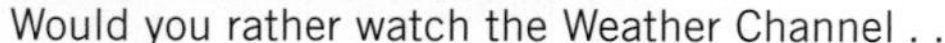
Would you rather watch the Weather Channel . . . . . . or SportsCenter?

preferences. For instance, in a competitive market you should be able to find a firm willing to sell only ESPN and the Weather Channel. In a monopoly situation, though, the cable company forces you to choose between buying a little more cable than you really need or going without cable altogether. Because the cable company has a good deal of market power, it can restrict your options and force you to buy more in order to get what you want. This is a profitable strategy for the company but a bad outcome for consumers.

Rent Seeking

Rent seeking occurs when resources are used to secure monopoly rights through the political process.

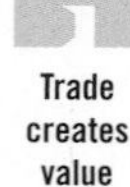
Trade creates value

The attempt to gain monopoly power encourages *rent seeking*. **Rent seeking** occurs when resources are used to secure monopoly rights through the political process. Throughout this text, we have seen the desirable effects of competition: lower prices, increased efficiency, and enhanced service and quality. However, rent seeking is a form of competition that produces an undesirable result. When firms compete to become monopolists, there is one winner without any of the benefits usually associated with competition. Consider the U.S. steel industry, which has been in decline for many years and has lost market share to steel firms in China, Japan, and Europe. If a U.S. steel company is losing money because of foreign competition, it can address the situation in one of two ways. It can modernize by building new facilities and using the latest equipment and techniques. (In other words, it can become competitive with the overseas competition.) Or it can lobby the government to limit imports. The domestic steel industry chose to lobby, and in 2002 the George W. Bush administration imposed tariffs of up to 30% on imported steel. Here is the danger: when lobbying is less expensive than building a new factory, the company will choose to lobby! If politicians give in and the lobbying succeeds, society is adversely affected because the gains from trade are smaller.

A former steel plant in Bethlehem, Pennsylvania.

PRACTICE WHAT YOU KNOW

Problems with Monopoly: Coffee Consolidation

A community has many competing coffee shops.

Question: How can we use the market demand curve to illustrate the consumer and producer surplus created by a competitive market?

When companies compete, consumers win.

Answer:

In a competitive market, supply and demand determine the price and quantity.

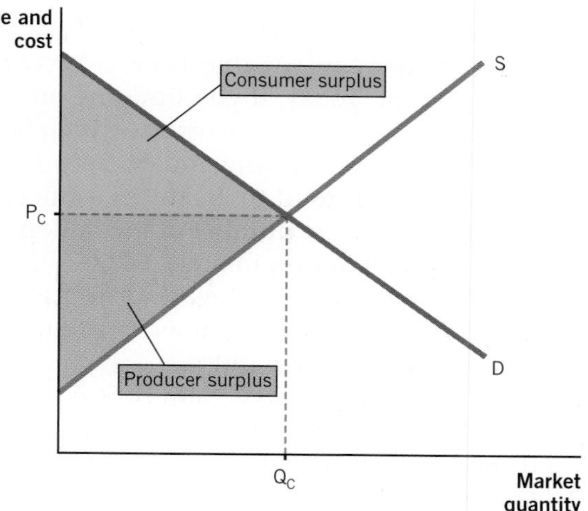

Question: Now imagine that all the independent coffee shops combine under one fictional franchise, known as Harbucks. How can we create a new graph that illustrates the consumer surplus, producer surplus, and deadweight loss that occur when a monopoly takes over the market?

Answer:

In this figure, we see that the consumer surplus has shrunk; the producer surplus has increased; and the higher price charged by Harbucks creates deadweight loss. Allowing a monopolist to capture a market does not benefit consumers and is inefficient for society.

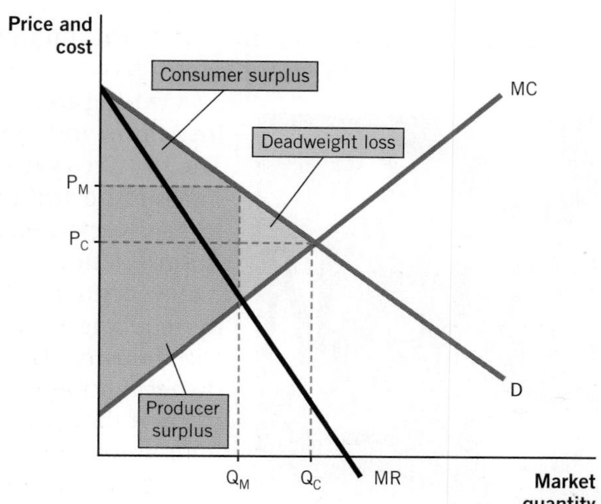

Supply and demand tell us that steel prices will rise in the absence of competition. This outcome is inefficient. Also, instead of pushing for legislation that grants market power, the lobbying resources could have gone into the production of useful products. As a result, the process of rent seeking benefits the rent seeker and yields little direct benefit for society.

ECONOMICS IN THE REAL WORLD

New York City Taxis

In 1932, during the depths of the Great Depression, New York City decided to license taxi cabs. The goal was to standardize fares, operating procedures, and safety requirements. At that time, a taxi cab license, or medallion, was available at no cost. Today, if you find one on the resale market, it costs over $300,000. The medallions are worth so much because the owners often make six-figure incomes from leasing and operating taxis in New York City.

The city did not intend to create an artificial monopoly, but it did. From 1932 until the 1990s, the number of medallions, which represents the supply of taxis, was fixed at approximately 12,000. During the same 60-year period, population growth and an increase in tourism caused the demand for taxi services to rise steeply. The number of medallions would have had to quadruple to keep up with demand.

In recent years, the city of New York has offered three auctions to introduce more medallions into the market. These auctions have netted the city over $100 million in revenue and have raised the number of medallions to slightly more than 13,000. Each of the current medallion holders owns a small part of an artificially created government monopoly. Collectively, the holders of medallions own a monopoly on taxi services worth 13,000 × $300,000, or about $4 billion. Yet demand for the medallions continues to far outpace the supply, and the market price has steadily climbed to an astonishing level.

Imagine what would happen if the city lifted restrictions on the number of available medallions and gave them out to any qualified applicant. Applications for licenses would increase, and profits for cab drivers and cab companies would fall until supply roughly equaled demand. Conversely, if taxi cab drivers experienced economic losses, the number of taxis operating would decline until the losses disappeared.

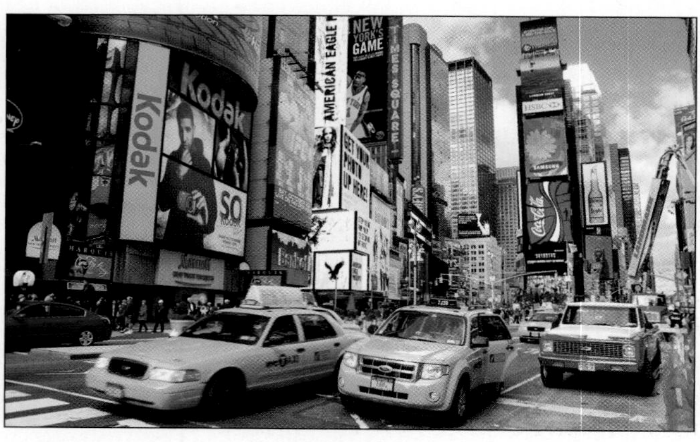

Medallion owners in New York City are protected from competition.

Owning and operating a taxi has all the makings of an industry with low barriers to entry. The only reason that medallions are worth so much is the artificially created barrier to entry—this protects medallion holders from competition. Restoring competitive markets would make each current medallion holder worse off by reducing the existing barriers to entry into the industry. This would cause the medallion owners' profits to fall. Therefore, it is not surprising that they seek to keep the number of medallions as low as possible. Since monopolists make profits by charging higher prices than firms in competitive markets do, no one who already has a medallion wants the supply to expand. ✷

The Problems of Monopoly

ECONOMICS IN THE MEDIA

One-Man Band

This Pixar short animation from 2005 tells the story of two street musicians competing for the gold coin of a young peasant girl who wants to make a wish in the town square's fountain.

When the short opens, there is only one street musician in the plaza. He performs a little bit and almost coaxes the girl to place her coin in his tip basket. Just as she is about to give it to him, another street musician starts playing. Since there is no longer a single performer, a spirited rivalry develops between the two very eager musicians vying to win the little girl's attention and money.

This clever story illustrates monopoly and competition in a number of compelling ways. The first street musician plays only halfheartedly in the beginning, when he does not face any competition. Indeed, lack of choice is one of the major criticisms of monopoly. But then the second musician's arrival changes the dynamic, inspiring a spirited competition for the gold coin. The "one-man band" is not really a monopolist; he is providing a service that has many good substitutes and lacks the ability to keep imitators from entering the market.

A little competition goes a long way to reduce monopoly.

Solutions to the Problems of Monopoly

We have learned that monopolies do not produce as much social welfare as competitive markets do. As a result, public policy approaches attempt to address this problem. The policy solutions include breaking up the monopolist, reducing trade barriers, and regulating markets.

Breaking Up the Monopolist

Eliminating deadweight loss and restoring efficiency can be as simple as promoting competition. From 1913 until 1982, AT&T had a monopoly on the delivery of telephone services. As the years passed, however, it became progressively harder for AT&T to defend its position that having a single provider of phone services was good for consumers. By the early 1980s, AT&T was spending over $300 million to fend off antitrust suits from the states, the federal government, and many private firms. The AT&T monopoly ended in 1982, when enormous pressure from the government led the company to split into eight smaller companies. Suddenly, AT&T had to compete to survive. The newly competitive phone market forced each of the phone companies to expand the services it offered—and sometimes even lower its prices—to avoid losing customers. For example, rates on long-distance calls, which were quite high before the break-up, plummeted.

Incentives

From this example, we see that the government can help to limit monopoly outcomes and restore a competitive balance. This is often accomplished through antitrust legislation. Antitrust laws are designed to prevent monopoly practices and promote competition. The government has exercised control over monopoly practices since the passage of the Sherman Act in 1890, and the task currently falls to the Department of Justice. We will discuss these regulations at greater length in Chapter 13.

Reducing Trade Barriers

Countries use tariffs, which are taxes on imported goods, as a trade barrier to prevent competition and protect domestic business. However, any barrier—be it tariffs, quotas, or prohibitions—limits the possible gains from trade. For monopolists, trade barriers prevent rivals from entering their territory. For example, imagine that Florida could place a tariff on California oranges. For every California orange sold in Florida, the seller would have to pay a fee. Florida orange producers might like this because it would limit competition from California. But California growers would cry foul and reciprocate with a tariff on Florida oranges. Growers in both states would be happy, but consumers would be harmed. For example, if a damaging freeze in Florida depleted the crop, Florida consumers would have to pay more than the demand-driven price for imported oranges from California. If, in contrast, Florida had a bumper crop, the tariff would keep prices artificially high and much of the extra harvest would go to waste.

Since 1994, reduced barriers to competition have transformed the Indian airline industry.

The United States has achieved tremendous growth by limiting the ability of individual states to place import and export restrictions on goods and services. The Constitution reads, "No State shall, without the consent of Congress, lay any imposts or duties on imports or exports." Rarely have so few words been more profound. With this simple law in place, states must compete on equal terms.

Trade creates value

Reducing trade barriers creates more competition, lessens the influence of monopoly, and promotes the efficient use of resources. For example, prior to 1994 private air carriers accounted for less than 0.5% of the air traffic in India. In 1994, Indian airspace was opened to allow private airlines to operate scheduled service. This move forced the state-owned Air India to become more competitive. These changes in Indian aviation policies had the effect of raising the share of private airline operators in domestic passenger carriage to over 70% by 2012. Two private companies, Jet Airways and IndiGo, are now the largest carriers in India, while Air India—which once controlled the market—has slipped to third place.

Regulating Markets

In the case of a natural monopoly, it is not practical to harness the benefits of competition. Consider the economies of scale that utility companies experience. Breaking up a company that provides natural gas, water, or electricity

SNAPSHOT

The Demise of a Monopoly

A monopoly can be broken up by the courts or by market forces. In the case of Microsoft, only one has worked. In November 1999, a federal judge declared Microsoft a monopoly of computer operating systems. The original decision underwent appeals that continue to this day, making the ruling largely ineffective in breaking up the monopoly. But market forces have had more success. New technologies have made the market much more competitive, meaning Microsoft is rarely considered a monopoly anymore.

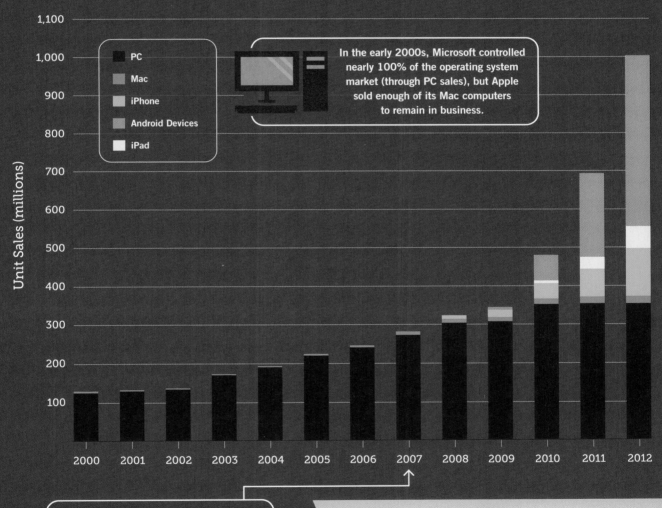

Unit Sales (millions)
1,100
1,000
900
800
700
600
500
400
300
200
100

Since 2007, the explosive growth of smartphone and tablet sales has tilted the operating system market toward Android (owned by Google) and Apple, eating into Microsoft's market share.

REVIEW QUESTIONS

Mac
iPhone
Android Devices
iPad
In the early 2000s, Microsoft controlled nearly 100% of the operating system market (through PC sales), but Apple sold enough of its Mac computers to remain in business.
2000
2001
2002
2003
2004
2005
2006
2007
2008
2009
2010
2011

- About what percentage of the operating system market did Microsoft (PC) control in 2012?
- Describe the demise of the Microsoft operating system monopoly using the following terms: competition, innovation, and market power.

would result in higher production costs. For instance, a second water company would have to build infrastructure to each residence or business in a community. Having redundant water lines with only a fraction of the customers would make the delivery of water extremely expensive, such that the final price to the consumer, even with competition, would be higher. Therefore, keeping the monopoly intact would be the best option. In this situation, policymakers might attempt to create a more efficient outcome and maximize the welfare of society by regulating the monopolist's prices. Theoretically, this would be a straightforward process—as we will see below. However, the reality is that few regulators are experts in the fields of electricity, natural gas, water, and other regulated industries, so they often lack sufficient knowledge to make the regulations work as designed.

When a natural monopoly exists, the government may choose to use the marginal-cost pricing rule to generate the greatest welfare for society. This is done by setting P = MC. Since the price is determined along the demand curve, setting P = MC guarantees that the good will be produced as long as the willingness to pay exceeds the additional cost of production. Figure 10.6 shows the difference in pricing and profits for a regulated and an unregulated natural monopoly.

To maximize profits, an unregulated monopolist sets MR = MC and produces Q_M at a price of P_M. Since P_M is greater than the average cost of producing Q_M units, or C_M, the monopolist earns the profit shown in the green rectangle. If the firm is regulated and the price is set at marginal cost, regulators can set P = MC and the output expands to Q_R. (The subscript R denotes the regulated monopolist.) In this example, since the cost of production is subject to economies of scale, the cost falls from C_M to C_R. This is a large improvement in efficiency. The regulated price, P_R, is lower than the unregulated monopo-

FIGURE 10.6

The Regulatory Solution for Natural Monopoly

An unregulated monopolist uses the profit-maximizing rule, MR = MC, and earns a small profit, shown in the green-shaded rectangle. If the monopolist is regulated using the marginal cost pricing rule, P = MC, it will experience the loss shown in the red-shaded rectangle.

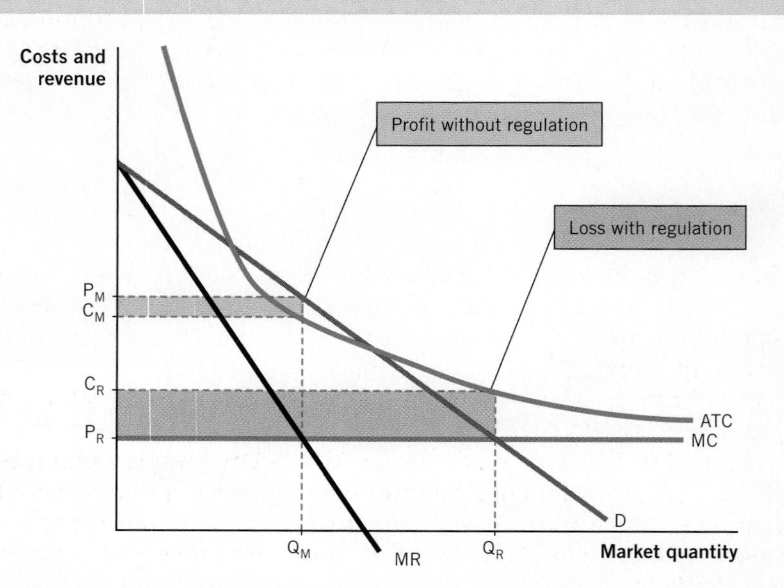

list's price, P_M, and production increases. As a result, consumers are better off. But what happens to the monopoly? It loses profits in the amount of the red rectangle. This occurs since the average costs under the marginal-cost pricing solution, C_R, are higher than the price allowed by regulators, P_R. This outcome is problematic because a firm that suffers losses will go out of business. That outcome is not desirable from society's standpoint, since the consumers of the product will be left without it. There are three possible solutions. First, to make up for the losses incurred at the higher output level, C_R, the government could subsidize the monopolist. Second, the regulated price could be set so that P = ATC at Q_R and the monopoly breaks even. (Remember that ATC is the average total cost.) Third, the government could own and operate the business in lieu of the private firm. This solution, however, has its own challenges, as we will explore in the next section.

Marginal thinking

A Caveat about Government Oversight

Firms with a profit motive have an incentive to minimize the costs of production, since lower costs translate directly into higher profits. Consequently, if the managers of firms do a poor job, they will be fired. The same cannot be said about government managers, or bureaucrats. Government employees are rarely let go, regardless of their performance. As a result, the government oversight and management of monopolies is problematic because there are fewer incentives to keep costs in check.

Consequently, the marginal-cost pricing rule is not as effective as it first seems. Regulated firms and government-owned businesses do not have the same incentives to keep costs down. Without the correct incentives in place, we would expect cost inefficiencies to develop.

Incentives

Public policy can mitigate the power of monopolies. But this outcome is not guaranteed. While monopolies are not as efficient as firms in competitive markets, this is not always the relevant comparison to make. We need to ask how the inefficiency of monopoly compares with the inefficiencies associated with government involvement in the market. Since good economists assess the benefits as well as the costs, when the costs of government involvement are greater than the efficiency gains that can be realized, the best solution to the problem of monopoly might be to do nothing.

Conclusion

It is tempting to believe that monopolies always earn a profit, but that is a misconception. The monopolist controls the supply, not the demand, so monopolies occasionally suffer losses despite the advantages they enjoy. Still, many monopolists do make profits.

In this chapter, we examined the monopoly model and, along the way, compared the result under monopoly with the competitive model that we developed in the previous chapter. While competitive markets generally yield welfare-enhancing outcomes for society, monopolies often do the opposite. Since monopolists do not produce an efficient outcome, government often seeks to limit monopoly outcomes and promote competitive markets.

Competitive markets and monopoly are market structures at opposite extremes. Indeed, we rarely encounter the conditions necessary for either a pure monopoly or a perfectly competitive market. Most economic activity takes place between these two alternatives. In the upcoming chapters, we will examine monopolistic competition and oligopoly—two markets that constitute the bulk of the economy. Fortunately, if you understand the market structures at the extremes, understanding the middle ground is straightforward. As a result, one way to think of how firms operate is to imagine a broad spectrum of industries ranging from those that are highly competitive to those for which competition is nonexistent. As we move forward, we will deploy the same tools we have used to examine monopoly in order to understand monopolistic competition (Chapter 12) and oligopoly (Chapter 13).

ANSWERING THE BIG QUESTIONS

How are monopolies created?

- Monopoly is a market structure characterized by a single seller that produces a well-defined product with few good substitutes.
- Monopolies operate in a market with high barriers to entry, the chief source of market power.
- Monopolies are created when a single firm controls the entire market.

How much do monopolies charge, and how much do they produce?

- Monopolists are price makers who may earn long-run profits.
- Like perfectly competitive firms, a monopoly tries to maximize its profits. To do so, it uses the profit-maximizing rule, MR = MC, to select the optimal price and quantity combination of a good or service to produce.

What are the problems with, and solutions for, monopoly?

- From an efficiency standpoint, the monopolist charges too much and produces too little. Since the monopolist's output is smaller than what would exist in a competitive market, monopolies lead to deadweight loss.
- Government grants of monopoly power encourage rent seeking, or the use of resources to secure monopoly rights through the political process.
- There are three potential solutions to the problem of monopoly. First, the government may break up firms that gain too much market power in order to restore a competitive market. Second, the government can promote open markets by reducing trade barriers. Third, the government can regulate a monopolist's ability to charge excessive prices.
- Finally, there are some circumstances in which it is better to leave the monopolist alone.

ECONOMICS FOR LIFE

Playing Monopoly Like an Economist

Monopoly is the ultimate zero-sum game. You profit only by taking from other players. The assets of its world are fixed in number. The best player drives others into bankruptcy and is declared the winner only after gaining control of the entire board.

Here is some advice on how to play the game like an economist.

- Remember that a monopoly is built on trade. You are unlikely to acquire a monopoly by landing on the color-groups you need; instead, you have to trade properties in order to acquire the ones you need. Since every player knows this, acquiring the last property to complete a color-group is nearly impossible. Your competitors will never willingly hand you a monopoly unless they get something of great value in return.
- Don't wait to trade until it is obvious what you need. Instead, try to acquire as many properties as you can in order to gain trading leverage as the game unfolds. Always pick up available properties if no other player owns one of the same color-group; purchase properties that will give you two or three of the same group; or purchase a property if it blocks someone else from completing a set.
- Think about probability. Mathematicians have determined that Illinois Avenue is the property most likely to be landed on and that B&O is the best railroad to own. Know the odds, and you can weigh the risks and rewards of trade, better than your opponents. This is just like doing market research before you buy: being informed matters in Monopoly and in business.

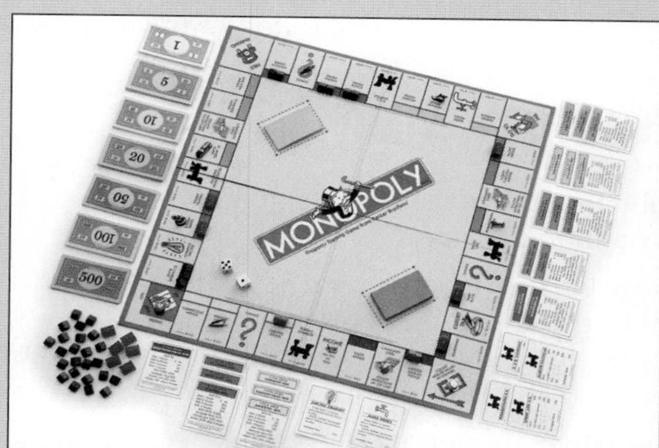

Apply some basic economic principles, and you can win big.

- When you get a monopoly, develop it quickly. Build as many houses as you can. That's sound advice in the board game and in life. Monopoly power is fleeting—you must capitalize on your advantages as soon as possible.
- Finally, if you gain the upper hand and have a chance to bankrupt a player from the game, do it. Luck plays a key role in Monopoly as it does in life. Although it may sound harsh, eliminating a competitor moves you one step closer to winning the game.

The decisions you make while playing Monopoly are all about cost-benefit analysis. You have limited resources and only so many opportunities to use them to your advantage. The skilled player understands how to weigh the values of tradeable properties, considers the risk-return proposition of every decision, manages money effectively, and eliminates competitors when given a chance.

CONCEPTS YOU SHOULD KNOW

barriers to entry (p. 304)
market failure (p. 315)
monopoly power (p. 304)
natural monopoly (p. 305)
price maker (p. 309)
rent seeking (p. 318)

QUESTIONS FOR REVIEW

1. Describe the difference between a monopoly and a natural monopoly.
2. What are barriers to entry, and why are they crucial to the creation of potential long-run monopoly profits? Give an example of a barrier that can lead to monopoly.
3. Explain why a monopoly is a price maker but a perfectly competitive firm is a price taker.
4. Why is a monopolist's marginal revenue curve less than the price of the good it sells?
5. What is the monopolist's rule for determining the profit-maximizing output? What two steps does the monopolist follow to maximize profits?
6. Why does a monopolist operate inefficiently? Draw a demand curve, a marginal revenue curve, and a marginal cost curve to illustrate the deadweight loss from monopoly.
7. Why is it difficult to regulate a natural monopoly?

STUDY PROBLEMS (✻ *solved at the end of the section*)

1. In the figure below, identify the price the monopolist will charge and the output the monopolist will produce. How do these two decisions on the part of the monopolist compare to the efficient price and output?

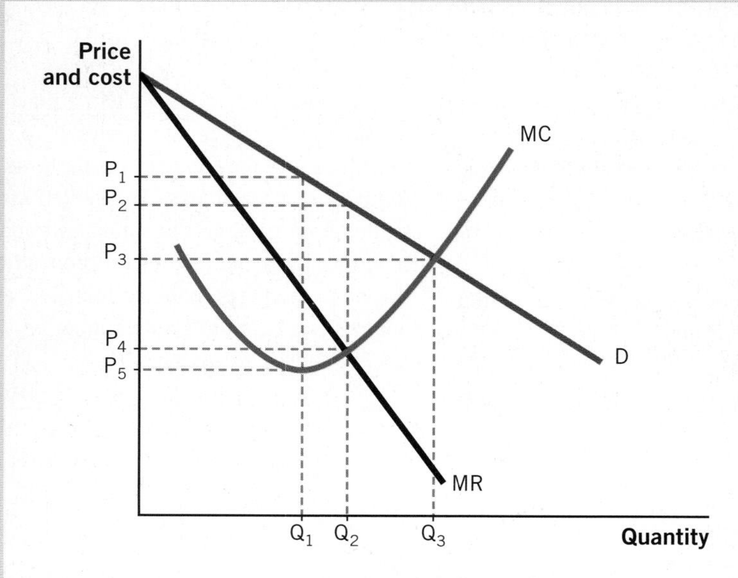

2. Which of the following could be considered a monopoly?
   a. your local water company
   b. Boeing, a manufacturer of airplanes
   c. Brad Pitt
   d. Walmart
   e. the only gas station along a 100-mile stretch of road

3. A monopolist has the following fixed and variable costs:

Price	Quantity	Fixed cost	Variable cost
$10	0	$8	$0
$9	1	8	5
$8	2	8	8
$7	3	8	10
$6	4	8	11
$5	5	8	13
$4	6	8	16
$3	7	8	20
$2	8	8	25

At what level of output will the monopolist maximize profits?

4. The year is 2278, and the starship *Enterprise* is running low on dilithium crystals, which are used to regulate the matter-antimatter reactions that propel the ship across the universe. Without the crystals, space-time travel is not possible. If there is only one known source of dilithium crystals, are the necessary conditions met to establish a monopoly? If the crystals are government-owned or -regulated, what price should the government set for them?

* 5. If demand falls, what is likely to happen to a monopolist's price, output, and economic profit?

* 6. A new musical group called The Incentives cuts a debut single. The record company determines a number of price points for the group's first single, "The Big Idea."

Price per download	Quantity of downloads
$2.99	25,000
$1.99	50,000
$1.49	75,000
$0.99	100,000
$0.49	150,000

The record company can produce the song with fixed costs of $10,000 and no variable cost.

   a. Determine the total revenue at each price. What is the marginal revenue as the price drops from one level to the next?
   b. What price would maximize the record company's profits? How much would the company make?
   c. If you were the agent for The Incentives, what signing fee would you request from the record company? Explain your answer.

7. Recalling what you have learned about elasticity, what can you say about the connection between the price a monopolist chooses to charge and whether or not demand is elastic, unitary, or inelastic at that price? (**Hint**: examine the marginal revenue curve of a monopolist. Since marginal revenue becomes negative at low prices, this implies that a portion of the demand curve cannot possibly be chosen.)

8. A small community is served by five independent gas stations. Gasoline is a highly competitive market. Use the market demand curve to illustrate the consumer and producer surplus created by the market. Now imagine that the five independent gas stations are all combined under one franchise. Create a new graph that illustrates the consumer surplus, producer surplus, and deadweight loss after the monopoly enters the market.

9. A local community bus service charges $2.00 for a one-way fare. The city council is thinking of raising the fare to $2.50 to generate 25% more revenue. The council has asked for your advice as a student of economics. In your analysis, be sure to break down the impact of the price increase into the price effect and the output effect. Explain why the city council's estimate of the revenue increase is likely to be overstated. Use a graph to illustrate your answer.

10. Suppose that a monopolist's marginal cost curve shifts upward. What is likely to happen to the price the monopolist charges, the quantity it produces, and the profit it makes? Use a graph to illustrate your answer.

SOLVED PROBLEMS

5. There is a two-part answer here. The first graph shows the monopolist making a profit:

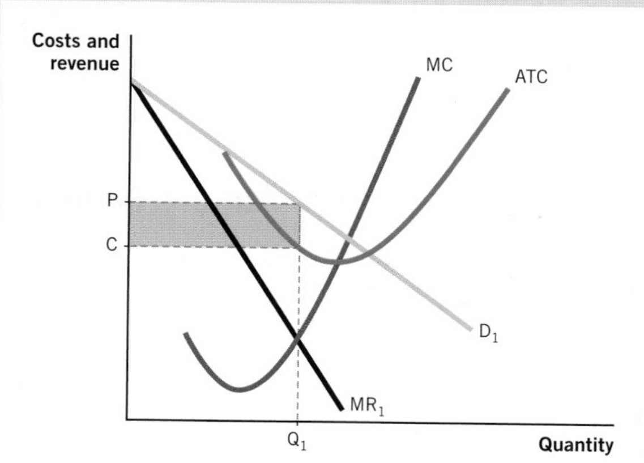

Now we show what happens if demand falls:

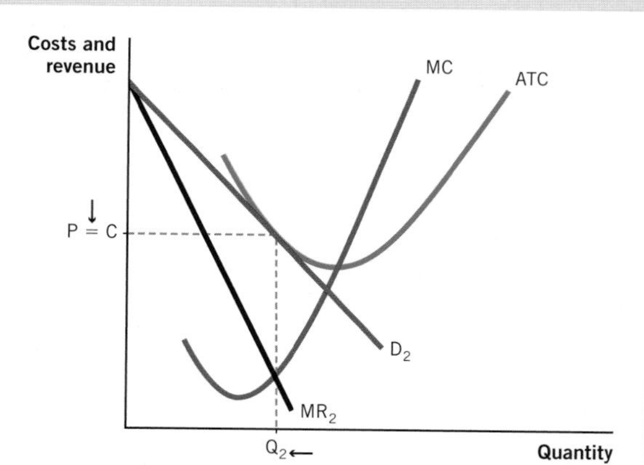

Lower demand causes the price to fall, the output to decline, and the profit to disappear.

6. a.

Price per download	Downloads	Total revenue	Marginal revenue
$2.99	25,000	$74,750	$74,750
$1.99	50,000	99,500	24,750
$1.49	75,000	111,750	12,250
$0.99	100,000	99,000	−12,750
$0.49	150,000	73,500	−25,500

b. Since marginal costs are $0, the firm would maximize its profits at $1.49. The company would make $111,750 − $10,000, or $101,750.

c. The company makes $101,750 from production, so as the agent you could request any signing fee up to that amount. Since determining a fee is a negotiation and both sides have to gain from trade, as the agent you should argue for a number close to $100,000, and you should expect the firm to argue for a much smaller fee.

CHAPTER

11 Price Discrimination

MISCONCEPTION

Charging different prices to different people is unfair and harmful.

Have you ever wondered why out-of-state students pay more than in-state students for the same education at many public universities? Or why private colleges have high sticker prices and then offer tuition discounts to some students but not others? Maybe you have noticed that many clubs let women in without a cover charge but require men to pay. And why do theaters charge more for adults and less for children when everyone sees the same movie? In each of these examples, some customers pay more and others pay less. Is this unfair and harmful? Not really. When a firm can charge more than one price, markets work more efficiently.

In this chapter, we examine many real-life pricing situations and how businesses can make additional profits if they charge more than one price to different groups of customers. The study of *price discrimination* adds a layer of complexity to the simple models of perfect competition and monopoly. A thorough understanding of how price discrimination works will be especially useful as we complete our study of market structure with monopolistic competition and oligopoly in the next two chapters.

Why do some clubs offer no cover charge to women but not to men?

BIG QUESTIONS

* What is price discrimination?
* How is price discrimination practiced?

What Is Price Discrimination?

Price discrimination occurs when a firm sells the same good at different prices to different groups of customers.

Price discrimination occurs when a firm sells the same good at different prices to different groups of customers. The difference in price is not related to differences in cost. Although "price discrimination" sounds like something illegal, in fact it is beneficial to both sellers and buyers. When a firm can charge more than one price, markets work more efficiently. Since price-discriminating firms typically charge a "high" and a "low" price, some consumers are able to buy the product at a low price. Of course, firms are not in business to provide goods at low prices; they want to make a profit. Price discrimination enables them to make more money by dividing their customers into at least two groups: those who get a discount and others who pay more.

We have seen that in competitive markets, firms are price takers. If a competitive firm attempts to charge a higher price, its customers will likely buy elsewhere. To practice price discrimination, a firm must be a price maker: it must have some market power before it can charge more than one price. Both monopolies and non-monopoly companies use price discrimination to earn higher profits. Common examples of price discrimination are movie theater tickets, restaurant menus, college tuition, airline reservations, discounts on academic software, and coupons.

Conditions for Price Discrimination

For price discrimination to take place, two conditions must be met. First, the firm must be able to distinguish groups of buyers with different price elasticities of demand. Second, the firm must be able to prevent resale of the product or service. Let's look at each in turn.

Distinguishing Groups of Buyers

In order to price-discriminate, the firm must be able to distinguish groups of buyers with different price elasticities of demand. Firms can generate additional revenues by charging more to customers with inelastic demand and less to customers with elastic demand. For instance, many restaurants offer lower prices, known as "early-bird specials," to people who eat dinner early. Who are these customers? Many, such as retirees and families with children, are on a limited budget. These early diners not only have less demand but also represent demand that is more elastic; they eat out only if the price is low enough.

Trade-offs

Early-bird specials work for restaurants by separating customers into two groups: one that is price-sensitive and another that is willing to pay full price. This strategy enables the restaurants to serve more customers and generate additional revenue.

Preventing Resale

For price discrimination to be a viable strategy, a firm must also be able to prevent resale of the product or service. In some cases, preventing resale is easy. For example, airlines require that electronic tickets match the passenger's government-issued photo ID. This prevents a passenger who received a discounted fare from reselling it to another passenger who would be willing to pay more. The process works well for airlines and enables them to charge more to groups of flyers with more inelastic demand. It also works well for restaurants offering early-bird specials, since the restaurants can easily distinguish between customers who arrive in time for the specials and those who arrive later.

One Price versus Price Discrimination

A business that practices price discrimination would prefer to differentiate every customer by selling the same good at a price unique to that customer—a situation known as **perfect price discrimination**. To achieve this, a business would have to know exactly what any particular customer would be willing to pay and charge them exactly that price. Many jewelry stores and automobile dealerships attempt to practice perfect price discrimination by posting high sticker prices and then bargaining with each customer to reach a deal. When you enter a jewelry store or a vehicle showroom, the salesperson tries to determine the highest price you are willing to pay. Then he or she bargains with you until that price is reached.

Perfect price discrimination occurs when a firm sells the same good at a unique price to every customer.

In practice, perfect price discrimination is hard to implement. To see why, let's look at a hypothetical example. Consider two small airlines, Flat Earth Air and Discriminating Fliers. Each airline has a monopoly on the route it flies, and each faces the same market demand curves and marginal costs. The costs of running a flight—fuel, pilots, flight attendants, ground crew, and so on—are about the same no matter how many passengers are on board. Both firms fly the same airplane, which seats 200 passengers. So the marginal cost of adding one passenger—the extra weight and the cost of a can of soda or two—is very small. What happens if one of the airlines price-discriminates but the other does not?

In Figure 11.1, Flat Earth Air charges the same price to every passenger, while Discriminating Fliers uses two different price structures. To keep our example easy to work with, the marginal cost (MC) is set at \$100, shown as a horizontal line.

Flat Earth sets its price by using the profit-maximizing rule, MR = MC. It charges \$300 for every seat and serves 100 customers (that is, passengers). Since the marginal cost is \$100, every passenger who gets on the plane generates \$200 in marginal revenue. The net revenue, represented by the green rectangle in the graph, is \$200 × 100, or \$20,000. At 100 passengers, this

Marginal thinking

FIGURE 11.1

One Price versus Price Discrimination

(a) A firm that charges a single price uses MR = MC to earn a profit. (b) When a firm price-discriminates, it takes in more revenue than a firm that charges a single price. The discriminating firm increases its revenue by charging some customers more and other customers less, as shown in blue. The increase in revenue is partly offset by the loss of revenue from existing customers who receive a lower price, as shown in red.

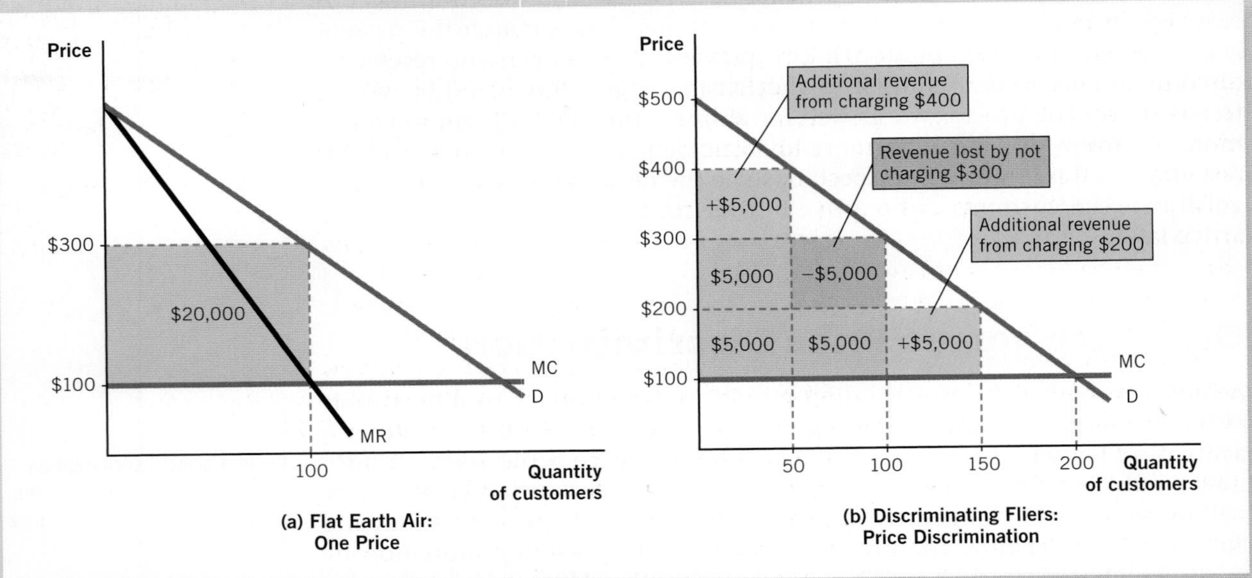

airline has done everything it can to maximize profits at a single price. At the same time, there are plenty of unsold seats in the plane, which holds 200 passengers. Those unfilled seats represent a lost opportunity to earn additional revenue. As a result, in cases like this airlines typically try to fill the plane by discounting the price of some seats.

In contrast, Discriminating Fliers experiments with two prices. It charges $400 for midweek flights or last-minute bookings, and $200 for weekend flights and to customers who book in advance. Let's look at the reasoning behind these two prices.

Since the firm faces a downward-sloping demand curve, the airline cannot sell every seat on the plane at the higher price. So it saves a number of seats, in this case 50, for last-minute bookings to capture customers with less flexibility who are willing to pay $400. These are travelers with inelastic demand, such as those who travel for business. The airline offers the rest of the seats at a low price, in this case $200, to capture customers with more elastic demand. The challenge for the airline is to make sure that the people who are willing to pay $400 do not purchase the $200 seats. To do this, it makes the low fare available to customers who book far in advance, because these customers are typically more flexible and shop for the best deal. It is common for a businessperson who needs to visit a client to make flight arrangements just days before the meeting, which precludes purchasing a $200 ticket available only weeks in advance. The customers who book early fill the seats that would otherwise be empty if the airline had only charged one price, as Flat Earth does. We can see this by comparing the total number of passengers under the two strategies. Discriminating Fliers, with its two-price strategy, serves 150 passengers. Flat Earth's single price brings in 100 passengers.

Airlines offer lower fares if you are willing to take the red-eye.

The net effect of price discrimination is apparent in the shaded areas of Figure 11.1b. By charging two prices, Discriminating Fliers generates more net revenue. The high price, $400, generates additional revenue equal to the upper blue rectangle—$5,000—from passengers who must pay more than the $300 charged by Flat Earth. Discriminating Fliers also gains additional revenue with its low price of $200. The less expensive tickets attract passengers with more elastic demand, such as college students, vacationers, and retirees. This generates $5,000, as shown by the lower blue rectangle.

Some customers would have paid Discriminating Fliers more if the airline had charged a single price. The group of customers willing to pay $300 is able to acquire tickets on Discriminating Fliers for $200. We see this in the red rectangle, which represents lost revenues equal to $5,000. The $10,000 in revenue represented by the blue rectangles more than offsets the $5,000 in lost revenue represented by the red rectangle. The airline that price-discriminates generates a net revenue of $25,000 in panel (b). The airline that charges a single price generates a net revenue of $20,000 in panel (a).

In reality, airlines often charge many prices. For example, you can find higher prices for travel on Friday and for midday flights. If your stay includes a Saturday night, or if you choose a red-eye flight, the prices will be lower still. Airlines also change prices from day to day and even from hour to hour. All these efforts price-discriminate on multiple fronts.

Since passengers cannot resell their tickets or easily change their plans, airlines can effectively price-discriminate. In fact, if an airline could charge unique prices for every passenger booking a flight, it would transform the entire area under the demand curve and above the marginal cost curve into more revenue.

The Welfare Effects of Price Discrimination

Price discrimination is profitable for the companies that practice it. But it also increases the welfare of society. How, you might ask, can companies make more profit and also benefit consumers? The answer: because a price discriminator charges a high price to some and a low price to others, more consumers are able to buy the good.

To illustrate this point, let's imagine an airline, Perfect Flights, that is able to perfectly price-discriminate. Perfect Flights charges each passenger a price exactly equal to what that passenger is willing to pay. As a result, some customers pay more and others pay less than they would under a single-price system. This is evident in Figure 11.2, where a profit-maximizing firm charges \$300. At this price, the firm captures the net revenue in the green rectangle, B. However, Perfect Flights charges each passenger a price based on his or her willingness to pay. Therefore, it earns significantly more net revenue. By charging higher prices to those willing to pay more than \$300 (P_{high}), the firm is able to capture additional net revenues in the upper blue triangle, A. Likewise, by charging lower prices to those not willing to pay \$300 (P_{low}), the firm is able to capture additional net revenues in triangle C. As a result, Perfect Flights is making more money and serving more customers.

By charging a different fare to every customer, Perfect Flights can also increase the quantity of tickets sold to 200. This strategy yields two results worth noting. First, in the long run, a perfectly competitive firm would charge a price

FIGURE 11.2

Perfect Price Discrimination

If the firm charges one price, the most it can earn is the net revenue in the green rectangle. However, if a firm is able to perfectly price-discriminate, it can pick up the additional revenue represented by the blue triangles.

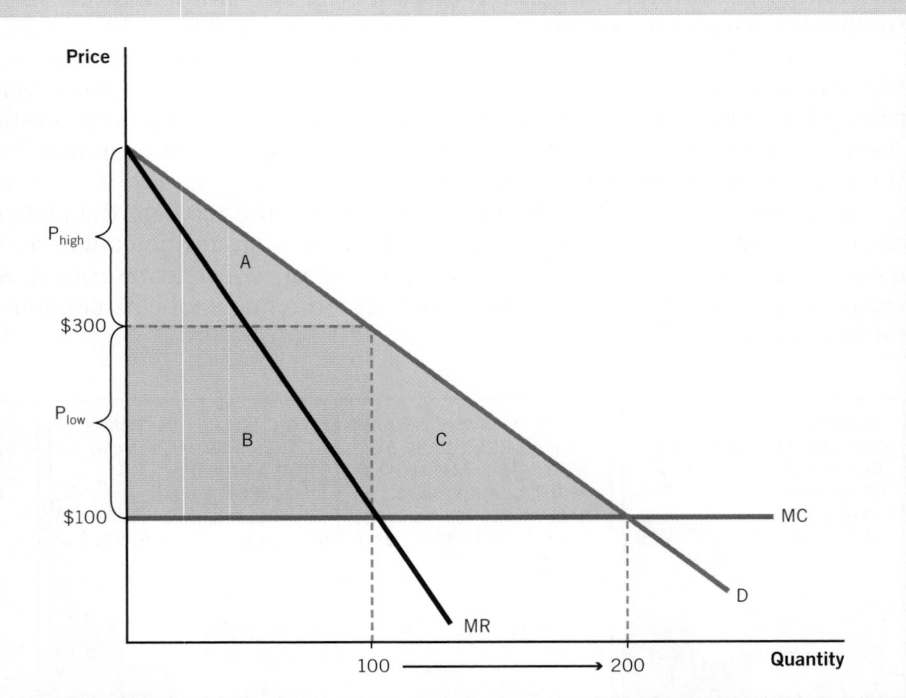

just equal to marginal cost. In the case of Perfect Flights, the last customer who gets on the plane will pay an extraordinarily low price of $100—the price you might find in a competitive market. Second, this outcome mirrors the result of a government-regulated monopolist that uses the marginal-cost pricing rule, P = MC, to enhance social welfare. Perfect Flights is therefore achieving the efficiency noted in a competitive market while also producing the output that a regulated monopolist would choose. This strategy provides the firm with the opportunity to convert the area consisting of the two blue triangles into more revenue. In other words, the process maximizes the quantity sold. The efficiency of the market improves, and the firm generates more revenue.

Comparing Perfect Price Discrimination with Perfect Competition and Monopoly

To understand the welfare effects of perfect price discrimination, we can compare the consumer and producer surplus in three scenarios: a competitive market, a market in which a monopolist charges a single price, and a market characterized by perfect price discrimination. The results, shown in Table 11.1, are derived by examining Figure 11.2.

First, in a "perfectly" competitive market, there are no barriers to entry and no firm has market power. In the long run, the price will be equal to the marginal cost. In our example of airline ticket prices, the price is driven down to $100. At this price, 200 tickets are sold. The entire area above the marginal cost curve (A + B + C) is consumer surplus, since the willingness to pay—as determined along the demand curve—is greater than the price. Because the ticket price is the same as the marginal cost, the producer surplus is zero. Also, since every customer who is willing to pay $100 or more can find a ticket, there is no deadweight loss. Under perfect competition, the market structure clearly favors consumers.

Marginal thinking

Second, a monopoly holds substantial market power, so the firm sets a price using the profit-maximizing rule, MR = MC, without having to worry about competition driving the price down to marginal cost. The monopolist's profit-maximizing price, or $300 in Figure 11.2, is higher than the $100 price under perfect competition. This higher price reduces the amount of consumer surplus to triangle A and creates a producer surplus equal to rectangle B. In addition, because the number of tickets sold falls to 100, there is now deadweight loss equal to triangle C. Economic activity associated with triangle C

TABLE 11.1

The Welfare Effects of Perfect Price Discrimination

	Perfect competition	A monopolist that charges a single price	Perfect price discrimination
Consumer surplus	A + B + C	A	0
Producer surplus	0	B	A + B + C
Deadweight loss	0	C	0
Total welfare	A + B + C	A + B	A + B + C

ECONOMICS IN THE MEDIA

Perfect Price Discrimination

Legally Blonde

In this 2001 film, Reese Witherspoon stars as Elle Woods, a sun-washed sorority girl who defies expectations. Believing that her boyfriend is about to propose to her, Elle and two friends go shopping to find the perfect dress for the occasion. They enter an exclusive boutique and start trying on dresses.

The saleswoman comments to another associate, "There's nothing I love more than a dumb blonde with daddy's plastic." She grabs a dress off the clearance sale rack and removes the "half price" tag. Approaching Elle, she says, "Did you see this one? We just got it in yesterday." Elle fingers the dress, then the price tag, and looks at the saleswoman with excitement.

ELLE: "Is this a low-viscosity rayon?"
SALESWOMAN: "Uh, yes—of course."
ELLE: "With half-loop top-stitching on the hem?"
SALESWOMAN (smiling a lie): "Absolutely. It's one of a kind."
(Elle hands the dress back to her, no longer pretending to be excited.)
ELLE: "It's impossible to use a half-loop top-stitch on low-viscosity rayon. It would snag the fabric. And you didn't just get this in, because I remember it from the June *Vogue* a year ago, so if you're trying to sell it to me at full price, you picked the wrong girl."

Do you know how to look good for the right price?

The scene is a wonderful example of an attempt at price discrimination gone wrong. Unbeknownst to the saleswoman, Elle is majoring in fashion merchandising in college and knows more about fashion than the saleswoman does. Her effort to cheat Elle fails miserably.

What makes the scene powerful is the use of stereotypes. When merchants attempt to price-discriminate, they look for clues to help them decide whether the buyer is willing to pay full price or needs an incentive, or discount, in order to make a purchase. In this case, Elle's appearance suggests that she is an uninformed buyer with highly inelastic demand. Consequently, the saleswoman's strategy backfires.

no longer exists, and the total welfare of society is now limited to A + B. From this, we see that monopoly causes a partial transfer of consumer surplus to producers and a reduction in total welfare for society.

Third, a firm that can practice perfect price discrimination is able to charge each customer a price exactly equal to the price that customer is willing to pay. This strategy enables the firm to convert the entire area of consumer surplus that existed under perfect competition into producer surplus (A + B + C). For the firm to capture the entire area of available consumer surplus, it must lower some prices all the way down to marginal cost. At that point, the number of tickets sold returns to 200, the market is once again efficient, and the deadweight loss disappears. Perfect price discrimination transfers the gains from trade from consumers to producers, but it also yields maximum efficiency.

Note that this gives us a better understanding of what economists mean when they use the word "perfect" in connection with a market. It can mean that consumer surplus is maximized, as it is under perfect competition, or that producer surplus is maximized, as it is under perfect price discrimination. It does not specify an outcome from a particular perspective; instead, it describes any market process that produces no deadweight loss. If society's total welfare is maximized, economists do not distinguish whether the benefits accrue to consumers or producers.

ECONOMICS IN THE REAL WORLD

Outlet Malls—If You Build It, They Will Come

Have you ever noticed that outlet malls along major roadways are often located a considerable distance from large population centers? Moreover, every item at an outlet mall can be found closer to home. The same clothes, shoes, and kitchenware are available nearby.

How far would you drive to visit an outlet mall?

Logic tells us that it would be more convenient to shop locally and forget the time and hassle of getting to an outlet center. But that is not how many shoppers feel.

Discount shopping is a big deal. How big? Here are a few statistics. Potomac Mills, 30 miles south of Washington, D.C., is Virginia's most popular attraction, with nearly 17 million visitors a year. (That figure rivals the number of annual visitors to Disney World's Magic Kingdom!) But Potomac Mills is not unique. Two adjacent outlet malls in San Marcos, Texas, attract over 6 million visitors a year—many more than the number that visit the Alamo. And in Pigeon Forge, Tennessee, over 10 million shoppers go to the outlets annually—more than the number of visitors to nearby Great Smoky Mountains National Park.

Outlet shopping is an example of price discrimination at work. Traditional malls are usually situated in urban settings and offer a wide variety of choices, but not necessarily low prices. If you want convenience, the local shopping mall is right around the corner. But if you want a bargain, shopping at a traditional, local mall is not the best way to go.

Incentives

What makes outlets so attractive are the discounts. Bargain hunters have much more elastic demand than their traditional mall-shopping counterparts who desire convenience. Moreover, the difference in the price elasticity of demand between these two groups means that traditional malls can more easily charge full price, while outlets must discount their merchandise in order to attract customers. This gives merchants a chance to price-discriminate on the basis of location—which is another way of separating customers into two groups and preventing resale at the same time. Retailers can therefore earn additional profits through price discrimination, while price-sensitive consumers can find lower prices at the outlets.

Opportunity cost

It is noteworthy that the convenience of finding discounts online threatens not only the traditional malls but also the outlets. When savvy shoppers can simply click to find the best deal, will they continue to drive to the outlets? ✷

PRACTICE WHAT YOU KNOW

How much would you pay to fly in a helicopter?

Price Discrimination: Taking Economics to New Heights

Consider the table below, which shows seven potential customers who are interested in taking a 30-minute helicopter ride. The helicopter has room for eight people, including the pilot. The marginal cost of taking on additional passengers is $10.

Customer	Maximum willingness to pay	Age
Amelia	$80	66
Orville	70	34
Wilbur	40	17
Neil	50	16
Charles	60	9
Chuck	100	49
Buzz	20	9

Question: If the company can charge only one price, what should it be?

Answer: First, create an ordered array of the customers, from those willing to pay the most to those willing to pay the least.

Customer	Maximum willingness to pay	Price	TR	MR
Chuck	$100	$100	$100	**$90**
Amelia	80	$80	160	**60**
Orville	70	$70	210	**50**
Charles	60	$60	240	**30**
Neil	50	$50	250	**10**
Wilbur	40	$40	240	−10
Buzz	20	$20	140	−100

(CONTINUED)

(CONTINUED)

If the firm charges $100, only Chuck will take the flight. When the firm drops the price to $80, Chuck and Amelia both buy tickets, so the total revenue (TR) is $80 × 2, or $160. Successively lower prices result in higher total revenue for the first five customers. Since the marginal cost is $10, the firm will benefit from lowering its price as long as the increase in marginal revenue is greater than, or equal to, the marginal cost. When the price is $50, five customers get on the helicopter, for a total of $250 in revenue. Adding the fifth passenger brings in exactly $10 in marginal revenue, so $50 is the best possible price to charge. Since each of the five passengers has a marginal cost of $10, the company makes $250 − (5 × $10), or $200 in profit.

Question: If the company could charge two prices, what should they be and who would pay them?

Answer: First, arrange the customers in two distinct groups: adults and children.

Adult customers	Willingness to pay	Age	Price	TR	MR
Chuck	$100	49	$90	$90	$90
Amelia	80	66	$80	160	60
Orville	70	34	$70	210	50

Young customers	Willingness to pay	Age	Price	TR	MR
Charles	$60	9	$60	$60	60
Neil	50	16	$50	100	40
Wilbur	40	17	$40	120	20
Buzz	20	9	$20	80	−40

As you can see, two separate prices emerge. For adults, total revenue is maximized at a price of $70. For children, total revenue is maximized at $40. The company should charge $70 to the adult customers, which brings in $70 × 3, or $210 in total revenue. The company should charge $40 for each child under age 18, which brings in $40 × 3, or $120. Note that if the company lowered the price of a child's ticket to $20 in order to entice Buzz to buy a ticket, it would earn $20 × 4, or $80, a lower total revenue.

Price discrimination earns the company $210 + $210 − (6 × $10), or $270 in profit. This is a $70 improvement over charging a single price. In addition, six passengers are now able to get on the helicopter instead of only five under the single-price model.

How Is Price Discrimination Practiced?

Price discrimination is one of the most interesting topics in economics because each example is slightly different from the others. In this section, we take a closer look at real-world examples of price discrimination at movie theaters and on college campuses. As you will see, price discrimination takes many forms, some that are easy to describe and others that are more nuanced.

Price Discrimination at the Movies

Have you ever gone to the movies early so you can pay less for tickets? Movie theaters price-discriminate based on the time of day, age, student status, and whether or not you buy snacks. Let's examine these pricing techniques to see if they are effective.

Pricing Based on the Time of the Show

Why are matinees priced less than evening shows? To encourage customers to attend movies during the afternoon, theaters discount ticket prices for matinees. This makes sense because customers who can attend matinees (retirees, people on vacation, and those who do not work during the day) either have less demand or are more flexible, or price elastic. Work and school limit the options for many other potential customers. As a result, theaters discount matinee prices to encourage moviegoers who have elastic demand and are willing to watch at a less crowded time. Movie theaters also discount the price of matinee shows since they pay to rent films on a weekly basis—so it is in their interest to show a film as many times as possible. Since the variable cost of being open during the day is essentially limited to paying a few employees relatively low wages, the theater can make additional profits even with a relatively small audience. On weekends, matinees also offer a discount to families that want to see a movie together—adding yet another layer of price discrimination.

Theaters charge two different prices based on show time because they can easily distinguish between high-demand customers and price-sensitive customers who have the flexibility to watch a matinee. Those with higher demand or less flexible schedules must pay higher show prices to attend in the evening.

Once the doors open, matinee prices will bring in moviegoers with elastic demand.

Pricing Based on Age or Student Status

Why are there different movie prices for children, seniors, students, and everyone else? This is a complex question. Income does not fully explain the discounts that the young, the old, and students receive. Movie attendance is highest among 13- to 24-year-olds and declines thereafter with age. Given the strong demand among teenagers, it is not surprising that "child" discounts are phased out at most theaters by age 12. But did you know that most "senior" discounts begin before age 65? In some places, senior discounts start at age 50. Now you might think that because people in their fifties tend to be at the peak of their earning power, discounting ticket prices for them would be a bad move. However, since interest in going to the movies declines with age, the "senior" discount actually provides an incentive for a population that might not otherwise go to a movie theater. However, as we have seen, age-based price discrimination does not always work perfectly. Theaters do not usually ask for proof of age, and it may be hard to tell the difference between a child who is just under 12 and one who is over 12. Nonetheless, price discrimination works well enough to make age or student status a useful revenue-generating tool.

Concession Pricing

Have you ever wondered why it is so expensive to purchase snacks at the movie theater? The concession area is another arena in which movie theaters practice price discrimination. To understand this, we need to think of two groups of customers: those who want to eat while they watch movies and those who do not. By limiting outside food and drink, movie theaters push people with inelastic demand for snacks to buy from the concession area. Of course, that does not stop some customers with elastic demand from sneaking food into the theater. But as long as some moviegoers are willing to buy concession fare at exorbitant prices, the theater will generate more revenue. Movie theaters cannot prevent smuggling in of snacks, and they don't have to. All they really want to do is separate their customers into two groups: a price-inelastic group of concession-area snackers and a price-elastic group of nonsnackers and smugglers who fill up the remaining empty seats. This is very similar to the problem we examined with airlines. Empty seats represent lost revenue, so it makes sense to price-discriminate through a combination of high and low prices.

If you have ever smuggled food into a movie theater, it is because your demand for movie theater concessions is elastic.

Price Discrimination on Campus

Colleges and universities are experts at price discrimination. Think about tuition. Some students pay the full sticker price, while others enjoy a free ride. Some students receive the in-state rate, while out-of-state students pay substantially more. And once you get to campus, discounts for students are everywhere. In this section, we consider the many ways in which colleges and universities differentiate among their students.

Tuition

Price discrimination begins before you ever set foot on campus, with the Free Application for Federal Student Aid (known as the FAFSA) that most families complete. The form determines eligibility for federal aid. Families that qualify are eligible for grants and low-interest loans, which effectively lower the tuition cost for low- and medium-income families. Therefore, the FAFSA enables colleges to separate applicants into two groups based on income. Since many colleges also use the FAFSA to determine eligibility for their own institutional grants of aid, the FAFSA makes it possible for colleges to precisely target

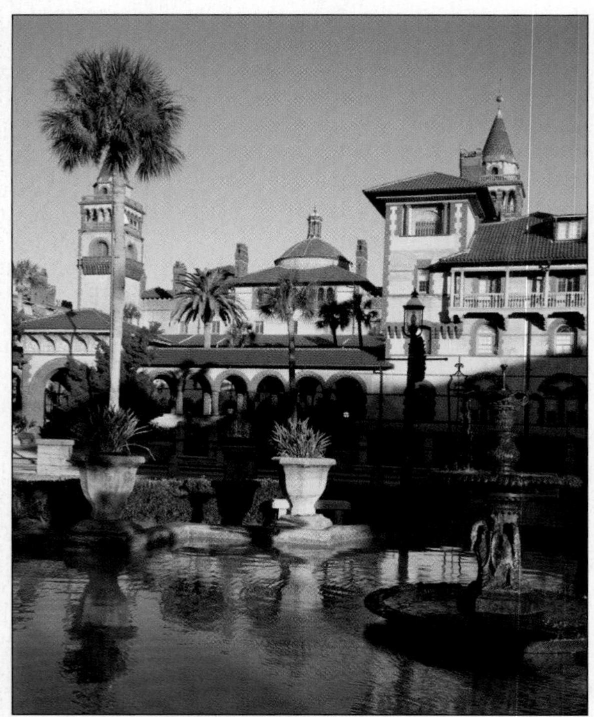
Resort or college? Sky-high tuition and room and board are one way to help pay for a beautiful campus.

grants and loans to the students who need the most help in order to attend.

Many state institutions of higher education have a two-tiered pricing structure. In-state students get a discount on the tuition, and out-of-state students pay a much higher rate. Part of the difference is attributable to state subsidies that are intended to make in-state institutions more affordable for residents. In-state students pay less because their parents have been paying taxes to the state, often for many years, and the state then uses those tax dollars to support its system of higher education.

This two-tiered pricing structure creates two separate groups of customers with distinctly different elasticities of demand. Students choose an out-of-state college or university because they like what that institution has to offer more than the institutions in their home state. It might be that a particular major or program is more highly rated, or simply that they prefer the location of the out-of-state school. Whatever the reason, they are willing to pay more for the out-of-state school. Therefore, out-of-state students have a much more inelastic demand. Colleges know this and price their tuition accordingly. Conversely, in-state students often view the opportunity to attend a nearby college as the most economical decision. Since price is a big factor in choosing an in-state institution, it is not surprising that in-state demand is more elastic.

Selective private colleges also play the price discrimination game by advertising annual tuition and room and board fees that exceed $50,000. With price discrimination, the "sticker" price is often discounted. Depending on how much the college wants to encourage a particular student to attend, it can discount the tuition all the way to zero. This strategy enables selective private colleges to price-discriminate by offering scholarships based on financial need, while also guaranteeing placements for the children of wealthy alums and others willing to pay the full sticker price.

Student Discounts

The edge of campus is a great place to look for price discrimination. Local bars, eateries, and shops all want college students to step off campus, so student discounts are the norm. Why do establishments do this? Think about the average college student. Price matters to that student. Knowing this, local merchants in search of college customers can provide student discounts without lowering their prices across the board. This means they can charge more to their regular clients, while providing the necessary discounts to get college students to make the trek off campus.

Price discrimination also occurs on campus. For example, students typically receive discounts for campus activities like concerts and sporting events. Since students generally have elastic demand, price discrimination provides greater student access to on-campus events than charging a single price does.

SNAPSHOT

Now Playing: Economics!

Have you ever gone to the movies early so you can pay less for tickets? Movie theaters price-discriminate based on the time of the movie and the age of the customer. In order to be able to practice price discrimination, theaters must be able to identify different groups of moviegoers, where each group has a different price elasticity of demand.

Demand for matinees is typically low. These showings attract groups with relatively elastic demand, like families and those on a budget, who decide to attend matinees because of lower prices.

EVENING
$13

Evening movie showings attract larger crowds that consist mainly of adults and couples on dates. This group has relatively inelastic demand, so price is not the determining factor of when and where they see a movie.

The concession counter also generates profit for the movie theater. The high prices mean that patrons who are price conscious (having relatively elastic demand) skip the counter or smuggle in their own snacks, while those who are more concerned about convenience than price (having relatively inelastic demand) buy snacks at the counter.

REVIEW QUESTIONS

- Does price discrimination hurt all consumers? Think about the example of movie theaters as you craft your response.
- Your local movie theater is thinking about increasing ticket prices for just the opening day of a blockbuster movie. How would you explain the economics behind this price increase to your friends?

PRACTICE WHAT YOU KNOW

Price Discrimination in Practice: Everyday Examples

Question: Test your understanding by thinking about the examples below. Are they examples of price discrimination?

a. **Retail coupons.** Programs such as discount coupons, rebates, and frequent-buyer plans appeal to customers willing to spend time pursuing a deal.

b. **Using Priceline to make hotel reservations.** "Naming your price" on Priceline is a form of haggling that enables users to get hotel rooms at a discount. Hotels negotiate with Priceline to fill unused rooms while still advertising the full price on their web sites.

c. **$5 footlong subs at Subway.** Customers who buy a $5 footlong get more sub at a substantially lower price per inch than a 6-inch sub.

d. **The Dollar Menu at McDonald's.** Customers who order off the Dollar Menu get a variety of smaller menu items for $1 each.

e. **Discounts for early shoppers on Black Friday.** Customers who line up in the early-morning hours after Thanksgiving get first dibs on a limited quantity of reduced-price items at many retailers.

Price discrimination or not?

Answers:

a. **Retail coupons.** Affluent customers generally do not bother with the hassle of clipping, sending in, and keeping track of the coupons because they value their time more than the small savings. However, customers with lower incomes usually take the time to get the discount. This means that coupons, rebates, and frequent-buyer programs do a good job of price discriminating.

b. **Using Priceline to make hotel reservations.** Priceline enables hotels to divide their customers into two groups: those who don't want to be bothered with haggling, and those who value the savings enough to justify the time spent negotiating. This is a good example of price discrimination.

c. **$5 footlong subs at Subway.** The $5 price is available to anyone anytime. Therefore, the $5 footlong is catchy marketing, but it does not strictly meet the definition of price discrimination. However, to get the deal customers must buy a 12-inch sub. This is an example of secondary price discrimination—that is, the price per unit varies with the quantity sold. Anyone could conceivably get the deal, but only those with big appetites or a willingness to eat leftovers will choose a footlong. Those with smaller appetites are stuck paying $3.50 for a 6-inch sub.

d. **The Dollar Menu at McDonald's.** Anyone can buy off the Dollar Menu at any time. Since McDonald's does not force customers to buy a large serving in order to get the deal, this is not price discrimination.

e. **Discounts for early shoppers on Black Friday.** The discounts are time-sensitive. Shoppers who arrive before the deadline get a lower price; shoppers who arrive after it do not. This is a clear-cut example of price discrimination.

Price Discrimination

ECONOMICS IN THE MEDIA

Extreme Couponing

Most of us use coupons from time to time, when it is convenient. The TV show *Extreme Couponing* showcases a small number of shoppers who plan their trips to the store with military precision. They clip coupons, scout out the stores that offer the best deals, and buy products in enormous quantities to save money. The returns are typically hundreds of dollars in savings each time they visit the store.

While these couponers often get groceries for practically nothing and appear to beat the system, they go to a lot of trouble to secure a deal. Some dive in dumpsters to get the discarded Sunday newspaper coupon sections. Others keep food stashes that take up most of the space in their homes. They use spreadsheets, folders, and calculators to determine how to save as much as possible.

Would you dumpster-dive to get coupons?

As good economists, we know that getting a really good deal on something doesn't make it free. The amount of time it takes to be an extreme couponer is staggering—equivalent to a part-time job. Clearly, the participants do not fully account for the time they spend on couponing. Saving $200 at the store sounds great unless it takes you 20 hours to do so; that's only $10 an hour. Many of the people on the show might find that they could earn substantially more by putting their organizational skills to use in the workforce. It is this very reason that causes many households not to clip coupons in the first place. After all, time is money.

ECONOMICS IN THE REAL WORLD

Groupon

Groupon is an organization that negotiates sizable discounts (typically 50% or more) with local businesses. It then sends the deals to local subscribers through email, Facebook, or Twitter. If enough subscribers decide they like the deal, Groupon sends—for a fee—a discount coupon to everyone who signed up. Both parties win: Groupon subscribers score a deal on something they might not otherwise purchase, and businesses generate additional revenue through price discrimination.

If enough people sign up, each one gets a discount.

Does Groupon price-discriminate perfectly? No. Some people who might have been willing to pay full price will occasionally score a discount. But on balance, since Groupon operates in many major cities, there are many residents who want to try something new. In addition, Groupon users tend to be more price-sensitive than nonusers. Because using Groupon requires some effort, not everyone will bother to become a subscriber, sign up for coupons, and remember to use them. This is imperfect price discrimination, but it is still good business. ✷

Conclusion

The word "discrimination" has negative connotations, but not when combined with the word "price." Charging different prices to different groups of customers results in more economic activity and is more efficient than charging a single price across the board. Under price discrimination, many consumers pay less than they would if a firm charged a single price. This has the effect of increasing social welfare, reducing deadweight loss, and creating a more efficient outcome. Perfect price discrimination occurs when a firm is able to charge a different price to every customer. The result is a socially efficient outcome in which most of the gains from exchange accrue to sellers.

Price discrimination also helps us understand how many markets actually function, since instances of highly competitive markets and monopoly are rare.

ANSWERING THE BIG QUESTIONS

What is price discrimination?

- Price discrimination occurs when firms have downward-sloping demand curves, can identify different groups of customers with varying price elasticities of demand, and can prevent resale among their customers.
- A firm must have some market power before it can charge more than one price.

How is price discrimination practiced?

- Under price discrimination, some consumers pay a higher price and others receive a discount. Price discrimination is profitable for the firm, reduces deadweight loss, and helps to restore a higher output level.

ECONOMICS FOR LIFE

Outsmarting Grocery Store Tactics

Throughout this chapter, we have considered the shopping experience in the context of price discrimination. Here we focus on how the typical grocery store is set up to manipulate buyers into spending more. Grocery stores carefully cultivate an enticing, multisensory experience—from the smell of the bread in the bakery, to the colorful cut flowers and fresh produce, to the eat-in restaurants and coffee bars, and the tens of thousands of other items to purchase. You need to be on your game so as not to overspend your budget. Here is some advice to help you save a few dollars.

Understand how grocery stores route you through the store. Have you ever wondered why the produce is displayed in a certain area? Or why most of the stuff you really need is at the back of the store? The grocery store has set things up to entice you to purchase more than you really need. Suppose that you are there to pick up a gallon of milk. In most stores, the refrigerated section is in the back, so that you have plenty of opportunities to impulsively grab something else that looks good.

Notice that popular items are placed at eye level. Believe it or not, supermarkets make more profits from *manufacturers* than from consumers. Manufacturers pay "slotting fees" to have their products placed in desirable locations. But the product you actually want may be on a higher or lower shelf—so it pays to look up and down.

Beware of sales. Stores know that shoppers gravitate to markdowns and sales. However, many shoppers are not very diligent in determining if the sale is a good value. Don't buy something simply because it is "on sale" and located at the end of the aisle. This is one way that groceries make extra money: you end up buying stuff you don't really need.

Find the loss leaders. To draw traffic to the store, groceries compete by offering a few fantastic promotions. Sometimes, the sale items are priced so low that the store actually loses money by selling them.

Grocery stores try to tempt you to buy more than you need.

But the store's management is counting on making up the difference when you buy other items throughout the store. The deal you get on one item should not cause you to let down your guard on other purchases.

Beware of coupons! Coupons aren't always the best deal either. Stores know which manufacturer coupons their customers have, so they rarely reduce the price on those products. If you have to pay full price in order to use a coupon, is it really a good deal? Consider store brands or other brands of the same item before you use a coupon.

Try the store brands. Generally, store brands are cheaper than name brands. The store brand is often exactly the same product as the name brand—it is just repackaged at the manufacturing plant and sold for less. You can save a lot of money by buying store brands.

Finally, get a smaller shopping cart. When their carts fill up, most shoppers instinctively ration the remaining space and become far more selective about what they pick up.

If you are aware of the tactics that grocery stores deploy, you can start beating them at their own game.

CONCEPTS YOU SHOULD KNOW

perfect price discrimination (p. 335)

price discrimination (p. 334)

QUESTIONS FOR REVIEW

1. What two challenges must a firm overcome to effectively price-discriminate?
2. Why does price discrimination improve the efficiency of the market?
3. Why is preventing resale a key to successful price discrimination?
4. If perfect price discrimination reduces consumer surplus to zero, how can this lead to the most socially desirable level of output?

STUDY PROBLEMS (✱ *solved at the end of the section*)

1. Seven potential customers are interested in seeing a movie. Since the marginal cost of admitting additional customers is zero, the movie theater maximizes its profits by maximizing its revenue.

Customer	Maximum willingness to pay	Age
Allison	$8	66
Becky	11	34
Charlie	6	45
David	7	16
Erin	6	9
Franco	10	28
Grace	9	14

   a. What price would the theater charge if it could only charge one price?
   b. If the theater could charge two prices, what prices would it choose? Which customers would pay the higher price, and which would pay the lower price?

2. Identify whether each of the following is an example of price discrimination. Explain your answers.
   a. A cell phone carrier offers unlimited calling on the weekends for all of its customers.
   b. Tickets to the student section for all basketball games are $5.
   c. A restaurant offers a 20% discount for customers who order dinner between 4 and 6 p.m.
   d. A music store has a half-price sale on last year's guitars.
   e. A well-respected golf instructor charges each customer a fee just under the customer's maximum willingness to pay for lessons.

3. At many amusement parks, customers who enter after 4 p.m. receive a steep discount on the price of admission. Explain how this practice is a form of price discrimination.

4. Name three products for which impatience on the part of the consumer enables a firm to price-discriminate.

✱ 5. Prescription drug prices in the United States are often three to four times higher than in Canada, the United Kingdom, and India. Today, pharmacies in these countries fill millions of low-cost prescriptions through the mail to U.S. citizens. Given that the pharmaceutical industry cannot prevent the resale of these drugs, are the industry's efforts to price-discriminate useless? Explain your answer.

✱ 6. Metropolitan Opera tickets are the most expensive on Saturday night. There are often a very limited number of "student rush" tickets, with which a lucky student can wind up paying $20 for a $250 seat. The student rush tickets are available first-come, first-served. Why does the opera company offer these low-cost tickets? How does it benefit from this practice? Why are students, and not other groups of customers, offered the discounted tickets?

SOLVED PROBLEMS

5. Buying prescription drugs outside the United States is increasingly common. Since the pharmaceutical companies charge three to four times more for drugs sold domestically than they do in most other countries, it would seem that the drug industry's efforts to price-discriminate aren't working, but that is not true. Not everyone fills their prescriptions from foreign sources—only a small fraction of U.S. customers go to that much effort. Since most U.S. citizens still purchase the more expensive drugs here, the pharmaceutical companies are benefiting from price discrimination, even though some consumers manage to navigate around their efforts.

6. The Met hopes to sell all of its $250 tickets, but not every show sells out and some tickets become available at the last minute. The student rush tickets benefit both the opera company and the students: the company can fill last-minute seats, and the students, who have elastic demand and low income, get a steep discount. The Met is able to perfectly price-discriminate, since the rush tickets require a student ID. Other groups of operagoers are therefore unable to buy the rush tickets. This practice effectively separates the customer base into two groups: students and nonstudents. Students make ideal rush customers because they are more willing to change their plans in hopes of obtaining last-minute tickets than other groups. Some opera companies also open up the rush tickets to seniors, another group that is easy to identify and generally has significant flexibility.

CHAPTER

12 Monopolistic Competition and Advertising

MISCONCEPTION

Advertising increases the price of products without adding value for the consumer.

If you drive down a busy street, you will find many competing businesses, often right next to one another. For example, in most places a consumer in search of a quick bite has many choices, and more fast-food restaurants appear all the time. These competing firms advertise heavily. The temptation is to see advertising as driving up the price of a product, without any benefit to the consumer. However, this misconception doesn't account for why firms advertise. In markets where competitors sell slightly differentiated products, advertising enables firms to inform their customers about new products and services; yes, costs rise, but consumers also gain information to help make purchase decisions.

In this chapter, we look at *monopolistic competition,* a widespread market structure that has features of both competitive markets and monopoly. We also explore the benefits and disadvantages of advertising, which is prevalent in markets with monopolistic competition.

Want something to eat quickly? There are many choices.

BIG QUESTIONS

- What is monopolistic competition?
- What are the differences among monopolistic competition, competitive markets, and monopoly?
- Why is advertising prevalent in monopolistic competition?

What Is Monopolistic Competition?

Monopolistic competition is characterized by free entry, many different firms, and product differentiation.

Product differentiation is the process that firms use to make a product more attractive to potential customers.

Some consumers prefer the fries at McDonald's, while others may crave a salad at Panera Bread or the chicken at KFC. Each fast-food establishment has a unique set of menu items. The different products in fast-food restaurants give each seller a small degree of market power. This combination of market power and competition is typical of the market structure known as *monopolistic competition*. Indeed, **monopolistic competition** is characterized by free entry, many different firms, and *product differentiation*. **Product differentiation** is the process firms use to make a product more attractive to potential customers. Firms use product differentiation to contrast their product's unique qualities with competing products. The differences, which we will examine in detail, can be minor and can involve subtle changes in packaging, quality, availability, and promotion.

How does monopolistic competition compare to other market structures we have studied? As Table 12.1 shows, monopolistic competition falls between competitive markets and monopoly.

We have seen that firms in competitive markets do not have any market power. As a result, buyers can expect to find consistently low prices and wide availability. And we have seen that monopolies charge more and restrict availability. In markets that are monopolistically competitive, firms sell differentiated products. This gives the monopolistic competitor some market power, though not as much as a monopolist, who controls the entire market. Monopolistically competitive firms have a small amount of market power that enables them to search for the price that is most profitable.

To understand how monopolistic competition works, we will begin with a closer look at product differentiation.

TABLE 12.1

Competitive Markets, Monopolistic Competition, and Monopoly

Competitive markets	Monopolistic competition	Monopoly
Many sellers	Many sellers	One seller
Similar products	Differentiated products	A unique product without close substitutes
Free entry and exit	Low barriers to entry and exit	Significant barriers to entry and exit

Product Differentiation

We have seen that monopolistically competitive firms create some market power through product differentiation. Differentiation can occur in a variety of ways, including style, location, and quality.

Style or Type

A trip to a mall is a great way to see product differentiation firsthand. For example, you will find many clothing stores, each offering a unique array of styles and types of clothing. Some stores, such as Abercrombie & Fitch, carry styles that attract younger customers. Others, such as Ann Taylor, appeal to older shoppers. Clothing stores can also vary by the type of clothing they sell, specializing in apparel such as business clothing, plus sizes, or sportswear. Each store hopes to attract a specific type of customer.

When you're ready for lunch at the mall, you can go to the food court, where many different places to eat offer an almost endless variety of choices. Where you decide to eat is a matter of your personal preferences and the price you are willing to pay. Like most consumers, you will select the place that gives you the best combination of choice and value. This makes it possible for a wide range of food vendors to compete side by side with other rivals who provide many good substitutes.

Location

Many businesses attract customers because of their convenient location. Gasoline stations, dry cleaners, barber shops, and car washes provide products and services that customers tend to choose on the basis of convenience of location rather than price. When consumers prefer to save time and to avoid the inconvenience of shopping for a better deal, a firm with a more convenient location will have some pricing power. As a result, producers who sell very similar products can generate some market power by locating their businesses along routes to and from work or in other areas where customers frequently travel.

Quality

Firms also compete on the basis of quality. For instance, if you want Mexican food you can go to Taco Bell, which is inexpensive and offers food cooked

Would you like your Mexican food cheaper . . .

. . . or fresher?

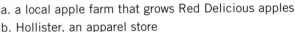

PRACTICE WHAT YOU KNOW

Product Differentiation: Would You Recognize a Monopolistic Competitor?

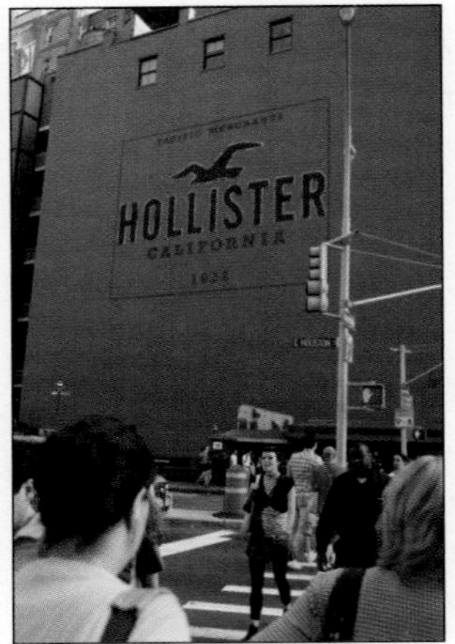

Is Hollister a monopolistic competitor?

Question: Which of the following are monopolistic competitors?

a. a local apple farm that grows Red Delicious apples
b. Hollister, an apparel store
c. your local water company

Answers:

a. Since Red Delicious apples are widely available at grocery stores, this local apple farm does not have a differentiated product to sell. In addition, it has many competitors that grow exactly the same variety of apples. This apple farm is part of a competitive market; it is not a monopolistic competitor.

b. Hollister has a slightly different mix of clothes than competitors Abercrombie & Fitch and American Eagle Outfitters. This gives the brand some pricing power. Hollister is a good example of a monopolistically competitive firm.

c. Because water is essential and people cannot easily do without it, the local water company has significant monopoly power. Moreover, purifying and distributing water are subject to economies of scale. Your local water company is definitely a monopolist, not a monopolistic competitor.

in advance. In contrast, at Baja Fresh the food is freshly prepared and, as a result, is more expensive. This form of product differentiation serves consumers quite well. Budget-conscious consumers can feast at Taco Bell, while those with a larger budget and a taste for higher-quality Mexican food can consider Baja Fresh as another option.

What Are the Differences among Monopolistic Competition, Competitive Markets, and Monopoly?

Monopolistic competition occupies a place between competitive markets, which produce low prices and an efficient output, and monopoly, which produces high prices and an inefficient output. To help you decide whether monopolistic competition is desirable or not, we consider the outcomes that individual firms can achieve when facing monopolistic competition in the short run and in the long run. Once you understand how monopolistic competition works, we will be able to compare the long-run equilibrium result with that of competitive markets, and then determine if monopolistic competition is desirable from society's standpoint.

Monopolistic Competition in the Short Run and the Long Run

A monopolistically competitive firm sells a differentiated product; this gives it some market power. We see this in the shape of the demand curve for the monopolistic competitor, which is downward sloping. Like a monopolist, the monopolistic competitor uses the profit-maximizing rule, MR = MC, and locates the corresponding point on its demand curve to determine the best price to charge and the best quantity to produce. Whether the firm earns a profit, experiences a loss, or breaks even is a function of entry and exit of firms from the market. Recall that entry and exit do not take place in the short run. However, in the long run firms are free to enter an industry when they see a potential for profits, or leave if they are making losses. Therefore, entry and exit regulate how much profit a firm can make in the long run.

Marginal thinking

Suppose you own a Hardee's fast-food restaurant in Asheville, North Carolina. Your business is doing well and making a profit. Then one day a Five Guys opens up across the street. Some of your customers will try Five Guys and switch, while others will still prefer your fare. But your profit will take a hit. Whether or not you stay in business will depend on how much you lose. To understand how a business owner would make this decision, we now turn to the short-run and long-run implications of monopolistic competition.

Monopolistic Competition in the Short Run

Figure 12.1 depicts a firm, like Hardee's, in a monopolistically competitive environment. In 12.1a, the firm makes a profit. Figure 12.1b shows the same firm incurring a loss after a new competitor, like Five Guys, opens nearby. In each case, the firm uses the profit-maximizing rule to determine the best price to charge by locating the point at which marginal revenue equals marginal cost. This calculation establishes the profit-maximizing output along the vertical dashed line. The firm determines the best price to charge (Q_{max}) by locating the intersection of the demand curve with the vertical dashed line.

In Figure 12.1a, we see that because price is greater than cost (P > ATC), the firm makes a short-run economic profit. The situation in Figure 12.1b is different. Because P < ATC, the firm experiences a short-run economic loss. What accounts for the difference? Since we are considering the same firm, the marginal cost (MC) and average total cost (ATC) curves are identical in both panels. The only functional difference is the location of the demand (D) and marginal revenue (MR) curves. The demand in panel (a) is high enough for the firm to make a profit. In panel (b), however, there is not enough demand; perhaps too many customers have switched to the new Five Guys. So even though the monopolistic competitor has some market power, if demand is too low the firm may not be able to price its product high enough to make a profit.

Monopolistic Competition in the Long Run

In the long run, when firms can easily enter and exit a market, competition will drive economic profit to zero. This dynamic should be familiar to you from our previous discussions of competitive markets. If a firm is making an economic profit, it attracts new entrants to the business. Then the larger supply of competing firms will cause the demand for an individual firm's

FIGURE 12.1

The Monopolistically Competitive Firm in the Short Run

In this figure, we see how a single monopolistic firm may make a profit or incur a loss depending on the demand conditions it faces. Notice that the marginal cost (MC) and average total cost (ATC) curves are identical in both panels, since we are considering the same firm. The only functional difference is the location of the demand (D) and marginal revenue (MR) curves. The demand in (a) is high enough for the firm to make a profit. In (b), however, there is not enough demand, so the firm experiences a loss.

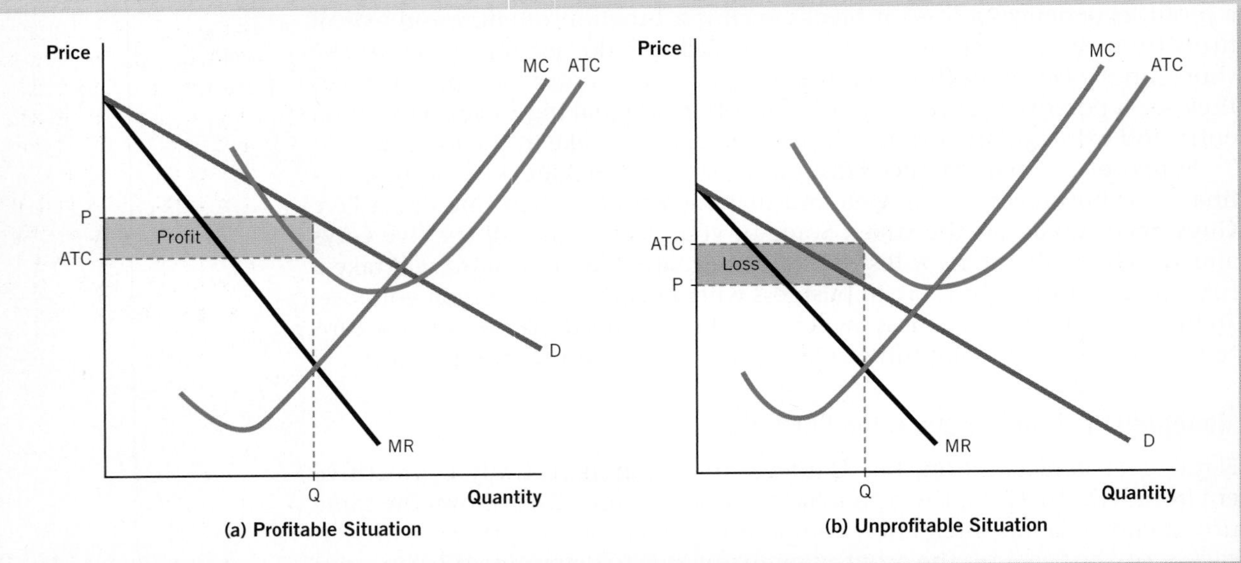

product to contract. Eventually, as more firms enter the market, it will no longer be possible for existing firms to make an economic profit. A reverse process unfolds in the case of a market that is experiencing a loss. In this case, some firms will exit the industry. Then consumers will have fewer options to choose from, and the remaining firms will experience an increase in demand. Eventually, demand will increase to the point at which firms will no longer experience a loss.

Figure 12.2 shows the market after the long-run adjustment process takes place. Price (P) is just equal to the average total cost of production (ATC) at the profit-maximizing rate of output (Q). At this point, firms are earning zero economic profit, as noted by P = ATC along the vertical axis; the market reaches a long-run equilibrium at the point where there is no reason for firms to enter or exit the industry. Note that the demand curve is drawn just *tangent* to the average total cost curve. If demand were any larger, the result would look like Figure 12.1a and firms would experience an economic profit. Conversely, if demand were any lower, the result would look like Figure 12.1b and firms would experience an economic loss. Where entry and exit exist, profits and losses are not possible in the long run. In this way, monopolistic competition resembles a competitive market.

Returning to our example of Hardee's, the firm's success will attract attention and encourage rivals, like Five Guys, to enter the market. As a result, the

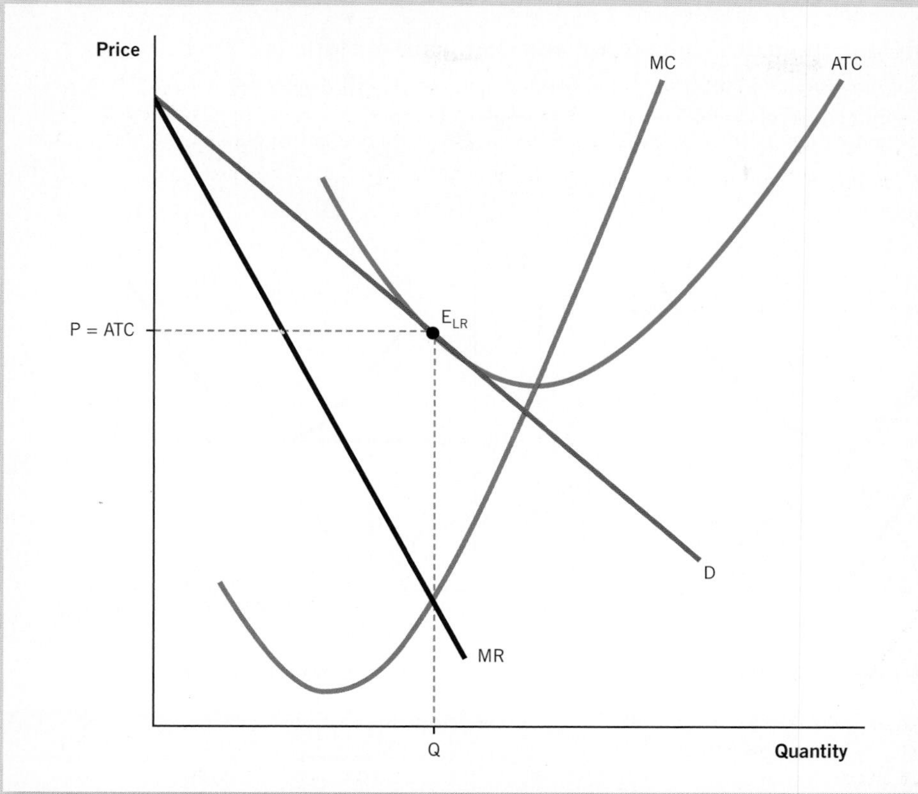

FIGURE 12.2

The Monopolistically Competitive Firm in the Long Run

Entry and exit cause short-run profits and losses to disappear in the long run. This means that the price charged (P) must be equal to the average total cost (ATC) of production. At this point, firms are earning zero economic profit, as noted by P = ATC along the vertical axis; the market reaches a long-run equilibrium (E_{LR}) at the point where there is no reason for firms to enter or exit the industry.

short-run profits that Hardee's enjoys will erode. As long as profits occur in the short run, this will encourage other competitors to enter, while short-run losses will prompt some existing firms to close. The dynamic nature of competition guarantees that long-run profits are not possible.

Incentives

Monopolistic Competition and Competitive Markets

We have seen that monopolistic competition and competitive markets are similar; both market structures drive economic profit to zero in the long run. But monopolistic competitors enjoy some market power, which is a crucial difference. In this section, we will compare pricing and output decisions in these two market structures. Then we will look at issues of scale and output.

The Relationship among Price, Marginal Cost, and Long-Run Average Cost

Monopolistically competitive firms have some market power, which enables them to charge slightly more than firms in competitive markets. Figure 12.3 compares the long-run equilibrium between monopolistic competition and

FIGURE 12.3

The Long-Run Equilibrium in Monopolistic Competition and Competitive Markets

There are two primary differences between the long-run equilibrium in monopolistic competition (a) and a competitive market (b). First, monopolistic competition produces markup, since P is greater than MC. In a competitive market, P = MC. Second, the output in monopolistic competition is smaller than the efficient scale. In a competitive market, the firm's output is equal to the most efficient scale.

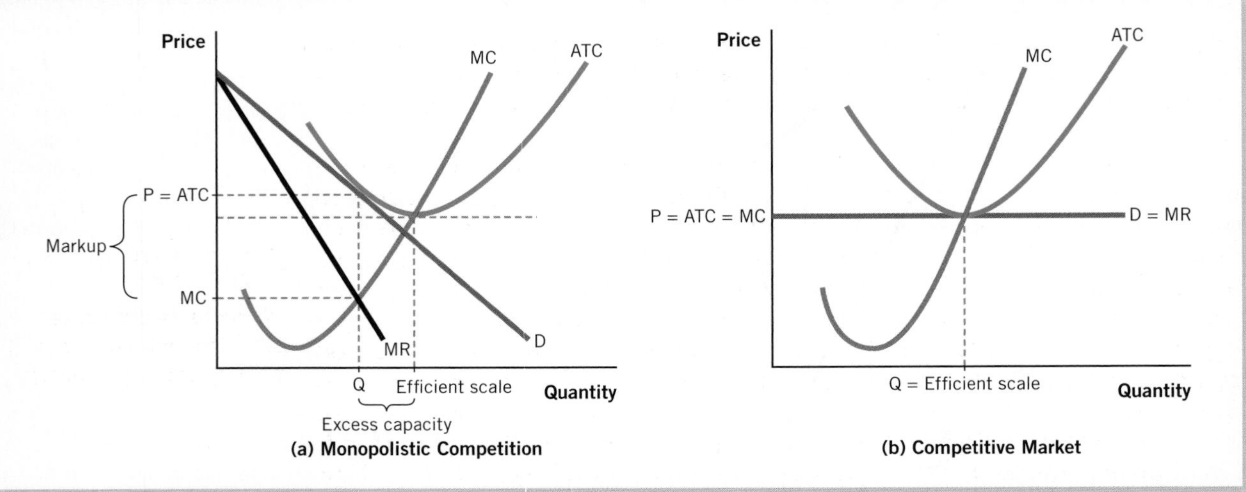

Markup
is the difference between the price the firm charges and the marginal cost of production.

a competitive market. Turning first to the firm in a market characterized by monopolistic competition, notice that the price (P) is greater than the marginal cost (MC) of making one more unit. The difference between P and MC is known as the *markup*, which is shown in Figure 12.3a. **Markup** is the difference between the price the firm charges and the marginal cost of production. A markup is possible when a firm enjoys some market power and sells a differentiated product. Products such as bottled water, cosmetics, prescription medicines, eyeglass frames, brand-name clothing, restaurant drinks, and greeting cards all have hefty markups. Let's focus on bottled water. In most cases, it costs just pennies to produce bottled water, but you're unlikely to find it for less than \$1; there is a lot of markup on every bottle! Some firms differentiate their product by marketing their water as the "purest" or the "cleanest." Other companies use special packaging. While the marketing of bottled water is unquestionably a successful business strategy, the markup means that consumers pay more. You can observe this result in Figure 12.3a, where the price under monopolistic competition is higher than the price in a competitive market, shown in Figure 12.3b.

Next, look at the ATC curves in both panels. Since a monopolistic competitor has a downward-sloping demand curve, the point of tangency between the demand curve and the ATC curve is different from the same point in a competitive market. The point where P = ATC is higher under monopolistic competition. Panel (b) shows the demand curve just tangent to the ATC curve at its lowest point in a competitive market. Consequently, we can say that monopolistic competition produces higher prices than a competitive market does. If this result seems odd to you, recall that entry and exit do not ensure the lowest possible price, only that the price is equal to the average total cost of production. In a competitive market, where the demand curve is horizontal, the price is always the lowest possible cost of production. This is not the case under monopolistic competition.

Perrier has a distinctive look—but how different is it from other mineral water?

Scale and Output

When a firm produces at an output level that is smaller than the output level needed to minimize average total costs, we say it has **excess capacity**. Turning back to Figure 12.3a, we see excess capacity in the difference between Q and the efficient scale.

This result differs from what we see in Figure 12.3b for a competitive market. In a competitive market, the profit-maximizing output is equal to the most efficient scale of operation. This result is guaranteed because each firm sells an identical product and must therefore set its price equal to the minimum point on the average total cost curve. If, for instance, a corn farmer tried to sell a harvest for more than the prevailing market price, the farmer would not find any takers. In contrast, a monopolistic competitor in a food court enjoys market power because some customers prefer its product. This enables food court vendors to charge more than the lowest average total cost. Therefore, under monopolistic competition, the profit-maximizing output is less than the minimum efficient scale. Monopolistically competitive firms have the capacity to produce more output at a lower cost. However, if they produced more, they would have to lower their price. Because a lower price decreases the firm's marginal revenue, it is more profitable for the monopolistic competitor to operate with excess capacity.

Excess capacity occurs when a firm produces at an output level that is smaller than the output level needed to minimize average total costs.

Monopolistic Competition, Inefficiency, and Social Welfare

Monopolistic competition produces a higher price and a lower level of output than a competitive market does. Recall that we looked at efficiency as a way to determine whether the decisions of a firm are consistent with an output level that is beneficial to society. Does monopolistic competition display efficiency?

In Figure 12.3a, we observed that a monopolistic competitor has costs that are slightly above the lowest possible cost. So the average total costs of a monopolistically competitive firm are higher than those of a firm in a competitive market. This result is not efficient. To achieve efficiency, the monopolistically competitive firm could lower its price to what we would find in competitive markets. However, since a monopolistic competitor's goal is to make a profit, there is no incentive for this to happen. Every monopolistic competitor has a downward-sloping demand curve, so the demand curve cannot be tangent to the minimum point along the average total cost curve, as seen in Figure 12.3a.

Incentives

Markup is a second source of inefficiency. We have seen that for a monopolistically competitive firm at the profit-maximizing output level, $P > MC$

by an amount equal to the markup. The price reflects the consumer's willingness to pay, and this amount exceeds the marginal cost of production. A reduced markup would benefit consumers by lowering the price and decreasing the spread between the price and the marginal cost. If the firm did away with the markup entirely and set P = MC, the output level would benefit the greatest number of consumers. However, this result would not be practical. At the point where the greatest efficiency occurs, the demand curve would be below the average total cost curve and the firm would lose money. It is unreasonable to expect a profit-seeking firm to pursue a pricing strategy that would benefit its customers at the expense of its own profit.

What if the government intervened on behalf of the consumer? Increased efficiency could be achieved through government regulation. After all, the government regulates monopolists to reduce market power and restore social welfare. Couldn't the government do the same in monopolistically competitive markets? Yes and no! It is certainly possible, but not desirable. Monopolistically competitive firms have a limited amount of market power, so they cannot make a long-run economic profit like monopolists do. In addition, regulating the prices that firms in a monopolistically competitive market can charge would put many of them out of business. Bear in mind that we are talking about firms in markets like the fast-food industry. Doing away with a significant percentage of these firms would mean fewer places for consumers to grab a quick bite. The remaining restaurants would be more efficient, but with fewer restaurants the trade-off for consumers would be less convenience and fewer choices.

Trade-offs

Regulating monopolistic competition through marginal cost pricing, or setting P = MC, would also create a host of problems like those we discussed for monopoly. A good proportion of the economy consists of monopolistically competitive firms—so the scale of the regulatory effort would be enormous. And since implementing marginal cost pricing would result in widespread losses, the government would need to find a way to subsidize the regulated firms to keep them in business. Since the only way to pay for these subsidies would be through higher taxes, the inefficiencies present in monopolistic competition do not warrant government action.

Varying Degrees of Product Differentiation

We have seen that products sold under monopolistic competition are more differentiated than those sold in a competitive market and less differentiated than those sold under monopoly. At one end of these two extremes we have competitive markets where firms sell identical products, have no market power, and face a perfectly elastic demand curve. At the other end we have a monopolist who sells a unique product without good substitutes and faces a steep downward-sloping demand curve indicative of highly inelastic demand. What about the firm that operates under monopolistic competition?

Figure 12.4 illustrates two monopolistic competitors with varying degrees of product differentiation. Firm A enjoys significant differentiation. This occurs when the firm has an especially attractive location, style, type, or quality of product that is in high demand among consumers and that competitors cannot easily replicate. H&M, Urban Outfitters, and Abercrombie & Fitch are good examples. Consumers have strong brand loyalty for the clothes these firms sell, so the demand curve is quite inelastic. The relatively steep slope of

FIGURE 12.4

Product Differentiation, Excess Capacity, and Efficiency

Firm A enjoys more product differentiation. As a result, it has more excess capacity and is less efficient. Firm B sells a product that is only slightly different from its competitors'. In this case, consumers have only weak preferences about which firm to buy from, and consumer demand is elastic. This produces a small amount of excess capacity and a more efficient result.

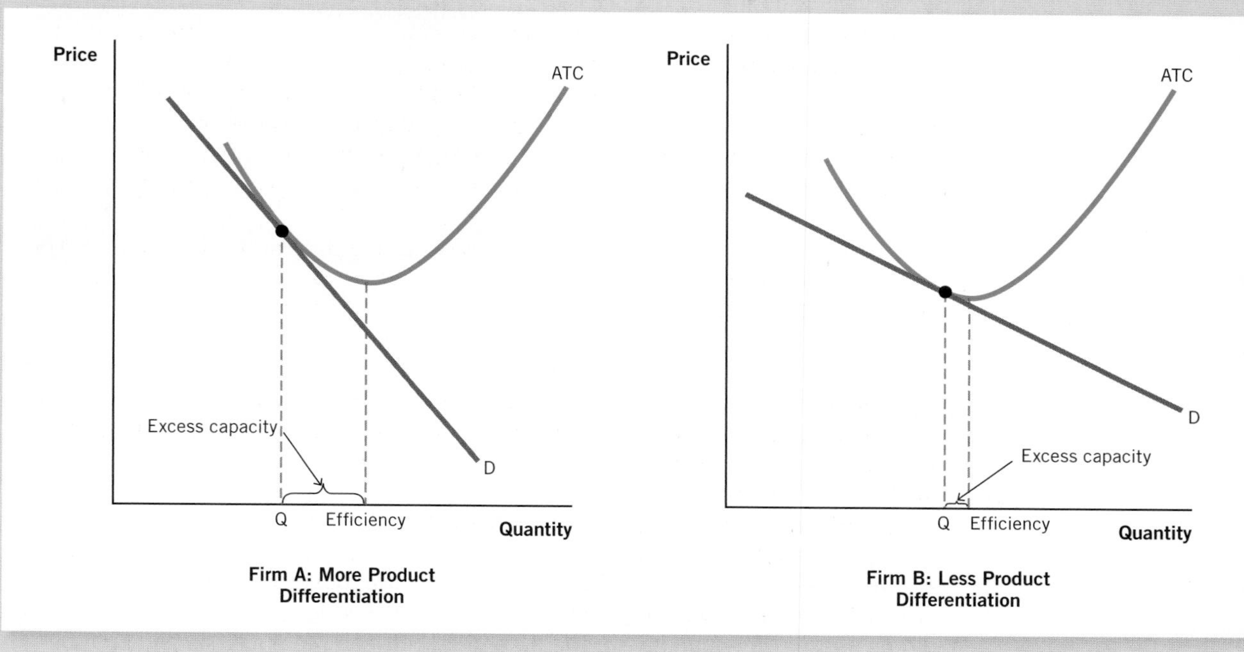

the demand curve means that the point of tangency between the demand curve (D) and the average total cost curve (ATC) occurs at a high price. This produces a large amount of excess capacity. In contrast, Firm B sells a product that is only slightly different from its competitors'. Here we can think of T.J.Maxx, Ross, and Marshalls—three companies that primarily sell discounted clothes. In this case, consumers have only weak preferences for a particular firm and consumer demand is elastic. The relatively flat nature of the demand curve means that the point of tangency between demand (D) and average total cost (ATC) occurs at a relatively low cost. This produces a small amount of excess capacity.

Monopolisitic competition leads to substantial product variety and greater selection and choice, all of which are beneficial to consumers. Therefore, any policy efforts that attempt to reduce inefficiency by

Would you want to dress like this every day? Product variety is something consumers are willing to pay for.

PRACTICE WHAT YOU KNOW

Markup: Punch Pizza versus Pizza Hut

Punch Pizza uses wood-fired ovens.

Question: Punch Pizza is a small upscale chain in Minnesota that uses wood-fired ovens. In contrast, Pizza Hut is a large national chain. Would one have more markup on each pizza?

Answer: If you ask people in the Twin Cities about their favorite pizza, you will find a cultlike following for Punch Pizza. That loyalty translates into inelastic demand. Punch Pizza claims to make the best Neapolitan pie. Fans of this style of pizza gravitate to Punch Pizza for the unique texture and flavor. In contrast, Pizza Hut competes in the middle of the pizza market and has crafted a taste that appeals to a broader set of customers. Pizza Hut's customers can find many other places that serve a similar product, so these customers are much more price-sensitive.

The marginal cost of making pizza at both places consists of the dough, the toppings, and wages for labor. At Pizza Hut, pizza assembly is streamlined for efficiency. Punch Pizza is more labor intensive, but its marginal cost is still relatively low. The prices at Punch Pizza are much higher than at Pizza Hut. As a result, the markup—or the difference between the price charged and the marginal cost of production—is greater at Punch Pizza than at Pizza Hut.

lowering the prices that monopolistically competitive firms can charge will have the unintended consequence of limiting the product variety in the market. That sounds like a small price to pay for increased efficiency. But not so fast! Imagine a world without any product differentiation in clothes. Part of the reason why fashions go in and out of style is the desire among consumers to express their individuality. Therefore, consumers are willing to pay a little more for product variety in order to look different from everyone else.

Why Is Advertising Prevalent in Monopolistic Competition?

Advertising is a familiar fact of daily life. It is also a means by which companies compete and, therefore, a cost of doing business in many industries. In the United States, advertising expenditures account for approximately 2% of all economic output annually. Worldwide, advertising expenses are a little

Advertising

ECONOMICS IN THE MEDIA

Super Bowl Commercials

The be-all of advertising spots is the televised Super Bowl. Because commercial time costs more than $3 million for a 30-second spot, examining the companies that advertise provides a useful barometer of economic activity. In 2013, three of the most popular commercials were by Best Buy, Taco Bell, and Anheuser-Busch. They joined the usual suspects Coca-Cola and Pepsi (soft drinks), Tide (detergent), Paramount (motion pictures), and Volkswagen, Audi, Toyota, Mercedes-Benz, Kia, and Hyundai (autos), in buying advertising time.

Super Bowl ads highlight sectors of the economy that are thriving. In addition, firms that advertise during the Super Bowl build brand recognition, which helps to differentiate their product from the competition.

"Ladies, look at me, now look at your man, now back to me."—Old Spice guy

less—about 1% of global economic activity. While the percentages are small in relative terms, in absolute terms worldwide advertising costs are over half a trillion dollars each year. Is this money well spent? Or is it a counterproductive contest that increases cost without adding value for the consumer? In this section, we will find that the answer is a little of both. Let's start by seeing who advertises.

Why Firms Advertise

No matter the company or slogan, the goal of advertising is to drive additional demand for the product being sold. Advertising campaigns use a variety of techniques to stimulate demand. In each instance, advertising is designed to highlight an important piece of information about the product. Table 12.2 shows how this process works. For instance, the FedEx slogan, "When it absolutely, positively has to be there overnight," conveys reliability and punctual service. Some customers who use FedEx are willing to pay a premium for overnight delivery because the company has differentiated itself from its competitors—UPS, DHL, and (especially) the United States Postal Service.

A successful advertising campaign will change the demand curve in two dimensions: it will shift the demand curve to the right and alter its shape.

TABLE 12.2

Advertising and Demand

Company / Product	Advertising slogan	How it increases demand
Quaker / Life cereal	*He likes it! Hey, Mikey!*	The slogan attempts to convince parents that children will like Life cereal, making it a healthy choice that their children will eat.
John Deere / tractors	*Nothing runs like a Deere.*	The emphasis on quality and performance appeals to buyers who desire a high-quality tractor.
Frito-Lay / Lay's potato chips	*Betcha can't eat just one.*	The message that one potato chip is not enough to satisfy your craving appeals to chip buyers who choose better taste over lower-priced generics.
Energizer / batteries	*He keeps going and going and going.*	The campaign focuses attention on longevity in order to justify the higher prices of top-quality batteries.
FedEx / delivery service	*When it absolutely, positively has to be there overnight*	Reliability and timeliness are crucial attributes of overnight delivery.
Visa / credit card	*It's everywhere you want to be.*	Widespread acceptance and usability are two of the major reasons for carrying a credit card.
Avis / rental cars 	*We're number two; we try harder.*	The emphasis on service encourages people to use the company.

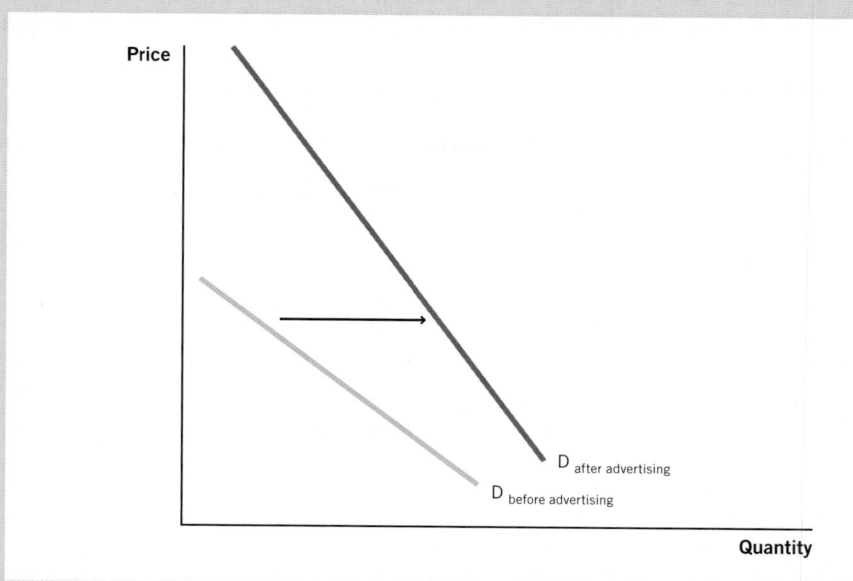

FIGURE 12.5

Advertising and the Demand Curve

A successful advertising campaign increases demand. Advertising also makes the demand curve more inelastic, or vertical, by informing consumers about differences that they care about. After advertising, consumers desire the good more intensely, which makes the demand curve for the firm's product somewhat more vertical.

Turning to Figure 12.5, we see this change. First, the demand curve shifts to the right in response to the additional demand created by the advertising. Second, the demand curve becomes more inelastic, or slightly more vertical. This happens because advertising has highlighted features that make the product attractive to specific customers who are now more likely to want it. Since demand is more inelastic after advertising, the firm increases its market power and can raise its price.

In addition to increasing demand, advertising conveys information that consumers may find helpful in matching their preferences. It tells us about the price of the goods offered, the location of products, and the introduction of new products. Firms also use advertising as a competitive mechanism to underprice one another. Finally, an advertising campaign signals quality. Firms that run expensive advertising campaigns are making a significant investment in their product. It is highly unlikely that a firm would spend a great deal on advertising if it did not think the process would yield a positive return. So a rational consumer can infer that firms spending a great deal on advertising are likely to have a higher-quality product than a competitor who does not advertise.

Advertising in Different Markets

Many firms engage in advertising, but not all market structures find advertising to be equally productive. In our continuum from competitive markets to monopoly, markets that function under monopolistic competition invest the most in advertising.

Advertising in Competitive Markets

As you know by now, competitive firms sell nearly identical products at an identical price. This means that advertising dollars raise a firm's costs without directly influencing its sales. Advertising for a good that is undifferentiated functions like a public good for the industry as a whole: the benefits flow to every firm in the market through increased market demand for the product. However, each firm sells essentially the same good, so consumers can find the product at many competing locations at the same price. An individual firm that advertises in this market is at a competitive disadvantage because it will have higher costs that it cannot pass on to the consumer.

This does not mean that we never see advertising in competitive markets. Although individual firms do not benefit from advertising, competitive industries as a whole can. For example, you have probably heard the slogan "Beef—it's what's for dinner." The campaign, which began in 1992, is recognized by over 80% of Americans and has been widely credited with increasing the demand for beef products. The campaign was funded by the National Cattlemen's Beef Association, an organization that puts millions of dollars a year into advertising. In fact, industry-wide marketing campaigns such as "It's not just for breakfast anymore" by the Florida Orange Juice Growers Association, or "Got milk?" by the National Milk Processor Board, generally

ECONOMICS IN THE MEDIA

Advertising

E.T.: The Extra-Terrestrial

The movie *E.T.* (1982) contains one of the most famous examples of product placement. In the movie, a boy leaves a trail of candy to bring E.T. closer to him. Originally, the filmmakers offered Mars the chance to have M&Ms used in the movie. Mars said no thanks. The filmmakers instead approached Hershey's, the manufacturers of Reese's Pieces—at that time a rival product of M&Ms that was not terribly successful. When *E.T.* became a blockbuster, the demand for Reese's Pieces suddenly tripled and firmly established the product in the minds of many Americans. How much did Hershey's pay for the product placement? It paid $1 million—not bad, considering how successful Reese's Pieces have become.

This is a great example of how firms must think beyond their advertising budgets and consider the strategic repercussions of possibly losing market share to a rival. Mars failed to protect its position in the market.

Hungry for a snack?

SNAPSHOT

Advertising and the Super Bowl

Super Bowl commercials are watched at least as closely as the football game itself. Fans love these usually creative and comedic ads. But economists pay close attention for different reasons. Who's advertising and what does it say about those industries? Are the ads money well spent, or do they increase business costs without making a noticeable difference in profits? Here we examine advertising over ten recent Super Bowls.

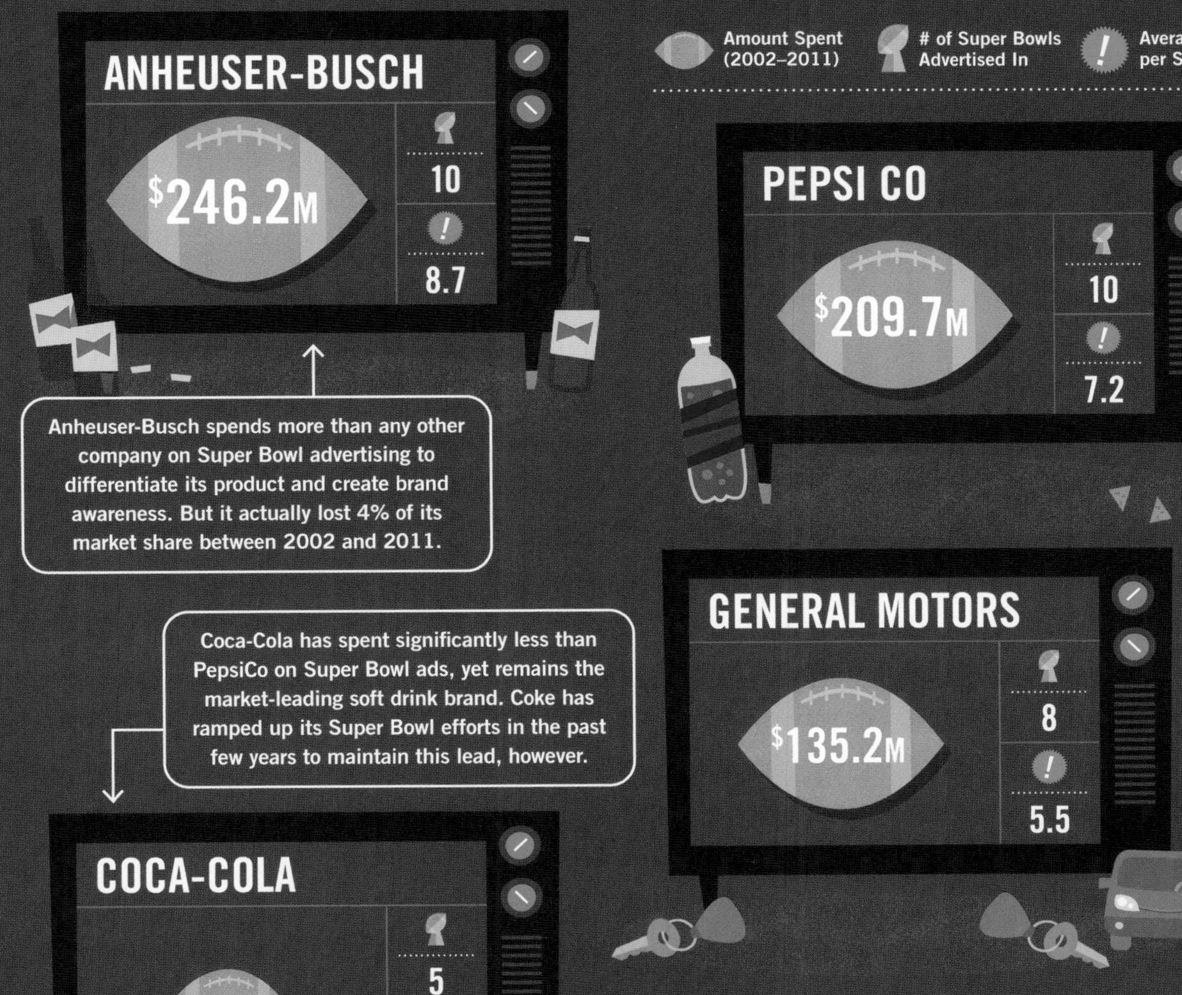

Amount Spent (2002–2011)
# of Super Bowls Advertised In
Average # of Ads per Super Bowl
ANHEUSER-BUSCH
$246.2M
10
8.7
PEPSI CO
$209.7M
10
7.2
GENERAL MOTORS
$135.2M
8
5.5
COCA-COLA
$61M
5
3
Anheuser-Busch spends more than any other company on Super Bowl advertising to differentiate its product and create brand awareness. But it actually lost 4% of its market share between 2002 and 2011.
Coca-Cola has spent significantly less than PepsiCo on Super Bowl ads, yet remains the market-leading soft drink brand. Coke has ramped up its Super Bowl efforts in the past few years to maintain this lead, however.

Some of these companies, especially Coca-Cola and Pepsi, are considered oligopolists rather than monopolistic competitors. We'll discuss oligopoly in the next chapter.

REVIEW QUESTIONS

- Draw what happens to a brand's demand curve when it successfully achieves product differentiation through advertising.
- Describe the risks and rewards of advertising from the perspective of both the brand and the consumer.

indicate that competitive firms have joined forces to advertise in an effort to increase demand.

Advertising under Monopolistic Competition

Advertising is widespread under monopolistic competition because firms have differentiated products. This is easy to observe if we look at the behavior of pizza companies. Television commercials by national chains such as Domino's, Pizza Hut, Papa John's, and Little Caesars are widespread, as are flyers and advertisements for local pizza places. Since each pizza is slightly different, each firm's advertising increases the demand for its product. In short, the gains from advertising go directly to the firm spending the money. This generates a strong incentive to advertise to gain new customers or to keep customers from switching to other products. Since each firm feels the same way, advertising becomes the norm among monopolistically competitive firms.

Incentives

Monopoly

The monopolist sells a unique product without close substitutes. The fact that consumers have few good alternatives when deciding to buy the good makes the monopolist less likely to advertise than a monopolistic competitor. When consumer choice is limited, the firm does not have to advertise to get business. In addition, the competitive aspect is missing, so there is no need to advertise to prevent consumers from switching to rival products. However, that does not mean that the monopolist never advertises.

The monopolist may wish to advertise to inform the consumer about its product and stimulate demand. This strategy can be beneficial as long as the gains from advertising are enough to cover the firm's cost. For example, De Beers, the giant diamond cartel, controls most of the world's supply of rough-cut diamonds. The company does not need to advertise to fend off competitors, but it advertises nevertheless because it is interested in creating more demand for diamonds. De Beers authored the famous "A diamond is forever" campaign and, more recently, has developed a new marketing campaign that suggests women should purchase a "right-hand ring" for themselves.

The Negative Effects of Advertising

We have seen the benefits of advertising, but there are also drawbacks. Two of the most significant are that advertising raises costs and can be deceitful.

Advertising and Costs

Advertising costs are reflected in the average total cost curve of the firm. Figure 12.6 shows the paradox of advertising for most firms. When a firm advertises, it hopes to increase demand for the product and sell more units—say, from point 1 at Q_1 to point 2 at the higher quantity, Q_2. If the firm can sell enough additional units, it will enjoy economies of scale and the cost will fall from ATC_1 to ATC_2. This return on the advertising investment looks like a good business decision.

However, the reality of advertising is much more complex. Under monopolistic competition, each firm is competing with many other firms selling somewhat different products. Rival firms will respond with advertising of their own. This dynamic makes advertising the norm in monopolistic competition. Each firm engages in competitive advertising to win new customers and keep the old ones. As a result, the impact on each individual firm's demand largely cancels out. This result is evident in the movement from point 1 to point 3 in Figure 12.6. Costs rise from ATC_1 to ATC_3 along the higher LRATC curve, but demand (that is, quantity produced) may remain at Q_1. The net result is that advertising creates higher costs. In this case, we can think of advertising as causing a negative *business-stealing externality* whereby no individual firm can easily gain market share but feels compelled to advertise to protect its customer base.

We have seen that advertising raises costs for the producer. It also raises prices for consumers. In fact, consumers who consistently favor a particular

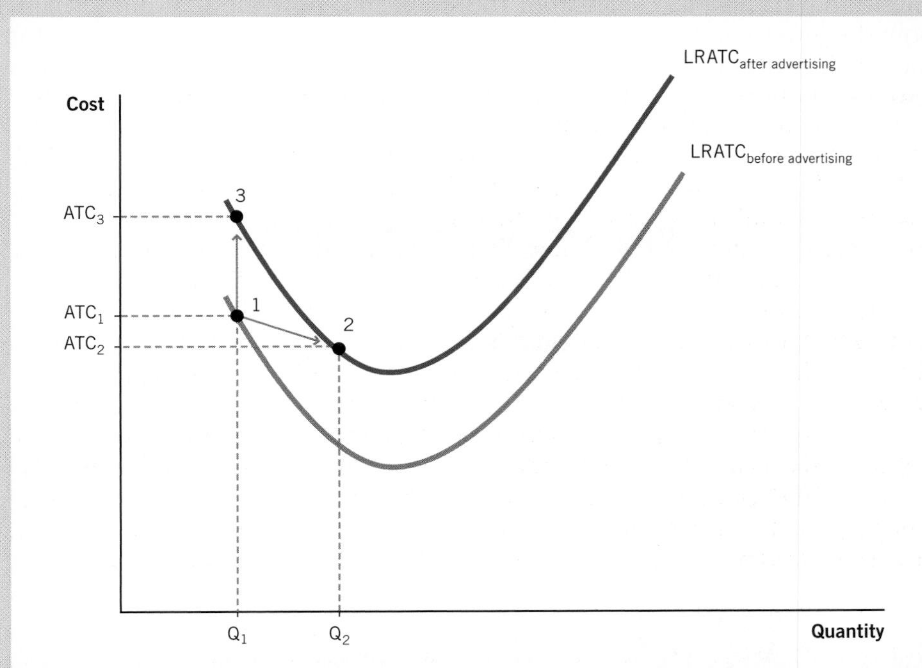

FIGURE 12.6

Advertising Increases Cost

By advertising, the firm hopes to increase demand (or quantity) from point 1 to point 2. In this scenario, the increase in demand from Q_1 to Q_2 is large enough to create economies of scale even though advertising causes the long-range average total cost curve (LRATC) to rise. Since monopolistically competitive firms each advertise, the advertising efforts often cancel each other out. This raises the long-range average total costs without increasing demand much, so the firm may move from point 1 to point 3 instead.

Pearl ear studs are a nice gift, but they are even better when they come in a . . .

. . . blue box.

brand of a product have more inelastic demand than those who are willing to switch from one product to another. Therefore, brand loyalty often means higher prices. Let's look at an example.

Suppose that you buy all your jewelry at Tiffany's. One day, you enter the store to pick up pearl ear studs. You can get a small pair of pearl studs at Tiffany's for $300. But it turns out that you can get studs of the same size, quality, and origin (freshwater) at Pearl World for $43, and you can find them online at Amazon for $19. There are no identifying marks on the jewelry that would enable you, or a seasoned jeweler, to tell the ear studs apart! Why would you buy them at Tiffany's when you can purchase them for far less elsewhere? The answer, it turns out, is that buying ear studs is a lot like consuming many other goods: name recognition matters. So do perception and brand loyalty. Many jewelry buyers also take cues from the storefront, how the staff dresses, and how the jewelry is packaged. Now spending $300 total is a lot of money for the privilege of getting the Tiffany's blue box. Consumers believe that Tiffany's jewelry is better, when all that the store is doing is charging more markup.

PRACTICE WHAT YOU KNOW

Advertising: Brands versus Generics

DiGiorno or generic?

Why do some frozen pizzas cost more than others, when brands that offer similar quality are only a few feet away in the frozen-foods aisle? To answer that question, consider the following questions:

Question: What would graphs showing price and output look like for DiGiorno and for a generic pizza? What is the markup for DiGiorno?

(CONTINUED)

(CONTINUED)

Answer: Here is the graph for DiGiorno.

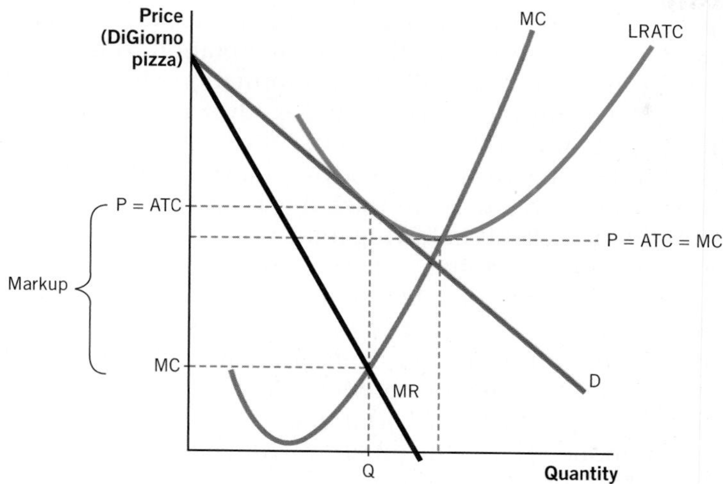

Answer: And here is the graph for the generic pizza.

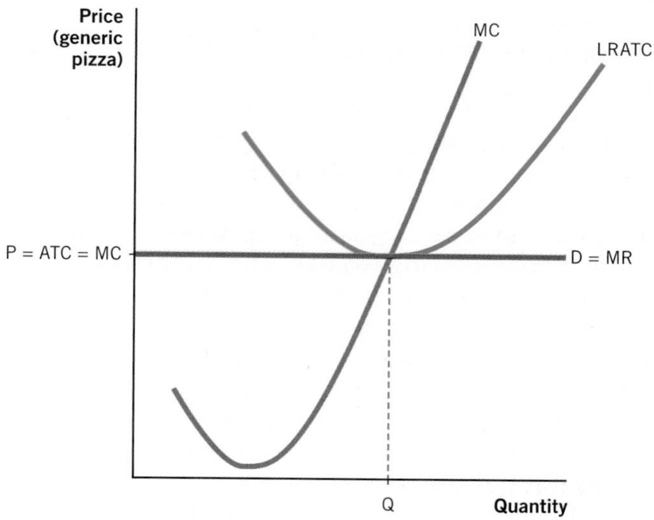

Question: Does DiGiorno or a generic brand have a stronger incentive to maintain strict quality control in the production process? Why?

Answer: DiGiorno has a catchy slogan: "It's not delivery. It's DiGiorno!" This statement tries to position the product as being just as good as a freshly delivered pizza. Some customers who buy frozen pizzas will opt for DiGiorno over comparable generics since they are familiar with the company's advertising claim about its quality. Therefore, DiGiorno has a stronger incentive to make sure that the product delivers as advertised. Since generic, or store-name, brands are purchased mostly on the basis of price, the customer generally does not have high expectations about the quality.

Truth in Advertising

Finally, many advertising campaigns are not just informative—they are designed to produce a psychological response. When an ad moves you to buy or act in a particular way, it becomes manipulative. Because advertising can be such a powerful way to reach customers, there is a temptation to lie about a product. To prevent firms from spreading misinformation about their products, the Federal Trade Commission (FTC) regulates advertising and promotes economic efficiency. At the FTC, the Division of Advertising Practices protects consumers by enforcing truth-in-advertising laws. While the commission does not have enough resources to track down every violation, it does pay particular attention to claims involving food, non-prescription drugs, dietary supplements, alcohol, and tobacco. Unsubstantiated claims are particularly prevalent on the Internet, and they tend to target vulnerable populations seeking quick fixes to a variety of medical conditions.

Of course, even with regulatory oversight, consumers must still be vigilant. At best, the FTC can remove products from the market and levy fines against companies that make unsubstantiated claims. However, the damage is often already done. The Latin phrase *caveat emptor*, or "buyer beware," sums up the dangers of false information.

ECONOMICS IN THE REAL WORLD

The Federal Trade Commission versus Kevin Trudeau

Channel flippers will surely recognize Kevin Trudeau, who has been a staple of infomercials for over a decade. Trudeau has a formula: he writes books about simple cures for complex medical conditions. He is an engaging, smooth talker. The infomercial is usually a "conversation" between Trudeau and a good-looking woman who seems very excited to learn more about the product. Unfortunately, Trudeau's claims are often unsubstantiated.

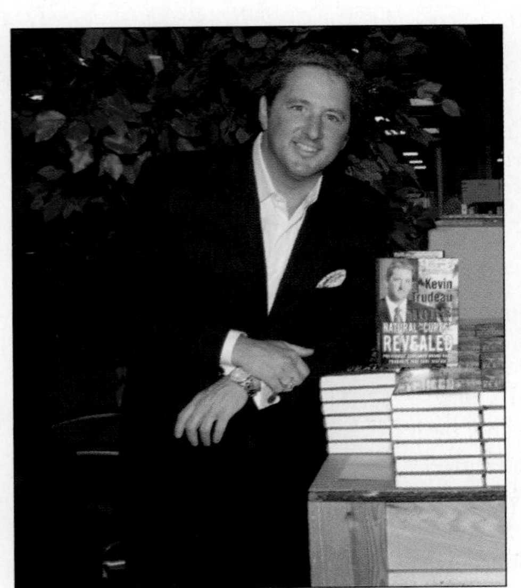

Do you trust this guy?

In 2009, a federal judge ordered Trudeau to pay more than $37 million for misrepresenting the content of his book *The Weight Loss Cure "They" Don't Want You to Know About* and banned him from appearing in infomercials for three years. This was not the first time Trudeau had been taken to task by the FTC. The commission first filed a lawsuit against him in 1998, charging him with making false and misleading claims in infomercials for products that he claimed could cause significant weight loss, cure drug addictions, and improve memory.

More recently, Trudeau has been offering his products for "free." Customers who call in receive a copy of one of his books and one issue of a monthly newsletter at no charge. However, those who fail to cancel the newsletter incur a monthly charge of $9.95 on their credit card. While there is nothing illegal about the 30-day free trial period, and while many other firms use this tactic, it has sparked additional outrage. ✷

ECONOMICS FOR LIFE

Product Differentiation: Would You Buy a Franchise?

Franchises are valuable in markets where product differentiation matters. McDonald's, Panera Bread, and KFC each has a different take on serving fast food. But what does it mean to own a franchise?

Franchises are sold to individual owners, who operate subject to the terms of their agreement with the parent company. For instance, purchasing a McDonald's franchise, which can cost as much as $2 million, requires the individual restaurant owner to charge certain prices and offer menu items selected by the parent corporation. As a result, customers who prefer a certain type and quality of food know that the dining experience at each McDonald's will be similar. Most franchises also come with non-compete clauses that guarantee that another franchise will not open nearby. This guarantee gives the franchise owner the exclusive right to sell a differentiated product in a given area.

Suppose that you want to start a restaurant. Why would you, or anyone else, be willing to pay as much as $2 million just for the right to sell food? For that amount, you could open your own restaurant with a custom menu and interior, create your own marketing plan, and locate anywhere you like. For example, Golden Corral and Buffalo Wild Wings are two restaurants with high franchising fees that exceed $1 million. Golden Corral is the largest buffet-style restaurant in the country, and Buffalo Wild Wings is one of the top locations to watch sporting events.

How much do different franchises cost?

You might think that it would make more sense to avoid the franchising costs by opening your own buffet or setting up a bank of big-screen TVs. However, failures in the restaurant industry are high. With a franchise, the customer knows what to expect.

Franchise owners are assured of visibility and a ready supply of customers. Purchasing a franchise means that more potential customers will notice your restaurant, and that drives up revenues. Is that worth $2 million? Yes, in some cases. Suppose that you'll do $1 million in annual sales as part of a franchise, but only $0.5 million on your own. That half-million difference over 20 years means $10 million more in revenue, a healthy chunk of which will turn into profits. This is the magic of franchising.

Conclusion

We began this chapter by discussing the misconception that advertising increases the price of goods and services without adding value for the consumer. Advertising does cost money, but that does not mean it is harmful. Firms willingly spend on advertising because it can increase demand, build brand loyalty, and provide consumers with useful information about differences in products. Monopolistic competitors advertise and mark up their products like monopolists, but, like firms in a competitive market, they cannot earn long-run profits. While an economic profit is possible in the short run for all three, only the monopolist, who has significant barriers to entry, can earn an economic profit in the long run. Entry and exit cause long-run profits to equal zero in competitive and monopolistically competitive firms.

Monopolistic competitors are price makers who fail to achieve the most efficient welfare-maximizing output for society. But this observation does not tell the entire story. Monopolistic competitors do not have as much market power or create as much excess capacity or markup as monopolists. Consequently, the monopolistic competitor lacks the ability to exploit consumers. The result is not perfect, but widespread competition generally serves consumers and society well.

In the next chapter, we continue our exploration of market structure with *oligopoly*, which produces results that are much closer to monopoly than monopolistic competition.

ANSWERING THE BIG QUESTIONS

What is monopolistic competition?

* Monopolistic competition is a market characterized by free entry and many firms selling differentiated products.
* Differentiation of products takes three forms: differentiation by style or type, location, and quality.

What are the differences among monopolistic competition, competitive markets, and monopoly?

* Monopolistic competitors, like monopolists, are price makers who have downward-sloping demand curves. Whenever the demand curve is downward sloping, the firm is able to mark up the price above marginal cost. This leads to excess capacity and an inefficient level of output.
* In the long run, barriers to entry enable a monopoly to earn an economic profit. This is not the case for monopolistic competition or competitive markets.

Why is advertising prevalent in monopolistic competition?

* Advertising performs useful functions under monopolistic competition: it conveys information about the price of the goods offered for sale, the location of products, and new products. It also signals differences in quality. However, advertising also encourages brand loyalty, which makes it harder for other businesses to successfully enter the market. Advertising can be manipulative and misleading.

CONCEPTS YOU SHOULD KNOW

excess capacity (p. 363)
markup (p. 362)
monopolistic competition (p. 356)
product differentiation (p. 356)

QUESTIONS FOR REVIEW

1. Why is product differentiation necessary for monopolistic competition? What are three types of product differentiation?
2. How is monopolistic competition like competitive markets? How is monopolistic competition like monopoly?
3. Why do monopolistically competitive firms produce less than those operating at the most efficient scale of production?
4. Draw a graph that shows a monopolistic competitor making an economic profit in the short run and a graph that shows a monopolistic competitor making no economic profit in the long run.
5. Monopolistic competition produces a result that is inefficient. Does this mean that monopolistically competitive markets should be regulated? Discuss.
6. Draw a typical demand curve for competitive markets, monopolistic competition, and monopoly. Which of these demand curves is the most inelastic? Why?
7. How does advertising benefit society? In what ways can advertising be harmful?

STUDY PROBLEMS (*∗ solved at the end of the section*)

∗ 1. At your high school reunion, a friend describes his plan to take a break from his florist shop and sail around the world. He says that if he continues to make the same economic profit for the next five years, he will be able to afford the trip. Do you think your friend will be able to achieve his dream in five years? What do you expect to happen to his firm's profits in the long run?

2. Which of the following could be considered a monopolistic competitor?
   a. local corn farmers
   b. the Tennessee Valley Authority, a large electricity producer
   c. pizza delivery
   d. grocery stores
   e. Kate Spade, fashion designer

3. Which of the following produces the same outcome under monopolistic competition and in a competitive market in the long run?
   a. the markup the firm charges
   b. the price the firm charges to consumers
   c. the firm's excess capacity
   d. the average total cost of production
   e. the amount of advertising
   f. the firm's profit
   g. the efficiency of the market structure

4. In competitive markets, price is equal to marginal cost in the long run. Explain why this is not true for monopolistic competition.

5. Econoburgers, a fast-food restaurant in a crowded local market, has reached a long-run equilibrium.
   a. Draw a diagram showing demand, marginal revenue, average total cost, and marginal cost curves for Econoburgers.
   b. How much profit is Econoburgers making?
   c. Suppose that the government decides to regulate burger production to make it more efficient. Explain what would happen to the price of Econoburgers and the firm's output.

∗ 6. Consider two different companies. The first manufactures cardboard, and the second sells books. Which firm is more likely to advertise?

7. In the diagram below, identify the demand curve consistent with a monopolistic competitor making zero long-run economic profit. Explain why you have chosen that demand curve and why the other two demand curves are not consistent with monopolistic competition.

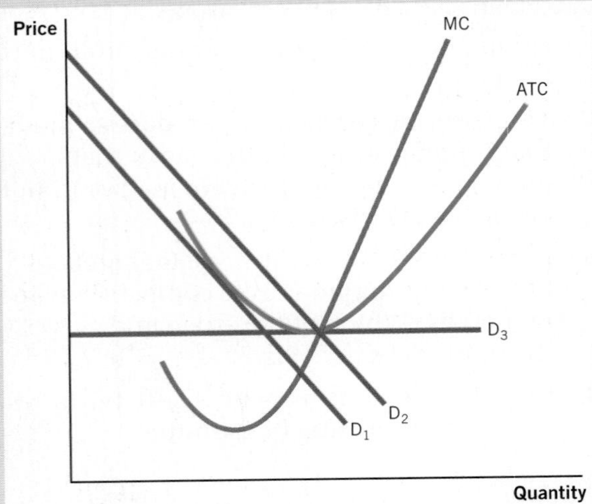

8. Titleist has an advertising slogan, "The #1 ball in golf." Consumers can also buy generic golf balls. The manufacturers of generic golf balls do not engage in any advertising. Assume that the average total cost of producing Titleist and generic golf balls is the same.
   a. Create a graph showing the price and the markup for Titleist.
   b. In a separate graph, show the price and output for the generic firms.
   c. Who has a stronger incentive to maintain strict quality control in the production process—Titleist or the generic firms? Why?

SOLVED PROBLEMS

1. The florist business is monopolistically competitive. This means that firms are free to enter and exit at any time. Firms will enter because your friend's shop is making an economic profit. As new florist shops open, the added competition will drive prices down, causing your friend's profits to fall. In the long run, this means that he will not be able to make an economic profit. He will only earn enough to cover his opportunity costs, or what is known as a fair return on his investment. That is not to say that he won't be able to save enough to sail around the world, but it won't happen as fast as he would like because other firms will crowd in on his success and limit his profits going forward.

6. The cardboard firm manufactures a product that is a component used mostly by other firms that need to package final products for sale. As a result, any efforts at advertising will only raise costs without increasing the demand for cardboard. This contrasts with the bookseller, who advertises to attract consumers to the store. More traffic means more purchases of books and other items sold in the store. The bookstore has some monopoly power and markup. In this case, it pays to advertise. A cardboard manufacturing firm sells exactly the same product as other cardboard producers, so it has no monopoly power and any advertising expenses will only make its cost higher than its rivals'.

CHAPTER 13

Oligopoly and Strategic Behavior

MISCONCEPTION

Cell phone companies are highly competitive.

If you have a cell phone, chances are that you receive service from one of four major cell phone carriers in the United States: AT&T, Verizon, Sprint Nextel, or T-Mobile. Together, these firms control 85% of all cellular service. In some respects, this market is very competitive. For example, cell phone companies advertise intensely, and they offer a variety of phones and voice and data plans. Also, there are differences in network coverage and in the number of applications users can access. But despite outward appearances, the cell phone companies are not a good example of a competitive, or even a monopolistically competitive, market. How can we explain this misconception? An important reason is the expense of building and maintaining a cellular network. The largest cell phone companies have invested billions of dollars in infrastructure. Therefore, the cost of entry is very high. And as we learned in Chapter 10, barriers to entry are a key feature of monopolies.

The cell phone industry has features of both competition and monopoly: competition is fierce, but smaller firms and potential entrants into the market find it difficult to enter and compete. This mixture of characteristics represents another form of market structure—*oligopoly*. In this chapter, we will examine oligopoly by comparing it to other market structures that are already familiar to you. We will then look at some of the strategic behaviors that firms in an oligopoly employ; this will lead us into a fascinating subject known as game theory.

Lots of advertising and regular promotions lead most people to view cell phone companies as highly competitive firms—is that true?

BIG QUESTIONS

- What is oligopoly?
- How does game theory explain strategic behavior?
- How do government policies affect oligopoly behavior?
- What are network externalities?

What Is Oligopoly?

Oligopoly
exists when a small number of firms sell a differentiated product in a market with high barriers to entry.

Oligopoly exists when a small number of firms sell a product in a market with significant barriers to entry. An oligopolist is like a monopolistic competitor in that it sells a differentiated product. But, like pure monopolists, oligopolists enjoy significant barriers to entry. Table 13.1 compares the differences and similarities among these three market structures.

We have seen that firms in monopolistically competitive markets usually have a limited amount of market power. As a result, buyers often find low prices and wide availability. In contrast, an oligopoly sells in a market with significant barriers to entry and fewer rivals. This gives the oligopolist more market power than a firm operating under monopolistic competition. However, since an oligopolistic market has more than one seller, no single oligopoly has as much market power as a monopoly.

Our study of oligopoly begins with a look at how economists measure market power in an industry. We will then work through a simplified model of oligopoly to explore the choices that oligopolists make.

Measuring the Concentration of Industries

In markets with only a few sellers, industry output is highly concentrated among a few large firms. Economists use *concentration ratios* as a measure of the oligopoly power present in an industry. The most common measure, known

TABLE 13.1

Comparing Oligopoly to Other Market Structures

Competitive market	Monopolistic competition	Oligopoly	Monopoly
Many sellers	Many sellers	A few sellers	One seller
Similar products	Differentiated product	Typically differentiated product	Unique product without close substitutes
Free entry and exit	Easy entry and exit	Barriers to entry	Significant barriers to entry

TABLE 13.2

Highly Concentrated Industries in the United States

Industry	Concentration ratio of the four largest firms (%)	Top firms
Search engines	98.5	Google, Yahoo, Microsoft
Wireless telecommunications	94.7	Verizon, AT&T, Sprint Nextel, T-Mobile
Satellite TV providers	94.5	DIRECTV, DISH Network
Soda production	93.7	Coca-Cola, PepsiCo, Dr Pepper Snapple
Sanitary paper products	92.7	Kimberly-Clark, Procter & Gamble, Georgia-Pacific
Lighting and bulb manufacturing	91.9	General Electric, Philips, Siemens
Tire manufacturing	91.3	Goodyear, Michelin, Cooper, Bridgestone
Major household appliances	90.0	Whirlpool, Electrolux, General Electric, LG
Automobile manufacturing	87.0	General Motors, Toyota, Ford, Daimler-Chrysler

Source: Highly Concentrated: Companies That Dominate Their Industries, www.ibisworld.com. Special Report, February 2012.

as the four-firm concentration ratio, expresses the sales of the four largest firms in an industry as a percentage of that industry's total sales. Table 13.2 lists the four-firm concentration ratios for highly concentrated industries in the United States. This ratio is determined by taking the output of the four largest firms in an industry and dividing that output by the total production in the entire industry.

In highly concentrated industries like search engines, wireless telecommunications, soda production, and tire manufacturing, the market share held by the four largest firms approaches 100%. At the bottom of our list of most concentrated industries is domestic automobile manufacturing. General Motors, Daimler-Chrysler, Ford, and Toyota (which has eight manufacturing plants in the United States) dominate the domestic automobile industry. These large firms have significant market power.

However, when evaluating market power in an industry, it is important to be aware of international activity. In several industries, including automobile and tire manufacturing, intense global competition keeps the market power of U.S. companies in check. For instance, domestic manufacturers that produce automobiles also must compete globally against cars that are produced elsewhere. This means that vehicles produced by Honda, Nissan, Volkswagen, Kia,

Competition from foreign car companies keeps the market power of the U.S.-based automobile companies in check.

and Volvo, just to name a few companies, limit the market power of domestic producers. As a result, the concentration ratio is a rough gauge of oligopoly power—not an absolute measure.

Collusion and Cartels in a Simple Duopoly Example

In this section, we explore the two conflicting tendencies found in oligopoly: oligopolists would like to act like monopolists, but they often end up competing like monopolistic competitors. To help us understand oligopolistic behavior, we will start with a simplified example: an industry consisting of only two firms, known as a *duopoly*. Duopolies are rare in national and international markets, but not that uncommon in small, local markets. For example, in many small communities the number of cell phone carriers is limited. Imagine a small town where only two providers have cell phone towers. In this case, the cell towers are a sunk cost (see Chapter 9): both towers were built to service all of the customers in the town, so each carrier has substantial excess capacity when the customers are divided between the two carriers. Also, since there is extra capacity on each network, the marginal cost of adding additional customers is zero.

Table 13.3 shows the community's demand for cell phones. Since the prices and quantities listed in the first two columns are inversely related, the data are consistent with a downward-sloping demand curve.

TABLE 13.3

The Demand Schedule for Cell Phones

(1) Price/month (P)	(2) Number of customers (Q)	(3) Total revenue (TR) (P) × (Q)
$180	0	$0
$165	100	16,500
$150	200	30,000
$135	300	40,500
$120	400	48,000
$105	500	52,500
$90	600	54,000
$75	700	52,500
$60	800	48,000
$45	900	40,500
$30	1,000	30,000
$15	1,100	16,500
$0	1,200	0

Column 3 calculates the total revenue from columns 1 and 2. With Table 13.3 as our guide, we will examine the output in this market under three scenarios: competition, monopoly, and duopoly.

Duopoly sits between the two extremes. Competition still exists, but it is not as extensive as you would see in competitive markets, which ruthlessly drive the price down to cost. Nor does the result always mirror that of monopoly, where competitive pressures are completely absent. In an oligopoly, a small number of firms feel competitive pressures and also enjoy some of the advantages of monopoly.

Marginal thinking

Recall that competitive markets drive prices down to the point at which marginal revenue is equal to the marginal cost. So, if the market is highly competitive and the marginal cost is zero, we would expect the final price of cell phone service to be zero and the quantity supplied to be 1,200 customers—the number of people who live in the small town. At this point, anyone who desires cell phone service would be able to receive it without cost. Since efficiency exists when the output is maximized, and since everyone who lives in the community would have cell phone service, the result would be socially efficient. However, it is unrealistic to expect this outcome. Cell phone companies provide a good that is non-rival and also excludable; in other words, they sell a club good (see Chapter 7). Since these firms are in business to make money, they will not provide something for nothing.

At the other extreme of the market structure continuum, since a monopoly faces no competition, price decisions do not depend on the activity of other firms. A monopoly can search for the price that brings it the most profit. Looking at Table 13.3, we see that total revenue peaks at $54,000. At this point, the price is $90 per month and 600 customers sign up for cell phone service. The total revenue is the monopolist's profit since the marginal cost is zero. Notice that the monopolist's price, $90, is more than the marginal cost of $0. In this case, the monopolist's marginal revenue is $1,500. The marginal revenue is determined by looking at column 3 and observing that total revenue rises from $52,500 to $54,000—an increase of $1,500. Since the firm serves 100 additional customers, the marginal revenue is $15 per customer. When the price drops to $75, marginal revenue is −$1,500, since total revenue falls from $54,000 to $52,500. Dividing −$1,500 by 100 yields a marginal revenue of −$15 per customer. The monopolist will maximize profit where $MC = MR = 0$, and the point closest to this in Table 13.3 is where $P = \$90$. Compared to a competitive market, the monopoly price is higher and the quantity sold is lower. This represents a loss of efficiency.

In a duopoly, the two firms can decide to cooperate—though this is illegal in the United States, as we will discuss shortly. If the duopolists cooperate, we say that they *collude*. **Collusion** is an agreement among rival firms that specifies the price each firm charges and the quantity it produces. The firms that collude can act like a single monopolist to maximize their profits. In this case, the monopoly would maximize its profit by charging $90 and serving 600 customers. If the duopolists divide the market equally, they will each have 300 customers who pay $90, for a total of $27,000 in revenue.

Collusion
is an agreement among rival firms that specifies the price each firm charges and the quantity it produces.

A **cartel** is a group of two or more firms that act in unison.

Antitrust laws
attempt to prevent oligopolies from behaving like monopolies.

When two or more firms act in unison, economists refer to them as a **cartel**. Many countries prohibit cartels. In the United States, **antitrust laws** prohibit collusion. However, even if collusion were legal, it would probably fail more often than not. Imagine that two theoretical cell phone companies, AT-Phone and Horizon, have formed a cartel and agreed that each will serve

Incentives

300 customers at a price of $90 per month per customer. But AT-Phone and Horizon each have an incentive to earn more revenue by cheating while the rival company keeps the agreement. Suppose that AT-Phone believes Horizon will continue to serve 300 customers per their collusive agreement, and AT-Phone lowers its price to $75. Looking at Table 13.3, we see that at this price the total market demand rises to 700 customers. So AT-Phone will be able to serve 400 customers, and its revenue will be 400 × $75, or $30,000. This is an improvement of $3,000 over what AT-Phone made when the market price was $90 and the customers were equally divided.

How would Horizon react? First of all, it would be forced to match AT-Phone's lower price, which would lower the revenue from its 300 customers to $22,500. But put in this position, there's no reason for Horizon to sit on the sideline and do nothing: if it decides to match AT-Phone's market share of 400 customers by lowering its price to $60, it would increase its revenue to 400 × $60, or $24,000. AT-Phone would match that price and make the same revenue, leaving each firm making $3,000 less than when they served only 600 customers.

From what we know about competitive markets, we might expect the competition between the two to cause a price war in which prices eventually fall to zero. But this is not the case. The duopolist will try to gain more market share and then wait to see its competitor's response. Once the market participants understand that a competitor is likely to match their movements, they will stop trying to increase production and end up at the second-best option. (This second-best option, often referred to as the Nash equilibrium, will be discussed in the next section.) For example, if AT-Phone is serving 400 customers and Horizon decides to serve 500 customers, the price of cell phone service will fall to $45. Horizon will make $45 × 500 customers, or $22,500. This is $1,500 less than what the company would have earned if it simply matched its rival's price at $60. As a result, duopolists are unlikely to participate in an all-out price war, and the result of their competition is more efficient than a monopoly's output. In the end, each firm will serve 400 customers, for a total of 800 customers—or 200 more than the monopolist would serve.

Mutual interdependence is a market situation where the actions of one firm have an impact on the price and output of its competitors.

Table 13.4 summarizes the different results under competition, duopoly, and monopoly, using our cell phone example. From this example, we see that a market with a small number of sellers is characterized by **mutual interdependence**, which is a market situation in which the actions of one firm have

TABLE 13.4

Outcomes under Competition, Duopoly, and Monopoly

	Competitive markets	Duopoly	Monopoly
Price	$0	$60	$90
Output	1,200	800	600
Socially Efficient?	Yes	No	No
Explanation	Since the marginal cost of providing cell phone service is zero, the price is eventually driven to zero. Since firms are in business to make a profit, it is unrealistic to expect this result.	Since each firm is mutually interdependent, it adopts a strategy based on the actions of its rival. This leads both firms to charge $60 and serve 400 customers.	The monopolist is free to choose the profit-maximizing output. In the cell phone example, it maximizes its total revenue. As a result, the monopolist charges $90 and serves 600 customers.

an impact on the price and output of its competitors. As a result, a firm's market share is determined by the products it offers, the price it charges, and the actions of its rivals.

ECONOMICS IN THE REAL WORLD

OPEC: An International Cartel

The best-known cartel is the Organization of the Petroleum Exporting Countries, or OPEC, a group of oil-exporting countries that have a significant influence on the world crude oil price and output of petroleum. In order to maintain relatively high oil prices, each member nation colludes to limit the overall supply of oil. While OPEC's activities are legal under international law, collusion is illegal under U.S. antitrust law.

What would oil prices be like if OPEC didn't exist?

OPEC controls almost 80% of the world's known oil reserves and accounts for almost half of the world's crude production. This gives the cartel's 12 member nations significant control over the world price of oil. OPEC's production is dominated by Saudi Arabia, which accounts for approximately 40% of OPEC's reserves and production. As is the case within any organization, conflict inevitably arises. In the 50 years that OPEC has existed, there have been embargoes (government prohibitions on the exchange of oil), oil gluts, production disputes, and periods of falling prices. As a result, OPEC has been far from perfect in consistently maintaining high prices. In addition, it is careful to keep the price of oil below the cost of alternative energy options. Despite the limitations on OPEC's pricing power, the evidence suggests that OPEC has effectively acted as a cartel during the periods when it adopted output rationing in order to maintain price. ✷

Oligopolists want to emulate the monopoly outcome, but the push to compete with their rivals often makes it difficult to maintain a cartel. Yet the idea that cartels are unstable is not guaranteed. In the appendix to this chapter, we explore two alternative theories that oligopolists will form long-lasting cartels. When a stable cartel is not achieved, firms in oligopoly fall short of fully maximizing profits. But they do not compete to the same degree as firms in competitive markets either. Therefore, when a market is an oligopoly, output is likely to be higher than under monopoly and lower than within a competitive market. As you would expect, the amount of output affects the prices. The higher output (compared to monopoly) makes oligopoly prices generally lower than monopoly prices, and the lower output (compared to a competitive market) makes oligopoly prices higher than those found in competitive markets.

The Nash Equilibrium

As we have discussed in earlier chapters, the market price is the price at which the quantity of a product or service demanded is equal to the quantity supplied. At this price, the market is in equilibrium. In oligopoly, the process

ECONOMICS IN THE MEDIA

Nash Equilibrium

A Brilliant Madness and *A Beautiful Mind*

A Brilliant Madness (2002) is the story of a mathematical genius, John Nash, whose career was cut short by a descent into madness. At the age of 30, Nash began claiming that aliens were communicating with him. He spent the next three decades fighting paranoid schizophrenia. Before this time, while he was a graduate student at Princeton, Nash wrote a proof about non-cooperative equilibrium. The proof established the Nash equilibrium and became a foundation of modern economic theory. In 1994, Nash was awarded a Nobel Prize in Economics. The documentary features interviews with John Nash, his wife, Alicia, his friends and colleagues, and experts in both game theory and mental illness.

A Brilliant Madness conveys the essentials about Nash without taking liberties with the facts, as Ron Howard did in his 2001 film *A Beautiful Mind,* based on the life of Nash. If you watch *A Brilliant Madness* and then watch the famous bar scene in *A Beautiful Mind,* you should be able to catch the error Ron Howard made in describing how a Nash equilibrium works!

Russell Crowe playing John Nash, who revolutionized modern microeconomics.

that leads to equilibrium may take on a special form referred to as a *Nash equilibrium,* named for mathematician John Nash.

A **Nash equilibrium** occurs when an economic decision-maker has nothing to gain by changing strategy unless it can collude.

A **Nash equilibrium**, or second-best outcome, occurs when an economic decision-maker has nothing to gain by changing strategy unless it can collude. The theoretical phone example we just explored was an example of a Nash equilibrium. The best strategy for AT-Phone and Horizon is to increase their output to 400 customers each. When both firms reach that level of output, neither has an incentive to change. Bear in mind that the rivals can do better if they collude. Under collusion, each rival serves 300 customers and their combined revenues rise. However, as we saw, if one rival is willing to break the cartel, it will make more revenue if it serves 400 customers ($30,000) while the other firm continues to serve only 300 ($22,500). The firms continue to challenge each other until they reach a combined output level of 800 customers. At this point, the market reaches a Nash equilibrium and neither firm has a reason to change its short-term profit-maximizing strategy.

Oligopoly with More Than Two Firms

We have seen how firms behave in a duopoly. What happens when more firms enter the market? The addition of a third firm complicates efforts to maintain a cartel and increases the possibility of a more competitive result.

We can see this interaction in the cell phone market. The four major companies are not all equal. AT&T and Verizon are significantly larger than Sprint Nextel and T-Mobile. If AT&T and Verizon were the only two providers, the market might have very little competition. However, the smaller Sprint Nextel and T-Mobile play a crucial role in changing the market dynamic. Even though Sprint Nextel and T-Mobile have significantly less market share, they still have developed extensive cellular networks in order to compete. Since Sprint Nextel and T-Mobile have networks with smaller subscriber bases and significant excess capacity, they both aggressively compete on price. As a result, in many respects the entire cell phone industry functions competitively.

To see why this is the case, consider what the addition of a third firm will do to price and output in the market. When the third firm enters the market, there are two effects to consider—price and output. For example, if the third firm builds a cell phone tower, it will increase the overall capacity to provide cell phone service. As we observed in the duopoly example, if the total number of cell phone contracts sold (the supply) increases, all the firms must charge a lower price. This demonstrates the **price effect**, which occurs when the price of a good or service is affected by the entrance of a rival firm in the market. But since the marginal cost of providing cell phone service is

A **price effect** occurs when the price of a good or service is affected by the entrance of a rival firm in the market.

PRACTICE WHAT YOU KNOW

Oligopoly: Can You Recognize the Oligopolist?

Question: Which firm is the oligopolist?

a. Firm A is in retail. It is one of the largest and most popular clothing stores in the country. It also competes with many rivals and faces intense price competition.

b. Firm B is in the airline industry. It is not the largest carrier, but significant barriers to entry enable it to serve a number of very profitable routes.

c. Firm C is a restaurant in a small, isolated community. It is the only local eatery. People drive from miles away to eat there.

Answer: Firm A sells clothing, a product with many competing brands and outlets. The competition is intense, which means that the firm has little market power. As a result, firm A is a player in a monopolistically competitive market. It is not an oligopolist. Firm B has market power on a number of routes it flies. Since barriers to entry often prevent new carriers from securing gate space, even smaller airlines are oligopolists—as is Firm B. Firm C is a monopolist. It is the only place to eat out in the isolated community, and no other restaurant is nearby. It is not an oligopolist.

Are airlines a good example of an oligopolist?

essentially zero, the price that each firm charges is substantially higher than the marginal cost of adding a new customer to the network. When the firm sells an additional unit, it generates additional revenues for the firm. This is known as the **output effect**, which occurs when the entrance of a rival firm in the market affects the amount produced.

An **output effect** occurs when the entrance of a rival firm in the market affects the amount produced.

The price effect and output effect make it difficult to maintain a cartel when there are more than two firms. Generally, as the number of firms grows, each individual firm becomes less concerned about its impact on the overall price level, because any price above marginal cost creates a profit. Therefore, individual firms are more willing to lower prices since this creates a large output effect for the individual firm and only a small price effect in the market.

Of course, not all firms are the same size. Therefore, smaller and larger firms in an oligopolistic market react differently to the price and output effects. Increased output at smaller firms will have a negligible impact on overall prices because small firms represent only a tiny fraction of the market supply. But this is not true for firms with a large market share—decisions at these firms will have a substantial impact on price and output because the overall amount supplied in the market will change appreciably. In other words, in an oligopoly the decisions of one firm directly affect other firms.

How Does Game Theory Explain Strategic Behavior?

Decision-making under oligopoly can be complex. Recall that with a Nash equilibrium, participants make decisions based on the behavior of others around them. This is an example of **game theory**, a branch of mathematics that economists use to analyze the strategic behavior of decision-makers. In particular, the techniques of game theory can help us determine what level of cooperation is most likely to occur. A game consists of a set of players, a set of strategies available to those players, and a specification of the payoffs for each combination of strategies. The game is usually represented by a payoff matrix that shows the players, strategies, and payoffs. It is presumed that each player acts simultaneously or without knowing the actions of the other.

Game theory is a branch of mathematics that economists use to analyze the strategic behavior of decision-makers.

In this section, we will learn about the prisoner's dilemma, an example from game theory that will help us understand how dominant strategies often frame short-run decisions. We will use the idea of the dominant strategy to explain why oligopolists often choose to advertise. Finally, we will come full circle and argue that the dominant strategy in a game may be overcome in the long run through repeated interactions.

Strategic Behavior and the Dominant Strategy

We have seen that in oligopoly there is mutual interdependence: a rival's business choices affect the earnings that the other rivals can expect to make. In order to learn more about the decisions firms make, we will explore a fundamental problem in game theory known as the *prisoner's dilemma*. The dilemma takes its name from a famous scenario devised by pioneer game theorist Al Tucker soon after World War II.

Incentives

The scenario goes like this: two prisoners are being interrogated separately about a crime they both participated in, and each is offered a plea bargain to cooperate with the authorities by testifying against the other. If both suspects refuse to cooperate with the authorities, neither can be convicted of a more serious crime, though they will have to spend some time in jail. But the police have offered full immunity if one cooperates and the other does not. This means that each suspect has an incentive to betray the other. The rub is that if they both confess, they will spend more time in jail than if they had both stayed quiet. When decision-makers face incentives that make it difficult to achieve mutually beneficial outcomes, we say they are in a **prisoner's dilemma**. This situation makes the payoff for cooperating with the authorities more attractive than the result of keeping quiet. We can understand why this occurs by looking at Figure 13.1, a payoff matrix that shows the possible outcomes in a prisoner's dilemma situation. Starting with the white box in the upper-left-hand corner, we see that if both suspects testify against each other, they each get 10 years in jail. If one suspect testifies while his partner remains quiet—the upper-right and lower-left boxes—he goes free and his partner gets 25 years in jail. If both keep quiet—the result in the lower-right-hand corner—they each get off with one year in jail. This result is better than the outcome in which both prisoners testify.

The **prisoner's dilemma** occurs when decision-makers face incentives that make it difficult to achieve mutually beneficial outcomes.

Since each suspect is interrogated separately, the decision about what to tell the police cannot be made cooperatively; thus, each prisoner faces a

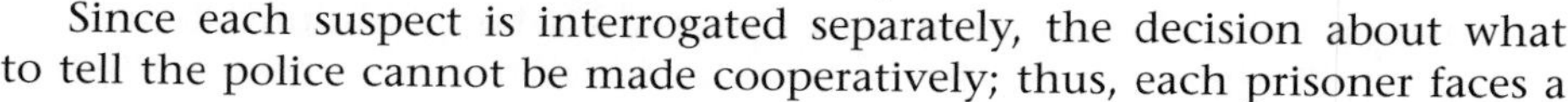

FIGURE 13.1

		Tony Montana	
		Testify	**Keep quiet**
Manny Ribera	**Testify**	10 years in jail (Tony Montana); 10 years in jail (Manny Ribera)	25 years in jail (Tony Montana); goes free (Manny Ribera)
	Keep quiet	goes free (Tony Montana); 25 years in jail (Manny Ribera)	1 year in jail (Tony Montana); 1 year in jail (Manny Ribera)

The Prisoner's Dilemma

The two suspects know that if they both keep quiet, they will spend only one year in jail. The prisoner's dilemma occurs because the decision to confess results in no jail time for the one who confesses if the other does not confess. However, this outcome means that both are likely to confess and get 10 years.

dilemma. The interrogation process makes it a non-cooperative "game" and changes the incentives that each party faces.

Under these circumstances, what will our suspects choose? Let's begin with the outcomes for Tony Montana. Suppose that he testifies. If Manny Ribera also testifies, Tony will get 10 years in jail (the upper-left box). If Manny keeps quiet, Tony will go free (the lower-left box). Now suppose that Tony decides to keep quiet. If Manny testifies, Tony can expect 25 years in jail (the upper-right box). If Manny keeps quiet, Tony will get 1 year in jail (the lower-right box). No matter what choice Manny makes, Tony is always better off choosing to testify. If his partner testifies and he testifies, he gets 10 years in jail as opposed to 25 if he keeps quiet. If his partner keeps quiet and he testifies, Tony goes free as opposed to spending a year in jail if he also keeps quiet. A similar analysis applies to the outcomes for Manny.

A dominant strategy exists when a player will always prefer one strategy, regardless of what his opponent chooses.

When a player always prefers one strategy, regardless of what his opponent chooses, we say it is a **dominant strategy**. We can see this at work in the case of our two suspects. They know that if they both keep quiet, they will spend one year in jail. The dilemma occurs because both suspects are more likely to testify and get 10 years in jail. This choice is obvious for two reasons. First, neither suspect can monitor the actions of the other after they are separated. Second, once each suspect understands that his partner will save jail time if he testifies, he realizes that the incentives are not in favor of keeping quiet.

Incentives

The dominant strategy in our example is a Nash equilibrium. Recall that a Nash equilibrium occurs when economic decision-makers choose the best possible strategy after taking into account the decisions of others. If each suspect reasons that the other will testify, the best response is also to testify. Each suspect may wish that he and his partner could coordinate their actions and agree to keep quiet. However, without the possibility of coordination, neither has an incentive to withhold testimony. So they both think strategically and decide to testify.

Duopoly and the Prisoner's Dilemma

The prisoner's dilemma example suggests that cooperation can be difficult to achieve. To get a better sense of the incentives that oligopolists face when trying to collude, we will use game theory to evaluate the outcome of our cell phone duopoly example.

Recall that our duopolists, AT-Phone and Horizon, produced an output of 800 customers, an amount that was lower than would occur under perfect competition (1,200) but higher than under monopoly (600). Figure 13.2 puts the information from Table 13.3 into a payoff matrix and highlights the revenue that AT-Phone and Horizon could earn at various production levels.

Incentives

Looking at the bottom two boxes, we see that at high production Horizon can earn either $30,000 or $24,000 in revenue, depending on what AT-Phone does. At a low production level, it could earn either $27,000 or $22,500. The same reasoning is true for AT-Phone. Now look at the right-hand column, and you will see that AT-Phone can earn either $30,000 or $24,000, depending on what Horizon does. At a low production level, it could earn either $27,000 or $22,500. So, once again, the high production levels dominate. The two companies always have an incentive to serve more customers because this strategy yields the most revenue. A high level of production leads to a Nash

FIGURE 13.2

The Prisoner's Dilemma in Duopoly

Each company has a dominant strategy to serve more customers because it makes the most revenue even if its competitor also expands production. A high level of production leads to a Nash equilibrium at which both firms make $24,000.

		AT-Phone	
		Low production: 300 customers	High production: 400 customers
Horizon	Low production: 300 customers	AT-Phone: $27,000 revenue; Horizon: $27,000 revenue	AT-Phone: $30,000 revenue; Horizon: $22,500 revenue
	High production: 400 customers	AT-Phone: $22,500 revenue; Horizon: $30,000 revenue	AT-Phone: $24,000 revenue; Horizon: $24,000 revenue

Prisoner's Dilemma

ECONOMICS IN THE MEDIA

Murder by Numbers

There is an especially compelling example of the prisoner's dilemma at work in *Murder by Numbers* (2002). In this scene, the district attorney's office decides to interrogate two murder suspects. Without a confession, they don't have enough evidence and the two murderers are likely to go free. Each is confronted with the prisoner's dilemma by being placed in a separate room and threatened with the death penalty. In order to get the confession, the detective tells one of the suspects, "Just think of it as a game. Whoever talks first is the winner." The detective goes on to tell one of the suspects that his partner in the other room is "rolling over" (even though the partner is not actually talking) and that the partner will get a lighter sentence because he is cooperating. This places added pressure on the suspect.

Would you rat on your partner in crime?

equilibrium; both firms make $24,000. However, if the companies operate as a cartel, they can both earn $27,000. Therefore, the Nash equilibrium is their second-best outcome.

Advertising and Game Theory

Incentives

We have seen that oligopolists function like monopolistic competitors in that they sell differentiated products. We know that advertising is commonplace in markets with a differentiated product. In the case of an oligopoly, mutual interdependence means that advertising can create a contest among firms looking to gain customers. This may lead to skyrocketing advertising budgets and little, or no, net gain of customers. Therefore, oligopolists have an incentive to scale back their advertising, but only if the other rivals also agree to scale back. Like all cooperative action among competitors, this is easier said than done.

Figure 13.3 highlights the advertising choices of Coca-Cola and PepsiCo, two fierce rivals in the soft drink industry. Together, Coca-Cola and PepsiCo account for 75% of the soft drink market, with Coca-Cola being the slightly larger of the two firms. Both companies are known for their advertising campaigns, which cost hundreds of millions of dollars. To determine if they gain anything by spending so much on advertising, let's look at the dominant strategy. In the absence of cooperation, each firm will choose to advertise, because the payoffs under advertising ($100 million or $150 million) exceed those of not advertising ($75 million or $125 million). When each firm chooses

FIGURE 13.3

The Prisoner's Dilemma and Advertising

The two companies each have a dominant strategy to advertise. We can see this by observing that Coca-Cola and PepsiCo each make $25 million more profit by choosing to advertise. As a result, they both end up in the upper-left box earning $100 million profit when they could have each made $125 million profit in the lower-right box if they had agreed not to advertise.

		Coca-Cola: Advertises	Coca-Cola: Does not advertise
PepsiCo	Advertises	Coca-Cola: $100 million profit; PepsiCo: $100 million profit	Coca-Cola: $75 million profit; PepsiCo: $150 million profit
PepsiCo	Does not advertise	Coca-Cola: $150 million profit; PepsiCo: $75 million profit	Coca-Cola: $125 million profit; PepsiCo: $125 million profit

SNAPSHOT

Airlines in the Prisoner's Dilemma

American Airlines and Delta Airlines once found themselves in a classic prisoner's dilemma. It all started when Delta wanted to expand its share of the lucrative Dallas-to-Chicago route, where American was the dominant carrier. Delta offered a substantial fare cut on that route to attract new travelers. American threatened a price war by offering its own fare cut on the Delta-dominated Dallas-to-Atlanta route.

Worst

Both airlines had a dominant strategy to cut their fare on the targeted route. Why? If one airline cut its fare and the other did not, the airline that did would gain market share. This was each airline's best possible outcome.

Best

3rd Best

Even if the rival cut its fare too, lowering the price was still the right move—the dominant strategy—for each airline. Why? Because if an airline failed to match the fare of its rival, it would lose market share. This scenario, where both rivals would cut fares and maintain the same market share, was the third-best outcome.

3rd Best

		American: Discount	American: No Discount
Delta	Discount	American: 3rd Best Delta: 3rd Best	American: Worst Delta: Best
	No Discount	American: Best Delta: Worst	American: 2nd Best Delta: 2nd Best

The hallmark of a prisoner's dilemma is when two rivals follow their dominant strategy and the result is the third-best situation for both. It would have been better if no fare discounts were ever considered.

What happened? Fortunately for both airlines, they posted their planned fare cuts on a computer system that allowed them to see what their rival was doing. They each saw the price war starting, backed down, and escaped the prisoner's dilemma!

REVIEW QUESTIONS

- Which expected outcome in the matrix reflects the outcome of this American/Delta pricing war?
- Explain how the ability to communicate can allow two parties to escape a prisoner's dilemma.

to advertise, it generates a profit of $100 million. This is a second-best outcome compared to the $125 million profit each could earn if neither firm advertises. The dilemma is that each firm needs to advertise to market its product and retain its customer base, but most advertising expenditures end up canceling each other out and costing the companies millions of dollars.

ECONOMICS IN THE REAL WORLD

The Cold War

The idea that companies benefit from spending less on advertising has an analogue in warfare. Countries benefit from a "peace dividend" whenever war ends. There is no better example of this than the Cold War between the Soviet Union and the United States that began in the 1950s. By the time the Cold War ended in the late 1980s, both countries had amassed thousands of nuclear warheads in an effort to deter aggression.

The Cold War created a prisoner's dilemma for the United States and the Soviet Union.

This buildup put enormous economic pressure on each country to keep up with the other. During the height of the Cold War, each country found itself in a prisoner's dilemma in which spending more in an arms race was the dominant strategy. When the Soviet Union ultimately dissolved, the United States was able to spend less money on deterrence. In the post–Cold War world of the 1990s, the U.S. military budget fell from 6.5 to 3.5% of gross domestic product (GDP) as the nation reaped a peace dividend. Of course, the prisoner's dilemma cannot account for all military spending: following the terrorist attacks of 2001, U.S. military spending increased again to nearly 5% of GDP by 2004. ✷

Escaping the Prisoner's Dilemma in the Long Run

We have seen how game theory can be a useful tool for understanding strategic decision-making in non-cooperative environments. When you examine the prisoner's dilemma or the Nash equilibrium, the solution represents an outcome that yields the largest gain in the short run. However, many decisions are not made in this way. The dominant strategy does not consider the possible long-run benefits of cooperation.

Game theorist Robert Axelrod decided to examine the choices that participants make in a long-run setting. He ran a sophisticated computer simulation in which he invited scholars to submit strategies for securing points in a prisoner's dilemma tournament over many rounds. All the submissions were collected and paired, and the results were scored. After each simulation, Axelrod eliminated the weakest strategy and re-ran the tournament with the remaining strategies. This evolutionary approach continued until the best strategy remained. Among all strategies, including those that were solely cooperative

ECONOMICS IN THE MEDIA

Prisoner's Dilemma

The Dark Knight

In what is arguably the greatest superhero movie of all time, *The Dark Knight* (2008), the Joker (played by the late Heath Ledger) always seems to be one step ahead of the law. The strategic interactions between the police and the conniving villain are an illustration of game theory in action.

Near the end of the movie, the Joker rigs two full passenger ferries to explode at midnight and tells the passengers that if they try to escape, the bomb will detonate earlier. To complicate matters, one of the ferries is carrying civilian passengers, including a number of children, while the other ferry is transporting prisoners. Each ferry can save itself by hitting a detonator button attached to the other ferry.

The Joker's plan sets up a prisoner's dilemma between the two boats and an ethical experiment. Are the lives of those on the civilian boat worth more than those of the prisoners? The Joker's intention is to have one of the ferries blow up the other and thereby create chaos in Gotham City.

In the payoff matrix, the dominant strategy is to detonate the other boat. Failing to detonate the other boat results in death—either one ferry blows up at midnight, or the other boat detonates it first. In this scenario, the only chance of survival is if one ferry detonates the other ferry first. As the scene unfolds and the tension builds, the passengers on both boats realize their plight and wrestle with the consequences of their decisions. Gradually, everyone becomes aware that the dominant strategy is to detonate the other boat. What is interesting is how the civilians and prisoners react to this information.

What actually happens? Passengers on each boat decide that they would rather be detonated than willingly participate in the Joker's experiment. Watching the scene as a game theorist will give you a new appreciation for the film.

		Prisoner ferry	
		Detonate other boat	**Do not detonate other boat**
Civilian ferry	**Detonate other boat**	Cannot simultaneously happen Cannot simultaneously happen	Die Survive
	Do not detonate other boat	Survive Die	Die Die

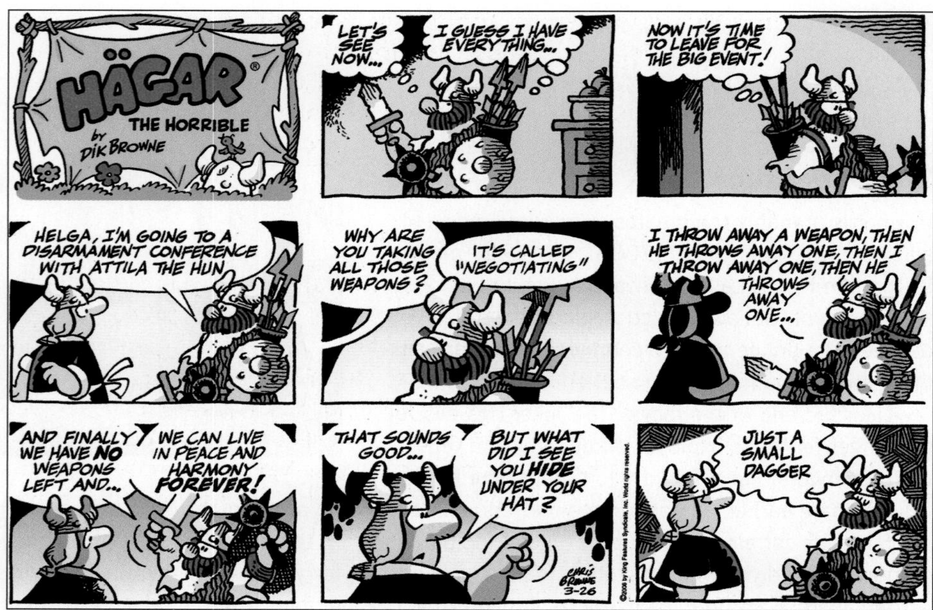

Tit-for-tat is a long-run strategy that promotes cooperation among participants by mimicking the opponent's most recent decision with repayment in kind.

or non-cooperative, *tit-for-tat* dominated. **Tit-for-tat** is a long-run strategy that promotes cooperation among participants by mimicking the opponent's most recent decision with repayment in kind. As the name implies, a tit-for-tat strategy is one in which you do whatever your opponent does. If your opponent breaks the agreement, you break the agreement too. If the opponent behaves properly, then you behave properly too.

Since the joint payoffs for cooperation are high in a prisoner's dilemma, tit-for-tat begins by cooperating. In subsequent rounds, the tit-for-tat strategy mimics whatever the other player did in the previous round. The genius behind tit-for-tat is that it changes the incentives and encourages cooperation. Turning back to our example in Figure 13.3, suppose that Coca-Cola and PepsiCo want to save on advertising expenses. The companies expect to have repeated interactions, so they both know from past experience that any effort to start a new advertising campaign will be immediately countered by the other firm. Since the companies react to each other's moves in kind, any effort to exploit the dominant strategy of advertising will ultimately fail. This dynamic can alter the incentives that the firms face in the long run and lead to mutually beneficial behavior.

Incentives

Opportunity cost

Tit-for-tat makes it less desirable to advertise by eliminating the long-run benefits. Advertising is still a dominant strategy in the short run because the payoffs with advertising ($100 million or $150 million) exceed those of not advertising ($75 million or $125 million). In the short run, the firm that advertises could earn $25 million extra, but in every subsequent round—if the rival responds in kind—the firm should expect profits of $100 million because its rival will also be advertising. As a result, there is a large long-run opportunity cost for not cooperating. If one firm stops advertising and the other follows suit, they will each find themselves making $125 million in the long run. Why hasn't this happened in the real world? Because Coke and PepsiCo don't trust each other enough to earn the dividend that comes from an advertising truce.

The prisoner's dilemma nicely captures why cooperation is so difficult in the short run. But most interactions in life occur over the long run. For example, scam artists and sketchy companies take advantage of short-run opportunities that cannot last because relationships in the long run—with businesses and with people—involve mutual trust. Cooperation is the default because you know that the other side is invested in the relationship. Under these circumstances, the tit-for-tat strategy works well.

A Caution about Game Theory

Game theory is a decision-making tool, but not all games have dominant strategies that make player decisions easy to predict. Perhaps the best example is the game known as Rock, Paper, Scissors. This simple game has no dominant strategy: paper beats rock (because the paper will cover the rock) and rock beats scissors (because the rock will break the scissors), but scissors beats paper (because the scissors will cut the paper). The preferred choice is strictly a function of what the other player selects. Many situations in life, and business, are more like Rock, Paper, Scissors than the prisoner's dilemma. Winning at business in the long run often occurs because you are one step ahead of the competition, not because you deploy a strategy that attempts to take advantage of a short-run opportunity.

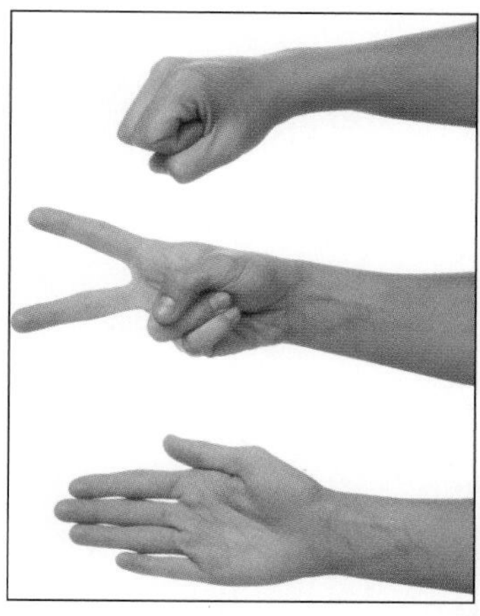

Rock, Paper, Scissors is a game without a dominant strategy.

Consider two friends who enjoy playing racquetball together. Both players are of equal ability, so each point comes down to whether the players guess correctly about the direction the other player will hit. Take a look at Figure 13.4. The success of Joey and Rachel depends on how well each one guesses where the other will hit.

		Rachel	
		Guesses to the left	Guesses to the right
Joey	Hits to the left	Rachel wins the point Joey loses the point	Rachel loses the point Joey wins the point
	Hits to the right	Rachel loses the point Joey wins the point	Rachel wins the point Joey loses the point

FIGURE 13.4

No Dominant Strategy Exists

Neither Rachel nor Joey has a dominant strategy that guarantees winning the point. Any of the four outcomes are equally likely on successive points, and there is no way to predict how the next point will be played. As a result, there is no Nash equilibrium here.

In this competition, neither Rachel nor Joey has a dominant strategy that guarantees success. Sometimes Joey wins when hitting to the right; at other times he loses the point. Sometimes Rachel wins when she guesses to the left; at other times she loses. Each player only guesses correctly half the time. Since we cannot say what each player will do from one point to another, there is no Nash equilibrium. Any of the four outcomes are equally likely on successive points, and there is no way to predict how the next point will be played. In other words, we cannot expect every game to include a prisoner's dilemma and produce a Nash equilibrium. Game theory, like real life, has many different possible outcomes.

How Do Government Policies Affect Oligopoly Behavior?

When oligopolists in an industry form a cooperative alliance, they function like a monopoly. Competition disappears, which is not good for society. One way to improve the social welfare of society is to restore competition and limit monopoly practices through policy legislation.

Antitrust Policy

The **Sherman Antitrust Act** was the first federal law limiting cartels and monopolies.

Efforts to curtail the adverse consequences of oligopolistic cooperation began with the **Sherman Antitrust Act** of 1890. This was the first federal law to place limits on cartels and monopolies. The Sherman Act was created in response to the increase in concentration ratios in many leading U.S. industries, including steel, railroads, mining, textiles, and oil. Prior to passage of the Sherman Act, firms were free to pursue contracts that created mutually beneficial outcomes. Once the act took effect, however, certain cooperative actions became criminal. Section 2 of the Sherman Act reads, "Every person who shall monopolize, or attempt to monopolize, or combine or conspire with any other person or persons, to monopolize any part of the trade or commerce among the several States, or with foreign nations, shall be deemed guilty of a felony."

The **Clayton Act** targets corporate behaviors that reduce competition.

The **Clayton Act** of 1914 targets corporate behaviors that reduce competition. Large corporations had been vilified during the presidential election of 1912, and the Sherman Act was seen as largely ineffective in curbing monopoly power. To shore up antitrust policy, the Clayton Act added to the list of activities that were deemed socially detrimental, including:

1. *price discrimination* if it lessens competition or creates monopoly
2. *exclusive dealings* that restrict a buyer's ability to deal with competitors
3. *tying arrangements* that require the buyer to purchase an additional product in order to purchase the first
4. *mergers and acquisitions* that lessen competition, or situations in which a person serves as a director on more than one board in the same industry

As the Clayton Act makes clear, there are many ways to reduce competition.

PRACTICE WHAT YOU KNOW

Dominant Strategy: To Advertise or Not—That Is the Question!

Question: University Subs and Savory Sandwiches are the only two sandwich shops in a small college town. If neither runs a special 2-for-1 promotion, both are able to keep their prices high and earn $10,000 a month. However, when both run promotions, their profits fall to $1,000. Finally, if one runs a promotion and the other does not, the shop that runs the promotion earns a profit of $15,000 and the other loses $5,000. What is the dominant strategy for University Subs? Is there a Nash equilibrium in this example?

How much should a firm charge for this sandwich?

		University Subs: Runs a 2-for-1 promotion	University Subs: Keeps price high
Savory Sandwiches	Runs a 2-for-1 promotion	University Subs: Makes $1,000 Savory Sandwiches: Makes $1,000	University Subs: Loses $5,000 Savory Sandwiches: Makes $15,000
Savory Sandwiches	Keeps price high	University Subs: Makes $15,000 Savory Sandwiches: Loses $5,000	University Subs: Makes $10,000 Savory Sandwiches: Makes $10,000

Answer:

If University Subs runs the 2-for-1 promotion, it will make either $1,000 or $15,000, depending on its rival's actions. If University Subs keeps the price high, it will make either –$5,000 or $10,000, depending on what Savory Sandwiches does. So the dominant strategy will be to run the special, since it guarantees a profit of at least $1,000. Savory Sandwiches has the same dominant strategy and the same payoffs. Therefore, both companies will run the promotion and each will make $1,000. Neither firm has a reason to switch to the high-price strategy since it would lose $5,000 if the other company runs the 2-for-1 promotion. A Nash equilibrium occurs when both companies run the promotion.

Over the past hundred years, lawmakers have continued to refine antitrust policy. Additional legislation, as well as court interpretations of existing antitrust law, have made it difficult to determine whether a company has violated the law. The U.S. Justice Department is charged with oversight, but it often lacks the resources to fully investigate every case. Antitrust law is complex and cases are hard to prosecute, but these laws are essential to maintain a competitive business environment. Without effective restraints on excessive market power, firms would organize into cartels more often or would find other ways to restrict competition. Table 13.5 briefly describes the most influential antitrust cases in U.S. history.

TABLE 13.5

Influential Antitrust Cases in U.S. History

Defendant	Year	Description
Standard Oil	1906	Standard Oil was founded in 1870. By 1897, the company had driven the price down to 6 cents a gallon, which put many of its competitors out of business. Subsequently, Standard Oil became the largest company in the world. In 1906, the U.S. government filed suit against Standard Oil for violating the Sherman Antitrust Act. Three years later, the company was found guilty and forced to break up into 34 independent companies.
ALCOA	1937	The Aluminum Company of America (ALCOA), founded in 1907, maintained its position as the only producer of aluminum in the United States for many years. To keep that position, the company acquired exclusive rights to all U.S. sources of bauxite, the base material from which aluminum is refined. It then acquired land rights to build and own hydroelectric facilities in both the United States and Canada. By owning both the base materials and the only sites where refinement could take place, ALCOA effectively barred other firms from entering the U.S. aluminum market. In 1937, the Department of Justice filed suit against ALCOA. Seven years later, the Supreme Court ruled that ALCOA had taken measures to restrict trade and functioned as a monopoly. ALCOA was not divested because two rivals, Kaiser and Reynolds, emerged soon thereafter.
AT&T	1974	In 1974, the U.S. Attorney General filed suit against AT&T for violating antitrust laws. It took seven years before a settlement was reached to split the company into seven new companies, each serving a different region of the United States. However, five of the seven have since merged to become AT&T Incorporated, which is now one of the largest companies in the world.
Microsoft	1995	When Internet Explorer was introduced in 1995, Microsoft insisted that it was a feature rather than a new Windows product. The U.S. Department of Justice did not agree and filed suit against Microsoft for illegally discouraging competition to protect its software monopoly. After a series of court decisions and appeals, a settlement ordered Microsoft to share application programming interfaces with third-party companies.

Predatory Pricing

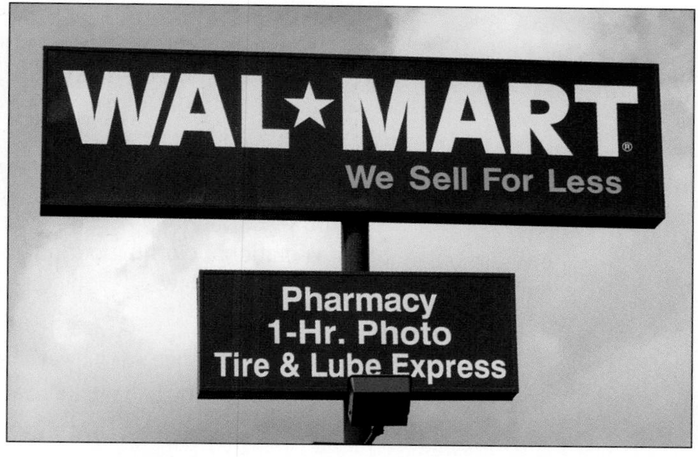

Though Walmart keeps its prices low, there is no evidence that it engages in predatory pricing.

While firms have a strong incentive to cooperate in order to keep prices high, they also want to keep potential rivals out of the market. The practice of setting prices deliberately below average variable costs with the intent of driving rivals from the market is known as **predatory pricing**. When this occurs, the firm suffers a short-run loss in order to prevent rivals from entering the market or to drive rival firms out of business in the long run. Once the rivals are gone, the firm should be able to act like a monopolist.

Predatory pricing is illegal, but it is difficult to prosecute. Neither the court system nor economists have a simple rule that helps to determine when a firm steps over the line. Predatory pricing can look and feel like spirited competition. Moreover, the concern is not the competitive aspect or lower prices, but the effect on the market when all rivals fail. To prove that predatory pricing has occurred, the courts need evidence that the firm's prices increased significantly after its rivals failed.

Predatory pricing occurs when firms deliberately set their prices below average variable costs with the intent of driving rivals from the market.

Walmart is often cited as an example of a firm that engages in predatory pricing because its low prices effectively drive many smaller companies out of business. However, there is no evidence that Walmart has ever systematically raised prices after a rival failed. Therefore, its price strategy does not meet the legal standard for predatory pricing. Similarly, Microsoft came under intense scrutiny in the 1990s for giving away its browser, Internet Explorer, in order to undercut Netscape, which also ended up giving away its browser. Microsoft understood that the key to its long-term success was the dominance of the Windows platform. Bundling Internet Explorer with Microsoft Office enabled the company not only to gain over 80% of the browser market but also to keep its leadership with the Windows operating system. Eventually, Microsoft was prosecuted by the government—but not for predatory pricing, which could not be proved because Microsoft never significantly raised the price of Internet Explorer. Instead, the government prosecuted Microsoft for tying the purchase of Internet Explorer to the Windows operating system in order to restrict competition. The Microsoft case lasted over four years, and it ended in a settlement that placed restrictions on the firm's business practices.

What Are Network Externalities?

We end this chapter by considering a special kind of externality that often occurs in oligopoly. A **network externality** occurs when the number of customers who purchase or use a good influences the quantity demanded. This means that firms with many customers often find it easier to attract new customers and to keep their regular customers from switching to other rivals. In the early days of social networking, for example, MySpace and Friendster

A **network externality** occurs when the number of customers who purchase or use a good influences the quantity demanded.

PRACTICE WHAT YOU KNOW

Predatory Pricing: Price Wars

You've undoubtedly encountered a price war at some point. It could be two gas stations, clothing outlets, or restaurants that are charging prices that seem unbelievably low.

Question: Is a price war between two adjacent pizza restaurants evidence of predatory pricing?

Predatory pricing? Check out the two competing signs above!

Answer: One essential element for proving predatory pricing is evidence of the intent to raise prices after others are driven out of business. That is a problem in this example. Suppose one of the pizza places closes. The remaining firm could then raise its price substantially. But barriers to entry in the restaurant industry are low in most metropolitan areas, so any efforts to maintain high prices for long will fail. Customers will vote with their feet and wallets by choosing another pizza place a little farther away that offers a better value. Or a new competitor will sense that the victor is vulnerable because of the high prices and will open a new pizza parlor nearby. Either way, the market is competitive, so any market power created by driving out one rival will be fleeting.

The aggressive price war is not evidence of predatory pricing. Instead, it is probably just promotional pricing to protect market share. Firms often price some items below their variable costs to attract customers. These firms hope to make up the difference and then some with high profit margins on other items, such as beverages and side dishes.

had many more users than Facebook. How did Facebook gain over 2 billion users when it had to play catch-up? Facebook built a better social network, and MySpace was slow to respond to the threat. By the time MySpace did respond, it was too late: Facebook was on its way. Now the tables are turned, as Facebook is the dominant social-networking platform. Moreover, the sheer size of Facebook makes it a better place to do social networking than MySpace or Google+. However, even though Facebook now enjoys significant network externalities, it must be mindful to keep innovating or else it might end up like MySpace someday.

Most examples of network externalities involve the introduction of new technologies. For instance, some technologies need to reach a critical mass before consumers can effectively use them. Consider that today everyone seems to have a cell phone. However, when cell phones were introduced in the United States in 1983, coverage was quite limited. The first users could not surf the Internet, roam, text, or use many of the applications we enjoy today. Moreover, the phones were large and bulky. How did we get from that situation in 1983 to today? As additional people bought cell phones, networks expanded and manufacturers and telephone companies responded by building more cell towers and offering better phones. The expansion of networks brought more users, and the new adopters benefited from the steadily expanding customer base.

Users of the first-generation cell phone, the Motorola DynaTAC 8000X, created a positive network externality for future users.

Other technologies have gone through similar transformations. The Internet, fax machines, and Blu-ray disks all depend on the number of users. If you were the only person on the Internet, or the only person with the ability to send and receive a fax, your technical capacity would have little value. Likewise, the owner of a Blu-ray machine depends on the willingness of movie studios to create content in that format. In a world with ever-changing technology, first adopters pave the way for the next generation of users.

Positive network externalities are also generated by the **bandwagon effect**, which arises when a buyer's preference for a product increases as the number of people buying it increases. Fads of all sorts fall into this category. North Face jackets, oversized handbags, Uggs, and Bluetooth headsets are in vogue today, but how long that will remain true is anyone's guess.

The **bandwagon effect** arises when a buyer's preference for a product increases as the number of people buying it increases.

In addition to the advantages of forming a larger network, firms find that many of their customers face significant *switching costs* if they leave. **Switching costs** are the costs incurred when a consumer changes from one supplier to another. For instance, the transition from listening to music on CDs to using digital music files involved a substantial switching cost for many users. Today, there are switching costs among the many digital music options. Once a consumer has established a library of MP3s or uses iTunes, the switching costs of transferring the music from one format to another create a significant barrier to change. When consumers face switching costs, the demand for the existing product becomes more inelastic. As a result, oligopolists not only leverage the number of customers they maintain in their network, but also try to make switching to another network more difficult.

Switching costs are the costs incurred when a consumer changes from one supplier to another.

There is no better example of the costs of switching than cell phone providers. First, contract termination fees apply to many cell phone agreements if the contract is broken. Second, many providers do not charge for calls inside the network or among a circle of friends. This means that if you switch and your friends do not, you will end up using more minutes on a rival network. These two tactics create high switching costs for many cell phone customers. To reduce switching costs, the Federal Communications Commission in 2003 began requiring that phone companies allow customers to take their cell phone numbers with them when they change to a different provider. This change in the law has reduced the costs of switching from one provider to another and has made the cell phone market more competitive.

Oligopolists are keenly aware of the power of network externalities. As new markets develop, the first firm into an industry often gains a large customer base. When there are positive network externalities, the customer base enables the firm to grow quickly. In addition, consumers are often more comfortable purchasing from an established firm. These two factors favor the formation of large firms and make it difficult for smaller competitors to gain customers. As a result, the presence of significant positive network externalities causes small firms to be driven out of business or forces them to merge with larger competitors.

ECONOMICS FOR LIFE

Why Waiting Is Generally a Good Idea

If you are like a lot of people when you hear about something new and cool, you check it out. There is no harm in doing that. But what happens when you decide to purchase the latest gadget or join a new social media web site? You've made an investment of money or time. The fruitfulness of that investment often depends on how many other people do the same thing.

Consider the first people to get a 3D television—the first purchasers paid well over $5,000 for the new technology, but what exactly could they watch? The amount of 3D programming to start was tiny. Those early purchasers had very expensive TVs that they could rarely use to watch 3D because the content was playing catch-up. In contrast, consumers who waited could buy a 3D unit with greater clarity at a lower price, and more content was available to watch. That meant a win-win-win for procrastinators. The early adopters got penalized for paving the way.

The same is true today with many social media sites. Waiting for a web site to gain traction will save you from setting up a profile and investing your time and effort only to find out that other people are not nearly as excited about the features as you are. You end up wasting a lot of time, and because other online users never show up, you don't get the benefits that come from network externalities. If you wait until a platform is already established, then you can be fairly confident that your return on investment will be rewarded. This is certainly true with Facebook, Twitter, and LinkedIn—all of which have come to dominate segments of the social media market.

Google glasses? Should you buy the newest gadget when it comes out?

Network externalities are also important on dating sites. Just consider the overwhelming number of choices in this market: Match.com, Zoosk, eHarmony, OurTime, Chemistry.com, and many other sites. You could sign up for dozens of dating sites or simply choose the largest site, Match.com, because it offers the biggest database. Since dating sites charge member fees, waiting and seeing which sites are more popular is one way to use network externalities to improve your odds of success.

PRACTICE WHAT YOU KNOW

Examples of Network Externalities

Question: In which of these examples are network externalities important?

a. college alumni
b. Netflix
c. a local bakery that sells fresh bread

Does Netflix benefit from network externalities?

Answers:

a. Colleges and universities that have more alumni are able to raise funds more easily than smaller schools, so the size of the alumni network matters. The number of alumni also matters when graduates look for jobs, since alumni are often inclined to hire individuals who went to the same school. For example, Penn State University has the nation's largest alumni base. This means that each PSU graduate benefits from network externalities.
b. Netflix's size enables it to offer a vast array of DVDs and downloads. If it were smaller, Netflix would be unable to make as many obscure titles available. This means that Netflix customers benefit from network externalities by having more DVDs to choose from.
c. The local bakery is a small company. If it attracts more customers, each one will have to compete harder to get fresh bread. Since the supply of bread is limited, additional customers create congestion, and network externalities do not exist.

Conclusion

We opened this chapter with the misconception that cell phone companies are highly competitive—that is, that they compete like firms in competitive markets or monopolistically competitive markets do. The reality is that cell phone companies are oligopolists. Firms in oligopoly markets can compete or collude to create monopoly conditions. The result is often hard to predict. In many cases, the presence of a dominant short-run strategy causes firms to compete on price and advertising even though doing so yields a lower economic profit. In contrast, the potential success of a tit-for-tat strategy suggests that oligopolistic firms are capable of cooperating in order to jointly maximize their long-run profits. Whether oligopoly mirrors the result found in monopolistic competition or monopoly matters a great deal because society's welfare is higher when more competition is present. Since oligopoly is not a market structure with a predictable outcome, each oligopolistic industry must be assessed on a case-by-case basis by examining data and utilizing game theory. This makes the study of oligopoly one of the most fascinating parts of the theory of the firm.

In the next section of the book, we will examine how resource markets work. After all, each firm needs access to resources such as land, labor, and capital to produce goods and services. As a result, understanding how resource markets work will deepen our grasp of the theory of the firm. We will pay special attention to the labor market going forward since it determines workers' job prospects and the amount of income inequality within society.

ANSWERING THE BIG QUESTIONS

What is oligopoly?

* Oligopoly exists when a small number of firms sell a differentiated product in a market with significant barriers to entry. An oligopolist is like a monopolistic competitor in that it sells differentiated products. It is also like a monopolist in that it enjoys significant barriers to entry. The small number of sellers in oligopoly leads to mutual interdependence.
* Oligopolists have a tendency to collude and to form cartels in the hope of achieving monopoly-like profits.
* Oligopolistic markets are socially inefficient since price and marginal cost are not equal. The result under oligopoly falls somewhere between the competitive-market and monopoly outcomes.

How does game theory explain strategic behavior?

* Game theory helps to determine when cooperation among oligopolists is most likely to occur. In many cases, cooperation fails to occur because decision-makers have dominant strategies that lead them to be uncooperative. This can cause firms to compete with price, advertising, or research and development when they could potentially earn more profit by curtailing these activities.
* A dominant strategy ignores the possible long-run benefits of cooperation and focuses solely on the short-run gains. Whenever repeated interaction occurs, decision-makers fare better under tit-for-tat, an approach that maximizes the long-run profit.

How do government policies affect oligopoly behavior?

* Antitrust law is complex, and cases are hard to prosecute. Nevertheless, these laws are essential in providing oligopoly firms an incentive to compete rather than collude.
* Antitrust policy limits price discrimination, exclusive dealings, tying arrangements, mergers, and predatory pricing.

What are network externalities?

* A network externality occurs when the number of customers who purchase a good or use it influences the quantity demanded. The presence of significant positive network externalities can cause small firms to go out of business.

CONCEPTS YOU SHOULD KNOW

antitrust laws (p. 387)
bandwagon effect (p. 407)
cartel (p. 387)
Clayton Act (p. 402)
collusion (p. 387)
dominant strategy (p. 394)
game theory (p. 392)
mutual interdependence (p. 388)
Nash equilibrium (p. 390)
network externality (p. 405)
oligopoly (p. 384)
output effect (p. 392)
predatory pricing (p. 405)
price effect (p. 391)
prisoner's dilemma (p. 393)
Sherman Antitrust Act (p. 402)
switching costs (p. 407)
tit-for-tat (p. 400)

QUESTIONS FOR REVIEW

1. Compare the price and output under oligopoly to that of monopoly and monopolistic competition.
2. How does the addition of another firm affect the ability of an oligopolistic industry to form an effective cartel?
3. What is predatory pricing?
4. How is game theory relevant to oligopoly? Does it help to explain monopoly? Give reasons for your response.
5. What does the prisoner's dilemma indicate about the longevity of collusive agreements?
6. What is a Nash equilibrium? How does it differ from a dominant strategy?
7. What practices do antitrust laws prohibit?
8. What are network externalities? Describe why network externalities matter to an oligopolist.

STUDY PROBLEMS (*✱ solved at the end of the section*)

1. Some places limit the number of hours that alcohol can be sold on Sunday. Is it possible that this sales restriction could help liquor stores? Use game theory to construct your answer. **Hint:** even without restrictions on the hours of operation, individual stores could still limit Sunday sales if they wanted to.

2. Which of the following markets are oligopolistic?
   a. passenger airlines
   b. cereal
   c. fast food
   d. wheat
   e. golf equipment
   f. the college bookstore on your campus

✱ 3. At many local concerts, the crowd stands for some songs and sits for others. You are a fan of the concerts but not of having to stand; you prefer to stay seated throughout concerts. What would be your tit-for-tat strategy to encourage other concertgoers to change their behavior?

4. After teaching a class on game theory, your instructor announces that if every student skips the last question on the next exam, everyone will receive full credit for that question. However, if one or more students answer the last question, all responses will be graded and those who skip the question will get a zero. Will the entire class skip the last question? Explain your response.

5. For which of the following are network externalities important?
   a. gas stations
   b. American Association of Retired Persons (AARP)
   c. eHarmony, an Internet dating site

6. Your economics instructor is at it again (see question 4). This time, you have to do

a two-student project. Assume that you and your partner are both interested in maximizing your grade, but you are both very busy and get more happiness if you can get a good grade with less work.

You \ Your partner	Work hard	Work less hard
Work hard	Your partner: Grade = A, but you had to work 10 hours. Happiness = 7/10. You: Grade = A, but you had to work 10 hours. Happiness = 7/10.	Your partner: Grade = A, and you only worked 5 hours. Happiness = 9/10. You: Grade = A, but you had to work 15 hours. Happiness = 4/10.
Work less hard	Your partner: Grade = A, but you had to work 15 hours. Happiness = 4/10. You: Grade = A, and you only worked 5 hours. Happiness = 9/10.	Your partner: Grade = B, but you only worked 5 hours. Happiness = 6/10. You: Grade = B, but you only worked 5 hours. Happiness = 6/10.

a. What is your dominant strategy? Explain.
b. What is your partner's dominant strategy? Explain.
c. What is the Nash equilibrium in this situation? Explain.
d. If you and your partner are required to work together on a number of projects throughout the semester, how might this change the outcome you predicted in parts (a), (b), and (c)?

7. Suppose that the marginal cost of mining gold is constant at $300 per ounce and the demand schedule is as follows:

Price (per oz.)	Quantity (oz.)
$1,000	1,000
$900	2,000
$800	3,000
$700	4,000
$600	5,000
$500	6,000
$400	7,000
$300	8,000

a. If the number of suppliers is large, what would be the price and quantity?
b. If there is only one supplier, what would be the price and quantity?
c. If there are only two suppliers and they form a cartel, what would be the price and quantity?
d. Suppose that one of the two cartel members in part (c) decides to increase its production by 1,000 ounces while the other member keeps its production constant. What will happen to the revenues of both firms?

* 8. Trade agreements encourage countries to curtail tariffs so that goods may flow across international boundaries without restrictions. Using the following payoff matrix, determine the best policies for China and the United States in this example.

United States \ China	Low tariffs	High tariffs
Low tariffs	China gains $50 billion U.S. gains $50 billion	China gains $100 billion U.S. gains $10 billion
High tariffs	China gains $10 billion U.S. gains $100 billion	China gains $25 billion U.S. gains $25 billion

a. What is the dominant strategy for the United States?
b. What is the dominant strategy for China?
c. What is the Nash equilibrium for these two countries?
d. Suppose that the United States and China enter into a trade agreement that simultaneously lowers trade barriers. Is this a good idea? Explain your response.

9. A small town has only one pizza place, The Pizza Factory. A small competitor, Perfect Pies, is thinking about entering the market. The profits of these two firms depends on whether Perfect Pies enters the market and

whether The Pizza Factory—as a price leader—decides to set a high or a low price. Use the payoff matrix below to answer the questions that follow.

		Perfect Pies	
		Enter	Stay out
The Pizza Factory	High price	Perfect Pies makes $10,000 The Pizza Factory makes $20,000	Perfect Pies makes $0 The Pizza Factory makes $50,000
	Low price	Perfect Pies loses $10,000 The Pizza Factory makes $10,000	Perfect Pies makes $0 The Pizza Factory makes $25,000

a. What is the dominant strategy of The Pizza Factory?

b. What is the dominant strategy of Perfect Pies?

c. What is the Nash equilibrium in this situation?

d. The combined profit for both firms is highest when The Pizza Factory sets a high price and Perfect Pies stays out. If Perfect Pies enters the market, how will this affect the profits of The Pizza Factory? Would The Pizza Factory be willing to pay Perfect Pies not to enter the market? Explain.

SOLVED PROBLEMS

3. Since standing at a concert imposes a negative externality on those who like to sit, the behavior is non-cooperative by nature. When one person, or a group of people, stands up, it forces those who would prefer to sit to have to stand up as well to see the performance. When this happens repeatedly, it diminishes the enjoyment of those who like to sit—especially when others nearby dance, sway, scream, and raise their arms. A concert typically consists of two sets of music with 20 to 25 songs played over the course of a few hours. As a result, your behavior has the potential to influence the behavior of those nearby. Think of this as a game in which you utilize tit-for-tat, or your behavior when the next song is played mimics what the other concertgoers did during the previous song. If you stand, dance, sway, scream, and raise your arms when everyone else is seated, eventually they will get the message that their actions impose a cost on everyone else. Once they understand this and remain seated, you can sit down as well and everyone can see the performance.

8. a. The dominant strategy for the United States is to impose high tariffs, because it always earns more from that strategy than if it faces low tariffs no matter what policy China pursues.
   b. The dominant strategy for China is to impose high tariffs, because it always earns more from that strategy than if it faces low tariffs no matter what policy the United States pursues.
   c. The Nash equilibrium for both countries is to levy high tariffs. Each country will earn $25 billion.
   d. China and the United States would each benefit from cooperatively lowering trade barriers. In that case, each country would earn $50 billion.

Two Alternative Theories of Pricing Behavior

APPENDIX

13A

Two alternative theories argue that oligopolists will form long-lasting cartels. These are the kinked demand curve and price leadership.

The Kinked Demand Curve

Imagine that a group of oligopolists has established an output level and price designed to maximize economic profit. The **kinked demand curve** theory states that oligopolists have a greater tendency to respond aggressively to the price cuts of rivals but will largely ignore price increases. When a rival raises prices, the other firms all stand to benefit by holding their prices steady in order to capture those customers who do not want to pay more. In this scenario, the firm that raises its price will see a relatively large drop in sales. However, if any of the rivals attempts to lower the price, other firms in the industry will immediately match the price decrease. The price match policy means that the firm that lowers its price will not gain many new customers. In practice, since a price drop by one firm will be met immediately by a price drop from all the competitors, no one firm will be able to attract very many new customers. This is the case at any price below the agreed-to price.

The **kinked demand curve** theory states that oligopolists have a greater tendency to respond aggressively to the price cuts of rivals but will largely ignore price increases.

The firms' behavior creates a demand curve that is more elastic (or flatter) at prices above the cartel price and more inelastic (or steeper) at prices below the cartel price. The junction of the elastic and inelastic segments on the demand curve creates a "kink" that we see in Figure 13A.1.

This illustration begins with each of the firms in the industry charging P and producing Q. Since demand is more elastic above P and less elastic below P, the marginal revenue curve (MR) is discontinuous. The gap is illustrated by the dashed black vertical line. The presence of the gap in marginal revenue means that more than one marginal cost curve intersects marginal revenue at output level Q. This is evident in marginal cost curves MC_1 and MC_2. As a consequence, small changes in marginal cost, like those shown in Figure 13A.1, will not cause the firms to deviate from the established price (P) and quantity (Q).

Price Leadership

The kinked demand curve explains why firms generally keep the same price, but it cannot explain how prices change. In that regard, the theory of price leadership provides some insight.

FIGURE 13A.1

The Kinked Demand Curve

At prices above P, demand is relatively elastic. At prices below P, demand is relatively inelastic. This creates a kink in the demand curve that causes the marginal revenue curve to become discontinuous. As a result, small changes in marginal cost do not cause firms to change their pricing and output. Therefore, firms are generally slow to adjust to changes in cost.

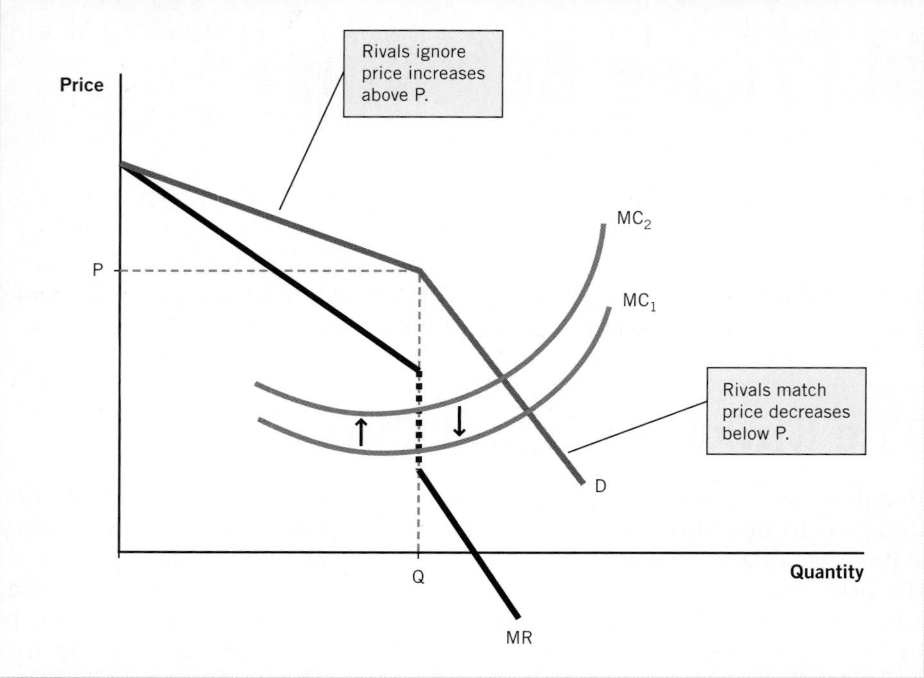

Price leadership occurs when a dominant firm in an industry sets the price that maximizes profits and the smaller firms in the industry follow.

In many industries, smaller firms may take a cue from the decisions made by the price leader. **Price leadership** generally occurs when a single firm, known as the price leader, produces a large share of the total output in the industry. The price leader sets the price and output level that maximizes its own profits. Smaller firms then set their prices to match the price leader. Since the impact on price is small to begin with, it makes sense that smaller rivals tend to follow the price leader.

Price leadership is not illegal since it does not involve collusion. Rather, it relies on an understanding that an effort to resist changes implemented by the price leader will lead to increased price competition and lower profits for every firm in the industry. Since the firms act in accordance with one another, this practice is commonly known as *tacit collusion.*

One well-known example of price leadership is pricing patterns in the airline industry. On almost any route with multiple-carrier options, a price search for flights will reveal almost identical prices on basic economy-class flights. This happens even though the firms do not collude to set a profit-maximizing price. Rather, when one firm sets a fare, the other carriers feel compelled to match it. Airlines are very good at matching low prices, just like the model predicts. They are much less successful in implementing across-the-board fare increases, since that involves the leader sticking its neck out and trusting that the other firms will follow suit.

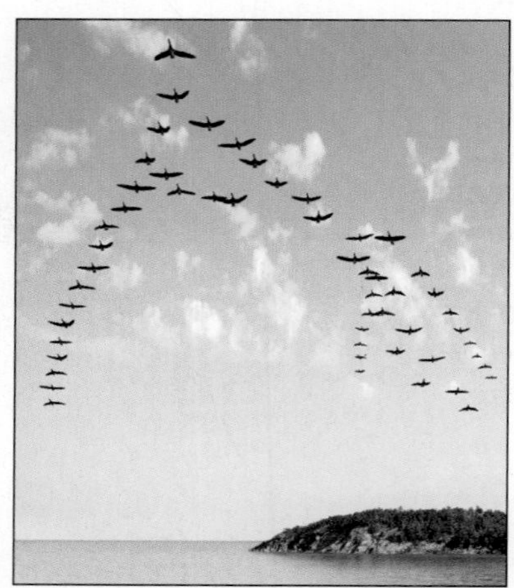

The airline industry is often cited as a market where price leadership is at work behind the scenes.

CONCEPTS YOU SHOULD KNOW

kinked demand curve (p. 415)

price leadership (p. 416)

STUDY PROBLEMS

1. A parking garage charges $10 a day. Whenever it tries to raise its price, the other parking garages in the area keep their prices constant and it loses customers to the cheaper garages. However, when the parking garage lowers its price, the other garages almost always match the price reduction. Which type of oligopoly behavior best explains this situation? If the parking garage business has marginal costs that generally vary only a small amount, should it change the price it charges when its marginal costs change a little?

2. Most large banks charge the same or nearly the same prime interest rate. In fact, banks avoid changing the rate; they try to do it only when market conditions require an adjustment. When that happens, one of the major banks announces a change in its rate and other banks quickly follow suit. Is this an example of price leadership or the kinked demand curve? Explain.

BLR04

PART

4

Labor Markets and EARNINGS

CHAPTER

14 The Demand and Supply of Resources

MISCONCEPTION

Outsourcing is bad for the economy.

When U.S. jobs are outsourced, workers in the United States lose their jobs. People commonly think that this means outsourcing is bad for the economy, but that is misleading. Outsourced jobs are relocated from high-labor-cost areas to low-labor-cost areas. Often, a job lost to outsourcing creates more than one job in another country. In addition, outsourcing lowers the cost of manufacturing goods and providing services. Those lower costs translate into lower prices for consumers and streamlined production processes for businesses. The improved efficiency helps firms compete in the global economy. In this chapter, we will examine the demand and supply of resources throughout the economy. The outsourcing of jobs is a very visible result of these resource flows and an essential part of the market-economy process.

In earlier chapters, we have seen that profit-maximizing firms must decide how much to produce. For production to be successful, firms must combine the right amounts of labor and capital to maximize output while simultaneously holding down costs. Since labor often constitutes the largest share of the costs of production, we will begin by looking at the labor market. We will use the forces of supply and demand to illustrate the role of the labor market in the U.S. economy. We will then extend the lessons learned about labor into the markets for land and capital. In Chapter 15, we will expand our understanding of the labor market by examining income inequality, unemployment, discrimination, and poverty.

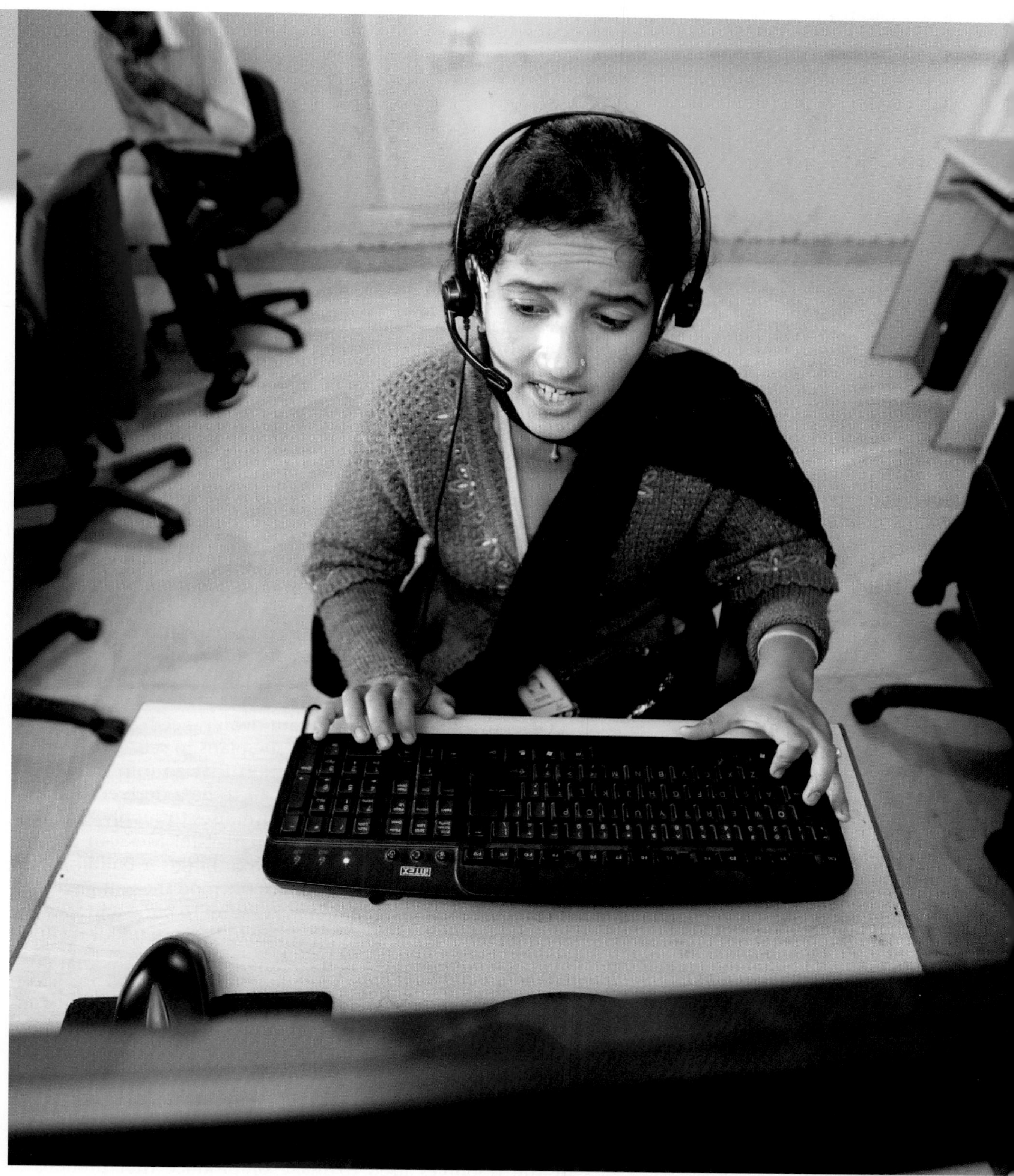

If jobs are relocated to low-labor-cost areas like rural India, is it good or bad for the economy?

BIG QUESTIONS

- What are the factors of production?
- Where does the demand for labor come from?
- Where does the supply of labor come from?
- What are the determinants of demand and supply in the labor market?
- What role do land and capital play in production?

What Are the Factors of Production?

Wages and salaries account for two-thirds of all the income generated by the U.S. economy. The remaining one-third of income goes to the owners of land and capital. Together, labor, land, and capital make up the factors of production, or the inputs used in producing goods and services.

Derived demand is the demand for an input used in the production process.

For instance, let's imagine that Sophia wants to open a Mexican restaurant named Agaves. Sophia will need a dining room staff, cooks, dishwashers, and managers to coordinate everyone else; these are the labor inputs. She also will need a physical location; this is the land input. Finally, she will need a building in which to operate, along with ovens and other kitchen equipment, seating and tableware, and a cash register; these are the capital inputs.

A lack of customers is an ominous sign for restaurant workers.

Of course, Sophia's restaurant won't need any inputs if there is no demand for the food she plans to sell. The demand for each of the factors of production that go into her restaurant (land, labor, and capital) is said to be a **derived demand** because the factors are inputs the firm uses to supply a good in another market—in this case, the market for Mexican cuisine. Let's say that Sophia secures the land, builds a building, and hires employees in order to produce the food she will serve. She is willing to spend a lot of money up front to build and staff the restaurant, because she expects there to be demand for the food her restaurant will make and serve.

Derived demand is not limited to the demand for a certain type of cuisine. For example, consumer demand for iPads causes Apple to demand the resources needed to make them. The switches, glass, memory, battery, and other parts have little value alone, but when assembled into an iPad they become a device that many people find very useful. Therefore, when economists speak of derived demand, they are differentiating between the demand for a product or service and the demand for the resources used to make or produce that product or service.

PRACTICE WHAT YOU KNOW

Derived Demand: Tip Income

Your friend waits tables 60 hours a week at a small restaurant. He is discouraged because he works hard but can't seem to make enough money to cover his bills. He complains that the restaurant does not have enough business and that is why he has to work so many hours just to make ends meet.

Question: As an economist, what advice would you give him?

Answer: Since labor is a derived demand, he should apply for a job at a more popular restaurant. Working at a place with more customers will help him earn more tip income.

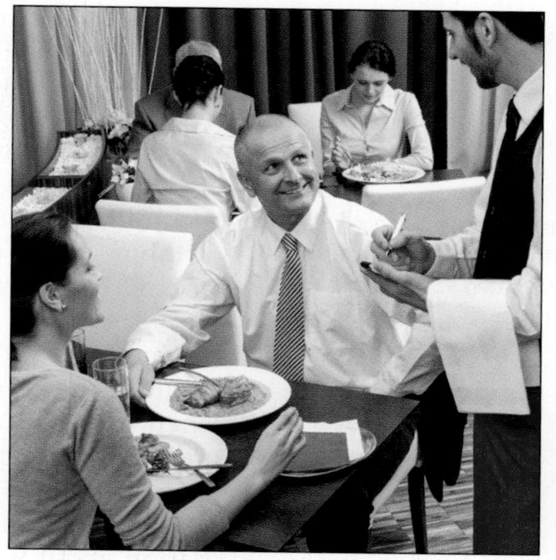

Want more tip income? Follow the crowd.

Where Does the Demand for Labor Come From?

As a student, you are probably hoping that one day your education will translate into tangible skills that employers will seek. As you choose a major, you might be thinking about potential earnings in different occupations. Have you ever wondered why there is so much variability in levels of salary and wages? For instance, economists generally earn more than elementary school teachers but less than engineers. Workers on night shifts earn more than those who do the same job during the day. And professional athletes and actors make much more for jobs that are not as essential as the work performed by janitors, construction workers, and nurses. In one respect, the explanation is surprisingly obvious: demand helps to regulate the labor market in much the same way that it helps to determine the prices of goods and services sold in the marketplace.

To understand why some people get paid more than others, we will explore the output of each worker, or what is known as the *marginal product of labor*. In fact, the value that each worker creates for a firm is highly correlated with the demand for labor. Then, to develop a more complete understanding of how the labor market works, we will examine the factors that influence labor demand.

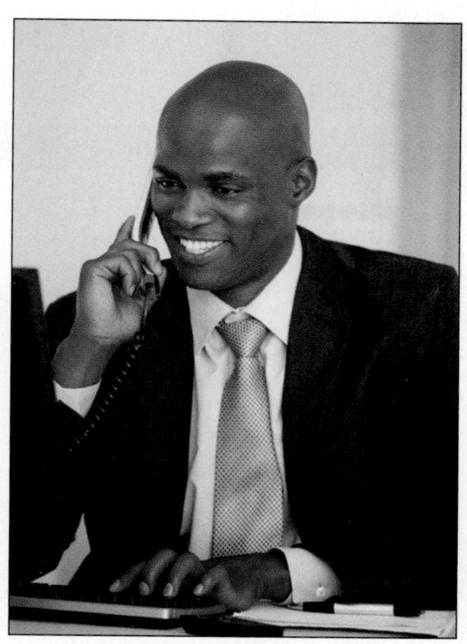

Why do economists generally earn more than elementary school teachers?

The Marginal Product of Labor

To gain a concrete appreciation for how labor demand is determined, let's look at the restaurant business—a market that is highly competitive. In Chapter 8, we saw that a firm determines how many workers to hire by comparing the output of labor with the wages the firm must pay. We will apply this analysis of production to the labor market in the restaurant business. Table 14.1 should look familiar to you; it highlights the key determinants of the labor hiring process.

The **marginal product of labor** is the change in output associated with adding one additional worker.

Let's work our way through the table. Column 1 lists the number of laborers, and column 2 reports the daily numbers of meals that can be produced with differing numbers of workers. Column 3 shows the **marginal product of labor**, or the change (Δ) in output associated with adding one additional worker. For instance, when the firm moves from three employees to four, output expands from 120 meals to 140 meals. The increase of 20 meals is the marginal product of labor for the fourth worker. Note that the values in column 3 decline as additional workers are added. Recall from Chapter 8 that when each successive worker adds less value, this is known as diminishing marginal product.

Marginal thinking

It is useful to know the marginal product of labor because this tells us how much each additional worker adds to the firm's output. Combining this information about worker productivity with the price the firm charges gives us a tool that we can use to explain how many workers the firm will hire. Suppose that Agaves charges $10 for each meal. When the firm multiplies the marginal product of labor in column 3 by the price it charges, $10 per meal, we see the *value of the marginal product* in column 4. The **value of the marginal product (VMP)** is the marginal product of an input multiplied by the price of the output it produces. The firm compares the gain in column 4 with the cost of achieving that gain—the wage that must be paid—in column 5. This reduces the hiring decision to a simple cost-benefit analysis in which the

The **value of the marginal product (VMP)** is the marginal product of an input multiplied by the price of the output it produces.

TABLE 14.1

Deciding How Many Laborers to Hire

(1) Labor (number of workers)	(2) Output (daily meals produced)	(3) Marginal product of labor	(4) Value of the marginal product of labor	(5) Wage (daily)	(6) Marginal profit
Formula:		Δ Output	Price × marginal product of labor		Value of the marginal product of labor − wage
0	0				
		50	$500	$100	$400
1	50				
		40	400	100	300
2	90				
		30	300	100	200
3	120				
		20	200	100	100
4	140				
		10	100	100	**0**
5	150				
		0	0	100	**−100**
6	150				

wage (column 5) is subtracted from the value of the marginal product (column 4) to determine the marginal profit (column 6) of each worker.

You can see from the green numbers that the marginal profit is positive for the first four workers. Therefore, the firm is better off hiring four workers. After that, the marginal profit is zero for the fifth worker, shown in black. The firm would be indifferent about hiring the fifth worker since the marginal cost of hiring that employee is equal to the marginal benefit. The marginal profit is negative for the sixth worker, shown in red. Therefore, the firm would not hire the sixth worker.

Figure 14.1 plots the value of the marginal product (VMP) from Table 14.1. Look at the curve: what do you see? Does it remind you of a demand curve? The VMP is the firm's willingness to pay for each laborer; in other words, it is the firm's labor demand curve.

The VMP curve slopes downward due to diminishing marginal product—which we see in column 3 of Table 14.1. As long as the value of the marginal product is higher than the market wage, shown as \$100 a day, the firm will hire more workers. For example, when the firm hires the first worker, the VMP is \$500. This amount easily exceeds the market wage of hiring an extra worker and creates a marginal profit of \$400. We illustrate this additional profit in Figure 14.1 with the longest green arrow under the demand curve and above the market wage. The second, third, and fourth workers generate additional profit of \$300, \$200, and \$100 respectively, represented by the progressively smaller green arrows. As the value of the marginal product declines, there will be a point at which hiring additional workers will cause profits to fall. This occurs because labor is subject to diminishing marginal product; eventually, the value created by hiring additional labor falls below the market wage.

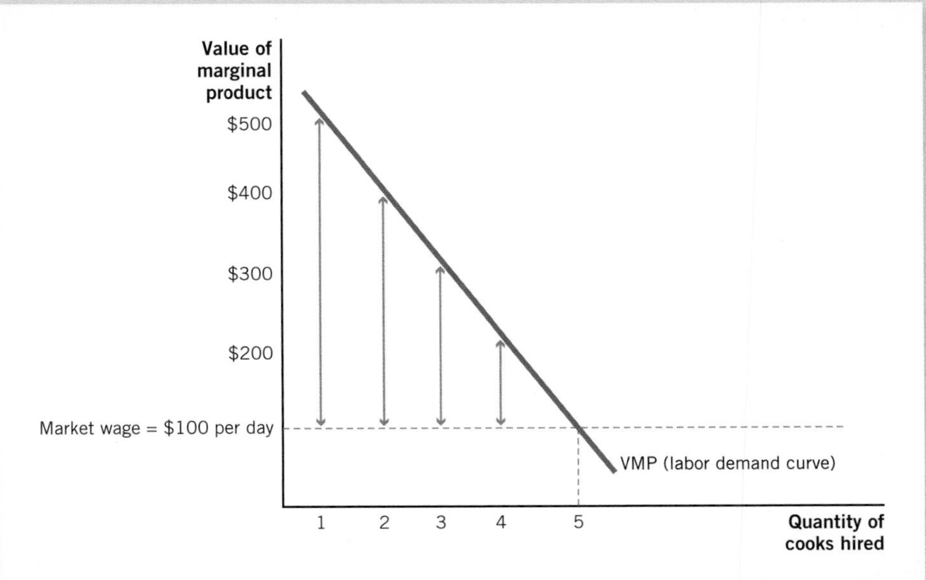

FIGURE 14.1

The Value of the Marginal Product

The firm will hire workers as long as the value of the marginal product (VMP) is greater than the wage it must pay. The value of the marginal product is the firm's labor demand curve. When the value of the marginal product is higher than the market wage, the firm will hire more workers. However, since labor is subject to diminishing marginal product, eventually the value created by hiring additional labor falls below the market wage.

Changes in the Demand for Labor

We know that customers desire good food and that restaurants like Agaves hire workers to satisfy their customers. Figure 14.2 illustrates the relationship between the demand for restaurant meals and restaurant workers. Notice that the demand for labor is downward-sloping; this tells us that at high wages Agaves will use fewer workers and that at lower wages it will hire more workers. We illustrate this with the orange arrow that moves along the original demand curve (D_1). Recall from Chapter 3 that this relationship is known as a change in the quantity demanded. In addition, the demand for workers depends on, or is derived from, the number of customers who place orders. So changes in the restaurant business as a whole can influence the number of workers that the restaurant hires. For example, if the number of customers increases, the demand for workers will increase, or shift to D_2. Likewise, if the number of customers decreases, the demand for workers will decrease, or shift to the left to D_3.

Two primary factors shift labor demand: a change in demand for the product that the firm produces, and a change in the cost of producing that product.

Changes in Demand for the Product the Firm Produces

A restaurant's demand for workers is derived from the firm's desire to make a profit. Because the firm is primarily interested in making a profit, it only hires workers when the value of the marginal product of labor is higher than the cost of hiring labor. Consider Agaves. If a rival Mexican restaurant closes down, many of its customers will likely switch to Agaves. Then Agaves will

FIGURE 14.2

The Labor Demand Curve

When the wages of workers change, the quantity of workers demanded, shown by the gold arrow moving along the demand curve, also changes. Changes that shift the entire labor demand curve, shown by the gray horizontal arrows, include changes in demand for the product that the firm produces, in labor productivity, or in innovation.

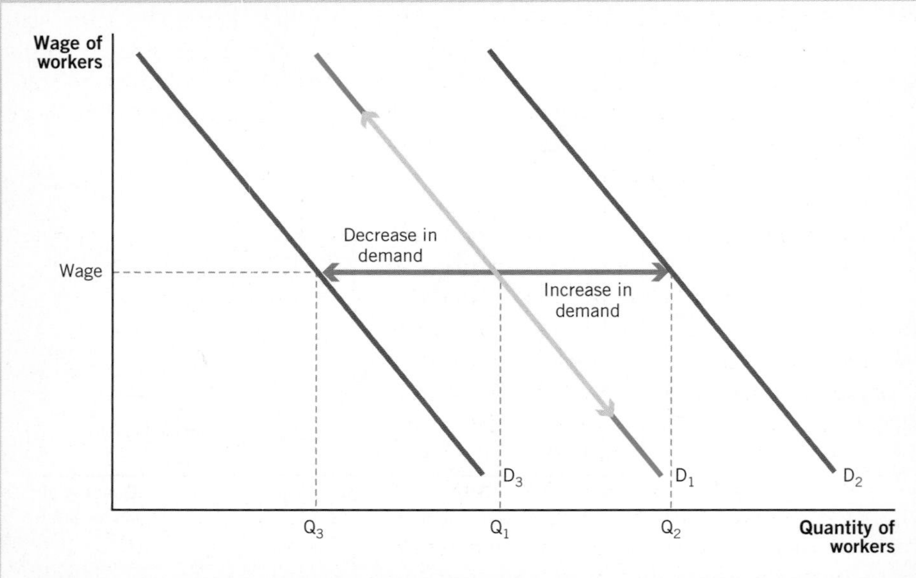

need to prepare more meals, which will cause the entire demand curve for cooks, table clearers, and waitstaff to shift outward to D_2.

A machine at McDonald's helps to fill the drink orders.

Changes in Cost

A change in the cost of production can sometimes be positive, such as when a new technology makes production less expensive. It can also be negative, such as when an increase in the cost of a needed raw material makes production more expensive.

In terms of a positive change for the firm, technology can act as a substitute for workers. For example, microwave ovens enable restaurants to prepare the same number of meals with fewer workers. The same is true with the growing trend of using conveyor belts and automated systems to help prepare meals or even serve them. Therefore, changes in technology can lower a firm's demand for workers.

In the short run, substituting technology for workers may seem like a bad outcome for the workers and for society in general. However, in the long run that is not typically the case. Consider how the demand for lumberjacks in the forestry business is affected by technological advances. As timber companies invest in new harvesting technology, they can replace traditional logging jobs, which are dangerous and inefficient, with equipment that is safer to use and more efficient. By deploying the new technology, the lumber companies can cut down trees faster and more safely, and the workers are freed up to work in other parts of the economy. In the short run, that means fewer timber jobs; those workers must find employment elsewhere. Admittedly, this adjustment is painful for the workers involved, and they often have difficulty finding jobs that pay as well as the job that they lost. However, the new equipment requires trained, highly skilled operators who can fell more trees in a shorter period than traditional lumberjacks can. As a result, harvester operators have a higher marginal product of labor and can command higher wages.

For every harvester operator employed at a higher wage, there are perhaps ten traditional lumberjacks displaced and in need of a job. But consider what happens after the short-run job losses. Overall production rises because while one worker harvests trees, the nine other workers are forced to move into related fields or do something entirely different. It might take some of these displaced workers many years to find new work, but when they eventually do, society benefits in the long run. What once required ten workers to produce now takes only one, and the nine other workers are able to complete other jobs and grow the economy in different ways.

One John Deere 1270D harvester can replace ten lumberjacks.

PRACTICE WHAT YOU KNOW

Value of the Marginal Product of Labor: Flower Barrettes

Question: Penny can make five flower barrettes each hour. She works eight hours each day. Penny is paid $75.00 a day. The firm can sell the barrettes for $1.99 each. What is Penny's value of the marginal product of labor? What is the barrette firm's marginal profit from hiring her?

Answer: In eight hours, Penny can make 40 barrettes. Since each barrette sells for $1.99, her value of the marginal product of labor, or VMP_{labor} is 40 × $1.99, or $79.60. Since her VMP_{labor} is greater than the daily wage she receives, the marginal profit from hiring her is $79.60 − $75, or $4.60.

How many flower barrettes could you make in an hour?

To summarize, if labor becomes more productive, the VMP curve shifts to the right, driving up both wages and employment. This is what occurs with the demand for harvester operators. There is the potential for substitution as well, causing the demand for traditional labor to fall. This is what has happened to traditional lumberjack jobs, leading to a decrease in those workers' wages.

Where Does the Supply of Labor Come From?

In this section, we examine the connection between the wage rate and the number of workers who are willing to supply their services to employers. Since workers also value leisure, the supply curve is not always directly related to the wage rate. Indeed, at high wage levels some workers may desire to cut back the number of hours that they work. Other factors that influence the labor supply include the changing composition of the workforce, migration, and immigration; we explore these factors below as well.

The Labor-Leisure Trade-off

People work because they need to earn a living. While it is certainly true that many workers enjoy their jobs, this does not mean they would work for nothing. In other words, while many people experience satisfaction in their work, most of us have other interests, obligations, and goals. As a result, the supply of labor depends both on the wage that is offered and on how individuals want to use their time. This is known as the *labor-leisure trade-off*.

Trade-offs

In our society today, most individuals must work to meet their basic needs. However, once those needs are met, a worker might be more inclined to use his or her time in leisure. Would higher wages induce an employee to give up leisure and work more hours? The answer is both yes and no!

At higher wage rates, workers may be willing to work more hours, or substitute labor for leisure. This is known as the **substitution effect**. One way to think about this is to note that higher wages make leisure time more expensive, because the opportunity cost of enjoying more leisure means giving up more income. For instance, suppose that Emeril is a short-order cook at Agaves. He works 40 hours at $10 per hour and can also work 4 hours overtime at the same wage. If Emeril decides to work the overtime, he ends up working 44 hours and earns $440. In that case, he substitutes more labor for less leisure.

The **substitution effect** occurs when laborers work more hours at higher wages, substituting labor for leisure.

Opportunity cost

But at higher wage rates, other workers may work fewer hours, or substitute leisure for labor. This is known as the **income effect**. Leisure is a normal good (see Chapter 3), so as income rises some workers may use their additional income to demand more leisure. As a consequence, at high income levels the income effect may overwhelm the substitution effect and cause the supply curve to bend backward. For example, suppose that Rachael chooses to work overtime for $10 per hour. Her total pay (like Emeril's) will be $\$10 \times 44$, or $440. If her wage rises to $11, she may continue to work the overtime at a higher wage. However, if she does not work overtime, she will earn as much as she earned before the wage increase ($\$11 \times 40 = \$440$), and she might choose to discontinue the overtime. In this case, Rachael enjoys more leisure.

The **income effect** occurs when laborers work fewer hours at higher wages, using their additional income to demand more leisure.

Figure 14.3 shows what can happen to the labor supply curve at high wage levels. When the supply of labor responds directly to wage increases, the wage rises progressively from W_1 to W_2 to W_3, and the number of hours worked increases from Q_1 to Q_2 to Q_3, along the curve labeled S_{normal}. However, at high wage rates workers might experience diminishing marginal utility from the additional income and, thus, might value increased leisure time more than increased income. In this situation, workers might choose to work less. When this occurs, the normal supply curve bends backward beyond W_2 because as the wage goes up, the hours worked go down.

The **backward-bending labor supply curve** occurs when workers value additional leisure more than additional income. This happens when the income effect is large enough to offset the substitution effect that typically causes individuals to work more when the wage rate is higher. Since most workers do not reach wage level W_2 (that is, a wage at which they might begin to value leisure more than labor), we will draw the supply curve as upward-sloping throughout the chapter. Nevertheless, it is important to recognize that the direct relationship we normally observe does not always hold.

A **backward-bending labor supply curve** occurs when workers value additional leisure more than additional income.

Changes in the Supply of Labor

If we hold the wage rate constant, a number of additional factors determine the supply of labor. Immigration, migration, demographic shifts in society, and job characteristics and opportunities all play important roles in determining

FIGURE 14.3

The Labor Supply Curve

At high wage levels, the income effect may become larger than the substitution effect and cause the labor supply curve to bend backward. The backward-bending supply curve occurs when additional leisure time becomes more valuable than additional income.

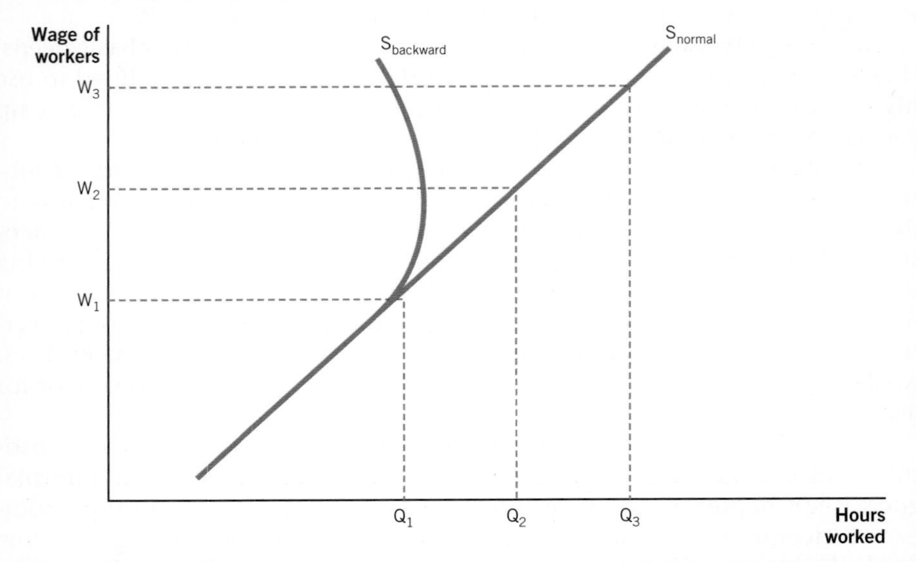

the number of workers who are willing to perform various jobs. In this section, we look beyond the wage rate to other forces that govern the supply of labor.

Turning to Figure 14.4, the gold arrow along S_1 shows that the quantity of workers increases when the wage rate rises. But what will cause a shift in the supply curve? Three primary factors affect the supply curve: other employment opportunities, the changing composition of the workforce, and migration and immigration.

Other Employment Opportunities

The supply of workers for any given job depends on the employment opportunities and prevailing wage in related labor markets. Let's consider the supply of labor at Agaves. Notice that the supply curve for labor in Figure 14.4 is upward-sloping; this tells us that if Agaves offers higher wages, more workers, such as table clearers, would be willing to work there. We illustrate this situation with the gold arrow that moves along the original supply curve (S_1). Moreover, the supply of table clearers also depends on a number of nonwage factors. Since table clearers are generally young and largely unskilled, the number of laborers willing to work is influenced by the prevailing wages in similar jobs. For instance, if the wages of baggers at local grocery stores increase, some of the table clearers at Agaves will decide to bag at local grocery stores instead. This will decrease the supply of table clearers and cause a leftward shift to S_3. If the wages of baggers were to fall, the supply of table clearers would increase, or shift to the right to S_2. These shifts reflect the fact that when jobs that require comparable skills have different wage

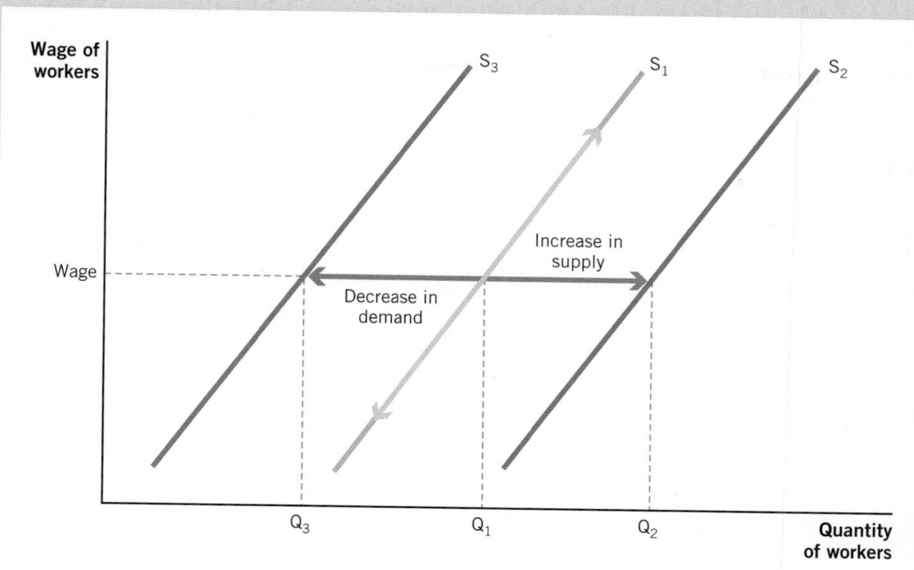

FIGURE 14.4

The Labor Supply Curve

A change in the quantity supplied occurs when the wages of workers changes. This causes a movement along the supply curve S_1, shown by the gold arrow. Changes in the supply of labor (the quantity of workers), shown by the gray horizontal arrows, can occur due to immigration, migration, demographic shifts in the workforce, and other employment opportunities.

rates, the number of workers willing to supply labor for the lower-wage job will shrink and the number willing to supply labor for the better-paid job will grow.

The Changing Composition of the Workforce

Over the last 30 years, the labor force participation rate (as measured by the female/male ratio) has increased significantly in most developed countries. Among that group, as measured by the United Nations Development Programme, the United States saw its female/male ratio rise from 66% to 81%, Switzerland from 67% to 82%, and New Zealand from 65% to 82%. Overall, there are many more women employees in the workforce today than there were a generation ago, and the supply of workers in many occupations has expanded significantly as a result.

Immigration and Migration

Demographic factors, including immigration and migration, also play a crucial role in the supply of labor. For example, immigration—both legal and illegal—increases the available supply of workers by a significant amount each year.

In 2010, over one million people from foreign countries entered the United States through legal channels and gained permission to seek employment. Today, there are over 40 million legal immigrants in the United States. To put this in perspective, the United States accepts more legal immigrants as permanent residents than the total number of legal immigrants accepted into all other nations in the world combined. In addition, illegal immigrants account for close to 20 million workers in the United States, many of whom enter the country to work as hotel maids, janitors, and fruit pickers. Every time a state passes a tough immigration law, businesses in food and beverage, agriculture, and construction protest because they need inexpensive labor to remain competitive, and U.S. citizens are reluctant to work these jobs. Many states have wrestled with the issue, but policies that address illegal immigration remain controversial and the solutions are difficult. The states need the cheap labor but don't want to pay additional costs such as medical care, as well as schooling for the illegal immigrants' children.

For the purposes of this discussion, we will consider migration to be the process of moving from one place to another within the United States. Migration patterns also affect the labor supply. Although the U.S. population grows at an annual rate of approximately 3%, there are significant regional

ECONOMICS IN THE MEDIA

Immigration

A Day without a Mexican

This offbeat film from 2004 asks a simple question: what would happen to California's economy if all the Mexicans in the state suddenly disappeared? The answer: the state economy would come to a halt.

Indeed, the loss of the Mexican labor force would have a dramatic impact on California's labor market. For example, the film makes fun of affluent Californians who must do without low-cost workers to take care of their yards and homes. It also showcases a farm owner whose produce is ready to be picked without any migrant workers to do the job.

In addition, the film adeptly points out that migrants from Mexico add a tremendous amount of value to the local economy through their purchases as well as their labor. One inspired scene depicts a television commercial for a "disappearance sale" put on by a local business after it realizes that most of its regular customers are gone.

A Day without a Mexican illustrates both sides of the labor relationship at work. Because demand and supply are inseparably linked, the disappearance of all of the Mexican workers creates numerous voids that require serious adjustments for the economy.

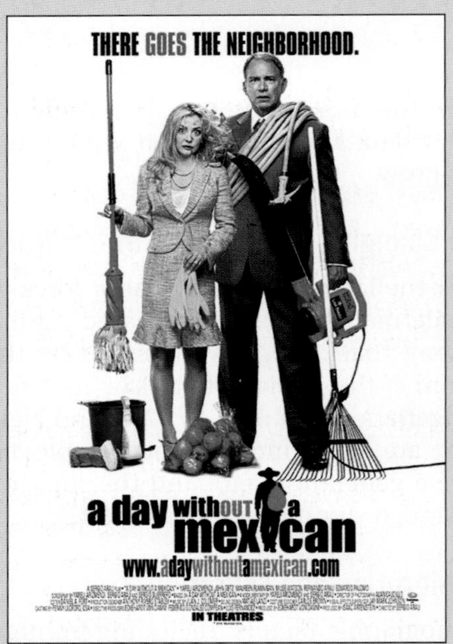

What would happen to an economy if one-third of the workers suddenly disappeared?

differences. Indeed, large population influxes lead to marked regional changes in the demand for labor and the supply of people looking for work. According to the U.S. Census Bureau, in 2010 the 10 fastest-growing states were in the South or West, with some states adding as much as 4% to their population in a single year. States in these areas provided 84% of the nation's population growth from 2000 to 2010, with Nevada, Utah, North Carolina, Idaho, and Texas all adding at least 20% to their populations.

It is worth noting that statewide data can hide significant localized changes. For example, census data from 2010 indicate that a number of counties experienced 50% or more population growth between 2000 and 2010. The biggest population gain was in Kendall County, Illinois, a far-flung suburb of Chicago that grew by nearly 100% between censuses. The county has been transitioning from an agricultural area to a bedroom community. Most of the fastest-growing counties are, like Kendall, relatively distant suburbs of major metropolitan areas. These are areas where new homes are available at comparatively reasonable prices.

PRACTICE WHAT YOU KNOW

The Labor Supply Curve: What Would You Do with a Big Raise?

Question: Your friend is concerned about his uncle, who just received a big raise. Your friend doesn't understand why his uncle wants to take time off from his job to travel. Can you help him understand why his uncle might want to cut back on his hours?

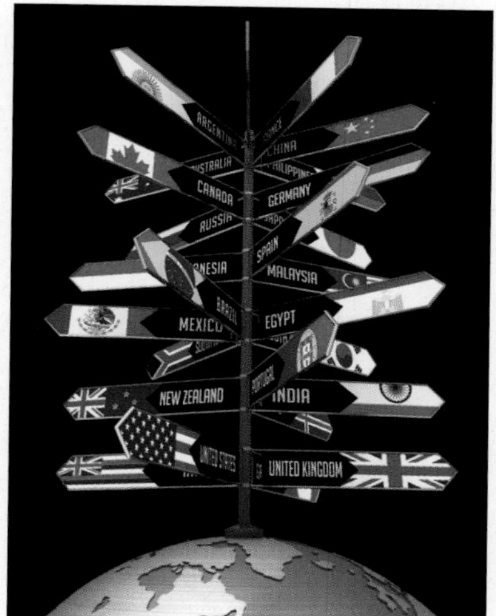

Would you travel the world?

Answer: Ordinarily, we think of the labor supply curve as upward-sloping. When this is the case, higher wages translate into more hours worked and less leisure time. However, when the wage rate becomes high enough, some workers choose to substitute leisure for labor because they feel that enjoying free time is more valuable than earning more money. When this happens, the labor supply curve bends backward, and the worker spends fewer hours working as his wage rises. Your friend's uncle is reflecting this tendency.

What Are the Determinants of Demand and Supply in the Labor Market?

In earlier chapters, we have seen how markets reconcile the forces of demand and supply through pricing. Now that we have considered the forces that govern demand and supply in the labor market, we are ready to see how the equilibrium wage is established. This will enable us to examine the labor market in greater detail and identify what causes shortages and surpluses of labor, why outsourcing occurs, and what happens when there is a single buyer. The goal of this section is to provide a rich set of examples that help you become comfortable using demand and supply curves to understand how the labor market operates.

How Does the Market for Labor Reach Equilibrium?

We can think about wages as the price at which workers are willing to "rent" their time to employers. Turning to Figure 14.5, we see that at wages above equilibrium (W_E), the supply of workers willing to rent their time exceeds the

FIGURE 14.5

Equilibrium in the Labor Market

At high wages (W_{high}), a surplus of workers exists. This drives the wage rate down until the supply of workers and the demand for workers reach the equilibrium. At low wages (W_{low}), a shortage occurs. The shortage forces the wage rate up until the equilibrium wage is reached and the shortage disappears.

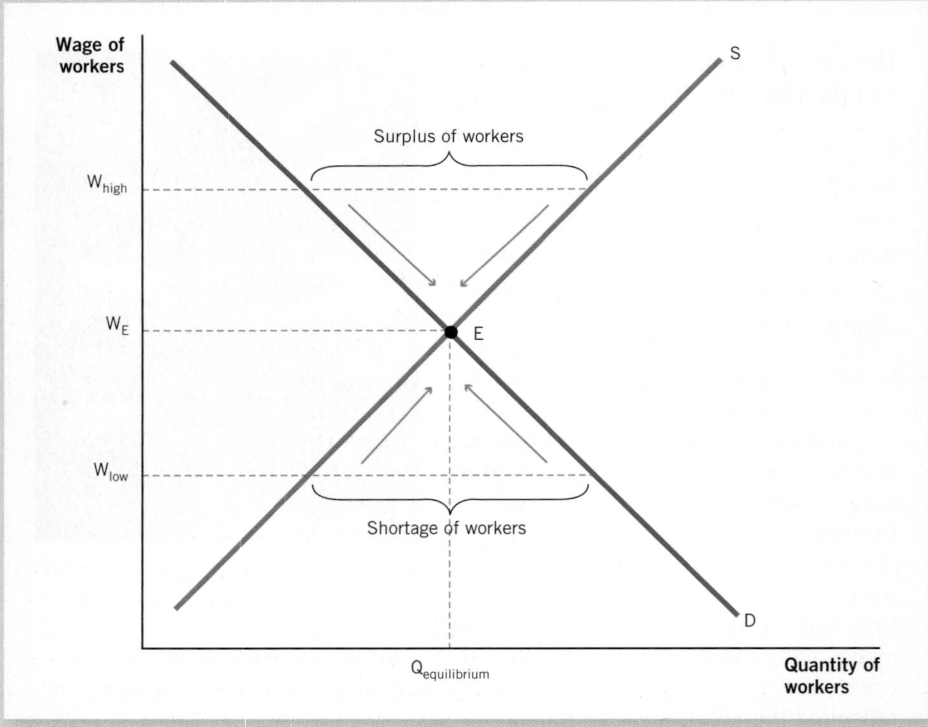

demand for that time. This causes a surplus of available workers. The surplus, in turn, places downward pressure on wages. As wages drop, fewer workers are willing to rent their time to employers. When wages drop to the equilibrium wage, the surplus of workers is eliminated; at that point, the number of workers willing to work in that profession at that wage is exactly equal to the number of job openings that exist at that wage.

A similar process guides the labor market toward equilibrium from low wages. At wages below the equilibrium, the demand for labor exceeds the available supply. The shortage forces firms to offer higher wages in order to attract workers. As a result, wages rise until the shortage is eliminated at the equilibrium wage.

ECONOMICS IN THE REAL WORLD

Where Are the Nurses?

The United States is experiencing a shortage of nurses. A stressful job with long hours, nursing requires years of training. As baby boomers age, demands for nursing care are expected to rise. At the same time, the existing pool of nurses is rapidly aging and nearing retirement. By some estimates, the shortage of nurses in America will approach one million by 2020. This makes nursing the #1 job in the country in terms of growth prospects, according to the Bureau of Labor Statistics.

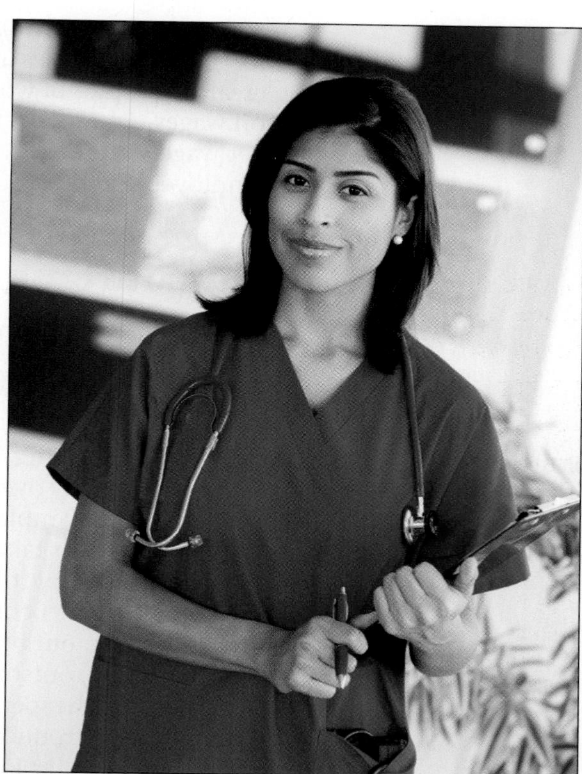

Entering an occupation with a shortage of workers will result in higher pay.

However, economists are confident that the shortage of nurses will disappear long before 2020. After all, a shortage creates upward pressure on wages. In this case, rising wages also signal that nursing services are in high demand and that wages will continue to rise. This will lead to a surge in nursing school applications and will also cause some practicing nurses to postpone retirement.

Since the training process takes two or more years to complete, the labor market for nurses won't return to equilibrium immediately. The nursing shortage will persist for a few years until the quantity of nurses supplied to the market increases. During that time, many of the tasks that nurses traditionally carry out—such as taking patients' vital signs—will likely be shifted to nursing assistants or technicians.

Economics tells us that the combination of more newly trained nurses entering the market and the transfer of certain nursing services to assistants and technicians will eventually cause the nursing shortage to disappear. Remember that when a market is out of balance, forces are acting on it to restore it to equilibrium. ✷

Change and Equilibrium in the Labor Market

Now that we have seen how labor markets find an equilibrium, let's see what happens when the demand or supply changes. Figure 14.6 contains two graphs: panel (a) shows a shift in labor demand, and panel (b) shows a shift in labor supply. In both cases, the equilibrium wage and the equilibrium quantity of workers employed adjust accordingly.

Let's start with a shift in labor demand, shown in panel (a). Imagine that the demand for medical care increases due to an aging population and that, as a result, the demand for nurses (as we noted in the Economics in the Real World feature) increases and the demand curve shifts from D_1 to D_2. This creates a shortage of workers equal to $Q_3 - Q_1$. The shortage places upward pressure on wages, which increase from W_1 to W_2. As wages rise, nursing becomes more attractive as a profession; additional people choose to enter the field, and existing nurses decide to work longer hours or postpone retirement. Thus, the number of nurses employed rises from Q_1 to Q_2. Eventually, the wage settles at E_2 and the number of nurses employed reaches Q_2.

Turning to panel (b), we see what happens when the supply of nurses increases. As additional nurses are certified, the overall supply shifts from S_1 to S_2. This creates a surplus of workers equal to $Q_3 - Q_1$, which places downward pressure on wages. As a result, the wage rate falls from W_1 to W_2. Eventually, the market wage settles at E_2, the new equilibrium point, and the number of nurses employed reaches Q_2.

Outsourcing

Why would a firm hire someone from outside if it has a qualified employee nearby? This practice, known as *outsourcing*, has gotten a lot of attention in recent years. In this section, we explain how outsourcing works, why companies engage in it, and how it affects the labor market for workers.

Outsourcing of labor occurs when a firm shifts jobs to an outside company, usually overseas, where the cost of labor is lower.

The **outsourcing of labor** occurs when a firm shifts jobs to an outside company, usually overseas, where the cost of labor is lower. In the publishing industry, for example, page make-up (also known as composition) is often done overseas to take advantage of lower labor costs. This outsourcing has been facilitated by the Internet, which eliminates the shipping delays and costs that used to constitute a large part of the business. Today, a qualified worker can lay out book pages anywhere in the world.

Sometimes, outsourcing occurs when firms relocate within the country to capitalize on cheaper labor or lower-cost resources. For example, when General Motors introduced its Saturn division in 1985, it built an entirely new production facility in Tennessee, where wages were substantially lower than those in Detroit.

When countries outsource, their pool of potential workers expands. But whether a labor expansion is driven by outsourcing, which is an external factor, or by an increase in the domestic supply of workers, those who are already employed in that particular industry find that they earn less. As a result, a rise in unemployment occurs in the occupation that can be outsourced.

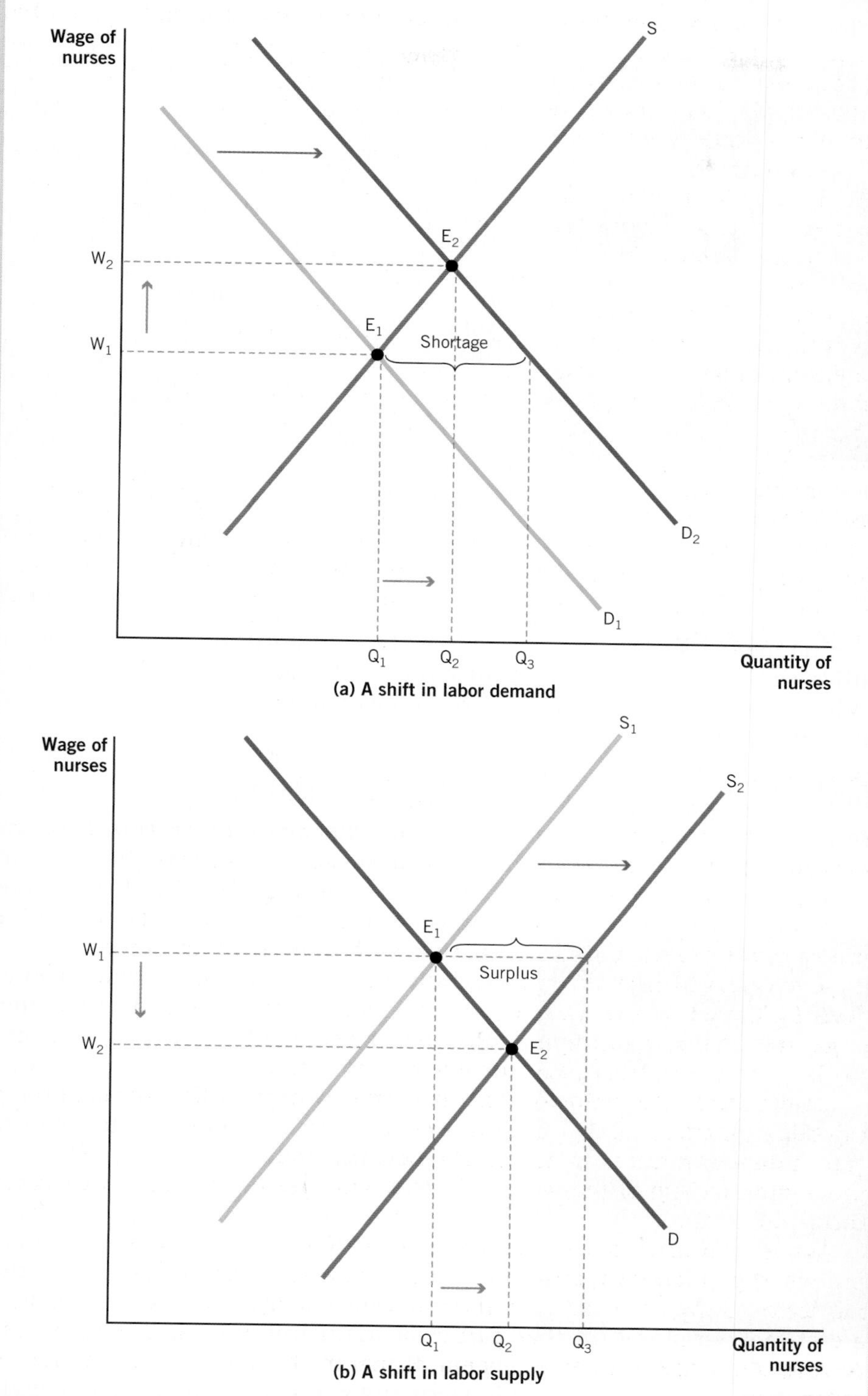

FIGURE 14.6

Shifting the Labor Market Equilibrium

In panel (a), the demand for nurses increases. This creates a shortage of workers equal to Q_3–Q_1, which leads to a higher equilibrium wage (E_2) and quantity of nurses employed (Q_2) than before. In panel (b), the supply of nurses increases. This leads to a surplus of workers equal to $Q_3 - Q_1$, and causes the equilibrium wage to fall (E_2) and the number of nurses employed to rise (Q_2).

ECONOMICS IN THE REAL WORLD

Pregnancy Becomes the Latest Job to Be Outsourced to India

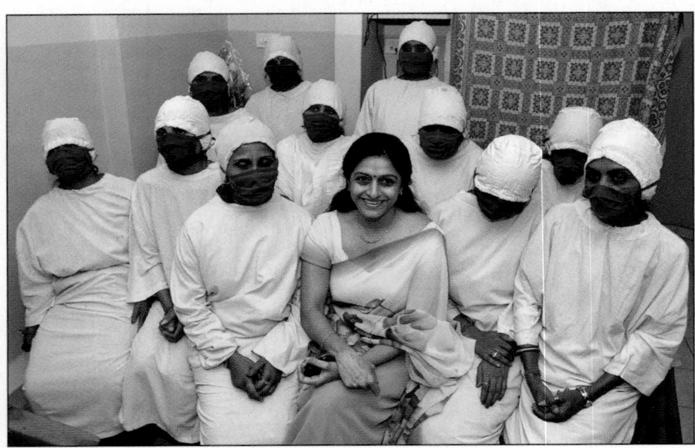

Kaival Hospital in Anand, India, matches infertile couples with local women, such as these surrogate mothers.

When we think of outsourced jobs, we generally think of call centers, not childbirth. But a growing number of infertile couples have outsourced pregnancy to surrogate mothers in India. The process involves surrogate mothers being impregnated with eggs that have been fertilized in vitro with sperm taken from couples who are unable to carry a pregnancy to term on their own. Commercial surrogacy—"wombs for rent"—is a growing industry in India. While no reliable numbers track such pregnancies nationwide, doctors work with surrogates in virtually every major city in India.

In India, surrogate mothers earn roughly $5,000 for a nine-month commitment. This amount is the equivalent of what could take 10 or more years to earn in many low-skill jobs there. Couples typically pay approximately $10,000 for all of the costs associated with the pregnancy, which is a mere fraction of what it would cost in the United States or Europe.

Commercial surrogacy has been legal in India since 2002, as it is in many other countries, including the United States. However, the difference is that India is the leader in making it a viable industry rather than a highly personal and private fertility treatment. ✷

The Global Implications of Outsourcing in the Short Run

Recall our chapter-opening misconception that outsourcing is bad for the economy. Many people hold that opinion because when they think of outsourcing they immediately imagine the jobs that are lost in the short run. However, the reality is more complex. Outsourced jobs are not lost; they are relocated from high-labor-cost areas to low-labor-cost areas. Outsourcing also creates benefits for firms in the form of lower production costs. The lower costs translate into lower prices for consumers and also help the firms that outsource to compete in the global economy.

The Mercedes-Benz plant near Tuscaloosa, Alabama, illustrates that outsourcing is more than just a one-way street.

Outsourcing need not cost the United States jobs. Consider what happens when foreign countries outsource their production to the United States. For example, the German auto manufacturer Mercedes-Benz currently has many of its cars built in Alabama. If you were an assembly line worker in Germany who had spent a lifetime making cars for Mercedes, you would likely be upset if your job was outsourced to North America. You would feel just like the American technician who loses a job to someone in India or the software writer who is replaced by a worker in China. Outsourcing always produces a job winner and a job loser. In the case of foreign outsourcing to the United States, employment in this country rises. In fact, the Mercedes-Benz plant in Alabama employs more than 3,000 workers. Those jobs were transferred to the United States because the company felt that it would be more profitable to hire American workers and make the vehicles in the United States rather than constructing them in Germany and shipping them across the Atlantic.

Figure 14.7 shows how outsourcing by foreign firms helps to increase U.S. labor demand. In panel (a), we see the job loss and lower wages that occur in Germany when jobs are outsourced to the United States. As the demand for labor in Germany falls from D_1 to D_2, wages drop to W_2 and employment declines to Q_2. Panel (b) illustrates the corresponding increase in demand for U.S. labor in Alabama. As demand shifts from D_1 to D_2, wages rise to W_2 and employment rises to Q_2.

Since each nation will experience outsourcing flows out of and into the country, it is impossible to say anything definitive about the overall impact of outsourcing on labor in the short run. However, it is highly unlikely that workers who lose high-paying jobs toward the end of their working lives will be able to find other jobs that pay equally well.

The Global Implications of Outsourcing in the Long Run

Although we see mixed results for outsourcing in the short run, we can say that in the long run outsourcing benefits domestic consumers and producers. In fact, outsourcing is a key component in international trade. In earlier chapters, we have seen that trade creates value. When companies and even countries specialize, they become more efficient. The efficiency gains, or cost savings, help producers to expand production. In the absence of trade barriers, lower costs benefit consumers in domestic and international markets through lower prices, and the outsourcing of jobs provides the income for foreign workers to be able to purchase domestic imports. Therefore, the mutually interdependent nature of international trade enhances overall social welfare.

Trade creates value

FIGURE 14.7

Shifting the Labor Market Equilibrium

Outsourcing creates more demand in one market at the expense of the other. In panel (a), the demand for German labor declines from D_1 to D_2, leading to lower wages and less employment. Panel (b) shows the increase in the demand for labor from D_1 to D_2 in Alabama. This leads to higher wages and more employment.

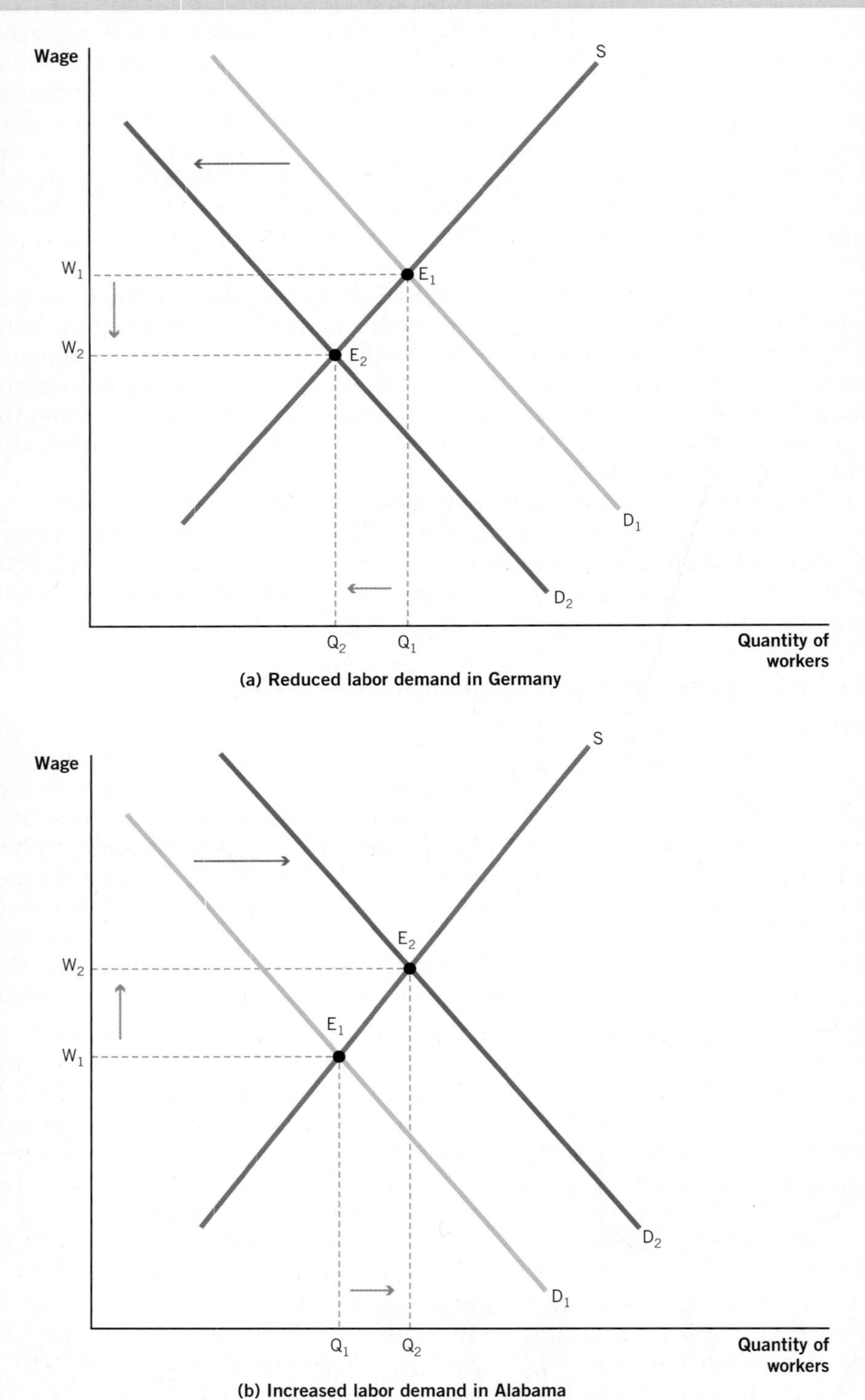

Outsourcing

ECONOMICS IN THE MEDIA

Outsourced

In this film from 2006, an American novelty products salesman from Seattle heads to India to train his replacement after his entire department is outsourced.

Some of the funniest scenes in this charming movie occur in the call center. The Indian workers speak fluent English but lack familiarity with American customs and sensibilities, so they often seem very awkward. In one memorable phone call, an American caller becomes irate when he learns that the product he is ordering was not made in the United States. He gives the voice on the other end of the line an earful about the loss of jobs in America. However, the call center supervisor devises a clever tactic to convince the disgruntled customer to buy the product despite his objections. She tells him that a manufacturer in the United States offers the same product for $20 more. He pauses and after some thought decides that he would rather buy the cheaper, foreign-made product.

Because *Outsourced* humanizes the foreign workers who benefit from outsourced domestic jobs, we learn to appreciate how outsourcing affects consumers, producers, domestic workers, and foreign laborers.

Outsourcing can connect different cultures in positive ways.

Monopsony

In looking at supply, demand, and equilibrium in the labor market, we have assumed that the market for labor is competitive. But that is not always the case. Sometimes, the labor market has only a few buyers or sellers who are able to capture market power. One extreme form of market power is **monopsony**, which occurs when a only single buyer exists. Like a monopolist, a monopsonist has a great deal of market power. As a consequence, the output in the labor market will favor a monopsonist whenever one is present.

Monopsony
is a situation in which there is only one buyer.

In Chapter 10, we examined how a monopolist behaves. Compared to a firm in a competitive market, the monopolist charges a higher price for the product it sells. Likewise, a monopsonist in the labor market can leverage its market power. Because it is the only firm hiring, it can pay its workers less. Isolated college towns are a good example. Workers who wish to live in such college towns often find that almost all the available jobs are through the college. Since it is the chief provider of jobs, it is said to have a monopsony in the labor market. The college can use its market power to hire many local workers at low wage levels.

ECONOMICS IN THE REAL WORLD

Pay and Performance in Major League Baseball

What is the correlation between winning and revenues?

Gerald Scully was the first sports economist. In his seminal work, "Pay and Performance in Major League Baseball," published in 1974 in the *American Economic Review,* Scully used economic analysis to determine the value of the marginal product that each player produced during the season. Scully's work was important because at that time each player's contract had a "reserve clause" stating that the player belonged to the team for his entire career unless he was traded or released.

If a player was unhappy with his contract, his only option was to withdraw from playing. Since most players could not make more than they were earning as baseball players in their next-most-productive job, the teams knew that the players would stay for the wage that the team was willing to pay. Therefore, under the reserve clause each team was a monopsonist. The teams used their market power to suppress wages and increase their profits.

In this context, Scully's work changed everything. He used two baseball statistics—slugging percentage for hitters, and the strikeout-to-walk ratio for pitchers—to evaluate the players' performance and then estimate how much player performance affected winning. Next he examined the correlation between winning and revenues, which enabled him to estimate how many dollars of revenue each player generated for his team. The results were stunning. The top players at that time earned about $100,000 per season but generated nearly $1,000,000 in revenue for their teams, or approximately 10 times more than they were being paid. However, since each player was tied to a particular team through the reserve clause, no matter how good the player was he lacked the leverage to bargain for higher wages.

Scully's work played a key role in the court decisions of two players, Andy Messersmith and Dave McNally, whose cases led to the repeal of the reserve clause in 1975. The reserve clause was struck down because the practice was deemed anti-competitive. Today, because players have gained limited free agency, salaries have steadily increased. Top professional baseball players can earn over $30 million a year, and the average salary is slightly more than $3 million. ✳

Why Do Some Workers Make More Than Others?

While most workers generally spend 35 to 40 hours a week at work, the amount they earn varies dramatically. Table 14.2 presents a number of simple questions that illustrate why some workers make more than others.

The table shows how demand and supply determine wages in a variety of settings. Workers with a high-value marginal product of labor invariably earn more than those with lower-value marginal product of labor. It is important to note that working an "essential" job does not guarantee a high income. Instead, the highest incomes are reserved for jobs that have high demand and a low supply of workers. In other words, our preconceived notions of fairness take a backseat to the underlying market forces that govern pay. In the next chapter, we will consider many additional factors that determine wages, including wage discrimination.

TABLE 14.2

Why Some Workers Make More than Others

Question	Answer
Why do economists generally earn more than elementary school teachers?	Supply is the key. There are fewer qualified economists than certified elementary school teachers. Therefore, the equilibrium wage in economics is higher than it is in elementary education. It's also important to note that demand factors may be part of the explanation. The value of the marginal product of labor of economists is generally higher than that of most elementary school teachers since many economists work in industry.
Why do people who work the night shift earn more than those who do the same job during the day?	Again, supply is the key. Fewer people are willing to work at night, so the wage necessary to attract labor to perform the job must be higher. (That is, night shift workers earn what is called a compensating differential, which we discuss in Chapter 15.)
Why do professional athletes and actors make so much when what they do is not essential?	Now demand takes over. The paying public is willing, even eager, to spend a large amount of income on entertainment. Thus, demand for entertainment is high. On the supply end of the equation, the number of individuals who capture the imagination of the paying public is small, and they are therefore paid handsomely to do so. The value of the marginal product that they create is incredibly high, which means that they can earn huge incomes.
Why do janitors, construction workers, and nurses—whose jobs are essential—have salaries that are a tiny fraction of celebrities' salaries?	Demand again. The value of the marginal product of labor created in these essential jobs is low, so their employers are unable to pay high wages.

PRACTICE WHAT YOU KNOW

Labor Supply: Changes in Labor Supply

Labor is always subject to changes in demand.

Question: A company builds a new facility that doubles its workspace and equipment. How is labor affected?

Answer: The company has probably experienced additional demand for the product it sells. Therefore, it needs additional employees to staff the facility, causing a positive shift in the demand curve. When the demand for labor rises, wages increase and so does the number of people employed.

Question: A company decides to outsource 100 jobs from a facility in Indiana to Indonesia. How is labor affected in the short run?

Answer: This situation leads to two changes. First, a decrease in demand for labor in Indiana results in lower wages there and fewer workers hired. Second, an increase in demand for labor in Indonesia results in higher wages there and more workers hired.

ECONOMICS IN THE MEDIA

Value of the Marginal Product of Labor

Moneyball

Moneyball, a film based on Michael Lewis's 2003 book of the same name, details the struggles of the Oakland Athletics, a major league baseball team. The franchise attempts to overcome some seemingly impossible obstacles with the help of their general manager, Billy Beane, by applying innovative statistical analysis, known as Sabermetrics, pioneered by Bill James.

Traditional baseball scouts utilize experience, intuition, and subjective criteria to evaluate potential players. However, Beane, formerly a heavily recruited high school player who failed to have a successful professional career, knows firsthand that this method of scouting does not guarantee success. The Oakland A's lack the financial ability to pay as much as other teams. While trying to negotiate a trade with the Cleveland Indians, Beane meets Peter Brand, a young Yale economist who has new ideas about applying statistical analysis to baseball in order to build a better team. Brand explains that evaluating a player's marginal product would be a better tool for recruitment.

In the key scene in the movie, Brand briefly explains his methodology for evaluating players and how the A's can build a championship team:

> It's about getting things down to one number. Using the stats the way we read them, we'll find value in players that no one else can see. People are overlooked for a variety of biased reasons and perceived flaws: age, appearance, and personality. Bill James and mathematics cut straight through that. Billy, of the 20,000 notable players for us to consider, I believe that there is a championship team of 25 people that we can afford, because everyone else in baseball undervalues them.

The A's go on to have a remarkable season by picking up "outcasts" that no other team wanted.

Can a young economist's algorithm save the Oakland A's?

Thanks to Kim Holder of the University of West Georgia.

What Role Do Land and Capital Play in Production?

In addition to labor, firms need land and capital to produce goods and services. In this section, we complete our analysis of the resource market by considering how land and capital enter into the production process. Returning to the restaurant Agaves for a moment, we know that the business hires labor to make meals, but to do their jobs the workers need equipment, tables, chairs, registers, and a kitchen. Without a physical location and a host of capital resources, labor would be irrelevant.

The Market for Land

Like the demand for labor, the demand for land is determined by the value of the marginal product that it generates. However, unlike the supply of labor, the supply of land is ordinarily fixed. We can think of it as nonresponsive to prices, or perfectly inelastic.

In Figure 14.8, the vertical supply curve reflects the inelastic supply. The price of land is determined by the intersection of supply and demand. Notice the label on the vertical axis, which reflects the price of land as the rental price necessary to use it, not the price necessary to purchase it. When evaluating a firm's economic situation, we do not count the entire purchase price of the land it needs. To do so would dramatically overstate the cost of land in the production process because the land is not used up, but only occupied for a certain period. For example, consider a car that you buy. You drive it for a year and put 15,000 miles on it. Counting the entire purchase price of the car would overstate the true operating cost for one year of service. The true cost of operating the vehicle includes wear and tear along with operating expenses such as gasoline, maintenance, and service visits. A similar process is at work with land. Firms that own land consider the rent they could have earned if they had rented the land out for the year. This nicely captures the opportunity cost of using the land.

Opportunity cost

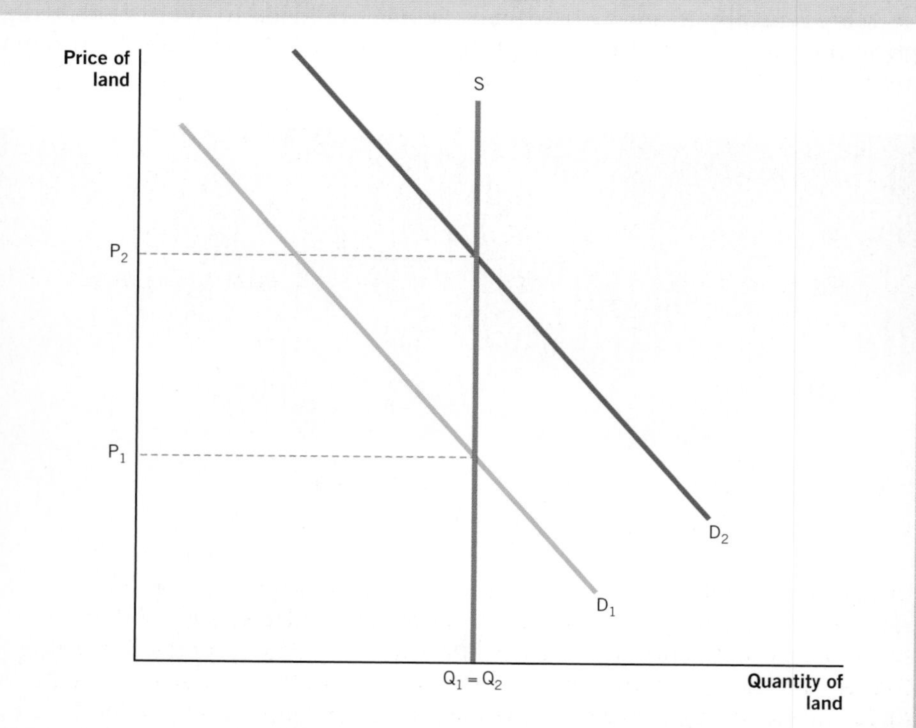

FIGURE 14.8

Supply and Demand in the Market for Land

Since the supply of land is fixed, the price it commands depends on demand. If demand increases from D_1 to D_2, the price will rise from P_1 to P_2.

Since the supply of land is usually fixed, changes in demand determine the rental price. When demand is low—say, at D_1—the rental price received, P_1, is also low. When demand is high—say, at D_2—the rental price of land is high, at P_2. Apartment rentals near college campuses provide a good example of the conditions under which the demand for land is high. Since students and faculty want to live near campus, the demand for land is often much higher there than even a few blocks away. Like labor, the demand for land is derived from the demand for the products that it is used to produce. In this case, the demand for apartments, homes, and retail space near campus is very high. The high demand drives up the rental price of land closer to campus because the marginal product of land there is higher.

Marginal thinking

Economic rent is the difference between what a factor of production earns and what it could earn in the next-best alternative.

When we see the term "rent," most of us think of the rental price of an apartment or a house. But when economists talk about an **economic rent**, they mean the difference between what a factor of production earns and what it could earn in the next-best alternative. Economic rent is different from *rent seeking*. Recall from Chapter 10 that rent seeking occurs when firms compete to seek a monopoly position. In contrast, "rent" here refers to the ability of investors to beat their opportunity cost. For instance, in the case of housing near college campuses, a small studio apartment generally commands a much higher rent than a similar apartment located 10 miles away. This occurs because the rent near campus must be high enough to compensate the property owners for using their land for an apartment instead of in other ways that might also be profitable in the area—for example, for a single residence, a business, or a parking lot. Once you move 10 miles farther out, the number of people interested in using the land for these purposes declines.

More generally, in areas where many people would like to live or work, rental prices are often very high. Many places in the United States have high rental

A satellite photo shows manmade islands in Dubai—an exception to our assumption that the amount of land is fixed.

SNAPSHOT

Outsourcing

Outsourcing, though painful for those whose jobs are outsourced, is simply the application of a fundamental economic principle—keep costs as low as possible. Labor is usually the most expensive input for a business, so all managers must seek to pay the lowest wage that still ensures an effective workforce. Firms seek the right balance of costs and relevant skills when outsourcing jobs. Here is a look at three representative jobs in the United States, Mexico, China, and India, with salaries measured as a percentage of the typical U.S. salary.

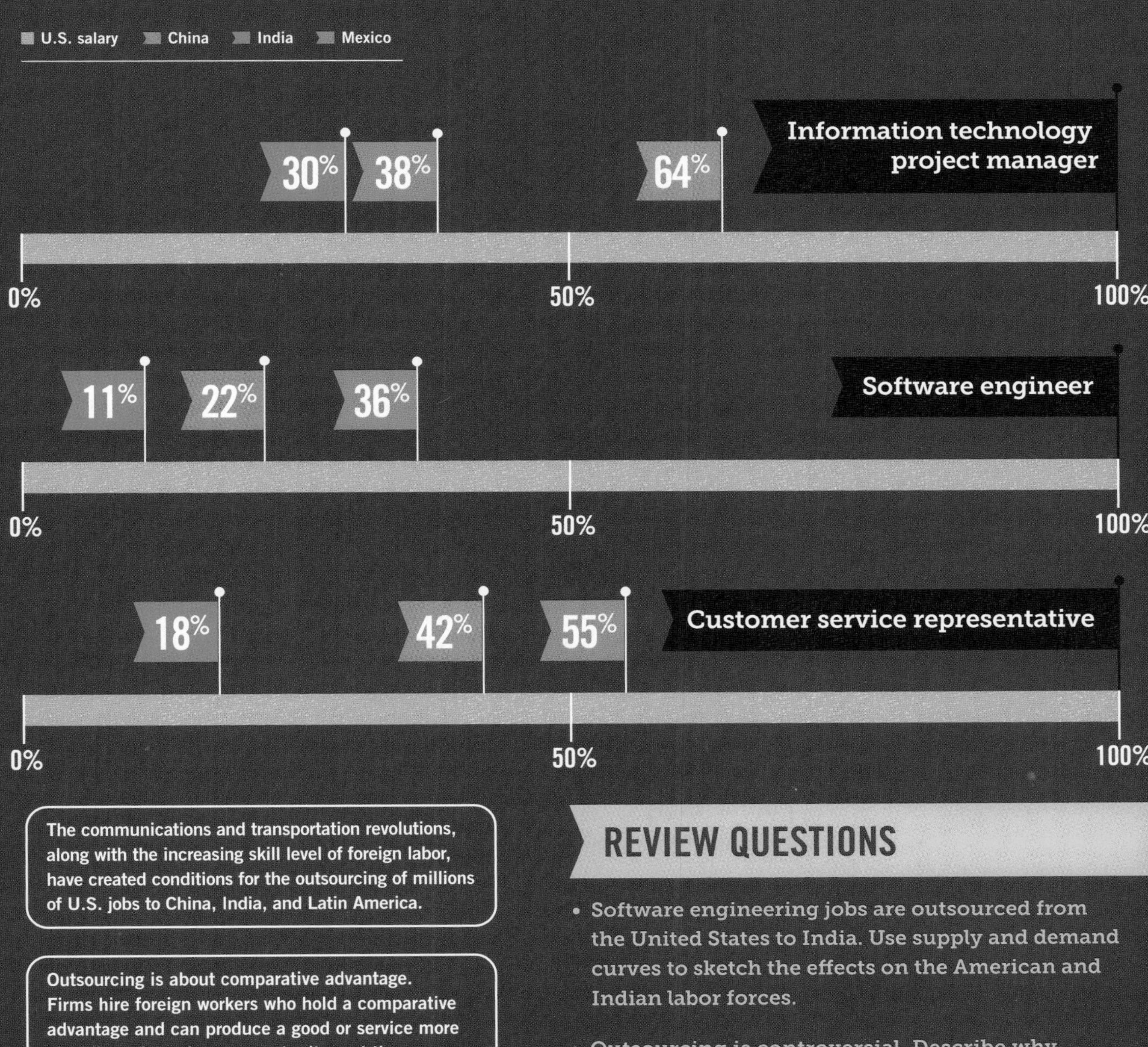

The communications and transportation revolutions, along with the increasing skill level of foreign labor, have created conditions for the outsourcing of millions of U.S. jobs to China, India, and Latin America.

Outsourcing is about comparative advantage. Firms hire foreign workers who hold a comparative advantage and can produce a good or service more cheaply and at a lower opportunity cost than domestic workers.

REVIEW QUESTIONS

- Software engineering jobs are outsourced from the United States to India. Use supply and demand curves to sketch the effects on the American and Indian labor forces.
- Outsourcing is controversial. Describe why by citing effects to the economy both in the short run and in the long run.

prices, but none of those compare with Hong Kong, where an average two-bedroom apartment rents for almost $7,000 a month. That staggering amount makes most apartment rental prices in the United States seem downright inexpensive. While not as high as Hong Kong, owners of property in Moscow, Tokyo, London, and New York all receive more economic rent on properties than those who own similar two-bedroom apartments in Peoria, Idaho Falls, Scranton, or Chattanooga. The ability to earn a substantial economic rent comes back to opportunity costs: since there are so many other potential uses of property in densely populated areas, rents are correspondingly higher.

Opportunity costs

The Market for Capital

Capital, or the equipment and materials needed to produce goods, is a necessary factor of production. The demand for capital is determined by the value of the marginal product that it creates. Like land and labor, the demand for capital is a derived demand: a firm requires capital only if the product it produces is in demand. The demand for capital is also downward-sloping; this reflects the fact the value of the marginal product associated with its use declines as the amount used rises.

When to Use More Labor, Land, or Capital

Firms must evaluate whether hiring additional labor, utilizing more land, or deploying more capital will constitute the best use of their resources. In order to do this, they compare the value of the marginal product per dollar spent across the three factors of production.

Let's consider an example. Suppose that a company pays its employees $15 per hour, the rental rate of land is $5,000 per acre per year, and the rental rate of capital is $1,000 per year. The company's manager determines that the value of the marginal product of labor is $450, the value of the marginal product of an acre of land is $125,000, and the value of the marginal product of capital is $40,000. Is the firm using the right mix of resources? Table 14.3 compares the ratios of the value of the marginal product (VMP) of each factor of production with the cost of attaining that value (this gives us the bang per buck for each resource), or the relative benefit of using each resource.

TABLE 14.3

Determining the Bang per Buck for Each Resource

(1) Factor of production	(2) Value of the marginal product ($)	(3) Wage or rental price ($)	(4) Bang per buck ($)
Labor	$450	$15	$450 ÷ 15 = 30
Land	125,000	5,000	125,000 ÷ 5,000 = 25
Capital	40,000	1,000	40,000 ÷ 1,000 = 40

Looking at these results, we see that the highest bang per buck is the value $40 created by dividing the VMP of capital by the rental price of capital in column 4. When we compare this value for capital, it tells us that the firm is getting more benefit per dollar spent from using capital than it is from using labor ($30) or land ($25). Therefore, the firm would benefit from using capital more intensively. As it does so, the VMP of capital in column 2 will fall due to diminishing returns. When this happens, the bang per buck for capital will drop from $40 in column 4 to a number that is more in line with bang per buck for labor and land. Conversely, the firm is using land ($25) too intensively, and it would benefit from using less. Doing so will raise the VMP it produces and increase its bang per buck for land. By using less land and more capital, and by tweaking the use of labor as well, the firm will eventually bring the value created by all three factors to a point at which the revenue per dollar spent is equal for each of the factors. At that point, the firm will be utilizing its resources efficiently.

Why does all this matter? Because the world is always changing: wages rise and fall, as do property values and the cost of acquiring capital (interest rates). A firm must constantly adjust the mix of land, labor, and capital it uses to get the largest return for its resources. Moreover, the markets for land, labor, and capital are connected. The amount of labor a firm uses is a function not only of the marginal product of labor, but also of the marginal product of land and capital. Therefore, a change in the supply of one factor will alter the returns of all factors. For instance, if wages fall, firms will be inclined to hire more labor. But if they hire more labor, they will use less capital. Capital itself is not any more, or less, productive. Rather, lower wages reduce the demand for capital. In this situation, the demand curve for capital would shift to the left, lowering the rental price of capital as well as the quantity of capital deployed.

Marginal thinking

ECONOMICS IN THE REAL WORLD

The Impact of the 2008 Financial Crisis on Labor, Land, and Capital

The financial crisis of 2008 led to the loss of 40% of all global wealth. By most measures, $10 trillion in wealth was lost in just a few months. The results are evident in the land, labor, and capital markets. Since demand in the factor markets is derived from the demand in the final goods and services market, it is not surprising that the underlying factor markets felt the impact of the crisis. Unemployment rose from under 6% to over 10% due to the drop in demand for labor. Home prices and land values plummeted by more than 30% since the peak in 2007. Finally, the cost of acquiring, or renting, capital dropped to historic lows.

Our understanding of the factor markets teaches us that workers and land-owners alike were vulnerable to systemic changes in the capital markets. As a result, both Main Street and Wall Street shared the pain. ✷

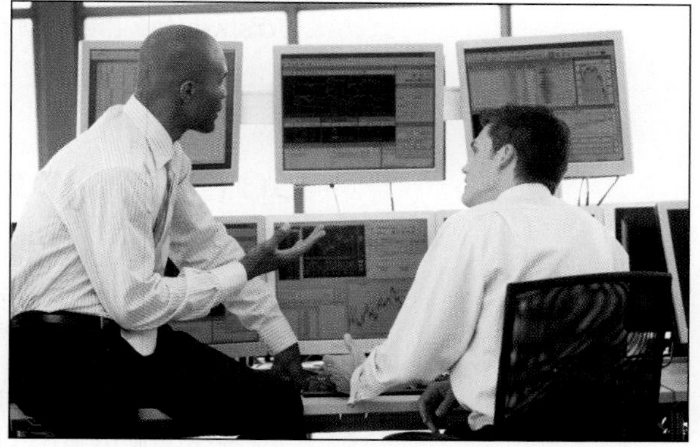

Market analysts know that the land, labor, and capital markets are interconnected.

PRACTICE WHAT YOU KNOW

How are all those dishes going to get clean?

Bang for the Buck: When to Use More Capital or More Labor

Suppose that Agaves is considering the purchase of a new industrial dishwasher. The unit cleans faster, uses less labor and less water, but costs $10,000. Should the restaurant make the capital expenditure, or would it be better off saving the money and incurring higher operating costs? To help decide what Agaves should do, consider this information: the dishwasher has a usable life of five years before it will need to be replaced. It will save the restaurant $300 a year in water and 10 hours of labor each week.

Question: Should Agaves purchase the new dishwasher?

Answer: This is the kind of question every business wrestles with on a regular basis. And the way to answer it is very straightforward. A firm should invest in new capital when the value of the marginal product it creates per dollar spent is greater than the value of the marginal product per dollar spent on the next-best alternative. In other words, a firm should invest in new capital when the bang per buck exceeds that of labor or other investments.

Let's compare the total cost of purchasing the dishwasher with the total savings. The total cost of the dishwasher is $10,000, but the savings are larger.

Item	Amount saved	Total for five years
Water	$300/year	$1,500
Labor	10 hours per week × $8/hour = $80/week × 52 weeks = $4,160/year	20,800
Total		22,300

The total savings over five years is $22,300. This makes the investment in the dishwasher the best choice!

Conclusion

We began this chapter with the misconception that outsourcing is bad for the economy. Indeed, outsourcing destroys some jobs in high-labor-cost areas, but it also creates jobs in low-labor-cost areas. As a result, it lowers the cost of manufacturing goods and providing services. This improved efficiency helps firms that outsource by enabling them to better compete in the global economy.

Throughout this chapter, we have learned that the compensation for factor inputs depends on the interaction between demand and supply. Resource demand is derived from the demand for the final product a firm produces, and resource supply depends on the other opportunities and compensation level that exists in the market. As a result, the equilibrium prices and outputs in the markets for land, labor, and capital reflect, in large part, the opposing tensions between the separate forces of demand and supply.

In the next chapter, we will examine income and poverty. As you will discover, there are many factors beyond the demand for and supply of workers that explain why some workers make more than others. For instance, wages also depend on the amount of human capital required in order to be hired, as well as location, lifestyle choices, union membership, and the riskiness of the profession. Adding these elements will enable us to deepen our understanding of why workers earn what they do.

ANSWERING THE BIG QUESTIONS

What are the factors of production?

* Labor, land, and capital constitute the factors of production, or the inputs used in producing goods and services.

Where does the demand for labor come from?

* The demand for each factor of production is a derived demand that stems from a firm's desire to supply a good in another market. Labor demand is contingent on the value of the marginal product that is produced, and the value of the marginal product is equivalent to the firm's labor demand curve.

Where does the supply of labor come from?

* The supply of labor comes from the wage rate that is offered, and it is determined by each person's goals and other opportunities. At high wage levels, the income effect may become larger than the substitution effect and cause the supply curve to bend backward.

What are the determinants of demand and supply in the labor market?

* Labor markets reconcile the forces of demand and supply into a wage signal that conveys information to both sides of the market. At wages above the equilibrium, the supply of workers exceeds the demand for labor. This causes a surplus of available workers that places downward pressure on wages until they reach the equilibrium wage, at which point the surplus is eliminated. At wages below the equilibrium, the demand for labor exceeds the available supply of workers, and a shortage develops. The shortage forces firms to offer higher wages in order to attract workers. Wages rise until they reach the equilibrium wage, at which point the shortage is eliminated.
* There is no definitive result for outsourcing of labor in the short run. In the long run, outsourcing moves jobs to workers who are more productive.

What role do land and capital play in production?

* Land and capital (as well as labor) are the factors of production across which firms compare the value of the marginal product per dollar spent.

ECONOMICS FOR LIFE

Will Your Future Job Be Outsourced?

When you select an academic major and learn a set of skills, you hope they will enable you to find stable employment. This becomes more challenging in an environment where labor is easily outsourced. So as you seek employment, you need to consider the long-term likelihood that your job could be replaced. To help you think about this, let's consider jobs that are likely to be outsourced and jobs that are more likely to remain in the United States.

Jobs with a high risk of outsourcing

Let's begin with computer programmers, who typically earn $70,000 per year. Programming is not location specific; that is, it can be done from anywhere. This makes programmers susceptible to outsourcing. Similarly, insurance underwriters, who earn approximately $60,000 per year, are increasingly being outsourced because the mathematical algorithms involved in estimating risk can be analyzed from any location. Also at risk are financial analysts. When we think of financial analysts, who make roughly $70,000, we typically think of Wall Street. However, crunching numbers and evaluating prospective stock purchases do not require residence in New York City. As a result, financial positions are increasingly being outsourced. The same is true of biochemists, who make $85,000, and physicists, who make $95,000. Even jobs in architecture, management, and law are under pressure. Having a high-paying job does not guarantee that it is safe from outsourcing.

Jobs with a low risk of outsourcing

Conversely, it is good to be a dentist because fillings, crowns, and root canals have to be done locally. Most jobs in medical care are also safe. Physicians, nurses, technicians, and support staff are all part of the medical delivery process. More broadly, most service-sector jobs are safe from outsourcing because they require someone to be nearby to assist the client. Real estate and construction jobs, which have typical salaries of $40,000 and $45,000 respectively, function in the same way: houses must be built and sold in the local community, so outsourcing is not possible. Also, despite the increase in online courses, education remains primarily a brick-and-mortar enterprise. Likewise, public-sector jobs such as police protection and administration of government programs cannot be outsourced.

More important, the best way to ensure that your future job is not outsourced is to be valuable to your organization. Developing new skills and knowledge is integral to maintaining and increasing the value of the marginal product of your labor. When you are highly valued, it will be difficult to replace you, especially from overseas.

Might your future job be outsourced? Then what would you do?

CONCEPTS YOU SHOULD KNOW

backward-bending labor supply curve (p. 429)
derived demand (p. 422)
economic rent (p. 446)
income effect (p. 429)
marginal product of labor (p. 424)
monopsony (p. 441)
outsourcing of labor (p. 436)
substitution effect (p. 429)
value of the marginal product (VMP) (p. 424)

QUESTIONS FOR REVIEW

1. Why is the demand for factor inputs a derived demand?
2. What rule does a firm use when deciding to hire an additional worker?
3. What are the two labor demand shifters? What are the three labor supply shifters?
4. What can cause the labor supply curve to bend backward?
5. If wages are below the equilibrium level, what would cause them to rise?
6. What would happen to movie stars' wages if all major film studios merged into a single firm, creating a monopsony for film actors?
7. If workers become more productive, what would happen to the demand for labor, the wages of labor, and the number of workers employed?
8. How is economic rent different from rent seeking?

STUDY PROBLEMS (*✱solved at the end of the section*)

1. Maria is a hostess at a local restaurant. When she earned $8 per hour, she worked 35 hours per week. When her wage increased to $10 per hour, she decided to work 40 hours. However, when her wage increased again to $12 per hour, she decided to cut back to 37 hours per week. Draw Maria's supply curve. How would you explain her actions to someone who is unfamiliar with economics?
2. Would a burrito restaurant hire an additional worker for $10.00 an hour if that worker could produce an extra 30 burritos and each burrito made could add $0.60 in revenues?
3. ✱ Pam's Pretzels has a production function shown in the following table. It costs Pam's Pretzels $80 per day per worker. Each pretzel sells for $3.

Quantity of labor	Quantity of pretzels
0	0
1	100
2	180
3	240
4	280
5	320
6	340
7	340
8	320

   a. Compute the marginal product and the value of the marginal product that each worker creates.
   b. How many workers should Pam's Pretzels hire?

4. Jimi owns a music school that specializes in teaching guitar. Jimi has a limited supply of rooms for his instructors to use for lessons. As a result, each successive instructor adds less to Jimi's output of lessons. The following table lists Jimi's production function. Guitar lessons cost $25 per hour.

Quantity of labor	Quantity of lessons (hours)
0	0
1	10
2	17
3	23
4	28
5	32
6	35
7	37
8	38

   a. Construct Jimi's labor demand schedule at each of the following daily wage rates for instructors: $75, $100, $125, $150, $175, $200.
   b. Suppose that the market price of guitar lessons increases to $35 per hour. What does Jimi's new labor demand schedule look like at the daily wage rates listed in part (a)?

5. In an effort to create a health care safety net, the government requires employers to provide health care coverage to all employees. What impact will this increased coverage have in the following labor markets in the short run?
   a. the demand for doctors
   b. the demand for medical equipment
   c. the supply of hospital beds

6. A million-dollar lottery winner decides to quit working. How can you explain this behavior using economics?

7. Illustrate each of the following changes by using a separate labor supply and demand diagram. Diagram the new equilibrium point, and note how the wage and quantity of workers employed changes.
   a. There is a sudden migration out of an area.
   b. Laborers are willing to work more hours.
   c. Fewer workers are willing to work the night shift.
   d. The demand for California wines suddenly increases.

* 8. A football team is trying to decide which of two running backs (A or B) to sign to a one-year contract.

Predicted statistics	Player A	Player B
Touchdowns	7	10
Yards gained	1,200	1,000
Fumbles	4	5

The team has done a statistical analysis to determine the value of each touchdown, yard gained, and fumble lost to the team's revenue. Each touchdown is worth an extra $250,000, each yard gained is worth $1,500, and each fumble costs $75,000. Player A costs $3.0 million, and Player B costs $2.5 million. Based on their predicted statistics in the table above, which player should the team sign?

9. How does outsourcing affect wages and employment in the short run and the long run?

10. Farmers in Utopia experience perfect weather throughout the entire growing season, and as a result their crop is double its normal size. How will this bumper crop affect the following factors?
    a. the price of the crop
    b. the marginal product of workers helping to harvest the crop
    c. the demand for the workers who help harvest the crop

11. What will happen to the equilibrium wage of crop harvesters in Dystopia if the price of the crop falls by 50% and the marginal product of the workers increases by 25%?

12. Suppose that the current wage rate is $20 per hour, the rental rate of land is $10,000 per

acre, and the rental rate of capital is $2,500. The manager of a firm determines that the value of the marginal product of labor is $400, the value of the marginal product of an acre of land is $200,000, and the value of the marginal product of capital is $4,000. Is the firm maximizing profit? Explain your response.

SOLVED PROBLEMS

3. a.

Quantity of labor	Quantity of pretzels	Marginal product	Value of the marginal product
0	0	0	$0
1	100	100	300
2	180	80	240
3	240	60	180
4	280	40	120
5	310	30	90
6	330	20	60
7	340	10	30
8	320	−20	−60

b. The VMP of the fifth worker is $90 and each worker costs $80, so Pam should hire five workers. Hiring the sixth worker would cause her to lose $20.

8.

Predicted statistics	Player A	VMP of Player A	Player B	VMP of Player B
Touchdowns	7	$1,750,000	10	$2,500,000
Yards gained	1,200	1,800,000	1,000	1,500,000
Fumbles	4	−300,000	5	−375,000
Total value		3,250,000		3,625,000

Player A has a value of $3.25 million and a cost of $3.0 million, so he is worth $0.25 million. Player B has a value of $3.625 million and a cost of $2.5 million, so he is worth $1.125 million. The team should sign Player B.

CHAPTER

15 Income, Inequality, and Poverty

MISCONCEPTION

It's unfair that some jobs pay so much more than others.

Many people believe that the structure of compensation in the working world is unfair. After all, why should someone who does backbreaking work digging holes for fence posts make so much less than someone who sits behind a desk on Wall Street? Why do such large differences in income exist? In the last chapter, we learned that two primary factors govern wage income: productivity and the forces of supply and demand. You may be an outstanding babysitter or short-order cook, but because these jobs are considered unskilled, many other workers can easily replace you. And neither occupation will ever earn much more than the minimum wage. In contrast, even an average neurosurgeon gets paid very well, since few individuals have the skill and training to perform neurosurgery. In addition, society values neurosurgeons more than babysitters because the neurosurgeons are literally saving lives.

If you wish to earn a sizable income, it is not enough to be good at something; that "something" needs to be an occupation that society values highly. What matters are your skills, what you produce, and the supply of workers in your chosen profession. Therefore, how hard you work has little to do with how much you get paid.

In this chapter, we will continue our exploration of labor by examining income and inequality in labor markets, including the characteristics of successful wage earners and the impediments the poor face when they try to escape poverty. Examining those at the top and the bottom of the income ladder will help us to understand the many forces that determine income. In addition, we will explore the reasons for poverty. These include low worker productivity, insufficient training and education, cyclical downturns in the economy, employment discrimination, single-wage earners, and bad luck.

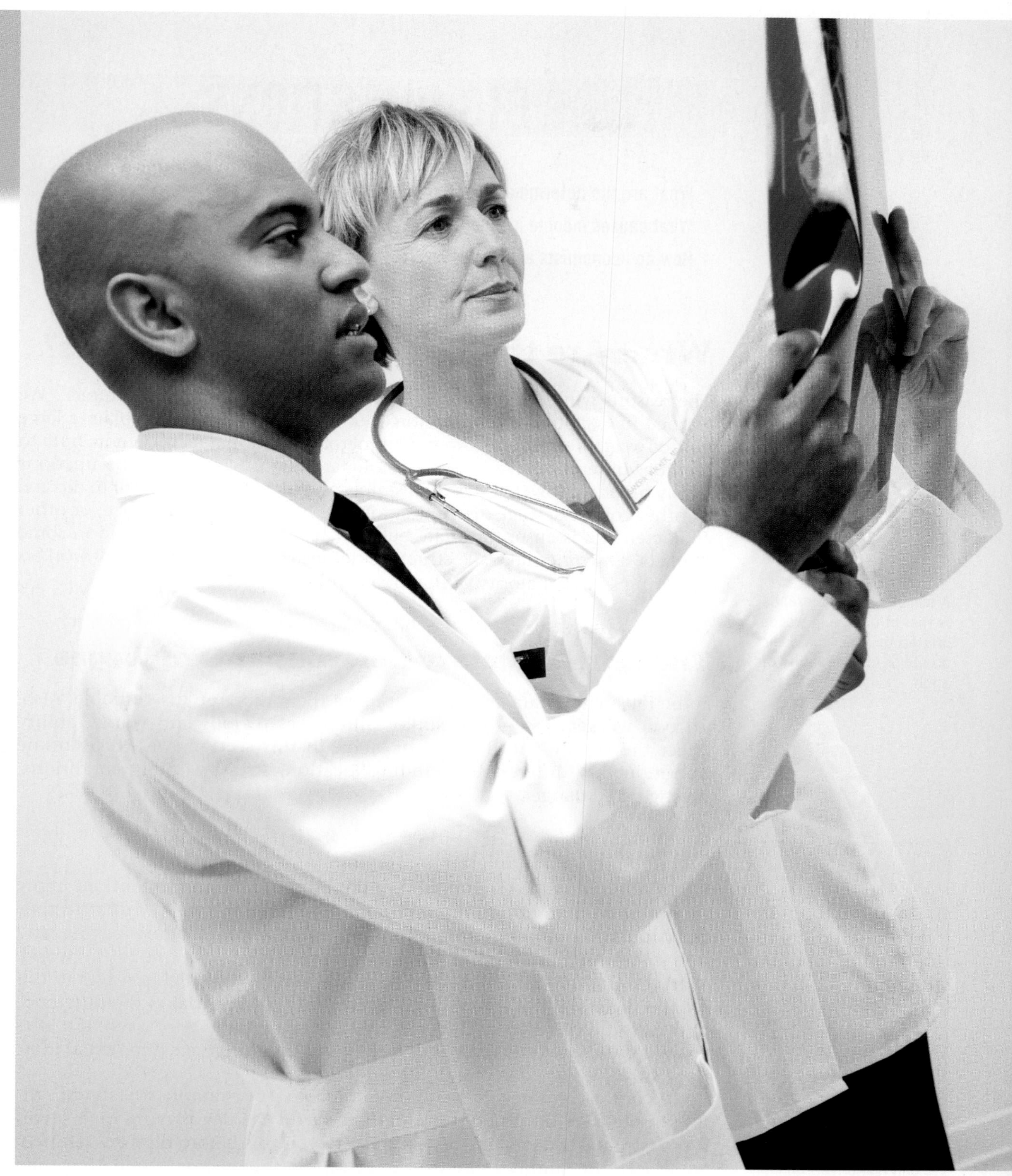

Why do neurosurgeons earn more than short-order cooks?

BIG QUESTIONS

* What are the determinants of wages?
* What causes income inequality?
* How do economists analyze poverty?

What Are the Determinants of Wages?

The reasons why some workers get paid more than others are complex. We learned in Chapter 14 that the forces of supply and demand explain a large part of wage inequality. However, numerous additional factors contribute to earnings differences. Various non-monetary factors cause some occupations to pay higher or lower wages than supply and demand would seem to dictate. In other contexts, wage discrimination on the basis of gender, race, or other characteristics is an unfortunate but very real factor in wages. And in some markets, a "winner-take-all" structure can lead to a small number of workers capturing a large majority of the total earnings.

A **compensating differential** is the difference in wages offered to offset the desirability or undesirability of a job.

The Non-Monetary Determinants of Wages

Incentives

Some jobs have characteristics that make them more or less desirable. Also, no two workers are exactly alike. Differences in jobs and worker ability affect the supply and demand of labor. In this section, we will examine non-monetary differences including location, stress, working conditions, prestige, and danger.

Are you being paid enough to risk a fall?

Compensating Differentials

Some jobs are more unpleasant, risky, stressful, inconvenient, or more monotonous than others. If the characteristics of a job make it unattractive, firms must offer more to attract workers. For instance, roofing, logging, and deep-sea fishing are some of the most dangerous occupations in the world. Workers who do these jobs must be compensated with higher wages to offset the higher risk of injury. A **compensating differential** is the difference in wages offered to offset the desirability or undesirability of a job. If a job's characteristics make it unattractive, the compensating wage differential must be positive.

In contrast, some jobs are highly desirable. For example, restaurant critics sample a lot of great food, radio DJs spend the day playing their favorite music, and video game testers try beta versions before they are released. Some jobs are simply more fun, exciting, prestigious, or stimulating than others. In these cases, the compensating differential is negative and the firm

TABLE 15.1

The Relationship between Education and Pay

Education level	Median annual earnings in 2010 (persons age 25 and over)
Advanced (master's or doctoral) degree	$68,350
Bachelor's degree	52,550
Some college or associate degree	37,700
High school degree (includes GED)	32,650
Less than high school diploma	22,500

Source: Bureau of Labor Statistics, Current Population Survey, April 2012.

offers lower wages. For example, newspaper reporters and radio DJs earn low pay. Video game testing is so desirable that most people who do it are not paid at all.

Education and Human Capital

Many complex jobs require substantial education, training, and industry experience. Qualifying to receive the specialized education required for certain occupations—for example, getting into medical school—is often very difficult. Only a limited number of students are able to pursue these degrees. In addition, such specialized education is expensive, in terms of both tuition and the opportunity cost of forgone income.

The skills that workers acquire on the job and through education are collectively known as **human capital**. Unlike other forms of capital, investments in human capital accrue to the employee. As a result, workers who have high human capital can shop their skills among competing firms. Engineers, doctors, and members of other professions that require extensive education and training can command high wages in part because the human capital needed to do those jobs is high. In contrast, low-skill workers such as ushers, baggers, and sales associates earn less because the human capital required to do those jobs is quite low; it is easy to find replacements.

Human capital is the skill that workers acquire on the job and through education.

Table 15.1 shows the relationship between education and pay. Clearly, attaining more education leads to higher earnings. Workers who earn advanced degrees have higher marginal products of labor because their extra schooling has presumably given them additional skills for the job. But they also have invested heavily in education. The higher marginal product of these workers helps to create high demand for their skills. In addition, the time required to complete more advanced degrees limits the supply of workers with a high marginal product. Taken together, the firm's demand for workers with a high marginal product and the limited supply of such workers causes earnings to rise. Higher wages represent a compensating differential that rewards additional education.

ECONOMICS IN THE REAL WORLD

Does Education *Really* Pay?

An alternative perspective on the value of education argues that the returns to increased education are not the product of what a student learns, but rather a signal to prospective employers. According to this perspective, the degree itself (specifically, the classes taken to earn that degree) is not evidence of a set of skills that makes a worker more productive. Rather, earning a degree and attending prominent institutions is a signal of a potential employee's quality. That is, prospective employers assume that a student who gets into college must be intelligent and willing to work hard. Students who have done well in college send another signal: they are able to learn quickly and perform well under stress.

It is possible to test the importance of signaling by looking at the returns to earning a college degree, controlling for institutional quality. At many elite institutions, the four-year price tag has reached extraordinary levels. For example, to attend Sarah Lawrence College in Yonkers, New York, the most expensive institution in the country, it cost $61,236 in 2012–2013. Over four years, that adds up to almost a quarter of a million dollars! What type of return do graduates of such highly selective institutions make on their sizable investments? And are those returns the result of a rigorous education or a function of the institution's reputation? This is difficult to determine because the students who attend more selective institutions would be more likely to have higher earnings potential regardless of where they attend college. These students enter college as high achievers, a trait that carries forward into the workplace no matter where they attend school.

Economists Stacy Dale and Alan Krueger used data to examine the financial outcomes for over 6,000 students who were accepted or rejected by a comparable set of colleges. They found that 20 years after graduation, students who had been accepted at more selective colleges but who decided to attend a less selective college earned the same amount as their counterparts from more selective colleges. This finding indicates that actually attending a prestigious school is less important for future career success than the qualities that enable students to get accepted at a prestigious school.

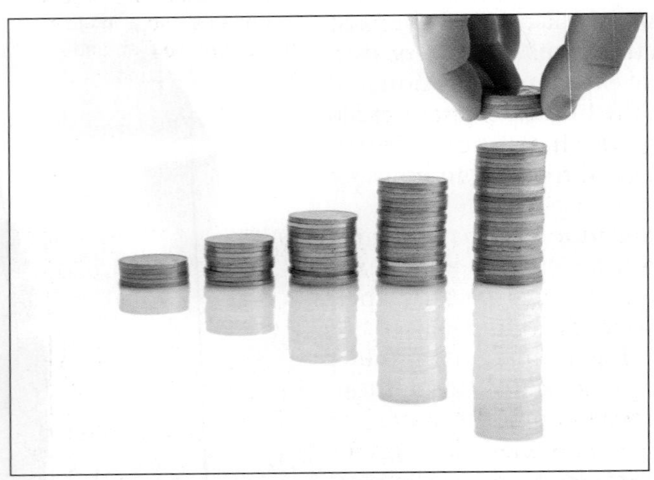

Does an advanced degree mean you learned more or were simply smarter anyway?

Although Table 15.1 shows that additional education pays, the reason is not simply an increase in human capital. There is also a signal that employers can interpret about other, less observable qualities. For instance, Harvard graduates presumably learn a great deal in their time at school, but they were also highly motivated and likely to be successful even before they went to college. Part of the increase in income attributable to completing college is a function of a set of other traits that the student already possessed independent of the school or the degree. ✱

Location and Lifestyle

How much more would you pay to live near here?

For most people, sipping margaritas in Key West, Florida, sounds more appealing than living in Eureka, Nevada, along the most isolated stretch of road in the continental United States. Likewise, being able to see a show, visit a museum, or go to a Yankees game in New York City constitutes a different lifestyle from what you'd experience in Dodge City, Kansas. People find some places more desirable than others. So how does location affect wages? Where the climate is more pleasant, all other things being equal, people are willing to accept lower wages because the non-monetary benefits of enjoying the weather act as a compensating differential. Similarly, jobs in metropolitan areas—where the cost of living is significantly higher than in most other places—pay higher wages as a compensating differential. This helps employees to afford a quality of life similar to what they would enjoy if they worked in less expensive areas.

Choice of lifestyle is also a major factor in determining wage differences. Some workers are not particularly concerned with maximizing their income; instead, they care more about working for a cause. This is true for many employees of nonprofits or religious organizations, or even for people who take care of loved ones. Others follow a dream of being a musician, writer, or actor. And still others are guided by a passion such as skiing or surfing. Indeed, many workers view their pay as less important than doing something they are passionate about. For these workers, lower pay functions as a compensating differential.

Unions

A **union** is a group of workers that bargains collectively for better wages and benefits. Unions are able to secure increased wages by creating significant market power over the supply of labor available to a firm. A union's ability to achieve higher wages depends on a credible threat of a work stoppage, known as a **strike**. In effect, unions can manage to raise wages because they represent labor, and labor is a key input in the production process. Since firms cannot do without labor, an effective union can use the threat of a strike to negotiate higher wages for its workers.

A **union** is a group of workers that bargains collectively for better wages and benefits.

A **strike** is a work stoppage designed to aid a union's bargaining position.

Some unions are prohibited by law from going on strike. These include many transit workers, some public school teachers, law enforcement officers, and workers in other essential services. If workers in one of these industries reach an impasse in wage and benefit negotiations, the employee union is required to submit to the decision of an impartial third party, a process known as binding arbitration. The television show *Judge Judy* is an example of binding arbitration in action: two parties with a small claims grievance agree in advance to accept the verdict of Judith Sheindlin, a noted family court judge.

Does going on strike result in higher wages?

The effect of unions in the United States has changed since the early days of unionization in the late 1800s. Early studies of the union wage premium found wages to be as much as 30% higher for workers who were unionized. At the height of unionization approximately 60 years ago, one in three jobs was a unionized position. Today, only about one in eight workers is a member of a union. In a 2003 study, David G. Blanchflower and Alex Bryson found the wage premium to be around 16.5%. The demise of many unions has coincided with the transition of the U.S. economy from a manufacturing base to a greater emphasis on the service sector, which is less centralized.

While union membership in the private sector has steadily declined, membership in the public sector has increased to almost 40%. This asymmetry is explained by competitive pressure. In the private sector, higher union labor costs prompt firms to substitute more capital and use more technology in the production process. Higher union labor costs also spur firms to relocate production to places with large pools of non-union labor. These competitive pressures limit unions' success at organizing and maintaining membership, as well as the wage premium they can secure. However, competition in the government sector is largely absent. Federal, state, and local governments can pay employees according to union scale without having to worry about cost containment. As a result, unions are common among public school teachers, police, firefighters, and sanitation workers.

Efficiency Wages

Efficiency wages are wages higher than equilibrium wages, offered to increase worker productivity.

In terms of paying wages, one approach stands out as unique. Ordinarily, we think of wages being determined in the labor market at the intersection of supply and demand. When the labor market is in equilibrium, the wage guarantees that every qualified worker can find employment. However, some firms willingly pay more than the equilibrium wage. **Efficiency wages** exist when an employer pays its workers more than the equilibrium wage. Why would a business do that? Surprisingly, the answer is: to make *more* profit. That hardly seems possible when a firm that uses efficiency wages pays its workers more than its competitors do. But think again. Above-equilibrium wages (1) provide an incentive for workers to reduce slacking, (2) decrease turnover, and (3) increase productivity. If the gains in overall productivity are higher than the increased cost, the result is greater profit for the firm.

Incentives

Automaker Henry Ford made use of efficiency wages to generate more productivity on the Model T assembly line. In 1914, Ford decided to more than double the pay of assembly-line workers to $5 a day—an increase that his competitors did not match. He also decreased the workday from nine to eight hours. Ford's primary goal was to reduce worker turnover, which was frequent because of the monotonous nature of assembly-line work. By making the job so lucrative, he figured that most workers would not quit so quickly. He was right. The turnover rate plummeted from over 10% per day to less than 1%. As word of Ford's high wages spread, workers flocked to Detroit. The day after the wage increase was announced, over 10,000 eager job seekers lined up outside Ford's Highland Park, Michigan, plant. From this crowd, Ford hired the most productive employees. The resulting productivity increase per worker was more than enough to offset the wage increase. In addition, reducing the length of each shift enabled Ford to add an extra shift, which increased productivity even more.

Henry Ford developed a visionary assembly process and also implemented efficiency wages at his plants.

We have seen that wages are influenced by factors that include compensating differentials, human capital, location and lifestyle, union membership, and the presence of efficiency wages. Table 15.2 summarizes these non-monetary determinants of income differences.

TABLE 15.2

The Key Non-monetary Determinants of Wage Differences

Determinant	Impact on wages	In pictures
Compensating differentials	Some workers are eager to have jobs that are more fun, exciting, prestigious, or stimulating than others. As a result, they are willing to accept lower wages. Conversely, jobs that are unpleasant or risky require higher wages.	
Human capital	Many jobs require substantial education, training, and experience. As a result, workers who acquire additional amounts of human capital can command higher wages.	
Location and lifestyle	When the location is desirable, the compensating wage will be lower. Similarly, when employment is for a highly valued cause, wage is less important. In both situations, the compensating wage will be lower.	
Unions	Since firms cannot do without labor, unions can threaten a strike to negotiate higher wages.	
Efficiency wages	The firm pays above-equilibrium wages to help reduce slacking, decrease turnover, and increase productivity.	

PRACTICE WHAT YOU KNOW

Efficiency Wages: Which Company Pays an Efficiency Wage?

You are considering two job offers. Company A is well known and respected. This company offers a year-end bonus based on your productivity that can substantially boost your income, but its base wage is relatively low. Company B is less well known, but its wages are higher than the norm in your field. This company does not offer a year-end bonus.

Question: Which company, A or B, is the efficiency wage employer?

Answers: Efficiency wages are a mechanism that some companies use to reduce turnover, encourage teamwork, and create loyalty. Company A's bonus plan will reward the best producers, but the average and less-than-average workers will become frustrated and leave. Company A is not paying efficiency wages; it is simply using incentives tied to productivity. Company B is the efficiency wage employer because it pays every worker somewhat higher wages to reduce turnover. You should work for this company.

Forbes magazine calls Google the best company to work for—and not just because you can bring your dog to work.

Wage Discrimination

Wage discrimination occurs when workers of the same ability are not paid the same as others because of their race, ethnic origin, sex, age, religion, or some other group characteristic.

Wage discrimination occurs when workers of the same ability are not paid the same as others because of their race, ethnic origin, sex, age, religion, or some other group characteristic. Most economic studies of wage discrimination indicate that the amount of discrimination today accounts for only small wage differences. However, less than 40 years ago it was a serious problem. Economists and policymakers continue to study the issue in order to understand its effect in the past and to help address any remaining discrimination today.

Most of us would like to believe that employers no longer pay men more than women for doing the same job. However, wage discrimination does still exist. In 2009, President Obama signed the Lilly Ledbetter Fair Pay Act, which gives victims of wage discrimination more time to file a complaint with the government. The act is named after a former employee of Goodyear who sued the company in 2007. The courts determined that she was paid 15% to 40% less than her male counterparts. The fact that a major U.S. corporation was violating the Equal Pay Act of 1963 almost 50 years after its passage was a poignant reminder that wage discrimination still occurs in our society.

Determining Wage Discrimination

Determining discrimination is no longer as simple or obvious as it once was. Table 15.3 presents median annual earnings in the United States by sex, race or ethnic group, age and experience, and location. Looking at the data, we see large earnings differences across many groups in U.S. society. You might be tempted to conclude that the gap reflects employer discrimination. However, although female workers earn 23% less than their male counterparts, much of this gap reflects compensating differentials and differences in human capital. Let's explore this point in more detail.

The types of jobs that women and men typically work are different. For example, men are more likely to work outdoors. The higher wages offered for jobs such as road work and construction reflect, in part, a compensating differential for exposure to extreme temperatures, bad weather, and other dangers. Also, more women than men take time off from work to raise a family, meaning that they have fewer years of work experience, put in fewer work hours per year, are less likely to work a full-time schedule, and leave the labor force for longer periods. Because of these differences, women generally earn less than men. These factors—the jobs that men and women undertake, experience, and employment history—explain most of the female-male wage gap.

For every $1 men make, women make, on average, 77 cents.

However, the gender gap is shrinking. In 2009, for example, more women than men in the United States received doctoral degrees. The number of women at every level of academia has been rising for decades. Women now hold a nearly 3-to-2 majority in undergraduate and graduate education. Over time, this education advantage will offset some of the other compensating differentials that have kept the wages of men higher than those of women.

Similarly, wide gaps in earnings data by race or ethnic group largely reflect differences in human capital. Asians often have

TABLE 15.3

Median Annual Earnings by Group

Group	Median earnings in 2011	Percentage difference within each group
Males	$48,202	–
Females	37,118	−23%
White	$55,412	–
Black	32,229	−42
Asian	65,129	18
Hispanic	38,624	−30
Early-career workers (25–34)	$50,774	−19
Mid-career workers (35–54)	62,889	–
Late-career workers (55–64)	55,937	−11
Inside a metropolitan area	$51,574	–
Outside a metropolitan area	40,527	−19

Source: U.S. Bureau of the Census, "Income, Poverty, and Health Insurance Coverage in the United States: 2011," *Current Population Reports,* September 2012.

much higher education levels than whites, who in turn generally have much higher levels than blacks and Hispanics. Much of the difference in educational attainment is related to cultural values: some groups place more emphasis on formal education than others. We would expect the wage disparities among groups to decrease as these cultural differences become less pronounced. Socioeconomic factors also play a significant role. For instance, the low quality of many inner-city schools limits the educational attainment of many minorities.

The earnings gap between mid-career workers and others also reflects differences in human capital. After all, workers who are just starting out have limited experience. As these workers age, they accumulate on-the-job training and experience that make them more productive and enable them to obtain higher wages. However, for older workers the gains from increased experience are eventually offset by diminishing returns. For example, workers nearing retirement are less likely to keep up with advances in technology or learn new approaches. Consequently, wages peak when these workers are in their fifties and then slowly fall thereafter. This pattern, known as the **life-cycle wage pattern**, refers to the predictable effect that age has on earnings over a person's working life.

The **life-cycle wage pattern** refers to the predictable effect that age has on earnings over the course of a person's working life.

As we noted earlier, location is also a source of wage differentials. Workers who live outside metropolitan areas make, on average, 19% less than their counterparts who live in cities (see again Table 15.3). This gap occurs because the cost of living is much higher in metropolitan areas.

Clearly, broad measures of differences in earnings do not provide evidence of wage discrimination. Since no employer will admit to discriminating, researchers can only infer the amount of discrimination after first correcting for observable differences from compensating differentials and differences in human capital. The unobservable differences that remain are presumed to reflect discrimination. Because these unobservable differences are small, estimates generally put discrimination at less than 5% of wage differences.

ECONOMICS IN THE REAL WORLD

The Effects of Beauty on Earnings

According to research that spans the labor market from the law profession to college teaching, and in countries as different as the United States and China, beauty matters. How much? You might be surprised—as related by economist Daniel S. Hamermesh in his book *Beauty Pays*, beautiful people make as much as 10% more than people with average looks, while those whose looks are considered significantly below average may make as much as 25% below normal.

Jennifer Lopez, Zac Efron, and Katie Holmes—three of the decade's most beautiful people.

The influence of beauty on wages can be viewed in two ways. First, it can be seen as a marketable trait that has value in many professions. Actors, fashion models, waiters, and litigators all rely on their appearance to make a living, so it is not surprising to find that beauty is correlated with wages in those professions. If beautiful people are more productive in certain jobs because of their beauty, then attractiveness is simply a measure of the value of the marginal product that they generate. In other words, being beautiful is a form of human capital that the worker possesses.

However, a second interpretation finds evidence of discrimination. If employers prefer "beautiful" people as employees, then part of the earnings increase associated with beauty might reflect that preference. In addition, the success of workers who are more beautiful could also reflect the preferences of customers who prefer to work with more attractive people.

Since it is impossible to determine whether the beauty premium is a compensating differential or the result of overt discrimination, we have to acknowledge the possibility that the truth, in many situations, could be a little bit of both. ✷

Occupational Crowding: How Discrimination Affects Wages

Occupational crowding is the phenomenon of relegating a group of workers to a narrow range of jobs in the economy.

Discrimination is not as overt or widespread today as it was a few generations ago. Today, doors that were once closed are now open, and this trend has helped to equalize wages among qualified workers. Still, the impact of wage discrimination continues. For example, in many jobs *occupational crowding* continues to suppress wages for women. **Occupational crowding** is the phenomenon of relegating a group of workers to a narrow range of jobs in the economy. To understand how this works, imagine a community named Utopia with only two types of jobs: a small number in engineering and a large number in secretarial services. Furthermore, everyone is equally proficient at

TABLE 15.4

Where the Men Aren't

Job	Percentage female
Kindergarten teachers	98%
Dental hygienists	98
Secretaries	98
Childcare workers	97
Nurses	93
Bank tellers	87
Librarians	86
Legal assistants	84
Telephone operators	83

Source: Bureau of Labor Statistics, 2010.

both occupations, and everyone in the community is happy to work either job. Under these assumptions, we would expect the wages for engineers and secretaries to be the same.

Now imagine that not everyone in Utopia has the same opportunities. Suppose that we roll back the clock to a time when women in Utopia are not allowed to work as engineers. Women who want to work can only find employment as secretaries. As a result of this occupational crowding, workers who have limited opportunities (women, in this example) find themselves competing with one another, as well as with the men who cannot get engineering jobs, for secretarial positions. As a result, wages fall in secretarial jobs and rise in engineering. Since only men can work in engineering, they are paid more than their similarly qualified female counterparts, who are crowded into secretarial positions and earn less. Furthermore, since women who want to work can only receive a low wage as a secretary, many decide instead to stay at home and produce non-market services, such as child-rearing, with a higher value to the women than the wages they could earn as secretaries.

Of course, in the real world women today are not restricted to secretarial jobs. However, women still dominate in many of the lower-paying jobs in our society. Table 15.4 shows a number of female-dominated occupations in the United States. Not surprisingly, given the low wages, men have not rushed into these jobs. However, because women have not exited them to the extent one might expect, wages have remained low. Rigidity in changing occupations, social customs, and personal preferences all help to explain why this is the case. The same forces are at work in traditionally male-dominated jobs, where men have enjoyed higher wages due to a lack of female employees. Engineers, auto mechanics, airline pilots—to name a few—are career areas that have begun to admit women in large numbers over the last 20 years. As the supply of workers expands, the net effect will be to lower wages in traditionally male-dominated jobs.

ECONOMICS IN THE MEDIA

Occupational Crowding

Anchorman: The Legend of Ron Burgundy

This film from 2004 depicts the television news industry in the early days of women anchors—the 1970s! Stations were diversifying their broadcast teams and beginning to add women and minorities to previously all-white, all-male lineups.

In one scene, Veronica Corningstone, a news anchor, introduces herself: "Hello, everyone. I just want you all to know that I look forward to contributing to this news station's already sterling reputation."

The added competition for air time does not sit well with Ron Burgundy and his male colleagues: "I mean, come on, Ed! Don't get me wrong. I love the ladies. They rev my engine, but they don't belong in the newsroom! It is anchorman, not anchor lady! And that is a scientific fact!"

Veronica overhears the conversation, and after leaving the office she begins a monologue: "Here we go again. Every station it's the same. Women ask me how I put up with it. Well, the truth is, I don't really have a choice. This is definitely a man's world. But while they're laughing and carrying on, I'm chasing down leads and practicing my non-regional diction. Because the only way to win is to be the best."

Do you think Veronica's strategy of trying to be the best would help her to be accepted in a real-world work environment?

"You stay classy, San Diego."

Winner-Take-All

In 1930, baseball legend Babe Ruth demanded and received a salary of $80,000 from the New York Yankees. This would be approximately $1,000,000 in today's dollars. Babe Ruth earned a lot more than the other baseball players of his era. When told that President Herbert Hoover earned less than he was asking for, Ruth famously said, "I had a better year than he did." In fact, the annual salary of the president of the United States is far less than that of top professional athletes, movie stars, college presidents, and even many corporate CEOs.

Why does the most important job in the world pay less than jobs with far less value to society? Part of the answer involves compensating differentials. Being president of the United States means being the most powerful person in the world, so compensation is only a small part of the benefit of holding that office. The other part of the answer has to do with the way labor markets function. Pay at the top of most professions is subject to a form of competition known as **winner-take-all**, which occurs when extremely

Winner-take-all occurs when extremely small differences in ability lead to sizable differences in compensation.

small differences in ability lead to sizable differences in compensation. This compensation structure has been common in professional sports and in the entertainment industry for many years, but it also exists in the legal profession, medicine, journalism, investment banking, fashion design, and corporate management.

Alex Rodriguez has 27.5 million reasons a year to smile, but not all professional baseball players are as fortunate.

In a winner-take-all market, being a little bit better than one's rivals can be worth a tremendous amount. For example, in 2007 baseball player Alex Rodriguez received a 10-year contract worth $275 million, or $27.5 million a year. As good as Rodriguez is, he is not 10 times better than an average major league baseball player, who makes almost $3 million. Nor is he a thousand times better than a typical minor league player, who earns a few thousand dollars a month. In fact, it is hard to tell the difference between a baseball game played by major and minor leaguers. Minor league pitchers throw just about as hard, the players run almost as fast, and the fielding is almost as good. Yet major league players make hundreds of times more.

Winner-take-all has also found its way into corporate America. For example, exploding CEO pay is a relatively recent phenomenon in U.S. history, growing from an average of 35 times the salary of the average American worker in 1975, to 150 times by 1990. According to some estimates, CEO salaries today are more than 300 times greater than that of the average worker.

Paying so much to a relatively small set of workers may seem unfair, but the prospect of much higher pay or bonuses motivates many ambitious employees to exert maximum effort. If we look beyond the amount of money that some people earn, we can see that winner-take-all creates incentives that encourage supremely talented workers to maximize their abilities while at the same time helping to maximize social welfare.

Incentives

What Causes Income Inequality?

Income inequality occurs when some workers earn more than others. Compensating differentials, discrimination, corruption, and differences in the marginal product of labor all lead to inequality of income. Would it surprise you to learn that we shouldn't want everyone to have the same income? Income inequality is a fact of life in a market economy. In this section, we first examine why income inequality exists. Once we understand the factors that lead to income inequality, we examine how it is measured. Because income inequality is difficult to measure and easy to misinterpret, we explain how observed income inequality statistics are constructed and what they mean. We end by discussing income mobility, a characteristic in many developed nations that lessens the impact of income inequality on the life-cycle wage pattern.

Factors That Lead to Income Inequality

To illustrate the nature of income inequality, we begin with a simple question: what would it take to equalize wages? For all workers to get the same wages, three conditions would have to be met. First, every worker would have to have the same skills, ability, and productivity. Second, every job would have to be equally attractive. Third, all workers would have to be perfectly mobile. In other words, perfect equality of income would require that workers be clones who perform the same job. Be glad we don't live in a world like that! In the real world, some people work harder than others and are more productive. Some people, such as aid workers, missionaries, teachers, and even ski bums, choose to earn less. What makes us unique—our traits, our desires, and our differences—is also part of what leads to income inequality. In fact, income inequality is perfectly consistent with the forces that govern a market economy.

The Role of Corruption in Income Inequality

One notable area of concern is the influence that corruption has on trade. In this section, we examine why corruption slows trade and simultaneously increases income inequality.

Trade creates value

All economic systems require trust in order to exact gains from trade. However, some societies value the rule of law more than others. Many less developed countries suffer from widespread corruption. Consider Somalia, a country without a functional central government. This situation has led to lawlessness in which clans, warlords, and militia groups fight for control. The situation is so dire that international aid efforts often require the bribing of government officials to ensure that the aid reaches those in need.

Corruption can play a large role in income inequality. In societies where corruption is common, working hard or being innovative is not enough; getting ahead often requires bribing officials to obtain business permits or to ward off competitors. Moreover, when investors cannot be sure their assets are safe from government seizure or criminal activity, they are less likely to develop a business. Under political systems that are subject to bribery and other forms of corruption, dishonest people benefit at the expense of the poor. Corruption drives out legitimate business opportunities and magnifies income inequality.

ECONOMICS IN THE REAL WORLD

5th Pillar

Widespread corruption leads to more income inequality.

Recognizing the damage that corruption causes has prompted some people to fight back. For example, 5th Pillar, an independent organization, has developed zero-rupee notes in India, where corruption is rampant. The notes provide a way for persons who are asked for a bribe to indicate that they are unwilling to participate. Presenting a zero-rupee note lets the other person know that you refuse to give or take any money for services required by law or to give or take money for an illegal activity. Since 5th Pillar reports attempted bribery to the authorities, individuals who are brave enough to use them know that they are not alone in fighting corruption. ✷

Measuring Income Inequality

When is income inequality a serious concern, and when is it simply a part of the normal functioning of the market? To answer this question, we begin with income inequality in the United States. Economists study the distribution of household income in the United States by quintiles, or five groups of equal size, ranging from the poorest fifth (20%) of households to the top fifth. Figure 15.1 shows the most recent data available, for the year 2011.

According to the U.S. Bureau of the Census, the poorest 20% of households makes just 3.2% of all income earned in the United States. The next quintile, the second fifth, earns 8.4% of income. This means that fully 40% of U.S. households (the bottom two quintiles) account for only 12% of earned income. The middle quintile earns 14.3%, the second-highest quintile 23.0%, and the top quintile 51.1%. Being a pie chart, Figure 15.1 vividly shows the wide disparity between the percentage of total U.S. income earned by the poorest households (3.3%) and by the richest households (51.1%). If we divide the percentage of income earned by households in the top fifth (51.1%) by the percentage of income earned by households in the bottom fifth (3.3%), we get about 15.8. Looking at the numbers this way, we can say that households in the top fifth have approximately 15.8 times the income of those in the bottom fifth. Viewing that number in isolation makes the amount of income inequality in the United States seem large.

However, to provide some perspective, Table 15.5 compares the income inequality in various other countries. The countries above the dashed line are more developed, and those below are less developed.

As you can see, the U.S. income inequality ratio of 15.8 is high compared to that of other highly developed nations but relatively low compared to that of less developed nations. In general, highly developed nations have lower degrees of income inequality. This occurs because more developed countries

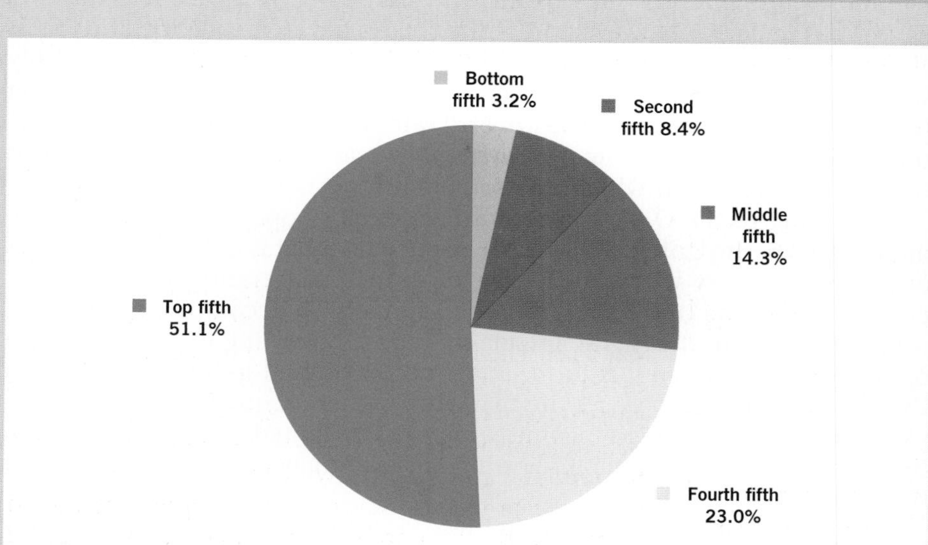

FIGURE 15.1

The Distribution of Income in the United States by Quintile

The top fifth of income earners makes 51.1% of all income, an amount equal to the combined income of the four remaining quintiles. Income declines across the quintiles, falling to 3.3% in the lowest fifth.

Source: U.S. Census Bureau.

TABLE 15.5

Inequality in Selected Countries

Country	Inequality ratio (richest 20% ÷ poorest 20%)
Japan	4.1
Germany	6.3
Canada	8.6
United Kingdom	12.7
United States	15.8
Mexico	19.3
Brazil	37.0
Bolivia	85.5
Namibia	98.2

Source: Adapted from United Nations Development Programme, *Human Development Report,* 2009, Table M.

have less poverty, so those individuals who are at the bottom of the income ladder there earn more than those at the bottom in other countries.

Understanding Observed Inequality

Translating income inequality into a number, as we've done with the income quintiles, can mask the true nature of income inequality. In this section, we step back and consider what the income inequality ratio can and cannot tell us.

Since the inequality ratio measures the success of top earners against that of bottom earners, if the bottom group is doing relatively well, then the inequality ratio will be smaller. This explains why many highly developed countries have ratios under 10. However, the United States has an inequality ratio that is close to 15. What is driving the difference? The United States has many highly successful workers and a *poverty rate* that is similar to those found in other highly developed countries. The **poverty rate** is the percentage of the population whose income is below the *poverty threshold.* The **poverty threshold** is the income level below which a person or family is considered impoverished.

The **poverty rate** is the percentage of the population whose income is below the poverty threshold.

The **poverty threshold** is the income level below which a person or family is considered impoverished.

According to the Organization for Economic Cooperation and Development (OECD), the United States has a poverty rate that is quite similar to that of Japan, a country with a markedly lower inequality ratio. Given that the poverty rate in the United States is not unusually large compared to Japan's, we cannot explain the higher inequality ratio by pointing to the percentage of poor people. Rather, it is the relative success of the top income earners in the United States that causes the markedly higher inequality ratio. In other words, there are more high income earners in the United States than in Japan. In this case, the inequality ratio is quite misleading because of the success of high-income earners.

High levels of income inequality also occur when the poorest are *really* poor. For example, there are many successful people in Mexico, Brazil, Bolivia, and Namibia. The problem in these countries is that the success of some people is benchmarked against the extreme poverty of many others. Therefore, high inequality ratios are a telltale sign of a serious poverty problem. Suppose that the poorest quintile of the population in Bolivia has an average income of \$500, while those in the top quintile earn \$42,750. The income inequality ratio is \$42,750 ÷ \$500 ≈ 85.5. By comparison, consider Canada. If the poorest quintile of the population in Canada has an average income of \$5,000, while those in the top quintile earn \$42,750, the income inequality ratio there is \$42,750 ÷ \$5,000 = 8.6. In both countries the top quintile is doing equally well, but the widespread poverty problem in Bolivia produces an alarming income inequality ratio. In this example, inequality ratios signal a significant poverty problem.

A high income inequality ratio can occur if people at the bottom earn very little or if the income of high-wage earners is much greater than the income of others. The key point to remember is that even though income inequality ratios give us some idea about the degree of inequality in a society, a single number cannot fully reflect the sources of the underlying differences in income.

Difficulties in Measuring Income Inequality

Not only can income inequality numbers be misinterpreted, but they can often be unreliable. Because inequality data reflects income before taxes, it does not reflect disposable income, which is the portion of income that people actually have to spend. Nor does the data account for **in-kind transfers**—that is, goods and services that are given to the poor instead of cash. Examples of in-kind services are government-subsidized housing and the Subsidized Nutrition Assistance Program that provides food supplements to 35 million low-income citizens in the United States. In addition, the data does not account for unreported or illegally obtained income. Because less developed countries generally have larger underground economies than developed countries do, their income data is even less reliable.

In-kind transfers are transfers (mostly to the poor) in the form of goods or services instead of cash.

Many economists also note that income data alone does not capture the value created from goods and services produced in the household. For example, if you mow your own lawn or grow your own vegetables, those activities have a positive value that is not expressed in your income data. In less developed countries, many households engage in very few market transactions and produce a large portion of their own goods and services. If we do not count these, our comparison of data with other countries will overstate the amount of inequality present in the less developed countries. Finally, the number of workers per household and the median age of each worker differ from country to country. When households contain more workers or those workers are, on average, older and therefore more experienced, comparing inequality across countries is less likely to be accurate.

Individually, none of these shortcomings poses a serious measurement issue from year to year. However, if we try to measure differences in income across generations, the changes are significant enough to invalidate the *ceteris paribus* ("all other things being equal") condition that allows us to assume that outside factors are held constant. In short,

Growing your own vegetables is an activity that is not counted in official income data.

comparing inequality data from this year with last year is generally fine, but comparing inequality data from today with data from 50 years ago is largely meaningless. For instance, we might note that income inequality in the United States increased slightly from 2011 to 2012. However, since this is just a single data point, we must be cautious about interpreting it as a trend. To eliminate that problem, we can extend the time frame from 1962 to 2012. That data shows an unmistakable upward trend in income inequality but also violates *ceteris paribus*; after all, the last 50 years have seen dramatic shifts in the composition of the U.S. labor force, changes in tax rates, a surge in in-kind transfers, a lower birthrate, and an aging population. It is a complex task to determine the impact of these changes on income inequality. A good economist tries to make relevant comparisons by examining similar countries over a relatively short period during which there were no significant socio-economic changes.

Finally, the standard calculations and models that we have discussed assume that the income distribution is a direct reflection of a society's welfare. However, we must be very careful not to infer too much about how well people are living based on their income alone. Indeed, income analysis does not offer a complete picture of human welfare. In Chapter 16, we will see that income is only one factor that determines human happiness and well-being. People also value leisure time, non-wage benefits, a sense of community, safety from crime, and social networks.

Income Mobility

Income mobility is the ability of workers to move up or down the economic ladder over time.

When workers have a realistic chance of moving up the economic ladder, each person has an incentive to work harder and invest in human capital. **Income mobility** is the ability of workers to move up or down the economic ladder over time. Think of it this way: if today's poor must remain poor tomorrow and 10 years from now, income inequality remains high. However, if someone in the lowest income category can expect to experience enough economic success to move to a higher income quintile, being poor is a temporary condition. Why does this matter? It matters because economic mobility reduces inequality over long periods of time.

The dynamic nature of the U.S. economy is captured by income mobility data. Table 15.6 reports the income mobility in the United States over a series of 10-year periods from 1970 to 2005. We can see that mobility increased through the late 1980s, but thereafter it declined for both the poorest and the

TABLE 15.6

Income Mobility in the United States, 1970–2005

(1) Ten-year period	(2) % Poorest quintile that move up at least one quintile	(3) % Highest quintile that move down at least one quintile	(4) % Poorest quintile that move up at least two quintiles	(5) % Highest quintile that move down at least two quintiles
1970–1980	43.2	48.8	19.1	22.8
1975–1985	45.3	50.9	20.6	24.8
1980–1990	45.2	47.6	21.3	25.7
1985–1995	41.8	45.8	17.8	21.5
1990–2000	41.7	46.7	15.2	20.7
1995–2005	41.9	45.0	15.4	20.2

Source: Katharine Bradbury, *Trends in U.S. Family Income Mobility, 1969–2006,* Working Paper, Federal Reserve Bank of Boston, No. 11-10. Data for 1990–2000 was interpolated.

highest quintiles. Columns 4 and 5 show the percentage of households that moved up or down at least two quintiles.

Mobility data enables us to separate those at the bottom of the economic ladder into two groups: (1) the *marginal poor,* or people who are poor at a particular point in time but have the skills necessary to advance up the ladder, and (2) the *long-term poor,* or people who lack the skills to advance to the next quintile. The differences in income mobility among these two groups provide a helpful way of understanding how income mobility affects poverty.

For the marginal poor, low earnings are the exception. Since most young workers expect to enjoy higher incomes as they get older, many are willing to borrow in order to make a big purchase—for example, a car or a home. Conversely, middle-aged workers know that retirement will be possible only if they save now for the future. As a result, workers in their fifties have much higher savings rates than young workers and workers who are already retired. On reaching retirement, earnings fall; but if the worker has saved enough, retirement need not be a period of low consumption. The life-cycle wage pattern argues that changes in borrowing and saving patterns over one's life smooth out the consumption pattern. In other words, for many people a low income does not necessarily reflect a low standard of living.

Marginal thinking

When we examine how people actually live in societies with substantial income mobility, we see that the annual income inequality data can create a false impression about the spending patterns of young and old. This occurs because the young are generally upwardly mobile, so they spend more than one might expect by borrowing; the middle-aged, who have relatively high incomes, spend less than one might expect because they are saving for retirement; and the elderly, who have lower incomes, spend more than one might expect because they are drawing down their retirement savings.

In the next section, we turn our attention to the long-term poor, who do not have the skills to escape the lowest quintile. Members of this group spend their entire lives near or below the poverty threshold.

PRACTICE WHAT YOU KNOW

The good life: so near, yet so far . . .

Income Inequality: The Beginning and End of Inequality

Consider two communities, Alpha and Omega. Alpha has ten residents: five who earn $90,000, and five who earn $30,000. Omega also has ten residents: five earn $250,000, and the other five earn $50,000.

Question: What is the degree of income inequality in each community?

Answer: To answer this question, we must use quintile analysis. Since there are ten residents in Alpha, the top two earners represent the top quintile and the lowest two earners represent the bottom quintile. Therefore, the degree of income inequality in Alpha using quintiles analysis is $90,000 ÷ $30,000, or 3. In Omega, the top two earners represent the top quintile and lowest two earners represent the bottom quintile. Therefore, the degree of income inequality in Omega is $250,000 ÷ $50,000, or 5.

Question: Which community has the more unequal distribution of income, and why?

Answer: Omega has the more unequal distribution of income because the quintile analysis yields 5, versus 3 for Alpha.

Question: Can you think of a reason why someone might prefer to live in Omega?

Answer: Each rich citizen of Omega earns more than each rich citizen in Alpha, and each poor citizen earns more than each poor citizen of Alpha. Admittedly, there is more income inequality in Omega, but there is also more income across the entire income distribution. So, depending on one's preferences, one could prefer Omega if the absolute amount of income is what matters more, or Alpha if relative equality is what matters more.

How Do Economists Analyze Poverty?

The United States does not have a wealth problem, but it does have a poverty problem. According to the Census Bureau, close to 15% of all households are below the poverty threshold. To help us understand the issues, we begin with poverty statistics. Then, once we understand the scope of the problem, we examine policy solutions.

The Poverty Rate

For the last 50 years, the U.S. Bureau of the Census has been tracking the *poverty rate,* or the percentage of the population whose income is below the *poverty threshold*. The United States sets the poverty threshold at approximately three

SNAPSHOT

Income Inequality around the World

"The rich get richer, and the poor get poorer" is a simple yet profound way to think about income inequality. As top earners make more and bottom earners make less, the inequality rate increases. It's a combination of these factors, not just extreme wealth or extreme poverty, that leads to huge gaps between those at the very top and those at the very bottom.

$$\text{Inequality ratio} = \frac{\text{Wealth controlled by top 20\%}}{\text{Wealth controlled by bottom 20\%}}$$

- Wealth controlled by top 20%
- Wealth controlled by bottom 20%
- Inequality ratio
- Poverty rate

Namibia 98.2

Brazil 37

Less developed countries, like Namibia, have high rates of inequality. Why? Because the poor are extremely poor and earn just a fraction of the income of the affluent.

United States 15.8

17.3%

Poverty is not the only factor of inequality, however. When the top earners are highly successful, the gap between rich and poor grows. The United States has a poverty rate similar to Japan's but a top 20% who earn more than Japan's top class.

Japan 4.1

15.7%

REVIEW QUESTIONS

- Suppose the top 20% of Brazilian earners make, on average, the equivalent of $100,000 a year. What does the average earner in the bottom 20% make?
- A friend tells you he wants to live in a world without income inequality. Discuss the pros and cons using at least one of the five foundations of economics from Chapter 1.

Those below the poverty threshold are unable to make ends meet.

times the amount of income required to afford a nutritionally balanced diet. To keep up with inflation, the poverty threshold is adjusted each year for changes in the level of prices. However, an individual family's threshold is calculated to include only the money that represents income earned by family members in the household. It does not include in-kind transfers, nor is the data adjusted for cost-of-living differences in the family's specific geographic area. For these reasons, poverty thresholds are a crude yardstick. Figure 15.2 shows the poverty rate for households in the United States from 1959 to 2011.

In 1964, Congress passed the Equal Opportunity Act and a number of other measures designed to fight poverty. Despite those initiatives, the rate of poverty today is slightly higher than it was 40 years ago. This result is surprising, since the economy's output has roughly doubled in that time. One would have hoped that the economy's progress could be measured at the bottom of the economic ladder, as well as at the top. Unfortunately, the stagnant poverty rate suggests that the gains from economic growth over that period have accrued to households in the middle and upper quintiles, rather than to the poor. Poverty has remained persistent, in part, because many low-income workers lack the necessary skills to earn living wages and, at the same time, investments by firms in automation and technology have reduced the demand for these workers. This situation cannot be easily solved by public-sector jobs initiatives; it will require a long-run investment in education programs targeted at the poor and retraining programs designed to help unemployed workers obtain jobs in growing segments of the economy.

Table 15.7 illustrates that children, female heads of household, and certain minorities disproportionately feel the incidence of poverty. When we combine at-risk groups—for example, black or Hispanic women who are heads of household—the poverty rate can exceed 50%.

FIGURE 15.2

Poverty Rate for U.S. Households, 1959–2011

Poverty rates for households fluctuated from 1959 through 2011. Since 2008, the poverty rate has climbed due to the recession that began in that year.

Source: U.S. Bureau of the Census.

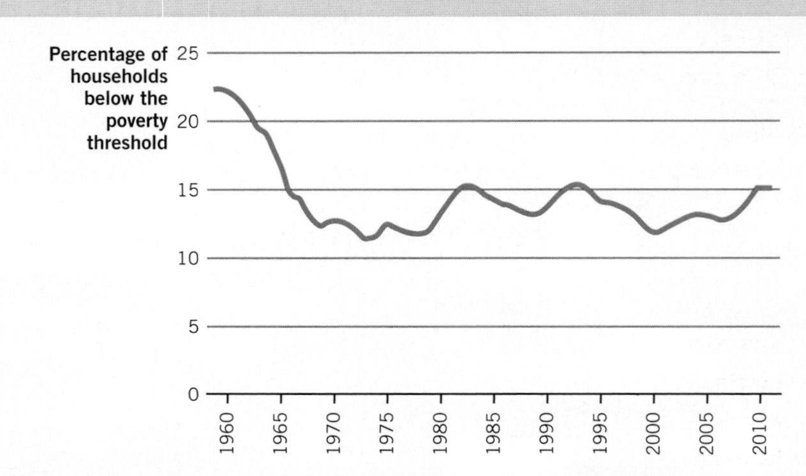

In the next section, we consider how public policy can address the issue of poverty. As Table 15.7 shows, poverty is a wide-ranging and multifaceted problem. Therefore, constructing policies that are targeted at specific groups will be more effective than taking a one-solution-for-all approach.

Poverty Policy

In this section, we outline a number of policies related to the problem of poverty. Because each policy carries both costs and benefits, efforts to help the poor must be considered carefully. Policies do not always distinguish between the truly needy and those who can help themselves. Therefore, in seeking to help the poor, we encounter two conflicting motivations: we want to give generously, but we also want the poor to become self-sufficient and eventually contribute to society. Almost everyone agrees that both goals are vital. Unfortunately, achieving both simultaneously has proven to be almost impossible.

Trade-offs

Welfare

"Welfare" is not a government program, but rather a term that describes a series of initiatives designed to help the poor by supplementing their income. Welfare can take a variety of forms, such as monetary payments, subsidies and vouchers, health services, or subsidized housing. Welfare is provided by the government and by other public and private organizations. It is intended

TABLE 15.7

The Poverty Rate for Various Groups

Group	Poverty rate (percentage)
Age	
Children (under 18)	21.9
Adults (18–64)	13.7
Elderly (65 or older)	8.7
Race/Ethnicity	
White	9.8
Asian	12.3
Hispanic	25.3
Black	27.6
Type of household	
Married couple	6.3
Male head only	15.8
Female head only	31.7

Source: U.S. Bureau of the Census, 2011.

to help the unemployed, those with illnesses or disabilities that prevent them from working, the elderly, veterans, and households with dependent children. An individual's eligibility for welfare is often limited to a set amount of time and is valid only as long as the recipient's income remains below the eligibility cutoff. Some examples of welfare programs include: Temporary Assistance for Needy Families (TANF), which provides financial support to families with dependent children; the Supplemental Security Income (SSI) program, which provides financial support to those who are unable to work; and the Subsidized Nutrition Assistance Program (SNAP), which gives financial assistance to those who need help to purchase basic foods.

In-Kind Transfers

In addition to financial assistance, the poor receive direct assistance in the form of goods and services. Local community food banks, housing shelters, and private charities like Habitat for Humanity and Toys for Tots all provide

ECONOMICS IN THE MEDIA

Welfare

Cinderella Man

The 2005 film *Cinderella Man* portrays the story of James Braddock, a boxing contender in the late 1920s before the stock market crash wiped him out and a busted right hand caused him to lose his license to box. Desperate to earn a living and support his family, Braddock secures a job working on the docks in New Jersey. However, he is unable to make ends meet, and his family is forced to move in with relatives. Braddock swallows his pride and goes to the welfare office, where he receives $19 in relief. Despite the sudden loss of income, separation from his family, and no clear end in sight, Braddock tries to remain upbeat. But the Great Depression begins to defeat him.

At this point, Braddock gets a break to fight in a preliminary match in Madison Square Garden when another fighter cancels the day before. Braddock wins with a stunning knockout, and his comeback begins. As money rolls in, he returns to the relief office and hands the same lady a roll of bills to pay back all that his family had been given.

That gesture might seem like a byproduct of an age of innocence, but there is an important message that is worth recalling. Welfare assistance represents an ethical obligation from the state to its citizens, but in any meaningful ethical arrangement the process must be two-sided. Welfare recipients also have an ethical obligation to look for work and not exploit welfare assistance.

Russell Crowe as a reluctant welfare recipient.

in-kind benefits to the poor. Moreover, the government gives out food stamps and provides health care to the poor through Medicaid.

The idea behind in-kind transfers is that they protect recipients from the possibility of making poor decisions if they receive cash instead. For example, some recipients may use cash transfers to support drug or alcohol addictions, to gamble, or to spend frivolously on vacations, expensive clothes, or fancy meals. None of those poor decisions will alleviate the recipients' future need for food, clothing, and shelter. To limit the likelihood of such poor decisions, in-kind transfers can be targeted at essential services.

The Earned Income Tax Credit (EITC)

The Earned Income Tax Credit (EITC) is a refundable tax credit designed to encourage low-income workers to work more. At very low income levels, the EITC offers an incentive to work by supplementing earned income with a tax credit that can reduce the amount of taxes owed by as much as $6,000 a year. The amount is determined, in part, by the number of dependent children in the household and the location. Once a family reaches an income level above its earnings threshold, the EITC is phased out, and workers gradually lose the tax credit benefits. Under many welfare and in-kind transfer programs, the qualifying income is a specific cutoff point; an individual or household is either eligible or not. In contrast, the EITC is gradually reduced, which means that workers do not face a sizable disincentive to work as the program is phased out.

The EITC helps over 20 million families, making it the largest poverty-fighting program in the United States. EITC payments are sufficient to lift more than 5 million households out of poverty. In addition, the EITC creates stronger work incentives than those found under traditional welfare and in-kind transfer programs.

Incentives

The EITC is a form of *negative income tax*. A **negative income tax** is a tax credit paid to poor households out of taxes collected from middle- and upper-income taxpayers. For example, suppose that a household's tax liability is computed on the basis of the following formula:

A negative income tax is a tax credit paid to poor households out of taxes received from middle- and upper-income households.

$$\text{Taxes owed} = (0.25 \text{ of household taxable income}) - \$10{,}000$$

Table 15.8 shows taxes that would be owed according to this formula at various income levels.

At any income below $40,000, the government pays a credit. Households with incomes above $40,000 owe taxes. Although taxes in the real world are far more complex, economists have long admired the simple elegance of the negative income tax, and this is essentially how the EITC (with a few extra wrinkles) works in practice.

The Minimum Wage

The minimum wage is often viewed as an anti-poverty measure. However, we learned in Chapter 5 that the minimum wage cannot generate more jobs or guarantee higher pay. Predictably, firms respond to higher minimum wages by hiring fewer workers and utilizing more capital-intensive production processes, such as self-checkout lanes. Since the minimum wage does not guarantee employment, the most it offers to an individual worker is a slightly

TABLE 15.8

How the Negative Income Tax Works

Income	Calculation	Tax owed/Credit
$80,000	($80,000 × 0.25) – $10,000	$10,000
60,000	($60,000 × 0.25) – $10,000	5,000
40,000	($40,000 × 0.25) – $10,000	0
20,000	($20,000 × 0.25) – $10,000	–5,000
0	($0 × 0.25) – $10,000	–10,000

larger paycheck. At the same time, a higher minimum wage makes those jobs more difficult to find. Despite rhetoric that trumpets the minimum wage as a potential cure to poverty, the real problem remains: some workers lack skills, motivation, or both. In that case, they cannot improve their earning ability by means of a minimum wage law.

Problems with Traditional Aid

Many welfare programs create work disincentives. In fact, a serious incentive problem arises when we examine the combined effects of welfare and in-kind transfer programs. Many benefits are severely reduced or curtailed altogether at certain income thresholds. This creates an incentive for low-income workers to work less in order to maintain eligibility for government assistance.

To see why this matters, consider a family of five with a combined income of $20,000 a year. Suppose that the family qualifies for public assistance that amounts to another $10,000 in benefits. The family's combined income from employment and benefits thus rises to $30,000. What happens if another family member gets a part-time job and income from wages rises from $20,000 to $30,000? Under the current law, a maximum income of $30,000 disqualifies the family from receiving most of the financial assistance it had been getting. As a result, the family's benefits fall from $10,000 to $2,000 per year. Now the family nets $32,000 total. The person who secured part-time employment may feel that this isn't worth it because even though the family earned an additional $10,000, they lost $8,000 in "welfare" benefits. Since they are only able to raise their net income by $2,000, they have effectively returned $8,000. The loss of those benefits feels like an 80% tax, which creates a large disincentive to work.

Incentives

This is a basic dilemma that poverty-reducing programs face: those that provide substantial benefits discourage participation in the workforce because a recipient who starts to work, in many cases, no longer qualifies for the benefits and loses them. Among the three options we have discussed so far, the EITC does the best job of addressing the work incentive problem by phasing out assistance at a gradual rate.

While few people dispute that welfare programs are well intentioned, many economists are concerned about the programs' unintended consequences. A society that establishes a generous welfare package for the poor will find that it faces a *samaritan's dilemma*. A **samaritan's dilemma** occurs when an act of charity creates disincentives for recipients to take care of themselves. President Bill Clinton addressed this concern in 1996 when he vowed "to end welfare as we know it." As part of the TANF program, Clinton changed the payout structure for federal assistance and encouraged states to require employment searches as a condition for receiving aid. In addition, the TANF program imposed a five-year maximum for the time during which a recipient can receive benefits. This strategy changed welfare from an entitlement under the law into a temporary safety net program, thereby reducing the samaritan's dilemma.

A **samaritan's dilemma** occurs when an act of charity causes disincentives for recipients to take care of themselves.

Incentives

ECONOMICS IN THE REAL WORLD

Muhammad Yunus and the Grameen Bank

One economist, Muhammad Yunus, stands alone. In 2006, he received the Nobel Peace Prize for his work helping poor families in Bangladesh. What did Yunus do to win that honor? He founded the Grameen Bank, which was instrumental in creating a new type of loan that has extended more than $8 billion to poor people in Bangladesh in an effort to eliminate extreme poverty.

The Grameen Bank gives out very small loans, known as *microcredit*, to poor Bangladeshis who are unable to qualify for conventional loans from traditional lenders. The loans are provided without collateral, and repayment is based on an honor system. By conventional standards that sounds preposterous, but it works! The Grameen Bank reports a 99% repayment rate, and according to one survey over 50% of the families of Grameen borrowers have moved above the poverty line.

It all started with just a few thousand dollars. In 1974, Yunus, who was trained as an economist in the United States, returned to Bangladesh and lent $27 to each of 42 villagers who made bamboo furniture. The loans, which were all paid back, enabled the villagers to cut out any middlemen and purchase their own raw materials. A few years later, Yunus won government approval to open the Grameen Bank, named for the Bengali word for "rural."

Yunus had a truly innovative idea. In order to receive a loan, applicants must belong to a five-member group. Once the first two members begin to pay back their loans, the others can get theirs. While there is no group responsibility for returning the loans, the Grameen Bank believes it creates a sense of social responsibility, ensuring that all members will pay back their loans. More important, Yunus trusted that people would honor their commitments, and he was proven right. With just a relatively few dollars, Yunus changed the perception about how to effectively fight poverty in underdeveloped nations—a truly remarkable achievement! ✱

In 2006, Yunus received the Nobel Peace Prize.

PRACTICE WHAT YOU KNOW

Welfare is an economic means of lending a helping hand.

Incentives

Samaritan's Dilemma: Does Welfare Cause Unemployment?

The state you live in is considering two different welfare programs. The first plan guarantees $8,000 for each person. The second plan does not guarantee any payments, but it doubles any income earned up to $12,000.

Question: Which program creates the lesser amount of unemployment?

Answer: Think about incentives. Under the first plan, recipients' benefits are not tied to work. The $8,000 is guaranteed. However, the second plan will pay more if recipients do work. This policy acts as a positive incentive to get a job. For instance, someone who works 20 hours a week and earns $10 per hour would make $200 per week, or about $10,000 a year. Under the second plan, that person would receive an additional $10,000 from the government. Therefore, we can say that the second program reduces the amount of unemployment.

Conclusion

Some jobs pay much more than others, but that is not inherently unfair despite what many people believe. Income inequality is often misunderstood. People and jobs differ in many dimensions, and wages respond accordingly. Wages are determined by supply and demand along with many non-monetary factors, such as compensating differentials, location, and union membership, all of which create significant income inequality. As we have seen, income inequality is neither good nor bad; it simply reflects the way the economic world works. Any effort to equalize incomes would have a very serious unintended consequence: the incentive to work hard would be reduced.

In addition, since the long-term poor are perpetually below the poverty threshold, welfare policies must differentiate between those who are temporarily impoverished and those who need more long-term assistance. The EITC program gives the marginal poor the correct incentives to escape poverty, while welfare and other in-kind transfers provide a safety net for those who need more assistance. The challenge for policymakers is to design aid programs so that they provide a safety net for the long-term poor while creating disincentives for the marginal poor to remain on welfare.

ECONOMICS FOR LIFE

Donating to Charity More Effectively

The samaritan's dilemma is not unique to public assistance; it also applies to private charitable donations. Here the dilemma occurs with the stewardship of the donations. Donors want their gifts to benefit the largest possible set of needs. However, charitable organizations have overhead expenses that limit how much of the gift actually reaches the hands of the needy. In addition, not all charities are aboveboard. Here are a few tips to ensure that your donations make a difference.

1. Ask for a copy of the organization's financial report. Find out how much of your money actually will be used for charitable programs. If the organization is reluctant to share this information upon request, walk away.
2. Be careful of charities with copycat names. Some organizations use names similar to those of well-known organizations in order to confuse donors.
3. Be wary of emotional appeals that talk about problems but do not explain how donated monies will be spent. Do not succumb to high-pressure tactics or solicitations made over the phone; donating should be a reasoned and thoughtfully considered process. Step back, and ask for written materials containing information about the charity.
4. Ask if donations are tax deductible. Do not pay in cash, but instead pay by check so you have proof that you gave if you are ever audited.
5. Finally, after you have done your due diligence, give confidently and generously.

How can you make sure your donation gets to those that need it?

ANSWERING THE BIG QUESTIONS

What are the determinants of wages?

* Supply and demand play a key role in determining wages, along with a number of non-monetary determinants of earnings such as compensating differentials, human capital, location, lifestyle, union membership, and efficiency wages.
* Economic studies of wage discrimination have found that the amount of discrimination is relatively small, accounting for only 3% to 5% of wage differences.
* Despite recent gains, women still earn significantly less than men. Occupational crowding partially explains the wage gap. As long as supply imbalances remain in traditional male and female jobs, significant wage differences will persist.

What causes income inequality?

* Compensating differentials, discrimination, corruption, and differences in the marginal product of labor all lead to income inequality.
* Economic mobility reduces income inequality over long periods. Due to the life-cycle wage pattern, distinct borrowing and saving patterns over an individual's life smooth out his or her spending pattern. Therefore, in societies with substantial income mobility, the annual income inequality data overstates the amount of inequality.

How do economists analyze poverty?

* Economists determine the poverty rate by establishing a poverty threshold.
* The poverty rate in the United States has been stagnant for the last 40 years despite many efforts (welfare, in-kind transfers, and the EITC) to reduce it.
* Efforts to reduce poverty are subject to the samaritan's dilemma because they generally create disincentives for recipients to support themselves.

CONCEPTS YOU SHOULD KNOW

compensating differential (p. 458)
efficiency wages (p. 462)
human capital (p. 459)
in-kind transfers (p. 473)
income mobility (p. 474)
life-cycle wage pattern (p. 465)
negative income tax (p. 481)
occupational crowding (p. 466)
poverty rate (p. 472)
poverty threshold (p. 472)
samaritan's dilemma (p. 483)
strike (p. 461)
union (p. 461)
winner-take-all (p. 468)
wage discrimination (p. 464)

QUESTIONS FOR REVIEW

1. Why do garbage collectors make more than furniture movers?
2. What are efficiency wages? Why are some employers willing to pay them?
3. Why is it difficult to determine the amount of wage discrimination in the workplace?
4. Discuss some of the reasons why full-time working women make, on average, 77% as much as full-time working men.
5. How does the degree of income inequality in the United States compare to that in similarly developed countries? How does U.S. income inequality compare with that in less developed nations?
6. Why do high rates of income mobility mitigate income inequality?
7. Which anti-poverty program (welfare, in-kind transfers, or the Earned Income Tax Credit) creates the strongest incentive for recipients to work? Why?

STUDY PROBLEMS (*✱solved at the end of the section*)

1. Suppose that society restricted the economic opportunities of right-handed persons to jobs in construction, while left-handed persons could work any job.
   a. Would wages in construction be higher or lower than wages for other jobs?
   b. Would left-handed workers make more or less than right-handed workers?
   c. Now suppose that right-handers were allowed to work any job they like. What effect would this change have on the wages of right-handers and left-handers over time?
2. Internships are considered a vital stepping-stone to full-time employment after college, but not all internship positions are paid. Why do some students take unpaid internships when they could be working summer jobs and earning an income? Include a discussion of human capital in your answer.
3. Consider two communities. In Middletown, two families earn $40,000 each, six families earn $50,000 each, and two earn $60,000 each. In Polarity, four families earn $10,000 each, two earn $50,000 each, and four earn $90,000 each. Which community has the more unequal distribution of income? Explain your response.
4. The United States has attracted many highly productive immigrants who work in fields such as education, health, and technology. How do these immigrants affect the income inequality in this country? Is this type of immigration good or bad for the United States, and why? What impact is this type of immigration having on the countries that are losing some of their best workers?

✱5. Suppose that a wealthy friend asks for your advice on how to reduce income inequality. Your friend wants to know if it would be better to give $100 million to poor people who will never attend college or to offer $100 million in financial aid to students who could not otherwise afford to attend college. What advice would you give, and why?

6. What effect would doubling the minimum wage have on income inequality? Explain your answer.

* 7. Suppose that a company has 10 employees. It agrees to pay each worker on the basis of productivity. The individual workers' output is 10, 14, 15, 16, 18, 19, 21, 23, 25, and 30 units, respectively. However, some of the workers complain that they are earning less than the other workers, so they appeal to management to help reduce the income inequality. As a result, the company decides to pay each worker the same salary. However, the next time the company measures each worker's output, they find that 6, 7, 7, 8, 10, 10, 11, 11, 12, and 12 units are produced. Why did this happen? Would you recommend that the company continue the new compensation system? Explain your response.

8. The government is considering three possible welfare programs:
   a. Give each low-income household $10,000.
   b. Give each low-income household $20,000 minus the recipient's income.
   c. Match the income of each low-income household, where the maximum they can receive in benefits is capped at $10,000.

   Which program does the most to help the poor? Describe the work incentives under each program.

SOLVED PROBLEMS

5. The return on your wealthy friend's investment will be higher by giving the money to students with the aptitude, but not the income, to afford to go to college. After all, college students earn substantially more than high school graduates do. Therefore, an investment in additional education will raise the marginal revenue product of labor. With the higher earning power that a college degree provides, more people will be lifted out of poverty, thereby reducing the amount of income inequality in society.

7. Begin by calculating the average output when each worker's wage is based on the amount that he or she produces: 10 + 14 + 15 + 16 + 18 + 19 + 21 + 23 + 25 + 30 = 191 ÷ 10 = 19.1. Then compute the average output when the company decides to pay each worker the same wage: 6 + 7 + 7 + 8 + 10 + 10 + 11 + 11 + 12 + 12 = 94 ÷ 10 = 9.4. The output has dropped by one-half! Why did this happen? The company forgot about incentives. In this case, an attempt to create equal pay caused a disincentive problem (since hard work is not rewarded), and the workers all reduced their work effort. The new compensation system should be scrapped.

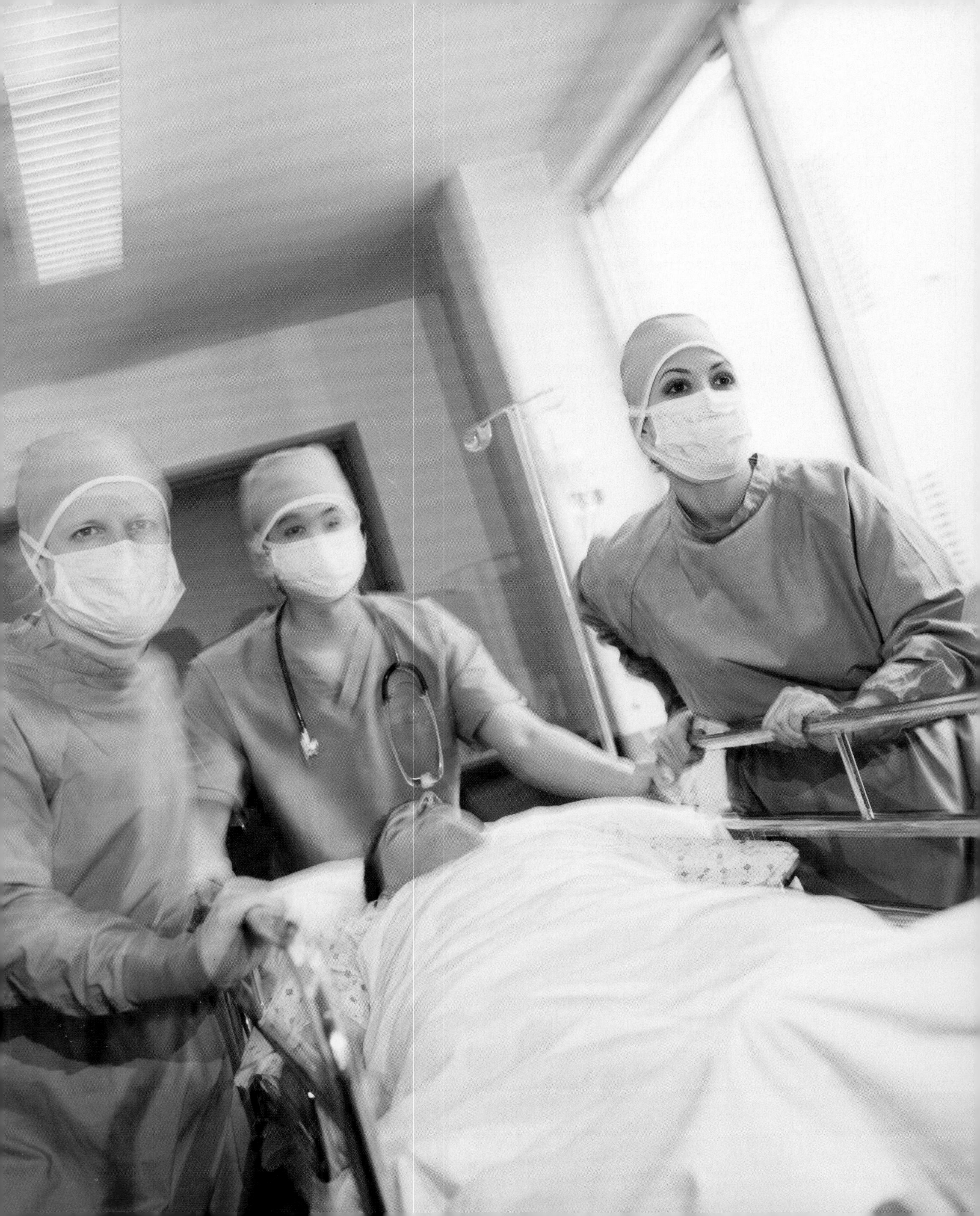

PART

5

Special Topics in MICROECONOMICS

CHAPTER

16 Consumer Choice

MISCONCEPTION

The more money you have, the happier you'll be.

Did having more money make Ebenezer Scrooge happier? How about Montgomery Burns from *The Simpsons*? Or Mr. Potter from *It's a Wonderful Life*? The answer is *no*. All three fatally flawed characters hoarded money and, in the process, missed out on many of the good things that life has to offer. Then there is Jack Whittaker, a real-life millionaire who won a $315 million Powerball jackpot in 2002. He is now completely broke, is divorced from his wife, has been arrested for DUI, and was robbed on two separate occasions while carrying $500,000. (Who does *that*?) Worst of all, he lost his daughter and granddaughter to drug overdoses. Do you think Jack Whittaker regrets winning the lottery? "If only I could win the lottery" may be one wish you don't want granted.

Money can be used in ways that lift the spirit. For one thing, more money means more opportunities to strengthen your connections with others and contribute to your community. It also means you can afford to travel, experience the diverse wonders of nature, and spend more time with family and friends instead of collecting material possessions. Moreover, saving money for a goal, such as a special trip, can make the experience more rewarding. Money is best spent when it invokes strong positive feelings and creates memories. So can more money buy more happiness? We say yes, but only if you are careful about what you buy and do not become consumed by the pursuit of money.

In this chapter, we will use our understanding of income constraints, price, and personal satisfaction to determine which economic choices yield the greatest benefits.

Can money really buy happiness?

BIG QUESTIONS

* How do economists model consumer satisfaction?
* How do consumers optimize their purchasing decisions?
* What is the diamond-water paradox?

How Do Economists Model Consumer Satisfaction?

Trade-offs

Utility
is a measure of the relative levels of satisfaction that consumers enjoy from the consumption of goods and services.

A **util** is a unit of satisfaction used to measure the enjoyment from consumption of a good or service.

Imagine that it is a hot afternoon and you decide to make a quick stop at a convenience store for a cold drink. While you're there, you decide to get a snack as well. Brownies are your favorite, but apple pie is on sale and you choose that instead. You may not think about these purchases very carefully, but they involve several trade-offs, including the time you could use to do something else and the money that you could be spending on something else. If brownies are your favorite snack, why do you sometimes choose to eat apple pie? Why do many people pay thousands of dollars for diamond jewelry, which is not essential for life, and yet pay only pennies for water, which is essential for life? These are the kinds of questions we must answer if we are to understand how people make personal buying decisions.

To better understand the decisions that consumers make, economists attempt to measure the satisfaction that consumers get when they make purchases. **Utility** is a measure of the relative levels of satisfaction that consumers enjoy from the consumption of goods and services. Utility theory seeks to measure contentment, or satisfaction. To understand why people buy the goods and services they do, we need to recognize that some products produce more utility than others and that everyone receives different levels of satisfaction from the same good or service; in other words, utility varies from individual to individual. To quantify this idea of relative satisfaction, economists measure utility with a unit they refer to as a **util**.

Do you prefer a slice of apple pie . . .

. . . or a fudge brownie?

There is tremendous value in modeling decisions this way. When we understand utility, we can predict what people are likely to purchase. This process is similar to the way we used models in earlier chapters to describe how the firm makes decisions or how the labor market works. We expect the firm to maximize profits, the laborer to accept the best offer, and the consumer to find the combination of goods that gives the most utility. For example, a brownie lover may get 25 utils from her favorite snack, but someone who is less susceptible to the pleasures of chewy, gooey chocolate may rate the same brownie at 10 utils. However, even this is not a completely accurate measurement of relative utility. Who can say whether one person's 25 represents more actual satisfaction than another person's 10? Even if you and a friend agree that you each receive 10 utils from eating brownies, you cannot say that you both experience the same amount of satisfaction or happiness; each of you has a unique personal scale. However, the level of enjoyment one receives can be internally consistent. For example, if you rate a brownie at 25 utils and a slice of apple pie at 15 utils, we know that you like brownies more than apple pie.

Utility, or what most of us think of as happiness, is a balance between economic and personal factors. Even though there is an inherent problem with equating money and happiness, this has not stopped researchers from exploring the connection.

In the next section, we explore the connection between total utility and marginal utility. This connection will help us understand why more money does not necessarily bring more happiness.

ECONOMICS IN THE REAL WORLD

Happiness Index

Since 2006, the Organisation for Economic Co-operation and Development (OECD) has compiled the Better Life Index—popularly called the "happiness index"—that includes social variables alongside economic data for 34 highly developed countries. The OECD measures well-being across these countries, based on 11 topics it has identified as essential in the areas of material living conditions and quality of life.

"Down under" is a satisfying place to live!

Which countries are happiest? The OECD doesn't rank them, and the results depend on the relative importance assigned to the different measurements. Giving each category equal weight, Australia currently comes in first, followed closely by Norway and the United States. What makes Australians so happy? It's not their income, which averages only $26,000 per year. However, Australians live to an average age of 82 (two years longer than typical in developed countries), experience low amounts of pollution, display a high degree of civic engagement, and enjoy a very high life satisfaction rating.

In contrast, the OECD identifies the United States as having the highest income, but it scores substantially lower in work-life balance than many of the other top countries do. At the opposite end of the list, we find Mexico. In Mexico, safety concerns, poor education, and low levels of income combine to produce a very low rating among the countries surveyed. ✳

Total Utility and Marginal Utility

Thinking about choices that consumers make can help us understand how to increase total utility. Consider a person who really likes brownies. In this case, the **marginal utility** is the extra satisfaction enjoyed from consuming one more brownie. In the table on the left-hand side of Figure 16.1, we see that the first brownie eaten brings 25 total utils. Eating additional brownies increases total utility until it reaches 75 utils after eating five brownies.

Marginal utility is the additional satisfaction derived from consuming one more unit of a good or service.

The graph in panel (a) of Figure 16.1 reveals that while the total utility (the green curve) rises until it reaches 75, the rate of increase slowly falls from 25 utils for the first brownie down to 5 additional utils for the fifth. The marginal utility values from the table are graphed in panel (b), which shows that marginal utility declines steadily as consumption rises.

Marginal thinking

FIGURE 16.1

Total Utility and Marginal Utility

The relationship between total utility and marginal utility can be seen by observing the dashed line that connects panels (a) and (b). Since the marginal utility becomes negative after five brownies are consumed, the total utility eventually falls. To the left of the dashed line, the marginal utility is positive in panel (b) and the total utility is rising in panel (a). Conversely, to the right of the dashed line, the marginal utility is negative and the total utility is falling.

Number of brownies eaten	Total utility (utils per brownie)	Marginal utility (utils per brownie)
0	0	
		25
1	25	
		20
2	45	
		15
3	60	
		10
4	70	
		5
5	75	
		0
6	75	
		25
7	70	
		210
8	60	
		215
9	45	
		220
10	25	

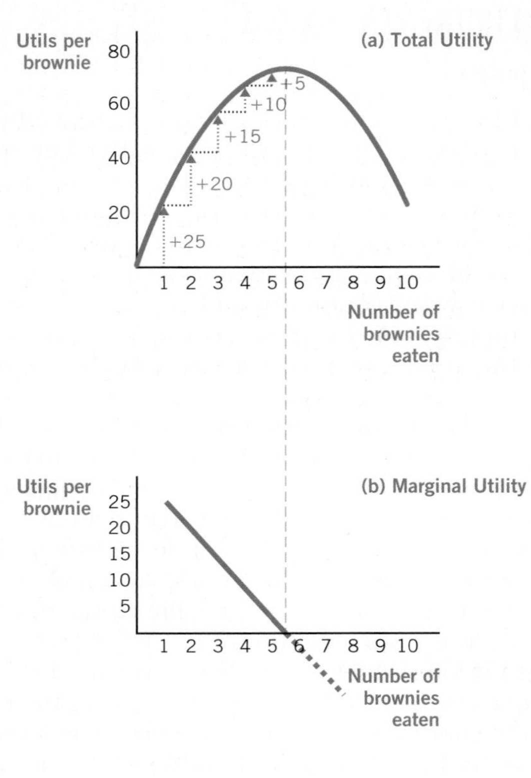

The relationship between total utility and marginal utility is evident when we observe the dashed line that connects panels (a) and (b). Since the marginal utility becomes negative after five brownies are consumed, the total utility eventually falls. To the left of the dashed line, the marginal utility is positive in panel (b) and the total utility is rising in panel (a). Conversely, to the right of the dashed line, the marginal utility is negative and the total utility is falling.

When marginal utility becomes negative, it means that the consumer is tired of eating brownies. At that point, the brownies are no longer adding to the consumer's utility, and he or she will stop eating them.

Diminishing Marginal Utility

As you can see in Figure 16.1b, the satisfaction that a consumer derives from consuming a good or service declines with each additional unit consumed. Consider what happens when you participate in a favorite activity for an hour and then decide to do something else. **Diminishing marginal utility** occurs when marginal utility declines as consumption increases. The concept of diminishing marginal utility is so universal that it is one of the most widely held ideas in all of economics.

Diminishing marginal utility occurs when marginal utility declines as consumption increases.

In rare cases, marginal utility can rise—but only temporarily. Consider running. Many people choose to run for recreation because it is both healthy and pleasurable. Often, the first mile is difficult as the runner's body gets warmed up. Thereafter, running is easier—for a while. No matter how good you are at distance running, eventually the extra miles become more exhausting and less satisfying, and you stop. This does not mean that running is not healthy or pleasurable. Far from it! But it does mean that forcing yourself to do more running after you have already pushed your limit yields less utility. Your own intuition should confirm this. If increasing marginal utility were possible, you would find that with every passing second you would enjoy what you were doing more and never want to stop. Since economists do not observe this behavior among rational consumers, we can be highly confident that diminishing marginal utility has tremendous explanatory power.

Table 16.1 highlights how diminishing marginal utility can serve to explain a number of interesting real-world situations.

Running is fun for only so long.

PRACTICE WHAT YOU KNOW

Diminishing Marginal Utility

Question: A friend confides to you that a third friend has gradually lost interest in watching *Gossip Girl* with her and has begun saying she's too busy. How would you advise your friend to handle the situation?

Answer: Tell your friend about diminishing marginal utility! Even the best television show runs its course. After a while, the same humor or drama that once made the show interesting no longer seems as interesting. Then suggest to your friend that they mix it up and do something different together. If that doesn't work, it may not be *Gossip Girl* that is the problem—it may be that your friend's friend has grown tired of her.

Would you watch a *Gossip Girl* marathon?

TABLE 16.1

Examples of Diminishing Marginal Utility

Example	Explanation using diminishing marginal utility
Discounts on two-day passes to amusement parks	The excitement on the first day is palpable. You run to rides, don't mind waiting in line, and experience the thrill for the first time. By the second day, the enthusiasm has worn off and the lower price entices you to return.
Discounts on season tickets	Over the course of any season, people anticipate some games and concerts more highly than others. To encourage patrons to buy the entire season package, venues must discount the total price.
All-you-can-eat buffet	All-you-can-eat buffets offer the promise of unlimited food, but the average diner has a limited capacity. Eating more eventually leads to negative marginal utility. Restaurants assume that diminishing utility will limit how much their customers eat.
Unlimited night and weekend minutes on cellphone plans	Cellphone companies rely on the diminishing marginal utility of conversation. Because of unused capacity at night and on the weekends, cellphone companies offer "unlimited" plans; they know that consumers will not stay on their phones indefinitely.
Newspaper vending machines	A person rarely wants a second copy of the same newspaper. Since the value of the second paper is close to zero, most people do not steal additional copies from vending machines. (Sunday papers with money-saving coupons are a possible exception.)
Nathan's Famous Hot Dog Eating Contest	Many people enjoy eating a hot dog or two or three, but Nathan's Famous Hot Dog Eating Contest is very difficult to watch.

How Do Consumers Optimize Their Purchasing Decisions?

Maximizing utility requires that consumers get the most satisfaction out of every dollar they spend, or what is commonly called "getting the biggest bang for the buck." When this is accomplished, we say that the consumer has optimized his or her purchasing decisions. However, this is easier said than done. Over the course of the year, each of us will make thousands of purchases of different amounts. Our budgets are generally not unlimited, and we try to spend in a way that enables us to meet both our short-run and our long-run needs. The combination of goods and services that maximizes the satisfaction, or utility, we get from our income or budget is the **consumer optimum**. In this section, we examine the decision process that leads to the consumer optimum. We start with two goods and then generalize those findings across a consumer's entire income or budget.

The **consumer optimum** is the combination of goods and services that maximizes the consumer's utility for a given income or budget.

Consumer Purchasing Decisions

Let's begin by imagining a world with only two goods: Pepsi and pizza. This will help us to focus on the opportunity cost of purchasing Pepsi instead of pizza, or pizza instead of Pepsi.

Pepsi is available for \$1 per can, and each pizza slice costs \$2. Suppose that you have \$10 to spend. How much of each good should you buy in order to maximize your satisfaction? Before we can answer that question, we need a rule for making decisions. To reach your consumer optimum, you must allocate your available money by choosing goods that give you the most utility per dollar spent. By attempting to get the biggest bang for your buck, you will end up optimizing your choices. This relationship, shown below in terms of marginal utility (MU), helps quantify the decision. So if you get more for your money by purchasing Pepsi than pizza, then you should buy Pepsi—and vice versa.

$$\frac{MU_{Pepsi}}{Price_{Pepsi}} \quad \textbf{Which is larger?} \quad \frac{MU_{Pizza}}{Price_{Pizza}}$$

If we divide the marginal utility of a good by its price, we get the utility per dollar spent. Since you wish to optimize your utility, a direct comparison of the marginal utility per dollar spent on Pepsi versus pizza gives you a road map to your consumer satisfaction. Table 16.2 shows the marginal utility for each can of Pepsi (column 2) and the marginal utility for each slice of pizza (column 5).

To decide what to consume first, look at column 3, which lists the marginal utility per dollar spent for Pepsi, and column 6, which lists the marginal utility per dollar spent for pizza. Now it's time to make your first spending decision—whether to drink a Pepsi or eat a slice of pizza. Since the marginal

TABLE 16.2

The Consumer Optimum with Pepsi and Pizza

(1) Pepsi consumed (cans)	(2) Marginal utility (MU Pepsi)	(3) MU Pepsi / Price Pepsi (Pepsi \$1/can)	(4) Pizza consumed (slices)	(5) Marginal utility (MU pizza)	(6) MU pizza / Price pizza (pizza \$2/slice)
1	9	9/1 = 9	1	20	20/2 = 10
2	8	8/1 = 8	2	16	16/2 = 8
3	7	7/1 = 7	3	12	**12/2 = 6**
4	6	**6/1 = 6**	4	8	8/2 = 4
5	5	5/1 = 5	5	4	4/2 = 2
6	4	4/1 = 4	6	0	0/2 = 0
7	3	3/1 = 3	7	−4	−4/2 = −2
8	2	2/1 = 2	8	−8	−8/2 = −4
9	1	1/1 = 1	9	−12	−12/2 = −6
10	0	0/1 = 0	10	−16	−16/2 = −8

utility per dollar spent for the first slice of pizza (10) is higher than the marginal utility for the first can of Pepsi (9), you order a slice of pizza, which costs $2. You have $8 left.

After eating the first slice of pizza, you can choose between having a second slice of pizza, which brings 8 utils per dollar spent, and having the first can of Pepsi, which brings 9 utils per dollar spent. This time you order a Pepsi, which costs $1. You have $7 left.

Now you can choose between having a second slice of pizza, representing 8 utils per dollar spent, and having a second can of Pepsi, also 8 utils per dollar spent. Since the two choices each yield the same amount of utility per dollar spent and you have enough money to afford both, we'll assume you would probably purchase both at the same time. This costs another $3, which leaves you with $4.

Your next choice is between the third slice of pizza at 6 utils per dollar spent and the third can of Pepsi at 7 utils per dollar spent. Pepsi is the better value, so you buy that. This leaves you with $3 for your final choice: between the third slice of pizza at 6 utils per dollar spent, and the fourth can of Pepsi at 6 utils per dollar spent. Since you have exactly $3 left and the items are of equal utility, you end your purchases by buying both.

Let's see how well you have done. Looking at column 2 in Table 16.2, we calculate that the four Pepsis you consumed yielded a total utility of (9 + 8 + 7 + 6) = 30 utils. Looking at column 5, we see that three slices of pizza yielded a total utility of (20 + 16 + 12) = 48 utils. Adding the two together (30 + 48) gives 78 total utils of satisfaction. This is the most utility you can afford with $10. To see why, look at Table 16.3, which reports the maximum utility for every affordable combination of Pepsi and pizza.

The optimum combination of Pepsi and pizza is highlighted in orange. This is the result we found by comparing the marginal utilities per dollar spent in Table 16.2. Notice that Table 16.3 confirms that this process results in the highest total utility. All other affordable combinations of Pepsi and pizza produce less utility. Table 16.3 also illustrates diminishing marginal utility. If you select either pizza or Pepsi exclusively, you would have a much lower total utility: 60 utils with pizza and 45 utils with Pepsi. In addition, the preferred outcome of four Pepsis and three pizza slices corresponds to a modest amount of each good; this avoids the utility reduction associated with excessive consumption.

TABLE 16.3

The Maximum Utility from Different Combinations of Pepsi and Pizza

Affordable combination of pizza and Pepsi	Total utility
5 pizza slices (20 + 16 + 12 + 8 + 4)	60 utils
2 Pepsis (9 + 8) and 4 pizza slices (20 + 16 + 12 + 8)	73 utils
4 Pepsis (9 + 8 + 7 + 6) and 3 pizza slices (20 + 16 + 12)	**78 utils**
6 Pepsis (9 + 8 + 7 + 6 + 5 + 4) and 2 pizza slices (20 + 16)	75 utils
8 Pepsis (9 + 8 + 7 + 6 + 5 + 4 + 3 + 2) and 1 pizza slice (20)	64 utils
10 Pepsis (9 + 8 + 7 + 6 + 5 + 4 + 3 + 2 + 1 + 0)	45 utils

SNAPSHOT

The OECD Better Life Index

The OECD Better Life Index attempts to measure 11 key factors of material well-being in each of its 34 member countries. The goal of the index is to provide member governments with a snapshot of how its citizens are living, thus providing a road map for future policy priorities. Some factors are objectively measured, such as average household income. Others are more subjective, such as "life satisfaction," and are measured from survey responses. Below is a look at the results in three countries.

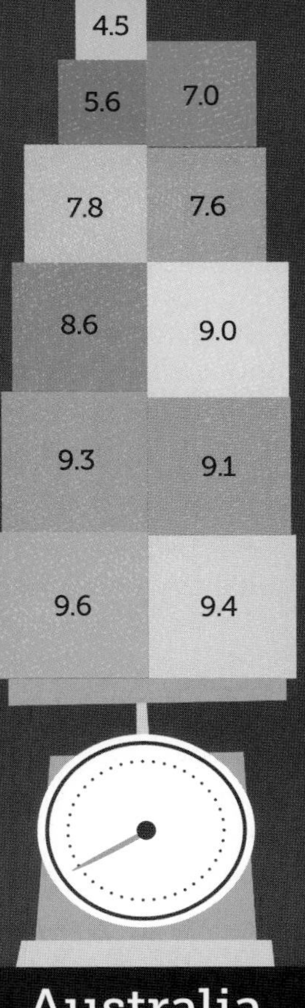

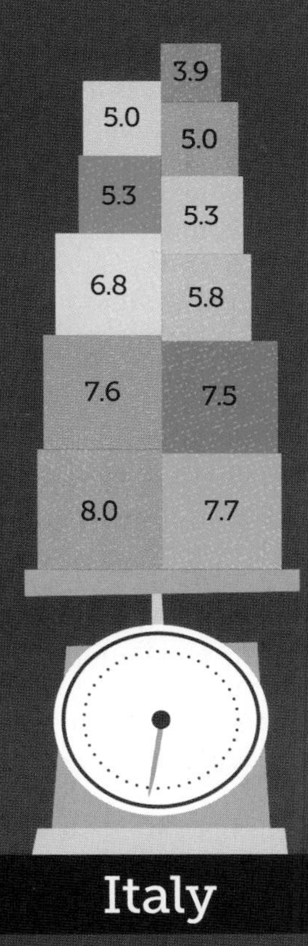

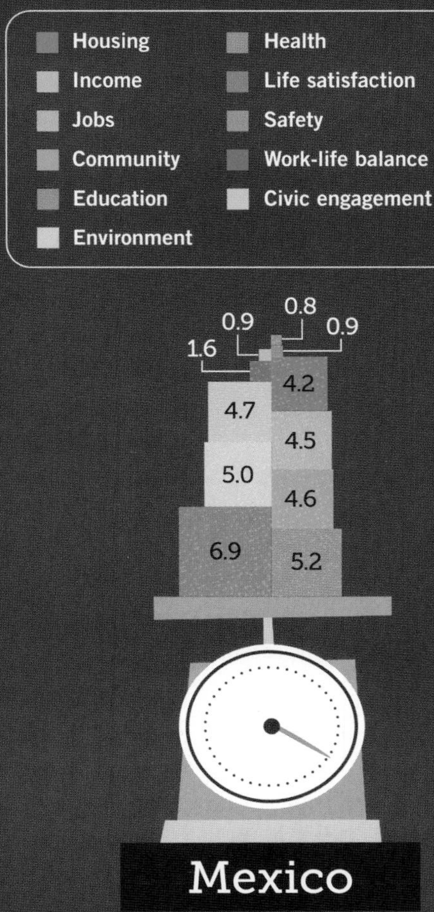

10.0 Each factor is ranked on a scale of zero to 10, with 10 being the highest. One to three indicators go into each measurement. For instance, "Jobs" is measured through the unemployment rate, job security, and personal earnings.

What do these numbers say about a nation's quality of life? It depends on which factors you think are most important. At www.oecdbetterlifeindex.org you can weight the different categories, create an index, and see how nations compare.

REVIEW QUESTIONS

- Mexico has four glaring challenges to the well-being of its citizens. What are they?
- Visit the OECD website and create your own index. Are any of the 11 factors trade-offs?

Marginal thinking

By thinking at the margin about which good provides the highest marginal utility, you also maximize your total utility. Of course, most people rarely think this way. But as consumers we make choices like this all the time. Instead of adding up utils, we think "that isn't worth it" or "that's a steal." Consumer choice is not so much a conscious calculation as an instinct to seek the most satisfaction. Next we extend our analysis by generalizing the two-good example.

Marginal Thinking with More Than Two Goods

The idea of measuring utility makes our instinctive sense more explicit and enables us to solve simple optimization problems. For instance, when you travel without the aid of GPS you instinctively make choices about which route to take in order to save time. The decision to turn left or right when you come to a stop sign is a decision at the margin: one route will be better than the other. If you consistently make the best choices about which way to turn, you will arrive at your destination sooner. This is why economists focus on marginal thinking.

Marginal thinking

In reality, life is more complex than the simple two-good model implies. When you have $10 to spend, you may choose among many goods. Since you buy many items at all kinds of prices over the course of a year, you must juggle hundreds (or thousands) of purchases so that you enjoy roughly the same utility per dollar spent. Consumer equilibrium captures this idea by comparing the utility gained with the price paid for every item a consumer buys. This means that a consumer's income or budget is balanced so that the ratio of the marginal utility (MU) per dollar spent on every item, from good A to good Z, is equal. In mathematical terms:

Left or right? One way will get you to your destination sooner.

$$MU_A \div Price_A = MU_B \div Price_B = \dots = MU_Z \div Price_Z$$

In the next section, we explore the relationship between changes in price and changes in the consumer optimum.

Price Changes and the Consumer Optimum

Recall our example of pizza and Pepsi: you reached an optimum when you purchased four Pepsis and three slices of pizza. At that point, the marginal utility per dollar spent for Pepsi and pizza was equal:

$$MU_{pizza} \text{ (12 utils)} \div \$2 = MU_{Pepsi} \text{ (6 utils)} \div \$1$$

In the earlier example, the prices of a slice of pizza ($2) and a can of Pepsi ($1) were held constant. But suppose that the price of a slice of pizza drops to $1.50. This causes the ratio of $MU_{pizza} \div Price_{pizza}$ to change from 12 ÷ 2, or 6 utils per dollar, to 12 ÷ 1.5, or 8 utils per dollar. The lower price for pizza increases the quantity of slices that the consumer will buy:

$$MU_{pizza} \text{ (12 utils)} \div \$1.50 > MU_{Pepsi} \text{ (6 utils)} \div \$1$$

As a result, we can say that lower prices increase the marginal utility per dollar spent and cause consumers to buy more of a good. Higher prices have

PRACTICE WHAT YOU KNOW

Consumer Optimum

Question: Suppose your favorite magazine, *The Economist*, costs $6 per issue and *People* magazine costs $4 per issue. If you receive 20 utils when you read *People*, how many additional utils would you need to get from reading *The Economist* to cause you to spend the extra $2 it costs to purchase it?

Answer: To answer the question, you first need to equate the marginal utility (MU) per dollar spent for both magazines and solve for the missing variable, the utility from *The Economist*:

$$MU_{\text{The Economist}} \text{ (X utils)} \div \$6 = MU_{\text{People}} \text{ (20 utils)} \div \$4$$
$$X \div \$6 = 20 \div \$4$$
$$X = \$120 \div \$4$$
$$X = 30$$

When the $MU_{\textit{The Economist}}$ is equal to 30 utils, you are indifferent between purchasing either of the two magazines. Since the question asks how many additional utils are needed to justify purchasing *The Economist*, you should then subtract the utils from *People*, or 20, to get the difference, which is 30 − 20, or 10 utils.

the opposite effect by lowering the marginal utility per dollar spent. If that sounds an awful lot like the law of demand, it is! We have just restated the law of demand in terms of marginal utility.

We know that according to the law of demand (see Chapter 3), the quantity demanded falls when the price rises, and the quantity demanded rises when the price falls—all other things being equal. If we think of consumer desire for a particular product as demand, it makes sense to find a connection among the prices that consumers pay, the quantity that they buy, and the marginal utility that they receive.

When a price changes, there are two effects. First, because the marginal utility per dollar spent is now higher, consumers substitute the product that has become relatively less expensive—a behavior known as the **substitution effect**. Second, at the same time, a price change can also change the purchasing power of income—that is, the **real-income effect**. (For a basic discussion of the trends behind these effects, see Chapter 3).

The **substitution effect** occurs when consumers substitute a product that has become relatively less expensive as the result of a price change.

The **real-income effect** occurs when there is a change in purchasing power as a result of a change in the price of a good.

Let's go back to our Pepsi and pizza example to separate these two effects. A lower price for a slice of pizza makes it more affordable. If slices are $2.00 each, a consumer with a budget of $10.00 can afford five slices. If the price drops to $1.50 per slice, the consumer can afford six slices and still have $1.00 left over.

When the price of a slice of pizza is $2.00, your optimum is three slices of pizza and four Pepsis. If we drop the price of a slice of pizza to $1.50, you save $0.50 per slice. Since you are purchasing three slices, you save $1.50—which is enough to buy another slice. Looking back at column 5 in Table 16.2, we see that the fourth slice of pizza yields an additional 8 utils. Alternatively, you could use the $1.50 you saved on pizza to buy a fifth can of Pepsi—which has a marginal utility of 5—and still have $0.50 left over.

The lower price of pizza may cause you to substitute pizza for Pepsi since it has become relatively less expensive. This is a demonstration of the substitution effect. In addition, you have more purchasing power through the money you save from the lower-priced pizza. This is the real-income effect.

The real-income effect only matters when prices change enough to cause a measurable effect on the purchasing power of the consumer's income or budget. For example, suppose that a 10% price reduction in peanut butter cups occurs. Will there be a substitution effect, a real-income effect, or both? The secret to answering this question is to consider how much money is saved. Most candy bars cost less than a dollar, so a 10% reduction in price would be less than 10 cents. The lower price will motivate some consumers to switch to peanut butter cups—a substitution effect that can be observed through increased purchases of peanut butter cups. However, the income effect is negligible. The consumer has saved less than 10 cents. The money saved could be used to purchase other goods; but very few goods cost so little, and the enhanced purchasing power is effectively zero. Thus, the answer to the question is that there will be a modest substitution effect and essentially no real-income effect.

What Is the Diamond-Water Paradox?

The **diamond-water paradox** explains why water, which is essential to life, is inexpensive while diamonds, which do not sustain life, are expensive.

Now that you understand the connection between prices and utility, we can tackle one of the most interesting puzzles in economics—the diamond-water paradox. First described by Adam Smith in 1776, the **diamond-water paradox** explains why water, which is essential to life, is inexpensive while diamonds, which do not sustain life, are expensive. Many people of Smith's era found the paradox perplexing. Today, we can use consumer choice theory to answer the question.

Essentially, the diamond-water paradox unfairly compares the amount of marginal utility a person receives from a small quantity of something rare (the diamond) with the marginal utility received from consuming a small amount of additional water after already consuming a large amount.

We know that marginal utility is captured in the law of demand and, therefore, by the price. For example, when the price of diamonds increases, the quantity demanded declines. Moreover, total utility is determined by the amount of consumer surplus enjoyed from a transaction. We learned in Chapter 6 that when thinking graphically the consumer surplus is the area under the demand curve and above the price, or the gains from trade that a consumer enjoys. Therefore, if the price of diamonds rises, consumers will enjoy less surplus from buying them.

Figure 16.2 contrasts the demand and supply equilibrium in both the market for water and the market for diamonds. Notice that the consumer surplus is the area highlighted in light green for water and the triangular area highlighted in dark green for diamonds. The light green area of total utility for water (TU_w) is much larger than the dark green area of total utility for diamonds (TU_d)

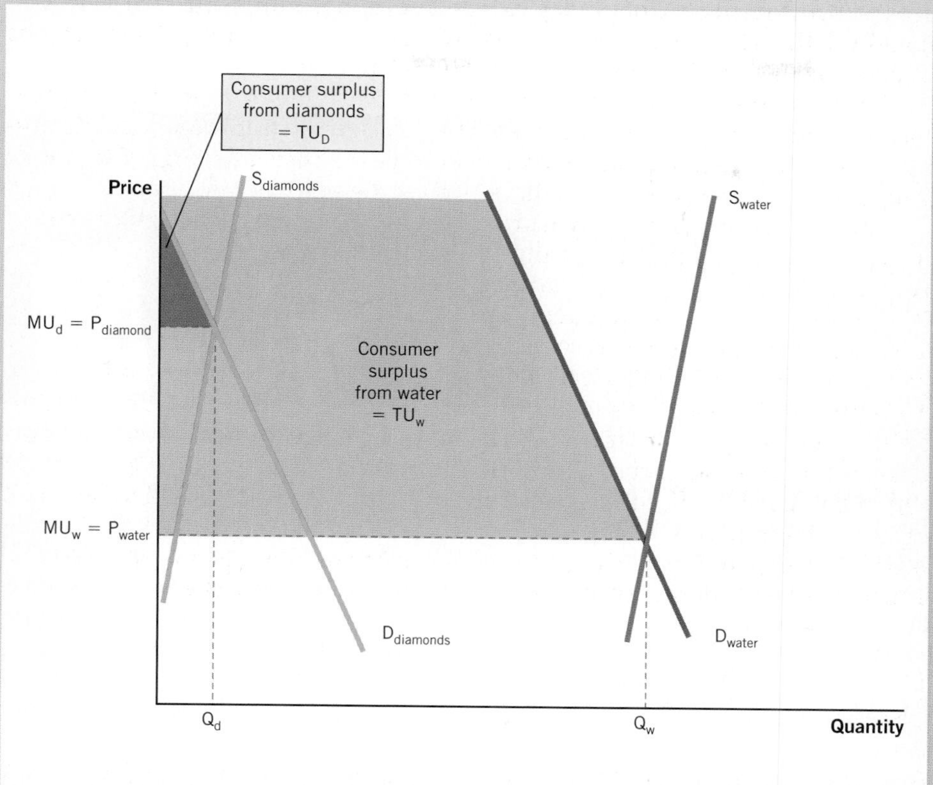

FIGURE 16.2

The Diamond-Water Paradox

The diamond-water paradox exists because people fail to recognize that demand and supply are both equally important in determining the value a good creates in society. The demand for water is large, while the demand for diamonds is small. If we look at the amount of consumer surplus, we observe that the light green area (TU_w) is much larger than the dark green area (TU_d), because water is essential for life. As a result, water creates significantly more total utility (TU) than diamonds. However, since water is abundant in most places, the price, P_{water}, is low. In contrast, diamonds are rare and the price, $P_{diamond}$, is high.

because water is essential for life. Therefore, water creates significantly more total utility than diamonds do. However, in most places in the United States water is very plentiful, so people take additional units of it for granted. In fact, it is so plentiful that if someone were to offer you a gallon of water right now, you would probably hesitate to take it. But what if someone offered you a gallon-size bucket of diamonds? You bet you would take that! Therefore, it should not surprise you that something quite plentiful, water, would yield less marginal utility than something rare, diamonds ($MU_w < MU_d$).

Let's consider how we use water. We bathe in it, cook with it, and drink it. Each of those uses has high value, so the marginal utility of water is high. But we also use it to water our lawns and fill our fish tanks. Those uses are not nearly as essential, so the marginal utility of water for these uses is much lower. The reason we use water in both essential and non-essential ways is that its price is relatively low, so low-value uses, like filling fish tanks, yield enough utility to justify the cost. Since water is abundant in most places, the price (P_{water}) is low. In contrast, diamonds are rare and their price ($P_{diamond}$) is high. The cost of obtaining a diamond means that a consumer must get a great deal of marginal utility from the purchase of a diamond to justify the expense. This explains why diamonds are given as gifts for extremely special occasions.

ECONOMICS IN THE MEDIA

The Diamond-Water Paradox

Super Size Me

What would happen if you ate all your meals at McDonald's for an entire month—without ever exercising? *Super Size Me*, a 2004 documentary by Morgan Spurlock, endeavored to find out. It is the absurd nature of Spurlock's adventure that pulls viewers in. No one would *actually* eat every meal at the same restaurant for a month, because diminishing marginal utility would cause the utility from the meals to plunge. (This is especially true with McDonald's, which is not known for quality.)

Why did Spurlock take aim at McDonald's, and more generally the fast-food industry? His aim was to reveal how unhealthy fast food really is, but the documentary also happens to unintentionally offer a modern parallel to the diamond-water paradox.

The key is the business model that many fast-food restaurants follow. These restaurants provide filling food at low cost, a combination that encourages consumers to eat more than they would if the price was higher. Eating a lot of food causes diminishing marginal utility; often, the last bite of a sandwich or fries, or the last gulp of a 32-ounce drink, brings very little additional utility, so it is not uncommon for consumers to discard the excess.

In contrast, consider fine dining. Fancy establishments serve smaller portions by design. A five-course meal is meant to be savored, and the experience trumps price. What makes someone willing to pay significantly more when dining out at such places? Upscale restaurants are creating high marginal utility by making every bite mouthwatering. They do not want to diminish the marginal value through overeating.

A Big Mac a day for 30 days! What could possibly go wrong?

To summarize, McDonald's is a lot like water in the diamond-water paradox. It is easy to find a McDonald's restaurant almost anywhere, and the chain serves close to 50 million customers a day. Therefore, the total utility the chain creates is high, despite the fact that the marginal utility of an individual bite is low. Upscale restaurants are a lot like diamonds: they are uncommon, and the number of customers they serve is small. The total utility that upscale restaurants create is low compared to McDonald's, but the marginal utility of an individual bite at an upscale restaurant is quite high.

Conclusion

Does having more money make people much happier? The answer is no. More money enables people to buy more goods, but because of diminishing marginal utility the increases in happiness from being able to buy more goods, or higher-quality goods, become progressively smaller with rising income. So we could say that having more money makes people somewhat happier. But it seems more appropriate to add that the relationship between quality of life and money is not direct. More money sometimes leads to more utility, and at other times more money means more problems.

As we have seen in this chapter, prices play a key role in determining utility. Since consumers face a budget constraint and wish to maximize their utility, the prices they pay determine their marginal utility per dollar spent. Comparing the marginal utility per dollar spent across many goods helps us to understand individuals' consumption patterns. Diminishing marginal utility also helps to describe consumer choice. Since marginal utility declines with additional consumption, consumers do not exclusively purchase their favorite products; instead, they diversify their choices in order to gain more utility. In addition, changes in prices have two different effects: one on income, and a separate substitution effect that determines the composition of the bundle of goods that are purchased.

In the next chapter, we will question how much individuals use consumer choice theory to make their decisions. An alternative approach, known as behavioral economics, argues that decision-makers are not entirely rational about the choices they make.

Finally, in the appendix that follows we refine consumer theory by discussing indifference curves. Please read the appendix to get a glimpse into how economists model consumer choice in greater detail.

ANSWERING THE BIG QUESTIONS

How do economists model consumer satisfaction?

* Economists model consumer satisfaction by examining utility, which is a measure of the relative levels of satisfaction that consumers enjoy from the consumption of goods and services.
* An important property of utility is that it diminishes with additional consumption. This property limits the amount of any particular good or service that a person will consume.

How do consumers optimize their purchasing decisions?

* Consumers optimize their purchasing decisions by finding the combination of goods and services that maximizes the level of satisfaction from a given income or budget. The consumer optimum occurs when a consumer balances income or budget, so that the marginal utility per dollar spent on every item in the budget is equal to that of every other item.
* Changes in price have two distinct effects on consumer behavior. If the price falls, the marginal utility per dollar spent will be higher. As a result, consumers will substitute the product that has become relatively less expensive. This move reflects a substitution effect. If the lower price also results in substantial savings, it causes an increase in purchasing power known as the real-income effect.

What is the diamond-water paradox?

* The diamond-water paradox explains why water, which is essential to life, is inexpensive, while diamonds, which do not sustain life, are expensive. Many people of Adam Smith's era, in the eighteenth century, found the paradox perplexing. We can solve the diamond-water paradox by recognizing that the price of water is low because its supply is abundant and, at the same time, the price of diamonds is high because their supply is low. If water were as rare as diamonds, there is no doubt that the price of water would exceed the price of diamonds.

ECONOMICS FOR LIFE

The Economic Calculus of Romance: When Do You Know You've Found the "Right" Person?

We all know that finding your soul mate can create more happiness in your life than anything else. Being with the right person can bring you joy, meaning, and a sense of personal strength. But—if you'll forgive us for being a bit unromantic—isn't there also something to say about all this happiness in terms of utility? In this box, we give some "economic" advice about love and marriage.

1. Recognize that your choice in a partner is being made in a market (the dating market), but the market doesn't use money, it uses barter. You offer someone the qualities that they're looking for—love, support, shared life goals—and hope that they are willing to trade those things back to you. (And that they don't get a better offer from someone else!) You find someone you want who feels the same way about you.
2. Partnerships often work best when the partners have characteristics and skills that are quite different from one another. Maybe one person manages the household finances while the other takes care of the yard. In other words, a couple can make gains from trade by using their comparative advantages in the production of household services.
3. Consumption complementarities also exist in a strong relationship. When doing things together makes them more enjoyable than doing them alone, you've found someone special. It can be as simple as taking walks, making dinner together, having a common passion for animals, or belonging to the same religious organization. A beneficial partnership isn't just about getting more done through gains from trade. It's also about having more fun because each partner enjoys "consuming" life more when the other one is around.
4. Finally, when you think of marriage, think of a business contract between two people about how they will organize their lives together. As with any contract, you'll need to set some terms. Will you both need to work to support your lifestyle together? Where will you live, and will you plan to have children? How will you organize your financial affairs—will you use separate or joint bank accounts? How much will you set aside for retirement? The effort you make to understand decisions like these is time and energy well spent, because you can avoid serious conflicts later.

There you have it. All you need to do is to find someone who is willing to enter into a binding contract with you. Or in the words of this chapter, you just need to find someone with a consumer optimum that matches yours!

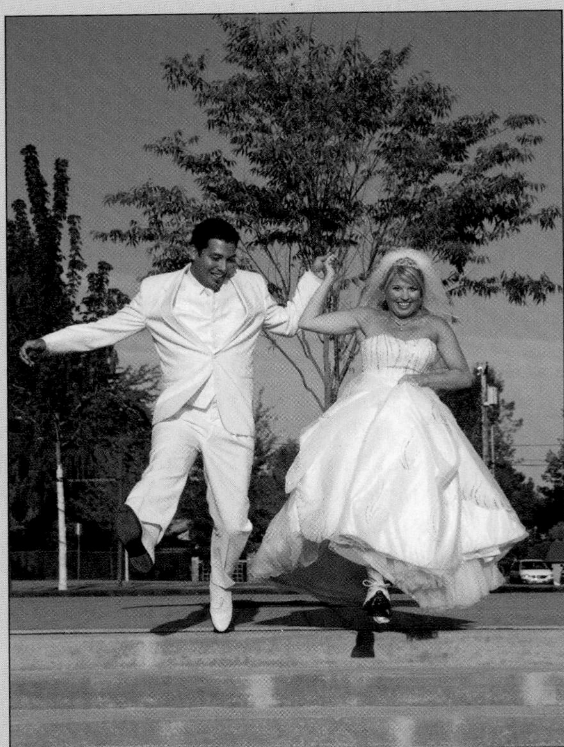

Do you suppose this couple has found their consumer optimum in the market for romance?

CONCEPTS YOU SHOULD KNOW

consumer optimum (p. 498)
diamond-water paradox (p. 504)
diminishing marginal utility (p. 497)
marginal utility (p. 495)
real-income effect (p. 503)
substitution effect (p. 503)
util (p. 494)
utility (p. 494)

QUESTIONS FOR REVIEW

1. After watching a movie, you and your friend both indicate that you liked it. Does this mean that each of you received the same amount of utility? Explain your response.
2. What is the relationship between total utility and marginal utility?
3. How is diminishing marginal utility reflected in the law of demand?
4. What does it imply when we say that the marginal utility per dollar spent is equal for two goods?

STUDY PROBLEMS (*∗solved at the end of the section*)

1. A local pizza restaurant charges full price for the first pizza but offers 50% off on a second pizza. Using marginal utility, explain the restaurant's pricing strategy.
2. Suppose that the price of trail mix is $4 per pound and the price of cashews is $6 per pound. If you get 30 utils from the last pound of cashews you consume, how many utils would you have to get from the last pound of trail mix to be in consumer equilibrium?
3. Fill in the missing information in the table below:

Number of cookies	Total utility of cookies	Marginal utility of cookies	Number of pretzels	Total utility of pretzels	Marginal utility of pretzels
0	0	25	0	0	—
1	—	15	1	10	—
2	—	10	2	18	—
3	—	5	3	24	4
4	—	—	4	—	2
5	55	—	5	—	0
6	50		6	—	

4. Use the table in problem 3. Suppose that you have a budget of $8 and that cookies and pretzels (in problem 3 above) cost $1 each. What is the consumer optimum?
5. Use the table in problem 3. What is the consumer equilibrium if the price of cookies rises to $1.50 and the price of pretzels remains at $1.00?
6. You are considering either dining at Cici's, an all-you-can-eat pizza chain, or buying pizza by the slice at a local pizzeria for $2 per slice. At which restaurant are you likely to obtain the most marginal utility from the last slice you eat? Explain your response.
7. In consumer equilibrium, a person buys four cups of coffee at $2 per cup and two muffins at $2 per muffin each day. If the price of a cup of coffee rises to $3, what would you expect to happen to the amount of coffee and muffins this person consumes?
8. How do dollar stores survive when *none* of the items sold brings a high amount of total utility to consumers?

* 9. Imagine that the total utility from consuming five tacos is 10, 16, 19, 20, and 17 utils, respectively. When does marginal utility begin to diminish?

10. You and your friends are considering vacationing in either Cabo San Lucas or Cancun for spring break. When you first researched the cost of your hotel and flights, the total price was $1,000 to each destination. However, a sale has lowered the total cost of going to Cancun to $800. Does this change create a substitution effect, a real-income effect, or both? Explain.

* 11. Everyone wears underwear, but comparatively few people wear ties. Why are ties so much more expensive than underwear if the demand for underwear is so much greater than the demand for ties?

SOLVED PROBLEMS

9. The key to answering this question is to realize that the data is expressed in total utils. The first taco brings the consumer 10 utils. Consuming the second taco yields 16 − 10, or 6 additional utils. Since there are fewer extra utils from the second taco (6) than the utils from the first taco (10), diminishing marginal utility begins after the first taco.

11. Recall that demand is only half of the market. The other half is supply. Far fewer ties are produced than items of underwear. The supply of ties also plays a role in determining the price. In addition, ties are a fashion statement. This makes ties a luxury good, whereas underwear is a necessity. As a result, ties are a lot like diamonds: there is a small overall market, and prices are high. Underwear is a lot like water: there is a very large overall market, and prices are low. The fact that ties generally cost more does not mean that ties are more valuable to society. Rather, people get more marginal utility from purchasing the "perfect" tie as opposed to finding the "perfect" underwear.

APPENDIX 16A Indifference Curve Analysis

There is much more to economic analysis than the simple supply and demand model can capture. Chapter 16 considered how consumers can get the biggest bang for their buck, or the greatest utility out of their purchases. Here we explore the question in more detail, using the tool of indifference curve analysis. The purpose of this appendix is to get you thinking at a deeper level about the connections between price changes and consumption decisions.

Indifference Curves

Indifference curves are a tool that economists use to describe the trade-offs that exist when consumers make decisions.

An **indifference curve** represents the various combinations of two goods that yield the same level of satisfaction, or utility.

A **maximization point** is the point at which a certain combination of two goods yields the most utility.

An **indifference curve** represents the various combinations of two goods that yield the same level of satisfaction, or utility. The simplest way to think about indifference curves is to envision a topographical map on which each line represents a specific elevation. When you look at a topographical map, you see ridges, mountains, valleys, and the subtle flow of the land. An indifference curve conveys the same complex information about personal satisfaction. Indifference curves visually lead upward to a top called the **maximization point**, or the point at which utility is maximized. The only limitation of this analysis is that this book is a two-dimensional space that we use to illustrate a three-dimensional concept. Let's set this concern aside and focus on achieving the maximization point, where total utility is highest.

Returning to our example of pizza and Pepsi, recall that you had $10 to spend and only two items to purchase: Pepsi at $1 per can, and pizza at $2 per slice. Like all consumers, you will optimize your utility by maximizing the marginal utility per dollar spent, so you select four Pepsis and three slices of pizza. But what happens if your budget is unlimited? If you're free to spend as much you like, how much pizza and Pepsi would you want?

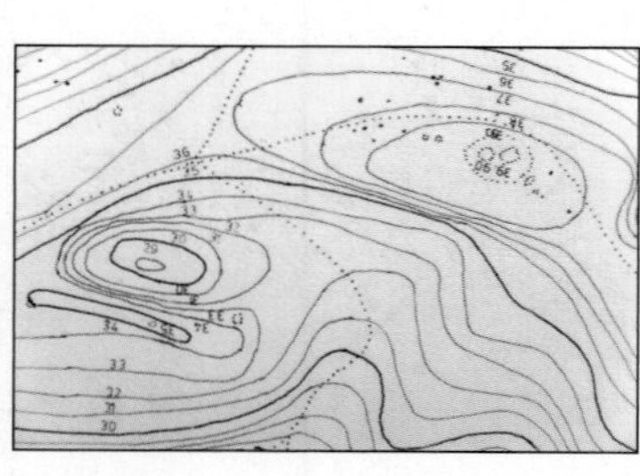

A topographical map and indifference curve analysis share many of the same properties.

Economic "Goods" and "Bads"

To answer the question posed above, we'll start with another question. Are Pepsi and pizza always economic goods? This may seem like a strange question, but think about your own consumption habits. Would you keep eating something after you felt full? Would you continue to eat even if your stomach ached? At some point, we all stop eating and drinking. In this sense, economic goods, like Pepsi and pizza, are "good" only up to a point. Once we are full, however, the utility from attaining another unit of the good becomes negative—a "bad."

Each indifference curve represents lines of equal satisfaction. For simplicity, Figure 16A.1 shows the indifference curve as circles around the point of maximum satisfaction. The closer the indifference curve is to the maximization point, the higher the consumer's level of satisfaction.

Indifference curves are best seen as approaching the maximization point from all directions (like climbing up a mountain on four different sides). In any hike, some paths are better than others. Figure 16A.1 illustrates four separate ways to reach the maximization point. However, only one of the paths makes any sense. In quadrants II, III, and IV, either pizza or Pepsi is a "bad," or both are "bads" (because at those levels of consumption one or both of them make the consumer feel too full or sick). Since the consumer must pay to acquire pizza and Pepsi, and since at least one of them is reducing their utility,

FIGURE 16A.1

Indifference Curves

The maximization point indicates where a consumer attains the most utility. In quadrant I, both Pepsi and pizza are "goods" (because their consumption involves the reactions of either tasting great or getting full), so attaining more of each will cause utility to rise toward the maximization point. In quadrants II, III, and IV, either pizza or Pepsi is a "bad," or both are (because at those levels of consumption they make the consumer feel either too full or sick). Since the consumer must pay to acquire pizza and Pepsi, and since at least one of the items is reducing the consumer's utility in quadrants II, III, and IV, the most affordable path to the highest utility—that is, the maximization point—is quadrant I. (Notice that the labels are qualitative and reflect decreasing utility with additional consumption.)

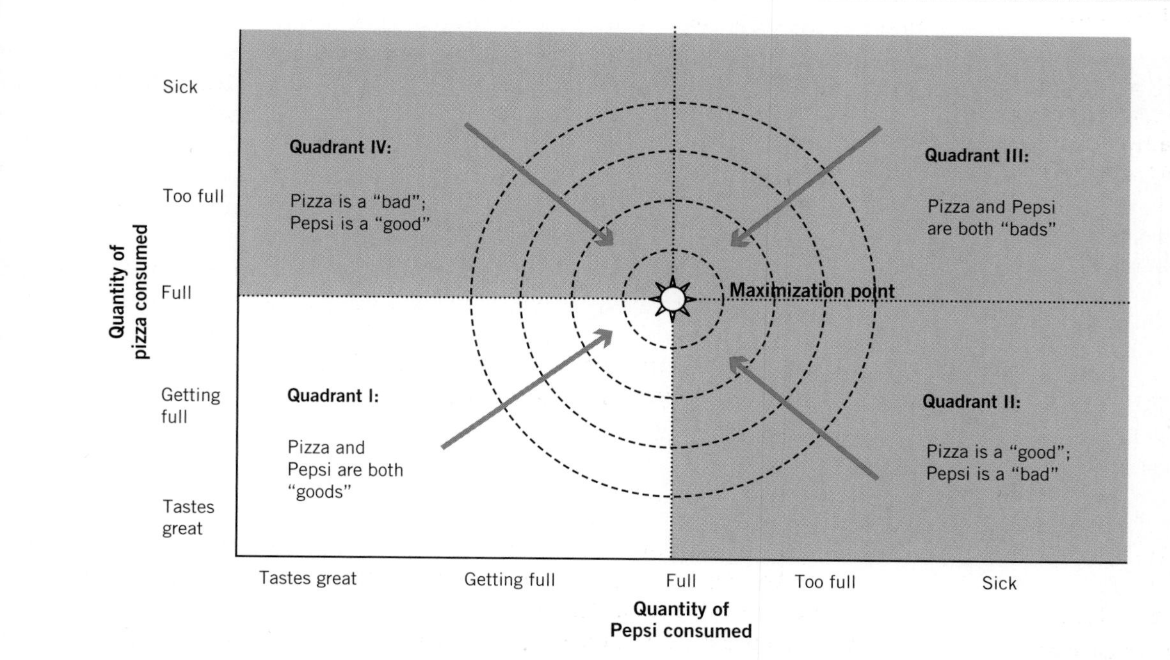

the consumer's satisfaction will increase by purchasing less of the "bad." In other words, why would anyone willingly pay in order to feel worse? Quadrants II, III, and IV are highlighted in red because people are unlikely to choose an option that makes them feel too full or sick. That leaves quadrant I as the preferred path to the highest utility. In quadrant I, increasing amounts of pizza and Pepsi produce more utility. (Notice that the labels in Figure 16A.1 are qualitative and reflect decreasing utility with additional consumption.)

The Budget Constraint

Figure 16A.1 illustrates the choices facing a consumer with an unlimited budget and no opportunity costs. However, in real life the money spent on Pepsi and pizza cannot be spent elsewhere. We need to account for a person's budget and the cost of acquiring each good. The amount a person has to spend is the **budget constraint**, or the set of consumption bundles that represent the maximum amount the consumer can afford. If you have $10 to spend on pizza ($2 per slice) and Pepsi ($1 per can), you could choose to purchase ten cans of Pepsi and forgo the pizza. Alternatively, you could purchase five slices of pizza and do without the Pepsi. Or you could choose a number of different combinations of pizza and Pepsi, as we saw in Chapter 16. The budget constraint line in Figure 16A.2 delineates the affordable combinations of pizza and Pepsi.

The **budget constraint** is the set of consumption bundles that represent the maximum amount the consumer can afford.

There are many different affordable combinations of the two goods. Let's take the pairs along the budget constraint line first. If you spend your entire $10 on Pepsi, the combination of coordinates would be the point (10,0), which represents 10 cans of Pepsi and 0 slices of pizza. If you spend your

FIGURE 16A.2

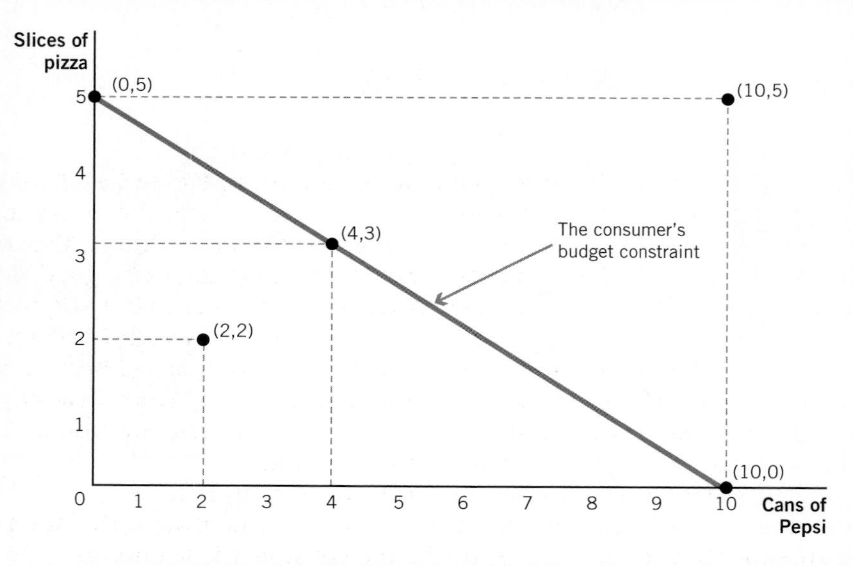

The Budget Constraint

The budget constraint line shows the set of affordable combinations of Pepsi and pizza with a budget of $10. Any point inside the budget constraint—for example (2,2)—is also affordable. Points beyond the budget constraint—for example (10,5)—are not affordable.

entire budget on pizza, the coordinates would be (0,5). These two points are the extreme outcomes. By connecting these two points with a line—the budget constraint—we can see the many combinations that would fully exhaust $10. As a consumer, your goal is to pick the combination that maximizes your satisfaction, subject to your budget constraint. One possibility would be to spend the $10 on four slices of pizza and three cans of Pepsi (4,3), which happens to be the point of utility maximization we discovered in the chapter (see Table 16.3).

What about the points located below and above the budget constraint? For example, looking again at Figure 16A.2, at the point (2,2) you would be spending $6—that is, $2 on Pepsi and $4 on pizza. You would still have $4 to spend on more of either good. Since both goods are desirable, spending the leftover money in your budget will increase your level of satisfaction. So the combination (2,2) represents a failure to maximize utility. On the other side of the budget constraint line, we find the point (10,5). This combination, which would cost you $20 to attain, represents a lack of funds in your budget. Since you only have $10, you cannot afford that combination. From this example, you can see that the budget constraint is a limiting set of choices, or a constraint imposed by scarcity.

In the next section, we examine the indifference curve in greater detail. Once we fully understand the properties that characterize indifference curves, we can join them with the budget constraint to better describe how consumers make choices.

Properties of Indifference Curves

It is useful to keep in mind several assumptions about indifference curves. The properties described below help to ensure that our model is logically consistent.

Indifference Curves Are Typically Bowed Inward

A rational consumer will only operate in quadrant I in Figure 16A.1. Within that quadrant, the higher indifference curves (those nearer the utility maximization point) are preferred to the lower ones (nearer the origin). Also, nonsatiation, or the idea that consumers cannot get too much of a good thing, requires that indifference curves bow inward with respect to the origin. This convex shape eliminates any outcome in quadrants II through IV by requiring that goods be "good," not "bad." Non-satiation is modeled here because economists assume that people make rational decisions. Since quadrants II through IV result in less utility and greater expenditures, no rational consumer would ever willingly operate in these regions.

Trade-offs

Figure 16A.3 shows an indifference curve that reflects the trade-off between two goods. Since the indifference curve bows inward, the **marginal rate of substitution**, or the rate at which a consumer is willing to trade one good for another, varies. This is reflected in the slope of the indifference curve in the figure. Points A and B are both on the same indifference curve, so

The **marginal rate of substitution** is the rate at which the consumer is willing to purchase one good instead of another.

FIGURE 16A.3

The Marginal Rate of Substitution

The marginal rate of substitution (MRS) along an indifference curve varies. This is reflected in the slope of the indifference curve. Since Pepsi and pizza are both subject to diminishing marginal utility, it takes more of the plentiful good to keep the consumer indifferent when giving up another good that is in short supply.

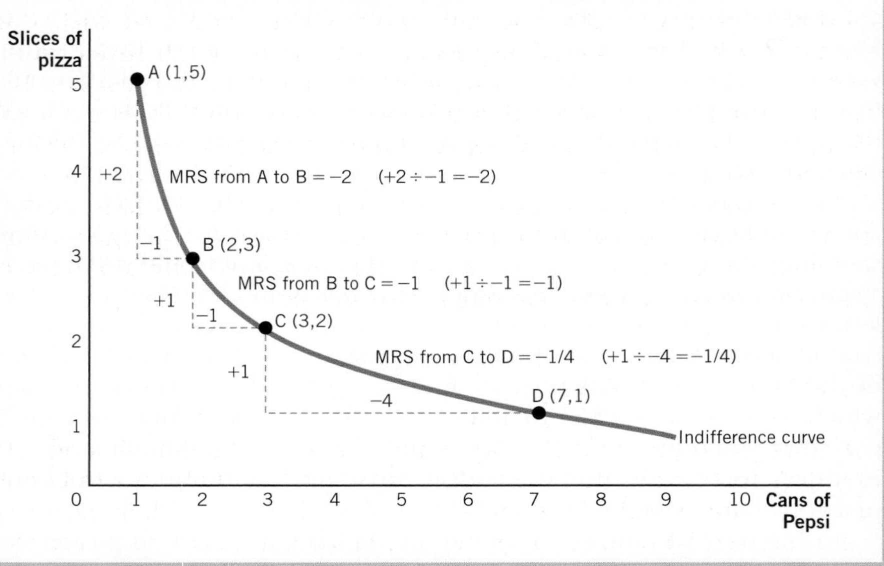

the consumer finds the combinations (1,5) and (2,3) to be equally attractive. Between points A and B, the consumer must receive two slices of pizza to compensate for the loss of a can of Pepsi. We can see this in the figure by observing that the consumer chooses only two cans of Pepsi and three slices of pizza at (2,3). Since the marginal utility from consuming Pepsi is high when the amount consumed is low, giving up an additional Pepsi requires that the consumer receive back two slices of pizza to reach the point (1,5). Therefore, the marginal rate of substitution (MRS) is 2 to −1, or −2 (because +2 ÷ −1 = −2).

Marginal thinking

However, if we examine the same indifference curve between points C and D, we see that the consumer is also indifferent between the combinations (3,2) and (7,1). However, this time the consumer is willing to give up four cans of Pepsi to get one more slice of pizza, so the MRS is 1 to −4, or −1/4 (because +1 ÷ −4 = −1/4). Why is there such a big difference between (3,2) and (7,1) compared to (2,3) and (1,5)? At (7,1), the consumer has a lot of Pepsi and very little pizza to enjoy it with. As a result, the marginal utility of the second pizza is so high that it is worth four Pepsis! We can see the change in the marginal rate of substitution visually, since the slope between points A and B is steeper than it is between points C and D.

What explains why Pepsi is more valuable between points A and B? The consumer starts with only two cans. Pizza is more valuable between points C and D because the consumer starts with only two slices of pizza. Since Pepsi and pizza are both subject to diminishing marginal utility, it takes more of the plentiful good to keep the consumer indifferent when giving up another good that is in short supply.

Indifference Curves Cannot Be Thick

Another property of indifference curves is that they cannot be thick. If they could be thick, then it would be possible to draw two points inside an indifference curve where one of the two points was preferred to the other. Therefore, a consumer could be indifferent between those points. This is evident in Figure 16A.4. Points A, B, and C are all located on the same (impossible) indifference curve. However, points B and C are both strictly preferred to point A. Why? Because point B has one extra slice of pizza compared to point A, and point C has two extra cans of Pepsi compared to point A. Since non-satiation is assumed, more pizza and Pepsi adds to the consumer's utility, and the consumer cannot be indifferent among these three points.

Indifference Curves Cannot Intersect

Indifference curves, by their very nature, cannot intersect. To understand why, let's look at a hypothetical case. Figure 16A.5 shows two indifference curves crossing at point A. Points A and B are both located along the light orange curve (IC_1), so we know that those two points bring the consumer the same utility. Points A and C are both located along the darker orange curve (IC_2), so those two points also yield the same utility for the consumer. Therefore, the utility at point A equals the utility at point B, and the utility at point A also equals the utility at point C. This means that the utility at point B should also equal the utility at point C, but that cannot be true. Point B is located at (1,3), and point C is located at (2,4). Since (2,4) strictly dominates (1,3), point C is preferred to point B. Therefore, we can say that indifference

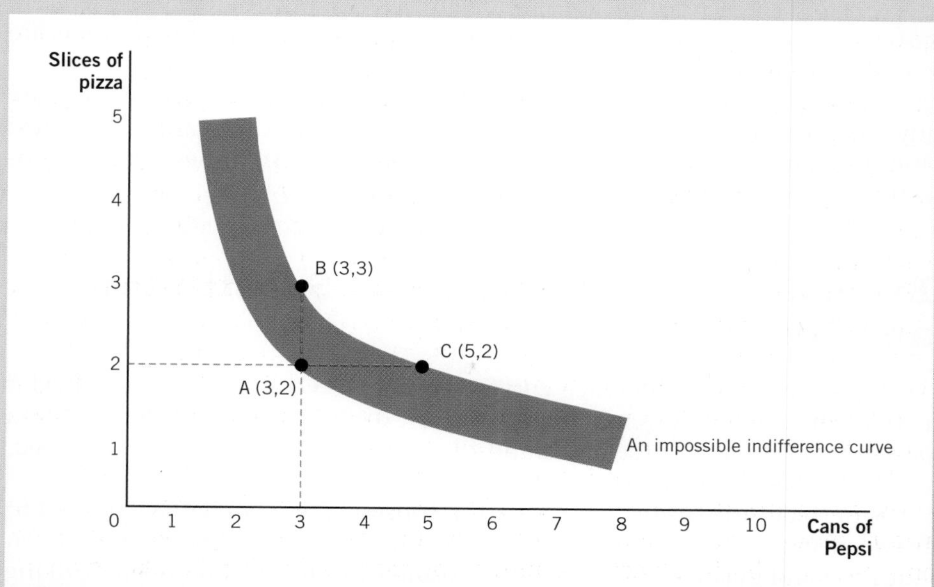

FIGURE 16A.4

Indifference Curves Cannot Be Thick

If indifference curves could be thick, it would be possible to draw two points inside the curve in a way that indicates that one of the two points is preferred to the other. Point B has one extra slice of pizza and point C has two extra cans of Pepsi compared to point A. Therefore, the consumer cannot be indifferent among these three points, and the indifference curve cannot be thick.

FIGURE 16A.5

Indifference Curves Cannot Intersect

The utility at point B should equal the utility at point C, but that cannot be true even though the utility at point B is equal to the utility at point A (along IC_1) and the utility at point C is equal to the utility at point A (along IC_2). Point B is located at (1,3) and point C is located at (2,4). Since (2,4) strictly dominates (1,3), point C is preferred to point B.

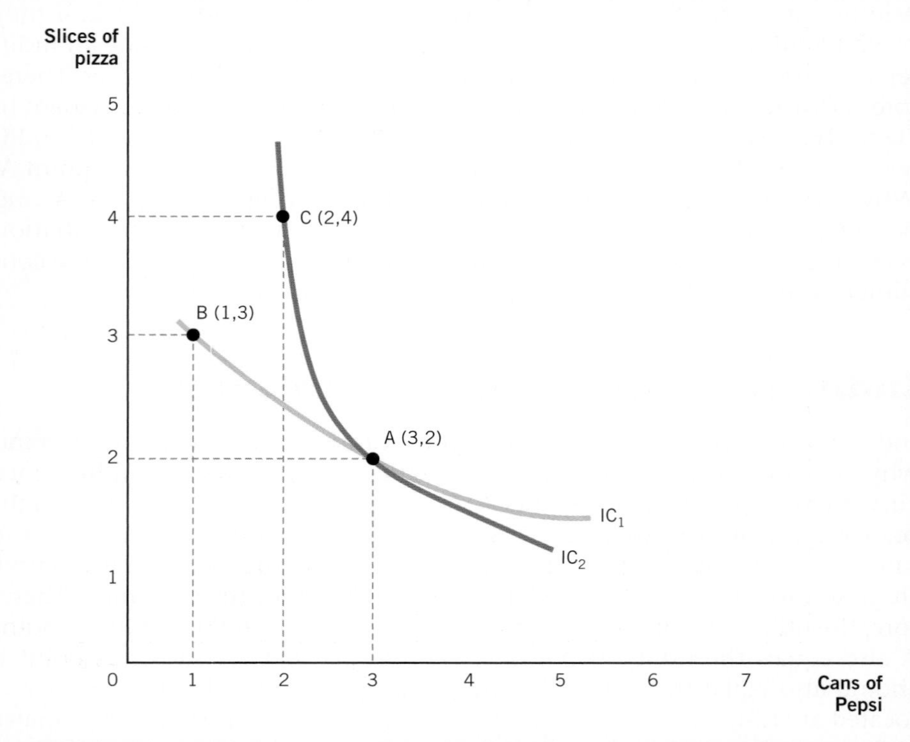

curves cannot intersect without violating the assumption that consumers are rational utility maximizers.

We have seen that indifference curves have three properties: they are inward-sloping, or convex with respect to the origin; they cannot be thick; and they cannot intersect. These properties guarantee that they take the general shape shown in quadrant I of Figure 16A.1.

Extreme Preferences: Perfect Substitutes and Perfect Complements

As we saw above, indifference curves typically are convex and bow inward toward the origin. However, there are two exceptions: *perfect substitutes* and *perfect complements*. These are found on either side of the standard-shaped, convex indifference curve.

A **perfect substitute** exists when the consumer is completely indifferent between two goods, resulting in straight-line indifference curves.

A **perfect substitute** exists when a consumer is completely indifferent between two goods. Suppose that you cannot taste any difference between Aquafina and Evian bottled water. You would be indifferent between drinking one additional bottle of Aquafina or one additional bottle of Evian. Turning to Figure 16A.6a, you can see that the indifference curves (IC_1, IC_2, etc.) for these two goods are straight, parallel lines with a marginal rate of substitution, or

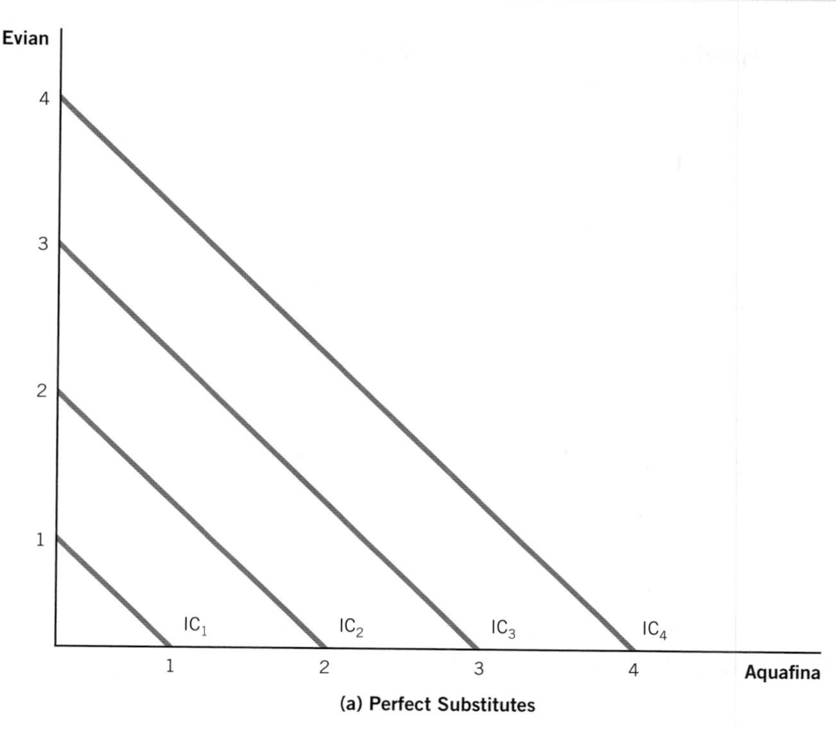

(a) Perfect Substitutes

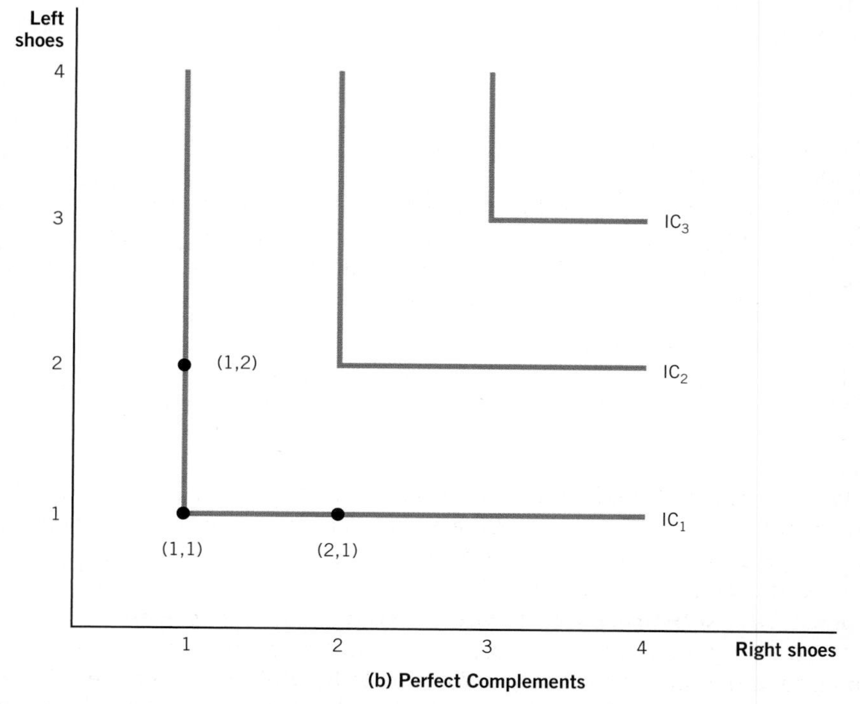

(b) Perfect Complements

FIGURE 16A.6

Perfect Substitutes and Perfect Complements

(a) Since perfect substitutes have a marginal rate of substitution that is constant, they are drawn as straight lines. In this case, the MRS, or slope, is -1 everywhere along the lines, or curves.

(b) Perfect complements are drawn as right angles. A typical indifference curve that reflects the trade-off between two goods that are not perfect substitutes or perfect complements has a marginal rate of substitution that falls between these two extremes.

slope, of −1 everywhere along the curve. However, it's important to note that the slope of an indifference curve of perfect substitutes need not always be −1; it can be any constant rate. Since perfect substitutes have a marginal rate of substitution with a constant rate, they are drawn as straight lines.

A **perfect complement** exists when the consumer is interested in consuming two goods in fixed proportions, resulting in right-angle indifference curves.

A **perfect complement** exists when a consumer is interested in consuming two goods in fixed proportions. Shoes are an excellent example. We buy shoes in pairs because the left or right shoe is not valuable by itself; we need both shoes to be able to walk comfortably. This explains why shoes are not sold individually. An extra left or right shoe has no marginal value to the consumer, so the indifference curves are right angles. For instance, left and right shoes are needed in a 1:1 ratio. Let's look at indifference curve IC_1 in Figure 16A.6b. This curve forms a right angle at the point (1,1) where the person has one left and one right shoe. Now notice that the points (1,2) and (2,1) are also on IC_1. Since an extra left or right shoe does not add utility, the points (1,2), (1,1), and (2,1) are all connected.

Perfect complements can also occur in combinations other than 1:1. For instance, an ordinary chair needs four legs for each seat. In that case, the indifference curve is still a right angle, but the additional chair legs do not enhance the consumer's utility unless they come in groups of four.

Using Indifference Curves to Illustrate the Consumer Optimum

Figure 16A.7 shows the relationship between indifference curves and the budget constraint. As the indifference curves move higher, the consumer moves progressively closer to the maximization point—that is, the point at which he or she has reached the consumer optimum. At some point, the consumer will run out of money. Therefore, the area bounded by the budget constraint (shaded in purple) represents the set of possible choices. The highest indifference curve that can be attained within the set of possible choices is IC_3, where the budget constraint is just tangent to IC_3. Even though all the points on IC_4 are more desirable than those on IC_3, the consumer lacks the purchasing power to reach that level of satisfaction. Moreover, the point (4,3) is now clearly the preferred choice among the set of possible decisions. Other choices that are also affordable—for example, the combination (2,4)—fall on a lower indifference curve.

Progressively higher indifference curves bring the consumer closer to the maximization point. Since the budget constraint limits what the consumer can afford, the tangency of the budget constraint with the highest indifference curve represents the highest affordable level of satisfaction—that is, the consumer optimum.

Using Indifference Curves to Illustrate the Real-Income and Substitution Effects

The power of indifference curve analysis is its ability to display how price changes affect consumption choices. Part of the intuition behind the analysis involves understanding when the substitution effect is likely to dominate the real-income effect, and vice versa.

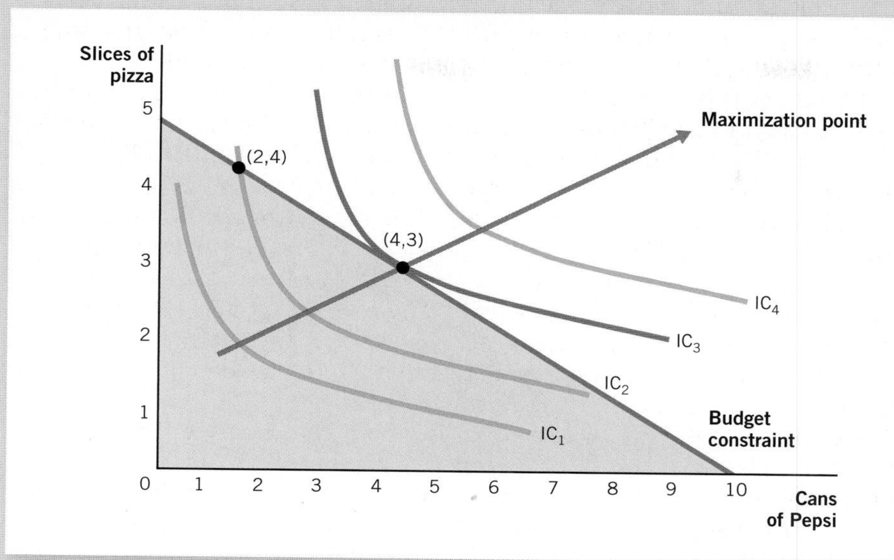

FIGURE 16A.7

Consumer Optimum

Progressively higher indifference curves bring the consumer closer to the maximization point. Since the budget constraint limits what the consumer can afford, the tangency of the budget constraint with the highest indifference curve represents the highest level of affordable satisfaction—that is, the consumer optimum. In this case, the point (4,3) represents the consumer's preferred combination of Pepsi and pizza.

In our example you have only $10, so when the price of Pepsi increases from $1 to $2 per can, it represents a financial burden that significantly lowers your real purchasing power. However, we can easily think of cases in which a change in the price of Pepsi wouldn't matter. Suppose yours is a typical American household with a median annual income of $50,000. While out shopping, you observe that a local Toyota car dealer is offering 10% off new cars and a nearby grocery store is selling Pepsi at a 10% discount. Since the percentage saved on each product is the same, the substitution effect will be of an equal magnitude: more people will buy Toyotas instead of Hondas, and more people will buy Pepsi instead of Coca-Cola. However, the real-income effects will be quite different. Saving 10% on the price of a new car could easily amount to a savings of $3,000 or more. In contrast, saving 10% on a 2-liter bottle of Pepsi will only save a couple of dimes. In the case of the new car, there is a substantial real-income effect, while in contrast the amount you save on the Pepsi is almost immaterial.

Changes in prices can have two distinct effects. The first is a substitution effect, under which changes in price will cause the consumer to substitute toward a good that becomes relatively less expensive. In our example, suppose that the price of Pepsi rises to $2 per can. This price increase reduces your marginal utility per dollar of consuming Pepsi. As a result, you would probably buy fewer Pepsis and use the remaining money to purchase more pizza. In effect, you would substitute the relatively less expensive good (pizza) for the relatively more expensive good (Pepsi).

However, this is not the only effect at work. The change in the product price will also alter the purchasing power of your money, or income. And a change in purchasing power generates a real-income effect. In this case, your $10 will not go as far as it used to. In Figure 16A.8, we can see that the inward rotation of the budget constraint along the *x* axis from BC_1 to BC_2 is a result of the rise in the price of Pepsi. At $2 per can, you can no longer afford to buy

FIGURE 16A.8

How a Change in Price Rotates the Budget Constraint

The inward rotation of the budget constraint along the *x* axis from BC_1 to BC_2 is a result of the rise in the price of Pepsi. At \$2 a can, you can no longer afford to buy ten cans; the most you can purchase is five. Therefore, the budget constraint moves inward along the *x* axis to five units (causing utility to fall from IC_1 to IC_2) while remaining constant along the *y* axis (since the price of pizza slices did not change).

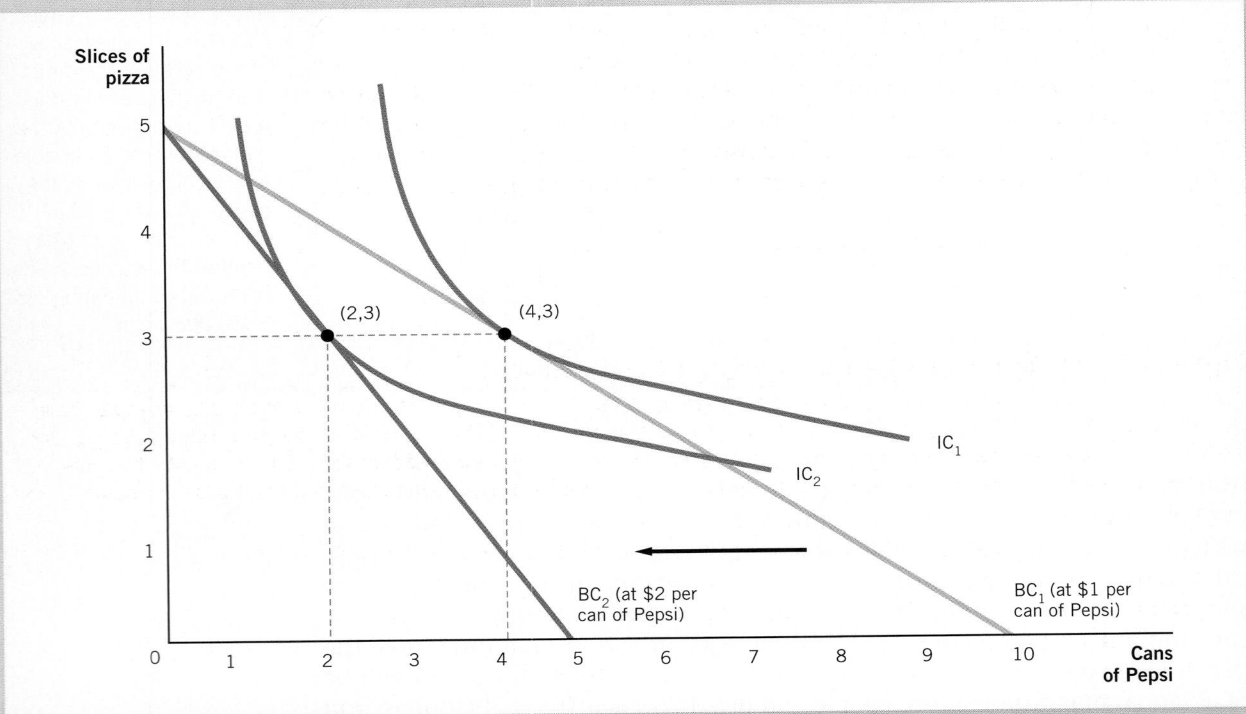

ten cans; the most you can purchase is five. Therefore, the budget constraint moves inward along the *x* axis to five units while remaining constant along the *y* axis (since the price of pizza did not change). As a result, the combination (4,3) is no longer affordable. This produces a new consumer equilibrium at (2,3) along IC_2. The end result is predictable: a rise in the price of Pepsi causes you to purchase less Pepsi and yields a lower level of satisfaction at IC_2 than your former point on IC_3 did, which is no longer possible. (See Figure 16A.7 for your former point on IC_3.)

Separating the Substitution Effect from the Real-Income Effect

Sometimes, the substitution effect and the real-income effect reinforce each other; at other times, they work against each other. In this section, we separate the substitution effect from the real-income effect.

Breaking down the movement from IC_3 to IC_2 into the separate real-income effect and substitution effect enables us to see how each effect impacts the consumer's choice. Imagine that you were given just enough money to attain IC_2 in Figure 16A.9 with the original prices of pizza and Pepsi intact. The new budget constraint ($BC_{real\ income}$) will now be parallel to BC_1 but just tangent to IC_2. The change from BC_1 to $BC_{real\ income}$ separates the real-income effect from the substitution effect. Since the slope of the new budget constraint, $BC_{real\ income}$, is less steep than that of BC_2, the point of tangency between $BC_{real\ income}$ and IC_2, point A, is lower. Furthermore, since the slopes of $BC_{real\ income}$ and BC_1 are equal, we can think of the movement from (4,3) to point A as a function of the real-income effect alone. This occurs because we have kept the slope of the budget constraint constant. Keeping the slope constant reflects the fact that the consumer has less money to spend, while the prices of Pepsi and pizza are held constant. The subsequent movement along IC_2 from point A to (2,3) results from the substitution effect exclusively,

FIGURE 16A.9

Separating the Substitution Effect from the Real-Income Effect

Breaking down the movement from IC_3 to IC_2 into the real-income effect and the substitution effect enables us to see how each effect impacts the consumer's choice. The real-income effect causes the budget constraint to shift to $BC_{real\ income}$, and the loss of purchasing power lowers the consumption of both Pepsi and pizza, as noted by the green arrows. At the same time, the substitution effect reduces the amount of Pepsi consumed and increases the consumption of pizza, as noted by the orange arrows.

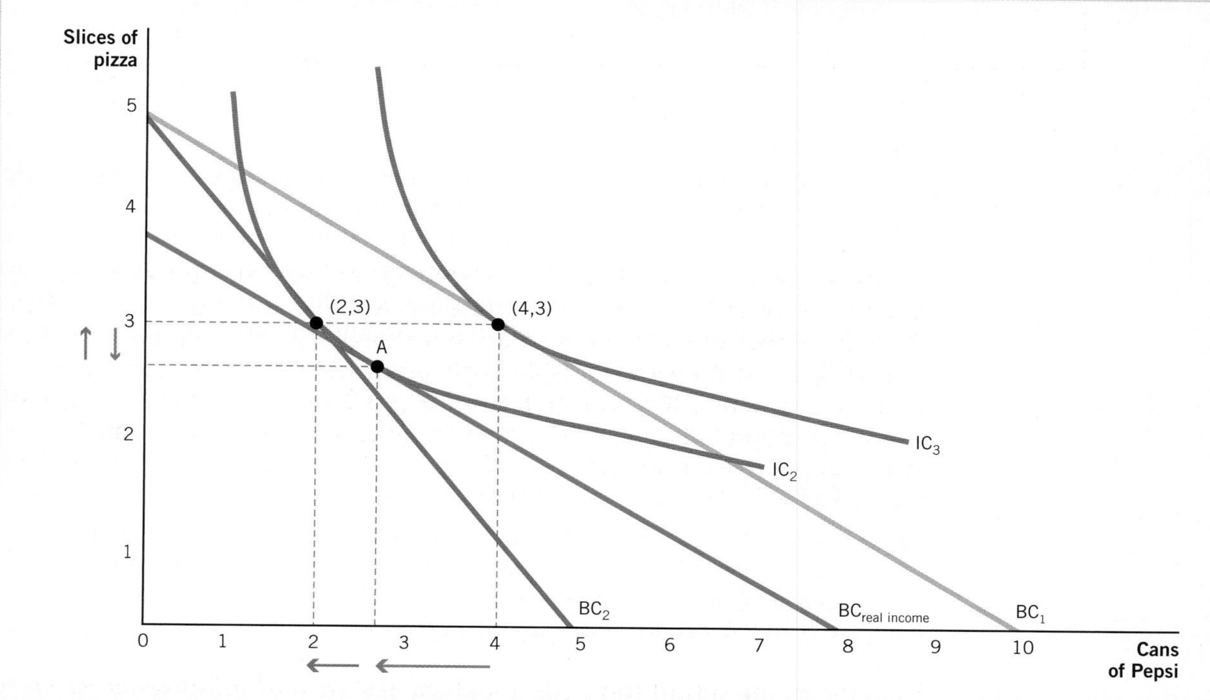

and it occurs because the price of Pepsi is now higher. This outcome causes BC_2 to become steeper.

Beginning with the real-income effect, we see that the impact of a loss of purchasing power lowers consumption of both Pepsi and pizza. The green arrows in Figure 16A.9 highlight this outcome. At the same time, the substitution effect reduces the amount of Pepsi consumed and increases the consumption of pizza. The orange arrows in the figure highlight this outcome. Since Pepsi is now relatively more expensive, you reallocate your consumption toward pizza. Overall, your consumption of Pepsi falls dramatically while your consumption of pizza remains constant.

More generally, whenever the price of a good increases (as Pepsi does in this example), this will lead to a reduction in the amount consumed since both the income and substitution effects (as represented by the orange and green arrows along the *x* axis) move in the same direction. However, since the real-income effect and substitution effect move in opposite directions with respect to the good whose price has not changed (pizza in this example), the result is ambiguous for that good (pizza), and any change in consumption depends on which effect—the substitution effect or the real-income effect—is greater.

In our example, when the price of Pepsi rose to $2 per can, it produced a large real-income effect (the green arrow along the *x* axis). Prior to the price increase, you were spending $4 out of your $10 budget on Pepsi, so Pepsi expenditures represented 40% of your budget. When the price doubled, it was like finding out that your rent just doubled from $800 a month to $1,600 a month! Since Pepsi is a big component of your budget, a doubling of its price causes a sizable real-income effect. This is not always the case, however. For example, if the price of a candy bar were to double, the typical household would barely notice this change. When this happens, the real-income effect is negligible and the substitution effect tends to dominate.

Conclusion

Economists use indifference curve analysis to gain additional insights into consumer behavior. This analysis extends the basic understanding found in supply and demand by incorporating utility theory. Because indifference curves are lines of equal utility, we can impose a budget constraint in order to describe the bundle of goods that maximizes utility. This framework enables us to illustrate the effect of price changes and budget constraints on the decisions that consumers make.

Summary

- The point of maximum consumer satisfaction is found at the point of tangency between an indifference curve and the budget constraint line.
- Indifference curves share three properties: they are inward-sloping with respect to the origin (non-satiation), they cannot be thick, and they cannot intersect.
- Indifference curves can be used to separate the substitution effect from the real-income effect.

CONCEPTS YOU SHOULD KNOW

budget constraint (p. 514)
indifference curve (p. 512)
marginal rate of substitution (p. 515)
maximization point (p. 512)
perfect complement (p. 520)
perfect substitute (p. 518)

QUESTIONS FOR REVIEW

1. If your budget increases, what generally happens to the amount of utility you experience?
2. If your budget increases, is it possible for your utility to fall? Explain your response.
3. What is the difference between an economic "good" and an economic "bad"?
4. Describe what happens to your budget constraint if the price of one item in your budget becomes less expensive. Show this on a graph.
5. A friend mentions to you that the campus coffee shop offers a 10% discount each Thursday morning before 10 a.m. Is this more likely to cause a significant substitution effect or a significant real-income effect? Explain.

STUDY PROBLEMS

1. Kate has $20. Fish sandwiches cost $5, and a cup of espresso costs $4. Draw Kate's budget constraint. If espresso goes on sale for $2 a cup, what does her new budget constraint look like?
2. When you head home for dinner, your mother always sets the table with one spoon, two forks, and one knife. Draw her indifference curves for forks and knives.
3. Frank's indifference curves for movies and bowling look like this:

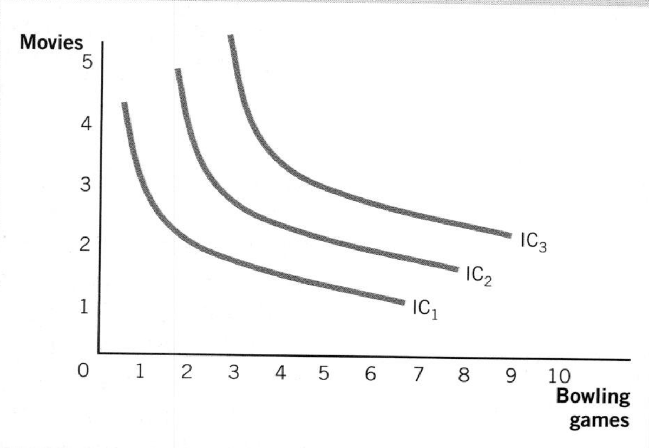

Each game of bowling costs $4, and each movie costs $8. If Frank has $24 to spend, how many times will he go bowling? How many times will he go to the movies?

CHAPTER 17

Behavioral Economics and Risk Taking

MISCONCEPTION

People always make rational decisions.

In this textbook, we have proceeded as if every person were *Homo economicus*, or a rationally self-interested decision-maker. *Homo economicus* is acutely aware of opportunities in the environment and strives to maximize the benefits received from each course of action while minimizing the costs. What does *Homo economicus* look like? If you are a fan of *Star Trek: The Next Generation*, you'll recall Data, the android with perfect logic. Data was not capable of human emotion and didn't face the complications that it creates in making decisions.

We don't want to leave you with the misconception that we're all like this! As human beings, we love, laugh, and cry. Sometimes, we seek revenge; at other times, forgiveness. We can be impulsive and shortsighted, and we can fail to see the benefits of pursuing long-run gains. Each of these behaviors is real, although they do not fit squarely within our economic models. Human decision-making is far more complex than the standard economic model of behavior implies. In this chapter, we step back and consider why people don't always make rational decisions. To fold the broadest possible set of human behavior into economic analysis, we must turn to the field of *behavioral economics*, which will enable us to capture a wider range of human motivations than the rational-agent model alone affords.

Data, the android in *Star Trek: The Next Generation*, exemplifies fully rational behavior.

BIG QUESTIONS

* How can economists explain irrational behavior?
* What is the role of risk in decision-making?

How Can Economists Explain Irrational Behavior?

The study of psychology, like economics, endeavors to understand the choices that people make. One key difference is that psychologists do not assume that people always behave in a fully rational way. As a result, psychologists have a much broader toolbox at their disposal to describe human behavior. **Behavioral economics** is the field of economics that draws on insights from experimental psychology to explore how people make economic decisions.

Behavioral economics is the field of economics that draws on insights from experimental psychology to explore how people make economic decisions.

Bounded rationality proposes that although decision-makers want a good outcome, either they are not capable of performing the problem-solving that traditional theory assumes, or they are not inclined to do so.

Until relatively recently, economists have ignored many human behaviors that do not fit their models. For example, because traditional economic theory assumed that people make optimal decisions like robots, economic theorists did not try to explain why people might make an impulse purchase. Behavioral economists, however, understand that many behaviors contradict standard assumptions about rationality. They employ the idea of **bounded rationality**, which proposes that although decision-makers want a good outcome, either they are not capable of performing the problem-solving that traditional theory assumes, or they are not inclined to do so.

Bounded rationality, or limited reasoning, can be explained in three ways. First, the information that the individual uses to make the decision may be limited or incomplete. Second, the human brain has a limited capacity to process information. Third, there is often a limited amount of time in which to make a decision. These limitations prevent the decision-maker from reaching the results predicted under perfect rationality.

Will you say "yes" to the dress?

For example, suppose you're about to get married and find yourself at Kleinfeld Bridal with your bridesmaids. You enter the store to begin your search for the perfect wedding dress. You find a dress that you like, but it's for a price higher than you were planning to spend. Do you make the purchase or not? The decision to buy depends on whether you believe that the value is high enough to justify the expense. But there is a problem: you have a limited amount of information. In a fully rational world, you would check out alternatives in other stores and on the Internet and then make the decision to purchase the dress only after you were satisfied that it is the best possible choice. Full rationality also assumes that your brain is able to recall the features of every dress. However, a dress you tried on at one location often blurs into another dress you tried on elsewhere. Wedding dresses are selected under a binding deadline. This means that you, the bride, must reach a decision quickly. Collectively, these three reasons often prevent a bride from achieving the result that economists' rational models predict. In reality, you walk into a store, see something you love, and make the purchase using partial information. Whenever people end up making decisions without perfect information, the decisions reflect bounded rationality.

We will continue our discussion of behavioral economics by examining various behaviors that do not fit assumptions about fully rational behavior. These include misperceptions of probabilities, inconsistencies in decision-making, and judgments about fairness when making decisions. The goal in this section is to help you recognize and understand many of the behaviors that lead to contradictions between what economic models predict and what people actually do.

Misperceptions of Probabilities

Economic models that assume rationality in decision-making do not account for the way people perceive the probability of events. Low-probability events are often over-anticipated, and high-probability events are often under-anticipated. To understand why this is the case, we will consider several familiar examples, including games of chance, difficulties in assessing probabilities, and seeing patterns where none exist.

Games of Chance

Playing games of chance—for example, a lottery or a slot machine—is generally a losing proposition. Yet even with great odds against winning, millions of people spend money to play games of chance. How can we explain this behavior?

For some people, the remote chance of winning a lottery offers hope that they will be able to purchase something they need but cannot afford, or even to escape from poverty. In many cases, people have incomplete information about the probabilities and prize structures. Most lottery players do not calculate the exact odds of winning. Lottery agencies typically highlight winners, as if the game has a positive expected value, which gets people excited about playing. Imagine how sobering it would be if every headline trumpeting the newest lottery millionaire was followed by all the names of people who lost. In fact, almost all games of chance have negative expected values for the participants, meaning that players are not likely to succeed at the game.

Players often operate under the irrational belief that they have control over the outcome. They are sure that playing certain numbers or patterns (for example, birthdays, anniversaries, or other lucky numbers) will bring success. Many players also feel they must stick with their favorite numbers to avoid regret; everyone has heard stories about players who changed from their lucky pattern only to watch it win.

In contrast, some gaming behaviors are rational. For example, the film *21* depicts how skilled blackjack players, working in tandem, can beat the casinos by betting

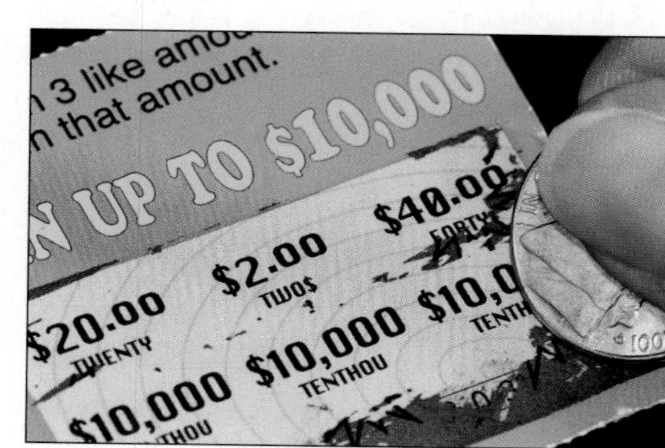

Many games of chance only return about 50 cents for every dollar played.

strategically and paying close attention to the cards on the table. In fact, some individuals are able to win at blackjack by counting the cards that have been dealt. Anytime the expected value of a gamble is positive, there is an incentive to play. For instance, if a friend wants to wager $10.00 on the flip of a coin and promises you $25.00 if you guess right, the expected value is half of $25.00, or $12.50. Since $12.50 is greater than the $10.00 you are wagering, we say that the gamble has a positive expected value. In other words, the more you play, the more you are likely to make.

Incentives

Gambles can also make sense when you have very little to lose or no other options. And some people find the thrill of gambling enjoyable as entertainment whether they win or lose. However, most gambling behaviors do not have rational motivations.

The Difficulties in Assessing Probabilities

In our discussion of games of chance, we saw that people who gamble do not usually evaluate probabilities in a rational way. But this irrational decision-making also happens with many other behaviors besides gambling. For example, on a per mile basis, traveling by airplane is approximately 10 times safer than traveling by automobile. However, millions of people who refuse to fly because they are afraid of a crash do not hesitate to get into a car. Driving seems to create a false sense of control over one's surroundings.

The 1970s television game show *Let's Make a Deal* provides a well-known example of the difficulties in assessing probabilities accurately. At the end of the show, the host asked a contestant to choose one of three curtains. Behind each curtain was one of three possible prizes: a car; a nice but less expensive item; or a worthless joke item. Contestants could have maximized their chances of winning the car if they had used probability theory to make a selection. However, contestants rarely chose in a rational way.

Opportunity cost

Suppose that you are a contestant on a game show like *Let's Make a Deal*. You pick curtain number 3. The host, who knows what is behind the curtains, opens a different one—say, curtain number 1, which has a pen filled with chickens (the joke prize). He then offers you the opportunity to switch your choice to curtain number 2. According to probability theory, what is the right thing to do? Most contestants would stay with their original choice because they figure that now they have a 50/50 chance of winning the car. But the probability of winning with your original choice remains 1/3 because the chance that you guessed correctly the first time is unchanged. Equally, the chance that one of the other curtains contains the car is still 2/3–but with curtain number 1 revealed as the joke prize, that 2/3 probability now belongs entirely to curtain number 2. Therefore, the contestant should take the switch, because it upgrades their chance of winning the car from 1/3 to 2/3. Few do, though. Almost all contestants think that each of the two remaining unopened curtains has an equal probability of holding the car, so they decide not to switch for fear of regretting their decision. Not switching indicates a failure to understand the opportunity costs involved in the decision.

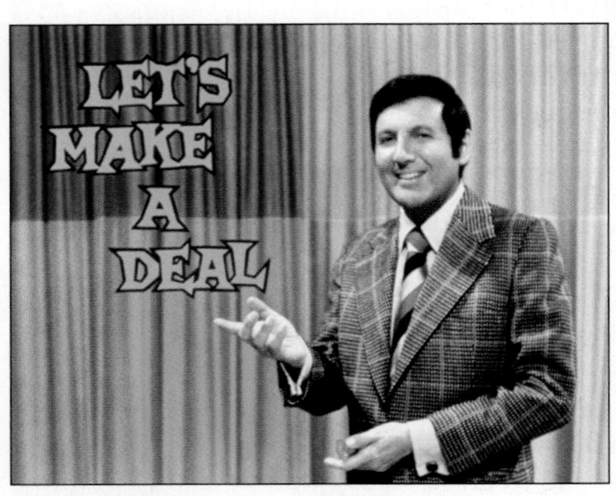

If you were a contestant, would you make a rational choice?

The difficulty in recognizing the true underlying probabilities, combined with an irrational fear of regret, leads to many poor decisions. Understanding these tendencies helps economists to evaluate why some decisions are difficult to get right.

Don't let your emotions fool you. There is no such thing as a "hot hand" in sports.

Seeing Patterns Where None Exist

Two fallacies, or false ways of thinking, help to explain how people make decisions: the *gambler's fallacy* and the *hot hand fallacy*.

The **gambler's fallacy** is the belief that recent outcomes are unlikely to be repeated and that outcomes that have not occurred recently are due to happen soon. For example, studies examining state lotteries find that bets on recent winning numbers decline. Because the selection of winning numbers is made randomly, just like flipping coins, the probability that a certain number will be a winner in one week is not related to whether the number came up in the previous week. In other words, someone who uses the gambler's fallacy believes that if many "heads" have occurred in a row, then "tails" is more likely to occur next.

The **gambler's fallacy** is the belief that recent outcomes are unlikely to be repeated and that outcomes that have not occurred recently are due to happen soon.

The **hot hand fallacy** is the belief that random sequences exhibit a positive correlation. The classic study in this area examined perceptions about the game of basketball. Most sports enthusiasts believe that a player who has scored several baskets in a row—one with a "hot hand"—is more likely to score a basket with his next shot than he might be at another time. However, the study found no positive correlation between success in one shot and success in the next shot.

The **hot hand fallacy** is the belief that random sequences exhibit a positive correlation.

ECONOMICS IN THE REAL WORLD

How Behavioral Economics Helps to Explain Stock Price Volatility

Let's examine some of the traps that people fall into when they invest in the stock market. In a fully rational world, the gambler's fallacy and the hot hand fallacy would not exist. However, in the real world, people are prone to seeing patterns in data even when there are none. Investors, for example, often believe that the rise and fall of the stock market is driven by specific events and by underlying metrics such as profitability, market share, and return on investment. But, in fact, investors often react with a herd mentality by rushing into stocks that appear to be doing well—reflecting the hot hand fallacy—and selling off stocks when a downward trend seems to be occurring. Similarly, there are times when investors believe the stock market has run up or down too rapidly and they expect its direction to change soon—reflecting the gambler's fallacy.

Some segments of the market are driven by investor psychology instead of metrics that measure valuation. Research has also shown that mood matters: believe it or not, there is a small correlation between the weather and how the stock market trades on a particular day. The market is more likely to move higher when it is sunny on Wall Street than when it is cloudy! The very fact that the weather outside in Lower Manhattan could have anything to do with how the overall stock market performs is strong evidence that some market participants are not rational. ✱

The stock market can give investors a wild ride.

PRACTICE WHAT YOU KNOW

Gambler's Fallacy or Hot Hand Fallacy? Patterns on Exams

Do you ever wonder what it means when the same answer comes up many times in a row?

Your instructor is normally conscientious and makes sure that exam answers are randomly distributed. However, you notice that the first five answers on the multiple choice section are all C. Unsure what this pattern means, you consider the next question. You do not know the answer and are forced to guess. You decide to avoid C because you figure that C cannot happen six times in a row.

Question: Which is at work: the gambler's fallacy or the hot hand fallacy?

Answer: According to the gambler's fallacy, recent events are less likely to be repeated again in the near future. So it is the gambler's fallacy at work here in your decision to avoid marking another C. If you had acted on the hot hand fallacy, you would have believed that random sequences exhibit a positive correlation and therefore would have marked the next answer as C.

Inconsistencies in Decision-Making

Trade-offs

If people were entirely rational, they would always be consistent. So the way a question is asked should not alter our responses, but research has shown that it does. Likewise, rational decision-making requires the ability to take the long-run trade-offs into account: if the returns are large enough, people should be willing to sacrifice current enjoyment for future benefits. Yet many of us make shortsighted decisions. In this section, we examine a variety of decision-making mistakes, including *framing effects, priming effects, status quo bias*, and *intertemporal decision-making*.

Framing and Priming Effects

Framing effects occur when people change their answer (or action) depending on how the question is asked.

We have seen a number of ways in which economic models do not entirely account for the behavior of real people. One common mistake that people make involves the **framing effect**, which occurs when an answer is influenced by the way a question is asked or a decision is influenced by the way alternatives are presented. Consider an employer-sponsored retirement plan. Companies can either (1) ask employees if they want to join or (2) use an automatic enrollment system and ask employees to let them know if they do not wish to participate. Studies have shown that workers who are asked if they want to join tend to participate at a much lower rate than those who are automatically enrolled and must say they want to opt out. Surely, a rational economic decision-maker would determine whether to participate by evaluating

Misperceptions of Probabilities

ECONOMICS IN THE MEDIA

π

This psychological thriller from 1998 tries to make sense out of chaos. The title refers to the mathematical constant π (pi). In the film, Max Cohen is using his supercomputer to find predictable patterns within the stock market. What makes the film especially interesting are the three assumptions that rule Max's life:

1. Mathematics is the language of nature.
2. Everything around us can be represented and understood from numbers.
3. If you graph the numbers in any system, patterns emerge.

Based on these assumptions, Max attempts to identify a mathematical pattern that will predict the behavior of the stock market. As he gets closer to uncovering the answer, he is pursued by two parties: a Wall Street firm that wishes to use Max's discovery to manipulate the market, and a religious person who believes that the pattern is a code sent from God.

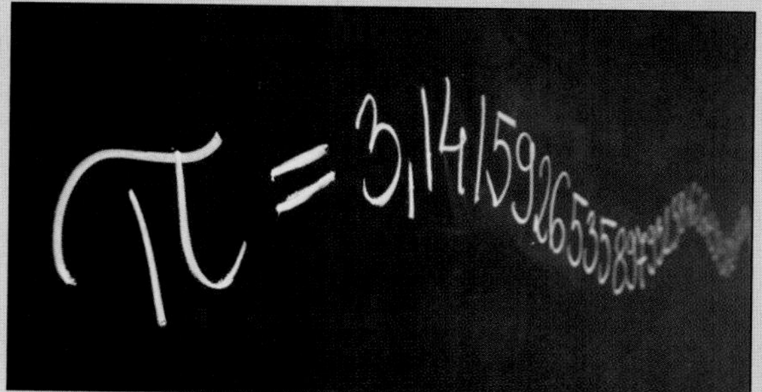

Can we use mathematical patterns to predict what will happen next?

Max's quest reminds us that the average investor lacks full information, but nevertheless irrationally believes that he or she knows more than others. As a result, widespread investor misperceptions about the true probability of events can lead to speculative bubbles and crashes in the stock market.

the plan itself, not by responding to the way the employer presents the option to participate. However, people are rarely that rational!

Another decision-making pitfall, known as the **priming effect**, occurs when the order of questions influences the answers. For example, consider two groups of college students. The first group is asked "How happy are you?" followed by "How many dates have you had in the last year?" The second group is asked "How many dates have you had in the last year?" followed by "How happy are you?" The questions are the same, but they are presented in reverse order. In the second group, students who had gone out on more dates reported being much happier than similar students in the first group! In other words, because they were reminded of the number of dates first, those who had more dates believed they were happier.

Priming effects occur when the ordering of the questions that are asked influences the answers.

Status Quo Bias

When people want to maintain their current choices, they may exhibit what is known as the **status quo bias**. This bias leads decision-makers to try to protect what they have, even when an objective evaluation of their circumstances suggests that a change would be beneficial. In behavioral economics,

Status quo bias exists when people want to maintain their current choices.

Are you on Team Dollar Bill or Team Dollar Coin?

Loss aversion
occurs when individuals place more weight on avoiding losses than on attempting to realize gains.

the status quo bias is often accompanied by **loss aversion**, which occurs when a person places more value on avoiding losses than on attempting to realize gains.

Loss aversion causes people to behave conservatively. The cost of this behavior is missed opportunities that could potentially enhance welfare. For example, a loss-averse individual would maintain a savings account with a low interest rate instead of actively shopping for better rates elsewhere. This person would lose the potential benefits from higher returns on savings.

Status quo bias also explains why new products and ideas have trouble gaining traction: many potential customers prefer to leave things the way they are, even if something new might make more sense. Consider the $1 coin. It is far more durable than the $1 bill. It is also easier to tell the $1 coin apart from the other coins and bills in your wallet, and if people used the coin, the government would save about $5 billion in production costs over the next 30 years. That sounds like a slam-dunk policy change, but it is not. Americans like their dollar bills and rarely use the $1 coin in circulation even though they repeatedly use nickels, dimes, and quarters to make change, to feed parking meters, and to buy from vending machines. Introducing more of the $1 coin and eliminating the $1 bill would be rational, but the status quo bias has prevented the change from happening.

ECONOMICS IN THE REAL WORLD

Are You An Organ Donor?

More than 25,000 organ transplants take place every year in the United States, with the vast majority coming from deceased donors. Demand greatly exceeds supply. Over 100,000 people are currently on organ-donation waiting lists. Most Americans are aware of the need, and 90% of all Americans say they support donation. But only 30% know the essential steps to take to be a donor.

There are two main donor systems: the "opt-in" system and the "opt-out" system. In an opt-in system, individuals must give explicit consent to be a donor. In an opt-out system, anyone who has not explicitly refused is considered a donor.

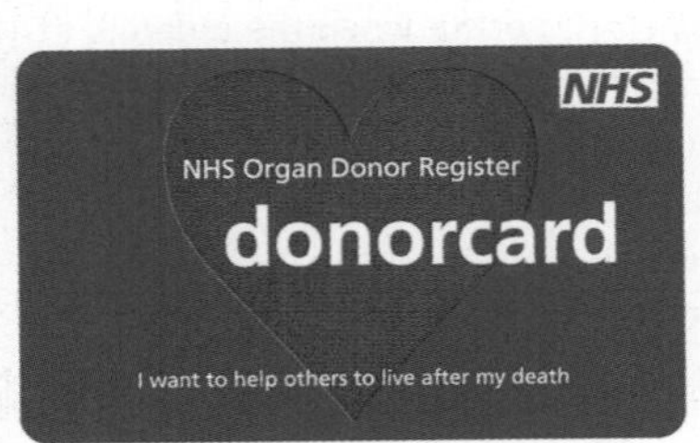

In the United Kingdom, organ donors must opt in.

In the United States, donors are required to opt in. Since opting in generally produces fewer donors than opting out, many states have sought to raise donation awareness by allowing consent to be noted on the individual driver's licenses.

In Europe, many countries have opt-out systems, where consent is presumed. The difference is crucial. After all, in places with opt-in systems, many people who would be willing to donate organs never actually take the time to complete the necessary steps to opt in. In countries like France and Poland, where people must opt out, over 90% of citizens do not explicitly opt out, which means they give consent. This strategy yields organ donation rates that are significantly higher than those of opt-in programs.

According to traditional economic analysis, opting in or opting out should not matter—the results should be the same. The fact that we find strong evidence to the contrary is a compelling illustration of the framing effect. ✷

SNAPSHOT

Opt-Out Is Optimal

Some of the most successful applications of behavioral economics are "opt-out" programs, which automatically enroll eligible people unless they explicitly choose not to participate. The incentives and freedom of choice are exactly the same as in "opt-in" programs, where members must choose to participate, but enrollments are significantly higher under opt-out. Here's a look at three remarkable results.

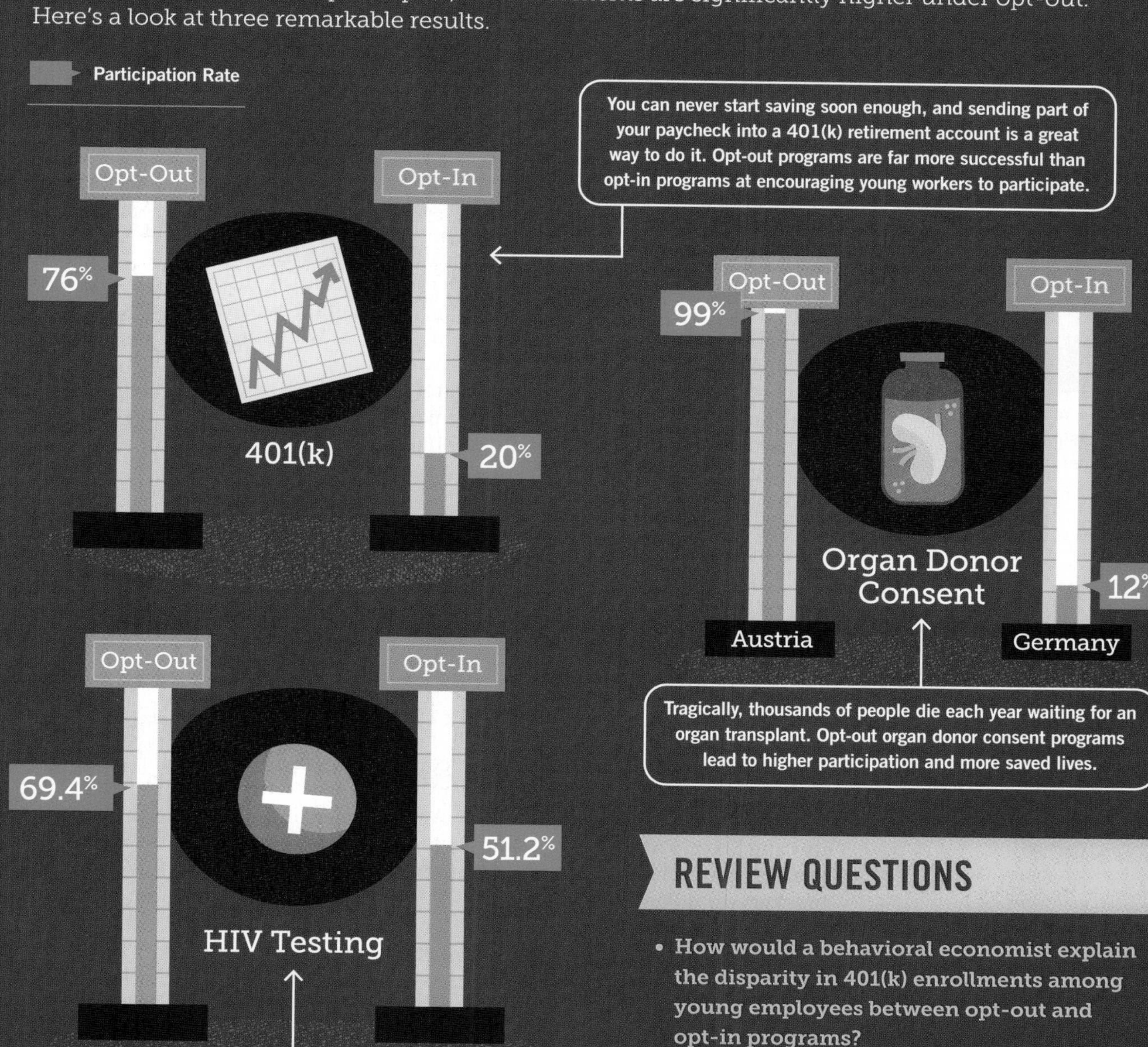

Participation Rate
You can never start saving soon enough, and sending part of your paycheck into a 401(k) retirement account is a great way to do it. Opt-out programs are far more successful than opt-in programs at encouraging young workers to participate.
Opt-Out
Opt-In
76%
20%
401(k)
Opt-Out
Opt-In
99%
12%
Organ Donor Consent
Austria
Germany
Tragically, thousands of people die each year waiting for an organ transplant. Opt-out organ donor consent programs lead to higher participation and more saved lives.
Opt-Out
Opt-In
69.4%
51.2%
HIV Testing
HIV screening remains a crucial public health need. Evidence from one study indicates that opt-out consent at emergency rooms leads to substantially more individuals agreeing to be tested.

REVIEW QUESTIONS

- How would a behavioral economist explain the disparity in 401(k) enrollments among young employees between opt-out and opt-in programs?
- Opt-in and opt-out programs ask us to make the same decisions, but achieve different results. Use the concepts of the framing effect and non-rational behavior to explain why.

Intertemporal Decision-Making

Intertemporal decision-making involves planning to do something over a period of time; this requires valuing the present and the future consistently.

Intertemporal decisions occur across time. **Intertemporal decision-making**—that is, planning to do something over a period of time—requires the ability to value the present and the future consistently. For instance, many people, despite their best intentions, do not end up saving enough for retirement. The temptation to spend money today ends up overwhelming the willpower to save for tomorrow. In a perfectly rational world, a person would not need outside assistance to save enough for retirement. In the real world, however, workers depend on 401(k) plans and other work-sponsored retirement programs to deduct funds from their paycheck so that they don't spend that portion of their income on other things. It may seem odd that people would need an outside agency to help them do something that is in their own long-term interest, but as long as their intertemporal decisions are likely to be inconsistent, the additional commitment helps them to achieve their long-run objectives.

Can you resist eating one marshmallow now, in order to get a second one later?

The ability to resist temptation is illustrated by a classic research experiment conducted at a preschool at Stanford University in 1972. One at a time, individual children were led into a room devoid of distractions and were offered a marshmallow. The researchers explained to each child that he or she could eat the marshmallow right away or wait for 15 minutes and be rewarded with a second marshmallow. Very few of the 600 children in the study ate the marshmallow immediately. Most tried to fight the temptation. Of those who tried to wait, approximately one-third held out long enough to earn the second marshmallow. That finding is interesting by itself, but what happened next is truly amazing. Many of the parents of the children in the original study noticed that the children who had delayed gratification seemed to perform better as they progressed through school. Researchers have tracked the participants over the course of 40 years and found that the delayed-gratification group had higher SAT scores, more savings, and larger retirement accounts.

Judgments about Fairness

The pursuit of fairness is another common behavior that is important in economic decisions but that standard economic theory cannot explain. For example, fairness is one of the key drivers in determining tax rate structure for income taxes. Proponents of fairness believe in progressive taxation, whereby the rich pay a higher tax rate on their income than those in lower income brackets do. Likewise, some people object to the high pay of chief executive officers or the high profits of some corporations because they believe there should be an upper limit to what constitutes fair compensation.

The **ultimatum game** is an economic experiment in which two players decide how to divide a sum of money.

While fairness is not normally modeled in economics, behavioral economists have developed experiments to determine the role of fairness in personal decisions. The **ultimatum game** is an economic experiment in which two players decide how to divide a sum of money. The game shows how fairness enters into the rational decision-making process. In the game, Player 1 is given a sum of money and is asked to propose a way of splitting it with Player 2. Player 2 can either accept or reject the proposal. If Player 2 accepts, the sum is split according to the proposal. However, if Player 2 rejects the proposal, neither player gets anything. The game is played only once, so the first player does not have to worry about reciprocity.

Consider an ultimatum game that asks Player 1 to share $1,000 with Player 2. Player 1 must decide how fair to make the proposal. The decision tree in Figure 17.1 highlights four possible outcomes to two very different proposals—what the figure shows as a fair proposal and an unfair proposal.

Traditional economic theory presumes that both players are fully rational and wish to maximize their income. Player 1 should therefore maximize his gains by offering the minimum, $1, to Player 2. The reasoning is that Player 2 values $1 more than nothing and so will accept the proposal, leaving Player 1 with $999. But real people are not always economic maximizers because they generally believe that fairness matters. Most of the time, Player 2 would find such an unfair division infuriating and reject it.

Player 1 knows that Player 2 will definitely accept an offer of $500; this division of the money is exactly equal and, therefore, fair. Thus, the probability of a 50/50 agreement is 100%. In contrast, the probability of Player 2 accepting an offer of $1 is close to 0%. Offering increasing amounts from $1 to $500 will continue to raise the probability of an acceptance until it reaches 100% at $500.

Player 2's role is simpler: her only decision is whether to accept or reject the proposal. Player 2 desires a fair distribution but has no direct control over the division. To punish Player 1 for being unfair, Player 2 must reject the proposal altogether. The trade-off of penalizing Player 1 for unfairness is a complete loss of any prize. So while Player 2 may not like any given proposal, rejecting it would cause a personal loss. Player 2 might therefore accept a number of unfair proposals because she would rather get something than nothing.

Trade-offs

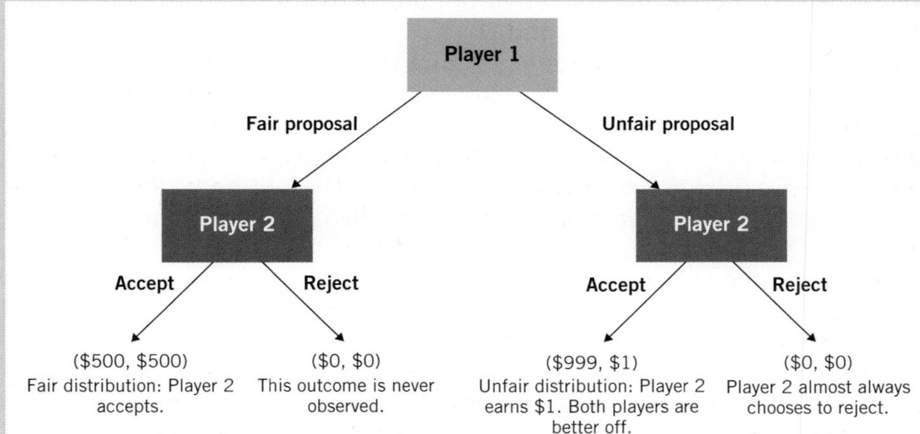

FIGURE 17.1

The Decision Tree for the Ultimatum Game

The decision tree for the ultimatum game has four branches. If Player 1 makes a fair proposal, Player 2 will accept the distribution and both players will earn $500. However, if Player 1 makes an unfair proposal, Player 2 may reject the distribution even though this means receiving nothing.

Each of the ideas that we have presented in this section, including misperceptions of probability, inconsistency in decision-making, and judgments about fairness, represent a departure from the traditional economic model of rational maximization. In the next section, we focus on risk taking. As you will soon learn, not everyone evaluates risk in the same way. This fact has led economists to reconsider their models of human behavior.

What Is the Role of Risk in Decision-Making?

In this section, we examine the role that risk plays in decision-making. The standard economic model of consumer choice assumes that people are consistent in their risk-taking preferences. However, people's risk tolerances actually vary widely and are subject to change. Thus, risk-taking behavior is not nearly as simple, or predictable, as economists once believed. We begin with a phenomenon known as a *preference reversal*. We then consider how negative surprises can cause people to take more risk, which is explained by *prospect theory*.

Preference Reversals

Risk-averse people prefer a sure thing over a gamble with a higher expected value.

Risk-neutral people choose the highest expected value regardless of the risk.

Risk takers prefer gambles with lower expected values, and potentially higher winnings, over a sure thing.

As you know, trying to predict human behavior is not easy. Maurice Allais, the recipient of the 1988 Nobel Prize in Economics, noticed that people's tolerance for risk appeared to change in different situations. This observation did not agree with the standard economic model, which assumes that an individual's risk tolerance is constant and places the individual into one of three distinct groups: **Risk-averse people** prefer a sure thing over a gamble with a higher expected value. **Risk-neutral people** choose the highest expected value regardless of the risk. **Risk takers** prefer gambles with lower expected values, and potentially higher winnings, over a sure thing.

Allais developed a means of assessing risk behavior by presenting the set of choices (known as the Allais paradox) depicted in Table 17.1. Individuals were asked to choose their preferred options between gambles A and B and then again between gambles C and D.

TABLE 17.1

The Allais Paradox

Choose gamble A or B	
Gamble A	**Gamble B**
No gamble—receive $1 million in cash 100% of the time.	A lottery ticket that pays $5 million 10% of the time, $1 million 89% of the time, and nothing 1% of the time.
Choose gamble C or D	
Gamble C	**Gamble D**
A lottery ticket that pays $5 million 10% of the time.	A lottery ticket that pays $1 million 11% of the time.

Economic science predicts that people will choose consistently according to their risk preference. As a result, economists understood that risk-averse individuals would choose the pair A and D. Likewise, the pair B and C makes sense if the participants wish to maximize the expected value of the gambles. Let's see why.

1. *Risk-Averse People:* People who select gamble A over gamble B take the sure thing. If they are asked to choose between C and D, we would expect them to try to maximize their chances of winning something by selecting D, since it has the higher probability of winning.
2. *Risk-Neutral People:* Gamble B has a higher expected value than gamble A. We know that gamble A always pays $1 million since it occurs 100% of the time. Calculating gamble B's expected value is more complicated. The expected value is computed by multiplying each outcome by its respective probability. For gamble B, this means that the expected value is ($5 million × 0.10) + ($1 million × 0.89), which equals $1.39 million. So a risk-neutral player will select gamble B. Likewise, gamble C has a higher expected value than gamble D. Gamble C has an expected value of ($5 million × 0.10), or $0.5 million. Gamble D's expected value is ($1 million × 0.11), or $0.11 million. Therefore, a risk-neutral player who thinks at the margin will choose gambles B and C in order to maximize his or her potential winnings from the game.

Marginal Thinking

PRACTICE WHAT YOU KNOW

Risk Aversion: Risk-Taking Behavior

Question: In the following situations, are the choices evidence of risk aversion or risk-taking?

1. You have a choice between selecting heads or tails. If your guess is correct, you earn $2,000. But you earn nothing if you are incorrect. Alternatively, you can simply take $750 without the gamble. You decide to take the $750.

Answer: The expected value of a 50/50 outcome worth $2,000 is $1,000. Therefore, the decision to take the sure thing, which is $250 less, is evidence of risk aversion.

2. You have a choice between (a) predicting the roll of a six-sided die, with a $3,000 prize for a correct answer, or (b) taking a sure $750. You decide to roll the die.

Answer: The expected value of the roll of the die is 1/6 × $3,000, or $500. Therefore, the $750 sure thing has an expected value that is $250 more. By rolling the die, you are taking the option with the lowest expected value and also the most risk. This indicates that you are a risk taker.

How do you handle risky decisions?

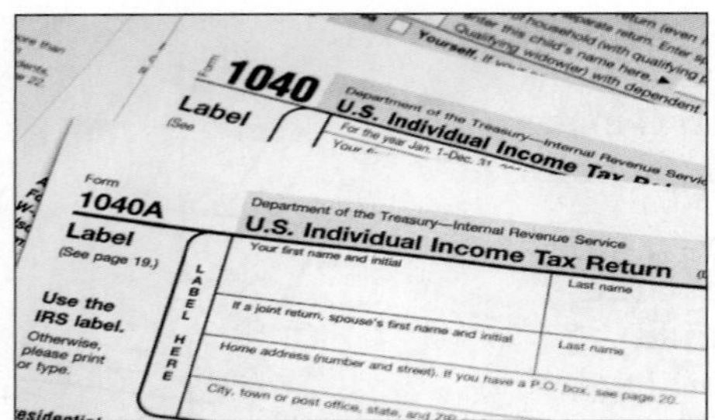

Withholding too much in the previous year and then paying your accountant to file for a rapid refund is a good example of a preference reversal.

While we would expect people to be consistent in their choices, Allais found that approximately 30% of his research population selected gambles A and C, which are contrasting pairs. Gamble A is the sure thing; however, gamble C, even though it has the higher expected value, carries more risk. This scenario illustrates a *preference reversal*. A **preference reversal** occurs when risk tolerance is not consistent. Allais argued that a person's risk tolerance depends on his or her financial circumstances. Someone who chooses gamble A over gamble B prefers the certainty of a large financial prize—the guarantee of $1 million over the uncertainty of the larger prize. Choosing gamble A could be seen as similar to purchasing insurance: you pay a fee, known as a premium, in order to protect your winnings. In this case, you forfeit the chance to win $5 million. In contrast, gambles C and D offer small chances of success, and therefore the choice is more like playing the lottery.

A **preference reversal** occurs when risk tolerance is not consistent.

People who play games of chance are more likely to participate in games with large prizes—for example, Powerball—because the winnings will measurably improve their financial status. Allais showed that people care about how much they might win and also how much they stand to lose. This distinction causes people to choose gambles A and C. By establishing that many people behave this way, Allais reshaped traditional economists' view of risk-taking behavior.

It turns out that preference reversals are more common than economists once believed. For example, approximately 80% of all income tax filers expect to get a refund because they overpaid in the previous year. This behavior is odd, since there is an opportunity cost of waiting to get money back from the government when it didn't need to be paid in the first place. Employees could have asked their employers to withhold less and enjoyed their money sooner. Individuals who choose to wait to receive their money later are said to have a time preference that is weakly positive. In most circumstances, people have strongly positive time preferences: they prefer to have what they want sooner rather than later. So what do these taxpayers do when they learn the amount of their refund? In many cases, they pay their tax preparers an additional fee to have their refunds sent to their bank accounts electronically so they can receive the money sooner! Traditional economic analysis is unable to explain this behavior; but armed with Allais's insights, we now see this behavior as a preference reversal.

Deciding when to take the "deal" makes the show compelling.

Prospect Theory

The television game show *Deal or No Deal* provides an opportunity for economists to examine the risk choices that contestants make in a high-stakes setting. *Deal or No Deal* has created particular excitement among researchers who study game shows because it involves no skill whatsoever. Taking skill out of the equation makes it easier to analyze the contestants' strategy choices. Other TV game shows, such as *Jeopardy!* and *Who Wants to Be a Millionaire?*, require skill to win prizes. Highly skilled players may have different risk tolerances than their less-skilled

Preference Reversals

ECONOMICS IN THE MEDIA

"Mine"

Taylor's dream illustrates one version of a preference reversal.

The music video for Taylor Swift's 2010 hit begins with Swift walking into a coffee shop. When she sits down, she notices a couple arguing at a nearby table. This reminds Swift about her parents arguing when she was very young. Just then, the waiter drops by to take Swift's order. She looks up and dreams of what life would be like with him: we see them running together in the waves at the beach, then unpacking boxes as they move in together. Later, the two argue, resulting in Swift running away from their house and crying, just like she did when she was young and saw her parents arguing. Her boyfriend follows her, and they reconcile. They get married and have two sons. The video ends with Swift re-emerging from her dream and ordering her food at the coffee shop.

In the song's refrain, Swift sings, "You made a rebel of a careless man's careful daughter." Think about that line, keeping in mind that a "rebel" is a risk-taker. Does that remind you of a concept from this chapter? It should—this is a preference reversal. The entire song is about someone (Swift) who is normally risk averse but falls for this guy so hard that she lets her guard down and acts differently. Instead of running away when it comes time to fall in love, she stays in the relationship. In other words, the song is about finding someone who would make you believe in love, so much that you were willing to take a chance for the first time in your life.

counterparts. As a result, part of the beauty of studying *Deal or No Deal* is that the outcome is a pure exercise in probability theory.

For those who are unfamiliar with *Deal or No Deal,* here is how the show works. Each of 26 models holds a briefcase that contains a sum of money, varying from one cent to \$1 million. The contestant picks one briefcase as her own and then begins to open the other 25 briefcases one at a time, slowly revealing a little more about what her own case might hold. Suspense builds, and the contestant's chance of a big payoff grows as small sums are eliminated and the \$1 million case and other valuable cases remain unopened. As cases are eliminated, a "banker" periodically calls the host to offer the contestant a "deal" in exchange for quitting the game.

At the start of the game, the expected value (EV) of the chosen briefcase is determined as follows:

$$EV_{\text{briefcase}} = \$.01 \times (1/26) + \$1 \times (1/26) + \$5 \times (1/26) + \cdots + \$1M \times (1/26)$$

This value computes to approximately \$131,000. As the game progresses and cases are opened, the "banker" offers a settlement based on whether the expected value of the briefcase has increased or decreased.

Some contestants behave as the traditional model of risk behavior predicts: they maximize the expected value of the briefcase while remaining risk neutral. Since contestants who are risk neutral don't make for exciting television, the "banker" typically offers a "deal" that is far less than the expected value of the remaining cases throughout the early part of the game. This move encourages contestants to play longer so that the excitement and tension have a chance to build.

But not all contestants do what the traditional model expects them to do. For example, some contestants take more risks if they suffer setbacks early in the game, such as opening the $1 million briefcase. This behavior is consistent with *prospect theory* from psychology. **Prospect theory**, developed by Daniel Kahneman and Amos Tversky, suggests that people weigh decisions according to subjective utilities of gains and losses. The theory implies that people evaluate the risks that lead to gains separately from the risks that lead to losses. This result is useful because it explains why some investors try to make up for losses by taking more chances rather than by maximizing the utility they receive from money under a rigid calculation of expected value.

Prospect theory suggests that individuals weigh the utilities and risks of gains and losses differently.

ECONOMICS IN THE REAL WORLD

Why Are There Cold Openings at the Box Office?

The line for tickets is long. Do you suppose this movie was cold-opened?

Movie studios generally make a film available for review if the screenings are expected to generate a positive buzz. Also, access to movie reviews provides moviegoers with a measure of a film's quality. So a rational moviegoer should infer that if a movie studio releases a film without reviews, it is signaling that the movie is not very good: the studio didn't want to risk negative reviews, so it didn't show the movie to reviewers.

Economists Alexander L. Brown, Colin F. Camerer, and Dan Lovallo studied 856 widely released movies and found that cold openings—movies withheld from critics (that is, not screened) before their release—produced a significant increase (15%) in domestic box office revenue compared with poor films that were reviewed and received predictably negative reviews. Most movie openings are accompanied by a marketing campaign to increase consumer demand. As a consequence, cold openings provide a natural field setting to test how rational moviegoers are. Their results are consistent with the hypothesis that some moviegoers do not infer low quality from a cold opening as they should.

The authors showed that cold-opened movies earned more than pre-screened movies after a number of characteristics were controlled for in the study. An important point is that the researchers also found that cold-opened films did not fare better than expected once they reached foreign film or video rental markets. In both of those cases, movie reviews were widely available, which negated any advantage from cold-opening the films. This finding is consistent with the hypothesis that some moviegoers fail to realize that no advance review is a signal of poor quality. The fact that moviegoer ratings from the Internet Movie Database are lower for movies that were cold-opened also suggests that in the absence of information, moviegoers overestimate the expected quality.

Over time, distributors have learned that there is a certain amount of moviegoer naiveté, especially among teenagers. As a result, distributors have overcome their initial reluctance and have cold-opened more movies in recent years.

These findings provide evidence that the best movie distribution strategy does not depend entirely on generating positive movie reviews. Cold openings work because some people are unable to process the negative signal implied by incomplete information, despite what traditional economic analysis would lead us to expect. ✳

ECONOMICS FOR LIFE

Bounded Rationality: How to Guard Yourself against Crime

Suppose that a recent crime wave has hit your community and you are concerned about your family's security. Determined to make your house safe, you consider many options: an alarm system, bars on your windows, deadbolts for your doors, better lighting around your house, and a guard dog. Which of these solutions will protect you from a criminal at the lowest cost? All of them provide a measure of protection—but there's another solution that provides deterrence at an extremely low cost.

The level of security you need depends, in part, on how rational you expect the robber to be. A fully rational burglar would stake out a place, test for an alarm system before breaking in, and choose a home that is an easy target. In other words, the robber would gather full information. But what if the burglar is not fully rational?

Since criminals look for the easiest target to rob, they will find a house that is easy to break into without detection. If you trim away the shrubs and install floodlights, criminals will realize that they can be seen approaching your home. A few hundred dollars spent on better lighting will dramatically lower your chances of being robbed. However, if you believe in bounded rationality, there is an even better answer: a criminal may not know what is inside your house, so a couple of prominently displayed "Beware of dog!" signs would discourage the robber for less than $10! In other words, the would-be thief has incomplete information and only a limited amount of time to select a target. A quick scan of your house would identify the "Beware of dog!" signs and cause him to move on.

Beware of dog!

This is an example of bounded rationality since only limited, and in this case unreliable, information is all that is easily available regarding possible alternatives and their consequences. Knowing that burglars face this constraint can be a key to keeping them away.

Conclusion

Behavioral economics helps to dispel the misconception that people always make rational decisions. Indeed, behavioral economics challenges the traditional economics model and invites a deeper understanding of human behavior. Armed with the insights from behavioral economics, we can answer questions that span a wider range of behaviors. We have seen this in the examples in this chapter, which include the "opt in" or "opt out" debate, the economics of risk-taking, the effects of question design, and the status quo bias. These ideas do not fit squarely into traditional economic analysis. You have learned enough at this point to question the assumptions we have made throughout this book. In the next chapter, we will apply all of the tools we have acquired to examine one of the most important sectors of the economy—health care and health insurance.

ANSWERING THE BIG QUESTIONS

How can economists explain irrational behavior?

* Economists use a number of concepts from behavioral economics to explain how people make choices that display irrational behavior. These concepts include bounded rationality, misperceptions of probabilities, the status quo bias, intertemporal decision-making, judgments about fairness, and prospect theory.
* Folding the behavioral approach into the standard model makes economists' predictions about human behavior much more robust.

What is the role of risk in decision-making?

* Risk influences decision-making since people can either be risk averse, risk neutral, or risk takers.
* In the traditional economic model, risk tolerances are assumed to be constant. If an individual is a risk taker by nature, he or she would take risks in any circumstance. Likewise, if an individual does not like to take chances, he or she would avoid risk.
* Maurice Allais proved that many people have inconsistent risk preferences, or what are known as preference reversals. Moreover, he showed that simply because some people's preferences are not constant does not necessarily mean that their decisions are irrational.

  Prospect theory suggests that individuals place more emphasis on gains than on losses, and they are therefore willing to take on additional risk to try to recover losses caused by negative shocks.

CONCEPTS YOU SHOULD KNOW

behavioral economics (p. 528)
bounded rationality (p. 528)
framing effects (p. 532)
gambler's fallacy (p. 531)
hot hand fallacy (p. 531)
intertemporal decision-making (p. 536)
loss aversion (p. 534)
preference reversal (p. 540)
priming effects (p. 533)
prospect theory (p. 542)
risk-averse people (p. 538)
risk-neutral people (p. 538)
risk takers (p. 538)
status quo bias (p. 533)
ultimatum game (p. 536)

QUESTIONS FOR REVIEW

1. What is bounded rationality? How is this concept relevant to economic modeling?
2. What are the hot hand fallacy and the gambler's fallacy? Give an example of each.
3. How does the status quo bias reduce the potential utility that consumers enjoy?
4. Economists use the ultimatum game to test judgments of fairness. What result does economic theory predict?
5. What is prospect theory? Have you ever suffered a setback early in a process (for example, seeking a job or applying for college) that caused you to alter your behavior later on?

STUDY PROBLEMS (*✱solved at the end of the section*)

✱ 1. You have a choice between taking two jobs. The first job pays $50,000 annually. The second job has a base pay of $40,000 with a 30% chance that you will receive an annual bonus of $25,000. You decide to take the $50,000 job. On the basis of this decision, can we tell if you are risk averse or a risk taker? Explain your response.

2. Suppose that Danny Ocean decides to play roulette, one of the most popular casino games. Roulette is attractive to gamblers because the house's advantage is small (less than 5%). If Danny Ocean plays roulette and wins big, is this evidence that Danny is risk averse or a risk taker? Explain.

3. Many voters go to the polls every four years to cast their ballot for president. The common refrain from those who vote is that their vote "counts" and that voting is important. A skeptical economist points out that with over 100 million ballots cast, the probability that any individual's vote will be decisive is close to 0%. What idea, discussed in this chapter, explains why so many people actually vote?

4. Your instructor is very conscientious and always makes sure that exam answers are randomly distributed. However, you notice that the first five answers on the true/false section are all "true." Unsure what this pattern means, you consider the sixth question. However, you do not know the answer. What answer would you give if you believed in the gambler's fallacy? What answer would you give if you believed in the hot hand fallacy?

✱ 5. Suppose that a university wishes to maximize the response rate for teaching evaluations. The administration develops an easy-to-use online evaluation system that each student can complete at the end of the semester. However, very few students bother to complete the survey. The Registrar's Office suggests that the online teaching evaluations be linked to course scheduling. When students access the course scheduling system, they are redirected to the teaching evaluations. Under this plan, each student could opt out and go directly to the course scheduling system. Do you think this plan will work to raise the response rate on teaching evaluations? What would traditional economic theory predict? What would behavioral economics predict?

6. Ray likes his hamburgers with American cheese, lettuce, and ketchup. Whenever he places an order for a burger, he automatically orders these three toppings. What type of behavior is Ray exhibiting? What does traditional utility theory say about Ray's preferences? What would a behavioral economist say?

7. Many people give to charity and leave tips. What prediction does utility theory make about each of these activities? (Hint: think of the person's narrow self-interest.) What concept from behavioral economics explains this behavior?

8. Given a choice of an extra $1,000 or a gamble with the same expected value, a person prefers the $1,000. But given a choice of a loss of $1,000 or a gamble with the same expected value, the same person prefers the gamble. How would a behavioral economist describe this decision?

SOLVED PROBLEMS

1. The first job pays $50,000 annually, so it has an expected value of $50,000. The second job has a base pay of $40,000 with a 30% chance that you will receive an annual bonus of $25,000. To determine the expected value of the second job, the calculation looks like this: $40,000 + (0.3 × $25,000) = $40,000 + $7,500 = $47,500. Since you decided to take the job with higher expected value, we cannot tell if you are a risk taker or risk averse.

5. Since students who access the course scheduling system are redirected to the teaching evaluations, they are forced to opt out if they do not wish to evaluate the instructors. As a result, behavioral economists would predict that the new system will raise the teaching evaluation response rate. Traditional economic theory predicts that the response rate will not change simply based on whether or not students opt in or opt out.

CHAPTER

18 Health Insurance and Health Care

MISCONCEPTION

Providing national health care would be a simple solution to the healthcare crisis.

We have come a long way in our exploration of microeconomics. In this chapter, we will apply our economic tool kit to one particular industry—health care. The goal of this chapter is not to sway your opinion but to provide you with a simple set of tools to help focus your thinking about how medical care can best serve individuals and society as a whole.

The debate over healthcare spending is at the core of the healthcare crisis in this country. Many people believe that national health care (also called universal health care) would be the solution to the healthcare crisis because it would help to control costs. For example, the Affordable Care Act (or the federal healthcare law) passed under President Obama argues that expanding healthcare coverage will lower healthcare costs. But can we really get more coverage for less? Supporters and opponents vehemently disagree.

The healthcare debate is about trade-offs. The misconception that national health care will solve our healthcare crisis ignores the complex trade-offs that society faces and that drive the healthcare debate. In this chapter, we describe how the healthcare industry works and how the government and the market can each make the delivery of health care more efficient. We will consider how health care is delivered, who pays, and what makes the provision of medical care unlike the delivery of services in any other sector of the economy. Then we will use supply and demand analysis to look at how the medical market functions. One important aspect of medical care is the role that information plays in the incentive structure for patients and providers. Finally, we will

The healthcare debate has many sides.

examine a number of case studies to pull all this information together so you can decide for yourself where you stand on one of the most important issues of the twenty-first century.

Health care is big business. If you add the education and automobile sectors together, they represent about 10% of national economic output. But health care alone accounts for more than 17% of the nation's economic output. That's 1 out of every 6 dollars spent annually in the United States—more than \$2 trillion, or almost \$8,000 for every citizen. No matter how you slice it, that is a lot of money!

BIG QUESTIONS

- **What are the important issues in the healthcare industry?**
- **How does asymmetric information affect healthcare delivery?**
- **How do demand and supply contribute to high medical costs?**
- **How do incentives influence the quality of health care?**

What Are the Important Issues in the Healthcare Industry?

In this section, we examine the key issues in health care: how much is spent on it, where the money goes, and who the key players in the industry are. The goal is to give you a sense of how the sector functions. Then we will turn our attention to supply and demand. First, though, we take a brief look at how health care has changed over the past hundred or so years.

At the start of the twentieth century, life expectancy in the United States was slightly less than 50 years. Now life expectancy is close to 80 years—a longevity gain that would have been unthinkable a few generations ago. Let's go back in time to examine the way medical care was delivered and see some of the advances that have improved the human condition.

Early in the twentieth century, infectious diseases were the most common cause of death in the United States. Typhoid, diphtheria, gangrene, gastritis, smallpox, and tuberculosis were major killers. Today, because of antibiotics, they have either been completely eradicated or are extremely rare. Moreover, the state of medical knowledge was so dismal that a cure was often far worse

Cutting-edge medical equipment: then . . .

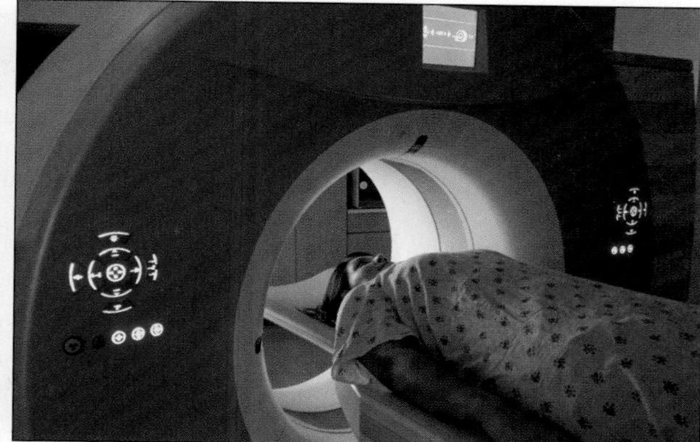

. . . and now.

than the condition it was supposed to treat. For instance, tobacco was recommended for the treatment of bronchitis and asthma, and leeches were used to fight laryngitis. Throughout the first half of the twentieth century, a trip to the doctor was expensive and painful, and it rarely produced positive results.

Since 1950, advances in cellular biology and discoveries in biochemistry have led to a better understanding of the disease process and more precise diagnostic tests. In addition, discoveries in biomedical engineering have led to the widespread use of imaging techniques such as ultrasound, computerized axial tomography (CAT scans), and nuclear magnetic resonance imaging (MRI). These and other procedures have replaced the medical practices of the past and made medical care safer, gentler, and more effective. In addition, pharmaceutical companies have developed a number of "miracle" drugs for fighting many conditions, including high blood pressure, leukemia, and bad cholesterol, thereby limiting the need for more invasive treatments. Each of these amazing medical advances costs money—sometimes, lots of money. As a society, we have made a trade-off: in exchange for a dramatically longer life expectancy, we now devote much more of our personal and government budgets to health care.

Trade-offs

Healthcare Expenditures

We have noted that health expenditures in the United States are more than 17% of economic output. As you can see in Table 18.1, this is quite a bit higher than similar expenditures in Canada and Mexico. Canada spends about 11% of its economic output on health care, and Mexico spends slightly more than 6%.

The United States spends significantly more on health care than our neighbors to the north or south, but life expectancy in the United States is lower than that in Canada. How does Canada achieve a higher life expectancy while spending less money? And why doesn't Mexico, which spends only about one-tenth of what we do on health care, trail farther behind the United States than it does? To answer those questions, consider the usual assumption of *ceteris paribus*, or other things being constant. We all agree that increased healthcare expenditures are making people healthier, probably happier (since they feel better), and more productive—this is true for most

TABLE 18.1

Selected Health Care Facts

Country	Total expenditure on health (percentage of economic output)	Per capita expenditure on health (in U.S. dollars)	Life expectancy at birth, total population (in years)
Mexico	6.2%	$916	75.5
Canada	11.4%	$4,445	80.8
U.S.	17.6%	$8,223	78.7

Source: OECD Health Division, *Health Data 2012: Frequently Requested Data.*

countries. However, longevity is also a function of environmental factors, genetics, and lifestyle choices—variables that are not constant across countries. The question we should be asking is not how much money we are spending, but whether we are getting our money's worth. In other words, what concerns economists in this context are the impediments to the efficient delivery of medical care.

Why does health care take up so much of our budget? There are a number of reasons. Health insurance plays a contributing role. When private insurance covers most treatment costs, many patients agree to tests or medical visits that they wouldn't be willing to pay for out of pocket. Also, doctors are more willing to order tests that might not be necessary if they know the patient isn't paying directly. Medicare and Medicaid, the two government-sponsored forms of health insurance, add to the overall demand for medical services by providing medical coverage to the elderly and poor. And we know that anytime there is more demand for services, the market price rises in response.

Another reason for high healthcare costs is the number of uninsured—close to 50 million in the United States. When uninsured people need immediate medical treatment, they often seek care from emergency rooms and clinics. This raises costs in two ways. First, emergency care is extraordinarily expensive—much more so than routine care. Second, waiting until one has an acute condition that requires immediate attention often requires more treatment than would occur with preventative care or an early diagnosis. For example, an insured person who develops a cough with fever is likely to see a physician. If the patient has bronchitis, a few days of medicine and rest will be all it takes to feel better. However, an uninsured person who develops bronchitis is less likely to seek medical help and risks the possibility of a worsening condition, such as pneumonia, which can be difficult and costly to treat.

Medical demand is quite inelastic, so when competition is absent (which is usually the case), hospitals and other providers can charge what they want and patients will have to pay. In addition, people are not usually proactive about their health. Many health problems could be dramatically reduced and costs contained if people curbed habits such as cigarette use, excessive alcohol consumption, and overeating, and if they exercised more. Finally, heroic end-of-life efforts are extraordinarily expensive. These efforts may extend life for a few months, days, or hours, and they come at a steep price.

Diminishing Returns

In the United States, it has become the norm to spare no expense in efforts to extend life for even a few days. However, providing more medical care is subject to diminishing returns, as we can see in Figure 18.1. The purple curve shows a society's aggregate health production function, a measure of health reflecting the population's longevity, general health, and quality of life. This function initially rises rapidly when small amounts of health care are provided, but the benefits of additional care are progressively smaller. This is made evident by looking at points A and B. At point A, only a small amount of medical care is provided (Q_A), but this has a large impact on health. The slope at point A represents the marginal product of medical care. However, by the time we reach point B at a higher amount of care provided (Q_B), the marginal product of medical care (the slope) is much flatter, indicating that diminishing returns have set in.

Higher medical care expenditures, beyond some point, are unlikely to measurably improve longevity and quality of life. This is because many other factors—for example, disease, genetics, and lifestyle—also play a key role in determining health, quality of life, and longevity. As we move out along the medical production function, extending life becomes progressively more difficult, so it is not surprising that medical costs rise appreciably. Given this pattern, society must answer two questions. First, what is the optimal mix of expenditures on medical care? Second, could society get more from each dollar spent by reallocating dollars away from heroic efforts to extend life, and allocating monies toward prevention and medical research instead?

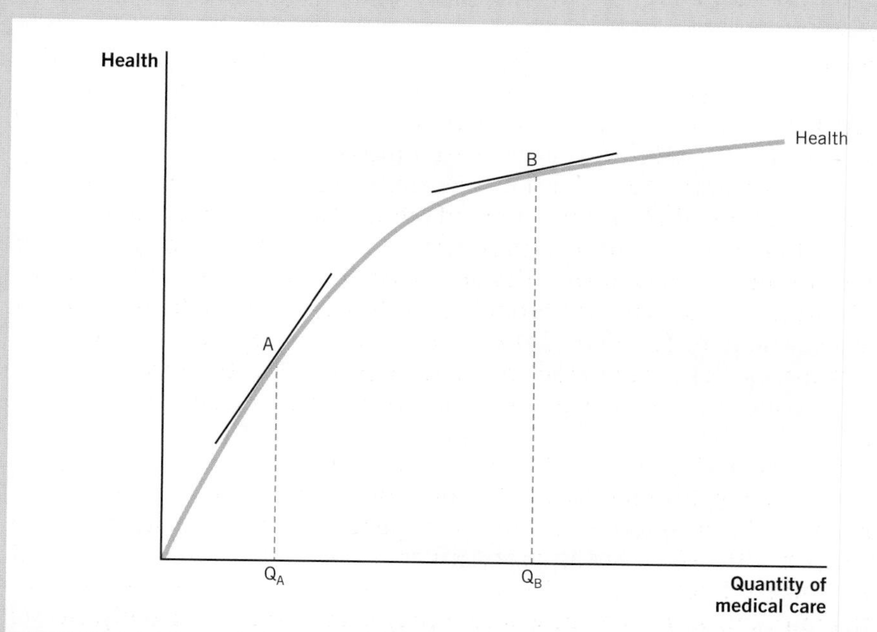

FIGURE 18.1

Health Production Function

The marginal product of medical care, indicated by the slope of the health production function, is higher at point A than at point B.

Figure 18.2 shows where the typical health dollar goes. Hospital care, physicians, and clinics account for half of all medical expenses. After that, prescription drugs, dental care, home health care, and nursing homes each represent smaller parts of healthcare expenditures. Here we note a paradox. On the one hand, medical care has become much more efficient as medical records are increasingly computerized and many procedures that required days of hospitalization a generation ago can now take place on an outpatient basis. Thus, reducing medical costs through efficiency gains is ongoing. Yet, on the other hand, costs continue to rise. What is going on? In the next section, we examine the incentives that patients, providers, and insurance companies face when making medical decisions and how the incentive structure contributes to escalating costs.

Who's Who in Health Care

Incentives

Healthcare consumption is different from that of most other goods and services. Like the others, healthcare services have consumers and producers; but because of intermediaries, such as insurance companies, the two rarely interact directly. This situation generates a unique set of incentives and leads to distortions in the standard supply and demand analysis. It is important to understand how medical care is delivered and paid for, as well as the incentives that patients, medical providers, and insurers face when making decisions.

FIGURE 18.2

The Nation's Health Dollar

Hospital care, physicians, and clinics make up over half of all healthcare expenditures, which totaled $2.6 trillion in 2010. (Dollar amounts shown in parentheses are in billions.)

Source: Centers for Medicare and Medicaid Services, Office of the Actuary, National Health Statistics Group. See "National Health Expenditure Data," cms.gov.

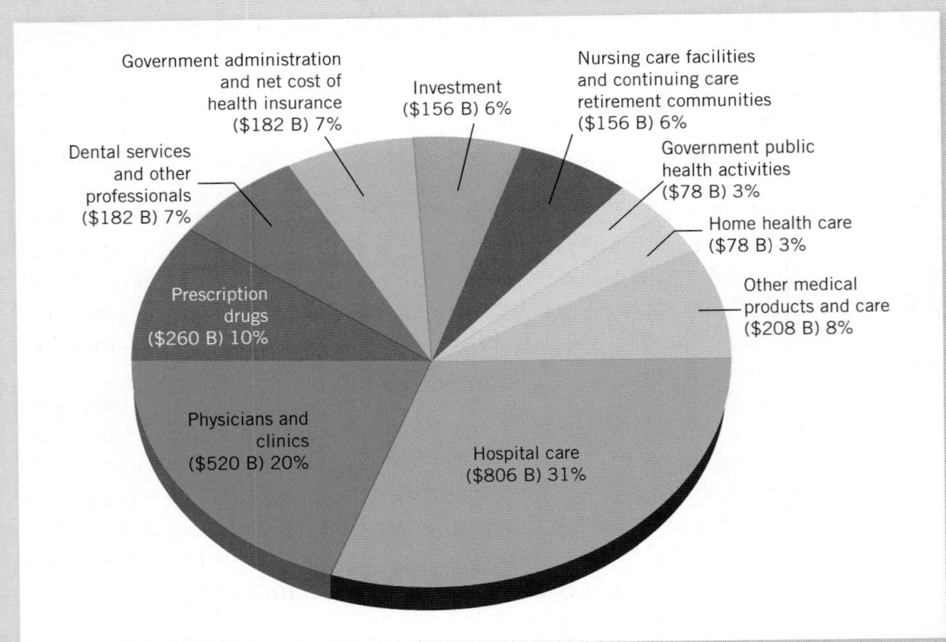

Consumers

The two biggest consumers of medical care are patients and the government. Patients demand medical care to prevent and treat illness. The federal government runs Medicare, a program that provides medical assistance to the elderly, and Medicaid, a program that provides medical assistance to the poor. Medicare and Medicaid are social insurance programs that each serve over 40 million enrollees. The two programs account for approximately one-third of all medical spending in the United States and represent about one-fifth of all U.S. government expenditures.

Producers

The medical care industry employs millions of workers, including doctors, nurses, psychologists, technicians, and many more. There are also over 500,000 medical facilities in this country, including small medical offices, large regional hospitals, nursing homes, pharmacies, and stores that supply medical equipment. In addition, pharmaceutical companies generate over $300 billion in annual sales in the United States.

Intermediaries

Intermediaries—for example, insurance companies—cover certain medical expenses in exchange for a set monthly fee, known as a premium. Medical insurance enables consumers to budget their expenses and limit what they will have to pay out-of-pocket in the event of a serious condition.

In addition to the premium, a *co-payment* or *deductible* is typically required. **Co-payments** are fixed amounts that the insured pays when receiving a medical service or filling a prescription. Insurance companies use co-payments in part to share expenses with the insured. In addition to covering a small portion of the costs, the co-pay serves to prevent most people from seeking care for common conditions that are easy to treat at home. **Deductibles** are fixed amounts that the insured must pay before most of the policy's benefits can be applied. Deductibles are sometimes subject to exceptions, such as a necessary visit to the emergency room or preventative physician visits and tests. Some policies also require **co-insurance payments**, or a percentage that the insured pays after the insurance policy's deductible is exceeded up to the policy's contribution limit. These services vary with each type of plan. Like co-insurance, co-payments and deductibles work to encourage consumers to use medical services judiciously.

Co-payments
are fixed amounts that the insured must pay when receiving a medical service or filling a prescription.

Deductibles
are fixed amounts that the insured must pay before most of the policy's benefits can be applied.

Co-insurance payments
are a percentage of costs that the insured must pay after exceeding the insurance policy's deductible up to the policy's contribution limit.

Insurance companies use the premiums, co-payments, deductibles, and co-insurance they receive from their customers to pay medical suppliers. For example, you may not need an appendectomy this year, but a predictable number of insured customers will. Using statistical techniques, an insurance company with millions of customers can accurately predict how many of its customers will visit the doctor and require hospitalization and other services. This enables the company to estimate its costs in advance and set premiums that generate a profit for the company.

Many people receive medical care through *health maintenance organizations*, or HMOs—another example of an intermediary. HMOs provide managed care for their patients by assigning them a primary care physician who oversees their medical care. The HMO then monitors the primary care provider to ensure that unnecessary care is not prescribed. HMOs earn revenue from premiums, co-payments, deductibles, and co-insurance.

Another kind of insurance company sells insurance against medical malpractice, or negligent treatment on the part of doctors. The doctor pays a set fee to the insurer, which in turn pays for the legal damages that arise if the doctor faces a malpractice claim. By analyzing statistics about the number of malpractice cases for each type of medical procedure performed each year, insurers can estimate the probability that a particular physician will face a malpractice claim; the insurers then incorporate that risk into the fee they charge.

Pharmaceutical Companies

Constituting another major player in the healthcare industry are the many pharmaceutical companies that develop the drugs used to treat a wide variety of conditions. Global pharmaceutical sales are almost $1 trillion—that's a lot of prescriptions! Pharmaceutical companies spend billions of dollars developing and testing potential drugs, which can take years for even just one drug. Once a drug is developed, it must receive approval by the Federal Drug Administration before it can be sold. The development cost, time required, and risk that a drug may turn out to be problematic or ineffective combine to make the development of new drugs an expensive proposition.

Medical Costs

Incentives

To understand why medical costs are so high, we must look at the incentives that drive the decisions of the major players. Consumers want every treatment to be covered, providers want a steady stream of business and don't want to be sued for malpractice, and the insurance companies and pharmaceutical companies want to make profits. This dynamic showcases the inherent conflict that exists among consumers, producers, and intermediaries, and it helps explain the difficulty of containing medical care at a reasonable cost.

Since patient co-payments are only a tiny fraction of the total cost of care, the effective marginal cost of seeking medical treatment is quite low. This causes consumers to increase the quantity of medical care they demand. Some physicians prescribe more care than is medically necessary in order to earn more income and to avoid malpractice lawsuits. Meanwhile, insurance companies, which are caught in the middle between patients and medical providers, do their best to contain costs, but they find that controlling the behavior of patients and providers is difficult. Consequently, escalating costs result from a system with poorly designed incentive mechanisms. In the case of Medicare and Medicaid, the government attempts to control costs by setting caps on the reimbursements that are paid to providers for medical treatments. An unintended consequence of government price-setting is that it forces physicians and medical centers to raise costs for other procedures that are not covered by Medicare and Medicaid.

PRACTICE WHAT YOU KNOW

Physical Fitness

"I work out . . ."

Question: You go in for a physical, and your doctor suggests that you get more exercise. So you decide to start working out. The increased physical activity has a big payoff and soon you feel much better, so you decide to double your efforts and get in even better shape. However, you notice that the gains from doubling your workout effort do not make you feel much better. What economic concept explains this effect?

Answer: More of a good thing isn't always better. Physical activity extends longevity and increases quality of life up to a point. This occurs because working out is subject to *diminishing returns*. In other words, a small amount of physical activity has a big payoff, but lifting more weights or running more miles, after a certain point, does not increase your overall health—it simply maintains your health.

How Does Asymmetric Information Affect Healthcare Delivery?

We have seen that incentives play an important role in the delivery of medical care. Another important element is the information and lack of information available to participants. Imbalances in information, known as **asymmetric information**, occur whenever one party knows more than the other. Asymmetric information has two forms: *adverse selection* and the *principal-agent problem*.

Asymmetric information is an imbalance in information that occurs when one party knows more than the other.

Adverse Selection

Most of us know very little about medicine. We know when we don't feel well and that we want to feel better, so we seek medical attention. Because we know very little about the service we are buying, we are poor judges of quality. For example, how can you know your provider is qualified or better than another provider? **Adverse selection** exists when one party has information about some aspect of product quality that the other party does not have. As a result, the party with the limited information should be concerned that the other party will misrepresent information to gain an advantage.

Adverse selection exists when one party has information about some aspect of product quality that the other party does not have.

When one side knows more than the other, the only way to avoid an adverse outcome is to gather better information. Suppose that you are new in town and need medical care. You haven't had a chance to meet anyone and find out whom to see or where to go for care. Fortunately, there is a way to avoid the worst doctors and hospitals: websites like ratemds.com and ratemyhospital.com provide patient feedback on the quality of care that they have received. Armed with knowledge from sources like these, you can request to be treated by doctors who you know to be competent and at facilities that have strong reputations. This helps prevent new residents from unknowingly receiving below-average care. More generally, it is important for patients to take charge of their own health care and learn all they can about a condition and its treatment so they are prepared to ask questions and make better decisions about treatment options. When patients are better informed, adverse selection is minimized.

Adverse selection also applies when buyers are more likely to seek insurance if they are more likely to need it. Consider a life insurance company. The company wants to avoid selling an inexpensive policy to someone who is likely to die prematurely, so before selling a policy to that applicant, the insurance company has to gather additional information about the person. It can require a medical exam and delay eligibility for full benefits until it can determine that the applicant has no pre-existing health conditions. As a result, the process of gathering information about the applicant is crucial to minimizing the risk associated with adverse selection. In fact, the process is similar for automobile insurance, in which drivers with poor records pay substantially higher premiums and safe drivers pay substantially lower ones.

The Principal-Agent Problem

A **principal-agent problem** arises when a principal entrusts an agent to complete a task and the agent does not do so in a satisfactory way.

Patients generally trust doctors to make good treatment decisions on the basis of medical welfare. Unfortunately, in our current medical system, *the principal-agent problem* means this is not always the case. A **principal-agent problem** arises when a principal entrusts an agent to complete a task and the agent does not do so in a satisfactory way. Some non-medical examples should be familiar to you. When parents (the principal) hire a babysitter (the agent), she might talk on the phone instead of watching the children. A company manager (the agent) might try to maximize his own salary instead of working to increase value for the shareholders (the principal). Finally, a politician (the agent) might be more likely to grant favors to interest groups than to focus on the needs of his constituents (the principal).

In a medical setting, the principal-agent problem occurs whenever patients cannot directly observe how medical providers and insurers are managing their (the patients') interests. The lack of oversight on the part of patients gives their agents, the physicians and insurance companies, some freedom to pursue other objectives that do not directly benefit patients. In the case of medicine, doctors and hospitals may order more tests, procedures, or visits to specialists than are medically necessary. The physician or the hospital may be more concerned about making profits or avoiding medical malpractice lawsuits than ensuring the patient's health and well-being. At the same time, insurance companies may desire to economize on treatment costs in order to maximize the bottom line. In both cases, the patient's desire for the best medical care conflicts with the objectives of the agents who deliver their care.

Moral Hazard

Moral hazard occurs when a party that is protected from risk behaves differently from the way it would behave if it were fully exposed to the risk. Moral hazard does not necessary mean "immoral" or "unethical." But it does imply that some people will change their behavior when their risk exposure is reduced and an "it's insured" mentality sets in. This can lead to inefficient outcomes, such as visiting the doctor more often than necessary. Likewise, physicians may prescribe more care than is medically necessary if they stand to make more money from insurance company payouts.

Moral hazard
occurs when a party that is protected from risk behaves differently from the way it would behave if it were fully exposed to the risk.

In each of the examples mentioned above, there is a moral hazard problem that can be lessened by restructuring the incentives. For the patient, a higher co-payment will discourage unnecessary visits to the doctor. For the physician, a hospital might tie a portion of the doctor's salary to periodic performance evaluations.

Incentives

To solve a moral hazard problem in medical care, it is necessary to fix the incentive structure. Many health insurance companies address moral hazard by encouraging preventative care, which lowers medical costs. They also impose payment limits on treatments for preventable conditions, such as gum disease and tooth decay.

ECONOMICS IN THE MEDIA

Moral Hazard

"King-Size Homer"

In this episode of *The Simpsons*, a new corporate fitness policy is intended to help the power plant workers to become healthier. Morning exercises are instituted, and the employees are whipped into shape. But Homer hates working out, so he decides to gain a lot of weight in order to claim disability and work at home. In order to qualify, he must weigh at least 300 pounds. This means that he must go on an eating binge. Of course, his behavior is not what the designers of the fitness policy had in mind.

This amusing episode is a good example of moral hazard, and it showcases how well-intentioned policies can often be abused.

Moral hazard makes Homer decide to gain weight.

PRACTICE WHAT YOU KNOW

Asymmetric Information

Question: In each of the following situations, is adverse selection, the principal-agent problem, or moral hazard at work?

Is she for real, or has she been Photoshopped?

1. You decide to use an online dating site, but you are not entirely sure if the posted picture of your date is accurate.

Answer: Adverse selection is at work. The person you are interested in knows more about himself than you do. He can, and probably would, post a picture of himself that is flattering. When you finally meet him, you are likely to be disappointed.

2. You hire a substitute tutor for your sister and agree to pay $40 up front. Later, you find out that the tutor spent more time texting on his phone than helping your sister.

Answer: Since you paid up front for a one-time session, the substitute tutor has much less incentive to help compared to your sister's regular tutor, who expects repeat business and a tip. The poor outcome is a result of moral hazard.

3. You hire a friend to feed your cat and change the litter twice a day while you are on spring break. However, your friend only visits your apartment every other day, and your cat shows his disapproval by using your bedspread as a litter box.

Answer: This is a principal-agent problem. Since you are out of town, there is no way to tell how often your friend goes to your house. Your friend knows that cats are largely self-sufficient and figures that you won't be able to tell how often she changed the litter.

How Do Demand and Supply Contribute to High Medical Costs?

Now that we have a basic understanding of how the healthcare industry functions and who the key players are, we can examine the way demand and supply operate in the market for health care. On the demand side, we consider what makes healthcare demand stubbornly inelastic. Health care, when you need it, is not about the price—it is about getting the care you need. When you consider this fact and the presence of third-party payments, or payments made by insurance companies, you can begin to understand why medical expenses have risen so rapidly. On the supply side, medical licensing requirements help to explain why the supply of medical services is limited. The combination of strongly inelastic demand and limited supply pushes up prices for medical services.

Healthcare Demand

Health care is usually a necessity, without many good alternatives. This explains why the demand for health care is typically inelastic. For example, going without a heart transplant when you need one isn't an option. In fact, a 2002 RAND Corporation study found that health care has an average price elasticity coefficient of −0.17. This means that a 1% increase in the price of health care will lead to a 0.17% reduction in healthcare expenditures. Recall that as an elasticity coefficient approaches zero, demand becomes more inelastic. So we can say that the demand for medical care is quite inelastic. (For a refresher on elasticity, see Chapter 4.)

But there are some situations in which healthcare expenditures can be reduced. For example, otherwise healthy people with minor colds and other viruses can use home remedies, such as drinking fluids and resting, rather than making an expensive visit to the doctor. So the price elasticity of demand depends on the severity of the medical need and the sense of urgency involved in treatment. Urgent needs have the most inelastic demand. As the time horizon expands from the short run to the long run, the demand for health care becomes progressively more elastic. Non-emergency long-term treatments have the greatest price elasticity. For instance, a significant portion of the adult population postpones routine dental visits, despite the obvious benefits. Later, when a tooth goes bad, some people choose extractions, which are less expensive (though less attractive) than root canals and crowns.

In recent years, demand for health care has grown. As people live longer, demand rises for expensive medical goods and services, including hearing aids, replacement joints, assisted living and nursing home facilities, and so on. In an aging population, the incidence of certain illnesses and conditions—for example, cancer and Alzheimer's disease—rises. In addition, new technologies have made it possible to treat medical conditions for which there previously was no treatment. While these medical advances have improved the quality of life for many consumers, they drive up demand for more advanced medical procedures, equipment, and specialty drugs.

Third-Party Participation

People who are risk averse (see Chapter 17) generally choose to purchase health insurance because it protects them against the possibility of extreme financial hardship in the case of severe illness or other medical problems. But when people have insurance, it may distort their idea of costs and cause them to change their behavior, which creates a potential moral hazard problem. For example, if an insurance policy does not require the patient to pay anything, or requires very little, to see the doctor, the patient may wind up seeing the doctor more often than necessary.

ECONOMICS IN THE MEDIA

Inelastic Healthcare Demand

John Q

The 2002 feature film *John Q* follows John Quincy Archibald's quest to help his son receive a heart transplant. His son suddenly collapses while playing baseball and is rushed to the emergency room. Doctors inform John Q (played by Denzel Washington) that his son's only hope is a transplant. Since the child will die without the transplant, John Q's demand for this surgery is perfectly inelastic. Unfortunately, due to an involuntary work reduction at his job, John Q's insurance won't cover his son's transplant.

The tagline of the film is "give a father no options and you leave him no choice." This statement summarizes the dilemma that many people without insurance face. However, it does not stop the uninsured from demanding medical care when the situation is life threatening. This is problematic on two fronts. First, when those without insurance turn to the emergency room as their only source of medical care, their medical conditions are treated in the most expensive manner possible. Second, hospitals transfer the cost of treating the uninsured by raising fees for the other services that they provide. As a result, society picks up the tab for the uninsured indirectly through higher insurance premiums.

Inelastic demand for his son's heart transplant drives John Q to take desperate steps.

No one wants to risk a child possibly dying because his family lacks health insurance. After exploring every available financial option, John Q takes matters into his own hands and takes the emergency room staff hostage until the hospital agrees to do the transplant. Of course, this plot line sensationalizes the problem, but it also makes a very powerful point about the costs and benefits of life-saving care.

Consider how this situation affects two patients. Abigail does not have insurance and therefore must pay the full cost of medical care out-of-pocket. Brett has an insurance policy that requires a small co-payment for medical care. Figure 18.3 illustrates the difference between how Abigail (point A) and Brett (point B) might react. Let's suppose that they both get sick five times during the year. Because Abigail pays the full cost of seeking treatment ($100 per physician office visit), she will only go to the doctor's office three times. She ends up paying $300. Brett pays $10 per visit, so he will go to the doctor's office five times for a total cost to him of $50. The insurance company picks up the rest of the cost for Brett, or $90 per visit.

The overall impact of a $10 co-payment on healthcare costs is large. In the scenario described above, since each visit costs $100, total healthcare costs for the office visit are only $300 when a patient is uninsured, but they increase

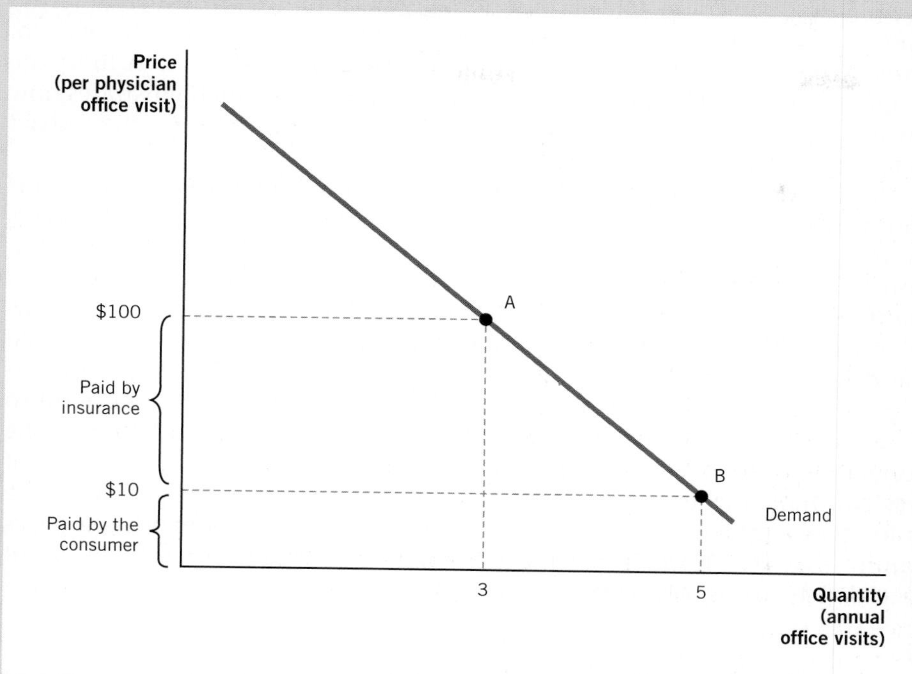

FIGURE 18.3

Price and the Quantity Demanded of Medical Care Services

Without insurance, the consumer bears the entire cost of an office visit, or $100. At this amount, the consumer might think twice about whether the medical care is truly necessary. As a result of these costs, the consumer makes 3 office visits per year, represented by point A. However, when a consumer has insurance and pays only a $10 co-payment per visit, the marginal price drops and the quantity demanded increases. This consumer makes 5 office visits per year, represented by point B.

to $500 with healthcare coverage—a $200 increase in total healthcare costs just for the initial office visit. Since in our example the insurance companies are paying 90% of the cost, the consumer has little reason not to seek medical attention, even for minor problems that will respond to home treatment. The two extra visits per year illustrate a change in consumer behavior as a result of the lower co-payment. This demonstrates one simple reason insurance costs are so high.

Healthcare Supply

While consumers worry about the price, or premium, they pay for health insurance, producers are concerned about profits. As much as we might like to think that medical providers care only about our health, we must acknowledge that they are providing a service for which they expect to be paid. Therefore, it is more accurate to think of healthcare providers in the same way we think of any other producers: when the price rises, they are willing to supply additional health care. Producers of medical care such as physicians and hospitals also enjoy significant market power. In this section, we consider how licensing requirements limit the supply of certain healthcare providers and the effect this has on the market.

Becoming a skilled medical provider is a lengthy process that requires extensive training, education, and certification. Physicians must secure licenses from a medical board before they can practice, and nurses must become registered. Thus, restrictions associated with entering the medical profession limit the supply of workers. This point is captured in Figure 18.4, which illustrates how barriers to entry limit the number of physicians and nurses and the impact that this outcome has on their wages.

Barriers to entry in the medical profession restrict the supply of physicians and nurses. The subsequent decrease in the supply of these medical workers (from Q_1 to Q_2) causes their wages to increase (from W_1 to W_2). In addition, many medical facilities do not face direct competition. For example, many small communities have only one hospital. In these cases, familiarity, the need for immediate care, and convenience make the nearest hospital the default option for most patients. Since economies of scale are important in the provision of medical care, even large metropolitan areas tend to have only a few large hospitals rather than many smaller competitors. As the population base expands, larger hospitals can afford to offer a wider set of services than smaller hospitals do. For instance, the need for pediatric care units, oncology centers, organ transplant centers, and a host of other services require that the hospital develop a particular expertise. The availability of specialized care is, of course, a good thing. However, as hospitals become

FIGURE 18.4

Barriers to Entry Limit the Supply of Certain Medical Workers

Restrictions associated with entering the medical profession limit the supply of certain workers. This causes a decrease in the supply of physicians and nurses from Q_1 to Q_2 and an increase in wages from W_1 to W_2.

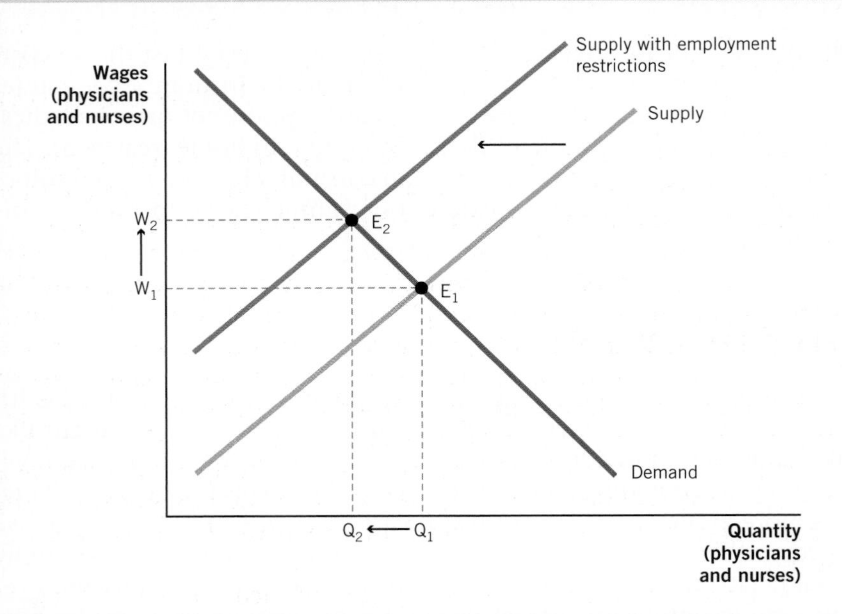

larger and more highly specialized, competitive pressures subside and they are able to charge higher fees.

The market power of suppliers is held in check to some extent by insurance companies and by the Medicare and Medicaid programs. Also, some services are not reimbursed by insurance. And the insurance companies push back against certain other medical charges by limiting the amount they reimburse, as do Medicare and Medicaid for certain treatments. In contrast, elective medical services, such as Lasik eye surgery, are typically not reimbursed by insurance plans. As a result, consumer demand is quite elastic. Still, overall medical costs have continued to rise.

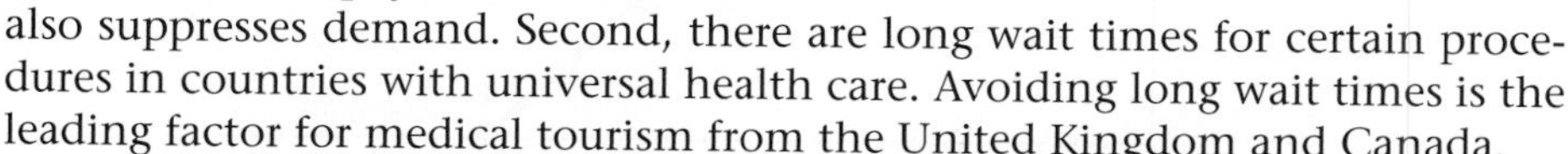

ECONOMICS IN THE REAL WORLD

Medical Tourism

Medical tourism has grown explosively over the last 20 years as the quality of medical care around the globe has improved rapidly and international travel has become more convenient. Today, it is possible for a patient to have cardiac surgery in India, a hip replacement in Egypt, and a face-lift in Rio de Janeiro. Supply and demand helps explain the rapid growth of medical tourism. People seek medical care abroad for two reasons: costs and wait times.

Recovery from surgery doesn't get any better than this!

First, the cost of medical care is as much as 90% lower in a developing country than in a developed country such as the United States. This is a function of lower costs of living, less administrative overhead, a favorable currency exchange rate, and lower malpractice premiums. Also, health insurance is not readily available in many locations, which leads to a policy of cash payment for healthcare services and also suppresses demand. Second, there are long wait times for certain procedures in countries with universal health care. Avoiding long wait times is the leading factor for medical tourism from the United Kingdom and Canada.

In the United States, the main reason for medical tourism is the lower cost. Indeed, many procedures performed abroad cost a fraction of the price in developed countries. For example, a liver transplant in the United States can cost more than $250,000, but it costs less than $100,000 in Taiwan. Some insurance plans offer incentives to have orthopedic surgery, such as knee and hip replacements, performed in Panama and Costa Rica, where the cost of the surgery is a quarter of the cost in the United States. Patients agree to leave the country for this type of surgery because their insurance company will pay all their travel-related expenses and waive the typical out-of-pocket expenses that would be incurred from co-pays and deductibles.

Medical tourism has even led to the creation of medical "safaris," where patients go to South Africa or South America for cosmetic surgery, stay in luxurious accommodations, and take in the savanna or rain forest while recuperating. ✷

PRACTICE WHAT YOU KNOW

Demand for Health Care: How Would Universal Health Care Alter the Demand for Medical Care?

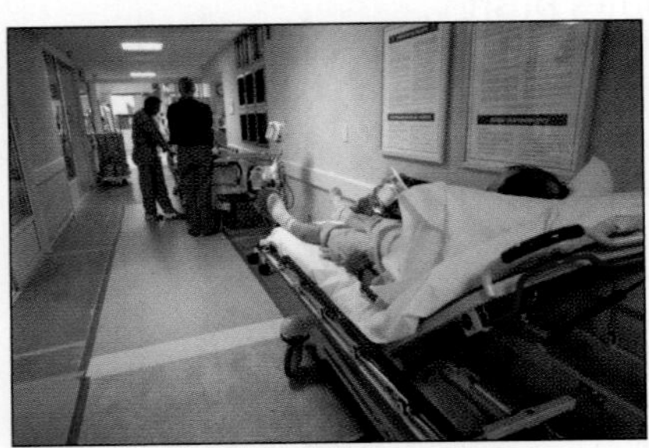

Increased demand for services might mean that "Hurry up and wait" becomes a common experience for most patients.

Question: Suppose that the United States scraps its current healthcare system and citizens are 100% covered for all medical care with no co-payments or deductibles. How would the new system affect the demand for medical care? Illustrate your answer on a graph.

Answer: Without any co-payment or deductibles, each patient's out-of-pocket expense would be zero. Society would pick up the tab through taxes. As a result, the quantity of medical care demanded by each patient would increase from point A to point B.

At point B, demand is no longer contingent on price, so this represents the largest potential quantity of care demanded.

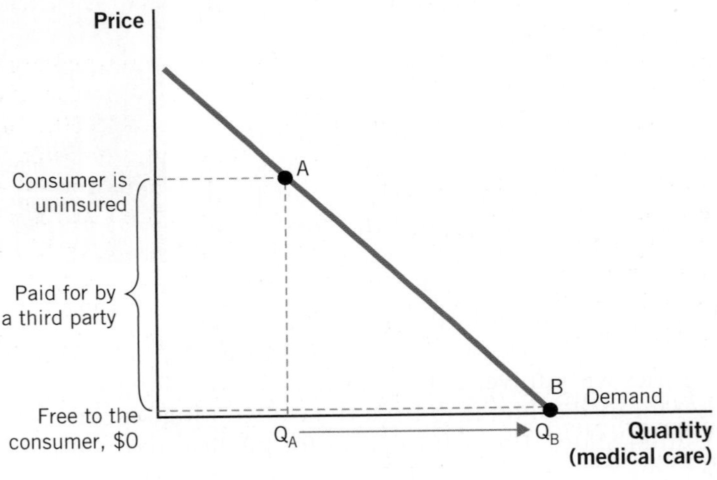

How Do Incentives Influence the Quality of Health Care?

In this section, we apply what we've learned about health care. First, we look at the universal healthcare debate by comparing the healthcare systems in the United States and Canada. Then we examine the shortage of human organs available for transplant. By considering these two issues, we can see how incentives influence the quality of health care that patients receive.

Single-Payer versus Private Health Care

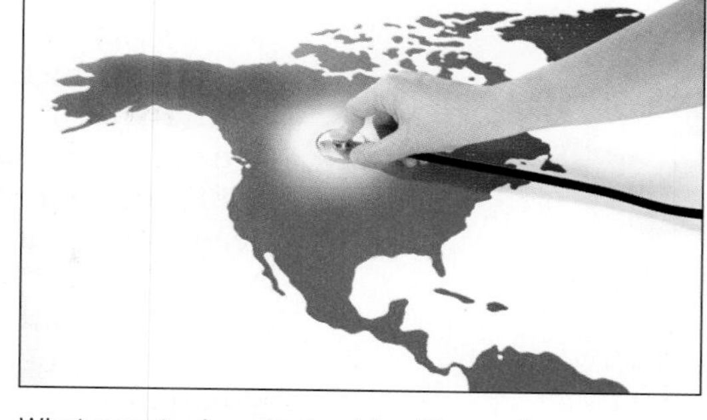

What country has the best health care?

Rationing is a fact of life because we live in a world of scarcity. The simplest way of thinking about the health-care issue is to understand how different rationing mechanisms are used in medical care. In the United States, the primary rationing mechanism is the consumer's ability to pay. One consequence of using prices to ration medical care is that close to 50 million U.S. citizens forgo some medical care because they lack insurance or the means to pay for care on their own. In Canada, no citizen lacks the means to pay because medical care is paid for by taxes. This does not mean that medical care there is unlimited, however. In Canada, rationing occurs through wait times, fewer doctors, and limited availability of certain drugs.

As in almost all things economic, there is a trade-off. No medical system creates the perfect set of incentives. In the United States, a large majority of citizens have the means to pay for medical care, have access to some of the best medical facilities in the world, and face relatively short wait times. However, under the current U.S. system, the poorest members of the society have reduced access to health care.

In Canada, each citizen is treated equally, but access to immediate medical treatment is more restricted. We have seen in Table 18.1 that Canada spends far less than the United States per capita ($4,363 versus $7,960). How does Canada provide medical care to every citizen at approximately half the price of the U.S. system? There are several ways. First, the government sets the rates that are paid to medical providers. Second, physicians are not permitted to have private practices. Third, to eliminate outside competition and to prevent wages from rising with the market, physicians' salaries are capped. Fourth, hospitals receive grants from the government to cover the costs of providing care. This system, in which there is only a *single payer*, makes the government the single buyer, or monopsonist, of most medical care. (See Chapter 14 for a discussion of monopsony.) In other words, in a **single-payer system** the government covers the cost of providing most health care, and citizens pay their share through taxes.

In a **single-payer system**, the government covers the cost of providing most health care, and citizens pay their share through taxes.

The Canadian government uses its leverage as a monopsonist to set compensation levels for physicians below the competitive market wage rate. Under Canada's Health Act, government funding is required for medically necessary care, but only if that care is delivered in hospitals or by certified physicians. This means that the Canadian government funds about 70% of all medical expenses, with the remaining 30% of costs being generated by prescription medications, long-term care, physical therapy, and dental care.[3] In these areas, private insurance operates in much the same way it does in the United States.

Predictably, cost containment measures have an influence on physician flows. Medical schools in the United States produce a relatively constant number of physicians each year, but the new supply is not enough to keep up with the demand in the United States. In fact, U.S. demand exceeds the supply by approximately 30% annually. As a result, physicians flow into the

United States each year from beyond its borders, and one of the major suppliers is Canada.

Patients seeking medical care in Canada are also far more likely to seek additional care in the United States than U.S. patients are to seek care in Canada. This fact might strike you as odd. After all, Canada has national health care, and health services there are covered under the Canadian Health Act. However, there is a difference between access and availability. Because Canada keeps tight control over medical costs, people with conditions that are not urgently life-threatening often face extended waits. Ironically, closely related services that are not regulated—for example, veterinarian visits—provide access to medical care without waiting. Dogs in Canada have no trouble getting MRIs and chemotherapy quickly—unlike their human counterparts, who have to wait—but of course the pet owner has to pay the full expense.

ECONOMICS IN THE REAL WORLD

Health Care in France

In 2000, the World Health Organization (WHO) ranked every country's health-care system.* France came in first. The United States finished 37 out of 191 nations. When the WHO study was questioned, researchers in London decided to control for longevity by separating out deaths caused by accidents and homicides from those by natural causes to determine how effective each system was at preventing deaths with good medical care. In the second study, conducted in 2008, researchers looked at health care in 19 industrialized nations. France, again, finished first. The United States was last. More recent studies continue to confirm these findings.

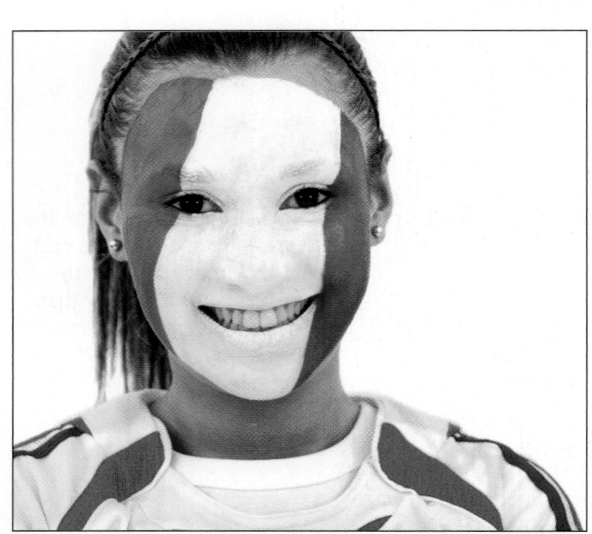

France is #1 in health care, according to the World Health Organization.

What separates the United States from France? Not as much as you might think. The French balk at any notion that they have socialized health care. France, like the United States, relies on both private insurance and government insurance. In both countries, people generally get private insurance through their employer. Both healthcare systems value choice, and patients can choose preferred providers and specialists. The chief difference is that 99.9% of French citizens have health insurance, as opposed to 85% in the United States. This occurs because in France there is mandatory national health insurance, alongside supplemental private insurance that most people purchase.

Another difference between the French and U.S. systems is in the way coverage works for the sickest patients. In France, the most serious conditions

---

* Material adapted from Joseph Shapiro, "Healthcare Lessons from France," *National Public Radio,* July 11, 2008. Transcript available at www.npr.org.

are 100% covered. In contrast, in the United States patients' out-of-pocket expenses for the most serious conditions often require supplemental insurance, and experimental procedures and drugs are rarely covered. As a result, the French report that they are quite satisfied with their healthcare system, while similar surveys in the United States find a much more mixed reaction, with roughly half the population happy and the other half concerned.

Of course, none of this is inexpensive. In France, the average person pays slightly over 20% of his or her income to support the national healthcare system. Since French firms must pick up a large chunk of the healthcare tab, they are more reluctant to hire workers. In the United States, workers do not pay as much in taxes, but they do pay more for medical care than the French do when we add in the costs of private insurance and higher out-of-pocket expenses. The lower overall costs of providing medical care in France can be traced to the government control of the amount of compensation that hospitals and providers receive. In other words, the French do a better job of using monopsony power to control costs. Nevertheless, healthcare costs in France have risen rapidly, which has led to cuts in services in order to keep the system solvent. ✳

The Human Organ Shortage

Many altruistic people donate blood each year to help save the lives of tens of thousands of other people. Their generosity makes transplants and other surgeries possible. Unfortunately, the same cannot be said for organ donations. The quantity of replacement organs demanded exceeds the quantity of replacement organs supplied each year, resulting in thousands of deaths. Many of these deaths would be preventable if people were allowed to sell organs. However, the National Organ Transplant Act of 1984 makes it illegal to do so in the United States. Restrictions do not cover the entire body: people can sell platelets, sperm, and ova. In those markets, prices determine who donates. With blood, kidneys, livers, and lungs, the donors are not paid. This discrepancy has created two unintended consequences. First, many people die unnecessarily: in the United States, more than 6,000 patients on transplant waiting lists die each year. Second, the demand for human organs has created a billion-dollar-a-year black market.

Let's consider the market for kidneys. Figure 18.5 illustrates how the supply and demand for human kidneys works. Almost everyone has two kidneys, and a person's life can continue almost normally with only one healthy kidney. Of course, there are risks associated with donation, including complications from the surgery and during recovery, as well as no longer having a backup kidney. However, since there are roughly 300 million "spare" kidneys in the United States (because the population is 300 million), there is a large pool of potential donors who are good matches for recipients awaiting a transplant.

Since kidneys cannot be legally bought and sold, the supply curve shown in Figure 18.5 does not respond to price. As a result, the curve becomes a vertical line at point Q_S (quantity supplied). Notice that the quantity supplied is not zero. This is because many people donate kidneys to friends and family members in need, and others participate in exchange programs under which they donate a kidney to someone they don't know in exchange

FIGURE 18.5

The Supply and Demand for Human Kidneys

Restrictions on selling kidneys limit the supply of organs as shown by $S_{restricted}$ and cause the shortage noted between Q_d and Q_s. A black market develops with an illegal price of $125,000.

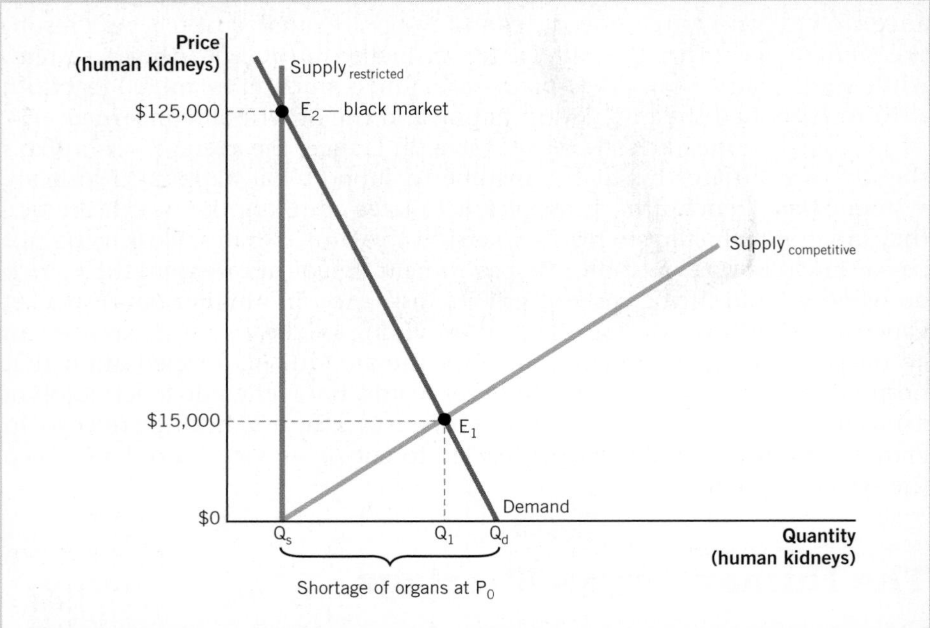

for someone else agreeing to donate a kidney to a friend or family member. (Exchange programs help to provide better matches so that the recipient is less likely to reject the kidney transplant.) Moreover, a few altruistic persons donate their kidneys to complete strangers. Nevertheless, the quantity supplied still falls short of the quantity demanded, since $Q_d > Q_s$ at a price of $0.

Markets would normally reconcile a shortage by increasing prices. In Figure 18.5, an equilibrium market price of $15,000 is shown ($E_1$). Economists have estimated that this would be the market price if the sale of kidneys were legal in the United States. Since it is illegal, the nation faces the shortage illustrated in Figure 18.5. Over 3,000 people die each year in this country waiting for a kidney transplant. Many others have a low quality of life while waiting to receive a kidney. Because patients waiting for human organs eventually die without a transplant, a black market for kidney transplants has developed outside the United States. However, the price—typically, $125,000 or greater—requires doctors, hospitals, staff, and patients to circumvent the law. As a consequence, the black market price (at E_2) is much higher than it would be if a competitive market for human kidneys existed.

SNAPSHOT

Health: United States vs. Canada

Is the healthcare dollar being spent as efficiently as possible to maintain the health of Americans? To answer this question, it's helpful to compare our situation to other countries, such as Canada. The United States and Canada have very different healthcare systems. Canada's is primarily a publicly funded, single-payer system with the government paying 71% of all health-related expenses. The United States' is primarily a privately funded, multi-payer system with the government paying 48% of all health-related expenses.

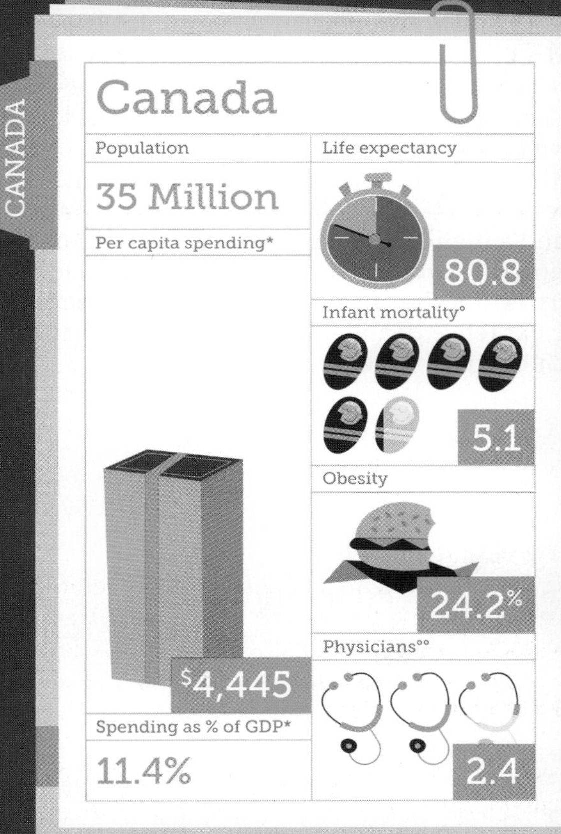

CANADA
Canada
Population
35 Million
Per capita spending*
$4,445
Spending as % of GDP*
11.4%
Life expectancy
80.8
Infant mortality°
5.1
Obesity
24.2%
Physicians°°
2.4

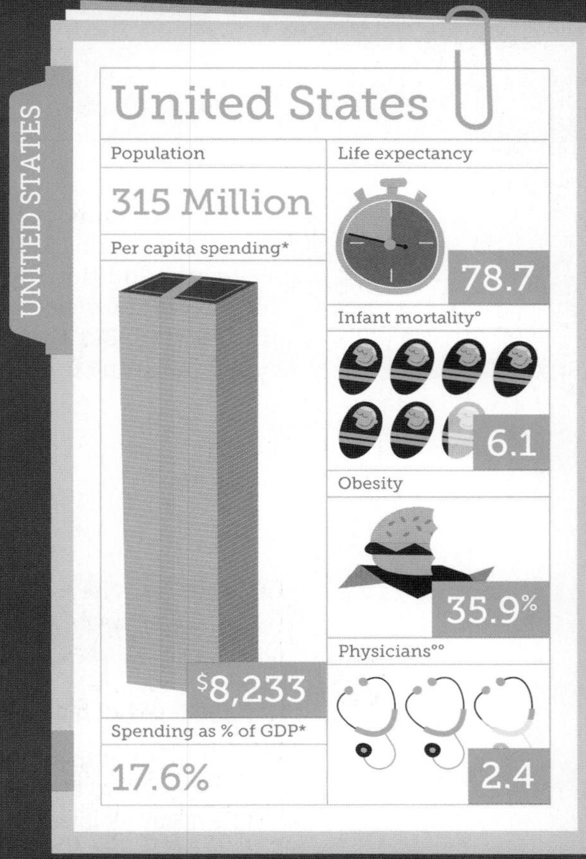

** Total expenditure, public and private   ° Per 1,000 live births   °° Per 1,000 people*

Both countries achieve similar health outcomes, but health care is a clear example of trade-offs. The Canadian system cuts costs, while patients in the United States benefit from shorter wait times for care and the best medical facilities in the world.

REVIEW QUESTIONS

- How do you think the obesity level in the United States contributes to healthcare costs?
- What are the benefits and costs of a private versus a public healthcare system?

ECONOMICS IN THE REAL WORLD

Selling Ova to Pay for College

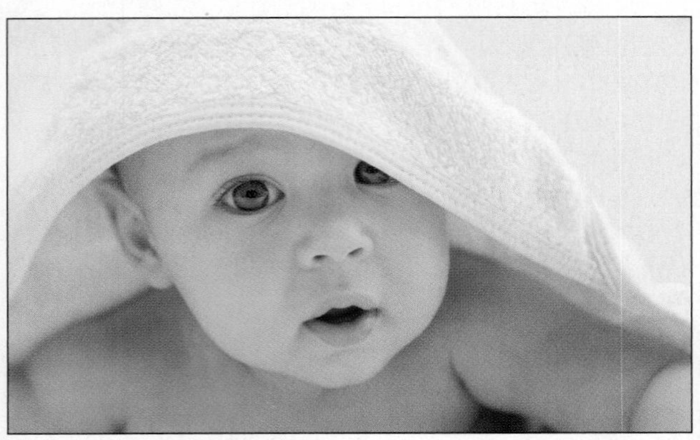

"Baby, baby, baby, oh."

Did you know that young, bright, American women with college loans can help pay off their debts by donating their ova? The process is relatively simple. The donor is paid to travel to a fertility clinic, and several weeks of hormone treatments are begun. After this, pairs of the donor's ova are removed surgically, then fertilized in a laboratory and implanted inside the womb of a woman who is infertile. With careful lab work and a little luck, the procedure works. The donor receives between $5,000 and $15,000, depending on her track record as a donor. Those whose ova have been successfully implanted and led to the birth of a healthy child are in high demand.

The procedure is not without risks, including rare but potentially serious complications for donors and a high incidence of multiple births among recipients; additionally, long-term risks are not well understood. And, clearly, volunteering for elective surgery isn't a choice everyone would feel comfortable making. But that said, the existence of a market allows a trade that can benefit both the donor and recipient greatly. ✷

PRACTICE WHAT YOU KNOW

Human Organ Shortage: Liver Transplants

Most liver transplants make use of organs from cadavers. However, liver transplants are also possible from live donors, who give a portion of their liver to a needy recipient. Donating a live liver involves major surgery that lasts between 4 and 12 hours. The complication rate for the donor is low, but the recovery time is typically two to three months. Not surprisingly, there is still a shortage of live livers for transplant.

Question: What solutions can you think of that would motivate more people to donate part of their liver to help save the life of someone else?

Answer: One answer would be to repeal the National Organ Transplant Act. This move would create a market for livers and establish a price that would eliminate the shortage. Other ways to increase donations would be to allow donors to claim a tax deduction equal to the value of the liver donated, or to receive scholarships for themselves or members of their family.

The Human Organ Black Market

ECONOMICS IN THE MEDIA

Law & Order: Special Victims Unit

In one episode of *Special Victims Unit*, the officers try to track down a sleazy kidney dealer. What makes the episode compelling is the tension between doing what the law requires—stopping an illegal kidney transplant mid-surgery—and subsequently wrestling with watching the patient suffer as a result. In addition, the officers interview the dealer, the physician, patients on kidney waiting lists, and an administrator of the national kidney wait list. Their opinions, which run a wide gamut, allow the viewer to experience all of the emotions and arguments for and against the purchase of kidneys.

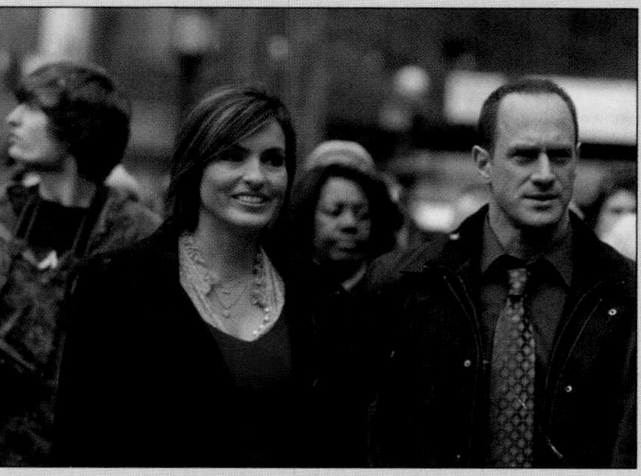

On the track of a black-market kidney dealer.

Each character tugs on viewers' emotions in a different way. The sleazy dealer proudly proclaims that he is making his customers happy and that the officers wouldn't be so judgmental if one of their own family members needed a kidney. The physician who does the transplant explains that he is not driven by making money but by saving lives. The patients all know where they can get an illegal kidney, but most accept their fate within the current system. The administrator of the wait list argues that "they have enough trouble getting people to volunteer as it is. What would happen if donors learned that we had made an exception and approved the transplant of an illegally purchased kidney?" By the end of the episode, we see that the economic and ethical dimensions of the issue are not clear-cut.

Despite the success of ova donations, concerns about equity and ethics have made the sale of many vital organs illegal. In its simplest form, the issue is essentially this: why should the affluent, who can afford to pay for organ transplants, continue to live, while the poor, who also need organ transplants, die? That hardly seems fair. Unfortunately, altruism alone has not provided enough organs to meet demand, leading to a shortage of many vital organs. Since we continue to experience shortages of human organs, the supply must be rationed. Whether the rationing takes place through markets, waiting in line, or via some other mechanism is a matter of efficiency. As a result, using markets, in some form, may be one way to prevent avoidable deaths. However, the ethical considerations are significant. For example, if organs can be bought and sold, what would prevent the use of coercion to force people to sell their organs?

Of course, the ethical dilemma becomes moot if viable artificial organs can be created. And in fact, in this regard medical science is making progress toward someday solving the organ shortage. In the meantime, if you are uncomfortable with markets determining the price, remember that relying solely on altruism is not enough. If we really want to increase the supply

ECONOMICS FOR LIFE

Getting the Right Insurance

Many young people go without health insurance after they age out of their parents' plans, figuring that their health will continue to be good. You might be one of these young people. But what happens if, for example, you break a wrist on a weekend ski trip? Do you have $8,000 to pay the medical bill? Going without medical insurance is a high-risk proposition. As an alternative, high-deductible health insurance policies provide a middle ground for healthier consumers who want to insure against catastrophic illness but can handle out-of-pocket expenses for minor treatments. Likewise, going without life insurance is also a high-risk decision once you have a family.

Life insurance protects your family in the event of your death. Most people try to purchase enough life insurance to provide financial security for the family they leave behind. Typically, this means buying enough insurance to pay off the mortgage on the house they own, set up a fund so their children will be able to attend college, and provide a reserve fund for other expenses.

Buying the right life insurance is usually presented as a choice between term insurance and whole life insurance. But don't be fooled. You should buy term insurance. Let's review the differences between these two types of policies.

A term policy includes only life insurance, whereas a whole life policy combines a term policy with an investment component. The term policy provides a fixed benefit upon the death of the insured and covers a specific term that may range up to 30 years, after which the policy expires. A whole life policy buys a specific amount of coverage that does not expire and combines this insurance with an investment component. Whole life policies are typically sold as investment vehicles that the insured can tap into if it becomes necessary to borrow cash later in life. This option may sound appealing, but it is a bad idea because commission rates and fees are very high. If you want to invest your money, you can look on your own to find stock and bond funds with far lower fees and, correspondingly, much higher rates of return.

Premiums for term insurance are low for anyone in good health before age 50. Beyond age 50, the premiums rise quickly as the rate of death for any given age group rises. By the time you reach age 65, term insurance is very expensive.

Wouldn't you want to protect your family's financial future?

We can illustrate the real value of term insurance by making a direct comparison. Suppose you are a 30-year-old in great health. You can purchase a $1 million policy for a 20-year term for under $1,000 annually or a $1 million whole life policy for $10,000 annually. If you invest the difference, or $9,000, your investment will grow faster than it would as part of a whole life policy. After 20 years, you would have an extra $75,000 saved up due to lower fees alone! If you are also making smart moves by paying down your mortgage and saving for your children's college expenses, there will come a point at which you will need less insurance. In a sense, you will become self-insured. Term insurance is the least expensive bridge to that point. Whole life forces you to save; for some people, that commitment mechanism may be worth pursuing. For others, though, term insurance is the path to greater long-term wealth.

of organs, we need to try incentives. Some proposals along this line include allowing people to receive tax deductions, college scholarships, or guaranteed health care in exchange for donating an organ. All these suggestions would reduce the ethical dilemma while still harnessing the power of incentives to save lives.

Incentives

Conclusion

When people speak about health care, they often debate the merits of universal health care versus private medical care as if the issue involved just those two factors. That misconception, which frames the political debate about health care, obscures the important economic considerations at work on the micro level. The reality is that the healthcare debate exists on many margins and requires complex trade-offs. The way the various participants deal with different healthcare issues affects how well our nation's overall healthcare system functions. Supply and demand works just fine in outlining the incentives that participants face when considering healthcare options; what complicates the analysis is the impact of third parties on the incentives that patients face.

Health care straddles the boundary between microeconomic analysis, which focuses on individual behavior, and macroeconomics, in which society's overarching concern is how to best spend so large an amount of money. Moreover, health decisions are an unavoidable part of our individual lives. Medical expenditures account for one out of every six dollars spent in the United States. Therefore, understanding the micro forces that lead to fundamental changes to the healthcare system will have a large impact—a macro effect—on our economy.

ANSWERING THE BIG QUESTIONS

What are the important issues in the healthcare industry?

* The healthcare debate is about efficiency and cost containment. Increases in longevity and quality of life are subject to diminishing returns and require choices with difficult trade-offs.
* The widespread use of insurance alters the incentives that consumers and producers face when making healthcare decisions. Consumers pay premiums up front and much smaller deductibles and co-payments when seeking medical care. Producers receive the bulk of their revenue from intermediaries such as insurance companies. The result is a system in which consumers demand more medical care because they are insured and many providers have an incentive to order additional tests or procedures that may not be absolutely necessary.

How does asymmetric information affect healthcare delivery?

* Asymmetric information (adverse selection, moral hazard, and the principal-agent problem) complicates the way medical insurance is structured. Insurance companies try to structure their plans to align the patient's incentives to seek care only when it is needed and also to seek preventative care. The companies can achieve this by making many preventative care visits free and establishing deductibles and co-payments that are high enough to discourage unnecessary trips to the doctor or the seeking of additional procedures.
* Inelastic demand for many medical services, combined with third-party payments that significantly lower out-of-pocket expenses to consumers, gives rise to a serious moral hazard problem in which patients demand more medical care than is medically advisable. As a consequence of the way health care is structured and the moral hazard it creates, the United States devotes a far larger share of its national output to health care than is optimal. To solve a moral hazard problem, it is necessary to fix the incentive structure. This explains why many insurance companies encourage preventative care: it lowers medical costs. This also explains why insurance companies impose payment limits on preventable conditions.

How do demand and supply contribute to high medical costs?

* Inelastic demand and third-party payments help explain why medical expenses have risen so rapidly, while licensing helps explain why the supply of medical services is limited. The combination of third-party payments and inelastic demand for medical care increase the quantity of medical care demanded; both factors also result in increased expenditures. As we learned previously, more demand means higher prices.
* In addition, licensing requirements limit the supply of key healthcare providers. This provides a supply-side explanation leading to increased medical expenditures. In addition, hospital charges are rarely subject to competitive pressures. In many small communities, there is only one local hospital, clinic, or specialist nearby. This gives providers market power, which they can use in setting prices.

How do incentives influence the quality of health care?

* The demand for many replacement organs exceeds the supply made available each year. However, because of the National Organ Transplant Act of 1984, it is illegal to sell most organs in the United States. This restriction results in thousands of deaths annually, many of which would be preventable if people were allowed to sell organs in legal markets.
* A single-payer system makes the government the single buyer, or monopsonist, of most medical care. The government uses its leverage as a monopsonist to set compensation levels for providers below the competitive market wage rate.
* Single-payer systems ration medical services through increased wait times, whereas private healthcare systems ration medical care through prices.

CONCEPTS YOU SHOULD KNOW

adverse selection (p. 557)
asymmetric information (p. 557)
co-insurance payments (p. 555)
co-payments (p. 555)
deductibles (p. 555)
moral hazard (p. 559)
principal-agent problem (p. 558)
single-payer system (p. 567)

QUESTIONS FOR REVIEW

1. What is asymmetric information? Why does it matter for medical care?
2. Give one example each of adverse selection, moral hazard, and the principal-agent problem.
3. For each of the examples you gave in question 2, discuss a solution that lessens the asymmetric information problem.
4. Describe why the marginal product of medical care declines as medical expenditures rise.
5. What are two primary reasons why healthcare demand has increased dramatically over the last 20 years?
6. What is a supply-related reason for high medical care costs?
7. What are the two primary ways in which health care is rationed?

STUDY PROBLEMS (** solved at the end of the section*)

1. Suppose that a medical specialist charges $300 per consultation. If your insurance charges you a $25 co-pay, what is the marginal cost of your consultation? Suppose that a second patient has a different policy that requires a 25% co-insurance payment, but no co-pay. What is the second patient's marginal cost of the consultation? Which patient is more likely to see the specialist?

* 2. Newer automobiles have many safety features, including antilock brakes, side air bags, traction control, and rear backup sensors, to help prevent accidents. Do these safety features lead the drivers of newer vehicles to drive more safely? In your answer, consider how an increased number of safety features affects the problem of moral hazard.

3. A customer wants a new health insurance policy. Even though the customer's medical records indicate a good health history, the insurance company requires a physical exam before coverage can be extended. Why would the insurance company insist on a physical exam?

4. Describe whether the following medical services have elastic or inelastic demand.
   a. an annual physical for someone between the ages of 20 and 35
   b. an MRI used to detect cancer
   c. the removal of a non-cancerous mole on your back
   d. seeing a physician when your child has a 104-degree temperature

5. Most people have two working kidneys, but humans need only one working kidney to survive. If the sale of kidneys was legalized, what would happen to the price and the number of kidneys sold in the market? Would a shortage of kidneys continue to exist? Explain your response.

* 6. An isolated community has one hospital. The next closest hospital is two hours away. Given what you have learned about monopoly, what prices would you expect the hospital to charge? How much care would you expect it to provide? Compare the prices and amount of care provided to those of a comparably sized

hospital in a major metropolitan area where competition is prevalent.

7. One insurance plan costs $100 a month and has a $50 co-payment for all services. Another insurance plan costs $50 a month and requires patients to pay a 15% co-insurance. A customer is trying to decide which plan to purchase. Which plan would the customer select with an anticipated $200 per month in medical bills? What about $600 per month in medical bills? Set up an equation to determine the monthly amount of medical expenses at which the consumer would be indifferent between the two plans.

8. For each of the following situations, determine whether adverse selection, moral hazard, or the principal-agent problem is at work.
   a. You decide to buy a scalped ticket before a concert, but you are not entirely sure the ticket is legitimate.
   b. A contractor takes a long time to finish the construction work he promised after you gave him his final payment.
   c. You hire a neighborhood teenager to mow your grass once a week over the summer while you are traveling. The teenager mows your grass every three weeks instead.

SOLVED PROBLEMS

2. When drivers feel safer, they drive faster—not more safely. The higher speed offsets the safety gain from safety features that help prevent accidents or make them survivable. Drivers of vehicles who feel especially safe are more likely to take on hazardous conditions and become involved in accidents. In other words, they alter their behavior when driving a safer car. The change in behavior is evidence of a moral hazard problem.

6. Since the demand for medical care is quite inelastic, an isolated hospital with significant monopoly power will charge more and will offer fewer services. In contrast, a comparably sized hospital in a major metropolitan area where competition is prevalent is forced to charge the market price and offer more services to attract customers.

GLOSSARY

absolute advantage: the ability of one producer to make more than another producer with the same quantity of resources

accounting profit: calculated by subtracting a firm's explicit costs from total revenue

adverse selection: phenomenon existing when one party has information about some aspect of product quality that the other party does not have

antitrust laws: attempts to prevent oligopolies from behaving like monopolies

asymmetric information: an imbalance in information that occurs when one party knows more than the other

average fixed cost (AFC): determined by dividing a firm's total fixed costs by the output

average total cost (ATC): the sum of average variable cost and average fixed cost

average variable cost (AVC): determined by dividing a firm's total variable costs by the output

backward-bending labor supply curve: supply curve occurring when workers value additional leisure more than additional income

bandwagon effect: condition arising when a buyer's preference for a product increases as the number of people buying it increases

barriers to entry: restrictions that make it difficult for new firms to enter a market

behavioral economics: the field of economics that draws on insights from experimental psychology to explore how people make economic decisions

black markets: illegal markets that arise when price controls are in place

bounded rationality: concept proposing that although decision-makers want a good outcome, either they are not capable of performing the problem-solving that traditional theory assumes, or they are not inclined to do so

budget constraint: the set of consumption bundles that represent the maximum amount the consumer can afford

cap and trade: an approach used to curb pollution by creating a system of pollution permits that are traded in an open market

capital goods: goods that help produce other valuable goods and services in the future

cartel: a group of two or more firms that act in unison

causality: condition existing when one variable influences another

***ceteris paribus*:** the concept under which economists examine a change in one variable while holding everything else constant

club goods: goods with two characteristics: they are nonrival in consumption and excludable

Clayton Act: law of 1914 targeting corporate behaviors that reduce competition

Coase theorem: theorem stating that if there are no barriers to negotiations, and if property rights are fully specified, interested parties will bargain to correct any externalities that exist

co-insurance payments: a percentage of costs that the insured must pay after exceeding the insurance policy's deductible up to the policy's contribution limit

co-payments: fixed amounts that the insured must pay when receiving a medical service or filling a prescription

collusion: an agreement among rival firms that specifies the price each firm charges and the quantity it produces

common-resource goods: goods with two characteristics: they are rival in consumption and nonexcludable

comparative advantage: the situation where an individual, business, or country can produce at a lower opportunity cost than a competitor can

compensating differential: the difference in wages offered to offset the desirability or undesirability of a job

competitive market: one in which when there are so many buyers and sellers that each has only a small impact on the market price and output

complements: two goods that are used together; when the price of a complementary good rises, the demand for the related good goes down

constant returns to scale: condition occurring when costs remain constant as output expands in the long run

consumer goods: goods produced for present consumption

consumer optimum: the combination of goods and services that maximizes the consumer's utility for a given income or budget

consumer surplus: the difference between the willingness to pay for a good and the price that is paid to get it

cost-benefit analysis: a process that economists use to determine whether the benefits of providing a public good outweigh the costs

cross-price elasticity of demand: measurement of the responsiveness of the quantity demanded of one good to a change in the price of a related good

deadweight loss: the decrease in economic activity caused by market distortions

deductibles: fixed amounts that the insured must pay before most of the policy's benefits can be applied

demand curve: a graph of the relationship between the prices in the demand schedule and the quantity demanded at those prices

demand schedule: a table that shows the relationship between the price of a good and the quantity demanded

derived demand: the demand for an input used in the production process

diamond-water paradox: concept explaining why water, which is essential to life, is inexpensive while diamonds, which do not sustain life, are expensive

diminishing marginal product: condition occurring when successive increases in inputs are associated with a slower rise in output

diminishing marginal utility: condition occurring when marginal utility declines as consumption increases

diseconomies of scale: condition occurring when costs rise as output expands in the long run

dominant strategy: in game theory, a strategy that a player will always prefer, regardless of what his opponent chooses

economic profit: calculated by subtracting both the explicit and the implicit costs of business from a firm's total revenue

economic rent: the difference between what a factor of production earns and what it could earn in the next-best alternative

economic thinking: a purposeful evaluation of the available opportunities to make the best decision possible

economics: the study of how people allocate their limited resources to satisfy their nearly unlimited wants

economies of scale: condition occurring when costs decline as output expands in the long run

efficiency: an allocation of resources that maximizes total surplus

efficiency wages: wages higher than equilibrium wages, offered to increase worker productivity

efficient scale: the output level that minimizes a firm's average total cost

elasticity: a measure of the responsiveness of buyers and sellers to changes in price or income

endogenous factors: the variables that can be controlled for in a model

equilibrium: condition occurring at the point where the demand curve and the supply curve intersect

equilibrium price: the price at which the quantity supplied is equal to the quantity demanded; also known as the *market-clearing price*

equilibrium quantity: the amount at which the quantity supplied is equal to the quantity demanded

equity: the fairness of the distribution of benefits within the society

excess capacity: phenomenon occurring when a firm produces at an output level that is smaller than the output level needed to minimize average total costs

excise taxes: taxes levied on a particular good or service

excludable goods: goods that the consumer must purchase before being able to use them

exogenous factors: the variables that cannot be controlled for in a model

explicit costs: tangible out-of-pocket expenses

external costs: the costs of a market activity paid by people who are not participants

externalities: the costs or benefits of a market activity that affect a third party

factors of production: the inputs (labor, land, and capital) used in producing goods and services

fixed costs: costs that do not vary with a firm's output in the short run

framing effects: a phenomenon seen when people change their answer (or action) depending on how the question is asked

free-rider problem: phenomenon occurring when someone receives a benefit without having to pay for it

gambler's fallacy: the belief that recent outcomes are unlikely to be repeated and that outcomes that have not occurred recently are due to happen soon

game theory: a branch of mathematics that economists use to analyze the strategic behavior of decision-makers

hot hand fallacy: the belief that random sequences exhibit a positive correlation

human capital: the skill that workers acquire on the job and through education

incentives: factors that motivate a person to act or exert effort

incidence: the burden of taxation on the party who pays the tax through higher prices, regardless of whom the tax is actually levied on

income effect: phenomenon occurring when laborers work fewer hours at higher wages, using their additional income to demand more leisure

income elasticity of demand: measurement of how a change in income affects spending

income mobility: the ability of workers to move up or down the economic ladder over time

indifference curve: a graph representing the various combinations of two goods that yield the same level of satisfaction, or utility

inferior good: a good purchased out of necessity rather than choice

inputs: the resources (labor, land, and capital) used in the production process

immediate run: a period of time when there is no time for consumers to adjust their behavior

imperfect market: one in which either the buyer or the seller has an influence on the market price

implicit costs: a firm's opportunity costs of doing business

in-kind transfers: transfers (mostly to the poor) in the form of goods or services instead of cash

internal costs: the costs of a market activity paid by an individual participant

internalization: condition occurring when a firm takes into account the external costs (or benefits) to society that occur as a result of its actions

intertemporal decision-making: decision-making that involves planning to do something over a period of time; this requires valuing the present and the future consistently

investment: the process of using resources to create or buy new capital

kinked demand curve: theory stating that oligopolists have a greater tendency to respond aggressively to the price cuts of rivals but will largely ignore price increases

law of demand: the law that, all other things being equal, quantity demanded falls when prices rise, and rises when prices fall

law of increasing relative cost: law stating that the opportunity cost of producing a good rises as a society produces more of it

law of supply: the law that, all other things being equal, the quantity supplied of a good rises when the price of the good rises, and falls when the price of the good falls

law of supply and demand: the law that the market price of any good will adjust to bring the quantity supplied and the quantity demanded into balance

life-cycle wage pattern: the predictable effect that age has on earnings over the course of a person's working life

long run: a period of time when consumers have time to fully adjust to market conditions

loss: the result of total revenue being less than total cost

loss aversion: phenomenon occurring when individuals place more weight on avoiding losses than on attempting to realize gains

macroeconomics: the study of the overall aspects and workings of an economy

marginal cost (MC): the increase in cost that occurs from producing additional output

marginal product: the change in output associated with one additional unit of an input

marginal product of labor: the change in output associated with adding one additional worker

marginal rate of substitution: the rate at which the consumer is willing to purchase one good instead of another

marginal thinking: the evaluation of whether the benefit of one more unit of something is greater than its cost

marginal utility: the additional satisfaction derived from consuming one more unit of a good or service

market: a system that brings buyers and sellers together to exchange goods and services

market-clearing price: see *equilibrium price*

market demand: the sum of all the individual quantities demanded by each buyer in the market at each price

market economy: an economy in which resources are allocated among households and firms with little or no government interference

market failure: condition occurring when the output level of a good is inefficient

market supply: the sum of the quantities supplied by each seller in the market at each price

markup: the difference between the price the firm charges and the marginal cost of production

maximization point: the point at which a certain combination of two goods yields the most utility

microeconomics: the study of the individual units that make up the economy

minimum wage: the lowest hourly wage rate that firms may legally pay their workers

monopoly: condition existing when a single company supplies the entire market for a particular good or service

monopolistic competition: a situation characterized by free entry, many different firms, and product differentiation

monopoly power: measurement of the ability of firms to set the price for a good

monopsony: a situation in which there is only one buyer

moral hazard: phenomenon seen when a party that is protected from risk behaves differently from the way it would behave if it were fully exposed to the risk

mutual interdependence: a market situation where the actions of one firm have an impact on the price and output of its competitors

natural monopoly: a situation when a single large firm has lower costs than any potential smaller competitor

Nash equilibrium: in game theory, a phenomenon occurring when a decision-maker has nothing to gain by changing strategy unless it can collude

negative correlation: condition occurring when two variables move in the opposite direction

negative income tax: a tax credit paid to poor households out of taxes received from middle- and upper-income households

network externality: condition occurring when the number of customers who purchase or use a good influences the quantity demanded

normal good: a good consumers buy more of as income rises, holding other things constant

normative statement: an opinion that cannot be tested or validated; it describes "what ought to be"

occupational crowding: the phenomenon of relegating a group of workers to a narrow range of jobs in the economy

oligopoly: condition existing when a small number of firms sell a differentiated product in a market with high barriers to entry

opportunity cost: the highest-valued alternative that must be sacrificed in order to get something else

output: the production the firm creates

output effect: phenomenon occurring when the entrance of a rival firm in the market affects the amount produced

outsourcing of labor: a firm's shifting of jobs to an outside company, usually overseas, where the cost of labor is lower

perfect complements: two goods the consumer is interested in consuming in fixed proportions, resulting in right-angle indifference curves

perfect price discrimination: the practice of a firm selling the same good at a unique price to every customer

perfect substitutes: goods that the consumer is completely indifferent between, resulting in straight-line indifference curves

price ceilings: legally established maximum prices for goods or services

price controls: an attempt to set prices through government involvement in the market

price discrimination: the practice of a firm selling the same good at different prices to different groups of customers

price elasticity of demand: a measure of the responsiveness of quantity demanded to a change in price

price elasticity of supply: a measure of the responsiveness of the quantity supplied to a change in price

price effect: phenomenon seen when the price of a good or service is affected by the entrance of a rival firm in the market

price floors: legally established minimum prices for goods or services

price gouging laws: temporary ceilings on the prices that sellers can charge during times of emergency

price leadership: phenomenon occurring when a dominant firm in an industry sets the price that maximizes profits and the smaller firms in the industry follow

price maker: a firm with some control over the price it charges

price taker: a firm with no control over the price set by the market

predatory pricing: the practice of a firm deliberately setting its prices below average variable costs with the intent of driving rivals from the market

preference reversal: phenomenon arising when risk tolerance is not consistent

priming effects: phenomenon seen when the ordering of the questions that are asked influences the answers

principal-agent problem: a situation in which a principal entrusts an agent to complete a task and the agent does not do so in a satisfactory way

prisoner's dilemma: a situation in which decision-makers face incentives that make it difficult to achieve mutually beneficial outcomes

private goods: goods with two characteristics: they are both excludable and rival in consumption

private property: provision of an exclusive right of ownership that allows for the use, and especially the exchange, of property

producer surplus: the difference between the willingness to sell a good and the price that the seller receives

product differentiation: the process that firms use to make a product more attractive to potential customers

production function: description of the relationship between inputs a firm uses and the output it creates

production possibilities frontier: a model that illustrates the combinations of outputs that a society can produce if all of its resources are being used efficiently

profit: total revenue minus total cost; a negative result is a *loss*

profit-maximizing rule: the rule stating that profit maximization occurs when the firm chooses the quantity that causes marginal revenue to be equal to marginal cost, or MR = MC

property rights: an owner's ability to exercise control over a resource

prospect theory: a theory suggesting that individuals weigh the utilities and risks of gains and losses differently

positive correlation: condition occurring when two variables move in the same direction

positive statement: an assertion that can be tested and validated; it describes "what is"

public goods: goods that can be jointly consumed by more than one person, and from which nonpayers are difficult to exclude

poverty rate: the percentage of the population whose income is below the poverty threshold

poverty threshold: the income level below which a person or family is considered impoverished

quantity demanded: the amount of a good or service that buyers are willing and able to purchase at the current price

quantity supplied: the amount of a good or service that producers are willing and able to sell at the current price

real-income effect: a change in consumption when there is a change in purchasing power as a result of a change in the price of a good

rent control: a price ceiling that applies to the housing market

rent seeking: behavior occurring when resources are used to secure monopoly rights through the political process

reverse causation: condition occurring when causation is incorrectly assigned among associated events

risk-averse people: those who prefer a sure thing over a gamble with a higher expected value

risk-neutral people: those who choose the highest expected value regardless of the risk

risk takers: those who prefer gambles with lower expected values, and potentially higher winnings, over a sure thing

rival goods: goods that cannot be enjoyed by more than one person at a time

samaritan's dilemma: a situation in which an act of charity causes disincentives for recipients to take care of themselves

scale: the size of the production process

scarcity: the limited nature of society's resources, given society's unlimited wants and needs

scatterplot: a graph that shows individual (x,y) points

Sherman Antitrust Act: the first federal law limiting cartels and monopolies
short run: a period of time when consumers can partially adjust their behavior
shortage: market condition when the quantity supplied of a good is less than the quantity demanded
signals: information conveyed by profits and losses about the profitability of various markets
single-payer system: government coverage of most healthcare costs, with citizens paying their share through taxes
slope: the change in the rise along the *y* axis (vertical) divided by the change in the run along the *x* axis (horizontal)
social costs: the internal costs plus the external costs of a market activity
social optimum: the price and quantity combination that would exist if there were no externalities
social welfare: see *total surplus*
status quo bias: condition existing when decision-makers want to maintain their current choices
substitutes: goods that are used in place of each other; when the price of a substitute good rises, the quantity demanded falls and the demand for the related good goes up
substitution effect: (1) the decision by laborers to work more hours at higher wages, substituting labor for leisure; (2) a consumer's substitution of a product that has become relatively less expensive as the result of a price change
sunk costs: unrecoverable costs that have been incurred as a result of past decisions
supply curve: a graph of the relationship between the prices in the supply schedule and the quantity supplied at those prices
supply schedule: a table that shows the relationship between the price of a good and the quantity supplied
surplus: market condition when the quantity supplied of a good is greater than the quantity demanded
strike: a work stoppage designed to aid a union's bargaining position
switching costs: the costs incurred when a consumer changes from one supplier to another
third-party problem: a situation in which those not directly involved in a market activity nevertheless experience negative or positive externalities
tit-for-tat: a long-run strategy that promotes cooperation among participants by mimicking the opponent's most recent decision with repayment in kind
total cost: the amount a firm spends in order to produce the goods and services it produces
total revenue: (1) the amount that consumers pay and sellers receive for a good; (2) the amount a firm receives from the sale of the goods and services it produces
total surplus: the sum of consumer surplus and producer surplus; also known as *social welfare*
trade: the voluntary exchange of goods and services between two or more parties
tragedy of the commons: the depletion of a good that is rival in consumption but nonexcludable
ultimatum game: an economic experiment in which two players decide how to divide a sum of money
union: a group of workers that bargains collectively for better wages and benefits
util: a unit of satisfaction used to measure the enjoyment from consumption of a good or service
utility: a measure of the relative levels of satisfaction that consumers enjoy from the consumption of goods and services
value of the marginal product (VMP): the marginal product of an input multiplied by the price of the output it produces
variable: a quantity that can take on more than one value
variable costs: costs that change with the rate of output
wage discrimination: unequal payment of workers because of their race, ethnic origin, sex, age, religion, or some other group characteristic
welfare economics: the branch of economics that studies how the allocation of resources affects economic well-being
willingness to pay: the maximum price a consumer will pay for a good
willingness to sell: the minimum price a seller will accept to sell a good or service
winner-take-all: phenomenon occurring when extremely small differences in ability lead to sizable differences in compensation

CREDITS

The Economics in the Real World feature in Chapter 5, pp. 165–66, eprints "Efforts Meant to Help Workers Squeeze South Africa's Poorest," by Celia W. Dugger. From *The New York Times*, Sept. 26, 2010. © 2010 The New York Times. All rights reserved. Used by permission and protected by the Copyright Laws of the United States. The printing, copying, redistribution, or retransmission of this Content without express written permission is prohibited.

SOURCES FOR SNAPSHOT GRAPHICS

Chapter 4, p. 133: Elasticity values from H. S. Houthakker and Lester D. Taylor, *Consumer Demand in the United States: Analyses and Projections* (Cambridge, MA: Harvard University Press, 1970), and Joachim Moller, "Income and Price Elasticities in Different Sectors of the Economy: An Analysis of Structural Change for Germany, the UK and the USA," in *The Growth of Service Industries: The Paradox of Exploding Costs and Persistent Demand*, edited by Thjis ten Raa and Ronald Schettkat (Northampton, MA: Edward Elgar Publishing, 2001).
Chapter 5, p. 169: Minimum wages as of January 2013, from "Minimum Wage Laws in the States," U.S. Department of Labor, www.dol.gov/whd/minwage/america.htm.
Chapter 6, p. 201: Adapted from "The 10 Strangest State Taxes," *U.S. News and World Report*, money.usnews.com/money/personal-finance/slideshows/the-10-strangest-state-taxes. For British window tax, see the original tax act at British History Online, www.british-history.ac.uk/report.aspx?compid=46825#s1.
Chapter 7, p. 223: The original account is in R. H. Coase, "The Problem of Social Cost," *Journal of Law and Economics* Vol. 3 (1960): 1–44, available at www.jstor.org/stable/724810.
Chapter 9, p. 287: Stadium capacities are approximate. All stadium capacities and attendance records from Baseball Almanac, www.baseball-almanac.com.
Chapter 10, p. 323: All Apple product sales figures from Bare Figures, barefigur.es. PC and Android sales figures from Gartner, Inc., www.gartner.com.
Chapter 12, p. 371: Data from 24/7 Wall St., "Eight Brands That Wasted the Most on the Super Bowl," 247wallst.com/2012/02/01/the-eight-brands-that-wasted-the-most-on-the-super-bowl/2/.
Chapter 13, p. 397: Adapted from an example in David McAdams, *The Game Changer* (New York: W. W. Norton, 2014).
Chapter 14, p. 447: Data from SourcingLine, www.sourcingline.com/country-data/cost-competitiveness.
Chapter 15, p. 477: Income inequality data adapted from United Nations Development Programme, Human Development Report, 2009, Table M. Poverty rates for United States and Japan calculated by OECD as households earning <50% of national median income, for late 2000s: see "Income Distribution—Poverty," at OECD.StatExtracts, http://stats.oecd.org/Index.aspx?DatasetCode=POVERTY.
Chapter 16, p. 501: Adapted from the OECD Better Life Index, www.oecdbetterlifeindex.org (accessed April 2013).
Chapter 17, p. 535: 401(k) data from Robert Strauss, "How Opt Out Keeps People In," *Business Week*, Aug. 23,2012, www.businessweek.com/articles/2012-08-23/how-opt-out-keeps-people-in. Organ donation numbers from Richard Thaler, "Opting In vs. Opting Out," *New York Times*, Sep. 26, 2009, www.nytimes.com/2009/09/27/business/economy/27view.html. HIV screening data from Rob Goodier, "'Opt-Out' Program for HIV Screening in the ED Gets More Patients Tested," Oct. 16, 2012, at Modern Medicine, www.modernmedicine.com/legacy/article/793039.
Chapter 18, p. 571: All data from OECD Health Division, *Health Data 2012: Frequently Requested Data*.

PHOTOGRAPHS

p. 2: © Pancaketom | Dreamstime.com; **p. 5:** John Lund/Stephanie Roeser/Getty Images; **p. 6 left:** © Phang Kim Shan | Dreamstime.com; **p. 6 right:** © Nguyen Thai | Dreamstime.com; **p. 8:** Visions of America, LLC / Alamy; **p. 9:** © Haywiremedia | Dreamstime.com; **p. 12:** PARAMOUNT / The Kobal Collection/Art Resource, NY; **p. 13:** © Linqong |

Dreamstime.com; **p. 14 top:** Joe Robbins/Getty Images; **p. 14 bottom:** © Seanyu | Dreamstime.com; **p. 15:** © Yusputra | Dreamstime.com; **p. 16:** Jacqueline Larma / AP Photo; **p. 18:** Stockbyte/Getty Images; **p. 20:** © Andres Rodriguez | Dreamstime.co; **p. 25:** Wizards of the Coast and Magic: The Gathering are trademarks of Wizards of the Coast LLC. Images used with permission of Wizards of the Coast LLC; **p. 27:** Archive Holdings Inc. /The Image Bank/Getty Images; **p. 28:** M.L. Watts / Wikimedia Commons; **p. 29:** © Nikolai Sorokin | Dreamstime .com; **p. 30:** Paul Springett / Alamy; **p. 36:** Lou-Foto / Alamy; **p. 44:** © Philcold | Dreamstime.com; **p. 45:** DREAMWORKS / Album/Newscom; **p. 46 left:** Teraberb | Dreamstime.com; **p. 46 right:** Yuri Arcurs | Dreamstime.com; **p. 48:** © Globe photos/ ZUMAPRESS.com/Newscom; **p. 49:** © Monkeybusiness | Dreamstime.com; **p. 50:** © Boeing; **p. 66:** Bruce Lonngren/iStockphoto.com; **p. 69:** AP Photo/The Day, Sean D. Elliot; **p. 70:** All Canada Photos / Alamy; **p. 71 top:** Getty Images/First Light; **p. 71 bottom:** Peter Horree/Alamy; **p. 72:** © William Perry | Dreamstime.com; **p. 74:** Maren Caruso/Photodisc/Getty Images; **p. 78:** © Edith Layland | Dreamstime.com; **p. 80:** © John DeFeo/ iStockphoto.com; **p. 81 left:** Radius Images / Alamy; **p. 81 right:** © Showface | Dreamstime.com; **p. 83:** POLYGRAM/WARNERS/SILVER PICTURES/THE KOBAL COLLECTION/JAMES BRIDGES/Art Resource, NY; **p. 87:** © Lucian Coman | Dreamstime.com; **p. 89:** AP Photo/Ted S. Warren; **p. 91:** AP Photo/IBM; **p. 92:** Stockbyte/Getty Images; **p. 95:** CRANKSHAFT(NEW) © 2005 MEDIAGRAPHICS, INC. NORTH AMERICA SYNDICATE; **p. 97:** © R. Gino Santa Maria | Dreamstime.com; **p. 106:** © Hugoht | Dreamstime.com; **p. 109:** AP Photo/Reed Saxon; **p. 110:** © Columbia Pictures/courtesy Everett Collection; **p. 111:** Allstar Picture Library/Alamy; **p. 112 top:** Evan-Amos/Wikimedia Commons; **p. 112 bottom:** © Cobalt88 | Dreamstime.com; **p. 113:** © Seanyu | Dreamstime.com; **p. 114 top:** © Wisconsinart | Dreamstime.com; **p. 114 second from top:** © Oleksiy Mark | Dreamstime.com; **p.114 second from bottom:** Lisa Thornberg/iStockphoto .com; **p. 114 bottom:** IFCAR/Wikimedia Commons; **p. 115:** © 20th Century Fox Film Corp. All rights reserved. Courtesy: Everett Collection; **p. 117:** © Mathew Hayward | Dreamstime.com; **p. 118 top left:** © Mathew Hayward | Dreamstime.com; **p. 118 top right:** © Rick Rhay/iStockphoto.com; **p. 118 bottom left:** © Johnfoto | Dreamstime.com; **p. 118 bottom right:** Wikimedia Commons ; **p. 119 top:** © Rick Rhay/iStockphoto.com; **p. 119 bottom:** © Johnfoto | Dreamstime.com; **p. 120:** Wikimedia Commons; **p. 121 top:** © Mathew Hayward | Dreamstime.com; **p. 121 second from top:** © Rick Rhay/iStockphoto.com; **p. 121 second from bottom:** © Johnfoto | Dreamstime.com; **p. 121 bottom:** © Wikimedia Commons; **p. 126:** ©20th Century Fox. All rights reserved/courtesy Everett Collection; **p. 127:** © Eliza Snow/iStock-photo.com; **p. 128 top:** © Barbara Helgason | Dreamstime.com; **p. 128 bottom:** Geoffrey Kidd/ Alamy; **p. 129:** © Aleksandar Mijatovic | Dreamstime .com; **p. 130 top:** © Svetlana Foote | Dreamstime .com; **p. 130 middle:** © Steven von Niederhausern / iStockphoto.com; **p. 130 bottom:** © Ragoarts | Dreamstime.com; **p. 131, table, top left:** © Steve Shepard/iStockphoto.com; **p. 131, table, top right:** © Steve Shepard/iStockphoto.com; **p. 131, table, middle left:** © Chaoss | Dreamstime.com; **p. 131, table, middle right:** © Ljupco Smokovski | Dreamstime.com; **p. 131, table, bottom left:** © Olga Lyubkina/iStockphoto.com; **p. 131, table, bottom right:** © Daniel R. Burch/iStockphoto.com; **p. 131 bottom:** http://www.flickr.com/photos/ turkeypants/135934601/sizes/m/in/photostream/; **p. 132 top:** JACK GUEZ/AFP/Getty Images; **p. 134:** Daniel Bendjy/iStockphoto.com; **p. 135 top:** Yuri Arcurs | Dreamstime.com; **p. 135, table, top:** Yuri Arcurs | Dreamstime.com; **p. 135, table, middle:** Ildar Sagdejev/Wikimedia; **p. 135, table, bottom:** © Julie Feinstein | Dreamstime.com; **p. 137:** © George Peters/iStockphoto.com; **p. 138:** PSL Images/ Alamy; **p. 140:** © Rich Legg/iStockphoto.com; **p. 141:** © Jeffry W. Myers/CORBIS; **p. 147:** © The Gallery Collection/Corbis; **p. 148:** © Chhobi | Dreamstime.com; **p. 149 top:** © Chhobi | Dreamstime.com; **p. 149 second from top:** PR NEWSWIRE/AP Photo; **p. 149 third from top:** © Inga Nielsen | Dreamstime.com; **p. 149 second from bottom:** Justin Sullivan/Getty Images; **p. 149 bottom:** Rebecca Kohn; **p. 150:** Andres Rodriguez/ Alamy; **p. 153 right:** http://englishrussia .com/2006/10/13/more-soviet-stuff/; **p. 153 left:** AP Photo/Liu Heung Shing; **p. 154 top:** Scott Legato/ Getty Images; **p. 155:** Alex Craig/Photolibrary/Getty Images; **p. 157:** © Lisa F. Young | Dreamstime.com; **p. 159 top:** © Yuri Arcurs | Dreamstime.com; **p. 159 bottom:** © Steven von Niederhausern / iStockphoto

.com; **p. 160, table, top:** © Julie Feinstein | Dreamstime.com; **p. 160, table, middle:** Courtesy of Andrew Le; **p. 160, table, bottom:** Chris Graythen/Getty Images; **p. 160 bottom:** © Anthony Aneese Totah Jr/Dreamstime.com; **p. 163:** © Peter Booth/iStockphoto.com; **p. 166:** EPA/NIC BOTHMA/ Newscom; **p. 168 top:** © FX Networks/ Courtesy:Everett Collection; **p. 168 bottom left:** © John Carvalho; **p. 168 bottom right:** Kyoungil Jeon/iStockphoto.com; **p. 170:** © Robert Churchill/ iStockphoto.com; **p. 173:** AP Photo/Kathy Kmonicek; **p. 177:** © Milosz7 | Dreamstime.com; **p. 178:** © DreamWorks/Courtesy Everett Collection; **p. 183:** Dee Cercone/Newscom; **p. 185 top:** Image Source/Getty Images; **p. 185 bottom:** © Chuck Place/istockphoto.com; **p. 186 top:** © DreamWorks/ Courtesy Everett Collection; **p. 186 bottom:** © Grublee | Dreamstime.com; **p. 187:** © Jen Grantham/ iStockphoto.com; **p. 188 left:** © Versluis Photography/iStockphoto.com; **p. 188 right:** © Dan Van Den Broeke | Dreamstime.com; **p. 192:** Photos 12/Alamy; **p. 193:** Jason Brindel Commercial/Alamy; **p. 194:** HAGAR © 2005 KING FEATURES SYNDICATE; **p. 198:** © Uros Petrovic | Dreamstime .com; **p. 199:** © Rui Matos | Dreamstime.com; **p. 202:** © apcuk/iStockphoto.com; **p. 204:** © RonTech2000/iStockphoto.com; **p. 211:** © Frederic Prochasson/iStockphoto.com; **p. 213:** © Christophe Testi | Dreamstime.com; **p. 214:** © Charlieb34 | Dreamstime.com; **p. 216:** © Alistair Laming/Alamy; **p. 217:** © Sean Locke/iStockphoto.com; **p. 218 top left:** © Charlieb34 | Dreamstime.com; **p. 218 middle left:** © Steve Lovegrove | Dreamstime.com; **p. 218 bottom left:** © Stef Bennett | Dreamstime .com; **p. 218 top right:** © Yarinca/iStockphoto .com; **p. 218 middle right:** © Jonathan Cohen/ iStockphoto.com; **p. 218 bottom right:** RiverNorthPhotography /iStockphoto.com; **p. 219:** © Denis Raev | Dreamstime.com; **p. 220:** © Charlene Key | Dreamstime.com; **p. 221 top left:** Stephen Ausmus/ARS/USDA; **p. 221 top right:** Michael Thompson/ARS/USDA; **p. 221 bottom:** © Vplut | Dreamstime.com; **p. 222:** © Annie Su Yee Yek | Dreamstime.com; **p. 224 top:** http://www.youtube .com/watch?v=hnOPu0_YWhw; **p. 224 bottom:** U.S. Navy photo by Mass Communication Specialist 3rd Class John Grandin; **p. 225 top:** FAMILY CIRCUS © 2006 BIL KEANE, INC. KING FEATURES SYNDICATE; **p. 225 bottom left:** © Crystal Kirk | Dreamstime.com; **p. 225 bottom right:** © Jeff Greenberg / Alamy; **p. 226, table, top left:** © Annie Su Yee Yek | Dreamstime.com; **p. 226, table, bottom left:** © Jeff Greenberg/Alamy **p. 226, table, top right:** © Crystal Kirk | Dreamstime.com; **p. 226, table, bottom right:** U.S. Navy photo by Mass Communication Specialist 3rd Class John Grandin; **p. 226 bottom:** © Realimage/Alamy; **p. 227:** © Kenneth Sponsler/iStockphoto.com; **p. 228:** Wikimedia Commons; **p. 230 top:** Stockbyte/Getty Images; **p. 230 bottom:** Karl Dolenc /iStockphoto; **p. 231:** NASA/Goddard Space Flight Center; **p. 232 top:** Robert Nickelsberg/Getty Images; **p. 232 bottom:** © kali9/iStockphoto; **p. 233:** © June M. Sobrito | Dreamstime.com; **p. 238:** © Geoffrey Kidd/Alamy; **p. 241:** Marc F. Henning/ Alamy; **p. 242:** HO/UPI/Newscom; **p. 243:** ZITS © 2002 ZITS PARTNERSHIP, KING FEATURES SYNDICATE; **p. 246:** © YinYang/iStockphoto.com; **p. 247:** Justin Sullivan/Getty Images; **p. 251:** San Antonio Express-News/ZUMA Press/Newscom; **p. 256:** FOXTROT © (2005) Bill Amend. Reprinted with permission of UNIVERSAL UCLICK. All rights reserved; **p. 257:** © NBC Universal, Inc./Chris Haston/ZUMA Press/Newscom; **p. 258:** © John Verner/iStockphoto.com; **p. 259 top:** © Sandra Nicol/iStockphoto.com; **p. 259 bottom:** © JillKyle/ iStockphoto.com; **p. 260 top:** © Sandra Nicol/iStock-photo.com; **p. 260 middle:** © JillKyle/iStockphoto .com; **p. 260 bottom:** © John Verner/iStockphoto .com; **p. 262:** akg-images/Newscom; **p. 263:** © Antonio Jodice | Dreamstime.com; **p. 265:** © Columbia/courtesy Everett Collection; **p. 271:** © Graça Victoria | Dreamstime.com ; **p. 273 top:** Neilson Barnard/iStockphoto.com; **p. 273 second from top:** © Manon Ringuette | Dreamstime.com; **p. 273 second from bottom:** © Raine Vara / Alamy; **p. 273 bottom:** © Russell Shively/iStock-photo.com; **p. 274:** Michel Porro/Getty Images; **p. 275:** Henry M. Trotter/Wikimedia Commons; **p. 277 top:** © 20th Century Fox. All rights reserved/ courtesy Everett Collection; **p. 277 bottom:** © Michael Shake | Dreamstime.com; **p. 280:** Courtesy of Dirk Mateer; **p. 284:** © Kevinpepper | Dreamstime .com; **p. 285:** © Alexandr Mitiuc | Dreamstime.com; **p. 286:** Laura Farr//Time Life Pictures/Getty Images; **p. 289 top:** © Judy Ledbetter/iStockphoto.com; **p. 289 bottom:** © adrian beesley/iStockphoto.com; **p. 293:** CBS-TV /The Kobal Collection/Art Resource, NY; **p. 294:** © hywit dimyadi/iStockphoto.com; **p. 295:** © Chrisyates | Dreamstime.com;

p. 298: © DNY59/iStockphoto.com; **p. 303:** © kali9/iStockphoto.com; **p. 306 top:** © GYI NSEA/iStockphoto.com; **p. 306 bottom:** Michelle Del Guercio/Photo Researchers/Getty Images; **p. 307:** © Howard Harrison/Alamy; **p. 308:** PARAMOUNT PICTURES/Album/Newscom; **p. 314:** Tom Strickland/Bloomberg via Getty Images; **p. 315:** © desuza communications/iStockphoto.com; **p. 318 left:** AP Photo/Ric Feld; **p. 318 right:** AP Photo/Jessica Hill; **p. 318 bottom:** © Paul Souders/Corbis; **p. 319 left:** © Debbi Smirnoff/iStockphoto.com; **p. 319 right:** © jfmdesign/iStockphoto; **p. 320:** © rabbit75/iStockphoto.com; **p. 321:** ONE MAN BAND, 2005. ©Buena Vista Pictures/courtesy Everett Collection; **p. 322:** AFP/Getty Images/Newscom; **p. 327:** John Mutrux/MCT/Newscom; **p. 333:** © Arne9001 | Dreamstime.com; **p. 337 top:** Nacivet/Photographer's Choice/Getty Images; **p. 337 bottom:** FOXTROT © (2006) Bill Amend. Reprinted with permission of UNIVERSAL UCLICK. All rights reserved; **p. 340:** M.G.M / TRACY BENNETT / Album/Newscom; **p. 341:** © Cynthia Farmer | Dreamstime.com; **p. 342:** © vau902/iStockphoto.com; **p. 344:** © Kyoungil Jeon/iStockphoto.com; **p. 345:** Picasa; **p. 346:** © Benkrut | Dreamstime.com; **p. 348:** TRIPPLAAR KRISTOFFER/SIPA/Newscom; **p. 349 top:** © TLC/Courtesy of Everett Collection / Everett Collection; **p. 349 bottom:** Scott Olson/Getty Images; **p. 351:** AP Photo/Charles Agel; **p. 355:** ZUMA Press/Newscom; **p. 357 left:** © swalls/i-Stock.com; **p. 357 right:** Emile Wamsteker/Bloomberg via Getty Images; **p. 358:** © Geraint Lewis / Alamy; **p. 363:** ShutterWorx/iStockphoto.com; **p. 365:** © Monkey Business Images | Dreamstime.com; **p. 366:** © Serafino Mozzo/iStockphoto; **p. 367:** Robin Platzer/ Twin Images/LFI/Photoshot/Newscom; **p. 368 (Life cereal):** Photo by Rebecca Kohn; **p. 368 (John Deere tractor):** © Anthony Seebaran/iStockphoto; **p. 368 (Lay's chips):** © Stanley Marquardt/Alamy; **p. 368 (Energizer bunny):** AP Photo/Tom Gannam; **p. 368 (FedEx truck):** © Lynn Watson | Dreamstime.com; **p. 368 (Visa cards):** © Carlos Gawronski/iStockphoto; **p. 368 (Avis sign):** David Paul Morris/Bloomberg via Getty Images; **p. 370:** Universal/The Kobal Collection/Art Resource, NY; **p. 372:** PEANUTS ©1966 Peanuts Worldwide LLC. Dist. By UNIVERSAL UCLICK. Reprinted with permission. All rights reserved; **p. 374 top left:** © Atm2003 | Dreamstime.com; **p. 374 top right:** © Pedro Antonio Salaverría Calahorra | Dreamstime.com; **p. 374 bottom:** BOB FILA AND JAMES F. QUINN KRT/Newscom; **p. 376:** RW3 WENN Photos/Newscom; **p. 377:** Johnny Rockets/PRNewsFoto/AP Photo; **p. 383:** PAK IMAGES/Newscom; **p. 385:** iStockphoto; **p. 389:** © Jack Sullivan / Alamy; **p. 390:** Mary Evans/UNIVERSAL PICTURES/DREAMWORKS/IMAGINE ENTERTAINMENT/Ronald Grant/Everett Collection; **p. 391:** © Icholakov | Dreamstime.com; **p. 395:** MURDER BY NUMBERS, Ryan Gosling, 2002, © Warner Brothers/courtesy Everett Collection; **p. 398:** AP Photo/ Sergey Ponomarev; **p. 399:** THE DARK KNIGHT, Heath Ledger as The Joker, 2008. © Warner Bros./Courtesy Everett Collection; **p. 400:** HAGAR © 2006 KING FEATURES SYNDICATE; **p. 401:** © Nickilford/iStockphoto; **p. 403:** © TheCrimsonMonkey/iStockphoto; **p. 405:** Scott Olson/Getty Images; **p. 406:** © Richard Levine/Alamy; **p. 407:** Tim Boyle/Bloomberg/Getty Images; **p. 408:** Google/ZUMA Press/Newscom; **p. 409:** © Brandon Alms | Dreamstime.com; **p. 416:** © Stephen Strathdee/iStockphoto; **p. 418:** Picture Alliance/ZUMApress/Newscom; **p. 421:** AP Photo/Saurabh Das; **p. 422:** Ernesto Diaz /iStockphoto.com; **p. 423 top:** © Candybox Images | Dreamstime.com; **p. 423 bottom:** Daniel Laflor /iStockphoto.com; **p. 427 top:** AP Photo/The Daily Dispatch, Ashley Steven Ayscue; **p. 427 bottom:** © South West Images Scotland/Alamy; **p. 428:** © Pzaxe | Dreamstime.com; **p. 432:** The Everett Collection, Inc.; **p. 433:** © Kts | Dreamstime.com; **p. 435:** Eric Hood/iStockphoto.com; **p. 438 top:** AP Photo/Ajit Solanki; **p. 438 bottom:** © The Protected Art Archive/Alamy; **p. 439:** GRAND AVENUE ©2003 Steve Breen and Mike Thompson. Reprinted by permission of Universal Uclick for UFS. All rights reserved; **p. 441:** OUTSOURCED, Josh Hamilton, Ayesha Dharker, 2006/The Everett Collection, Inc.; **p. 442:** jonathansloane /iStockphoto.com; **p. 443:** EPA/Newscom; **p. 444:** ©Columbia Pictures/courtesy Everett Co/Everett Collection; **p. 446:** MCT/Newscom; **p. 449:** © Monkeybusiness | Dreamstime.com; **p. 450:** jez gunnell/iStockphoto.com; **p. 452:** iStockPhoto; **p. 457:** © Redbaron | Dreamstime.com; **p. 458:** Pete Collins/iStockphoto.com; **p. 460:** Ljupco/iStockphoto.com; **p. 461 top:** Pete Collins/iStockphoto.com; **p. 461 bottom:** Matthew Simmons/Stringer/WireImage/Getty Images; **p. 462:** Getty Images; **p. 463, table, top:** Pete Collins/iStockphoto.com; **p. 463, table, second from top:**

Stockbyte/Getty Images; **p. 463, table, third from top:** Pete Collins/iStockphoto.com; **p. 463, table, second from bottom:** Matthew Simmons/ Stringer/WireImage/Getty Images; **p. 463, table, bottom:** Getty Images; **p. 463 bottom:** © National Geographic Image Collection/Alamy; **p. 464:** © Nyul | Dreamstime.com; **p. 466 left:** GYI NSEA /iSTockphoto.com; **p. 466 center:** © Featureflash | Dreamstime.com; **p. 466 right:** GYI NSEA /iStockphoto.com; **p. 468:** DREAMWORKS SKG/ MASI, FRANK/Album/Newscom; **p. 469:** AP Photo/ Reinhold Matay; **p. 470:** Courtesy of 5th Pillar; **p. 473:** Nilgun Bostanci/iStockphoto.com; **p. 474:** THE BORN LOSER ©2005 Art and Chip Sansom. Reprinted by permission of Universal Uclick for UFS. All rights reserved; **p. 476:** Design Pics/Carson Ganci/Getty Images/Perspectives; **p. 478:** © Ken Backer | Dreamstime.com; **p. 480:** Mary Evans/ Universal Pictures/Miramax Films/Imagine; Entertainment/Ronald Grant/Everett Collection; **p. 483:** AFP/Getty Images/Newscom; **p. 484:** © Zhang Bo/iStockphoto.com; **p. 485:** Daniel Loiselle/iStock-photo.com; **p. 490:** Tom Grill/Photographer's Choice RF/Getty Images; **p. 493:** Cristian Baitg/iStockphoto .com; **p. 494 top:** Stephen Walls /iStockphoto.com; **p. 494 bottom:** John Shepherd/iStockphoto.com; **p. 495:** Sarah Salmela/iStockphoto; **p. 497 top:** Mathias Wilson/iStockphoto.com; **p. 497 bottom:** PacificCoastNews/Newscom; **p. 498 top:** © Christian Degroote | Dreamstime.com; **p. 498 second from top:** Robert Billstone/iStockphoto.com; **p. 498 third from top:** Juanmonino/iStockphoto.com; **p. 498 third from bottom:** iStockPhoto; **p. 498 second from bottom:** Joe Potato Photo/ iStockphoto.com; **p. 498 bottom:** © Cal Vornberger/Alamy; **p. 502:** © Vividpixels | Dreamstime.com; **p. 506:** SUPER SIZE ME, Morgan Spurlock, 2004, © Samuel Goldwyn/courtesy Everett Collection; **p. 508:** © Catonphoto | Dreamstime .com; **p. 512:** © Ying Feng Johansson | Dreamstime .com; **p. 527:** STAR TREK: THE NEXT GENERATION, Brent Spiner as "Data," 4th season, 1987–94. Paramount/Courtesy: Everett Collection, Paramount Pictures; **p. 528:** LifesizeImages/iStockphoto.com; **p. 529:** © Jennifer Pitiquen | Dreamstime.com; **p. 530:** © Everett Collection, Inc.; **p. 531 top:** slobo/ iStockphoto.com; **p. 531 bottom:** © Corbis RF/ Alamy; **p. 532:** Ryan Balderas/iStockphoto .com; **p. 533:** Laszlo Sovany/iStockphoto.com; **p. 534 top:** © Filmfoto | Dreamstime.com; **p. 534 bottom:** © Presselect/Alamy; **p. 536:** © Westend61 GmbH/Alamy; **p. 539:** Alex Slobodkin/iStockphoto .com; **p. 540 top:** Mark Stahl/iStockphoto.com; **p. 540 bottom:** Jason Merritt/FilmMagic/Getty Images; **p. 541:** © Everett Collection Inc / Alamy; **p. 542:** Alamy; **p. 543:** © Yuri Arcurs | Dreamstime .com; **p. 549:** © Peter Gridley/Photographer's Choice/Getty Images; **p. 551 left:** Brown - Brooks/ Photo Researchers/Getty Images; **p. 551 right:** Mark Kostich/iStockphoto.com; **p. 557:** Jamie McCarthy/ WireImage/Getty Images; **p. 559:** Michael Germana/ Everett Collection; **p. 560:** © Wendy White/Alamy; **p. 562:** JOHN Q, Denzel Washington, 2002 © New Line, courtesy Everett Collection; **p. 565:** © RCWW, Inc./Corbis; **p. 566:** © ZUMA Wire Service / Alamy; **p. 567:** Jovan Jaric/iStockphoto.com; **p. 568:** © Andres Rodriguez | Dreamstime.com; **p. 572:** Vesna Andjic/iStockphoto.com; **p. 573:** © John Barrett/Globe Photos/ZUMAPRESS.com/ Newscom; **p. 574:** omgimages/iStockphoto.com.

INDEX

Page numbers where key terms are defined are in **boldface**.

Aalsmeer flower auction, 274
Abercrombie & Fitch, 357, 364
absolute advantage, **39**
accounting profit, **244,** 244–46
Adobe, 213
adverse selection, **557,** 557–58
advertising, 366–76
  in competitive markets, 370, 372
  and game theory, 396–98, 400, 403
  in monopolistic competition, 366–67, 372
  by monopolists, 372
  negative effects of, 372–76
  and price vs. value of products, 354
  reasons for, 367, 369
  Super Bowl commercials, 367, 371
  and tit-for-tat strategy, 400
  truth in, 376
Affordable Care Act, 548
age
  and earnings gap, 465
  and poverty rate, 478
Air India, 322
airline industry, 322, 397, 416
Allais, Maurice, 538, 540
Allais paradox, 538
All the President's Men (film), 11
Aluminum Company of America (ALCOA), 304, 404
Amazon, 307
Anchorman: The Legend of Ron Burgundy (film), 468
Android, 323
Anheuser-Busch, 367, 371
Ann Taylor, 357
antitrust laws, **387,** 389, 402, 404
Apple, 11, 213, 323, 422
assumptions, faulty, 29
asymmetric information, **557,** 557–60
  adverse selection, 557–58
  in healthcare industry, 557–60
  and moral hazard, 559
  principal-agent problem, 558–59
AT&T, 321–22, 382, 404
auctions, 274, 320
Audi, 367
Australia, 10–11, 495, 501
average fixed cost (AFC), 253, **253,** 255, 256
average total cost (ATC), 253–56, **254,** 362–63
average variable cost (AVC), **252,** 252–53, 255, 256
Avis, 368
Axelrod, Robert, 398

backward-bending labor supply curve, **429,** 430
Baja Fresh, 358
bandwagon effect, **407**
Bangladesh, 483
barriers to entry, **304**
  in competitive markets, 272
  government-created, 305–7
  in medical profession, 564
  natural, 304–5
Beatles, the, 192
Beautiful Mind, A (film), 390
Beauty Pays (Daniel S. Hamermesh), 466
behavioral economics, 526–44, **528**
  bounded rationality in, 528–29
  and inconsistencies in decision making, 532–36
  and judgments about fairness, 536–38
  and misperceptions of probabilities, 529–32
  preference reversals, 538–40
  prospect theory, 540–43
  and risk in decision making, 538–43
Bell, Joshua, 224
Bell Labs, 213
Best Buy, 367
Better Life Index, 495, 501
Bieber, Justin, 306
binding minimum wage, 164, 166, 167
binding price ceilings, 150–52
binding price floors, 160–62
black markets, **149,** 153
  creation of, 95
  for human organs, 569–70, 573
  and price controls, 149
  and price floors, 162
  and supply and demand, 151
Blanchflower, David G., 462
Blockbuster, 284
Boeing, 40
Bolivia, income inequality in, 472, 473
bounded rationality, **528,** 528–29, 543
brands, costs of generics vs., 374–75
Brazil, income inequality in, 472
Brilliant Madness, A (film), 390
British Petroleum (BP), 212
broadband monopoly, 314
Brown, Alexander L., 542
Bryson, Alex, 462
budget constraint, **514,** 514–15, 520–22
Budget Reconciliation Act (1990), 198–99
budgets, 112, 141
buyers
  distinguishing groups of, 334–35
  in monopsony, 441–43
  price and number of, 82–83

cable companies, 317–18
California, labor market in, 432
Camerer, Colin F., 542
Canada
  healthcare expenditures in, 551, 552, 571
  healthcare system of United States vs., 566–68, 571
  income inequality in, 472, 473
  medical tourism from, 565
cap and trade, **230,** 230–31
capital
  determining bang per buck for, 448–50
  as factor of production, 247, 422
  human, 459
  market for, 448
  problems in raising, 305
  and productivity of additional labor, 248
capital goods, **46,** 46–49
Carlyle, Thomas, 4

cartels, **387,** 387–89, 415–16
causality, **63,** 63–64
cell phones, 382, 407, 498
ceteris paribus, **28**
  and healthcare expenditures, 551–52
  and income inequality, 473, 474
  and opportunity cost, 44
change, dynamic nature of, 284
Chaplin, Charlie, 262
charitable donations, 485
children, cost of raising, 265
China, 12–13, 48, 49, 447
Cinderella Man (film), 480
Cinergy Field (Cincinnati), 287
Cisco, 213
Citizens Bank Park (Philadelphia), 287
Clayton Act, **402**
Clinton, Bill, 483
club goods, 225, 226
Coase, Ronald, 220
Coase theorem, 220–22, **221**, 223
Coca-Cola Co., 55–56, 168, 367, 371, 396
cod populations (Newfoundland, Canada), 229–30
co-insurance payments, **555**
cold-opened movies, 542–43
Cold War, 398
college degrees, midcareer salaries by, 20
collusion, **387,** 387–89, 416
Comcast, 72, 314
commercial surrogacy, 438
common property, 228–29
common-resource goods, **225,** 226, 228–32
comparative advantage, **17,** 40–41, 42, 43
compensating differential, **458,** 458–59, 463
competition
  in duopolies, 387
  predatory pricing vs., 405
  promoting, 321–22
  winner-take-all, 468–69
competitive advantage, 298
competitive markets, **71,** 71–72, 270–96
  advertising in, 370, 372
  almost perfect, 273
  consumer and producer surplus in, 339
  and duopolies, 387, 389
  entry to, 272
  equilibrium price in, 178
  monopolies vs., 312, 313
  and monopolistic competition, 356, 361–63
  price takers in, 272
  and profit maximization, 274–86
  supply curve in, 286–96
  surpluses and shortages in, 95
complements (complement goods), **80,** 130, 131
concentration ratios, 384, 385
congestion charges, 216
constant returns to scale, **259**
consumer choices, 492–507
  complexity of, 526; *See also* behavioral economics
  and consumer satisfaction modeling, 494–98
  and diamond-water paradox, 504–6
  and indifference curve analysis, 512–24
  with monopoly, 317–18
  for purchasing decision optimization, 498–504
consumer goods, **46,** 46–49
consumer optimum, **498**
  and indifference curve, 520–24
  with more than two goods, 502
  and price changes, 502–4
  in purchasing decisions, 499–500, 502
consumer preferences, price elasticity of demand and, 111–12
consumers, health care, 555
consumer satisfaction, 494–98
consumer surplus, **179**
  and demand curve, 179–80
  in markets, 178–80
  and price discrimination, 339–41
  and total surplus, 184–85
coordinate system (graphs), 57–58
co-payments, **555,** 562–63
copyright laws, 11, 228, 306
corruption, income inequality and, 470
cost-benefit analysis, **227,** 227–28, 298
costs, 240–65
  accounting profit vs. economic profit, 244–46
  and advertising, 373–74
  of brands vs. generics, 374–75
  decision making about, 250–52
  explicit and implicit, 243–44
  external, 212–13
  internal, 212, 213
  labor needs and changes in, 427, 428
  long run, 257–60
  marginal, 16
  and marginal product, 249–51
  medical, 556
  in monopolistic competition, 363
  opportunity, *See* opportunity cost
  private, 212
  and production function, 247–49
  profit and loss calculation, 242–43
  of raising children, 265
  relative, 33–34
  short run, 252–57
  of smaller vs. larger firms, 240
  social, 212–14, 227
  start-up, 298
coupons, 348–50
crime, guarding against, 543
cross-price elasticity of demand, **130,** 130–31
Crowe, Russell, 390, 480
currency trading, 273

Daimler-Chrysler, 385
Dale, Stacy, 460
Dark Knight, The (film), 399
Day without a Mexican, A (film), 432
deadweight loss, **191**
  balancing tax revenues and, 199–200
  created by taxes, 191–200, 202
  and externalities, 215, 218
  with highly elastic demand, 195–97
  with inelastic demand, 192–94
  of monopoly, 317
  with more elastic demand, 194–95
Deal or No Deal (television show), 540–42
De Beers, 136, 372
decision making; *See also* behavioral economics; consumer choices
  bang per buck of production resources, 448–50
  complexity of, 526
  cost-benefit analysis in, 227–28
  about costs, 250–52
  game theory in, 392–402
  incentives in, 7–12
  inconsistencies in, 532–36
  long run costs in, 257–60
  long-term, 45
  marginal thinking in, 15–17
  about market entry/exit, 290–91, 294
  about operating or shutting down, 280–84
  opportunity cost and, 13–15
  optimizing purchasing decisions, 498–504
  about pollution, 210

private and social, 215–16
about production inputs, 247, 248, 250
risk in, 538–43
short run costs in, 252–57
trade-offs in, 12–13
decision tree, for ultimatum game, 537
deductibles, **555**
deforestation, in Haiti, 231
delayed gratification, 536
demand, 72–83; *See also* supply and demand
for capital, 448
changes in both supply and, 103–6
demand curve, 75
derived, 422, 423
determinants of, 72, 74
and diamond-water paradox, 504–6
and differences in wages, 442–43
for health care, 560–63, 566
income elasticity of, 127, 129–30
for labor, 423–28
for land, 445
law of, 75, 110, 302
market, 75–77
market adjustment to decrease in, 291–95
market effects of shifts in, 93–96
perfectly elastic, 120
perfectly inelastic, 119, 123
price elasticity of, 110–28
and price gouging, 157
and price of health care, 552
relatively elastic, 119
relatively inelastic, 119
responsive and unresponsive, 110
shifts in demand curve, 76–83
and short- and long-run supply, 139
unitary, 124
demand curve, **75,** 75–76
and advertising, 369
and consumer surplus, 179–80
and elasticity of demand, 118
factors affecting, 78
and monopolies, 309, 310
of perfectly competitive firms and monopolists, 309–10
with price ceilings, 152, 153
and price floors, 162–63
and price–total revenue trade-off, 124–27
shifts in, 76–83, 95–96
slope and elasticity on, 121–23
and taxes, 193–97
time and elasticity over, 121, 122
demand schedule, **75**
derived demand, **422,** 423
DHL, 367
diamond-water paradox, **504,** 504–6
DiGiorno, 374–75
Digital Equipment Corp. (DEC), 40
diminishing marginal product, 249–51, **250**
diminishing marginal utility, **497,** 497–98
diminishing return, on health care spending, 553–54
direct incentives, 9
disaster preparedness, 173
discounts, diminishing marginal utility of, 498
discount shopping
Black Friday, 348
with coupons, 348–50
outlet malls, 341–42
student discounts, 346
diseconomies of scale, **258**, 261
dismal science, economics as, 4
Disney World, 70
division of labor, 247–48
dominant strategy, **394**
and advertising, 403
lack of, 401–2
and long-run benefits, 398, 400
as Nash equilibrium, 394, 396
Dominican Republic, 231
Domino's, 240, 372
Dr. Pepper Snapple, 55–56
Dubai, 446
duopolies, 386–89
and cartels, 387–88
collusion in, 387–88
and prisoner's dilemma, 394–96
Dutch auctions, 274

Earned Income Tax Credit (EITC), 481, 482
eBay, 17
economic activity
and market distortions, *See* deadweight loss
and price ceilings, 154–58
and price floors, 164–68
and taxes, 191
economic growth, 34–35, 48
economic models, 28–29
ceteris paribus concept in, 38
production possibilities frontier, 31–37
economic profit, **244**
accounting profit vs., 244–46
and competitive markets, 290
and output, 247
economic rent, **446,** 448
economics, **6**
as the "dismal science," 4
foundations of, 4, 6, 7, 19; *See also individual foundational concepts*
incentives, 7–12
macroeconomics, 7
marginal thinking, 15–17
microeconomics, 7
models used in, 28–30
opportunity cost, 13–15
positive and normative analysis in, 27, 30
scientific method in, 26–27
trade, 17–18
trade-offs, 12–13
welfare, 178
economic thinking, 13, **15**
economies of scale, **258,** 262, 305, 564
education
as form of capital, 46
and human capital, 459
pay and, 459, 460
positive externality created by, 213–14
price discrimination on campus, 345–46
to reduce poverty rate, 477
tuition prices, 332
and wage discrimination, 464, 465
women's levels of, 464
efficiency, **185**
equity vs., 185, 187–88
market, 184–88, 212, 219
and product differentiation, 365
efficiency wages, **462,** 462–63
efficient scale, **256**
Efron, Zac, 466
elastic demand
deadweight loss with, 194–97
perfectly elastic, 120
relatively elastic, 119
elasticity, 108–41, **110**
cross-price, 130–31
and demand curve over time, 121, 122
income, 127–30
price elasticity of demand, 110–27, 133, 138–41
price elasticity of supply, 134–41
and slope of demand curve, 121–23
and total revenue, 124–26
unitary, 120
elastic supply (relatively elastic), 135
electronics, drop in prices of, 91
Emergency Price Control Act (1943), 155

Empire State Building, New York City, 72
employment opportunities, labor supply and, 430–31
endogenous factors, 28–29, **29**
Energizer, 368
entering markets, 272, 289–91, 294; *See also* barriers to entry
environmental degradation, 210
Equal Opportunity Act (1964), 477
Equal Pay Act (1963), 464
equilibrium, **93**
  and change in both supply and demand, 104
  and externalities, 218
  in labor market, 434–37, 440
equilibrium price, **93**
  in competitive markets, 178
  on Internet service, 170–71
  and price ceilings, 150
  and price floors, 150, 160–61
  and taxation, 189, 190
equilibrium quantity, **94**
equity, 185, **187,** 187–88
E.T. (film), 370
ethics, of selling organs, 573
ethnicity, income and, 464, 465, 478
Europe, organ donor system in, 534
excess capacity, **363,** 365
excise taxes, **188,** 188–89, 193–94, 204
excludable goods, **222,** 225, 226
exiting competitive markets, 289–91, 294
exogenous factors, 28, **29,** 50
expectations, regarding future price, 80, 90
expenses, 242–44
explicit costs, **243,** 243–44
external costs, **212,** 213
externalities, **212,** 212–19
  and Coase theorem, 221
  correcting for, 214–18
  internalized, 215, 216
  negative, 213–16, 218
  network, 405–9
  positive, 213, 216–18
  and property rights, 219–20
  and third-party problem, 212–18
Extreme Couponing (television show), 349

Facebook, 213, 406, 408
factors of production, **247,** 422, 448–50; *See also* capital; labor; land
fairness, judgments about, 536–38
farmers' markets, 273
Federal Communications Commission, 407
Federal Trade Commission (FTC), 376
FedEx, 367, 368
Ferris Bueller's Day Off, 12
5th Pillar, 470
financial crisis of 2008, 449
fiscal policy, 8
fishing, 229–30
fixed costs, **252**
  average, 253, 255
  total, 252, 253, 255
flexibility, of producers, 136
Florida, price gouging law in, 156
flower markets, 271
Ford, Henry, 462
Ford Motor Company, 262, 385, 462
Forrest Gump (film), 308
framing effects, **532,** 533
France, 534, 568–69
franchises, 377
Free Application for Federal Student Aid (FAFSA), 345–46
free-rider problem, **224,** 225, 228, 231
Friendster, 405, 406
Frito-Lay, 368

gambler's fallacy, **531,** 532
gambling, 530, 540
games of chance, 529–30, 540
game theory, **392,** 392–402
  advertising and, 396–98
  caution about, 401–2
  escaping prisoner's dilemma, 398–401
  prisoner's dilemma, 392–96
Gates, Bill, 68
gender
  and occupational crowding, 466–67
  wage discrimination by, 464–68
General Motors, 371, 385, 436
Germany, income inequality in, 472
gifts, 186
globalized trade, 18
global warming, 229–31
Goodyear, 464
Google, 213, 463
government
  and externality issues, 222
  lobbying, 318
  natural monopoly regulation by, 324–25
  oligopoly and policies of, 402–5
  public goods provided by, 224–25
  regulation by, 364
Grameen Bank, 483
graphs, 31, 55–64
  area formulas for rectangles and triangles, 62–63
  consisting of one variable, 55–57
  consisting of two variables, 57–63
  interpreting, 63–64
  with omitted variables, 63–64
  slope of curves on, 59–61
  time-series, 57
Great American Ballpark (Cincinnati), 287
Great Recession (2007–2009), 29
grocery store tactics, 351
Groupon, 349–50
Gulf of Mexico oil spill, 212

Haiti, deforestation in, 231
Hamermesh, Daniel S., 466
happiness index, 495, 501
Hardin, Garrett, 228
Harrison, George, 192
health care, 548–76
  and asymmetric information, 557–60
  demand and medical costs, 560–63
  in economic output, 550
  health insurance, 574
  incentives and quality of care, 566–73, 575
  industry issues in, 550–57
  national, 548
  and organ shortage, 569–70, 572–73, 575
  single-payer vs. private, 567–69
  supply and medical costs, 563–65
  United States vs. Canada, 571
health insurance, 561–63, 567–69, 574
health maintenance organizations (HMOs), 555–56
Hershey's, 370
Hewlett Foundation, 214
Hewlett-Packard, 213
Hindenburg disaster, 26, 27
H&M, 364
Holmes, Katie, 466
Honda, 385–86
Hong Kong, 448
Hoover, Herbert, 468
hot hand fallacy, **531,** 532
household types, poverty rate and, 478
housing market, 97
Howard, Ron, 390
Hudsucker Proxy, The (film), 83
human capital, **459,** 463
hybrid cars, 106
Hyundai, 367

IBM, 40
Ice Cream Float, 280
I Love Lucy (television show), 293
immediate run, **113,** 136
immigration, labor supply and, 431–32
imperfect markets, **72**
implicit costs, **243,** 243–44
incentives, **7,** 7–12
  for black markets, 151
  direct and indirect, 9
  in games of chance, 530
  in healthcare services, 554, 556, 559
  and innovation, 11
  at outlet malls, 341–42
  patents as, 306
  positive and negative, 8, 9
  for poverty reduction, 482
  for price gouging, 157
  in prisoner's dilemma, 393, 394
  for property owners, 219, 220, 229
  and quality of health care, 566–73, 575
  for sugar growing/use, 167, 168
  taxes as, 199
  in tragedy of the commons, 228
  unintended consequences of, 9–11, 168
  to violate copyright law, 228
  with winner-take-all competition, 469
incidence (of taxation), **188,** 188–91
income; *See also* salaries; wages
  and beauty, 466
  demand curve and changes in, 79–80
  and happiness, 492, 495
  midcareer salaries by college degrees, 20
  and occupational crowding, 466–67
income effect, **429**
income elasticity of demand, **127,** 127–30, 134
income inequality, 468–75
income mobility, **474,** 474–75
income tax, negative, 481, 482
inconsistencies in decision making, 532–36
India
  airline industry in, 322
  capital goods investments in, 48
  commercial surrogacy in, 438
  corruption in, 470
  outsourcing to, 447
indifference curve, **512,** 512–24
  and budget constraint, 514–15
  and consumer optimum, 520–24
  and economic "goods" and "bads," 512–14
  and perfect complements, 519, 520
  and perfect substitutes, 518–20
  properties of, 515–20
IndiGo, 322
indirect incentives, 9
industry concentration, measuring, 384–86
inefficiency, in monopolistic competition, 363–64
inelastic demand
  deadweight loss with, 192–94
  for health care, 561, 562
  perfectly inelastic, 119, 123
  relatively inelastic, 119
inelastic supply, 135
inferior goods, **79,** 129–30, 134
information, preferences influenced by, 80
in-kind transfers, **473,** 480, 481
innovation, incentives and, 11
inputs, **89,** 247
insurance companies, 555–56, 558, 565
intellectual property, 11, 228, 306
intermediaries, in health care, 555–56
internal costs, **212,** 213
internalized externalities, **215,** 216, 218, 221–22
Internet, bandwidth control for, 314
Internet piracy, 228, 306
intertemporal decision making, **536**
inventory, production and, 248
investment, **46,** 46–47
invisible hand, 70, 73
iPads, 422
irrational behaviors, *See* behavioral economics
Italy, 82, 501

Jagger, Mick, 14
James, Lebron, 307
Japan, income inequality in, 472, 477
Jingle All the Way (film), 115
Jobs, Steve, 11
John Deere, 368
John Q (film), 562
Judge Judy (television show), 461
judgments about fairness, 536–38

Kahneman, Daniel, 542
KFC, 377
Kia, 367, 385–86
kidneys, sale of, 569–70
king crab protecting, 230
kinked demand curve, **415,** 416
Knight's Tale, A (film), 48
Krueger, Alan, 460

labor
  changes in demand for, 426–28, 436
  changes in supply of, 429–33, 436
  demand for, 423–28
  determining bang per buck for, 448–50
  determining need for, 248–49
  division of, 247–48
  as factor of production, 247, 422
  labor-leisure trade-off, 428–29
  largest bang per buck for, 448–50
  marginal product of, 423–25
  outsourcing of, 436–41, 447
  in starting a business, 298
  supply of, 428–33
labor-leisure trade-off, 428–29
labor market
  changes in demand, 426–28
  changes in supply, 429–33
  determinants of supply and demand in, 434–43
  equilibrium in, 434–37, 440
  and outsourcing, 436–41
labor supply curve, 429–31
labor unions, 461–62
land
  determining bang per buck for, 448–50
  as factor of production, 247, 422
  market for, 445–48
larger firms, 240
law of demand, **75,** 110, 302
law of increasing relative cost, 33–34, **34**
law of supply, **84,** 135
law of supply and demand, **94**
Law & Order: Special Victims Unit (television show), 573
Ledbetter, Lilly, 464
Ledger, Heath, 48
Legally Blonde (film), 340
Let's Make a Deal (television show), 530
leverage, for larger firms, 240
Lewis, Michael, 444
licensing, 305, 320, 321
life-cycle wage pattern, **465,** 475
life expectancy, 550
life insurance, 574
lifestyle, as wage determinant, 461, 463
Lilly Ledbetter Fair Pay Act (2009), 464

LinkedIn, 408
Little Caesars, 372
liver transplants, 572
lobbying, 318
location
  differentiation by, 357
  as wage determinant, 461, 463, 465
London, congestion charges in, 216
long run, **113**
  costs in the, 257–60
  escaping prisoner's dilemma in, 398–401
  implications of outsourcing in, 439
  and market price changes, 113
  monopolistic competition in, 359–61
  price ceilings in, 152–53
  and price elasticity of supply, 139
  price floors in, 162–65
  profit maximization in, 283–85
  rent control in, 156
long-run average total cost (LRATC) curve, 259–60
long-term poor, 475
Lopez, Jennifer, 466
loss aversion, **534**
losses, **242**
  calculating, 242–43
  minimizing, 274
  signals of, 289
Louisiana, sugar cane in, 167, 168
Lovallo, Dan, 542
lumberjacks, 427
luxury goods, 112, 127, 129–30
luxury taxes, 198–99

macroeconomics, **7,** 8
Major League Baseball, 442
Malthus, Thomas, 4
margin, 15
marginal analysis, 15
marginal benefit, 16
marginal cost (MC), 16, 253–57, **254,** 263, 362
marginal poor, 475
marginal product, **248,** 248–50
  diminishing, 249–51
  of factors of production, 449
  of medical care, 553
  and number of workers, 248–49
marginal product of labor, 423–25, **424**
marginal rate of substitution, **515,** 515–16
marginal thinking, **15,** 15–17, 250, 502
marginal utility, **495,** 495–96
  in consumer purchasing decisions, 499–504
  and diamond-water paradox, 504–6
  diminishing, 497–98
margin-cost pricing rule, 324–25
market-clearing price, 93, 94
market demand, 75–77, **76**
market economy, **70**
market efficiency, 184–88, 212, 219
market failure, **315**
market forces, 270
market inefficiencies, 210–34
  externalities, 212–19
  nonexcludable goods, 226–33
  private goods and public goods, 219–26
market power
  in healthcare industry, 563, 565
  measuring, 384–86
  of monopolists, 302, 304
  of monopsonists, 441
market price, 70–72
markets, **17,** 68–72; *See also specific topics, e.g.:* demand
  changes in number of firms in, 90
  cleared, 94
  competitive, *See* competitive markets
  consumer surplus in, 178–80
  effects of supply and demand shifts on, 93–96
  efficiency of, 184–88
  imperfect, 72
  producer surplus in, 181–83
  regulating, 324–25
market supply, **86**
markup, **362,** 362–64, 366
Mars (company), 370
Marshalls, 365
Match.com, 408
maximization point, **512,** 513
McDonald's, 242, 247–48, 348, 377, 506
McNally, Dave, 442
measuring income inequality, 471–74
Medicaid, 552, 556, 565
medical care, *See* health care
medical tourism, 565
Medicare, 552, 556, 565
Medina, David, 156
Mercedes-Benz, 367, 438–39
Merck, 306
Messersmith, Andy, 442
Met Airways, 322
Mexico
  happiness rating of, 495, 501
  healthcare expenditures in, 551, 552
  income inequality in, 472, 477
  outsourcing to, 447
microcredit, 483
microeconomics, **7,** 8
Microsoft, 68, 302, 323, 404, 405
midpoint method (elasticity of demand), 116–17, 131
migration, labor supply and, 432–33
"Mine" (music video), 541
minimum wage, 146, **164,** 164–69, 481, 482
minimum wage laws, 166–67, 169
Modern Times (film), 262
money, 492
Moneyball (film), 444
monopolistic competition, 354–66, **356**
  advertising in, 366–67, 372
  characteristics of, 356
  and competitive markets, 361–63
  inefficiency in, 363–64
  in the long run, 359–61
  and other market structures, 356
  price differentiation in, 364–66
  product differentiation in, 357–58
  in the short run, 359, 360
Monopoly (game), 327
monopoly(-ies), **72,** 302–26
  advertising by, 372
  competitive markets vs., 312, 313
  consumer and producer surplus in, 339, 340
  creation of, 304–7
  and demand curve, 309, 310
  and duopolies, 387
  government-created, 320
  and Microsoft, 323
  and monopolistic competition, 356
  natural, 305
  and perfect price discrimination, 339–41
  as price makers, 309–10
  problems with, 315–21
  profit-maximizing rule for, 310–15
  solutions to problems of, 321–25
monopoly power, **304**
monopsony, **441,** 441–43, 567, 569
moral hazard, **559**
Moscow on the Hudson (film), 153
movies
  cold openings, 542–43
  price discrimination at the, 344–45, 347
Msango, Nokuthula, 165
Mumbai, India, rent control in, 154, 155
Murder by Numbers (film), 395
music industry, 284, 407
mutual interdependence, **388**

MySpace, 405, 406
MythBusters (television show), 26

Namibia, income inequality in, 472, 477
Nash, John, 390
Nash equilibrium, 389, **390,** 394, 396
Nathan's Famous Hot Dog Eating Contest, 498
national defense, 224–25
National Football League, 302
national health care, 548
National Organ Transplant Act (1984), 569
Natural Bridge Park, Virginia, 226
natural monopoly, **305,** 324–25
necessities, 112, 127, 129–30
negative correlations, **58,** 58–59
negative externalities, 213, 218
  correcting for, 214–16, 218
  markets' reactions to, 218
  putting a price on, 216
  and social optimum, 214–15
  in tragedy of the commons, 228–29
negative incentives, 8, 9
negative income tax, **481,** 482
negative slope, 61
Netflix, 314
Netscape, 405
network externalities, **405,** 405–9
Newfoundland, Canada, cod populations, 229–30
New York City, 155, 320, 321
Nintendo, 132
Nissan, 385–86
nonbinding minimum wage, 166–67
nonbinding price ceilings, 150, 157
nonbinding price floors, 160, 161
nonexcludable goods, 225–33
  and cost-benefit analysis, 227
  and tragedy of the commons, 228–31
nonlinear relationships, 60
nonrival goods, 225, 226
Nordstrom, 68
normal goods, **79,** 127, 129–30, 134
normative analysis, **27**
normative statements, 27, 30
Norway, happiness rating of, 495
nurse shortage, 435, 437

Oakland Athletics, 444
Obama, Barack, 232, 464, 548
occupational crowding, **466,** 466–67
Office, The (television show), 257
Old School (film), 186
oligopoly, 382–410, **384**
  duopolies, 386–89
  game theory in decision making under, 392–402
  government policies affecting, 402–5
  and measurement of industry concentration, 384–86
  with more than two firms, 391, 392
  Nash equilibrium in, 389, 390
  network externalities in, 405–8
  and other market structures, 384
  and theories of pricing behavior, 415–16
Olive Garden, 259
Olson, Ken, 40
O'Neal, Shaquille, 42, 43
One-Man Band (short animation), 321
online ticket auctions, 273
opportunity cost, **13,** 13–15
  ceteris paribus and, 44
  in consumer purchase decisions, 499
  example of, 45
  and fair-trade coffee, 163
  in game shows, 530
  as implicit cost, 243–44
  of labor, 296
  law of increasing relative cost, 33–34
  and market entry/exit, 290–91
  of out-of-date facilities, 286
  pricing and, 41–42
  and specialization, 40–41
  of taxes, 188
opt-in and opt-out systems, 534, 535
organ donors/organ transplants, 534, 535, 565, 573, 575; *See also* organ shortage
Organisation for Economic Co-operation and Development (OECD), 495, 501
Organization of the Petroleum Exporting Countries (OPEC), 389
organ shortage, 569–70, 572–73, 575
outlet malls, 341–42
output, **247**
  and economic profit, 247
  inefficient, 316–17
  and marginal product, 248–50
  of monopolies, 302
  in monopolistic competition, 363
  and variable costs, 252
output effect, 311, **392**
Outsourced (film), 441
outsourcing of labor, 420, **436,** 436–41, 447, 452
ova, selling, 572
ownership, common vs. public and private ownership, 229

Panera Bread, 377
Papa John's, 240, 372
Paramount, 367
Parnell, Chris, 130
patents, 11, 306
"Pay and Performance in Major League Baseball" (Gerald Scully), 442
PepsiCo Inc., 55–56, 367, 371, 396
perfect competition, perfect price discrimination and, 339–41
perfect complements, 519, **520**
perfectly elastic demand, 120
perfectly inelastic demand, 119, 123
perfectly inelastic supply, 135
perfect price discrimination, **335,** 339–41
perfect substitutes, **518,** 518–20
pharmaceutical companies, 556
phone market, 321–22
physical fitness, 557
π (film), *533*
Pike Place Market, Seattle, 71, 76, 84, 87, 272
Pizza Hut, 240, 366, 372
PNC Park (Pittsburgh), 287
Poland, organ donor system in, 534
policy decisions, trade-offs in, 12
pollution, 210, 215, 230–31
positive analysis, 27
positive correlations, **58,** 58–59
positive externalities, 213, 216–18
positive incentives, 8, 9
positive slope, 61
positive statements, **27,** 30
Potomac Mills (Washington, D.C.), 341
poverty, 476–84
  and marginal vs. long-term poor, 475
  policies related to, 478–82
  poverty rate, 476–78
  and problems with traditional aid, 482–84
  in the United States, 471, 477
poverty rate, **472,** 476–78
poverty threshold, **472,** 476–77
predatory pricing, **405,** 406
predictions, 50
Preece, Sir William, 40
preference reversal, 538–40, **540**
preferences, changes in, 80

president of the United States,
compensation for, 468
price ceilings, **148,** 148–58
and economic activity, 154–58
effect of, 150–51
in the long run, 152–53
on student rental apartments, 158
understanding, 148–49
price controls, 146–71, **148**
minimum wage, 146
price ceilings, 148–58
price floors, 158–68
on sugar, 167
price differentiation, in monopolistic competition, 364–66
price discrimination, 332–50, **334**
on campus, 345–46
conditions for, 334–35
and coupons, 349–50
at the movies, 344–45, 347
one price vs., 335–37
perfect, 335–41
value of, 334
welfare effects of, 338–42
price effect, 311, **391,** 392
price elasticity of demand, 110–28, **111,** 133
and car purchases, 141
computing, 113–17
determinants of, 110–13
developing intuition for, 114
graphing, 117–23
and price, 120–21
and price elasticity of supply, 138–41
and total revenue, 123–27
price elasticity of supply, **134,** 134–41
calculating, 136–37
and car purchases, 141
determinants of, 135–38
and price elasticity of demand, 138–41
price floors, 158–68, **159**
and binding minimum wage, 164
and economic activity, 164–68
effect of, 159–62
in the long run, 162–63
understanding, 159
price gouging laws, **155,** 155–57, 173
price leadership, 415, **416**
Priceline, 348
price maker, **309,** 309–10
price(s)
black-market, 151
and budget constraint, 521–22
and change in both supply and demand, 105
in competitive markets, 71–72
consumer optimum and changes in, 502–4
control over, 270
and demand curve, 77
elasticity of, 110
of electronics, 91
equilibrium, 93, 94
established in markets, 70
expectations regarding, 80, 90
in imperfect markets, 72
and law of demand, 110–11
market-clearing, 93, 94
with monopolies, 302, 316–17
in monopolistic competition, 361–63
and price elasticity of demand, 120–21
and quantity demanded, 74, 75
and quantity supplied, 84
and rationing of medical care, 567
of related goods, 80
and shifts in supply/demand, 95–96
of “specials,” 81–82
and taxes, 188
and total revenue, 124–27
value of products vs., 354
willingness to pay, 178
willingness to sell, 181
price takers, **272,** 275
price wars, 406
pricing
to facilitate trade, 41–42
one price vs. price discrimination, 335–37
predatory, 405, 406
priming effects, **533**
principal-agent problem, **558,** 558–59
prisoner’s dilemma, 392–401, **393**
and advertising, 396, 398
and duopoly, 394–96
escaping, 397, 398–401
incentives in, 393, 394
private costs, diverged from social costs, 212
private goods, **222,** 226
private healthcare plans, 567–69
private property, **220,** 220–22, 229
probabilities, 529–32
producers, 136, 181, 555
producer surplus, **181**
in markets, 181–83
and price discrimination, 339–41
and supply curve, 181–83
and total surplus, 184–85
product differentiation, **356**
degrees of, 364–66
and franchises, 377
in monopolistic competition, 357–58
production
in competitive markets, 278–79
and costs, 250, 252
factors of, 247–50, 444–50
and marginal product, 249–50
production function, 247–49
scale of, 257–58, 261
production function, **247,** 247–49
production possibilities frontier (PPF), **31,** 31–37
and economic growth, 34–35
and investment in capital vs. consumer goods, 47
with no trade, 38
and opportunity cost, 32–34
with trade, 40
in a two-goods society, 31–32
production process, 89
products, changes in demand for, 426, 427
profit maximization, 274–86
deciding on production output for, 278–79
in the long run, 283–85
profit-maximizing rule, 275–78
in the short run, 279–83
and sunk costs, 286
profit-maximizing rule, **278**
for competitive markets, 275–78, 285
for monopolies, 310–15
profits, **242**
accounting vs. economic, 244–46
calculating, 242–43
of monopolies, 302
signals of, 289
and trade-offs, 14
property rights, **219**
for environmental protection, 231
intellectual property, 11, 228, 306
and Internet piracy, 228
private property, 220–22
property values, 97
Property Virgins (television show), 97
prospect theory, 540–43, **542**
public goods, **222,** 222–28
public policy, for poverty reduction, 478–82
public sector, union membership in, 462
Punch Pizza, 366
purchasing decisions, optimizing, 498–504

Quaker foods, 368
quality, differentiation by, 357, 358
quantity, and change in both supply and demand, 105
quantity demanded, **72,** 74
  and equilibrium price, 93, 94
  and price, 74, 75, 96, 110–11
quantity supplied, **84,** 96

race, income and, 464, 465, 478
real estate market, 97
real-income effect, **503,** 503–4, 520–24
rectangles, determining formula for, 62–63
Red Sox, 15
regulation
  of advertising, 376
  of markets, 324–25
  and monopolistic competition, 364
relationships
  causal, 63–64
  in cross-price elasticity of demand, 130–31
relative cost, law of increasing, 33–34
relatively elastic demand, 119
relatively elastic supply, 135
relatively inelastic demand, 119
relatively inelastic supply, 135
rent, economic, 446
rent control, **154,** 154–56
rent seeking, **318**
Republic of Ireland, 199
reservation price, 178
resources, 6, 304
responsive demand, 110
revenues
  difference between expenses and, 242
  total, 123–27, 242–43
reverse causation, **64**
rise (slope), 59
risk
  in decision making, 538–43
  and moral hazard, 559
  of outsourcing, 452
  protection from, 298
risk-averse people, **528,** 539
risk aversion, 539
risk-neutral people, **528,** 539
risk takers, **528**
risk taking, 539
risk tolerance, 538–40
rival goods, **222,** 225, 226, 228
Rodriguez, Alex, 469
Ross, 365
run (slope), 59
Ruth, Babe, 468

salaries, 423, 442; *See also* wages
samaritan's dilemma, **483,** 483–85
Samberg, Andy, 130
Sarah Lawrence College (Yonkers, New York), 460
Sarnoff, David, 40
Saturday Night Live (television show), 130, 131
Saving Private Ryan (film), 34
scale, **257,** 257–59, 262, 363
scarcity, **6,** 504–6
scatterplots, **58**
scientific method, 26–27
Scully, Gerald, 442
Sheindlin, Judith, 461
Sherman Antitrust Act, **402**
shortages, **94,** 95
  of human organs, 569–70, 572–73, 575
  and price gouging, 157
short run, **113**
  costs in the, 252–57
  implications of outsourcing in, 438–39
  and market price changes, 113
  monopolistic competition in, 359, 360
  and price elasticity of supply, 136, 139
  price floors and minimum wage in, 164–65
  price floors in, 159–60
  profit maximization in, 279–83
  rent control in, 156
short-run average total cost (SRATC) curve, 259
shut-down decisions, 280–81
signals (of profits and losses), **289**
Simpsons, The (television show), 126, 277, 559
single-payer system (health care), **567,** 567–69
slope, **59,** 59–61, 515–16
smaller firms, costs of larger firms vs., 240
Smith, Adam, 70, 504
social costs, **212,** 212–14, 227
social optimum, **214,** 214–18, 227
social welfare, **184,** 364, 402; *See also* total surplus
Sony, 132
South Africa, wage laws in, 165–66
South Park (television show), 232
Soviet Union, Cold War and, 398
specialization, 17–18
  and gains from trade, 37–40
  labor, 247–50
  in medical care, 564
Sprint, 382
Spurlock, Morgan, 506

stadiums, 286, 287
Standard Oil antitrust case, 404
Stanford University, 213–14, 536
Starbucks, 68, 87, 89
starting a business, 298
status quo bias, **533,** 533–34
steel industry, 318
Stockholm, congestion charges in, 216
stock market, 273
stock price volatility, 531
street performances, 224
strikes, **461**
style, differentiation by, 357
subsidies, 90, 176
Subsidized Nutrition Assistance Program (SNAP), 480
substitutes (substitute goods), **80**
  and cross-price elasticity, 130, 131
  and price elasticity, 111–12
  for taxes luxury goods, 198–99
substitution effect
and labor-leisure trade-off, **429**
and price changes, **503,** 503–4, 520–24
Subway, 348
sugar incentives, 167, 168
sunk costs, **286,** 287
Super Bowl commercials, 367, 371
Super Size Me (documentary), 506
Supplemental Security Income (SSI), 480
supply, 84–92; *See also* supply and demand
  changes in both demand and, 103–6
  and diamond-water paradox, 504–6
  and differences in wages, 442–43
  of labor, 428–33
  of land, 445–46, 448
  law of, 84, 135
  market, 86
  market effects of shifts in, 93–96
  and medical costs, 563–65
  perfectly inelastic, 135
  price elasticity of, 134–41
  relatively elastic, 135
  relatively inelastic, 135
  shifts in supply curve, 87–91
  supply curve, 84–85
supply and demand, 71, 92; *See also* price controls
  and black markets, 151
  changes in both supply and demand, 103–6
  and consumer electronics prices, 91
  market effects of, 93–96

supply curve, **84,** 84–85
  in competitive markets, 286–96
  determinants of supply elasticity on, 136, 137
  factors shifting, 88
  labor, 429–31
  long-run market, 283–84
  with price ceilings, 152
  and price floors, 163
  and producer surplus, 181–83
  and profit maximization, 282–84
  shifts in, 87–91, 95–96
  short-run market, 282–83
  and taxes, 89–90, 197–99
supply schedule, **84,** 85
surpluses, **94,** 94–95
  of agricultural products, 159
  consumer, 178–80, 339–41
  of labor, 435
  and price floors, 162
  producer, 181–83, 339–41
  total, 184–85
surrogate mothers, 438
Swift, Taylor, 541
switching costs, **407**

tacit collusion, 416
Taco Bell, 357, 358, 367
Target, 69
tariffs, 322
tastes, changes in, 80
taxes
  benefits of, 188
  bizarre taxes, 201
  deadweight loss from, 191–200, 202
  Earned Income Tax Credit, 481
  excise, 188–89, 193–94, 204
  gasoline, 176
  incidence of taxation, 188–91
  luxury, 198–99
  negative income tax, 481, 482
  on plastic bags, 214
  politics of, 202
  and supply curve shifts, 89–90
"Taxman" (song), 192
technologies
  medical, 551
  substituted for workers, 427
  supply and demand for, 91
  waiting to buy new technologies, 408
Temporary Assistance for Needy Families (TANF), 480, 483
textbooks, buying, 16–17
third-party problem, **212,** 212–18
30 Days (television show), 168
3Com, 213
Three Rivers Stadium (Pittsburgh), 286, 287
Tide (detergent), 367
time
  elasticity and the demand curve over, 121, 122
  and price elasticity of supply, 135, 136
  and response to market price changes, 112–13
time-series graphs, 57
tit-for-tat, **400**
T.J.Maxx, 365
T-Mobile, 382
total cost (TC), **242**
  average, 253–56
  and explicit and implicit costs, 243–44
  fixed, 252, 253, 255
  variable, 252, 253
total fixed cost (TFC), 252, 253, 255
total revenue
  and calculating a firm's profit and loss, **242,** 242–43
  and price elasticity of demand, **123,** 123–27
total surplus, **184,** 184–85
total utility, 496, 504–6
total variable cost (TVC), 252, 253, 255
Tournament Players Club at Sawgrass (Florida), 111–12
Toyota, 262, 367, 385
trade, **17,** 17–18, 24
  bystander effects of, *See* externalities
  and comparative advantage, 40–41
  globalized, 18
  incentives for, 220
  and opportunity cost, 41–45
  and outsourcing, 439
  pricing and, 41–42
  production possibilities frontier model, 31–37
  and specialization, 37–40
  specialization and gains from, 37–40
trade barriers, reducing, 322
trade-offs, 12–13
  with cap and trade, 231
  in consumer choices, 494
  in healthcare debate, 548, 550
  in healthcare systems, 567
  labor-leisure, 428–29
  long-run, 45–49
  with monopolistic competition, 364
  in production possibilities frontier, 31–37
  in setting minimum wage, 171
  between taxes and prices, 199
  between total revenue and price elasticity of demand, 124–27
  with unfair proposals, 537
tragedy of the commons, **228,** 228–32
triangles, determining formula for, 62–63
Trudeau, Kevin, 376
truth in advertising, 376
Tucker, Al, 393
tuition prices, 332, 345–46
Tversky, Amos, 542
21 (film), 529–30
Twitter, 408
type, differentiation by, 357

ultimatum game, **536,** 536–37
unemployment
  in financial crisis of 2008, 449
  and minimum wage, 165–67
  and outsourcing, 436
  in South Africa, 165–66
  and welfare, 484
unintended consequences (of incentives), 9–11, 168
unions, **461,** 461–63
unitary demand, total revenue and, 124
unitary elasticity, 120
United Kingdom, 472, 565
United States
  birthrate in, 11
  causes of death in, 550, 551
  Cold War, 398
  happiness rating of, 495
  healthcare expenditures in, 551, 552, 554, 571
  health care in economic output of, 550
  healthcare system of Canada vs., 566–68, 571
  healthcare system of France vs., 568–69
  immigration to, 431
  income inequality in, 472–74, 477
  income mobility in, 474–75
  life expectancy in, 550
  medical tourism from, 565
  organ donor system in, 534
  outsourcing to and from, 438–39, 447
  poverty rate in, 477
  poverty threshold in, 476–77
  regional populations in, 432, 433
  uninsured in, 552
United States Postal Service, 302, 367
unresponsive demand, 110
UPS, 367

Urban Outfitters, 364
used goods, buying, 233
util, **494,** 494–95
utility, **494**
  and consumer choices, 494–95
  and indifference curve, 512
  and romance, 508
utility theory, 494

value
  of education, 460
  price of products and, 354
value creation
  in buying/selling textbooks, 17
  by markets, 178
  in trade, 17, 40–41
value of the marginal product (VMP), **424,** 425, 428, 444
variable costs, **252**
  average, 252–53, 255, 256
  total, 253–55
variable(s), **55**
  graphs consisting of one variable, 55–57
  graphs consisting of two variables, 57–63
  in supply and demand changes, 104
Varian Associates, 213
Verizon, 382
Veterans Stadium (Philadelphia), 286, 287
video game industry, 132
Visa, 368
Volkswagen, 367, 385–86
Volvo, 386

wage discrimination, **464,** 464–68
wage laws, in South Africa, 165–66
wages
  and education level, 459, 460
  efficiency, 462–63
  equalizing, 470
  equilibrium, 434–35
  and income inequality, 469–76
  and labor-leisure trade-off, 429
  and labor shortages, 435
  non-monetary determinants of, 458–63
  for physicians in Canada, 567
  for professional baseball players, 442
  reasons for differences in, 442–43
  variability in, 423
  and wage discrimination, 464–68
  and winner-take-all competition, 468–69
Walmart, 240, 241, 405
Washington, D.C., 214
Washington, Denzel, 562
Watergate scandal, 11, 12
welfare economics, **178**
  and price discrimination, 338–42
  total surplus, 184–85
welfare programs, 9, 478, 480, 482–84
Whittaker, Jack, 492
Wii rollout, 132
willingness to pay, **178,** 178–79
willingness to sell, **181**
winner-take-all, **468,** 468–69
Witherspoon, Reese, 340
women
  and occupational crowding, 466–67
  and wage discrimination, 464–68
Woodward, Bob, 11, 12
workforce composition, labor supply and, 431
Wright, Orville, 28–29
Wright, Wilbur, 28–29

Xerox, 213

Yunus, Muhammad, 483

Zwane, Thoko, 165

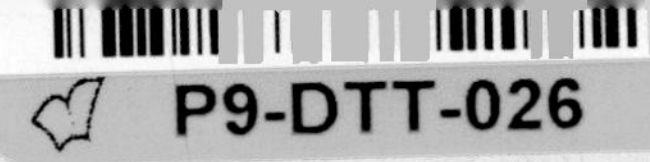

PRAISE FOR

THE EMANCIPATOR'S WIFE

"A COMPELLING FICTIONAL PORTRAIT OF ONE OF THE MOST MALIGNED AND MISUNDERSTOOD FIRST LADIES IN AMERICAN HISTORY." —*Booklist*

"Hambly fleshes out the historical record to put before us a compassionate and evenhanded portrait of the 16th First Lady. . . . [She] summons the languorous gentility of the antebellum South as persuasively as she does the clamor, filth and meat-packing stench of post–Civil War Chicago. And she manages to capture, with a light hand, the elusive bond between 'Molly' and Mr. Lincoln that endured the snowballing hardships of their lives." —*Washington Post Book World*

"Hambly injects compassion and empathy into the story of a complicated woman living in a difficult time. Like any good historical novelist, Hambly keeps her eye on the record, inventing characters and scenes which are plausible and not at odds with the generally agreed-upon facts. . . . Compelling." —*Rocky Mountain News*

"Just as Lincoln is seduced in the book, Barbara Hambly seduces the reader with a brilliantly crafted opening account of Mary's 1875 insanity trial. . . . Excellent." —*Seattle Times*

"Hambly has a knack for bringing historical figures to life in all their flawed humanity. This touching portrait of Mary Todd . . . paints a full, nuanced picture of a talented, tormented woman."
—*Publishers Weekly*

"Hambly gets inside Mary Lincoln's head. . . . Though a fictional account, the book makes you realize that presidents are just men, their wives are just women, and both have their own demons."
—*Sunday Oklahoman*

"From its perfect title to its beautiful, poignant last scenes, this is a wonderful portrait of one of the most important, complex and misunderstood figures in American history—a brilliant novel of the Civil War!" —Max Byrd

"Mary Todd Lincoln was an enormous pain in the ass to everyone in the world, including herself. Barbara Hambly has pulled off the impossible, by encompassing this obnoxious, annoying, and completely fascinating woman in a fashion that fills us simultaneously with drop-jawed astonishment, cringing horror . . . and wrenching empathy. A real tour de force of historical fiction!" —Diana Gabaldon

"A skilled historical novelist limns an absolutely convincing portrait of Mary Todd Lincoln." —*Kirkus Reviews*

"*The Emancipator's Wife* may be a work of 'historical fiction,' but its facts are impeccable and its fictions most believable. . . . Long considered the hag behind the hero, Mary Todd Lincoln finds space in this novel for her historic idiosyncrasies to be interpreted differently—as symptoms of a 19th-century struggle for her own financial and personal freedom. Hambly's novel faithfully describes the factual enslavement and emancipation of a nation. Its fiction details the same cycle of rebirth for one woman."
—*Wichita Falls (TX) Times Record News*

AND PRAISE FOR BARBARA HAMBLY'S BENJAMIN JANUARY MYSTERIES

DEAD WATER

A *Deadly Pleasures* Best Mystery/Crime Novel of 2004

"A historian by training, Hambly knows how to make us live her scenes. . . . We hear the clangs of bells and slave-chains and practically smell the ash from the wood-burning boilers. *Dead Water* is a lively read, with one of Hambly's best plots ever."
—*New Orleans Times-Picayune*

"Hambly's brilliantly crafted eighth historical brings the antebellum South so alive you could swear the author traveled back in time to observe her settings firsthand. . . . This riveting novel of suspense is sure to win Hambly many new fans."
—*Publishers Weekly* (starred review)

"The novels in this series are clever mixtures of scholarship and imagination. . . . Hambly keeps things moving, always focused on her characters and her story. . . . Keep 'em coming!" —*Booklist*

DAYS OF THE DEAD

"Sumptuous." —*New York Times Book Review*

"Hambly's historical research adds the right touches. . . . There's plenty of Low Country color—from the washing of collard greens to the dancing of the shag—to keep the story firmly rooted in its locale, making for a fast, fun read." —*Boston Globe*

"Hambly doesn't just write period mysteries; she engages in literary time travel. Few historical novels are as textured, as tactile, as the January mysteries." —*Booklist*

"Hambly puts us smack-dab into the streets and haciendas of Mexico in the same way she gives us 19th-century New Orleans, with fine detail that seems casual but can only come from painstaking scholarly research." —*Charlotte Observer*

WET GRAVE

"Barbara Hambly continues to delight us with her sensuous evocation of life in New Orleans in the turbulent era of the 1800's."
—*New York Times Book Review*

"Fans of historical mysteries will savor every word of Barbara Hambly's beautifully written *Wet Grave*. . . . Astonishing." —*Miami Herald*

"Hambly's characters are complex and her descriptive ability is astonishing." —*Chicago Sun-Times*

"Along with the faithful, readers new to the series will find this installment as bracing as chicory-laced coffee." —*Kirkus Reviews*

DIE UPON A KISS

"Ravishing."
—*New York Times Book Review*

"Dazzling. January is a wonderfully rich and complex character."
—*Chicago Tribune*

"Fine entertainment." —*Boston Globe*

SOLD DOWN THE RIVER

"A masterly piece of historical storytelling . . . haunting."
—*New York Times Book Review*

"The darkest time in American history comes alive in Hambly's unforgettable series. . . . [A] fiercely burning picture of the horrors of slavery . . . astonishing." —*Publishers Weekly*

GRAVEYARD DUST

"Seductive . . . Sweeps from lavish balls on elegant river plantations to voodoo rites in Congo Square and savage brawls in men's waterfront dives . . . January proves the ideal guide through these treacherous social strata." —*New York Times Book Review*

"A richly detailed murder mystery with a little bit of voodoo mixed in for flavor. Don't miss this powerful series."
—*Mystery Lovers Bookshop News*

FEVER SEASON

A *New York Times* Notable Book of the Year

"A notable writer of mystery fiction . . . This one grips the reader from start to finish." —*Washington Times*

"From the highborn Creoles in their river mansions to the uncivilized Americans brawling on the levee, Hambly speaks all their languages, knows all their secrets, and brings them all to life."
—*New York Times Book Review*

A FREE MAN OF COLOR

"Magically rich and poignant . . . In scene after scene researched in impressive depth and presented in the cool, clear colors of photography, Hambly creates an exotic but recognizable environment for January's search for justice." —*Chicago Tribune*

"A darned good murder mystery." —*USA Today*

Also by Barbara Hambly

A Free Man of Color

Fever Season

Graveyard Dust

Sold Down the River

Die Upon a Kiss

Wet Grave

Days of the Dead

Dead Water

And coming soon in hardcover from Bantam:

Patriot Ladies

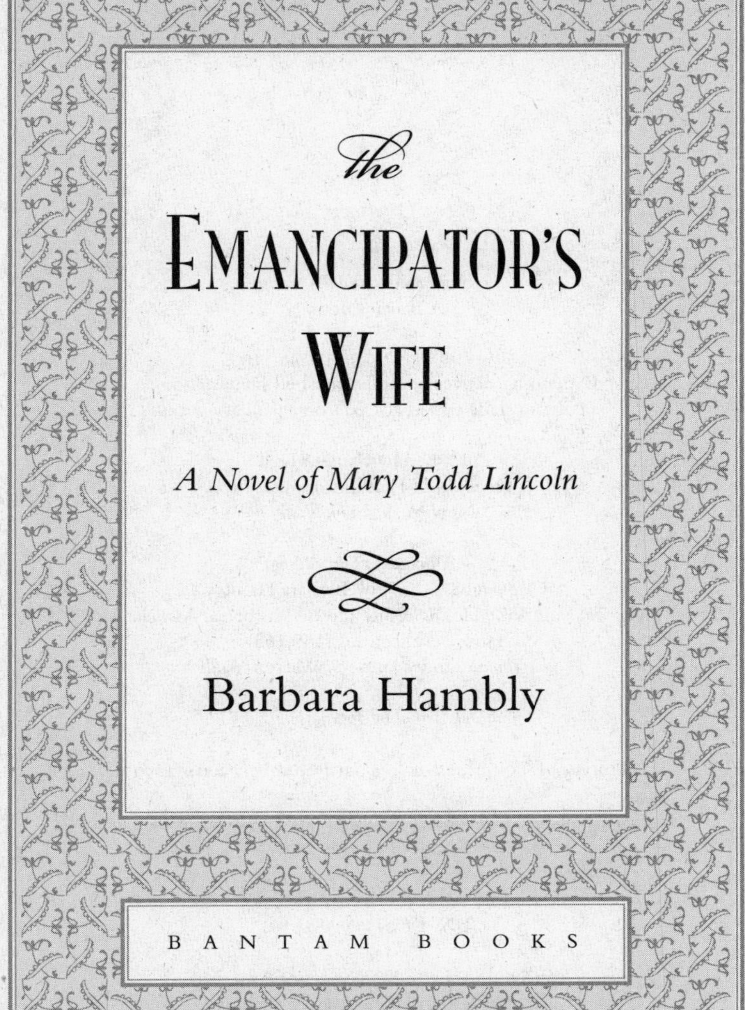

the Emancipator's Wife

A Novel of Mary Todd Lincoln

Barbara Hambly

BANTAM BOOKS

THE EMANCIPATOR'S WIFE
A Bantam Book

PUBLISHING HISTORY
Bantam hardcover edition published January 2005
Bantam trade paperback edition / January 2006

Published by Bantam Dell
A Division of Random House, Inc.
New York, New York

Cover image by Katherine Helm/White House Historical Association (White House Collection) (165,165)
Cover design by Jamie S. Warren Youll

Book design by Laurie Jewell

Library of Congress Catalog Card Number: 2004048797

ISBN-13: 978-0-553-38193-1
ISBN-10: 0-553-38193-8

Printed in the United States of America
Published simultaneously in Canada

www.bantamdell.com

BVG 10 9 8 7 6 5 4 3 2 1

For Kate

Special Thanks

Are due (in no particular order) to

Kathy Tabb at the Mary Todd Lincoln House in Lexington, KY; James Patton and Barbara Guinan at Lincoln's New Salem; Ed Russo at the Sangamon Valley Collection; Tom Schwartz at the Old Capitol Building in Springfield, IL; John Eden, proprietor of the Long Nine Museum in Athens (pronounced AY-thens), IL; Mr. Wayne Temple for our long phone conversation on the circumstances of the Lincoln marriage; the staff of the library at the Old Capitol Building; the staff of the Library of Congress.

Extra-special thanks to

Roger and David at the Mischler House Bed and Breakfast in Springfield; to Managing Editor Kathleen Baldonado for her usual wonderful job of shepherding my manuscript through the production process; to my long-suffering mother for retyping the manuscript when the hard drive crashed; and, as usual, to Kate, for the genesis of the whole project.

A Note on Nomenclature

Confederates and Rebels

Because it was Lincoln's contention that the Confederate States of America had no legal existence—that his reason for assembling an army was to put down a rebellion, not to invade another nation—I have, in all sections written from the viewpoint of Mary Todd Lincoln, referred to the Confederacy and Confederates as "rebels."

That is her opinion, not mine, and I extend my apology to those whom it offends.

When writing a historical novel, a writer takes as much as possible the voices of those whose lives the book is trying to re-create. It would be as inappropriate to ascribe recognition of the Confederacy to Mrs. Lincoln as it would be to have General Sheridan refer to the Sioux Nation as "Native Americans" instead of "Indians."

All stories are true, and some actually happened.

—ANONYMOUS,
twentieth century

It is very hard to deal with someone who is sane on all subjects but one.

—ROBERT TODD LINCOLN,
writing about his mother

Prologue

Washington 1862

Encountering Mary Todd Lincoln was the nicest thing that happened to John Wilamet on his first day in the Promised Land. This fact did not speak well for his other experiences in that first twenty-four hours of freedom.

For three weeks he'd been working his way north from his master's plantation in Halifax County, Virginia. As a boy he'd been as far as Richmond twice—once, terrifyingly, when Mr. Henry Wilamet, who owned Blue Hill Plantation, had decided to sell him, but he had changed his mind when he couldn't get the price he wanted. Runaways who'd passed through Blue Hill on their way north to Washington City after the fighting started had told John the route. Such knowledge was a whispered undercurrent among the unfree: which back-roads were safest, what the scrawled marks were on back-fences and sheds that meant, *They'll give you food here.* John could have made the journey quicker, but he had his mother with him, two younger sisters, and a tiny brother.

He was fifteen.

It was October, and the corn had long since been harvested. Mounted patrols seemed to be everywhere, north and south of the river, making it far too perilous to thieve from the houses and the barns they passed. Because Southern troops were camped around the railway junction at Manassas John and his family swung wide and crossed the river in a stolen rowboat near Leesburg, then moved cautiously down the Maryland side: John had been warned that most Marylanders were slaveholders who would as soon secede as not. Just because they'd crossed into Union-held territory did not mean they were safe.

"I'm hungry," whimpered Isaac, who was five. "We gonna have food when we get to Promise Land?"

"We sure will, baby," their mother assured him, a dangerous sparkle in her eyes. John caught his sister Cassy's wary sidelong glance. Their mother's touchwood temper and bizarre whims had already cost them several days' travel time. Aside from the fact that John had no desire to deal with her ranting herself to exhaustion about what the Promised Land was supposed to be like, you could hear her for miles when she got going. Trying to hush her only made matters worse.

"We'll have food, and shoes, and a cabin all to our own," she added, her voice rising, and Lucy, who was eight, asked,

"How we know which one's ours?"

"Don't you back-talk your mama! John'll find him some work, cuttin' wood or drivin' a wagon"—John had never driven a wagon in his life and had no idea where his mother had gotten the idea that he could—"and we'll all have chicken an' biscuits, an' quilts on the beds. You girls'll have pretty new dresses. . . ."

Hooves ahead. The woods here were thin, already blazing with the golds and maroons of autumn. The hard blue of uniforms stood out vivid as jewels. John put a hand on his mother's arm to steer her to the cover of the nearest thicket, but she pulled from him, strode toward the soldiers shouting, "What we got to hide? We here in the Promise Land of Freedom!"

No we not, Mama, we in Maryland. . . .

One of the soldiers reached for his rifle at the sight of movement, but holstered it again the next moment. John panted, trying to keep up with his mother—she could go damn fast when she had a head of steam in her—while Cassy drew Lucy and Isaac to the side of the road, ready to vanish like bunnies if they had to.

"This here the road to Washington, sir?" demanded his mother, looking up at the officer. His mother—Phoebe was her name—was a beautiful woman, and even ragged and disheveled had a fey loveliness that drew the men's eyes. John was used to seeing that.

Used, too, to the way most drew back after a closer look.

One of the men spit tobacco over the side of his horse and mumbled, "Damn contrabands. How many does this make today?"

The officer pointed back along the road. "Left-hand fork," he said, in a curious yapping voice: *fork* sounded almost like *fahk*. "When you cross Rock Creek, follow the road till you come to the fort: Ask anyone you meet for Fort Barker. You contrabands? Runaways?"

"No, sir," began John quickly, with a story he'd used before about searching for a lost master, but his mother shook off the hand he'd put on her arm and shrilled,

"Yes, sir! We have run away, run away to freedom!" She swept her arms wide about her, like a raven-haired goddess of the woods.

John flinched—he had no idea what instructions Northern soldiers might have received about runaway slaves—but the officer only shook his head with an air of annoyance. John drew his mother as gently—and as firmly—as he dared along the road in the direction the man had pointed, and said, "Thank you, sir."

The rider in the back ranks spit again. "Damn contrabands." The riders went on.

"Why you pullin' me away?" The sharpness of the slap that accompanied the words was less worrisome to John than that hard crazy glitter in Phoebe's eyes. Looking for an argument. Hungering for someone to shout at, the way Mr. Henry's brother Clive would hunger for liquor. "You shouldn't be treatin' your mother like that, when you coming into the Promised Land."

They smelled Washington City miles before they reached it. Richmond had smelled like that, when they'd circled past it cautiously in the night, and the camps around Manassas railway junction: the reek of thousands of latrine trenches, of countless corrals of horses, cattle, Army mules.

Washington City was a thousand times worse. As they crossed the Rock Creek bridge the first of the Army camps lay jumbled and dirty to the right of the road, row after row after *row* of little round white tents like dirty mushrooms straggling down the brushy hillside. Men in blue uniforms slopped around in mud up to their booted ankles, amid goods-boxes and ambulance-wagons and iron pots slung over campfires. Smoke gritted in the throat. Beyond the camps—and they seemed endless—John saw houses and trees, and farther off a big domed building three-quarters built against the hazy noon sky.

"So this the Promise Land, hunh?" muttered Cassy, though she was careful not to let her mother hear. She was twelve, thin and fine-boned like John, and like John (he reflected gloomily) too smart for her own good. "Don't look so promisin' to me." On the other side of the road, in weedy fields among thin stands of bright-leaved yellow poplar, lay other camps, smaller and dirtier and less organized than those of the soldiers. Through the open sides of some tents John glimpsed makeshift barrooms, planks laid over barrels and card-games going at crude tables. In other places slatternly women loitered, or lines of laundry hung to dry.

Camp Barker, when they reached it at last, turned out to be like these lesser, unofficial establishments, a vast, messy agglomeration of shanties and rude tents—some no more than blankets stretched over ropes—clustered around the packed earth embankments that in their turn surrounded half a dozen wood buildings. The snubby brown snouts of cannon protruded over the earthen walls and the weedy, trash-littered ground stank of garbage and piss.

There seemed to be no order anywhere. Men crouched over smoldering fires among the ragged willows, arguing in the desultory fashion of those who have little else to do. In a rough board shelter a young woman was suckling a baby.

"This here Camp Barker?" asked John, and she nodded.

"They done give out the food this mornin' already, though," she added. Her dress was ragged, the faded calico stained by tobacco leaves, like every garment John had ever owned. He guessed she'd been a field hand, like his mother. "It was just soup, and they was so many, most people didn't even get none of that." She wasn't much older than he, but her eyes were like a tired crone's. Beaten, like those of someone who has come a long hard journey for nothing.

"So what do we do?" John forced cheer into his voice against a dread he could not name. "Where do we go?"

The girl shrugged. "You here."

"And what you all sittin' around here for?" His mother shoved past him, jabbed a knotted finger at the young woman. "You folks all lazy or somethin'? This here Washington City! This here the Promise Land! Land of milk and honey! You free, and you just sittin' here on your lazy ass?"

The young woman stared at Phoebe in shock, as well she might, reflected John, catching his mother by the arm. "Mama . . ."

She jerked free of his grip. "Don't you *Mama* me! And don't you grab on to me like I was a child!" Her voice pitched high as she rounded on the woman with the baby. "It stink around here! This here the Promise Land, and all you can do is sit out here makin' it stink! We come a thousand miles through the night and through the storm, an' for what? To see a bunch of shiftless folks settin' in the woods . . ."

People were gathering and John and Cassy tried to pull their mother away. "You turn my own children against me! You gonna call the pate-rollers on us? You gonna send us back?" Phoebe's voice rose to a scream as she fought them. She seemed to get these spells of quick fury more frequently when she was hungry, or worried, or tired. God knew they were all three. Sometimes it seemed to John that his entire life wrapped around his mother's moods like a vine on a stake.

Two or three other runaways came over to them, but backed off when his mother lunged at them, bending to snatch up handfuls of mud, her black Medusa hair tumbling around her shoulders. "Where we get food around here, hunh? This here the Promise Land, they gotta give us food!" Isaac, clinging to Lucy's hand, began to cry.

John and Cassy walked their mother to the outskirts of the camp. In back of the fort near the stink of the sheep-pens, they settled her under a sycamore tree. John talked her quiet, then left her with Cassy and walked down the main road into town. "There got to be some way we can get food," he reasoned. "Cuttin' kindling or cleaning some white folks' yard, somethin' they'll just give me a little food for." He felt light-headed with hunger and too tired to go far, but he knew once their mother got an idea in her head, she'd harp and harp at him until he did what she demanded. It was easier to just do it at once.

He didn't think they could get sent back to Halifax County, anyway, and the soldiers hadn't seemed in any tearing hurry to turn them over to Maryland slaveholders.

But after he passed through the muddy Army camps along the road, and came into Washington City itself, he discovered that he wasn't the first contraband to come looking for food or a little work to get food, not by a good long way.

"We fixed here just fine," said a man curtly—a slave, John thought, or a servant, anyway—who was cleaning gardening tools in the shed of the first yard he asked at.

"There anyplace you know where I could do work for some food?"

The man grunted. The big yellow house, set among shady oak-trees, was a nice one, like the houses in Richmond, though the street in front of it was like a hog-wallow. "I get four–five niggers a day askin' for food, or work if they honest. Ain't the Army take care of you?"

John shook his head, reflecting that it didn't sound like the Army was taking care of those "four–five niggers" a day either.

"Well, we can't take care of you, neither," the man snapped. He jerked his head back toward the house again. "With all the Army in town food costs somethin' scandalous. My missus say we can't be handin' out no food to them that comes beggin'."

"I ain't beggin' for food." John prickled with anger, but kept his voice even. "I'm askin' for work."

"An' I'm tellin' you we don't got food nor work. An' I'm wore out with people like you comin' up all the time when the Army's supposed to be takin' care of you. Now get along."

In the alley again John stood still for a moment, his heart beating so hard he could feel it in his ears. He knew his mother's ideas of the

Promised Land of Freedom might be exaggerated—a lot of her ideas were—but it had never occurred to him that when they got there, there might not be enough milk and honey to go around.

Or that those who had it wouldn't want to share.

By sunset he'd been turned away from dozens of big white houses along those astonishingly wide streets and any number of the humbler two-room cottages of the free colored in the alleys. Sometimes roughly, sometimes politely, or with sympathy and pity, and admonitions to "let the Army take care of you"—presumably with the small amount of soup the woman at the camp had spoken of. Two or three housewives gave him food—heel-ends of bread and table-scraps—but it wasn't enough to satisfy one person, let alone five. The autumn afternoon had turned chilly, with a nip to the wind. Harsh cookfire smoke mingled with the ever-present stench of the Army camps that lay everywhere over the city, and as he trudged the wide sloppy street back to where he hoped the fort and Camp Barker lay, he felt a stab of longing for the simplicity of life on the run.

After weeks in the variegated stillness of the woods, he found the constant rumbling passage of wagons and ambulances confusing, almost painful. Raised on a rural plantation where he saw no one but the same hundred and fifty people he'd known all his life, he felt as if time had somehow speeded up. There were people everywhere, strangers walking and riding and driving buggies and carriages that he had to watch out for, stray dogs snapping at him, walls and fences like a dizzying dirty labyrinth. Too much movement, too many new things coming at him too fast. The stink of the town was awful, the noise a disorienting clamor in his ears.

He'd been hungry and frightened, all those nights and weeks up from Halifax County. But he was hungry here and—though he didn't like to admit it to himself—frightened too, in a different fashion that he couldn't describe. In the woods at least there was peace.

He was concentrating so hard on remembering all the turns and streets he'd taken that he didn't even notice the little group of young white men until they crossed the street to surround him.

They were dressed roughly, wool trousers and coarse calico shirts powdered all over with dust. They wore thick boots and slouch hats and two of them carried whips, the long blacksnake kind that teamsters used. When two of them pointed at him he hastily sprang off the footpath into the ditch—they were in a street of rough little houses not too far from the camps on the edge of town, small unpaved streets darting with half-naked white children who screamed in a language John had never heard.

But the stockiest of the young men moved to block his way: "What you doin' hereabouts, then, boy-o?" He shoved John hard on the shoulder, so that he staggered and almost fell.

"I'm lookin' for work, sir." John lowered his eyes, his heart pounding. He'd had to do with few enough white men in his short life and they always scared him, for they had power and a cruel need to prove their power to anyone around them.

"You a runaway, then, boy-o?" The white youth wasn't much older than John, nor were any of his friends, but he was squat and stocky, with hair the color of a fox and tawny eyes that seemed yellow against the mask of dust. His body stank of sweat and his breath of liquor.

"No, sir. My ol' Miss, she died, an'—"

Without change of expression the young man slashed him across the face with the rolled-up whip. "Don't you be lyin' to me, boy."

John staggered back, and one of the others must have come around behind him and tripped him. His memories weren't clear after that. A boot cracked into his ribs and another into the soft meat below them, and he curled himself together, clenched his thighs to protect his balls and wrapped his arms around his head. He heard someone shout something about going back to where he came from. Weeks later he remembered seeing a Union soldier stroll over across the street to them with his rifle, but he never did remember the actual blow that knocked him cold.

"Are you all right, young man?" A small, gentle hand brushed his forehead. A white lady's voice, with the honeyed inflection of the South.

Even before he opened his eyes the midday light went through his skull like an ax.

He mumbled, "I'm fine, ma'am," out of the sheer habit of never admitting to a white that there was a problem—you never knew what they'd choose to do about it. But when he opened his eyes the pain in his skull cleft him down to his belly, and he rolled over fast, feeling bile flood up his throat, drowning him.

He tried to roll away; the movement only made it worse. Vomit exploded from his lips like the seeds from a squished tomato. The woman was sitting on the ground beside him with her black skirts spread around her and she got a lapful—*How the hell can I throw up so much when I ain't eaten anything?*

Then he was heaving helplessly, conscious of nothing except those small hands holding him steady, agony in his ribs with every spasm, and the smell of vomit that seemed to fill the world.

He sank back to the rough blanket spread on the ground, whispering frantically, "I'm sorry, ma'am, I'm so sorry—I didn't mean it. . . ." Mr. Henry at Blue Hill had beaten a servant for passing wind while waiting at table. John knew perfectly well that white ladies—particularly Southern ladies—did not appreciate niggers vomiting on their skirts.

"Good heavens, don't be silly," she said briskly. Beneath the overwhelming halitus of the vomit he smelled the musk-rose sachet in her clothing as she leaned around him with a wet kerchief, and wiped his mouth and chin.

He opened his eyes, and met her worried gaze, the most beautiful shade of green-touched blue he'd ever seen, like the heart of a flower.

And genuinely concerned that he was all right.

He looked away at once—Mr. Henry would box a pickaninny's ears for being "uppity," i.e., looking a white in the face—but this woman only went on briskly, "If anyone owes me an apology it's the louts who did this to you. Lizabet . . . thank you."

She held out a tin cup of water to him and in taking it he immediately upset it all over her tightly corseted bosom. She rocked back but caught the cup deftly—"Oh, dear, you *did* take a bad hit, didn't you?"—and put a steadying hand on his shoulder. "Do you want to lie down again?"

"No, ma'am. Thank you, ma'am." He glanced shyly up again at her face, her tone of matter-of-fact friendliness sponging away his fear and his shame. He saw a square, motherly face with a short nose and a determined chin, older than her girlish voice would lead you to think—his mother's age at least and probably more. The flesh around those beautiful eyes was discolored with sleeplessness, netted with fine lines of grief and pain, and he saw she wore the black of deepest mourning.

"I'm all right now, ma'am."

A woman leaned down behind her with another cup of water.

"Thank you, Lizabet. Shall we try this again?" And she gave John an encouraging smile as he took the second cup.

They were under the shelter of an Army marquee. John could see the sloped weedy wall of the fort nearby, yellowing in the autumn heat. It was nearly midday. It had been growing dark when he had been jumped. Lizabet, who had handed down the second cup, was a tall creamy-dark mulatto woman. In Virginia, John would have guessed her to be a housekeeper or uppermost lady's maid, but she was too elegantly dressed in clothes that obviously weren't her dumpling-shaped friend's cast-offs. In a lovely low alto Lizabet said, "He was brought in last night, beaten up by some Irish teamsters, and at least one soldier." She handed her white friend a damp towel to wipe her skirts.

John didn't remember the soldier, but he touched gingerly the pounding nexus of pain on the left side of his forehead and felt a bandage there. His face felt puffy as a blown-up bladder; his ribs and belly ached from blows.

"Even before the fighting brought refugees into town, the Irish seemed to think every black man a personal threat to their livelihood," Lizabet added in a voice like cold bitter coffee.

The white woman turned back to John, shocked. "Is what Mrs. Keckley says true?"

"Yes, ma'am," said John, sitting up—cautiously—and sipping the water. "But I wasn't askin' for a job drivin' no team, I swear. Just cuttin' wood or somethin' so's I could get a little food." His hands shook so badly he spilled the water he held, and his left eye was swollen almost shut. His clothes stank of the ditch where he'd been knocked down. "I didn't start nuthin'."

The marquee around them seemed to be jammed with people, with more pressing in around its open sides. Three or four women at the other end of the big shelter dipped flour and cornmeal and cups of beans from sacks on a rough table before them. They, like the elegant Lizabet Keckley, were people of color, mostly lighter-skinned than the runaways—the contrabands, the soldiers had called them—who shoved each other to get near them, holding out dishes and gourds and empty sacks to receive the food.

"Well, I should hope not," said the white lady briskly. "If you *had* started something with a gang of Irish teamsters and an armed soldier I should be obliged to question your sanity. It's a complete disgrace, Lizabet. Something must be done about it! I'm sure this boy... What's your name, son?"

"John," he said. "John Wilamet."

"And I am Mrs. Lincoln," she told him, holding out a small gloved hand to shake. "I'm sure John here could do as good a job driving horses as any of those Irish louts." She scrubbed at her fouled skirt with the matter-of-fact touch that made John guess that she'd nursed the sick before—and in spite of the stylish cut of her mourning dress, that she'd washed clothes, too. "Do you have family here, John?"

"Yes, ma'am—Mrs. Lincoln." At least the name was easy to remember, for it was the same one as the Union President whose election Mr. Henry had gotten so worked up about last year. John wondered if she was any relation, though he couldn't imagine how she could be. She was very much a Southern lady. She would have been much more at home among the friends of Mr. Henry's wife Miss Daphne, he thought, than in this Northern place looking after him. "My mama, and the girls an' Isaac. They'll be worried about me. I left 'em yesterday afternoon, under a tree out by the sheep-pens. . . ."

"You rest for a few minutes more, then, dear, and let me know when you're feeling well enough to get up. I'll see you back there. I'm sure your dear mother—oh!" Her head snapped sharply around at the sound of rising voices from the food-tables.

A man—a contraband—was thrusting his gourd back at one of the serving women, shaking it about angrily, demanding more. At the sight of this, Mrs. Lincoln's eyes flared with abrupt fury. "Oh, this is ridiculous! I've told them about keeping order here!"

She got to her feet with surprising speed for a lady of her girth and swept in the direction of the tables, hoops and drapes and ribbons all flouncing like a peony in a tempest. "I *told* that Mrs. Durham that it was no good handing things out piecemeal like this, not that anyone ever listens to *me*...."

John sat up, watching in a kind of horrified fascination, as his stout little friend thrust her way into the middle of the altercation between contraband and server. The nearly instantaneous change in her, from worried kindliness to hot rage, was so total as to be shocking.

Another woman of color, neatly clothed in blue-and-white calico, had already come over to speak to the angry contraband, but Mrs. Lincoln pushed between them. "Stop that at once! You should be grateful you're getting anything at all, rather than demanding more!" When the woman in blue—presumably Mrs. Durham—spoke quietly to her, Mrs. Lincoln whirled upon her.

"Let *you* handle it? I've let you handle the whole of this distribution, and to what end? Nothing organized properly, people shoving in any old how..." She positively spit the words, her small black-gloved hands balled into fists. "If you'd done as I suggested and worked through the Army, I daresay in time I could have gotten men in my husband's Cabinet to improve the allotment. I know men in Congress, and I daresay I'm not without *some* influence, in spite of what people like you seem to think. But instead we have only this piddling tent, and people thrusting in as if they owned the whole concern...."

"The only one who's acting as if she owned the whole concern," retorted Mrs. Durham, her voice arctic, "is *you,* Mrs. Lincoln."

"How *dare* you!" Mrs. Lincoln's face went from blotchy red to a furious pallor. "*Mrs.* Durham—if that *is* your name, and I daresay I've often wondered why there isn't a *Mr.* Durham anywhere in sight..."

By this time John was on his feet and almost to her side, heedless of the pain jabbing his ribs. He acted without thinking, recognizing with deadly accuracy in her voice, in her stance, in the narrow blazing focus of her eyes, the echo of his own mother's flash-fire rages. Mrs. Keckley was right beside him, reaching out to touch Mrs. Lincoln's swagged black sleeve before the outraged Mrs. Durham could collect her breath to respond.

"Mrs. Lincoln," Lizabet said, and John put in,

"Mrs. Lincoln, 'scuse me, ma'am, but I feel well enough if you'd take me on back to my family now."

Her blind momentum broken, Mrs. Lincoln stopped, gasping, seemingly dazed by the onslaught of her own emotions. Mrs. Keckley flashed John a grateful look and put in gently, "Come, Mrs. Lincoln, we must help this young man."

For a moment it was touch and go whether she'd respond—whether she'd even heard them—for she was trembling with anger. But she blinked, and looked again at John's ashy face, and the hot wrath in her eyes changed to concern.

"Of course," she said, her voice uncertain. "Of course, poor boy..."

As if it were the most natural thing in the world—as if she were one of his own aunties back at Blue Hill instead of a white lady in an expensive dress—she took his arm and put it around her shoulder to take some of his weight. Exhausted, discouraged, and hungry—and sick with the sense of having once more failed to meet his mother's expectations—John could have wept at her kindness.

As they made their way through the crowded tents and makeshift shelters of the contraband camp, Mrs. Lincoln alternated between watchful concern for John and leftover fulminations concerning Mrs. Durham: "The *impudence* of the woman! Who does she think she is?"

Lizabet nodded and made gentle noises that neither agreed nor disagreed, from which John deduced that Mrs. Keckley was also used to this abrupt transformation from lady to Gorgon and back. And whatever the right and the wrong of the matter was, Mrs. Keckley clearly valued her volatile friend too much to sever the relationship.

"Obviously she regards herself as cleverer than a mere *smatterer* like myself, who has *only* been around men organizing major military and political campaigns. I—" Mrs. Lincoln broke off, pressed her hand to the bridge of her nose. When she took it away her eyes had lost their glitter, and seemed to see him again. "Are you quite sure you can walk, John? You look dreadful."

John felt dreadful, struggling to stay on his feet. But what he felt mostly was deep gratitude for her care and friendship at what was probably the nadir of his short life, coupled with awed fascination. Later, looking back on the incident, he was never sure what shook him up more:

that this snub-nosed, haunted-eyed Southern belle, who could show such kindness one moment and such termagant fury the next, was in fact the wife of the notorious President Lincoln—

—or that she was quite clearly as crazy as his mother.

JOHN SAW MRS. LINCOLN MANY TIMES DURING THAT BITTER COLD winter of 1862.

She often came to the contraband camp with Elizabeth Keckley—who, Cassy told him a few days after their first encounter, was her dressmaker and one of the most prominent free colored residents of Washington City. Mrs. Keckley had helped found the Freedmen's Relief Association, and had enlisted her friend and employer to help her distribute food and blankets, to find homes for the runaways who continued to flood into Washington City, and jobs they could work at to earn their keep.

John quickly became a sort of page for Mrs. Lincoln when she came. He ran her errands, or helped her unload the bundles of blankets and clothing that she would collect from the wives of Senators, Cabinet members, and officers. Long experience in dealing with his own mother had given John the knack of letting her quick, spit-cat angers slide off his back; had taught him how to talk her out of her rages when it seemed that she did not know or care what words came out of her mouth.

"I really don't know what gets into me," she said, upon one occasion when she returned to the camp a few days after an outburst directed at the commander of Fort Barker that had finished with her departing in tears. "I hear myself saying these *terrible* things, see myself . . . it's almost like watching someone else." She made a quick gesture as if pushing the memory away. "*So* mortifying . . ."

Mrs. Keckley put a hand on her shoulder as if to say that she understood. But in fact John guessed that the quiet-voiced, supremely reasonable seamstress didn't understand, any more than he understood why his mother would rant and shriek at total strangers—or, worse, at people who could do her harm if annoyed. They were standing beside Mrs. Lincoln's carriage, a handsome open barouche, in which Mrs. Lincoln had brought clothing collected for the camp children: John guessed that without the necessity of delivering these, she wouldn't have come at all.

"But the Commander really was at fault," Mrs. Lincoln declared, rallying. "He had *no* call to speak to me as he did and *certainly* no call to question my judgment about shelter for the contrabands. He just wants to save himself trouble. If he could find a way not to provide shelter for his *own* soldiers here he'd prefer that, too. *Or* food . . . 'Surely the men could just go into town for their suppers.' " She aped the Commander's pinched Maine accent with such devastating accuracy that both John and Mrs. Keckley dissolved into laughter.

Later in the winter, when John's little brother, Isaac, fell ill with fever, Mrs. Lincoln helped care for him in the rude shack on M Street that the family occupied. She brought him meat and milk unobtainable in the camp, and when Isaac died, she wept so bitterly that Cassy had to lead her outside, for her stricken wailings only fanned their mother's howling grief.

Later, Lizabet Keckley told John this was because Mrs. Lincoln had only recently lost her own son—and indeed, John noticed, when he next saw Mrs. Lincoln at a troop review with the tall, gawky President, that her husband, too, wore the black of deepest grief.

In the spring the armies began to move. Mrs. Lincoln found John a job with an Army surgeon in General Ord's corps. By that time his family was living with a free colored family named Gordon, in a tiny cottage not far from the unfinished Capitol Building: the Gordons had taken in five other contrabands already and the house was bursting at the seams.

At sixteen, John was small and wiry, but working for Dr. Brainert was less physically taxing than picking tobacco leaves for seventeen hours a day. He and the sturdy, red-faced surgeon got along well.

John still had blinding headaches, especially in cold weather, and the cut he'd taken from the rifle-butt had healed to a curved scar that pulled one eyebrow to a peak and turned his thin, clerkish face oddly ferocious.

He was in Richmond two years later, when President Lincoln came by steamboat to view the captured Southern capital.

Never, in after years, did John forget the host of men, women, children, former slaves—wearing the ragged garments that were all their masters could afford to give them in these days of privation and defeat—pressing up around the President's horse as he rode with his Generals through the rubble of bricks, the soot-black broken walls. Women held up their babies for Lincoln to touch, as if he were a god in one of the books John had begun so voraciously to read. Men struggled through the crush to grasp his boots in the stirrups.

Everything seemed vividly clear to John that day, for he'd recently gotten his first pair of spectacles from the Army, and was still dazzled at being able to distinguish leaves on trees, the letters in his books, the faces of people at a distance with such magical, crystalline brightness. He had glimpsed Mr. Lincoln often at Headquarters—a gangly, almost comical figure, cracking his knuckles as he slouched in a camp-chair with his feet on the table, telling funny stories in that high husky scratchy voice. But today that tall man looked grave and a little shaken, as if shocked by light streaming in from the opened doors of the future, light that only he could see. He had made all these people free, John thought, watching the tall black figure over the heads of the crowd. Had given them not only the rights, but the terrible burdens of the free. That responsibility would rest on his bony shoulders forever.

Ten days later he was dead.

In Richmond John had hoped to renew his acquaintance with Mrs. Lincoln, for he'd heard she was coming with the President. But she quarreled publicly and hysterically with the wives of General Grant and General Ord, and went back to Washington, prostrate with dudgeon and migraine. When she returned a few days later to tour the captured city John was at one of the Army hospitals, puzzling over the case of a Massachusetts soldier who'd been brought in after the fighting at Petersburg, unwounded but paralyzed and unable to speak.

Thus he had had only a glimpse of Mary Todd Lincoln one evening as he passed the steamboat *River Queen* at its dock: saw her stubby black form beside the stooped, beanpole outline of her husband, silhouetted against the lucid sky. He saw her reach out her hand for his, apologizing maybe for the scene she'd made the week before. He watched Lincoln take off his tall hat and bend—a long way down—to kiss her.

Like Lizabet Keckley, thought John, Mr. Lincoln—he'd learned right off never to call him "Abe" or "Old Abe," names he apparently hated—valued his volatile bride too much to hold her outburst against her. In their touch, in their kiss, it was clear to the young man that they were old friends and partners, who'd come a long, hard road together. And because he was very fond of Mary Lincoln himself, John felt glad that she had at least that faithful lover, those faithful friends.

That far-off image, almost like a picture in a book, was the last John saw of her, until ten years later when he was locking her into a cell.

Chapter One

Chicago May 19, 1875

She was surrounded by enemies.

For the dozenth time Mary Lincoln glanced sharply behind her, heart hammering in her throat with both panic and rage.

Nothing. Bowler-hatted businessmen in natty suits bought newspapers from scruffy boys, barefoot in the spring heat. Tight-corseted women, the ruffled swags that trailed from their bustles sweeping the dirty sidewalk, paused by the windows of shops to admire and chat. Immigrant vendors in grubby corduroy yelled their wares from pushcarts—apples, kerchiefs, mousetraps, toys. A cab darted by along Clark Street, hooves clattering, iron tires banging, as it dodged around trolleys, carriages, drays of barreled beer.

Downtown Chicago on a spring morning. Heat swimming up from the sidewalk bricks; the stink of horse-droppings.

She knew she was being followed. For weeks now she'd been certain of it.

Who? she wondered. *Why?*

And quickened her step. The fear that had shadowed her all her fifty-seven years breathed again at her shoulder. Her feet were swollen in her tight black kid shoes and the snip of breeze that whispered from Lake Michigan died away, leaving her sweating beneath the thick black veils. Why didn't people get out of her way? She dodged past a dawdling woman by a shop window. *Can't they see I'm a widow? I'm entitled to consideration on that score, aren't I? Even if they don't know whose widow I am.*

Thinking about him, even after all these years, made her throat constrict with the grief that had never eased.

She had to get home.

She gazed longingly after another cab that rattled by—they all drove like lunatics in this town! There was money in her purse, and even more hidden in secret pockets of her petticoats, in case of emergencies. But cabs were so expensive. She'd spent enough that morning as it was. Nine pairs of lace curtains at Gossage's, so beautiful! *But I really will have to save after this.*

So no cabs.

And the crowds on the trolleys filled her with nameless but familiar dread.

Why were people following her?

Why that elusive half-familiar glimpse of bulk and movement that she'd seen again and again during the past eight weeks?

Newspapermen? Those vile vampires who'd dogged her every step, twisted her every word . . . called her Confederate spy and worse?

Or was someone plotting to kill her as they'd killed her husband?

Or was it all something she imagined?

She pushed that troubling suspicion away.

Movement in the corner of her vision—were things starting to appear and disappear again? *Not another migraine,* she thought in weary despair. *I had one only yesterday, or was it the day before?* Was the blazing shimmer that came and went only the reflection of the noon sun on the windows of the high buildings? Or the herald of yet another bout of nausea, blindness, pain?

Anxiety swamped the worry about being followed in a greater wave of panic. *I have to get home!* In her room she'd be safe. She could take her medicine before those kinked burning lines started to creep across her vision, before sick disorientation overtook her. The room would be hot and unbearably stuffy—mentally she calculated the cost of even the most modest chamber in the Grand Pacific Hotel against what her husband had left her, against the pension she had finally pried out of those tight-fisted ungrateful liars in Congress. But at least there she would be safe.

She could barely remember a time when she had not felt herself in danger.

A pack of ragamuffin boys flurried past her, like blown leaves among the crowd. Their treble laughter brought back the laughter of her own sons and the stab of grief was as piercing as if they had each died yesterday. Eddie scarcely more than a baby, crying with fever as he clung to her hand. Sweet-faced, sweet-natured Willie, gentle and always so worried about her, bringing her flowers from the weedy lots behind the Capitol. And Tad, flighty and willful, growing daily more like his father...

She squeezed her mind shut against Mr. Lincoln's image. She'd never thought of him as anything but Mr. Lincoln—or Father, when they were alone. His shadow rose behind the shadows of her sons: the looming gawky height, as if his body had been put together from a bundle of slats, the deft lightness of his touch. His hands had been huge, nearly twice the length of hers when they'd press them palm to palm and laugh....

After his death she'd given away everything he'd possessed, lest the sight of even his reading-glasses in a drawer surprise her with heart-crushing pain. In the ten years since then she'd visited hundreds of mediums, speakers with and summoners of the dead, begging for only a glimpse of him. Desperate to hear his voice again, to hear him call her "Mother," and see his smile.

Father, she thought, *how could you have left me in this awful place alone?*

The Grand Pacific Hotel loomed before her, story after story of stone and glaring glass. Only ten years, she thought wonderingly, since Washington's muddy unpaved streets, since the tumult of soldiers tramping by in the sticky night. Ten years since she'd heard the thunder of enemy guns beyond the river. Chicago with its macadam-paved streets, with its trolley cars and bustles and advertising posters and its thousands and thousands of immigrants, seemed like another world, as if she had somehow missed her way coming back from Europe in '71 and fetched up in some bewildering alien land.

Her anxiety lessened somewhat as she climbed the Grand Pacific's marble steps and crossed the lobby's acres of red plush carpet like a determined black bug scuttling for the baseboard. Almost home. Almost safe.

The Grand Pacific was expensive, with its French chef and its conservatory garden. But Abraham Lincoln's widow couldn't be seen to live in common lodgings. That much she owed his memory. And boarding-houses had always been abominations to her.

Mr. Turner, the manager, was understanding and kind. When she'd wake in terror in the night, he'd provide a reliable chambermaid to stay in her room with her at only a very modest charge. He was reassuring and helpful, if occasionally maddeningly stupid, during those spells when voices seemed to be speaking to her out of the walls and floor, when during her migraines she could see the spirit of an Indian warrior pulling the bones out of her face; when she'd wake in panic and terror, thinking she smelled smoke—when she'd see the city in flames, the wall of fire approaching....

Mary shook her head at herself as she climbed the stairs. The Grand

Pacific was equipped with modern elevators but she'd never trusted such things. The reminder of her spells of confusion made her headache worse. Maybe it was all only her imagination. Though she only cloudily recalled what she did and said in her spells, it did seem to her they mostly came on her in the afternoons. All she had to do, really, was be a little careful about staying inside.

She pushed the thought out of her mind. Her heart was thudding and her feet, her back, her head were in agony. Her medicine would make her feel better.

And sometimes during her spells—especially at night—one or another of her sons would come to her, beautiful shining figures, smiling and holding out their hands in comfort.

Only Robert was left, of the four beautiful boys she had borne.

Mary paused on the stairs to get her breath, to rest the searing ache in her back. She supposed her shoes were not really made for walking long distances in, but she would *not* be like those absurd suffragist women who went around in Bloomer costumes and ugly boots. Her friend Myra had often expounded on "rational" dress. *That really would give Robert a seizure,* she thought, and smiled a little despite her discomfort at the recollection of her chronically disapproving eldest son. *He thinks I'm eccentric enough without that.*

Poor Robert. As she resumed her climb she wondered whether he suffered from an overdeveloped sense of his own importance, or merely a complete lack of imagination. *Probably both,* she thought. *Such a stuffy man, even before he married that horrid girl . . .*

Yet her heart ached with love for him, and for her granddaughter . . . Mr. Lincoln's granddaughter. Beautiful little Mamie. The terrible dream she'd had in Florida two months ago, the dream of Robert lying ill, dying just as Tad and Eddie and Willie had died, had brought her flying back here, desperate to save him, to push that terrible shadow away if she could. Desperate that he not leave her, as all the others had left her . . .

Mary paid a quick, grateful visit to the ladies' lavatory on the way down the hall. Hot weather always brought back the burning itches that had tormented her since Tad's birth, over two decades ago. Then at last, with a sense of having safely negotiated an unknown battlefield yet again, she unlocked her own room.

It was small, and, as she'd feared, already appallingly stuffy. Since Tad's death she'd found daylight almost too harsh to stand, but even the single gas jet burning in the heavily curtained room added to the already intolerable summer heat. She'd insisted on the least expensive room available in the hotel—really, her money disappeared so quickly!—but for that reason it was already too crowded for comfort. In addition to the eleven trunks she'd brought back from Florida with her—such a beautiful place, and the doctors there most sympathetic and helpful—she'd done a good deal of shopping in these past weeks. Mostly to pass the time, to get herself out—really, what else was there for a woman to do?—but there was no telling when she might get a house of her own, a home of her own, again.

Her plump hands shook as she put aside the packages from yesterday's shopping expedition (an album of poetry and twelve yards of exquisite jade-green satin, and shoes to match) and opened the cupboard, barely to be reached behind the trunks. She was definitely getting a migraine, and she could scarcely see the bottles as she took them out. Not that it mattered which was which. *They're all the same, really. And Dr. Somers in Florida said they're all beneficial.* Godfrey's Cordial, Ma-Sol-Pa Herbal Indian Balm, Dr. Foote's Sanitary Medical Tonic, Nervine, Hunt's Female Revivifier...

She poured them all in a tumbler and drained it, savoring the musky intensity, the burning comforting warmth that rose through her. She'd begin to feel better in a few moments....

A knock sounded on the door.

The delivery boy from Gossage's. That was quick. But it wasn't the delivery boy who stood in the hall when she opened the door. For a flashing, confusing moment, between the uncertain light of the curtained chamber and her own slightly blurred eyesight, Mary thought it was her husband.

Mr. Lincoln...

Was it, impossibly, him? As the others had appeared to her, had he finally come?

She blinked, then said uncertainly, "Mr. Swett?"

"Mrs. Lincoln." Leonard Swett took off his hat. It was the high silk hat of a professional that had deceived her migraine-dazzled eyes by adding to his six-foot height. Swett's face was lean, and he wore the same kind of beard that Mr. Lincoln had during the last few years of his life, a jawline Quaker beard without a mustache. Memories flared through her mind, of Swett and his wife, Laura—before Laura's incapacitating illness—coming to dinner at that little cottage on Eighth Street in Springfield. Of Swett laughing with Mr. Lincoln over this lawsuit or that, like boys who've trounced each other behind the schoolhouse, then dusted themselves off and shaken hands.

What was Mr. Swett doing here at her room? Why hadn't he sent up a card? *Had* he sent up a card, and she just didn't remember? No, of course not, she'd just gotten here herself....

"I do apologize." Mary spread her lace-mitted hands across the sable crape of her skirts and wondered how quickly she could get rid of him. She was exhausted, her head was throbbing, and, having taken her medicine, she wanted only to lie down.

Why hadn't he sent up a card and asked her to meet him in the lobby? A gentleman *never* came up to a lady's room.

But it was a basic tenet of Southern womanhood that a lady always gives a gentleman the benefit of the doubt. So instead of asking tartly if he'd been born in a barn, Mary explained, "I've just come in, and have not had time to change. What might I do for you?" She saw now that the boy from Gossage's *was* there, waiting in the hallway gloom, with two men in uniforms she did not recognize. Big men. A problem about the curtains? Probably the fault of that stupid clerk...

"I regret exceedingly that it is I who must perform this office, Mrs. Lincoln." Swett drew a folded sheet of paper from his coat. He held it out to her in his neatly gloved hand. "This is a writ of arrest from the State of Illinois. You are being charged with lunacy."

If he'd slapped her face she could not have been more surprised. In that first instant she wasn't even taken aback, merely confused, wondering if this were a dream. One of those weird visions, like the Indian spirit who tortured her during her migraines, or the voices that spoke to her out of the walls. Goodness knew she felt unreal enough, as if she'd put her foot down what she'd thought was a step in a familiar staircase, only to find no footing there.

But in Swett's pale eyes she saw that expression with which she was so familiar from a lifetime around lawyers and politicians. That gauging look, waiting for a reaction as a hunter waits for a turkey to step out from behind a bush.

"Lunacy?" Mary thrust her hands behind her. Time and time again she'd heard Mr. Lincoln say to clients, *Whatever you do, don't take any paper they try to hand you.*

Swett was still talking.

"...courtroom today—this afternoon, in fact—" He took out his watch, as if to emphasize to her how valuable everybody's time was. "—to defend yourself at a hearing..."

"What hearing?" She blinked at him, feeling nonplussed in the most literal sense of the word: at a point from which one cannot go on. He couldn't really be charging her with lunacy. She had to be mistaken about that. She was Abraham Lincoln's wife! "How can it be this afternoon? I need a lawyer...."

"A lawyer has already been arranged for you, Mrs. Lincoln."

"By whom?" Her voice sounded astoundingly calm in her own ears. She remembered all those times back in Springfield, when people would come to Lincoln's office asking for help. You could get a lawyer in a day, but seldom in an hour.

Robert, she thought. *Robert will know how to get me a lawyer. He's a lawyer himself. He'll probably defend me; that way I won't have to spend any money.* Her mind was working slowly, clogged with a dreamlike confusion. It was hard not to simply stare at the pattern of Mr. Swett's silver silk waistcoat. She must keep her mind focused.

Then Swett's next words hit her like a spear in the chest. "By your son Robert, Mrs. Lincoln. Now please." He held out the writ to her and she fell back another step, still refusing to touch it. Refusing to believe.

"Robert knows?" Her mouth felt like someone else's mouth as she said the words. *Robert knows,* her mind repeated, like a litany that was crucially important for reasons she couldn't recall. *Robert knows. How could Robert know, unless . . . ?*

A portion of Swett's vulpine face disappeared behind a fragment of migraine fire. His beard waggled, temporarily with nothing above it. "Now, Mrs. Lincoln, please. Surely you yourself must admit that much of your behavior is not that of a sane woman."

"I 'must admit' nothing of the kind!" Her mind snapped clear and fury bloomed in her, the blind rage that had all her life lain just beneath the surface, taking her breath away. In a staggering vision of lucid clarity she saw that all her fears had always been true, all her suspicions, all her wariness of betrayal. . . . She heard her own voice rise to a scream of hatred for them all. "How *dare* you speak to me this way? It's Robert who put you up to this, isn't it? It's Robert who thinks I'm insane, isn't it? He always has! Because I won't put up with that cold little sourpuss he married! Because I want to travel and see the world! Because he wants my money—"

"Mrs. Lincoln, please!"

"Because I see more of the world of the spirits than he does, and he believes that only *his* view of our world can be right!"

"Mrs. Lincoln," said Swett patiently, "all of this can be discussed at the courthouse. That's what a hearing is for. Your son has consulted doctors, and the doctors believe you to be insane."

"What *doctors*?" Her voice twisted at the word. "They don't know me, they haven't even spoken to me!"

"Mrs. Lincoln, look at this room—" He gestured around at the tight-drawn curtains, the trunks piled high against the walls, the packages stacked on the floor, on the table, on the bed all around the small area where she slept, when she slept.

"You come into a lady's room unannounced and pronounce upon her sanity because you did not give her the opportunity to make it presentable for callers? Because you did not give her the option of replying that she was not at home? For shame, sir! Did no one ever teach you that a *gentleman* sends up his card to ask if his arrival is entirely convenient?"

"None of this is to the point." Swett's voice had hardened. Mary, backing from him like a mouse from a cat, saw him suddenly as an alien creature, alien to her as Lincoln had sometimes appeared alien on those few occasions when she'd seen him with other lawyers, wearing his calculating lawyer-face. Hastily she pushed that memory of his cold craftiness from her. Of course he hadn't been like them ever in any way! He'd been a saint. . . .

"The judge and the jury are waiting for us at the courthouse. Your lawyer, too, and the doctors who have heard an account of your case." He took out his watch again, and glanced at it significantly, as if, thought Mary, there weren't four other clocks in the room, one of them purchased only last week. . . .

"An account that *you* saw fit to give!" She hurled the words at him like knives. "God knows what lies you've told them! Or did you even have to tell them lies? Just bribe them, the way you have all your life bribed juries to rob the poor!"

He didn't so much as flicker an eyelid at the barb. "You can come with me, or these officers"—he gestured to the stone-faced men in the hall behind him—"will bring you, whether you will or no. There are two carriages downstairs. Unless you yield to me I will either have to seize you forcibly myself, or these men will have to take you and bring you in handcuffs. Now please, Mrs. Lincoln, put on your bonnet and come with me, as you usually would. I'm sure you don't want there to be a scene in the lobby—"

"You are a scoundrel and a coward, and if my husband were alive he would deal with you! Go home and take care of your own wife—about whom God knows I've heard enough tales!—and leave *me* alone!"

She was trembling, and clutched at the corner of the cluttered dresser for support. *This has to be a dream,* she thought, *a nightmare.* And, *Robert knows. Robert is having them do this thing.* She felt the same nauseating fury that she had when the stylish Washington hostesses would whisper behind her back—or Washington newspapers would print, for all the world to read—that she was a Confederate spy. That she slipped into Lincoln's office late at night to steal Army plans to send to her brothers in Lee's forces across the river. That she should be locked up.

She was surrounded by her enemies, as she had been all her life.

Through blinding tears she screamed, "Let me at least change my dress!" for she was revoltingly conscious of the muck splattered on the hem of her skirt and the stale smell of sweat in her bodice and chemise.

But Swett's hand was on her elbow, and Swett—glancing pointedly at his watch again—was escorting her out the door. She yanked free of him, barely able to see, her hands fumbling with the veils on her bonnet. Mr. Lincoln, she wondered in rising panic, where was Mr. Lincoln? When the big prairie lightning-storms frightened her, in that little cottage in Springfield, he'd come striding home from his office through the pounding summer rain to be with her. . . .

He's dead, she remembered, the memory like yesterday, like a dagger in her guts.

He's dead.

For a minute she smelled his blood on the shoulder of her dress.

The iron elevator doors clattered open. She wanted to explain to Swett how dangerous elevators were, but caught herself: *They'll use that to call me insane.* She held her breath in terror as the car rattled down.

Every word, every action, every glance will give them ammunition, as it did in Washington when they all said I was a spy.

They passed through the lobby, Mary holding herself bolt upright, though her head felt ready to explode. She pulled away, walked ahead of Swett as though he were a servant, hiding her terror under scorn. It was early afternoon: ladies in walking-dresses of summer silk clustered like flowers around the doorway to the conservatory. She felt their glances like knives in her back.

Enemies.

As Swett had promised, there were two carriages at the curb, though it wasn't more than a street or two to the Cook County Courthouse. Single-horse broughams, such as doctors drove—she could guess which was Swett's by the spanking-new paint, the glossy youth of the well-mannered horse. What did the novels all say? *The poor thing was taken away in a closed carriage. . . .*

This can't be happening to me. . . .

She was a Todd of Lexington, whose grandfathers had fought and defeated British and Indians.

This can't be happening to me. . . .

The terrible, agonizing realization of how alone she was.

Swett held out a gloved hand to help her in, for the step was high. It was as if even the inanimate wood and steel mocked the shortness of stature that had all her life been a bitter unchangeable fact.

Mary pulled her hand away. "I ride with you from compulsion," she said coldly, keeping her voice steady with an effort, "but I beg you not to touch me."

Swett climbed in. The carriage moved off with a jolt.

Chapter Two

Lexington, Kentucky July 1825

A child cried in the dark of a silent house.

The breathing of the four other children in the bed was a presence more felt than heard, but Mary knew they were asleep. Twelve-year-old Elizabeth, dark and slim and efficient, had whispered reassuringly to the others as Mammy Sally put them to bed, "Now the doctors are here Ma will be all right." Six-year-old Mary wasn't so sure of it.

On other nights in summer the house smelled of lamp-oil and the straw matting on the floors, of the wet scent of the chestnut-trees behind it and now and then smoke from the kitchen. Now the sticky darkness stank of medicines and blood.

Just before Mammy Sally put the children to bed—Elizabeth, fragile eight-year-old Frances, Mary, and tiny, fretful Ann, with little Levi in the trundle-bed—their Granny Parker had come to the house, something she rarely did after the sun had set. Their father had come down out of their mother's bedroom with a branch of candles in hand, and had embraced his mother-in-law with desperate intensity.

Dr. Warfield had arrived shortly after that, and Dr. Dudley; Mary had heard their voices downstairs as Mammy was tucking the children in. As soon as the old black nurse's candle disappeared down the stairs, Levi had crept up into the bed with the girls, like a frightened puppy seeking the comfort of its litter-mates. When the footsteps of the men vibrated on the stairs, and the door of their mother's room opened and shut, Elizabeth had done her whispered best to comfort them all.

Now Mary stared at where she knew the open door had to be in the darkness, gaping into the still-deeper dark of the hall. Their new brother—George, Elizabeth said his name was—still wailed untended, which meant that Mammy had to be in the sickroom, too.

In time she could stand the uncertainty no longer. She feared the dark—Mammy was full of tales about African demons and the Platt-Eye Devil that lurked under beds—but she feared even more this state of not knowing. Carefully, Mary slipped from Elizabeth's comforting arm and slithered to the floor, a little white ghost in her nightdress, her auburn-bronze braids hanging down her back. Silently she tiptoed to the door, and sat beside it in the pitch-dark hall, listening to her infant brother cry, to the occasional half-heard mumblings behind the closed sickroom door.

Once she heard her mother groan, and smelled fresh blood above the stale odors of sickness. Elizabeth had told her that bleeding would bleed out the sickness, but the smell made Mary's heart quake. Then after a long time the scrape of a chair on the floor, and her father's voice, saying her mother's name. . .

A thump, indistinct and dreadful, like something unknown and unspeakable groping its way toward her in the dark. Mary pressed her hands to her mouth and in her heart whispered the litany with which she'd tried on other nights to keep the Platt-Eye Devil at bay: *Hide me, oh my Savior, hide*. . .

But whatever it was that the future held, it was rushing toward her and there was no way she could hide.

The door down the hallway opened. Candlelight, and the redoubled smells of sickness and blood. One of the doctors emerged with the candlestick in his hand, and Granny Parker, bony and upright in her black dress. Then Mary's father and another doctor, carrying between them a woman's body in a white shift, her long dark braids trailing down to the floor. The shift was spattered with blood and there were bandages on both arms. When Mary's father stumbled a little, the woman's head lolled and Mary saw for the last time her mother's face, pale with the ravages of sickness and death.

MARY'S EYES SNAPPED OPEN, THE TERROR OF THAT HOT DARK HALL jolting back hard into the sticky-hot terror of the carriage as it stopped.

Leonard Swett said, "Here we are, Mrs. Lincoln."

Mary had passed the massive gray stone walls of the Cook County Courthouse almost daily since coming back to Chicago in March, and still felt disoriented at the sight. Like everything on the street—in the whole of downtown—it was unfamiliar to her, and the shock of seeing it made her clench her small hands tight until her nails pinched the palms through the silk-fine black kid of her gloves. *I mustn't let them see. I mustn't let anyone see me break down.*

She was a Todd of Lexington, whose grandfathers had fought and defeated British and Indians.

I won't give them that satisfaction.

The tension of her clenched jaw-muscles fired blinding snakes of light through her vision. Her head swam—in addition to the migraine, she was definitely having one of her "spells"—*Why does it have to be now? I must focus my mind, do something. . . . They said I have a lawyer. . . .*

But terror of the blaze that had destroyed the city seemed to be branded into her brain, tangling thoughts of the present with images of the past. Her mother . . . the Fire . . . and Tad had died only weeks before the Fire. Choking out his life, imploring her with sunken eyes, so like her husband's.

He'd left her to face the Fire alone. As they all had left her.

She pulled her hand away again from Mr. Swett's proffered help, hoping she wouldn't stagger on her swollen feet as she stepped down that too-long drop to the curb.

Preceded him in silence from the blinding heat of the sidewalk into the dense gloom of the Courthouse's side door. She had to use the toilet again and didn't dare ask for it, couldn't endure reducing herself before these haughty, scornful men.

The courtroom was full of people.

She heard their voices as Mr. Swett and his guards led her along the corridor, and her heart sank.

She should have realized there'd be an audience to her shame. Of course word would get to the papers. It always did. And of course people would show up, to gape, to listen, to have all the gossip to carry home to their families or their cronies at the saloon. Gossip about the Confederate spy. About Mr. Lincoln's crazy widow who never could keep her temper. *Vampires, ghouls, all of them . . .*

Every chair in the room was full. An usher was already bringing in more from other courtrooms, for those who waited, standing, around the doors.

Mary's whole body turned hot, then icily cold. She wanted to scream at them, to curse them. How dared they treat her this way? She was Abraham Lincoln's wife. . . .

"Mrs. Lincoln . . ." Mr. Isaac Arnold came down the aisle between the wooden chairs, a stringy grim-faced man with an untidy gray goatee. Her heart leaped at the sight of him. He was her friend, Mr. Lincoln's old legal colleague from his circuit-riding days.

"Mr. Arnold, what is the meaning of—?"

And she broke off as she saw the man behind him. A neat-featured man, young and tall and becoming burly, his pouting rosebud mouth nearly hidden under an immense light-brown mustache and his eyes, blue-green like hers—like so many of the Todds'—filled with a calm neutrality in which wariness flickered ever so slightly, his own version of the hated lawyer-face.

Of course it had to be, she thought with despair that held no surprise. *Of course he would be the one to betray me, to drive the knife into my heart.*

A square, firm hand immaculately gloved in gray kid took hers, propelled her toward the front of the room while Mr. Arnold hastened to join Swett by the doors. Robert Todd Lincoln said nothing to her, and she was not going to give the entire population of Chicago the satisfaction of screaming at her son in front of them.

How dare you?

How could you?

Robert would have an explanation. He always did.

At the back of the courtroom Mr. Arnold was in conference with Swett, and with a man whom Mary had recognized vaguely as Mr. Ayer, Swett's partner. *So he's on their side,* she thought bitterly, *and not my lawyer at all. Who have they got for me, then?*

For a ludicrous moment she wondered if Robert would be defending her after all.

To save money, naturally. *Her* money, of which he was sole heir.

Robert, she thought, *I am sorry. . . .*

Robert sat down next to her, at the small table that, in the United States, constituted the "dock." Though she would not look at him, Mary could smell the pomade with which he combed his hair. She looked around the courtroom, narrowing her eyes a little, trying desperately to discern faces through the flashing scrim of migraine.

There were faces she knew—faces and forms, for as age blurred her sight she had relied more and more on shape, color, and movement as much as on features. Surely that was Mr. Turner of the Grand Pacific! He couldn't possibly think she was insane! He'd said himself, those nights she'd gone to him after nightmares, that several women of his acquaintance needed a hotel maid to stay in their room through the dark hours. . . . When things she heard or saw in her strange spells of confusion frightened her, he'd said he understood, had agreed that it was all perfectly normal. . . .

And that was Mary Gavin, the stout maid who'd usually stay with her on those terrifying nights when, all too often, she'd hear voices speaking out of the walls and the floor. When dreams of fire would be so real to her that she had to fight not to run out into the streets again, panting with terror. And Mrs. Harrington, the housekeeper of the Grand Pacific, with her gray hair piled in a pompadour eked out as usual with false switches . . . .

The shock of seeing them turned Mary cold. Her fury snatched at all her trusty weapons of sarcasm and mockery, all the secrets about them that she had gleaned: *For a girl whose brother is a simpleton you have little room to talk. . . . Why should the jury believe Irish trash? I never met an Irish servant who didn't lie like Satan. . . . Why don't you tell them about your father's bankruptcy instead of about me?*

But then they will say I'm crazy, she thought, forcing her rage back. *If I stand up and say Mrs. Harrington skims money to invest in railroad schemes, I've seen Mr. Turner corner the housemaids in the linen-room, it won't help me. It will just give Robert a chance to twist my words, to point out to them how little self-control I have. I have to think. . . .*

There was one of those moments of quiet that sometimes fall on buzzing rooms, and she heard Mr. Arnold say quite clearly, ". . . doubt the propriety of my being on this case at all."

"May I remind you," said Swett icily, "of the necessity to have this case over with swiftly? Before there is further embarrassment for all? Back out, and you will put into her head that she can get some mischievous lawyer to make us trouble and defend her. Do your duty."

But it was only when she saw Mr. Arnold coming back down the aisle toward the dock that Mary understood that this friend of her husband—this man to whom she had recently given a complete set of Shakespeare, in gratitude for his support of her during her grief—was in fact going to be her defender.

Do your duty, Swett had ordered him. . . .

Arnold sat on the other side of Robert, so that to speak to him, Mary would have to speak across her son.

The bailiff was saying, "All rise for Judge Wallace . . . the Court of Cook County is now in session. . . ."

Some of the pounding in Mary's head had now diminished, buried under the warm featherbedding of medicine. Even the itching, the burning pain in her privates didn't seem so bad. But it was hard to concentrate; her mind kept slipping to other thoughts, old memories and dreams, then pulling back in shock so intense that it was easy to slide away again.

I am not insane!

She felt as if, for some inexplicable reason, everyone had started saying she was a black woman, when she could look at her hands, look at her face in the mirror, and see herself as white as she had been yesterday, as white as they. . . .

"I was first called to attend to Mrs. Lincoln in November of 1873 at the home of her son, Mr. Robert Todd Lincoln," declared Dr. Willis Danforth, a stubby and businesslike little man whom Mary chiefly remembered for nodding offhandedly throughout her account of her physical symptoms ("Nervousness is only to be expected of the female system," he'd said, and hadn't taken a single note), and the unquestionable garishness of his watch-fobs.

"She was at the time suffering from a derangement of the nervous system, and a fever in her head."

I was suffering every day from blinding headaches, you self-important dolt, as I've suffered all my life!

"She said that the spirit of a dead Indian was at work inside her head, drawing wires from her eyes—especially the left one—and from the bones of her cheeks. She said that she saw him quite clearly...."

I did! He was there! He's there now, waiting for me with his pincers....

Of course the spirits of the dead are present, are all around us. If the benevolent ones help us and aid us, is it not just as reasonable to suppose that there are spirits of malice who torment us?

"These symptoms were undoubtedly rooted in a physical cause, and under my care they decreased gradually and I ceased to see her. In March of last year, however, I was called back to attend upon Mrs. Lincoln, who was again suffering from a debility of the nervous system, with hallucinations. She claimed that her deceased husband had told her that she would die on the sixth of September, and this time I could discern no physical cause for her symptoms beyond an abnormal nervous state."

Mary flinched, recalling as if through clouds of gauze the desperate obsession that had possessed her all through that grilling summer. Mr. Lincoln *had* told her, she thought. Had whispered it in her ear, when the candles' light lengthened in her darkened parlor. She would die when she reached the age that he had been when he died. *I will see you on the sixth of September,* he'd said, and her heart had leaped with joy.

She had been alone, and frantically lonely that summer. Her mind had turned and turned again to that date, with a nervous terror and readiness that would not let her sit still....

She'd been afraid—not of death, but of dying. How could she not be, when she remembered with such clarity the horror of his face, like old ivory in the candlelight of that crowded little bedroom, the immense black-red bruise around his right eye where the bullet lodged? When she woke up in the night hearing at the edge of her consciousness the ragged, painful gasps of his failing breath? When she remembered poor Tad, trying to breathe, remembered how Willie had cried and twisted with the fever that ate him like a monster on those stormy icy nights . . .

And then nothing had happened. The sixth of September came and went. She didn't know why. For weeks she had stayed in her room at the Grand Pacific, with the curtains drawn, nursing her headaches and her anxiety—her disappointment—with Godfrey's Cordial and Nervine.

"At Mr. Robert Lincoln's request I called upon his mother again on the eighth of May 1875, ten days ago, at her room in the Grand Pacific Hotel," Danforth droned on. "She spoke of her stay in Florida, of the scenery and the pleasant time she had had there, of the manners and customs of the Southern people. She appeared at the time to be in excellent health, and her former hallucinations appeared to have passed away. She said that her reason for returning from Florida was that she was not well."

"And no mention was made of her fears for her son's health?" asked the lawyer Ayer. "Nor of the telegrams she had sent begging him to 'hold on' until she could reach his side?"

"No, none. I was somewhat startled when she told me that an attempt had been made to poison her on her journey back. She said she was very thirsty, and at a way-station not far from Jacksonville she took a cup of coffee in which she discovered poison. She said she drank it, and took a second cup, that the overdose might cause her to vomit. . . ."

Mary felt her whole face and body grow hot at the bald relation of her story. She remembered vomiting at that station, after two cups of coffee, and remembered wondering if the coffee had been poisoned. But for the life of her could not remember why she'd spoken of it to Danforth, of all people. During his visit she'd felt on the edge of one of her spells, she recalled, and her recollection was hazy, like watching someone else. Like so many things she said, that she wished later with all her heart she hadn't said. . . .

"I could see no traces of her having taken poison, and on general topics her conversation was rational."

"But you are of the opinion that Mrs. Lincoln is insane?"

"Yes," said Dr. Danforth. "I am of the opinion that Mrs. Lincoln is insane."

"Your witness," said Mr. Ayer, bowing to Arnold as he walked back to his seat.

"No questions," said Mr. Arnold.

Mary was so breathless with shock and outrage—*No questions after that?*—that she could not speak, could not take it in, could think of nothing to do or say.

"On April first of this year I encountered Mrs. Lincoln in the third-floor hallway of the hotel at ten o'clock in the evening," said Mr. Turner, the manager of the Grand Pacific Hotel. "She was very carelessly dressed, with a shawl over her head...."

Of course I was carelessly dressed. I was probably on my way to the toilet down the hall! Mary made the trip sometimes seven or eight times a night, to her aching humiliation. All her life she had been one of those people who needed the toilet frequently, especially at night. One could use a chamber pot in the room only so many times. Then those awful, agonizing minutes of listening and surreptitious watching for the corridor to be vacant, the hasty sneaking down the hall....

One of her greatest grievances in the stinginess of Congress in the matter of her husband's pension—one of her deepest resentments at Robert and that fat oily moneybag Judge Davis, who'd probated her husband's estate—had been that their combined machinations had prevented her from having enough money to own her own house and dispense with such humiliating nighttime expeditions.

But that, too, was something she could not say to anyone. The newspapers had mocked her so viciously at the time—"So much for womanly gentleness and obedience," one had commented—that she dreaded even to think about bringing the matter up again.

"...insisted that the whole South Side of Chicago was in flames. She asked me to accompany her back to her room, and complained that a man was communicating with her through the wall of her room."

Mary stared at him, shocked. She dreamed often of voices speaking to her through the walls and the floor, but could remember nothing of actually telling Turner this. *He's making it up,* she thought. *He has to be making it up....*

"She said that she had a note from a Mr. Shoemaker in room 137, asking her to visit him. Although there is no room 137 in the hotel, she insisted that we seek him: we went to rooms 127, 107, and 27. Then she asked me if she could be allowed to stay in some other lady's room, as she feared that the hotel was going to burn down...."

It's a lie! Mary screamed within her mind, baffled and aghast. *I never said such things.*

Dreamed them, yes, sometimes...Shoemaker was the name of that sad-eyed graying gentleman who had been at the Spiritualist gatherings in St. Catherine's, in Canada, the summer before last. She remembered him quite well, for he, like her, had lost his wife and all but one of his children. He, like her, had been seeking, desperately, for years, to hear them speak, to know they remembered him beyond the grave....

"So great was Mrs. Lincoln's conviction that the city was on fire that she ordered me to dispatch her trunks to the shipping-office in Milwaukee to be safe."

The Fire, thought Mary, shivering as fear rolled over her again in a blinding wave. The memory of running through the night streets, blind with smoke. Of shrieking voices, and the crash of shop windows breaking. Of men staggering from empty houses with bedsheets bulging with silver and jewelry. Of a man hurling a glass of liquor at a girl whose hair was on fire. Of a corpse in the gutter with his head smashed in, staring up at her with accusing eyes.

"Your witness," said Mr. Ayer.

"No questions."

Another surge of sick terror washed through Mary, as she stared disbelievingly at Arnold. He didn't even look at her. Nor did Robert, staring resolutely ahead of him, his hands folded and his mouth set. *They're not going to ask any questions,* Mary realized. *Robert hired Arnold the way he hired Swett and Ayer—to make it look like a trial. Arnold thinks I'm as mad as the others do.*

She felt as if the chair—slightly too tall for her short legs, as all chairs were—swayed under her with the force of this shock. She couldn't imagine what she could do in this situation. For a moment the hilarious irony of it struck her. *All my life I've been surrounded by lawyers—all Mr. Lincoln's friends were lawyers. . . . Why can't I get a lawyer when I need one?*

A man she'd never seen before was on the stand. She hadn't caught his name, but he was relating how the symptoms described to him by Robert two days previously in Robert's office were definitely the symptoms of madness. Her extravagant spending not only bordered on mania, it was a *symptom* of mania. . . .

Then go arrest John D. Rockefeller for lunacy! Or John Jacob Astor! Put Potter Palmer the millionaire on trial, with his purchase of all those paintings and statues!

Her uncontrollable rages, long attested in the public press, her uncontrollable grief . . . tragic, yes . . .

Tragic? You have the brains blown out of the one you most love on earth, his shattered head falling bloody to your shoulder, and see what it does to your nerves, sir!

Other doctors followed one another to the stand. The symptoms Robert had described to them undoubtedly pointed to madness. The crazed alternation between parsimony and extravagance, the attempt—which all in the court would clearly remember—to sell off the used and soiled gowns she'd worn as First Lady, and the scandal that had followed in the newspapers. Her monomania about trying to contact the spirits of her husband and sons. *(And Robert's embarrassment—let's not forget that!)* "The false sensuous impressions of the mediums force too much blood to the brain, predisposing Spiritualists to lunacy. And it is well known that the female system is by its very nature more prone to nervous debility than the male, being far more intimately connected with the organs of generation...."

The heat in the courtroom was like an oven. Even the men on the jury—stern-faced respectable-looking men in heavy frock-coats and tight cravats—were sweating, and under her layers of black mourning crape and whalebone corsetry, Mary's body was consumed with itches and pain.

"...unnatural fear of fire gives great cause for concern, for the insane will frequently leap from windows in a delusional attempt to escape..."

"No questions."

Unnatural fear? Were none of you driven out of your homes by the Fire? Didn't any of you have to flee to the lakeside, to be crushed and shoved by those screaming crowds as they waded out into the black stinking water?

Am I the only one who remembers that?

"Mrs. Lincoln's closet is piled full of packages, which she has never opened, but are just as they came from the store...."

"Mrs. Lincoln goes out shopping once a day and sometimes twice, and her closet and her room are filled with packages which she never opens. Yes, on the nights when she has me sleep in her room she says that she hears voices coming through the walls, and she's scared to go to sleep. When she goes to the washroom she says people watch her through a tiny little window there....No, sir, there's no window in that washroom...."

"...called me to Mrs. Lincoln's room, and she asked me to take her down and show her the tallest man in the dining-room...."

"On the twelfth of March of this year"—this was Mr. Edward Isham, Robert's law partner—"I received a frantic telegram from Mrs. Lincoln, who was then in Florida. The telegram stated her belief that her son was ill and dying, and that she would start for Chicago at once. Of course Mr. Lincoln was nothing of the kind, and though the telegraphers and superintendent at the Western Union office in Jacksonville attempted to dissuade Mrs. Lincoln, she and her nurse boarded a train to return to this city."

Face crimson with shame, Mary stole a glance at Robert. That obsession, like the desperate belief that she would die last year, seemed so strange to her now. Yet she remembered the intensity of her conviction, the frantic fear that Robert—the only one she had left—would leave her. Someone had warned her in a dream....

I only did it from fear that you would leave me, too!

That you would leave me the way everyone has left me....

Last of all, Robert Todd Lincoln took the stand.

"For a long time I have suspected that my mother is not sane. She has shown signs of hysteria and nervous disability for as long as I can remember. . . ."

He looked very pale but extremely composed, and spoke absolutely without the hesitations, the nervous interpolations of "um" and "you see" that so many of the other witnesses had used. It was the professional fluency of a lawyer, of a man supremely used to public speaking—of a man who has planned out in advance his every word and his every pause. Mary remembered Abraham Lincoln speaking before juries, every word honed and ready and without the slightest impression of being prepared in advance—speaking the way everyone wished they could speak in an argument.

"On one occasion she spent $600 on lace curtains; on another, $450 on three watches which she gave to me, for which I had no use. She spent $700 on jewelry last month, $200 on soaps and perfumes, though she has no home in which to hang curtains, trunks full of dresses which she never wears, and she has not worn jewelry since my father's death, ten years ago."

And while we're on the subject of money, thought Mary, *why don't you mention the nearly $10,000 in real estate that I've given you? The $6,000 in bonds from Tad's inheritance from his father? The $5,000 for your law library? Why don't you mention the interest-free loans I've made to you for your real-estate speculations?*

Surely I can buy curtains for a house that I don't yet own?

Not that it's any of your business, or anyone's, what I spend my money on. . . .

Her eyes burned with tears. Robert's image blurred and only his voice remained, the voice of the chilly, reasonable boy who had seemed so apart from his younger brothers, who had spoken to her even as a child with such formality.

The boy who had begged to be allowed to go into the Army, because so many others at Harvard had gone. Because people looked at him, and whispered: *Lincoln started this war and yet he keeps his son back where it's safe.*

How could I let him go into the Army to die?

The boy whose whole life she had shaped, with that single lie that she would give anything not to have told.

The heat in the courtroom was so intense she felt she would die. Her head pounded, and rising through the pain the anxiety and depression that always followed on one of her dreamy spells; the frantic desire to hide in darkness, to be alone, to quaff one more spoonful of medicine to take the edge off her pain and her grief.

"Certainly I was in excellent health on the twenty-fifth of March and remain so. I met my mother's train and urged her to stay with me at my home on Wabash Avenue, at least while my wife was away, for admittedly my wife and my mother do not get along."

As if anyone could get along with that sneaking, cold-blooded hussy!

"She refused and took a room instead at the Grand Pacific Hotel, much against my wishes. Mr. Turner was so good as to give me the room next to hers, where I remained until early in April. I observed many times my mother wandering about the halls in a very disordered state. . . ."

I was on my way to the toilet, you ignorant blockhead! Doesn't that precious wife of yours ever piss?

"On the night of the first of April I stopped her when she would have gone down into the lobby in such a state, and she screamed at me, 'You are going to murder me.' "

"Oh, that is a lie!" gasped Mary, though in fact she had only the dimmest recollections of wandering in the halls. So often she dreamed of such searchings—such fears . . .

"I told her that if she continued such proceedings that I would leave the hotel; and so at length I did. However, since I knew that my mother habitually went about with at least $10,000 in bonds concealed in a purse sewn into her petticoats—"

And how did you know I still did that, unless you were paying the hotel servants to spy on me?

"—I hired detectives of the Pinkerton Agency to follow her and make sure that she came to no harm."

I knew it! Through the hammering of the heat, through the blinding pain and the sick waves of anxiety and shock, betrayal was only beginning now to penetrate to her inner thoughts. *I knew I was being followed, being watched!*

You spy on me and then you call me crazy for believing that I am being spied on!

She looked around her, wondering if any of the men on the jury—those cold-featured respectable men who hadn't the imagination to realize that there were worlds of spirit beyond what could be bought and sold, those grim-hearted brokers and bankers who thought that a woman was insane if she believed that love endured beyond death—understood what had just been said. They were too far off for her to read their faces clearly, but one or two of them were nodding wisely, approving of this evidence of Robert's care for her.

Or his care for her $10,000 in bonds, which would be subtracted from his inheritance if she were to be robbed.

"Any implication that I might be seeking to obtain control of my mother's affairs is unreasonable, because I already manage her affairs. In fact, I telegraphed her the money that enabled her return from Florida."

Another lie! She shook her head angrily.

"I have no doubt my mother is insane. She has long been a source of great anxiety to me. She has no home and no reason to make these purchases."

Always money, she thought. Robert's mind always returned to money. His, hers, what Mr. Lincoln had left to them—which Robert had held on to as long as he possibly could, Robert and Robert's obese and crafty mentor Judge Davis. Was that because his first memories must be of those earliest days of her marriage to Mr. Lincoln, when they lived in a single rented room in the Globe Tavern in Springfield and she was in constant fear of further destitution, in constant shame when she saw her former friends rattle by in carriages?

Money, and the fact that she would not do as he wanted her to.

"Your witness, Mr. Arnold."

Mary turned in fury to her attorney—now separated from her only by Robert's vacated chair—but Arnold wasn't looking at her. He was looking at Robert, meeting his eyes across the small space of the front of the courtroom that separated them.

"No questions," he said.

Chapter Three

The jury deliberated for barely ten minutes. When Robert stepped down from the stand and returned to his seat beside her he held out his hands to her; Mary turned her face from him. His face was pale and streaked with tears—Robert had always, she reflected, been able to talk himself into feeling whatever emotion was most appropriate for the situation.

Of course a man who's been forced to hold his mother up to the scorn and ridicule of the entire city of Chicago—the entire nation, thanks to the press—would shed tears on the witness stand. How else could he make himself the victim, instead of me?

She could imagine—as Robert undoubtedly could, too—what the newspapers would say of a son who *didn't* shed tears on the witness stand as he asked the Court to lock his mother up.

"To think that my son would do this to me," she said.

The courtroom was like a slow oven. Beneath layers of wool crape and black veiling Mary felt her flesh sticky, and burning as if dipped in acid. As the gentle effect of the medicine subsided the pain in her head mounted, confusing her. She couldn't bear the thought of asking Arnold—*traitor, Judas, hypocrite!*—if she might seek out the toilets. . . . Would they have a Pinkerton agent follow her there?

Just get back to my room, she thought desperately. *Just get away, out of the light, into the comforting dimness. . . .* The frantic anxiety she had felt in the street that morning returned, the aching need for medicine, the terror of more pain to come. *Back to my room . . .*

And she startled in shock. *What if I can't go back?*

What if they find me insane?

Until this moment it had never truly occurred to her that this hideous ordeal, this hotbox redolent of the stinks of sweaty wool suiting and cheap pomade, was anything more than a single awful afternoon. . . .

What if they lock me up? Put me in a cell like a prisoner, chained to the walls like the people in pictures I've seen? Hide me and forget me, like Mr. Rochester's wife in Jane Eyre*?*

Her eyes shot to Robert—who was talking to Swett and Ayer and casting venomous glances at the reporters—and into her mind flashed a memory, the memory of those awful months after her son Willie's death. Willie had died in February: Mary had remained in bed herself for weeks, and as much as six months later the grief had still returned in blinding waves of incapacitating weeping. She remembered how after trying vainly to comfort her, her husband had led her gently to the window of the summer cottage where they were staying.

Mother, do you see that large white building on the hill yonder? She could still hear that high, husky voice, that could carry like a trumpet when he spoke to a crowd, soft now like a troubled lullaby. Could still conjure back the light firmness of that enormous hand on the small of her back. The new lunatic asylum was only partially visible from the windows of the Soldiers' Home—the stone cottage to which the President's family retired during the sticky horrors of Washington summers—but Mary knew what it was.

She could hear beneath the gentleness of Lincoln's voice how frightened he was, how helpless in the face of a grief whose blackness he understood himself, far too well. *You must try to control your grief, or it will drive you mad and we may have to send you there.*

He never would have. She knew that as clearly as she knew her name.

Not to an asylum. Like those hideous reports she had read of patients being doused with icy water or chained behind bars like animals, or like that dreadful story by Mr. Poe . . .

And I'm not mad. . . .

At first she thought nothing of the scraping of chairs, the sudden rise of voices. *It has to be the reporters getting excited about something.*

But when she saw Robert hastily return to his seat, and Arnold gathering his papers, she swung around and saw the jury filing back into their box.

But they only just left!

The horrible suspicion seized her that one of her spells had come on her again. Time telescoped during those episodes. Hours could pass in the daydream of what felt like moments. But a glance at the courtroom clock, at the hot gold angle of light high on the wall, showed her that no, in fact only ten minutes had gone by.

"Gentlemen, have you reached a verdict?" The judge didn't look at her. Mary found herself trembling all over, struggling not to scream, not to start flinging things at Robert—books, pens, Arnold's useless and untouched papers. . . .

"We have, Your Honor. This jury finds that Mrs. Lincoln is insane—"

No.

"—and though she is neither suicidal nor homicidal—"

No!

"—she is a fit person to be confined to an asylum."

Reporters came crowding up. Swett, Arnold, Robert, and the two Pinkerton men—*Where were you when my husband was killed?* she wanted to scream at them—formed up around her, thrust their way through them to the back of the room. Mary stumbled in that circle of male shoulders, dark frock-coats smelling of tobacco and Macassar oil, the faces around her a blur.

Robert was speaking to her. Introducing her to a grave-faced man with a splendid chestnut beard, who had testified so learnedly about the vicious effects of Spiritualism and "theomania." *I believe Mrs. Lincoln to be insane from the account given to me by Mr. Robert Lincoln in his office. . . .*

". . . Dr. Richard Patterson," Robert was saying. "Dr. Patterson operates a private sanitarium in Batavia."

"You mean a madhouse." Mary's voice sounded flat in her own ears, and queerly alien, as if someone else were speaking.

Robert's eyes shifted, but Dr. Patterson said, "Bellevue Place is a pleasant house where people can rest and get better, Mrs. Lincoln. We think you'll be very comfortable there."

She opened her mouth to snap, *And it doesn't matter what I think?*

And then realized, *No, it doesn't.*

You're a madwoman. You must go where they send you, and do what you're told. Forever.

Trembling, she said, "You set this up between you, didn't you? You had a prison all ready for me before we ever walked into this courtroom."

While her heart whispered to her, *It was my doing. my punishment. My shame. No more than my deserving. . .*

Reporters were craning to listen. Calmly, as if she had said nothing, Robert said, "Mr. Arnold and I will escort you to Bellevue Place tomorrow, Mother. I've taken a room next to yours at the Grand Pacific for tonight. But first, Mother, I must insist that you turn over to me the bonds that you have been carrying with you—"

"The ones you bribed chambermaids to tell you about? Or did you peek through the keyholes at me yourself? That's what you wanted all along, wasn't it? To get hold of my money?"

Robert raised his voice just slightly, though he didn't even glance at the purposefully loitering members of the press. "You're talking foolishly, Mother. You know I've always had the management of your affairs. And you also know that it's dangerous to carry them on your person as you do. Of course I will write you a proper receipt. . . ."

"Surely," put in Swett in his silky voice, "you would wish to spare yourself the humiliation of having the sheriff take the bonds from you by force, Mrs. Lincoln?"

She rounded on him. "Robert will never have anything of mine!"

"Then perhaps you would prefer to hand them over to Mr. Arnold?"

"I will not hand them to anyone! And I'm sure," she added, "that since—as all the world *now* knows, thanks to *your* paid testimony, sir—I carry the bonds in my underclothing, even my son wouldn't wish me to be indelicate in the presence of all the people in the courtroom. Now I'm hot, and tired, and I wish to go back to my room—or do you propose to chain me now in a cage, and feed me through the bars?"

"Of course you will be allowed to go back to your room, Mother," said Robert unhappily.

"Once you promise to give Mr. Arnold the bonds when we arrive there," added Swett.

"He can have what he likes." Mary's voice cracked and she forced it steady, forced herself not to give them even the smallest satisfaction. Hating them, and hating Robert most of all. "Take from me what he likes. Only let me go back."

Leaving the courthouse was like those dreams she'd had as a girl, of attending her classes at Ward's Academy and discovering in the midst of recitation that she was still in her nightgown. . . .

They used to let people tour madhouses and stare at the lunatics, she thought, dizzily sinking into the upholstery of Swett's closed brougham, sweating in pain at every jolt of the pavement. *Do they still?* Evening was beginning to come on, though the bustle of pedestrians and vehicles on Clark Street was worse, if anything, than it had been in the heat of the afternoon. A breath of breeze from the lake brought a little freshness, but not one jot of relief. *We think you'll be comfortable there. . . .*

No. Not that.

She closed her eyes and wondered how much it would hurt to die.

With stony dignity she stepped out of her group of escorts—Swett, Arnold, the two faithful Pinkertons, and a very uncomfortable-looking

Mary Gavin, whom they'd gathered up on their way through the Grand Pacific lobby—and into the ladies' toilets down the hall from her room. Blessed relief—blessed, blessed silence, stillness, privacy away from staring eyes and whispering men . . .

They were all waiting in the hall for her when she came out. She almost laughed at their clumsy unease.

"The bonds," Swett reminded her as she unlocked the door of her room. He reached to take the key from her but she closed it tight in her palm.

"You shall have nothing from me, sir. My husband left me those bonds. . . ."

"I'm sure Mr. Lincoln would not have left them to you had he known you were going to walk around Chicago with ten thousand dollars' worth pinned in your petticoats!"

Her head splitting, her stomach queasy with the aftermath of migraine and medicine, her whole body trembling with exhaustion, Mary shouted at them, raged at them, backed into a corner of the dark suffocating room with its crowded packages and high-piled trunks. But they did not leave, would not leave. They stayed, argued, insisted, and refused to listen when she begged them to leave, begged them to let her alone, to let her rest. At last, sick and dizzy and shaking, Mary retreated to a corner among the trunks and pulled up her heavy overskirt, so that Arnold could tear the bonds out of the pocket sewn to her petticoat.

Then they left, all except Mary Gavin, who settled in her usual chair, as she did all those nights when Mary could not sleep and paid the stolid Irishwoman to spend the night in her room with her.

The bonds were gone.

Her money was gone.

She was helpless. She was exactly where she had all her life feared she would one day be: penniless. And alone.

This is what it is, she thought, frantic, exhausted, fighting with all her strength not to collapse in tears, *to be a madwoman.*

It is to be a child again, without a penny, with no place to live but what they give you and no place to go but what they permit.

I am not insane!

She lay for a long time on the bed, her hands pressed to her mouth, her face turned to the wall, burningly conscious of the woman on the other side of the cluttered room.

Always watched. Never alone.

The sharp curve of her stays gouged her ribs as she drew in a breath, let it out.

She thought, with aching longing, of the medicines in the cabinet, of their promise of sweet sleep and oblivion.

But if she slept, she thought, she'd only wake in the morning with Robert and that hateful Dr. Patterson at the door, waiting to take her to the madhouse.

If she slept, she'd lose whatever time she had to act before Robert arrived to spend the night in the next room.

She took another breath, and sat up. "I'm going down the hall," she announced.

Mary Gavin hastily screwed the top back onto the little flask she'd withdrawn from her reticule, tucked it away out of sight.

"You don't have to come with me," added Mary, getting to her feet. "I won't be long." She knew the maid never liked to get out of her chair once she'd settled in with her little nips of gin. Through the curtained window, light still lingered in the airshaft. It was seven o'clock. Here downtown, most shops remained open until eight, and those within the hotel itself until ten.

Her heart beat fast as she opened the door, praying the maid didn't see—black against the black of her mourning dress, in the dense dimness of the room's single gas jet—that she had her reticule with her, her reticule that had in it, now, all the money she had in the world.

She prayed it would be enough.

The Pinkerton men got to their feet and one of them hastily stashed the *Police Gazette* in his pocket. Coldly, Mary informed them, "I am going down to Squair's Pharmacy in the lobby, to get some medicine for my neuralgia. I shall be back in a few minutes."

The two men glanced at one another uncertainly and she walked off down the corridor, head high. One of them put on his bowler hat and followed her; Mary stopped, turned back and leveled a freezing glare at him, a glare that only the students of a select Female Academy such as Madame Mentelle's of Lexington, Kentucky, could muster.

Cowed, the man hesitated, fell back, and though he followed her—lumbering rapidly down the stairs as she steeled herself to take the elevator—he kept his distance.

And that, Mary knew, would be enough.

"I WOULD LIKE TWO OUNCES EACH OF LAUDANUM AND CAMPHOR, SIR." Her voice sounded reasonable, if rather flat and distant—it was astonishing, she thought, how difficult it was to sound normal when one was trying to sound normal. What was "normal-sounding," anyway? The doctors in the courtroom that afternoon had seemed to be very sure of it. She thought Mr. Squair's clerk looked at her oddly—had she sounded too normal?—and she added, "I suffer from neuralgia of the shoulder, and bathe it in laudanum and camphor for relief."

"Of course, Mrs. Lincoln. Just a moment, please."

The clerk, a young man with a mustache that made him look like a terrier, disappeared through a white-painted door into the room behind the counter. Mary stared at her reflection in the mirrors that caught the last daylight from the lobby, the gas jets that were just beginning to be lit throughout the Grand Pacific Hotel. For two months now she'd been in and out of Mr. Squair's pharmacy, which opened out of the lobby. It was more expensive than Dole's Pharmacy three blocks down Clark Street, but when her migraines were upon her she was willing to pay almost anything, just to be able to purchase medicine and go quietly to her room. In the mirrors she could see the Pinkerton agent—the fatter of the two, like an immense squash in his cheap mustard-colored suit—in the lobby, looking around him unhappily.

Let him look, she thought. *He can't stop me. If he tries to come in here I shall complain. . . .*

To whom?

She was a madwoman. She was going to be sent to an asylum in the morning. She had only tonight left to her.

Had she dreamed that hideous trial, the way she dreamed and redreamed about the Fire? About her mother's death? About that last night in the theater . . .

It would not be the first time that she'd acted on some too-vivid dream.

No. The Pinkerton man was proof of that.

"I'm sorry, Mrs. Lincoln." The clerk re-emerged from the white door. "We—er—the medicine will take a half hour to make up. If you can—please come back in thirty minutes."

"Thirty minutes?" Mary's temper snapped. "That's outrageous! I can't possibly wait thirty minutes! I'm in pain. . . . Thirty minutes for something you only have to pour out of a bottle? Is Mr. Squair here?"

"No, ma'am. He just—he's having his supper—he went home to have his supper. . . ."

The clerk was trying to sound normal, too.

Mary caught at her temper, breathing hard. Waiting infuriated her, but lashing out at Mr. Squair would only cost her time and draw attention to her. Much as she would have liked to get this officious young lout fired, she knew time was what she did not have. Robert might arrive any minute. If he came before she could procure the laudanum, he would never let her go. . . .

He would never let her go anywhere again.

She drew a deep breath and said—still trying to sound normal—"When I come back, young man, I shall have some words to say to Mr. Squair about your incompetence and rudeness to a good paying customer! I have never been so ill-treated in my life!"

There were two entrances to Squair's, which formed a corner between the main lobby and the hotel's side entrance onto Quincy Street. Mary stormed out the secondary door before the Pinkerton in the squash-colored suit could react—*really, it was no wonder that murdering beast was able to shoot my husband, with blockheads of that stamp for his defense!*—and through the hotel's side door.

There was the usual line of cabs drawn up along the curb on Clark Street and it was no time to count pennies. Mary climbed into one and said, "Rogers and Smith drugstore, please." It was only about a block, but this wasn't the first time she'd taken a cab that short distance. The cabmen didn't like it, but there was no time to waste.

"Shall I wait for you, ma'am?" The driver's voice had the flat vowels of Kentucky. One of the legs propped on the cab's dash was wooden, gone just below the knee. Mary wondered which side he had fought on.

"Of course you shall wait; I'm not in any condition to walk back to the hotel." With traffic as heavy as it was this time of the evening she would have done better to walk, but she was exhausted and in her tight shoes her swollen feet felt as if someone were trying to cut them off at the ankles. The clerk at Rogers and Smith was even stupider and more incompetent than the one at Mr. Squair's. He was gone so long in the back room that Mary left before he even came out, consumed with the fear that the Pinkerton agent would come in, would stop her, would drag her back to the hotel and her guards.

Of course, she thought, *I can always tell him the truth, that Squair's stupid young man wasn't able to fill the order. That my shoulder was hurting so badly I had to seek relief elsewhere. They can't quarrel with that. Even Robert can't quarrel with that. . . .*

"Dole's Pharmacy," she told the cab driver, and the cab lurched away into the thick mill of carriages and drays in the street.

It was dark now, the white glare of the gaslights making the faces of passersby seem harsh, and alien beyond belief. Staring out the cab window, Mary shuddered at that wall of humanity—going where? Doing what? Tomorrow it would be in all the newspapers: "Wife of Lincoln

Found Insane." That morning she had cursed at them for not knowing who she was—such unfeeling anonymity seemed a blessing to her now.

And by tomorrow afternoon, she thought, it would be "Emancipator's Widow Dead."

She pressed her hands to her lips, and closed her eyes. They said suicides went straight to Hell. But in the dark parlors where spirits knocked and whispered in the shadows, she had heard the souls themselves give the lie to those joyless preachers and their mistaken ideas of faith. *I will not go,* she thought. *Robert wants my money, well, he may have it: it's all going to him in my will in any case. Rather than be a prisoner for the rest of my life—rather than be stared at, pointed at, hear them whisper "That is Abraham Lincoln's widow, and now she's gone mad, poor thing," I will simply depart. It can't be so terribly difficult. Everyone says that one just slips away.*

And it is no more than I deserve. . . .

And for an instant she was twenty-four again, with the heavy strength of a man's body lying on top of hers. Feeling the rough power of those enormous hands caressing her, seeing firelight reflected in the desperate darkness of deep-set gray eyes.

At Dole's they refused her outright. Time was passing—Robert might arrive at the hotel at any minute—so she did not argue. Would an account of her lunacy have come out in the newspapers already? Why else would they look at her that way, would refuse to sell her laudanum when they'd done so before? She didn't argue. She returned to her cab and ordered him back to the hotel, praying that Mr. Squair wouldn't give her any more trouble.

He didn't, though the cab driver as usual demanded far more than a ride of three blocks was worth: "You'll take fifty cents and like it," snapped Mary, feeling as if her skull were about to split. "In my day gentlemen did not haggle with ladies over the cost of services. Your mother would be ashamed of you." She turned and swept up the steps of the hotel before he could reply, trembling with anxiety and rage.

The bottle Mr. Squair gave her was labeled LAUDANUM—POISON and she drank it on the second-floor landing. She hadn't eaten since lunch and her head throbbed, her feet stabbed with pain as if every small bone in them had been broken. As always she felt, as she climbed the stairs, that she'd safely negotiated some terrible countryside filled with dangers, that she was approaching the place where she was safe, where she could rest. . . .

From the top of the stair she could see the remaining Pinkerton man by the door of her room, talking with Mary Gavin. *Gossiping about me,* she thought. *Whispering how I did or said this, that, or the other. They're all the same.*

Mary Gavin's testimony on the stand stung her, how she'd blithely babbled to everyone in Chicago about Mary's nightmares, and the things she'd confided to her in the dim spells of confusion. . . .

Haven't you ever heard about keeping confidences? Mary wondered bitterly as she forced herself to walk, head high, along that endless hallway. *Or is it customary among you slum-Irish to chat to the neighbors about your friends' secrets and troubles, and how much they spent at the department stores?* She'd given the woman presents, too, and money—which she'd doubtless spent on gin. . . .

"That mentally deficient clerk at Squair's was taking so long to fill my order that I was forced to go down the street to Rogers and Smith," said Mary as the Pinkerton man opened his mouth to admonish her. "Your partner will bear me out, sir, if you suppose that I'm a liar . . . or insane," she added, with a vicious glance at Mary Gavin. "Provided he didn't stop at a saloon on his way."

She thrust past Mary Gavin, adding over her shoulder, "Please close the door. And please ask those two *gentlemen* in the corridor to keep their voices low. I am, as you may suppose, very tired, and would like to lie down. Since you must be in here, please see to it that I'm not disturbed."

She took off her bonnet, and lay down fully clothed on her bed, wondering how long it would take the poison to work. Everyone was always telling her how dangerous laudanum was, as if she hadn't been taking it without the slightest ill effect for years. But at the moment it didn't seem to be doing much, not even taking away her headache. The room was hateful to her, with Mary Gavin's gin-bottle and newspapers crumpled on the chair, and the empty purse that Mr. Arnold had torn out of her petticoats only a few hours ago lying flat on the table.

How dared he? The shame and humiliation flooded back at having pulled up her skirts in front of all those men—at having been forced to go through what she had been through that day. *How dared Robert subject me to that. . . .*

Shame tore at her, the frantic shame that had followed her all her life, and the burning torment of guilt. The old feeling overwhelmed her, of wishing she could go back in time and scrub out events and scenes; make them be gone, have never happened. *A single lie . . .*

How could God be said to forgive, when events followed you through life that way, stacking up more events like tokens in some hellish game?

She sat up, and fished from the cupboard as many bottles as she could reach—Nervine and Catawba Indian Balsam—and poured a dollop of each into her glass, as she had that afternoon. After drinking it she lay down again. The familiar sweet warmth steadied her, lessening her anxiety. With luck when Robert got here they'd tell him she was resting. She pictured his shock and grief when they told him she was dead, when they found the empty bottle—LAUDANUM—POISON—in her handbag, when he realized what he'd driven her to.

Though of course he'd find some way of keeping it out of the newspapers.

Or maybe he wouldn't. Maybe he'd tell the reporters all about it, as proof that she was insane. Only insane people committed suicide, after all.

No, she thought, as sleep stole on her—final sleep, she thought, endless sleep. *One doesn't have to be insane to want to die.*

One only has to be lonely for long enough.

"Oh, my darling," she whispered to that tall shadow that she could half-see, where the dim pink-amber of the lamplight did not reach. "Oh, my beloved, forgive me."

Though as she slipped over into darkness she could not have said whether she wanted forgiveness for taking her own life, or for keeping him waiting so long.

Chapter Four

It was a Friday afternoon in April, muggy and hot. Though the curtains of that large oval parlor on the White House's second floor were closed, still the sharp yellow light pierced the chinks. Sitting in the dimness, Mary tried to summon enough energy to go over and close them more firmly.

But it did not seem worth the effort of getting to her feet, crossing the room.

The darkness comforted her. In the darkness, in the quiet, she could feel that Willie hovered near her. She could almost see the child's sweet spirit tiptoeing out of the shadows, flowers in his hands. He had been her boy, her treasure, the most intelligent of her sons and the most loving. Even when the boys were small, it was Tad who'd go crashing outside at a run to play, Willie who'd stop his headlong rush after him to ask, "Is there anything you need, Mama?"

Is there anything you need?

I need you, my darling! I need your cheer to make me laugh, your smile to make me know I'm alive! When she thought of herself in old age, it was Willie she had pictured at her side. Dear God, the sight of his face, wax-white and so thin, on the satin pillows of his coffin!

"Mother?"

It was her husband. He stood in the doorway of the secret hall that he'd had put in between his offices and the family rooms. For four years he'd had to go through the public hallway on the Executive Mansion's second floor to get from one place to the other, the hallway so crowded with people bringing petitions or seeking favors or asking for jobs for themselves or their family members that it sometimes took him an hour and a half to walk a few dozen feet. He still had a boyish glee about using the inner door, as if it were a secret passage designed to thwart the grown-ups. . . .

His head came within a few inches of the lintel. In the light that came through from his secretary's office beyond, flecks of gray showed in that coarse Indian-black unruly hair that had begun its stealthy retreat back up his forehead. She saw, too, how thin he'd become, not that he'd ever been stout before. But the dark suit that had fit him two years ago hung baggy over his shoulders, and his eyes had a bruised look in hollows under the heavy brow.

"I'm sorry I am late," he said. "Will you come driving with me after all?" He spoke diffidently and a little stiffly, and did not move from the door, as if he feared yet another half-sobbed demand to be left alone.

He was indeed late, and Mary felt a flash of anger at him, for she had looked forward all day to the ride, and now he had spoiled it with his endless meetings. "I thought you had forgotten," she said, "and had gone with Mr. Stanton?" She hated the nervous, masterful Secretary of War who was so often Lincoln's companion on his drives. Couldn't he see the man was dangerous?

"Or perhaps you'd rather go with Julia Grant?" She remembered how her husband had laughed at some witticism of his chief General's bosomy wife, and the attentions he'd paid the woman when they'd gone down to Richmond last week. They were going to the theater with the Grants tonight, too, and she didn't know how she'd manage to sit in the same box with Julia all night, not to mention that coarse drunkard brute of a husband of hers. . . .

The minute the words were out of her mouth she regretted them. Tears flooded her eyes. Her temper had gotten worse since Willie's death and she knew it. As whose wouldn't, she thought defensively, in the face of her husband's growing silences, his absence for eighteen hours out of twenty-four. He had used to share things with her, talk over his plans and his hopes, the cases he had in the courts. He used to ask her advice about his speeches: Would "supremacy of law" offend the Southern moderates she'd grown up with, or should he soften it to "primacy"? Now he talked of nothing but commonplaces, left her out of the circles of power, pushed her aside. . . .

She looked back at the doorway, expecting it to be empty. But he still stood there, though by the deepened lines of his face she could see she'd hurt him. *Good,* she thought. *Maybe next time he'll take to heart what I say. Maybe he'll leave me alone. . . .*

"I'd like your company best, Mother," he said. "As I always have."

Her mouth opened to rage at him—*A pretty poor way you've had of showing it lately!*

But something in the weariness of his eyes stopped her, the silence like a man who takes a whipping without a sound. For a moment she saw, not a tired man of fifty-six with gray in his beard, but a gawky, gaunt, and painfully shy Kentucky barbarian in a suit that didn't fit, standing in the doorway of her sister Elizabeth's house under Elizabeth's withering gaze....

She smiled at that far-off young man, and said instead, "Pretty poor company I've been, too," and watched the tension melt out of his eyes. She got up and took his hand. "I'd like to go driving with you, Mr. Lincoln. Thank you."

Outside the air was cooler than she'd feared it would be, the first stirrings of breeze wafting across the Potomac to rustle the dogwoods. The dappled sun on her face felt like a blessing, dissolving her disappointed anger. It dissolved even some of the terrible grief over Willie's death that seemed to have turned her heart to stone. The small escort of cavalry that followed the carriage kept their distance. "A lot of use they'll be if a rebel assassin shoots at you from the trees," she said, glancing over her shoulder.

"The only way they could prevent a rebel assassin from shooting from the trees is to surround us like a wall," Lincoln pointed out, in a tone of academic observation, as if he had not been receiving death-threats and letters filled with unbelievable hatred for nearly five years. "And even then they couldn't stop a man from flying overhead in a balloon and dropping a brick on my head."

"*Will* you be serious?"

"No," said Lincoln, and smiled—that sweet lightening of his whole ugly face that the photographers never caught. "I have been serious all morning and I am mighty weary of it." He curled his enormous hand around her small, plump fingers. "Besides, what point would there be in murdering me now? The war is over, all but the shouting—of which I'm afraid there'll be plenty, once Congress hears that there are to be no war trials or hangings or firing-squads for men who were only following their consciences. I want a carriage-ride with the woman I love, not a military parade."

Mary blushed, and tightened her hand over his. How could he still love her? A few days ago she had apologized for the scene she'd made on their trip to Richmond—an apology she wasn't sure she'd have offered if she'd known it would lead to the invitation to spend this evening in a theater-box with General and Mrs. Grant—and things had been easy between them, easier than they'd been in months. It was good, she thought, to have her husband back, at least for an hour or two...

"By the way," he said, "the Grants have been forced to beg off from the theater this evening. Robert's given his excuse as well. . . ."

Mary's lips tightened at this newest evidence of their oldest son's estrangement from his father.

"But we could ask Senator Harris's daughter Clara and her fiancé. . . . Or we could cry off ourselves, which I've half a mind to do. We've both seen the play before, after all."

"Oh, no!" said Mary quickly, the prospect of an evening at the theater *without* Julia Grant and her cigar-stinking husband beckoning like a circus-treat in her childhood. "We've already announced to the newspapers that we would be there; it would be a shame to disappoint them. And it would do me good to get out." She sighed, and settled back on the cushions, looking out over the open barouche's sides at the lush sweetness of the woods north of the last houses of the town, the silver sparkle of far-off water among the trees.

As the carriage rattled along the dusty roads in the slanted evening light they talked of small things: how Jip the dog kept trying to convince one of the kitchen cats to play with him, and the scheme their just-turned-twelve-years-old Tad had evolved to trap the last holdouts of the rebel army in North Carolina. The fighting was over, and Mary reveled in Robert's safe return—not that he'd ever been in real danger, as a member of Grant's staff, but one never knew. It was good beyond computation to see how the years melted away from her husband's face, to see the mischief and the old delight sparkle in his somber gray eyes.

Good to have him to herself, as she had used to do in their old home in Springfield, before office-seekers and Generals and Cabinet members and, as he would put it, "every man and his little black dog" had a claim on his time and attention and energy. For five years now, all she had wanted was to have him to herself.

Good to hear him laugh when she mimicked Julia Grant, conjuring up a scene of the woman measuring the White House for her own furniture. Good to laugh almost to tears at his own imitation of the barely literate brother-in-law of some Ohio Representative's cousin who'd come requesting to be made military governor of New Orleans on account of his services to the Republican Party back home in Cincinnati. . . .

As they came back into town again, and the walls of the White House made a pale blur in the gathering gloom, Lincoln said, "Mother, it has been such a joy only to be ourselves again. We must both be more cheerful in the future; between the war and the loss of our darling Willie, we have both been very miserable."

Mary nodded. "I know. And I have been as guilty of it as you. With the war over now it will be easier."

"I hope so. I find myself looking forward to the end of my term as much as any of the poor slaves looked forward to Freedom. Where shall we go, when I finally get my own emancipation papers? I know you've always said you wanted to travel."

"Oh, yes! Paris first, and then Rome... Oh, and we must visit Venice...." She checked herself in her visions of the Opéra and the shops along Rue de la Paix, and asked, "Where would *you* like to go?" And was surprised at herself, because she realized—even after twenty-three years of marriage—that she didn't know.

"I'd like to go to Jerusalem," he replied, and she thought, *Of course.* For a skeptic who stayed as far away as he could from anything resembling a Church, he knew the Bible, as if it were some marvelous storybook. Of course he would want to see David's city, and the remains of Solomon's Temple....

"And after that," he said, "I think I would like to go to California."

"California?" The name had an almost mythical ring to it, a place at the farthest end of creation.

"To see the goldfields," he explained. "When the men are done in the Army, many of them will go there to find jobs in the mines. And after that," he smiled, "I think the place I look forward most to seeing is Springfield again, and the inside of my old law office. To having things be as they used to be... Except with Emancipation, you can bet there'll be more litigation over it than if I'd put a tax on air."

She laughed over that, and in her dream Mary clutched at the happiness she felt; clutched at the white clouds of the dogwood against the graying evening sky, and the sweetness of the air on her face. She knew what was coming next and she tried to run from it, tried to put it aside, like a book whose ending she didn't wish to read. *Let it end here,* she begged. *This is all I want to remember....*

But of course she found herself in the carriage again, later that night, the fog so thick she could see nothing beyond the carriage windows. Senator Harris's daughter Clara was a pretty young thing and her fiancé, Major Rathbone, was overwhelmingly jolly, like some character out of Dickens. But Mary didn't care. In the dark of the carriage she held her husband's hand.

We must both try to be more cheerful, she thought, knowing what he had said was true. She had put off her mourning for Willie that night, and wore a gown of stiff gray silk that rustled like silver as Lincoln helped her down from the carriage, led her up the theater steps and through the dress circle to their box above the stage. The play had already begun, but the conductor of the orchestra spotted them, and broke into "Hail to the Chief." Lincoln—whose main objection to a cavalry guard was that it embarrassed him to be treated like an emperor—nodded gravely and gestured his thanks to the conductor, and to the actors smiling up at them from the stage; Mary basked in the music, as if in that afternoon's sun.

Maybe it embarrassed him to be treated like an emperor, she thought, half-smiling at him. But she felt such pride in him that she knew she must be visibly glowing. Those evenings when he'd come to her sister's house returned to her, that shy tall awkward-looking man whose arms were too long for his sleeves. *That bumpkin,* Elizabeth had called him. *You can't possibly be seriously thinking of marrying that hayseed?*

I showed you, Mary thought, remembering Elizabeth's nearly successful efforts to discourage the match. *I showed you all. . . .*

The Republican Queen, the newspapers had called her.

She hoped Elizabeth had read them, back in Springfield. Hoped everyone had read them who'd looked out their carriage-windows at her walking in the snow, that first poverty-stricken winter of their marriage. One reason she'd wanted to come tonight was her delight in reading about her own smallest movements in the papers the next day, like admiring herself in the mirror back in the days when she'd been the belle of Lexington.

Down on stage, the actor Harry Hawks ad-libbed, "This reminds me of a story, as Mr. Lincoln would say," and the audience roared with laughter and applause. Just as if, thought Mary, half-angry and half-smug, they hadn't been calling her husband nigger-lover, fool, despot, coward, a thousand hateful things during the years of war. . .

As if every day hadn't brought mail telling him to say his prayers and threatening his life.

But all that was forgotten now. The theater was packed, and a mood of infectious jollity and goodwill rose out of parterre and stage with the usual hot chow-chow of theater smells: pomade and perfume and the stink of the gaslights. The play was delightfully preposterous, with the haughty English grande dame Mrs. Mountchessington conniving to try to wed her unprepossessing daughter Augusta to the homespun backwoodsman she mistakenly believed was a wealthy Yankee.

As sister Elizabeth might have done, thought Mary gleefully, if she'd ever believed that tall skinny lawyer Mr. Lincoln had had two nickels to rub together. . . .

She slipped her hand into Lincoln's, leaned her head on his shoulder: "What will Miss Harris think of my hanging on to you so?"

There was a smile in his voice. "She won't think anything of it."

Maybe he was remembering sister Elizabeth, too.

On stage, Mrs. Mountchessington reeled in horror as she learned the ghastly truth: Asa Trenchard was not rich! Outraged, she sent daughter Augusta from the room, and after a few well-chosen admonitions to the bemused backwoodsman, flounced off herself.

"Don't know the manner of good society, eh?" Trenchard retorted. "Wal, I guess I know enough to turn *you* inside out—you sockdologizing old mantrap!"

Lincoln was just starting to lean down, to make some wiseacre remark in Mary's ear—she never afterwards knew what it was. The crack of a gunshot was hideously loud in the enclosed space of the dark box, and his arm jerked convulsively, wrenching from her hand. Mary caught him as he slumped, smelled the gunpowder and the hot smell of blood. . . .

There was a man in the box, springing out of the cloud of powder-smoke, shouting something. Mary screamed when she saw that he held a dagger, her mind stalled, refusing to understand, her husband's weight bearing down on her heavier and heavier, blood glistening darkly in his black hair.

HER SCREAM PLUNGED HER OUT OF SLEEP, DROPPED HER INTO waking—her scream, the smell of his blood, the weight of him on her shoulder and the knowledge that he was gone, he had left her alone. . . .

And seeing the shadows of her cluttered, crowded room in the Grand Pacific, the looming shadow of Mary Gavin starting up from her chair, Mary screamed again, and again, and again.

She was alive.

It hadn't been laudanum or camphor in Mr. Squair's bottle at all—only one more trick.

And she was going to the madhouse in the morning.

Chapter Five

Lexington 1832

Strangely, what kept going through Mary's mind on the train ride from Chicago across to Batavia, Illinois, was that this felt exactly like being sent away from home at the age of thirteen for putting spiders in her stepmother's bed.

She had detested her stepmother from the time that fair, thin, decisive woman had first entered her father's house when Mary was eight. Elizabeth, even then on the threshold of young-ladyhood, could smile at "Betsey" and call her "Ma," as she and their father demanded. Frances, a pale, quiet-tempered nine-year-old, was exquisitely and impenetrably polite as she was to everyone. From the first, Mary loathed that fragile, steely woman who looked at her with so pointed an eye and said, "It takes seven generations to make a lady," and from the first it was Mary who led Levi, Ann, and little Georgie in mischief, petty thefts, and finely-calculated never-quite-disobedience. "She's not our Ma and nobody can make me say she is!"

The spider incident had its roots two days before Elizabeth's wedding, in the icy February of 1832.

It was a Wednesday, and Nelson, the Todd family coachman, had driven Betsey and the elder girls of the household downtown, for a final fitting of the girls' new dresses with Madame Deauville, and to pick up the creamer and sugar-boat Betsey had ordered for a wedding-gift. Under ordinary circumstances this would have filled Mary with unalloyed delight: there were few things in the world she enjoyed more than new dresses. It was not quite a mile from the brick house on Short Street to the paved streets and stylish shops of Cheapside downtown, and the girls could walk it easily, but taking the carriage imparted a sense of style and importance to the expedition, and Mary loved to wave to her friends from Mr. Ward's school when they passed them on the streets.

She loved, too, the hurry and importance of downtown. Lexington wasn't a great city, like Philadelphia or New York, but around the Courthouse square, and along Main Street and Broadway, brick buildings reared two and three stories tall, and it was possible to buy almost anything: breeze-soft silks from France that came upriver from New Orleans, fine wines and cigars, pearl necklaces, and canes with ivory handles shaped like parrots or dogs'-heads or (in the case of Mary's older friend Cash Clay) scantily dressed ladies (but Cash was careful not to carry that one in company). Downtown, every sort of person could be seen walking along the wide flagways that bordered the streets, from her father's friends—planters and bankers in well-fitting fiddleback coats of brown or blue and high-crowned beaver hats—to the young belles of the town, Elizabeth's cronies, in their bright dresses that rustled with petticoats and dangled with a thousand extravagancies of ribbon and lace. Backwoods farmers in homespun shirts brushed shoulders with young gentlemen from the University, studious Yankees who never seemed to have any fun, the swaggering sons of the local planters in their ruffled shirts and varnished boots, and slaves doing the marketing or sweeping the sidewalks in front of their masters' shops, drab dark notes in the colorful scene.

Madame Deauville had the dresses finished—exquisite white silk festooned with blond lace for Mary, Frances, and Mary's cousin Eliza Humphreys, twelve years old and Betsey's cousin, who was living at the Todd house because the schools were better in Lexington than in Frankfort. They would do, her father had said, for the "second day" party as well. This would be given for those who couldn't make the twenty-mile drive out to Walnut Hill, where Elizabeth had gone to live with their Aunt Liza Carr: It was from Aunt Liza's house, and not their father's, that she would be wed. It was almost a day's drive by carriage—the "second day" party would in fact take place on the third day of Elizabeth's married life—and even the acquisition of a new frock did not erase the anger in Mary's heart, that she had lost the sister who had been like a mother to her a month earlier than she had to, because of her stepmother Betsey.

Elizabeth—unlike Mary—had never breathed a word one way or the other about her feelings toward the woman who'd come to take over the household and Robert Todd's six motherless children, five years ago. But about the time Betsey's first baby, Margaret, was born, Elizabeth had started going to Aunt Liza's for "visits" of a week at a time. After Betsey produced little Sam, and tensions in the now-crowded house on Short Street grew, these visits had lengthened. From the final one, a few weeks after Christmas, Elizabeth had simply neglected to come back.

She still called Betsey "Ma," and kissed the older woman's thin cheek whenever they met. But Mary knew that Elizabeth had left rather than let her father's new wife run her life.

And this thought was in her heart as she, Frances, and Cousin Eliza waited in the carriage for Betsey to pick up the wedding-gift from Blanchard the silversmith.

Betsey was taking her time in the shop—"I'll bet she's going over every square inch of it, as if she thought Mr. Blanchard would give her silver-painted tin," she whispered to Frances—and across the street Mary saw a group of her school friends from Ward's. "Will you look at that *beautiful* mantle Mary Jane's wearing?" gasped Mary. "Is that velvet?" Without waiting to hear Frances's speculation on the garment, Mary pulled her own mantle around her and sprang from the carriage in a froufrou of petticoats.

"Now, Miss Molly," called Nelson from the box. "Miss Betsey told you girls to stay in the carriage."

Eliza and Frances drew back at once. "Don't be a baby, Eliza, come on!" called Mary, halfway across the street already. "I'll only be a minute!" she added, turning to wave at Nelson. She knew perfectly well the gray-haired coachman could not abandon either the horses or the other girls. Then she darted across the ice-slick pavement, to Mr. Sotheby's tall brick store.

"Mary Jane, how gorgeous!" she cried, swirling into the lamplit gloom on the heels of the group of girls. "Where did you get the velvet? Who made it up? Will you wear it to the second-day party Sunday?"

The girls surrounded her, exclaiming in their turn over Mary's description of her own new dress, which lay snug in its cardboard box on the seat of the carriage: "Is it true her sweetheart Ninian is the son of the governor of Illinois?" asked Mary Jane Warfield, the doctor's daughter, and Meg Wickliffe chimed in, "What luck, to get a dress from Madame Deauville! Papa simply won't hear of my going to anyone but old Miss Barney!"

The other girls giggled and exclaimed—Miss Barney was in fact every bit as stylish and expensive as her French counterpart—and Arabella Richardson turned from Mr. Sotheby's small case of jewelry and purred, "You couldn't have done better than Deauville, Mary. She can cut a dress so that even fat girls look lovely. My aunts absolutely *swear* by her."

Mary felt the heat of rage scorch her face, since this wasn't the first time the sylphlike Arabella had publicly remarked on Mary's plumpness. But before Mary could make a retort about the provenance of Arabella's dress, the blonde girl turned back to the jewel-case and inquired sweetly, "Mr. Sotheby, could I just have a look at that sapphire pendant? Papa's getting me a new blue silk and it would be just the thing to go with it."

Searing with anger one moment, Mary felt her face grow cold. The chatter of her friends around her seemed to fade into nothingness, as her consciousness focused on Arabella, Mr. Sotheby, and the pendant now in Arabella's pink-gloved hands. Mary had coveted that pendant for weeks, since it had first come into the store, trying to figure out some way of talking her father into getting it for her. It was a beautiful piece, sapphire and tourmaline flowers clustering on golden leaves, more beautiful than anything Mary had seen in her life. But it was a woman's jewel, not a schoolgirl's, and Mary was only thirteen. Arabella—whom Mary had airily referred to as "that blockhead who can't even spell 'cat' " in the hearing of half their class at the Reverend Mr. Ward's school—held it up to her throat as Mr. Sotheby angled the lamp to make it sparkle: "What do you think, Molly dear?" she asked archly. "Does it go with my eyes?"

Nearly strangling with fury, Mary replied evenly, "It does make them look less squinty." The other girls laughed.

"You know," crooned Arabella to Meg Wickliffe, with deliberate thoughtfulness as the girls rustled out of the shop like an ambulatory flower garden, "it's so pretty, I'll just bet I can get Papa to buy it for me. My birthday's next week."

Following them out, Mary was almost too upset to breathe. Her father wasn't due back from the Legislature in Frankfort until tonight, and then he'd be taken up with preparations for tomorrow's day-long drive to Walnut Hill, and Mary had begged a new pair of party-gloves only last week from her other source of fashionable necessities, Granny Parker. What's more, she knew that Mr. Richardson would buy anything for his lovely and stuck-up daughter. Though in Mary's class, Bella was fifteen, and ready for her come-out. On impulse Mary doubled back into the shop, heart hammering with fear that Betsey would come out of Blanchard's and cross the street looking for her. She would not—*could* not—permit Arabella of all people to take that pendant away from her.

Anyone but her, thought Mary, as her small feet thumped hollowly on the plank floor. . . .

But in her heart she knew, that what she really meant was, *No one but me.*

In the instant that she turned back she'd thought, *Maybe I can get him to hold it for me until I can coax Granny Parker.* But she knew already that Mr.

Sotheby dealt cash-in-hand. The thought that flashed through her mind shocked her, but her anger at Arabella—and her sense of grievance that Arabella didn't have to share her things with sisters or a stepmother's niece—burned stronger in her, and as she walked up to the counter and looked up into Mr. Sotheby's horsey face she opened her mouth and said the first words that came to her.

"I didn't want to say so while the others were here, sir, but Papa wrote me from Frankfort, that if I truly wanted that pendant—and I *truly* do—to tell you to put it on his account."

Her stomach gave a jar of dread as she heard herself—*How could I* SAY *that?*—but even as the storekeeper's eyebrows went up in pleasure and surprise she knew she couldn't take it back. Then excitement flashed through her like fire on a powder-trail, erasing her first horror at herself. It was hers now! That beautiful, beautiful thing was *hers. . . .*

And she'd taken it right out from under Arabella's nose.

I'll talk to Papa tonight, she promised herself frantically, watching with huge eyes as Mr. Sotheby wrapped the pendant up for her (beautiful exquisite gems, coyly hiding in rustling white paper!). *I'll beg him . . . I'll cry.* (Tears usually worked). *And I'll keep it hidden until after he's said I can get it, and then pretend I got it a few days later, and there's no difference, really.*

Then I'll wear it to the Washington's Birthday Dance at Giron's Ballroom and just see that stuck-up Bella's face. . . .

She suspected, as she crossed the street again—Betsey, as she'd hoped, was still searching for minute nicks and imperfections on the wedding-present—that God probably wouldn't think much of this line of reasoning. *But I can't back out now! And what's the difference, if Papa says it's all right . . . ?*

"I thought I told you to stay in the carriage." Betsey emerged from Blanchard's with the silversmith carrying her parcels at her heels. She was increasing *again,* Mary noticed resentfully, and her thin face looked sallow against the old gold plush of the pelerine around her shoulders.

"I'm sorry, ma'am, but I just needed some air, and I thought it would be all right."

Betsey clicked her tongue and allowed Nelson to hand her in, then took the parcels from Mr. Blanchard. The old coachman cocked an eye at Mary as he helped her up the carriage's high step, but didn't comment on the fact that that purported breath of air had involved a trip to Sotheby's and had occupied a good twenty-five minutes.

Mary's father returned to Lexington well after dinner that night, for the roads down to the state capital at Frankfort were icy in this season. Through dinner—always a tumultuous meal, with Ann sulking because she wouldn't be allowed to stand up with Elizabeth at the wedding Friday (and wouldn't get a new dress on the strength of it, as Mary and Frances had) and George and Levi plaguing their tutor, the stiff-backed and bespectacled young Mr. Presby of New England—Mary had almost to shout to make herself heard when she talked to Cousin Eliza. And throughout the meal she was listening, listening for her father's knock at the door.

But when he finally came in he was mud-slathered and cold. "Horse threw a shoe, poor fellow," he said, as his children crowded clamoring around him. "Thank you, Pendleton—" He handed the butler his gloves, riding-cloak, and hat. "Has Nelson got the carriage packed for tomorrow?" Six feet tall, powerfully built, dark-haired and blue-eyed, Robert Todd was in Mary's eyes the handsomest man in all of Kentucky and she would have died for him.

The others were all shouting at once to be heard ("Did you bring me something, Papa?" demanded Ann), and Mary saw at once that he was too tired to listen properly to tear-stained cajoleries about jewelry. She ducked into the dining-room while Betsey clapped her hands and ordered the others up to bed, then found her father's slippers and brought them to him in the small parlor where Pendleton had stirred up the fire.

Betsey glanced impatiently up as Mary came in, but said, "Thank you, Mary," as Mary sat on the footstool to place them on his feet.

As the butler knelt to pull off Robert Todd's boots, Betsey asked, "Are those fools in Washington still talking of letting the National Bank's charter lapse?"

"They're talking of it. Though what they think is going to happen to the country's credit abroad if they do, I can't even begin to guess."

"Aren't they going to shift the country's specie to state banks, at least?" asked Mary. "That's what it said in the *Kentucky Gazette.*"

"That's my clever girl." Her father reached out a hand to stroke the bronze-gold curls that fell forward over her shoulder. "State banks and private banks, which means more power for Jackson's friends, when they've got control of the money to do favors."

"But you run the Bank of Kentucky," pointed out Mary, her concerns about the pendant currently hidden in her jewelry-box vanishing in the double joy of talking politics and having her father's attention. "Won't that give *you* power?"

"Really, Mary. Your father's just come in from a day in the saddle, and I'm sure he's too tired to explain the National Bank to a schoolgirl. Why don't you just run along to bed? Goodness knows we all have to be up early enough in the morning." And Betsey put her arm through her husband's, squeezed it possessively. Robert Todd smiled at her, and covered her hand with his.

"Goodnight, Molly." In his fond eyes she saw herself change from a friend and political partner back into a schoolgirl.

As if the golden joy she'd had in his company had been glass, it shattered in her hands. And left her bleeding.

"Goodnight, Papa," she said tonelessly. "Goodnight . . . ma'am."

She was trembling as she left the parlor, and Betsey closed the door behind her, leaving her in the icy gloom of the candlelit hall. Too hurt, too furious to go up to bed, Mary snatched her shawl from where it hung over the bottom of the bannister and, pulling it tight around her, crossed through the darkened dining-room and out through the butler's tiny pantry, to the blackness of the yard.

It was bitterly cold out there, last week's patches of snow still dotting the ground. Her Granny Parker's tall brick house, catercorner from her father's on the same big lot, was dark already, but rosy light beckoned from the kitchen, and as she crossed the yard Mary heard the slaves' mellow laughter. The door opened as she approached it, Pendleton coming out with a tray of cold supper for his master. Welcoming warmth puffed out around him, the clatter of dishes and the scents of cooking and soap.

"Lord, child, you should be in bed!" Mammy Sally looked up from the hearth, where she was stirring milk-puddings for the little ones—*Betsey's* little ones—in the nursery.

"You got a long trip tomorrow," added Nelson, sitting at the battered table in the middle of the crowded little room, drinking the watered-down remains of the coffee from dinner. "As do we all." He glanced across the table at Saul, Granny Parker's stableman, a good-natured young fellow who'd managed to keep himself out of the subtle power-struggles between the slaves who'd served the first Mrs. Todd and those that Betsey had, five years ago, brought to the household.

"I think he's talkin' to me," sighed Saul. He put his arm around Jane, who sat beside him. Jane was Betsey's slave, the housekeeper who acted as her right hand and, Mary knew, was resented by most of the others because her mistress had taken the place of Granny Parker's daughter. The house that Robert Todd lived in had been given to him by Granny Parker—the continued occupation was not the most comfortable of situations.

Jane—whom Mary had expected to look down on a mere stableman because she was a housekeeper, and far lighter of skin—wrapped her fingers around Saul's, and gently kissed his knuckles.

"What's the matter, child?" Mammy Sally beckoned Mary to the hearth, under cover of the murmur and activity as Chaney the cook finished scouring out the pans, and Betsey's maid Judy came in for Betsey's herb tea. "You been quiet all afternoon. . . . Careful—stand back from the smoke. You get one speck of soot on your dress and neither you nor me'll hear the end of it from *someone* in this house." She glanced across the kitchen at Judy and Jane.

"What's always the matter?" Tears burned Mary's eyes as she drew up one of the kitchen stools. "Mammy, she's poisoning Papa's mind against us! She's keeping him away from us! She told me to run away and not talk to him, because he's too tired, but she doesn't think he's too tired for *her.* She calls me a limb of Satan to my face, or says I'm too fat or will never catch a husband. She's got to be saying that to Papa, too! And he goes along with it!"

She brought up one small white short-fingered hand, dashed the tears away from her eyes.

"I haven't seen him for weeks! He's always gone at the Legislature in Frankfort, and right after the party Sunday he's going back again!" Desolation filled her at the thought of losing him, of always losing him. "She doesn't like to hear me talking politics with him. And I *don't* need it explained to me! I know what we're talking about, I read the newspapers! I'm not stupid, like she thinks I am—like she tells Papa and everyone I am."

"No, child, I've never heard her say to anyone you're stupid," corrected Mammy.

"She says to everyone I'm a limb of Satan."

"That's not the same thing." An expression of gentle amusement pulled the corner of the old nurse's mouth. "Takes brains, to be a limb of Satan." With an almost absentminded motion she continued to stir the thickening custard in its pan.

"Lord, Miss Mary," added Jane, coming to the hearth to tilt steaming water into the tea-pot, "why you take everythin' so hard? Why can't you be sweet, like Miss Frances?"

Mary pulled in her breath in a ragged sob, but if there was one thing her Granny Parker—and her elegant Granny Humphreys, Betsey's mother, in Frankfort—had inculcated into her, it was that you didn't put out your tongue at darkies. So she waited until Jane had gone back to tidying up her account-book at the table before she said, in a low mutinous voice, "If Jane's so smart, let *her* tell *me* why I can't be sweet like Frances. Frances is just a mealy-mouthed wall-flower . . . and I *am* sweet. Or I want to be."

"Miss Frances is what she is." Mammy Sally raised her eyebrows at the scowling girl beside her. "And you are what you are. Wipe your eyes, child." And she took a clean bandanna from her pocket, lest Mary sully the small square of lace and lawn pinned to her pink silk sash.

Mary obeyed, hands trembling. As always, the sudden swing from the sense of power and gladness that she had in her father's presence, to the rage and tears of having him taken from her yet again, left her exhausted and feeling strange, as if some part of her had separated from herself and couldn't quite fit back together. At such times she had a sensation, almost a fear, of losing herself: an uneasy sense that she was about to start doing or saying things that she didn't want to, couldn't help.

Was that, she wondered, for the flashing split-second before she buried the thought, why she'd lied to Mr. Sotheby?

No. I'll make it all right.

Why *couldn't* she be like Frances? Frances would never have told such a lie. Or like gay Meg Wickliffe, or giggling Mary Jane Warfield, or even Arabella Richardson, who might be a conniving blockhead but never seemed to lose control of either her temper or her tears. Why couldn't she be like any of her other friends and cousins in Lexington, who seemed to get on with their lives with little more than minor heartaches and occasional anxieties over what dress to wear?

She didn't know, and the loneliness of this isolation—worse now that Elizabeth had gone—was like a fish-hook, forever embedded in her heart.

Mammy Sally's heavy-jowled face glistened with sweat as she hooked the pot on its chain down closer to the heat, quickened the gentle rhythm of her stirring. Mary knew she should get to bed—Eliza, who shared her room, would be wondering where she was—but lingered. She felt comforted by the soft clanking of dishes, by the murmur of talk in this familiar room, with its sieve hung on the door to keep the witches away.

She wished she could hang a sieve on the door of the house, to keep Betsey out forever.

"Sometimes when I hears them old stories about wicked stepmothers, I wonder how the poor stepmothers feel," said Mammy Sally at last, still so low that the others could not hear. "Can't be easy for Miss Betsey, you know, coming down here from Frankfort where she had her own property and her family was just about kings and queens of that town. Coming away from being free, to marry a man with six children already and your grandmother lookin' over her shoulder..." She shook her head. "That'd be enough to give *me* headaches all the time like she gets, and to make me spit poison in all directions."

"How dare you take her side?" The betrayal cut Mary's heart like a knife.

"Child, I'm not taking her side." Mammy Sally turned from her stirring to give Mary a hug, her uncorseted flesh yielding as a feather mattress under the faded calico of her dress. "I'm just sayin' she *has* a side."

"Well, I have a side, too. Why couldn't she stay in Frankfort, and be free and queen of everybody there like you say? Why did she have to come here?"

Mammy Sally smiled, and poured out the cooling milk into the shallow ramekins for Patty the nurse-girl to take up to little Margaret and baby Sam. "Maybe she wonders that now, too. But she got to make the best of things as they are, the way we all do."

The door opened into the frosty night and Saul came back in, breath blowing steam. "Everythin' loaded up ready to leave in the mornin'," he reported, and went to put his arms around Jane's waist. The housekeeper turned, startled, then closed her eyes and with a motion that went straight to Mary's heart leaned her head back against the man's heavy shoulder, as if relaxing into the pillow of a bed.

"Because you know she can't go back," Mammy Sally's quiet voice went on. "Can't none of us ever go back."

Chapter Six

Mary left the pendant hidden in her jewel-box at home the following morning, when the family set out on the daylong drive to Aunt Liza Carr's. She knew she'd be sharing a room that night not only with Eliza, but with Ann, who kept a ruthless eye on Mary's trinkets to make sure their father never gave Mary more than she herself got. Mary had meant to take her pony and ride beside her father's tall horse—a ploy she used whenever she could, to get time alone with him—but Betsey ruled that ladies didn't spend all day in the saddle the way men did. A few hours was all that was proper for a girl.

So Mary and Eliza were drafted into the chore of looking after little Georgie, who chose that morning to act up, racing wildly around the house, refusing to dress, and shrieking at the top of his lungs.

Betsey's babies, mercifully, were left back at home with Mammy Sally. Only those whom Mary thought of as Robert Todd's "real children"—Frances, herself, Levi, Ann, and George—plus Cousin Eliza, of course—would be with their father to witness the wedding of Elizabeth, who had stood in as a mother to them all.

Even in wintertime, Mary loved the hilly bluegrass country, with its sharp outcrops of granite, its shadowy thickets and dense woods. The dangers from Indians, from cougar and bears, that had given this land the name "The Dark and Bloody Ground" fifty years ago, had given place to plantations of tobacco and hemp, where blood-horses looked mildly over pasture fences, but the shape of the land remained, dramatic and untamed. Though pale sunlight filtered through the leafless boughs of tulip and paw-paw trees, the silence of the woods seemed to hold secrets that tugged at Mary's heart.

The ceremony at Walnut Hill was quiet, and small by Southern standards, meaning fewer than a hundred people: Todds and Parkers and Logans and Russells and all the other connections that made such unbreakable chains all across the South. In addition to Mary and her brothers and sisters, several of her father's brothers and their wives were present, and her exceedingly handsome cousin John Stuart, who had recently gone to practice law in the recently-admitted state of Illinois. The bridegroom himself had come from Illinois to study law at Transylvania University in town, and it was understood that though he would take up residence with Elizabeth at Walnut Hill until he finished his studies, he would (*what else?* thought Mary) be welcome in Robert Todd's house as an overnight guest several times a week.

Her throat ached with renewed desolation as she watched Elizabeth speak her vows in Aunt Liza's parlor. All those years of going to Elizabeth for comfort against Betsey's sharp tongue, all those years of knowing her oldest sister was her refuge, and now Elizabeth was leaving her for good. Even the fantasy that somehow, some way, Betsey would disappear and Elizabeth would come back from Walnut Hill dissolved in the glowing happiness of Elizabeth's words, "I do." Elizabeth would go with Ninian, wherever Ninian decided to go.

No quantity of sapphire pendants would ever assuage that hurt.

The second-day party held at Robert Todd's house in Lexington on the following Sunday was four times as big as the wedding, and wildly more gay. The house, which wasn't even large enough for the family (not to mention the cousins, brothers, and family connections Betsey unhesitatingly invited to take up residence from time to time), was jammed to the doors with well-wishers and friends. Arabella Richardson showed up in the promised new dress of blue silk so elaborate, and so much more beautiful than Mary's new white frock, that Mary darted back upstairs and put on the sapphire pendant, on a blue velvet ribbon around her neck.

The blazing chagrin on Bella's face was everything Mary had hoped it would be.

Robert Smith Todd was a popular man in Lexington, and his friends crowded the parlor. From the chattering circle of her school-friends, their voices drew her like the Pied Piper's magic music toward them around the refreshment table. Fond as she was of Meg Wickliffe and Mary Jane and the others, their conversation was centered wholly around beaux and earbobs . . . subjects all very fine in their place, but nothing to the headier mental delights of politics. Her father was saying,

"...just because Jackson fought the British and can hold his liquor doesn't mean he has honest friends."

"The voters will find their mistake if Jackson does do away with the bank." Mr. Henry Clay took a julep from the tray Pendleton offered, a tall man, thin and hawk-faced and leonine, and also the handsomest man in Kentucky, Mary thought, right after her father. "Think about some of the bankers you know, gentlemen... present company excepted." Clay's warm gray eyes twinkled as he raised his glass toward Robert Todd. "Can you imagine putting the finances of the *country* into their hands?"

Mary edged closer, and the man beside her glanced down at her with an understanding flash of a grin: Mr. Clay's cousin Cash, who'd stayed at the Todds'—naturally, at Betsey's invitation—when he and his body-servant had managed to inadvertently burn down the dormitory of Transylvania University a few years before. Though everyone was crowding close to hear Henry Clay speak, Cash squeezed aside to make room for Mary. He was a big handsome young man with black hair and a devil in his green-eyed smile.

Mary's new brother-in-law Ninian Edwards said, "And every one of them can make as many friends as he needs for votes, just by extending credit...."

"Hell," snorted Cash, "Old Hickory's idea of raising money is betting everything he owns on a horse-race and hoping for the best—not that I mean to disparage a single one of his horses."

"I daresay some of them have more sense than some of the men Mr. Jackson's been putting into office," remarked Mary impulsively, and that got an even bigger laugh.

"You have a smart little girl there, Todd," approved Old Duke Wickliffe, Meg's father and the wealthiest of the planters near-by Lexington. He spit—with perfect politeness and excellent aim—into the cuspidor half-concealed among the ferns at the end of the refreshment table.

Mary looked up at Mr. Clay, who had served in the government under every President from George Washington on, who had been one of the last to flee the capital in the face of the invading British, who was as close to a fighting hero as Kentucky had. "You *will* run for President against Mr. Jackson again, won't you, sir?" And, with her dimpled, one-sided smile, she added archly, "I still hold you to your promise of an invitation to your inaugural ball."

Henry Clay laughed at the reminder of the old jest between them. Mary had known Mr. Clay for most of her life, admiring him with her father's admiration, and later loving him as a friend when she'd go riding out to the gates of his plantation, Ashland, along the Richmond road outside of town. Only gradually had she understood that he was something more than a kingly, lion-haired family friend with a voice like an avenging god's. She'd heard her father talk of Mr. Clay being elected President of the United States long before she had any clear idea that President of the United States was very different from state Assemblyman or state Senator, both offices her father had held.

"My dear." Clay bowed over her hand. "Since you remind me of my promise, you give me no choice but to run."

The men applauded, and Cash likewise bowed to Mary and said, "Then you have my personal thanks, Miss Mary, for spurring my cousin on to his duty again...."

"Like he needed it," commented Meg's brother Young Duke Wickliffe with a cheeky grin at the tall statesman.

"And I, in turn," said Clay, with becoming gravity, "claim *your* invitation, Miss Mary, to your husband's inaugural ball... whoever the lucky gentleman may be."

Cash and the other men laughed again, and Mary fluttered her fan and glanced up at Mr. Clay sidelong, as she'd seen Elizabeth and Meg Wickliffe glance at their beaux. It was another old joke between her and Mr. Clay that if she couldn't grow up and marry him, whoever she *did* marry would have to become President to even things out. Even at thirteen Mary understood how to flirt as well as talk politics, how to look shyly under her lashes, and which angles of her head best became her. This knowledge was almost second nature among the well-born belles of the South. In fact, for a woman to talk politics, she was almost obliged to flirt, to take the edge off what she said so that men wouldn't think her mannish.

Besides, Mary had always enjoyed flirting.

"Elizabeth, you'd best go fetch that good-looking husband of yours away if you're ever to get started on your wedding journey," said Granny Parker, leading Elizabeth into the parlor and fixing Ninian with a beady dark eye. Old Elizabeth Parker had come over the Cumberland Gap in a wagon and had lived in a blockhouse among the canebrakes before Lexington was founded. She had scant regard for husbands, having buried her own decades ago. "I take it you'll still be with Liza when you get back from White Sulphur Springs?"

"Until Ninian's done at the University, yes." Elizabeth's gaze followed her grandmother's, to where Ninian's dramatic raven curls could be seen over the crowd around Mr. Clay and her father. Something in her face, in the way her expression softened, brought back to Mary the way Jane had settled into Saul's shoulder in the kitchen, like the same passage of music, played in a different key.

"Where's she put you these days, Frances?" inquired Granny Parker of the second sister, who trailed along behind Elizabeth, holding her hand. "In the attic?"

"I think I heard her tell Nelson to move a blanket out to one of the sheds," provided Mary archly, which got another laugh. "That way she can rent out the room."

Frances, who had no sense of the ridiculous, only said, "Oh, no, ma'am, I share the small room at the top of the stairs with Ann." But Betsey, making her way to her husband's side, stopped and stiffened with anger, and her narrowed gaze focused on Mary as if seeing her clearly for the first time in that very crowded day.

Mary turned quickly, and looked around for her father. She had to catch him now, had to make it all right.... *I'll tell him I don't know what came over me*—that was true enough.... *I'll tell him Bella Richardson said she deserved to have the pendant because her father is richer than Papa.... And I... and I got so angry that I couldn't let that pass....*

She began to tremble as she nerved herself up for the interview.

But the group of men had shifted, Ninian and Cash coming over to the knot of girls around Granny Parker, Ninian to put an arm around Elizabeth and Cash to sidle as close to Mary Jane Warfield as he could without her father seeing them. Mary slipped away as soon as she could, joining the group of girls who accompanied Elizabeth up to Frances's room, to collect the last of Elizabeth's things as the carriage that would take her and Ninian to White Sulphur Springs was brought to the door. The girls hugged Elizabeth as they mounted the rather narrow stairway, blocking the way completely with their wide mountains of petticoats: Frances and Meg were already in tears and Arabella Richardson was pretending to be.

Mary saw Betsey emerge from the parlor and come toward them, and tried to get up the stairs before her, but there were simply too many girls in the way. Her stepmother reached out and caught the sapphire pendant in her hand, jerking so hard Mary thought either the ribbon or her neck would snap.

"Why don't you tell me which is worse, Miss: to hold household in the face of needless expenditure, or to lie to tradesmen in order to get something you want?"

She spoke in a level tone, but quietly, so quietly Mary wasn't sure, afterwards, how many of her friends heard. Mary's stomach gave one sickening heave under her tight-laced corsets and she felt her face grow cold. Then blood flamed to her cheeks and her throat and her chest, and she retorted, "At least I don't spy on people behind their backs!"

With a gesture as smooth and swift as swatting a fly, Betsey dealt her a stinging box on the ear, and every girl on the stairway stopped dumb, staring down at the two of them at its foot. "You can go to your room, Miss," said Betsey, "and stay there. I think I've seen enough of you for the day."

As Mary thrust her way blindly up through what felt like a patchouli-scented forest of petticoats, she heard the voices behind her, whispering questions....

Whispering answers.

She slammed the door of her room like a wordless curse flung at her stepmother, then stood hanging on to the handle, her knees trembling so hard she didn't think she could make it to the bed. Shame washed over her like the waves of a bottomless ocean.

Shame and terror. *She'll tell Papa.* The words hammered the inside of her ribcage until she felt she would die if she did not scream.

Liar. Liar. Mary Todd is a liar.

The whole town would know about it and nobody would ever speak to her again.

Her father...

She felt sick, as if she were going to throw up. *I didn't mean it. I only wanted something pretty!*

Thief. Liar and thief.

Please, God, don't have everybody in town be whispering that. Papa will be disgraced, too. He'll never speak to me again.

And then I really will die.

Somehow she made it to the bed, and lay trembling, listening to the hushed whispers of the girls in Frances's room next door. *Thief, liar.* Mary dragged the pillow over her head, heedless of Mammy Sally's careful hours with the curling-irons. She lay that way for a long time, her mind blank to everything except dread and shame.

Betsey would tell everyone. Betsey had practically announced it to all her friends, right there on the stairway. What would Eliza and Frances say? They'd never be able to hold up their heads at Ward's again, unless they joined in the cry against Mary....Mary knew exactly how those alliances worked. Her heart curled up at the thought, like a giblet in a dry oven.

Daylight was fading from the windows when Mammy Sally knocked on the door. Mary snatched the pillow from her head. "Go away!" And, when Mammy knocked again and opened the door, "Don't you say a word to me! I don't want to talk about it!" She was shaking all over. Somehow that was almost worse than her father being disgraced for having a liar and a thief in his family: that every darky in town was going to be whispering her name in kitchens, tack-rooms, garden sheds. *Did you hear what that Mary Todd did . . . ?*

Mammy's eyebrows went up, but she only said, "Turn round, child, let me unlace you. No sense gettin' that pretty dress all creased up layin' on it."

Mary obeyed in silence, too angry—and too humiliated—to further humble herself by crying. When Eliza came up a few hours later Mary pretended to be asleep. When she did sleep, her dreams were of walking down Broadway hearing everyone she knew whispering behind her: *Liar. Liar and thief.*

The next morning Mary stayed in her room. She heard the voices of the family going down to breakfast, but knew better than to even try it herself. All she'd need would be Betsey dragging out the whole story in front of them. She trembled at the thought of the upcoming interview with her father. He would ask her why she'd done it—with the look of hurt in his eyes, as he'd asked her about countless acts of disobedience over the years—and she had nothing, literally nothing, that she could tell him.

She didn't know why she'd done it. Just thinking about saying that made her want to cry.

But she wanted above all things to have it over with, done. *He will never speak to me again,* she thought, and the next moment, *He has to say it's all right. He has to say it or I'll die.*

She strained her ears for the sound of his boots on the stairs, and wondered if she should pray. But she could think of nothing God would even consider granting her.

Boots at the bottom of the stairs. Muffled voices, her father's and Betsey's. She held her breath: *It's going to be now. . . .*

I'll cry. He'll forgive me if I cry. . .

Then, very dimly, the sounds of hooves in the street. A saddle-horse being brought around to the front of the house. The sound of the front door opening . . . "I'll be back on the first," said her father's voice.

The door closed. Betsey's light decisive step retreated to the parlor. A moment later, the sound of hooves rattled down Short Street as her father rode away.

Mary sat up, her mouth literally ajar with shock and, a moment later, outrage. There would be no confrontation. No bargaining, no tears, no forgiveness.

He had left without any of them. Without saying good-by.

"She told him you weren't feeling well," reported Eliza, when she came up an hour later after helping Betsey and Frances wash the good breakfast china—a task never relegated to darkies. "She said you were still asleep."

And SHE *called* ME *a liar!* The hairs on her head prickled with wrath.

Her father was going to be gone for almost two weeks, and Betsey had taken it upon herself to step between them, and prevent them from even having the chance to say good-by.

"What did she say to you yesterday, anyway?" asked Eliza, digging through her own little painted tin box for a ribbon to go in her yellow curls. "Is your ear all right?"

Mary barely remembered Betsey hitting her in front of her friends. All she could think was, *She told him in private. Of course—she doesn't want to hear the darkies in every kitchen in town saying, "That Mary Todd's a liar and a thief," any more than I do. Not because she cares one single thing about me, but because of Papa's reputation at the Legislature and the bank.*

But she'd told him. Betsey wouldn't pass up the chance to drive the wedge more firmly between Robert Todd and his "real children." She had taken him from Mary, and had driven Elizabeth from the house, Elizabeth who had been like a mother to Mary, to make way for her own children. She had struck Mary in front of all her friends, and had lied—*lied* to keep her husband away from his daughter before he rode back to Frankfort.

Mary managed to whisper, "My ear is fine."

Later that day she made it her business to linger in the kitchen, and when Betsey's back was turned abstracted a handful of coffee-beans from the tin caddy that was usually kept locked. These she used to bribe Saul to procure for her a dozen live spiders, an astonishing number considering it was the middle of winter. The result was everything Mary had hoped it would be, Betsey's voice screaming wildly in the darkness a few minutes after bedtime—she was always too stingy to carry a bedroom candle—and Patty, who had her own reasons for disliking her mistress, reporting the next day in the kitchen that she'd found Miss Betsey standing on a chair naked as a jaybird, shrieking and trying to claw the confused arachnids out of her long unbraided hair.

She can't prove I did it, thought Mary, with a kind of burning complacency as she lay listening to the cries and thumps. *She can't prove a thing.*

But Betsey didn't need or want proof. Despite the fact that Mary had sworn Saul to secrecy and dropped down the outhouse the candy-tin in which the spiders had been delivered, Betsey confined Mary to her room for the ten days intervening before her father's return from Frankfort—days of anxiety, loneliness, and alternating waves of defiance and agonizing shame.

Worse still, she refused to let her have any books, not even the Bible. Only sheets to hem.

So there was nothing to do but wait for her father's return.

She wished there were something she could do to punish herself, so that he would forgive her. Wished there was some way she could go back in time and rub out everything that had happened since that Wednesday afternoon in Mr. Sotheby's store. Make it all not have happened, make everything go back to what it had been before.

She knew she mustn't wish for Betsey to die before her father got home—she could just imagine what God would have to say if she prayed for it—but the thought was frequently in her mind.

Sometimes, when she thought of what her father would say to her, she wished she could simply die herself.

Her father came home just before suppertime on the first of March. Mary was so exhausted with shame, with remorse, with anger at herself and Betsey and all the world, that she started sobbing the moment she heard the hooves of his horse in Short Street, and was still weeping after supper, when Betsey came into her room—wordlessly and without knocking—and escorted her down to his study.

"Your mother and I have been talking," said Robert Todd, when Betsey had closed the door and went to stand beside him at his desk.

Mary protested, "She's not my mother!" Then she clapped her hands over her mouth and stood, tears streaming down her face, looking from Betsey's stony countenance to her father's weary one. She saw in his eyes only a kind of tired peevishness. There wasn't even anger, she realized, with a sick shock of disappointment. Only that he didn't want to be troubled with the conflict between his first wife's children and their stepmother.

He just wants everything to be all right, so he can be like his friends and not worry about it.

The knowledge was like opening a beautifully-wrapped present and finding it empty. Like biting into a delicious-looking piece of cake that had been made without sugar or salt.

And I'm the one who's hurting him.

It seemed that there was nothing that she could do or feel that was not wrong.

"Your mother and I have been talking," he said again, and Mary flinched, waiting for the words of anger, of disappointment, of rejection. *Liar. Thief.* She wished she could shrink in on herself and disappear. Then he said, "And we've agreed that you're old enough now to go away to school."

Mary looked up. This was so unexpected that she was caught breathless, as if she'd stepped through her familiar bedroom door and found herself falling down the backyard well. Then the meaning of his words sank in, and her disappointment evaporated, her volatile spirits leaped.

School . . .

Mary had listened in hungry envy when the Reverend John Ward had spoken to his classes about the seminaries for higher education that girls could go to, in Philadelphia and New York. Meg Wickliffe—who at sixteen was almost finished at Ward's—said she might go to Sigoigne's very prestigious Female Academy in Philadelphia, next year or the year following, and Mary's soul had ached with the desire to go, too. To learn more of history than the Reverend and Mrs. Ward could teach. To have access to all the literature of England and France that she'd only just heard about . . . to learn to speak French properly, and maybe Italian, maybe even Latin like the boys.

The sudden shift from shame and dread to the great longing of her heart was so unexpected that for the first few moments while her father was speaking, Mary only felt confused, as if she were dreaming. *Betsey didn't tell him. She can't have told him. . . .*

". . . know that we don't have the money to send you to Philadelphia or New York. But Madame Mentelle at Rose Hill teaches a very fine course of studies. . . ."

Madame Mentelle! Mary's thoughts came crashing back to earth. She'd seen the tall, rangy Frenchwoman striding about Lexington's muddy streets in her hopelessly old-fashioned, high-waisted dresses. In the frame of her short-cropped hair her angular face and pale eyes had a decisive expression even more witchlike than Betsey's.

Mary's glance shot to Betsey's face, and she understood. This was Betsey's way of getting her out of the house. Of having Robert Todd that much more to herself.

She, Mary, had handed her the wherewithal to convince him to do it. . . .

And because of the pendant—because of the falsehood she had told—she couldn't even protest.

"You'll like it there," said her father, with encouraging cheer.

How do you know?

She managed to say, "Yes, Papa. Thank you, Papa."

He held out his arms to her, and Betsey moved aside a half step, as if giving permission for Mary to sit on her father's knee. "That's my little girl," he said, rocking her, holding her—taking comfort, she felt, though it was something never said between them, in her nearness and her unquestioning love.

Betsey didn't tell him, Mary thought again, disbelieving. Her heart ached with gratitude—not to Betsey, but to God.

Betsey was getting exactly what she wanted, spiders notwithstanding.

Mary was still her father's little girl, his child for whom he could make everything all right without effort when she wept, and not a liar and a thief.

But the price of that miraculous salvation was exile.

"Mary," said her father's deep voice in her ear, "I want you to apologize to your mother for what you did."

Mary nodded, and at his urging slipped down off his knee. She curtsied to Betsey, whispered, "Ma, I'm so sorry."

Betsey's face was enigmatic. "I accept your apology, Mary. We will say no more of it." A formula? A promise? A simple acknowledgment that certain things were best kept quiet for the good of the family's reputation? Mary's eyes searched her stepmother's face briefly, then fell before the cold gaze. Betsey had kept her secret, and Mary, now, was obliged to keep it, too. The shame of being caught in a lie—of being trapped by her lie—burned in her like the scar of a red-hot knife, sealed in her secret heart. She knew she would never, ever speak of what she had done.

Not even to obtain forgiveness.

"Run along now," said Betsey, "and tell Chaney to give you some supper."

As Mary backed from the little book-crammed study she saw her stepmother take the place she had had moments ago on Robert Todd's knee. "Well," said Betsey, as Mary shut the door, "now maybe we'll have some peace."

Chapter Seven

Rose Hill was a low, rambling house built in a grove of locust trees, out on the Richmond Pike. From earliest childhood Mary would pass the place when she'd ride her pony to Mr. Clay's graceful stucco house at Ashland, which stood nearby. She'd seen Madame Mentelle in town, too, and had overheard Betsey and her bosom-bow Sophonisba Breckenridge talking about her—"virago" and "bluestocking," and "very well educated I *suppose,* but those *dresses* she wears..." The roll of Sophy's eyes had been worth a thousand words. "I'll bet that poor husband of hers lives under the cat's foot." And the two women had giggled like malicious girls.

Now the tall Frenchwoman stood at the top of the front door's three brick steps: "Dulcie will show you where to put Miss Mary's things," she told Nelson, as the old coachman unstrapped the trunk from the back of the carriage. The slave woman of whom she spoke stepped down to help Nelson carry in Mary's many boxes, and Madame herself glanced sidelong at Mary, her pale eyes unreadable. "Take the books into the library. *La bibliothèque de votre père, c'est renommé ici à la ville.*" Her French was so fast, and so slurred, that Mary had to grope for the words addressed to her, picking the sentence apart.

La bibliothèque... the library... *de vot' père*... your father's library...

"Merci, Madame," she replied carefully, meeting that disconcerting gaze unflinchingly. Understanding that this woman was testing her—probing to see how much work her French would need to achieve the

proficiency of a truly accomplished young lady, she went on in that language. "Papa says you are a scholar."

Madame winced, as at the scraping of a nail on tin. "*Une scholaira?* This isn't Latin! I was afraid all you'd learned here was American French. Good God, the Chickasaws speak it better than those imbeciles at Ward's."

Mary's spine stiffened, for she liked the Reverend Ward and his wife. "Maybe the Chickasaws learned it while selling American scalps to the French before the Revolution," she retorted.

Madame's eyebrows shot up at this impertinence. Then, slowly, she smiled, revealing long yellow teeth like a horse's. "From what I hear, your grandfather kept the local market in such commodities fairly scanty."

And as they crossed the threshold into the dim entryway Mary's heart flooded with warmth, that this forbidding woman knew something of her family. That she wasn't just another nameless schoolgirl to be pushed aside, as she was always pushed aside at home unless she raised a fuss or made them laugh. And at the same time it burst upon her like sunlight that French was a language in which one could talk about things that were important and fun, not just about the pen of the gardener's aunt.

"Grandpa Todd held off the Indians at Blue Licks, Madame." She had no idea what the French word for a salt-lick was, so simply gave the vowel a Gallic twist. "My Great-Uncle John was killed in that battle."

" 'My Great-Uncle John, *he was* killed in that battle,' " Madame corrected. "This is how it is said in Paris. I too had an uncle killed in battle, fighting for the King of France against the rabble." She paused in the hallway; through a door on her right Mary glimpsed dark bookshelves and busts of bronze and marble and gilt-trimmed porphyry in niches; through another, wide windows and dappled light. Somewhere in the house a woman sang as she worked, a light air, and in French. There was a smell of wood-smoke, and of pine boughs brought in to freshen the winter stuffiness. The quiet felt like the blessing of God, after the constant turmoil and children crying of her father's house—her stepmother's house.

"I understand you are something of a scholar yourself."

"Yes, ma'am."

"And I suppose you've been told all your life not to tax your poor little female brain with such heavy matters as history and mathematics." Madame led the way down a passageway, and across a narrow court tucked in like an open-air hallway between the main block of the house and its western wing. Plum-colored nubbins of new canes punctuated the thorny stems of roses along the brick of the wall. A green film of moss on the bricks underfoot showed where the shadows lay longest. "At least that's what people were always telling me."

"Did they call you a bluestocking, ma'am?" It was the worst thing Betsey and Sophy Breckenridge could say of another woman, and Mary was astonished she remembered the phrase for it in French.

"Bluestocking? To hear them tell it, I was blue all the way up to my chin." Madame walked beside her down the court, which had several doors opening onto it and a little iron gate at the end. "And do you know what? It didn't change how I felt. One cannot change what one feels, child. Any more than one can change what one loves." She paused with her hand on the door-latch. "We're a bit crowded this season. I hope you don't mind a room in the family wing, instead of over on the east side with the other boarders? Dinner is in the main house at five, and perhaps we'll have a little music afterwards—do you play?"

Before Mary could reply Madame opened the door, to reveal a room every bit as constricted—and as innocent of a fireplace—as her own on Short Street. The two small beds it contained seemed to fill it. Mary's own three trunks were piled at the foot of one, with hatboxes and satchels stacked neatly on top. Beside the other, just removing an armful of folded linen from a stylish portmanteau, was Meg Wickliffe, a smile of welcome and delight on her face.

"I shall see you girls at dinner," said Madame. "Don't put spiders in my bed, and I daresay you and I shall get along fine."

WITH THE POSSIBLE EXCEPTION OF MAMMY SALLY'S KITCHEN, MARY had never known a place where she felt so profoundly at home as she did at Rose Hill. She missed Frances and Eliza—missed Mammy Sally and even months later missed Elizabeth—but she had never known a sense of peace like the peace she knew at the rambling, tree-shaded house on the Richmond Pike.

For all Lexington's brick shops and paved streets, for all its University and bustling little downtown, it was still only a few minutes from the hilly bluegrass meadows, from the dark woods and the fields of tobacco and corn. When Nelson came with the carriage on Friday evenings to bring Mary back to Short Street, they drove for the most part through groves and woodland before the houses of the town rose around them, windows glowing amber in the freezing winter dark, or, later, somnolent in the grass-scented twilight of summer. Mary would wave to friends both black and white as they passed them, and then they'd be on the other edge of town, where the hills started up again and the trees clustered thick.

Mary settled quickly into the sleepy rhythm of those days, the peculiarly Southern blending of countryside and town.

During the week, Meg Wickliffe was like a sister to her. They'd braid each other's hair at night, and laugh over the running feud between Madame Mentelle's parrot Xenophon and Dulcie the maid—Xenophon had learned to imitate the sound of the silver bell Madame used to summon Dulcie, and called the exasperated woman into the parlor a dozen times a day. Xenophon also swore in Italian—"I shall never be able to teach Italian so long as that bird is in the house," remarked Madame.

At sixteen Meg was very much a belle, and would be sent, she said, to Sigoigne's next year, as soon as her French was up to Philadelphia standards. Her beaux would come to Rose Hill in the evenings and make careful conversation in the drawing-room with Meg and the older girls, under Madame's watchful eye. Meg instructed Mary in the intricacies of curling-irons, chignons, and how to wire one's braids into the latest and most fashionable styles as seen in fashion plates from France; they giggled over the courtships of their friends, designed elegant dresses for one another, and stayed up far too long after bedtime reading *The Monk* to one another by the light of a single shielded candle.

Mary would flirt with Meg's beaux in the parlor, when Madame's back was turned.

When she was home on Saturdays, she would stroll down to Cheapside to shop with Frances and Eliza, with Elizabeth if she was in town, and sometimes with Ann. Mary had learned her lesson and never lied to Mr. Sotheby again, though she found that she didn't feel quite right about the sapphire pendant and seldom wore it. Still, her father bought her other things, earbobs and slippers and gloves, as if deep in his heart he understood that he'd really sent her away to buy peace with his wife. Mary sensed the guilt that lay behind his unwillingness to see her cry, and occasionally used it, if there was something she really, really wanted . . . though whenever she did this, she always felt ashamed.

Sometimes after Nelson brought her back to Rose Hill on Sunday evenings, Mary would sit in her room and take her special things out of the little casket where she kept them: brooches, necklaces, handkerchiefs bordered in lace. Proof that her father loved her.

Hope that he loved her best of all.

Frances, at fourteen, had finished Ward's school and was already a belle, her fair hair dressed up in elaborate side-curls and serpentine plaits adorned with silk flowers from Sotheby's. As far as Mary could see, she did little but shop, and stroll, and chat with her friends, and sew dresses to wear at the dances held in the long salon above M'sieu Giron's confectionary. On those rare occasions when their father was home from the Legislature, he would shake his head and say, "Now, a girl must be able to amuse her husband, and to raise intelligent sons for the nation," but Mary observed how Robert Todd would puff with pride when planters' sons like Nate Bodley or Young Duke Wickliffe would come calling.

And though there was nothing Mary liked better than to shop and stroll and chat with Frances and Elizabeth—nothing that excited and interested her more than the selection of lace for a pelerine, or of silk for a dancing-dress, or being made a fuss over by Mr. Sotheby or Mr. Fowler when she'd come into their stores—she loved, too, the peaceful stillness of the library of Rose Hill, away from the noise and confusion of too many children in too few rooms. There she could savor in peace the way Shakespeare's words sounded in her mind: *If I profane with my unworthiest hand / this holy shrine, the gentle fine is this / My lips, two blushing pilgrims ready stand / to smooth that rough touch with a tender kiss. . . .*

She had to be careful, of course, not to speak of it too much—no gentleman liked a bluestocking—but she found great pleasure in being able to talk sensibly about Shakespeare if the subject arose.

Spring advanced and the dogwood bloomed. The high tide of summer transformed the hills to lush green, the shade of the thick groves to mysterious blue-black. Like the savor of burgoo against the sweetness of toffee, the social delights of dances and picnics were flavored with politics that were the heartbeat of the South, as men wrangled with the framework of power and law to shape and enable their quest for money and the comforts of life.

Henry Clay was running for President. An ardent Whig like Robert Todd, Ninian took Mary, Frances, and Elizabeth out to hear the candidates speak at a picnic at Trotter's Grove. Elizabeth joined at once with the other matrons, young and old, of Lexington, in directing their slaves to set out the tables and the food—cornbread, Brunswick stew, imported oysters, homemade jams—and Frances, who cared little who became President, gravitated at once to the young gentlemen who'd come to listen, but Mary found herself a place by the speakers' platform. Cheap draperies of red, white, and blue bunting adorned it; the American flag had had a couple of extra stars scootched into its blue field for Maine and Missouri, and looked a bit ragged and out of balance. Ninian, also maneuvering his way through the crowd to stand close, caught her eye and winked.

Mary had followed the campaign closely in the several journals available in Lexington, both Democrat and Whig, and wanted to hear what men from elsewhere in the state were saying about Clay's American System of public works and strong currency. But when she tried to edge closer, Elizabeth gestured to her to come to the food-tables.

"Really, Mary," she whispered, as soon as Mary came close. "You mustn't push yourself in among the men that way."

"I was close to Ninian," protested Mary. And then, when Elizabeth simply pursed her lips and handed her a dish of beans to set out, she added in annoyance, "I'm not going to flirt with him, if that's what's worrying you."

"The things you do say." Elizabeth's expression was that of a woman requesting a servant to remove a dead mouse from the soup tureen. "A gentleman never *seems* to mind anything a lady does, but what he *thinks* of a young lady who has so few qualms about unsexing herself is another matter. In any case," she added, "gentlemen are more comfortable talking politics *without* ladies present . . . if you know what I mean."

Mary scowled rebelliously, but when she looked back in the direction of the platform, it was pretty clear to her what Elizabeth meant. She could hear Old Duke Wickliffe's voice rising in anger about the God-damned bill to forbid the importation of slaves to the state, see his son Young Duke lashing the air with his riding-whip. Cash Clay was squaring off with the bull-like young Nate Bodley, gesticulating furiously. By the sound of it, Nate—whose father owned Indian Branch, one of the wealthiest plantations in Fayette County—was already half drunk.

Before nightfall, thought Mary uneasily, somebody would call somebody out, or someone would end up thrashed with a cane behind the line of carriages where black grooms walked the blood-horses to be raced later in the afternoon. And the young ladies of her acquaintance, Frances and Meg, Eliza and Mary Jane and Isabelle, all clustered together, giggling at Arabella Richardson's jokes or crying out admiringly at Meg's new walking-dress of pleated jaconet, as if nothing more serious existed in all the world.

Don't they remember that Isabelle's brother KILLED Meg's brother three years ago, over a letter written to a newspaper? Mary wondered, puzzled and angry. *Don't they care who gets elected, who runs the nation?*

Of course, it didn't do for a girl to thrust herself in among the gentlemen once the talk got heated, for fear of hearing words no young lady should hear. But that didn't mean girls had to act like imbeciles, just to get young men to like them.

She realized that the sun-dazzle in her eyes was growing brighter, that sections of leaves were disappearing from the chestnut trees, appearing and disappearing, as things do in dreams. Her stomach curled with dread. In a small voice she said, "I think I'm getting a headache," and Elizabeth's annoyance changed swiftly to her old protective sympathy.

"Maybe if you sit down in the carriage where it's shady it'll go off." She put her arm comfortingly around Mary's shoulders, though Mary knew perfectly well that her headaches never "went off."

She had had them, on and off, for a year or more; it seemed to her that since she'd begun having her monthlies they'd become more frequent, and worse. Sometimes Mammy Sally's remedies of bitter herbs would stave them off. More frequently nothing helped.

"Well, I'm not going back home," Frances hastened to put in. "You just sit still and be quiet, Mary." And as if to emphasize her words she fluttered off in the direction of Arabella and her cronies. Even in her agony, Mary felt a stab of furious resentment, that she could not be joining her as the center of the boys' attention. Wittier and quicker-tongued than the fairy-like Frances, she surreptitiously enjoyed the game of drawing beaux away from her sister.

It was like the knowledge that her father sent her more presents than he sent Frances or Ann.

"I'll get you a wet napkin to put on your eyes." Elizabeth guided Mary gently to the carriage, with clearly no intention of leaving the speaking either. "Ninian, I think I saw Dr. Warfield over near the tables. Do you think he might come and see Mary?"

By the time Ninian came to the carriage, with the gray-haired professor of obstetrics and surgery from the University in tow, old Nelson had fetched a glass of ginger-beer and had put up the hood of the barouche in a vain effort to approximate by shade the darkness that Mary's throbbing head craved. As Mary heard the voices approach, she heard Nelson offer, "I can take Miss Mary on home and be back in an hour, Miss Elizabeth."

"That's probably best," agreed Elizabeth.

And Dr. Warfield—whose daughter Mary Jane had been shyly slipping away all afternoon to speak to Cash Clay among the trees of the groves—asked, "How often does your sister have these nervous headaches, Mrs. Edwards?"

"Sometimes two or three a week. Sometimes she'll go a few weeks without one."

Old Dr. Warfield climbed into the carriage, making it rock like a ship in the storm and bringing Mary's lunch heaving back into her throat. She wanted to scream at him to go away, to leave her alone. . . . Elizabeth and Ninian climbed in also *(rock, sway, lurch!)*, Elizabeth taking her seat beside Mary and the two men opposite. It would have been, of course, completely improper for any man to have been in the carriage alone with her. "May I take your pulse, Miss Mary?"

Elizabeth turned down the cuff of Mary's glove; the medical man's gloved fingers felt warm on her icy wrist.

"Your sister is of a nervous disposition, is she not, Mrs. Edwards?" There wasn't a soul in town who hadn't heard of Mary's alternating charm and tantrums.

"Yes," replied Elizabeth, "very much so."

"And I believe Mr. Edwards told me that this is your little family politician?"

"She has a very lively mind." Much as Elizabeth might disapprove of Mary's unladylike zest for politics and study, she would never admit this to even so prominent an acquaintance as the professor.

Just let me alone! Mary wanted to scream at them, and began to weep as the hammering in her head increased. She opened her eyes a slit: Dr. Warfield looked like a buzzard, with unhealthy skin and a straggling beard. As she watched, half his head and a portion of his right shoulder disappeared into a fiery cloud of migraine light.

"That explains it," said the doctor wisely. "A female's constitution is far more nervous than a boy's would be. The entire system of the female is rooted in the nerves and the generative functions rather than in the higher organs of thought and reason. For this reason mental activity tends to overload and debilitate her, resulting in these headaches, which are much more characteristic of the female system than the male."

"But what can we do about them?" asked Ninian.

Her brother-in-law might be a blockhead about tariffs, thought Mary, but that was the first practical remark she'd heard concerning her headache from any white person that afternoon.

"Personally, I would recommend that she be bled, to lower her constitution. If bleeding does not relieve the pressure on the overactive nervous system we shall try a blister, to draw the heat away from her brain."

There's nothing wrong with my brain! Just take me home and leave me alone in the dark! Get Mammy Sally to make me some of her herbs. . . .

But of course nothing would do for it but that Dr. Warfield and Ninian accompanied Mary and Elizabeth back to the house—and to Betsey, who was sent for and who was less than pleased about being obliged to leave the picnic and her friends to tend to a stepdaughter whom she half-suspected was putting on this show of pain simply to gain attention.

Mary was put to bed, swathed in her green-and-gold-flowered wrapper. Dr. Warfield came in with a china bleeding-bowl and a sharp little knife. He was brusque and rough-handed, his breath smelling of bourbon, and the blade gouged deep. In the stuffy, curtained bedroom the blood stank. Mary wept, wondering if she were going to die as her mother had died, but her headache didn't go away.

"Do you feel better, darling?" asked Elizabeth, and Mary had the good sense to nod. The last thing she wanted was a blister to draw the heat away from her brain.

"I'm afraid that as long as she is kept in school, she will run the risk of continuing to suffer in this fashion," she overheard Dr. Warfield say, outside the bedroom door, as Elizabeth made sure no chink of light came through the curtains and Ninian tucked her in with brotherly affection. "Education, and the mental overstimulation of attending a political speaking, invariably react thus on the female organism."

"Well, I know how much Mary loves school. . . ." Her father's voice. He must have ridden back from the political speaking too. He sounded doubtful, because it was true that the headaches had become much worse in the three months Mary had been at Mentelle's. But before Mary could do much more than think in panic, *Don't take me out of the school . . . !* Betsey's crisp voice cut in.

"We shall speak to Madame Mentelle about modifying Mary's course of study, but I see no reason why she cannot continue to attend. I've heard wonderful things of her there, and of course her French has improved tremendously."

Of course, thought Mary. *She doesn't want me here.*

She desperately hoped her father would come in and see her, maybe sit on the edge of the bed and hold her hand a little. But he didn't.

"We'll keep you informed of Mary's progress, Dr. Warfield." Tongue click. "Now we really must be getting back—folks will wonder what's become of us. . . ." The voices trailed away down the stairs.

Hooves and the jingle of carriage-harness in the street, dimly perceptible even through the shut curtains, the closed windows.

Mama wouldn't have left me alone, thought Mary, grief welling up in her, almost worse than the pain. *Mama wouldn't have sent me away—or made me share a room with her cousin.* She barely remembered her mother, barely remembered sitting on her lap, enfolded and safe, in the days before Levi came along. But the memory was precious. After Levi's birth—and then Ann's and George's—her mother had had little time to give to her. But what she had had, Elizabeth Parker Todd had given. As always when she felt sick and alone, Mary tried to picture what life would be like now if her mother had not been carried out of her room like that in the dead of night, never to return again.

The anger she felt made her head hurt worse, swamping her grief in pain.

After a little time soft bare feet creaked on the hall floor, and Mammy Sally came in, bearing a cup that smelled sharply and sweetly of hot ginger and sugar. Mary drank it thirstily, and lay back in the darkness while those warm strong hands unbraided her hair, gently brushed out the long, heavy curls. She whispered, "Thank you," and slipped over into sleep.

THAT WAS ALMOST THE LAST OCCASION ON WHICH MARY STAYED IN that small room. The following Saturday, when Nelson brought her home for dinner, her father announced that he had "closed the deal" on Palmentier's Tavern on Main Street, and would be converting it into a house for the family—he cast a significant eye at Betsey as he spoke, and she simpered in acknowledgment of what the novelist Mrs. Radclyffe would have called the "token of his affection" that currently swelled the front of her white lawn gown. *You didn't even ask us,* thought Mary resentfully, as Eliza gasped, "May I have my own room?" and Betsey heaved a visible sigh of relief.

"Now maybe we'll be able to entertain properly."

Robert Todd said quietly, "Now maybe my family can come and go from our own front door without crossing paths with coffles of Mr. Pullum's slaves."

And young Mr. Presby the tutor said, "Amen."

Mary glanced sharply at her father from beneath her lashes, then across at Elliot Presby, the theology student who hailed from some tiny rock-ribbed village in New England. Bespectacled, skinny, with a face like a saint who's just bitten a sour lemon, young Mr. Presby had little that was good to say about the South or Southerners, and on more than one occasion had reacted to Mary's teasing with sharp anger.

Above all he detested the institution of slavery, and looked upon all slaveholders—including Mary's father—with ill-concealed disapproval. When she was younger Mary had teased him mercilessly, but now she was more and more conscious herself of the brick-walled yard on the corner near her father's house, of the men and women who sat on benches under Pullum's awnings out front, with chains around their ankles. . . .

And of old Nelson's silence when he drove her past the place on the way to and from Rose Hill.

Cash Clay had returned from his year at Yale an abolitionist, afire to end slavery, or at least forbid the importation of more slaves to Kentucky. According to Frances, after Mary had left the political-speaking Nate Bodley had attempted to cane Cash over it.

Of course it isn't the same with our people, thought Mary, watching as

Pendleton circulated the table with a platter of boiled ham. The darkies were slaves, yes, in that they were legally her father's property—or more properly Granny Parker's property—but she knew he treated them well. Slavery in Kentucky wasn't at all like slavery in the deeper South. She'd been in and out of the kitchen all her life, listening to Nelson tell his stories, or watching Mammy Sally make her custards for the children, as lovingly as if they were her own.

Her father would never sell Nelson or Mammy Sally or Jane or even grumpy old Chaney. They were part of the family.

And where would they go if they didn't live with us? That was something that had always bothered her about Cash's wild insistence that all slaves be freed immediately, for their own good and that of the owners' souls. *What would they do? Who would take care of them?*

Then she thought, *If we move down to Palmentier's Tavern, it will be harder for Jane and Saul to meet.* It was only a few streets up from Main Street to Granny Parker's big house, of course; but she knew Granny Parker was strict about keeping her people at their duties, as was Betsey.

And she, Mary, had been consulted about the move no more than had been the slaves.

Why should I care? she wondered, as Nelson drove her back to Rose Hill early Monday morning, with the horses' breath and her own a faint mist in the chill. *It isn't as if it were my home anymore.* She had shared a bed with Eliza, because Ann had taken over her old bed. Though they all laughed and giggled as they always did when she came home, she felt like an interloper. Ann and Eliza had to move their things around to admit her, cheerfully as they always did. But she felt, as she always felt, that things went on without her. That if she did not return, she would not be much missed.

Still, the thought of complete strangers sleeping in that bedroom, of another family reading the newspaper by lamplight in the study where she had read on those rare, precious evenings with her father, filled her with desolation. As if she were invisible, and no one cared if she lived or died. She stayed away from the house on the Saturday when the furniture was moved, joining instead with Meg and the Trotter sisters, with Mary Jane and her sisters Julia and Caroline, and her other friends from Ward's, to gather hickory-nuts in the woods along the Richmond Pike.

It was a warm day at summer's end. The leaves of the maples had begun to turn and the air within the woods felt heavy, mysterious with the coming of the year's change. The girls were joined by several of Meg's numerous beaux—Nate Bodley, Jim Rollins, Buck Loveridge, and a few others, sons of the local planters or the gentlemen of the town—and there was a great deal of laughter and chasing around the laurel thickets among the trees, under the benevolent eye of Isabelle's widowed Aunt Catherine. Mary, with her curls bobbing under a new hat of pink straw and a new dress of pink-sprig voile, flirted with Nate and let him hold in his handkerchief the nuts she gathered, a curiously exhilarating experience. In the dappled green light his handsome face looked different, gentler than it did when she'd seen him among the cronies at the political speakings. His brown eyes caressed her when he called her "Miss Mary," and she realized, for the first time in her young life, that something might lie beyond flirting.

That instead of the delight in being the center of attention in a ring of young men held by her saucy wit, she might draw to her a single man, who would love her as Saul loved Jane.

It was a revelation to her, and one that confused her, as she had lately been confused by the stirrings in her body of feelings she didn't understand. She pulled her hands away from Nate and he chased her, laughing, through the sun-dappled woods.

They came out of the undergrowth to see Cash Clay sitting alone in the clearing, his long legs stretched out on the grass, hulling the hickorynuts the others had gathered, striking them on an outcrop of rock. Nate and Mary stopped, unseen, for at that same moment Mary Jane came into the clearing by herself, her bonnet gone, her fair hair undone and lying over her shoulders. She was looping it up and working a hair-pin into it when she saw Cash; Mary caught Nate by the sleeve and tugged him deeper into the laurel, touching a finger to her lips. Nate nodded, his eyes bright. He knew, as Mary knew, the trouble Cash had in getting a word alone with Mary Jane. Since Cash's return from Yale as a new-fledged abolitionist ("He'll get over it," Nate had sighed. "With Cash it's always some damn thing"), Dr. Warfield had barely been able to tolerate the young man's presence in his house.

By all rules of propriety, of course, Mary Jane should have gone immediately to seek the others, for even the slaves had left to set up the picnic-baskets by the spring. Betsey—and certainly Mary Jane's mother, the formidable Maria Warfield—were quite clear on what a young lady must and must not do. Watching her, Mary thought, *Go to him!* As if she watched a play—like reading *Twelfth Night* and whispering to Viola, *Tell him who you are!*

And slowly, Mary Jane crossed the clearing, her long hair falling unnoticed down over her shoulders again, and stood above Cash, who held out his hand to her, and moved his long legs aside. She hesitated for an endless moment, then settled beside him, her butter-yellow skirts billowing as she sank down, covering his shins in a froth of tucking and lace. Nate's hand closed around Mary's behind the screening laurels, and she was suddenly, profoundly conscious of the warmth of his grip, the soft whisper of his breath on her hair. Like actors in the green-and-golden proscenium of the glade, Cash laid his hands on either side of Mary Jane's face and kissed her; her own hands closed briefly, hungrily, on his arms.

Then quickly she was on her feet, and hurrying away.

CASH AND MARY JANE WERE MARRIED IN FEBRUARY, AT DR. Warfield's house in Lexington near the University. For two days before, there had been whispers, panic, excitement. Another of Mary Jane's suitors had sent a letter to Mary Jane—which her mother had then passed along to Cash for reasons best known to herself—calling Cash a rake, an abolitionist, and a traitor, and Cash had ridden down to Louisville and publicly caned the man. The result, predictably, was a duel, to be fought on the eve of the wedding.

"Cash is really going to *fight*?" demanded Mary, aghast, when she and Elizabeth went to call on Mary Jane on the afternoon before. Elizabeth would be Mary Jane's matron of honor. They'd found the distraught bride with her sister and four other friends, pacing the parlor and fighting not to weep.

"What else can he do?" demanded Bella Richardson, widening her long-lashed violet eyes. "After the things Dr. Declarey called him in that letter..."

"And getting himself killed is going to help Mary Jane?" retorted Mary. She remembered how her friend had looked up at Cash in the clearing in that hazy autumn light, the way she'd held his arms, wanting and yet afraid. On the back of the parlor sofa, where the light from the bow-window fell, Mary Jane's bridal gown lay in a cascade of ivory-colored silk and point-lace. Mary felt sick at the thought of not knowing whether in the morning she would put on that dress, or black mourning for what was never to be.

"It's a matter of honor," protested Bella. "I couldn't marry a man who would not fight for his honor."

"That's the stupidest thing I've ever heard," snapped Mary, rounding on her fiercely, and Elizabeth said, *"Hush!"*

Elizabeth put her arms around Mary Jane, almost forced her to sit in one of the parlor chairs. Mary Jane was visibly trembling, her face waxen, but she held herself calm. In her place Mary knew too well that she herself would be in hysterics. Meg Wickliffe knelt beside the chair, gripping Mary Jane's hands. Not speaking the name of the brother who had been shot.

"The matter is in God's hands," said Elizabeth quietly. "Very often in such affairs no one is hurt at all."

Meg turned her face away.

But in the morning Cash appeared at McChord's Presbyterian Church, muddy from his hard ride back from Louisville but otherwise none the worse for wear. The matter vanished as if it had never been, save for the tears Mary saw in Mary Jane's eyes, and the way she trembled as she stood at the altar with her dark-haired, savage bridegroom. Mary, just turned fourteen and clothed in her own new status as a budding belle, wondered if she were the only person still troubled by the implications of the duel. At the reception in the Warfield parlor afterwards, she watched Mary Jane and her friends laugh and chatter and felt as alien from them as if they were characters in some fantastic book. *Isn't anyone going to ask Mary Jane if she has second thoughts about marrying Cash?* From the group of men around the punch-bowl she heard Cash's booming voice:

"...of course the news had spread of the duel, and the whole state had turned out to watch, it seemed like—Lord, it was like a fair! So I said to Declarey..."

Could you marry a man who would stake his life—and your happiness—on a letter written in anger, that should simply have been put on the fire?

Her eyes traveled the room, picking out the way Elizabeth touched Ninian's sleeve as she murmured something to him; the way Mary Jane's gaze turned, again and again, in mingled love and pain, toward Cash's dark, tousled head among the crowd around the punch-bowl. She saw Nate Bodley in the crowd, and saw how he turned also to scan the big double-parlor...seeking her? She remembered the way he'd taken her own hands in the woods, the whisper of his breath on her hair. She had dreamed last night that she was Mary Jane, sinking down to be kissed in the green and gold of the glade.

Nate had come often to Rose Hill in the evenings, when the older girls would sit in the parlor or, in warm weather, on the pillared porch, exchanging shy commonplaces with the sons of planters, the students at the University. He'd laughed uproariously with the rest at Mary's jokes and witticisms, and had shown a marked disposition to seek the chair beside hers.

I will marry, Mary reflected again. The feelings stirred that day in the woods had changed the words' meaning for her. It had always been, *I will marry someday, when I'm grown. . . .*

But she was grown, or close to it. She'd coaxed a new dress from her father for today, white tarlatan that rustled and whispered with silvery sweetness, the sleeves so wide they were held out with hoops and everything trimmed with green velvet ribbons. More and more young men were riding out to Rose Hill to see her, and she had become adept at the secret language of sidelong glances and gentle laughter, of kisses promised or withheld.

But it came to her that this was more than a pleasant game, a way to collect beaux as tokens of her beauty and to score off her sisters. It was a hunt, to find a husband. To not be an old maid, scorned and pitied by all.

To hear Meg talk, or Bella or Isabelle, any husband was better than having people whisper about you in that sweetly hateful way, and urge their brothers or cousins to dance with you so you wouldn't be a wall-flower.

Even a husband who would leave you a widow on your wedding-day because some other man called him an abolitionist in a private letter that was intended for no one's eyes but yours.

There was Nate of course, whose quest for her seemed to have been sidetracked by a promising discussion of the proposed railroad between Lexington and Frankfort. A golden Hercules, and well-off—stupid as a brick, Mary thought, and not likely to get anywhere in the world except to be a slaveowner and raise tobacco and horses.

When I marry, she decided, *it will have to be to a man who's going somewhere. A man like Father, or Mr. Clay.*

Her old jest with Mr. Clay, about marrying a man who would be President of the United States, returned to her. Naturally there was no way of guaranteeing that, though it would be intensely gratifying to stand at the center of power, to shine as first among all the women of the land. But it occurred to her that marriage to someone who just stayed at home and minded his slaves and his business would be appallingly dull.

And what if I don't want to get married at all? She thought of Betsey, always pregnant, more and more frequently ill, confined to the quiet of her room. *What if by the time I'm nineteen*—the last possible outpost of bellehood before people started calling you an old maid—*I haven't met anyone I love the way Mary Jane loves Cash, the way Elizabeth loves Ninian or Jane loves Saul! What if I don't meet someone like that at all? What then?*

As soon as Cash and Mary Jane left in the carriage for Crab Orchard Springs for their wedding-trip, Mary took the opportunity to walk home with Elizabeth, Frances, Eliza, and Ann. There would be dancing that night, and while the men lingered over the punch-bowl and their cigars the girls retreated, to change clothes and have a beauty-nap, for the dancing would last most of the night. The other girls' chatter saved Mary from having to talk. She felt troubled and lonely, doubly so because she had never felt completely at home in the tall-fronted brick house on Main Street.

The other girls went rustling up the stairs, but Mary passed through the dining-room and pantry to the big kitchen in the back of the house, where she knew the servants would be gathered, taking advantage of the warmth there on this icy day and also of the fact that the family was out.

But coming into the pantry she saw Nelson and Pendleton standing in the kitchen door, and beyond them, heard the sound of a woman weeping.

"What is it?" Mary slipped between the two men and into the brick-floored room. "What's wrong?"

Nelson turned, and Mary saw that his eyes burned with impotent rage. Past him in the kitchen Jane sat huddled on a stool beside the big brick hearth, her face buried in her hands. Mammy Sally held her, rocked her gently, tears running down her face.

Softly, Nelson said, "Your Granny Parker took Saul to Mr. Pullum, to help your Uncle David out for having backed a bill for one of his friends. Saul's gone. Taken away with a coffle for Louisville this morning."

"Saul..." Mary fell back a step. After the biting air of the street the kitchen was warm, the smell of vanilla and steaming cider incongruously sweet. Jane leaned her head back against Mammy Sally's shoulder, still hugging herself, as if without the binding strength of the older woman's arms her heart would tear itself out of her ribcage and flee to some land where things like this didn't happen. Where a man couldn't be taken away and sold just to raise a little extra cash, without anyone once asking if he had family or loved ones.

Saul was gone, just like that. Without warning, without good-by.

Not because of some stupid dispute about honor, thought Mary, that he would have had the choice to take up or leave alone. But because it suited her grandmother to help out Uncle David, and this was the quickest and easiest way.

Marriage, and honor, and sapphire pendants, and not being an old maid—even having a stepmother who sent one away from home for putting spiders in her bed—suddenly seemed insults to the silent agony on Jane's face. The petty luxuries of the free.

Mary gathered up her skirts and went quietly back through the pantry, and up the stairs.

Chapter Eight

After Cash's wedding, Mary understood there were two worlds in Lexington. She had always been aware of the division between them, but had slipped back and forth across it with the blithe malleability of a child, to whom the fairies in the garden are as real as the horses in the stable. Besides the storybook tales of King Arthur and his knights, and the heroes of Troy, Mary had grown up on Nelson's narrations of talking foxes and clever rabbits and of little boys and their conjure-wise grannies; of the Platt-Eye Devil who waited for bad children in the dark and of the jay-bird who'd fly to Hell every Friday night to tell Satan of little girls' iniquities.

Everyone always said that slavery in Kentucky "wasn't like it was deeper south," and that, to Mary's mind, had made it all right.

When Granny Parker sold Saul, the division between the worlds sharpened into focus for her: how narrow the gap was, and how abysmally deep.

The world of the whites was itself divided into two: the world of men, of politics, of speculation for new lands opening in the West, of horse-racing and money-making and the casual, noisy, whiskey-smelling friendships of men; and the world of women. Mary wasn't sure which she liked best. She reveled in gossip, in shopping, in flirtations on the porch of Rose Hill and beautiful new dresses—she'd grown adept at coaxing promises from her father, and at holding him to them, if necessary, with tears. She loved afternoon-calls and the intricate ritual of who was at home to whom and who left cards on whom. But she understood that the ultimate power lay with the men.

And the men, who would gallantly offer their arms to help women cross puddles that they assumed the women didn't have the brains to walk around, guarded their power jealously. To get drunk, to shoot or thrash one another, to whip any darky who needed it or gamble the fortunes on which their families depended, were prerogatives not to be shared with addlepated females or Northerners like Mr. Presby who couldn't comprehend what things were like in the South.

Yet it was also a world of enchantment, of sultry evenings on the porch listening to the cry of the crickets, a world of taffy-pulls and dances in the big ballroom above Giron's Confectionary. A world of writing letters to friends and brushing Meg's hair and frantically trying to sneak time to get back to the literary adventures of the blameless Isabelle and her flight from the loathsome and doomed Duke Manfred . . .

A world of sweet peacefulness where day succeeded quiet day, and season gentle season, in a land where the rules were always clear—if sometimes byzantine and never spoken—and people could be counted on.

On the other side of that narrow abyss lay the world of kitchens, backyards, and dusty alleys in the deep shade of elm-trees, refuges for whoever could get away from their unceasing work for a quick chat with friends who might disappear tomorrow. It was a world of back-fences and the tiny economies of vegetable-plots, fish-hooks, second-run coffee-grounds, and dresses too worn for "the missus" to want anymore.

A world where there was no power, and no redress. Ever.

For weeks after Saul's departure Mary thought of him. She would see him in her mind, chained to the deck of the steamboat going down the Ohio to the Mississippi, and down the Mississippi to New Orleans, and thence to harsh labor and early death in the sugar and cotton lands of the deeper South. In her dreams he would gaze silently at the dark walls of trees gliding past, and Mary would sometimes hear the wailing slave-songs that would drift from behind the brick walls of Pullum's slave-yard.

"I'm goin' away to New Orleans,
Good-by, my love, good-by,
I'm goin' away to New Orleans,
Good-by, my love, good-by,
Oh, let her go by."

Papa would never sell any of our people, she thought, and most of the time truly believed it. But in fact, Mammy Sally and Nelson and Chaney and Pendleton belonged, not to her father, but to Granny Parker. As Saul had done. When that thought came to her, Mary would close her eyes in panic, her heart hammering at the fear of losing her friends.

At the idea of her friends losing their homes and each other, weeping as Jane had wept.

And there was nothing she could do about it, as there had been nothing she could ever do about her mother's death.

When Cash came back from Crab Orchard Springs with Mary Jane, Robert Todd gave a reception for the newlyweds at the new Main Street house. At this party Mary took Cash aside and asked, "*Are* you an abolitionist, Cash?" She'd heard the word bandied about a great deal, usually as a deadly insult. Even her father would argue that, though opposed to slavery in principle as Mr. Clay was, he was not an abolitionist. Cash looked down at her with his arms folded, his piercing eyes grave.

He said, "Yes, I am."

"But you own slaves." He had been left fatherless young, at sixteen inheriting the plantation of White Hall, where they grew tobacco and hemp.

"That will only be until I can establish my brothers in some profession where they can make their own way, and until I can establish myself in a way that will not do injustice to Mary Jane." He glanced across the spacious double-parlor that had once been the common-room of Palmentier's Tavern. Mary Jane, clothed in the brighter colors and more modish styles of a young wife, laughed with her friends as if she had never felt fear in her life. The company overflowed the double-parlor and filled the family parlor across the hall, and the dining-room beyond that. "Then I will free the people whom my father left to me—and in freeing them, will free myself."

Mary was quiet. She had heard this before, from Elliot Presby—and had gotten into screaming arguments with the tutor on the strength of it. But from Cash it was different. Cash *did* understand the South, as the sanctimonious young New Englander never could.

"People in this country talk about slavery as if it were a matter of choice," Cash went on. "Like the decision whether or not to keep a carriage, or whether to become a Methodist or a Baptist. We have lived with it so long that it seems like that to us, and not what it really is. Not what Mr. Lloyd Garrison has shown us—showed *me,* when I went to hear him speak at Yale—that it is."

Cash's voice had grown grave, without his usual edge of theatrical anger. "And it is a sin, Mary. It is an evil, the most wicked of injustices, perpetrated and carried on simply because it is profitable to *us* to buy and sell black men and make them do work for us. Garrison describes it for what it is, and describes slaveholders—myself still numbered among them—for what they—*we*—really are: oppressors beside whom Herod and the Pharaoh of Egypt were fiddling amateurs. It cannot be allowed to continue."

A few days later Cash rode out to Rose Hill in the evening, at the time when young gentlemen customarily called on the girls. In warm weather, chairs would be brought out onto the lawn beneath the chestnut-trees, for Madame frowned on such visits, but in the bitter cold of early spring she relented, and admitted them to the fire-warmed parlor. There she would take out her violin and play, to the accompaniment of her daughter Marie on the piano. Most of the young gentlemen were terrified of her.

Madame had long ago ceased to frighten Mary. When the school-day was done and the day-students went home, Madame and her husband seemed more human, like parents to the handful of boarding-students. Evenings in the big parlor were like the family that Mary had always wished she had; they made up, in part, for the desolation she still felt each time she left her father's house.

That evening Cash brought her a note from Mary Jane, a commonplace invitation to tea the following week. When Mary walked him out to the porch, he slipped her a closely folded packet of papers: "Mr. Garrison's newspaper, *The Liberator,*" he whispered. "Read it yourself, Mary, and see if you do not agree with us, that slavery is a moral issue, and not merely a question of white man's property and white man's law."

She stowed the papers under her mattress, where she was fairly certain no one would find them. The girls made up their own beds each morning, and changed their own sheets on Tuesday nights, the linen fresh-washed and fresh-pressed by Dulcie and Caro. It did not seem, thought Mary, that you could get away from slaves. Once she'd read *The Liberator,* tucked between the pages of *A Young Lady's History of the United States,* it seemed to her that slaves were everywhere, in every corner of Lexington.

They did all the laundry. They cut all the wood, for kitchen fires, bedroom fires, heating water to wash clothing and dishes. They ironed sheets and napkins in every house she knew of, from the wealthy plantations like the Wickliffes' Glendower and Dr. Warfield's The Meadows to houses like her father's and Granny Parker's. They worked on road-gangs, cutting trees and leveling grades so that wagons could come and go from Louisville on the river, taking hemp and tobacco down to market or hauling up the *batiste de soie* and *gros de Naples,* the feathers and ribbons and buttons of mother-of-pearl that made shopping-expeditions in Cheapside so entrancing. They milked everyone's cows and shoveled out everyone's stables; they spread the manure on everyone's gardens so that roses and carrots and potatoes would grow.

She realized she didn't know anyone—except old Solly, the town drunk and gravedigger—who didn't own a slave.

Yet it was clear to her, reading Mr. Garrison's impassioned writings, that the owning of slaves, the selling of slaves, did more than just make a mockery of the liberty that the United States had claimed as a birthright in separating from England. It was evil in and of itself, in the eternal eyes of God. The men who owned other men were tyrants, the men who sold other men were kidnappers, the men who punished other men for not accepting bondage as their lot were no better than robbers who beat their victims. Garrison's words burned her, left her breathless and deeply troubled.

Because she knew in her heart that they were true. But if she accepted them, she understood that she would have to accept that her father was a tyrant and kidnapper. That Mr. Clay, whom she both admired and loved, was, in Garrison's words, "a patriotic hypocrite, a fustian declaimer of liberty, a highway robber and a murderer."

Then she would look around her at the friends chatting of beaux and dresses—good people, dear and sweet (except maybe Arabella Richardson)—and she wouldn't know what to feel or think.

She would have liked to talk to her father about this, but on those Saturdays and Sundays when she returned to the Main Street house, her father, if he was home at all, was always surrounded by family: always talking to Ninian—who frequently came up with Elizabeth from Walnut Hill if the couple weren't staying outright at the Main Street house for a few weeks—or admonishing Levi and George, or playing with little Margaret, little Sam, or baby David. . . . Or if he were doing none of those things, Betsey was there, and Mary felt robbed and abandoned all over again.

Even a new pair of slippers or the promise of a new dress did not entirely make up for the ache—and confusion—in her heart.

Nor could she bring the matter up to M'sieu Mentelle without opening the subject of where she'd gotten hold of copies of *The Liberator.* No young lady at Rose Hill was permitted to receive correspondence that had not been scrutinized by Madame. The parents of her boarders expected her to be aware of such things. And in any case the rule about speaking only French within the house was strict, and Mary did not feel up to discussing "the popular fury against the advocates of bleeding humanity" in French.

One Saturday evening in the summer of her second year at Mentelle's—1833—Mary found her chance. Supper at the Main Street house was done—a reduced group around her father's table, for Ninian had received his law degree not long ago, and had taken Elizabeth north to his family home in Springfield, Illinois, leaving Mary bereft. Mr. Presby had returned to Boston to visit his family, and the Todds had begun to make plans to retreat to Crab Orchard Springs—or perhaps to Betsey's small country house, Buena Vista, five miles outside town, as soon as Mary was out of school for the summer.

Mary herself felt depressed and strange, as if she were going to have a headache later. She had had a nightmare the night before, about the town being flooded with water that shone ghastly green with poison, and the thunderclouds building over the mountains filled her with uneasy dread.

After supper she'd followed her father out onto the rear porch that overlooked the small formal garden that was Betsey's pride, and beyond it the woodland that bordered the stream at the rear of the property. In buying Palmentier's, Robert Todd had also purchased the three town lots surrounding it—practically the only vacant lots remaining near the center of Lexington—so that this green and pleasant prospect would remain his.

This evening he sat smoking in the gloom, listening to the muted burble of the creek. Betsey had retreated early to bed with a headache—she was, Mary suspected, increasing yet again—and Mary herself shivered at the far-off sounds of thunder.

But she sat on one of the cane-bottomed chairs beside her father, and said, "Is Mr. Clay going to run for President again, when Mr. Jackson's term is up?"

Her father grinned, and pinched her cheek. "Always the little politician, eh?" He sighed. "Maybe. Jackson's a sick old man. Even if he could, I don't think he'd court accusations of being a dictator by running for a third time when Washington was content with only two."

"Mr. Clay is against slavery, isn't he, Papa?" Mary leaned against her father's arm, taking comfort in his bulk and size, in the scent of tobacco and Macassar oil and horses, the faint sweaty smell of manhood in his coat. "Yet he owns slaves, the way you do."

Her father sighed again. "A man can be against slavery and still not be a crazy abolitionist, Molly," he said. The darkness, broken only by the faint glow of light from the kitchen windows, seemed to bring them closer; Mary treasured the delicious quiet of the moment, the man-to-man matter-of-factness of her father's voice as he spoke to her. Like a woman and a friend, not like a child.

A closeness better than all the sapphire pendants in the world.

"Slavery is evil. I don't think you can argue that. But simply turning all the slaves loose would bring down a greater evil, in terms of poverty, and chaos, and lawlessness. Darkies aren't like you and me, daughter. They don't understand principles—you know how you have to keep instructions to Chaney or Judy very simple, if you're going to get anything like what you're asking for—and in most ways they're like children. Even a smart darky like Jane isn't more than a few generations removed from the jungle, you know. It wouldn't be any kindness to them to turn them loose to fend for themselves, any more than it would be to let loose your sister Frances's pet canary in the woods."

Thunder rumbled above the hills. The metallic drumming of the cicadas in the trees seemed to accentuate the heat and closeness of the dark. Mary shivered, hating the electric feel of the air that pressed so desperately on her skull, as if the lightning itself flickered in her brain. Nelson emerged from a side door, descended the back steps, and crossed through the garden to the coach house, in whose attic he and Pendleton had their rooms while the women slaves slept above the kitchen. "But couldn't they do their same jobs at wages?"

He shook his head. "It doesn't work that way, sweetheart. No planter could make a profit if he had to pay wages, and if the wages were low the darkies would go looking for higher ones, and drive white men out of work. No, Mr. Clay's scheme is best. You don't free the Negro race until you're able to provide a home for them. Either colonize them out in the West beyond the Mississippi—which would certainly spark problems with the Indians or the Spanish—or set up colonies for them in Africa, where the benefits of what they've learned in this country will gradually civilize the heathen tribes around them."

"Wouldn't that be like letting loose a canary in the woods?" asked Mary.

"Of course it would, baby." Her father patted her gently, and glanced longingly at the cigar he'd stamped out the moment Mary had appeared in the dark door to the house. "That's why we have to do this slowly. It's only the abolitionists who want to rush pell-mell into things, to solve the problem *their* way, in *their* time, the minute they think they see a solution. They're not thinking about the consequences, to the country or to the darkies themselves."

Lightning leaped white across the sky, blanching the leaves of the chestnut-trees. Mary screamed—at the same moment the trees bent in the rushing wind, as if reaching for the walls of the house, and thunder ripped the darkness that dropped like a smothering blanket in the lightning's wake. Trembling, she retreated to the house as a second blast of lightning split the night, and torrents of rain began to fall. Her head aching in earnest, she ran up the stairs to the guest-room, flung herself fully clothed on the bed, covered her head with the pillow so she would not hear.

But she did hear. And she saw, through the pillow and her shut eyelids, the white blasts of lightning that ripsawed the night. She heard, too, the hammering of the rain, until it seemed to her that the house and the whole town would wash away. Once she crept from her bed and looked out the window, to see the spring at the bottom of the garden overflowing, its waters spilling everywhere, glittering in the lightning's blue flare. She remembered her dream, of overspilling water bringing poison, bringing death.

The following day, Sunday, the bells of McChord's Church were tolling. Her father came in while the family was seated at breakfast and said, "That was Jim Rollins outside, coming up from the University. There's a woman down on Water Street, where the Town Branch flooded last night, down sick. They're saying it's cholera."

Betsey clicked her tongue. "Nonsense. They can't tell so quickly."

But Mary glanced over at Eliza, cold terror gripping her. Last summer's newspapers had been filled with reports of the cholera that had killed thousands in New York and New Orleans, like the ravenous plagues of medieval Europe. Frances set down her spoon rather quickly, and said, "I know Mary has a few weeks of school yet, but if some of us could go down to Crab Orchard Springs early this year she could join us as soon as she's done."

And little Margaret, glancing from face to face of her shaken seniors, asked, "What's cholera?"

"It's a sickness, sweetheart." Betsey stroked her eldest daughter's blond curls. "A sickness that only bad people and poor people get."

"Aunt Hannah wasn't bad, or poor," pointed out Mary, "and she died of it last year." Betsey looked daggers at her, but Mary turned to her father, whose sister Aunt Hannah had been. He didn't admonish her for contradicting her stepmother.

Instead he said, "I think I'll just ride over to the University, and see what they're saying at the Medical College. I won't be long—and I think it's probably best if no one goes outside for now."

Just before dinner he was back, with the news that ten other cases of cholera had been reported in the town. Nelson was sent to the market to buy tar and lime: "The disease seems to spread through the night air, according to Dr. Warfield," said Robert Todd, to his wife and children assembled in the family parlor. "Until we can get packed, and get out of town, I think the safest thing we can do is stay indoors, keep the windows shut, spread lime on all the windowsills and thresholds and burn tar to cleanse the air. I think the Mentelles will understand if you leave school a few weeks early this term, Molly," he added, glancing over at Mary. "I understand the air is better in Crab Orchard Springs. If we leave now, we can probably get a cabin there, until the epidemic is over."

But the next morning Mary came down to breakfast to hushed whispers and bad-news voices. "Pendleton is sick," her father told her. "We've got him isolated and I've called Grant Shelby to take a look at him"—Grant Shelby was the local veterinarian, who also handled slaves—"but Mammy Sally says it looks like the cholera, and from what I've seen I agree with her. I'm afraid there's no question of leaving town now—or of leaving this house."

There followed three of the most nightmarish weeks Mary had spent in her life. The summer's heat lay on the city like a soaked blanket. The air was unbreathable from the white streaks of lime on every window- and doorsill, and from the flambeaux of tar that Nelson made up and burned all around the house. In the dark of the shuttered house the smells thickened daily, hourly, in every stuffy, shadowy room. Mary felt the stink of it would never leave her throat. Yet she was forbidden to so much as venture out into the yard, though Betsey crossed back and forth to the coach house a dozen times a day, to help with Pendleton's nursing.

Mary herself felt very little fear that she would catch the disease. She feared it far less than she feared lightning-storms, or the silence that lay over the stricken town. Generally the creak of wagons and carriages, the clop of hooves and clamor of voices from Main Street, reached to every corner of the big house, shutters or no shutters. Now Lexington was silent, and under the summer's heat the only sounds that could be heard through the shutters were the occasional creak of a single wagon passing, or the tolling of a funeral bell. If she had no fear for herself, she was frantic with fear that Frances, or Ann, or Eliza would come down sick, or that, when the quarantine was over, she would hear the news that Mary Jane or Meg or Nate Bodley was dead. Every night when she prayed—as Granny Parker had instructed her from earliest childhood—she added to the rote litany of OurFatherWhoArtinHeaven . . . the fervent request that her friends be spared.

But she had no sense that God heard her. The last time that she had truly petitioned God was when she was six, that her mother return to comfort her, for she needed her so.

God apparently had not heard.

Nearly as bad as the smells was David's crying, which went on and on, sawing at the terrible silence. That, and the fact that as fruits and vegetables were thought by some to cause the disease, in the height of the season of peaches and mulberries the family lived on beaten biscuits and beef tea. After the first week there was no more newspaper, for so many of the men who printed it were either sick or tending the sick in makeshift hospitals. Betsey, wraith-thin, took to her own bed with exhaustion, and was snappish and impatient, and Robert Todd spent most of his days at her side. Mary kept to the semi-dark of her shuttered bedroom, reading books from her father's library to shut out her fears, or peering through the chinks in the shutters to watch the dead-carts rumble by below. One afternoon the noise of clumping and thumping in the hall brought her to the door, and she saw her father and Nelson bringing trunks down the attic stairs.

"What is it?" she asked. "What's happening?"

"Old Solly the gravedigger's outside," said Nelson. "He's asking for whatever trunks and boxes folks have, since the coffin makers can't make enough coffins for those that're dead."

Shoulder to shoulder in the lamplight, both men were dirty and dusty, shirtsleeved and daubed with the smuts of burned tar: black man and white man, of the same age, in the same household, feeling the same fear—helping others as well as they could. Mary opened doors for them and helped them maneuver the heavy trunks down the stairs, with a sense of seeing the front-parlor world of the whites, the shadow-world of the back alleys and kitchen-yards, merge. . . .

Do men like Papa and Dr. Warfield think they're going somewhere different than Pendleton and Nelson when they die?

Pendleton recovered, though he was weeks in bed and lost a good thirty pounds. By July the funeral-bells had quit tolling, and Robert Todd packed up his family and took them, belatedly, to Crab Orchard Springs. Later Mary heard that five hundred people had died in Lexington, including half the patients at the lunatic asylum that stood beside the University.

COMING BACK THAT FALL TO LEXINGTON, MARY HAD THE SAME unsettled feeling that she had had at Mary Jane's wedding: a sense that fear and upheaval were all being swept tidily away out of sight. Fate had asked questions about the two dusty men bringing trunks down from the attic, and those questions were put aside unanswered. White men and black men had died, but when the shadow of death withdrew, business at Pullum's Exchange revived more quickly than at any other establishment in town. When Mary would go down to the perfumers and milliners on Cheapside with Frances or Mary Jane, she would see the hickory whipping-post beside the Courthouse, the place where disobedient slaves were chained and flogged, and she would sometimes look at her companions and think, *Don't you see? Don't you understand?*

But how could they, when she didn't really understand herself? All the argument that year was about the National Bank, and Andrew Jackson's iniquities, and the takeover of Indian lands in the West. Perhaps her father and Mr. Clay were right, she thought, and freedom was something to be given to the darkies only with due care, and not handed out rashly. . . .

But the sight of slavery still sickened her.

One night shortly after the family's return, just before Mary was to go back to Mentelle's, she was waked again by the distant rumble of thunder. Her sleep was never sound, and some nights she would lie awake until nearly dawn, listening to the soft breathing of Eliza and Ann, whose room she shared in summer so that the guest room could be kept ready for visitors. Neither of the other girls stirred. For a time Mary lay silent, listening to the slow ticking of the clock in the hall and wondering what time it was and what had wakened her. . . .

Voices, she thought. Voices, and the sound of a door opening in the yard.

Silently, she slipped out of her low trundle-bed. The night was hot, the smooth old wood of the floor cool under her feet as she stole to the bedroom door and out into the hall. The door was a bone of contention between herself and the other two girls, for since childhood Mary had been unable to endure an open door—even of a closet or armoire—in a room where she slept. She opened it now, and slipped into the upstairs hall, knowing that if she opened the bedroom shutters they would awaken, too.

Moving by touch in the dark she unlatched the shutters of the window in the hall. There was no light in the yard below, but by the moon's gleam she could see figures moving at the bottom of the high kitchen stairs. Mammy Sally, Mary thought, identifying the woman's figure though she wasn't wearing the headrag that kept kitchen soot and grease out of the hair of the women servants. And the tall man with short-cropped silver hair could be no one other than Nelson. They faded back into the shadows of the wall, but having seen them, Mary could see them still.

Waiting.

Curious, and wide-awake, Mary eased the shutter back into its place. She knew she ought to go back into the bedroom for a wrapper or a shawl—Betsey had repeated over and over that for a lady to move about in her nightgown was only a half-step above walking about naked—but to do so would risk waking Eliza and Ann. Besides, Mary frequently made surreptitious nocturnal expeditions to the outhouse clothed only in her nightgown—when she'd already used the chamber pot two or three times in the night and didn't want to risk Ann or Eliza deriding her—and didn't think it so horrible. She was covered, after all.

Crickets and cicadas made a strident chorus outside as she crept down the wide staircase, her long braids lying thick down her back. Somewhere a dog barked.

Hoodoo? she wondered. Though Mammy Sally would deny it to every white member of the household, the old slave knew more about nursing than the herbs and willow-bark she'd employed to get Pendleton through the cholera. More than once, on her stealthy trips to the outhouse, Mary had seen the old nurse out at midnight, drilling a hole in the south side of one of the chestnut-trees at the bottom of the yard, to "blow the chills" out of her own body and into the tree. Mary knew, too, that servants from other households would sometimes come to their kitchen, asking for a conjure of peace-plant and honey to sweeten up a harsh mistress, or balls of black wax and pins to send an importunate master away. These they'd deny wanting, if they saw Mary watching.

The dining-room with its graceful table and glass-fronted cabinet of silver service was a cavern of nameless shadow. Mary kept to the wall, feeling her way along, till she reached the pantry door, and slipped through into the kitchen, smelling of grease and ashes, warm as a bake-oven even hours after the big hearth-fire had been banked.

From there she stepped out at last into the blackness of the porch. Shadows stirred in the dark beneath the house's tall brick walls, and Mary saw the harlequin squares of a man's gingham shirt, the brief flash of eyes.

"Lou?" came Mammy's voice, and a whisper replied, " 'S'me." A moment later Lou stepped across to the bottom of the kitchen steps. In the moonlight Mary identified him; one of Mrs. Turner's slaves, whom she rented out as a day laborer to the hemp and bagging factory in which Robert Todd was a partner.

Mammy stepped out of the shadows, handed Lou a bundle. Not bulky enough for blankets, Mary guessed; it had to be food or clothes. "There's a hay-barn five miles down the Louisville road," Mammy whispered. "Don't sleep there, they always look there, but there's a cave in the creek-bank just behind it."

"Patrols ride that road mostly early in the night," added Nelson. "Whatever you do, you keep away from them."

"With Mrs. Turner behind me," said Lou, "you got no worry there." In the kitchen Mary had heard talk of Mrs. Turner, things the white folks of Lexington never knew. The chill-eyed Boston woman was hated and feared throughout the slave community. If even half of what Mammy and Nelson and Jane had whispered was true, Mary wasn't surprised Lou would run away.

"When you get to Louisville keep to the edge of town. There's a tavern on the south side called Bridges, the owner don't care who sleeps in his sheds. Look for Mrs. Chough that lives behind the Quaker meeting-house there, she'll get you across the river. You see this sign on a fence, it means they'll take you in." Kneeling, Mammy sketched something in the dust of the yard, smoothed it over at once. "You see that sign, it means they'll give you food at least. When you been gone three days, I'll let Tina know you got away."

Lou bent quickly to kiss Mammy's sunken cheek. "Tell Tina I'll send for her, I swear it. . . ." Tina must be the woman he loved, thought Mary, in some other household, some other kitchen in the town. "Tell her I'll find a way somehow."

Nelson said, "She knows you will."

"God bless you." The runaway clasped Nelson's hand, kissed Mammy again. "God bless you both."

The two Todd slaves waited until Lou had disappeared into the dark of the trees. Like a ghost Mary fleeted away before Mammy could reach the top of the steps from the yard. In the dark of the downstairs hall she paused for a moment, overwhelmed with a wild urge to laugh, to cheer, to dance.

She felt she had learned a secret, and the secret was this:

That the people most concerned in the subject of freedom weren't sitting around tamely waiting for the abolitionists and the colonizers to quibble the matter out between them. The people most concerned didn't really care whether Mr. Clay and his friends were thinking "what was best for the darkies," or whether the issue was moral or political, or whether, as Nate Bodley's father claimed, abolitionist pamphlets stirred up slave revolts.

They were doing whatever they had to, to be free.

Chapter Nine

For the most part, however, Mary's awareness of the shadow-world that underlay the gracious brick houses of Lexington, the horse-races and picnics and the ubiquitous network of kinship ties that spread from Kentucky to the Virginia tidewater, was simply that: an awareness, like her awareness of the earth underfoot. Cash, and Mr. Clay, and increasing numbers of men in the town might be preoccupied with the subject of that earth—might see everything in terms of mud and worms and stones—but except on those occasions when the veil between the worlds of black and white lifted, Mary's days were shaped and colored by other things.

She turned sixteen. Nate Bodley kissed her in the shadows of the cherry orchard behind Rose Hill; she slapped him, and burst into tears, as a young lady must (Betsey said), but the sensation of being held, of being touched, of being wanted stirred her deeply. She found herself watching for opportunities to engineer such a scene again.

Along with the girls she'd gone to Ward's Academy with—some of whom were now day-students at Rose Hill as well—she and her sisters were part of the vast web of Todd cousinry that stretched back into Virginia and extended its tentacles across the river into Illinois: Porters and Parkers and Stuarts, Logans and Russells and Richardsons and ramifications still more distant. Girls and young men, they had known each other from childhood parties, from picnics in the woods and on the banks of the Town Branch and the Kentucky River, chasing each other through the trees as Nate Bodley had chased her. And as she now looked at Nate, they all looked at one another with changed eyes.

It was a happy time. In addition to Nate—and half a dozen other beaux—Mary had her studies and her beloved books at Rose Hill. She had Frances and Eliza and her friends, friends she'd known all her life. No longer forced to live under Betsey's roof, she came to dearly love the small half-brothers and half-sisters whom she had formerly so resented. Secure in the knowledge that she would be returning to her own pleasant room at Rose Hill on Sunday afternoon, she could hold little David on her lap, play with small Margaret and small Sam, and bask in their uncomplicated love.

There were balls and cotillion parties almost every week, either in the long room above Giron's Confectionary or in the private houses of friends. Summer lemonade or Christmas eggnog, crickets calling in the warm nights or the diamond glow of silent winter stars. Her father and the other men arguing cotton and politics. There were lectures at the Lyceum about nitrous oxide, galvanic batteries, cold-water cures for fever, and the Reverend Zaccheus Waverly's talks on travel in the Holy Land, from which Nate or one of the young law students at Transylvania would beg for the privilege of walking her home.

There were exhibitions of waxworks, and rides under the lilac trees of Ashland, Mary straight and graceful in a rifleman-green riding habit that flowed down over the left side of the neat-stepping little hackney her father had bought for her. There were student plays at Rose Hill, not amateur fit-ups but careful productions with elaborate props and scenery: *Pizarro, Hernani, Macbeth* in which everyone exclaimed over the passion with which Mary played the mad scene to a couple of tall, thin senior students grimly bedight in false beards. There was the true theater too, with troupes visiting from New York or Philadelphia. There were bonnets and coiffures, and the always-delightful challenge of extracting promises for new frocks from her father, and holding him to them with tears; there was *La Belle Assemblée* and the *Royal Ladies Magazine.*

The second Monday of every month was Court Day, when the justices of the peace would assemble in the County Courthouse. But most of the people who crowded the square before the Courthouse had little interest in what went on inside. Peddlers, horse-traders, trappers from the hills would set up their pitches, shouting the virtues of bloodstock or coonskins, milk-cows or Old Sachem Medicinal Bitters. Slave-dealers would be there, too, to buy up debtors' Negroes at the Courthouse door: stony-faced black men tricked out in blue coats and plug hats and women in neat-pressed calico ("Strip off, gal, let the gennleman have a look at yuh. . . ." "See his back? Not hardly a stripe on 'im; he don't need much whippin'. . . .").

On the benches along the iron fence, idlers spit and whittled, smoked and swapped tales: Nate Bodley in his ruffled shirt bought a peg of hard cider for ragged old Solly the gravedigger, who had once been so drunk and disorderly that in desperation the town council had sold the old white man to a free Negro woman for thirty cents so he'd have someone to look after him.

Even young Mr. Presby would stop to hear the news and ask what was being said in New York and Philadelphia. The young ladies went in rustling groups with aunts or brothers or fathers to shop for ribbons and silk flowers, but Mary found herself drawn as always to the men who argued about improvements and the National Bank.

"Good gracious, Mary, you don't want gentlemen to think you're a bluestocking!" exclaimed Frances, and Mary flipped her fan at her and lowered her long eyelashes, and said, "Silly!" Mary was always meticulously careful not to "parade" her learning more than was seemly for a girl, and in any case a girl with as many beaux as she had was in no danger of being considered "blue."

But afterwards at the Court Day cotillion, Mary was hard-pressed to keep her mouth shut when Buck Loveridge or Jim Rollins speculated on possibilities of government contracts and the jobs that could be traded for favors, votes, and influence. Her newspaper reading gave meaning to chance fragments of conversation overheard at dances: "What the hell we need some Yankee Congressman takin' money from us, every time we turn around?"

"Because if Congress didn't build a road down to Louisville with its taxes you'd sit on your tobacco and starve," Mary retorted. The men all laughed, but later, as she edged her way to the lemonade table through a flowerbed of petticoats and gowns, she heard Arabella Richardson purr to Nate Bodley, "Honestly, Mary's so quick with a comeback, I just don't know how she does it! Myself, I never could tell a demi-crat from a demi-john." And Bella smiled meltingly up into Nate's bedazzled eyes, like a trusting child.

A few evenings after this, Mary treated the other boarding-students at Mentelle's to a hilarious imitation of Bella's simpering, during one of those quiet evenings when the handful of boarders gathered after supper in the library to study their lessons. From the secretaire in the corner where she was doing the household books, Madame observed her without comment. But when the other boarders went to bed, she crossed to where Mary sat reading at the marble-topped circular table beneath the chandelier, and said gently, "It hurt, didn't it?"

"What did?" Mary looked up from *Les Trois Mousquetaires.* "Little Miss

Demi-crat?" And she mimed Arabella's languishing flutter of eyelashes—then had to turn her face aside at the sudden sting of tears.

Growing from girl to woman hadn't lessened the wild swings of her moods. At balls and cotillions she still burned with the wild glow of exultation, simply at the pleasure of dancing; from this she could pass almost instantly into volcanic anger that left her ill and shaking. She still had those strange periods in which it seemed to her that she was two people, that she stood on the edge of saying and doing some unthinkable word or deed. And try as she would to control her temper, in her anger she would still say cutting things that had to be apologized for later, with agonies of anxiety and tears. She had wept on and off, in secret, for two days, for Quasimodo and Esmeralda when she'd finished *Notre Dame de Paris;* sometimes it only took a caring look or a gentle query if she felt all right, to bring on tears she could neither explain nor control.

But she refused to weep for the "slings and arrows," as she scornfully termed them, aimed at her by the other girls in the town, the ones who said she was a bluestocking, or who raised their eyebrows or rolled their eyes when she'd quote from Shakespeare. She shrugged and replied, "As if I care what that little—" She fished in her French vocabulary for the word for "knothead" "—imbecile thinks."

"You are right not to care, child," said Madame gently. "In five years what will she be? The wife of some planter who fritters his money away on pretty dresses and jeweled earbobs, with nothing to look forward to in this life but the squalling of children and listening to her husband talk of horses and slaves."

Mary's mind returned to the cotillion, and Bella in her gown of shell-pink silk, surrounded by young gentlemen. To herself, likewise the center of a group who vied to get their names on her dance-card. To the sheer sensual thrill of the fiddles, the sweet scents of the night outside. To Nate in his ruffled shirt and coat of black superfine, swinging her out onto the dance-floor with such gay strength. To the joy of being held, and the empty ache when she looked through her little chest of her father's gifts.

"And in five years," she asked softly, "what will I be, Madame?"

Madame's hand rested gently on her shoulder. With her angular face and mannishly short-cropped hair, she looked like the embodiment of all those sniggering warnings: *virago, harridan, bluestocking.*

If you're not careful you'll end up like that. . . .

Mary didn't even know whose voice it was, speaking that warning in her mind. Because in a way she envied Madame. Madame was happy, with her husband and her daughter and her books and her fiddle, doing exactly what she pleased and not caring what others said.

Mary wondered what it would be like, not to be always looking over her shoulder, wondering if Betsey or Elizabeth or Granny Parker were approving of what she did.

"The world is an enormous place, Mary, and there is a great deal in it. Good plays by actors a notch above the strolling players who come to Mr. Usher's theater. Opera, sung by men and women of talent and long training. Buildings that are older than your grandmother and that speak of the ages they have seen."

For a moment the schoolmistress's pale eyes softened, remembering perhaps those gray streets of Paris in the days of the kings, where lush moss grew on stones that had been set into place before the first Pilgrims boarded the *Mayflower.* Then she smiled, and shook her head: "Somehow, child, I cannot see a girl of your intelligence spending the whole of her life within a dozen miles of the Kentucky River."

No, thought Mary. And yet sometimes as Nelson would drive her to her father's house on Main Street on Friday evenings, and back to Rose Hill on Monday mornings, and she'd watch the slaves sweeping down the board sidewalks in front of McCalla's Pharmacy, or old Mrs. Richardson gossiping with Mr. Ritter—M'sieu Giron's cook—in front of the confectionary, she'd wonder how she was ever going to leave this place.

Meg was gone, at Sigoigne's Select Female Academy in Philadelphia. Her letters were full of playhouses and opera and dazzling dresses. Frances and Eliza were fully occupied with the leisurely lives of helping Betsey run the household, making dresses, riding out with their friends to pay "morning-calls." Though Mary loved her studies at Rose Hill, loved the exhilaration of taking first in recitations and of knowing more about history than any other girl, she sometimes wondered what Betsey's reaction would be if she said some Sunday evening, "I don't want to go back."

Would she reply, "You must"?

Rose Hill was her home, and Madame Mentelle like a mother to her, giving her what no one ever had. But as the years flowed stealthily by, and her father and Mr. Clay started talking of who would run for President again—as Mary realized that from being among the younger girls at the school she was now eighteen and the oldest—she began to feel a kind of desperation.

It wasn't that there had been any falling-off of her suitors. A belle to her lace-gloved fingertips, she knew how to make the most of her rosy prettiness, and had the advantage of being sharply intelligent, well-read, and with a name for witty repartee. She was skilled enough on the dance-floor to follow even the most awkward gentleman and make him feel he was actually dancing rather well; she used a variation of the same technique in conversation.

Nate Bodley continued to seek her out at subscription dances and cotillions and balls, and there had been a number of kisses stolen in quiet parlors and secluded woods.

If she had loved any of the regiment of town boys and sons of planters whose names filled her dance-cards, she knew it wouldn't be difficult to find a husband.

But she didn't. And a husband wasn't what she wanted to find.

She didn't know the name for what she wanted to find.

Increasingly, it was dawning upon her that many of the Lexington boys frightened her. It wasn't that she disliked them, although she considered a number of them complete idiots on the subject of paper currency. Some, like Cash and Nate, she was deeply fond of.

But the first time Cash got into a duel after his wedding—with Mary Jane expecting their first child—Mary was shocked, and furiously angry. The whole scene in the parlor, this time of White Hall, was repeated, except without the wedding-dress lying like a mute and gorgeous intimation of tragedy over the back of the sofa. Mary Jane weeping, Frances and Mary and Mary Jane's sisters all gathered around to comfort her—old Mrs. Warfield, too, muttering, "I told you how it would be. . . ." in the background, and Cash, of course, nowhere to be found.

And just as well, thought Mary, stroking her friend's icy hand. She didn't think she could have seen Cash without screaming at him, "How can you do this to Mary Jane?"

Four years had changed her view of what it was for a man to defend his honor. It was no longer a case of the romantic agony of a bride widowed upon her wedding-night, trading bridal white for somber veils of woe. Cash's death would leave Mary Jane a widow and his unborn child an orphan, to be raised by the gloomily triumphant Mrs. Warfield and whatever new husband Mary Jane might eventually find. Their suffering was the price Cash would cheerfully pay, thought Mary, for his precious honor.

Yet no one—not even Mary Jane—seemed to share Mary's awareness. When she spoke her thought to Frances in the carriage on the way out to White Hall, Frances stared at her and said, "For God's sake, Mary, keep your mouth shut! Don't you think Mary Jane is suffering enough?" As if Cash had come down with cholera, and had not chosen to make his wife suffer rather than let some other man call him "nigger-lover" unpunished.

And Mary, sitting mute beside Frances as the team pulled the vehicle up one of the long steep hills by the river, had the queer, sudden sensation of kinship with Mr. Presby. She felt a stranger in an alien land, wanting to shout things in a language that nobody there understood.

That night, at her father's house, after the exhausting afternoon comforting Mary Jane, Mary had dreamed of Cash and the other man both firing into the dirt at their feet. In the dream it was the earth that bled, as if in justification of the Indian name of Kentucky, "The Dark and Bloody Ground." On her way down to breakfast a few hours later Nelson caught her with the news that both Cash and his opponent had shot deliberately wide, and Mr. Presby subjected everyone at the breakfast-table to a scathing sermon on the evils of dueling, a practice never engaged in in the North. ("Except by Alexander Hamilton and Aaron Burr," remarked Mary, shaking out her napkin, which earned her a bespectacled glare from the tutor.)

But every man Mary knew—including her father and both her uncles—carried weapons when he left his front door. In the glass showcases of half the shops, braces of pistols were displayed along with silk scarves and necklets of pearls. Men showed off their knives to one another, which they carried sheathed beneath their superfine swallow-tailed coats, and spoke with pride of the swords concealed within the hollow shafts of their canes. During the election of 1836 feelings ran high, and there were shouting-matches at political-speakings, the hot tempers fueled by Kentucky bourbon. The ladies mostly kept clear of these—as ladies must—but unlike most ladies of her acquaintance, Mary could not pretend she didn't see what she saw: red faces, mouths stretched by shouted oaths, the vicious blaze of violence in men's eyes.

Men spoke admiringly of the "code duello" of the South, but there was little of that punctilious tradition in the brawling that broke out at Court Days. On one occasion Mary saw Cash holding back the crowd while his friend Jim Rollins kicked and lashed a Louisville Democrat who'd sung a song insulting Henry Clay: *"In spite of his running he never arrived. . . ."*

Dust stinging her eyes and the smell of blood in her nostrils, Mary thought, *I can't live like this. I can't.*

She turned her face aside and found herself looking down a quiet street near the Courthouse, in time to see her neighbor Mrs. Turner being helped by her coachman into a carriage. There was a slave boy with them, carrying two small parcels his mistress had bought from the peddlers in front of the Courthouse. At the sound of the ruckus around the fight the boy checked his steps and craned his neck, and without word or admonition Mrs. Turner took the coachman's light whip from beside the dashboard and caught the youth a savage lick across the backs of his legs that dropped him to his knees. The parcels went tumbling into the dust.

Mrs. Turner lashed the boy a second time, this time across the face, and stood quiet as a schoolmistress in her walking-dress of lavender-gray while the boy picked up the parcels and staggered to his feet, blood running down his face.

Then she handed the whip back to her coachman, and got into her carriage, the boy handing in her packages and scrambling up behind.

Where will I be in five years?

That year, Frances went to Springfield, Illinois, to visit Elizabeth and Ninian.

"I daresay it won't be long till Elizabeth finds a husband for her," remarked Betsey in a tone of deep satisfaction, when Frances's first letter reached them in Lexington, speaking of her warm welcome to Ninian's big house on the hill, and the cheerful entertainments planned by the best of Springfield society. Like Lexington, Springfield was a new town, rough and raw on the bluffs above the Sangamon River, but growing fast. Like Lexington, it was a hotbed of state and local politics, with money to be earned and money to be grabbed in land-dealing and political patronage.

Like Lexington, too, Springfield seethed with Todd cousins and Todd connections. Half of southern Illinois was populated by Kentuckians who had crossed the river rather than compete, in industry or agriculture, with the slaves the Virginians brought in. Mary's uncle John Todd was a physician in town; another uncle there was a judge. Her handsome cousin John Stuart was a lawyer there, as was her cousin Stephen Logan from the other side of the Parker family: both were active in the Legislature in Vandalia, and there were female cousins as well, Lizzie and Francy and Annie. In her letters Frances sounded very much at home.

"And high time," Betsey added, folding up the letter and glancing along the table at Mary. Margaret, Sammy, David, and Martha had been joined in Mammy Sally's care by beautifully dimpled little Emilie, and Mary suspected her stepmother was increasing yet again. Robert Todd was as usual in Frankfort at the Legislature. "A girl who isn't married by the time she's nineteen just isn't trying." Mary would be nineteen in December. "I don't know what she's waiting for."

"Maybe to fall in love?" Mary dusted sugar over the dish of mulberries and cream that Pendleton had handed her. She didn't look up, but felt her stepmother's glare.

"Girls fall in love every other week—most girls do, that is. I hope your sister isn't too high in the instep for the Springfield boys."

"And in any case," added Mr. Presby disapprovingly, "the whole idea of young females 'falling in love' and marrying willfully whoever takes their fancy is, I believe, responsible for a great deal of heartache and unhappy matches." He spooned a frugal pinch of salt onto the oatmeal he'd requested Betsey have Chaney make for him—everyone else in the household ate cornbread or grits. "The writers of romantic novels have a great deal to answer for."

"Surely you aren't advocating the selection of husbands by professional matchmakers, as they do in China, Mr. Presby?" Mary fluttered her eyelashes. "Or perhaps by the lawyers of the young ladies' families?"

Mr. Presby's upper lip seemed to lengthen with disapproval. Over the years their relations had not improved—once they had nearly come to a screaming-match over molasses. "It is to be hoped that Mrs. Edwards, with a certain amount of experience in the world, will be able to guide Miss Frances's choices and make sure that she marries a gentleman, and a man of means sufficient to support her in the comfort to which she is accustomed. I am sure that otherwise there is no happiness to be expected."

She would miss him, Mary thought, when he returned to New England to take up a parsonage in one of those gray little towns where no one seemed to have any fun.

Already she missed Frances. Ann—now fifteen and finished with whatever the Reverend Ward could teach her—she had never liked, bearing her an obscure grudge from the days when she'd learned that her own name would be shortened from Mary Ann to simply Mary... as if Ann had willfully stolen half her name. Ann was a tale-bearer, a crybaby, and had a temper almost as bad as Mary's—without Eliza to keep the peace between them, they had come to hair-pulling more than once.

Eliza finished her schooling and had returned to Frankfort. Mary wrote to her weekly, as she wrote to Frances and Elizabeth and Meg in Philadelphia, but it wasn't the same. One by one the friends Mary had made at Ward's school had married, or were engaged. When she went to the dances at Giron's, the talk among them was all of servants and babies, or the latest of them to be engaged. There were new young belles "coming out"—including Ann—girls four and five years younger than Mary. Though Mary laughed and flirted, she felt increasingly alone.

It was her last year at Rose Hill. She was the oldest girl in all the classes, and helped Madame Mentelle with the younger ones. She still had the room she'd shared with Meg, at the end of the narrow courtyard on the family side of the house, but she now occupied it alone. More than once Madame had said to her, "You are like a daughter to me." Her own daughters were married, Marie to the son of Henry Clay ("A drunkard who'll break his father's heart," predicted Betsey, with gloomy satisfaction).

"It is a shame and a disgrace that there is no possibility for a young woman to attend college the way a young man does," declared Cash, when he encountered Mary at a Court Day in the spring of 1837. "You're a perfectly intelligent person—God knows more intelligent than half the men of my acquaintance. You're well read, well informed, politically astute." He frowned, his black brows plunging down over the slight hook of his nose. "Yet this country can find no better use for you than to marry you off to a bucolic ignoramus like Nate Bodley."

He jerked his head in the direction of the planter's son, standing with half a dozen of his cronies around Bill Pullum. Pullum had a young slave woman with him, and by the sound of their voices, and the stony expression of the girl's face, there was bargaining going on. Nate's voice rose over the others: "Yeah, but will she breed, that's what I want to know." He grabbed the front of the girl's yellow calico dress in both hands, pulled it open and down over her arms, to squeeze her breasts.

"Yet what choice does a woman have in this country—or in any country?" went on Cash, not quite rhetorically, but with his usual habit of preaching to Mary about her rights. " 'Female seminaries' . . . 'young ladies' academies' . . . Faugh! Marriage-marts by another name!"

Cash had recently expanded his interest in abolition into what he sometimes termed "the rational treatment of females"—something Mary Jane laughed gently over, because her husband still hadn't the faintest idea what it cost to run a household. "This country will remain in bondage until women as well as men free their slaves, make up their own beds, wash their own clothes, throw away their corsets. . . ."

"Why, Cash," purred Mary, flipping open her fan and widening her eyes at him over its lacy brim, "I never *dreamed* you wore corsets."

Caught off-guard in mid-tirade, Cash burst into laughter, his eyes twinkling: "You, young lady, are a minx," he said. "Now you tell me whether you don't think women should have the same rights to be educated as well as men—to hold property in their own names—even to vote!"

"I'm not sure," said Mary in a judicious tone, "that I'd sleep well at night knowing Arabella Richardson could vote for the President of the United States," and Cash laughed again.

"I don't sleep well knowing Nate Bodley can. You aren't going to marry him, are you, Molly?"

Mary sighed, and turned her eyes away in sick distaste from the sight of Nate and his friends clustered around Bill Pullum and the slave girl in yellow. "He's rich," she said. "And Betsey has been trying to push us together. When he comes to the house on Saturday evenings she always finds some reason to leave us alone in the parlor, and whenever I go to the theater or the Lyceum, it's 'Why don't you send a note to Indian Branch?' I don't..." She hesitated, looking up at the man by her side, the eagle profile, the lively sparkle of his mad green eyes.

There was a man, she thought, who was going somewhere, who was going to make something of himself.

Maybe she wouldn't end up marrying the President, she reflected. But a man who wasn't in politics at all—who only followed what all his friends proclaimed—seemed to her not wholly a man. And though she knew that other men examined female slaves in the same fashion in the open markets, she also knew it wasn't the same.

Then she tossed her head again, making the ribbons dance on her bonnet and her bronze curls bounce. "I can't imagine spending the rest of my life listening to Nate Bodley go on about his racehorses and his slaves....Not that there's anything the matter with his racehorses, of course."

But when Cash had conducted her back to where her father and Betsey stood on the Courthouse steps, and she asked—hesitantly—about going on with her education, her father frowned in puzzlement, and said, "Do you mean to be a schoolteacher, then?" in a voice of disappointment and disbelief.

As if, thought Mary, she had expressed an interest in becoming a nun. A Presbyterian one, presumably...

Levi and George snickered and nudged one another. George, at thirteen, had already been in half a dozen brawls at Court Days and political-speakings. Levi, four years older and living now in a boarding hotel, was drunk, though it was early in the afternoon.

"I think it's an excellent idea." There was something in Betsey's tone of a woman in a shop slapping down a coin to buy the last packet of pins before a rival's hand can touch it. "The Reverend Ward was telling me only the other day what an exemplary student Mary was when she attended the Academy, and how he would have loved to have her return for further study and to teach the younger children. Although really," she added, with a titter of laughter and a sharp look at Mary under her bonnet-brim, "now that Frances has gotten engaged up in Illinois I bet it won't be long until *you* catch a husband—"

"I didn't say I wanted to be a teacher," Mary interrupted, feeling as if her stepmother had given her a shove toward the door of the house.

"Then what did you say?" Betsey's glance was like steel. "Honestly, Mary, I'm only trying to help you...."

"You're only trying to get me out of the house," retorted Mary hotly, "so there'll be more room for your own children. Don't think I don't know that's why you've been shoving Nate Bodley at me like that purple fright of a hat you made for me—"

"Mary!" exclaimed her father, with a fast look around to make sure none of his friends had heard this outburst. Mary clapped her hands over her mouth, tears of shame flooding her eyes.

"I'm sorry," she gasped in a stifled voice. She turned and, springing down from the Courthouse steps, darted into the crowd.

"Mary, come back!" called out her father, and Betsey added her voice to his:

"Come back here this minute!"

She dodged around a gaggle of skinny cows, caught up her green-striped skirts, fled between a countrywoman hawking lettuces and a trader trying to sell a farmer a donkey, ran from the square down Main Street. . . .

And stopped, shocked, seeing behind the shelter of two drawn-up carriages a little knot of men beating another, savagely, with their canes. Two of the attackers held the victim's arms as a third struck him, over and over. Mary first saw the struggling shapes, almost without meaning: the figure bent under the blows, the glint of the brass cane-head, the white straw hat lying in the mud near the wheels of the Breckenridge carriage, the glint of broken spectacle-glass. A fourth man stood apart, his hands on the shoulders of a young black woman in a yellow dress.

The silence was eerie, broken only by the thwack of the cane, the grunt of the wielder as he raised it above his golden-blond head.

Nate. The man with the cane was Nate Bodley.

And the man he and his friends were beating was Mr. Presby.

They flung the tutor to the ground and Nate said, "Goddamn Yankee abolitionist, you keep out of my business after this, you hear?" He kicked him, then turned, grabbed the slave girl roughly by the arm, and thrust her ahead of him down the street, trailed by his friends. Presby lay in the dirt where he'd fallen, blood gleaming in his hair.

Mary ran to him, fell on her knees beside him, turned him over. Panic filled her, blind terror. . . . He wasn't dead, he moved his hand, *thank God, thank God. . . .*

And all the while she repeated, over and over in her mind, *I must get out of this place. I must get out.*

Chapter Ten

Bellevue Place, Batavia, Illinois May 20, 1875

"A very sad case." Dr. Richard Patterson laid the slim bundle of papers on the worktable in John Wilamet's little cubicle off the sunny parlor of Bellevue House. John drew a clean folder from the drawer, scanned the top page of the bundle—a letter in his mentor's careful, tidy handwriting—for the new client's name, then raised his eyes to Dr. Patterson's in startled shock.

Dr. Patterson nodded at the unspoken question—*Yes, it really is who you think it is.* "A most tragic case. And one which requires special consideration, of course."

"Of course," John murmured, and let his body settle back in his chair again. His long fingers flicked through the correspondence and doctors' opinions that would make up the basis of the file. A letter from Robert Todd Lincoln dated April tenth: "*. . . If you would meet with me and Drs. Jewell, Danforth, Isham, Smith, Davis and Johnson at my Chicago office on the twentieth . . .*" A much longer letter from Dr. Patterson's younger brother DeWitt, also—like Patterson's son—a physician: "*I treated Mrs. Lincoln during her husband's tenure of office as President of the United States, for weakness of the bladder and for head and back injuries resulting from a carriage accident on the second of July 1863. I do not believe any permanent injury was sustained in the carriage accident, though for the remainder of her residence in Washington she complained of increased headaches. . . .*" Several letters from Dr. Danforth, whom John had met now and then during the past two years, when he came to Bellevue Place to consult.

He looked up at Patterson again. "Is she violent?" Thinking of that stout little black-clothed figure in the Army tent by the walls of Fort Barker years earlier, screaming imprecations at the ladies of the Freedmen's Relief Association.

Thinking of his mother.

"Good heavens, no." Patterson sounded vaguely horrified at the idea, although even some of his own carefully selected patients had their moments. Through the open door of his cubbyhole, John could see Miss Judd and Mrs. Goodwin, two of the twenty or so well-to-do white ladies who were the only people Dr. Patterson would admit to Bellevue, both writing letters.

Miss Judd, fragile and ethereal-looking in the shaft of sunlight from the wide windows, looked better than she had a few nights ago, when John had settled down to the tedious task of coaxing her to eat. She'd entered Bellevue at less than seventy pounds and there had been times John had feared she would die simply because her heart would not endure the deprivation that she seemed to so desperately crave. Mrs. Goodwin was thumbing through the notepaper in the box, looking for a sheet that was sufficiently clean not to repel her.

That bore watching.

"No," Patterson repeated, and drew up another of the cane-bottomed chairs that furnished—barely—the stark little room off the parlor. "Nothing of that kind, dear boy. Mr. Lincoln—Mr. *Robert* Lincoln—is of the opinion that his mother's insanity dates to her husband's death. Scarcely surprising, given the terrible circumstances of her widowhood. And a woman's nervous system naturally suffers from the burden of modern civilization more than does that of a man. Greater noise, greater stimulation, the greater stresses engendered by a need for order and punctuality..." He shook his head.

"In my opinion Mrs. Lincoln should have retired to some country retreat following her husband's assassination, and lived quietly, instead of choosing such over-stimulating venues as Chicago and Europe. Mr. Robert Lincoln concurs with me on that. Her mental powers, already dangerously overtaxed, seem to have been further irritated by the death of her youngest son four years ago. Again, she followed this bereavement not with the total rest that is the only possible amelioration of such a condition, but with further travel and stimulation that eventually deteriorated her nervous tissue. Her attachment to Spiritualist séances, and the excitation engendered by their rejection of the divine authority of Scripture, only hastened the inevitable."

In the parlor, Mrs. Goodwin finished her search through the small packet of notepaper at the rosewood desk, sat back, her narrow, rectangular face pursed with pent emotions. Then she leaned forward and began to thumb through again. Her movements were quicker now and she'd begun to rock a little in her chair. Bad signs.

Dr. Patterson went on, "According to Drs. Danforth and Isham, Mrs. Lincoln suffers from a hysterical bladder and frequent urination, as well as from spinal irritation, and theomania. Of course all of this must be confirmed by observation. According to Mr. Lincoln there's no family history of insanity or alcoholism, certainly no syphilis or epilepsy involved. I'm afraid, if indeed her illness is of ten years' standing, that she may be with us for some time."

John held up a finger, caught Patterson's eye and nodded out the door to where Mrs. Goodwin had just sat back a second time, trembling now and looking restlessly around. Patterson smiled a little at John and said, "You go speak to her." John got to his feet, crossed the parlor without appearance of hurry or deliberateness to the woman's side.

"Maybe it's time for a little walk in the garden, ma'am?" he suggested, and she turned on him, her face contorted with anger.

"Why can't this filthy place provide clean paper?" Mrs. Goodwin's gloved fists bunched together on the table's waxed and polished top. Unlike Miss Judd, who wore lace house-mitts of the kind wealthy ladies often did in company—and who was regarding the stout stockbroker's wife with more alarm than was usual in her lackluster blue eyes—Mrs. Goodwin had on kid gloves of the sort usually worn for visiting and outdoors. She took them off only to bathe. "Every single one of those pieces of paper is disgusting!"

"Dr. Patterson does the best he can here, ma'am," said John in his most reasonable voice. "Let's talk about this outside in the garden. . . ." He had observed that Mrs. Goodwin generally calmed down and felt better after a few minutes among Mrs. Patterson's roses with the sun on her face. "When we come back, I'll help you find one that's clean."

Mrs. Goodwin got to her feet—John carefully moved her chair aside without touching her—and, he thought later, would have walked outside with him had not Dr. Patterson, who had been watching from the cubicle door, come over and said, "Now, Mrs. Goodwin, surely you know those notepapers are for everyone. We can't bring in paper specially to suit your tastes."

"They're dirty!" She whirled, her cheeks reddening and her eyes unnaturally bright. "I couldn't write to my children on those disgusting rags! There's a spot—look at it!" She jabbed a gloved forefinger at a nearly invisible speck on the small, clean buff sheets. "Every page is like that! Goodness knows what they'd catch!"

"But no one here is sick," pointed out Patterson in his deep, reasonable voice. "The papers are quite clean, you know. . . ." He touched the top of the stack, at which Mrs. Goodwin drew back as if he'd spit on it. "And we can't make special cases for everyone."

"You can give your patients something that's clean enough to touch without giving them every disease from smallpox to cholera, and passing them along to their families!" And with that she turned and fled up the wide stairs in a storm of blue faille ruffles. Minnie Judd pressed a clenched fist to her mouth and burst into silent tears.

"I suspect hydrotherapy is what she needs," said Patterson to John. "You'd best tell Peter to prepare the tub. She's been progressively excited for the past two days. I've only been waiting for an outburst like this. But you did quite well," he added. "We shall make an alienist of you yet."

"Thank you, sir," said John. He wondered whether, if he had been allowed to take Mrs. Goodwin for a short stroll in the sunlight before bringing her back to the subject of the notepaper, the whole scene could have been avoided. As Dr. Patterson climbed the stairs after his recalcitrant patient, John went to reassure Minnie Judd, who was trembling like a whipped greyhound and weeping without a sound.

JOHN HAD BEGUN CORRESPONDENCE WITH DR. PATTERSON THREE years earlier, when he'd written to him asking for copies of the proceedings of the Fox River Medical Association, of which Patterson was president. At the time John had been working as a secretary for the resident surgeon of the state asylum in Jacksonville. He read old journals, and the proceedings of medical associations, whenever he could lay hands on them in the offices. The overworked white men who ran the institution spoke approvingly of John's "desire to improve himself," but it never seemed to cross anyone's mind to put him in a position of any responsibility. Those positions—or more probably the salaries that went with them—were the purview of white men.

At times during those years at Jacksonville, John had wondered why he didn't simply become a carpenter, or work in a brewery, or shovel horse-shit in the streets—God knew Chicago's streets could use more full-time shovelers. Lionel Jones—whose family shared the rear cottage of a two-house lot on Maxwell Street with Cassy, Cassy's children, Lucy's children, John's wife, Clarice, and their daughter, and Phoebe—was a laborer at the Armour stockyards and made enough to pay his share of the rent and keep body and soul together, something John was not always able to do. Lionel lived day to day, ate and slept and walked out with his family along the shores of the lake on Sundays, and sometimes fought with his wife, Lulu, and sometimes loved her. . . .

Why, John wondered, did he want more?

Why did anyone want more?

Why this driving curiosity to learn what insanity *was*? To help the insane?

As Cassy put it, "Don't you got enough to do lookin' after one insane lady?" with a sharp nod at their mother.

John had no answer to that. For the first few years after the War's end he had worked for Dr. Brainert, under whom he'd served in the Army; the red-faced Army surgeon had resumed his private practice in Chicago, specializing increasingly in diseases of the nerves. Working as his assistant, John had studied the works of Greisinger, Charcot, and Johann Reil, trying to fathom the shadowy world of lunacy while at the same time trying to cope with his mother's intermittent hysterical rages, her long periods of silent refusal to get out of bed, to wash or dress herself—her increasing tendency to seek release from her inner demons in drunkenness or opium or "hop."

During those first few years in Chicago, immediately after the War, John had felt a good deal of hope. In spite of living in a rattletrap cottage "back of the yards," and being refused service in all but "Negro" stores, he had a sense of being given a chance to prove what he could do.

When Brainert had died, suddenly, of heart-failure—struck down as if smitten by lightning as he stepped from the trolley-car near his house—John had learned how illusory that sense of well-being actually was.

That was in 1869; the first optimistic flush of Reconstruction was over. The sense of rebuilding a new nation, of educating and helping the freedmen to "take their places in American society," had faded before the realization that those freedmen wanted the same jobs that white men held. By the common consensus of everybody but the former slaves themselves—who weren't asked—their "places in American society" seemed to be doing exactly the kind of jobs they'd been doing before the War: that is, anything that was too nasty, too backbreaking, or too time-consuming for anybody but slaves to undertake, and for not much more profit than they'd had as slaves. Less, in most cases, because at least slave-owners *had* to provide shelter and food, or their neighbors would talk.

After months of finding no work at all, John had secured a place as assistant to a surgeon attached to a private sanitarium in Lake Forest, for a third what a white man would be paid. The sanitarium had closed in '71; that was when he'd gone to work at Jacksonville, after yet more months of helping Cassy do white people's laundry, and rolling cigars in the Maxwell Street room by the light of a single kerosene lamp to make the rent. When the banks all failed in '73 he'd been let go from Jacksonville—not that they could spare a single man from that overcrowded and hellish warehouse for the permanently insane—and with that failure, it seemed to him, even the nasty and backbreaking employment tended to go to the white men, who mostly had brothers-in-law or cousins or friends in city government or the packing-yards or the railroads. At least they got paychecks.

And he was, for all intents and purposes, back on that street in Washington being beaten up by the Irish teamsters, who feared that newly freed slaves would take their jobs.

The recollection of that day was clear in John's mind as he read over the reports from Mrs. Lincoln's trial, and the evaluations of Drs. Jewell, Isham, Danforth, et al. concerning the sanity of the President's widow. For years John had regarded Abraham Lincoln with skepticism for backing the colonizers, the men who'd wanted to free the slaves only if they could be shipped out of the country where they wouldn't interfere with the white men. Now, he wondered if the man hadn't simply guessed what would likely happen if all black men were given their liberty at once, as the abolitionists had demanded: that in such numbers, most black men would be unable to find jobs.

John lowered the papers, looked out through the window of his tiny office—like a dressing-room off Dr. Patterson's handsome study, with its shelves of books, painted lamp-globes, and imposing rosewood desk—and thought about the stout little Southern belle who would come to the contraband camps with boxes of clothing or blankets, brisk and busy and bossy. The woman who would give such wickedly funny accounts of the reactions of the pro-Southern society matrons of the town to her requests for help. Swinging from energy to tears to hysterical rage with the same unexpected violence, fragile in the same way that his mother was fragile.

But Mr. Robert Lincoln—and Drs. Jewell, Danforth, Isham, etc.—were wrong if they thought her insanity began when her husband's blood had been splattered over her gray silk dress at Ford's Theater that Friday night in 1865.

Whatever was wrong with Mary Lincoln, it started long before that.

Dr. Patterson had Argus—the attendant who doubled as coachman—harness the team and rode down to the train-station late in the afternoon. They returned in the evening, an hour before supper, when the first cooling breezes rustled the trees around Bellevue Place. Mrs. Patterson shut her daughter, Blanche, into her room in the family wing—Blanche was simpleminded and often kept out of the way—and with her son, also named John but referred to throughout Bellevue as Young Dr. Patterson, went out onto the steps.

John Wilamet watched from the window of his cubbyhole as Peter opened the iron lodge gates to admit the vehicle. When it reached the steps, two men—one lean and bearded with a mouth like a bracket, the other burly, mustachioed, and dressed with the finicking care of a dandy—helped a stout black figure out. Dr. Patterson made a sweeping gesture with one arm, taking in the three-story brick house, with its lower wings and comfortable-looking bow windows. Mrs. Patterson came down the steps and held out her hands to the veiled widow; Mrs. Lincoln pulled her hand sharply from the other woman's grip. John saw Mrs. Patterson's back stiffen, and knew Mrs. Lincoln had already made an enemy, before she even crossed the threshold.

Somehow, that didn't surprise him.

A number of the other patients were in the parlor when Mrs. Lincoln was escorted in. Mrs. Goodwin, of course, was still confined to her hydrotherapy tank, wrapped in wet sheets with a steady stream of water flowing over her to calm her spirits. But Minnie Judd was there, sharing the green-tufted sofa with Mrs. Edouard—up and around for once—and the restless-eyed Lucretia Bennett. By herself at the table sat Mrs. Johnston, to whom most of the other ladies gave a wide berth. Mrs. Munger quietly brooded in a corner. Mrs. Patterson made introductions, not mentioning that "Mrs. Lincoln" was in fact the wife of the man whose idealized image, decorated with an incongruous halo, was appearing coast-to-coast on china souvenir plates and allegorical paintings of apotheosis in Heaven.

Behind them, in his study, Dr. Patterson was saying to Mrs. Lincoln's two escorts, "I know your mother will be comfortable and happy here." So one of them—it had to be the younger man, in the natty gray suit, with the watchful, suspicious eyes—was Robert, Abraham Lincoln's oldest—and only surviving—son.

"Here at Bellevue we offer the modern management of mental disease through moral treatment, not restraint. Rest, proper diet, baths, fresh air, occupation, diversion, change of scene, an orderly life, and no more medicine than is necessary are all that are required, we believe, to restore the failing reason to health, if in fact it can be restored. And I believe we have had a good deal of success in that field."

"As to that," said Robert Lincoln in a light voice that reminded John at once of his father's, "I'm not sure how much success anyone could have with my mother. The important thing is that she is placed somewhere safely, where she can do no harm to herself. Beyond that..."

If in fact it can be restored, thought John, quietly leaving the cubicle and following Young Doc, Mrs. Patterson, and Mrs. Lincoln into the hall that led to the family wing. *Aye, there's the rub.* At Jacksonville, where he'd sometimes doubled as an attendant, he'd seen those upon whose restoration to reason family, doctors, state had given up: the maniacs pounding on walls, writhing in the metal-barred cribs to which they were confined, shrieking or weeping as they were held down for "water cures" considerably more rough-and-ready than Mrs. Goodwin's hydrotherapy. He'd watched the delusional confined to "tranquilizing chairs"; the melancholy wasting silently away unnoticed, except when force-fed through tubes; the syphilitic screaming in pain and the filthy avoided by everyone.

Many of them hadn't seemed worse than some of the ladies here—only poorer, long ago abandoned by families who could deal with them no longer, and picked up on the streets by police or strangers who turned them over to the courts.

Could some of them be cured, he wondered, if treated with *rest, proper diet, baths, fresh air* and all the rest of it instead of the Utica crib or the metal collar? How could you reach them if they barely heard you? What could you do?

"Now, I'm sure you'll find this room very comfortable." Mrs. Patterson's voice drifted around the corner from the hall that ran down the center of the wing where she, Dr. Patterson, Blanche, and Young Doc had their private rooms. John had guessed, a few days ago, when one of the small patient rooms on that wing—and its next-door "attendant's room"—had been aired and made up, that someone of some importance, a "special case," was being brought in. "You'll be free, of course, to walk around the grounds and in the garden—I'm quite proud of my garden—and of course you'll have the use of the carriage for riding anytime you care to. Our grounds are quite extensive. We encourage our ladies to walk in the fresh air."

Argus had brought in Mrs. Lincoln's trunks already, five of them, and half a dozen carpetbags. They crowded the bright, bare little room with its single iron-framed bed, its white curtains that did not hide the window-bars, its small barred judas-hole in the door. Mrs. Lincoln put back her black veils and regarded Mrs. Patterson with those large, tourmaline-blue eyes John remembered: eyes red with weeping now, and settled into unhealthy-looking pouches of pale flesh. In Washington, struggling to regroup from the death of her beloved son, Mrs. Lincoln had struck John as brittle, changeable, volatile.

Now she looked beaten. In her small, silvery voice she said, "I don't suppose anyone in this place has bothered to tell you that I'm not a well woman? I suffer from headaches—not that my son will admit that they're anything but a *figment of my imagination,* as he wishes they were—and from pain in my back."

"Of course Dr. Danforth has been over all that with us—"

"Dr. Danforth," retorted Mrs. Lincoln witheringly, "would undoubtedly prescribe poison for me—if he thought he could get away with it. And my son would thank him for it, always supposing he didn't request it to begin with."

"Now, Mrs. Lincoln," smiled Mrs. Patterson, "you know you don't mean that. You're just tired. Of course you'll have medicine here, all the medicine you need. This is John Wilamet. . . ." She gestured toward him as he stood in the doorway. "John helps my husband, and he will bring you whatever you ask for."

John supposed there were worse things than being treated like an attendant by Mrs. Patterson. At least Dr. Patterson consulted with him over treatment of patients, and taught him what he had learned in over twenty years of dealing with those troubled in their minds. And it certainly beat rolling cigars until your fingers bled, or ironing shirts that white folks' servants brought to be washed.

But such an attitude didn't bode well for his chances of becoming a doctor of minds himself.

Mrs. Lincoln regarded him bleakly. He couldn't tell whether she recognized him or not.

"Supper will be at six," said Mrs. Patterson. "You'll want to wash up, of course, and change your dress. You shall take your meals with the family, rather than with the other patients. . . ." She smiled in what she'd probably been told was a kindly way. John wasn't sure her square, expressionless face was capable of much else. "Someone will knock on your door."

She rustled off down the hall, like a solid rectangle of corsetry. John knew what was expected of him. His hand on the door, he asked, "Can I bring you anything, Mrs. Lincoln, or do anything for you?" He had to check on Mrs. Goodwin before supper, and look in on Mrs. Wheeler, who frequently became disoriented at this time of the evening. But he could not, he thought, simply leave this woman here without a word. There was something in the way she looked around the small room in the graying light that reminded him of a child, sent to a strange place alone.

She snapped, "No." And then, as he began to withdraw, her square, heavy face softened infinitesimally, and she added, "Thank you, Mr. Wilamet."

John closed the door, and bolted it from the outside.

Chapter Eleven

On Friday afternoons, Dr. Patterson was driven in the carriage to the railway station to take the Chicago and Northwestern to the city. John had learned to lie low and stay quiet until the superintendent's return. Though neither Young Dr. Patterson nor Mrs. Patterson had ever spoken a word of disapproval about taking a man of color to train as an assistant—and though neither was ever anything but polite—neither treated him in any way different from Gunther, Peter, and Zeus, the men who made the rounds of the rooms with the door-keys every night and were ready at call to restrain unruly or hysterical patients, or from Amanda, Katie, Gretchen, and Louise, who were in charge of making up beds and walking with the patients in the gardens. John had once overheard Mrs. Patterson say to her husband, "I don't see what the point is, since there are no Negro doctors anyway," and had been unable to hear what Patterson replied. Her tone had carried the self-evident inflection of one who says, *You know they don't enter sheep in the Kentucky Derby.*

John knew that there were, in fact, black doctors, most of them trained overseas. But there weren't many of them, and those there were made an extremely poor living, as few blacks had the money to call a doctor when they were sick.

And no blacks that he knew had the money to seek out help for the terrifying agonies of the mind.

So on the Fridays and Saturdays while Dr. Patterson was gone, John slipped into the invisibility he had perfected most of his life. He mixed medicines for the patients—camphor, laudanum, morphine, saline draughts, chloral hydrate, belladonna, ergot, cannabis indica . . . despite Dr. Patterson's assurances about "no more medicine than is necessary." Croton oil for those who stubbornly refused to move their bowels and tartar emetic for those whose frenzies or obsessions were best controlled by keeping them semi-nauseated most of the time. He helped Gunther and Gretchen with the hydrotherapy patients, making sure the water in which they lay was tepid—Dr. Patterson at least didn't believe in such "stimulating" treatment as "the bath surprise," unexpectedly pouring ice water down a patient's sleeve in the hopes of snapping their mind back to sanity, a favorite at Dr. Marryat's sanitarium in Lake Forest. He helped Young Doc in leeching those patients like Mrs. Wheeler who had exhibited signs of over-excitement and mania, and took his turn at observing those who were confined.

He prepared a blister for the back of Mrs. Johnston's neck—as a counter-irritant to the irritations of her brain—and more tartar emetic to puke Miss Canfield out of her lethargy. Young Doc gave an electrical treatment to Mrs. Hill, who was also slipping into a lethargy, but unlike Patterson he did not permit John to observe.

At least, John reflected, Patterson's refusal to deal with the chronically violent precluded such techniques as refrigeration—or maybe it was only that the wealthy gentlemen who installed their female relatives here didn't wish to see them going about with their heads shaved.

In any case, John didn't see Mrs. Lincoln again until late Friday afternoon, twenty-four hours after her arrival.

Bellevue Place, before Dr. Patterson had purchased it, had been a school. Although most of its sixteen-acre grounds were occupied by graveled paths, green lawns, and little copses of trees, there was a formal garden to one side of the main house. This Mrs. Patterson had had put into shape again, so that the twenty or so ladies under Dr. Patterson's care—he admitted neither epileptics nor syphilitics, no "furiously insane" nor of "filthy habits" (except of course Mrs. Johnston)—could have at least a chance of regaining the balance of their minds by fresh air and quiet. After the hellhole stench and noise of the state asylum at Jacksonville, John wholeheartedly agreed with this treatment. He loved the garden, though he did not walk there or sit there except in attendance on one of the patients.

It would not do for these wealthy ladies to think that the silence and repose being paid for by their families were being shared—and gratis at that—with a black man.

So on Friday afternoon he stepped out the side door as he usually did, and stood near it where the corner of the wall shielded him. Feeling the sun on his face, listening to the silence and birdsong and drinking in the scents of warm mulch, of grass, of sweet alyssum and June roses. Thinking of those, like Mrs. Wheeler, or Mrs. Edouard who had spent most of the night screaming and who now lay in opiated sleep, so lost in their lightless inner labyrinths that they were cut off from this beauty, this peace.

The door creaked behind him and he straightened, turned back to the house with the air of one hurrying from one duty to the next, as a stout crape-clad figure stepped out. "Excuse me," she said, "I was looking for—" Mary Lincoln stopped on the threshold, gazing out at the brilliant green, the neat hedged squares, and the exuberant colors—Ispahan and La Noblesse, Painted Damask and Ville de Bruxelles. Her face, puckered a little with annoyance, relaxed into her slightly crooked smile.

"How beautiful," she sighed, and looked up at him, shading her eyes with her hand though she wore the black bonnet of a widow. "We had a rose garden, when we lived in Washington. . . . Will you walk with me, John? Mr. Wilamet, I should say now. It's good to see you after all these years." She seemed relaxed and cheerful—as well she should be, thought John, considering the amount of laudanum she'd had that morning for back pains, headache, and what Mrs. Patterson had described as "agitation." Her voice had the slight dreaminess with which he was well familiar. "I had no idea that being clapped up as a madwoman could be so pleasant."

"I wish I could say I was delighted to see you, ma'am." John smiled and offered her his arm. "And I would be, under other circumstances, I hope you know."

"What a dilemma for the writers of etiquette books." Mrs. Lincoln laid a small plump hand on his elbow, and with her other hand opened her fan. Her black straw bonnet—worn without a veil—was in the latest style, John observed. He knew she'd been assigned Amanda as a permanent attendant and wondered how that quiet, matter-of-fact quadroon woman had dealt with the contents of those five trunks and numerous hatboxes and carpetbags in the confines of the small room. He'd already heard from Peter that another eleven trunks were expected later in the week.

"I'm sure my husband would have come up with a dozen formulae for introductions and greetings when one meets an old friend in a madhouse, or in jail, or in the gutter outside a tavern: 'Why, whatever are you doing here?' seems somehow inadequate to the task. Is there any possibility of getting a decent novel to read here rather than the collection of moralizing tracts they have in the library? Or will I be put in a straitjacket only for asking?" Her voice was careless, with an echo in it of a Southern belle's ineradicable flirtatiousness, but John heard the tension hidden beneath. *She doesn't know the rules,* he thought. *She is in a new place, and, in spite of the laudanum, watchful.*

She may, too, have heard some of the commotion last night when Mrs. Edouard started beating the walls and screaming.

"You won't be put in a straitjacket," he replied. "Dr. Patterson practices what they call moral treatment, rather than chaining up lunatics the way they used to. . . ." *The way they still do,* he reflected, *in every institution but those wealthy enough to hire the staff needed for adequate attention to their patients.* "In a way it's almost like letting the mind heal itself, the way the body heals itself, provided there is no infecting agent poisoning the system. There are lectures every Sunday night, and concerts—and of course you may call for the carriage to go riding anytime you wish."

Beyond the garden, he could see Mrs. Johnston walking with young Miss Canfield and ignoring the nurse Louise, who walked in attendance behind, as if she weren't there. Maybe to Mrs. Johnston she wasn't. At the far end of the aisle of roses, Mrs. Hill sat alone on a bench, rocking back and forth and presumably communing with the voices that spoke to her out of the air. With a kind of wry bitterness John reflected on the filthy brick wards of Jacksonville, on the never-ending smells, on the notorious "swing" that the few overworked doctors there told themselves and each other was actually calming and therapeutic . . . and had the added benefit of being a threat that all but the most frantic lunatic understood.

"There seem to be lectures night and morning here." Mrs. Lincoln's light, silvery voice was dry. "I got a good one from Dr. Patterson before breakfast concerning my 'will to insanity,' as he called it. And another about my dear son's concern for me. Is that part of moral treatment, as well?"

"It's part of Dr. Patterson's system to instruct and convince patients in changing their ways."

"And to censor what they read, the way they do in Russia?"

And in Virginia, reflected John, *if you happened to be black there sixteen years ago.* "I admit the library isn't the most modern in the Western Hemisphere," he answered. "If you asked for a book I think it would depend on what it was, whether Mrs. Patterson would procure it for you or not. They're cautious about anything that would affect the balance of the mind. . . ."

"The balance of my mind is perfectly fine!" She rounded on him, her cheeks flushing red. She almost shouted the words.

John was silent.

"I'm not a child." Her voice was trembling. "Or a lunatic." Turning her back on him, she burst into tears and strode away down the path. John started after her. Swinging back, she shouted, "Let me alone!" and quickened her steps, almost running—running in any direction that presented itself, because within the wall that surrounded Bellevue Place, all directions were ultimately the same.

Chapter Twelve

Chicago May 1875

On Wednesday afternoons John walked into town and took the train to Chicago. An hour and a quarter through flat warm prairies, green with summer's advance, combed by wind and broken by the emerald tufts of woodlots. Then a quarter-hour through thickening lines of brown brick workingmen's cottages—white workingmen—that eroded into a ring of shacks and shanties, boardinghouses and clapboard saloons, the streets dirtier and more crowded and the steel rails doubling and trebling and quadrupling and the stench of the packing-yards growing until it was impossible to believe that the stink could still be invisible: John always felt that somewhere it stood in a glowing green wall of filth, he was only looking in the wrong direction. . . .

And that was Chicago.

He knew most of the people who rode on Wednesday afternoons in the third-class "Negro" car. These were men who worked as gardeners or stablemen during the week in Batavia or Geneva, and women who were maids in Wheaton. There wasn't much work for blacks in Chicago, let alone out in the white peaceful towns of the prairie countryside. Those few who had it, tended to leave their families in the city where they had friends to help them if anything went wrong. Amanda, the attendant at Bellevue, had two children in town whom she left with her parents, and would visit every other Tuesday when she had the night off. The Germans and Poles and Hungarians who crossed through the rattletrap car for their own less-than-palatial third-class accommodations—men who'd flocked west in search of jobs that simply weren't to be had in

New York—regarded the black enclave with occasional curiosity, occasional suspicion, when they regarded them at all. Mostly the blacks were invisible, as long as they stayed quiet, which they did. Nobody wanted any trouble. The week was hard enough as it was.

All the car windows were open—those that weren't jammed permanently shut—and still the air was hot. Sweat ran down the sides of John's thin face, itched in his close-cropped hair under his mouse-brown derby and stuck his shirt to his back. The thick lenses of his spectacles slipped down heavy on his nose. As the train slowed down flies came in, the flies that seemed to hang over Chicago in the summer like a roaring, glittering cloud.

Once they got into the city itself the noise of the other trains, coming and going all around them as the tracks converged, drowned any attempt at conversation. John gritted his teeth, bracing against the din as he always did, as if it were a physical pain. Once he was out of the train he hurried through the echoing immensity of the half-built station to the platform where the southbound local would depart, chugging its slow way through the crowded neighborhoods south of downtown. The shriek of train-whistles, the yelling of the porters, the clamor of the engines, even after all these years, still made his chest feel as if it would burst.

Since the War's end he had lived in cities. In Richmond, briefly and terrifyingly, knowing that his blue uniform and his black skin made him a potential target whenever he stepped outside the Army Headquarters; then this nightmare metropolis where everyone seemed to be rushing, scrambling, fighting at all times amid the unending stink of factory-smoke, horse-dung, and the all-drowning stench of decaying meat. The moments he could snatch in the garden at Bellevue were the more precious, in contrast to this. No wonder women sometimes got well there, away from these hideous streets.

No wonder Dr. Patterson was of the often-expressed opinion that "the Negro race is constitutionally unable to adapt itself to the pace and demands of civilized life." Most representatives of "the Negro race" that John knew had come, like himself, from the quiet of country plantations.

Chicago was enough to drive anyone, black or white, insane.

From the Twelfth Street station he turned west again, picking his careful way across and through the mazes of tracks. This whole neighborhood between the Galena yards and those of the Illinois Central—which included the river levee and the lower end of Satan's Mile—lay under a permanent pall of sooty smoke, rasping in his lungs. Dead cats and dead dogs lay by the rails, some cut nearly in half. Now and then the trains would claim a child, or a drunk. This close to the river the stink of the packing-houses, of the soap and turpentine plants, was enough to knock you down. Constant, unending, the squeals of the dying pigs, the lowing of cattle terrified and in agony made an aural curtain as palpable as that green, rotting wall of smell.

The houses here, cramped two on a lot along the unpaved streets, sweltered in the clammy heat. The Great Fire of four years ago hadn't reached this far and this part of Satan's Mile was much as it had been for a dozen years: clapboard cottages of two and three stories that had started life as sheds; stables and shacks that still housed goats and pigs; muck-filled alleys and rough frame houses whose very kitchens and hallways were sub-sub-sub-let to make the exorbitant rents. Elsewhere in the city it had been as bad or worse, but the vile "patches"—neighborhoods so rough they were a law unto themselves, like Hell's Half-Acre or Hairtrigger Row—had been supplanted by endless dreary zones of clapboard cottages.

The inhabitants of those ramshackle dwellings still grouped according to nationalities, as they had before the Fire—why live among people you couldn't talk to, even supposing they wouldn't beat you up on sight? But there was a sort of neutrality accorded to the main thoroughfares. John walked quickly as everyone walked in Chicago, tired and hot with his coat slung over his shoulder and his little carpetbag of laundry in his other hand. He mentally counted his way through the neighborhoods: Judd Street, Russians; O'Brien Street, Hungarians; Kramer Street, *now we're down to the Italians*—skinny children with glossy black curls chasing one another through the alleys behind saloons where the kerosene lamps had begun to throw their orange glow over shirtsleeved men in derbies and the thick blue pall of cigar-smoke . . .

Griffe Moissant's on Maxwell Street—red-peeling paint, shutters thrown wide to the reeking heat—marked the last two blocks before the dump where refuse from a nearby packing-house was thrown. In heavy rains the runoff was the color of coffee, the texture of phlegm, and smelled like nothing of the human earth. The neighbors here were mostly like John, born slaves and either runaways during the War or freed in its wake. Many of the men had fought, in the 22nd C.I. or the 107th or the 2nd Light Artillery. Many more of them had been told, when news of Lee's surrender reached their home plantations, that the government would prefer it if they'd stay put on the same land they'd worked for their former masters, and work it for a wage.

"Funny thing about that," had said Lionel Jones, when John and his family had first moved in with Lionel, whose brother had still been alive then and married to Cassy. "Once Marse Barton finished takin' out the rent for the cabin, an' the bill for food from the plantation store, an' new shoes for wintertime, an' hire of his hoes an' his plows an' his mules, *we* owed *him* money. . . . But he was nice enough to let us stay on an' work for free."

"What a good man," John had replied drily, and Lionel gave him a wink and a savage, broken-toothed grin.

Most had stayed in the South. Seeing some of those who lived along Maxwell Street—none of whom could read and few of whom had any training or experience at anything except agricultural work, much less the connections with police and city politics that were so vital to borrowing money and establishing businesses—John understood why. The devil you knew, in the quiet world of familiar faces and familiar countryside, be it ever so stricken by poverty, was infinitely less terrifying than the grinding, bewildering, many-visaged unknown demons that waited grinning at the end of the tracks.

There were times, when the hammering of the train-engines and the stink of the smoke and the rotting meat seemed about to crush him like a spider between two stones, when he wondered if he shouldn't have gone back to Virginia himself.

John passed Griffe's, and then Cuff's Grocery, where another gaggle of drinkers sat on the porch sipping the stale dregs that Cuff bought from the downtown saloons for a few cents a barrel. As he did so John felt his stomach begin to tighten with dread. It was nearly dark and above the smells of privies and stockyards he could scent the drift of side-meat and beans, cornbread and red-eye from the open doors of those weathered shacks. Could hear old Aunt Machie singing through her open door as he passed her house, singing at the top of her lungs as always, sweet and beautiful as an angel:

"Shoo, shoo turkey, throw your feather way yonder,
Shoo, shoo turkey, throw your feather way yonder. . . ."

He was almost home. That cold quivering behind his breastbone tightened up like a fist around his heart, wondering what the hell he'd find.

Every week—every Wednesday night when he came home to spend his half-holiday with Clarice and Cassy and the rest of his family—it was a toss-up whether he'd have rest and joy, or an agony of chaos and awfulness.

As he walked past the Bonfreres' house in the front of the lot, he found himself listening for his mother's screaming voice.

Nothing.

But no sound of the children either, and they always made a noise as they went about their chores. Cassy and Nando Jones had had three:

Selina, Abe, and Miranda, before Nando's death from pneumonia in '71—'71 had been a bad year all around. John's little sister Lucy had grown up wild all her short life, refusing to work with Cassy as a laundress and taking up with a gambling man when first they'd come to Chicago. She'd died birthing her second child, Josephine—Cassy had taken in Josie and Josie's sister, Geraldine. You didn't turn family out-of-doors. Then there were the brothers and sisters John's mother, Phoebe, had borne in Washington during the War, and in Chicago afterwards, those who had survived: Rowena, Sharon, Ora, Ritchie.

With the children of Lionel and his wife, Lulu—George, Tom, Ish, and baby Dellie—that made enough and more than enough to support, and most of them too young to be of much help. A year and a half ago, against every resolution not to do anything of the kind, John had fallen in love with a girl named Clarice, and now their child, Cora, was just learning to walk. Clarice helped Cassy with her laundry business, her sweetness and tact increasing the number of their clients in times when nearly everyone else was losing them to hard times, tight money, the closing of factories and shops.

But it was backbreaking work, and it took every minute of daylight for the four grown women while nine-year-old Selina looked after the babies and marshaled the younger children to the household chores. When times were good John could hear Selina's sharp, sweet voice calling out commands, encouragement, teasing, sometimes getting Tom and Abe to sing part-songs with her as she swept and they hauled wood for the boilers set up in the narrow yard, just the way Cassy had done, he remembered, with Blue Hill Plantation's "hogmeat gang" all those years ago.

But there was only silence now and the silence went to the pit of John's stomach as he came into the yard. Clarice and Lulu were gathering in washing from the lines that strung back and forth, taking up the whole of the yard between the Bonfreres' house and his own. In the cobalt dark of the porch the open door shone with red-gold kerosene light. Clarice saw him, laid the shirts and sheets carefully back over the line and ran to him, caught him in her arms—"God, I'm so glad to see you!" and their lips met, hard. Hers tasted of sweat, with the slightest whisper of honey. He could have stood there kissing her in the dark all night among the wavering lines of sheets. "Your Mama's gone off."

Shit. "Where?"

She shook her head. She was a few inches short of John's own five-foot, eight-inch height, and like John and Cassy built slim; darker than they, nearly full-blooded African, like Lionel and Lulu, but delicate-featured, a coal-black gazelle. She had her hair wrapped up for work and he wanted nothing more than to tear off her headscarf and gather those great, soft, scrunchy handfuls of her hair in his hands, and to hell with Phoebe....

"The kids have gone out after her." Meaning Selina, Rowena, Abe, and Tom.

"And Cassy didn't?"

"Cassy maybe got other things to do." His sister appeared at the top of the porch steps, her sleeves pushed up and her arms folded, slim as a strap. He could only see her silhouette, but knew what her expression was from the sound of her voice. "I got ten sets of sheets that need to be delivered tonight if we're going to eat next week, and I'm just starting into the ironing now, brother. Mama was in and out all morning, saying how she had a headache, and a backache, and a bellyache, and how she was just going to stay in bed and get herself better, and then just before the sun started going down she lit out of here, said she was gonna go buy medicine."

Shit. John was perfectly familiar with his mother's "medicine-buying" expeditions. "I'll go look for her."

"Get yourself something to eat first."

"Save me some." Though with the youngest nine children home and the three grown women—and Lionel coming in God knew when from Griffe's—whatever would be left by the time John located his mother wouldn't be much. "I'll be back when I can, baby," he whispered to Clarice, cupping the side of her face for one more kiss, the anger and weariness of going through all this yet again tight in his chest.

Then he set out on his search.

If Phoebe were a simple drunk, he reflected, taking a quick look through the door at Griffe's—where as he suspected Lionel was having a couple with his friends from the stockyard—the matter would be an easy one. Even the drunks in the neighborhood knew enough not to stray across Kramer Street, and that was a piece of wisdom just about impervious to liquor.

But for Phoebe, liquor was only an adjunct to whatever dark things inhabited her skull. When her voices started talking to her, there was no telling where they would lure her, or what would appear to her to be a good idea at the time.

So he worked his way south and east, making for the dives and flophouses and tawdry saloons of the levee. This was the way his mother had gone last time she'd wandered away, when she'd been picked up, with a blacked eye and a bloodied lip, naked in an alley behind the Eagle of the Republic saloon on Grove Street and telling the cops at the Twenty-second Precinct House about the revelation God had given her—John winced at the memory. For weeks at a time she'd be more or less the woman who had raised him, who had fled with her children from Blue Hill, with her wry sense of humor and her bitter, sardonically funny observations, telling amazing tales to the children of princesses and warriors and the serial adventures of the Hebrew Children in the wilderness that had nothing to do with any Bible story John had ever read. . . .

And then she'd be gone. Even when she was there, she was gone. Abusive, angry, shouting, or simply silent, staring at the wall. For the past four years he'd been keeping a log of her moods, and knew she was getting worse, much worse.

He didn't know what to do about that.

He hunted for her until nearly midnight, through steamy dark streets illumined only by the smoky glare of the barroom doors. A one-legged white beggar in the shabby remains of a blue Union uniform claimed he'd seen her, on the plank sidewalk outside Dapper Dan's on Judd Street. The man, though drunk himself, was good enough to go into the saloon to ask after her and thus prevent John from getting his head broken by the men inside. Dapper Dan's was one of those places where the "regulars" were all white. Through the door John saw him pause long enough to pull off his wooden leg, untie his real leg from among his rags, park prosthesis and crutches in a locker, and ask the other plug-uglies in the place about her—he came back out, said she'd been seen and thrown out.

From there John asked for her at the shabby dives along the levee, where merchant sailors were incapacitated with chloral hydrate and relieved of their pay, their shoes, and frequently their lives; at the catacombs that doled out needled beer and murder. He went to the lakefront bagnios where the clap was probably the mildest and most benign thing that would happen to you. . . . His sister Lucy, John knew, had died in one of the places along here.

One of the waterfront gangs shoved him up against a wall, drunk and looking for sport: "Christ, you mean that nigger bitch who went on about the river of flamin' locusts pourin' down out of the moon?" marveled the bulldog Irishman who led them.

"She's my mother," said John, keeping his voice steady with an effort. The man who pinned him against the wall had on brass knuckles and there were blackjacks, sticks, and chains dimly visible in the gang's shadowy hands. John knew if you showed fear you were dog's meat.

"Let 'im go, boys. He got trouble enough."

The men passed on, bawling with laughter.

In time John found her, where the tracks of the Illinois Central ran into the lakefront yards. It was a nightmare world of darkness and lights, like a shooting-gallery of trains switching back and forth, engines clattering, bells hammering, all night long without cease. The night was still hot and the occasional chuff of breeze off the lake like smelly glue, mosquitoes roared and swarmed around the railroad lanterns that hung before the doors of dark little dens where crooked games, camphor-laced wood-alcohol, and whores too far gone to work even the levee beckoned to those with nowhere else to go. John heard Phoebe's voice singing, cracked and beautiful and silvery, the skipping, almost childlike march the Union soldiers had sung, with words that always raised the hair on his nape:

"Mine eyes have seen the glory of the coming of the Lord. . . ."

John always wondered what that woman had actually seen, the one who had written that song. What the glory of the coming of the Lord had looked like, in the deep of the night.

Phoebe was staggering along the tracks in the middle of what looked like a river of ties and steel. Her black hair hung down her back to her hips and her pink dress lay torn and ragged over her shoulders and she sang full-out as if she were in a choir.

"I have seen Him in the watchfires of a hundred circling camps,
They have builded Him an altar in the evening dews and damps,
I can read His righteous sentence by the dim and flaring lamps—
His day is marching on."

The groaning shriek of pistons and wheels drowned her voice and a train clanked by between them, medium fast. Steam blasted John in the face. He stopped on the tracks, aware that if another engine bore down on him the noise was so great all around that he wouldn't hear it; he kept looking over his shoulders, left and right. There was an engine there, lamp burning, but unmoving as of yet—at least he could perceive no movement, in the shifting shadows and dark. Two cars went by, tramps dimly perceived in their open doors, and the lights beyond framed Phoebe's body and caught like dark fire in the ends of her hair. She was walking toward another moving engine, her arms outspread as if welcoming a lover.

"I have read a fiery gospel writ in lines of burnished steel,
As ye deal with my contemners, so with you my grace shall deal,
Let the hero born of woman crush the serpent with his heel,
While God comes marching on. . . ."

With one panicky look over each shoulder—and yes, there was another train coming, though not fast—John darted over the tracks. His eye was caught by the rats swarming between the ties, by the dark slumped form of a drunk asleep or dead on the ground with a bottle glistening under his hand.

"Get your hand off me!" ordered Phoebe, when John caught her, pulled her from the track. "I don't got to go with you! I don't got to go anywhere with *you*!" Her breath smelled of oil of turpentine, a favorite tipple at the rough joints along the tracks.

"It's me, Mama, it's John."

"No it ain't. John wouldn't come look for me. John too good to go out lookin' for his own mama. John thinks he's too *good* to speak to her, when he see her on the street."

"Ain't you got no place to take her?" One of the train-men emerged from the dark at the edge of the switch-yard. "State asylum or someplace? She sure crazy."

The way the man looked at her—the familiar way he helped her over the last couple of ties and over the filth-swimming ditch into Water Street—John suspected the man had had her, in the shadows of one of the alleyways. Maybe six or eight of his friends as well. He always suspected that was how she'd ended up bearing Sharon, Ritchie, and her last baby, who had died.

John said shortly, "State asylum don't take colored."

"Oh." The man nodded vaguely. "Damn shame."

Yes, thought John, escorting his mother back through the now-quiet streets. *It certainly is a damn shame.*

About halfway home Phoebe abruptly decided that he was who he said he was after all, and commenced on a rambling account of why she'd had to go looking for medicine for her back and her belly and to shut up the ants running through her brain. John murmured, "Yes, Mama," and "No, Mama," as she spoke of the things she'd done.

At home he found Clarice had saved out some supper for him, but Phoebe announced, "I'm hungry," and took the pot from her. When John tried to get a share she shouted at him so loudly that, mindful of Lionel and Lulu and the older kids asleep in the next room—or out on the porch, draped in makeshift tents of sheeting against the mosquitoes—he let her have it. As she gorged down all that remained of the beans and rice, Clarice took him quietly aside and showed him what she'd found under the house beneath the corner of the room where his mother's bed was: twelve patent medicine bottles, all of them new and all empty.

"How much pain is she in, to need that much medicine?" asked his wife worriedly. John sniffed the necks of one bottle and then another, and glanced back through the door at his mother in the single candle's quavering light. All her favorites, Godfrey's Cordial and Nervine and Pritchard's Female Elixir. Two definitely had the bitter smell of laudanum and two more the pong of alcohol beneath the mingling sweetness of herbal tonic. "You think if you ask your Dr. Patterson about her, to have a look at her . . . ?"

"That's all I'd need," sighed John. "To tell the man I work for that my mother's crazy? That anytime she might take it into her head to come out to Batavia and look for me?" All the way out to the levee, and all the way back, the anger had been building in him, anger and grief and shame that he'd hold her craziness against her. Shame even that he'd hold her drunkenness against her, for it clearly was no fault of hers.

He knew those ants had been running through her brain long before she'd started trying to shut them up with alcohol.

Clarice asked softly, "What are we going to do?" She too raised her head, looked back through the doorway at the packing-box in which Cora slept. At Cassy curled in a tight ball on her mattress with Miranda and Ritchie. Though Cassy kept a hand on her money-box and slept with it under her pillow at night, still Phoebe had managed to raid it two or three times in the past few years, spending the rent-money inexplicably on toys for all the children, or games of keno. "You know this can't go on."

"I know."

By the time they got Phoebe to bed—after an endless argument during which she refused to lower her voice—it was nearly dawn. John could do no more than lie on the mattress with Clarice in his arms, trembling with anger and frustration, listening to the clanging of the switchyards in the dark.

Chapter Thirteen

Slanting sunlight dappled through the dogwood trees along Pennsylvania Avenue; the horse of one of the Union Light Guard shied at a passing dog and snorted, tossing its head. Mary glanced over her shoulder at the sudden clatter of hooves, then back at Lincoln in the carriage beside her: "A lot of use they'll be if a rebel assassin shoots at you from the trees."

Lincoln leaned back against the leather of the carriage-seat: "The only way they could prevent a rebel assassin from shooting from the trees is to surround us like a wall. And even then they couldn't stop a man from flying overhead in a balloon and dropping a brick on my head." And he looked up, shading his eyes as if to search for such a craft.

"*Will* you be serious?"

"No." Lincoln smiled, and put his arm around Mary's shoulders. "I have been serious all morning and I am mighty weary of it."

Deep in her dream, feeling as if she were trapped in quicksand, Mary thought, *No . . . Let me out. Let me wake up.*

I know what's coming and I don't want to see it. Not again.

But she couldn't wake—couldn't put from her the happiness of each relived second in his company, even if she knew that each one was a knife in her heart.

". . . I want a carriage-ride with the woman I love, not a military parade. . . ."

Sometimes—tonight was one of those times—Mary caught fragments of other events in her dreams: hurrying downstairs to the carriage in her silver-gray dress, her tippet of black and ermine wrapped around her shoulders. Hearing Lincoln in the hall behind her knock at Robert's door. "We are going to the theater, Bob; don't you want to go?"

She didn't hear Robert's reply, but in the carriage, on the way to Fifteenth Street to pick up young Major Rathbone and Miss Harris, Lincoln shook his head and said, "I can't blame him, the poor boy hasn't slept in a bed in two weeks. I told him to do just what he felt most like."

And then they were in the theater. Mary was conscious of the damp cold of Lincoln's coat-sleeve as he escorted her up the dark little stair, of the scent of Major Rathbone's hair-pomade and of Miss Harris's lavender sachet. Her heart was crying *No! Let me out!* but she tightened her grip on the sinewy arm, still strong enough, after all these years, to pick up an ax by the last inch of its handle and hold it out straight before him. . . .

Strong enough to swoop her up in his arms as easily as he'd swoop Tad.

The Pinkerton guard John Parker, burly and disheveled and smelling faintly of liquor, rising hastily from the wooden chair beside the door of the box to salute; Lincoln stopping for a moment to say something to him as Major Rathbone opened the door and bowed Mary and Miss Harris through. The box itself, dark and a trifle stuffy, with its drapery of red, white, and blue, and the glow of the stage lights beyond it outlining the rocking chair the management always brought in for Lincoln. The band breaking into "Hail to the Chief," and Lincoln moving the draperies aside a little to bow to the audience.

Laughter and cheering gusted up from below, warming Mary with a glowing satisfaction—a sense of deep vindication—that she felt even through her rising panic, her desperate struggle to get out of the dream before the end. Six months previously every newspaper in the country had been calling him "that giraffe from Illinois" and claiming that re-electing him would damage "the cause of human liberty and the dignity and honor of the nation." "There was never a truer epithet applied to a certain individual than that of 'Gorilla.' "

He had suffered—not from those slurs, but from the grinding toll of the War itself. She could see it in his face, in the shadowy glow of the gaslights. The deep lines, the sadness in his eyes, made her want to weep. The cheers from the audience were a balm, to her and, she thought, to him. At least there was the lightness in his movement that he'd had during their carriage-ride, the relaxation, as he sat beside her, that she hadn't seen in him in months. Major Rathbone and Miss Harris settled in the other two seats, hand in hand, heads together: the young soldier's mother had married Miss Harris's father, an irascible and sharp-tongued Senator from New York, and now it looked like the children of their separate first unions would themselves unite. Mary's hand stole into Lincoln's, and down onstage the sprightly Florence tried to tell a joke to Lord Dundreary, with predictably sparse results.

Florence: "Why does a dog wag its tail?"

Lord Dundreary: "Good heavens, I have no idea."

Florence: "Because the tail can't wag the dog."

"There's Charlie Taft," murmured Lincoln, looking down into the audience below them, and Mary hid a smile; in any crowd, Lincoln was always looking for people he knew. And the other Mary, the Mary who lay locked in the dream of these minutes, felt the minutes passing as if she heard the ticking of a clock. . . .

Ten more minutes to go. Nine. As if she walked with him down the road to a ferry, dreading the sight of every tree, every path-side stone that told her it was getting closer, and there was nothing she could do to stop the approach of the crossing-over point, when he was with her one moment, and the next. . . .

Maybe if I scream I can wake myself. . . .

"Don't know the manner of good society, eh?" sniffed the bumpkin Asa Trenchard, down on the stage. "Wal, I guess I know enough to turn you inside out—you sockdologizing old mantrap!"

Lincoln leaned down, to make some wiseacre remark in Mary's ear; she felt the brush of his beard against her temple.

NOOOO . . . !!!

The gunshot was like the cracking boom of thunder, like the lightning that had always so terrified her. Lincoln's arm jerked convulsively in her grip, and Mary caught him as he slumped sideways in the rocking chair. Gunpowder stink filled her nostrils, gunpowder and the horrible hot smell of blood.

Someone was shouting, rushing forward through the smoke. Major Rathbone tried to seize him, struggling in the reflected glow from the stage, and a knife flashed in the gaslight gleam. Miss Harris fell back against the box rail, screaming, and on Mary's shoulder Lincoln's weight grew heavier and heavier as he sagged against her. She saw the blood in his hair and began to scream too, screaming as all that she had feared for four years came rushing to catch her, to sweep her into the darkness that lay on the other side of that dividing-line of her life. . . .

THERE MUST BE SOMETHING I COULD HAVE DONE.

Mary looked back on the dream—like looking back into a room, through a window from the outside—as she sat beneath the elm-trees of

Bellevue's parklike grounds the following morning. Beside her on the bench sat Mrs. Olivia Hill, black-clothed like herself, a widow like herself, who had come up to her last Friday, after she'd run away from John Wilamet in the rose garden: "Is there anything I can do, my dear?" she had asked.

There wasn't, of course, and both of them knew there wasn't. But it was good at least to know that someone in this place actually cared. Like John... Imagine meeting John here, after all those years! Olivia had sought her out again after breakfast this morning, and offered to walk with her, the gray-clad form of Amanda trailing inconspicuously behind. "They don't like to see us in conversation, you know," whispered Mrs. Hill, and widened her enormous blue eyes at Mary. "Especially not those of us who were put here for our beliefs."

Mary turned her head sharply, met that gentle gaze. There was something in Mrs. Hill's voice that told her exactly what "beliefs" her family had considered marked her as insane, and she lowered her voice before she asked, "Do you think it might be possible to speak to our loved ones here?"

Olivia glanced back at Amanda, then at Mary again.

"Have you ever tried it?" Mary persisted. "Since you've been here, I mean?"

Olivia's thin, intent face grew troubled in its frame of black veiling. "The problem is the daylight," she explained, and Mary nodded. Every medium she'd ever spoken to had emphasized that the yellow vibrations of sunlight were absolutely inimical to the materialization of ectoplasm. "You notice how careful the good doctor is, to keep us separated once it grows dark."

Mary looked up at the trees overhead: elms like the clouds of a prairie thunderstorm, even in the brightness of morning casting a dense blue shade. "Surely," she urged, "we can at least try. Is there anyone else here, who might form a circle with us? Who might lend their strength, to summoning the spirits across the Veil?"

"Oh, yes. Lucretia Bennett was put in here for exactly that reason—because, her husband says, she believes that their sons speak to her from the Land Beyond. And that, of course, must be madness." She smiled her sweet, sardonic smile. "And little Miss Judd as well, though I'm afraid, poor child, she does have a terribly nervous constitution.... She says she knew you when she was a little girl."

Mary smiled at the recollection of that fairy-like child she'd known in Chicago, in the chaotic days of 1860 before the Republican Convention. "She did. Her father was one of my husband's great supporters.... The President of the Illinois Central Railroad, you know. My husband did a great deal of work for them, in his lawyer days. *And* had to sue them to get paid, I might add."

"Oh, well, one can understand how the *poor* Illinois Central Railroad would be so *poverty-stricken* that they wouldn't have the money to pay their lawyer. . . ."

And both women laughed. Bellevue Place, Mary thought, looking out past her companion to the thick green lawns, the winding graveled carriage-drive that circled the grounds, did not seem so very different from the Spiritualist camps she'd attended in the green country of upstate New York. There was that same relaxed air of not having anywhere else to be, of having all arrangements for room and meals taken care of in advance. . . .

The difference, of course, being that in those places one was treated like an adult capable of making decisions despite one's grief, and not like a willful and deluded child.

And even when she was a child, Mary didn't recall this horrible sense of being always watched, always spied upon, tattled on for the slightest deviation from what Dr. Patterson considered "normal" behavior.

It was worse than living with her sister Ann.

"I've never had success in materializing the spirits since I've been here," went on Olivia, with a sigh of regret. "It's what one can expect, of course, in this atmosphere of concentrated skepticism—I should think the look on Mrs. Patterson's face would send any spirit fleeing. But if nothing else, we can transmit to our loved ones the assurance that *we* are thinking of *them,* even if they cannot come to us."

"But they know that anyway," Mary pointed out.

"Of course," agreed Olivia, with a beatific smile. "But is it not good to receive a letter full of love and cheerful thoughts, even from one to whom you are prevented from writing?"

No, thought Mary crossly. *Mr. Lincoln hears me speak to him every day, hears me tell him how much I love him, need him. . . . My sons hear my words of love daily, hourly. One holds séances in order to hear from THEM. In order to see their dear faces again, to hear their words, touch their beloved hands. It isn't that I don't think they hear, there in the Summer Land. But I miss them so!*

"When those medical lackeys my husband hired came with their statements about conversing with the dead being proof of madness, I told them, if belief in the survival of the soul in Heaven is madness, then I claim the sisterhood of madness with Christ and all his saints." Scorn flicked in Mrs. Hill's voice and she squared her slim shoulders. "If it is madness to believe that love survives death, and that my precious boys in Heaven still love and comfort the mother they loved on earth, then how I pity your bleak and loveless sanity!"

Mary assumed there was some kind of grapevine telegraph in operation, as soldiers exchanged from rebel prison camps during the War had assured her existed in Andersonville and Libby Prison under the very noses of the guards. She was certainly aware that every darky in Lexington had known news and information long before a single white was aware of it, apparently by telepathy. In any case, the following morning directly after breakfast, she and Olivia Hill made their way to the densest copse of elm-trees, that stood farthest from the house at a corner of the grounds, and found Minnie Judd and the white-haired Mrs. Bennett waiting for them there.

"It's *good* of you to come with us here," said Lucretia Bennett in her oddly-inflected voice. "*Good* of you to *help* us in trying to reach out to our *loved* ones on the Other Side."

"I don't hold much hope." Olivia took Mary's other hand and drew her down onto the bench in the secluded shade. "We have twice attempted to hold gatherings here—mostly at this early hour, when the sunlight is not so harsh. Perhaps there were not enough of us to invoke the energies needed to build a bridge of thoughts for the souls to pass from the Summer Land to this world. We can only trust, and pray."

In the dense shade the four women recited, very softly, the Lord's Prayer, and just as softly, sweet voices harmonizing, sang "Shall We Gather at the River." Despite her misgivings about the daylight, Mary felt herself relaxing with the familiar words, the peaceful sense that these circles always brought her. Others over the years had included more prayers, and many had incorporated more music, drawing the Seekers together into calm and ready thought.

But always was that awareness that they understood her loss. Who young Minnie might have lost, Mary did not know—a friend, perhaps? She was too young to have given a sweetheart to the War. But Mrs. Bennett's black dress told her at least that this woman, like Olivia Hill, had walked the road she had walked. And all of them, she knew, had this in common: that they had found life without their loved ones literally beyond bearing.

In her mind Mary painted the darkness of those shuttered, curtained parlors, the enclosed sense of comfort and safety. The flicker of candles that always recalled the dim parlors of her girlhood, before the pallid glare of gaslight chased shadows away.

Please come, beloved, she whispered in her heart. *Please speak to me through these kindly women. Rest your hands on my shoulders, let me know that even here you're with me. That you've forgiven me . . .* The dreams of the night before last, and of last Wednesday night—was it only a week ago?—were the clearest she had seen him in many months. Even the knowledge that they would end with his head slumping down to her shoulder, blood gleaming blackly in his hair, wasn't enough to make her thrust them aside, even if she could have. They were all she had.

Give me something to live on, something to hold! I miss you so.

"Now, ladies." Dr. Patterson's deep voice broke the sweet silence that succeeded the song. Mary's eyes snapped open and Olivia and Mrs. Bennett dropped her hands at once, like guilty schoolgirls. The superintendent strode across the grass toward them, with his wife and Amanda striding purposefully behind. "You know this kind of excitement isn't at all good for you. Mrs. Hill, I'm surprised at you."

Mary replied, since Olivia seemed unable to answer. "Are we not then even permitted to pray? I should think *you,* of all people, would approve."

The doctor smiled, that impenetrable and eternal smile that she was coming to hate. "Of course you may pray, my dear Mrs. Lincoln. But prayer is for Sunday in chapel, or quietly and privately in your room, as St. Paul recommends, and in a spirit of Christian resignation. Mrs. Bennett, Mrs. Hill, I have a little treatment I'd like to try on you now before lunch, to see if we can make you feel better. . . ."

"He always does that," whispered Minnie Judd, in her soft thread of a voice as the doctor and his wife led the two other women away. "He doesn't like to see us gathered together. Not even in daytime."

"And you put up with it?" Mary's voice snapped with scorn for this thin girl in the dazzlingly fashionable dove-gray gown, scorn that reflected the surge of rage burning through her. Minnie regarded her with surprise in her cornflower-blue eyes.

"We must put up with it, ma'am. What choice do we have?"

What choice indeed? thought Mary, shaking with anger as Minnie, too, walked away under the trees toward the big stone house, her demi-train rustling on the grass. *When you have been judged a madwoman, you have no choice. You must take what they give you, and rejoice that it is no worse.*

And all the peace beneath those lush trees, all the pleasant treatment and hollow professions of understanding, could never make up for that indignity.

THAT NIGHT MARY TOOK SUPPER WITH THE PATTERSON FAMILY. MRS. Patterson smiled her wooden smile and tried to make gracious small-talk, but the fourth time she broke off to berate her daughter for not "behaving like a lady" when the poor young woman was clearly doing her best not to upset her food in company, Mary was hard put not to slap the doctor's wife.

Dr. Patterson had just returned from his bi-weekly visit to Chicago, and though he spoke kindly to his daughter he said nothing in her defense. Mostly, he chatted with his son about the affairs of his practice in Chicago. All her girlhood Mary had been ingrained with the idea that Yankees had no manners, and though she'd found that in many cases this was an exaggeration, she'd never been able to get used to this particularly Yankee combination of sanctimoniousness and preoccupation with work to the exclusion of one's company. Even after all these years, even in this situation, it annoyed her.

After supper Dr. Patterson mixed Mary a glass of medicine to take before she went to bed, for her back had begun to ache again, and her head, and she found herself both depressed and unable to rest. But when Amanda had helped her change into her nightgown and wrapper, and had locked the door for the night, Mary sat up for a time in the chair beside her bed, her eyes closed in the silence.

She whispered the Lord's Prayer, as the women had done that morning in the shade, and sang softly under her breath, *"Shall we gather at the river / the beautiful, the beautiful river. . . ."*

Prayer and song were an incantation, like Mammy Sally's hoodoo rhymes. Hoping against hope that even without the circle of loving hands and hearts, the spirits would come. The gas hissed softly, its flame turned down low behind a painted globe of glass—never since childhood had Mary been able to sleep in a completely dark room. Through the pink mosquito-bar tacked over the window a whisper of breeze stirred the dense, hot air. The big house was silent around her. Even the woman who had screamed last night—screamed so loudly that she could be heard here on the family side of the house—made no sound.

How many nights she had sat thus in her great bedroom in that cold dreadful mansion on Pennsylvania Avenue, that fraudulent white-painted sepulchre of her dreams. . . . Had sat late, so late that even the incessant noise of soldiers marching in the street, of bugle calls from the camps on the near-by Mall, had ceased. Her husband was absent, as he was so often absent, having slipped down the service stairs and out of the house through the basement, to walk alone through the chilly fog to the War Department to wait for dispatches. Sometimes he'd even sleep there on the sofa in the telegraphers' room. Or coming back, he would go to his office, his stockinged footfalls passing her door, to read petitions or pleas or the papers related to a thousand and one details of the

War that only he could decide upon, until he fell, exhausted, asleep at his desk.

In that silence—Mary remembered it so clearly now, called it back to her, *willed* it back—it had seemed to her that the gaslight had burned blue, just as candles did in the romances she read, and she had seen those beautiful, glowing forms pass through the closed door of her bedroom and come to her, holding out their hands.

Willie. . . ! She had seen him so clearly. His face—a round Todd face, just beginning to lengthen as he passed his eleventh birthday—wore that expression of thoughtful calm that had nothing in it of solemnity. A Todd face and his father's gray eyes. Sometimes he wore the gaudy little uniform the militia Zouaves had given him, along with an honorary commission of Colonel; sometimes the dark wool suit in which he'd been buried. He did not seem ghostly at all, only wrought of a pale light, and he led a smaller child by the hand, little Eddie in the long toddler's dress of tucked linen that Mary had sewed for him.

Her dearest boys! She had clasped them to her heart, though now she could not remember whether their flesh had felt solid in her arms. *Yet it wasn't a dream!* she told herself. It happened, just as Nettie Colburn, and Lord Colchester, and the other mediums of the spirits had assured her it would!

She breathed deep, the swoony warmth from Dr. Patterson's medicine enfolding her. If Dr. Patterson had not interrupted them, would not a few more minutes have sufficed for the Circle they'd formed? Even in daylight, even in the midst of this terrible place? Would not the spirits have found some way of communicating with those they loved? In her mind she formed the scene, Mr. Lincoln shyly smiling as he walked toward her through the deep shadows of the elms, with Eddie on one hip and Willie clinging to his hand, and Tad—young thin tall Tad like a half-grown Thoroughbred colt—striding alongside.

Could she not at least have felt on her shoulders the pressure of strong hands, as occasionally happened in the darkness of those séance rooms, when the medium would tell her that he sensed the presence of a tall and bearded man?

She sat awake—or mostly awake—in the gloom for what felt like hours, before lying down on top of the covers, and crying herself to sleep.

Chapter Fourteen

Springfield 1837

In June of 1837 Mary packed her many trunks and hatboxes, and in company with her father and Judy, made the jolting coach journey down to Louisville, to take one of the Ohio River steamers to Cairo.

Her father hired a stateroom for her, barely big enough to swing a mouse in, let alone a cat. He himself took a curtained bunk in the men's cabin, and spent a good portion of each day in the gentlemen's parlor, smoking long nine cigars, playing vingt-et-un and talking politics with the highly assorted crowd of slave-traders, land-speculators, cotton- and sugar-brokers, merchants, and lawyers who journeyed up and down the Ohio from Cairo all the way up to Pittsburgh. "I don't believe you talk politics with them at all," teased Mary, when her father took her for a walk around the upper deck in the evening cool after supper. "I believe you just use that as an excuse to gossip, the way you always accuse us poor women of doing." And she twinkled a smile at him from beneath her bonnet-brim.

"And isn't that just what you do?" he countered with a grin.

And Mary laughed, for she didn't want to complain of the company in the ladies' parlor. But in fact she found it excruciatingly dull, consisting as it did of a New England woman whose husband was engaged in "something to do with land" in Mississippi, a merchant's wife whose whole soul was occupied in the cost and difficulties of running her husband's business (and his life as well, in Mary's opinion), and the wife and daughter of an Ohio state Assemblyman who weren't entirely clear whether the husband/father of the family was a Democrat or a Whig.

The talk was all of servants, and of the expense of running a household, and the best way to get wine-stains out of damask. Why was it, Mary wondered, that married people became so *dull*? When Mary said she was from Kentucky the Yankee woman had asked disapprovingly if her father owned slaves, and had proceeded to lecture her—in Mr. Presby's best style—on the evils of slavery without bothering to ask first what her own views on the subject were.

"You'll like Springfield," prophesied her father, leaning his elbows on the upper-deck rail. "With your taste for politics you'll feel right at home there." On the stern-deck below them hogs squealed in their pens among high-piled sacks of corn, bushels of oats, barrels of whiskey and apples. Now and then above the incessant pound and splash of the two great paddles, Mary could hear the voices of the slaves who'd come onboard at Louisville, chained to the walls along the narrow walkways on either side of the engine-room. Sometimes singing, sometimes calling out in whatever gambling-games it was they played to pass the time and take their minds off where they were going. Sometimes, from the starboard where the women were chained, she would hear a child cry.

"It's going to be the state capital now, isn't it?" Elizabeth had mentioned that in her latest letter, in the midst of a host of Ninian's concerns, as if it were important only because it raised the value of Ninian's town lots.

"If Ninian and the Long Nine have anything to say about it, it will."

"The Long Nine?" Mary raised her brows. "So my brother-in-law has become a cigar? It's a guarantee of popularity, I suppose. . . ."

Her father laughed. "That's the name someone gave the representatives of the Sangamon County delegation at the Legislature. There are nine of them—the biggest county delegation in the state—and every man of 'em's over six feet tall, the tallest six feet four. Springfield's already the center of trade and farming in the state, and the biggest town. Vandalia's a mere village by comparison."

He shifted his broad-brimmed straw hat on his head, and looked out, as if he could see, beyond the wall of forest along the riverbank, the small settlements marked by pluming smoke, the tiny farms. "Illinois is one of the fastest-growing states of the Union, daughter. The key to our nation's future lies in the West. You'll meet the best of the coming men there."

"Are you trying to marry me off, Pa?" Mary regarded him coquettishly.

He pinched her chin. "I just want my girl to be happy."

She turned her eyes away to the green monotony on either side of the river, the forest that seemed to stretch on forever, trying to unthink the thought that had sliced across her mind: *You want to be happy knowing you've done your duty by "your girl."*

Happy with Betsey. And Betsey's children.

With the problem of those she supplanted all happily gone away at last, and no man to say you didn't do your duty.

She had so looked forward to this journey—to seeing Elizabeth and Frances again, and Elizabeth's new baby—Julia, named for the first tiny daughter, who had died. She still felt wild, dancing excitement at the sound of the churning paddlewheels, a bursting exhilaration at these new lands, this new *world*. But the suspicion that this was only a farther-away version of Mentelle's snagged in her mind. It caught on her thoughts like a burr in a petticoat, filling her with unthinkable shame.

At Cairo they transferred to another steamboat, this one going upriver on the Mississippi, which even in those high reaches was a broad yellow-brown stream whose banks were a tangle of snags and bars that the pilot had to negotiate with care. Sometimes they'd pass a flatboat, wide rafts a hundred feet long and laden with pumpkins and corn and hogs, riding the current all the way down to New Orleans. The paddles would churn the water and the men working the sweeps would shake their fists, sun-browned men who looked like they'd been braided out of strips of rawhide, with their faded hair and faded shirts and heavy Conestoga boots. Mary made the acquaintance of a French lady from New Orleans and her even-more-French aunt from Paris, and had a good time speaking to them in their native language of the cities she longed more than anything to see. She had a sense, riding the river, of profound delight, of moving out of the lush hollows of Kentucky and into a wider world.

They debarked at St. Louis, and then truly the world did change.

All of her life Mary had lived in Lexington, traveling no farther than Frankfort to visit Betsey's haughty, thin-nosed old mother. Her world had been a rolling verdant world of dense forests and granite outcrops, of patches of laurel, paw-paw, tulip trees. When the stagecoach climbed from the river-valley where St. Louis lay, the full harsh sweep of the prairie wind struck them, and she saw for the first time the prairie emptiness: green, flat, endless, unbroken to the horizon, baking with that indescribable scent of curing grasses under the morning sun.

Clinging to the strap in the swaying coach, Mary gazed at the stage-ruts sweeping away into the unimaginable distance and thought, *I'm going in the wrong direction! I should be going south, to New Orleans, or east to New York and Europe. Where am I going, and why?*

At least there were trees in Springfield. For two days on the stage, jolting through that vast untenanted world of tall grass and meadowlarks, Mary had had terrible visions—her sister's letters to the contrary—of yet another desolate constellation of board shacks, weathering slowly to grayness in the hot wind and unending glare of the sun.

But Springfield stood on the bluffs above the Sangamon River, and the fertile country along the bottomlands was settled up with scattered farms and cattle grazing contentedly in the waist-deep prairie grass. It was late in the day when the stage pulled into the yard of the Globe Tavern, an unpromising quadrangle of whitewashed buildings whose long porch sheltered an assortment of the local bumpkins and a pair of sleepy dogs. A bell clanged from the cupola on the roof, to announce the arrival. Dust and smoke hung in the air, as did the smell of livestock.

"What do you want to bet that's Ninian's carriage?" Robert Todd helped his daughter from the big high-wheeled coach and nodded toward the lower-slung and more elegant vehicle that stood waiting. "I wrote him the night we arrived in St. Louis, that we'd be on the next stage. The team certainly looks like Ninian's taste in horseflesh," he added, with an admiring glance at the glossily-groomed bays. "Have a seat and I'll go find him. He'll be inside."

He handed Mary into the carriage and signed to the stagecoach guard to pile their luggage beside it, then crossed the yard and climbed the plank steps to vanish into the inner darkness of the porch. The slave girl Judy, exhausted and intimidated by the journey, retreated to a bench near the woodpile. Mary put up her parasol against the slanting light of the afternoon sun and looked eagerly around her, taking in what she could see of the town that Elizabeth—and now, apparently, Frances—had chosen for their home.

The tavern yard certainly didn't look promising, and the street visible beyond—rutted and unpaved under a miasma of yellow dust—even less so. In addition to the carriage in which Mary sat, the yard contained half a dozen infinitely more plebeian vehicles, mostly farm-wagons, and a decrepit buggy, as well as a number of saddle horses hitched to the porch railing. Dogs snored in the shade. Chickens scratched. An occasional hog wandered in from the so-called street.

Whereas in Lexington there would have been a variety of people in evidence—wealthy planters, students of law and medicine from the University, slaves on errands for their masters, and young ladies in silks and fine muslins shopping in the Cheapside stores—here there seemed to be nothing but farmers and teamsters. In the shadows of the tavern porch a gang of rough-looking idlers drank, spit tobacco, and laughed uproariously over some tale being spun for them by a tall skinny idler sitting on a barrel with his long legs sprawled out before him. Presumably, reflected

Mary, sitting up quite straight in her new pink ruffled dress, there was a better class of citizen farther into town.

Movement in the tavern doorway. Mary turned, hoping it was her father and Ninian. But instead a blocky, broad-shouldered man in the tattered remains of a black long-tailed coat, bewhiskered and filthy, staggered across to the carriage, jabbed a grimy finger up at her, and declared, "And another thing, Missy: if slavery was to be expanded into the Western territories, how long would it be before the white slave-lords of the South would demand white slaves as well as black? How long before the wealthy factory-lords would take the indifference of the government for license to enserf the luckless laborers who are already de facto slaves, by further robbing them of what little liberty they still enjoy? Eh?" He glared up at Mary, red-faced with anger. "You answer me that, Miss!"

Mary looked away, cheeks burning. The man reeked of cheap liquor and clearly was incapable of taking—or even recognizing—a hint that his conversation was not wanted. Judy, who'd gotten to her feet, was looking around in an agony of uncertainty, not about to go up and tell a white man to go away. In Lexington, of course, it simply wouldn't have happened. Too many people knew Mary—any shopkeeper or clerk in town would have headed off the drunkard from a girl they'd waited on since her earliest childhood.

But since the alternative was to take refuge in a public tavern—presumably among this man's equally inebriated comrades—and since Mary wasn't sure she could make a dismount from the rather high carriage without providing every idler on the porch with a glimpse of petticoats, pantalettes, and ankles—she remained where she was. Her frozen silence seemed to enrage her interrogator still further.

"A government system which condones the domination of any man by any other man has automatically doomed to destruction all those it pretends to protect!" bellowed the whiskered man. "Of course the government will permit the extension of slavery into the newly formed territories and of course the result will be—"

"Professor Kittridge, come on up here on the porch and let me buy you a beer." The storyteller unfolded himself from off his barrel and ambled over to the carriage. Mary had an impression of enormous stringy height, of coarse black hair sticking out in all directions and high, sharp cheekbones. The stranger's features all seemed too big for his face—nose, brow, mouth—and his eyes were deep-set and gray as winter rain. He was dressed like the men on the flatboats in what seemed to be the uniform of the country, a faded calico shirt and linsey-woolsey trousers tucked into Conestoga boots, and there was a small straight knife-scar on his right temple.

His voice was a husky tenor, high without being reedy, and underlaid, Mary thought, by a soft Kentucky flatness about the vowels.

"Lay not your hand upon me, servant of the servants of Mammon!" Professor Kittridge swung around and lashed at the storyteller with a punch that would have stopped an ox in its tracks. "Pettifogger! Serpent! *Diabolos!*"

The storyteller met this barrage of invective by putting his hand on his attacker's forehead and holding him off at the length of his gorilla-like arm, Kittridge's frenzied punches slashing inches short of his ribs. At the same time he backed off, so that Kittridge's own momentum propelled him by degrees to the porch. As he did so, the storyteller glanced up over Kittridge's head to Mary, checking to make sure she wasn't harmed or alarmed. His gray eyes met hers, and when he saw that far from fainting with affront she was struggling not to laugh aloud, they sparkled with a deep answering delight.

Barely had the Professor and the servant of the servants of Mammon vanished into the darkness of the porch when Robert Todd, Ninian Edwards, and a skinny little man carrying a coachman's whip appeared from around the corner, quickening their pace as they crossed the yard. "Miss Mary, I beg your pardon," called out Ninian. "I thought I'd have time to pick up sugar and coffee from Irwin's. Can you ever forgive me?" His eyes twinkled as he, the coachman, and his father-in-law loaded the trunks onto the back of the carriage and strapped them into place. Judy, looking infinitely relieved to have the world return to situations with which she was familiar, hurriedly crossed to join them.

"Shall I horsewhip Jerry here for leaving the carriage?" Ninian indicated the coachman with a grin, and the black man grinned back.

"I should think it massively unjust to punish the servant for a sin he shares with the master." Mary put on her most pious expression, and all three men laughed. "Just don't you dare let it happen again."

Ninian and her father sprang into the carriage, Judy climbing up to the coachman's box. Jerry unhitched the team and swung himself up beside her. "You are just, as well as beautiful, Miss Mary," said the coachman gravely, and clicked to the horses. Ninian leaned forward to point something out to her father about his team. As the carriage turned, Mary saw the tall storyteller emerge from the porch again, a couple of saddlebags over one bony shoulder, making for the saddle-horses tethered on the other side of the yard. He stopped a stride beyond the porch steps, seeing her with the men of her family.

Mary met his eyes, raised her hand in a little gesture: *I'm well. Thank you.* And he lifted his enormous hand to her in return.

The wheels of the carriage threw dust on him as it pulled out of the yard.

Chapter Fifteen

Mary was three months in Springfield. It was heaven, to be with Elizabeth again, mothered and fussed over as she had been when she was a child. Heaven to share the second-floor front room of Ninian's handsome brick house with Frances, instead of with the whining tattletale Ann. Frances slept promptly and soundly, and didn't make a fuss when Mary sat up reading: didn't moan and mumble, "What, again?" on those nights when Mary had to use the chamber pot half a dozen times. It was heaven not to spend all day, every day in a battle of wills with Betsey; heaven not to have a gaggle of little half-brothers and -sisters playing in the library when she wanted to read.

That made up for a lot.

And Springfield was lively. Ninian's house—the "House on the Hill," though personally Mary wouldn't have called that *hill* more than a bump—was the center of all the best society there, the young lawyers and politicians who were starting to flood into town, now that it would be state capital. As a member of the influential Long Nine, and the son of the former governor, Ninian had connections with all the spider-threads of influence and favors and promises of government jobs in the county.

For the first time in her life she could discuss politics freely, without Betsey throwing up her hands and making remarks about schoolgirls and bluestockings, and Mary reveled in this like a cat in catnip.

She had plenty of chances to talk politics. With the State Legislature coming to Springfield, single gentlemen were ten to a lady, and a girl had to be really trying, not to have her dance-card filled days before a ball.

That, too, made up for a lot.

But it didn't make up for the prairie thunderstorms, whose violence Frances hadn't lied about. When the forks and sheets of lightning drove down out of the blackness, when thunder ripped the sky as if the whole of the universe were tearing to pieces, Mary could do nothing but hide herself in bed, weeping with a fear she didn't understand and sometimes screaming inconsolably as if Death itself stood just outside the bedroom door.

And it didn't make up for the fact that Ninian's modest collection of books was one of the finest libraries in Sangamon County: Its few volumes of edifying fiction Mary either had already read or made short work of in the first week. The only bookstore in town, C. Birchall and Company, refused to stock novels on the grounds that they were immoral, and thus she spent her three months in Springfield engaged in a constant quest for something—*anything*—to read.

Professional theatricals were immoral, too. No amount of picnics and buggy-rides in company with admiring young gentlemen could make up for that.

If Lexington was provincial, Springfield was rustic.

Much as she enjoyed that summer, she could not rid herself of the feeling that she should have gone in the other direction when she got on the steamboat at Cairo.

Though Springfield was officially now the state capital of Illinois—with a cleared field for the new State House and ox-teams hauling stones through the unpaved streets to prove it—the Legislature still met in Vandalia, a sleepy village sixty miles to the south. Teamsters, laborers, and ruffians associated with the building jostled along the few board sidewalks that dignified the downtown, and clogged the barrooms of the shabby and unprepossessing taverns that dotted the outskirts of town.

On Mary's second evening in Springfield, when Ninian gave a party for the regiment of Todd and Stuart cousins—and their most privileged friends—Mary couldn't help missing the students and professors who had added a note of sophistication and learning to Lexington parties. The talk was either gossip concerning all the Todd, Logan, and Stuart cousins, or of state politics, of government contracts, and of who had influence with the state's Congressmen and Senators in Washington—fascinating topics enough, but not to the exclusion of everything else.

"Of course it's not much," grinned her cousin John Stuart, as they stood together on the porch in the semi-darkness, with the dim glow of the oil-lamps within shining on the bower of polished honeysuckle leaves. "It's rough and raw compared to Kentucky—and I'll say it myself, though I love this place. But that's why we're all here. To be in on a good thing from the beginning."

From within, Elizabeth's voice lifted, calling for a game of Speculation. There was warm laughter, and the scraping of chairs. "Can I help you, Eppy?" asked Frances's voice—Eppy had been introduced to Mary as "our cook," and though legally Illinois was free soil, it was quite clear to Mary that Elizabeth regarded the handsome young black woman in the same light that she'd regarded Mammy Sally, as a well-loved slave.

Springfield was, Mary reflected, in some ways very like home.

"Sure, you can walk three blocks and be out on the prairie . . . now." Cousin John tucked a thumb into his waistcoat pocket, and turned his head, a strong, blunt profile against the dark masses of the trees. The air felt dense, and even this far from the river the occasional mosquito whined. Mary felt the preliminary ache behind her eyes that whispered of a thunderstorm somewhere, over those endless grasslands.

"But you mark my words, Mary, in five years, Springfield is where everything will be happening in this section—maybe in this country. The prairies are the best farmland there is. Land that people are trading around now as if it were shoelaces is going to settle up. Town lots that people give me to pay bills with will be worth what they are in Boston or Philadelphia. The State of Illinois will swing a lot of power in the country. You could do worse than to settle here and make it your home."

"Are you trying to hitch me up with someone already, Cousin John?" Mary forced aside fears of the coming storm and gave him a sidelong look.

John Stuart merely laughed. "I don't think you'll need any help from me, Cousin Molly."

He might even be right, thought Mary, as she let the big man take her arm and lead her back into the parlor, though she'd heard far too many land-speculators and schemers in her father's parlor in Lexington to be dazzled by encomiums about "this section's going to go far. . . ." She'd heard much the same about the proposal to run a railway line from Frankfort to Lexington, which had ended up in disastrous failure when it was discovered that the grade was too steep and that the weight of the trains very quickly destroyed the granite ties between the tracks.

The section may indeed have been destined for greatness, but the thought of living in a town with no bookstores and no circulating library filled her with dismay.

And if her destiny in life was to marry the President of the United States, Mary reflected, with a wry nod to her early passion for Mr. Clay, it was pretty clear she wasn't going to meet him here.

It was enough, on the occasion of that first party, to sort out relatives she'd only met upon occasion years ago, if at all: the courtly cousin John Stuart and his wife; Uncle John Todd—a doctor—and his schoolgirl daughters, tall Lizzie and chubby Francy; Ninian's brother Benjamin and *his* wife Helen; the Leverings, who lived nearby on the Hill; quiet, saturnine Dr. Wallace, who was Frances's leading beau. Then there was Senator Herndon—another of Ninian's Long Nine—and his chinless and pompous cousin Billy, and a short, dandified little lawyer with the manners of a dancing-master and the voice of Jove speaking from Olympus, Mr. Stephen Douglas.

"I thought your partner was going to make one of us this evening, Stuart," remarked Dr. Wallace, when the rather extended family party settled down in the parlor for a game of Speculation.

John Stuart shook his head and grinned again. "He's ridden over to New Salem, courting."

"What, still?" laughed Ninian. "Is he never going to bring himself to the scratch?" And Elizabeth rapped his elbow with her fan and scolded, "Shame!"

"Your sister's been trying for months to get Mr. Lincoln married off," said Mercy Levering, a fair and rather reserved girl of Mary's age to whom Mary had taken on sight. "Mr. Lincoln is Mr. Stuart's law partner. . . ."

"It would challenge any matchmaker in the world," teased Frances. "Which is why Elizabeth is so keen on it. . . ."

"I am not," replied Elizabeth, with the matronly dignity she'd already begun to assume back in Lexington, and went on handing out the little mother-of-pearl fish tokens for the game.

"Is he that ugly?" asked Mary, and Mercy put her hand over her mouth so as not to be seen giggling.

"He is ugly as Original Sin," replied Frances grandly. "*And* he eats with his knife."

"Frances . . . ," reproved Elizabeth, who would have taken the lead in the gossip if she didn't have her position to uphold.

"Well then, dearest," said Mary judiciously, "I can only say that your encouragement of the match is terribly irresponsible, both for the sake of the poor woman *and* whatever children they'll bear. . . ."

"That is unjust." Elizabeth was struggling not to burst out laughing. "He isn't *that* ugly."

"But you must admit he *does* eat with his knife," pointed out Frances, amid gales of chuckles around the table.

"He's a backwoodsman," protested Ninian. "It's taken Cousin John a year to teach him not to sit on the floor."

"Stuart met him in the militia during the Black Hawk War," provided Uncle Dr. John, "and taught him to read. . . ."

"I didn't *teach* him," laughed Cousin John, turning to Mary as Elizabeth went back primly to handing out counters. "I just encouraged him to read law. He was a captain under me, elected by his men, a gang of toughs from the rough side of New Salem. . . ."

"As if New Salem had a polite side," added Frances, rolling her eyes.

"I remember one day Lincoln was marching them across a field someplace in the north of the state, beating the bushes for Black Hawk and his braves, and they come up on a fence. It's clear across their line of march and there's a gap of about three feet in the fence; I could see the look on Lincoln's face when he realized he didn't remember the command to form a column—to get in a single line to pass through the gap. He looked aghast for about half a minute as the fence gets closer and closer, then he yells out: 'Company to fall out for two minutes and reassemble on the other side of that fence!' I almost fell off my horse laughing."

"Mr. Lincoln is engaged to a Miss Owens from Kentucky," supplied Elizabeth, seating herself at the head of the parlor table in a demure rustle of taffeta petticoats. "I'm hoping—we're all hoping, for he is really the best-natured soul on the planet—that she'll succeed in teaching him a few social niceties."

Frances shuffled the cards. "He'll always be ugly."

"Well, there *is* that."

Mary's father returned to Kentucky the following day—or more probably, she reflected wryly, he returned to Frankfort, or Louisville, or some other town where there was business that would keep him from the too-crowded house in Lexington, and the sharp-voiced demands of his wife. The bitterness that flavored her old grief at being left behind Mary hid, as she tried always to hide it, beneath flirtation and jests and fun.

And it was fun. Frances had already formed around herself and Elizabeth a coterie of the young men and girls of Springfield—with more young men coming in all the time—and there was no more talk of being an old maid at nineteen. On the afternoon of Robert Todd's departure, Mr. Douglas appeared in a buggy to take Mary riding out on the prairies, and as if Elizabeth had hoisted a flag from the topmost gable of the House on the Hill, every eligible bachelor in Springfield put in an appearance that first week.

Mary was usually accompanied by Frances, and by Mercy Levering, with whom she quickly became fast friends. Lively, dark-haired Julia Jayne often joined them, the daughter of yet another town doctor: The four of them went together to the orgy of militia reviews and barbecues that surrounded the great Daniel Webster's visit to Springfield, and the ceremonies and speeches that accompanied the laying of the State House cornerstone on the Fourth of July.

Mr. Douglas was a dandified little dynamo, barely an inch taller and only a few years older than Mary and already registrar of the land-office of Springfield, a position of considerable power. Of all the men in Springfield, Mary felt that he was the only one who had potential to go beyond the small politics of state and county. When he would take her to picnics and cotillions, his talk was of the close maneuverings of money and land, and the promise of new inventions that would open the frontier country to men of enterprise and resource.

"Douglas is a Democrat," said Ninian, over supper one night. "And a demagogue, with his eye always on the main chance. I don't trust him."

"Just because he votes for Van Buren doesn't mean he's going to break my heart." Mary smiled a little as she said it, because charming as he was, she found something about Douglas's Yankee single-mindedness slightly repellant.

"Doesn't it?" Ninian glanced sharply at her from beneath those level black brows. "Could you really love a man whose politics were that different from yours, Molly? You take politics seriously, as all intelligent people should. Could you really live with a man for whose intellectual mainspring you had contempt?"

Mary delicately buttered one of the beaten biscuits that were Eppy's pride before replying. At home she would have dodged the question, since most of Betsey's questions had some ulterior motive, but in Ninian's eyes—and Elizabeth's peaceful silence—she read only interest in what she actually thought. At length she said, "I hope I'll never be put to the test of falling in love with a man whose ideas differ radically from mine."

"That would hardly be possible, would it?" asked Frances. Mary and Frances had spent the day—a Saturday, hot with the breathless humidity of high summer—picnicking with Dr. Wallace, Mr. Douglas, and Mercy Levering, in the woods that fringed Sutton's Prairie to the east of town. That huge expanse of empty grassland, rising imperceptibly to a too-close horizon, filled Mary with a kind of panic, and she had been glad for the company of her sister and her friends.

Having watched the matter-of-fact understanding, the peaceful teamwork, of Frances and William Wallace—having seen her sister's obvious happiness with the soft-voiced young doctor—Mary wasn't sure what to answer. *Could* she wholeheartedly love someone whose mind was alien to hers? She had certainly not loved Nate Bodley.

She felt a lump of envy in her chest, and the lump of loneliness that never quite ever went away. She said, "Would you love Dr. Wallace, if his ideas differed from what you believed was right?"

"Of course." The prompt self-evidentness in her sister's voice told Mary that Frances had never given the matter a thought and hadn't the slightest idea of why Mary hesitated.

"Which I suppose is why," smiled Elizabeth, "everyone says that women should stay out of politics. In how many households do you think there's really room for *two* politicians?"

By her tone of voice that ended the matter, but Mary persisted. "Next you'll be saying that women shouldn't have an education."

"Of course not, dear," said Elizabeth. "I know how you love your books. Just don't let your education interfere with your happiness."

Mary opened her mouth, and shut it again, overwhelmed with the familiar sense of speaking to people from some unknown land.

In any case the point was a moot one, because much as Mary enjoyed flirting with Stephen Douglas—and he, clearly, with her—she felt in his presence no such stirring of the senses as she'd experienced with Nate Bodley, let alone the delicious and instantaneous raptures occasioned by the heroes of *Belinda* and *Glenarvon*. What she did experience—with more and more frequency as the summer drew on—was an odd sense of desperation.

"Elizabeth is less insistent about it than Betsey," sighed Mary a few nights after that conversation, as she and Mercy sat on the porch of Ninian's house watching their escorts for the evening drive off in a rented buggy. Merce had been asked to a lecture on Phrenology at the Mechanics' Institute hall by Josh Speed, a partner in Speed and Bell's Dry Goods—a twinkly-eyed Kentuckian who had the gift of getting along with nearly everyone in town—and Mary had been escorted along by Mr. Shields, a bantam Irish lawyer who quite plainly considered himself God's gift to the female sex. "But she wants to marry me off, too."

Mary felt a twinge of anger as she said the words—at Elizabeth, at Betsey, at her father. At the world that was so constituted that an unmarried girl would, when she died, spend Eternity leading apes around Hell.

"They just want you to be happy," pointed out Mercy, breaking off a spray of the sweet-smelling honeysuckle to twine around her fingers. She spoke a bit diffidently, for in spite of their friendship Mary had lost her temper at her once or twice over trifles, and though they'd made up with tears and apologies, Mercy now tended to pick her words carefully.

"Can't they see I'm happy as I am? Why does a woman need to marry some *man* to be happy?"

Mercy replied, her voice peaceful in the thickening twilight, "I suppose because we can't stay forever in our fathers' houses." Sitting straight-backed on the rush-bottomed porch chair, she seemed to give off an aura of quiet from her rustling lavender muslin skirts, her smooth fair hair. "Because if we're not part of some household—father's, brother's, brother-in-law's, husband's—we won't be comfortable, and will have to make our livings at some horrid task like sewing or ironing or teaching school. And because without a husband or children of her own, I don't think any woman can truly be happy."

Mary was silent, thinking of her mother, thin and worn with child-bearing. Of Betsey, always pregnant, always angry, more and more often ill and confined to her room... With a flash of insight Mary realized her stepmother felt the same anger she did, at the husband and father who found it so easy to be away for weeks at a time with the Legislature.

"Elizabeth sees Mr. Speed, or Mr. Shields, and sees they'll be rich, and have nice homes, and that as Mrs. Shields you'll never want for nice dresses or a carriage."

"As if that mattered!" retorted Mary. "I should rather marry a poor man whom I loved, a man who is going someplace—even a Yankee—than an old rich one with all his fortune secure. I've told Elizabeth that."

"And I think Elizabeth doesn't see why you can't love a wealthy man as easily as a poor one," responded Mercy. "Or why you can't love Mr. Douglas, who is certainly going someplace. He's used his position as registrar to buy up some of the choicest property in the state, Mr. Speed tells me, up near Chicago...."

"Chicago?" exclaimed Mary, startled. "You mean that village where the lumber boats come in?"

"Mr. Speed said Chicago will be a major city one day, and that Mr. Douglas will end as a very rich man."

Mary sniffed, amused. "If I paid ten cents for one town lot in every village someone told me was going to be a major city one day, I'd be bankrupt tomorrow. And Ninian doesn't trust Mr. Douglas." She hesitated, turning her fan over in her hands. "To tell you the truth I don't either, after the way he went on about Mr. Sampson's Ghost."

Sampson's Ghost was the pseudonym used by a writer of letters to the *Sangamo Journal* during a local campaign for probate justice that had been closely followed by every inhabitant of the House on the Hill. The Democratic candidate, a General Adams, lived on land deeded to him by the deceased Mr. Sampson; the letter-writing Ghost offered proof that not only had Adams forged the deed to Mr. Sampson's land, he had earlier forged a judgment to gain title to the land of a man named Anderson, robbing Anderson's widow and son. The letters were entertaining, written with a wry satiric humor that had most of the town laughing. Stephen Douglas had bristled when Mary had laughed at them, however, and had defended Adams hotly.

"A fool can write whatever he likes to the papers, and get another fool to print it." Douglas, Mary had learned already, had little use for the editor of the *Journal,* the bespectacled and cheerful Simeon Francis. Then he had added—fatally, if he'd ever had any intention of winning Mary's hand—"What does a pretty girl like you need to go reading that farrago for, anyway?"

"I think," said Mary slowly now, looking back from her vantage-point on the porch with Mercy in the scented dusk, "that Ninian is right about Mr. Douglas. He probably wouldn't appreciate two politicians in one household. Certainly not if the other one wasn't a Democrat."

A mosquito whined in her ear, and she swept at it with her fan. It was time to go inside. She gave Mercy a hug and a kiss, and the girls exchanged promises to meet the next day to go downtown to look at ribbons at Birchall's Store. Within the house the hall was dark, though lamps burned in the dining-room where Frances helped Eppy to set the table. Mary ascended the dark stair to her room, Mercy's placid words lingering uncomfortably in her heart.

We can't stay forever in our fathers' houses. . . .

What if Father dies? She hastily pushed the thought from her mind, turning from it as she'd physically have averted her face.

But the image of him standing in the upstairs hall with Nelson rose out of the shadow, both men covered with dust, the stink of lime and gunpowder hanging heavy in the stuffy heat of the enclosed house and the glowing green ghost of cholera flitting from window to window, just waiting to slip inside.

One day he will die. What then?

Live with Betsey? Mary shuddered.

With Levi? Or George?

Father will be fine!

But panic whispered to her, nevertheless. *What then? What then? What then?*

A letter lay on her dressing-table, its green sealing-wafers cracked across. Of course it was Ninian's right—and Elizabeth's, as her guardians this summer—to read letters that came to her under their roof. But the sight of the opened correspondence filled Mary with the sudden desire to go storming downstairs and inform her sister that she would not stand to be treated like a child.

But until I marry, she thought furiously, *I am only a child in her house-*

hold. . . . Elizabeth certainly read Frances's letters. As Merce's sister-in-law read Merce's.

And there was nowhere but Betsey's house to go back to.

Her hands trembled as she carried the letter to the window, where the last twilight gave enough of a faint blue flush for her to read.

It was from the Reverend John Ward, her old Lexington schoolmaster.

My dear Miss Todd,

I hope this letter finds you in full health and happiness. Often in the years since you left my tutelage I have spoken of you as the best and most promising pupil I have ever had the pleasure and privilege to educate; and frequently my good wife and I have wondered whether, in fact, you might find your calling in the education of the young.

Owing to my wife's illness this summer, she has been unable to assist me as she formerly did, making it necessary for us to seek help in the education of the younger students here at Ward's. Yours was the first name that rose to both of our minds. Your deep love of learning, combined with your affection for small children, impressed us both deeply. I have already spoken to your father and your stepmother concerning the propriety of your returning here to board and to teach. . . .

Mary's hand tightened hard on the paper and she thought, *Oh, I'll just bet Betsey leaped to tell Papa how proper it is, as long as it keeps me out of the house. . . .*

But as she sat in the window, looking out into the last of the twilight, she thought again, *We can't stay forever in our fathers' houses.*

A schoolmistress.

The thought made her smile. She remembered Madame Mentelle. Maybe an eccentric and happy schoolmistress, who did as she pleased and could stay up all night reading if she wished, and whose letters no one would read without her permission.

One who did not have to live in this desolate and book-less hog-wallow in the midst of the empty prairies, waiting in terror for the next storm.

Still she leaned in the window, her forehead against the glass that was no cooler than the stifling air. A man walked by in the street, a tall skinny silhouette, whistling an old backwoods tune. Darkness settled thick.

After a long time Mary got up, shook her petticoats straight, and went downstairs, to ask Ninian if, when he journeyed to Lexington next month to investigate railroad stocks, she could return with him.

It was time to go home.

Chapter Sixteen

Bellevue Place May 1875

"Mrs. Lincoln."

A soft tap at the door of her room. John's voice—it was hard for her to think of him as Mr. Wilamet, though he was so grown-up now, with his thin, serious face and his spectacles. They changed so, boys. . . .

Mary pressed her hands to her face, unwilling to think about the boys who would change no more.

"Mrs. Lincoln?"

She didn't even look at the curtained judas on the door, the curtain that could be nudged aside by anyone in the corridor.

"What is it?"

"Your son is here to see you."

Mary's voice rang hard as flint in her own ears. "I have no son."

John Wilamet said nothing in reply to that. But he didn't go away. Mary had learned the distinctive creak of the floorboards in the quiet downstairs hall of the family wing, even through the muffling of the Turkey carpets. When she couldn't sleep—as often she couldn't, this past week that she'd been here—it seemed to her sometimes that the comings and goings of Mrs. Patterson and Young Doc shook the house, forcing her to demand paregoric or chloral hydrate to help her drift off. How anyone could be so inconsiderate . . .

She repeated, raising her voice, "I have no son!"

Still Mr. Wilamet remained. Mary watched the curtain on the door, waiting for it to move, as it did when Gretchen or Mrs. Patterson would peep in on her—believing they were so clever and subtle! But it didn't stir.

She got impatiently to her feet and went to the door, yanked the curtain aside to face the young man through the wooden bars. "Didn't you hear me?"

"I heard you, ma'am." John still retained the gentle burr of the South that Mary had not heard about her in years. "But the man who's here seems to think he has a mother."

Mary put a hand to her head; a tear leaked from her eye. She wasn't even sure why she wept—Robert never had any patience with tears. But it had become such a habit with her to weep that she did it almost without thinking. "Get me some paregoric, then, if you will," she said fretfully. "I have such a headache. If I'm to see him I must be at my best."

"Of course," agreed John. "But if I may say so, ma'am—he'll be watching for that."

"Watching for what?"

"Watching for you to be a little sleepy, the way paregoric makes you. Maybe a little less sharp. More forgetful."

Mary opened her mouth to snap that paregoric never had that effect on her, but closed it. It *did* make her a little drowsy and more than a little forgetful—so much so that she'd sometimes sit for many hours gazing into the dimness of her hotel-room, and come out of a dream to discover she'd drunk half the bottle without being aware of it. But she'd hoped that no one had noticed.

The thought that Robert would be watching for weakness had never occurred to her. But of course he was a lawyer. He'd watch, as lawyers all watched. And use everything she did and said.

"Just a little, then—water it down. I won't give him that satisfaction. And send Amanda in here to me, so I can change my dress."

"Good for you, ma'am," grinned John. "Don't give him a thing."

As she dressed, Mary's anger rose, sharpened by the sense of restless unhappiness that had so frequently attacked her over the years. In her mind she saw Robert in the courtroom again, tears in his eyes as he announced to the entire world that his own mother was a lunatic.

But when, at last, she entered the parlor and saw him sitting there, physically so like her father, tall and barrel-chested, with wariness in his Todd-blue eyes, her rage overflowed into tears again and she could only sob, "How could you?"

He was on his feet at once, to conduct her to a chair. She jerked her arm away. "Mother, you know you are not well," he said, in his even, rather light-toned voice. "You know you haven't been well—"

"I haven't been well for twenty-three years!" Mary lashed at him. "You try living with headaches, neuralgia, back pains, and internal complaints for that long and see what it does to *you*! But I am not insane!"

"No one is saying you are *completely* insane, Mother. . . ."

"You are. A week ago, in a public courtroom, you said exactly that!"

"I didn't come here to argue with you." Robert took her hands, his tone indicated that he didn't want to discuss the matter further—Mary was familiar with that from a lifetime of dealing with her own father. "I came to see how you are feeling. You look more rested than you did, more at peace. How has your week been passed here?"

Mary started to snap back at him that it had been passed in much the fashion anyone would expect, for a woman locked up unjustly by her own family, but she hesitated, his words penetrating past her fury.

How *had* she passed the week here?

And she realized, with a sense of panicked shock that shook her to her core, that she did not exactly know.

It was a realization that took her breath away. It was not that she had been unconscious: she remembered small incidents quite clearly, like the attempt at a séance in the garden with Mrs. Hill, and the carriage-rides—twice? three times?—with Mrs. Patterson and Blanche. But they all came back to her as if part of a cloudy and pleasant dream, without anxiety or pain. She recalled telling Mrs. Bennett—that haunted-eyed old woman with the extraordinary delusion that parts of her body had been taken away and replaced by parts of someone else's—that she had not been so happy or comfortable in her life.

Except when she slept.

She wasn't even sure if her conversation with Mrs. Bennett had been real, or on what day it had taken place.

Was that madness?

"Mother?" Robert was still holding her hands.

"I'm so sorry, dear," said Mary automatically, and made herself smile. She added, because Robert was looking at her as if she'd begun talking about her tormenting Indian spirit again, "Things go along so quietly here I was just trying to remember what I *have* done all week." And she laughed, the light sweet conversational laughter of an accomplished belle.

But her heart had begun to pound and her thoughts to race, and she thought, *I must keep his suspicions at bay.*

And then, *I can ask Mr. Wilamet. He will know about such things, and he won't betray me.*

"I'm delighted to hear it, Mother," Robert was saying, in the pleased tone of one who has put everything into its proper drawer. "That's precisely why I wanted you to come to Bellevue Place—so that you could rest."

No, thought Mary, looking into her son's face and seeing only a stranger's. *You wanted me to come to Bellevue Place so you wouldn't be worried that I'd embarrass you in public. You wanted me to come here so that I wouldn't have to live with YOU. So that you wouldn't have to think about me again, except maybe to say to yourself, "Poor Mama."*

And in her secret heart of hearts, a voice whispered: *You wanted me to come to Bellevue because of what I did to you, all those years ago.*

Because of the lie I told.

The lie that had made, and destroyed, his life and hers.

Lexington 1837

MARY RETURNED TO LEXINGTON IN THE COLD AUTUMN RAIN OF 1837, jolting up the hill in the stagecoach with Ninian and almost in tears with the pleasure of those craggy familiar hills, the dripping tangled trees. She spent a week at her father's house—which was still hard for her to think of as "home"—sharing the upstairs front bedroom with Ann. Then Nelson loaded her trunks and hatboxes into the carriage and took them over to Ward's school, where she would occupy a room of her own five nights a week for what turned out to be the next twenty-five months.

Ward's school being ten minutes' brisk walk down Main Street and up Market Street, it was seldom that Nelson would bring the carriage, as he had to Mentelle's. Instead Mary would walk—shaded by a ruffled parasol or muffled in a stylish coat of her favorite hunter green—to the big brick house on Main Street every Friday afternoon, and back after Sunday dinner. Under these circumstances she could be pleasant and friendly with Betsey, and have the patience to teach Margaret and Martha—Mattie, they all called her—their sewing-stitches while her stepmother looked after golden-haired little Emilie.

It was good to be back in the South, back in the world whose rules she instinctively knew.

Yet that world had changed, and the subtleness of the changes made the alteration more, not less, disturbing.

There were still the dances in the long room above Giron's Confectionary, and laughter and French gallantries from the little Frenchman who was so delighted to be able to hold conversation in his native tongue. There were plays at Usher's Theater—heaven after three months in the wilds of Springfield!—and danceables at the Meadows and in the big double-parlor at Ashland. There were picnics at race-meetings in the spring, and young men jostling discreetly to sit beside her while the horses galloped down the long green turf, glistening like polished bronze and copper in the sun. There was the wonderful gossip that only Southerners could understand, of vast tangled family trees and acquaintance that went back generations.

But many of the shops in Lexington were closed up now, owing to the collapse of the banks in the wake of President Jackson's economic woes. Girls Mary had known no longer came to the dances, or they came in dresses that bore the mark of discreet refurbishment from last season, and people like Bella Richardson were extra-sweet to them and whispered, "Poor things . . ." when she thought they didn't hear. Many of Mary's former beaux no longer raced their own horses, and wore a look of grimness, as if they'd grown suddenly old.

Mary Jane Warfield Clay had a son, and was expecting another child soon. Though Mary delighted in little Elisha's soft curls and bright, knowing blue eyes, she found Mary Jane almost wholly preoccupied with servants, high prices, and the household budget. Meg and Mary Wickliffe were likewise both married, and talked exactly like the Yankee women who'd ridden with her on the steamboat down the Ohio, of teething babies and the shocking cost of lamp-oil. When Mary stood at the dances among the single girls, she was disconcerted to realize that some of them were in the upper year or two at Ward's—as she herself had been, when first she'd put up her hair and entered the fascinating world of a belle.

They seemed so *young.* Mary laughed about it with Isabelle Trotter and Julia Warfield, before one of Mr. Clay's sons came over and swept her into a cotillion on his arm. Then for a time she could dimple and laugh and be once again the belle of the ball. But that night, listening to Ann's soft breathing beside her in the dark of the upstairs front bedroom, Mary stared at the ceiling with panic racing in her heart.

Nate Bodley came to call on her, the second or third afternoon after her return from Springfield. "What is it?" he asked, when she stood up and stepped away from his attempt to clasp both her hands, and they both glanced at Betsey, who smiled pointedly and said,

"Well, I'll leave you two young people to get re-acquainted." She rustled out into the hall, leaving them alone together in the double-parlor. Mary heard her sharp voice call out to Chaney about laying another plate for dinner.

"I've missed you, Mary." Nate stepped closer, smiling his old devilish smile, and still Mary didn't answer. In her mind she saw the brass head of his cane flying up and down, smelled the mud of the gutter, and the bitter tang of Mr. Presby's blood. "What is it, sweetheart? Now, don't you freeze up on me. . . ."

At that she glanced up at him, her eyes bright with anger. "Do you honestly need to ask that, sir, since Mr. Presby lived here under our roof?" The young tutor had returned to his family's New England home at the same time Mary had gone to Springfield. He had not returned.

Nate's face flushed. Mary wondered whether it was because of guilt over the caning, or because the caning involved the pretty quadroon slave girl he had bought. She wondered too whether that girl was still in Nate's father's household. "That was politics," he protested. "You gotta understand, Mary, there's things a man can't put up with another man layin' on him."

A well-bred young lady would have simply said, *Then we can only agree to differ, Mr. Bodley*—with or without shyly downcast eyes—and left it at that. If she really wanted to sever the connection, there were a thousand social ways to avoid Nate without fuss. Mary felt her *own* cheeks flame.

"It was not politics, sir," she replied in a steady voice. "A righteous man accused you of evil and you had no argument in your favor but violence. That doesn't sound like politics to me."

"What it doesn't sound like to me is any of your business, begging your pardon, Miss Todd, or any woman's business. . . ."

"It is every right-thinking person's business—"

"It is not!" Nate cut her off, jabbing his finger at her, his eyes blazing with the gunpowder violence that had so frightened her that spring day half a year ago. "I see you've become an abolitionist in the North, talking to people who haven't got the slightest idea what it's like here—"

"I didn't need to travel to the North to see what's right under my eyes here, Mr. Bodley!"

"But it's no man's right to tell me what I can and can't do with my own property in my own house!"

"And not the right of the woman you'd make your wife, either, whether or not you have a concubine under your roof?" Mary lashed back.

Nate's mouth flew open with shock at hearing her say the word; for an instant he was silenced. Then he laughed harshly. "God help the man that makes *you* his wife, Mary Todd!" Turning on his heel, he strode from the room. Mary heard Betsey call out, "Mr. Bodley . . ." as the front door slammed.

Mary stood by the hearth, trembling, tears of anger blurring her vision and her head starting to pound as her stepmother came into the parlor. "Mary, honestly, how can you quarrel with Mr. Bodley so soon after your return? You really must strive to get the better of your temper, my dear, or you stand in grave danger of ending an old maid."

"Oh, leave me alone!" Mary turned in a whirl of turkey-red skirts. "What woman wouldn't be better off an old maid, than living with a yellow rival beneath her husband's roof?"

"Mary!" gasped Betsey. "You didn't say such a thing to Mr. Bodley?"

"It's true!"

The older woman's lips pursed impatiently. "A good many things are true in this world, Miss, but that doesn't mean that a lady ever speaks of them. If you don't curb your temper, men will say—"

Mary screamed, "Leave me alone! I don't care what men say!" And pushing past her, she blundered into the wide hall and up the stairs. Her vision was beginning to dissolve into jagged lines of flaming wire. She wanted to curse, to beat on the walls, to shriek at them for a parcel of fools. Later, lying in her room on the big four-poster bed, she felt sick and depleted. Frightened, too, and half-nauseated with guilt. Nate would tell everyone he knew—all the young men in Lexington—that Mary had become a termagant and an abolitionist since she'd been in the North.

And Betsey. . . !

She remembered screaming at Betsey—who would be certain to tell her father when he came home, not to mention all her gossipy friends. . . .

The floorboards outside the bedroom door creaked. There was a gentle knock, familiar from a lifetime of tantrums and headaches and darkened rooms, and Mary whispered, "Come in. Please come in," without turning her face from her pillow.

She heard Mammy Sally enter, and cross at once to the windows, pulling the curtains against the light that Mary had been too angry and too sick to block out. The day was hot for September, and Mary heard the dim voices of children in the street—Sam and David and Margaret and Mattie and little Emilie all shrieking at one another like baby birds. She peered dolefully up from beneath the tangle of her disordered hair as the elderly nurse looked down at her for a moment, then sighed and shook her head, and sat on the bed at her side.

"Your head ache, child?"

Mary nodded. Even with the curtains shut the light in the room seemed blinding.

The strong hand stroked back the tumbled chestnut curls. "Nelson told me you took up for that poor yeller gal Serena, that Mr. Bodley bought last spring, and thrashed Mr. Presby over. That was good of you, child, but it wasn't any business of yours. Not to lose a beau over. And not to get yourself into trouble with Miss Betsey, so soon after you come home."

"He wasn't my beau," said Mary softly. "Not from the minute I saw it happen." She sighed, and dropped her head back down to her arm, wondering that her skull didn't split. Mammy Sally reached to the bedside table, where she'd set a cup of her herbal tea. Mary managed to sit up, took it with trembling hands and sipped the sharp-tasting, nasty brew. In the day's heat the steam only made her head feel worse. "And Betsey would marry me off to the Sultan of Turkey, if she thought it would get me out of the house."

She turned over, tangled in her petticoats and stiff with corset-bones, and Mammy Sally, instead of saying—as Betsey certainly would—that she would crumple her dress and rip a sleeve-seam by lying on the bed fully clothed, merely helped straighten the heavy volutes of fabric around her, and brought up the other pillow for her head.

"Why can't I keep my temper, Mammy?" Mary whispered. "Betsey talks like she thinks I *like* to shout and scream and feel sick the way I do. I can't help it—I don't mean to get angry like this. I know what I'm supposed to do and say, and I just . . . I just *can't.*"

"I know you can't, child," the older woman said softly, reaching out a gentle, work-roughened hand to wipe the tears away. "All you can do is watch yourself, and do what you can so you'll have less to fix later. And maybe the Sultan of Turkey likes a wife with a little temper to her, to keep him from getting bored."

And in spite of her pain, and the sickness rising in her stomach, Mary laughed, and hugged the old woman.

It was truly good to be home.

NATE BODLEY BECAME ENGAGED TO ARABELLA RICHARDSON THE FOLLOWING week. For the next year, in between teaching French and listening to the smaller girls at Ward's read their lessons in the chill of early dawn, Mary periodically suffered the spectacle of the radiant Bella shopping for her trousseau, or comparing notes about it with the other unmarried girls of the town.

Mary had not been the only girl whom Nate had squired to picnics, Court Days, and danceables, and Nate had been far from Mary's only beau. Still, when young gentlemen who were slaveholders or the sons of planters asked Mary to dance, or came to sit beside her beneath the trees of Trotter's Grove, there was a note in their voices, a difference in the way they disposed their legs and arms and bodies, that told her—and every other girl in town as clearly as an announcement taken out in the newspaper—that they no longer considered her marriage material.

She was a good friend from childhood, and would of course go on being a good friend. She was Robert Todd's daughter, cousin or second cousin or kin to most of them, and there was no question of cutting her: people were entitled to be abolitionists if they wanted to, they supposed. It was a free country, wasn't it?

But none of them danced more than one dance with her, and only after the younger girls' dance-cards were full.

And because—of course—nobody would speak of the scene between her and Nate, she never had the opportunity to explain to anyone whether she was actually an abolitionist or not.

Gentlemen who believed, with her father, that the slaves should be one day freed—when they'd been sufficiently educated and prepared for freedom, or when they could be relocated to some other country suitable for them—continued to court her. The older students at Transylvania University were joined by some of the younger professors. If Mary had to suffer the spectacle of Bella Richardson hanging possessively on Nate Bodley's arm, at least—for a time—she could contemplate it from within a circle of her own admirers.

For two years she was happy at Ward's, happier than she had been at any time since she'd left Madame Mentelle's in 1837. She loved her pupils, who ranged in ages from seven to eleven—girls and boys both, for the Reverend believed that if the two sexes mingled in the backyards, nursery wings, and parties of the town, there was no reason they shouldn't do so in the classroom. She loved, too, having her own room, having access to all the books she wanted—being able to travel, in thought at least, to those places where she longed to visit: Venice, Constantinople, Paris, Scotland. When Elizabeth wrote the following summer inviting her back to Springfield, Mary passed it by in favor of a visit with the family to Crab Orchard Springs, as they had done in her girlhood.

There were good times even with her family, helping to look after the littler children when baby Alex was born, in '39, almost two years after her return. She would sit in the kitchen as she used to, watching the stir and bustle of the big house. Elizabeth's Eppy had taught her some cookery in Springfield—Chaney began to instruct her in more.

Yet during those two years Mary found herself lying awake more and more, either in her small pretty room in Mr. Ward's house or at her father's house—with her father gone to the Legislature in Frankfort yet again—wondering if this was what she wanted. If this was all there was.

All there was going to be. Sometimes she'd take out her casket of jewels, as she'd done at Mentelle's, and turn over the earbobs, the gold chains, the sapphire pendant in her fingers, as if the sight of them were reassurance that though she didn't live in her family's house, still she was loved.

Sometimes this worked.

Sometimes it didn't.

She was perfectly aware of it, when people first started treating her as a spinster.

That was at Christmas of 1838, shortly after she turned twenty-one. Nellie Clay—who had been one of her senior pupils at Ward's when first Mary returned from Springfield—got married then, in a huge party held at Ashland, Nellie being a twice-removed cousin of Mr. Henry Clay's. Mary had coaxed a new dress of pink and green silk from her father for the occasion, and her curls, threaded with dark-green velvet ribbon, shone like copper in the light of the candles in the octagonal central hall as the bride descended the stair. And it gave her a sense of pride, almost as if Nellie were a daughter she had raised, when Nellie ran to hug her after the ceremony—girls wed young in Kentucky, and Nellie was seventeen.

Yet at the reception afterwards, hearing the babble of voices and seeing so many familiar faces—Mr. Clay a bit grayer than he'd been at Elizabeth and Ninian's second-day party, Nate already getting thick under the chin—Mary felt a sudden stricken, shaken fear, as if the ground beneath her feet had been rocked by an earthquake.

All the belles, in their rustling skirts of ivory or rose or pale-blue silk, were now decidedly younger than she, some by nearly five years. The young men crowded around them, offering cups of punch and slices of cake; eyelids were fluttered, blushes half-concealed behind blond lace fans. The young matrons—Mary Jane Clay, and Margaret Preston, who had been Meg Wickliffe when she'd shared a room with Mary at Rose Hill—were gathered in the rear parlor, watching with the satisfied air of soldiers whose battle has already been won as the fiddles struck up a dance-tune. Madame Mentelle glanced around from conversation with Mr. Clay and M'sieu Giron, and beckoned Mary to join them, but halfway there Mary was intercepted by Nate Bodley.

"Will you dance with me, Mary?" he asked. "For old times' sake?"

Nellie, in the arms of her bridegroom—a planter from Louisville—was smiling dewily at her, gratified, Mary realized with a flare of alarm, that anyone was dancing with her teacher at all.

It was then she realized she was becoming someone that other people had to look after socially.

She danced with Nate, but she talked to him as if she were talking with a stranger, asking after his horses, his plantation, his wife—all the polite small-talk that rose so easily to her lips. He replied in kind, perfectly happily, as if he'd never taken her in his arms in the orchards behind Rose Hill, or chased her through the green-and-golden woods. She wondered if he still had the quadroon girl in his household, or if he'd sold her off.

It was something a lady wasn't supposed to ask, or even think about.

In May Elizabeth wrote to her again, announcing Frances's wedding to Dr. Wallace and asking if Mary would like to come back to Springfield when the Legislature finally opened there in the fall.

Mary wrote back, saying that she would be delighted to come.

Even then she knew that, books or no books, theater or no theater, thunderstorms or no thunderstorms, she would never live in Lexington again.

Chapter Seventeen

Springfield 1839

Springfield had grown in two years. The State House was nearly finished, though the earth around it was the same hog-wallow of mud, torn-up rubble, and trampled gravel—scummed now with ice—that it had been, and the Legislature would be meeting in shop-fronts all over town because none of the building's rooms were finished inside. The State Supreme Court had been given quarters in a commercial building across the street. But the town swarmed with lawyers, clerks, minor officials eager to get government jobs or government patronage. Ninian's house was always full of men, eager to do favors or to buy small gifts—flowers for his wife and sisters-in-law, a stick-pin or a pair of gloves—to curry his good opinion. Political wives were now bringing their daughters to husband-hunt in the man-heavy town.

Springfield's atmosphere had changed, from bucolic sleepiness to the aggressive sparkle of power. It went to Mary's head like drink.

Mr. Douglas called on Mary's first afternoon in Elizabeth's house, to bespeak a waltz at the upcoming cotillion to be held for the legislators at the new American House Hotel. He wore a well-tailored tobacco-colored coat and a yellow silk waistcoat, and looked like a man who was going places in the world.

"He's still a Democrat," remarked Ninian, and Mary laughed.

Elizabeth had spoken of holding a ball to celebrate Mary's return, but since her arrival was so soon before the American House cotillion, they settled on a festive supper for all their friends before going *en masse* to the more general fête. "Somehow it doesn't surprise me," remarked Dr.

Wallace, helping Frances and Mary into the carriage after supper, "that Mary would manage to get the entire Legislature to welcome her to town."

In the long, lamp-lit common room of the American House, Mary, clothed in a ruffled gown of fawn and rose silk—her father's parting gift—was again the center of a court of gentlemen, laughing behind her fan and teasing them as they vied to bring her up-to-date on all that had happened in the town in the two years since her departure. Since she'd had Ninian send her both the *Sangamo Journal* and the *Illinois Republican,* there was little she didn't already know about the wild mudslinging that had gone on between the *Journal*'s claque of "Young Whigs" and the *Republican*'s "Young Democrats" over every conceivable subject from the State Bank to the digging of local canals. Legislators and would-be government employees from Chicago to Cairo clustered around her, and nobody even asked what her opinions on slavery were or how old she was.

She danced two waltzes with Mr. Douglas, who was her height to an inch, so that their steps matched beautifully. He was a wonderful dancer, light on his feet and firm in his lead—"Of course that's how he'd dance," she giggled to Frances later, over a cup of punch. "That's what his politics are like, too—leading you right along and making you like it."

"I don't know, Mary," teased Frances. "If you really want to marry the President of the United States, maybe you'd better think about changing your politics." But she laughed when she said it, knowing—as all of them knew—that Mary took her politics far more seriously than she took Mr. Douglas.

Senator Herndon's chinless cousin Billy—who after a number of opening shots at various careers was currently a clerk at Speed and Bell's Dry Goods—asked her to dance too, declaring that she moved as gracefully as a serpent; Mary rolled her eyes, and replied, "That's rather severe irony, sir, especially to a newcomer. Now I think I've torn a flounce, and need to go repair it." As she retreated upstairs with Merce and Julia she added, "Remind me to wear a torn flounce next time, in case he ever asks me again." All three of them were still laughing over this—and over Billy's newly-grown whiskers, which resembled nothing so much, in their patchy fairness, as socks hanging on a clothesline—when they returned to the dancing a few minutes later.

Merce's new sweetheart, a patrician New Yorker named Jamie Conkling, came up and claimed Merce with a bow—"If you'll excuse me, Miss Todd, I think I need Miss Levering to keep me from dying of loneliness out on the floor. . . ." Across the room, Dr. Wallace caught Mary's eye and started to approach, but beside her a quiet, very light voice asked, "Miss Todd?"

She turned, looked up—and up and up—and saw to her enormous surprise the tall stringy storyteller who'd rescued her from Professor Kittridge in the Globe Tavern yard over two years before.

He wore a suit now of very ill-fitting dark wool, and a black string tie, and his black hair was firmly pomaded to his narrow, rather bird-like head. In his eyes was the look of an unarmed man about to go into single combat with a Gorgon.

"If you please . . . Miss Todd . . . That is, if you don't mind . . ."

Beside him Josh Speed gave him a nudge closer to her, and whispered, "Just ask her, Lincoln."

Lincoln swallowed hard. He had an Adam's apple like a lime on a string. Mary realized this had to be Cousin John Stuart's partner. Frances certainly hadn't lied about his looks.

He blurted out, "Miss Todd, I'd sure like to dance with you in the worst way."

Speed shook his head and groaned.

Fighting to keep from laughing, Mary held out her hand and answered, "I'd be delighted, Mr. Lincoln."

He did, in fact, dance with her in the worst possible way. But while Mary would have been merciless about someone like Billy Herndon—who had done himself no good with his "serpent" remark—she felt oddly protective of this gangly backwoodsman, and did her best to keep her new slippers out from under the Conestoga boots that she guessed were Lincoln's only footwear.

The fact that the dance was a schottische didn't help the situation any. Halfway through Lincoln stopped abruptly, abashed, with all the other couples swirling around them. "I guess I better let you go 'fore I kill you, Miss Todd. I thank you. . . ."

"Mr. Lincoln." She looked up into his eyes, clear gray under the overhang of his brow, and smiled. "How dare you slight a lady's courage, sir? I'm made of hardier stuff than that. *Lay on, Macduff. . . .*"

His whole gargoyle face transformed with delight at the quote. "*And curs't be he that first cries 'Hold, enough.'* But let's sort of get ourselves out of the main channel here, and practice a little in the shallows."

In a corner of the common room away from the main ring of dancers Mary took him carefully through the steps: hop-hop, slide-slide, hop-skip-slide. . . .

"Like tryin' to learn to march in the Army," Lincoln said, gravely studying the toes of Mary's pink Morocco-leather slippers, which she made just visible with the tiniest lifting of the hem of her skirt. "Only then it was just right and left, and once I'd tied a string around my right wrist I could remember it most of the time. I guess folks would just laugh at us if I was to ask you to lead."

"You did all right leading old Professor Kittridge across the yard the way you did. *What* did he call you? For two years now I've been dying to ask. . . ."

Lincoln laughed, and scratched the back of his head, a habitual gesture that made rapid inroads on the pomaded neatness of his hair. His smile transformed his face, dissolving its gravity into comic mobility, and lightening it like sunlight on stones. "*The servant of the servants of Mammon.* Bad enough, he says, that humanity has enslaved itself to the Devil of Property. But lawyers who haggle over other men's property for pay are the lowest of the low. Lookin' at it that way, I reckon he's got a point." He gingerly held out his hands to her. "Can we slow down to half-speed, till I get the blame thing figured out?"

"Of course." Mary took his hands—the biggest hands she'd ever seen, straining at the seams of his much-mended kid gloves. "Everyone else in the room is so busy minding their own feet, they'll never notice."

It robbed the dance utterly of the reason that one did a schottische—the exhilaration of its flying speed—but it did give Mary enough time to get her toes clear of his boots. Now and then, when she glanced up, she could see his lips move as he counted the steps.

"Did he ever marry his lady from New Salem?" asked Mary, after Lincoln had bowed awkward thanks, fetched her a cup of punch (at Speed's whispered reminder), and beaten a hasty retreat to join the men in the hall. The musicians—a German, a free black farmer, and Ninian's quadroon coachman Jerry—were likewise refreshing themselves before the next dance: Mary, her sisters, Merce and Julia clustered at the rear of the room, all except Elizabeth flushed and rumpled.

Elizabeth heaved a long-suffering sigh. "No. After all our urging . . ."

"Well, you could hardly blame him," retorted Frances. "Apparently Miss Owens didn't trouble to watch her figure and got enormously fat."

"*I* heard *she* was the one who called it off," put in Julia Jayne, tossing her dark curls. "One *can* have enough of a man who falls into brown studies and can't be troubled to converse with a woman for hours on end. Not to mention leaving the poor thing to fend for herself when a group of their friends went riding and had to cross a stream on horseback. . . ."

"Lincoln's trouble," observed Josh Speed, who had joined them, "—other than not having a lick of sense about women—is that he's risen out of the world he was born into, and so cannot marry the kind of woman he grew up with. Yet he's still enough of a backwoodsman that he's never learned how to talk to ladies of this new world that he hopes to make his."

"I'd say," remarked Frances, looking over at the unruly black head rising above the jostling group in the hall, "that he's never going to learn to talk to ladies at the rate he's going. He must be thirty if he's a day."

There were shouts of laughter from among the men: *". . . so about the third time the top of the hogshead fell down inside the barrel, the cooper figured he'd put his son inside the barrel, to hold the top up while he fixed on the hoops. . . ."*

Mary remembered Court Days at Lexington, and the backwoodsmen who'd come in from their rough cabins in the canebrakes. Most held a few acres of corn which they chiefly made into whiskey, their herds of cattle and pigs which they let rove wild in the woods. Illiterate, coarse, woodcrafty as the Indians they had supplanted, they lived from hand to mouth and from day to day, their women barefoot in faded calico with trains of tow-headed silent children.

What became of those children? Mary wondered, comparing them with her well-mannered little pupils at Ward's, with Betsey's little ones at home. What became of the ones who yearned for something beyond the woods, who looked about them at men dying of pneumonia or accidents or sheer hardship at thirty-five or forty, when their strength gave out? The ones who thought—as she had thought—*There must be something else*?

She glanced across at Speed, and she saw the deep, amused affection in the young storekeeper's eyes as he watched his lanky friend: a servant of the servants of Mammon, in his shabby suit and rough boots and mended gloves, an ungainly interloper in the world of gentility and power. "Mr. Lincoln's come a long way," she said softly, and Speed's gaze shifted to her.

"That he has."

"And he'll have to go a long piece farther," sniffed Frances, "before he's likely to come across a woman willing to put up with him."

ABRAHAM LINCOLN WAS LIKE NO MAN MARY HAD EVER MET. FRANCES still made fun of him, but when they encountered one another at dances that winter, he would awkwardly maneuver to speak to Mary, to dance with her if he could. She was used to having beaux jockeying for her attention and trying to cut one another out for dances, but Stephen Douglas, and the elderly widower Edwin Webb, Josh Speed, cocky little Jimmy Shields, handsome Lyman Trumbull—for whom Mary had a passing *tendre*—and the suave John Gillespie were men who knew how to play the game, with women and with one another.

Lincoln was different. He was agonizingly shy, laboring under the double burden of his very odd looks and his excruciating awareness of social backwardness. Mary guessed, from the hesitant way he spoke to her, the way he would hang back when Douglas or Shields deftly claimed her attention from under his nose, that he'd had harsh rebuffs from women before, and had no idea how to make a neat riposte. Mostly he just retreated to the world of men, a world in which he was a quite different man.

Across the room at Ninian's or the Leverings' she would watch him with Ninian, with Jamie Conkling or Ed Baker—a brisk little cock-sparrow Englishman and another of her Coterie, as their circle of friends came to be called—or others who knew him through Legislature and the courts. The shyness fell off him there like an ill-made coat, and he'd joke, and listen to other men's stories, and speak with a sharp and quiet acuteness that vanished utterly the moment one of the Springfield belles addressed him.

Elizabeth referred to him as a "cracker from the canebrakes'" but he had, despite deficiencies in table manners, an inherent dignity that went far beyond which fork to use, and a genuine kindly consideration for others. Moreover, Mary knew perfectly well that a man couldn't become a lawyer, much less a member of the State Legislature, without being able to read and write. "No, it's perfectly true," Josh Speed told her, one freezing January afternoon when Mary came into Speed and Bell's to buy ribbons. "Most of what Lincoln knows he taught himself. I don't think he's had more than a year of schooling in his life. He really did grow up in a log cabin, in the Indiana woods. His father used to hire him out to the neighbors to cut wood and husk corn, and keep the money he made—which is legal," he added, as Mary opened her mouth in indignant protest. "Up until a boy's twenty-one. It's just most fathers don't do that kind of thing anymore."

"So that's what they mean when they speak of a 'gentleman of the old school,' " sniffed Mary, and Speed laughed, and came around the end of the counter to hold out his hands to the iron heating-stove.

"Well, Lincoln left Indiana the minute he could, and I haven't seen him in any tearing hurry to get back. He told me once his pa used to thrash him for reading. When he was living in New Salem, about a day's ride from here up the Sangamon River, he used to walk ten or twelve miles to borrow books, if he heard of people who had them."

Speed and Bell, Mary knew, generally had a small stock of books, whatever could be brought in from the East. These were mostly almanacs and volumes of sermons, though once they did get in a volume of Shakespeare's sonnets, which Mary bought. The store was built of sawn lumber and whitewashed inside and out. It smelled of wood and soap, and now the heavy scent of smoke and burnt coffee. Barrels and bins ranged the center of the room near the stove, where men would sit through the winter evenings talking politics and spitting tobacco. Shelves occupied every foot of wall with bright bolts of calico and sheeting, pots of white-and-blue enamel, caddies of tea and coffee and dishes to whose edges packing-straw still clung. They didn't stock the variety of fancy goods and ribbons that Birchell and Irwin did, but Mary liked Josh Speed.

"Is he in?" she asked impulsively, because she knew Lincoln lived upstairs with Speed, in the big loft. Speed shook his head.

"He'll be at your cousin's law offices if he isn't in the Legislature—Stuart left him in charge of the whole practice when he went to take his seat in Congress. Lincoln's a devil for work: between riding the circuit courts all summer, and now working to organize the Whig Party the way the Democrats are organized, my guess is once the snow melts I won't see much of him."

"That must be what happens," remarked Mary lightly, "when you're allowed to keep some of the money you make."

Speed laughed, then glanced at the empty wooden chairs around the stove with a reminiscent grin. "He'll be here tonight—the whole bunch of them, Baker and Conkling and Douglas . . ." He shook his head, with a kind of wonder and delight in his eyes. "I've never heard arguing the way it is when Lincoln and Douglas get after each other over the State Bank or divorce or Indian lands or anything that's on their minds. It's amazing, like watching two gods throwing lightning-bolts at each other. One night Douglas wasn't here and Lincoln did an imitation of him, and argued with himself. That's the closest I've come in my life to dying laughing."

Mary chuckled at just the thought of it—by this time she'd seen Lincoln do imitations of people. But as Joshua escorted her across the muddy plank sidewalk to Ninian's carriage she felt a pang of bitterest jealousy, that this world of politics and power and informal alliances around the stove was something she would never be permitted to join. For a moment she was a child again, seeing the shoulders of her father's guests close in a rank against her.

Hearing Betsey say, *Really, Mary. . . .*

And being relegated to conversation about earbobs and beaux.

The next time she saw Lincoln, at a Washington's Birthday ball given by the Leverings, Mary caught his eye and edged from the group of her admirers to stand with him in the corner by the stairway. "Mr. Speed tells me you're an admirer of Robert Burns, sir," she said, glancing up at the tall man who towered over her. "I have a book of his poems, if you'd ever care to borrow it. Mr. Speed says come spring you'll be riding all over the state to the circuit courts—that has to be unbelievably dreary."

The lined gargoyle face lit up first with surprise, then with pleasure, and the uncertainty he always had around women vanished from his eyes.

"Why, thank you, Miss Todd. You're right, it's tiresome and lonely, riding the circuit courts, and Burns would be the best companion I could ask for, aside from Mr. Shakespeare. It's kind of you to think of me, Miss Todd."

Any other man of her acquaintance would have spoken the words as a formula: It's-kind-of-you-to-think-of-me-Miss-Todd, with a bow and a knowing smile. But the way Lincoln said them, Mary knew that it was not only kind, but almost unheard-of in the lawyer's experience.

"I promise I won't let it come to harm."

"Good heavens, I never thought you would!" She smiled. "I can tell you're a man who knows how to take care of books. God knows I've spent enough of my time here in Springfield trying to find things to read to have sympathy for someone cast ashore in places like Petersburg and Postville!"

He laughed at that, his nose wrinkling up and his big horselike teeth flashing. "And in some of those places I feel cast ashore, like Mr. Crusoe—and wasn't it just lucky for him that ship of his didn't sink under him at the outset, and leave him without any of those guns and axes and ropes and the rest of his plunder."

"Which I think was just a *little* providential on Mr. Defoe's part," remarked Mary consideringly. "On the other hand, if he hadn't provided him with all that 'plunder,' as you say, poor Mr. Crusoe would probably have starved in the first week, and Mr. Defoe couldn't have made much of a story out of that."

Lincoln laughed again, and scratched his head, augmenting the crazy ruin of his hair. Seeing the way his whole frame relaxed, Mary understood that this sad-eyed man truly loved to laugh. "Though I will say, you'd be surprised what you can do with just an ax. Still, there should have been an almanac someplace on that boat, and if you're real desperate you can get some good reading out of an almanac."

After that Mary would lend Lincoln books, which he consumed like a child devouring candy. He usually returned them on Sunday afternoons, when Elizabeth held open house for the Coterie at the House on the Hill. Frances would act as co-hostess for these gatherings, for she and Dr. Wallace were still living in a rented room at the Globe Tavern. Mary—who was becoming quite a notable cook under Eppy's tutelage—would assist with the refreshments, but for the most part she was free to mingle with her guests, and many of those freezing winter afternoons ended with her and Lincoln lingering in the darkening parlor, long after the others had departed.

They talked of the books she lent him, and Mary was surprised at the scope of his reading, and the depth and acuteness of his mind. Her other suitors—Douglas and Shields, Trumbull and Webb—were educated men, familiar as a matter of course with Shakespeare and Homer. Lincoln, uneducated, had discovered the stories for himself, and had read them as Mary read Gothic novels, with an almost sensuous pleasure. On one occasion he recited to her "John Anderson, My Jo," which he had memorized as he casually and easily memorized entire speeches and scenes from Shakespeare, and she thought she heard a catch in his voice on the ending line, *"We'll sleep together at its foot, John Anderson, my jo."*

"I got to memorizing poetry for when I travel," he said. "It's three days' ride down to Carthage, and four days to someplace like Belleville, and most days you don't meet a soul on the roads. Back when I didn't have a horse I'd walk, sometimes two and three days, if I'd delivered a load of goods by raft and had to get back home."

On other evenings they spoke of the issues in the Legislative committees he was on, or of the suits he had before the courts. "Yes, the state needs a strong central bank, but if it has one, who's going to run it?" pointed out Mary, one lamp-lit evening when they sat, half-forgotten by the other guests, in the dim rear parlor. "What if you get a scoundrel in charge, like Biddle in the National Bank, who spent his time buying influence and manipulating credit to favor his own supporters? Wouldn't that discredit the bank and cause more ruin than it amends?"

"Oh, I would love to see some politician go to the polls sayin' he's gonna tell the banks what to do," sighed Lincoln, with a comical shake of his head. "He'd be the first man in the country's history to not only get *no* votes, but to have 'em taken away from him, so he'd be a vote-debtor and have liens against him for the next six times he runs.... But this whole mess the state's in now, with no money for canals or railroads or anythin' else we need, is because there's nuthin' sayin' what money is and what it ain't, which is all banks really do, when you think of it...."

When she spoke of her father's slaves, he asked if she were an abolitionist: "I hate slavery—one trip to New Orleans was enough to do that for me—but the way the abolitionists are goin' about their business will surely tear this country apart. When I see the violence that's come about in the last few years, that printer Lovejoy murdered over in Alton, and the mob in St. Louis that burned that poor Negro sailor to death—when I hear that some state governments have put bounties on the heads of abolitionist publishers—all I see is that *both* sides are turnin' their backs on reason, turnin' into a mob."

"It's easy enough for us to say," replied Mary softly, "because we're white. For us it *is* a matter of reason. People like the slaves of that horrible Mrs. Turner who lived back in Lexington, who would beat them literally to death over things like a broken teapot, don't really care about what the Founding Fathers intended. They just want to be able to leave a place where they're being mistreated, and not have their husbands and wives taken away from them to pay for someone's gambling debts."

If he spoke easily and earnestly of how the state could raise money for internal improvements through the sale of federal lands, or at what point Macbeth could have turned aside from his disastrous course, he did not speak of his family, or the Kentucky canebrakes where he'd been born. The stories he told were of people he'd met on the road, or folks he'd known in New Salem or Cairo or points between. And Mary remembered what Josh Speed had said of Lincoln's father on that winter afternoon in the store, and of Lincoln himself on the night of the Legislature's cotillion: that he was an exile from the world he'd grown up in, who had found no place yet in the world for which his starved mind yearned.

And Lincoln was ambitious. That was one of the first things Mary learned about him, and one of the most surprising: that behind his diffidence in polite company, his razor-sharp wit and his deep, gentle love for animals and children, he had his eyes on political power and studied how to achieve it the way he had once, he told her, studied to become a surveyor.

"Which you don't expect, when you speak to him in company," said Mary to Speed, on a rainy day in early March. She'd heard the rumor that there was a new shipment of Irish lace—the first of the spring—and because Elizabeth was out paying calls with the carriage, she had convinced Merce to walk downtown through the slushy muck of the streets, hopping from plank to plank of building material dropped off the construction drays and carrying a bundle of shingles they'd found to bridge the gaps. Speed was astonished to see her—the weather had been foul all morning and promised worse—but, as she'd calculated, Mary had first pick of the lace, and put money down on the two best pieces for herself, plus gifts for Elizabeth, Frances, Merce (who was thumbing through the books), and Julia.

"He appears so humble—like Duncan, *he hath borne his faculties so meek*—but I notice he doesn't put a foot wrong when he's negotiating with delegates from the other districts for Legislative votes, and at Court Days I don't think there's a man he doesn't speak to." Mary dimpled, and shook her head. "Yet he likes to present himself as a bumpkin who couldn't tell a wooden nutmeg from a barleycorn."

"Only when it suits him." Speed leaned on the counter and scratched the ears of the fat marmalade tomcat who shared the building with Lincoln and himself. "People like to hear that, when he makes a speech—Lincoln's figured that out. It lets him slip his point across when their minds aren't closed to argument by highfalutin' words. I think his ambition springs from a different root than, for instance, our little Stephen's—though they're both poor boys who want to end up richer than their fathers were. But Lincoln's ambition goes beyond that. He wants power so that he can do the job right, while other men want it only so they can collect the job's pay."

He glanced at the windows, gray with dreary afternoon light. The brown puddles in the street lay still as glass, but the sky lowered sullenly above the wet board buildings of the town. Work had resumed on the State House the week before and the downtown streets were rivers of half-frozen slush. "You two had best get home, if you're going to do it without getting wet. Would you like to wait here where it's warm, and I'll see if I can find someone to take word to Ninian's house to get the carriage here?" And after one look at the ocean of goo beyond the plank sidewalk's edge, he added, "I'd take you home myself but the canoe's got a hole in it."

"We'll manage," laughed Mary. "We got here, didn't we?" But when she and Mercy reached the edge of the sidewalk Mary saw, to her alarm, that most of the dropped planks and shingles that they'd used for stepping-stones had already sunk in the mud.

A few wagons creaked past, hauling roof-slates to the State House before the rain should start again.

Mercy looked around her anxiously as they retreated toward the shop's door again where Joshua waited. "I promised my sister-in-law I'd be home. Jamie's coming to dinner. . . ."

"And Mr. Gillespie's coming to our house," said Mary consideringly. "And goodness knows if Elizabeth's back yet with the carriage . . . Oh!" she called out, hurrying back to the edge of the sidewalk and waving her handkerchief at the driver of a passing dray. "Oh, Mr. Hart!" For she recognized the man as a laborer whom Ninian had hired on several occasions to fix fences and mend the stable.

"Mary!" cried Merce, shocked. "What are you . . . ?"

The little Irishman drew rein and touched his soaked hat-brim, and Mary gave him her most flirtatious smile. "Mr. Hart, could I possibly, *possibly* trouble you to drive past my brother-in-law's house on your way back to the freight depot? It isn't so very much out of your way. . . ."

"Miss Todd . . . !" said Speed, half-shocked and half-laughing, and Merce gasped, "Mary, don't you *dare*! Everyone will talk!"

"Oh, pooh. We need to get home."

"*We* nothing! That dray is . . ." She visibly bit back the word *filthy,* out of consideration for Mr. Hart, and finished with, "My sister-in-law will *kill* me!"

"Well," laughed Mary, "I think I'm a match for my sister. I can't make poor Mr. Speed go hunting someone to take a message for me, Mr. Speed, I really couldn't. . . . And I think we can trust Mr. Hart, can't we, Mr. Hart?" She turned to the carter appealingly, with a helpless flutter of her lashes, and the unshaven, stocky little man laughed good-naturedly and held out a dirty-gloved hand.

"I'm not too proud if you're not, Miss Todd."

Speed rolled his eyes. "Your sister will skin me for letting you do this. Here," he added, pulling off his apron, "you'd better put this over the seat. . . ."

"Are you sayin' the seats of me vehicle aren't all they should be?" Hart bristled with mock indignation, as if the plank on which he sat wasn't wet with rain and slick with spattered mud, and all four burst into laughter. As they jolted through the streets—Merce having remained, like a stranded mariner, on the boardwalk outside Speed's store—Mary saw Douglas and Lincoln emerging from Birchall's store, Douglas natty in a new broadcloth coat and Lincoln looking like he'd dressed in a high wind in some scarecrow's hand-me-downs. Mary lifted her hand like a queen and waved as Betsey had admonished her for years: move the wrist, never the elbow.

Douglas looked shocked, and as if he asked himself if he really wanted as a Senatorial—or Presidential—wife a woman who'd ride unchaperoned on a construction dray through the middle of town.

Lincoln removed his dilapidated hat and executed a profound bow.

Chapter Eighteen

It was through letters that their love first grew.

Even with Mary—who had reason to believe that she was the woman he talked to most easily—Lincoln was often silent as a clam, as if at some time in the past he'd been told that he mustn't speak to women as he spoke to men and had no idea how one *did* speak to women. He was not, Mary noticed, a good speaker extempore, even on politics, and needed to prepare his notes carefully. Had they not shared an interest in both politics and poetry, she thought he'd never have been able to put two words together with her at all.

Writing freed his thoughts.

In his letters she had the feeling of seeing the man, and not what his awkward body or his barren upbringing had made of him.

And Mary, as quick with witty repartee as she could be with defensive sarcasm, found that she, too, could write of deeper thoughts than she could express aloud . . . certainly than she could express to Elizabeth and Ninian. Not only was Lincoln different from any man she had ever met—*she* was different, with him.

Through the winter of 1839 they met each other socially, at the House on the Hill or the homes of friends: the Leverings, or the Englishman Edward Baker, the acerbic Dr. Anson Henry or Simeon Francis, who published the *Sangamo Journal*. The *Journal*'s little one-room board building, or Simeon's big house on Sixth Street near-by, were de facto clubhouses for the Young Whigs of the capital, of whom Lincoln was acknowledged chief. Mary became very fond of the sturdy editor and his forthright wife, Bessie, and read the *Journal* regularly. Any trace of romantic possibility between herself and Stephen Douglas was swept away when in the wake of a particularly nasty round of political mudslinging Douglas lost his temper and tried to cane Simeon in the street.

Lincoln was one of those who pulled the two men apart. Mary, who had just stepped from Diller's drugstore when it happened, flattened back against the wall, her gloved hand pressed to her mouth, almost in tears with the wave of unreasoning terror that washed over her at the sight.

"What is it?" asked Lincoln, crossing the street to her when Douglas had jerked himself free of other men's restraining hands, and stormed on his way. "Are you all right, Miss Todd?"

"Yes." Mary's voice was a toneless whisper, but she was shaking as if she, not Simeon—not Elliot Presby—had been attacked. Lincoln just stood there, looking down at her as if he hadn't the slightest idea of what to do in the face of feminine emotion. Mary fumbled in her reticule for a handkerchief and guessed, wryly, that if Lincoln had a bandanna in his pocket it probably wasn't clean. "No. It's just . . . a friend of mine was caned in the street, back home, and . . . and hurt very badly. And one of my cousins . . . shot his best friend, over an article printed in the newspaper. . . ." She fought to keep her face from crumpling into weeping again.

Nothing really happened! she reminded herself desperately.

Why did she feel the panic terror, smell again the mingling of gutter-mud and blood?

She tried to draw a deep breath.

Douglas of course would have had a clean handkerchief and dabbed away her tears with it.

Douglas with his cane flashing through the air . . .

But it was Lincoln who'd seen her pressed against the wall, her face white with shock, while everyone else went about their business.

"Would you like me to take you home, Miss Todd?" he asked gently, and she nodded, and laid her hand on his offered arm.

THE MUDSLINGING, OF COURSE, HAD BEEN PART AND PARCEL OF THE CAMPAIGN to elect General William Henry Harrison President come November.

As soon as the roads were clear in spring, Lincoln was on them, making speeches in support of General Harrison and debating political issues with every Democrat in every corner of the state. He wrote to Mary from Jacksonville, from Alton and Belleville: brief notes, mostly concerning the political debates, in which he knew she was interested. *(Catch*

Stephen Douglas telling me what his *rivals said about* him, she thought.) Though the tall, gawky man was almost as reticent about stating his thoughts on paper as he was on Ninian's porch, his feelings came through in those simple, lucid paragraphs, his deep sense of politics as service, as the duty that must be taken up as the price of power. Mary, who like her father and Ninian and nearly everyone she knew, had only thought of government in terms of privileges, perquisites, favors, and contracts, felt surprised and a little ashamed: it was as if she had mistaken a woodland pond for the Atlantic Ocean.

She had, she realized, operated under the assumption that men who'd lived most of their lives in the backwoods, if not invariably stupid, were certainly simple.

There was nothing simple at all about Abraham Lincoln.

When the Legislative session closed for the summer, Mary accepted the invitation of her two uncles—the Honorable North Todd and Judge David Todd—to spend the summer in Columbia, Missouri. She packed her trunk and Ninian escorted her on the two-day stage-ride to St. Louis, then by steamboat up the Missouri to Rocheport. Ninian had his own reasons for going to Rocheport, for there was going to be a gathering of Missouri Whigs there in a few weeks.

Mary had always held a little grudge in her heart against her uncle David, because it was to pay his debts that, long ago, Granny Parker had sold poor Saul. But the feeling dissolved when the big, jovial man sprang down from the buggy where he'd been waiting for her at the landing, and gathered her into his arms. "What, you haven't got our girl married off yet?" demanded Uncle David of Ninian, and pinched Mary's cheek. "What's that wife of yours been doing?"

"Fending off suitors with a broadsword and shield," returned Ninian with a grin, and shook Uncle David's hand. "And she needs to, sir, with the way this girl draws 'em."

Mary gave him her sidelong smile, said, "I'm quite capable of fending off my own suitors, thank you, sir," and flipped open her fan. A drift of breeze came off the river, but the air felt thick and hot, damper than the dry prairie winds of Springfield.

And Uncle David laughed and shook his head.

It was curious, after even a few months in Springfield, to be back in a slave state again. And though Mary was as strongly opposed to slavery as ever, she could not deny that she loved the gentler pace of the lands where scrabbling competition was tempered by a more easygoing outlook on life. Uncle David's house in Columbia—most of a day's buggy-ride from Rocheport—though roughly built by even Springfield standards, ran with quiet efficiency. Mary reveled in being brought coffee in bed by the housemaids, and in knowing that if the ribbons on her pink muslin needed pressing before a party, they'd be pressed without arguments from the maids about how much other work they had to do.

And there were parties. It was twenty miles back down to Rocheport, but when the Whig Convention opened with a grand ball on the night of June 16th, Mary and her cousin Annie were there, strictly chaperoned by Annie's mother, plump Aunt Bet. The town was crammed with delegates and only the fact that cousins on the other side of the family had a house in Rocheport guaranteed the David Todd party anyplace to stay—every boardinghouse and hotel was jammed. Mary was secretly disappointed that Lincoln wasn't among the Illinois delegates—he'd written her he had a court case on the seventeenth—but on Sunday morning, after the closing of the convention, when Mary was just wondering whether Rachel the cook's wonderful pancakes were worth pulling herself out of bed for, she heard the far-off sound of knocking downstairs.

The creak of footfalls—one of the housemaids running, Abigail or Kessie. Cousin Annie was already awake and brushing her hair—Mary didn't understand how she did it, after both girls had danced until nearly four in the morning at a party given for the delegates who'd come up to Columbia after the convention closed. "Oh, my goodness, if that's that Mr. Teller from Hannibal, who kept asking me to dance last night...," moaned Annie, with a comical grimace, and listened.

Mary listened too, and heard, unmistakably, that light, husky voice saying, "I am terribly sorry to disturb you, Miss, but is this where I might leave a note for Miss Mary Todd?"

She jolted upright in bed, coppery braids tumbling. "Get Abigail and tell her not to let him leave." It didn't occur to her until later to ask herself why it was *his* voice that elicited such a reaction. Had it been James Shields, or Lyman Trumbull, or any of her other suitors, she'd simply have rolled over and thanked God for servants to tell them to go away. "Where are my stays?"

"I do beg your pardon for not sending a note," apologized Lincoln, when Mary—in an unbelievably brief half-hour—appeared, corseted, dressed, washed, and not a curl out of place, in the parlor. "I didn't know how long it would take to get the judgment, but I figured if I could get to Rocheport in time to have a talk with some of the delegates before they left town, it'd be a good idea to try."

"So faithful in love, and so dauntless in war / There never was knight like the young Lochinvar?" And then, a little shyly, she added, "You must have ridden all night."

Lincoln scratched his long nose. "Pretty near," he admitted. "I've got to be in Shelbyville Saturday to speak. If we can't *dance but one measure, drink one cup of wine,* I thought maybe I might at least walk you to church, Miss Todd? If it's all right with your uncle, that is."

They lagged behind the rest of the family party all the way to the Presbyterian church, comparing notes about the delegates and their positions, and lingered under the trees until the lifted notes of the first hymn dragged them unwillingly indoors. Then they had to run the gauntlet of eyes. In Missouri there was no slipping unobtrusively through the door and onto the nearest bench and pretending they'd been there all along. Lincoln started to do this and Mary tugged him sharply by the sleeve; it was only on a second glance that it apparently dawned on him that those rear benches were entirely the province of the slaves.

The laundresses, gardeners, kitchen girls all grinned good-naturedly and slid over to make room for them, since Miss Molly was already known all over town as the young cousin staying with Judge Todd and they were used to seeing young couples sneak in late, but Mary pulled him down the aisle to the Todd family pew.

As they walked back to the house afterwards for Sunday dinner—still far in the rear of the rest of the family—Lincoln mused, "I spent most of yesterday evening catching up on the platform for the election, and I never saw so many men dodgin' and skirtin' an issue in my life. It was like watching folks tryin' to dance under a leaky roof in a rainstorm. You'd think to listen to 'em nobody'd ever heard the word *slavery* in their lives."

Mary rolled her eyes in sympathy. "I thought Kentucky was bad," she sighed. "*Nobody* here will talk about it, not even if they're *not* trying to avoid offending delegates. Like at home," she added. "Betsey—my stepmother—always impressed on us that we call darkies 'servants,' or 'our people.' Even her mother did—Granny Humphreys—and she was against slavery like my father. But if you can sell someone, they're not a *servant.*"

Lincoln shook his head. He'd sat beside her in her uncle's pew—the first time Mary had ever heard of him entering a church—listening respectfully to the sermon ("Render unto Caesar those things that are Caesar's") but mostly, she'd thought, he watched the faces of the congregation around them. As he always watched, wherever he was.

"They can't go on pretendin' forever that slavery doesn't exist," he replied quietly. "Not with the abolitionists callin' every slaveholder a murderer, an' the slaveholders claiming the abolitionists are incitin' rebellion, and working men in the North gettin' into the act by killin' Negroes in the streets. Here we're choosing a man to run the country for the next four years, we're putting on the line for the world to see what we, the Whigs, believe in an' don't believe in, and all most Whigs want to say about General Harrison is that he's a plain honest man who drinks hard cider an' lives in a log cabin, unlike that frippery fop Van Buren. What kind of election is *that*? It's like we're in a runaway buggy headin' straight for a brick wall. Sooner or later, we're gonna have to do *somethin'* about that wall."

"I cannot tell you," said Mary quietly, when they sat alone on the porch again after dinner, "how good it is to talk to someone. . . ." She hesitated. What was it about Lincoln that she found so restful? Why did she feel that, alone among all the people of the world, she could speak her mind to him, be her true self?

Of course, she never discussed slavery with any of Uncle David's family—it wouldn't have been polite. Nor with any of the young gentlemen of the town who, in the weeks before the Whig Convention, had given such promise of a summer rich with dances, flirtations, compliments, and proposals of marriage. And as she'd found in Lexington, once slavery as a topic became forbidden ground, there was very little of politics that *could* be discussed. The unspoken darkness permeated every thread and corner of life.

But most of those young gentlemen—clerks and land speculators, young farmers or the sons of the small cotton-planters and dealers who made up the town—who'd come calling as potential beaux hadn't even offered to discuss politics. Not with a lady. It was unheard-of. With them, Mary had been all that a lady should be: flirtatious and clever, laughing at their jokes and twinkling at their wit (such as it was), lively and breathless and filled with energy. . . .

And only half herself.

Impulsively she said now, in the quiet shade of the porch, "How good it is to talk to you, Mr. Lincoln. I've missed you."

He studied her for a moment, as if weighing up how much to say about himself. Then he said, "And I you, Miss Todd."

She held out her hand to him, plump white fingers emerging from a mitt of lace. Uncle David's house was of squared logs, added to and clapboarded over, and its wide porch boasted only a bench to sit on, to take the hot feathers of breeze that floated from the hills beyond the town. "You can make that Molly," she said softly, "if you want."

He hesitated, then his big hand closed gently around hers. She remembered Speed telling her how Lincoln's father had handed him an ax at the age of eight and put him to work; he had the hands and arms of a laborer. "It's a pretty name," he said. "Molly." He smiled uncertainly, like a man stepping over the threshold of an unknown room in the dark, then bent his head suddenly and pressed his lips to her fingers.

At the touch of them, and the sight of the dark rumpled head bending over her hand, Mary felt a kind of a calm shock, as if she understood something she had only known intellectually before, like the first time she'd dreamed in French. And she thought, *I love him.*

And it was in her eyes, as he raised his head and met her gaze. Her heart felt clear, and peaceful, and as if all things had suddenly simplified in her life: *I love you.*

His big hands caught her arms, crushed her to him, as if she weighed nothing. His mouth was hot on her lips and his breath burned her cheek. Then the next second he thrust her away, or thrust himself away from her. For a moment he sat half turned from her, his breath fast and thick as if he'd been running, then he stood up abruptly and had made one long stride toward the porch steps before Mary sprang up and caught his sleeve.

He turned, and looked down into her face. "Miss Todd," he whispered, "I am sorry. . . ."

"It's all right." She could feel the shivering tension in his arm. Could see, for one instant, the naked desire in his gray eyes, before he looked aside. As if he feared, she thought, that if he didn't hold himself in check with a rein of iron he would back her to the wall and devour her.

And it was hard to remember any reason on earth not to let him.

She said again, "It's all right, Mr. Lincoln. And you may still make that Molly, if you'd like."

He drew a shaky breath, held it for a moment, and let it out; his shoulders relaxed a little as he looked back at her. The expression in his eyes was of a man who expects to have his face slapped hard.

On a similar occasion back in Springfield, Stephen Douglas had made a gallant remark about how a woman ought to forgive a poor man's gesture prompted only by her beauty, and had begged debonair forgiveness on his knees. And James Shields had protested—rather smugly—that he did not know how it had come about that he'd been overwhelmed enough to steal a kiss. . . .

But Mary knew that love was something Lincoln—the perpetual jester—did not joke about. And he wasn't going to say he didn't know how it had come about when he knew very well.

He said again, more collectedly, "I am sorry. . . Miss Molly."

"You understand that every girl has to *say* she is sorry, too." Her twinkling eyes belied her words, and under his deep tan his cheekbones colored. The corner of his big mouth moved in a smile.

"I can step down off the porch if you'd like to slap me," he offered, in the grave voice he used for jests, and suited the action to the word, bringing his face down almost on level with hers.

Mary reached out with her folded fan and touched him—like the breath of a butterfly—on his cheek. "There," she said. "Don't let it happen again."

They both knew it would.

Lincoln was on the road the rest of the summer and fall. His letters came to her from Carlinville, from Belleville, from Shawneetown. He mostly spoke of rallies and speeches, of the discreet horse-trading that went on among the delegates: *I promise to throw contracts your way if your friends vote for me.* Mary had told him that her Aunt Bet read her letters, as Elizabeth read them back in Springfield—he'd been horrified at this and even more shocked when Mary had told him that this was customarily done in all polite households—so he was circumspect in what he wrote, both about his own feelings and about the careful jockeyings among the politicians on the issue of slavery.

But under his wry observations and astute commentary, she sensed his pleasure in having someone with whom he could share his thoughts. "Man does not live by politics alone," he wrote her from Waterloo, after ten days of travel and political meetings in southern Illinois, "and sometimes I wish I could only sit beside a stream in the woods as I used to, watching to see what leaves would float past." The decision on the part of the Whig leaders to evade the issue of slavery completely, for fear of offending Southern, slave-owning Whigs like the Todds, annoyed him: "The sole argument of this election seems to be that General Harrison doesn't use gold dessert-spoons like President Van Buren does. By this argument I too would be qualified for the Presidency, and I don't see anyone rushing out to vote for me."

Because even sleepy little Columbia—which made Springfield look like New Orleans in comparison—was galvanized by the election, there was plenty for Mary to write to him about, and between her accounts of rallies and excursions and parades, she wrote of her affection for him, and her hopes to see him in Springfield in the fall. "Julia writes me that in October there will be a grand circus and menagerie coming to Springfield, which will display a gigantic elephant, the *first ever* seen in the State, as well as a giraffe and exhibitions of horsemanship and trapeze artistry," she wrote. "I do hope that, even amid the final stages of General Harrison's campaign, we can take the time to behold such a *spectacle*."

Of course, knowing that she loved Lincoln did not keep her from flirting with half a dozen of the Columbia beaux. She made herself the life and soul of the entertainments surrounding the Presidential campaign, kept her mouth properly shut about both Shakespeare and politics, and in the three months she was in Missouri received two proposals of marriage, one from a young cotton-planter and another from a delegate from one of the southern counties. She walked out with a number of gentlemen and received posies and danced whenever she could, and this almost—but not quite—made up for the fact that there wasn't a book in the town besides a couple of Bibles and what she'd brought in her own trunks, and there was nothing resembling a theater closer than St. Louis, a hundred miles away.

During a political campaign, one didn't really need plays.

With the dances and parties attendant on the campaign there were always refreshments—pies and taffy, picnics of burgoo and barbeque—and, a little to Mary's alarm, she found her sleeves getting tight and her corset-laces harder to pull close. "Oh, it's nothing, everyone gets a little plump in the summer," consoled Annie—no sylph herself—and the two girls talked Uncle David into an expedition down to St. Louis on the steamboat for new dress-goods. Mary laughed about this, and made jokes with Annie and her other girl-friends in the town as they cut and fitted lettuce-green sprig muslin and pink dimity, but her recollection of Betsey's remarks about fat girls never finding husbands gnawed at her mind.

Yet the food was so good! Sweet and comforting, and doubly so because Elizabeth wasn't always looking over her shoulder, making remarks about the need to catch a beau.

Nevertheless, when Mary was packing her trunk to return to Springfield, it was with a pang of horrified shock that she realized how many of the dresses she'd brought with her at the beginning of summer she hadn't worn in some weeks—and how many of her favorites had had the seams let out two, or in one case three, times. Even as she ate a last breakfast of Aunt Bet's justifiably famous blueberry-maple pancakes before Quincy the coachman brought the buggy up to drive her and Uncle David to Rocheport, she quailed at the thought of facing Elizabeth. Quailed, too, at the recollection of Josh Speed's humorous account of Lincoln's reaction when he discovered that the Miss Owens he'd been tepidly engaged to a couple of years ago had grown enormously stout in his six-month absence.

I'm not enormously *stout,* Mary told herself, as she got into the buggy. Her heart began to pound with guilty apprehension, though it would be a good four days' travel before she'd have to face her family and friends. *And that'll soon disappear, once I get back to Springfield. If I just don't eat much on the steamboat. . . .*

But almost the first thing Elizabeth said to her, when Mary came downstairs the morning after her arrival in Springfield four days later, was, "Good God, Molly, you've put on flesh! I would scarcely have recognized you, now that I see you in the light." The stage had been late coming into town, and Mary, her head aching from its swaying, had been glad only to come home and go upstairs after a swift embrace to Ninian, Elizabeth, little Julie, and Eppy in the kitchen.

She flushed now to the roots of her hair. "Well, and I'm *delighted* to see you too, Elizabeth! Thank you for making me feel *so much* at home already."

It was Elizabeth's turn to color up. She said, "I'm sorry. You're right, it wasn't my place to say anything. . . ."

"I should say not!"

"But if your own sister can't give you a hint, who can? I can see we're going to have some work cut out for us, letting out your winter dresses." She spoke in a mollifying tone, but Mary, stung to tears, was in no mood to forgive and forget.

"Well, thank you *very much,*" she retorted. "Please don't hesitate to use the tape-measure so you can have the most *accurate* information when you tell your friends about it."

"I'm sure no one in town," replied Elizabeth icily, "is going to need *my* word that you've gotten stout, once they see you. I only say this for your own good, dear, for you are twenty-one now and as you know, gentlemen as a rule don't ask fat girls to marry them."

"Well, I wouldn't know about *that*! As it happens, I got *four* perfectly decent proposals of marriage in Columbia—not that I had the *slightest* interest in any of them! And Mr. Lincoln finds me attractive enough to come to an understanding with me."

"Mr. Lincoln?" Elizabeth stared at her, appalled. "Molly. . ."

"What's wrong with Mr. Lincoln?"

"He is a bumpkin," stated Elizabeth, with cold finality. "A backwoodsman, and a penniless bankrupt to boot. Why don't you accept a proposal of marriage from Mr. Hart the carter while you're at it?"

"And why don't *you* admit—while you're at it—that you have no use for a man unless he's wealthy and high-born! That you'd as soon have married some crippled old dotard, if he'd had a big house and land and wealth—"

"Molly!"

"—and have whistled Ninian down the wind if it weren't that he was the son of the governor!" All Mary's pent-up resentments about having her letters read, about being called fat, about her father's long absences, frothed to the surface. "*You* have no more notion of love than does that snippy old harpy our father married! Only love of money. . ."

Elizabeth—who had never had any trouble holding her own in the noisy Todd household—reddened with anger, but as usual her voice remained cuttingly level. "If you marry that backwoods pumpkin-roller with his load of debts you'll find out soon enough what money means!"

"Money means nothing beside love!" Mary screamed at her. She felt as if she were burning up inside. "I'd rather by far marry a poor man who's going somewhere than a rich incompetent who couldn't even get on the electoral ballot of his own party in his own state!" (Ninian hadn't.)

"Honestly!" Elizabeth threw up her hands. "There's no talking to you when you get like this! I'd hoped that a little time away would cure your temper. . . ."

"There is nothing wrong with my temper!!!" Mary shrieked. "It's you who don't want to admit that you're—"

Movement caught Mary's eye and she turned—they both turned—to see Eppy frozen in the parlor doorway.

And behind her, his eyes bulging out of his head with horror, was Mr. Lincoln.

Chapter Nineteen

Lincoln and Mary went to the circus together a few days later, and tried to pretend everything was still all right. Mary tried hard—and succeeded well—in being her usual bright, flirtatious self, but the excursion was not a success.

Lincoln marveled over the elephant—Sultan, his name was—and asked the dour Scotsman in charge of him all kinds of questions about what elephants ate and how they worked. "I never did see anything like it," he remarked, in one of his rare relaxed moments that day. "Though my ma told me of them—my stepmother," he corrected. "I'll have to write her of this. She'd tell me tales of wonderful things, things I'd never seen, growin' up in the woods; the only person back then who treated me like a human being."

But for the most part Mary felt, all that day, that Lincoln was studying her uneasily. He had little to say to either Elizabeth or Ninian and she wondered exactly how much Lincoln had heard of what she and Elizabeth had said to one another, and how much of a shock it was to him, to see how her bust and waist and hips had expanded since their last meeting in June. Wondered if he were re-thinking, in that new light, all the local gossip that Mary Todd "had a temper." Certainly Elizabeth never went beyond glacially exquisite politeness to him, and when they returned to the house that evening, he was not asked to stay to dinner.

Mary had another screaming-match with Elizabeth and cried herself to sleep.

Lincoln left town soon after that, and was gone almost a month.

His journeys up and down the state all summer in the cause of the Whig Party and William Henry Harrison showed on his face and his form, during the few October days before his latest departure. While Mary had grown plumper from the thrill and jollity of campaigning, Lincoln had grown more lean. Even in repose, he looked tired. The skin over his high cheekbones was tanned dark from riding long distances between the prairie towns, and lines were settled around his eyes. His notes to her were short, and when he did see her, he was very quiet. Mary tried to convince herself that this was only the result of days and weeks spent exerting himself to charm and convince voters.

She failed. And as usual when she felt fear, it transformed itself to anger. When Lincoln left for Pontiac to take cases at the DeWitt County Circuit Court—because of his campaign journeys he hadn't worked all summer—Mary returned, almost defiantly, to the round of rallies and speeches, balls and barbeques, attendant on the final throes of the election, culminating in a glorious, dazzling, torchlit procession on Election Night.

Tippecanoe and Tyler, too!

But she wished Lincoln were in town at her side.

After making speeches, trading favors, promising votes, talking to delegates, crisscrossing the state on horseback for six solid, weary months—to the total neglect of the work that might buy him new clothes or would pay his board bill at Butler's, where he and Speed both ate—Mary wasn't even sure whether Lincoln himself cast a vote.

She flirted with Douglas, danced with Gillespie and Trumbull, walked out with Jimmy Shields and sweetly tried to discourage—but not discourage too much—the attentions of the avid and elderly Mr. Webb, all the while trying to eat as little as possible. But she found her temper was shorter on short rations and her headaches, which had plagued her on and off through the summer, grew worse. She longed for Mammy Sally's mouth-wringing tisanes, for the gentle care of Uncle David's old cook Rachel . . . for something other than Elizabeth's tart remarks about "overcoming her tendency" to headaches, as she admonished her to "overcome" her temper.

On the ninth of November, the Sangamon County Circuit Court would begin its session. On the twenty-third, the Legislature would begin meeting, in the Springfield Methodist Church, since the State House was still not done. Mary was determined that when Lincoln returned to town, she'd demonstrate to him that she wasn't a girl to wait sighingly for a man's attention. He'd see how popular she was—plump or not, spirited or not, twenty-one or not—with every other bachelor in that man-filled town, and she wrote to her father in Lexington for the money for three new dresses to make sure the point was carried across.

And on the seventh of November, Ninian's Uncle Cyrus arrived in town, with his daughter Matilda.

Mary liked Matilda Edwards immediately. She and Elizabeth waited impatiently in the parlor, on the evening that Ninian had Jerry harness up the carriage and rode to meet the stage at the American House Hotel—a total of three blocks, but there would be luggage and the streets were unpaved and soupy after the first of the autumn rains. Cyrus came in with Ninian, big-shouldered and tall like all the Edwards men, elegantly dressed, even for travel. He was a prominent politician and man of business, and one of the wealthiest citizens of Alton, which lay just upriver from St. Louis. He bowed over Elizabeth's hand, smiled at Mary: "Here's my girl Tilda," he told her. "I know you'll be great friends."

Matilda Edwards was sixteen years old, tall for her age and blonde and ethereally slender. She was exquisitely dressed in dark-blue delaine and what appeared to be at least ten petticoats beneath her rustling skirts, and had the gentlest, most natural smile Mary had ever seen. "Oh, dear, I hope you'll be able to put up with me," she murmured guiltily to Mary, as Mary led her up to show her the bedroom they would share. "I sleep like a cat—up and down and moving all around. . . ."

"It's all right, I get up about a dozen times a night. . . ."

"Oh, dear, neither of us will get any sleep. . . ."

"Do you read in bed?"

"Shhh! Papa would *slay* me if he knew. . . Oh, you have a copy of *Belinda* . . . !"

The two girls stayed awake, whispering and giggling, until nearly dawn.

Every man in Springfield fell instantly and violently in love with Matilda Edwards on sight.

Including Abraham Lincoln.

And no girl could be really angry with her because she was so sweet.

"Oh, Papa will be *so* pleased," Tilda sighed, after the first small party at the House on the Hill—to which Mr. Lincoln was not invited—at which Cyrus renewed his political connections with the wealthier inhabitants of Springfield and his daughter was introduced to the Coterie. It was nearly two in the morning; she and Mary were brushing out each other's hair and getting into their nightgowns, while the rain pattered gently on the leaves outside. "He wants me to meet other gentlemen. That's why he brought me here."

"*Other* gentlemen?" Mary cocked her head at the significance of the modifier. Any other girl would have driven her wildly jealous, the way the young men had clustered around her—including several of Mary's own beaux.

Tilda turned her enormous blue eyes upon Mary. "You won't tell?"

Mary shook her head.

"There's a . . . a gentleman." Self-possessed and matter-of-fact as she had been all evening, the girl blushed. "Back home. Mr. Strong." She could barely bring out his name above a whisper, as if the syllable was a precious thing. "Papa thinks I must look about me a little—he says I am too young. A girl must have beaux, you know," she assured Mary anxiously, as if she thought that after flirting with a dozen men herself Mary would somehow object. "But . . . I could *never* truly look at another man, you know."

Mary gave her a smile that beamed with understanding. "I know." And made a resolve to encourage her young cousin in exactly that course of action, no matter how long she should stay beneath Ninian's roof.

The fact that at no time did she worry about losing Lincoln to Tilda did not, however, make it any easier to watch him follow the girl with his eyes, and stand talking with her for fifteen minutes at a time at the American House ball that marked the opening of the Legislative session. In response, Mary flirted and danced with every other suitor she could attract. Back in Lexington, she had learned that if a girl wanted to gain and hold a man's attention, all she had to do was lavish her smiles upon another man. Stephen Douglas danced as divinely as ever; Jimmy Shields was most assiduous in bringing her cups of punch (with superhuman resolve, she eschewed the cake).

And Lincoln, hovering at the edge of the cluster of young clerks and delegates around that slim, blonde vision in pink silk, barely seemed to notice Mary was in the room.

As far as Mary could see—and she kept as much of an eye on the group around Matilda as she could while engaged in holding as many other men as possible on her own string—Lincoln never worked up the courage to so much as approach the girl as a suitor. That could have had something to do with whatever he might have overheard Elizabeth snap at Mary about him during their quarrel.

And it could have been because Josh Speed had also fallen—apparently quite seriously—in love with Matilda, too.

Mary's temper shortened as the evening progressed, until she finally lashed out at Julia Jayne over some casual jest about Mary's new dress. She left the assembly-room in tears. Jamie Conkling—who had become great friends with her, since their mutually beloved Mercy had returned to her parents in Baltimore—escorted her home.

After that Mary saw little of Lincoln. As a practicing attorney and a member of the State House of Representatives he was, she knew, frenziedly busy. With his party in the minority in both Houses and the whole state's finances in disarray he was fighting an uphill battle to salvage the internal improvement measures that the Whigs had put through. With banks and businesses closing right and left, nobody was about to release funds to build roads, no matter how badly they were needed.

Sometimes he would call after supper in the evenings, or walk with her on those few Sundays before rain—and then snow—closed in on the prairies. Once, he took her sledding.

But he was always withdrawn, as if struggling with his own thoughts. On the sledding excursion he spent a good deal of the time talking with Matilda, who had accompanied them in company with Josh Speed.

Even before Tilda had appeared on the scene—even before Lincoln had walked into Elizabeth's parlor to discover that the prettily plump, high-spirited girl he'd danced with and written to was now a fat, shrieking termagant—there had been times when Mary had wanted to hit him over the head with a book. He was abstracted, absentminded, and perpetually late through becoming absorbed in whatever case he was working on or story he was telling to the loafers who hung around Diller's drugstore. He would drift away into thought and pay no attention to what Mary or anyone else was saying to him. On some occasions, when she was late coming down to the parlor, she'd find him so engrossed in one of Ninian's books that he'd been unaware of her entering the room.

And if there was something on his mind—and she would take oath, as the winter days advanced toward Christmas, that there was—he was as tight as an oyster about saying what it was.

Raised in a vociferous family where everyone spoke their mind and if you didn't ask for what you wanted you certainly wouldn't get it, Mary found this silence maddening.

Yet when, after Lincoln had walked her home one snowy night from a Missionary Society lecture on the South Sea Islands, she asked him what the matter was, he turned the question aside with a story he'd heard about what the native ladies of those islands actually did with the dresses the missionaries sent them: "And I don't know whether the moral of that story has to do with innocence, modesty, or only just the weather there." Mary had to laugh, in spite of her annoyance, and stepped up on the porch, two steps up so that their faces would be on level when he kissed her, gently, on the cheek. Her hands tightened over his, big and awkward in his mended gloves, and his fingers returned the pressure.

But he turned away hastily as Ninian came out onto the porch, and as she rustled into the hall to shed her jacket and muff, she heard her brother-in-law say, "A word with you, if I may, Lincoln."

Mary froze. She was starting to turn back toward the door when

Elizabeth appeared from the parlor: "How was the lecture, dear?" And, when Mary took an impulsive step toward the door, Elizabeth purposefully crossed the room to head her off. "Come into the parlor, dear, and get warm. You must be frozen."

"What's Ninian talking to Mr. Lincoln about?" She could hear Ninian's voice on the porch, but he'd closed the door. An understandable thing to do—the night was freezing—but anger and panic stirred in her heart at this exclusion.

"Good heavens, dear, I don't know." Elizabeth's usually soft laugh was tinny. "Politics, I suppose. . . ."

"Ninian sees Mr. Lincoln every day at the State House."

Elizabeth put a hand on Mary's elbow to guide her into the parlor, and when Mary balked, her hand tightened. "Darling . . ."

Mary tried to yank her elbow away and Elizabeth's grip closed like a claw.

"Darling," she repeated, and closed the door of the parlor behind them. There was an edge to her voice, and a wariness in her eyes, bracing for another storm. "Ninian and I have your best interests at heart, you know that. Mr. Lincoln is a very fine man, a very honorable man. But you cannot deny that he is a very cold man, a man who has no particular liking for women. . . ."

"He is not!" cried Mary, who had the best of reasons to know the volcanic physical desires masked by the lawyer's wary reserve. "Just because he doesn't say a lot of pretty words—"

"And you cannot deny," cut in Elizabeth inexorably, "that he is a man ten thousand dollars in debt due to poor business practices. You keep saying that wealth doesn't matter, but you have never been poor."

"And I suppose *you* have?"

Elizabeth's lips tightened. "Your happiness is my duty, Mary. I assure you, you would not be happy with Mr. Lincoln, even if he should ask for your hand. . . . Which I doubt he will do, the way he's been dangling after Tilda."

"That isn't true!" Mary flashed back. "We have an understanding. . . ."

Elizabeth rolled her eyes.

"Tilda isn't the slightest interested in him. . . ."

"Good God, I should hope not!" cried Elizabeth, clearly startled that Mary would even consider an idea so grotesque. "Her father left her here to make a decent match, not to ally herself with a bankrupt clod-crusher, never mind how clever he is. He has no family, Mary, and no—"

"If you tell me again how he has no money I shall scream!" Mary screamed at her. She pulled free of Elizabeth's grip and slammed through the parlor door and into the hall just as Ninian came in from outside, his sharp nose red with cold. Mary jerked open the front door and stumbled onto the porch.

"Mr. Lincoln!" she called out into the coal-sack blackness of the snowy night. The glow of the parlor lamps touched the drifting flakes, a foot or two beyond the edge of the porch, but there was no sign of any tall figure in the blackness.

Sick dread in her heart and tears flowing from her eyes, Mary thrust past Elizabeth and Ninian, and ran up the stairs to her room.

"Darling..." Matilda turned from the mirror where she was brushing her hair as Mary slammed into the big front bedroom. "I'm worried about Mr. Speed." Speed was the beau who had escorted Matilda to the lecture. "He's become so serious about me—about himself and me—and this evening he said he couldn't endure to remain in Springfield, if he and I could not be together. I'm afraid that—"

"Oh, leave me alone!" cried Mary, and flung herself down on the bed in a huge storm of crushing petticoats, and buried her face in the pillows. She was crying.

Matilda, being Matilda, took her at her word and left her alone. For nearly forty minutes she brushed and braided her own lovely flaxen hair while Mary sobbed. Only after Mary's grief began to subside did she wrap every shawl in the unheated room around her for warmth, and cross to the bed and silently take Mary in her arms. Mary held on to her and wept afresh. After a long time, her head aching, she finally consented to be helped to undress.

She dreamed she was trying to catch up with Mr. Lincoln on an overgrown woodland path; running and stumbling through the sun-splashed green shadows, calling out to him again and again. But her legs were too short, and she was fat and out of breath, and her head ached too terribly. She saw him ahead of her, the flecks of sunlight mottling his coarse Indian-black hair and the faded blue of the homespun shirt he wore, and his long legs carried him away from her, out of sight.

NEW YEAR'S EVE CAME, AND WITH IT A GIANT COTILLION AT THE American House. Though Lincoln spent most of the evening talking with the men, he was standing beside Mary when midnight tolled, and like every other young couple with an understanding, they kissed. His hands closed tight over hers, though his lips scarcely brushed her cheek.

Not much else was possible, with Elizabeth and Ninian only feet away. But as always, Mary felt the hunger in him, the powerful physical desire of an active man coupled with the desperation of an unwanted child. She wanted to drag his mouth down to hers, to let his embrace overwhelm her as it had on her uncle's porch in Columbia, to revel in it as she had then. That physical desire, unspoken of by either, held taut between them, as much a part of their understanding as any amount of Shakespeare and Whig politics.

Her eyes closed, Mary didn't even see who Matilda kissed as midnight struck.

But when Lincoln went back immediately to the men, gathered around the long tables that had been set up to the left of the great common-room fireplace, Mary decided he needed a lesson, and proceeded to flirt, turn and turnabout, with every man of the dozen gallants who preferred dances with the ladies to speculation about who President Harrison would appoint to government jobs. With the Legislature and the courts both in session, even the presence of the Vandalia political matron Mrs. Browning and her daughters didn't lessen the ratio of men to women much. Clerks, delegates, and lawyers jockeyed and nudged for a chance to dance with the flaxen Matilda, black-haired Julia, and plump, lively, fascinating Mary Todd.

Josh Speed danced with them all, but as she circled the room with him in a gay polka, Mary saw Speed's dark eyes follow Matilda's graceful white form. "Mr. Speed," said Mary worriedly, her small hand resting on his arm as they lilted through the figures.

The dark gaze returned to her. She saw the marks of sleeplessness in the lined lids, the crease between nostril and mouth, and remembered Matilda's words in their bedroom after the South Sea Islands lecture, and later gossip of Elizabeth's.

"Tilda . . . is very fond of you. I know she wouldn't want to think that you would . . . would do anything rash or foolish because of her."

"You mean, like selling up my half of the store and leaving town?" Speed's smile, usually light as sunshine, seemed tired, with the wryness of a beaten man. "Word gets around fast. No." He shook his head. "Miss Edwards isn't why I decided to sell up, *if* I sell up . . . and I still haven't completely made up my mind to do it. Though since Pa's death they do need me now at home." He managed a chuckle. "God knows what'll become of Lincoln if I do."

It was something that had gone through Mary's mind, too. Not that Lincoln couldn't have found someplace—even in the overcrowded boardinghouses of the new state capital—to live. But she knew he depended on Speed's friendship far more than most people suspected. For a man as gregarious as Lincoln was, very few people pierced the iron wall of isolation he kept around his heart.

Then Speed sighed, and shook his head. "But it's time for a change, Molly... Miss Todd. Time to... I don't know. Fish or cut line on a lot of things. What better time than the New Year?"

So when Lincoln knocked at the door of the House on the Hill late on New Year's afternoon, when the curtains of cinder-colored twilight were winding themselves thick beyond the windows, Mary thought only that he brought news concerning Speed's decision—or perhaps sought solace for the separation he knew would come.

New Year's dinner at the House on the Hill was always a special occasion. They had spent the morning, like everyone else in town, in obligatory calls, leaving their cards at every house. Elizabeth was justly proud of her hospitality, and Eppy had worked like the Israelites in Egypt to prepare cakes, pies, gingerbread, and an enormous savory ham for the Leverings, for Ninian's brother Ben and sister-in-law Helen, for Dr. Wallace and Frances, Uncle John Todd and his daughters, plus the thin, red-haired, and irascible Cousin Stephen Logan. After dinner there had been open house, for all the wealthy and fashionable of Springfield: Senator Herndon and the chinless, slightly inebriated, and now-married Billy; Dr. Merriman and Lincoln's friend Dr. Henry, and their wives; Dr. Jayne and his wife with Julia and her brother William; Stephen Douglas and Jimmy Shields and a whole train of other bachelors come to pay court to Mary and Matilda....

Elizabeth and Eppy had spent the afternoon and evening darting back and forth to the kitchen for claret cups, platters of gingerbread, and cups of coffee, resolutely refusing all offers of help from the girls.

The last suitors had been gone for an hour. Matilda—who had been extremely quiet all day—had gone upstairs. When the clock struck six, Mary guessed that there would be no more callers, and with a grateful sigh took off her gloves—which were still too tight for her, much to her annoyance—and stood to see what help she could give in the kitchen.

Then there was a knock on the door. After a long time—Lina, the housemaid, was back in the kitchen helping Eppy clear up—Mary heard the girl's swift feet running to the hall to answer.

"Is Miss Todd here?" asked the familiar voice.

And Mary thought, *Thank God, Elizabeth's in the kitchen. . . .*

And there he stood, the top tousle of his unruly hair seeming to reach for the wooden archway that separated front parlor from rear.

She melted into a smile. "Mr. Lincoln! Do sit..."

He held up his hand to silence her. In the firelight—only a single lamp had been lit in the other parlor—she saw his face was haggard, his eyes filled with the last extremities of wretchedness.

"Miss Todd," he said.

And Mary felt the tears rush to her eyes at the formality of his address. Had it been another man who had gone back to calling her by her surname after the more intimate "Miss Molly," she would have twitted archly on the defection, fluttered her eyelids, and made her dimples peep. . . .

Her heart was sick within her. She could say nothing.

Lincoln took a deep breath and went on, as if he were speaking from memorized notes, as he did in court and on the political platform.

"Miss Todd, I had meant to communicate with you by letter, setting forth all the reasons why our understanding—if understanding it is—cannot any longer endure. But a better man than I am put that letter on the fire, and convinced me that I was honor-bound to speak to you in person. . . ."

Mary began to tremble uncontrollably. Her vision of him blurred with tears but she heard the miserable desperation in his voice as he said, "Molly. . ."

"I didn't mean to flirt!" she sobbed frantically. "Oh, the deceiver is deceived! I never meant . . ."

"Molly, it hasn't got anything to do with you flirting!" The formal tone broke from his voice as he abandoned his rehearsed lines. "Good Lord, I know you flirt with everything in britches! That's just how you are!"

"I've played fast and loose with you, and now you turn from me. . . ." Shudders wracked her whole body. She collapsed back on the sofa, hands pressing to her face, praying, desperate her tears would change his mind, as they so often changed her father's. "I never, never meant to—"

"No!" She heard him cross the room to her, felt his arms, so astonishingly strong, gather her to him. Felt the warmth of his body through the wet cold of the coat he still wore. "Molly, it's just it would never work out between us! I'm . . . I'm saddled with debts. . . ." He stumbled, groping for words. "Poverty is the only thing I'd have to offer any woman. . . ."

And I can't keep my temper, thought Mary, pressing against him, her hands locked around his lapels, *and I let myself get fat. . . . No wonder he wants to run away!* Terror of losing him—of losing the one man she could talk to easily, the one man who understood her—ripped at her like the shock of a wound, and she sobbed, "I love you! And you said that you loved me, too!" *Don't leave me. . . .*

"Molly. . . !"

He lifted her onto his lap, cradled her to him like a child. The physical power that had shocked her, drawn her on the porch in Columbia, now comforted her and she clung to him, her face against his chest, sobbing that it was all her fault and wanting to hold him and never let him go. *There has to be something I can say, some way I can undo the damage. . . .* "You promised me," she sobbed again and again, as she had sobbed to her father, to coax dresses out of him. "You said you loved me! I trusted you, I believed you—was your love a lie, then?"

"No!" He wiped her eyelids, and kissed her cheek, and turning in his arms she pulled his mouth to hers, frantic for reassurance of love. He tried to pull away and she wept harder, refusing to let him go. The next moment he was holding her close, kissing her, not with the passionate hunger of before, but with great gentleness, as if he understood how deep ran her need to be loved.

Footsteps in the hall.

Mary stumbled to her feet, Lincoln rising above her. "I must go," he said tonelessly, and Mary nodded, clutching one final time at his hand. He strode from the house just as Elizabeth came into the front hall. Mary fled past her, up the darkness of the stairs. *Let her make of that what she pleases. If she thinks I'm weeping because he said good-by, so much the better.*

She knew that above all else, she didn't want to see Elizabeth's satisfied face.

Matilda was sitting in bed, reading by the light of a branch of candles, her fair hair shining in the amber light. She looked up and saw Mary's face. "Dearest . . ."

Mary shook her head violently, and went to stand by the window, though the cold seeped through the panes and made that whole side of the room as icy as outdoors. She pressed her forehead to the glass, hoping that the pounding pain starting behind her eyes would subside. Hoping that she'd catch a glimpse of that tall form striding away into the night. But there was only darkness outside.

"It has been a day, hasn't it?" came Matilda's voice softly behind her. "I'm so sorry, dearest. And I'm afraid I hurt Mr. Speed terribly this morning. . . ."

"Mr. Speed?" Mary turned back from the window, remembering how Speed had seemed to see no one but Matilda, all through the ball last night.

Speed, she recalled then, had been one of the few members of the Coterie who had not passed through the parlor that day.

"He came by just after breakfast, while you were still upstairs," said Matilda softly, shutting her book. "He asked me to marry him, so tenderly—it quite broke my heart to tell him that I could not."

Mary whispered, "Poor Speed." And turned to look out once more into the darkness.

So Lincoln had heard that Matilda had turned down Speed—and that he was now free to court her without fear of hurting his friend.

And had rushed immediately to end whatever existed between Mary and himself.

Mary closed her eyes and knew she hated all men.

"Not a very good start for the year 1841, is it?" Matilda's voice was sad.

"No," said Mary, softly. "Not a very good start."

Chapter Twenty

Within a week, Joshua Speed sold out his share in Bell's dry-goods store and made arrangements to return to his family in Kentucky. If Tilda shed any tears at the prospect of his departure, she didn't do so in Mary's presence.

When Lincoln neither called on Mary nor sent her a note by the second week of January, she made an excuse and had Jerry drive her down to the offices of the *Sangamo Journal*.

Any lady who was a proper lady would, of course, have sent in her card to Simeon Francis and waited in the carriage. But by the standards of Lexington society, no true lady would have gone seeking word of Lincoln in the first place—certainly no self-respecting belle would have *dreamed* of letting herself be seen wearing the willow for any man—and Mary had always been a believer in the sheep-and-lamb principle.

She could just imagine what Betsey, or Betsey's redoubtable mother, would have to say about the single big room of the print-shop, with its bare wooden floor reeking of ink and spit tobacco. Though the *Sangamo Journal* was the leading Whig newspaper of the state, Simeon Francis still couldn't afford to hire a clerk or turn down job-printing work to make ends meet. When Mary entered, the stocky editor was setting type for calling cards for the wealthy Mrs. Iles, working as close to the iron heating-stove as he could in the bitter cold.

"Miss Todd!"

"I realize it's not terribly ladylike of me to come here, sir," said Mary, with a wan twinkle. "But it wouldn't have been ladylike of me to make you come out to the street and freeze to death, and..." She hesitated, holding out her hands to the stove, wondering what Springfield gossip had spread so far about herself and Lincoln.

She finished, "...and there were reasons that I couldn't write you, to come to the house."

"I take it—" Simeon wrapped an inky rag around his fist to pick up the tin coffee-pot and pour her a cup "—this concerns Lincoln?" Mary flushed, and looked down into the black depths of the liquid he handed her, unable for a moment to reply. "Since I understand your sister and Ninian aren't exactly in favor of your engagement?"

"Did Mr. Lincoln tell you this?"

She glanced up as she spoke, saw the compassion in his blue eyes, and wondered what Lincoln had told him. Wondered for the thousandth time what Ninian had said to Lincoln, back on that snowy night in November.

She sipped the coffee. It was utterly poisonous.

"I've heard nothing from him, sir," she said, in what she hoped was a matter-of-fact voice. "I was concerned he'd been taken sick. I haven't wanted to...to ask Ninian."

"No." Simeon sighed and propped his small square spectacles up onto the bridge of his nose. "No, I understand."

"*Is* he ill?"

Dear God, she thought, suddenly aghast, *don't let Mr. Francis say he's been fancy-free and happy as a lark and going about his business. . . .*

"Not in body, no, I don't think so," replied the editor slowly. He drew up a wooden chair for her, of the several that stood around the stove, silent reminders of the male political camaraderie from which Mary was forever excluded. "As far as I know he's been hauling himself down to the Methodist Church to vote in the Assembly most days. I'm glad he has, to tell you the truth, for it gets him out of his room. He and Speed are both rooming at Bill Butler's these days, while Speed gets his affairs together. When Lincoln's not actually in the Assembly he's up there alone. Pacing, sometimes, Speed tells me. Sometimes just sitting staring out at the sleet."

Mary was silent, shocked. Lincoln had told her he was subject to fits of sadness—hypochondria, he called them deprecatingly. But he had jested about them, as a man might jest about breaking out in a rash when he ate strawberries.

To her mind, unbidden, rose the desperation in his voice as he'd cried, "Molly..." The passion of his kisses and the shocked horror in his eyes as he'd seen her for the first time in the full spate of her fury against

Elizabeth. *I've driven him away,* she thought, and tried to push the thought from her mind. *He loves me, but . . .*

Or have I killed his love for me?

Yet how could he have kissed me with such frenzy, if he didn't love me?

Had he kissed Matilda that way? Had he dreamed of doing so? Was he only waiting for his best friend to leave town so he could have his chance to try?

She felt her eyes fill with tears, not knowing whether they were of sorrow or blind, screaming rage at the man she loved. She fought them back: *I must not, must not, have a tantrum, or a fit of crying, for Mr. Francis to tell him about. . . .*

Are they all talking about me like that?

The recollection of every spurt of rage, every sharp-tongued retort, speared through her mind like a rainstorm of daggers: remorse, panic, shame. Then murderous anger at everyone for talking of her when it wasn't their business, for laughing at her behind her back.

Very carefully, she said, "May I . . . would you take him a note, sir?" She fought the impulse to run out to the carriage, to tell Jerry to take her to Butler's boardinghouse. To rush into that dark and lonely—and probably icily cold—room and tell the tall, silent man there how much she loved him, how much she needed him. . . .

To beg his forgiveness, to make him say that he loved her, too.

To hear him say that he wasn't really in love with Matilda, that he wasn't really in torment of mind because Matilda was really the one he wanted to wed.

But of course it was ridiculous. No young woman *ever* called on a bachelor in his room.

Ever.

No matter how much she needed to hear his voice.

Tears began to flow down her cheeks, hot against her chilled skin. If she'd ever doubted she loved him, she knew now that she did.

Simeon said gently, "Of course, Miss Todd." He moved toward the end of the table closest to the stove. Mary guessed that the ink at the far end would be frozen.

She brought her hand from her muff, held it up to stay him: "Thank you, Mr. Francis. I'll . . . I'll send one over later, if you'd be so kind."

Back in her room Mary prayed, *Dear God, don't let him be really in love with Matilda.* But she felt as always that she was speaking the words into an empty room. She had always been able to move her father by her desperate tears of contrition, and to move Lincoln.

She'd never managed to move God.

Sitting at the little vanity—profoundly thankful, cold as it was, Matilda was out paying calls with Elizabeth—Mary tried to compose a note to Lincoln. But again and again her mind turned to the thought of that tall skinny storyteller sitting alone in his room—the new room that he now occupied alone—with a blanket around his shoulders, staring out at the driving sleet.

An exile from the world he sought to leave behind, and an unaccepted sojourner in the world of ideas, power, and the responsibility for not only his own actions but the well-being of others.

And she could find nothing to say to him except, *I love you. Don't leave me.*

The following day she still hadn't found the words to write. The weather was foul, snowing and sleeting, and she sat in the parlor with Elizabeth and Matilda, drinking tea and making a brown challis dress for the St. Valentine's Day ball that would be held at the American House . . . annoyed because she still couldn't fit into last winter's ball-dresses even though the seams had been let out as far as they'd go. "It absolutely isn't fair," she declared archly, stitching lace to the low swoop of the corsage. "You eat *one* piece of cake and you get *enormously* fat, and then it takes *years* of nibbling on bread and water before all is well again . . . that can't be right, can it? Why don't we ever have a lecturer at the Mechanics Institute on why *that* happens?"

And both Elizabeth and Matilda—who appeared to be able to consume tarts and gingerbread all day without gaining an ounce—went into peals of laughter.

Lina appeared in the door. "Miss Molly? Dr. Henry's here to speak to you."

Shabby-looking as always, the angular physician bowed as he came into the room. Elizabeth rose graciously and said, "You must be frozen, Dr. Henry," in a voice that Mary had heard her use on other occasions when she was being gracious to people she considered beneath the notice of Todds. "Lina, please fetch another cup for Dr. Henry."

"Please don't trouble. . . ."

"It's not a bit of trouble. . . ."

He's here from Mr. Lincoln. Mary knew it, for Dr. Henry was, like Simeon, one of the closest friends Lincoln had in Springfield. Her heart seemed to shrink in her breast to the size of an apple-seed.

She wondered whether Speed would have come, if he hadn't feared meeting Matilda.

She set aside the yards of soft snuff-colored fabric and sat with folded hands, saying all the proper things in the long rigamarole ritual of tea and welcome and "Oh, Matilda and I can go sit in the front parlor..." which was freezing cold, no fire being kindled there on days when Elizabeth was not receiving company....

And wanting to scream.

After byzantine maneuverings, Elizabeth and Matilda left the parlor for the kitchen. Dr. Henry sat quiet for a time in the upholstered velvet chair Elizabeth had vacated, and Mary, hands still folded, waited, feeling as if the room echoed with the hammering of her heart.

She knew she should make some further inane inquiry about Dr. Henry's health, or how was dear Mrs. Henry...? Or offer him sugar or a slice of gingerbread. No young lady—as Betsey, and Elizabeth, and Mammy Sally had always impressed upon her—ever came at things brashly with a man, letting him know what you thought or wanted.

But she felt too lost to go on.

"How is Mr. Lincoln?"

"Not well," said Dr. Henry.

I will not cry.

"He is... in terrible torment of mind. And the body can endure only so much, when the mind is torn, as his is, between scruples, and honor, and desire."

What a tidy formula, thought Mary bitterly. She shut her lips on the question, *What is his desire, and exactly where does he think his honor lies?*

"You should remember, too," Henry went on, turning Elizabeth's silver sugar-tongs over and over in his thin fingers, "that for nine months now he has worn himself out physically, campaigning. And the Legislature rescinding all those motions and plans he fought so hard for, I think only added to this crisis in him. You know how deep his passions are, behind that bumpkin façade."

Mary nodded silently, remembering the power of his arms around her, the naked hunger of his kiss.

"He is a man whose heart is stronger than his body." Dr. Henry set the tongs down, finally met her eyes. "And it is wearing him away. Speed looks after him as well as he can, and his new landlady Mrs. Butler, but we are all concerned."

Mary drew a deep breath. "Does he want me to release him from our engagement?" She wondered whose voice it was that she heard saying those words. It sounded astonishingly calm.

Henry leaned forward, and took her hands.

That means yes, thought Mary, despairing, even before he replied.

"Miss Todd, Mr. Lincoln holds you in highest esteem. Too high to put you in the position you would be in, he says, were you to go through with this match. His debts weigh heavily on his mind, and the . . . the disapproval of your family. . . ."

"He says," repeated Mary, and looked helplessly into those kind and worried blue eyes. "What do you say, Dr. Henry?"

Did he tell you about Matilda Edwards?

Would you say so, if he had?

She remembered Lincoln telling her he'd written a letter, which someone—probably Speed—had put on the fire. Had he written because he knew that he couldn't face a woman's tears? Because he knew he was no good speaking without notes, and would end up giving in if she cried?

Or because, as she'd learned in their correspondence over the summer, he could write what was truly in his heart?

She remembered Speed telling her that Lincoln had broken up with his last fiancée—the portly Miss Owens over in New Salem—by letter. Had he seen her face-to-face—had she wept as Mary had wept on New Year's Day—would he be married now?

I'm twenty-two! she wanted to scream. *How much longer can I go on waiting?*

"I'm a doctor of people's bodies, Miss Todd," said Henry gently. "Not their minds, and not their hearts."

"His heart?" she asked, trying to keep the anger out of her voice. "Or mine?"

She wrote the letter sitting in the parlor before the fire, while Dr. Henry sipped his tea and Elizabeth and Matilda undoubtedly dissected Lincoln's character and prospects in the kitchen and prayed that Mary would come to her senses. Mary forced herself to pretend she was writing a practice composition at Madame Mentelle's: *My dear Mr. Lincoln, it is with deep sorrow (deepest sorrow?) that I take pen in hand. . . .*

Her usual method of writing was to write as she spoke, tumbling, hurried, thoughts sparking other thoughts in a welter of ellipses, parentheses, and underlines. Now she forced herself to consider every word, to remain formal and contained. *I release you, I wish you well, but remember that my feelings toward you have in no way changed. I will always be . . . Your Mary.*

Her hands shook as she put down the pen and, contrary to Elizabeth's repeated admonitions of thrift, she thrust the three botched attempts into the fire. Let Elizabeth guess what she might have said rather than find it on the back of a sheet on which she wrote her grocery-lists.

She was still staring into the fire as Dr. Henry took his departure. "Is everything all right?" she heard Elizabeth inquire in the hall, and despair flared in her at the note of smug satisfaction she detected in her sister's voice.

Cold flowed through the room with the opening and closing of the outer door.

SPEED LEFT SPRINGFIELD QUIETLY BEFORE THE END OF JANUARY. Dances were held in the big common-room of the American House in honor of St. Valentine's Day and Washington's Birthday: Lincoln attended neither. There was a rumor—which Mary heard through Jamie Conkling, Mercy's fiancé—that the new President, Mr. Harrison, was considering Lincoln for chargé d'affaires of Bogotá, in return for the prodigious efforts Lincoln had put forth during the campaign. Mary's heart was sick at the thought of Lincoln leaving Springfield—leaving the country!—but it came to nothing. President Harrison died in April, and his Vice-President, former Virginia governor John Tyler, was a compromise nomination whom no one had taken seriously. Tyler took over as President, owing no favors to anyone.

Ninian and others, who had expected great rewards from a successful Whig candidate, were considerably miffed.

A more serious rumor—and one that Mary tried to push from her mind—was that Lincoln, in addition to wearing the willow for Matilda Edwards, was shyly courting his landlady's young sister: "A much better match, if you ask me," sniffed Elizabeth. "Though what a child of sixteen would want with marrying a man of thirty-two, I'll never know. Not that there's anything wrong with a young girl marrying a man of maturer years," she added hastily—she and Mary were in the ladies' cloakroom at the American House, Mary having been press-ganged into pinning up a torn petticoat-flounce at the Washington's birthday dance. "Was that Mr. Webb I saw you dancing with earlier, dear?"

"It was." Mary concentrated on pinning the stiff taffeta—not easy, between the uncertain dimness of the single oil-lamp, the arctic temperature of the cloakroom, and the shrieks of laughter from Mrs. Browning's daughters nearby as they compared notes about a friend's engagement. Her breath was a cloudy puff of gold. "Trying to be gallant and to pretend that he hasn't two darling little objections to any sane woman taking her place as the second Mrs. Webb."

"Now, dearest," coaxed her sister, "you know how you like children. You always said how you loved your little pupils at Ward's. And you're just a marvel, Betsey writes me, with the little ones at home. As for Mr. Lincoln, marrying the Rickard girl will do him no good politically. She's quite common, I understand, as one could expect. But then, for all Mr.

Lincoln's undoubted virtues, his background and manner are such that no one can or would take him seriously for any post higher than the State Legislature." Disinterested as she was in politics, Elizabeth was still Ninian's wife.

Mary bent her face down over her sister's petticoat-frill, unable to trust herself to meet Elizabeth's eyes.

"Don't tell me he *fell* for that?" gasped one of the Browning girls, and the other said, "Darling, men have no idea how long it takes for a woman to know she's with child! They don't know what's happening when we get our monthlies, or anything about women, really. You can tell them almost any tale and they'll believe it."

I drove him away, thought Mary dully. *Not just to Matilda, who of course isn't interested in him, but to this . . . this sly little chit of a girl.* It was all she could do not scream, to leave the American House that night and go at once to the Butler house, where Lincoln was boarding.

To throw herself, sobbing, into his arms again? To promise as she promised Elizabeth and Mercy and Julia and everyone else who knew her, at one time or another, that she didn't mean the things she said when she was in a temper? *I don't want to be this way . . . !*

Or to pull Sarah Rickard's hair out in black handfuls and fling it into Lincoln's face?

For an interminable year, she waited for the news that Lincoln was going to marry Sarah Rickard.

And wondered what on earth she was going to do if he did.

Through the bitter days of winter she did daily battle with her pride not to write to him, to engineer a meeting. Instead she systematically kept every other beau in Springfield on her string and tried not to remember that she was now twenty-two. Only in Springfield was it possible for her to remain a courted belle—in Lexington she'd have been on the sidelines years ago, hearing the Arabella Richardson Bodleys of the world say "Poor dear," in hatefully sweet sympathy.

There was Mr. Webb, of course, faithful and paternal as ever.

And for a time she toyed with the idea of detaching the handsome Lyman Trumbull from his growing affection for Julia Jayne. Two years ago, in Lexington, she wouldn't have hesitated about it for an instant.

But the grip of Lincoln's hands on her shoulders—the slow deep twinkle in those gray eyes when she picked a hole in Douglas's tirade on states' rights, or made some sharp observation on a third party that amused him . . . How could she forget those and make herself settle for someone else?

When spring came and people started getting about the streets a little more, Mary would see Sarah Rickard coming and going from the Butler boarding establishment, a slender small girl with black hair and tilting dark eyes. It had hurt her, that Lincoln had asked for release from her the moment he knew that his best friend no longer had any claim on Matilda Edwards, but in her heart she'd known that Matilda was no threat. If Ninian frowned on Lincoln courting a mere Edwards sister-in-law like Mary, even had Matilda been willing, he would never have permitted a match between Lincoln and a full-blood Edwards.

But this black-haired sprite in flowered green calico was a girl of the world Lincoln had left, a girl of the farms and the backwoods, who sang the old ballads he loved as she went about her work.

So Mary waited. She never saw them in company, and listen as she would, there seemed to be no other gossip about them, one way or the other—where Elizabeth had picked up her information Mary didn't know. Lincoln dissolved his partnership with Cousin John Stuart, who since his election to Congress had been drifting further and further from him politically. Instead Lincoln went into partnership with Mary's elderly and irascible cousin Stephen Logan. When April opened the roads, Lincoln began riding the circuit again: Tazewell County, McLean County, Livingston County, DeWitt County, Champaign County, Logan County, Menard County. She saw him little in company, and wondered if, having been told that he was no fit mate for a Todd of Lexington and unwelcome in the Edwards family circle, he had withdrawn completely from the gay social circles of the town.

But ladies did not ask such things of their brothers-in-law.

In June, Springfield was shaken by the murder trial of the Trailor brothers, William, Henry, and Archibald. The three men had been seen entering town with the amiable and simpleminded Archibald Fisher, who had then vanished. The town hummed with anger and suspicion, posses going out to spend most of a week searching the brush along Spring Creek and tearing down Hickox's milldam so the stream could be dragged. Returning to town, Lincoln patiently asked questions of everyone in sight, combed the countryside, and eventually located Archibald Fisher in the care of a doctor who had found him wandering about the countryside after a mild head injury, much to the secret annoyance of everyone who'd come to the trial expecting it to end in a spectacular triple hanging.

Mary, personally, had to clap her hands over her mouth to keep from laughing when Lincoln rose to his full gangly height in the courtroom and said, in that high, rather hesitant voice, "Your Honor, I would like to call to the stand Mr. Archibald Fisher. . . ."

On the way out a spectator muttered, "It was too *damned* bad, to have so much trouble, and no hanging after all."

Ninian's only comment was "Jackanapes."

But she could see how the production of the supposed victim, alive and smiling mildly, in open court before a townful of would-be spectators to a hanging, would have been more than Lincoln could resist. Seeing him from the back row of the crowded courtroom, she thought he looked exhausted, like a man burning up inside with slow fever. If he saw her, he gave no sign of it.

The courts adjourned for the summer. Lincoln left for Kentucky, to spend some weeks with Speed at Speed's family plantation near Louisville. Thus he missed Mercy Levering's marriage to James Conkling, and the sight of a somewhat thinner Mary bedecked in a new frock of pink and copper sprig-muslin—her father had come through with a special gift yet again. She wondered if Lincoln would have stood up with Jamie, had Mary herself not been present.

Were people saying, behind her back, "Thrice a bridesmaid, never a bride"?

During that long summer, she thought often of that tall shy backwoodsman, encountering for the first time the slow-paced luxury of a Kentucky plantation. Wished she could be there, or at least read a letter of his impressions of the world she knew so well. She pictured him, sitting on the porch of the Big House with Joshua—though most of those "Big Houses" were not actually so big—listening to the singing of the field hands as they came home in the twilight. How would it look to him, that strange double world of white and black?

Christmas came, and spring again, and summer's heat and storms. Matilda Edwards departed gracefully for Alton, having broken every heart, male and female, in Sangamon County.

Mary was twenty-three.

We can't stay forever in our fathers' houses. . . .

She turned down another offer from Mr. Webb, put Mr. Gillespie off with smiles and dimples and eyelids fluttered behind her fan.

Elizabeth started to look at her with sharp sidelong glances, which did nothing for Mary's temper.

She was waiting. She did not know what she was waiting for.

"I would like to see him happy," she said, one afternoon in late August, when Bessie Francis, Simeon's stout motherly wife, came calling and found Elizabeth out. It wasn't often that Mary saw Bessie alone, but she liked the big woman, who shared her love of politics and, being Simeon Francis's wife, knew everything about everyone in Sangamon County. She asked Bessie to stay, and Eppy brought lemonade from the kitchen to the sweet-scented shade of the porch, for the day was grillingly hot.

Among the things the two women laughed about was the anonymous letter Lincoln had written to the *Journal,* hilariously funny as all Lincoln's political satires were and signed "Rebecca of the Lost Townships," poking fun at the political policies of the dapper Jimmy Shields.

"He writes these pieces that leave everyone laughing.... He was the one who wrote the Sampson's Ghost letters, wasn't he?"

"Couldn't you tell?"

"Once I got to know him, yes. And all those other silly aliases he uses, like John Blubberhead. And yet with that, and with all his jokes and jests, every time I look at him I see this... this terrible sadness. A darkness . . . *It goes so heavily with my disposition that this goodly frame, the earth, seems to me but a sterile promontory.* Is he . . ." Mary hesitated. "Is he happier now?"

Bessie didn't answer for a time, but in her eyes Mary saw an understanding, and another question entirely. Before her younger friends, Mary was careful to chatter of beaux and frolics, for there was nothing so dreadful as to be seen wearing the willow for a man who'd made a spectacle of himself following Matilda Edwards all around town . . .

But Bessie, in her forties, wasn't a frolic or a gossip.

After a little silence the older woman sighed. "No," she answered, "I don't think he's happier. I don't think Abraham has had much experience with happiness in his life. I suspect he's always been too intelligent not to see farther than is comfortable for a man." Bessie—and Mrs. Butler, Lincoln's landlady—were the only people in town who called Lincoln Abraham. "Are *you* happier now, Molly?"

Mary mutely shook her head.

Bessie said nothing, only plied her fan of stiffened newspaper. Around them, bees hummed in the honeysuckle.

"I know I should get over him and move on." Mary tried to force her voice not to tremble. "I know it's absurd to . . . to turn down what Elizabeth calls 'good offers,' as if they were pieces of land come up for sale. She asked me last night what my plans were, and I don't *know*! But the thought of marrying anyone else is . . . is simply impossible."

Bessie smiled, with gentle teasing, "That's not what Mr. Gillespie seems to think. Or Mr. Webb. Or Mr. Trumbull . . ."

"Well, a girl must have beaux." Mary plucked a sprig of the honeysuckle, turned it in her fingers, as Mercy had done that evening, five years ago. Then she asked, "I heard . . . that is, someone mentioned to me . . . that Mr. Lincoln was courting Sarah Rickard." She glanced quickly at her guest, then turned her eyes out to the shadows of the lawn again, to the sporadic passersby on Second Street. "Is that true?"

Bessie sighed. "That was over months ago." She looked as if she might have said something else, then held her peace, and said instead, "And since that time he's been on the road almost constantly, traveling between the courts."

Mary stroked the polished leaf in her hand, and said, "Indeed." Silence lay between them for a time, broken by the metallic throb of the cicadas in the trees.

"Well." The older woman rose to go. "Simeon tells me you speak and read French like a native—is that true? For he's gotten a box of the oddest old French books, and hasn't the faintest idea of what they are or what to do with them. Would you care to come over to dinner Saturday and help us look through them?"

"I'd love it!" Mary stood too, and walked her the few feet to the steps. "The one thing about Springfield that's the hardest to bear, is that I can never find a novel I haven't read before! It makes me glad I read French because that gives me that much more chance of finding *something*!"

"Well," smiled Bessie, "I hope we'll have something Saturday that will cheer you."

Accordingly, on Saturday evening Jerry harnessed the carriage and drove Mary the few streets to the Francis house. Though Springfield was still very much a frontier town, with woods and prairies only a few blocks from the new (and in places still unfinished) State House, Simeon Francis had a large and pleasant house, built of whitewashed lumber and surrounded by wide gardens of vegetables and flowers. Bessie was renowned as a cook, though like most of the housewives in Springfield she was in a constant quest to find and keep a servant girl from among the daughters of the itinerant population of Irish and Portuguese laborers. Guests of the Francises were just as likely to be pressed into service making gravy as entertained in the parlor.

Though it was nearly eight by the Courthouse clock, the sun had not yet set. The house was filled with the scent of boiled vinegar—Bessie had obviously been doing her pickling that day, even as Mary had spent most of the afternoon in the sweltering kitchen helping Eppy and Elizabeth put up preserves. Simeon greeted Mary on the porch and led her through to the parlor, where Bessie, red-faced and a little rumpled-looking, sat on a low pouf with a small box of books before her.

"Mr. Speed used to stock books at Bell's," the older woman said. "But that imbecile Irwin doesn't see the use in anything that isn't an almanac or a book on how to physic horses. . . . This looks like a novel."

"It's *Notre Dame de Paris*!" exclaimed Mary in delight. "Victor Hugo—the story of the hunchback and the gypsy-girl! Oh, put it aside for me . . . whatever it costs, I'll pay you . . . or I'll write Papa to pay you," she added with a laugh. "This one isn't French but Spanish: Lope de Vega. And *Manon Lescaut* . . . Oh, put this aside for me but don't *dare* tell Elizabeth. . . . Oh, and *Les Liaisons Dangereuses*!"

So absorbed was she in looking through the volumes—and trying to think of a way of getting *Les Liaisons* back to the house with her that evening without incurring Elizabeth's censure—that she didn't even hear Simeon leave the room until he returned. Then she only saw Bessie look up and smile, and turning her head to see who had entered, Mary—with her hair tumbled forward from its ribbons in her enthusiasm and book-dust all over her hands—found herself face-to-face with Lincoln.

"Simeon," commanded Bessie briskly, "I need help with the corn pudding." And she caught her husband's sleeve and dragged him bodily from the room.

Chapter Twenty-one

"I've missed you," said Lincoln bluntly, into the profound silence that followed.

You knew exactly where a letter would reach me, surged to Mary's lips—anger, pique, love, humiliation . . . the scared pain of eighteen months.

She took a deep breath and said, "I've missed you, too."

She started to rise from the hassock where she sat and Lincoln said, "No, don't get up, I'll come on down there. What have you got?" He folded his long legs, to sit on the floor beside her hassock.

"Books," said Mary, blessing Bessie—the scheming matchmaker!—from the bottom of her heart. And, when Lincoln picked up *Les Liaisons,* she added with a quick grin, "I'll have to smuggle that one into the house. It's supposed to be most improper for girls to read."

Lincoln grinned back. It was almost as if all the past year and a half had never been. "Well, there's chapters of the Book of Genesis—and Judges, too!—that wouldn't pass muster by half the ministers in this town."

"Oh, tell me which!" Mary bounced on the hassock and clapped her hands like a child.

"Now, I had enough hard names called me campaigning for Harrison, I'm not going to have 'corrupter of young maidens' added to the list." A door closed somewhere in the house; Simeon's voice called back to the kitchen.

". . . for goodness' sake, Bessie, there's only the four of us, unless you've got the Russian Army in the basement and didn't tell me about it. . . ."

Bessie was famous for the quantity, as well as the quality, of the food she served.

Lincoln's eyes warmed with affection at the overheard words. Then he looked back at Mary, and the amusement died away. Gently, he said, "Miss Todd . . ."

"You may make that Molly," said Mary softly. "If you like."

Lincoln was silent, no doubt turning over in his mind what it meant to call her by her nickname again. Then, very quietly, he said, "Molly. All these months I've owed you an apology that I wasn't man enough to make. I know I hurt you. I am sorrier for that than I have ever been for anything in my life."

Mary said, "It's all right."

"And I made a fool of myself."

You certainly did! In front of all Springfield, too. And of me . . . What are you saying, Mary Todd???

She took a breath again, thanking God that for once in her life she hadn't blurted her first, fatal, unconsidered thought.

Why was it that in novels, girls who loved and who passed through pain were always afterwards in perfect control of their hearts and thoughts and their nasty, flaying, ungovernable tongues?

"People do." She looked into his face, so close, for once, by her own. "Goodness knows I've gone through most of my life making a fool of myself. Saying things that I later wish I'd cut out my tongue before I said. Because I do wish that, I can't tell you how often."

Simeon came in then, with the announcement that dinner was on the table. If Mary had had a gun then, she would have shot him. Over dinner she asked Lincoln about Kentucky, and they were able to compare their thoughts concerning the divided world of the South. "I'd seen slaves being sold on the block in New Orleans," Lincoln told her. "Right out on the sidewalks of Baronne Street, like so many cattle. And comin' down the river on the flatboat, we'd see 'em in the sugar-fields, an' hear 'em sing, strange songs, African they must've been, like nuthin' human. But this was the first time I've lived with house-slaves fetchin' whatever I needed, an' cleanin' an' cookin'; first chance I'd had to actually talk to Mrs. Speed's servants. A couple evenin's I walked out to the quarters. Though I don't imagine they'd tell a white man the truth about what they really felt, I did hear some remarkable storytellin'."

"Did they tell you about the Evil Mr. Jaybird, who takes tales of bad children to whisper into Satan's ear in Hell?" asked Mary with a twinkle. "My Mammy used to scare me to death with that one."

His eyes widened in alarm. "Lord, I guess it would! No, I didn't hear that one . . . though I did get to pretend I was a Democrat for an hour and a half, so Speed could have the time alone with the young lady he was courtin', while I kept her pa busy rakin' me over about politics."

"That," laughed Simeon, "is nobility beyond the common run, Lincoln."

And Mary said, as lightly as she could, "It's good to know other people besides myself have families like dragons, that have to be fought."

At the end of the evening Lincoln helped Mary on with her light lace shawl, when the jingle of harness announced the arrival of the Edwards carriage. Mary cast a quick glance through the front window, praying that neither Ninian nor Elizabeth had decided to go for a little ride in the cool night air. But as far as she could see—the quarter-moon had risen late and it was very dark beyond the tiny yellow spots of the carriage lamps—only Jerry was on the box, so there would be no need to fear that that unmistakable tall silhouette would be seen in the lamplight of the door.

"Is there . . ." Lincoln hesitated, his big hands ever so slightly brushing her arms as he settled the lace wrap in place. "Is there any chance that we might meet again?"

Mary turned, her heart pounding suddenly, and looked up into his face. "I'm sure Bessie and Simeon could arrange it. Couldn't you?" Her glance went past him to their hosts. Bessie was smiling. Lincoln looked grave, and a little unhappy—Ninian had been a friend too long for him to feel comfortable about carrying on clandestine meetings with a member of his household. Mary wondered again what her brother-in-law had said to Lincoln, that night the winter before last, and told herself firmly that she'd only be arrested if she went straight home and brained him with the fire-shovel.

Not for separating them, she realized. But for hurting a sensitive man already so cruelly uncertain of himself.

A week later, Bessie Francis sent a note to Mary asking for her help in making over a dress—a task both of them knew Elizabeth loathed—on a night when they knew Elizabeth would be out with the ladies of the Episcopal Church sewing circle. Again Bessie dragged Simeon away to "help with supper" for nearly an hour and a half, and Mary and Lincoln sat in the parlor, talking and more at their ease than Mary could remember at any time in their earlier courtship. Had his sojourn in the world from which she'd come, she wondered, changed his perspective on her? She recalled his diffidence in company—and their earlier meetings had nearly always been in company. Recalled, too, how she had flirted with other men.

"It's just what one *does,* Mr. Lincoln," she explained earnestly, when the subject came up, and to her relief he laughed, as if she were some titled French lady explaining royal court procedure to an American. "One *must* have beaux."

"So I hear tell," he replied, scratching his deplorable hair. "And I've always thought the ladies should have just as much right to wag their tails as us men."

They helped clear up after supper, and sat in the warm darkness of the porch watching the fireflies. When Simeon and Bessie went inside Lincoln kissed her, gently at first and then with hungry urgency. Mary returned home that night shaken to her bones and profoundly glad that the single lamp in Ninian's front hall was too dim to give Elizabeth much of a look at her face.

Love grew in her like weeds in a wet, hot June. Love, and passion, for his roving touch waked in her a reciprocal sensuousness. She no longer wondered how the blameless heroines of so many novels "fell." Had not Lincoln been scrupulous of her honor, even in the midst of their most fevered embraces, Mary guessed how easy it would have been for them to slip from caresses that teetered on the edge of danger into coupling like animals in the hot darkness of the parlor.

She found herself thinking, for days on end, of the strength of his arms and the smell of his flesh, with an intensity that made her blush. She was aware, as the first sharp frost of September silvered the grass, that Elizabeth was watching her more closely. But it was hard now to hide her thoughts. Did Lincoln think of her, too? Daydream about her? When he was in the State House, or the brick building where the courts met, did he count the hours and the days until Bessie thought up some other excuse to invite them both to dinner?

Even when they were alone together, he was deeply self-contained. When he spoke with passion, that passion was often directed toward politics, toward justice and the purposes for which men united to govern themselves or toward the law.

His own passions he seemed to fear, thrusting her away from him sometimes with trembling abruptness, as he had the first time he'd kissed her. It was as if, for him, any middle ground between the clearheaded comradeship of two Whig politicians—one of whom happened to be a woman—and the brute lust that she tasted in his kisses was unexplored territory, in which he did not know his way. When he held her in his arms he whispered, "My God, Molly, I love you," but at other times he held himself back. Not aloof, but simply deflecting the issue, as he'd deftly dodge answers about road-tax legislation by coming up with some absurd story or jest that would have everyone laughing so hard they'd forget that he hadn't made a direct reply.

Was that because he was a lawyer? she wondered. Or because somewhere, sometime, someone had taught him to keep every feeling to himself?

It was at Simeon's that he read out loud to her the second of the "Rebecca" letters, describing, in an aside about Jimmy Shields's honesty in office, "I seed him . . . floating from one lady to another and on his very features could be read his thoughts: 'Dear girls, *it is distressing,* but I cannot marry you all. Too well I know how much you suffer; but do, *do* remember, it is not my fault that I am *so* handsome and *so* interesting.' " Mary, who had had enough of Shields's self-satisfied courtship, nearly choked with laughter, and the following week, when Lincoln disappeared into the case he was working on—something he was maddeningly wont to do—she and Julia spent an idle afternoon in Mary's room, gigglingly composing another letter from "Rebecca," enlarging upon Shields's supposed courtship of the author of the letters.

"I don't think, upon the whole, I'd be sich a bad match neither—I'm not over sixty, and am just four feet three inches in my bare feet, and not much more around the girth. . . ."

"Mary, you are *bad*!" Julia rapped her with the feather end of her quill, and Mary said, "Oh, wait, wait, I've got an idea, let's write a poem about their marriage!"

More suffocated laughter—goodness knew what Elizabeth thought the two young women were up to behind the closed bedroom door. But, Mary reflected, Elizabeth was used to Julia coming up to visit, and they did giggle like schoolgirls. . . .

Pardonably proud of their masterpiece, Mary presented the completed composition to Simeon, and it duly and anonymously appeared in the *Sangamo Journal* on Friday.

Reading it in Simeon's parlor at their next meeting, just before his departure for the Tazewell County Circuit Court, Lincoln only rolled his eyes and grinned. "You girls'll get me in trouble yet."

"I always said Lincoln's a fool and a jackanapes," snorted Ninian, over supper a week later. "It's one thing to call a man a liar and a thief in print—you saw what Lincoln and Douglas called each other during the election!—but it's another to make him a laughingstock, and he should know it. Well, he went too far with that poem. Jimmy Shields has called him out."

"Called him *out*?" Mary set down her fork, aghast. Even Eppy, carrying the platter of corn pudding in from the kitchen, paused in startled alarm.

Elizabeth said, "Good heavens," and Mary knew that her sister saw what she herself saw in her mind: Mary Jane Warfield crumpled weeping on the sofa of her father's parlor, with the sunlight falling through the bow window onto her unworn wedding-gown and veil. Panic seized her, and with it terrible dread. . . . "Does Mr. Lincoln even know how to use a dueling pistol?"

"More like squirrel-guns at twenty paces, I'd say. Or bowie knives."

"This is no joke," reproved Elizabeth, with a glance at Mary's ashen face. Ninian sighed.

"This is just what we don't need, with the Whigs in the minority all over the country and elections coming up," he said sourly. "They'll be lucky if they aren't jailed, the both of them. This isn't Kentucky or Louisiana! I understand Shields and General Whiteside went down to Tremont where Lincoln's trying a case and issued a challenge."

"They aren't really going to *fight*?" Mary felt tears burn her eyes. In her mind she saw from a great distance the dream she'd had the night before Cash's duel, of the two men firing into the earth, and the earth bubbling forth blood.

"Lincoln's named a second," said Ninian. "I hope and pray they'll have the sense to go kill each other across the river in Missouri, but even so . . ."

Mary got up and ran from the table, shaking with terror. Later in the afternoon, in spite of the towering storm clouds gathering, she had Jerry drive her to Bessie's. "I'm afraid it's true," said Bessie. "You *were* a little rough on Mr. Shields, Molly—but he was already hopping mad over Lincoln's earlier letter. Don't take it to yourself."

"What happened?"

The older woman shook her head, unwilling to speak. She'd taken off her apron and the day-cap that kept kitchen-soot and grease out of her hair, but the heavy folds of her skirt still bore the stains of boiled huckleberries. Looking through the open back door into the kitchen, Mary could see that she still hadn't found a girl to hire.

Then Bessie sighed. "Jimmy came flouncing over to the office last week, demanding to know who'd written the Rebecca letters. Simeon asked for twenty-four hours and went to Lincoln, and told him that Shields was ready to have blood for them. Lincoln said he'd written the four of them. I gather Jimmy went away and thought about it for a few days. Then he followed Lincoln down to Tremont with a second and demanded satisfaction."

"Dear God." Mary pressed her gloved hands to her face. For an instant she was thirteen again, standing at the foot of the stairway at Elizabeth's second-day party, caught in wrongdoing and aghast at what she had done. "Dear God, he will never speak to me again!"

I've lost him, she thought. *After we had just found one another. How could I have been so stupid . . . ?*

And then, *Dear God, what if he's killed?* Shields, for all his vanity, was an accomplished shot. Lincoln had told Mary of a youth spent in country wrestling-matches, but the only time he'd fought another man with weapons in his hands had been when his flatboat had been attacked by river-pirates on the way to New Orleans. He'd been twenty-two, and still carried the scar of that skirmish on his forehead.

Shakily, she asked, "When do they meet?" How could she get through the time, not knowing, hating herself, fearing that he would hate her for getting him into this mess . . . ?

"Wednesday," said Bessie. "Day after tomorrow. Lincoln came back from Tremont last night and left again for Jacksonville early this morning, with Dr. Merriman for his second, and Shields's second going along. He didn't want you to know."

"Does he . . . does he hate me?"

The older woman regarded her sharply for a moment, as if debating whether to tell a comforting lie. Then she poked her graying hair back into its knot at her nape, and said, "Molly, I could as easily read what a wooden post feels about things, as I can that man. You'll have to ask him yourself, when he comes back."

If he comes back.

Chapter Twenty-two

There was a thunderstorm that night, crashing over the huddled town like the wrath of a God who knew exactly the mess Mary Todd had gotten her beloved into. After a night of covering, screaming, and sobbing in her bed, Mary had a headache all of the following day, and the next—Wednesday—as well. She crept sick and shaken about the house, avoiding Elizabeth, avoiding Julia—whose wild excitement at the drama of the whole affair caused Mary to lash out at her in screaming fury—and wishing there was some way she could avoid herself. She dreamed she stood on the dueling ground on the river's bank, with Jimmy Shields beside her, and pools of blood soaking the ground. Dreamed she saw Lincoln walking away from her toward a small boat on the river where a solitary gray boatman waited, to carry him to the far, dark shore. Lincoln's face, and stiff wild Indian-black hair, were covered with blood. He neither looked back at her nor spoke, and she knew he was dead.

Friday a note reached her from Dr. Henry: *The duel was called off; Mr. Lincoln has gone on to the Woodford and McLean Circuit Courts.*

She burned the note in her bedroom fireplace, lest Elizabeth guess she had more than a passing concern about whether Shields shot Lincoln or not. It wasn't until over a week later that she was able to stroll, unnoticed, over to Bessie's house.

Lincoln was there, warming his big hands by the parlor fire. The leaves that strewed the mud of the streets were brilliant reds and brilliant gold, and one of them, adhering to the heel of Lincoln's boot, made a bright splash on that spare dark figure, like a tiny wound. Mary stood in the parlor doorway feeling as if her heart had stopped.

Then he looked up at her, and held out his hand. "Molly, you are just more blame trouble. . . ."

She caught his hand in both of hers, sank down onto the sofa beside him, certain her knees would no longer hold her up. He looked tired, his hair a wild tangle as usual, but he put his other hand on her shoulder and pulled her to him, kissed her hard.

"Oh, Mr. Lincoln, I am so *sorry*!" she sobbed, and began to cry. "I never, *ever* thought . . ."

He sighed. "Now, what am I going to do with you?" And dug in his pocket for a clean handkerchief—he was getting better about carrying spares. "Now, don't cry, Puss. It all came to nothing, like the raccoon that tried to wash a lump of sugar. . . ."

"What *happened*?"

"Well, as the challenged party, I had choice of weapons," said Lincoln. "Now, back when I was in New Orleans, I heard tell how this feisty little Creole once challenged an American blacksmith to a duel. The American bein' about my size, he stipulated that the duel was to be fought with sledge-hammers in six feet of water, which would have put the surface about six inches over the Creole's head. I figured this sounded like a good idea, so since Jimmy Shields stands about two inches taller than Steve Douglas, I said we would fight with cavalry broadswords, each of us to remain on the far side of two lines drawn six feet apart. . . ."

Mary's sobs dissolved abruptly into a hiccup of laughter. "Six feet apart? He wouldn't have been able to touch you!"

"And I'd barely have been able to touch him," added Lincoln. "It was the best I could do. I've had a little practice with the broadsword, with that fellow that teaches it over in the Delaney Building across from the State House, but I'd just as soon not have it on my record that I'd carved up a state auditor, even if he was a Democrat. That kind of thing gets around."

He shook his head, and gazed down into the fire. "And if that wasn't bad enough, it's like when two boys get into a fight behind the schoolhouse—boys run for miles to get their licks in. Now Shields has challenged Bill Butler to a duel. . . ."

"Your landlord? For what?"

"For laughing when he heard the conditions read off, I think, though Shields has it that it's something else—and *his* second is talking about challenging *my* second. . . . And of course all of this is all over the newspapers. I just wish everyone would forget the whole thing."

Mary looked down at his hand, still clasped in both of hers. Softly, she said, "Thank you. Thank you for saying you'd written all the letters. That was . . . very gallant of you. It was foolish of me, stupid beyond all measure. . . ." She looked up, and met his eyes, her own brimming with the tears of contrition that had always appeased her father.

He shook his head. "Molly, what *am* I going to do with you?"

There was a long silence. Then, hesitantly, she said, "I . . . I've been wondering that myself."

Bessie and Simeon, as usual, had disappeared to the back of the house. In the grate a log broke, sending down a whisper of glowing coals. Beyond the windows, the wind moaned softly in the trees.

Lincoln sighed, and put his hands gently on either side of her face. "Molly, I love you." It was the first time he had spoken the words in cold blood. "God help us both. But I would be the greatest scoundrel unhanged if I asked any woman to marry a bankrupt and a debtor, particularly a girl of your breeding, who's had ease and comfort all her life."

"You know money means nothing where love is true." Mary's hands came up to grasp his wrists. "I would love you if you were a beggar on the streets."

He smiled. "I don't doubt you would, Molly. But you'd also get darn tired of livin' on the few pennies I'd bring in. I love you," he repeated, as Mary opened her mouth to protest. "And one day, God help me, I shall be proud to look your brother-in-law in the eye and ask for your hand."

It was the most he had said on the subject, and so much did Mary burn with joy at the words that she said nothing more. But even as she threw her arms around him, even as they clasped one another tight by the sinking embers of the fire, she thought, *When?*

And what happens if you meet another slender young thing of sixteen before that time?

The mere thought of going through another eighteen months—or two years—or how much more?—like those she had just passed through made her breath come short. *And what if he died?* she asked herself, as Simeon drove her home through the cold darkness of the streets that night. *What if the glowing green rivers of cholera rose, even from this dry Western prairie? What if he fell sick, as my mother fell sick . . . ? What if some other lunatic Democrat calls him out and refuses to be put off with broadswords at six feet?*

What if, what if, what if?

October wind rolled handfuls of leaves through the small glow of the buggy lamps, like skittering goblins. Ahead of her she saw the glow of windows, the house where she had a single room, on sufferance.

We cannot remain forever in our fathers' houses. . . .

How old would she then be?

She was nearly twenty-four already. The belle of Lexington, the girl who'd collected beaux like they were buttons . . . would she really end as an old maid? With Bella Richardson Bodley saying sweetly, "Well, she let herself get so fat . . . and she never *could* learn to keep her temper. . . ." and her friends pushing their brothers and husbands to dance with her out of pity?

Her body flooded with sickened rage and terror at the picture of that future.

She loved Lincoln as she'd never loved anyone else, as she couldn't imagine loving another man. The dread of losing him, of the twin terrors of desolation and humiliation, kept her staring at the ceiling in darkness until she heard the soft clatter of Eppy in the kitchen at dawn.

Lincoln left on Thursday, for the DeWitt County Circuit. He was gone for a month. Winter was coming, and the prairies around Springfield wore their drabbest robes, the grass bleached a ghostly gray by the summer sun, the riot of flowers killed by the autumn frosts. Lincoln came home on a rainy Sunday night; rain was still falling on Monday afternoon, when Mary got a note from Bessie inviting her to dinner. She told Jerry as she got into the carriage, "Simeon will bring me home." She knew that in fact Simeon would be down at the newspaper until past midnight—Bessie had told her this earlier in the week—and that Bessie never emerged from her kitchen once she'd finished clearing up the dishes and usually simply retired to bed.

She trembled with the thought of what she intended—hoped—to do, but the recollection of the previous twenty-two months of waiting, of wishing, stabbed her like a goad. *It isn't as if he didn't love me, or I him. . . .*

Helena's words from *All's Well That Ends Well* circled in her mind:

Why then, tonight
Let us assay our plot; which, if it speed,
Is wicked meaning in a lawful deed. . . .

As Ninian's carriage jolted along Sixth Street through the gray world of falling rain, she closed her eyes. She wondered if she should pray, but knew not to whom or for what. She only knew she could not go on as she was.

Her heart felt very clear, knowing exactly what she had to do.

Lincoln was exhausted, and quiet during dinner. "It's nothing," he said, when Mary asked what troubled him. "I don't like to think of the rain fallin' on the grave of—" He hesitated . . . *over a name?* "—of those I've loved."

For a long time, after Bessie left them alone together, they sat on the couch before the fire, silent, in the circle of each other's arms. When Mary drew closer to him, and drew his head down to hers, he responded with a wordless gratitude, his big hands tangling in the thick coils of her hair. This they had done, many times before, this dance of passion, of kisses and touch, flirting with the heart-shaking borderlands of delight and need. She loved his strength, and he, she guessed, the fire of her response, holding him to her, gasping as he pressed her back against the arm of the couch.

It was nothing any true lady should do—no true lady should permit a beau more than a single chaste salute: Betsey, and Granny Humphreys, and Elizabeth had emphasized this, over and over.

Did they really, she wondered, believe it was possible to draw back from the seductive ambrosia of this? Sometimes it seemed to her that this was truly what she and this man sought: to see how deep they could sink into darkness and fire and still have the strength to draw back.

Always it was he who drew away, as if he could trust himself only so far and no further. When she felt him move to do so, instead of letting him go she clung tighter. He whispered her name, and she pulled him to her: "I want you. I want all of you."

"You don't know what you're asking. . . ." His voice was hoarse and she could feel his body trembling as it bent over hers.

"Do you think I'm a child?" she breathed. "Do you think I don't know? I know that you're the man that I love." All those conversations with Frances, with Mary Jane Warfield, and Merce—all those came back to her, about those things that girls only whispered about at night. The things that Elizabeth, and Betsey, never guessed that she had learned. Her hands tightened hard behind his neck and she slid her body down beneath his in a crushed sigh of petticoats, so that through them her legs pressed against his thighs. "I know that you're the man that I will marry, the only man I've ever loved or ever will love. Ever *can* love. Don't turn my love away."

He looked down into her face, his eyes hidden by the shadows of the dying fire, with his tangled hair hanging down over them. But he breathed like a man who had been running.

"Life is short," said Mary softly. "We don't know what the future will bring. I don't want never to have done this."

When they lay together later on the couch, locked in each other's arms in a tangle of disordered clothing, she touched his hair gently, wonderingly. Wondering how anyone could have thought him ugly. In repose the bony, mobile face recalled to her some vision of a prophet sleeping in the wilderness, at one with the silence and the stones.

At her touch his eyes opened, relaxed and infinitely at peace.

"Molly." He brought up his hand to cup her cheek. Seven years as a clerk, and a lawyer, and a legislator had not eradicated the frontiersman's hardness from his leathery palm. "I swear to you that I will be your husband. That I will not forsake you."

"I had no fear of that." So strongly she felt his love, and saw the tenderness in his eyes, that she honestly did not know whether what she said, at that moment, was a lie or not.

Lying in her own bed later, after Simeon had returned from the newspaper, and driven her home through the lessening rain, Mary turned the matter over in her heart and in her mind. Her body ached—Mary Jane had warned her about that—and she knew she'd have to inspect her petticoats closely and wash out the telltale spots of blood. Would have to do it early, before Lina was finished with the breakfast chores. Wet and muddy as last night had been, it would be easy to drop wet stockings or wet shoes on them, to cover dampness where dampness would not ordinarily be.

Mary Jane had told her about the blood, too.

What Mary Jane hadn't told her—or Merce, or Frances, when hushed questions and answers had been exchanged on darkened front porches during summer nights—was how profoundly the passage from girl to woman would alter her perceptions. How differently a woman looked at a man, once he became a lover instead of a beau.

Yesterday she had loved Lincoln with a girl's passionate yearning. Tonight, lying in her bed listening to the rain, she understood that with the fulfillment of that yearning, a new and wholly unsuspected dimension of love opened. She wanted him always, a part of her without which she was not—had never been—complete.

I will not forsake you, he had promised. *I will be your husband. . . .*

She wondered if, when the new day dawned, he would come to Ninian and ask for her in marriage.

In a novel, the lover would put aside his diffidence and his foolish concerns about money, and come striding up to the House on the Hill in the morning. *Your sister is of age,* he would say, *and you cannot hold her from her own course any longer. . . .*

Of course, in a novel, the lover wouldn't have spent eighteen months mooning after Tilda Edwards and Sarah Rickard.

Mary closed her eyes in the darkness, folded her hands on her breast over the remembered heat of his lips. *I will be your husband,* he had said, and her heart told her that once he had given his word, Lincoln was a man who could be trusted to the ends of the earth. She fell asleep not knowing whether she could carry through with what she had planned, or whether she would trust him and wait.

I will be your husband, he had said.

Only—an accident, or a lawyer's caution even in extremis?—he still had not mentioned when.

Lincoln did not come striding out of the raw mists at breakfast-time, to claim her from Ninian. Ninian wiped his mouth on his napkin and departed for the State House; Elizabeth disappeared into the kitchen in quest of a blancmange Eppy was making for Mrs. Irwin, who was down with *la grippe:* "You will come visiting with me, won't you, Mary? It's been an age since you did, and I'm sure everyone is asking where you've been. . . ."

The day passed in a blur and in the midst of an afternoon call on Mrs. Browning and her daughters at the American House, listening to their account of the negotiations with contractors over the marble floors of the new State-House lobby, Mary thought suddenly, *Dear God, what if I am with child?*

Even if he marries me as soon as I know for certain—three weeks from now—the baby will be early. Everyone in town will know! No one—nobody—will receive me in their houses again! We'll both be outcasts. And Elizabeth . . .

Panic filled her heart, blotting out all further discussion of how that particular contractor had come by his appointment. The faces of the Browning ladies, and of her sister, retreated to a dream, mouthing meaningless sounds. Mary debated feigning sick to return to the house but didn't dare—*What if Elizabeth asks just why I am sick? Can she read it in my face already? Did she not speak of it because we were just about to set out on her visits? Will Ninian send me home . . . back to Betsey?*

Dear God! Anything but that!

The visits seemed to last for months. The evening, after supper—waiting in the parlor while she and Elizabeth worked at their sewing—for decades. Mary's fingers trembled in the yellow light of the whale-oil lamp and she wondered again if Elizabeth was looking at her strangely, but she dared not plead a headache and go up to bed. What if Mr. Lincoln came by, and they said, "Oh, Mary has gone up to bed with a headache"?

At ten she knew he would not come.

In the morning, as early as she dared—meaning just after breakfast, and she flinched at Elizabeth's cheerful "You're up early, dear,"—she had Jerry harness the carriage, and drove to Bessie Francis's house. ("I was up all night trying to remember what I'd done with my coral bracelet, and I remember now I left it at Bessie's Wednesday. . . ." Did that sound convincing?) She only meant—she told herself later—to ask Bessie what she should do, what she thought. . . .

But Lincoln was there, having breakfast with Bessie and Simeon as he frequently did. She heard his trumpeting high-pitched laugh as she came up the porch steps. Try as she would she later had no recollection of any intervening process between that, and standing in the doorway of the kitchen, seeing the handwritten papers strewn on the table among the breakfast things, and Lincoln in his shirtsleeves rising, his face wreathed with delight at the sight of her.

"Molly . . ."

She took his hands, and drew him into the empty dining-room. Bessie and Simeon, as always, hung back to give them the time they sought with one another.

"I had to see you," she said, and Lincoln bent his tall height down, to kiss her lips.

"And I was plotting away with Simeon like Brutus and Cassius rolled into one, to come up with some reason Ninian would believe for you to come over here again soon, I . . ."

She squeezed his hands hard, shaking him a little; in the dimness of the curtained room, he looked down at her in consternation. "What is it? Did Ninian . . . ?"

She opened her mouth, and the words that came out were: "Mr. Lincoln, I'm with child."

And the next second, she would have given everything she possessed never to have spoken those words; would have traded her life not to have them emerge from her mind into reality, the reality of the rest of her life.

Lincoln's eyes widened with shock, like a man who has stepped unthinkingly around a corner in a friendly place, and been run through the heart with a spear.

Chapter Twenty-three

Bellevue 1875

Beyond Bellevue's window bars, and the white curtains that let in such maddening quantities of light, the summer day dimmed. Mary's head ached as she remembered the appalled shock in Lincoln's eyes, and anxiety began to overwhelm her, as it so often did at this hour of the day—the medicine she had had immediately after Robert left seemed to have had no effect at all. She understood Mr. Wilamet saying that she mustn't give Robert the advantage by being sleepy or forgetful, but Robert was gone now.

And she wanted to sleep, and forget the lie she had told, and all that came of it afterwards.

"Amanda," she called out, and a moment later the young woman was at the door of her room.

They both pretended Amanda didn't spend her days on the other side of the barred and curtained interior window, but Mary had only to get to her feet and walk to the door of her room—not locked, these days, for where was there for her to go?—for Amanda to meet her, smiling, in the hall.

"I'm still feeling quite ill," she told the younger woman. "Please ask Dr. Patterson to give me another dose of medicine."

"Of course, Mrs. Lincoln."

But it wasn't Dr. Patterson who came to her room, but John Wilamet.

"There's no need to go on watering down the medicine now," she said, at the first sip from the glass he gave her. "Robert is gone, and good riddance to him! How *could* he—how could *any* boy—do what he did . . . ?" She stopped herself, shook her head, hearing her own voice beginning to crack with anger and feeling her head throb.

"Robert is gone," she repeated. "And what I need now is to go to sleep." It was still afternoon, but what did that matter? The visit had exhausted her.

"Mrs. Lincoln," said John softly. "Do you know what's in the medicine?"

Mary blinked at him, startled at the question. His tone was the tone of a man who speaks to evade a request, and she'd had enough of that with her husband. She snapped, "What does it matter what's in it? Of course I don't know what's in it, it's a secret of the manufacturer! Manufacturers are entitled to their secret formulae. How else would they make any money? And what that has to do with—"

"This medicine contains opium," said John. "They all do."

"That's a lie!" Mary gasped the first words that came to her aching, buzzing brain. "I would *only* take opium under a doctor's advice, and then only a very little for my neuralgia!"

"You've been taking large quantities of opium for years," said John. "Your doctors have been giving it to you for years and you've been drinking twice, three times, five times as much on the side. Your whole system is habituated to it."

"What a thing to say!" Mary backed from him, her hand clutching the glass. "How dare you call me an opium-eater! Mr. Lincoln was the most strictly temperate man I knew. He would never have permitted my doctors to do anything so wicked!"

"Mrs. Lincoln." Patience and care tempered his voice far beyond the youth of his thin face. "May I ask you a favor? For old times' sake?"

Mary checked the fury rising in her, settled back into her chair. She remembered this young man as a boy in Camp Barker, remembered him driving her through the green trees of that hot foul city by the Potomac. Remembered laughing with him, in better times.

For old times' sake.

For the sake of times that had been sweet.

There were flecks of gray at his temples now and he looked careworn in the last fading daylight from the window. It crossed her mind suddenly to wonder what road had led him here, to this place, and whether his mother and sisters were still alive. His mother had been a strange woman, like a wild black Medea, but his sisters, especially little Lucy, had been dear to her, like so many of the contraband children in the camps.

The memories stilled her, drew her back to earth out of her rage.

"Of course," she agreed. But warily. She wasn't an opium-fiend! And if he thought he could call her one just because she took a little more medicine than pious hypocrites thought proper in a woman . . .

"Would you listen to me for a few minutes," said John, "while I talk about medicine? I'd like your thoughts on this, before I decide what to do."

He's going to take my medicine away from me! She could hear it in his voice. *For my own good, they all say . . . Wicked. Wicked like all the rest . . .*

"Most of the patent medicines you've been taking," he continued, "the ones they sell in the drugstores already bottled, contain opium. I've worked with medicines, I know what opium smells like and what it tastes like. It's there. Sometimes a lot of it. I don't know how much. Most doctors prescribe small amounts of purer opium for coughs, or headaches, or intestinal flux. It's the only thing that works. Most doctors don't know, or don't want to know, how quickly a patient can become habituated. Many doctors I know are opium-takers themselves, and don't want to admit how harmful it is. Beyond that, nearly all those medicines contain alcohol as well."

"Well, a little bit, of course . . ."

"I don't think it's a little bit. They put in bitter herbs, or sweet syrups, to change the taste. But I think most of these medicines are stronger than saloon rum."

"What are you telling me?" Mary set down her glass on the bedside table behind her, her black-mitted hands closed into fists. The headache behind her left eye gave a sudden agonizing throb—old Chief Lightning-Wires getting his tomahawk ready, she thought despairingly. Anger flashed through her on the heels of the pain. *I need that medicine.* . . . "That you think that as well as being insane, I'm a drunkard? An opium-eater?"

"Not of your own choosing . . ."

"Not under *any* circumstances or conditions! The very *idea* that because I have *occasionally* taken laudanum for my truly *agonizing* neuralgia and headaches, that I would . . . would *guzzle* such a thing of my own volition is an insult, the rankest implication that no gentleman would even consider in regards to any woman! I'll have you know that my husband was a member of the Washingtonian Society, that he was the most strictly temperate man who ever drew breath! And the kindest, and the best!"

Tears began to flow from her eyes and John reached out to her, but she whirled from him, strode to the window in the blind fury he recalled from other days. "I shall report you to Dr. Patterson. You will find yourself sweeping out saloons, where I daresay you belong! Now get out of here! Get out of my room or I shall scream!"

She was screaming already, and John, very quietly, got up and left.

Mary rushed to the door as he closed it and pounded on the panels, crying, "And don't you *dare* lock me in!" She yanked on the knob and the door came open with such violence that she staggered. He was walking away down the corridor, where the lamps had not yet been lit for the night. She screamed after him, "How can I rest here if you keep upsetting me? How can anyone rest in this place?"

She slammed the door behind him, opened it and slammed it again.

Then she went to the table and poured herself another glass of the medicine he had left. The whole bottle had been watered. She could tell how weak was the bitter taste that she was long used to associating with the strength—the warming comfort—of whatever medicine contained it.

She drank most of the bottle, and fell deeply asleep.

SHE DREAMED SHE WAS ATTENDING HER OWN WEDDING, IN NINIAN'S house, on that night in early November of 1842.

She stood in the back of the big double-parlor, nearly out of sight in the shadows in her black widow's dress. She was astonished at how young Ninian looked, the mass of his raven hair unfaded, glowering like a bear staked for baiting as the small group assembled in the lamplight. Elizabeth in her rose-colored dress, her hair still black instead of gray, alternated between seething indignation that her advice had not been taken, and annoyance that the wedding had been arranged with barely four hours' notice, and no time to do proper baking.

There was a cake, but it was still mildly warm from the oven and the frosting wouldn't set. The smell of ginger filled the room.

And Mary herself . . .

How pretty I was! She felt a kind of wonder at it, for it was something she had quite forgotten. That plump, bright-faced girl in her best dress of embroidered white muslin, with the collar of Irish lace, dancing with excitement one moment, then turning, suddenly, to look up at her groom with anxiety that amounted almost to fright in her eyes.

Trying to tell herself that she'd done right.

Lawful meaning in a lawful act . . .

Trying to convince herself that love was enough.

Praying that the words she'd said to him in Bessie Francis's dining-room that morning had not killed once and for all the love he bore her.

Even in the orange lamplight, and the hot glow of every candle Elizabeth could place in sconces and branches on table and sideboards, Lincoln looked ashen. His dark brows stood out sharply above the adze-blade nose. But it was the only sign he gave of whatever was going on inside. A politician—and a good one—he was never at a loss in company, shaking hands and chatting with the thirty-some friends and family who had been hastily gathered by word of mouth: Old Judge Brown and Lincoln's fellow-lawyer James Matheny, Frances and Dr. Wallace, Lincoln's landlord William Butler and his wife . . . But when the eddies of talk swirled away, and he took the hand of that plump, pretty little partridge in white to lead her to the Presbyterian minister, she could see that his eyes were haunted, as if he were mounting the steps of the scaffold.

He'd had a gold band inscribed that afternoon: *A.L. to M.T. Nov. 4, 1842, Love Is Eternal.* He held her hand, and spoke as if he'd memorized the words. "With this ring I thee endow," said Lincoln, "with all my goods and chattels, lands and tenements. . . ."

"Lord Jesus Christ God Almighty, Lincoln, the statute fixes that!" boomed Judge Brown from the crowd. "Get on with it!"

Everyone laughed, including, thank God, the groom himself. With laughter he put the ring on young Mary's finger. With laughter, they kissed.

Laughing herself in the shadows in her secret corner, Mary saw that young girl—for she *was* only a young girl, she understood now, no matter what others said or she feared about being an old maid of twenty-four—look up into the face of the man she adored to distraction. And she thought, *I'm glad I lied—if it was a lie. I'm glad I brought this about. I'm glad we had the time together that we had.*

All of it, good and bad.

Because good and bad, all put together, there wasn't so very much.

And if I had not lied as I did, there would have been less of it, or maybe none at all.

But she turned her head and glimpsed behind the backs of the crowd a young man in the natty gray suit of a different era, his burly body held stiff, his face with its drooping mustache a cold mask that revealed nothing of his thoughts.

You lied, Robert Todd Lincoln's eyes said.

And because of your lie, my father never loved me with the whole of his heart, as the firstborn son has a right to be loved.

Chapter Twenty-four

Springfield 1843

They lived in a single rented room in the Globe Tavern, at a cost of four dollars a week.

It took Jerry two trips in the carriage to bring five of Mary's trunks, plus hatboxes, valises, and books, to the plain two-story wooden boardinghouse on Adams Street. She spent the rest of the week going back and forth to Elizabeth's house, packing up what remained. Though Lincoln had left his room at William Butler's on his wedding morning without the slightest idea that he'd be moving in with a bride within twenty-four hours, he was able to walk over from Butler's the following morning with all his possessions crammed into two saddlebags and a cardboard box.

"Growin' up the way I did, I never did need much," he said, almost apologetically, as Mary, laughing, looked around the small room for places to put everything. The books—her novels, his law-books, and her volumes of Shakespeare and Burns—they stacked on top of the single bureau. There was no bookcase. "I see those big houses—your brother-in-law's among 'em—and they look so fine, an' I always end up wonderin', *what the blazes do them fill 'em up with*?"

"They fill them up," smiled Mary, turning back to her tall husband, "with the amenities of fine living. With the wherewithal to make music—for one's friends and for one's own peace of mind. With the space to entertain and give parties, for the pleasure of the friends one already has and to meet one's business and political acquaintances. With a healthy and happy environment in which to raise one's children."

Lincoln hesitated fractionally before putting his big hands on her shoulders. His grin was rueful. "And dear knows what our poor little codger's gettin' himself into, arrivin' early this way," he said, and bent to kiss her. His black hair hung down in his eyes—never, to the end of their days together, did Mary see it brushed back for more than five minutes at a time. *If he's to go anywhere in politics,* she thought, *we're going to have to invest in a little pomade.* "But we'll deal with that as best we can, Molly, and I reckon we'll brush by somehow."

He kissed her again, and then—Jerry having departed—folded her in his arms and carried her to the bed.

He left the next day for Taylorville, for a one-day session of Christian County Court. Mrs. Beck, who owned the Globe, found planks that could be put together to form a rough bookcase: Mary and Lincoln had already formed the habit of reading to one another in the evenings, Mary in this case reading *Les Liaisons Dangereuses* and translating as she went. ("Lord, that Valmont's a scoundrel!" exclaimed Lincoln, as if the whole thing were happening in Springfield instead of the Paris of the *ancien régime.)* Mrs. Beck was less than pleased when Mary complained about the curtains—which were faded and limp—and responded to Mary's suggestion that they be at least starched and ironed with a tart, "Well, my lady, I'll certainly send one of the slaves to take care of it right away!"

Mary flushed bright red, but Mrs. Beck had already turned on her heel and strode off down the stairs; Mary spent the rest of the rainy day with the six additional trunks of dresses, shoes, underwear, and books that Elizabeth had sent over, trying to arrange them in such a fashion that two people could at least get from the door to the bed without turning sideways. Julia arrived with Mary's cousins Lizzie and Francy, to sweep her off for tea at Uncle John Todd's, but that first night alone Mary lay for a long time awake, listening to the clamor of men's voices in the commonroom downstairs, to the clang of the bell that announced the arrival of the stages, to old Professor Kittridge's drunken harangues in the yard, and to the Bledsoe family arguing over money in the room next door.

Wondering how she, Mary Todd of Lexington, who could have been the wife of any planter in Kentucky and several states around, had come to be alone in this dreary place.

And trying to push from her mind the shame at her lie and the dread of what Lincoln would say if he ever found out.

He won't, she told herself frantically. *I can tell him I miscarried. . . .* She'd heard Mammy Sally speak of slave women who'd done so. *Or is it different for darkies than for whites?* Who could she ask?

The thought of him finding out—of standing revealed in his eyes as a liar and a cheat—was more than she could bear.

"You really must talk to that woman," said Mary, when Lincoln returned late Wednesday afternoon. "She's insufferable, and a slovenly housekeeper. I had to starch and iron the curtains myself, and I had a headache all the rest of the day. And her cooking leaves much to be desired as well. If we were to move to the American House . . ."

"It would cost us half again as much," said Lincoln gently, drawing Mary to his side where he sat on the bed. "And that we cannot afford."

"Oh." Mary looked down at her hands, filled with shame that she hadn't thought of that before getting into a quarrel with their landlady.

"I told you, didn't I, that you'd be marrying a poor man—"

"As if that mattered a whit to me!"

"Well, if it's true I'm grateful for it. And if it's not quite as true on closer examination as you thought it was when you said it, I'm glad you're still willin' to stand by it."

Mary opened her mouth to protest, then saw the twinkle in his eye and retorted, in mock primness, "You're not the only person in this household who stands by his word, Mr. Lincoln. I can be patient in a good cause."

"That's my Molly." He tightened his big hand on her shoulder, and bent to kiss the top of her head. "As for Mrs. Beck, I heard all about your hoo-rah from her on my way across the yard, an' I smoothed her feathers a trifle. You got to remember, she runs this place with just the two servant girls, when she can *get* a servant girl, and most of the work she does herself. Of course she'll get cross, when somebody tells her to do more. One day I'll be clear of the National Debt that landed on me when I took over my partner's half of that wretched grocery in New Salem, and then we'll be able to live . . . well, if not like Brother Ninian and Sister Elizabeth, at least as well as common folks. You think you got enough flub-dubs in them trunks to last you till then?"

Mary put on a considering expression as she studied the trunks, then glanced at him, smiling. "If you're not too long about it."

When the times were sweet, they were very sweet.

Lincoln had grown up in a man's world, and for years had associated mostly with men. With his agonizing shyness around women went a curiosity about them that few men had—as he was curious about all things, and all people. In the same spirit that he'd listened to the Speed slaves telling stories in the quarters, he would listen with a slow grin, cracking his knuckles, when Mary spoke of the intricacies of the Southern family feuds that had carried from Virginia to Kentucky and on into Illinois, and the inflexible rules about who left cards on whom, and why. He hadn't been joking when he'd said a woman should have the same right to sexual freedom as a man—he was also inclined to let women have the vote. "But God help you if you say so in this state."

For her part Mary had never known a man like him. Her experience had for the most part been with men of her own class, townsmen who saw the world in terms of making a living, and connecting with other men—and peripherally with their families—who would further their own careers.

Lincoln's countrified earthiness, that had so repelled Elizabeth, drew Mary. She felt that she was dealing with a man from a different age of history, a woodsman at heart who saw the world in terms of simpler survival, and who thus saw through the persiflage of town life and town ambitions to the bone and bedrock of politics and law.

At night they would read to one another from her books or from the half-dozen newspapers that were the party organs of Democrats, Whigs, Locofoco Democrats, "the conscience Whigs," anti-Tyler Whigs, and all phases of opinion in between. Or they would simply talk until the bedroom candle burned out. Shortly after they were married, as she brushed her hair before bed, he asked her shyly, "May I do that?" and she smiled at him sidelong:

"You heard the minister, Mr. Lincoln, and you know the laws of the state. It is now *your* hair, and you may do with it what you wish."

But the sweetness of those times didn't make up for her constant dread of being found out in her lie, and the galling humiliation of being truly poor. And Mary quickly found how right Elizabeth had been. From the first she hated poverty—hated it and all that it meant.

During that freezing winter, when she would struggle through the mud of Adams Street on foot and see Elizabeth pass in Ninian's carriage, she didn't even have the consolation of sympathy. She knew what Springfield gossip was. She had proclaimed, again and again, to every one of her friends that Lincoln's poverty and debt mattered nothing to her. She knew how Elizabeth would look down her nose, if word reached her that Mary did not actually like to be cold in their little boardinghouse room (Mrs. Beck charged extra to keep fires burning during the day), or disliked the appalling sameness of Mrs. Beck's uninspired cooking. She could almost hear Elizabeth say it: *You have no one to blame but yourself.*

To be poor was to be branded wrong in the eyes of the entire town.

When, in years past, Mary had pictured herself as married, she had always assumed she would have a home—perhaps not as elegant as that of Elizabeth and Ninian, but at least a place of comfort, like that of Bessie and Simeon Francis. A place in which to be "at home" when friends came calling, a place where she could give dinners and put up preserves.

But even with the little money from her mother's will that came to her on her marriage, Lincoln insisted that they had not the money for a house. So they remained at the Globe, where the noisy talk of the men in the common-room, the clang of the stagecoach bell, and the arguments of the Bledsoes next door kept Mary awake far into the nights.

What Lincoln had imagined marriage would be like, he did not say. Sometimes she wondered if he had ever pictured himself as being married at all. Or had he, she wondered, simply assumed that he would continue his bachelor existence of boardinghouses and courtrooms, arguing politics and swapping yarns with his male friends?

Whatever he'd been expecting—or not expecting—Mary found that Frances had been right in observing that at thirty-four, Lincoln was deeply set in his ways. She tried to remember this, when he'd stay out late at the law office, or the State-House library, or wherever it was he stayed until long after dark, leaving her to sit at the boardinghouse dinner-table with two dozen teamsters, laborers, clerks, and transients alone. Harriet Bledsoe and her six-year-old daughter Sophie were often the only other females at the table, and though some of the men were careful about their language, others weren't, and what Mary didn't learn about disgusting table-manners in that first winter could have been written on the back of a very small visiting-card.

Mary's resentment took the form of fits of rage; Lincoln's, of silence and absence, from which he'd return to apologies, embraces, and long sweet nights of lovemaking and talk. During the day when he was gone Mary would sometimes go calling on Julia or Bessie or Merce Conkling, but she found herself embarrassed, for they were now wealthier than she. They generally asked her to stay to luncheon or dinner ("Darling, everyone in town has heard about Mrs. Beck's cooking!") but she dreaded the thought that she was being looked upon as a cadger.

When she stayed at the Globe, she ran the risk of the equally idle Harriet Bledsoe knocking at her door, "for a chat." Harriet's husband was a new-fledged lawyer, just entering partnership with Lincoln's English friend Ed Baker, but Harriet herself read little but the Bible and had no conversation beyond her family back in New England and how much she missed the way things were done there. Mary's delight in dresses and jewelry she regarded as sinful; her newspaper-reading and interest in the question of Federal lands she considered simply bizarre. She'd bring Sophie to do her samplers in quiet beside the little fire—Mary sometimes suspected that Harriet was in the habit of letting the fire go out there, and brought her daughter over to Mary's room only so that the two of them could stay warm—at the Lincolns' extra expense.

"It seems like I saw more of you before we were married than I do now," Mary complained late one evening, when Lincoln finally came up the narrow wooden stair. It didn't help that she'd heard his voice downstairs in the common-room for a good hour already, talking to drunken Professor Kittridge and Billy Herndon. His high laughter was distinctive, and could pierce walls. She had waited, trying to read by the single candle that was all they could afford that week, with growing impatience—did the man have no concept of time?

Apparently not, because Lincoln looked mildly startled and said, "I'm only making hay while the sun shines, Molly. Mr. Logan's taken on more cases, with the Supreme Court sitting. . . ."

"Surely you can work on those while the sun is *actually shining,* and not leave me waiting for you alone in this wretched room in the dark!"

His face clouded in the candlelit gloom. "It's the work I do that will get us *out* of this room. . . ."

"*If* you do it! *If* you do it, and don't spend your days the way you've spent the past hour and a half, sitting around with those idlers downstairs while I waited up here!"

"Molly, I'm sorry. . . ."

"You've said you're sorry and you always end up doing the same thing! Sitting around in the common-room with every drover and law-clerk and pettifogger in town . . . !"

"A man is entitled to his friends, I guess," retorted Lincoln, "as you're entitled to running about all day with yours."

At that Mary lost her temper completely and lunged at him, hands striking out blindly. He caught her by the wrists and held her off with the same brutal, easy strength that five years before he'd used to hold off Professor Kittridge, while she screamed at him, words that she later could not even remember, words of reproach and fury that she wasn't even sure were directed at him. She didn't know who it was, at whom she wanted to scream, *You are always gone, always! You always leave me alone!*

He finally shouted at her, in anger of which she hadn't thought him capable, "Any man would leave you alone if he could!" and thrust her down onto the bed. Then he strode from the room, shutting the door behind him. Mary staggered to her feet and yanked the door open again, screamed after him,

"Get out of here! Get out!"

She slammed the door, then slammed it again. Then she stumbled to the bed, fell on her knees beside it, and barely had time to pull the chamber pot out from underneath before she began to vomit, her body spasming agonizingly in her stays. For a long time after that she simply lay on the floor beside the bed, sobbing and too exhausted to get up, her head throbbing and the room spinning around her.

They had quarreled before, but not like this. She had read in his anger the bitterness of his frustration at being tied down, as his father had tied him. *He didn't even need to know I lied, to turn against me,* she thought in despair. *He was afraid to marry me, afraid of my temper, and now he hates me. . . .*

She vomited again and sweat poured down her face, down her aching body. . . .

What is wrong with me?

And she thought, *What I told him was true.*

It wasn't a lie after all.

I really am going to have a child.

Lincoln was out nearly all night. Mary lay awake, waiting—listening to the voices downstairs. She thought she heard his laughter before she fell asleep. He must have come up sometime after midnight, with such silent animal stealth that he did not wake her, for she was wakened in the darkness by his voice sobbing out, crying confused words of terror, and she felt his body struggling at her side.

"Mr. Lincoln," she whispered, reaching over to shake his bony shoulder, "Abraham . . ."

He came awake with a choked cry and she felt him half sit up, bone and sinew trembling like a whipped horse beneath the coarse linen of his nightshirt. He gasped, "I done my best!" It was the hopeless plea of one who knows that one's best is no extenuation in the face of Fate.

"I'm here," she said, touching his arm again. "I'm here."

With a sob he caught her to him, clinging tight with arms and legs, like a drowning child. "Don't leave me," he implored her, and Mary locked her arms around his ribs.

"Never, my love."

His big hands closed in the thick handfuls of her hair.

SHE PASSED A WRETCHED SPRING AND SUMMER. LINCOLN WAS GONE all of April, for the circuit courts, and again for nearly three weeks in May and June. Her pregnancy was a difficult one, an exhausting cycle of migraines, queasiness, and alternating rage and tears. She quarreled repeatedly with Mrs. Beck, with Mrs. Bledsoe, and whoever else came within her range, including both Frances and Elizabeth. When Julia

Jayne came to her, breathless with delight, with the news that she was going to marry Lyman Trumbull, Mary burst into hysterical sobs.

Mary tried to explain, but couldn't understand herself, the blind rages that came over her, in which she would say anything and which left her ill with remorse. How could she explain, she wondered, to women who'd never felt the need for bright intellectual sword fights how dreary the feminized world of babies and pregnancy could be? After her quarrel with Elizabeth—from whose house she stormed back to the Globe on foot—she sent a note to her sister apologizing, but received only the briefest and coldest reply.

Only Lincoln seemed to understand. After that single outburst of frustrated anger he seldom lost his temper with her again. He'd do his best to talk or joke her out of her rages, but if he could not, he would simply leave. Sometimes he wouldn't come back till the small hours of the morning, though she would hear his voice, and his distinctive laugh, downstairs. Mary hated him at such times—she would infinitely have preferred a good fight—but the hatred vanished with her anger, clearing up the way her headaches cleared up, and she would apologize in the morning.

"I don't mean what I say," she promised anxiously, one hot June morning as Lincoln brought her up coffee, toast, and a copy of the *Sangamo Journal* from the dining-room before leaving for his office. It was her one consolation in the final stages of pregnancy, that even Mrs. Beck wouldn't expect her to come downstairs in her condition, and made up trays for her. If Harriet Bledsoe brought them up, the coffee was usually tepid and mouth-wringingly strong—the dregs of the pot—but Lincoln could always talk the landlady into making fresh.

Lincoln, Mary was finding, could talk just about anybody into just about anything.

"In fact I don't . . . sometimes I don't *know* what I say," she added, a little uncertainly, for this was something she'd never admitted to anyone else. "It's as if someone else is talking—someone I don't know . . . someone I hate. And I think, *Who's saying those terrible things?* And it's me." She leaned forward on the pillows, looked up at him as he rolled down his shirtsleeves and fetched a sock from the over-jammed drawers of the hotly-contested bureau. "Do you understand?"

He smiled down at her. She'd heard him at dawn in the yard, splitting Mrs. Beck's kindling for her—looking down from the little dormer window at the end of the hall she'd seen him in his shirtsleeves, handling the ax as casually as she herself would wield a crochet-hook.

"I understand there's folks that are that way," he said. "There was this feller in New Salem, used to pick a fight with anybody, just about.

Seemed to be nuthin' he could do about it. He'd only do it once a month or every six weeks, and you could tell he was spoilin' for it because he'd come out of his house without his hat on, so everybody knew. And everybody would just figgur, 'Here comes old Benson without his hat on, better get out of the way,' same as we say, 'Oops, it's rainin', better take an umbrella.' " He leaned down and put his hand on her night-gowned side, where the child that would be Robert slept within her flesh, and kissed her on the top of her head. "He wasn't near as sweet as you, between-times."

Then he was off, to the County Court or the Whig Party meetings, and Mary had to get through another day alone. Another day of wondering how she could possibly look after a child—how she could have been so stupid as to get herself "in a fix," as they said, and throw away comfort and friends.

She rarely felt well enough to go out, and few visited her. When one is in no position to entertain, Mary discovered, one gradually ceases to be invited. The gay Coterie of her Springfield friends seemed to have forgotten her in the flurry of picnics and dances and parties leading up to Julia Jayne's wedding.

Bessie Francis came, brought her books and newspapers, and helped her sew for the baby. Her talk of Legislative scandal and Locofoco enormities was the breath of life. But Bessie had her own house to run and half of Simeon's newspaper as well. Mostly Mary was left alone, with her resentment, her headaches, her swollen feet, and the everlasting, oven-like summer heat.

Twice she dreamed of crouching in the darkness of the upstairs hall at the old house on Short Street, listening to baby Georgie crying in the dark. Praying she'd wake up before the bedroom door opened and the men carried her mother's body out, her long dark hair trailing down to the floor.

Robert was born on the first of August, in the upstairs room of the Globe Tavern, with a midwife, Mrs. Beck, Bessie Francis, and Harriet Bledsoe in attendance. The labor seemed endless, the airless room filled with flies. Bessie closed the curtains on the wide windows, to cut down the grilling sun-glare, but the dimness was terrifying, and Mary, alternating between the bed and the birthing-stool that the midwife set up, lost track of time. Pain wrenched her, but no child came; only memories of the smell of blood and her mother's moans—and afterwards that terrible silence.

"Mammy Sally?" she whispered, clinging to Bessie's hands. "Where is she? Why doesn't she come?"

Bessie whispered, "Hush, dear. Hush."

Once, as if through a long tunnel of pain, she heard Lincoln's voice, and Bessie's replying, "Not yet. It's just taking longer. You go back downstairs."

"Is that the truth?" he demanded, his voice hoarse with raw fear. Then immediately, "I'm sorry, Bessie. Just—my sister died this way. Died because they wouldn't send for a doctor." From the bed Mary saw him in the doorway, framed by the gloom of the hall, sweat on his face and his black hair hanging in his eyes. Past Bessie's shoulder his eyes met hers, and Mary held out her hands to him.

"This is no place for a man," insisted the midwife firmly. "They only get in the way—and faint, like as not, at the sight of a little blood."

But Mary whispered, "Please," and in the end the midwife let him in. He might have no parlor conversation, but he held Mary's hands, stroked her hair and her back with the wordless gentle strength of a man encouraging a mare in foal.

"You'll be fine," he told her, and though she'd heard his fear about his sister's death, there was something in his voice that kindled belief, and Mary knew, then, that she would be fine.

A few hours later Robert was born.

Chapter Twenty-five

Bellevue 1875

"Is it true?" Mary asked Dr. Patterson, when the next afternoon, sluggish and aching, she came down to the wide parlor of Bellevue Place. "Is it true that the medicine that I've been taking is mostly opium?"

"Oh, not *mostly,* Mrs. Lincoln." Dr. Patterson seated himself on the chair across from her, and peered intently at her face. "There's only a little, for medicinal purposes, and of course if it's properly taken there is no more harm in it than a sip of after-dinner sherry. How do you feel this morning? You look tired."

"I don't feel well," she said. "I . . . I slept badly, and I'm afraid my neuralgia is acting up again." Waking, she had hidden the empty medicine bottle. She guessed that John would get into serious trouble for leaving it in her room, though she was honest enough to know that she'd have done everything in her power—up to and including physical violence—to keep him from taking it away from her, when she needed it so. She had been appalled to find it empty. Surely, *surely* she hadn't drunk the whole thing? She couldn't remember. She should have saved it, hidden it for the next time they wouldn't give her as much as she needed. . . .

But she felt the woozy aftermath of one of her "spells" still on her, even as she'd had Gretchen help her dress, and the urgency of her instinct to hoard the medicine frightened her.

"Would you like a little medicine to get you through the morning?"

Mary met Patterson's gaze, trying to read his intent, but in his brown eyes she saw only kindness and concern. *He truly believes that giving me opium is the best way to deal with me.* Her glance passed over his shoulder, to Mrs. Hill and Mrs. Johnston, who sat placidly near the window, gazing out into the grounds.

And what does he give to them?

"No, thank you, sir," she said. "I think a little walk in the garden will do me good."

"Splendid!" Patterson rose, and helped her to her feet. "Most of our troubles today arise out of irritated nerves, Mrs. Lincoln. Modern cities are no place for those of delicate constitutions. No wonder so many women find themselves prey to hysteria and delusions. All the hurrying and scurrying, all the clocks and traffic and noise! The best mode of life is quiet, without overstimulation. You do very well to take just a little mild exercise. Would you like Gretchen or Amanda to accompany you, Mrs. Lincoln?"

"Thank you, no. I'd like to be by myself."

He frowned at that, and gave her a grave talk about not permitting herself to fall into morbid reflection, but in the end let her go. As she walked out into the graveled terrace above the roses she could see Mrs. Wheeler and Mrs. Edouard sitting quietly on a bench beneath an elm-tree. Talking commonplaces, neatly dressed, just as if Rosemary Wheeler hadn't spent all day yesterday howling and pounding on the walls of her room, and Heloise Edouard hadn't been subjected to a "water treatment" every day for a week.

The best mode of life is quiet. *And if you're not sufficiently quiet yourself,* thought Mary, *a little medicine will make you so.*

Does Robert know?

Of course he does.

The smell of roses and grass washed over her, sun-warmed and soporific. Though it was high spring, the breezes from the Fox River flickered through the trees, cooling the blessed shade. It would be good, thought Mary, to stay here, to never worry about things again. To not be afraid; to not be sad; to feel neither humiliation nor grief—not for long at a time, anyway. The perfect life.

The resting-place she had been seeking for ten years.

"Live and lie reclined
On the hills like Gods together, careless of mankind.
For they lie beside their nectar, and the bolts are hurled
Far below them in the valleys, and the clouds are lightly curled
Round their golden houses, girdled with the gleaming world . . ."

She remembered reading Tennyson's "Lotos-Eaters" to her husband in bed, and the far-off look in his gray eyes as he savored the words. This was during the second winter of their marriage, which they'd spent in that tiny rented cottage on Fourth Street. Sleety wind howling outside the windows, Robert soundly asleep in his cradle at the foot of their bed. The lamp burning with a warm amber radiance and Lincoln crowded up close beside her under the heap of quilts: he was perpetually cold, and the room was freezing. One of the good times.

She'd set the book down on the counterpane, and they'd talked about that dreamy land, and what each would do, if offered the chance to live there.

"Surely, surely, slumber is more sweet than toil," he'd repeated, one big hand ruffling the fur of Lady Jane, the cat that lay on his stomach. *"The shore / Than labor in the deep mid-ocean, wind and wave and oar; / Oh rest ye, brother mariners, we will not wander more."*

AFTER A TIME MARY TURNED AWAY, FROM THE SUNLIGHT AND THE roses of Bellevue's garden, and from that cherished memory, and circled the house, to the corner where the side door was hidden behind a little wall. That was where she'd seen John Wilamet, more than once, standing where he could look out over the garden without being observed from the house. As she walked, she was conscious of Amanda, watching her from the parlor windows.

She supposed that was something that one became used to. Part of the price one paid for this ultimate peace.

As she'd thought, John was standing near the side door.

He saw her come around the corner of the house and made to go in. She called out softly, "Please don't go, Mr. Wilamet," and quickened her step to reach him. "I wanted to tell you . . . I wanted to ask your forgiveness for my losing my temper at you yesterday. I . . ." She hesitated, looking up at him. His eyes were grave and tired behind his spectacles.

She realized he'd probably spent a worried night, wondering if she really would complain about him to Dr. Patterson, and what she would say. In her Washington days she'd seldom hesitated to complain of fancied ill-treatment. She swallowed, and drew a deep breath.

"When one . . . ceases to take opium . . . what else can one take, for pain? Because I do have genuine pain, you know. All my life I have suffered from migraines, and twelve years ago I was in a carriage accident, and suffered injury to my back and shoulder. I cannot . . ."

The memory of the empty medicine bottle returned to her, and her frantic thoughts of hiding medicine. The memory, too, of the medicine she *had* hidden, in every room she'd inhabited, all those years. She felt her face grow red. In a suffocated voice, she went on, "I cannot be without *some*thing."

She had turned her eyes down to her small chubby hands as she spoke. Now, looking up again, she saw respect and pity mingled in the young man's face.

"I'll see that you get only as much as you really need," he said. "But I promise you, you're going to think you need more. And I promise you, too, that you're going to feel terrible."

"It's so . . . *humiliating,*" said Mary quietly. "To realize . . . to realize what one has become. In spite of oneself, one's best intentions. And you're quite right," she added, more briskly, "Dr. Patterson doesn't see any reason at all why every woman in this place shouldn't be opiated twenty-four hours a day. We're only lunatics, after all. I'm sure he considers it more restful for everyone concerned."

"It is," said John, and Mary stared at him, startled, before breaking into laughter. He laughed, too.

Of course it was. That was why Robert had sent her here.

It felt good beyond belief to laugh again.

Then she sighed, feeling the anxiety that was already beginning to gnaw at her grow stronger, the restlessness in hands and feet that at times could drive her to distraction. Remembering the migraines, and the nightmares from which she fled. The memories of guilt and shame. In a muffled voice she said, "I think I will need a great deal of help."

"I promise you," said John, "that I will give you all the help that I can."

THE REST OF THE DAY MARY SPENT IN HER ROOM, AND MANY DAYS after that. In part this was because she feared that, if Dr. Patterson pressed medicine of some kind on her for her restlessness and pain, she would swallow it gladly—would swallow anything, to be rid of the physical malaise and the horrible darkness.

And in part, it was because the grief that descended upon her was so incapacitating that she thought she would die of it. It was as if everything that she had fled and pushed aside, all those years, was returning, distilled and fermented by time. Everything that she had been unable to cope with then assailed her now, a night ocean in which she was adrift in the most fragile of canoes.

Without John coming to see her—coming to talk, to hold her hands, to give her small amounts of watered laudanum to hold the worst of the physical symptoms at bay—she did not think she could have endured it.

He came every few hours, sometimes so stealthily that she was certain Dr. Patterson did not know of the frequency of his visits and would not have agreed with either his diagnosis or his treatment. Mostly he simply let her talk, about Lexington, about Springfield—about Mr. Lincoln, and Elizabeth, and Betsey, and her boys. About the horror of her loneliness; about her anger that had all her life run like fire and poison in her veins.

But there were always those times at night, when all the house slept and she could not. When the door was locked and, far off, she could hear one of the other patients screaming. Then all she could hold on to was the memory of that windy night over thirty years ago, and Lincoln turning his head on the pillow to look at her:

"Would you go live in the land of the lotos-eaters, if you could, Molly?"

And she'd replied with the prompt optimism of twenty-five, "Of course not! It sounds flat dull to me."

His eyes twinkled. "You wouldn't notice how dull it was, you'd be so happy all the time." His hand stopped scritching Lady Jane's chin and the cat wrapped her paws protestingly around his wrist. One of the first things Mary had learned about her husband was that he always had a cat or two around him, and could never pass up even the straggliest stray. She'd fretted about one of the four currently in residence scratching the baby, but Lincoln had said, "Oh, I don't think they will," and so far they hadn't.

"Would you go there?" she asked. "To live where you could do nothing, and be happy all the time?"

"It's tempting," he admitted. "When I get the hypo—hypochondria, Dr. Henry calls it—it seems to me that if what I feel could be evenly distributed through the whole human race, there wouldn't be a smiling face left on the surface of the planet. But it's happened to me enough now for me to know that I won't die of it, and it *will* end—it always does. And it seems to me that if we were all to sit, every man under his own vine and fig-tree, we wouldn't do much to help those that need helping. And you notice, those lotos-eaters don't seem to have families, or children, or friends. Would you trade a whole bouquet of lotos-blossoms for Bobby, even when he's squalling his head off? Or for either of your sisters, even when they're hell-bound to tell you about what a mistake you made maryin' me?"

Mary feigned deep thought. "Ask me the next time Bobby's squalling," she said.

DESPITE HIS INITIAL DISMAY AT FINDING HIMSELF A HUSBAND AND A father, Lincoln worked hard to do his best at both. He still had his periods of bitter resentment at the loss of his easygoing bachelor life—his silences, his absences, an occasional flash of volcanic temper. But he adapted—outwardly at least—more quickly than did Mary.

When Bobby was wailing, or Mary had to leave some all-too-rare gathering of her friends to go home and care for him, she reflected that Lincoln could adapt because there was less change for him to adapt *to.* It was far easier for a man than for a woman, to be somewhere else.

Perhaps because of the tensions in that cramped boardinghouse room, Robert was a fussy, nervous child. He had been born, moreover, with a left eye that turned sharply inward, a deformation that Mary was sometimes able to ignore, and sometimes—to her abiding shame—was not. From the first heart-sinking moment she saw her son's eye, she felt certain that God had punished her lie by giving her a defective child. Every time she picked him up, in spite of all her will to feel something different, she was overcome by shame.

The infant felt it—she *knew* he felt it—and he would scream and would not be comforted.

But Lincoln had only to lift his son in his huge hands for the baby's cries to cease. With his great physical strength, and his calmly logical intelligence, he had a vast store of tenderness, and an almost womanly patience. He likewise exerted himself in caring for Mary, whether during one of her migraines or merely in her simple day-to-day conflicts with the world; caring quietly and without fuss, as he had the night she gave birth to their son. He would have been, in fact, the perfect husband, if he'd been around most of the time.

But he wasn't.

A month after Bobby was born, Lincoln was back on the circuit, leaving Mary to deal with Mrs. Beck and those other inhabitants of the tavern who didn't appreciate an infant's screams at all hours of the night. Mary knew they were right, but her shame at agreeing with them made her defensive, and she found herself in a number of sharp quarrels even with Harriet Bledsoe, who took care of her following the birth.

Knowing Lincoln couldn't afford to live anywhere but at the Globe, when her father came to Springfield to see his new grandson she swallowed her pride and asked him for money to set up housekeeping. With what he sent—ten dollars every month thereafter—they were able to move to the cottage on Fourth Street. Elizabeth, to whom Mary was speaking again by that time, thanks to their father's patient negotiations, sent Eppy to help nurse Bobby and deal with the heavier indoor chores.

The smiling freedwoman had been given as a gift to Ninian's father when she was seven, long years ago. Eppy undertook to teach Mary—who was already accounted a good cook—the heavier skills of day-to-day plain cooking, things the daughter of Robert Todd—or the sister of Elizabeth Edwards—had always been able to relegate to a servant: gutting and boning, and how to judge the amount of kindling and the heat on various portions of the cottage's old-fashioned open hearth.

She initiated Mary, too, into the never-ending routines of keeping house—the first time that Mary truly learned the sheer physical drudgery of being a poor man's wife. As with the cooking, she had helped out in Elizabeth's house, and knew what had to be done. But she'd always known that if there were morning-calls to make, or a picnic to go to, someone else would sweep the floors, clean the lamp-chimneys, clear the ash from the kitchen hearth, keep the boiler topped up with hot water, make sure the family chamber pot was clean and scoured, air the beds to keep the ever-present bugs at bay, keep up the kitchen fire, and cut up newspapers to furnish the out-house. This didn't even include the labor of washdays, and the tedious exertions involved in making sure that Lincoln had a clean shirt and her own petticoats were fresh and starched.

Eppy came over to help on those days—it was appalling how much linen a six-month-old baby went through in a week—but Mary always felt behind. She was not lazy, and when she felt well enough was perfectly willing to work, but life did not stop when she had a headache.

Then Bobby would cry, and Mary would have to go attend to him, leaving the rugs half-beaten or the few lunch dishes still sitting in their pan of cooling water. . . .

And at night, aching with fatigue, she would be too weary to open a newspaper or to care whether President Tyler had been drummed out of the Whig Party, or why. She would lie alone and listen to the far-off thunder of the prairie storms, trembling with panic and head throbbing with the onset of migraine, tensely waiting for Bobby to start shrieking again just when things looked to be finally settling into silence. . . . And she would hate Abraham Lincoln.

That was her second secret, never whispered to a soul—for to whom could she whisper it without admitting that she'd been wrong?

She hated him as she had hated her father when he was not there. And the shame of feeling what she felt was worse a thousand times than that of the lie she had told. Then he would come home, and the sweet times would return.

At winter's end, Lincoln started negotiating with Reverend Dresser, who had performed their wedding. In May—between the Champaign Circuit Court, the Moultrie Circuit Court, and a convention of the Seventh Congressional District Whigs in Tremont—they moved into Dresser's four-room frame cottage on the corner of Eighth and Jackson Streets: Lincoln, Mary, Bobby, six cats, Bob the Horse, and Clarabelle Cow in the stable out back.

They played hide-and-seek, laughing, in the bare whitewashed rooms, and made love on the naked planks of the bedroom floor.

It wasn't Ashland—or even the House on the Hill—but it was theirs.

Then Lincoln disappeared on the circuit again, leaving Mary to her own devices.

He made arrangements with the neighbor, Mr. Gurney, to do the heavy work of cutting kindling, hauling water from the well, and milking Clarabelle. He also wrote to his cousin Dennis Hanks, back in Coles County, Illinois, offering to house Dennis's young daughter Hetty so that the girl could come to Springfield and go to school. Mary welcomed this arrangement, in part because she felt so completely unable to cope with the physical toil of running even a small house unaided, and in part remembering what little Lincoln had told her of his own childhood—the hopeless childhood of the uneducated dirt-farmer.

If it had been so for him—like the snaggle-haired silent backwoods children Mary remembered from the Lexington Court Days, ill-clothed and illiterate as puppies—how much worse was it for a girl, who couldn't even leave her family's house to strike out on her own?

Hetty Hanks stayed for nearly eighteen months. Looking back on that time later, Mary supposed that if she herself had been more used to the demands of housework, less terrified about money, less resentful of Lincoln's absences, she and Hetty might have gotten along better than they did. Indeed, as it was she often enjoyed the company of this tall, quiet, skinny girl—as if Hetty were the daughter Mary one day hoped to have.

Elizabeth—and particularly the sarcastic Ann, who was now living in the front bedroom of the House on the Hill and cutting her own swath through Springfield's bachelors—rolled their eyes when they encountered this gawky backwoods girl in Mary's kitchen, calling a chair a "cheer" or saying she had a "heap sight" of chores. But Mary made the girl welcome, bought dress-goods at Irwin's and helped her make new clothes, bought her the first pair of shoes she'd ever owned.

Those were on her better days. But Hetty's ideas of "working for her keep" were very different from Mary's, and, like her cousin, she had a tendency to disappear when she didn't like what was going on. She also had an appetite like an anaconda (though she never appeared to gain an ounce, reflected Mary ruefully). In weeks when Lincoln had been too forgiving about his fees—or simply hadn't bothered to collect them—the perpetual theft of eggs, bread, butter, and sausages made a difference, particularly when Hetty would share them with her friends.

Quarrels were inevitable, and grew worse, rather than better, over time. Every time Lincoln would take his young cousin's side ("She treats me like she thinks I'm one of her daddy's slaves!"), Mary felt furious and betrayed. To her mind Hetty was simply lazy, as Lincoln was lazy. When he was away riding the circuit, as he so often was, there was no one to arbitrate at all, and there were days of silent sulking and resentment that defeated her best efforts to understand.

On days when migraine closed in on her, when Hetty didn't return from school till nearly suppertime and the kitchen fires went out, when Bobby's crying sawed at her pounding head, she would picture Lincoln as she knew he must be, arguing in some sweltering little courtroom about defaulting debtors or absconding seducers or divorcing farm-couples. Pictured him later repairing to the local tavern to sit telling yarns and talking politics with judge, opposing counsel, most of the jury, and upon occasion the defendant as well, before everyone went upstairs to sleep three to a bed and eight to a room, snoring and scratching like bears in wintertime.

And she would hate him, and every man who lived that way and left their wives behind with their babies and their silent slow-moving second cousin from Indiana.

It was not an easy year for any of them. At times during that miserable year of 1845 Mary would wonder, with tired amazement, how she who had been the belle of Lexington and the toast of half the Illinois Legislature had ended up here in a four-room cabin in last year's faded dress, washing greasy dishes. When she realized in September that she was with child again, she wept.

That despair was a low point, for Hetty was fascinated by the prospect of a new baby, and did her work more cheerfully thereafter. By the time Lincoln came home, full of enthusiasm at the possibility that had been discussed among the Illinois Whigs to nominate him for Congress, Mary had regained her good humor, and had begun to make plans for the new child.

But her pregnancy was accompanied as the first had been by devastating migraines. And as she chased the now-mobile Bobby around the house and through the vegetable garden in the back and out into the mud-wallow of Jackson Street, she could not rid herself of the feeling of being overwhelmed by events which she ought to have been able to manage, but was not.

Chapter Twenty-six

Lincoln was of little help to her at this time. In addition to riding the judicial circuit—he'd acquired a buggy to do it in, now, instead of simply going horseback with a couple of saddlebags—he was working the political circuit, and was gone most of the fall. The choice of Whig candidates for Congress came down to himself and Edward Baker, the cheerful little Englishman who had been one of Lincoln's partners in defending the Trailor brothers for the murder of the not-quite-dead Archibald Fisher.

That summer Baker was a frequent guest at the gatherings of politicians that took place in the little parlor of the Eighth Street house.

It was at such times that Mary was happiest: the mistress of her own house, however small, and a hostess whose burnt-sugar cake and intelligent conversation were not soon forgotten. Listening to the talk of the growing Democratic strength, and the threats of war with Mexico, Mary felt that she'd finally earned her chair around the stove—even if the stove was her own hearth and not the one in Speed and Bell's store or the *Sangamo Journal* offices.

From such discussions, and reading the newspapers, she was often able to help Lincoln hone his speeches—he would reword his thoughts a dozen times, and practice them on her: "Are you sure you want your prose to sound that purple?" she sometimes asked. Or, "Do you think it will help your cause to make a personal attack that way?" She recalled the aborted duel with Jimmy Shields. By Lincoln's thoughtful expression, so did he.

In his political dealings, Lincoln never forgot a face or mislaid a name, always remembered something to ask about family or acquaintances. He never told a lie, but, lawyerlike, committed himself rarely to any specific course of action. He never made a promise that he was not prepared to keep.

Even when, in the discussions of rotating the Whig Congressional seat among the several leading Whig Party members, he facetiously offered to name his unborn child after Baker if Baker agreed to step aside in his favor, he surprised Mary by holding to that promise when Baker did, in fact, decline the nomination. "I thought you'd want to name your son after Joshua Speed," she said, that evening after their guests were gone and he was helping her and Hetty clear away the coffee-things and brush the tablecloths. "He is still your best friend, isn't he, even away in Kentucky?"

"He is, and I do," he replied. "No, you sit down," he added, as Mary started to follow him into the little kitchen, "you been on your feet all evening." Mary sat obediently, in the chair that Baker had occupied. She had worked hard to set a good table, knowing from her own upbringing how good hospitality invisibly smoothed the edges of politics. This was probably the last gathering at the house before she began to show her condition to the point that it would be improper for a lady to appear in public.

Vexing, she thought resignedly, but it couldn't be helped. Betsey's pushiness in joining the men's discussions while visibly pregnant had always annoyed her.

"A rose by any other name is going to smell just as sweet," he said, and put his arm around her shoulders. "If Baker steps aside and I name my boy Joshua, that'll tell the entire state, Lincoln doesn't keep his promises."

Mary glanced up at him with a sidelong grin. "And if Baker steps aside and I have a girl, what are you going to do then, Mr. Smart Politician?"

"Name her Edwina," said Lincoln promptly. "Or shoot myself."

After that evening, as Mary expected, there were no further political suppers, but she felt satisfied in a way she hadn't, approaching Bobby's birth. She had learned, at her father's knee and at Henry Clay's elbow, the difference between a small-time politician and one whom state leaders and legislators took seriously. Her instincts told her that when she had met Lincoln, for all his brilliance he had been perceived as a backwoodsman, not only by Ninian and Elizabeth, but even by his friends. A man doesn't tell a man, *Don't say "ain't got" and don't wipe your hands down your front after a meal.* He only thinks, *What a hick!* And passes on, to vote for a man who looks like he knows what he's doing.

Teaching Lincoln the finer points of table-manners was a little like teaching Bobby (or Hetty)—only Lincoln understood why he needed them. "No one," Mary had told him once, "is going to campaign on behalf of a man who eats with his hands. Not for Congress, anyway."

At least Bobby didn't have thirty-five years of eating with his hands to unlearn.

But after that evening, though he was in town for the county court session, Lincoln was seldom at home. He opened his own law firm as a senior partner that year, with, of all people, the chinless Billy Herndon, who had previously been a clerk in Speed's store. As migraines added to the fatigue of advanced pregnancy and the exhaustion of trying to keep up with a very stubborn and active two-year-old, Mary noticed that Lincoln spent more and more time at his law office, often working on late into the night. More often, she suspected, yarning with Billy—who worshipped him with an irritating possessiveness—or stopping by Irwin's store to talk politics around the stove. Of course the house was small, she thought resentfully. And of course he could have no peace there, for reading or for thought. . . . Did he think *she* had any peace? Or was able to settle down with a newspaper or a book?

On Christmas Day there was a final, resounding quarrel with Harriet—with Lincoln caught in the middle as usual—and the girl returned to Coles County. Mary and Harriet made up before her departure and both shed tears as Harriet and Lincoln got on the stage, but Mary felt, along with loneliness and disappointment, relief that she was gone.

Living with Lincoln was difficult enough without the complications of a growing young woman in the house.

Even when he was home, Lincoln frequently wasn't home. His self-absorption when his mind was abstracted with some thought was absolute. Mary could stand a foot away from him and say, "Bring in the kindling," and he wouldn't turn his head, would simply go on gazing into space. Piecing together tomorrow's arguments for Court, or assembling points for a speech to deliver in Petersburg next week. When she wasn't tired out from cooking and cleaning, and when her head didn't ache, Mary was in awe of the amount of information her husband could deal with solely in his head.

But half an hour later, when after three more requests the kindling box was still empty, she'd go over and give his hair a hard twist, and he'd look up at her in surprise, as if he'd just realized he *had* a wife, let alone a house, a kitchen, an old-fashioned hearth that was wretched to cook on (unlike Elizabeth's new, modern iron stove), a kindling box, and a son whom he was supposed to be watching and who was nowhere in sight with darkness falling. . . .

There were times when Mary wondered if marriage to Edwin Webb—

or the handsome Nate Bodley and the demands of running Indian Branch plantation with a staff of slaves—would not have been an easier way to live.

Then some night she'd be tangled back in her old nightmare, of hiding in the dark hallway of her father's old house on Short Street, of hearing baby Georgie crying in the terrible stillness. The smell of blood and sickness, lamplight falling suddenly through an opening door. Her heart would hammer and she'd fight to wake up, fight not to be there when they carried her mother out of the room and away down the pitch-black hall—*If I scream maybe I'll wake myself up. . . .*

But no scream would come, only whimpering moans that echoed those from that other room in her dream. . . .

Then big gentle hands would shake her, and she'd roll over and clutch at those hard arms, that iron chest, and he'd rock her like a child, singing some old mountain ballad under his breath until she slept.

EDDIE'S BIRTH PASSED ALMOST UNNOTICED IN THE DOUBLE INTENSITY of the Supreme Court sessions and the beginnings of a campaign for the Congressional Session of 1847, over a year hence. This time in addition to the midwife, Frances's husband, Dr. Wallace, attended, and both Frances and Elizabeth were there. (Ann was at a taffy-pull at Julia Jayne Trumbull's.) While Mary rested, panting, between bouts of pain, Elizabeth came in with a cup of hot tea for her, aproned and pink-faced from the heat of the hearth, a shirtsleeved Lincoln at her heels. In spite of her pain Mary had to smile, wondering how the two of them got along, sharing work in that tiny kitchen. Afterwards Lincoln came in, holding Bobby by the hand, a tubby little boy of two and a half with that revolting, inward-turning blue eye.

"There, you see?" Lincoln told the child softly. "Your mother's just fine. And now you got a little brother to play with."

Bobby only looked doubtful, and reaching over Mary's sheltering arm, gave the tiny red bundle a sharp poke—which resulted in a most gratifying yowl. Bobby looked startled, but pleased.

As soon as Mary was on her feet again, and not in the same room with Eddie's cradle and Bobby's little bed, Bobby repeated the experiment whenever he could, prodding his brother out of sound sleep for the pleasure of hearing the noise. Of course, by this time Lincoln was on the road again, meeting with the Whig leaders in Jacksonville. Mary tried reasoning with her elder son, but finally dealt with the situation by giving him a sharp slap the next time she was brought from the kitchen by

Eddie's wails. It solved the Bobby-poking-Eddie problem—Bobby never did it again and indeed quickly came to feel protective of his brother—but thereafter Bobby developed the habit of simply disappearing.

She would be sweeping the floor—an endless task, in a town that was perpetually either fogged with dust or drowned in mud—or peeling potatoes in the kitchen, then suddenly turn in panic, realizing she hadn't heard the scurry of his steps since . . . when? "Bobby's run away!" she would cry, and pelt through the kitchen door, looking around the vegetable garden, the laundry shed, Clarabelle's stable. Jackson Street was often filled with wagons and horses, coming and going to the new construction of houses, offices downtown, the new church on Third Street. The thought of that sturdy little boy running into the muddy road, being struck, being carried home dead by strangers, sent her rushing into the yard. "Bobby will die! Bobby will die!"

She couldn't explain this fear, not even to Lincoln, any more than she could explain why thunderstorms turned her weak and sobbing. When Lincoln was in town she'd send whichever hired girl was working for them that week flying down to the law offices to fetch him. When he wasn't, she'd run next door and enlist young Jimmy Gurney in the search, and send out the hired girl, too. She lived in dread that she would be too late. That strangers would come to her and tell her that her son was dead, through her neglect. The son with whom she was never quite comfortable, whose deformed eye filled her with the double guilt of both responsibility and revulsion.

Hetty's presence at least had given Mary the illusion that she had "help," though she suspected her covert conflict with the girl hadn't helped Bobby's wary secretiveness any. Hetty's departure put Mary in the same position as every other woman in town she knew with the exception of Elizabeth: Frances, Julia Trumbull, Bessie, Merce Conkling, and all the rest were in constant quest for Irish or Portuguese girls who were willing to work and could be trusted not to steal silverware or entertain their boyfriends on the premises the moment their mistress's back was turned.

Yes, slavery was wrong, Mary reflected. Cash Clay, and Mr. Garrison of *The Liberator,* and the other abolitionists were correct when they said that the ownership of slaves destroyed the souls of the masters and eroded society from top to bottom. . . .

But obviously neither Cash nor Mr. Garrison had ever tried to find someone willing to help with the cleaning for a price that wasn't extortionate.

It was all very well for Elizabeth to look down her nose and make remarks like, "Oh, you haven't yet begun your spring-cleaning?" in a voice that implied that anyone who hadn't finished spring-cleaning by mid-April was an irredeemable slattern. Elizabeth's husband was rich, Elizabeth had three house servants and a coachman, and Elizabeth wasn't laid up for three days at a time with migraines. At times Mary looked back on her days as a belle in Lexington, and on those gay excursions with Stephen Douglas and James Gillespie and little cock-a-hoop Jimmy Shields—looked back on herself, in her gowns of pink silk and rose-colored velvet ribbons—and wondered who that was that she was looking at, and what had become of that girl.

Wondered what had ever possessed her to marry a man who was poor and in debt.

Except that she could imagine living with no one else. On those rare occasions—*extremely* rare, that summer of 1846—that she *did* live with him, she reflected wryly, or have more of him than his name on the nameplate of the front door.

And then suddenly it was September, and Lincoln was striding through the brown leaves of the kitchen walk calling out, "Molly! Molly!" to bring her to the door in her apron. "We're elected! It's official! I'm junior Congressman for Illinois and we're going to Washington!"

Chapter Twenty-seven

To Mary's intense gratitude, the Congressional term to which Lincoln was elected wouldn't start until December of 1847. She couldn't imagine trying to travel with an infant and a boy of three. "Are you sure you want to come?" asked Lincoln, once Mary's first spate of triumph, plans, and delight had run itself down. The current hired girl, Bridget, had joined them in the kitchen, leaning on her broom and beaming in vicarious delight. Bobby sat on Lincoln's knee, Mary being in occupation of most of his lap.

"Are you ashamed to be seen with a wife in tow, Mr. *Congressman*?"

"One so pretty, and dressed so fine as you? Never." He kissed her, something that always made Mary blush, for she had seldom seen Ninian kiss Elizabeth or her father kiss Betsey. It was one of the things Elizabeth considered ill-bred about her gangly, unwanted brother-in-law. "But we'll be living in a boardinghouse. Most Congressmen do."

"And what of that?" asked Mary. And, seeing a world of remembrances about Mrs. Beck in the lift of his brows, she added, "Pish, I was just a girl then, and didn't know how to go on. I hope I've learned a little more about the world by this time." She tousled Bobby's blond hair and kissed him, and leaned up to kiss her husband's hollow cheek. "To be able to attend Washington parties, to mingle with the makers of our country's law and policies, I daresay I could be happy living in a tent."

"And that's one in the eye for Mrs. Edwards," added Bridget—which of course had been the first thing Mary had thought, though she hadn't said it.

It seemed like there was so much to do, in the next year! Winter and spring, and a blazing-hot summer that seemed never-ending . . . She went shopping at Irwin's with Julia Trumbull and tall Cousin Lizzie—now Lizzie Grimsley, where *did* the time go?—and the three of them spent happy weeks studying *Godey's* and sewing and furbishing up dresses that would be fit for Washington parties.

That spring of 1847 the newspapers were filled with the war with Mexico, whose bellicose President Santa Anna had begun arming the moment the Republic of Texas applied for inclusion in the United States. Fighting broke out in April across the whole northern segment of Mexico that Congress had been trying to acquire by negotiation for years. The United States claimed the Mexicans had crossed the border to attack. Torchlight rallies were held. Militia companies formed overnight and rushed toward the Rio Grande. Southern slaveholders and land speculators pricked their ears at the prospect of new cotton lands to replace the worn-out soil of Alabama and the Carolinas.

One minute it seemed like forever until the Lincolns' projected departure, and the next, they were packing to leave. Lincoln found a renter for the house, and spent all of one October day moving their furniture up into the northernmost of the little slant-roofed attic rooms while Bobby did his best to get underfoot on the narrow attic stair and kill them both.

Then they were all getting on the stagecoach, under gray autumn skies.

Despite the proud dome of the sandstone State House, Springfield looked very small across the golden swell of the prairie.

At Scott's Hotel in St. Louis they were met by Joshua Speed, plumper now with the first flecks of gray in his beard, but with the same cheerful sparkle in his eye. "What's this I hear about you naming *my* namesake after some pettifogging politico, Lincoln?" The two men embraced, and Mary shook hands with the sweet-faced, dark-haired lady introduced to her as Fanny Speed.

"Now, I won't have you raking poor Mr. Lincoln down," said Mrs. Speed. "Your husband is a brave man, Mrs. Lincoln. When Joshua was courting me, Mr. Lincoln pretended to be a Democrat, so that my father could lecture him on the evils of his party while Joshua spoke to me on the gallery. I doubt that even David did that for Jonathan in Bible times."

"David would have thought King Saul heaving spears at him was a good trade, after ten minutes with your pa," grinned Lincoln, and Mrs. Speed tapped him on the elbow with her fan.

"Oh, the little darling!" Mrs. Speed added, tiptoeing to look at Eddie, whom Lincoln was carrying on one hip. The boy was, at nineteen months, solemn and long-faced and worrisomely thin, and looked for all the world like a miniature version of Granny Parker, except for his gray Lincoln eyes. Bobby, with his round face and watchful blue gaze, cock-eyed as it was, was all Todd. And for that matter, thought Mary suddenly, panic clutching her, where was Bobby . . . ?

She caught him just before he got out the hotel door and into the street. The traffic and bustle in St. Louis made Springfield look like a country village. The town was a river port, and the jumping-off point for the trading caravans that crossed the prairies and the Great American Desert to the Spanish colonies around Santa Fe.

Now with the Army to be supplied and militia companies streaming south, St. Louis jostled with merchants, bullwhackers, boatmen, and traders, in spite of the hardship of winter travel. In the crowded hotel dining-room Mary could barely make herself heard above the din as she gossiped with Fanny Speed over mutual acquaintances and kin all over Kentucky and Virginia. As for Lincoln and Joshua, immersed in discussion of the war, it was as if neither of their wives existed.

For some years, Mary knew, the two men's friendship had cooled—because of Joshua's management of his mother's plantation, she guessed, which put him in the position of owning and working slaves.

For all that Lincoln upheld the law of the land that permitted slavery to exist, on a personal level he both hated and feared it. She felt a pang of jealousy, watching them together now. Seeing there a past that she could never share.

From St. Louis all six of them took the steamboat to Louisville, and from there the Lincolns proceeded on to Frankfort. It required the efforts of all four adults to keep Bobby from coming to some kind of grief on the boat. The four-year-old proved just as prone to wandering on a boat of two hundred feet by forty as he had with all of Springfield to choose from, and Mary lived in constant terror of seeing him pitch himself over the rail of the high hurricane deck into the deadly swift currents of the river. Just above Cairo Bobby did disappear, and while Mary and Fanny Speed searched frantically among the boxes, bales, and crates of New Orleans merchandise on the fore-part of the lowest deck, Lincoln walked to the back along the promenades that ran along the sides of the boat, where coffles of slaves were chained, to be sold in Louisville.

Mary came hurrying aft with the news that she hadn't found a trace of Bobby, she was certain he'd gone overboard, to find her husband sitting on a keg of nails, their errant son at his side, talking to one of the chained blacks: ". . . couldn't take my eyes off the boat engines, even when we was flatboatin' and these things was the enemy an' the invention of the Devil."

"They still is, sir," agreed the slave equably. "We crunched up a flatboat in the fog not ten miles below Vicksburg—why don't they never hang lights on them things? Fog was so thick the pilot couldn't see the river below him. . . ."

"Ain't that just like a pilot, to keep goin' in a blind fog?"

"You ever get crunched by a steamboat, Pa? Father," Bobby corrected himself hastily, seeing Mary approach.

"Lord, yes! I thought I'd drown, stayin' under till the paddle went by overhead. . . . Mother," Lincoln added, turning to her with a smile. "I found the rascal just where I thought he'd be."

"I just wanted to see the wheel," explained Bobby.

"You just wanted to get yourself killed leanin' over that rail, li'l Marse," corrected the slave. "*And* give your poor Ma a conniption-fit. He's fine, ma'am," he added. Bobby was covered head to foot with splashed-up river-water and the soot of engine-smuts. "We kept him back off the rail."

Mary gave each member of the coffle a quarter, for whatever small luxuries might be bought in Louisville, and hauled the protesting Bobby back to the higher decks of the boat. But that night when she waked in their little stateroom in the rear of the boiler-deck to hear the muffled singing of the men chained below, she saw the moonlight shining in her husband's open, listening eyes.

THEY WERE FIVE DAYS TRAVELING UP THE OHIO RIVER TO CARROLLTON, where the Kentucky River flowed down from the dense green forest, and another day and a half going up the Kentucky to Frankfort. From the upper deck of the smaller stern-wheeler on that leg of the journey Mary watched the scenery transform itself into home: the gray rock of the banks becoming more jagged and fantastic, the trees darker and thicker than any Illinois woodland. This was The Dark and Bloody Ground, the violent land that the Todds had settled in the wake of the Revolution in the East, worlds distant from the clean-smelling grassy spaces of Illinois.

The land where she had flirted, and danced, and been hailed as the belle of Lexington.

The land she had fled eight years ago.

The land in which she still walked, most nights when she dreamed.

When Pendleton opened the door to the front hall of the big house on Main Street, Mary cried, "Pendleton!" and clasped the servant's hands, almost before she saw the rest of the family. She led Lincoln in, keeping a firm grip on Bobby's hand while Lincoln carried Eddie: The boys had nearly exhausted themselves running up and down the corridor of the train from Frankfort, and Mary, her head aching from the jolting and the noise of the train, was a little surprised that several of the passengers hadn't hurled the two obstreperous children out the windows.

And there they all were on the stairs, looking so changed. Her father coming down toward her, grayer even than he'd been four years ago. "Molly," he smiled, and bent gravely to take Bobby's hand. Mary braced herself, cringing, lest her father or Betsey draw back from Bobby's defective eye, but Robert Todd said only, "Well, now, sir, you've grown some since last I saw you. And got yourself a brother now, too, I see."

The others on the stair pushed forward. Betsey, so thin she looked like she'd break if she tripped, but still with that chill precise air: "What filthy things trains are, to be sure." She scrubbed at a smut of soot on Eddie's cheek, as if Mary should have been able to keep the boys clean on a conveyance that belched coal-smoke and churned dust with every yard it traveled.

Granny Parker, blue eyes still sharp though her hair was snow-white now: "Let the girl be, Betsey! You should have seen yourself last month when you came home on that thing from Frankfort!" Good heavens, was that stocky man with the receding hairline and red-veined nose *Levi*? And the shifty-eyed sallow malcontent beside him—smelling faintly of corn liquor—that couldn't be *George*?

They had to be, because the two young gentlemen of the ages Levi and George *ought* to have been—*were* still, in Mary's recollections—must be Sam and David, David, whose crying had nearly driven Mary crazy that horrible cholera summer of 1833. And the others were children she felt she'd never seen before: a coolly self-possessed girl of fifteen (not *Margaret,* surely!), a plump, vivacious girl a few years younger *(Mattie?!?),* a beautiful blond boy of nine who couldn't be anyone but Alec, Alec who'd been born while Mary was teaching at Ward's. . . .

"So you're my little sister?" asked Lincoln, looking down at the pretty golden-haired eleven-year-old who was the only one of them to come to him instead of hanging back.

Mary cried in delight, "Emilie!" and seized the little girl's hand as Lincoln picked Emilie up as easily as he'd have picked up a kitten, and gave her a kiss on the cheek. For years now Emilie had written to Mary—not often, but frequently and candidly enough to let Mary know that the child she'd taught her first samplers still remembered her with love.

The littler ones—Alec, Elodie, and Katherine—crowded around their tall new relative, clamoring to be picked up also and making the acquaintance of their rather overwhelmed small cousins, both of whom clung to their father's legs.

"That's going to be your President of the United States, is it?" Granny Parker folded her skinny arms beneath her shawl and stood beside Mary.

"He is," agreed Mary, a little defensively: Granny Parker had always been unpredictable.

"Not much to look at."

"On the contrary," replied Mary, "I think he's grand."

A door opened behind her. Warmth and familiar scents from the big kitchen enveloped Mary in a tide of the past so powerful that it brought tears. Even before she turned she knew who stood there, her smiling face more wrinkled than ever but her eyes as wise. "Mammy Sally!" Mary cried, and flung herself into the old woman's arms. "Oh, Mammy, I missed you! I missed you all!"

"Well, don't weep about it, child," said Granny Parker, both amusement and impatience in her voice.

"No need to weep, child," added Mammy Sally kindly. "You're home now."

YEARS BEFORE, WHEN LINCOLN HAD RETREATED IN EXHAUSTION TO Speed's plantation, Mary had pictured him in her home state, seeing close up for himself the conditions that so many Yankees fulminated against in self-righteous ignorance. In the three weeks they spent in the big front bedroom of her father's house that November, she had a chance at last to act as her husband's guide as he further explored the world of the South, this ambiguous double world of white and black.

Being Lincoln, of course, he would talk to anyone and listen to anyone, without the slightest sign that he even noticed whether they were white or black, male or female—he and Cash Clay were the only men she'd met in her life who had ever suggested that women as well as men ought to have the vote. She noticed that the house servants, who could be the sternest critics of "white trash" manners and pretensions, accepted him immediately—and not, she was sure, because he was a Congressman. They'd seen Congressmen before, and thought fairly poorly of some. One morning, waking early, Mary came downstairs and found Lincoln having breakfast in the kitchen, talking to Mammy Sally and Nelson. "You watch out for that one, sir," she heard Nelson's voice as she crossed the shadowy dining-room. "She get mad at Mammy Sally once, she put salt in her coffee—"

"Now, I can't *believe* my Molly would do a terrible thing like *that*!"

gasped Lincoln, in such exaggerated shock that both servants burst into the good-humored laughter of those—Mary reflected with wry affection—who knew her all too well.

Then she heard Mammy Sally say, more quietly, "She look happy, Mr. Lincoln. I always knew she'd need a strong man to take care of her; you're good for her."

Elizabeth might have her doubts about what was due a Todd of Lexington, Mary reflected, her heart warmed by joy. But it was wise Mammy Sally who saw more clearly what Mary needed.

It was good to know.

On the second night of their stay, Robert Todd held a party in their honor, and in the midst of flirting with old beaux (Nate Bodley had grown sadly stout and reeked of liquor) and catching up news from girlfriends (Mary Wickliffe had married the brother of Meg's husband, of all things), Mary glanced across the crowded room and saw Lincoln as usual in a knot of men, local politicians—listening with the air of a man who seeks to comprehend the place in which he finds himself.

He always listened more than he talked. She had heard him described as a jokester and a talker, but in fact he was more an observer. It was only that, when he talked, people remembered the tales and jests he told. She was intensely sorry Cash Clay was away—Cash had been among the first to volunteer, Meg Wickliffe (now Preston) had written her, and had gone with General Zachary Taylor to invade Mexico. He had been captured in January; "We just heard he's been freed," Meg now informed her breathlessly. Even without Cash's assistance, Lincoln and Robert Todd were engrossed in conversation hours after Betsey had gone yawning up to bed and the servants had cleaned up after the rest of the long-departed guests.

"I don't think you'll find a man in this country who'd argue that with Oregon settling up, we shouldn't have the rest of New Mexico as well," her father said. "Mexico can't hold the harbors of the California coast, for instance, and if we don't take them you know it's only a matter of time before Russia does."

After making sure Bobby and Eddie were tucked up in the trundle-bed in the corner of the guest-room, Mary crept silently back downstairs. The rear parlor was dim but for a single lamp, its amber light outlining her father's blunt features, Lincoln's long nose and jaw.

"I s'pose the average highway robber would make the same point about the contents of your pockets—that he's got a better use for 'em, an' if he don't take 'em the feller down the road will." Movement in the darker shadows of the front parlor, where Pendleton was loading the last of the abandoned punch-cups onto a tray. "But that aside, my question is: will the slaveholders in Congress try to make New Mexico into slave territories? An' then admit 'em as slave states?"

Robert Todd laughed. "We haven't even taken those places yet, Lincoln, and here you're worrying about what their status as *states* will be?"

"I am, yes. That's a flaw of my character. Because as long as slavery has a legal foothold in this country, it's gonna be like an alligator in your bathtub: every time you turn around, there the blame thing is. And the more I look at the problem, the more it seems to me that it's beyond my ability to come up with *any* solution that won't cause more damage than it remedies."

Mary slipped through the door, and settled on the black horsehair sofa, content to simply listen to the talk of these men that she loved. Lincoln was smiling, cracking his knuckles, his eyes very bright. In the forgiving warmth of the lamplight, her father's face shed years; it was as she remembered it from her childhood.

She was, again, her father's favored child, listening to the talk as she'd always listened, included in that circle of friendship and power.

If there was greater contentment in life, she couldn't imagine what it might be.

THREE WEEKS OF PEACE. THREE WEEKS OF BEING ABLE TO LIE ABED with her husband in the mornings, secure in the knowledge that Mammy Sally was looking after Eddie and that Bobby had been absorbed into the flock of younger Todds, playing noisily in the wide garden with Alec and Elodie, Mattie and Kitty. On the first day of their stay, she and Betsey had taken the children aside and ordered them on pain of death not to tease Bobby about his eye, and so far the threat seemed to be working. And even if Bobby ran away, Jane or Judy would find him, not she.

Three weeks of Chaney's marvelous cooking, of rides in the countryside with her father and her husband. Of watching Lincoln's utter bliss in browsing through her father's library and reading everything he could lay hands on, far into the night. Three weeks of listening avidly to talk of the war and the upcoming session of Congress. Of seeing the men of the district encounter Lincoln without the memory of the uncertain hick who had first come to Springfield in buckskin britches shrunken halfway up his shins. Here, he was, instead, a man who had been elected by the voters of his state.

A man who would one day have power.

And their approval shone back onto her, who had seen this man's promise and married him, when nearly everyone else had turned away.

They went to hear Henry Clay speak, first in the courtroom, then in the town's brick market-house while the rain pounded down outside. Thin and brittle-looking now, his hands stiff with arthritis, Clay blazed with his old intelligent fire as he denounced the war with Mexico, which had already claimed the life of his oldest son. Afterwards Mary fulfilled one of her deepest dreams by introducing Lincoln to Clay, beside the rough temporary stage that had been erected at one end of the hall. She flashed her old flirtatious smile at the statesman who had been like a second father to her: "And I promise you, Mr. Clay, he will be President one day. Though I'm still waiting for that invitation to *your* inaugural ball."

Clay laughed, "It may happen yet, Miss," and shook one long finger at her. His ginger hair was snowy now and this made his eyes seem pale as the wintry sky. He glanced across at Lincoln—there was not much difference in their heights. "I'm running for the Senate again this year—drives me crazy to see others making a mess of things up there."

"I'll try to keep things from going all to hell, sir," promised Lincoln, a little shyly, "till you arrive."

They took the stage to Winchester, Virginia, and from there the railroad to Washington City. They arrived late—the December night was bitterly cold and drizzly, the streets outside the depot swamps that rivaled the worst of Springfield's hog-wallows. Lincoln found porters for their four trunks, free blacks or, Mary guessed, slaves "working out" and bringing their owner part of whatever they earned for the day. As they walked down the dark street toward Brown's Hotel—recommended by Lincoln's legal colleague Judge David Davis—Lincoln gazed around him, as if sniffing the air in this, the largest city he'd seen in his life.

Far down one street the dark bulk of the Capitol loomed, lost in a maze of scaffolding. Brick houses stood among trees, some of them mellowed and elegant with years. Here and there newer buildings, taller and bulkier, shouldered each other in modern blocks. The streets were extravagantly wide, and gold lights shone in a few windows, blurred with mist.

"So this is Washington," said Lincoln softly. He carried both his sons, Eddie on his arm as easily as if the boy had been a parcel and Bobby on his shoulders, looking out wearily over his tall black hat. Both boys, after darting crazily up and down the aisle of the train car all day as was their wont, had suddenly crumpled with exhaustion, and Eddie was snoring softly in the circle of his father's arm.

Mary drew a deep breath, trembling all over with excitement, anticipation, triumph. "Yes," she said, and her breath misted amber in the lights of the hotel as they approached its doors. "We're finally here."

Chapter Twenty-eight

Washington 1848

They remained one night in Brown's Hotel. The following morning Lincoln went out and found them quarters at Mrs. Ann Spriggs's boardinghouse on First Street, just down the hill behind the Capitol, where both Cousin John Stuart and E. D. Baker had stayed.

And Mary remembered all over again why—and how much—she loathed boardinghouses.

She had met already Mr. Washburne, Lincoln's plump and pink-faced Congressional colleague from Galena. The first night at Mrs. Spriggs's, Mary could see the two men making a great effort to keep the conversation general at the common-table, before vanishing into the parlor to the more serious endeavor of hashing through what kind of political horse-trading each had had to do to get here, and comparing impressions of just how the land lay in the House of Representatives. Mary longed to join them as she'd joined Lincoln and her father but here there was no Mammy Sally to make sure Eddie was tucked up warmly and to keep Bobby in his bed. By the time overexcited Bobby was finally asleep—he wanted both a song and a story—it was quite late. Slipping down the stairs, she found Lincoln and Washburne still beside the parlor stove, with an elderly, ascetic gentleman who'd been introduced to her as Mr. Joshua Giddings—a name she recognized instantly from the abolitionist papers that Cash still sent her.

"You'll find within a day how it is in this city, sir," Giddings was saying, jabbing a skinny finger at Lincoln. "Slave pens within a hundred yards of the Capitol Building. Aside from the sheer disgrace of it, the traffic in Washington City represents a constant danger to every free man and woman of color who tries to go about their business here, for the slave-dealers do not scruple to kidnap men and women of color on these very streets, drug them with opium, and sell them south to Virginia and Georgia under the name of law. How anyone can hesitate to take a stand against such doings . . ."

"It all depends on what kind of stand you're fixing to take," replied Lincoln in his slow, light tenor. "I'll do my utmost to bring about whatever change in the law will mitigate the situation, but I can no more oppose the Constitution as it stands, than I can plead in court that my client should be permitted to break a law which I—or he—privately considers to be unjust."

Giddings's pale eyes glinted behind their spectacles, but for a moment he said nothing. Cash, Mary reflected, would have been on his feet and shouting.

"If nothing else," put in Washburne, "God help any man hopeful of being elected to anything who says the blacks should be freed. There are few enough jobs for white men in Illinois. You speak to any laborer on the street in Galena and he'll tell you there are too many Portuguese and Irish and Italians coming in as it is. And that in Illinois, let alone what it's like in New York. It wasn't more than a dozen years ago they were burning colored orphanages and beating free Negroes to death in the streets. They won't stand for it, sir—and a man who doesn't get elected loses his chance to do any good whatsoever for anyone."

"That reminds me of a story," remarked Lincoln, stretching out his long legs to the stove—which barely provided enough heat to encompass the three sitting near it, much less Mary in the darkness of the stairway arch, with her shawl of pink cashmere wrapped around her shoulders. "You ever hear about the Continental soldier after the Battle of Bunker Hill who scouted on ahead to the British lines? First he put on a red coat, so the British wouldn't shoot him, then he picked up a British musket, because it would shoot straighter than his own old piece, then he put on a pair of British boots so the British pickets wouldn't identify him by his old moccasins, and then a powdered wig for the same reason. . . . He ended up looking so much like a redcoat that he was finally obliged to shoot himself."

Listening to him—watching his exaggerated gestures, the way his face changed to the voice of this character or that, Mary had to smile. They would love him here in Washington. This was his place . . . and she would be here at his side.

From upstairs, Bobby's voice called out fretfully, "Mama!"

Elsewhere in the house another voice replied, "Can't someone shut that brat up?"

Mary tore herself away from the glow of the fire, the three men's faces, the laughter and the talk, and hastily ascended the stair to her child.

She got Bobby settled—the room was freezing cold, and Eddie was coughing—and then got into her nightdress behind the dressing-screen, brushed out her hair, and got into bed. She fell asleep still waiting for Lincoln to come upstairs.

LIVING IN WASHINGTON, EVEN IN A BOARDINGHOUSE, HAD ITS COMpensations. Their first Friday evening in the city, Lincoln bribed Mrs. Spriggs to look after Bobby and Eddie, and took Mary to a "drawing room" at the White House. The hack let them off some distance down Pennsylvania Avenue due to the crush of other hacks and polished town-carriages, all vying for position in the black sea of mud. Picking their way along the edge of the unpaved street through the raw mists under the shelter of her husband's big black umbrella ("And you *will* fold that thing up before we reach the steps.... What a sight we'll present to the President, coming up like a . . . a greengrocer and his wife . . . !") Mary saw its windows glowing through the darkness, and it seemed to her that her heart turned over in her breast.

The Executive Mansion.

We will live there. I know it.

Her grip tightened hard on the bony arm linked through hers and wild excitement shivered through her like a flame. In a way, she knew they were coming home.

"Whatever you say, Mother," Lincoln agreed, in his most placid bumpkin style, but she could tell that he was as excited as she. She glanced up at his face, saw the light in his eyes as he looked at the place, the hard eager folds at the corners of his mouth. He didn't speak much of his ambition—he didn't speak much, Mary knew, of anything that mattered deeply to him. But since they'd left Springfield under its gray prairie skies five weeks ago, she'd felt in his flesh and his bones and his breath the vibration of his exultation.

He was, at last, coming into the place where he could make some difference in the lives of men. Where he could use his abilities, and be recognized and heard.

And she was by his side, his partner before all the world.

She made a mental note to write Elizabeth all about "our evening at the Executive Mansion," "our conversation with Mr. Polk," even if Polk *was* a Democrat. That should teach her to call Mary's husband a hayseed.

The doors of the mansion stood open. Voices poured out, into the raw winter air.

The gathering, Mary realized with a pang of disappointment as they stepped into the lamp-lit hall, was not a select one. It seemed like everyone in Washington was there.

An endless reception line snaked from the front hall into the Red Parlor, where the diminutive President Polk and his dark-eyed imperious wife stood side by side, shaking hands with all comers. Mr. Polk smiled and nodded and spoke a few words of greeting to "our new colleague from Illinois," but passed on immediately to greet Mr. Washburne, in line behind them. Mrs. Polk expressed a polite hope that Mary was finding residence in the capital comfortable, while coolly evaluating: dress, hair, deportment, toilette, and jewelry in a single all-appraising glance. Ticked off on a mental list, filed for future reference, and the page turned. Mary wasn't even given a chance to say whether she was finding residence in the capital comfortable or not.

I'd like to see you try to put yourself together for a reception in a boardinghouse room with two boys underfoot and no one but your husband to lace you up, Mary reflected, looking back at the elegant, slim woman already exchanging affectionate greetings with a quiet-voiced Virginia lady, scion of one of the local planter families and—from the way everyone greeted her—hostess to half the government. Mary picked out the expensive sheen of Italian silk in the golden warmth of the chandelier, fabric unobtainable in Springfield, the tulle light as summer breath. The swagged double skirts made her own tiers of ruffles appear slightly dowdy and very much a remnant of last year or the year before.

Little Stephen Douglas came over to her, dandified as ever, and joked about old times. But he was drawn quickly back into the circles of the Southern Senators, whose wives all seemed to be cousins or schoolmates and have little interest in Illinois Whigs. Douglas had recently married the daughter of a North Carolina planter, and seemed to have been taken in as a brother by every slaveholding Democrat in Washington, she reflected.

Mary recognized at once who the influential hostesses were, around whom the men clustered; the talk was of politics, but politics as a closed club of who knew whom. The wives of the powerful Southern Senators, or of local bankers and landholders, had their townhouses here and could entertain such birds-of-passage as mere members of the House. They greeted Mary politely—when they noticed her at all—but spoke of politics in the context of long-standing personal alliances: who could be trusted and who could not, who was on the outside and who was on the in, and who was discreetly keeping a mistress in some little rented cottage in Alexandria across the river.

Five years of marriage had accustomed Mary—almost—to no longer being the belle of the ball, but in Springfield at least she was more and more being recognized as Abraham Lincoln's wife.

Here, no one seemed particularly to care what things were like in Illinois, or who her husband was.

Behind her, as she moved away from one chatty group in quest of her husband—who as the tallest man in the room wasn't hard to locate—Mary heard someone say, "Oh, she's from the West." She didn't know whether it was she whom the speaker meant or not.

In the chilly winter months that followed, she attended five more Friday "drawing rooms" at the Executive Mansion, and seldom spoke to a soul.

Dutifully, the day the family moved to Mrs. Spriggs's, Mary had gone to a printer's and had new cards made up: *Mrs. Abraham Lincoln*—gilt-embossed in the most handsome Germanic black-letter—and smaller ones with just *Abraham Lincoln.* She'd been warned by Cousin John's wife that Washington printers cost three times what Simeon Francis charged and were slow to boot, but there was no getting around them. With the most furious haggling Mary could do, she could not get any of the three printers she consulted to lower the cost by so much as ten cents on the hundred, and the dent they made in her monthly budget was painfully large.

When first Mary had married him, Lincoln had joked about morning-calls and visiting-cards as the flub-dubs of the rich, on par with President Van Buren's notorious golden spoons. He'd changed his tune, however, when Mary had started making morning-calls on the wives of those politicians who came to Springfield for the Legislative sessions, and the dinner parties she'd organized had smoothed the rough edges of acquaintanceship among men of power from different parts of the state.

He himself had commented—a little to his surprise—on how much difference it made, trying to talk a man into throwing his support to a road-building appropriation, whether you talked to him in a tavern's common-room or in your own comfortable parlor after a good dinner.

Leaving cards was another way of cementing ties—of marking yourself as someone to be taken seriously by people of wealth and power.

Thus, by the time they reached Washington, Lincoln was willing to do what all Congressmen did: spend an hour or two between breakfast and the start of the Congressional sessions at eleven, two or three days a week, in attendance on Mary as she made the rounds of the homes of Washington's elite, leaving a trail of cards in their wake. Two of Mr. Lincoln's (for Senator Useful and Mrs. Useful) and one of Mary's (for Mrs. Useful—God forbid even the implication that a lady should call upon a man!), with a corner folded down to indicate that Mrs. Lincoln had called in person. Mary deeply enjoyed this ritual, whether Lincoln accompanied her or not. If the hostess was "at home," it was a way of learning news and rumor, of getting the name Lincoln known, and of talking—if she was lucky—of something other than servants and children for fifteen minutes.

Many Congressmen made calls on Sundays as well, but Lincoln drew the line at that, preferring to take the boys down to the steamboat wharves on the Potomac while Mary attended St. John's Episcopal Church, or to take his sons to look at the ragged mudholes and heaped masonry where contractors were preparing to rear a granite obelisk as a monument to George Washington. As the winter advanced these outings became less possible. Washington was cold with a damp, clinging chill entirely foreign to the hard iciness of the Illinois prairies or Lexington's upland frosts. Few streets in the city were paved, and like Springfield's humbler ways, the vast and splendidly named avenues of the capital turned from aisles of dust to rivers of mud.

Now and then Mary would be invited to the handsome house Stephen Douglas and his wife had taken—with his father-in-law's money, she suspected—but few Washington ladies returned Mary's calls. It didn't seem to matter that so many of them—including the doyenne of them all, Dolley Madison—were connected in one way or another with the Parker/Todd clan. Mary left cards on everyone, from Mrs. Polk and the wife of the wealthy banker William Corcoran, on down to the Congressional wives in other boardinghouses. Although she knew that, naturally, one's own scope for entertaining in a boardinghouse parlor was sorely limited, she expected invitations, or at least the courtesy of returned visits.

But everyone seemed to be so busy laying cards on the tables of the great themselves that there was no time to so much as drive by—or send a servant by—Mrs. Spriggs's. Those who did visit, she gathered almost at once, were the wives of junior Congressmen, like herself, without power or influence. It would not do to be seen too often with them.

And indeed, with Bobby and Eddie to look after most days—and most nights, while Lincoln was out in informal after-session colloquies with his male colleagues in eating-houses, taverns, or other boardinghouse "messes," as they were called—Mary would have been hard-pressed to respond to an invitation from even Dolley Madison herself. She'd see the famous hostesses drive by in their carriages on the icy streets, or in the Capitol rotunda on those days when she could bribe Ann Spriggs to look after the boys so she could sit in the galleries with the most astonishing mélange of Congressional wives, town prostitutes, men-about-town, and what appeared to be half the colored population of Washington, slave and free, to listen to the debates. Like every other Congressional wife, Mary learned to recognize Dolley Madison, in her stylish gowns with her paint and powder fighting a rear-guard action against the years, or her queenly young niece Adele Cutts; heard the admiring whispers as people pointed out the Blair ladies—almost royalty in Maryland—or William Corcoran's wife Hannah.

Mary thoroughly enjoyed those rare visits to the Capitol itself, its lobby like a fair with journalists, spectators, *nymphes du pavé,* hawkers of hothouse oranges, and candidates for government pensions or government jobs lying in wait to ambush their Congressman the moment he put his head out the Chamber door. The United States had captured Mexico City, and terms of peace were being wrangled. Already abolitionists like Giddings were beginning to protest that slavery must not be allowed to spread. The atmosphere of power, influence, and rumor that tingled in the hallways and galleries filled her with delight and a sense of her own importance, and she reveled in writing knowingly to Elizabeth and Ninian, *They're all saying at the Capitol . . .*

One of her greatest triumphs was the evening when Lincoln brought John Quincy Adams to dinner at Mrs. Spriggs's "mess." The former President's wife entertained very little in the house they rented on Thirteenth Street. "Mrs. Adams has never quite gotten over the degradation of my choice to serve in Congress, after being President of the land," remarked the old gentleman, with a dry glance at Lincoln under his shelving white brow. "I cannot induce her to see that no man is degraded by seeking service in the government of his country—or in being elected as selectman of his hometown, for that matter."

Adams spoke in French to Mary, of Paris in the days before the Revolution, and of London and St. Petersburg in its wake. Mary recalled what Henry Clay had told her father about cold, stuffy, reserved, and charmless Adams: that he was like a very dry wine, that repels on first mouthful and only reveals its complexity to the thoughtful.

She made sure to include the quote in her next letter.

But most days, she spent alone in the boardinghouse room. The damp climate went to Eddie's chest, and the little boy was often sickly. Bobby, forced to remain indoors, was bored, noisy, and sullen, and Mrs. Spriggs referred to both boys as "those tiresome apes." By Bobby's increasing silence, and unwillingness to play with the few local boys he encountered, Mary suspected that the local boys called him "Cock-Eye," as a few of the Springfield children had.

Lincoln, as usual, was preoccupied. Though Mary tried to be patient, a good partner to him in his responsibilities, his habitual abstraction sparked stormy quarrels: "I'm here to do a job of work, not play dry-nurse to the boys!" he flared at her on one sleety Sunday afternoon, and Mary shot back with, "We'd be able to get Mrs. Spriggs to watch them more often if you'd act like a father and teach them a little discipline!" Lincoln went silent after that, and when Mary flung herself down on the bed in tears, he took Bobby and Eddie for a walk despite the cold. They came back just before dark, all three spattered from head to foot with mud and full of tales of seeing the war-hero Jefferson Davis's new town-carriage, driving up to the White House gates.

Just before Christmas, Lincoln enraged most of Congress with a resolution condemning the war with Mexico. Despite this, he confided to Mary, on one of the rare evenings that they spent reading in the warm downstairs parlor while the boys played at the hearth, he was being asked by other Whigs in Congress to support General Zachary Taylor for President.

"It'll mean a speaking tour, after Congress shuts up shop in summer," he told her, a little apologetically. "Through New England, they say. Now, you can go on back to Springfield with the boys, Molly—I'm sure Washburne would be glad to escort you. . . ."

"If you *dare* to go traveling through New England without me, Mr. Lincoln," said Mary, lowering her novel and regarding him with sparkling eyes, "after *martyring* myself in this *dreadful* city all winter, you'll come home to find the doors locked against you and all your clothes in a cardboard box on the porch."

Mrs. Penfold, the literal-minded and evangelistic lady who had the room next to theirs upstairs, looked up from her knitting, shocked. But Lincoln merely smiled and said, with deep satisfaction, "That's my Molly."

Eddie had a cold again after Christmas, and another in February. Lincoln would come in from sessions of the House, or meetings of the Postal Committee—to which he'd been appointed apparently on the grounds of his year's stint as postmaster of the village of New Salem—and would sit up nights with the feverish toddler so that Mary could get some sleep. Waking from a troubled doze—she seldom actually slept even when she could—Mary would see him, sitting on the edge of the trundle-bed with Eddie in his arms, rocking him and making the little rusty growls under his breath that passed, for him, for a lullaby:

"The water is wide, I cannot get o'er,
Nor do I have the wings to fly;
Give me a boat that can carry two,
And we both shall cross, my love and I. . . ."

Had the mother he never spoke of sung him that, she wondered, when he was ill?

He was up all the night, and gone in the morning to meet with Giddings on a bill to outlaw slavery within the District of Columbia, after going down to the yard in his shirtsleeves to chop kindling to keep Mrs. Spriggs sweet. So there passed another day, Mary reflected despairingly, that they couldn't make calls or set up connections, and that she would have no adult conversation and no time to read. How anyone could get along with Mrs. Spriggs she couldn't imagine, but Lincoln would do errands for her, and sweet-talk her out of extra firewood—for which she usually charged five cents extra, or ten if she had to cut kindling—or boiling water for poultices and tisanes.

Eddie was on the mend—and getting fractious—when Lincoln came in, late that night, with the news that John Quincy Adams had been felled by a stroke during the session, and was not expected to live. "The poor old gentleman!" exclaimed Mary, sitting on the edge of the trundlebed. She'd been trying to get Eddie to eat, but the child refused the porridge that was the only thing Mrs. Spriggs would cook for him.

"He had an apoplexy not long ago, and got over it," replied Lincoln, sitting on the other side of Eddie on the bed, with his big hands hanging down between his knees. Bobby, who'd been underfoot all day, ran to his father's side to be taken up on his knee. Lincoln hugged him, but absently, his mind still on the picture of that white-haired old gentleman toppling from his chair to the House floor, gasping for air. "They carried him into the Speaker's room, and there set up a cot; Douglas went to fetch a doctor. They say he'll stay there till he's fit to be moved, but myself, I think he'll end his life in the place where he spent it, in the house of service to his country. And that is not such a bad way to end," he added softly.

He sat silent, gazing into the shadows. How long he might have remained thus, oblivious to his surroundings, Mary didn't know; she'd seen him lost in one of his moods for hours. But Eddie seized the porridge-spoon from the bowl and whacked his father on the arm with it, leaving a long sticky smear. And, when Lincoln made no response whatsoever, piped up, "Papa, *nasty*!"

Mary pulled the spoon from him. Lincoln, roused from his thoughts, looked down at the boy, amusement flickering in his eyes: "I should say it is nasty, son—and you're bound to spread the nasty around until something gets done about it, aren't you?"

As Mary darted to the water-pitcher for a rag—her husband was perfectly capable of going into a debate on the floor of Congress with a smear of oatmeal on his sleeve—Bobby said, "Mama told Mrs. Spriggs to make Eddie a blancmange and Mrs. Spriggs said—"

"Never mind what Mrs. Spriggs said," snapped Mary, tears constricting her throat again at the recollection of that bitter exchange of personalities. Her head throbbed, with hunger as much as anything else, for in the wake of the quarrel with the landlady she'd been too exhausted to go down to supper. "Mr. Lincoln, that woman is impossible! I merely asked—a most *reasonable* request—that she make a blancmange for Eddie, or permit me the use of her kitchen to make one myself. In a most *disagreeable* voice she informed me that she could not spare the maid to help me or to go out for the almonds, of which she *said* she had none in the house. Though how any woman calling herself a cook could be without them . . ." She caught herself up, hearing her voice growing shrill. In the calmest tone she could, she added firmly, "We simply must find another place to live."

The light of the single lamp on the bedside table picked out the surge of jaw-muscle as Lincoln clenched his teeth. Resentment flooded through her, anger not only at the petty and avaricious Mrs. Spriggs, but the chewed-over details of the quarrel that she'd been waiting until nearly nine o'clock at night to present to her errant husband.

At the same time she saw his eyes travel to her—her hair loosened from its pins with Eddie's fitful pulling, the oatmeal-stains on her own dress and shawl, her eyes swollen with tears and headache. And past her, to the room, stuffy, cluttered with the boys' things, smelling faintly of mildew and chamber pots, two cans of the morning's wash-water still not carried out and a huge damp stain on the rug where a third can had been overturned by Bobby. The day had been rainy and Bobby bored to distraction and petulant. Mrs. Spriggs and her own husband were the only adults she had spoken to since she'd waked that morning.

Her eyes burned again and she felt the frustration blossom in her, turning her sick.

Very gently—in the same voice he'd used to try to conciliate her in her quarrels with his cousin Hetty Hanks—Lincoln said, "Mother, the town is as full as it can hold, with Congress sitting. But I will look—"

"When?" retorted Mary bitterly. "If you can't even come in time for supper, or to spend an hour with your wife and sons . . ." That hurt him—she saw him flinch like a man struck by an arrow—and felt a hateful spurt of pleasure that she'd at least gotten his attention. Did he realize that while he was politicking with his men friends and laying plans to elect Zachary Taylor President—on God knew what platform, since the

man had no opinions on anything that Mary had ever read!—his wife was cooped up in a twelve-by-fourteen room with two squalling children, waiting for a word with him?

"I'm going back to Lexington," she said.

Lincoln's eyes widened, stricken, but he said nothing.

"I'm writing to my father tomorrow. You don't care if I'm here or not. . . ."

"Now, Molly, that's not true. . . ."

"It is," she cried hotly, "and you know it is." The instant guilt in his face confirmed her words. Fury blinded her: at the mighty Washington hostesses who had no time for the wife of a mere Representative, at Mrs. Spriggs, at the other boarders who slurped soup through their whiskers or cleaned their ears at the table, at the poverty that would not let them take a house here, that for five years now had reduced her to the status of servant and drudge. Bobby and Eddie, as they generally did during their parents' quarrels, clung closer to Lincoln, making themselves invisible in his bony shadow. "You don't care. . . ."

Trembling, she forced herself to stop, hiccoughed, and stood, fumbling at her skirt pocket for a handkerchief.

Lincoln silently fished a clean one from his coat. Years of living with Mary had taught him to carry them.

She took it from him, feeling surprisingly, suddenly clear in her mind and heart. The poison-pain of resentment dissolved; it was as if a door had opened, in her life and in her mind. The words, flung at him in anger, showed themselves now as an actual solution, and it was as if an iron bond broke from around her chest.

She stretched out her hand, and laid it alongside his face. He looked up at her in surprise that was almost comical.

"You know Eddie hasn't been well," she said softly. "And poor Bobby is bored frantic, aren't you, darling?"

Bobby regarded her for a moment with those wide-set, mismatched blue eyes, gauging what she wanted him to say. Then he nodded.

Lincoln shut his eyes, drew in his breath, and let it out. Then he looked up at her again, and took her hand between both of his. "You truly don't mind?"

"Of course I mind." She bent to kiss his cheek. "And I'll be *miserable* away from you." The old rallying tone crept back into her voice. "But we're both miserable now. And if we're *both* going to be miserable anyway—and you had *better* be miserable while I'm away, Mr. Lincoln, and I'll write to Mr. Douglas and ask him to make *sure* that you are—at least the boys will have their cousins to play with, and be happy, and you'll get some work done without worrying about us."

Not, she reflected, that Lincoln *did* worry about her, much, when he got talking politics with his cronies. . . .

But he knew he ought to.

"You are a saint and a martyr, Mother." He scootched Eddie aside, to make room for Mary on his knee.

The following morning at breakfast he managed to sweet-talk Mrs. Spriggs into making a blancmange, too.

Chapter Twenty-nine

Inquiring among his Congressional colleagues, Lincoln found a respectable middle-aged clerk named Shepperton and his wife who were traveling to St. Louis via Lexington on family matters early in March. Mr. Shepperton proved a reliable and helpful traveling companion: laughing indulgently at the boys' obstreperousness, keeping track of the trunks and parcels, tipping porters just the right amount, and deferring to Mary in all things. Mrs. Shepperton adored him and agreed with everything he said, stupid or not, in the course of the four-day journey. She herself talked of nothing but the superiority of honey and onions for the cure of every ailment from catarrh to leprosy and Mary suspected that if, like Petruchio, he'd called the sun the moon his wife would have cheered his perception, but the couple were otherwise perfectly friendly and pleasant to travel with.

Mary was simply ecstatic at the thought of going home.

Chaney, Pendleton, Nelson, and Mammy Sally crowded to embrace her. Margaret and Mattie, Elodie and Emilie, gay young Alec and little Kitty, and the rest engulfed Bobby and Eddie into their midst; even Robert Todd beamed and Granny Parker gave her dry acerbic smile, and Betsey tried to look as if she were pleased.

It was heaven to be in Lexington again.

This was a true homecoming, she felt, coming home to be again someone she hadn't been in a long, long time. The woman she had become in Illinois—the poor man's wife who washed her own dishes and cowered from thunderstorms—faded almost at once. She felt, if not like a belle again, at least like her former self.

It was wonderful simply not to have a headache, something she'd suffered every spring she'd been on the Illinois prairies. It was wonderful beyond words not to be tied to the drudgery of housework. Wonderful, too, to know that the work of the house was being done by reliable slaves who knew their business instead of facing the daily exasperation of trying to explain to a sulky fourteen-year-old Irish girl that the *entire* floor of the parlor needed to be swept, and not just the parts that showed.

With Mammy Sally to look after the boys, Mary found her irritation at them dissolved. She could laugh and play with them, sympathize with Bobby's attempts to adopt a kitten (Betsey's hatred of the whole cat tribe remained as virulent as ever), and take the time to read to them each night. As Betsey's notion of bedtime didn't include bedside candles, much less chapters of *Young King Arthur,* the group around the trundle-bed in the guest-room rapidly expanded to include Kitty, Emilie, Elodie, and Alec—Betsey sniffed and clicked her tongue, but said only, "Well, just one chapter, and no talking afterwards." Sometimes, when he was home, Mary's father tiptoed in to listen, too.

With the improvement of the railway to Frankfort, Robert Todd was home most weekends, and that spring of 1848 was the most Mary had seen of him in her life. In the long mellow twilights, while the children dashed madly about the wooded lawns behind the house and down to the spring, she would sit with him on the gallery overlooking the garden, and talk of the upcoming election, and Lincoln's plans, and how to revive the flagging Whig Party in the face of the Democrats' war-time triumphs. He listened attentively to her descriptions of Washington, and spoke to her of his worries and doubts concerning the vexing issue of slavery: "The abolitionists are going to drive this whole country straight to perdition, with their disregard of facts as they are. Yes, slavery is wrong, but it exists! And there's no way you're going to keep it out of the territories. You can't just legislate it away, poof—and devil take the hindmost!"

Sometimes Betsey would join them, and Mary was surprised at her own ability to get along with her stepmother, now that she was no longer the unwanted stepdaughter who refused to marry the first man who would take her off Betsey's hands. They even laughed together about the Spider Incident, though Betsey never spoke of why Mary had been angry with her—Mary pretended she no longer recalled. That was all past and done now, and Mary was married to a Congressman, a fact, she knew, that made her father enormously proud.

Granny Parker and Emilie joined them too, those soft twilights when the air was filled with the smoke of lemongrass smudges. On several occasions Cash Clay and Mary Jane came, their own rowdy band of offspring joining the shrill-voiced shadows chasing back and forth among the trees beside the stream. Cash was full of descriptions of Mexico, and of its capital where he'd been held prisoner, like a gaudily-colored island in the midst of its shining lakes. He had, for over a year before the war, operated an abolitionist newspaper in Lexington, the *True American*. At the mention of it, Robert Todd rolled his eyes. "You could have got yourself killed," he said.

"If I had," declared Cash, leaning forward impetuously and jabbing with his finger, "I would have taken many a man of the forces of iniquity with me." With his black hair tumbled over his forehead, he seemed unchanged from the wild young man who'd smuggled Mary copies of *The Liberator* at Madame Mentelle's. He had, he related, reinforced with sheet iron the doors and windows of the *True American,* and installed two brass cannon on the table inside, pointed straight at the doors. To this he'd added a trapdoor on the roof and enough kegs of powder to blow the building and any invaders thereof sky-high. Mary knew this was not braggadocio: Abolitionist editors had been murdered before this, and their presses and offices wrecked.

"And I'd have stood them all off, and died in the attempt," he vowed, with a vast sweep of his arm, "had I not come down with typhoid fever, and had them destroy the newspaper in my absence."

Mary laughed, but in the dim light of the lamps and mosquito-smudges, she saw Mary Jane's glance slip sideways to her husband, and in her eyes there was no mirth. Cash was still, thought Mary, as ready to get himself killed without a moment's thought about how his wife and children might fare without him, as he had been when he'd accepted the challenge to a duel on his wedding-eve fifteen years before.

More than at Cash's egoism, Mary was shocked at the violence with which the town's slaveholding faction had greeted Cash's newspaper. She had always feared the readiness to lash out, that lay beneath the surface of Southern manhood; their willingness to destroy life or property to make a point. She remembered too vividly Elliot Presby's blood in the ditch of Main Street, and the men who had seen nothing wrong with beating him only for speaking to them of the evil of holding slaves. According to her father, the Legislature was increasingly in the hands of slaveholders, men whose factories, plantations, livery-stables, or sawmills simply could not operate without unpaid black labor.

Spring waxed warm. Eddie's sickliness abated, and with Chaney's cooking, his thinness filled out to pink-cheeked strength. Though he tired easily, her younger son was treated as a sort of beloved mascot by the other children, and showed signs of Bobby's—and his father's—insatiable curiosity, coupled with a sweet-tempered friendliness to all. Bobby—whose speech had picked up a marked Kentucky flatness of vowel—had become his protector and minor god.

Mary and Emilie spent long evenings together, talking of dresses, of hope, of love. Letters came from Washington, letters that brought pangs of loneliness, of longing to lie curled up against that long leathery bag of bones—longing for those endless wonderful talks after the candle was blown out, longing for the touch of those big callused hands, for the passionate strength of his kisses.

Pangs of guilt, too, because she hadn't the slightest wish to rejoin him in that horrible boardinghouse in that miasmic swamp of a town. Lincoln wrote of missing her terribly, wrote with longing of his sons, but she knew that if she were with him he'd go on his absentminded way just as before, not coming back from the House of Representatives until midnight, not giving a thought (or much of one) to what she might be doing all day, cooped up in a boardinghouse room with two small boys.

And sometimes—though she would never have admitted it to a soul—it was so good simply to have the luxury to sleep alone!

So she visited Mary and Margaret Wickliffe—now both Preston—quietly, because her father was engaged in a lawsuit with their father over a cousin's inheritance that was being claimed by Old Duke—and walked out to Rose Hill to have coffee and to laugh with Madame Mentelle. Her old teacher was as sharp as ever, and full of cynical comments about the new phenomenon that was sweeping the East, the conviction that certain persons could communicate with the dead.

"A mishmash of Swedenborgianism and plain superstition," Madame pronounced, and refused to participate when the Wickliffe-Preston girls, Mary, Emilie, and Madame's daughter Maria—who had married one of Henry Clay's sons—organized a séance in the Rose Hill parlor to communicate with the spirit of George Washington. The result was inconclusive, but everyone giggled and had a spookily good time.

There was talk, in May, of Mary going back to Washington, but in the end she decided to remain in Lexington. In June she went with the rest of the family out to Buena Vista, the summer home that was Betsey's property, riding and walking in the countryside as if she were a girl again.

Congress would adjourn in August—by which time, Mary knew, Washington City would be a sweating hellhole smothered in dust. Nevertheless, when Lincoln wrote her that he was going with the other Whig leaders to New England to campaign for Zachary Taylor, Mary wrote back immediately that she would come. *I look forward to being with you again on the sixth of September,* Lincoln wrote back; and in spite of the tediousness of the promised journey, and the wet heat of the capital, Mary found herself looking forward to it, too.

In the end, her desire to see him again got the better of her. She packed up her sons and her trunks (it was astounding how much extra clothing and luggage she'd accumulated over the summer!) in late July, and prepared to take the stage to Winchester, in company with her brother Levi, and thence to the weary succession of trains that would eventually lead to Washington.

In the dark before dawn on the day of departure old Nelson hitched up the carriage, and everyone except Betsey came down to breakfast by lamplight. Emilie hugged Mary: "I'll write to you, I promise. Tell Mr. Lincoln I hope his side wins." Robert Todd rode with Mary, Levi, Bobby, and Eddie to the Courthouse square, where the stage took its departure:

"You take care of those grandsons of mine, you hear?" he smiled, and gave Mary a hearty bear hug as he helped her from the carriage. In the dove-gray quiet of the square the six brown horses shook their heads, snuffing at the air and jangling their harness; black hostlers from the stage company held the leaders' heads. Two slaves belonging to Mr. Blanchard the silversmith sloshed buckets of water on the plank sidewalk and the smell of wet wood was strong in the warm air. "And tell that husband of yours not to let another seven years go by, before he brings you back here to call."

He pressed a roll of banknotes into her hand, and leaned down to kiss her. Then Levi helped her into the stage—Eddie and Bobby were already poking each other and the other passengers were starting to get annoyed—and the grooms sprang away from the horses' heads. Mary leaned out the window and twisted around backward, all her bonnet-ribbons fluttering, to get a last glimpse of her father's tall, burly shape, waving to her before he turned back to where Nelson waited with the carriage.

It was her last sight of him alive.

Chapter Thirty

Although her experience with Washington City had been ghastly—and Mrs. Spriggs hadn't improved any in the August weeks that Mary and the boys were back in the upstairs room on First Street—she hugely enjoyed the speaking tour. The weather was hot, but at least the boys weren't cooped up in hotel-rooms by rain and cold. She would take them sightseeing in the daytime in whatever town they were in—Boston, New Bedford, the small New England hamlets where the Yankee half of the Revolution was born.

In Illinois, and later in Washington, she'd grown accustomed to Yankee accents and the self-righteous pushiness of Yankee so-called manners, enough to deal with having them around her all the time, though at the hotels she sorely missed the gentle reliability of her father's slaves. The money her father had given her made it possible for her to pay hotel maids to look after the boys in the evenings, so that she could hear her husband speak.

Growing up where Henry Clay set the oratorical standard, she knew Lincoln was good. Even had he been a stranger to her, she reflected, looking up at that beanpole figure in the tin-sconced glow of the oil-lamps around the halls at Cambridge, at New Bedford, at Dorchester and Boston, he would have held her enrapt. And looking at the faces around her, listening to the murmur and stillness of the crowd that was like the sough of wind through leaves, she knew she wasn't the only one who thought so. She bought all the local newspapers and scanned them while riding the trains or the stages: *"He spoke in a clear and cool, and very eloquent manner... carrying the audience with him...."* *"The Hon. Abraham Lincoln made a speech, which for aptness of illustration, solidity of argument, and genuine eloquence, is hard to beat."* *"It was a glorious meeting."* In the hotel-rooms she clipped the articles out. Bobby and Eddie helped her file them away in envelopes, to be later pasted in albums.

In those few evenings when he was not meeting with local Whigs, or speaking, Lincoln and Mary would talk late into the nights, analyzing what those newspapers had said, as if through those journals they listened to the voices of the people in the crowd. As he had in Springfield, he practiced his speeches on her, and listened thoughtfully to her advice.

Mary had always loved the thrill and confusion of Presidential campaigns. Now she felt as she had during Harrison's campaign, when she and Merce and Julia had all gone to rallies wearing their banners, and cheered for hard cider and log cabins.

"Yes, and the cryin' shame of it is that we're runnin' another man on log cabins an' hard cider, or the next thing to it," sighed Lincoln, as the train chuffed out of New Bedford for Boston. Bobby and Eddie crowded to the window, craning to get a last sight of the harbor with its forest of masts: prairie boys, both had been riveted by their first glimpse of the open ocean the previous day. Despite his speech, and his meetings with the local Whig bosses, Lincoln had made the time to go with Mary and the boys to the harbor, where the whaling-ships stood in port, and the streets were filled with strange dark-faced men with savage tattoos. It had been, Mary realized, Lincoln's own first look at the sea—and hers as well.

"As good a man as Old Zack is," Lincoln went on, stretching his neck to look through the window for a final glimpse, "he doesn't stand for anything, much. People all over the country know his name and will vote for him, which they wouldn't for someone like Mr. Seward." He named the aristocratic former New York governor, who would share the platform with him at a huge mass meeting a week hence in Boston. "And Seward is by far the abler man. *He's* the one we should be electing." He drew about him the vast skirts of the brown linen duster he wore, against the smuts and fluffs of soot that floated through the car.

"And if the committee had nominated Seward instead of Taylor, he could make his own speeches, and not have me and the other local worthies do it for him. But you ask Mr. Gurley next door to us, or the Reverend Dresser or any of our neighbors in Springfield who William Seward is, and they won't know, nor any reason why they should elect him over Lewis Cass, who fought the British for the freedom of our nation back in 1812...."

"I'm still sorry," said Mary softly, "that the committee didn't stand behind Mr. Clay. He would outshine a dozen of Seward and Taylor put together." Past the window, the sea vanished behind the ghostly line of dunes. Then the train swayed, swinging westward, and that long gray shining promise vanished from view.

Lincoln sighed again, and settled back into his seat. "I too," he said. "Clay is a man I'd make speeches for gladly—not that I grudge a word of what I say for Old Zack. But Clay's made enemies. Too many people only remember that fool accusation of selling out his supporters in trade to be made Secretary of State. And he's old," he added quietly. "Seventy-one, older even than Cass."

Mary nodded. She recalled having a fight with one of her schoolmates at Ward's over who was handsomer, Andrew Jackson or Henry Clay . . . or Mary's father.

In her heart she knew Clay would not run again for the Presidency that he had so deserved.

"Taylor at least is hale and healthy," said Lincoln, and she thought she caught a trace of the same sadness in his voice. "He can be trusted to live out his term and put men of caution and principle in places where they can do some good."

"Yourself included." Mary squeezed his hand.

She saw the echo of her pride—and her hope—glint briefly in his eyes, but he only shook his head.

"But it is a chore," he added with a comical grimace, "coming up with reasons to vote for the man besides the fact that he'll appoint men who *do* know what they're doing. I certainly wouldn't vote for a man on those grounds alone, no matter what a great soldier he was. For that matter, *I* was a great soldier, too. I looked courageously behind every bush in northern Illinois for Black Hawk and his braves—who hid from me, knowin' how ferocious a fighter I was, so I never saw hide nor hair of 'em—not to mention sheddin' my blood to a thousand mosquitoes. . . ."

Mary clasped her hands over her heart in a burlesque of passion. "What woman could resist a Hector, a Hercules, a warrior such as you?"

Bobby and Eddie poked each other and giggled as their parents embraced and kissed, and the starchy Boston couple in the next seat tried to pretend they hadn't seen such shocking goings-on.

Lincoln made his final speech in Boston—clear and lucid arguments as to why votes for the Free-Soil splinter groups and so-called Conscience Whigs were in reality votes for the Democrats—and then they were en route for the home they had left nearly a year before. In Buffalo they booked a cabin on the steamer *Globe,* bound for the bustling little lumber-town of Chicago over the succession of canals and waterways that crossed the peninsula of Michigan. But before it steamed out into Lake Erie, the little ship took the occasion, to Mary's joy, to go upriver to Niagara Falls.

The sight of the water, pouring down endlessly, torrents of it, curtains of it, a world of vapor and rainbows, silenced even the boys. Lincoln stood on the deck of the little tourist steamer, openmouthed with shock, awe, and the most utter delight Mary had ever seen on his face. Not even the sight of the ocean had filled him with such wonder. "It's been falling like that—just like that—when there weren't even white men on this continent," he said wonderingly, as the *Globe* chuffed away back toward Buffalo. "When Christ walked the earth it was like that—thundering in the silence here, unseen by anyone but the Indians and God. It'll be falling like that when all of us are gone." He shook his head, trying to grasp the largeness of Time, with the mist of the falls beaded like raindrops in his hair.

In Chicago, they took a room in the Sherman Hotel. Mary was unimpressed by the city. It seemed to have been built and populated entirely by Yankees—pushing, mannerless, and valuing money before all other things. Balloon-frame houses of roughly sawn boards lined streets so deep in mud that there were signs posted on particularly soupy intersections: THE SHORTEST WAY TO CHINA. Regiments of pigs whose numbers would have put Springfield's swine population to blushing shame rooted vigorously for garbage or lay in wallows in alleys. Lincoln chuckled all the way to the hotel at a story the train conductor had told him, about a Chicago citizen who saw a man's head and shoulders sticking out of a mudhole at the intersection of State and Lake: "Can I help you, pilgrim?" "No, thanks," the mired man said cheerfully. "I've got a horse under me."

And it was crowded, frantic, jostling with activity. Mary remembered how, ten years ago, Stephen Douglas had spoken of his trips to Chicago to speculate in land—when she'd taken tea with him and his new wife in Washington, he'd told her that lots he bought for five thousand dollars were selling now for twenty thousand. Irish, Polish, Portuguese, and German immigrants slogged through the muddy streets or along the very few crude board sidewalks; the air stank from privies, sewage, and coal smoke.

Yet there was money here, business, power. Mary might wrinkle her nose, after all these years, at Northern accents, but from her years of poverty she understood what the Yankee way of life could bring. At the Sherman Hotel, while Mary took the boys out and doubtfully tried to find something in the overwhelming confusion for them to sightsee, Lincoln met with the leaders of the Chicago Whigs, businessmen who made her father's leisured graciousness seem laughably naïve. When she came back that afternoon Lincoln told her the Chicago bosses had asked him, at six hours' notice, to speak that night at a rally at the Cook County Courthouse.

They spent the rest of the afternoon in the hotel room together, drinking vile tea and working out what he'd say.

The rally turned out to be so huge that it adjourned to a nearby public square, where crowds stood in the mud by torchlight and listened for nearly two hours. The cheers when Lincoln finished were deafening; Mary stood near the stage, jostled by strangers who reeked of sweat and tobacco, looking up at her husband in the torchlight, transformed and seeming to blaze with his cold intelligence as he always did, when carried away by speaking before a crowd.

He will be President. In her bones she knew it. *Taylor will be elected, and will give him something, some office, that will get him known, and he will be on his way.* She longed to throw her arms around him as he descended the platform, to embrace him in her wild delight. But he was surrounded at once by men, those clever, crafty businessmen, lawyers, speculators, politicians who governed things. There was the florid-faced Mr. Judd, who was building railroads with Irish and German labor; their rosy friend Congressman Washburne from Mrs. Spriggs's; plus old friends from Springfield, Edward Baker and Lyman Trumbull . . .

And all of them, Mary observed with an inner smile, Lincoln greeted as if each was his special friend, his close confidant. She knew this did not spring from calculation or hypocrisy, but from genuine interest coupled with a very clear idea of how anyone, from lowest to highest, could help; could be knit together into a single fighting unit. It was as if he said to each, *I need you . . . I need you all.*

Around them in the square the crowd was still shouting, talking, a yammer of noise and torchlight in the cold October night. It was the sound of victory. Lincoln had fought the good fight for "Old Rough and Ready" Zack Taylor, and in time his reward would come. Douglas might have made a fortune here in this mudhole town and be the fair-haired boy of the slaveholding Senators, but Lincoln would have something more.

Around the narrow shoulder of Isaac Arnold—a skinny, bearded, watchful fellow lawyer—Lincoln caught Mary's glance, and the corners of his eyes crinkled in a smile.

RETURNING TO SPRINGFIELD ON OCTOBER 10, LINCOLN TOOK THEIR old room in the Globe Tavern, rather than put the Ludlum family out of the Jackson Street house. "Ludlum has asked me if you were intending to come back to Washington with me in November," Lincoln told Mary, on a windy night a day or so later, after they'd settled the boys to sleep in the trundle-bed. He'd spent the day with Billy Herndon, catching up all the legal business of the past year—tomorrow, Mary knew, he'd spend with Ninian, and Simeon Francis, and Cousin Stephen Logan, and Dr. Henry around the stove in the office of the *Sangamo Journal,* conferring about the recent state elections—which had been disastrous for the Whigs—and how they were going to organize to secure victory for Taylor.

But at least, she reflected, now she could visit Bessie Francis, and Julia, and Cousin Lizzie . . . and Elizabeth, who had Ann still living with her, and those two certainly deserved each other. . . .

She heard the query in her husband's voice, and glanced over at the sleeping boys. Eddie was sleeping, anyway. Bobby was pretending to sleep, as he usually did so he could listen to his parents' voices.

She paused, hairbrush in hand. Lincoln was sitting up in bed with the quilt over his knees, a book on his lap, and Charlotte, Mrs. Beck's calico cat, asleep on his feet. It didn't take more than a few hours for every cat in the house to make Lincoln's acquaintance and decide to sleep on his bed—at Mrs. Spriggs's there'd been four of them.

Lincoln went on, "Ludlum said he'd be pleased if he could rent the house until March, when the Congress adjourns again. I said I'd talk to you. I know you weren't much happy with Washington."

November to March. It wasn't much longer than he was gone when riding circuit. Mary thought about the little cottage on Jackson Street, about trying to deal with that horrendous succession of sulky Irish girls. Bobby and Eddie were older, and past the stage of disturbing everyone with squalling and crying, but they were still young enough to need constant minding, when she'd hoped to be attending sessions of the Congress or paying calls on the town's hostesses. During the weeks of August before the speaking tour, she'd been able to go to Congress only twice.

"I thought, Molly, that maybe you'd like to stay here at the Globe. I know you get along all right with Mrs. Beck these days." Which was true. Not being pregnant or exhausted, Mary had found, did wonders for her ability to deal with the Globe's no-nonsense landlady.

Mary felt as if a key had been turned, releasing her. Felt as she had when she'd finally said, *I'm going back to Lexington. . . .*

"Will you be all right on your own?" she asked him.

And saw, by the lightening of his eyes, that he, too, had suffered while the four of them were trying to live together in the Washington boardinghouse. That he'd felt guilty over leaving her to her own devices, torn between his ambition, his duty, and his love for and protectiveness of her.

"Well," he replied gravely, "since I'll be sending my whole salary here to pay Mrs. Beck, I won't have enough left to go chasing around bad women in Washington. . . ."

"Mr. Lincoln!" Mary swirled over to him in a flurry of white nightgown and unbraided hair, to rap his arm smartly with the hairbrush she held. "I have *never* been so shocked in all my life! Do you mean to tell me that *actual members* of the *government of the United States* even *know* what bad women *are,* much less chase around with them . . . ?"

"Only the Democrats," Lincoln assured her gravely, and pulled her giggling into bed at his side.

He was gone two days later, stumping the southern part of the state with Dr. Henry in a last-minute effort to rally the Illinois Whigs to Zachary Taylor's banner—a successful effort, for the General won the election handily. Mary was elated, and saw him off on the stage a few weeks later with a glow of pleasure, knowing there would be good things ahead. If he was given an appointment in Washington it would be for three or four years, longer than a single session of Congress. They could take a house there, and *then* she could be one of the hostesses, and not a petitioner leaving cards for other people's servants. One could get decent help in Washington, too, since it was possible to rent slaves or hire freedmen, who were *far* more reliable than the wild Irish. . . .

Her deepest regret about not accompanying Lincoln was that she couldn't be at Taylor's inaugural ball at her husband's side. He left early, he wrote her, and in the shoving and confusion of the gentlemen's cloakroom lost his hat, and had to walk back to his boardinghouse bareheaded in the rain.

While he was gone, that winter of 1848, Mary enrolled Bobby in school. She was beginning to feel deep concern about her older son, and hoped the schoolmistress could do with him what she herself could not. But the boy was forever in trouble with his schoolmates, partly because he was teased about wearing patched breeches, but mostly because the other children called him "Cock-Eye." When he wasn't in trouble he would simply run away, and even with Mary, his secrecy and his silent defiance were getting beyond what she could handle. After his fifth truancy, she took him to Dr. Wallace's small consulting-room behind the drugstore.

"It's a relatively simple problem." Dr. Wallace straightened up, gave Bobby a piece of peppermint, and drew Mary to the far corner of the office. "The muscle on the inner side of the eyeball is too short. It's a fast and easy operation to cut partially through it; in most cases the eye will return, if not to a completely normal position, at least to one that is barely obvious. There's a specialist here in town, Dr. Bell, who should be able to do it. Bobby will have to do eye exercises to restore the balance of the muscles, but I think that should solve the problem."

When Lincoln returned to Springfield in March, Mary told him what Dr. Wallace had said—told him, too, about Bobby's increasing quarrelsomeness and truancy at school. "If he's to get any education he mustn't be always fighting," she insisted. "Dr. Wallace promises that the earlier the surgery is done, the more normal his eye will appear when it heals.."

She tried to keep her anxiety out of her voice, to sound matter-of-fact. Try as she would, she could never completely push from her heart the ugly fact that the boy's inward-turning eye repelled her. Every time she saw her son's face, she heard the whisper in the back of her mind: *Mary Todd played the harlot. Mary Todd lied to get a husband. This is God's punishment.*

She could speak all she wanted about what was best for Bobby, but in truth, she would have done anything not to have a child whose imperfection trumpeted her shame. She wanted to love him wholeheartedly—to be *able* to love him wholeheartedly. With the defect gone, at least her lie would not be literally staring her in the face.

Lincoln nodded, though he didn't look happy at the thought of putting his son through the agony of surgery. That was the day they moved back into the cottage on Jackson Street, the boys dashing from room to echoing room in an atmosphere of soap and ironing and fresh paint. Lincoln carried the familiar furniture down from the attic room where it had been stored, reassembled their bed and put together small beds in the low-ceilinged attic bedroom for Bobby and Eddie ("Now, you boys remember I can hear every sound you make!" Mary warned). Eddie was dancing with joy at the prospect of sharing a room with his protector.

The surgery was set for June, when Lincoln would have built up his much-neglected law practice again. The eye specialist, Dr. Bell, would perform it, with Dr. Wallace assisting. Mary felt reassured by Wallace's presence—she trusted Frances's husband as if he were her own brother. For a month and a half Lincoln was busier, as he said, than a one-armed paperhanger, writing letters for men to whom he owed political favors on top of his legal work, juggling what little influence he had acquired in Washington.

Then in May he became entangled in what turned into a ferocious three-way tug-of-war over the one patronage office he truly desired, that of United States Land Commissioner. Though the flurries of letters and negotiations with Cyrus Edwards—father of the lovely Tilda, now long married to her handsome Mr. Strong—and other Whig leaders kept him preoccupied and absentminded, Mary understood, and followed the proceedings eagerly. As Land Commissioner, Lincoln would be able to dispense offices on his own and build up a network of influence that would lead to votes.

A few days before Bobby's surgery, word reached them that a Chicago man named Butterfield was being seriously considered for the post. Wrought up and torn between his complex negotiations and the day-to-day demands of his practice, Lincoln lost his temper, one of the few times since the early days at the Globe that Mary had seen him in a real rage.

"When I was sweating blood to get Taylor elected Justin Butterfield was all for Clay; when I was making speeches here, there, and yon he was sitting home with his feet on the fender! There isn't a Whig from central Illinois that's received any office, not *one*! Did someone forget to count our votes?"

After more letters—more nights of coming home late, of the dining-room lamp's glow dimly seen under the shut bedroom door—Lincoln packed his bags and took the stage for Indianapolis, whence the railroad cars would bear him to Washington. "You want to have Wallace put off the surgery?" asked Lincoln, the night before his departure, as Mary washed up the supper dishes.

She shook her head, aghast at the thought of further delay. Bobby had run away from school again that morning, after Lyman junior had taunted him, and the schoolmistress had informed her in private that one more problem and he would be dropped from her class. With Eddie down with another cold, and constantly underfoot, Mary couldn't imagine teaching her defiant elder son his letters herself at home. "We'll be all right," she said. "The longer we delay, the worse it will be."

But when Bobby was strapped down to the padded table in Dr. Bell's surgery—when Dr. Wallace gripped his head, and Dr. Bell pulled back the eyelid to expose the mucous membrane, and Bobby started screaming in terror and pain—her nerve failed her. She fled the room, sick and fainting. Crumpled on a chair in the empty outer office, she heard the little boy's screams through the open door; pressed her hands to her ears, knowing she must go back into the surgery to be with him but knowing that if she did she would start screaming, too. . . .

Before she could gather her strength to stand, Dr. Wallace emerged, spots of blood dabbling his clothes. "We're done, Molly." He gave her a few sips of brandy and then led her into the surgery and she held the sobbing, half-fainting boy in her arms, dizzy herself and terrified by the greenish pallor of his young face. But at least she was able to keep her composure. Dr. Wallace walked them home and Mary put Bobby to bed, then went to bed herself, trembling and shivering.

In the weeks after the bandages came off, Bobby did his eye exercises with diligence strange in a six-year-old, and after that time he was quieter, less quarrelsome but also far less communicative, even with Eddie.

He never spoke to either parent about the surgery.

As far as Mary could tell, he never mentioned it to a soul.

Chapter Thirty-one

On the third of July, Lincoln was home again. "Butterfield got it," he said, as Mary came into the lamplit kitchen from the dining-room where the boys were having their supper—as usual Lincoln had come in through the side door into the kitchen, dusty and tired from riding in the Indianapolis stage since dawn. He hugged Bobby—"Your uncle tells me you were a brave boy. Are you all right?" Then he turned to Mary. "I read the papers in Washington."

Mary nodded, though her head ached. She knew she looked terrible, haggard with sleeplessness and night after night of nightmares since first she'd read the news in the *Journal* a week earlier that cholera had broken out in Lexington. "Emilie wrote me," she said as Lincoln gently folded her into those long arms. "What a sweet child. She said she knew I'd be worried about Papa, and she says they're all well. They're out at Buena Vista, the house Betsey owned at their marriage, you remember. It's five miles out of town. Even Levi and his wife and their children are there. Catch Betsey thinking to write."

"News in Washington was that Mr. Clay was down sick."

"Emilie says he's better. Both he and his wife were ill. She says Papa's still campaigning for the Senate, in spite of the epidemic. He lived through one epidemic perfectly well," she added, a little shakily. "Of course they'll all do fine through this one."

Lincoln smiled, and kissed her on the top of the head. "That's my Molly." Bobby, his eye covered with a bandage, ate his soup and said nothing.

That night she dreamed of the cholera. Smelled again the thick choke of lime and gunpowder in her throat, and heard baby David crying, crying like an endless, steady machine-whistle. Dreamed of hearing thumping in the darkness, and of creeping out of her bedroom into the dark upstairs hall, to see Nelson and her father bringing down trunks from the attic to give to old Solly the gravedigger, because there were no more coffins to be had in the town.

And in her dream, both Nelson and her father were dead. Their faces were green with decay and their hair and clothes smelled of the mold of the graves. Outside in the streets the green, glowing essence of the cholera flowed like fouled water through the streets, shining sickly in the night.

Lincoln shook her awake in the darkness and she rolled over and clung to him, pressing her face to his bony chest, sobbing as if her heart would break. When she slept again she was back in the Winchester stagecoach, twisting around to get a final glimpse of her father as he stood waving to her in the Courthouse square.

But he wasn't there.

Two weeks later she got a letter from Emilie, telling her that her father was dead.

MARY WEPT UNTIL SHE WAS SICK. THE DEATH HIT HER DOUBLY HARD, for the same day she received Emilie's letter, Julia Trumbull's five-year-old son, Lyman, died as well, from scarlet fever. Lying in the dark of her bedroom, head throbbing with migraine, she was only dimly aware of comings and goings in the house. Lincoln would sit beside her for hours in the darkness, or stretch out next to her on the bed, quiet as one of the cats, and hold her as he did during a thunderstorm.

None of it seemed to touch the bottomless core of her grief.

Fanny and Dr. Wallace came in and out often during the daytimes. They'd taken Bobby and Eddie to stay at their home—Mary heard later that it was there that Lincoln ate, when and if he ate. Sometimes she would sleep, and would dream of her father. In her dreams she was still sitting on the porch with him in the mosquito-humming darkness, smelling the smoke of his cigars. Then she'd wake and remember that he was gone.

And she would weep again, as if she did not know how to stop.

Even when she was up and around again she felt dazed, and her father's image haunted her. Fanny, Merce, Cousin Lizzie, and Bessie Francis took it in turns for weeks to come calling, as they were taking it in turns to call on and care for Julia. They were almost the only outsiders she could stand to see, and sometimes she could not even endure being with them.

She emptied the little chest of trinkets her father had given her—pearl earbobs, silver combs, the sapphire pendant that she hadn't even unwrapped in years—and gave them to her friends, unable to look at them without seeing her father's face. During the days Lincoln took the boys to the office with him, and later she heard that Bobby and Eddie both came very close to driving Billy Herndon into murdering them and pitching their bodies into the street.

Mostly she simply couldn't believe that her father was gone. When Lincoln told her that he'd been offered the governorship of the Oregon Territory, she could only shake her head tearily and whisper, "No . . . no . . ." The thought of leaving her friends and family again, of months on a ship around Cape Horn and years of living in God knew what wild conditions in the forests, filled her with horror. Lincoln nodded—by the look in his eyes she could see he didn't think much of the idea himself—and no more was said of it. But she noticed that he was offered nothing else.

She was only beginning to believe her father was actually dead—only beginning to adjust—six weeks later, when her sister Ann came flouncing into the kitchen in red-faced fury with a letter in her hand and announced, "That *imbecile* brother of ours is trying to get Papa's will thrown out of court!"

Mary didn't need to be told which imbecile brother Ann meant. Levi was a sulky tosspot, but like his father tended to deal with problems by simply not being there. George—a young man who also, as they said, had a spark in his throat—was volatile and temperamental and generally in debt, and loathed Betsey perhaps most of all Robert Todd's "first children." Mary paused only long enough to instruct Ruth—the current "girl"—in getting dinner into the Dutch oven (God knew whether she would, or what would come out), then took off her apron, collected Eddie and Bobby from the yard, and followed Ann to Elizabeth's, where an indignation meeting was in progress in the parlor. The upshot—after several hours' free exchange of personalities about George and Betsey—was that when she returned home that evening, it was to ask Lincoln to go with her to Lexington, to safeguard the interests of the four Todd sisters when George's challenge of Robert Todd's will came to court.

They stayed with Granny Parker, in the big house Mary remembered so well from childhood. Long residence in Lexington had given her a front-row seat on the almost unbelievable viciousness of family quarrels in the large clans of the county, once the terms of some patriarch's will emerged. She herself had personally expected that Betsey would bag most of her father's money for herself and her children—that was what Betsey had all her life maneuvered to do—and had resigned herself to letting that happen rather than causing the kind of storm that had torn apart the various branches of Wickliffes, Bodleys, Crittendens, and Breckenridges over the years.

In this she'd guessed correctly. The bulk of the money—and all seven slaves—were to go to Betsey, with the surprising exception of Nelson. Nelson, it turned out, had bought his freedom years ago at a nominal fee and had simply continued as the Todd coachman because manumitted slaves were legally obliged to leave the state, and Nelson had too many friends in Lexington. The rest of the money was to be "equitably divided" between the "first and second children."

Which left only a pittance for George. With the invalidation of the will, and the resulting forced sale of all Robert Todd's property—including the slaves—all proceeds would be equally divided among all the heirs, Betsey and the fourteen Todd children getting equal shares. Even with six of those children's shares put in trust under her administration, this would leave Betsey barely able to continue housekeeping at Buena Vista and could entail the sale of Buena Vista itself.

"I always hoped the woman would get a comeuppance somehow," stated Granny Parker, folding her clawlike hands over the ivory head of her cane. "But damned if I don't feel sorry for her."

The situation was further complicated by the lawsuit Mary's father had been embroiled in against Old Duke Wickliffe at the time of his death. At issue had been the large estates of Duke's second wife, one of Mary's Russell cousins. "I never seen so much dirty laundry washed in public in my life," muttered Lincoln, turning over the forty pages of the closely written document defending Old Duke's right to the estates.

"Does it mention that octoroon boy, that was Mary Russell's only grandchild from her first husband?" demanded Granny Parker, who was having tea with Mary and Lincoln on the porch as Lincoln thumbed through the document. The autumn sun splashed the frowsty lawn between the old house and the small brick dwelling on Short Street where Mary had spent her first thirteen years. Levi and his wife lived there now, and their two older children dashed back and forth with Eddie and Bobby, with Elodie and Kitty and Alec, shrill laughter ringing in the hazy air.

"Oh, Molly knows all about it," stated Granny Parker, when Lincoln glanced over at Mary, with a gentleman's hesitancy about going into the whole sordid story in front of his wife. "Everybody in town knows Old Duke blackmailed his wife into conveying her property to him, under threat he'd sell that boy and his mother, who'd been mistress to Mary Russell's only son."

Lincoln lowered the document and stared at the old lady, baffled. "And there are still people in this state who claim that the institution of slavery is . . . is *beneficial*? That it doesn't corrupt everything and everybody it touches?"

Granny Parker let out a sharp crack of laughter, her eyes bright. She'd taken to Lincoln at once, and the gracious wealth of the Todds be damned. It might have had something to do with the number of his Lincoln cousins she'd encountered over the years—one of them had been Sheriff of Lexington for a time. But Mary guessed that the old lady saw in Lincoln the kind of men who'd come out to Lexington with her in her youth, back in 1790 when the only thing there had been a blockhouse in the canebrakes. "Thousands of them, boy, thousands of them." She nodded thanks as her elderly maid, Prudence, came out with more hot water for the teapot.

"You all right, Mr. Lincoln?" asked Prudence, holding up the pot, and Lincoln said,

"Yes, ma'am, thank you."

"The only reason I haven't freed Pru, Annie, and Cyrus so far," said Granny Parker as Prudence departed, "is that then they'd have to leave Kentucky, and I can't do without 'em. Besides, where would they go, that they wouldn't be in danger of some slicker like old Robards trapping 'em back?"

She jerked her head toward Short Street, across which the wall of Robards's slave jail was visible. As usual this time of the afternoon his common stock was out on benches beneath the awning, as Pullum's had been before, the men dressed in new blue coats and plug hats, the women and children in clean calico. Mary knew from Cash that Robards kept "choice stock"—coincidentally all of them light-skinned girls under the age of twenty—inside, where buyers could look at them in private.

Lincoln folded his hands and said nothing for a time, but his face was harsh with disgust. Mary knew he hadn't forgotten.

It took three weeks to draw up the documents for the division of Robert Todd's property, and to make sure that Betsey and her younger children would be comfortably settled at Buena Vista until such time as the estate could be sorted out. This process was made no easier by George's constant carping that his stepmother, as executrix of her husband's will, would cheat him out of his due share and had "poisoned our father's mind" against him and his siblings. Mary marveled at Lincoln's calm patience in pointing out to his brother-in-law that most of the slaves had been Betsey's personal property and not her husband's—or were

Granny Parker's, and not subject to sale for George's benefit. George and Mary got into more than one screaming-match, which ended with George storming out of Granny Parker's house in a fulminating rage.

During that time Lincoln also spent a number of days at Judge Robertson's office, taking depositions about the affairs of Old Duke Wickliffe and his wife amid a storm of conflicting testimony, character witnesses, and hearsay dating back twenty years. He said little about the squalid tangle of concubinage and blackmail, but Mary could tell, when they finally boarded the train for Frankfort and the long journey back to Springfield, that the whole business had left as sour a taste in his mouth as it had in hers.

"I never thought I'd live to feel sorry for Betsey," she sighed, as the depot and the last houses of the town gave way to the lush dark landscape of rock and trees that cloaked the hills. "And as for George—Bobby, stop it! Now, come sit down. . . . I don't fly into rages like that, do I?" She looked worriedly up at her husband, who was gazing out at the trees, still absently fingering the last late-blooming rose that thirteen-year-old Emilie had given him for a buttonhole. "I mean, not *that* badly?"

"Never," Lincoln assured her, with amusement deep in his eyes. "But at least now I see you come by it honestly—or *would* come by it honestly, if you ever was to do so."

"Well, I—Eddie, now, leave that lady alone . . . !" She sprang to her feet, to recapture her roving offspring.

Winter had settled in on Springfield when they returned. Iron-cold winds slashed across the gray prairies, bringing first rain, then snow. Lincoln returned to a stack of accumulated mail saved for him by Billy Herndon, a depressing agglomeration of criticism for his speech against the Mexican War, newspaper articles misquoting and misrepresenting everything he'd said, and the accumulating evidence that his recommendations for positions were being steadily ignored in Washington. Eddie, who had seemed to perk up in Lexington's warmth, came down sick again early in December. Mary and Lincoln moved his little cot back into their room, and took turns through the nights applying poultices and giving him the saline draughts and spikenard teas prescribed by Dr. Henry and Dr. Wallace. In the mornings Lincoln would walk to the law office in the dreary darkness on only a few hours of sleep, and Mary would return to the closed-up, stuffy room with mustard compresses for the boy's chest, or boiling water to make steam for him to breathe.

Bobby would sit with his little brother after school, reading stories from his primer or playing games. Now and then Mary would hear Eddie's thin voice speak to his brother in barely a whisper.

On the thirtieth of January, a letter reached Mary from Emilie telling her that Granny Parker had died. She was so exhausted from looking after Eddie, and so frightened by the child's worn-out weakness, that she could only retreat to the parlor, where she sat weeping by the fireplace while Ruth moved quietly about the kitchen, preparing dinner for Bobby. When Lincoln came home he listened to her news, read Emilie's letter, and said softly, "She was a fine lady, Mother, and had lived a good long life. You lie here on the sofa, and rest a little. You look done in."

He looked done in himself, but Mary leaned back and he went into the kitchen to get her a cup of what Mammy Sally had always called "headache tea." Her eyes closed, she heard him speak to Bobby, asking the boy about his day, and how his brother did. Bobby had grown very silent through that tense and worried Christmas as his brother grew no better. Then Mary heard Lincoln go quietly into the bedroom where Eddie lay. He moved with that catlike soft-footedness that was always so astonishing in so tall and loose-jointed a man.

Hours later—she never knew how many—she woke chilled, her neck cricked and aching from falling asleep in her corsets. It was nearly pitch dark, and only the tiniest glow of embers writhed on the unbanked hearth. The house was profoundly silent. Someone had laid a quilt over her, and she gathered it around her shoulders as she limped, stiffly, through the parlor door and across the hall to the bedroom. She opened the bedroom door carefully, so as not to introduce a chill or draft.

The single candle's flame had not been snuffed or trimmed and was smoking badly. By its juddering light she could just make out her husband, sitting on the edge of the bed with one hand pressed over his mouth, the other closed around the tiny clawlike fingers of their child. Eddie's breathing was a horrible, pain-wracked rasp, and beneath the little boy's lashes Mary could glimpse the wet glimmer of half-open eyes. Lincoln's eyes were closed. She could see his shirtsleeved shoulders tremble, and realized he hadn't been able to force himself to get up and fetch her.

Or he hadn't dared to leave his son's bedside.

She crossed the room silently and knelt beside him, put her hand on top of his and Eddie's.

About an hour later Eddie died.

Chapter Thirty-two

Bellevue June 1875

"Looking back, I realize I barely even thought at the time how terrible Eddie's death was for my husband." Mrs. Lincoln raised her forehead from her hand, turned to regard John Wilamet with tired eyes in the close gloom of her room. "I knew he grieved—sometimes in the night I would wake and hear him weeping. But he was always a man who would retreat with his griefs, like an injured animal. And I was . . . not much able to help."

For the fourth day in a row she had kept to her room, requesting the carriage only to feel too ill and depressed to take it. Every time John came in to check on her she clutched at his sleeve, talking, sometimes for hours, as if words could cleanse her mind of the shadows accumulated there.

He'd told Dr. Patterson that he was encouraging Mrs. Lincoln to put aside her delusions and to resign herself to a quieter life. She seemed to trust him, he said tactfully, because they'd known one another years ago.

Patterson had agreed, after a wise little lecture on the inadvisability of telling patients about the composition of their medicine: "I've never met one who didn't believe she knew more than a trained doctor, about what was best for her."

But in fact John only listened.

Sometimes he wondered what his mother would have said, if ever she spoke of her life instead of simply absorbing patent medicines in an effort to hide from its injustices.

But he couldn't imagine to whom his mother would speak.

The curtains were closed against the summer sunlight. Outside, the air was redolent of cut grass, of roses and warmed earth. This room, where Mrs. Lincoln sometimes lay all day in bed—though she had risen and had Amanda dress her both yesterday and today—was stiflingly warm, dim and enclosed as a womb. It could have been any room, in any year: bed, chairs, table, armoire. Nothing to tell whether it was 1875 or 1855 or 1835, except the tired lines in Mrs. Lincoln's face.

"I was . . . shattered," she went on softly. "I never knew such grief was possible. Coming on top of my father's death, and Granny Parker's . . . For months I caught myself wondering, in unguarded moments, why my father didn't write to me anymore. Wondering if he was angry or just busy . . . I'd look out the window and see Bobby playing and I'd panic, thinking Eddie was lost. . . . And he was." She shook her head sadly, wonderingly still, after all those years, that the too-thin child she'd chased down the aisles of so many train cars was not in the world anymore. "He was."

She folded her hands, plump soft hands that looked as if they'd never quite become accustomed to housework. The gold band placed there long ago by a diffident backwoods lawyer glinted through the somber lace of her house-mitt.

"So deep was my grief that it never crossed my mind what his death did to Mr. Lincoln. How it broke him. Changed him." Mrs. Lincoln's voice was calm, as if she looked on the events now from a great distance, from some shaded place of safety. "He never spoke of what moved him—of what hurt him, or what mattered most deeply to him. I think maybe when he was a child growing up there was no one to listen, the way Mammy Sally would always listen to me. And of course that winter—Eddie's death—followed hard on that terrible debacle in Washington. But for—I don't know, four years? five years?—he seemed to lose much of his interest in politics, and holding office, and the ambition that had all his life driven him. As if, like me, for a little while he simply couldn't see a reason to go on."

On a day-to-day basis it wasn't as profound or dramatic as that, of course. Lincoln continued to argue cases in court, to write up bills in chancery for clients, to send patient letters recommending political supporters for government jobs that seldom materialized. While Mary lay in bed for days, so sick with weeping that she could not even emerge for her four-year-old son's funeral, Lincoln managed the house as well as he could. He took Bobby to the office with him—a silent, withdrawn seven-year-old who seemed not so much dazed by his brother's death as simply puzzled. Dr. Wallace, and the ever-faithful Dr. Henry and his wife, made sure that someone dropped in on Mary several times a day, and there were many nights that Bessie Francis came over to cook supper for Lincoln and Bobby, and to make sure there was food in the house for breakfast.

The Reverend Dr. Dresser came too, and spoke of God's inscrutable mercy and of the joys of Heaven. But the words were like the food the fairy-folk were said to serve travelers who wandered into their realms: shining and aromatic, but providing no more nourishment to Mary's weeping heart than handfuls of twigs and leaves. She knew Lincoln had gone to speak to Dr. James Smith, of the Presbyterian Church, who had conducted Eddie's funeral, and found some comfort in the little Scot's simple faith. Sometimes, when she lay alone in the dimness, she heard Dr. Smith's voice in the parlor, and Lincoln's hesitant replies.

Sometimes Lincoln would read to her in the evenings from Smith's book, *The Christian's Defense.* The words helped a little, mostly while he was reading them—while he was there to speak to her of his own groping, painful thoughts concerning destiny and death. But always the darkness would return.

She would wake in the night, thinking she heard Eddie's gasping breath. She would hear Lincoln's footsteps on the steep attic stair as he went up to comfort Bobby—Bobby who never wept during the day. When Lincoln returned to bed she would grasp him frantically in the black hollow of the darkness, sometimes making love with a fierce desperation, as if the joining of their flesh would somehow negate the shadow of inevitable loss.

By March she was with child.

The newcomer was a Christmas baby and they named him William Wallace, after Fanny's husband. From the moment she knew she had conceived, Mary began to feel better, and Lincoln, too, seemed much more himself. But all that year, and in the years that followed, it seemed to her that Lincoln's heart was less in politics, and far more deeply involved in the raising and the care of his sons.

Maybe he understood, she thought—as her own father never had—that the time given to one had to be stolen from the other.

He was still gone for weeks and sometimes months at a time, six months out of the year. He was still maddeningly absentminded when he was present, retreating into that unreachable fortress of his thoughts to the exclusion of chores that needed doing, kindling that needed splitting, children who had fallen out of a toy wagon that he might continue to haul, oblivious, down Eighth Street.

But he was undeniably home more, and could not get enough of holding his new baby son, singing to him (if you could call the noise he made singing), changing his diapers and shirts. From the moment of his birth Willie was a sunny child, rosy, healthy, laughing and looking around him alertly. It was as if, Mary thought, God had relented at last, and given her a perfect infant to love.

Lincoln spent long hours at the office on the State House square. He would leave early in the morning, in his rusty black suit with a big gray shawl draped around his shoulders if the day was chill, and sometimes not return until late in the evening, having stopped to yarn with his cronies down at Dillard's store. On such occasions Mary—stranded at home with baby Willie and trying as usual to keep the house clean, the meals cooked, everyone's clothes washed and ironed, and the hired girl (if they had one that month) up to her work—frequently lost her temper with him, giving vent to her frustration in shrill vituperation that she barely recalled later. Afterwards, when he took Bobby with him to eat at a café downtown, or simply wrapped his old shawl around his shoulders and vanished into the night, she felt sick with remorse.

But she didn't know how to stop herself. Literally didn't know how to do it. And he would say, when she came to him weeping with apologies, "Everyone does the best they can, Mother." And he'd tell her some absurd story to make her laugh.

Part of her anger came simply from exhaustion. The small sum that finally came to her from her father's estate meant they were able to keep a hired girl more steadily—Ruth remained with them for some years. And after Willie's birth, when Lincoln devoted the whole of his time and attention to his law practice, money came a little easier. But Mary, for all her willingness to make a good home, had not been raised to housework, and never really got used to the endless physical labor involved. For many years she actively resented her sister Elizabeth, with her servants and her big house, her wealth and her tea-parties, her modern stove and her carriage which was so much finer than the dilapidated Lincoln buggy. Even Ann, who'd married one of the town's wealthiest storekeepers, had a finer house and did only the lighter housework.

Mary would sometimes see one or another of her sisters as she came and went to the market, afoot and sometimes with Bobby at her heels. She'd note the velvet bands on Elizabeth's wide bishop sleeves, or the vast extent of Ann's crinolines, or even Julia Trumbull's stylish rice-straw bonnet, and look back wonderingly on her days with the gay Coterie of the House on the Hill and the warm endless security of peaceful Lexington. Though her own dresses were neat and pretty, there was no denying their housewifey cotton fabric. No denying either that she made them herself, rather than paying a sewing-woman to do it.

Then when Lincoln would come home—two hours late to dry and shriveled chicken, or a week and a half later from the circuit court in Tazewell—her anger would boil over, not at him, but at the fact that she was no longer the daughter of a wealthy man, but only the wife of a poor one. Lincoln did what he could, for her and for the children, but this involved riding the entirety of the Eighth Judicial Circuit, something only the circuit court judge did—the fat and wealthy land speculator David Davis. Lincoln would come back, after three weeks or a month, with tales of cheap inns and moldering bedclothes, of sharing a bed with opposing counsel *and* the adjudicating justice—"We're lucky we didn't have the defendant and the clerk of the court in there with us"—with lawyers from half the state snoring in a pile on the other side of the room.

Mary would laugh, but those were nights she would spend alone, with insomnia or nightmares for company. Every few weeks, and sometimes oftener, she would be laid up with migraine: blinds drawn, sick with pain in semi-darkness, while Ruth whipped up meals for Bobby and Willie or took them over to the neighbors'. When the huge summer thunderstorms rolled across the prairie Mary would huddle under the sheets, sick and sweating and sobbing, pressing the pillows over her face so that Bobby wouldn't hear her scream.

Praying that Lincoln would come home.

Visions obsessed her that would not be argued away. Visions of Bobby being struck by lightning, of the house being struck and catching fire and Willie perishing in his cradle in the blaze. Of Old Buck being swept off his feet by a sudden rise while crossing some stream, and of Lincoln being swept away, drowning far from her.

Leaving her without a word of farewell.

Then her fear came out as anger, as fears often do. In her rage she would accuse Lincoln of leaving her, of not loving her, of pushing off onto her shoulders all the raising of their sons. He would disappear for a long walk or return to his office—sometimes past midnight, or in the driving rain, sometimes rubbing his forehead if she'd thrown a book at him or hit him with a piece of firewood—and be back with a joke or a story for her when she emerged, exhausted, from the spell of her rage in the morning. Often after he left she would sleep, and wake up filled with fear that he wouldn't return at all. At such times she couldn't imagine why he continued to love her, but in her heart—in the marrow of her bones—she knew he did.

There were compensations. They were sweet years.

Deep winter and early spring, and the hushed stifling heat of midsummer during the State Supreme Court session, Lincoln was hers, as much as he ever was anyone's. As often as he would spend sitting around Dillard's with his friends talking politics—and even in those years he was never completely separated from politics—there would be evenings when she would step out the side door and see him coming down Eighth Street with half the boys in the neighborhood tagging at his heels.

Lincoln was endlessly fascinating to the boys of the town, probably because he spoke to them exactly as he spoke to adults, except—Mary hoped—he kept his jokes a little cleaner. With a frontier boy's blithe estrangement from the entire concept of clocks and time, he would stop to spin them stories, to talk about his unsuccessful attempts at Indian fighting or his trips down the Mississippi to New Orleans on a flatboat, to listen to their speculations and opinions about the way their own small worlds worked.

On Sunday afternoons he'd take Bobby—and Willie, as soon as that intrepid little soul mastered the art of walking—and upwards of a dozen local boys of all ages, and, resplendent in his old Conestoga boots and rough wool pants with one suspender, would walk with them out onto the prairies, looking for birds' nests and lizards and June bugs. On Sunday evenings he and Mary would sit on the kitchen porch in a couple of broken-down cane-bottomed chairs, while the boys dashed madly up and down the rows of the vegetable garden and the luminous miracle of the prairie sky gradually lost its brilliance, and the stars appeared overhead and despite whatever smudges Mary could concoct they both got bitten to pieces by mosquitoes. When Bobby had gone up to his little attic room and Willie fell asleep—and Willie would always drop off as if he'd been hit over the head, within seconds of murmuring "G'night, Papa, g'night, Mama"—there would be long winter evenings of lying wrapped in each other's arms, sometimes reading, sometimes cuddling, sometimes only softly talking, with anywhere from one to six cats snoozing on their feet.

Sweet years.

Though the dinners she gave weren't instruments of politics anymore, there were still friends to entertain. Old friends departed: Julia and Lyman Trumbull for Alton, Dr. Henry for the far-off Oregon Territory. During Lincoln's second year in Washington, gold had been discovered in California—it seemed for a time that the whole of the country was on the move. New friends appeared. When she could, Mary sewed with the other ladies of the Episcopal Church, or hosted birthday parties or taffy-pulls. Their talk didn't have the intellectual headiness of local politics—which sometimes annoyed Mary—but they were far from stupid and seldom dull. In the summers they all helped each other bottle and pickle and preserve the bounties of the gardens. Willie would assist in these efforts from the moment he learned to walk, as cheery and open as Bobby was secretive, toddling into the kitchen with his arms full of tomatoes and squash.

When Willie was two and a half, Tad was born—Thomas, named after Lincoln's father, who had died, after years of whining letters asking for money, in Coles County, Illinois, in 1851. Mary felt, almost from the moment of Tad's conception, that all was not as it should be. Her pregnancy with Willie had been easy, or as easy as pregnancies ever were with her, for she suffered migraines sometimes for weeks at a time and her temper became more uncertain than ever. Dr. Wallace examined her and agreed that she carried a bigger baby than Willie had been.

Labor was an agonizing nightmare, to produce the longest, thinnest baby with the biggest head she'd ever seen: "Sort of like a tadpole," Lincoln told her later, when she woke up after falling into exhausted sleep. He was sitting beside her bed, the new-wrapped bundle of infant in his arms. Tad squalled and fussed when Lincoln gave him back to her, and was never, after that, really quiet except in his father's arms. Lincoln spoke to her gently and humorously, and addressed his new son as "Tadpole," but she could tell he'd been badly frightened.

It didn't stop him from leaving a week later for the McLean Circuit Court.

He was gone two months.

During those months her smoldering anger at him resurfaced, for she knew she'd been hurt by her son's birth, and she was a long time healing. Even when she was on her feet again, and able to get around, the pains and the cramps stayed with her, and the internal weakness that got her up a dozen times a night to use the chamber pot redoubled. After the birth, she suffered an agonizing infection of her bladder and privates that was months in easing: months of tepid sitz baths in her bedroom, while Bobby was at school and Willie called repeatedly for her from the parlor and Tad howled in his crib.

After Tad's birth, she never felt quite well again. It was nearly Christmas before she and Lincoln lay together as husband and wife, and then—probably at the advice of Dr. Wallace—Lincoln was careful with her, drawing back from anything that would get her with child again.

They both knew that this was not to be.

She missed the rough-and-tumble intimacy of their earlier relations, but with the internal troubles that followed on Tad's birth, she was grateful for Lincoln's understanding. And in many ways it was enough, just to lie with her head on his shoulder, quietly talking in the shadows.

Dr. Wallace prescribed Battley's Soothing Cordial for her, with the strict instructions that no more than a teaspoon of it be taken at a time, and never more than twice in any one day. The medicine was a lifesaver, dulling the throb of migraines and letting her drift into sleep, or taking the edge off the worst of her cramps and letting her tend to Willie or get out with her sewing circle or do whatever her work was that day.

She didn't like the sleepiness that followed on a dose—she had far too much to do. In addition to her work in the house, she had friends to visit with and neighbors to see, Cousin Lizzie or the Widow Black, and Mrs. Wheelock a few houses along Jackson. Though she still saw Merce and Julia, most of her friends were not the same bright gay crowd she had gone buggy-riding and picnicking with in her early days in Springfield. Instead they were neighbors, women who shared her current life of housewifery and children, and who certainly didn't look down their aristocratic Edwards noses at her because her husband was poor.

Then in June of 1854 Lincoln came home from the circuit with two-week-old copies of the *Chicago Herald* in his pocket, which had reached him in Urbana: "Congress has struck down the Missouri Compromise," he said, when Mary—with Tad on her hip and Willie orbiting her skirts—came across the deep grass of the yard to the stable where he was unsaddling Buck.

"I read that." Mary set Tad down but kept firm hold of his hand. The child would get into literally anything and she was trying to keep him away from large quadrupeds as long as she could. "They can't do that, can they?"

"No, they can't." Lincoln dropped the saddle over its sawbuck, slipped the bridle from his horse's head. He'd already shed his jacket—the rough corduroy one he wore for riding the long prairie roads—and in the shadows, in his shirtsleeves, with his black hair tumbled and standing up as usual in all directions, he looked like the hayseed storyteller who'd diverted old Professor Kittridge from her in the Globe Tavern's yard. "But they did. It's like every slaveholder in the South who wants to move into the Territories—and take his slaves with him—has been just waiting for Henry Clay to die, and Daniel Webster to die, and all those men to die who sweated to hammer out a compromise that would let this nation grow without tearin' ourselves apart over rich men ownin' slaves who run poor men out of work." He snatched up the currycomb and rucked it across Buck's back where the saddle had rested, working swiftly and automatically, the way Mary crocheted while concentrating on some piece of gossip with Cousin Lizzie. "So there *are* no free states or slave states anymore. Anytime some group of slaveholders wants to bring in slave labor to farm Illinois, they can do it, if they can get enough legislators to back them. And you bet the first man to do *that* is going to be *your* beau Mr. Douglas. . . ."

"He was not my beau!" cried Mary indignantly. "Not for very long, anyway. Oh, I was just a simple country girl." She put her knuckles to her forehead in imitation of every pure-hearted heroine in every play they'd ever seen, in Washington and Boston . . . even after sixteen years, Springfield still didn't have much in the way of theaters. "That Democrat blackguard broke my poor heart and went on to pass the Kansas-Nebraska Act. . . ."

"You're still a simple country girl." Lincoln came around the horse's hindquarters and out of the stall, one long arm extended to embrace her. Mary ducked aside with a squeak, since her husband was now covered with horsehair, road-dust, and sweat. He smiled, looking down at her; then his smile faded. "And in pushin' that Act through Congress, Douglas is goin' to be responsible for a lot more broken hearts than yours, Molly, before this is done."

He scooped out oats for Buck, retrieved his sons from under Clarabelle's feet, and, with Tad under one arm like a parcel and Willie on his shoulders, walked with her through the bean-rows and the tomatoes back toward the house.

All that summer, they followed the newspaper reports of what was taking place in Kansas. Thousands of squatters from slave-states—chiefly Missouri—flooded the huge territory, driving back the thousands of immigrants being sent to the state by abolitionist organizations in New England. In July, Cash Clay came on a speaking tour to Springfield, and under the spindly trees of the State House square spoke for two hours about what the forces of slavery would do in the way of intimidation, ballot-box stuffing, and outright bloodshed, to vote into Kansas a state constitution like Missouri's, under which no word against slavery could be legally spoken and under which the penalty for aiding a slave's escape was death.

For those two hours, Lincoln lounged on the ground under a tree whittling—Mary had never managed to teach him to use a chair, and even at home, if there was no company, he'd sit or lie on the floor. But afterwards he went to Clay, and Mary introduced them. Following supper at the house on Jackson Street, and after the boys were put to bed, she sat in the parlor with the two men, talking until far into the night.

Chapter Thirty-three

By fall Lincoln was campaigning again, on behalf of anti-Nebraska candidates for the Legislature.

"He's only making a fool of himself," declared Ninian, when Mary encountered him in the parlor of the House on the Hill as she waited for Elizabeth to come downstairs. "The Constitution defends the right of every man to his property, wherever that man may be or go within the country's boundaries. That's all the Kansas-Nebraska Act upholds. The right of every man to his property, and the right of self-government, which is why we fought to free ourselves from the British in the first place. Your husband has let his passions about slavery get the better of him, like far too many otherwise intelligent people in this country. He's going to find himself caught short."

"My husband," said Mary coolly, "*never* lets his passion about *anything* get the better of him—which as I recall was one of the arguments you and Elizabeth used against my marrying him. That he was *cold*."

"Don't chop logic with me, Mary." Her brother-in-law frowned down at her from his tall height. "The matter is too serious for that. If we want to preserve the Union we must find grounds upon which to end, once and for all, the bickering about slavery. The Kansas-Nebraska bill provides that."

"The Kansas-Nebraska bill truckles to Southerners who will not give up their slaves," she retorted, "and who hold the Union hostage in their demands to be allowed to keep them."

"Maybe." Ninian's face was hard, and sad; Mary forced herself to remember that this man had, like herself, walked daily past the Lexington whipping-post and auction-block. "The men who run the Legislatures of the cotton states are all slaveholders: it's not only their livelihood, it's their way of life, and they will not give it up. Is it worth giving up the Union, so that the abolitionists can congratulate one another on how righteous they are?"

Elizabeth came down then, and Ninian bowed and departed. With some difficulty Mary turned her mind back to the matter that had brought her to the House on the Hill: the letter she'd received from Emilie, now eighteen years old. "I wrote and asked her to come and make a long stay with us," she told her sister, unfolding the much-crossed sheets. "Since you'll be too much involved in matchmaking for Julie this season . . ."

"Julie is only seventeen," protested Elizabeth primly. "*Far* too young to be thinking of marriage."

"Of course!" Mary clasped her gloved hands before her bosom and nodded gravely. "And you were how old when you married Ninian?"

"Thirty," replied Elizabeth, who'd been seventeen. "Which makes me fifty-two now . . . and are *you* undertaking to find Emilie a husband?"

"Darling, I wouldn't *dream* of it." Mary winked. In fact, once Ann had married, Elizabeth had lost all interest in assisting any further sisters into Springfield matrimony. She maintained a polite interest in the affairs of Margaret, Mattie, and the rest of the Todd half-siblings back in Lexington, but it was Mary who wrote to them, not Elizabeth. Loyal and infinitely patient with her blood-sisters, Elizabeth—like Granny Parker whom she was more and more coming to resemble—never regarded Betsey or her eight children as anything more than interlopers.

"Well, with Mr. Lincoln back in politics," remarked Elizabeth, "at least Emilie won't be able to complain of having a dull winter."

By the end of an autumn of campaigning for various Whig state legislators opposed to the Kansas-Nebraska Act, Lincoln was beginning to talk about campaigning himself: for the United States Senate. The repeal of the Compromise that, thirty-four years earlier, had averted the breakup of the Union troubled him deeply. And the prospect of slavery spreading—and with it, the bloody conflicts between slaveholders and abolitionists—filled him with foreboding. When Lincoln entered a public debate over slavery at the Courthouse, Mary, in the audience, heard beneath his usual calm logic and clear, precise arguments a power that hadn't been there before. Over the years, she knew he'd improved. Partly at her urging, he'd discarded much of the clownishness, and personal satire that had characterized his earlier speeches. Now he renewed his ties with anti-Nebraska politicians, both Whigs and Northern Democrats. There were many nights when he and Mary would sit in the parlor reading newspapers from all over the country until the fire burned low in the grate; many more when she would go to bed, only to wake hours later alone and come across the hall in her wrapper to find him still staring into the glowing ash.

In September he challenged Stephen Douglas to a public debate on the subject of the Kansas-Nebraska Act. Douglas, in the midst of his own campaign to get another pro-Nebraska Democrat elected to the Senate from Illinois, refused to meet him. When most of the countryside was in town for the State Fair, and pouring rain turned the fairgrounds to glue, Douglas spoke in the State House, defending the Act and his own part in pushing it through, in terms of the sacred right of self-government for each state. When after Douglas's three-hour speech the crowds began to disperse, Lincoln shouted from the stairway outside the hall that he would rebut Douglas at the same time the following day.

Lincoln and Mary stayed up most of the night, Lincoln scribbling madly to incorporate the notes he'd taken into a rebuttal of the Act on which he'd worked long and thoughtfully since the summer. Mary and Emilie fixed supper, and Emilie got the boys to bed, reading Willie a story while Mary came into the parlor to listen to Lincoln practice it through. "That's a long introduction to your main point," she remarked.

"I have to show each link of the chain, Molly, for men to see how they've been bound by it."

"I understand," she agreed. "But it sounds less like the rebuttal you promised, and more like a polemical diatribe."

Lincoln said, "Hmmn."

The following day, Mary left the boys with the Wheelocks and joined the crowd that pressed into the Legislative assembly-room, watched the lanky figure take the rostrum.

He was almost like a stranger to her, seen that way by the unforgiving afternoon light, with his face running with sweat in the heat and his hair like a dark haystack. Was that really the man who would lie on the parlor floor propped on his elbows, arm-wrestling gently with the boys? The man who had told her that silly story about the old lady and her cat over breakfast that morning? The man she'd hit over the head with a stick of firewood only a few weeks ago?

"When a white man governs himself, that is self-government; but when he governs himself, and also governs another *man, that is* more *than self-government, that is despotism. . . .*

"Nearly eighty years ago we began by declaring that all men are created equal; but now from that beginning we have run down to the other declaration, that for some *men to enslave* others *is a 'sacred right of self-government.' . . .*

"Our republican robe is soiled, and trailed in the dust. Let us turn, and wash it white, in the spirit, if not the blood, of the Revolution. . . . If we do this, we shall not only have saved the Union, but we shall have so saved it, as to make, and to keep it, forever worthy of saving. . . ."

There was talk of forming a new free-soil party in opposition to the Nebraska Act—the Republican Party. Lincoln, who mistrusted splinter parties, remained a Whig, and began aligning and rallying his old connections among the Whigs. He was on the road again all October and most of November, meeting with this or that party leader, in between his appearances in the circuit courts. He started out running for the Legislature as well, but in his letters to her—some of them barely notes—Mary could tell he was more and more inclined to seek instead a Legislative nomination for the Senate.

"However you slice it, the Legislature is local," he said, on one of his rare visits to Springfield—she hadn't even known he was home until she'd looked out the front window of their neighbor Reverend Miner's house to see her husband, with his usual pack of boys trailing along at his heels, walking up Jackson Street in the icy twilight. "Any good I can do here is only local good."

He held out his hands to the kitchen fire, red and chapped. Mary, who'd run breathlessly across to the house, saw the gloves lying on her scrubbed kitchen table would have to be mended again. It was nearly impossible to find gloves for those immense hands. Eleven-year-old Robert was already dipping tea-leaves from the caddy into the pot, having, she saw, maneuvered the kettle on its gallows-hook over the fire. He moved with an economical neatness that was an echo of his father's movements, quiet-footed as a shadow.

"In the Senate I can do something that can actually help this country out of the mess it's heading straight for—the mess it's already in, if you read the newspaper reports from Kansas."

"Can you be in the Legislature and the Senate at the same time, Pa?" asked Robert, diffident as he always was around the father he seldom saw. His eye had completely healed and there was hardly anyone who even remembered that he'd been called Cock-Eye. But either the teasing he'd endured—or the hideous ordeal of terror, betrayal, and agony at the doctor's hands—had left a permanent wariness in him, a chilly barrier that Mary was never able to break.

"No," said Lincoln. "No, I can't . . . and if I'm elected I'll have to resign. But at least if I'm elected," he added with a grin, "the rest of the folks in the State House will remember my name."

He was elected, and he did resign—and, Mary learned a few days after the election, so did Lyman Trumbull, who had just won the Congressional seat for Alton. A Democrat, Trumbull had split with Douglas over the Nebraska Act—"He's the one we have to beat," growled the fat Judge Davis, when Lincoln held a strategy session in the parlor one sleeting December evening. Mary greeted the men at the door and made coffee and cake, enormously grateful that Emilie was keeping the boys out of the way in the kitchen.

Emilie, with her piquant face and beautiful red-gold hair, had only a passing interest in politics, but she was lively and funny and all three boys adored her. She had no trouble inventing a word-guessing game that interested both an inquisitive four-year-old and an eleven-year-old who considered himself too grown-up for such "baby" things, leaving Mary to listen quietly from the kitchen to the talk of the men.

Politicians, yes, but different from the drawling wealthy landholders and bankers who had thronged her father's parlors and argued about the National Bank over juleps. Different, too, from the smoothly powerful transplanted Southerners of Ninian's clique. These were lawyers and businessmen, harder and, Mary thought, shrewder than her father's friends or Ninian's cronies.

Judge David Davis was wealthy, but that wealth was self-made in land speculation. Immense and opulent, he occupied most of the sofa, plump hands folded over acres of subdued waistcoat—his eyes snapped with the single-minded attentiveness of a predator waiting to pounce. Ward Lamon, too, was massive, but instead of being fat like Davis he more resembled a grizzly who could kill with a swat—a lawyer from Danville, where he'd partnered Lincoln on any number of court cases. Lamon would play the banjo and tell jokes to the boys, when he'd come with Lincoln to Springfield, but Mary knew Elizabeth would never have had him in her parlor. Nor would she have had canny Simeon Francis—she had never forgiven the editor for fostering Lincoln's courtship of Mary and, in Elizabeth's eyes, making a fool of her before all Springfield. Stringy Leonard Swett reminded Mary of Cassius in *Julius Caesar,* too lean and hungry-looking to be completely trusted, and little Stephen Logan—the eccentric of the Todd-Edwards clan—was not a man who had patience with anything that was not life and death.

Mary understood that in the matter of the Kansas-Nebraska Act, they were, indeed, facing the possibility of the life or death of the United States. She knew instinctively she would not be welcome in their strategy session. They were like soldiers closing ranks for battle, wary of any outsider and of women most of all.

"Trumbull's got the Chicago Democrats behind him." Davis turned toward Lincoln, who—she was glad to see—sat in the chair nearest the fire, even though he sat with his long legs drawn up so that his knees were under his chin. "Norman Judd and John Palmer, railroad men."

"The Democrats are split," said Lamon dismissively. "Pro- and anti-Nebraska—half of them will waste their votes on Jimmy Shields, of all people. I hear Governor Matteson supports him."

"The one we need to watch out for," said Lincoln softly, "is Matteson himself. He runs his supporters like Wellington running the Battle of Waterloo. I watched him horse-tradin' all over the state. He's pro-Nebraska and pro-Douglas, and he'll support Douglas up to the steps of the White House . . . over the smokin' ruins of this nation."

Watching their faces from the door of the dark little dining-room, as Lamon waved aside the chances of Matteson being nominated and Davis outlined who should approach which legislators for support, she was reminded of men playing chess, or poker for high stakes. Gone was the camaraderie of the gentry who ran the countryside because they were the landowners and it was their taxes that supported the state. These were men gambling for position, for the control of patronage that would allow them to do favors for those who would help them to more power.

With the possibility of slavery spreading to all new states—and flowing back like blocked sewage into the established old ones—the stakes were too high for hesitation or mercy. Lincoln's face in the firelight was hard, almost a stranger's face to her. The face of a lawyer whose client stands in grave peril of hanging.

In the days that followed, Mary and Lincoln made endless lists of supporters, tallying whose votes in the Legislature were assured, and whose would require more work, more promises, more convincing. Mary pulled together her neatly organized envelopes of newspaper clippings: not only Lincoln's speeches, but records going back years of who supported whom and why. It was clear that Lincoln was the strongest of the anti-Nebraska contenders.

"We'll win this time," breathed Mary, as Emilie fixed her hair and laced her up for the New Year's Day reception at the House on the Hill. "We'll win. . . . This time we *will* take a house, for we'll be there six years . . . at the very least! One simply cannot do *anything* from a boardinghouse. . . . Of course Lafayette Square is the most fashionable, but it's quite expensive. . . . Though the neighborhood along Thirteenth and

Fourteenth Streets is perfectly genteel. . . . You will come visit us for the Congressional season, will you not?"

On the twentieth of January a blizzard dumped over a foot of snow on the town and hammered the small neat houses of clapboard and the brick mansions of the wealthy alike. Trains were stranded on the prairie, the rails buried under snow, trapping most of the Legislature and delaying the voting. Lincoln came in from chopping wood or milking Clarabelle shivering and half-frozen. He plowed his way across the knee-deep snow of the yard half a dozen times a day to make sure Buck and Clarabelle were warm enough in their snug stable, and dug out the path to the outhouse three and four times. On the third day of this he came in with something tucked in the front of his coat—

"What is it, Pa?" asked Robert, as Lincoln knelt by the kitchen stove, and Willie cried ecstatically, "It's a *puppy*!"

"Oh, the poor thing!" Mary knelt beside the wet ball of shuddering yellow fur. "Where did you find it?"

"In the stable." Lincoln tugged off his gloves and unwound his scarf. "Must have wandered there to get out of the wind—Bob, maybe you can break off a chunk of this morning's milk and heat it up for our little friend?"

Robert laughed—the milk had been thawed earlier in the day. There wasn't much of it, but Mary knew better than to protest that it should all be saved for baby Tad. The puppy lapped weakly and Willie, with great presence of mind for a four-year-old, fetched a clean towel and hung it in front of the hearth, to heat up as a bed for the newcomer. Emilie said, "One of those split-oak breadbaskets will do, won't it, Mary dearest?" and from beneath the kitchen table Sheba, Cinders, Little, and Bigger sneered as only cats can, as if to say they'd seen more impressive rats.

That night, while the wind screamed around the eaves, little Fido crept across the hall and scratched at the bedroom door, whining to be let in—which of course Lincoln did. He settled the pup on the foot of the bed by his feet, despite Mary's protests—"Those cats are bad enough. He's warm enough in the kitchen, surely?"

"He'll be no trouble," Lincoln promised, with the blitheness of one who hasn't had a cat spit up a hairball into his braids. He slithered back under the covers, shivering. Mary felt the pup curl itself confidingly as close to her feet as he could, and heard, from somewhere, one of the cats growl warningly. "Now, girls," her husband admonished. Then, to Mary, "The poor little fellow's probably lonely in the kitchen. When he's bigger he'll be fine there."

Mary sighed, knowing she'd acquired yet another bedmate for life. "You'll be sorry when he follows you into the Senate chamber, Father."

"I'll sic him on the Democrats," came Lincoln's voice out of the darkness, and strong arms wrapped around her waist. "I think even he could take on Jimmy Shields, don't you?"

Chapter Thirty-four

Jimmy Shields got forty-one Legislative votes on the first ballot when the Legislature finally assembled, after twelve snowbound days—Lincoln got forty-five. In the gallery of the Legislative chamber, Mary hugged her cloak around her and shivered with apprehension. All Lincoln needed to win was fifty-one votes.

Definitely, F Street between Thirteenth and Fourteenth. Or possibly Capitol Hill? For her first reception she'd serve quail, with the béchamel sauce M'sieu Giron had taught her the secret of, and perhaps a few touches of her good Kentucky specialties. . . .

She glanced beside her at Julia Trumbull, whose face was pink with the cold within the black fur of her coat-collar. Lyman Trumbull got exactly five votes. Mary squeezed her hand in sympathy, and on her other side, Emilie pressed her elbow in discreet congratulation.

The balloting began again. The crowd in the gallery up under the Legislative chamber's dome reminded her of the Washington Congressional audiences, only without the brightly dressed contingent of prostitutes. It certainly was as good as a theater—better, in some ways, because you knew everyone.

She watched from above as wizened little Cousin Stephen Logan moved among the legislators; watched his faded red head, his hands move as he spoke. A ladies' cloakroom had been set up off the lobby for the convenience of the spectators who'd come to watch the vote—ordinarily, of course, the building had facilities only for men. On her way downstairs, breathless so as not to miss the moment when Lincoln's victory would be announced, Mary saw Simeon Francis talking to big-shouldered Ward Lamon in the lobby. He tipped his hat to her and she came up to him and asked, "How goes it?"

"Sewn up," declared Lamon, and Mary clapped her hands in triumph.

"I'll be the first to tell Elizabeth. That will teach her to call Mr. Lincoln a bumpkin. She's just *torn,* you know, between admitting she was wrong about him and having a Senator for a brother-in-law. But pride won—it always does, with Elizabeth. She's doing the handsome thing, though, and is holding a victory reception for Mr. Lincoln at the House on the Hill tonight. . . ."

Simeon's eyes narrowed. "I think it'll be closer than your sister's counting on, Mrs. Lincoln. Governor Matteson's working to bring back Democratic votes, like your husband said he would. . . ."

"Matteson's had *one vote*!"

"He picked up support on this last ballot. . . ."

Drat, thought Mary, *I did miss the count. . . .*

"And Judd and Palmer say they won't vote for a Whig under any circumstances."

"They're afraid Mr. Lincoln won't pass along contracts to Democrats, is what they're afraid of," retorted Mary, and Simeon raised his grizzled brows.

"That's exactly what they're afraid of, Mrs. Lincoln," he answered. "We've got some of the anti-Nebraska Democrats voting for Lincoln now, but they're doing it looking over their shoulders, hoping they haven't guessed wrong."

By the sixth ballot most of Jimmy Shields's supporters had switched their allegiance to Governor Matteson. Mary saw Billy Herndon—chinless and self-important as ever, though nowadays he wore the dignity of the Mayor of Springfield—scuttle from the Representatives' chamber for the third or fourth time, hurrying, she knew, down the State House steps and across the trampled snow of the square to the office he and Lincoln shared. Lincoln would be there, she knew, pacing the worn carpet or stopping by the iron stove in the long room's center to warm his hands, his shabby shawl pulled close around his shoulders, waiting and listening for someone's step on the stair. Willie had protested at not being allowed to stay with his father while he waited—the two younger boys were at the Wheelocks' house, where Robert would go for supper when he got out of school. But Mary for once had been firm. The day would be nerve-wracking enough for Lincoln. At least he shouldn't have to play nursemaid as well.

On the next ballot, a number of Lincoln's Whig supporters—who on the whole either liked Matteson's noncommittal politics or hoped for public works contracts—voted for the governor.

"Why doesn't Lyman throw his votes to Lincoln?" demanded Mary, leaning over to tweak Julia's sleeve. "That would end this, and it would still get an anti-Nebraska candidate into the Senate. That's what Mr. Judd and the others want, isn't it? What difference does it make to them who it is?"

Julia's dark eyes avoided Mary's as she replied with forced lightness, "Good heavens, Molly, I don't know why politicians do what they do! I'd certainly never dream of asking Mr. Trumbull. Besides," she added, with a touch of smugness in her voice, "Mr. Trumbull is picking up votes, as you can see."

"I wonder if that could be because Mr. Trumbull is a rich man, and my husband a poor one."

Julia stared at her for one moment as the implication of that sank in; then her face turned crimson within the frame of dark hair and dark fur, and she whispered, "Oh—!" and turned away.

Mary scarcely noticed, because the tally had just been read out: Governor Matteson *(Another rich man,* thought Mary in fury, *with patronage to give out. . . .)* forty-seven, Lyman Trumbull thirty-five—she could not imagine how she had once thought he was so attractive! Abraham Lincoln, fifteen.

Billy Herndon left the chamber again. Mary knew exactly how long it took, for him to cross the snowy State House square, to climb those two flights of stairs. To come back, including a brief stop in the lobby to take a drink from his hip-flask, if he wasn't swearing Temperance this week . . .

She saw Logan, Francis, and Lamon huddled around the tall fair paunchy Herndon in a corner of the chamber, Logan shaking his head again and again. Her hands clenched hard, unbelieving, knowing what she saw, as the three men moved among the milling figures below, speaking now to one man, now to another . . . speaking only to those fifteen who still supported Lincoln.

No, Mary thought, NO . . .

Tears flooded to her eyes; she clung to the support of Emilie's hand.

On the tenth ballot, Lyman Trumbull was appointed to the United States Senate.

"You said yourself, what difference does it make who it is," said Julia.

"None, I suppose," retorted Mary, hot with fury for her husband's sake, "if both men are *honest.*"

She turned and flounced down the gallery stairs, brushed past Bessie Francis's extended hand of sympathy, strode out across the lobby to the icy night beyond the huge bronze State House doors.

The party at Elizabeth's that night was still held, in Lyman Trumbull's honor. "I know how disappointed you must be," sympathized Elizabeth as Lincoln entered the lamp-lit parlor, with Mary and Emilie on either arm. Lincoln smiled and shook his head.

"Not too disappointed to congratulate my friend Trumbull," he replied, stepping forward to shake the new Senator's hand. Afterwards he kept everyone at the party in a roar of laughter for hours with stories.

For her part, Mary could not bring herself to be so forbearing. She cut Julia Trumbull dead, and never spoke to her again.

THROUGHOUT THE FOLLOWING YEAR THERE WAS INCREASING BLOODshed in Kansas, as Missouri squatters forced a slaveowner's constitution and government on the state, and Free-Soilers set up their own, rival government in Topeka. Mary avidly read newspaper accounts all spring, of intimidation, ballot-stuffing, and outright fraud, while Lincoln was on the circuit and away in Chicago. More and more often he was called in on patent-infringement cases for the McCormick Reaper company, or for Norman Judd's Illinois Central Railroad. Meanwhile—according to Cash's letters—the Free-Soilers of Kansas began to import guns.

She found her time fully occupied, even had she not been giving small dinners for Lincoln's political friends, and introducing Emilie to every eligible bachelor in Springfield. To her despair, it was becoming clearer to her that Tad, like Robert, had been born with a deformity, in Tad's case a speech impediment that rendered his words nearly incomprehensible. Having seen what her distaste for imperfection had done to Robert, she worked hard to be patient in teaching the child, who in addition was nervous and cried at the slightest provocation.

Only Willie made up for her frustration and occasional despair, and Willie—perhaps because she was relaxed with him as she could not bring herself to be with his brothers—quickly took on himself the role of her protector, when his father was away.

In the spring Emilie returned to Lexington unbetrothed, and promptly fell in love with one of Mary's Hardin connections, a young lawyer named Ben Helm. Excited letters passed back and forth, Elizabeth temperately approved. . . .

But both Mary and Lincoln were aware that, in a sense, Lincoln was only marking time until the next Senatorial race.

Marking time, and praying that the sectional conflict would not explode before then.

When he returned to Springfield, they would talk of the bloody raids by one Kansas faction against another, of the horrors of retaliation and blood-feud. "It's like watchin' a fuse burn down," said Lincoln one night, dropping an armful of newspapers on the parlor table, "an' us sittin' on the keg." Billy Herndon—who to everyone's surprise had made an excellent Mayor—joined the antislavery forces with his usual headlong enthusiasm, arguing that any means, "however desperate," should be used against the enemies of freedom. Lincoln, who as his longtime partner was inevitably tarred with the same brush, was hard put to calm the radicals.

"We're fighting for freedom and for our country," he said to Mary later. "We can't do that by breaking our country's laws."

Billy, being Billy, signed Lincoln's name to a call for a meeting of Sangamon County anti-Nebraska supporters while Lincoln was away in May. Mary stormed over to the law office and screamed at him that he would ruin Lincoln with the more moderate voters, and—when Billy only looked down his nose at her and intoned, "This is politics, ma'am, and not something to discuss with ladies,"—went to Cousin John Stuart, who reprimanded Billy himself. By year's end, the anti-Nebraska Whigs had been absorbed into the Republicans: the more radical abolitionists, who objected also to foreigners and Catholics, formed the American Party, also known as the Know-Nothings.

By the middle of the following year—1856—Lincoln received over a hundred Republican nominations for Vice-President, to run in tandem with the flashy adventurer and hero of the Mexican War, John C. Frémont.

Lincoln was forty-seven, and seemed older—but then, even as a backwoods bumpkin there had always been something patriarchal about him. Mary was thirty-eight, a fact which surprised her. Lincoln still called her "my child bride" and though, to the boys, she referred to him as "Father," she sometimes caught herself thinking of him as exactly that: the father she still so sorely missed. He smiled when she called him that, and called her "Mother," which made her laugh. She pictured them sometimes as an old white-haired couple, surrounded by grandchildren . . . being invited to tea at the White House and pointed out in Washington society, as Dolley Madison was pointed out in her carriage, with love and respect.

In the same week as the Republican Convention, news reached Springfield that Missouri "border ruffians" had raided and sacked the free-soil city of Lawrence, Kansas. In retaliation the abolitionist John Brown and his men murdered and mutilated five pro-slavery men on

Pottawatomie Creek, and reading of it Mary shivered, as if at the sound of summer thunder.

Frémont and his eventual running-mate—a New Jersey Senator named Dayton—were defeated.

Mary felt no regrets at this. Though the victory of "Free Speech, Free Press, Free Soil, Free Men, Frémont" might have brought patronage, she believed that the cost would have been too high. In every newspaper that came to the house on Eighth and Jackson—and there were dozens, now—Southern Congressmen and Southern businessmen spoke angrily against the consolidation of anti-slavery forces into a single, Republican, party.

It was clear to her that if a Republican were elected President, there were those in the South who would demand that the Union be dissolved. The handwriting was on the wall. Only thus could they protect the institution upon which not only their economy, but their very society, was based.

Mary herself tried to talk Lincoln into voting for the Know-Nothing candidate Millard Fillmore, Zachary Taylor's Vice-President, who had filled out the end of "Old Rough and Ready's" incomplete term, and who had visited Lincoln a few years ago in Springfield, and spent a half-hour discussing roses with Mary.

She had other concerns that year. The Springfield town lot her father had left her finally sold, and to her immeasurable relief, Lincoln agreed to use the money to enlarge the house. Emilie's stay in the only spare nook available—Mary's sewing-room—had brought home to her the need for more space, particularly as Tad was old enough now to move into the overcrowded second attic with his brothers. The attics were transformed into a full-fledged second story, and—God be praised—a modern stove was acquired for the kitchen in place of the old assortment of roasters, gallows-hooks, Dutch ovens, and boilers on the kitchen hearth.

Robert got his own bedroom—suitable to both his fourteen-year-old dignity and his impatience with Tad's restlessness—with Willie sharing a smaller room with Tad. Tad adored Willie, who never treated him as a baby, as Robert often did. Imperious even at four, Tad would choose the games, and the easygoing Willie would fall in with whatever schemes his mischievous brother would devise.

Carried away with the joy of the new house, Mary bought new carpets, and a suite of parlor furniture, considerably over-running her budget. Lincoln's anger when he got the bills surprised and frightened her—she hadn't seen him that angry since the early days of their marriage. She'd far rather he'd shouted at her, as her father or brothers would have, rather than the cold silence that preceded his leaving the house. She half-guessed that he distrusted his anger, as he distrusted his sexual passions, and would pull away from it as he had pulled away from her during those feverish nights in Simeon Francis's parlor, after Bessie had gone to bed.

He was gone most of the night, and though he accepted her tearful apologies as always, she mentally swore never ever to spend money without telling him again.

One of the things Mary loved best about the new shape of the house was that she finally had the luxury of *her* own room, connected by a door to Lincoln's smaller bedroom where, if he had a case, he could stay up half the night writing without disturbing her often-fretful sleep.

She missed him sometimes waking her if she had a nightmare. But many times he would do so anyway, for he was a light sleeper himself. Hearing her whimpering in her sleep, even through the closed door, he would pad through in his nightshirt to gently shake her, usually climbing into bed beside her to hold her till dawn.

For her part she loved the luxury of sitting up reading by lamplight late into the night, without having to worry about whether Lincoln would be disturbed or when he might come in from his office. And though she didn't say so to him, she particularly enjoyed not having to sleep with Fido and six cats. Many nights he'd come in and sit in the chair beside her bed, reading the newspaper, with the dog curled confidingly at his feet.

Billy Herndon of course put the story around that Mary had had the second story put on without Lincoln's knowledge, because when Lincoln came home from the circuit and saw the second story had been completed, he'd facetiously asked a neighbor where the Lincolns lived: he didn't recognize the house, he said. It was the kind of thing Billy *would* take seriously. He'd gone around for weeks telling everyone that Lincoln had no appreciation for what he called the "Sacred Beauty of Nature" because Lincoln had replied, deadpan, to Billy's inquiry about Niagara Falls, "I just wondered where all that water came from."

Chapter Thirty-five

In March of 1857—only days after the elderly Democrat James Buchanan was inaugurated President—the United States Supreme Court handed down its decision that Dred Scott, a Missouri slave, had no right under the Constitution to seek his freedom because, as a Negro, he was not a citizen of the United States. Scott's master, an Army surgeon, had taken his slave first to Illinois, then to the Minnesota Territory. On his master's death, Scott had sued for liberty—as hundreds of other slaves had, over the years—on the grounds that he'd been resident of a free state and then of a territory from which slavery was banned.

Residence in a free state or a free territory meant nothing, Supreme Court Chief Justice Taney ruled, because Congress had no right to exclude slavery from either states or territories. The Missouri Compromise, over which fighting still continued in what men now called Bleeding Kansas, was in fact unconstitutional. The Founding Fathers had never intended blacks to be included in their definition of "liberty," since they had mentioned them neither in the Declaration of Independence, nor in the Constitution.

"Taney's wrong," said Lincoln softly, when he got back from the Clinton County Court, where he'd heard the news. "And there will be hell to pay."

Mary could almost feel sorry for Stephen Douglas, as the Senate race of 1858 drew near. As the architect of the Kansas-Nebraska Act, he was obliged to defend it, like a man trying to put out a prairie-fire with a teacup.

In the North.

In the South, Douglas was praised as a defender of the rights of states to govern as their people demanded, and as the friend of those who feared the abolitionists' increasingly strident demands. More and more, Southern slaveholders were proclaiming that slavery was the only condition suitable to the Negro race. It was beneficial to them, they insisted: it would be cruel to thrust inherently primitive and childlike intellects out into the cold, cruel world.

As Mary's father had once said of Frances's canary.

"And it isn't cruel to let people like that horrible Mrs. Turner back home in Lexington own them, I suppose?" fumed Mary. "The one who beat so many of her slaves that her coachman eventually killed her in self-defense? And was hanged for it?" She handed her husband a cravat. He'd come back to the house for an hour's rest and some supper, which he hadn't eaten, after a day spent at the State House, where the Republicans of Illinois had gathered to nominate their candidate for the Senate.

Norman Judd—of the "we won't vote for a Whig" group two years ago—had opened the convention with a banner saying, COOK COUNTY FOR ABRAHAM LINCOLN.

The papers that lay on Lincoln's small desk—Robert had twice kept Tad from shuffling them into a different order—were Lincoln's acceptance speech.

This time, thought Mary, he would win. He had to.

"Or that awful woman in New Orleans, back when I was a girl?" she went on. "I spent half my evenings in the kitchen, listening to Nelson and Mammy and Chaney talk. I know how everyone in town treated their darkies, and something tells me people haven't changed that much over the years. Some people—like Papa—treated them well. . . ."

"Except that they could be sold," reminded Lincoln softly, "to people who wouldn't treat 'em quite so well."

Mary was silent, thinking about Jane's tears, all those years ago when Saul had been sold to help pay Uncle David's debts. Remembering Pendleton, and Chaney, and Patty, sold as part of her father's property in the settlement, just because George didn't think he was getting enough of his father's money. Of Jane and Judy, sold too to help clear up Robert Todd's debts. When Emilie had come here—good God, was it four years ago already!—she had spoken of the financial hardship in which Betsey and all the younger ones were living; her latest letter informed Mary that Betsey had gone to live in Alabama with Mattie and her husband.

What had happened to Saul? To Jane and Judy? To Pendleton, whom

Betsey had nursed through the cholera; to grouchy old Aunt Chaney, who'd made such wonderful pastries; and the timid, good-natured Patty? Mary hadn't the faintest idea.

"Papa never would have sold them," she said at last.

But as President of the State Bank of Kentucky, Papa had sold hundreds of slaves when other men had died in debt, with as little thought as George had had, for where they went or what became of them.

"No," agreed Lincoln. He started to turn from the mirror—Mary handed him a hairbrush. As usual his hair was too long and looked as if a hurricane had passed across his head. "The Founding Fathers did what they had to do to make the Union, and I'm not about to undo their work. But they knew the evil they dealt with, and tried to limit it. And that we must do, or make a mockery of all they strove for."

Robert, Willie, and even Tad, who was just five but already knew the difference between the State Legislature and "We-uh Gongweth," as he called it, had wanted to go with their mother to hear their father accept the nomination. Mary had told them that children weren't allowed in the State House galleries, which was partly true—mostly, she wanted to hear Lincoln speak without worrying about Tad slipping away and ending up dancing a jig on the podium. Lincoln walked the three blocks to the State House square alone, through the falling summer twilight, to meet with Judd and Davis and the others before the convention re-convened at eight. She got the boys settled and followed later, taking her place in the crowded gallery with Cousin Lizzie, Dr. Wallace, and a new friend, Hannah Shearer, the lovely sister of their neighbor the Reverend Miner. The night was hot and smelled of far-off storm; Mary's head throbbed a little, and the itching discomfort of her old female complaint was back, but she'd forborne to take the usual two spoonfuls of Battley's Cordial: she wanted instead to savor every moment of triumph.

Lincoln stepped to the podium, and his voice cut the molten lamplight of the room like a silver knife. *"If we could first know where we are, and whither we are tending, we could then better judge what to do, and how to do it. . . ."*

In his black suit and black silk cravat he looked, if not exactly like other men, at least like a man of respect and education, not like some shambling backwoods lawyer. Mary had never quite taught him to sit in a chair when he wasn't being observed, and she despaired of ever breaking him of the habit of answering the door himself, in his shirtsleeves and like as not with a hammer in one hand and a mouthful of nails. . . .

But tonight he looked like a man voters could take seriously. He looked like a Senator.

And he spoke like a prophet whose God was justice.

"A house divided against itself cannot stand. I believe this government cannot endure, permanently half slave and half free.

"I do not expect this Union to be dissolved—I do not expect the house to fall—but I do expect it will cease to be divided. . . ."

"He should have cut that out." Dr. Wallace leaned across to Mary. "Lamon and the others told him to. He's going to lose any chance of getting into the Senate if he alienates all the Southerners living in the south part of Illinois."

"I think we've had enough of candidates who won't talk about what we're actually voting for," retorted Mary, whose opinion had been—Lincoln had asked her—to leave it in. "At least he's honest enough not to try to sell voters a pig in a poke."

Wallace raised his eyebrows, and shook his head. "Whether he's just won the election or cut his own throat," he mused, "you've got to admit he's come a long way."

A month later, with the campaign heating up, Lincoln issued a challenge to Stephen Douglas, for seven debates on the issue of slavery. Mary held her breath for the week it took Douglas to make up his mind. Ever since the days of hearing secondhand of Lincoln and Douglas arguing in Speed's store—"Like two gods throwing lightning at one another,"—she had longed to see these intellectual warriors meet.

Knowing Douglas, she knew exactly why he hesitated. Like Ninian, he would rather simply that the issue go away; he didn't want to alienate one side or the other. The object was to get into power first, *then* implement policy.

Maybe he suspected that his own position was false. That of the rights of states to choose their own path was less easy to defend than the biblical and patriotic echoes of that single word "liberty."

Maybe Lincoln's challenge was simply too public for him to back down.

Banners, posters, cartoons in newspapers spoke of the "Little Giant"—with his awe-inspiring presence and his voice of bronze and thunder—meeting the challenge of the "Giant Killer." There was much talk of David and Goliath, though newspapers differed on which combatant was on this occasion fighting on the side of the Lord. Through those seven weeks of campaigning Mary followed the debates in the *Illinois Journal,* with Robert reading over her shoulder and Tad, Willie, and Maria Francesca—the latest of the "girls"—listening eagerly, as if for news of a battlefront. When Lincoln came home—a day here, two days there—he was mostly occupied with the Republican leaders in Springfield, or in conference with newspapermen whose presence was increasingly a part of any major campaign. One of them, a young German named John Nicolay, became something of a fixture around Lincoln's law office and a fast friend of the new law clerk, dapper and supercilious John Hay.

In addition to debating Douglas, Lincoln crisscrossed the state, addressing meetings, rallies, audiences large and small, sometimes in towns he himself had staked out while a young surveyor struggling to make a living in New Salem. He remembered everyone's name, and the circumstances of previous meetings—Mary knew well his prodigious capacity, not only to recall everyone he had ever met, but to take a genuine warm interest in their doings, as if each man was a friend encountered across the stove of some country store.

Douglas was campaigning hard, too. But whereas he traveled by special train with an entourage including his second wife, Dolley Madison's niece the regal and beautiful Adele Cutts, Lincoln always rode the public cars, shaking hands with and listening to everyone he encountered. When at last Mary took the train to Alton to see them meet—when she finally stood in the heatless October sunshine of the Alton Courthouse square—the difference between the two candidates was even more pointed. Douglas radiated wealth and power, resplendent in a new blue suit and immaculate linen, every inch the respected Senator with offices in hand to bestow and bowing as gracefully to applause as he'd bowed to Mary, years ago in Elizabeth's parlor. Lincoln, following him up alone, looked like he did on any day in court, in his rusty black suit with the sleeves too short and the pants-hems hovering several inches above his worn black shoes.

She heard the cheers for "Old Abe," "Honest Abe," and her heart glowed—though she knew Lincoln hated the nicknames. He smiled and lifted his hand and the cheers swelled to a roar. A man who'd cut wood and slaughtered hogs for his living, a man who understood what it was to be poor. Last night at the Franklin Hotel, Lincoln had recounted how, during his first long-ago campaign for the Legislature, en route from one small village to another, he and Cousin John Stuart had passed reapers in a field, getting in the last of the wheat. The workmen had said they had little use for any candidate of either party, but would vote for any man who could do his share of the work; Lincoln had promptly climbed down from Cousin John's buggy, borrowed a scythe, and led the crew on a full round of the field.

"You can't pretend, with a scythe in your hands, Mother," he'd said to her. "Thank God they wasn't makin' shoes. It was as good a campaign speech as I ever made."

Mary, looking up at the platform now, couldn't imagine Stephen Douglas reaping wheat.

But it had been a fierce campaign. She saw it in Lincoln's lined face, heard it in Douglas's hoarse and nearly inaudible voice. Douglas started out speaking in defense of his policy toward Kansas: *". . . the signers of the Declaration of Independence . . . did not mean Negro, nor the savage Indians, nor the Fejee Islanders, nor any other barbarous race. . . ."*

He spoke for an hour, before Lincoln got up and replied. Mary had, in her luggage, transcripts of all the previous debates, from the ferocity of Douglas's first accusations that Lincoln had been "in conspiracy" to form an abolitionist Republican Party, through later baiting that he intended the Negro race to be either (a) extinguished or (b) amalgamated into the white race through interracial marriage.

Lincoln rose, with the sunlight slanting now, blinking a little in it with that deceptive bumpkin slowness that had fooled so many rival attorneys. But there was nothing of the bumpkin in the penetrating tenor that rang out over the crowd; nothing of the bumpkin as he spoke of the conflict "on the part of one class that looks upon the institution of slavery *as a wrong,* and of another class that *does not* look upon it as a wrong."

All his awkwardness, all the slightly comic effect of the scarecrow height and mud-fence ugliness, seemed to melt away, until only the voice was left, speaking words of silver and steel.

"That is the issue that will continue in this country when these poor tongues of Judge Douglas and myself shall be silent. It is the eternal struggle between these two principles—right and wrong—throughout the world. They are the two principles that have stood face to face from the beginning of time; and will ever continue to struggle. The one is the common right of humanity and the other the divine right of kings."

Mary closed her eyes, listening to the roar of applause. *They must elect him,* she thought. *If only they could elect him outright, and not put everyone through that horrible balloting in the Legislature. . . .* Hard to remember that neither Lincoln's name nor that of Douglas was anywhere on the ballot.

Only the names of men who would go to the Legislature, who would be favorable to one or the other.

On the second of November, in the pouring rain, Democrats won fifty-three percent of the seats in the Legislature. Much printer's ink was expended in accusations that illegal voters were brought in: "Thousands of roving—robbing—bloated pock-marked Catholic Irish were imported upon us," was how Billy Herndon put it. But in the end it made little difference.

At home, Lincoln was silent and deeply depressed, though he smiled when Willie presented him with an execrably spelled homemade "newspaper" article about the debates, complete with drawings. By the end of the week he was back in his office, with Billy and young John Hay—something for which Mary was deeply grateful, since an autumn on the campaign trail instead of the court circuit had reduced the household finances terrifyingly, and she'd overrun her credit at every shop in town. On the fifth of January, when the Legislature voted for Senator, Lincoln was in the Supreme Court chambers, arguing cases Herndon had filed.

By that time, the wildness of the campaign seemed a thousand years ago.

It was a winter of penny-pinching. Mary groaned with remorse every time she crossed those beautiful flowered rugs, sat on the new parlor chairs. She would wake in terror from dreams of being back at the Globe Tavern, hearing the clanging of the stagecoach bell, her heart hammering and her mind filled with desperation and the echoes of the Bledsoes arguing in the next room: *We have to get out of here! We have to get our own house. . . .*

"Things will be fine," Lincoln soothed, gathering her into his arms. "I just need to get back to real work, and God knows there's plenty of it out there. . . ."

"I should never have had the house enlarged!" Mary sobbed. "We could use that money now, and we don't need a place this big. . . ."

"Well, if you really feel that way," said Lincoln worriedly, "I'll start tearing it down tomorrow, but I think it might be better to wait for spring."

He could always make her laugh.

During one of their debates in Freeport, Lincoln had come out and asked Douglas if Popular Sovereignty meant that the people of a territory could *exclude,* as well as permit, slavery? Since that was what Popular Sovereignty was about, Douglas had been forced to answer yes . . . and had immediately begun losing support, not in Illinois, but in the Southern states that had looked to him to carry their banner to the White House.

By summer, Douglas was courting the Republicans to form a third party to elect him President in 1860. Between cases, between journeys, Lincoln worked to heal the rifts that his own defeat had left in the discouraged Republicans, juggling speeches against Douglas's still-catchy doctrine ("If one man chooses to make a slave of another man, neither that other man nor anybody else has a right to object") with vicious internecine squabbles between the wealthy Mr. Judd and Mayor Wentworth of Chicago about whose candidate (and whose pet newspaper) was going to wield power in the Republican Party. He went campaigning in Ohio, Indiana, Wisconsin, and Iowa, for Republican candidates and to strengthen the Republican Party. Mary and the boys went with him on one such journey, to Cincinnati and Indianapolis.

Mostly he went alone. In his absence her fears of poverty—of losing their home, of having to return to the nightmare of boardinghouse living—would return, and she found herself nervous, depressed, and easily angered. This anger frequently took the shape of quarrels with Robert, who, with one eye on his college education, would put forward tidy plans of how the family finances could be regularized.

Robert was a tall, big-shouldered boy of fifteen now, with blue Todd eyes, given to chilly silences and measured opinions. He did not appear to possess any sense of humor—Mary wondered how something that was so much a part of both parents had managed to be left out.

When Willie obtained, from God alone knew what source, four long, fat, black cigars, and talked Tad and two playmates into "blowing a cloud" behind the barn, it was Robert who was shocked. Mary took one look at the four green-gilled experimenters and nearly collapsed with laughter.

Robert, now a member of the Springfield Cadets, was applying to Harvard, with the intention of becoming a lawyer like his father—and a millionaire, he said. Mary grieved at the thought of losing him, but after Robert's carefully worded criticism of how she ran the household (*and let him try to keep five people decently clothed when his father forgets to collect his fees!* she thought) she sometimes had the despairing sense of never having known her oldest son at all.

After Robert's stinging criticism it was always Willie who would pull her out of her blues. Willie was as happy and open as his older brother was self-righteous and withdrawn. Willie, like his father, could always make her laugh. Like his father, Willie always knew when she needed arms put around her. It was Willie who'd come to sit beside her, when the prairie thunder hammered and his father was away.

"Really, Mother, it's no wonder Tad's a bundle of nerves, the way you take on," Robert would say, impatient, from the bedroom door.

And after he'd leave, Willie would tighten his small grip on her hand and whisper, "I'm here, Mama. Everything will be all right." It was he who'd make her "headache tea" when she had a migraine, or would hold her hand when she'd taken a couple of spoonfuls of Atkinson's Female Cordial and lay quiet in the dark, waiting for the pain to subside.

Robert took the train east to Massachusetts and failed—spectacularly and humiliatingly—in his Harvard entrance examinations. "I told him he wasn't working hard enough," fumed Mary, when they got the letter. "But he never would listen." She bit back the accusation, *If you'd only been around more . . .* "He just freezes on me and won't say a word."

"He's shy." Lincoln folded the letter and tucked it into the inner band of his hat, where he stowed most of his notes for speeches and the letters that had to be answered soonest, as if by proximity with his brain they'd remain "on his mind." He set the hat on the porch-rail beside them and settled back on the cane-bottomed chair, lifted a hand to wave at the minister's wife, Mrs. Smith, walking down Jackson Street in the summer twilight. Only last week, he'd helped her nail a new step on her back porch.

"There are preparatory academies back East. I know Douglas has influence with the President of Exeter. He'd write Robert a recommendation." Despite the drubbing they'd given one another on the campaign trail last fall, Lincoln and Douglas remained good friends, an attitude Mary found difficult to understand.

"And how much is that going to cost us?"

"Not more than we can afford, Mother."

"He should have studied harder. . . ."

"And maybe I should have campaigned harder," said Lincoln with a grin. "Then I'd be a Senator now."

Mary said nothing, torn between her worry about money—her worry that Lincoln would find out about the cost of her latest dress, the expense of the dinners she'd given to make an impression on Messrs. Judd and Palmer when last they'd been in town—and her genuine wish for Robert to get the kind of education his intelligence deserved.

Between campaigns and cases, Lincoln had given Robert what time he could. But there was always that wall around the boy, from behind which he would regard his parents with haughty, slightly accusing eyes.

Because his father left him home to deal with his mother's temper?

Because his mother had betrayed him into those moments of agony under the surgeon's knife?

Because he was old enough to remember Kentucky, and what it was like to live in a wealthy house with slaves instead of one in which pennies were counted when his father—again—let his law work slip in favor of political speeches?

Because Lincoln and Mary had spent the first year of his life resentfully adjusting to the loss of familiar comforts, familiar freedom?

Because, after all these years, he still missed Eddie, for whose loss Mary had been too grieved herself to give him comfort?

Mary didn't know.

In November, newspapers began to suggest that Abraham Lincoln might be the appropriate candidate for the Republicans to run for President in 1860.

"Me?" Lincoln roared with laughter that made Mary lower the paper—it was the *Sandusky Commercial Register*—and regard him across the kitchen table in miffed dignity. The day's rain had stopped, but the early-falling darkness was bitterly cold. Fido and the cats had called a temporary truce so they could all make space for one another in front of the stove.

"And why wouldn't you make a good President? A *great* President?"

"And what are they gonna run me on?" Lincoln grinned. "My Black Hawk war record, or the bang-up job I did on the House Post Office Investigatory Committee back in '48? 'Why, Mr. Secretary of War . . .' " He steepled his long fingers in mock conference with an imaginary Cabinet official, " 'I seem to recall just sech a problem back when I was on the Post Office Committee. . . . Only instead of bein' invaded by Britain, France, and Russia all at the same time, we had to investigate postmasters passin' mail free along to their friends. . . .' "

"You're being silly," said Mary severely, her own heart beating hard at the thought of what Elizabeth would say to the news that her "bumpkin" brother-in-law had been elected to the highest office in the land.

"Anybody who would elect *me* to the Presidency," Lincoln rose and fetched his old jacket from the cupboard behind the door, "is the one's bein' silly." But as he turned to go out into the dark yard to feed Buck, Mary saw the glint in his eye, like a traveler topping a rise of land, and looking out into new territory ahead.

Chapter Thirty-six

In February of 1860 Lincoln went to New York, to speak at a gathering of the Young Men's Central Republican Union—some of those "young men" being fairly venerable, like William Cullen Bryant, who was sixty-five, and Horace Greeley of the *Tribune,* New York's most influential Republican newspaper. Cash Clay would be speaking, too, and other anti-slavery luminaries. Already Mary could see, in the various journals that came to Jackson Street, the jostling among the men who sought power, like jockeys edging for position at the post. Chief among them was William Seward, senator and former governor of New York, a wily extremist whom she judged—and Lincoln judged—would scare off more voters than he'd draw in a national contest. Salmon Chase, the Republican governor of Ohio, was a less controversial but far less colorful contender: nobody knew ill of him because he really didn't have much to say. John C. Frémont was in the running, too, and an assortment of lesser fry, including an Associate Justice of the Supreme Court named MacLean, and the indefatigable Cash Clay.

None of them, she thought, could come up to Lincoln.

And Lincoln, she was well aware, wasn't unknown. He'd just had his debates with Douglas published in book form and they were selling smartly.

It was, of course, unthinkable that a man should campaign openly to become President. No man who boldly strove for the office was regarded as quite trustworthy. But Mary knew her husband well, and she knew he'd spent hours perfecting his New York address, and that he'd paid a hundred dollars for a new suit to give it in.

She later heard from Robert about his father's visit, how the other boys at Exeter had looked at each other in appalled astonishment at the sight of the immaculate and gentlemanly Robert's scarecrow progenitor. But when Lincoln rose to speak at the Cooper Union, when he passionately denounced the spread of slavery to new territories while upholding the Constitution that provided for it in existing states—when he argued for Union and compromise against the radicalism of either side—Robert's classmates could only whisper to him how proud he must be, that that man up there was his father.

What Robert himself felt, he did not say.

And by the time Mary got her son's account of the address—which was followed by a speaking tour of New England—she already knew that Lincoln had told his supporters to put his name in. He would run.

ALL SPRING THEY WATCHED THE NEWSPAPERS. AGAIN THEY MADE LISTS of supporters, spoke far into the night of what points to emphasize to whom. Mary clipped every article about Lincoln—or about Douglas, who was bidding for the Democratic Presidential nomination—that she could find, sticking them into a scrapbook with Willie's help. (Tad's "help" had resulted in large portions of Fido's fur being clipped off to get the glue out of it—thereafter part of Willie's job was to keep meticulous track of the glue-pot and of his younger brother.) Hannah Shearer and Cousin Lizzie came by nearly every day, to catch up on the latest word or speculate about Lincoln's chances. The whole town, it seemed, was watching and listening.

In April the Democrats met in Charleston, South Carolina, and roundly rejected Douglas—the question Lincoln had forced upon him in Freeport had had its lethal effect, like a slow-killing wound. The northern Democrats stormed out in a rage and set up their own convention in Baltimore. Without the necessity of nominating a Westerner—Lincoln—to counterbalance Douglas, William Seward pushed forward his Republican claims, or rather had his chief handlers push him forward ("Blushing and protesting all the way, I daresay," Mary sniffed) for President.

Lincoln was home for a week in March and another in April, between making speeches and arguing cases for the Illinois Central Railroad in Chicago. Those weeks, he spent much time at his law office and more writing letters or conferring with Judge Davis while Billy and John Hay dealt with his legal correspondence. As always, when he turned his energies toward politics instead of legal work, the family finances suffered. At other times, his absences would have been maddening; now, Mary scarcely noticed whether he was there or not.

It only mattered that he be nominated.

It only mattered that he win.

Mary recalled Henry Clay, one of the men who, thirty years before, had saved the Union through diplomacy and compromise, passed by again and again for President. Of all the statesmen she had ever heard of, he had deserved the Presidency most: *"For all of his running,"* the old song went, *"he never arrived. . . ."*

"Whoever gets the nomination in Chicago in May will win," said Lincoln softly, on one of those rare nights when he was home. "The Southern Democrats are for John Breckenridge, the Northerners for our friend Douglas—now here's a third Southern Union candidate stepping up, Bell. If the Republicans can pull *all* the anti-slavery votes together, they can take the election."

In Decatur and Chicago, "wigwams" were built—huge ramshackle temporary halls with canvas roofs—for the Republican Conventions, first the state and then the national a week later. Lying in bed reading, Mary would see Lincoln through the bedroom door in his own room, writing by lamplight at his little desk: letters to Norman Judd, letters to Judge Davis, letters to fellow attorneys and political supporters Ward Lamon, Leonard Swett, Isaac Arnold. Letters to the editors of every Republican newspaper in Illinois, and to the German-language papers that served that powerful minority. Even letters to Lyman Trumbull, whom she still considered perfidious and untrustworthy. Now and then he'd lean down to scratch Fido's silky yellow head, or would move aside whichever of the cats chose that moment to sit on his papers.

When he was finished with his work he'd come into Mary's room, and sit on the foot of the bed and talk until he'd tired himself out enough to sleep. On other nights, she fell asleep to the soft scratching of his pen.

He went to Decatur for the state convention: "Blamed if some band of fools didn't carry in a couple of fence-rails, all done up with streamers and flags, that I was supposed to have split down in Macon County thirty years ago, and put up a painting of me splittin' 'em." He shook his head, but Mary could see he was pleased, and moved closer to him on the sofa. He'd come home that evening on the train—the days when he'd ridden in the saddle all over the central portion of the state were long gone—and Tad and Willie and Fido all crowded as close around him as they could, as if like a fire he radiated both light and warmth.

"Does this mean you're going to be President, Pa?" Willie looked up into his face, gray eyes sparkling. Lincoln's eyes, Mary reflected, without that haunted shadow of sadness, the eyes of the child Lincoln had never been.

"Not yet, son." He ruffled Willie's thick, chestnut-brown hair—gold-flecked, like Mary's and Robert's. "It means I get to put my name in the hat, and if it gets pulled out of the hat, it means I get to stand on the starting-line and run the race."

"Oo gowa bead Dougwath?" Tad's combination of lisp and slur made any attempt at communication from him problematical—something that infuriated the boy in dealing with his playmates—but neither Lincoln nor Willie seemed to have the slightest problem understanding.

Lincoln smiled. "I'll beat him if I can, son. And that's *Mister* Douglas."

"And then will there be no more slavery?"

Lincoln and Mary exchanged a glance over Willie's head.

"That," said Lincoln softly, "is what remains to be seen."

Thanks to the skillful maneuvering by Norman Judd and David Davis—and a little judicious chicanery about the advance seating of Lincoln supporters in the Wigwam—the Republican delegates in Chicago nominated Lincoln on the third ballot. Seward was said to be seething, but in fact, Mary thought Lincoln was right when he said Seward would lose the moderate votes to Douglas in the Presidential race itself. "Seward's an abolitionist," he said, when he and Mary met briefly in his bedroom, where he repaired to put on a cravat, after the editor of the *Illinois State Journal*—none other than his old friend Edward Baker's son, now married to Elizabeth's Julie—brought the news to the house. "If Seward were elected, the whole South would secede from the Union. They're not about to sit still for a man who claims there's a Higher Law than the Constitution."

The booming crash of guns made Mary startle. She'd had a migraine the previous day, out of sheer nervousness, and her usual springtime headaches made her jumpy. She wished they could have gone up to Chicago, instead of remaining in Springfield pretending that election to the Presidency was of only minor concern to them. "That's for you, Lincoln!" cried young Mr. Baker, when Lincoln and Mary came down the stairs. "They're firing off the cannon at the Courthouse for Illinois's first Republican candidate for President!"

The gunfire went on all afternoon.

Nobody seemed to think it was an omen.

Henry Clay, Mary thought, remembering again that tall red-haired man in her father's parlor. Counting back the elections, the four-year wildness like a national quartan fever, the elation and the dizzy sense of power. Henry Clay, and old Hard Cider and Log Cabins Harrison . . . Then the intoxication of campaigning through New England for Zachary

Taylor, who owed Lincoln so much and who died before any patronage could be dispensed.

And now it was Lincoln—her own husband—whose name would be on the ballot.

In a way she couldn't believe it.

In a way, there was nothing else real in her life.

Elizabeth was full of faint praise and sidelong remarks about what would happen to the country if an avowedly anti-slavery candidate were elected. Ninian was a Douglas man, despite Mary's twits about certain conversations back in the days when the Little Giant was her beau. Cousin Lizzie Grimsley spent evening after evening in the kitchen with Mary, drinking tea and playing that agonizing, marvelous game of "What if . . . ?" Lincoln remained at home all the summer and fall, doing nothing, it seemed, but writing letters, endlessly. Everywhere his supporters made speeches, rallied voters. He took on young John Nicolay—the German-born journalist who'd helped get his name in so many southern Illinois papers—as a secretary, and still he'd spend all day at his office with correspondence, and into the night.

Mary chafed and fretted, kept up her books of clippings, gave dinners several times a week for Lincoln's supporters and struggled, with Maria Francesca's help, to keep the house spotless in between. In these days Lizzie was her mainstay. Bessie and Simeon had gone away to Oregon the year before—the *Illinois State Journal* being only a new name for the old *Sangamo Journal*—and her other close friend Hannah Shearer had moved to Pennsylvania with her ailing husband. Mary liked John Nicolay, and was inclined to like Lincoln's clerk John Hay, Nicolay's inseparable friend. Even more she liked the effervescent Chicago youth named Elmer Ellsworth who'd also come to work as Lincoln's clerk. Ellsworth had organized a prize-winning regiment of Zouave militia, who marched and drilled with nimble élan at pro-Lincoln rallies. Ellsworth was a born knight-errant, like an older version of Willie, and seemed to include in his clerkly duties that of looking after Mary and the boys when Lincoln was out of town.

Journalists came that fall too, like swarming bees. Sometimes they were polite, sometimes obnoxiously demanding. All wanted to see the man called "The Rail-Splitter" at home. Mary greeted them warmly, though she'd already begun to mistrust them; she refrained from remarking tartly that her husband hadn't split fence-rails in thirty years and hadn't liked doing it even then. They were delighted when they caught him in his shirtsleeves chopping kindling. Journalists in the South called him an ape and speculated that he had Negro blood in his own veins, since he loved that servile race so much.

Then it was November.

Lincoln's name wasn't even on the ballot in a number of Southern states.

He spent most of Election Day at the State House, in the small room off the rear hall usually reserved for the governor. He'd been there for days—coming out on the day before the election, he'd been stopped by a journalist who'd demanded how he was going to vote. "By ballot," Lincoln said—which he did, after cutting his own name off the card so that it could not be said that he had voted for himself.

All day she waited. Lizzie came in the morning, and helped her play hostess to a steady stream of callers, with occasional breaks to retrieve Tad from the polls, where he was standing outside waving an American flag and exhorting citizens—rather incoherently—to vote for his father. Darkness fell, though she could see the torchlight around the State House and the polling-places when she and Lizzie walked to the corner.

"Do you think there'll really be trouble with the Southern states, if Mr. Lincoln is elected?" asked Lizzie worriedly, pulling her shawl close around her shoulders. She was a big girl, taking more after the tall Todd men than the women of the family.

"I can't imagine why." Mary looked up at her quickly. "It isn't like Frémont running on a Free Soil ticket. Mr. Lincoln is a moderate. He's never been an abolitionist, in spite of what all those Southern newspapers keep insisting. He's *always* said that since the Founding Fathers permitted slavery to exist in the South he's not going to end it there, only keep it from spreading into the territories."

Yet she shivered. Emilie had written her from Lexington: *I think you ought to know what they're saying. . . .* And she received enough of the Lexington papers to feel a deep foreboding, deny it though she might.

Politics was a vicious business. She knew the lies that were being printed, and believed. She knew there were those in the South who'd scream that their rights were being violated by even the election of a Republican President. From the day she'd seen Nate Bodley cane Elliot Presby in the street, she'd known that the merest breath of criticism toward slavery could rouse some Southerners to bloody violence.

Like dark voices whispering in a dream, it came to her that if he won, Lincoln would have to face a hundred thousand Nate Bodleys.

That there was something beyond victory, other than a procession in triumph to the White House with Elizabeth gnashing her teeth in the background.

But he'll win, she thought, pushing that qualm aside with a rush of excitement. *He must win. . . .*

What came after could be dealt with then.

Lizzie and Maria Francesca helped her put Tad and Willie to bed. The boys were wild with excitement. It was impossible, in their eyes, that their father could be defeated.

Or that evil would come after victory.

She thought of Lincoln in the telegraph office, surrounded by the men who'd supported him through the campaign—Davis and Lamon, Swett and Arnold, hatchet-faced Lyman Trumbull and dapper little John Hay scuttling around like a banty rooster . . . Elmer Ellsworth as excited as her two sons and Billy Herndon running in and out with cups of coffee. Papers on the floor, telegraphic scrap, newspapers from here and there . . .

The atmosphere reminiscent of the days of argument around the stove at Speed's store—the political hearth tacitly forbidden to women. After all she had done, she was shut out of that, and her heart twinged with resentment and anger that had no place to settle.

Lizzie was still at the house at midnight when Mary heard Lincoln's stride on the kitchen steps. She sprang to her feet and the next instant heard his voice, high and clear in the night, "Molly . . ."

She and Lizzie dashed into the kitchen—of course he'd come in that way, he never used the front door. . . .

"Molly!" He stood in the kitchen door, breathless, beaming, cravat askew, smiling like the rising of the sun. "Molly, we're elected!"

She flung herself into his arms, Lizzie crowding to their side, Fido yapping excitedly around everyone's feet.

President, she thought.

President of the United States . . .

Even then, it crossed her mind that this was the end of their days of peace.

Chapter Thirty-seven

Bellevue July 1875

"Mrs. Lincoln." Dr. Patterson put aside his napkin, and folded his hands. "Now, is it true that you sent a letter out of here to a Dr. Swenson in New York?" He took a folded paper from beside his breakfast plate, crossed and re-crossed with Mary's blotted handwriting, held it up in the hot butter-colored sunlight of the family breakfast-room. Beside him his wife regarded Mary with a sad frown, as if she'd caught her urinating on the floor of her room as Mrs. Johnston was wont to do.

Mary could only stare, open-mouthed as much at his tone of gentle reproof—like an adult chiding a willful child—as at the postman's betrayal. "I am not in the habit of lying, Dr. Patterson, any more than I am in the habit of seeing my private correspondence in the hands of a person to whom it was not addressed."

"Now, Mrs. Lincoln," said Patterson soothingly. "The postman has orders to give me any letters that my guests send out without my knowledge. You are here to rest, and that means not overtaxing your nerves. I don't think that's so unreasonable, do you?"

"Not unreasonable!" Mary's hands clenched in her lap and the leaden ache that had settled on her head and belly for weeks since she'd cut down her medicine tightened its hold. "You forbid me to send letters—"

"But I don't, Mrs. Lincoln." Patterson's voice never wavered from its friendly warmth. "Don't you think you're being a little unfair to us here? I only ask that you limit your correspondence to those known to me. We must have rules. You can see how so many women write wild and unthinking letters to people who haven't any idea of their condition. . . ."

"I wrote Dr. Swenson, sir," said Mary, through gritted teeth, "because he *has* an idea of my condition—and his idea of my condition might not agree with those brutes my son bribed to declare me insane!" She had met Dr. Swenson at the Spiritualist camp on the shores of Lake St. Catherine, a few years before. He was a dreamy New Englander whose high-paying practice of medicine had been interrupted by his daughter's death.

Patterson merely looked mildly grieved, as if he heard no more than the further ravings of the insane. Behind him, Jenny the housemaid came in and cleared away the plates to the sideboard. On the other side of the table, Young Doc sat with folded hands, watching the scene between his father and Mary as if observing some clinical demonstration in a classroom. Only Blanche seemed to think there was something improper in the scene being played out before the family: she looked frightenedly from her brother to her father to her mother—like Fido would during Mary's quarrels with Robert back in Springfield—but said nothing.

"Mrs. Lincoln," said Dr. Patterson patiently, "you have to admit that you did agree not to correspond with people not known to myself and to your son, when you came to live here."

"What choice had I—?"

He held up his hand against her hot protest. "Now, you admit that you agreed. You are here to rest. Your son, as your legal conservator, is merely trying to see that you do so. Can't you see that your untruthfulness, your willfulness and lack of cooperation are only evidence of how badly you *do* need rest? All this changing your mind—" He gestured at the basket of cornbread still on the table before her, untouched. "This ordering cornbread at breakfast and then wanting to eat only rolls, or asking for griddle-cakes at supper which you then don't touch . . . Is that the activity of a sane woman?"

You obviously never met my sister, thought Mary savagely, recalling Ann's capacity for ordering food that was never eaten. Cornbread and griddle-cakes, the foods of her childhood, sounded so comforting, yet with her stomach still gripped by the periodic nausea that was the aftereffect of reducing her medicine, in fact rolls were all she actually wanted to eat.

"You order the carriage, then delay and delay . . . say you're going to go out walking and then stay in your room . . ." Patterson shook his head and sighed. "It is all part of your nervous condition, rebelling against the irritations of daily life. And of course I understand that much of the time you're not able to see it." He said it as if his understanding were a wise and forbearing favor. Mary wanted to fling her coffee-cup at him, though she supposed that, too, would be interpreted as willfulness and lack of cooperation.

"Your entire nervous system is like the most fragile of plants, which cannot withstand the shocks, the chills, the storms of the outside world, Mrs. Lincoln." Patterson rose from his place and came around the table to her, holding out his hand to help her up. "What is so bad about remaining with us and resting? We only want to help you."

"By reading my correspondence?" She pulled her hand from his gentle grip. "By having me watched every moment? By barring my window and forbidding me to seek the comfort of the spirits with my sisters in faith?"

"Now, you know that's only your insanity speaking. You know the spirits don't *really* visit people. What is so difficult about accepting the inspired authority of Scripture? You must learn to control your willfulness, and your tendency to deceit, Mrs. Lincoln. I fear you will be with us for a long time."

SITTING IN HER ROOM, MARY STARED OUT THE WINDOW. A JAYBIRD dove through a shaft of sunlight, wings a flash of sapphire against the green velvet of lawns and trees. The July heat brought her the scent of the roses, and the thick intoxication of the grass.

It brought her other things as well.

It brought her the memory of that sweltering Chicago July, four years ago now . . . four years almost to the day. The fifteenth, she thought, her heart beating fast—as it had been the fifteenth of April, that night in Ford's Theater. . . .

It brought her, with heart-tearing exactitude, the baking, breathless dryness of that summer of 1871, the way the air had pressed suffocatingly on that dark little furniture-cluttered room in the Clifton House where Tad sat, propped in that inquisitorial horror of a "therapeutic" chair, gasping for breath.

It brought the very feel of those worn impersonal hotel sheets over his emaciated body, their starchiness as she gripped them, as she crouched on her knees at Tad's side. Brought her the feel of that enormous hand, soft instead of callused but like Lincoln's down to the very shape of the bones. A young hand, a boy's hand. Tad was only eighteen. . . .

He squeezed her fingers gently, responding to her frantic clutch. Tried to smile.

"The doctor says he cannot live," Robert had said to her softly, in the hall outside the room. His voice was low and urgent and his grip on her arms had tightened, as if he would have put a hand over her mouth to keep her from crying out in grief. "The doctor says he cannot live, so please, please, Mother, don't make it worse for him!"

How like Robert, she thought bitterly, *not to understand.*

Yes, of course Tad, so sweet, so completely devoted to her all his short life, would be upset by her tears. . . . But Robert didn't understand what it meant for Tad to die! On her knees by the bed Mary had stared into her youngest son's face, twisted with the pain of struggling to breathe. In those bones she had seen so clearly another face, just emerging: the jutting nose, the high cheekbones, the heavy brow, and the sad gray eyes. Lincoln must have looked like that at eighteen, she thought. Or he would have looked like that if he'd had a decent home to grow up in, a proper education, someone who loved him. . . .

When Robert left the room to fetch fresh water in the pitcher, she had fallen to her knees beside the chair, gripped Tad's hand. "Don't die, Taddie!" she whispered, frantic tears streaming down her face. "Please don't die! Fight! Fight to stay alive! For me, for your mother! Taddie, I shall die without you, I shall die if you go too . . . !"

Tad had wept, and tightened his hand on hers. He had still been holding it a few hours later, when his life slipped away.

MARY CLOSED HER EYES, TEARS BLINDING HER AT THE MEMORY, AS IF IT had happened yesterday. She wanted to close the curtain, to retreat to her bed, but she wanted more than anything else to blot out that grief, with laudanum, Godfrey's Cordial, Nervine, chloral hydrate, anything. . . .

Tad was gone. Sorrow covered her like cindery darkness, familiar and comforting. She opened her mouth to call for Amanda, to say she had a headache—which she certainly did—and ask Dr. Patterson to give her an extra drink of medicine. He would, of course, and John would never know. . . . John was away for a few days, on business in New York.

Then she sighed, and closed it again. The jaybird was perched on the back of a bench beside the harsh gravel of the drive, visible around the corner of the house. *He will carry word of my weakness to Robert,* she thought, *and I will be that much further from getting out of here.*

I should have sent the letter to Dr. Swenson with John. Or does he, like the postman, have "instructions" to turn over all correspondence to Dr. Patterson?

Probably. What a fool she'd been, to think that women before her hadn't tried to suborn the postman, or bribe one of the attendants, to get letters out to their friends. One of the things Robert had taken when he'd cleared out her room at the Grand Pacific—one of the things he hadn't brought to her here—had been her memorandum-book which contained the addresses of friends. She'd met so many people over the years, and she couldn't call the addresses of more than a few dozen to mind. Of those, some were people who had no power, who obviously couldn't help her. What she needed were doctors, whose testimony would overturn those monsters Robert had bribed, or Congressmen, who could ask questions in the government, force those in power to make Robert—and Patterson—turn her loose.

Voices drifted to her through the window; she opened her eyes. Violet Goodwin and Olivia Hill were strolling along the gravel path, trailed by the ubiquitous Gretchen. Mrs. Goodwin was talking agitatedly, gesturing with her thickly gloved hands. Probably about the shortcomings of cleanliness in Bellevue, or Dr. Patterson's remissness in some detail. Mrs. Goodwin dwelled in a world of constant horror, of catastrophe held at bay only by the most rigid adherence to a thousand small rituals of her own invention, and was most tedious on the subject. Mrs. Hill nodded understandingly—her reaction to everything, Mary had discovered—and put out a hand to pat her companion, despite the fact that Mrs. Goodwin hated being touched and everyone at Bellevue knew it.

Mrs. Goodwin pulled away from her, shrilled, "Filthy slut, don't touch me!" loudly enough for Mary to hear her from her window. Gretchen sprang forward and seized Mrs. Goodwin by the arms, Mrs. Goodwin began to struggle in earnest at the contact, Gretchen shouted for assistance, Mrs. Hill—whom Mary had discovered had no common sense—waded in to try help "calm" the thrashing, sobbing woman....

And Dr. Patterson, Young Doc, Zeus, and Peter came running.

"Just don't touch me!" Mrs. Goodwin kept screaming. "Get your dirty hands off me! My God! My God!"

"Now, as soon as you learn to cooperate . . . ," began Dr. Patterson, and Mary closed the window. In a sort of dumb show she watched Mrs. Goodwin dragged back to the nearest door of the house, to the inevitable hydrotherapy and chloral hydrate. Last night Mrs. Munger had waked screaming from nightmares and was still slumbering under a combination of opium and chloral hydrate, something that happened several times a week.

The jaybird on his bench cocked his head and seemed to smile.

Mary pulled the curtain, walked back to sit on the end of her bed, hands gripping each other in the diffuse gloom.

How long will it be before I really lose my temper, and have Dr. Patterson decide that my "condition" is getting worse? Before I'm force-fed anodyne until I forget what freedom is or why I want it?

She remembered standing in the doorway between her room and Lincoln's, in that comfortable little house on Eighth and Jackson—the house that she could never bring herself to go into again, that she could barely bring herself to recall. It was the evening he'd been nominated for Senator, he was about to walk down to the State House in the misty gloom of evening. They'd been speaking of slavery, the key issue between himself and her old friend Stephen Douglas, the rock on which the Democratic Party had split . . . "Papa treated them very well," she'd contended.

And Lincoln had replied, "Except that they could be sold to people who wouldn't treat 'em quite so well."

And she had remembered her father's death, that had condemned so many of his slaves—so many of her friends—to the block and the coffle, to be shipped away to serve strangers, never to see those they loved again.

Robert was mortal.

If he dies while I'm in here, what then?

To whom would custodianship pass?

She understood now, exactly, why John Wilamet and his family had fled from Virginia, why Lizabet Keckley had humbled herself before her white friends, had begged and worked and borrowed money to obtain a freedom which offered her no guarantee of anything except more hard work.

She hadn't thought of Lizabet in a long time. Now she remembered the dressmaker's melodious alto voice saying, "I find helping others eases my grief."

Helping others, thought Mary. *Not "resting," as Dr. Patterson calls it.*

Without John there to talk to it was hard sometimes to remember why she shouldn't simply call for medicine. The thought *He'll never know, after all* crossed her mind with a frequency that horrified her.

But the memory of the time when she had been well enough, and free enough, to help others let her lie down on her bed in all her clothing, and close her eyes. To take her mind off the nagging ache in her heart and in her flesh, she counted up the addresses she knew—doctors, Congressmen, any man in power who might possibly owe her a favor from her days of success.

But if all of them had deserted her then, what made her think any of them would be of help to her now?

In her dream she was in the Cook County Courthouse in Chicago again, the heat so thick that she feared she would die. Her head pounded, her heart felt sick, her flesh itched like fire, and her mind reeled woozily. In a half-daze she looked from face to sweating face of those respectable citizens on the jury. "I am of the opinion that Mrs. Lincoln is insane," said Dr. Danforth on the witness stand, and beside her, her lawyer Isaac Arnold said, "No questions."

"On one occasion she spent $600 on lace curtains; on another, $450 on three watches which she gave to me, for which I had no use. . . ." Robert's mouth moved under his mustache, his eyes fixed at some spot on the cornice-molding above her head.

"No questions," Arnold said, and in her dream she leaped to her feet, screamed at them, "Cowards, blackguards and cowards!" They took no notice of her. Robert went on spouting prices and dates and opinions of her sanity. The jury—which included Dr. Patterson, now, and Young Doc, and President Grant and Nate Bodley—all nodded their heads wisely.

A firm hand took her elbow and drew her down into the chair. Turning her head she saw Lincoln beside her, dressed in the rather shabby black suit he wore on the circuit courts, his black hair rumpled and hanging in his eyes. He had a couple of legal briefs in front of him and his saddlebags lay on the floor beside his chair. "Do something!" she hissed. Lincoln was the best lawyer in the state. He'd argue rings around Ayers and Swett.

Lincoln listened to Robert for a few minutes more—"She spent $700 on jewelry last month, $200 on soaps and perfumes, though she has no home in which to hang curtains, trunks full of dresses which she never wears. . . ."

He leaned close and whispered, "I think you're going to have to get another lawyer, Molly."

"Why?" she demanded. "Who?"

But before he could reply there was the crack of a gunshot, hideously loud in the enclosed heat of the courtroom, and his arm jerked convulsively, wrenching away from her hand. Mary caught him as he slumped, smelled the gunpowder and the horrible hot smell of blood. . . .

SHE JERKED AWAKE, GASPING, HER WHOLE BODY TREMBLING. THE smell of blood lingered in her nostrils, on the shoulder of her dress. She could swear the smell of gunpowder gritted in the air. Her whole body ached for the comfort of the medicine, the comfort of darkness.

You're going to have to get another lawyer.

She knew exactly who he meant.

Someone whom she would not even have met, save for the long Calvary that followed the election of 1860: the Calvary that ended in nightmare.

Chapter Thirty-eight

Springfield January 1861

The picture was crudely drawn, and so vicious that it took Mary a moment to realize what it was.

It was her husband's nude body, hanging by the neck from a dead tree. His flesh was splotched with tar and feathers and his features were drawn so as to be almost Negroid, but there was a sign around his neck saying *Old Abe,* in case there was any question of identity. Under it was scrawled in brownish fluid that had powdered away in the paper's creases, SAY YOUR PRAYERS NIGGER-LOVER.

Mary recoiled in shock. Beneath that folded paper, on Lincoln's small desk beside his bedroom window, there were others, some of them drawings, some of them letters. She glimpsed only a word or two, but the hatred seemed to rise off the paper like a stench. *"Nigger-lover." "You are bound for Hell and we will send you there." "Liar." "Ignorant ape." "You will never live to reach Washington." "Word has reached us that there is an organization forming in New Orleans for the express purpose of your murder." "Say your prayers."*

"Molly."

She turned, breathless, to see Lincoln framed in the doorway of the hall, one of Sheba's new kittens in his huge hand. Her terrified face told him at once what she'd seen. He set the kitten on the bed in passing, strode to her side.

"It's all right," he said.

"All right? *All right?* Those—those *things* . . . that *filth* . . ." She stared up into his face. His battered trunk from his Congressional days stood open beside his dresser—he still owned little besides a few shirts and his books. He could almost have moved to Washington with his saddlebags, the way he'd come to Springfield twenty-five years ago. The new suit he'd purchased to go to New York in lay spread out on the bed, already acquiring a faint speckling of cat-hair. A dozen newspapers strewed the carpet.

"Why didn't you tell me?"

"I didn't think you needed to know."

"You didn't think I needed to know?" she screamed, her terror flaring into rage. "Someone threatens to murder my husband, calls him—"

"Mother!" He stepped close again, and she slapped his hands aside. "Mother, not so loud."

Sturdy footsteps shook the stairs. "Who's going to murder Pa?" Willie came tearing into the room, snow flecking his dark hair. Lincoln immediately scooped up the letters and slipped them into the drawer of his little writing-table. "Seceshes?"

On Willie's tenth birthday, four days before Christmas, news had reached Springfield that the State of South Carolina had voted to take itself out of the Union. Mississippi, Florida, and Alabama were all reported to be on the verge of secession as well, and President Buchanan—an elderly diplomat whose election four years ago had owed a great deal to the fact that he'd been in England during most of the sectional squabbling of the Fifties—had responded only by setting up various Congressional committees to look into compromise.

Lincoln grinned, and ruffled his son's hair. "They'll have to catch me first."

"Oh, my God," Mary whispered, as Willie went to the narrow bed to gather up the kitten. "I can't leave you at a time like this...."

Her own six trunks were already packed in her room, preparatory for departure for New York. For weeks—between visits from Congressmen and Senators, men whom Lincoln hoped to forge into a Cabinet—Mary had been trying to organize which of their furniture and possessions were to be sold, and which put in storage in the attic box-room for four years, until their return. When Philadelphia political boss Simon Cameron—to whom David Davis had promised a Cabinet position in return for Pennsylvania's votes, to Lincoln's outraged disgust—came to Springfield, he had spoken to her over dinner about the White House furnishings. Some things, like dishes, belonged to the house, but Presidents brought their own linens, bedside lamps, "everyday" dishes, small furnishings for the personal parlors upstairs.

A quick review of most of the contents of the house at Jackson and Eighth had convinced her that a shopping-trip to New York was in order.

Since Ann's husband, the jolly and diffident Mr. Smith, was about to embark on a buying-trip to New York for his store here in town, he'd offered to escort her and her sister. Mary still recalled, from their passing visit in '49, all those beautiful shops in New York, places she had barely glimpsed.

She recalled, too, with vivid envy, the hostesses of Washington: the glittering Mrs. Corcoran, the haughty Mrs. Clay of Alabama, the vivacious Varina Davis—the way those stylish uncrowned queens had looked down on the outdated ruffles of a Western Congressman's wife. She would not give anyone the opportunity to do so again. ("Definitely Stewart's," Cameron had purred, to her question. "I shall send a letter telling him you're coming.... And look in at Laurent DeVries's as well. Laurent's silks tend to be more à la mode, though *never* tell Alec Stewart I said so.")

But if anything should happen to Lincoln while she was gone...

"I'll be all right, Mother. You know you want to go and I think the change'll be good for you. Besides, Bob is expecting you to come back here with him. I'll be in a little more danger without your protection—" He dodged aside as she slapped at him. "—but I'll manage."

"We'll protect Pa." Willie's face was radiant at the prospect of standing guard. "Me and Tad and Fido." To demonstrate his readiness to die in his master's defense, Fido half-woke from his doze in the corner, sat up, and yawned.

Mary left two days later, nagged by the thought of what other threats her husband might be hiding from her, but elated to be gone. Since the election she had seen almost nothing of Lincoln, except when he came home, preoccupied and exhausted, from his makeshift office in the governor's room of the State House. Every few days he would have someone to the house, and Mary and Maria Francesca would put together a dinner to entertain them.

After reading about them for years in the newspapers, Mary felt she knew them all, even those who hadn't been pointed out to her in Chicago. Supporters like square-built Norman Judd, or men like myopic former Governor Chase of Ohio who had vied with Lincoln for the nomination. Lincoln spoke to Chase about a Cabinet post, which Mary thought a mistake: how could a rival be trusted? Simon Cameron thought—and had broadly hinted—that he would like to be made Secretary of the Treasury, despite the fact that his Philadelphia political machine was corrupt from top to bottom and he himself couldn't be trusted with twenty-five cents.

And elegant little William Seward, whom Lincoln wanted as Secretary of State, clearly envisioned himself as ruling the country with Lincoln as a mere figurehead.

Lincoln conferred with them all, patiently, keeping his thoughts to himself so well that none of them seemed to realize that he *had* thoughts. Which suited Lincoln just fine.

If Mary had thought the reporters were bad before the election, now they flocked like vampires in some Gothic novel. What would Old Abe do if President Buchanan surrendered the U.S. military installations in Charleston Harbor to the new South Carolina government? *(Do you think the secessionists don't read your newspaper, sir?)* Is the Rail-Splitter going to free the slaves? *(I suggest you review his speeches over the past fifteen years. . . .)* Mary would exert herself to be polite and gracious when she really wanted to chase them out of the house with a broom, and they'd smile and tip their hats and then go back to their home cities and print the most horrifying misquotations, misrepresentations, and outright lies.

Worse than any of these pests were the candidates for government jobs, great and small. "I voted for you and got all my friends to vote for you, now you make me assistant secretary of Nevada Territory. . . ."

It was her dream of patronage and power transformed to nightmare by sheer volume. It seemed as if everyone in the United States were making a pilgrimage to Springfield to talk to Lincoln, as if, with other states threatening to pull out of the Union, he had no more important things to deal with. And during all this, Tad and Willie ran wild with excitement, trying to make their own shrill voices heard by their distracted parents and refusing to be fobbed off with Aunt Lizzie or Lincoln's young clerk Mr. Ellsworth.

Mary felt intensely disloyal about the relief that filled her as the train pulled away for New York. For the time being, she could be away from the aggravation of the situation, and could revel in her dream of the future. Her dressmaker in St. Louis—Madame Blois to whom she'd begun going when Lincoln started working for the railroads—had been ecstatic when she'd heard, as she'd written to Mary: so much to prepare for, such a great office to fill.

True, Mary reflected, but though she'd have to start with several gowns appropriate to the wife of the President, she wasn't entirely certain that Madame Blois was up to the very latest styles. She'd have to see who the really elegant ladies of Washington—Mrs. Corcoran, and Mrs. Clay, and General Davis's wife—went to. Her luggage included an envelope of swatches: it was a certainty she'd never find jewelry appropriate to her new station anywhere but in New York.

She closed her eyes. Journeys were a world of their own, in which everyday care didn't exist. In the first-class car, with its plush seats and gold-trimmed hardware, she felt bathed in the old wild excitement of her girlhood. Her brother-in-law Clark was a bore, of course, and she couldn't imagine how she'd get through two days on a train with Ann without pulling every lock of her hair out, fistful by fistful, but . . .

"Mary!"

She looked up as Clark returned along the swaying aisle, a newspaper in his hand.

Wordlessly he held it out. Ann snatched it. "Good God," she cried. "Alabama, Mississippi, and Florida have seceded!" And she glanced at Mary in sisterly malice as Mary seized the paper back. "It looks like you won't be First Lady of the land after all, dear, but only First Lady of the North."

RUMORS SEETHED IN THE AIR OF NEW YORK. FOR THREE DAYS Clark—and Mr. Dorsheimer, the Treasurer of the State of New York—squired Mary from shop to shop, where, as Mr. Cameron had promised, even the great merchant prince Mr. Stewart bowed as they showed her silks, shawls, earbobs, trim, shoes of the very latest styles. In the evenings reporters came calling on her at the Astor House, and if it had occurred to any of them that she wasn't the wife of a "complete" President, nobody said anything.

Though in her heart Mary never forgave Ann for that "First Lady of the North" remark—and vowed to un-invite her from the Inauguration on the strength of it—she still felt pleased that Ann was there to witness this triumph. Everyone deferred to her—everyone asked questions and listened closely to her answers. Slick-haired young gentlemen from the *Times* and the *Tribune* and the *Herald*—even the London *Times*—leaped to their feet when she entered the lobby, and laughed heartily at her wit. It was like being the belle of Lexington again, without Betsey around to spoil her enjoyment.

"For the Lord's sake, Mary," said her brother-in-law, when she came down to breakfast in the hotel's handsome dining-room on their last morning in town, "did you have to go tell them Old Abe appointed Seward Secretary of State?"

"Nobody informed me that it was a state secret." Mary spread out her enormous skirts—twelve yards around the hem and rustling deliciously with taffeta—to take a seat at the small table that Mr. Astor himself had set aside for her and her party. Robert, across from her, looked uncomfortable. He'd come in last night, while she was still talking with the journalists, and they'd hailed him boisterously as "The Prince of Rails," a nickname by which he was known everywhere now and which he loathed quite as much as Lincoln hated "Old Abe."

He'd grown, in his eighteen months in the East. At seventeen and a half he was nearly six feet tall, his thick shoulders rendered less overpowering by the immaculately cut tweed of his suit and the subdued elegance of his collar and cravat. There was no trace of mis-alignment in his eyes, except a slight immobility when he was tired. He looked like he'd lived in Boston the whole of his life. He would be, she thought, an impressive man.

"Seward's an abolitionist," complained Clark peevishly, shaking out his napkin. "What are the Legislatures of Georgia and Virginia and Kentucky going to think, except that Old Abe means to abolish slavery after all?"

"Now, I'm sure if the legislators of those states read Mrs. Lincoln's remarks," soothed Mr. Drosheimer, "they'll also read the President's statements that he's only against the *extension* of slavery, that he won't touch it where it already exists. Are you feeling quite well, Mrs. Lincoln? It will be a long journey today." Throughout the journey—in fact since the day of the election—Mary had felt in jaggedly unequal spirits, torn between elation and anxiety without the steadying balance-wheel of home, neighbors, family.

The gaiety of travel enraptured her—the reaction, when it came, was crushing. The thought of Lincoln, alone and unprotected in Springfield, had preyed on her mind through a half-sleepless night. The images of those hateful letters and pictures returned to haunt her in terrible nightmares. New York was gorgeous, glittering, sophisticated—her new friends were delightful—but she found that at times the crowds frightened her, and she would return to her hotel room nervous and weepy. Sally Orne, the wife of a wealthy Philadelphia merchant to whom Simon Cameron had introduced her, recommended Uhrquart's Pacifying Indian Bitters for her nerves, and swore by its results. It did seem to help.

"I'm quite well, thank you for asking," Mary replied now to Mr. Dorsheimer. "As for the Legislatures of Virginia and Kentucky, you name two of the most loyal states of the Union, sir. I think we need hardly worry about a few radicals there, whatever the people of Georgia may choose to think."

"We'll need to worry about a few radicals in Maryland," said Robert grimly, "if they decide Father's going to interfere with *their* property. We have to cross *through* Maryland to get to Washington. There might be trouble with those Plug-Uglies they write about."

Mary shivered, and drew her new pink cashmere shawl from Stewart's more closely around her shoulders. Despite the two fireplaces in the Astor House's dining-room, the morning was cold. To no one in particular she murmured, "I shall be glad to get home."

At home, when they got there ten days later—three days late due to inclement weather, but free of charge from Buffalo to Springfield, thanks to a very friendly magnate of the State Line Railroad—the confusion was even worse. According to Lincoln, who met them at the railroad station, a tall black shadow in the falling snow, he had played host to delegation after delegation, from Indiana, Illinois, California, Pennsylvania; Cameron's supporters, Cameron's detractors, petitioners that he provide Cabinet posts for everyone from the Governor of Maryland to Cassius Clay. He looked exhausted, when he and Robert and Clark brought Mary's trunks into the house. The lines in his face had deepened, and he didn't look like he'd been sleeping well.

Or shaving.... "Really, Mr. Lincoln, you haven't been meeting all those delegations that way! You look like a savage!"

His old smile returned and he rubbed his stubbly jaw. "I had a letter from a little girl named Grace Bedell," he said. "She was of the opinion that I'd make a more impressive President if I had a beard."

Mary's mouth dropped open in disbelieving shock.

"An opinion shared by Davis and Trumbull and the others. Not to mention," added Lincoln in a lower voice; with a glance through the kitchen door to where Robert was exchanging mock cuffs with his two younger brothers, "it might be that on our way through Maryland to Washington, it would be better if quite so many people there weren't as able to recognize me."

"*I* think it looks swell," added Willie, coming into the kitchen—which was, she was relieved to note, still warm and orderly, in contrast to the shadowy glimpse of stacked boxes and half-wrapped parcels visible through the doors of dining-room and parlor. Lizzie and young Ellsworth had promised to make sure Tad and Willie stayed fed, warm, and out of trouble, and had, with the help of Lizzie's brother Lockwood, and the free colored valet whom Lincoln had recently hired, been organizing the furniture to be stored or sold. The much grander personal furnishings that she had bought in New York City were going to be shipped straight on to Washington. "He looks like a pirate!"

"Oh, thank you," sighed Lincoln. "Just the thing to give confidence to the South." But his eyes twinkled. "Looks like we're going to Washington the long way," he went on, pulling off his gloves and moving the gently steaming kettle to the front of the stove, to heat up for tea. "People need to be reassured, Mother. They want to see me and they want to hear everything's going to be all right—and God knows I need to see *them*. When a man asks help of someone," he added, "it comes better face-to-face."

He ran a hand over his jaws and through his hair, and she wondered despairingly how she was going to get him through four—or with luck, eight—years of the Presidency without letting him appear before the Prince of Wales or the Czar of Russia with his hair like a canebrake. "I've got invitations to stop and speak in half a dozen cities already—Cleveland and Cincinnati and Harrisburg and Honolulu for all I know—and more coming in all the time. It means leaving early, the eleventh. . . ."

"Of *February*? But I'll be in St. Louis! I've made an appointment for fittings for my dresses! That's two weeks from now! Madame Blois will never be able to have them ready. . . ."

"You and the boys can meet me in Indianapolis. The sale of the furniture's on the ninth—I think Mel Smith's buying most of it. Then we'll be staying at the Cheney House till we go."

"Good." Mary liked the Springfield druggist and his wife. "That gives us time for one last reception here, before we leave." She looked through the dining-room door and into the parlor again, seeing how dark the house was, and how cold and musty it already felt. Fido, curled up by the kitchen stove, raised his head worriedly, sensing that the world as he knew it was coming apart. Henry Rolls, whose yard backed the Lincolns', had already agreed to take the little yellow dog for the four years the Lincolns would be gone; she wondered if the boys would miss him.

If they would miss this house, as she would.

The reception was a splendid one, and lasted far into the night. Lizzie, Mary, and her two older sisters all turned the house upside-down, cleaning and sweeping and scrubbing. Elizabeth lent her Eppy and Lina, and came over to take charge of the baking herself. Then all the Todd girls turned out in their finest, to bid an official good-by.

Everyone in town put in an appearance—Merce and Jamie, the Reverend Smith, who'd spoken so kindly at Eddie's funeral; the ladies of the Episcopal Sewing Guild; Cousin John Stuart and Cousin Stephen Logan; the Gurleys and the Wheelocks and Mrs. Dall, whose infant Mary had nursed right after Tad's birth. . . . The house was crammed from parlors to attics and there was barely room for Eppy, William the new valet, and Maria Francesca to move about the kitchen. Robert, stiff and shy in his natty Eastern tailoring, stood with his parents, shaking hands and making sure to speak to everyone who filed in. Lizzie as usual tried to keep track of Tad and Willie and as usual succeeded only about two-thirds of the time.

To Mary's intense relief, Lizzie—who was accompanying her brother Lockwood, Elizabeth, the young Julie (now Baker), and Young Bess (as everyone called Julie's sister) to Washington City for the Inauguration—had promised to remain for a time as a guest in the White House and keep an eye on the boys until Mary found her feet. Harrison Grimsley shook his head over the plan and warned Lincoln, "I promise you, if my wife stays on with yours, you're going to have your hands full with the pair of them."

Lincoln grinned and ducked his head. "The boys'll keep 'em busy." He'd just returned from three days in Coles County. In all the time she'd known him—even when his Cousin Hetty was living in her sewing-room—she had seldom heard Lincoln speak of his family, though she was aware of the steady stream of ill-spelled and whining letters he'd received over the years, mostly asking for money. She remembered how he'd rushed down to Coles County when his stepbrother had written him that his father was dying: which had turned out to be a false alarm, but while he was there, could he loan them twenty dollars?

He had declined to rush down, the next time his stepbrother wrote. His father had died.

He had come back from this most recent visit to his stepmother sad and thoughtful: "They don't treat her well," he'd told Mary. "Like she was nothing, because she's of no use to them anymore."

She guessed, since they would be in Washington four years—if not, as she already hoped, eight—that Lincoln and old Mother Sarah would not meet again.

The reception was scheduled to last until midnight, but it was closer to two in the morning before the last guests finally left. Many of them were office-seekers, who had wangled their way into the party to speak to Lincoln. Towards the end of the evening, Robert, Ellsworth, and John Hay—like boisterous young Musketeers—were acting as discreet chuckers-out. Lincoln spent the next morning at the State House, but returned, exhausted, in the afternoon; she heard him lie down as she moved quietly about her own room, packing up the last of her things. In addition to Elizabeth, her daughters, and Lizzie, Dr. Wallace was going to be part of the Lincoln party—Frances was no longer healthy enough to undertake so long a journey—and her half-sisters Margaret and Mattie would be meeting them in Washington, to see her triumph *(and request government jobs for their husbands,* she reflected) as well.

Downstairs she could hear the boys—*too loud,* she thought, *they'll wake their father*—and Ellsworth's light, free laugh. But the house seemed strange, half-empty in the gray winter light.

From the next room she heard Lincoln call out, "Molly?" and there was fear in his voice.

She thought, *Nightmare,* and hurried to open the connecting door. *And no wonder . . .*

He was sitting up on the edge of his bed in his shirtsleeves, hair all tousled on his head, staring across the room at his shaving-mirror on the wall. "Look in that mirror," he said. "Do you see one reflection in it, or two?"

She angled her head, for the mirror was set high. "One." It looked, in fact, pretty much as it always had. "Are you all right?" His unshaven face looked waxen with shock.

"Yes. I guess." He shook his head, ran a hand through his hair. "It must have been a dream—one of those dreams when you dream you wake up."

"And you saw two reflections?" Her voice wavered a little—she knew from Mammy Sally the evil of seeing one's own face in a mirror in a dream.

Lincoln nodded. "One looked pretty normal—'cept for the beard, that is. But the other, the one behind it, was white, like a ghost's face. Like a dead man's. And it come to me—almost like hearin' someone say it—that was because I'd be elected twice."

She whispered, her heart like ice in her breast, "Elected twice—but you won't live through your second term."

He stood, and took her hands in one of his. "We don't know that." And his grip tightened a little when she tried to pull away. "It's only a dream, when all's said."

But he didn't believe it. She could hear that in his voice. And neither did she.

SHE DREAMED OF HIM HERSELF, A FEW NIGHTS LATER, WHEN SHE LAY asleep in the Wide Missouri Hotel in St. Louis after a day of fittings and shopping and chatter with Lizzie and with Madame Blois. Dreamed first of herself, burning her old papers the day before yesterday, her last day in Springfield. All those old letters, those quick-scribbled notes he'd sent her while on the circuit or in Washington. *Just cleaning house,* part of her said casually, and part of her admitted her fear that some journalist would get hold of them, and use them for God knew what. His views had changed over the years—in his letters he had not always been discreet.

In her dream she turned her head, to see Lincoln standing in the back door of the house, watching her as Mr. Smith the druggist and his men moved the last of their furniture away. Fido sat next to his boots, raised a worried paw to scratch his knee—*Will everything be all right?*

Then she dreamed of the bedroom at the Cheney House—the elegant bridal suite, the best in the hotel, where Tad and Willie had shared the trundle-bed and Robert had slept on the couch. Saw in her dream Lincoln there alone, roping up his single small trunk by himself: books, papers, a few shirts, and his new suit. Robert was already gone—*down to the station?* Robert was fanatically punctual and lived in terror of missing a train.

Outside the windows, the sky was bleakly dark, just staining with morning gray. Lincoln took one of the hotel's cards to the little marble-topped desk, wrote on the back, A. LINCOLN—WHITE HOUSE—WASHINGTON, and stuck it in the leather label-holder on the trunk. He carried the trunk downstairs himself, a tall man alone in the cold stillness of the morning, to join Robert and Ellsworth, Nicolay and Hay and the others waiting in the lobby. To go to the train station and start for Washington, not knowing when, or whether, he would return.

Chapter Thirty-nine

Philadelphia February 1861

"Mr. Lincoln?" Above the hubbub in the ballroom of the Continental Hotel in Philadelphia, Mary wasn't sure how she heard Norman Judd's murmur, but she did. She turned her head to see the railroad magnate touch Lincoln's sleeve, and the look on Judd's face was the iron look of a man who has received the worst kind of news.

Lincoln saw it, too, and knew it for what it was. He'd been shaking hands since eight-thirty with the cream of Philadelphia society, telling funny stories, remembering the names of everyone who was introduced to him and remembering too whatever contributions they'd made to Whig politics back twenty years. He bowed a little to a banker and his wife, with whom he'd been chatting under the chilly white glimmer of the gasoliers, and said, "If you good folks will excuse me, I think there's another crisis brewing." He kept his voice droll, so that the stout banker and his stouter wife both laughed. Mary, delightedly renewing her acquaintance with the vivacious Sally Orne, saw his tall black form edge away through the crowd toward the gilt-trimmed ballroom doors.

"Excuse me," she said, and began to thrust her way through the crowd after him.

There were times, during the ten days since they'd begun their journey to Washington, that she wondered if they were ever going to reach the capital at all. Every city they passed through, it seemed, had invited Lincoln to stop, to speak, to receive the local dignitaries—dignitaries whose support would be desperately needed, if the seceded Southern states should refuse to compromise or to return to the Union. Needed still more, if loyal and powerful Virginia, or worse yet, Maryland, should decide to join them.

Since meeting the Springfield party in Indianapolis, there had been days when she had barely spoken to her husband at all. Certainly she had not spoken to him alone. As if to remind the new Chief Executive of his obligations to Illinois Central, Norman Judd had provided them with a special Presidential car, decorated like a plush hotel suite with crimson curtains and gold tassels. Even in its privacy Lincoln was always surrounded by his supporters and advisors, that group of handlers she was coming to hate. It was as if the group around the stove at Speed's had taken over his life, leaving only crumbs of him for her. When he talked politics, he talked now with them. Judd was always there, and fat David Davis, the gigantic Ward Lamon, and crafty Orville Browning. Hay, Nicolay, and young Ellsworth added some lightness to the party, rushing about like squires to the political champions.

More than ever she was grateful for the company of Elizabeth and her daughters, and of Lizzie, and Lizzie's brother Lockwood. The atmosphere of alternating tension and elation, wearing enough on her, had turned her younger sons—never the quietest of souls to begin with—into frantic little dynamos. Frustrated at being shut out of the men's councils, Mary would slap the boys or shriek at them, something she knew did not help the situation but which she could not seem to keep herself from doing. What a blessing to have Elizabeth or Julie Baker, or Lizzie, scoop Tad up and say, "Your Mama's tired now, Taddie . . . ," and bear him screaming into another part of the car.

Moreover, she knew there were things she wasn't being told. Telegrams reached them at all stations, and Lincoln would go into conference with the men again, leaving her like a child shut out of her father's study.

She had heard of it, however, when Lamon came in from the train platform in Westfield, New York, with the news that Senator Jefferson Davis—hero of the Mexican War and fixture of Washington society and politics—had been sworn into office as President of the Confederate States of America. "Looks like they mean business," Browning had said, and Lincoln had only looked grim and sad.

Mary reached the door Lincoln had just passed through, to one of the smaller anterooms of the Continental's ballroom. John Hay stood beside it, smart-looking in new evening-clothes. The New York newspapers had had such a field day describing Lincoln as a hick, a bumpkin, an uneducated baboon who would make the United States ludicrous in the eyes of the world, that everyone, Lincoln included, was being very careful to be absolutely correct in all things.

"I'm sorry, Mrs. Lincoln," Hay said. Though he'd read law in Lincoln's office for over a year, he'd been officially taken on only days ago as John Nicolay's assistant. "Mr. Lincoln asked that he not be disturbed by anyone."

"What is it?" she demanded. "What's happened?"

Hay's dark eyes shifted. "It's nothing serious."

"Tell me!"

"Mother . . ." Robert appeared at her side, gently took her arm. "It's nothing serious. Everything's fine."

He was lying. They both were lying.

Trembling, she went back to the reception. She wanted to scream at them, to weep, to force them to let her into their secret councils. But she knew that with Lincoln out of the ballroom it was up to her to smile and greet all those Biddles and Mifflins and Rittenhouses. Elizabeth glanced over at her with warning disapproval for even inquiring about masculine business: Mary raised her chin defiantly and stared back. But when she finally returned to their suite and Lizzie unlaced her from the exquisite gown of lilac silk, she had a pounding headache and was so nervous she was ready to scream.

In Harrisburg the next day Lincoln went to the State House to address the Legislature. Mary was reading to Tad and Willie in the hotel parlor when she heard them return. Outside the door she heard Judd's deep voice, "Do you think it's wise?" and Lincoln's, "She'll wonder where I am, and there'll be no quieting her unless she knows what's going on."

The words went through her with a sickening jolt. She felt just as she did when thunder began to growl in the distance. She shut the book and got to her feet as the door opened. They were all around him: Judd and Davis, Browning and Robert and Ward Lamon, looking as grim as Judd had the night before. There was another man with them whom she vaguely recognized as Mr. Pinkerton, a solid little man like a knot of hardwood, with watchful dark eyes that never relaxed. Lincoln said, "It looks like there's definitely a plan to ambush me in Baltimore, Molly, while the railroad car's being hauled from one depot to the other to get on the Washington line. Fred Seward brought word last night that the local Plug-Uglies plan to rush the car, and Mr. Pinkerton here—he's Mr. Judd's railroad detective—says he's got proof."

The hate-letters flooded back to her mind: the vile drawing, the writing that had looked so much like blood. She put out her hand to steady herself on the chair and Willie stood up, protectively, at her side.

"Mr. Pinkerton," Lincoln went on, "says he's got it worked out for me to go into Washington by another train, alone, without fuss. . . ."

"Without fuss?" She felt panic rising in her. "What do you mean, without fuss? Alone? Without a guard?"

"If nobody knows it's me, nobody's going to attack me."

"And what if someone guesses?" She looked from one to the other of them—Judd, Pinkerton, Robert, Davis, fools, all of them, who were going to get her husband killed! She began to tremble, thoughts surging into her mind of rushing at them, striking them with her fists, with a broom, with a whip. . . . "It's all very well for you to grow that stupid beard, Mr. Lincoln, but you've been seen with it by thousands and thousands of people in every city along our way. What if someone's overheard your precious plan?"

"Molly—"

"Don't you 'Molly' me!" She jerked her hand from his touch. "What if you're murdered? What will happen to me, to our boys? What if *we're* murdered? Or doesn't that matter to your precious committee? What if we're caught and held for ransom?"

"I have to get to Washington," answered Lincoln quietly, "to be inaugurated as President. . . ."

"Don't leave me!"

"Molly . . ."

"Don't leave me!" She felt as if she would suffocate with terror. "Don't be a fool! You're protected here, with an escort—they're not really going to attack with Mr. Buchanan's soldiers on this train. . . ."

"Mrs. Lincoln," intervened Pinkerton, "believe me, they are. There are only twenty soldiers, and our reports indicate that there are hundreds in this plot. And with you and the boys and this whole . . ." He gestured impatiently, as if Elizabeth and Julie, Lizzie and Lockwood and Dr. Wallace, were all present as well. ". . . traveling road-show trailing along after him, those Baltimore secessionists are going to know exactly where to look for him."

"So you're going to send him out away from any protection and hope that nobody's going to notice a six-foot-four-inch man pussyfooting his way through Baltimore!"

"I've got that all arranged, ma'am. He'll be on a sleeper car, in a berth, as my sick relative. Nobody'll see him on his feet—"

"Well, that's a brave way to commence your administration!" She whirled on Lincoln, hearing her own voice rise to a termagant's shrillness. Any words, anything to make him change his mind . . . "Sneaking into your own capital city in disguise because you're afraid of a rumor—"

"It's not a rumor," snapped Judd.

"Don't you talk to me!" Mary screamed at him. "Don't you say a word to me!" Whipsawed by eleven days of travel, exhaustion, and uncertainty, she burst into frenzied tears. She struck at Lincoln's hands as he led her to the back of the parlor, tried to fight free of him, to flee. . . . Only there was nowhere to flee to. She was dimly aware of the men glancing at one another, of Robert's face wooden with embarrassment, of Willie coming up on her other side:

"It's all right, Ma. Things will be all right."

Of Lizzie's arms around her, gently easing her away from Lincoln, to whom she perversely clung the moment he tried to draw away and go back to his precious advisors—*may they all burn in Hell for eternity. . . .*

"Go back to them!" she screamed at him, shoving him suddenly away. "Go back to them and leave me! You don't care a thing about me and you never did! You'd sooner be inaugurated President than keep us safe, me and your sons!" And she flung herself, weeping, into Lizzie's arms.

Their suite at the Jones House Hotel included several bedrooms, though Governor Curtin had asked Lincoln and herself to spend the night at his house. Lizzie led her into the nearest one—assigned to Robert, Hay, and Nicolay, to judge by the leather gripsacks dumped on the beds and the scent of bay rum—and eased her into a chair. "So I won't disturb his precious advisors?" cried Mary resentfully. But it was good to be away from the men to weep, with Lizzie patting her hands and Elizabeth and the two girls hurrying back and forth with cold compresses and hartshorn. At least, she thought, *someone* cared. . . .

But the childishness of that thought tore her, as her paroxysms of tears subsided. *I've made a fool of myself,* she thought, bitterly, *and in front of them. . . .* Trembling, she blew her nose, and got to her feet.

"No," she said, when Lizzie tried to stop her. "I'm fine now. Let me go."

She could hear the voices of the men still in the parlor. Talking about her, she knew. About the scene she'd just made. About how right they were to keep her out of things. Her face grew hot with shame as she stepped past Lizzie and opened the door.

They all turned, faces wary—manlike, dreading another scene. Lincoln started toward her immediately but she said in her steadiest voice, "Mr. Lamon?"

The bearlike lawyer stood at once. Like Lincoln he was a frontiersman turned lawyer; in the plush comfort of the Presidential railroad car, he'd whiled away hours of travel playing the banjo and singing for Tad and Willie's delight.

"Please go with him, Mr. Lamon." She turned to Mr. Pinkerton, regarding her with suspicion in his reptilian eyes. "I understand your point, sir, about not drawing attention to my husband by a large entourage, and I apologize if I . . . if I let my feelings overcome me. But I beg you will allow at least one bodyguard, in the event of . . . of the unexpected."

Lincoln looked down at Pinkerton, then over at Lamon. "That's not a bad idea. I allow I'd feel a little better about it myself, knowing there's two of you."

"That's a good point, Mrs. Lincoln, and well taken." Pinkerton sounded like the admission cost him an effort to make. "Thank you."

"I won't leave his side, ma'am." Lamon opened his coat, to show her the two bowie knives he habitually wore at his belt. "You can count on me, Mrs. Lincoln."

SHE SLEPT LITTLE THAT NIGHT. AFTER SUPPER WITH THE GOVERNOR, Lincoln, Lamon, and Pinkerton took their departure. She lay awake most of the night fighting visions of the anonymous sleeping-car being stopped en route, being overswarmed by shouting men with clubs, ropes, tar and feathers; men who all had Nate Bodley's face. Then she would wake to hear the soft voices of Robert, Hay, Ellsworth, and Nicolay, continuing their endless card-game in the parlor.

Coming out to the parlor to breakfast the next morning she found Ellsworth beaming over the coffee-cups: "This came in around six, Mrs. Lincoln." He held out a telegram, unopened—an open one lay beside Nicolay's plate.

REACHED WASHINGTON SAFELY—WILLARD'S HOTEL

But it was a bad start, she thought, dropping sugar into her coffee, when a President could not enter his own capital city in triumph, for fear of being murdered by the very people he was taking an oath to protect.

Chapter Forty

The White House had changed greatly since Mary last had entered it for James K. Polk's receptions. Five days after her arrival in Washington—five days in which she barely saw her husband for more than a few minutes while he distractedly gulped down an egg and a cup of coffee for breakfast in their parlor at Willard's Hotel—she was received in the Blue Parlor by Harriet Lane, President Buchanan's niece.

Buchanan was a lifelong bachelor; Miss Lane, violet-eyed and beautiful and just edging past the final frontiers of even the most diplomatic definitions of "youth," had acted as hostess in his household since the death of her parents when she was a child. She had a slight British inflection to her voice and the well-schooled perpetual smile of a longtime member of the diplomatic corps, but behind it she watched Mary warily from the moment the gangly Irish doorman showed her into the Blue Parlor.

The newspapers—particularly the Democratic ones like James Bennett's *New York Herald*—had been merciless about the "Illinois gorilla" who was about to take over the Presidency, and his fat loud-mouthed vulgar wife. Mary had closely quizzed her escort that day—the white-haired Mrs. McLean, whose husband was an Associate Justice of the Supreme Court and had been one of the contenders for the Republican nomination—to make sure that her gown of magenta taffeta, with its flowing Isabeau sleeves, was, as Madame Blois had assured her, of absolutely the most fashionable style.

It apparently was, to judge by the infinitesimal relaxation in Miss Lane's cool greeting. The President's niece unbent a bit more at Mary's firm, polite handshake and quiet voice, and Mary silently blessed Madame Mentelle for schooling her, all those years ago, out of all but the slightest Bluegrass inflection in her speech. The Blue Parlor had at some time in the recent past been completely refurnished—she also noticed that the old glass-and-wood screen in the front hall that she remembered had been replaced by a new one of glass and iron—but the furnishings had a shabby look to them already; the brocatelle upholstery was worn and the brightly figured rugs threadbare.

"Housekeeping here is the most *appalling* challenge," drawled Miss Lane, with a gesture at the gaily painted blue ceiling, which was already peeling slightly over the fireplace and around the medallion of the Roman-style gasolier. "Rather like a cross between a palace and a hotel, with a subscription ballroom thrown in. Nothing really prepares one for it."

"I'm sure I'll manage," said Mary, detecting the patronage in the younger woman's light voice.

"Well, of course with so many of the town's hostesses leaving now over this horrible secession, goodness knows what your entertaining will be like. I understand the Corcorans left last week for Paris—that's their house across Lafayette Square, they gave the most astonishing parties—and the Taylors will be gone as well. And of course the Davises."

"I am sure," said Mary thinly, "that Washington will not suffer for lack of entertainments."

"Of course not," agreed Miss Lane, with the words *But who in their right senses would want to associate with the Republican riffraff coming in to take their places?* unfurling like an invisible banner in her restrained little smile.

Mary itched to slap her.

After tea Miss Lane showed her over the house and introduced her to the servants—"The doormen and the gardeners are the only ones employed by the government itself, you know. Will you be keeping on the rest of the staff? Mr. Vermereu, the butler, is a Belgian, but the rest are British. Uncle is a great believer in the British system of training servants, and I've found them quite reliable."

"Certainly I'll keep them on for the time being," replied Mary, determined to yield nothing to this flawless haughty woman, with her air of speaking to a country cousin.

If the downstairs of the house was shabby, with its tobacco-stained rugs, torn upholstery, and window-drapes that bore the scissor-marks of souvenir-hunters, the upstairs resembled a down-at-the-heels boarding-house. Her heart sank. The long central corridor was bare and gloomy, with gray filtered light leaking into it from the open doors of the bedrooms on either side. At the east end, through ground-glass doors, the shadows of men were visible in the vestibule of the President's office; the murmur of their voices and the vibration of their feet served as an uneasy reminder of those delegations that arrived, one after the other, at Willard's Hotel, demanding of Lincoln what he was going to do about the new Confederate States. Trunks were open in several of the bedrooms. A valet was packing one of them, a maid another.

In three days, this will be mine.

The wife of the President.

The First Lady of the land.

"Thank goodness, Mr. Pierce had all the plumbing modernized." Miss Lane's plummy voice broke into her private ecstasy. "Not that it works, half the time. But at least you have it. America does have *some* advantages over Britain—Uncle's house in St. James had only the most *primitive* bathing facilities and was absolutely *glacial* in the winters. The bathroom here has allegedly hot water piped in. . . ." She opened a door off the small private corridor in the southwest corner, to reveal a handsome dressing-room papered in imitation oak-graining, and floored with oilcloth printed to look like tile. "And there's another water-closet off the secretary's office, at the other end of the house. *Ghastly* number of bedrooms here to heat, but then you have quite a large family, haven't you?"

"I married young," lied Mary sweetly, with a glance at Miss Lane's ringless finger. *You old maid.*

"That's usual out West, isn't it?" *Where they haven't anything better to do with their lives, do they?* Miss Lane gathered her rustling skirts, and preceded her down the wide stairs.

Three days of delegations, of debates, of sitting beside Lincoln at dinners during which he was preoccupied in talk with political hosts. Suite Six at Willard's Hotel was besieged by office-seekers, whose determination and persistence made the jostling madness that had plagued him at Springfield look like a Presbyterian Church tea. Lincoln took to waking early and going for long walks before sunrise with Robert or Nicolay. Often he'd breakfasted before she woke, and was closeted all day with Congressmen trying frantically to reach a compromise to conciliate the Confederacy. "I will not extend slavery into the territories," he said, over and over, and the delegates went away.

In those days she received few calls from Washington hostesses, at least partly because the parlor of Suite Six was constantly in use by her husband. "The President's wife is never obliged to make calls," Adele Douglas informed her, when she invited Mary and her sisters and nieces for tea to the beautiful house she and Mary's old suitor owned on Lafayette Square. "It's a pity that all the really powerful hostesses were Southerners and slaveholders—which stands to reason, Washington being situated where it is. And of course nearly everyone else in Washington is here only temporarily."

Everyone but the Cuttses, who were related to the late and much-mourned Dolley Madison. Mary wondered, wryly, if one reason Douglas had fought so hard for re-election was because his wife didn't want to surrender her position as one of Washington's social leaders. "For the past seven years now everyone has agonized over their guest-lists, so as not to have fights breaking out over every dinner. Even before the election Mrs. Clay of Alabama would refuse to go in to dinner with anyone who'd been elected on an anti-slavery ticket, and she knew who they all were. Goodness knows what this season will bring."

"I daresay if Maryland secedes," replied Mary, "we'll all have other things to think of besides our guest-lists."

In fact she was far more interested in the horrors of the crisis that loomed over Washington—the desperate attempts to find some grounds of compromise between the Union and the secessionist states—than she was over the niceties of Washington's social scene. But as ever, she was excluded from the men's councils, and relegated to the task of forming the necessary social network with the wives of Cabinet members and influential Senators.

William Seward, whom she had distrusted from the days of the Chicago convention when the hawk-nosed little New Yorker had tried to take the nomination from Lincoln, had left his ailing wife in Albany. But Salmon Chase's daughter Kate—the ranking Cabinet hostess in town—made clear from her first visit that she intended to establish *herself* as the center of Washington society in her father's rented house, as she had been center of society in Columbus during her father's gubernatorial days.

Kate Chase was young, red-haired, breathtakingly pretty, highly educated, and keenly intelligent, and Mary loathed her at sight. To Mary's gracious invitation to call at the White House, Kate had replied, with an air of great innocence, "And I hope that *you* will call on *me,*" a slap in the face given the Washington custom that the President's wife did not make calls. Mary could not believe it wasn't calculated.

It did not help that it was obvious to Mary that both Seward and Chase regarded Lincoln as an uncouth barbarian who had to be "handled" as a pawn for their greater wisdom—though how much wisdom there was in Seward's plan to start a war with both Britain and France so that the Confederacy would leap back into the Union again, she was at a loss to determine.

The morning of the fourth of March dawned cloudy and raw. Rumor had flown around the previous afternoon that there would be an attempt to assassinate Lincoln during the inaugural parade, inflaming all Mary's fears anew. It had taken Willie and Lizzie hours to quiet her before the dinner that Lincoln was giving for the men he'd selected for his Cabinet. In addition to the hated Seward and the oleaginous Cameron, there was the sanctimonious Mr. Chase of Ohio; Mr. Welles, Secretary of the Navy, a newspaperman who sported a bad wig and had a beard like a holly-bush; Mr. Blair, whose extensive family had been virtual royalty in Maryland for generations; Mr. Caleb Smith, yet another of David Davis's political debtors; and Mr. Edward Bates, who had been appointed mainly because he came from Missouri and had political connections to every Democrat in that barely loyal tinderbox state.

On Inauguration Day, Army sharpshooters lined the parade route, and were stationed in the windows of the Treasury Building as well. She remembered the young Lexington blades of her youth, shooting apples off fence-posts at a hundred yards, or two hundred.

Any one of them could have sent that drawing, those letters. *"Say your prayers. . . ."*

She stood in the crowd of the diplomatic gallery, clinging to Lizzie's hand in the bitter cold of the day, waiting for the sound of a shot.

At one, James Buchanan and Abraham Lincoln emerged from the Capitol, followed by Mary's old friend from Lexington, John Breckinridge—Buchanan's Vice-President, whose wife hadn't called on Mary because Breckinridge was so violently opposed to the limitation of what he called "the rights of property"—and by swarthy, stocky Hannibal Hamlin, the Maine politician who'd been elected Lincoln's Vice-President.

Lincoln looked out over the crowd—as usual, he was the tallest man present—and removed his hat, looked around for somewhere to put it while he spoke. Behind him a man stepped out of the crowd, and held out his hand. "It would be my honor to hold that for you," he said.

It was Stephen Douglas.

"Apprehension seems to exist," Lincoln read, in a voice that seemed to carry like the note of a chime over the now-silent crowd, *"among the people of the Southern States, that by the accession of a Republican Administration, their property, and their peace, and personal security, are to be endangered. There has never been any reasonable cause for such apprehension. . . ."*

Mary closed her eyes, seeing again the vile drawings, the scribbled threats. Hearing in her mind Old Duke Wickliffe's voice thundering about the "damn abolitionists wanting to steal our property"; seeing Nate Bodley's cane rise and fall, splattered with blood.

Reasonable cause, she thought, has never had the slightest thing to do with politics.

Print a lie in a newspaper—whisper it across a Washington tea-table to your society friends—and there is no catching up with it.

And Lincoln knew this.

". . . there needs to be no bloodshed or violence; and there shall be none unless it be forced upon the national authority. . . ."

No mention of secession, or of the Confederate States of America. He was being a lawyer, always leaving the door open, pretending for as long as he could that he did not see. *No wonder people call him a fool,* Mary thought. *They don't see that until something is made official, it's possible to go back and pretend it all never happened.* That was a piece of politics she'd learned at her father's knee.

"One section of this country believes slavery is right, and ought to be extended, while the other believes that it is wrong, and ought not to be extended. This is the only substantial dispute."

No, Mary thought, and shivered. *One section of the country believes that neither the Federal government, nor any other section of the country, has the right to tell them what should be legal and what should not be legal.*

And one section of the country believes that it is their right to withdraw from the compact of Union that they entered willingly, eighty-five years ago.

And they are willing to fight for that right.

This, too, Lincoln knew.

The sound of his voice brought gooseflesh to her arms, though it had been so familiar to her for so many years. In courtrooms or in the State House, or across the kitchen table, laughing over Billy Herndon's latest fad. The words made her heart beat faster, even on this second hearing—despite the desperate press of business he'd made time to go over it with her. It was one of his best, and she knew it would not alter one single Southern heart.

Cold air breathed across her face, and with it the scent of rain. The murmur of the crowd was the echo of a thousand political-speakings of her girlhood, as they listened to Henry Clay or Old Duke Wickliffe or her father, so familiar that it was a part of her blood.

But everything was different now. It was no longer just arguments over patronage, bonds, whether or not the state would pay to build a railroad or dig a canal.

If compromise was not reached, blood would be shed.

"We must not be enemies," said Lincoln. *"Though passion may have strained, it must not break our bonds of affection. The mystic chords of memory, stretching from every battlefield, every patriot grave, to every living heart and hearthstone all over this broad land, will yet swell the chorus of the Union, when again touched, as surely they will be, by the better angels of our natures."*

Mary opened her eyes as Chief Justice Taney—the man who six years before had told Dred Scott that because he was black he had no right to seek his freedom—held out the Bible, for Abraham Lincoln to swear that he would uphold the Constitution and the laws of the land.

HARRIET LANE MAY HAVE THOROUGHLY DISAPPROVED OF A FAMILY OF Illinois hicks moving into the house that she had considered her own for four years, but she knew her duty as a hostess. Upon their arrival at the White House after the Inauguration, Mary found—to her intense gratitude—a hot dinner waiting, hot water in all the guest-rooms, and all the beds made up with fresh sheets. Young Ellsworth rose with glowing eyes from his place between Elizabeth's daughters and offered a toast: "To the President of the United States!"

Lincoln inclined his head, raised his glass—which contained water, Lincoln having seen, as he'd once said, enough drunkenness in his youth to last him a lifetime—and replied, "With the permission of all of my family, I will take this opportunity to say nothing at all."

Laughter, and thunderous applause from those around the table—Hay and Nicolay, Ellsworth and Lizzie, Lockwood and Mary's three sisters Margaret, Mattie, and Elizabeth, Dr. Wallace, the husbands of Mattie and Margaret, Elizabeth's daughters . . . all those who had come to see their kinsman and employer and friend put in charge, as Willie phrased it, of everything.

The windows were dark when they finished, bade a temporary *au revoir* to those of the party who were staying at hotels, and crossed through the hall for the first time, to climb the grand staircase, and seek their respective beds for what rest they could get before preparing for the Inaugural Ball at eleven. Large as the White House was, it was going to be a tight squeeze.

"I've put you and the girls in the Prince of Wales's bedroom," said Mary to Elizabeth, with rehearsed lightness. All her life, it seemed to her, she'd been waiting to say that with just the right degree of insouciance.

Elizabeth, being Elizabeth, said only, "I hope the sheets are properly aired."

Her girls at least looked deeply impressed.

But as they reached the landing and Mary fell back to ask Lincoln about the carriages to take them to the so-called Muslin Palace of Aladdin—set up for the occasion behind City Hall—he held up a folded note and told her, "This was handed to me as I came in. It's from Major Anderson at Fort Sumter. He says unless supplies get to him within the next few days, he'll have to surrender the fort to the government of South Carolina."

"What are you going to do?" she whispered, as they reached the top of the stairs, the family scattering before them down the dark central corridor with firefly candles in hand.

He sighed. "God knows, Mother."

Chapter Forty-one

Ever since Lincoln's nomination at the Illinois state convention, ten months previously, Mary had pictured in her mind what it would be like, to be the wife of the President. She had remembered the elegant and commanding Sarah Polk, standing at her unassuming husband's side; remembered the crowded reception rooms and the fashionable Washington hostesses, and the gossip of receptions, at-homes, dinners, evening parties that had trickled down to her at Mrs. Spriggs's.

And she had seen herself in command of it all.

Nothing had prepared her for the reality.

During the first week she only saw her husband at breakfast—if she rose early enough for it, which on most days was nearly impossible. When they found themselves together at a reception for the diplomatic corps—held at the rambling stone cottage that had once belonged to the governor of the Soldiers' Home on the high wooded ground on the outskirts of Washington—Lincoln tipped his hat to her and inquired straight-faced, "Do I know you, ma'am?" And her slow-steaming resentment dissolved into laughter.

They were together again for an hour at church. In Springfield Lincoln had been a lackadaisical church-goer; in Washington he was either more conscious of appearances, or felt a greater need of guidance and prayer. Perhaps he simply recognized that at the New York Avenue Presbyterian Church, not even the most persistent candidate for office would come up to him demanding to be made Minister to Belgium, and he would have a chance to spend a little quiet time with his children and his wife.

"I feel like an innkeeper," groused Lincoln at one point, "who is trying to live in one wing of his establishment while trying to put out a fire in the other."

Office-seekers had besieged him at Willard's Hotel, but in those first weeks, the White House was never without a line of men, in all stages of elegance or inelegance or downright odiferous decrepitude of person. They waited from dawn till long after nightfall in the office reception room, the outer office, the dark little vestibule at the top of the office stairs, and trailed in a line down the stairs themselves to the front hall, waiting to see the President, whom each one of them considered to be personally in his debt for his election. Only a set of ground-glass doors separated the vestibule from the upstairs hall. Occasionally one or two office-seekers would wander through in quest of a lavatory or a glass of water, or merely to "have a look at the house," as one furry-eared Missourian put it when he peered through Lizzie's bedroom door.

Between conferences with delegates from Maine, Oregon, Massachusetts, and California—between half-clandestine meetings with representatives of Virginia in a frantic attempt to keep that wealthy, powerful, and perilously nearby state from following South Carolina and the others out of the Union—between hectic arguments with the Cabinet about whether to supply Fort Sumter or abandon it to the rebels—Lincoln saw all these men.

Mary quickly came to hate them. She understood that Lincoln was now a public figure, and had his responsibilities to his constituents. *She* was now a public figure—it was what she had all her life wanted to be. But not *this* public. The lack of privacy—and of respect—made her nervous, knowing as she did that any one of those men might be a secessionist with a derringer in his coat, and the fact that they took Lincoln away from her, all day, every day, filled her with resentment.

That first month, though Margaret and her husband went on to Italy at the end of the week and Mattie and her husband returned to the rebel state of Alabama, she had Elizabeth, Lizzie, Lockwood, and the girls to keep her company and help her settle in. Elizabeth's undeniable talents for organization went a long way toward smoothing the transition from Harriet Lane's ways to Mary's, and it was good, when she gave her first reception on Friday night and her first "at-home" Saturday morning, to have her family around her, their elegant clothing and quiet demeanor a visible rebuke to those who called her a loud-mouthed and vulgar Westerner.

It was comforting, too, to know that she was undeniably the most elegantly dressed woman in the room. Adele Douglas gave her the name of the best seamstress in Washington ("She worked for Varina Davis, you know"), a tall and lovely mulatto woman named Lizabet Keckley. Mrs. Keckley arrived on Mary's first morning in the White House—Tuesday, with the reception looming Friday—took Mary's measurements with speedy competence, reviewed all the silks from Stewart's and Laurent's and selected a deep rose moiré, and promised to deliver it Thursday. In fact the dress wasn't ready until Mary was pacing the floor Friday evening in her petticoat and wrapper: it shouldn't have taken that long, Mary fumed, for Mrs. Keckley to make the alterations in trim that she had demanded at the fitting the day before. But after that initial hitch of nervous hysterics, apologies, and a contrite note from Mary the following morning, she settled in well with the dressmaker, who certainly had a better eye and a more up-to-date sense of fashion than Madame Blois.

But few Washington ladies came to her at-homes.

And most of those who did were lavish in their praise of Kate Chase's at-home the Wednesday before. When they spoke of the younger woman's lovely house and stylish furnishings, Mary writhed. The White House in its current run-down condition was an embarrassment, not only to the Lincolns personally (reflected Mary) but to the nation. What on earth would the French ministers think, or the British, who were openly negotiating to help the rebel government?

One of the first to call on her was Mrs. Taft, wife of the Chief Examiner of the Patent Office, who had left her card on Mary at Willard's. She had, it transpired in the course of the conversation, two sons, twelve-year-old Bud and eight-year-old Holly: "You must send them over to play with my boys," said Mary, consciously drawing back her envious attention from Mrs. Taft's extremely stylish blue velvet bonnet. "Poor things, Tad and Willie have been terribly lonely, now that all the excitement is dying down. I haven't yet had time to find them a tutor." The thought of sending them to school, even a private school, filled her with dread. What was to stop the same men who'd written those terrible letters to Lincoln from lurking outside the school, stealing his children?

Consequently Bud and Holly Taft—sturdy fair-haired boys accompanied by their pretty and excruciatingly well-behaved sister, Julia—appeared the following day, and immediately gave Tad and Willie the measles.

Dispatches continued to come from the besieged government forces in Fort Sumter—a tiny islet in Charleston Harbor still held by the United States—and Fort Pickens, off Pensacola in Florida. Gouty and ancient General Winfield Scott—Old Fuss and Feathers, Lincoln called him in private, on account of the gorgeousness of the older man's uniforms—

recommended the forts be abandoned, and turned over to the Confederate government. Frederick Blair of Maryland, the father of the new Postmaster and patriarch of the most powerful family in that critical border state, retorted that such an action would be treason on Lincoln's part. Cash Clay turned up and accepted Lincoln's offer of the post of Minister to Russia—Mary suspected that the Russians were just insane enough to get along well with him, though she wondered how poor Mary Jane would deal with St. Petersburg winters.

The Cabinet met late into the night.

Then at 4:30 in the morning of Good Friday, the twelfth of April, the Charleston garrison opened fire on Fort Sumter. Lincoln became even less visible than usual that day, and the next, except for a brief appearance at a gathering in the big oval family parlor upstairs. But though he looked grim and preoccupied, Mary could also see a springy lightness in his movements, as if a band of iron had been unlocked from around his chest. Coming up beside him, she whispered, "They fired the first shot, didn't they?"

And he grinned down at her, hearing the perfect understanding in her voice. "They certainly did," he replied. Mystic chords of memory and the better angels of Jefferson Davis's nature notwithstanding, she guessed that he had known all along that it would come to bloodshed. And since she had seen the hate-letters in his desk, she had known, too, that it was the South that would strike the first blow.

On Monday Lincoln issued a proclamation calling for seventy-five thousand militia troops for ninety days. Three months seemed long enough, everyone thought, to take care of the trouble. Effervescing with enthusiasm as usual, young Ellsworth quit his job in the War Department and hied off to New York to raise, he declared, a troop of volunteers among the city's fire companies.

Two days later Virginia voted to secede from the Union and establish its own government, and all eyes in the city turned north, to the railway lines that crossed the slave-state of Maryland.

The week that followed was one of the most nerve-wracking of her life. Militia troops were stationed around Washington, but even Tad could tell that they would be no match for a Confederate army. In the dark before dawn one morning, Mary overheard Lincoln say, "If I was Beauregard,"—he named the commander of the troops in Charleston—"I'd be on my way to take Washington now." He was speaking to Hay and Nicolay, in the chill, dark, and drafty upstairs corridor. *He probably thinks I'm asleep,* thought Mary, lying in the dimness of her bedroom, staring at the tall rosewood bedposts by the flickering whisper of the night-light in its painted glass shade. *As if anyone could sleep.*

She closed her eyes, vainly seeking the rest that had eluded her all night. *They'll kill him.* Earlier, she'd been wakened by Hay's soft knocking on Lincoln's door; had heard the young secretary tell him that yet another plot against his life had been uncovered.

Who knows what soldiers will do, if they burn the town?

Her head throbbed, as it had since the previous evening. She heard their steps fade down the hallway, to the office where Lincoln would read dispatches and write letters until the first of the endless delegations started to arrive. She heard Hay's lovely baritone voice, "You think Colonel Lee will accept your offer? He's a Virginian. . . ."

"I pray he does," answered Lincoln. "I'd hate to have to put our trust in Old Fuss and Feathers."

Aching for sleep, she crept from bed and dug in her cupboard for her bottle of Indian Bitters. She didn't like to take it—it sometimes left her drowsy in the morning and if she was absent from breakfast she wouldn't see Lincoln again all day—but at least it let her sleep.

General Scott ordered the strongest and largest of the government buildings to be fortified, as miniature redoubts to which the members of the government could retreat and hold off attackers if necessary. Mary could not keep from thinking of the men of the Texas Revolution, back in 1836, when she was still at Mentelle's, holding off a Mexican army for nearly two weeks in an old church, waiting for relief that never arrived.

Six hundred Kansas volunteers camped in the White House's huge East Room. Tad, Willie, Bud, and Holly pilfered cookies from the kitchen downstairs and took them to these uncouth guests, and spent most of their time among them, learning how to disassemble and clean rifles, how to cook on campfires on the lawn, and hearing tales of the bloody internecine warfare that had torn Kansas apart for the past seven years.

Night after night she would hear the shaggy young ruffians moving about downstairs, as she sat with Lizzie and Elizabeth in the oval parlor, waiting for Lincoln to return from conferences, delegations, meetings in the big office beyond the ground-glass doors. The clatter of boots vibrating the old bones of the mansion, the rough voices raised in occasional song, reminded her that morning might see rebel troops pouring across the river. Confederate flags could be seen flying over Alexandria, at the other end of the Long Bridge. It was a struggle not to give way to fear, and to the anger that fear always fuelled.

Without her family there she didn't know what she would have done.

Elizabeth's steely level-headedness always had a calming effect on her, and Lizzie did what she could to keep Tad and Willie entertained and out of everyone's way.

Not that they needed it, of course. When not in the East Room learning God-knew-what rude ditties from the Frontier Guards, the two boys had established a bastion on the White House roof—with a log for a cannon—and spent hours watching the hills of Virginia. Mary listened, through strained nerves and the renewed agonies of female itching, for shouting in the streets, for the crack of gunfire, for the running feet and the outcry that would herald inevitable disaster.

On the twenty-third of April, the Dominion of Virginia formally allied itself with the Southern Confederacy. Through the night Mary listened to Lincoln's footsteps, pacing his bedroom, or the corridor outside. Any troops coming to guard the capital must pass through Maryland, through which only two months ago Lincoln had had to be smuggled in disguise. Coming back indoors after he'd talked to General Scott in the White House drive—the elderly commander of the Union forces was so gouty he couldn't climb the stairs to the office—she overheard him say quietly to Nicolay, "I begin to believe that there is no North."

Then on the twenty-fifth, the Seventh New York Regiment arrived, marching through the rain down the muddy unpaved streets. Mary ran with the boys and Lizzie to join Lincoln on the White House steps to watch them pass; afterwards she went up to her room and burst into tears of relief.

Washington became an Army town. Regiments of ninety-day volunteers, hastily organized, camped on the swampy Mall between the Capitol and the White House, and the reek of their latrine-trenches hung like a permanent miasma in the air. The Seventh New York set up shop in the House Chamber of the Capitol. Cash Clay showed up with a battalion, and strutted through the White House halls adorned with three pistols and an "Arkansas toothpick"—a bowie knife as long as Mary's forearm—and for days her younger sons tried to imitate his walk and his extravagant drawl.

Lincoln wrote to Ben Helm, Emilie's young husband, who'd come to Springfield with her on her most recent visit. Since their weeks at the Todd house on the way to Washington in 1848, she and Lincoln had regarded Emilie as a daughter, and during her stays in Springfield Lincoln had come to treat her more as a younger sister. He had confided to Mary that he planned to offer Ben a good military post. *Please, please,* Mary prayed, *let Emilie come here, be here with me.* Lizzie and Elizabeth were both talking of returning home, and the thought of being left alone in this hostile town filled her with dread.

But when the young lawyer came down the stairs and into the Red Parlor where she was having tea, she saw the sadness in his dark eyes and knew it was not to be.

"Excuse me, please," she said to her guests—Elizabeth, the girls, Adele Douglas, and sixteen-year-old Julie Taft. Ben stepped with her into the hall: a slim man, darkly handsome as the hero of a Gothic novel.

"Your husband has just offered me the chance at a career," he said quietly. "Paymaster in the Army, with rank of major. It's something it would take me years to get to on my own. I've told him how much I appreciate it, beyond what words can say."

"But you won't take it."

"I asked him to give me a few days."

She saw the answer in his eyes. "Kentucky is still in the Union." She spoke sadly, as if to one standing already on the deck of a departing ship.

"Your husband is an honest man, Molly," said Ben in his soft voice. "I respect him, and you, too much to be less than honest with either of you." He put his hands on her shoulders, and bent a little to kiss her cheek. "I'll give your love—and his—to Emilie."

"I'd hoped to have you both here in Washington." Tears filled her eyes—of disappointment, and something far deeper. "You know Emilie would have been the belle of the town."

"Nobody's going to be the belle of this town more than you, Molly." Ben smiled, and pressed her hands in his. "Good-by."

She never saw him again.

That same day Colonel Lee—Lincoln's hoped-for choice for Commander in Chief—resigned his commission in the U.S. Second Cavalry, and crossed the river to Virginia, the land of his birth.

Washington waited for what was to happen next.

Simon Cameron, Secretary of War, reveled in the sudden influx of troops and started handing out plum contracts to all his supporters, regardless of the quality of the uniforms they were selling or the cost to Congress.

Salmon Chase met with Lincoln in frantic sessions to arrange financing for a war. Suddenly bankers—from New York, Philadelphia, and several European banking houses—became a part of Washington society.

The masses of office-seekers, which had begun at last to thin, redoubled. Good Republicans felt entitled to positions supplying the troops or selling things to the government or acting as clerks or marshals or quartermasters. Tad would trot up the stairs past them, greeting them in his almost incomprehensible lisp, on his way to finding some horrendous mischief to get into with his brother and the Taft boys.

With everything else that was going on, Mary tried desperately not to worry about Tad. From being a relatively normal seven-year-old, except for his speech, he now reverted to old, babyish behaviors, refusing to dress himself or pay the slightest attention to his beleaguered tutor. Lincoln said mildly, "He'll get over it," and Mary did her best to believe him.

On one occasion the four boys explored the attic and found the bell-wires that connected every room in the house with the servants' quarters in the basement. Lincoln, who was curious about things like bell-wires himself, tracked them down, amid servants scurrying up and down the stairs and unimaginable chaos. John Nicolay threatened to break their necks and throw them out the window—a sentiment that was heartily seconded by several members of the Presidential Cabinet but which did nothing for the feud that was beginning to smolder between Nicolay and Mary—but Lincoln only laughed. Another expedition to the attic yielded the cardboard boxes where all the visiting-cards of everyone who had ever crossed the White House's threshold were stored: the boys played "sled on the snow" and came downstairs filthy and dropping from every cuff and seam little squares of pasteboard engraved with the names of long-departed Washington luminaries: Dolley Madison, John Randolph, Aaron Burr.

"You want to watch your boys, goin' up to the attic that way," warned Johnny Watt, the smooth-faced Irishman who was head groundskeeper. "The house is riddled with rats, you know. Big ones, some of 'em, and worse now the Army camps are so near. We got one big tycoon up there I swear has been in office since Jackson's day, and Miss Lane not holdin' with cats." He shook his head, watching Mary with bright blue eyes.

Though Tad was the youngest of the four boys he was usually the ringleader in their enterprises. Alexander Williamson, the young Scotsman who came in every morning to tutor the boys, said that Tad's wild misbehavior and sudden, flaring rages might stem simply from frustration that no one understood his combination of mumble and lisp. Willie and Tad were the only two people in the house—perhaps in all of Washington—who weren't afraid constantly during that tense, waiting month of April 1861.

"Pa won't let anything happen to us," Willie said to Mary, one afternoon when anxiety and sleeplessness had driven her back to bed with an excruciating headache. He took her hand—it was another of those days when she had slept late and slept poorly, and so had missed seeing Lincoln even at breakfast. The constant murmur and grumble of men's voices from beyond the glass doors at the end of the corridor was a reminder that she probably wouldn't see him until late that night, if then.

"Ee'a bead-a sececheth," added Tad. "Ooo thee."

Mary sat up in bed, though the movement brought nausea and a dreamlike tickling sensation in her mind, as if she were about to start speaking in tongues as people did in the Bible. She hugged the boys close to her, praying they were right.

At the end of the month, when no one had yet attacked Washington and Federal troops had occupied Maryland to protect the railroad north, she came to the conclusion that a trip to New York could not be put off longer. The occupation by Federal troops of the East Room had ended, but it had reduced the already shabby carpet and draperies to mud-crusted and tobacco-stained rags.

And with the onset of hot weather, Mary found herself prey to "Potomac malaria," bouts of chills and fever that plagued many in the low-lying capital marshes.

What really spurred her on, however, was an editorial in the *Charleston Mercury:*

> If Washington was offered to us for nothing, the offer should be rejected. With a new Republic we should have a new Capital, erected in the heart of the South. Let Washington remain, with its magnificent buildings crumbling into ruin, a striking monument to future ages of the folly and wickedness of the people of the North. It would teach a lesson, in its silence and desolation, all the nations of the earth should learn and understand.

Fuming, she showed the paper to Lizzie, and that evening to Lincoln, when for the first time in days he put in an appearance at the family dinner-table rather than simply foraging around at midnight in the kitchen.

"We cannot let it be said, *anywhere,* that the Union suffers *any* diminution of its state or power," she pointed out, thrusting the paper into his hands. "On the ninth, as you know, there is to be a reception for the officers stationed here in the capital and their families. Though the servants have done wonders cleaning up the East Room I *cringe* to think of anyone going in there."

Least of all—as she didn't say—Kate Chase.

Chapter Forty-two

The thought of leaving Lincoln and the boys in a place of danger—the nightmare of reading in some newspaper that Beauregard had attacked unexpectedly after all, that the city was in flames and the President hanged—tormented her, but the recollection was stronger still of the way Kate Chase had surveyed the Red Room curtains and run her gloved fingers along the top of the mantle when she thought Mary wasn't looking.

Or perhaps when she thought she was.

By this time Adele Douglas and Mary Jane Welles—the kindly wife of the bushy-bearded Secretary of the Navy—had relayed to Mary some of the things the elegant Miss Chase had said about the President's wife at *her* at-homes.

A special session of Congress had been called for the first of July, and Mary knew that would entail a good deal of entertaining. There was the winter season to be thought of, too; truncated perhaps (as longtime Washington hostess Mrs. Eames pointedly lamented when she compared present-day Washington to the brilliance of that city under Buchanan and Pierce—"But of course you weren't here then, were you, Mrs. Lincoln?"), but critical.

After two more fittings with Mrs. Keckley, Mary, Elizabeth and her daughters, Lockwood Todd, and Lizzie—escorted by the very charming Federal Commissioner of Public Buildings William Wood—left by train for Philadelphia. Mary was ashamed of the relief she felt. Relief to be away from Washington. Relief to be on a journey again, under the different rules that applied to journeys. Relief not to be constantly terrified.

She was ashamed that she was *not* constantly terrified. She had, after all, left her husband and two of her sons in a city that (the *Charleston Mercury* notwithstanding) might be sacked and burned at any moment. But she loved traveling, and once they had bypassed Baltimore she found herself feeling better, and sleeping more soundly, even without the assistance of Atkinson's Cordial.

And New York City in the springtime was so lovely.

Alexander Stewart, white-haired and regal, met them himself at the train station and escorted them in his own carriage to the Metropolitan Hotel. For six days, Commissioner Wood conducted Mary and her relations through the shops and warehouses of New York, examining wallpapers, carpeting, furniture, crystal and dishes, dress silks and trim. The terror and stench of Washington seemed mercifully far away, as if the United States and the Confederacy (though Mary loyally refrained from referring to the rebel states as a separate nation) were two mythical lands about to do battle in a legend, like Greece and Troy.

The hurry and crowds of the New York streets had little to do with soldiers, artillery, preparations for invasion and death. Well-dressed businessmen strode along the paved flagways, coat-skirts flapping in the breeze from the river. Rough laborers in soft caps and corduroy jackets shouted to one another in Gaelic or German; well-dressed boys rolled hoops in the grassy lawns of Washington and Union Squares.

Reporters crowded about her every time she passed through the Metropolitan's lobby, tipped their hats to her, laughed at her imitations of Cameron and Seward. Commissioner Wood winked and flirted with her, and Mary flirted right back, despite Elizabeth's sharply whispered admonitions.

For the first time since her marriage—other than the months spent in Lexington—Mary felt truly young.

After all those years of counting pennies, of worrying what Mr. Lincoln's income might be, of wincing at the cheap lampshades and cheap upholstery and the patches on Robert's breeches that screamed failure to her and to anyone of decent breeding (like Elizabeth) who entered her house, Mary was finally able to relax and enjoy the exhilarating peace of knowing that she was buying the best. She conscientiously bought only American-made goods, even when she was purchasing for herself—except of course when there were no good American products, as with silk. She dickered endlessly with the merchants to make sure she was getting the best prices, and felt a warm surge of triumph each time she scored a victory.

So she reveled in her happy duty, weighing the relative merits of

Wilton and Axminster carpeting (Sally Orne in Philadelphia gave her good advice there), or deciding whether pristine white china with a gold rim would be more impressive than rich-toned solferino, and picking which of several grades of fancy straw matting would be best for the halls. The White House, when she was finished with it, would be truly the handsomest house in America, a palace that would proclaim the Union's confident strength to the British and the French.

And would, incidentally, put paid once and for all to those accusations of uncouthness and vulgarity that were still circulating in Washington and—via the *Herald* and its fellows—throughout the country.

The days were wonderful, the evenings exciting, as Commissioner Wood escorted her to the theater and restaurants. Men made much of her, and gave her presents, with the understanding that she'd "put in a good word" for them with her husband. Aside from the welcome sensation of being young and attractive again, this soothed the hurt of being shut out of the planning and politics she so enjoyed. She did, indeed, have a place as a shaper of policy—at least, these men seemed to think so.

Only at night would her fears return, the agitation and headaches and, twice, those strange spells of disorientation, as if she were in danger of becoming detached from her body and forced to watch herself doing and saying alien things. She telegraphed Lincoln daily at the War Department, shaking her head over the memory of how long it had taken for letters to pass between Columbia, Missouri, and all those small Illinois towns, once upon a long-ago time.

At the end of the week Elizabeth and her daughters took the train for Springfield under Lockwood Todd's escort, and Lizzie, Mary, and Commissioner Wood went on first to Boston, then to Cambridge to visit Robert, a very grown-up Robert with a new fuzz of pale mustache and much talk about "the men" of his hall and year. "There's a troop of them forming, if more volunteers are called up," he said, as he walked across the commons with Mary in the humid twilight after supper in the Hall.

She flinched, and put out her hand quickly to take Robert's. She had to force her voice into what she hoped was a semblance of normalcy. "Oh, darling, I'm sure that won't be necessary."

"It won't be necessary for my country to fight when it has been fired upon by an enemy?" Robert stopped, and looked gravely down at her. "Or it won't be necessary for *me* to fight for my country?"

"Let's not talk about it now, dearest." In her heart she saw young Ben Helm, walking out of the White House's marble-floored vestibule and down the steps in the sunlight. That night, in the cozy little Cambridge hotel, she dreamed of the White House, with black crape wreathed on its doors and all its windows darkened; dreamed of seeing it afloat in poisonous greenish mists that flowed up out of the ground.

All the way back to Washington two days later she struggled with a rising sense of dread, that she would return to find some terrible event had taken place. She chatted mechanically with Lizzie and Mr. Wood to take her mind from her fear, but every time the train slowed, her mind filled with confused visions of it stopping, of an officer in the blue uniform of the Army coming down the aisle to her: "I'm sorry, Mrs. Lincoln, the train can't go any farther. Washington has been taken. . . ."

John Nicolay met them at the station with the news that Virginia had officially become a part of the Confederacy, not merely an ally. Union troops had crossed the two bridges to the little town of Alexandria and had established bridgeheads there. The President, he told them, had been closeted with his Cabinet pretty steadily since the news had arrived on Tuesday.

Mary said, "Thank you," and settled her enormous, spreading crinoline over the carriage seats. It was Adele Douglas's carriage, on loan to the Lincolns. Mary could hardly wait to tell Lincoln of the beautiful open barouche she'd chosen, for which the businessmen of New York had agreed to pay! Nicolay asked politely after the journey, then dropped into conversation with Commissioner Wood, for which she was glad, for she had begun to see how deceived she had been in the thin young journalist with his faint German accent. Her blossoming dislike had flared into furious resentment when she'd been told that Nicolay, not she, would be in charge of social arrangements at the White House.

"It'll be more for consistency than for anything else," Lincoln had told her, when she'd gone storming into the parlor at Willard's—this had been a few days before the Inauguration—to demand why the State Department's point-by-point description of etiquette had been delivered to the young secretary instead of to herself. "You know how your headaches lay you out, Mother, and you've told me yourself there's never any knowing when you'll be struck by one. You wouldn't want, nor could we afford, for the purely mechanical arrangements of diplomacy to be put off by your illness."

"You think I can't be trusted?" she had demanded. "Is that it?" And, having no real argument against Lincoln's reasoning, had raged at him in a fury of tears fuelled by the exhaustion of that interminable journey from Springfield. The memory still rankled, against Nicolay, whom she suspected of putting himself forward with the argument and the suggestion, and against Lincoln himself, though her grudge had been mostly submerged in the tensions of the past few months. Riding back to the

White House now through the streets of town, already thick with rising clouds of dust, she reflected that her husband probably wouldn't even take the time to separate himself from his precious Cabinet to greet her. And the boys would be off somewhere with the Taft children. . . .

Tears of weary self-pity stung her eyes, and she took Lizzie's hand for comfort. Even in the twelve days she'd been gone, Washington had grown noticeably hotter, and the stench was incredible. Rows of tents covered the open Mall that stretched from the Capitol to the river. The reek of the latrine-pits vied with that of the horse-lines and the victualers' pens of cattle and swine.

More herds blocked the streets, en route to their destinies, and there seemed to be teamsters and wagons everywhere. Men in uniforms swarmed, no two companies arrayed alike. Blue, gray, young Ellsworth's gaudy scarlet-trousered Zouaves . . . country boys in twos and threes gawking about them as if Washington were a real city instead of the provincial Southern town that she knew it was. Bowery toughs from New York swaggered and cursed at the free blacks of the town, the first blacks that many of them had ever seen. In New York and Philadelphia Mary had seen for herself what she'd read of in the papers for years: the virulence of the hatred white working-men bore against the free blacks.

They would fight to preserve the Union, but newspapers, street-corner orators, broadsides all vociferously proclaimed that they would not fight to flood the Northern cities with men more impoverished—and willing to work for lower wages—than themselves.

And among the ninety-day militia soldiers, strode warriors of that secondary army that had followed on the first since the Greeks sat down before the walls of Troy: teamsters, sutlers, victualers, laundrywomen, harlots, bunco-artists, thieves. All coated with Washington's impenetrable dust, all waiting for the fighting to begin.

Two members of the Cassius Clay Battalion stood by the gate off Pennsylvania Avenue. The carriage-wheels crunched on the gravel of the circular drive. She glimpsed wizened Mr. McManus in the doorway, and the next moment the tall thin shape of her husband emerged from the dark hall behind him.

At least, she thought with relief, he wasn't in his shirtsleeves. Gladness swept her. Tad and Willie shoved past him and ran down the steps, followed almost at once by young Ellsworth, handsome in his Zouave uniform, ready to escort her up the steps. Bud and Holly, and young Julia in her white dress, grouped around Lincoln like a second family; Julia held a bouquet of welcoming flowers.

Home, Mary thought.

But the house itself, looming up behind them, even in the hot spring sunlight seemed to her to be shadowed, like the terrible house of mourning in her dream. *It's only because it's so shabby,* she thought, as Commissioner Wood helped her from the carriage. *And only because I'm tired.* Her head throbbed and she thought with longing of a few quiet hours in her room. *When the new furniture arrives, and we get a new coat of paint on it, it will be the finest in the city, in the nation. . . .*

Yet as she walked toward the steps, her sons romping around her like puppies—*Tad couldn't possibly have grown taller in less than two weeks!*—she shivered at the sight of it, as if, like the house in her dream, it was filled, not with the bustle of business and the noise of life, but with poison, and darkness, and the stench of death.

Chapter Forty-three

Two nights later she was waked from uneasy sleep by the tramp of men marching. Hair hanging down her back, she crossed to the window and put aside the curtains: dark figures, dark banners, gun-barrels catching cold dark gleams of moonlight. They were heading down the Mall toward the Long Bridge, which joined Washington to Alexandria. Only that day she had been driven past it in the carriage on the way to review the flag exercises of the Seventh New York Regiment, and Lincoln had pointed out how the planks of the bridge had been taken up to prevent rebel cavalry from charging across it.

The night was stifling, the window-glass tepid against her cheek. She had a horror of mosquitoes, and even with netting draped around the bed, the mere sound of one in the room was enough to keep her awake. The nights here were thick with them, like dust-motes around the lanterns of the guards by the White House gates.

She watched until the columns gave way to ambulance-wagons, supply-carts, remounts, and reserves. Still sitting beside the window an hour or so later, she heard the distant crackle of musket-fire, that told her the fighting had truly begun.

Because of being waked she slept late, until the day's heat woke her, sweating and itching. Her maid was just hooking her into one of her new dresses of pale-blue muslin when there was a knock on the door.

It was Lizzie. Her eyes were red and swollen and sick panic struck Mary to the heart, even before she spoke.

"Oh, darling, I'm so sorry," Lizzie whispered. "It's poor Ellsworth."

The two women went into the hall. Mary could see, beyond the ground-glass doors, Lincoln's tall shadow, struggling to get through the press of men in the vestibule without visibly thrusting them aside. She was familiar with this sight. It would take him an hour sometimes to get from his office to the doors that separated the business part of the White House from the family quarters, maybe another to get past the line between the doors and the stair. On this occasion, as had happened many times before, two men who evidently felt their affairs simply couldn't wait followed him down the hall, talking all the while: ". . . seein' as how it was me that got you the vote in Jackson County, you understand that I traded a lot of favors for it, and it's only right that I be given a quartermaster's post in return . . ."

She didn't hear what he answered. It seemed to take a long time. Why didn't that horrible man from Jackson County drop dead of the palsy as he spoke? When the man and his friend disappeared back through the ground-glass doors—nearly colliding with another office-seeker who was trying to come through into the hall and take advantage of this near glimpse of the President as well—Lincoln took Mary and Lizzie aside and drew them after him into the parlor. His lined cheeks were streaked with tears.

"The Zouaves were part of the force that took Alexandria last night." He spoke as if setting facts before a jury. "There was little fighting. Ellsworth and his men took the telegraph office first thing, to keep news from spreading farther south. They hoisted the flag there. When it got light they could see a rebel flag flying on top of the Marshall Hotel. Ellsworth led his men to pull it down—they were coming downstairs with it when the owner of the hotel shot him." His voice broke and he pressed his hand, very briefly, over his mouth.

Then he looked at his hand, as if he could see his friend's blood there, and said, very softly, "What have I done?"

"Exactly what you swore you would do," replied Mary steadily, though her own mind stalled on the fact that she would never see that ebullient young friend again. "Upheld the Constitution against those who would tear this nation apart."

And Lincoln sighed, like a man who feels the full weight of the cross settle at last on his shoulder, to be carried up the hill.

They were driven in the carriage to the Navy Yard that afternoon, to see the body. Someone had washed Ellsworth's face and covered him with a sheet, but some of the blood still soaked through. Spatters of it still clung to his hair and the gallant mustache he'd grown. Looking down at him, Mary saw him when he'd first come to Springfield, brimming with plans and enthusiasm for Lincoln's election; saw him all those evenings when he'd come home for supper with Lincoln and help with the dishwashing afterwards.

And looking down at him, she saw, as if with horrible double vision, Robert's face, waxy, bloodless, and flecked with gore.

She closed her eyes, and gripped Lincoln's arm until the wave of dizzy horror passed.

They held the funeral at the White House, a bier erected on the trampled and boot-scarred carpets of the dilapidated East Room. Lincoln wept again, as Mary placed a wreath and Ellsworth's photograph on the casket, that would be taken to the railroad station for the long journey back to his parents in New York. Feeling the convulsive grip of her husband's black-gloved hand seeking comfort in hers, she knew that guilt still tormented him.

His election had triggered the secession of the Southern states. His policy that the Union was indissoluble—that the Confederates were in fact rebels and no legitimate government at all—had dictated that they should not be let go in peace.

He had known there would be blood.

Even that of a young man who had, for a year, been like a son to him.

Not Robert, thought Mary frantically. *Never Robert . . .*

Robert arrived two days later from Harvard, wearing a black armband for the friend who had been like a brother. He was very quiet and made the time, between his father's conferences concerning the appointment of a Quartermaster General and long discussions with Seward, to have an interview with his father in his office. The following night, as Mary was getting ready for a Presidential levee, Lincoln came into her room and told her quietly, "Bob asked if he might leave school, and join the regiment some of his classmen are forming."

"You told him no!" She seized his sleeve in a death-grip. "You told him no!"

"I told him no," agreed Lincoln quietly. Mrs. Keckley, who had arrived to make sure her handiwork was most pleasingly arrayed on Mary and had remained to help her dress and fix her hair, retreated with soundless tact into the hall.

"He's too young," Mary gabbled, as if she had not heard him. Panic filled her, the same panic that had driven her, frantic, into the yard on Jackson Street screaming, *Bobby's run away! Bobby's run away!* "He isn't even eighteen. And he must finish his schooling, if he's to have any position, any hope of success, in the—"

"I told him no," Lincoln repeated, taking her hands. He'd written to Ellsworth's parents, she knew, trying to compose what words of comfort he could to people who had lost a son, when his own son of military age still lived.

It was the start of a nightmare, like a tour of Hell that only got worse the further they went, and from which there was no turning back.

When she looked back on it afterwards she wondered how she ever lived through it at all.

Less than ten days after Ellsworth's death, Stephen Douglas died in Chicago, where he'd been on tour to raise support for Lincoln's decision to fight for union against those who would divide the country. Ill before he started, he'd worn himself out in the campaign, tirelessly speaking in behalf of the man he'd battled so bitterly and known so long. He was a hard drinker, and his health had not been good for some time. When an attack of rheumatism hit, he had had nothing with which to fight the complications that followed.

Mary felt shocked, bereft. Even as she kept expecting to hear Ellsworth's footfalls leaping up the Grand Staircase two at a time, she could not imagine—literally could not form in her mind—that she'd never see those sparkly brown eyes again, or hear that gorgeous baritone voice dispensing his practiced compliments. She had herself driven to Adele Douglas's house—only a hundred yards away across the square—and wept with the widow, clinging to her in the red velvet dimness of the parlor.

He could have been my husband, Mary thought, dazed. The lovely Adele had known him first as a Congressman in Washington, a man famous already for the Kansas-Nebraska Act. But Mary's memories of the man went back to Springfield, and being swept along in that surprisingly strong light grip in cotillion dances at the American House; to his rolling laughter in the long prairie twilights as he drove her back from a picnic.

He couldn't be dead. It all had to be some terrible mistake.

In the evenings, when Lincoln could tear himself from the constant tormenting swarms of office-seekers, he sat in silence in the parlor. Remembering, Mary thought, those winter nights around the stove at Speed's store, hurling at one another the lightning-bolts of their minds.

And still troops poured into Washington. Volunteer companies on ninety-day enlistments from Massachusetts, Philadelphia, and New York, in all their varied uniforms or no uniforms at all. Companies composed entirely of Irishmen, or Germans, or of the inhabitants of single villages in Connecticut or Maine, all cousins and brothers and schoolmates. Camps sprouted up all around the perimeter of Washington, reenforcing its single old stone fort on the Potomac. Soldiers occupied the grounds of the old Custis mansion of Arlington on its bluff across the river, where the kindred of George Washington had once lived; the rattle of gun-limbers and ammunition wagons sounded in the streets day and night. Rumors proliferated about everything and anything. Half the population of Washington seemed to be secessionist spies, sending information nearly unchecked to the enemy via relatives in Maryland and Virginia. Nearly every permanent inhabitant of the town was related to someone in the rebel army.

Barrooms proliferated, many of them makeshift dispensaries of liquor under canvas tents. Fights proliferated, too, and all of a sudden, when Mary and Lincoln were driven to military reviews or the dedication of new camps, they saw women openly strolling the streets in gaudy dresses and hair of hues not found in nature.

Mary went abroad little in those days. She found solace in the conservatory that Buchanan had had added to the Executive Mansion, a fascinating indoor garden whose glass walls and steep-sided glass ceiling provided a comforting privacy. Roses grew there, and a hundred varieties of fern; camellias red, pink, and white; bougainvillea in hues to match the newest shades of fashion; peonies and fuchsias from China and Japan. Johnny Watt, the head groundskeeper, showed her around the long aisles of heavy, green-painted tables and told her stories of this plant or that, the bronze chrysanthemums that had been a gift from the Tycoon of Japan, brought back by Mr. Perry from his famous voyage; the intoxicating white jasmine that had been given, it was said, by Dolley Madison to Mr. Adams—the *first* Mr. Adams—and had now grown as thick as a man's arm.

Sometimes she would send down to the conservatory for bouquets, to be sent to Mrs. Taft or to Mrs. Fox, the sister of Postmaster Blair—her husband was helping to organize the coastal defenses. Sometimes she and Lizzie went to sit there in quiet talk, and at such times Watt would putter about with his shears or his watering-can, invisible as the bees that flew in when the hinged ceiling-panes were open. Far off the voices of her sons could be heard, riding their ponies in the rough ground between the house and the White House stables—cavalry-charging the Taft boys, who invariably got the task of being rebels.

Sleeping poorly, Mary almost never rose in time to encounter Lincoln at his spare breakfast. Lizzie would usually eat with her, when she came down mid-morning, but by that time the boys would be at their lessons and Lincoln would be in his office—with a long line of men stretching down the office stairway, across the vestibule, and out the front White House doors. Or he would be out with Seward, visiting the Army camps, shaking hands sometimes with every member of a newly come regiment and returning in the afternoon with fingers so tired and swollen that he could not hold a pen. When she did see him she could see that he was exhausted, distant, and preoccupied.

She didn't feel able to tell him how badly she needed him, but she did need him: for comfort at Douglas's death, for reassurance against her terror that Robert would steal away and enlist and be killed in another foray. When he went out for long walks through the streets of Washington alone, late at night or early in the morning, her temper would snap, for she knew the city was Southern in sympathy and even its Unionist citizens resented the government that had brought soldiers in to make the streets unsafe and raise the prices of everything.

Then there would be a scene, and Mary would retreat, weeping, to her room, and to Lizzie's comfort. By the time Mary had calmed down again and would have gone to him as she had in Springfield, he had returned to his office, where he would sit writing until late in the night. She would promise herself that she would keep her temper better, as she had promised herself—and him—a thousand times before.

He doesn't need this. His tasks are hard enough. Then some piece of Nicolay's officiousness or a bad day of itching would set her off again.

Congress met on the Fourth of July. The town was fuller, but because of fear of invasion most legislators did not bring their wives. It made for dull—and humiliatingly small—at-homes at first, but Mary had always preferred and enjoyed the company of men. One of her earliest and most welcome callers was the dandified bachelor abolitionist Senator Sumner of Massachusetts, with whom she could talk about slavery or Chinese silk brocades with equal enthusiasm. It was he who told her of the wrangling going on in Congress, how everyone there was calling for action, for a strike at the rebel armies, though the Generals themselves protested that their men were green recruits who could not keep discipline under fire.

"It's because of the enlistments, you see," Sumner explained. "On the fifteenth of July, the ninety days are up. The men will begin to go home, without a blow being struck."

He glanced toward the Blue Parlor's long windows, through which—past the low hedge and the stables—could be glimpsed the gaggle of tents, flags, corrals, and cook-fire smoke of the camps along the Mall.

"It will expose the capital to danger again, since you can be sure the rebels aren't going home. And it will make us, and our demands, look ridiculous, Mrs. Lincoln. Whatever state the soldiers themselves are in, you know that no politician is going to stand for that."

Chapter Forty-four

On the nineteenth of July the Army marched into Virginia under the command of Irvin McDowell, one of the few West Point officers who'd remained with the Army of the North. Their goal was the rebel force camped at Manassas Junction, where the railroad went down into the Shenandoah Valley and the heart of Virginia.

Mary woke in the small hours of the twenty-first, hearing what she first thought was distant thunder. But though the night had been close and hot, and the threat of storm seemed to hang in the air, she sensed that this was different even before she heard John Hay's step in the hall, the cautious whisper, "Mr. President?"

She opened her door a crack and saw the pair of secretaries, trousers pulled on over their nightshirts and braces hanging, Nicolay's Prince Albert beard a ruffle of disarray. The two young men shared a bedroom down at the end of the hall, near the glass doors.

Lincoln appeared in the dark of his bedroom door, still dressed, shirtsleeves and bare feet with his black hair standing out in all directions. He must have lain down and slept in his clothes, too exhausted to undress.

Nicolay said, "McDowell's men engaged the rebel forces just outside Manassas, sir, on the banks of Bull Run Creek."

"Too soon for any word, I suppose?"

Nicolay shook his head, but Hay grinned and said, "Anybody who can get a pass through the lines is heading out there in carriages with picnic-lunches, to watch the battle."

Lincoln stared at him, openmouthed. "Here I thought bein' a lawyer for twenty years I'd heard everythin'. Guess I was wrong."

He ducked back into his bedroom and returned a moment later with his coat, cravat trailing from his pocket and boots in his hand. He was back for breakfast, however, as Sunday church-bells began tolling over the city: "You heard, I guess?" he asked, after one glance at Mary's anxious expression.

"C'n 'ee go oud 'ere, 'oo?" demanded Tad, his face a single blaze of excitement, and Willie added eagerly, "We can ride our ponies. That's faster than the carriage."

"Nope." Lincoln dropped a kiss on top of Mary's head, then sat beside her. "It's comin' on to rain and all them Senators and their ladies in their carriages is just goin' to get wet." He turned to her again, asked softly, "You all right, Mother?"

Mary nodded. All she could see was Ellsworth's bloodless face, and the dark stains on the sheet that covered him, and, across the table, the discontented eagerness in Robert's blue eyes. In the morning stillness, with the windows open, the guns could be heard.

Lincoln went with her, Lizzie, and the boys to church, where she heard not a single word of the sermon, which she assumed to be on the subject of the battle being fought. She was conscious only of Robert beside her, and of her prayer, *Let the fighting end quickly, quickly, before he goes. . . .*

After church Lincoln went back to the War Department, to wait for telegrams that were, Hay reported, coming in at fifteen-minute intervals. A small company had captured a nearby telegraph office in Fairfax. In the evening he drove out to the Navy Yard, and while he was gone Seward arrived, breathless and grim-faced.

"The battle's lost," he said.

Rain started before Lincoln returned. Throughout the night he was in his office, while rain pounded on the windows and carriages arrived under the portico of the northern doors. Senators and Congressmen who'd driven out with picnic-baskets came in, bedraggled and shaken and scared. McDowell's men had been slow getting across Bull Run Creek itself; the rebel forces had rallied behind a Virginia colonel named Jackson, "as behind a stone wall," they said. Then more rebels had showed up, God knows from where—"Johnston's men, Mr. Seward thinks," John Hay told Mary, on one of his trips down the hall past the parlor where she and Lizzie sat up with the boys. "They could have come by train from the Shenandoah Valley."

The retreating Union forces had gotten tangled up in the rout of carriages, buggies, sightseers on horseback, panic spreading across the countryside under the driving rain.

"Are the rebels on their way here?" Lincoln kept asking. Nobody seemed to know.

Robert and John Hay acted as go-betweens, hurrying from Lincoln's office to the oval parlor, where Mary and Lizzie drank endless cups of tea and tried to keep Tad and Willie from running down the hall to join the Cabinet meeting. From the windows she could see torches and lanterns in the camps, and if they crossed the hall, from any of the bedrooms on that side—the guest-room where Lizzie slept, or Tad and Willie's—knots of wet, exhausted men were visible, limping weaponless down Pennsylvania Avenue, uniforms soaked with rain.

At two in the morning she heard the footsteps of many men: Lincoln, Seward, gouty General Scott hobbling on his cane. She stood as they came into the parlor. "I've advised the President that you and your sons be sent north, before Maryland takes it into its head to rise up and throw in their lot with the Virginians," the General told her. Red-faced, white-haired, fat, and lame, he had fought the British in 1812, and Santa Anna in '46. "Once the railroads are cut there'll be no getting you out, ma'am."

"There's no getting me out now, General." Mary put her arm around Tad's shoulders—Willie was sound asleep on the sofa. "My place is with my husband, and with the government that he represents."

"Told you so," Lincoln murmured.

"Are you leaving?" She looked across to meet his eyes.

He ran his hand through his hair, and shook his head. "Like the preacher said when the widow's house burned down and he came runnin' out in his nightshirt, this kind of thing doesn't look good."

She turned back to the old soldier. "Then I am staying, too." Hay and Nicolay traded a glance—expecting another scene like that in the Jones House Hotel in Harrisburg?

But Lincoln said, "I think that settles it, gentlemen."

He was up all night, and most of the following, talking with Charles Sumner, who was of the opinion that immediate emancipation of the slaves would both cripple the South and win hundreds of thousands of new soldiers to the Union cause. "To make up for the hundreds of thousands of men who'd desert if I did it, I suppose," he sighed to Mary the following day. "Not to mention bein' the last straw for Maryland." The city was in feverish tension, waiting for an attack from across the river or, worse yet, to hear news that Maryland had risen in revolt and that they were cut off.

Throughout that week Mary and Lincoln visited the wounded, in the makeshift hospitals set up all over Washington in the wake of the battle, in churches, in public buildings, and in private houses. She had to steel herself to see them, to walk between the beds through wards that stank of blood, of filth, of unwashed bodies, and of the horrible sweet rottenness of gangrene. The face on every dirty pillow was Ellsworth's. Or Robert's.

Still, the rebels did not attack. By seizing near-dictatorial powers as Commander in Chief, Lincoln put Maryland under what amounted to martial law and began systematically silencing the pro-rebel press. Sumner shook his head over this when he took tea with Mary in the Blue Parlor.

"It scarcely looks well, my dear Mrs. Lincoln, for a man who's declared war to uphold the Constitution to be so blithe in his disregard of the First Amendment."

He would have been a slightly ridiculous figure, with his long curly mane and extravagant waistcoats, to someone who didn't know his history: his fierce support of abolitionism in the Senate had gotten him caned—nearly fatally—in the Senate chamber in 1856.

"And in order to defend a Southern capital, his alternative is . . . ?"

Sumner pursed his lips, and held out his cup for more tea. "Shutting down rebel newspapers isn't going to silence criticism of his policies, you know." He regarded her for a moment in silence, then added, "Nor of you."

Mary stiffened. "If you mean that tiresome piece in the *Times* about me *'making and unmaking the political fortunes of men . . .'* "

"No," said Sumner. "I mean the rumors that you're sending information about troop movements to your three brothers in the rebel army."

Mary was silent, feeling as if her whole body were balling itself into a single fist. "Where heard you that?" she asked, very quietly. But her eyes must have had a dangerous sparkle, for the Massachusetts Senator raised his brows, and kept his tone light.

"Where does one hear anything, Mrs. Lincoln? It's being said around the town."

"You mean it's being said in Kate Chase's parlor." Mary heard the shrillness of anger in her voice and couldn't modulate it away. "By a woman who hopes to discredit my husband through me, so that her father can be elected. And it's being repeated by men who're looking for some reason besides themselves, that their lives and their country are a mess." She set down her cup, which was spilling. Her hand was shaking.

WITHIN A WEEK TENSIONS EASED ENOUGH FOR THE PRESIDENT TO GIVE a reception, and within two, to hold a formal dinner in honor of the visiting Prince Napoleon of France. Later Secretary Seward was quoted all over Washington as saying that he had given an exactly similar banquet for half the cost.

Robert made arrangements to return to Harvard, with Mary and Lizzie accompanying him north as far as the beach resort of Long Branch, New Jersey. After Prince Napoleon's dinner Lincoln came to her bedroom to unlace her and brush her hair, looking, for the first time in those hectic weeks, relaxed and in good spirits, though tired. He looked, in fact, very like the man she had known in Springfield, except for the beard.

"I saw you flirting with those hussies at last Friday's reception," she said severely. "That Mrs. Eames, and that General's wife, whatever her name is."

It had surprised her a little in the past weeks to see the number of ladies who flirted with Lincoln—surprised her and annoyed her. She knew better than anyone the strength of the desires that ran beneath the exterior of homespun humility and cool logic: she much preferred Lincoln when he was too shy to flirt back.

"I expect you to telegraph me every day while I'm away, and you can be sure I'll get a complete report on you from my spies."

"Why not you?" sighed Lincoln. "I'm sure Jeff Davis is."

It was good beyond words to be away from Washington. Good to know that Robert was going safely back to Harvard—good to feel healthy again, and to be fêted and fussed over again by reporters in New York. In Washington she felt invisible, like that child in Lexington, ignored among all the others, or, worse, pointed at and gossiped about. Robert of course looked down his nose and said, "You want to be more careful at what you say to the papers, Mother," but she merely laughed at him, giddy with relief at being able, finally, to laugh.

She'd written to her old Springfield friend Hannah Shearer, begging her to join them at Long Branch, promising anything, if only she would come and keep her company. The thought of losing Lizzie was hard to bear. "I've been away from poor Harrison for six months already, dearest." It didn't seem like six months, reflected Mary, as she boarded the train to return to Washington in September. Sometimes it seemed like years. Six months ago there had been no war.

Six months ago the sisters she'd helped raise, the brothers she'd played with, were not adherents to a cause that had sworn death to her husband and ruin to all he stood for.

Six months ago it wasn't being whispered all over town that she was a traitor.

Six months ago Ellsworth—and Stephen Douglas—had both been alive.

Returning to the White House was almost worth it, however. In the weeks she'd been gone, Lincoln had stayed at the little stone cottage at the Soldiers' Home by Rock Creek, where it was cooler, and the arrangements with the painters and decorators that Mary had made for the White House had all been carried out. She stepped across the threshold of the big mansion with a sense of exhilaration. The smell of fresh paint and plaster, the brightness of new wallpapers and carpets, made her spirits soar. The East Room was gorgeous, restored from the tattered wreckage of military occupation, the new carpet like a lake of soft green cut pile floating with pink roses.

She felt as she had at parties at her father's house, when she'd had a new dress to show off: the effervescent desire to rise on her toes and dance.

This, thought Mary, was truly the appropriate setting for the President and his Lady. The place to which she could have, with pride, invited Henry Clay.

Lincoln himself looked ill and tired, though he was glad to see her home. In Mary's absence Secretary Seward had made him and the boys a present of a basket of kittens, all of which had promptly gravitated to sleeping on Lincoln's bed when they should have been hunting rats in the White House attic. Sometimes when she couldn't sleep, or would steal down the hallway to the water-closet in the dressing-room, she would see, by the light of her candle, Lincoln stretched out on top of the sheets in his too-short yellow nightshirt, with kittens on his chest, pillow, and feet.

She worried about him a great deal, in that first fall and winter of the war. He would be in conference, with Generals and Cabinet members, sometimes until midnight; there were nights when she heard him pacing the floor of his room until she drifted off to sleep. With more and more troops assembling under the cocky little General McClellan—the Napoleon of the West, the Democratic newspapers called him—there were equipment and provisions to be decided on. Lincoln, fascinated as he was by gadgetry or machines of any kind, would go to the rifle-ranges to test new guns himself, or steam down the Potomac to watch demonstrations of new sorts of electro-mercury lamps.

With more and more troops—on enlistments of three years now, not three months—came fresh waves of rumor about rebel spies. During the summer the Mayor of Washington City had been arrested on suspicion of sympathy with the rebeling states, and one of Adele Douglas's aunts, the beautiful Rose Greenhow, was discovered to be running a ring of spies who passed information about troop movements to the rebel forces across the river. Mrs. Greenhow was incarcerated—along with many others—in the Old Capitol Prison, but the passing of information didn't cease. Half of the city's prostitutes engaged in a lively secondary traffic in military information, and newspapers blithely continued to print whatever plans and projections their reporters could learn.

More than one anti-Lincoln journal, in addition to snide editorials about *"entirely abolishing the Constitution of the United States, and substituting instead a naked philo-negro despotism,"* pointed out that Lincoln's wife, as yet another Southern lady, could not but be engaging in the same informational trade.

Reading the papers daily, Mary would be sick with anger, and with grief that she could not even speak of her fears for Ben Helm, for her half-brothers Alec, David, Sam.

Cold weather drew on. Rains laid the dust of the unpaved streets, then transformed it to mud. Congressmen came back to town and their wives left cards at the White House; Mary hugely enjoyed sorting through them to decide who should be invited to entertainments, and who not. With her long experience and strong instincts for social arrangements, it still infuriated her that John Nicolay would be in charge of the White House invitations and seating arrangements rather than herself. It angered her still more that Lincoln would not back down from this position: "Now, Mother, you know you couldn't have gone to Philadelphia, or New York, if you'd had to stay here and manage things."

"You don't trust me!" she shouted at him—this was on one of the rare evenings that he'd come into the oval parlor before eleven, when she retired to bed. "After the way I worked to make our home respectable, so you could get ahead . . . if it wasn't for *me* you'd be living in a cave and throwing bones on the floor for the dogs! And this is how you thank me!"

She stormed into her room and slammed the door, weeping—she found she wept far more easily now than she ever had in Springfield, and she had been, she knew, overly sensitive then. *It's the War,* she thought. *The War and this terrible house . . .*

But more than that—and in her heart she knew it—the source of her constant sense of panic these days was the bills that had begun to flood in from the merchants of Philadelphia and New York.

The bills! Mary's stomach churned when she thought of them. How could she *possibly* have spent over $5000 on upholstery fabrics? On the *fabrics,* not even counting what Mr. Alexander had charged to re-cover the furniture that years of hard wear and those dreadful Guards had spoiled. Seven hundred dollars for crystal glasses? But what would the French ambassador, the English minister, Prince Napoleon, say about being served in those old chipped ones that had been in the house when the Lincolns had arrived? Of course she'd spent a great deal at Stewart's on silks and dress-goods for herself, but no one, *no one,* was going to sneer at her. . . .

No one was going to say that the President's Lady was some countrified Westerner who didn't know how to dress!

I had to do it, she thought in despair. *I had to, and no one understands!*

She herself didn't understand how she could have spent that much. They must be cheating her, she thought. . . . But she remembered overspending when she'd bought furniture for the remodeled Springfield house, remembered not being quite aware of how that had happened, either.

Why couldn't money be like it had been for her father? Something you had and something you spent, a comfortable golden vagueness which no gentleman—and certainly no lady—ever discussed in specific terms. As a girl Mary had never had the slightest idea of what her clothes had cost. She'd just gotten what she wanted, and the shopkeepers sent their accounts to her father.

Why couldn't it still be that way?

Through the wall of her bedroom she heard Lincoln's footsteps in his own small bare chamber, and the faint creak of the bed as he lay down. Much later, in the dark pre-dawn, she heard him get up again, and go padding down the corridor to the bedroom where his secretaries slept. When the soft tread faded, she slipped on her wrapper and went to the door of her bedroom, and out to the main corridor, dark and terrifying and cold.

A faint stain of yellow lamplight showed through the secretaries' half-open door, and she could hear Lincoln's voice, reading aloud:

"What a piece of work is man! How noble in reason! How infinite in faculty! In form, in moving, how express and admirable. . . ."

And Nicolay's, answering, she couldn't hear what. Relaxed talk, of anything and nothing—of anything except the War that was tearing the country apart. Like the talk around the stove at Dillard's, or among the lawyers in those primitive country inns on the Eighth Judicial Circuit.

Lincoln's laughter: "That reminds me of a fellow in DeWitt County who married two wives. . . ."

The gentle talk that he'd come into the parlor that evening seeking, thought Mary, when she'd flown at him with demands about why she wasn't in charge of White House invitations, when she knew perfectly well that it had something to do with her refusal to invite that scheming hussy Kate Chase to dinner when Kate's father was a member of the Cabinet.

She stole quietly back into her room, her head throbbing, took a spoonful of Indian Bitters, and returned to her cold bed.

Chapter Forty-five

Mary begged Lincoln's pardon, sick with dread that he would simply turn cold on her—or worse, bring up the subject of the bills—and was forgiven.

But the matter of invitations still rankled, and John Nicolay still remained in charge of White House official entertainments.

There were so many people in Washington to whom one had to be polite, no matter what one knew they were saying behind one's back! "You're the President of the United States," said Mary, half-playful and half-earnest, over breakfast. "Surely that gives you the right to not have to put up with schemers and liars and hypocrites who would just as soon do you a dirty turn as not!"

"I surely wish it did," Lincoln sighed. Even the egg that was usually all he'd have for breakfast curdled untouched on the plate before him in the chilly sunlight. "But in fact it takes that right away."

Willie looked up at him, baffled. "Then what *do* you get, Pa, for being President?"

"I get to have an eagle embroidered on my napkin," replied Lincoln promptly. "And I get to have the band play when I come into the room."

Mary supposed he was right—that as President, he did not have the right to pick and choose whom he entertained. But the knowledge that Kate Chase's at-homes were better attended than hers—and that the Treasury Secretary's daughter lost no opportunity in advancing her father's chances for the next Presidential nomination by spreading gossip about Lincoln and Mary—made it difficult for Mary to be polite to the younger hostess.

She began to hold regular unofficial drawing-rooms in the Blue Parlor on her "off" afternoons, and, later, on Saturday nights as well, so that she could invite whom she chose. The company was mostly male, though Ginny Blair Fox was often present, and Sally Orne, when she was in town.

It was good to talk of literature and art as well as politics, to hear stories of foreign cities and the fashionable world outside the provincial circles of government. It was good to have a few hours in which she didn't have to worry, or watch what she said. It was good to feel that she was important—to push aside the troubling sense that Lincoln was avoiding her, and making plans and decisions in which she had no part.

Senator Sumner was a regular attendee, always ready to top her stories with his own or to give her pointers on the absolute newest styles in hats. Ben French was another, a gray-whiskered, fatherly man whom Mary had originally met back when he was a Democrat in 1848 and he'd come by Mrs. Spriggs's. He was a Republican now, and had replaced William Wood as Commissioner of Public Buildings, though he liked to say that the real Mr. French, dwelling like a little doll inside his skull, was a famous composer, trying to dig his way out. He played the piano beautifully in the Red Room, and wrote poems.

The Byronic General Dan Sickles came often, though there were some in Washington who frowned on him because of the scandal in his past, when he had shot the man who'd seduced his wife; the brooding darkness of that murder seemed to burn in his eyes, like a character from one of the novels Mary so loved. And for European dash and fashion there were Jacob and Henry Seligman, bankers from Frankfurt-am-Main.

Most fascinating of all was Chevalier Henry Wikoff. An American, Wikoff had moved like a graceful shadow through European courts for many years. The Chevalier seemed to have met everyone and to know amusing and slightly scandalous stories about them all, and his judgment on matters of etiquette and social usage was as impeccable as the cut of his waistcoats. He had a terrible reputation (Lizabet Keckley said), though to Mary he was never anything but gallant and deferential, and Mary—who'd developed her own hatred of the "vampire press" over those calculated innuendoes of Southern sympathy—was inclined to disbelieve half of what she heard. Even men who disapproved of him, like Charles Sumner, had to laugh at his tales of what the Sultan of Turkey had done with the French Minister to the Sublime Porte, and how the transplanted court of an Indian Royal Prince had comported themselves in a London bathhouse. It was Wikoff who gave her private entertainments and menus the last touch of Parisian elegance, the European flavor that made the diplomats nod approvingly. It was he who told her of what was being read in Paris, and what gossiped about in Madrid.

It was Wikoff who started calling her the "Republican Queen," a title swiftly picked up by the press.

Mary found it soothing beyond words to be treated like a belle again. When she looked in the mirror, although she dressed with great care, she was burningly aware that she was now forty-three, that her figure had thickened and her face had not only aged, but hardened. She looked forward eagerly to her salons in the Blue Parlor, where for a few hours she could forget that her husband spent fourteen hours a day talking to office-seekers and Generals, and preferred the company of his secretaries in the dark watches of the night.

In October word reached them that Lincoln's old Springfield friend Ed Baker—who had resigned from the Senate to take up command of the volunteer company he had raised in Oregon—had been killed in action at Ball's Bluff, and for a time her nightmares and grief returned. Willie wrote a poem about his father's friend, and it was published in the *Washington National Republican.*

No squeamish notions filled his breast,
The Union was his theme,
"No surrender and no compromise,"
His day thought and night's dream.

Meanwhile cocky General McClellan drilled his troops on the banks of the Potomac, asked for more men, and didn't go out to fight.

Late in November Lincoln proclaimed a national Day of Thanksgiving, and invited Josh Speed and his wife to the White House for turkey dinner. In the end they had Army beef instead, since Tad and Willie had taken to playing with the enormous turkey that the cook kept penned behind the stable to fatten; two days before Thanksgiving the boys appeared in Lincoln's office with a pardon for Jack the Turkey, asking him to sign, which of course he did. The cook complained to Mary about having to change the menu, Mary complained to Lincoln, and Lincoln—who didn't have much to laugh about those days—only laughed.

Mary also had very little to laugh about, as the New Year approached and bills poured in like a hemorrhaging wound. Fifteen thousand, one hundred and ninety-eight dollars from Carryl Brothers in Philadelphia. Three thousand dollars from Houghwont and Company in New York.

That was the solferino and gold dishes. Thousands more for Brussels velvet for new draperies in the Red Room. "This can't be right!" Mary sat back, aghast, her hand going to her throat; the next second she glanced up at young Mr. Stoddard, the assistant clerk who had been assigned to deal with her correspondence.

"I couldn't say, ma'am," replied the young man. "I can get Mr. Nicolay to double-check the bill with Alexander's—"

"No!" She reached as if to physically catch him, keep him in the parlor, then drew back her hand, ashamed. She made her voice light, the coquettish tone of a belle, denying something was important even as it burned a hole in her heart. "No, don't trouble Mr. Nicolay with it . . . or my husband. I . . . I will write to Mr. Alexander. . . ."

It couldn't possibly have cost $1700 to have new wallpapers in the East Room and the big State Dining Room downstairs! Why didn't she remember it costing that much?

Her hand began to shake as she looked through the other bills Stoddard had given her. Her mind simply blanked out the sums, dissolving them into a buzzing vagueness. There had been enough trouble over the $900 the dinner for Prince Napoleon had cost—the thought of going to John Nicolay for money to cover the overrun turned her sick to her stomach with dread.

The thought of what Lincoln would say was unthinkable.

"You can go, Mr. Stoddard. I will deal with these. I . . . I'm relying on your discretion. You know how the newspapers get hold of things."

"Of course."

I can't deal with this now, she thought, as the clerk's footsteps retreated down the cavern of the upstairs hall. Tears flooded her eyes.

Lincoln, she knew, would be beyond furious. Manlike, he had no idea how much redecoration cost, and no notion of the difference in appearance between the best materials and inferior goods. It was the Springfield house all over again. Few men she knew understood that one never knew how much work would cost until it was actually done. *Nor should he have to worry about this,* she thought wretchedly. He was already obliged to entertain hundreds of people several times a week out of his own salary.

She couldn't let anyone know.

Even as she couldn't let anyone know of her grief and fears for Ben Helm and her brothers.

Alone in the curtained dimness of the parlor, she could hear the voices of the men beyond the glass doors. Careless voices, loud and coarse. Cursing sometimes, as if they didn't even realize that the President's wife and children might be within earshot; or talking about the women who had swarmed to the city in such numbers, following the Army, women with names like Short Annie and Lucy Twenty-Three.

He didn't need this evidence of Mary's fecklessness, on top of everything else.

She thrust the bills into her secretaire and locked it. Her head ached and she fled the dark room, seeking someplace where there wasn't a chance that Nicolay or Hay would walk in on her as she wept.

Like a fugitive shadow, her silk taffeta skirts rustling, she descended the wide stair, slipped through the dining-room where servants were already laying the table for dinner, and down the short corridor of glass that led to the conservatory. Even in the corridor, the humid warmth of the greenhouse enfolded her in its comforting embrace. Southward through the wavy panes of the corridor's glass Tad and Willie were visible on their ponies, galloping back and forth across the cropped grass of the paddock. Their tutor, Mr. Williamson, sat on the fence and watched them good-naturedly. It was he who'd named the ponies Caesar and Napoleon (though Tad pronounced his mount's name "Teeda"—and Williamson still hadn't had the slightest success in teaching the boy to read).

Silence and sweetness, and the thick scents of greenery and earth. She sank down onto one of the heavy green benches, pressed her hands to her face. Five thousand dollars! And another $3000 . . . plus that bill for the rose-colored silk for the new gown for next week's reception . . . but she could just imagine what the newspapers would say if she made an appearance in the same gown she'd worn to entertain Prince Napoleon!

But this was all her fault, nevertheless. She always swore not to spend any more money and this always happened. She didn't quite know how or why. She lowered her head to her hands, and began to cry.

"Now, then, Mrs. L.," said a gentle Irish voice, "we can't have you makin' those lovely blue eyes red."

She raised her head. Johnny Watt stood before her, in his rough boots and mud-stained shirtsleeves, his honest countenance grave with shared sorrow. The groundsman had a trowel in one hand and hanks of string dangling from his pocket, for tying up vines. Gossip attributed him with years of corrupt bookkeeping and chicanery, but Mary couldn't believe that was true any more than some of the vile rumors being circulated about the elegant Chevalier Wikoff. Certainly no more true than the abominable absurdities ascribed to *her.* A quiet and unalarming presence, Watt was always willing to take time from his work to show her the new blooms.

"Sure, Mrs. L., it's no great thing to run over the amount you was given," he said, when Mary had sobbed out her trouble to him. "Why,

Congress does it all the time, and you don't see them fine gentlemen in tears over it, not that nine-tenths of 'em would know what a tear was if they was to drown in an ocean of 'em. . . . All they do is shift over money from some other fund."

Mary blew her nose, folded her handkerchief, and looked across into those bright, understanding eyes.

"It's like a man shiftin' change from one pocket to the other, that's all," Johnny went on encouragingly. "Nothing to grieve yourself over, or to go showin' a long face to poor Mr. Lincoln, and him with so much else to worry him nowadays. Why, it's what Congress does payin' that stuck-up laddybuck Hay to be the secretary of your husband's secretary, when he's on the books as a clerk in the Department of the Interior."

He snipped a pink rose from the bush nearby, neatly trimmed off the points of the thorns with his shears and wrapped the stem in a square of tissue from the box on the bench.

"Now, what's to keep you from turnin' that smooth English scoundrel Goodchild out, that was Mr. Buchanan's steward, who's been sellin' the food you pay for out the back door? You could do his books yourself, and have Mr. Nicolay pay over his salary to you. I'm sure you'd run the place better than Goodchild ever did." He grinned his leprechaun grin. "It's what you do, after all, when you've overspent your dress allowance back home. You turn off the cook and do your cookin' yourself for a month or so, till the dibs get back in tune."

She laughed shakily. "So it is! Not that half of those wretched cooks we had in Springfield could make a sauce as well as I. I think Mr. Lincoln always ate better in their absence."

"That's the spirit, Mrs. L.!" Johnny gave her a boisterous thumbs-up. "A few months of old Goodchild's salary, and things will be right as rain."

But Nicolay regarded her with frosty suspicion when she suggested that she keep the departing steward's salary herself, and the interview ended—as had so many with the secretary—with her temper snapping, and Mary screaming vituperation at him and then fleeing back to her parlor in tears. Nicolay distrusted Watt, and believed every tattled rumor of his raising produce on the White House grounds to sell to the local grocers. He claimed the groundsman was a Southern sympathizer, though Mary guessed he'd have claimed anyone a Southern sympathizer who didn't sympathize with John Nicolay.

When turning off the steward didn't produce enough of a surplus to cover the bills, and Watt offered to order several thousand dollars' worth of trees and roses for the garden and hand over the allotted money to her instead, Nicolay began to make investigations—"Not that it's any of his business, the schemin' German," muttered Watt. "It's all money for the house, after all."

At last, when the creditors became insistent, Mary sent a note to Ben French, begging him to come at once. Instead he sent a note saying he was otherwise engaged—it being Sunday afternoon—and that he'd wait on her first thing in the morning. She passed the rest of the day in panic and tears, and retired to bed with Indian Bitters and a headache, to be roused with difficulty by her maid Mrs. Cuthbert the next morning at nine with the news that Mr. French was waiting in the Red Parlor.

It was on the tip of Mary's tongue to demand just who he thought he was, to arrive at this hour of the morning and expect a lady to see him all of a crack.... But the memory of the bills drove her out of bed. "Just get me my wrapper," she instructed, stumbling groggily to the vanity to brush her hair, "and ask him to come up to the parlor."

"Mrs. Lincoln . . . !" The maid was scandalized.

"Just tell him, and hurry!" Her head still throbbed from last night's headache, and she felt woozy. "I'm sure I'm perfectly decent in my wrapper." It was new, silk velvet, and of a sumptuous burgundy hue. "Certainly it covers more of me than an evening gown."

Mr. French half-rose from the parlor sofa as she rushed into the room, the bills in her hands. Merely the sight of that stocky, heavy-shouldered gentleman, and the thought of confessing, released another flood of tears: she could barely get the words out. "Please, please tell the President that it's a common thing, to over-run appropriations. Everyone does it! The money can be taken from some other place, like a man shifting his coins from one pocket to the other, but he must sign to have it done."

French's eyes bulged slightly when he saw the bills. He shuffled through them, as if hoping that some of them were duplicates, then looked at Mary again with startled awe. She sniffled, and wiped her eyes. "Please," she whispered. "Please, I shall be ruined if you don't get him to sign—but don't tell him that I spoke to you! Don't tell him that I asked you to help me! Swear it! Promise me!"

When French was gone, she sank down on the sofa, trembling with remorse and humiliation. She heard the Commissioner's footfalls traverse the hall. Heard the glass doors open, and close.

He will hate me, she thought, her hands tangling in her long hair. *He will hate me forever.* The thought of Lincoln's coldness, his silence, was more than she could bear. How could her life have changed so drastically, when she had achieved her lifelong goal? What had she done wrong?

In time, when French did not return, she summoned Mrs. Cuthbert, dressed, and went down to the conservatory again. As she crossed through the hall she saw Lincoln's thin form silhouetted against the daylight of the open front doors, descending the steps to where his horse waited. Hay and Nicolay stood on either side of the door until he was gone. Then Hay whistled, and rolled his eyes: "What a blow-up! I don't think I've ever seen the Tycoon that mad! What was it about? Did you hear?"

"The Hellcat's spending," replied Nicolay grimly. "An elegant, grand carpet for $2500. . . ."

"Did anybody tell him what that pink-and-green monstrosity in the East Room cost?"

"He called me in and asked who let that upholsterer Carryl into the house. I said I didn't know at first, then said it has to have been Mrs. Lincoln. . . ."

"Who approved it in the first place?"

"That idiot Wood, who went to New York with her."

"You think there was ever anything really between them?"

Standing behind the doors of the Blue Parlor, Mary clenched her hands in fury. How *dare* that puppy insinuate that there had been anything in Mr. Wood's escorting her to New York? Was that what the newspapers were saying, too? What Kate Chase was whispering in her so-fashionable parlor? The man was gallant, that was all. God knew Mr. Lincoln was gallant enough to the ladies to make Mary want to tear his hair out.

"The man's an imbecile, but he's not crazy." Nicolay shrugged impatiently. "And of course Frenchie would swear he'd never seen a requisition for so much as a teaspoon. 'It will never have my approval,' Father Abraham said. 'I'll pay out of my own pockets first—it would stink in the nostrils of the American people to have it said that the President had approved a bill over-running an appropriation of $20,000 for flub-dubs for this damned old house, when the soldiers cannot have blankets. . . .' "

Their voices faded, up the office stairs.

Chapter Forty-six

Worse was to come. Chevalier Wikoff took her aside during the next Saturday evening soiree and murmured, "Please forgive my mentioning this, Mrs. Lincoln—only the wish to be of assistance to a lady in distress would prompt me to so much as mention a matter which must be extremely painful to you. But it happens that I might be in a position to help you. I have friends. . . ."

His voice dipped discreetly—he'd already mentioned and hinted at his connections with the French embassy, and his work for the English government in India and Turkey. "Friends who would pay a good deal for advance notification as to what your husband intends to say in his message to Congress next week. Nothing to do with our friends south of the river," he added hastily, as Mary opened her mouth to protest. "And nothing to do with anything that would come out in this country. Purely for internal consumption only. By the time it reaches Eng—the home country," he corrected himself modestly, "the address would have been given here already."

He glanced around him, though the groups in the oval salon were all engaged in animated talk: General Sickles bowing over the hand of Ginny Fox. Sumner and the Seligman brothers laughing over one of Sumner's stories.

"They offered me eight hundred dollars," Wikoff murmured. "I told them I no longer played that little game. But when a mutual friend spoke of your need, I realized at once it may be a way out of your difficulty. And it's surely no crime to 'spoil the Egyptians,' as Moses says, and carry away money from a rival government who wants to hear things the day before they come out in the newspapers anyway. I only offer it for your consideration."

And Mary thought, *Eight hundred dollars!* As if she'd been tossed a rope in a stormy sea. There was the traditional New Year's reception to be thought of—which had to impress diplomats and Senators alike—and her cherished hope of holding a grand private ball in the White House—perhaps for Lincoln's birthday?—one to which she would have to invite no one but those who supported and honored her husband.

And it wasn't as if his Congressional message contained military plans, or anything that would aid the Secessionist rebels if it leaked out. Surely there was no harm in showing the text, "for internal consumption only," to some domestic department in England? In the back of her mind, all the way over to the government printing office on an invented errand a few days later, some small voice kept screaming, *You know he would be furious—he would hate you for this. . . .*

But Lincoln's scrupulous honesty, particularly where money was concerned, was one of the things that had always annoyed her about him, especially when they needed the money so badly. Wikoff had recently sold her a quantity of stock in the Nevada silver-mines, and had proven himself honorable in that transaction. He could be trusted.

And it was Lincoln's fault, really, for refusing to consent to sign an appropriations bill. . . .

How often, in their Springfield days, had he neglected his practice for politics, but objected when Mary prevaricated with storekeepers over credit unredeemed? He simply didn't understand.

When the text of the Congressional message appeared in the *New York Herald* two days before Lincoln delivered it to Congress, it was as if someone had set off a bomb in the White House. Wikoff—probably because of his former reputation, thought Mary indignantly—was immediately suspected and called before a Congressional Judiciary Committee; she was sick with dread until word came back to her that Wikoff claimed that Johnny Watt had stolen the address. Watt, to Mary's astonishment and relief, assented to the lie, and in heartfelt gratitude she wrote a letter furiously denouncing those who claimed the gardener was a Confederate sympathizer.

Something must have gone wrong, she thought, *with Wikoff's transfer of the information to his contacts in the British Ministry. He must be trying to protect his sources. Or perhaps he, too, is afraid of retaliation . . . ?*

Wikoff was put in the Old Capitol Prison for a month, with the notorious Mrs. Greenhow and the other rebel sympathizers. He sent Mary a thoroughly amusing note apologizing for his inattendance at the New Year's reception. The *Evening Star,* the *National Intelligencer,* the *Boston Advertiser,* the *Telegraph,* all had a field day, trumpeting corruption and inefficiency, and segueing into speculation about Mrs. Lincoln's extravagance and parsimony, including a ridiculous tale that she was cutting up the outworn White House sheets to make drawers for "Old Abe" and her family.

Further and far juicier rumors circulated by mouth, spread, Mary was certain, by the servants she'd discharged and fanned by Kate Chase's malicious gossip.

Lincoln accepted the story of Watt's responsibility, and asked Mary nothing of the matter. But his chilly silence terrified her more than shouting ever could. The rainy nights passed sleepless, or clouded with dreams of trying to explain to him that she'd needed the $800 to pay Carryl of Philadelphia for a sapphire pendant.

"My dearest, dearest Mrs. Lincoln, can you ever forgive me?" whispered Wikoff, when, on the first of February, he appeared again in her Blue Room salon. He looked not a hair the worse for his month of incarceration, immaculately turned out as usual and resplendent in a new waistcoat of yellow silk. He fell to one knee in front of the chair where she sat, and kissed her hands. From the other side of the room General Sickles and Senator Sumner looked shocked. "I was aghast, horrified.... I'd warned the Minister over and over about a certain one of his clerks...."

"It wasn't you who sent the address to the paper?"

"Good God, no!" Wikoff gazed up at her with dark, ardent eyes. "How could you suspect . . . ? Except of course that it is what everyone *did* suspect...."

"I *knew* there had to be some mistake!"

Wikoff shook his head solemnly. "Never make a social misstep, Mrs. Lincoln. Even those mistakes one makes in the passion of one's youth, the world never forgives, nor ever again regards your actions with anything but suspicion! All I could do was keep quiet—and trust to Watt's good nature. What," he asked suddenly, peering into her face. "Not crying?"

Mary dabbed quickly at her eyes.

"My dearest Mrs. Lincoln, staying in the Old Capitol Prison wasn't pleasant, but I'd go back there for another month rather than cause you pain...."

She half-laughed, turned her face aside. "No, it's just that my son has come down sick—Willie—and I'm worried about him, a little...."

And my husband barely speaks to me, much less reads me his speeches any-

more. And the young men he spends his days with—and his nights—call me "Hellcat" behind my back. . . .

And I'm so alone.

She drew a deep breath, and called on all those years of hiding her heartaches from her old Lexington nemesis Arabella Richardson. "I'm quite all right. I'm doing what I can for Mr. Watt, for of course he cannot be simply turned out of his job here. I've written to—"

The door of the Blue Room opened. Lincoln stood framed in it, wearing his coat but no tie, the way he often worked in the evening. His face was grave, but she instantly saw the anger burning deep in his gray eyes.

"Mr. Lincoln," she said, rising, a welcoming lilt in her voice. "To what do we owe . . . ?"

Lincoln quietly crossed the room, nodding to Sumner and Sickles, and bowing deeply to Ginny Fox. He got close enough to Wikoff so that no one else could hear except Mary, and said softly, "Please come with me, Chevalier." In the doorway she glimpsed Nicolay watching, and beside him another one of the reporters who were around so often—Smith or Jones, she didn't remember the name, only that he wrote for a Boston paper. . . .

Lincoln took Wikoff by the elbow and walked him out of the room. The whole of the salon flooded after them at a discreet distance into the vestibule, hanging back behind the glass windscreen that shielded the doors, to see and not be seen. Mary heard Nicolay's voice behind her: ". . . of course he's a spy! Smith showed the President the evidence—Wikoff's been in the pay of the *Herald* all along. . . ."

At the outside doors, Mary heard Lincoln say quietly, "Chevalier, I don't want ever to hear of your coming into this house again."

Wikoff started to say, "You wrong me, sir. . . ." But Lincoln had already turned away. McManus, the Scots gnome who kept the doors, closed them in the Chevalier's face.

Lincoln paused beside Mary in the gaslit front hall, the other members of her salon crowded around and staring, aghast. With great gentleness—considering how furious she could see he was—he bent down from his height and kissed her cheek, then walked across the hall, and disappeared through the doorway of the servants' stair.

THE GRAND PRIVATE BALL THAT SHE HAD COAXED AND SCRIMPED AND maneuvered for—and, some said, committed minor treason for—took place four nights later, and was one of the most splendid in the history of

Washington. Since it was private, and not official, the invitations were out of Nicolay's control for once. She had given a great deal of thought to the guest-list. The Marine Band played, and Washington's finest restauranteur, M'sieu Gautier, outdid himself on the provision of refreshments at the midnight supper: sweetened replicas of Chinese pagodas and the Goddess of Liberty; a sugar Fort Pickens and an edible frigate *Union,* guns, smokestacks and all; pâté de foie gras and beehives full of charlotte russe.

But for Mary the night had a hollow, unreal quality, like attending a party in a dream. Even Lincoln's gentle teasing, as Lizabet Keckley put the finishing touches on Mary's scarf, gown, and hair, had a subdued note, as if he were trying to resume the old lightness of their conversations, before he'd thrown the Chevalier out of the house. "My cat's got a long tail tonight," he said, smiling at the length of her white satin train, and Mary tapped at his elbow with her fan. "Maybe if some of that tail were up around the head it would have a better appearance," he added—he always professed to be shocked at the low cut of her ballgowns, though they were certainly no lower than, for instance, those of Harriet Lane or Kate Chase.

She had also noticed he didn't animadvert on the propriety of other women's dresses.

Mostly, as they descended the stairs and crossed through the wide State Floor corridor to the East Room, her thoughts were with Willie, lying sick upstairs. He'd seemed to feel a little better that day, when Lincoln came into the guest bedroom to tell him about the offer he'd had from the King of Siam of a corps of elephants for his army. ("C'n 'ee hab un?" demanded Tad at once. " 'Fraid not, Tadpole," said Lincoln gravely. "It'd scare your ponies if we kept it in the stables, and we need the East Room for your mother's fandango.") But the pale skin of the boy's forehead had still felt feverishly hot to Mary's lips, and today he'd seemed worse, tossing restlessly between sleep and waking.

Between Lizabet Keckley's ministrations, Mary had gone back to the guest-room a dozen times to see him, and had always found Lincoln there. He'd reached out to her and taken her hand, and the shadow of the Chevalier—and of the eighty couples who had returned their invitations as inappropriate in days of war—retreated before the shadow of still greater fear.

That shadow followed them down to the East Room, like an uninvited guest. The great reception hall glittered with gaslight, the air redolent with the masses of hothouse flowers with which it was decked. Through the evening Mary was torn between concern for Willie and bursting pride in the beauty of the place. She and Lincoln made the promenade of the room, shaking hands with officers, diplomats, Senators. The midnight supper in the State Dining-Room was admitted to be superb, even by the fussy old Lord Lyons, the British Minister. But Mary excused herself two or three times, and, gathering her vast skirts in hand, hurried up the stairs, to where Lizabet Keckley sat by Willie's bed.

The next day Willie was worse, and by Saturday the doctors were saying that it was typhoid fever, the same disease that had some ten days ago killed Queen Victoria of England's Prince Consort Albert. The usual Saturday reception at the White House was canceled, and Mary spent all the day sitting beside the bed, changing the cold compresses on Willie's head, and reading to him when he woke. Lincoln hired an Army nurse—a Quaker lady named Mrs. Pomeroy—to look after Willie and take some of the burden from Mary's shoulders. He himself came in as often as he could, and Lizabet was there every night. Bud and Holly Taft also spent much time in the sickroom, and young Julia brought flowers—Holly went to play with Tad, but Bud remained beside Willie's bed. Lincoln had a cot moved into the guest-room, so that he could be with his son at night.

On Monday Tad came down sick. Lincoln spent most of the day sitting beside one or the other of the boys, though Hay and Nicolay brought telegrams from the War Department about the fighting now raging in Tennessee. Willie's throat was so swollen that he could eat little, and it seemed to Mary, when she came into the room over the course of the next week, that her son was wasting away before her.

As the days went by she forced herself not to see the looks the doctors gave one another, when they thought her back was turned.

He can't die! she thought frantically. *Not Eddie and Willie too!* His delirium terrified her, when he would mumble fragments of games, or call out for his Springfield friends, Jimmy Gurley or Delie Wheelock, or for Fido. Bud Taft was there almost constantly, holding his hand.

"He'll get better," said Bud, rubbing the waxy little claw in his grip. "My uncle was sicker than this last year, and he got better."

Bud looked exhausted; he had been there most of the night, and come back again that morning. But he only shook his head when Lincoln came in and said gently, "You should get some rest, Bud." The afternoon light was beginning to fade from the windows, and by its pallor Willie's face looked gray against the pillows, like a tired little old man's.

"If I go he'll call for me," said the boy. "I want him to know I'm here."

Mary, who had sat up most of the night also, let Lincoln ease her into her room, loosen her stays and take the pins from her hair. "We'll call you," whispered Lizabet, "if there's any change."

Lincoln drew the coverlet over her, and bent to kiss her. "He'll be fine," he said.

For an hour Mary lay, listening to the mutter of the petitioners for office who, even at this time, still lined the hallway and the stair. Once she heard Nicolay's voice, asking how the boys were; now and then Lizabet's step in the hall would have her sitting bolt upright, heart pounding in panic. When the twilight shadows began to gather she heard Lincoln's step in the hall, and coming to the door of her room, saw her husband emerge from the sick-room, carrying the sleeping Bud as lightly as a baby in his arms. He took the boy across the hall to his own bedroom and laid him on the bed, then went back to stand in the sick-room doorway, framed in the wan silvery shadows.

Mary wrapped her shawl around her shoulders, went to slip her arm around his waist. Beyond the doorway, Lizabet wrung out a towel with lavender-water, mopped Willie's face; no lamp had been kindled, but the remaining daylight showed up the glitter of the tears flowing down her face. She looked up and said, "He seemed better about an hour ago, ma'am. Stirred a little, and smiled, and held Bud's hand. Now. . . ."

Astonished at how calm her own voice sounded, Mary said, "Go lie down, Lizabet. Mrs. Pomeroy will be here at six. I shall watch until then. You look all in."

Lizabet embraced her silently, and Lincoln led the seamstress down the hall to the cot that had been fixed up for her in Mary's room. Mary heard his steps retreat toward his office; she drew her shawl more closely about her, and sat in the chair that had been Lizabet's, beside the bed with its drapings of purple and gold. Her little protector, she thought, looking down at his face, her champion, whose faithful presence had gotten her through all those years of Illinois thunderstorms.

He'll be fine, Lincoln had said. She repeated the reassurance to herself—he had to be fine. She could not imagine . . . Her mind hesitated over even forming the words. She could not imagine anything else.

She supposed she should light the lamp, for the room was growing dark, but could not bring herself to turn away from the bed, or to let go of her son's fingers. She was still sitting there, holding that thin little hand, about an hour later when Willie died.

Chapter Forty-seven

New York and Washington July 1875

There were very few places in the world where John Wilamet felt safe, and New York City wasn't any of them.

His initial contact with Irish teamsters on his first day in Washington during the War had been followed by a hundred potentially similar incidents in his years with the Medical Corps. Whole regiments of the Union Army had been Irish, and the Irish, in general, had no use for black men, free or otherwise. New York had always been an Irish city, and as far as John could see, as he came down the granite steps of the Grand Central Depot on Forty-second Street, it hadn't changed.

The city was as squalid now as it had been just after the War, the streets clogged with the dung of a hundred thousand horses and humming with flies in the sweltering heat. He left his grip at the railroad hotel Zeus had told him about—it catered mostly to the colored waiters and railroad porters—and took the elevated train up Third Avenue, glancing repeatedly at the address on one of the two letters in his pocket. The city had grown, spreading above Forty-second along both sides of the wild green woodlands of the Park. Rows of neat brownstones were broken by occasional giant blocks of European-style apartments. Did squatters still camp in shacks on the broken ground around Harlem Heights? Once upon a time there'd been hundreds of them, black and white, eking a living from vegetable-patches, free-roving swine, and theft.

The address he'd been given, however, was a respectable small wooden house on East Ninety-second Street, set high above the street and brightly painted. Dr. Jacob Sunderhof registered only the slightest surprise to see that the John Wilamet who'd written him about his "Guaranteed Cure for Drug and Alcohol Inebriety" was a black man. He stepped around the desk in his consulting-room and shook hands with John warmly, and if he looked surprised at least his face didn't fall into that expression of disappointed annoyance with which John was so familiar in dealing with Americans.

"It is so difficult to convince doctors in this country that there is any *need* for a cure for inebriety," sighed the German doctor, gesturing him to a chair. "They point out—quite correctly—that as long as an opium-taker continues to take opium in moderation, there is no problem. His symptoms are suppressed, and laudanum is inexpensive and easily obtainable. A patient can live for decades, for the rest of his life, in fact, with no ill effects whatsoever." He shrugged. "So where, they ask, is the problem?" He was a little ginger-haired man of about fifty, with a Prince Albert beard that was darker than his hair. His consulting-room, with its matched suite of blue plush chairs and its charts of physiognomical regions and "types," spoke of a prosperous practice.

"Where the problem always lies with alcohol and drugs," said John softly. "With those who don't take them moderately. Who seemingly can't take them moderately."

"Exactly." Sunderhof nodded sadly. "They would like to stop, but their bodies have become so habituated, and their characters so degenerated, that the physical effects of withdrawal drive them back to their bad habits. It is a much more widespread problem than you would think, especially since the War. Men come to me all the time, men who were wounded, or who contracted the flux, which was terribly prevalent in both the armies of the North and the South. . . ."

"I know," said John. "I was in the Medical Corps at Crown Point and at Richmond."

"Were you?" Sunderhof's eyebrows shot up. "I didn't know. . . . Well, then you understand whereof I speak."

"All we had was opium," agreed John. "I don't think anyone even thought about how difficult it was to quit."

"But now," beamed the doctor, reaching into his desk, "the problem has been solved." He opened the little rosewood box with its mountings of brass. Within was a glass-and-steel hypodermic syringe and needle, and a vial of clear liquid. "My system is simple, and makes use of regular injections of morphine. It works for both drunkards and opium-takers. No patient who has been treated with this system has shown the slightest inclination to return to his old ways."

John shut his eyes, trying not to imagine what his mother would do if given access to regular injections of morphine. Then he looked at Sunderhof again. "And they are able to quit using morphine, too?"

"Dear heavens, why should they?" asked Sunderhof, genuinely surprised. "Morphine is part of the treatment. While undergoing my morphine treatment, I have never had a patient relapse."

FROM NEW YORK IT WAS A HALF-DAY DOWN TO WASHINGTON BY train—the capital had changed, if anything, more than New York.

Both cities seemed to John not only bigger, but heavier, more clogged with stone and brick and humanity. There were more buildings in downtown Washington, and the streets in the center of the city had been paved. Gaslights and sidewalks gave the place more the air of a true city than it had had during the War. But as John walked away from the center of town toward the streets above K Street, he was conscious of more grime, of more loafers both white and black along insalubrious streets, of a deeper sense of desperation and poverty.

During the long ride down from New York that morning, he'd tried to digest his disappointment, and the cold tiredness that settled on his heart. Maybe there was no answer for his mother, no way to break her desperate predilection for the drunkenness of gin or paregoric. As the handsome houses of downtown gave way around him to run-down cottages and weedy ditches, his mind roved back to his childhood. To his mother's constant quarrels with the other women in the quarters at Blue Hill, to her inexplicable rages that alternated with periods of childlike sweetness.

Maybe there was no answer for him, or for any of those who had to live with her.

Lizabet Keckley still lived in the same neighborhood where she had before the War, but the neighborhood itself had deteriorated. The wooden cottages of the free colored servants and artisans were dilapidated and mostly needed paint. Porches and porch-roofs sagged. The streets were unpaved, and nobody had bothered to clear dead dogs, dead cats, dead rats out of the gutters. Flies glittered in the hammering heat.

But the big wooden house from which Mrs. Keckley's letter to him had been addressed was as spotlessly neat as any John had been in, painted fairly recently, the porch in good repair, although laundry hung prominently in the yard. As he came up the steps to the porch Mrs. Keckley rose from the wickerwork chair where she'd been watching for him, setting aside her sewing. She took his hands in hers, kissed his cheeks, and smiled her familiar smile.

"Mrs. Keckley," he said.

"John, you're a grown man now and you can certainly call me Lizabet."

"I wouldn't dare," he said, and they both laughed. When he had first read Dr. Sunderhof's article about a cure for drunkenness and drug-taking, he had written to Elizabeth Keckley, telling her he was coming to New York, and asking if she would see him.

She occupied two rooms at the back of the house. She had lived with the owners—the Lewises—in half a dozen successive boardinghouses that they had owned, and the rooms were spacious, airy, and as comfortable as any rooms could be in Washington in the summer. From the wide windows they could look down on the yard, which though weedy and hung with still more laundry, at least hadn't degenerated into a trash-pile the way so many did in this neighborhood, where the demands of making ends meet took precedence above the time required to keep some absentee landlord's property neat.

As they drank lemonade by the open window he answered her kindly questions about his mother's health and mental state as well as he could, and about Clarice and little Cora, Cassy and Lucy's children, and what it was like in Chicago. He found himself, a little to his surprise, telling far more than he'd meant to. There was something about this calm, strong woman that engendered trust. She listened without putting in any opinions, any remarks—listened gently and givingly.

No wonder the wives of two rival Presidents had taken her into their confidence.

While they talked she kept working, stitching tiny jet buttons on a bodice of pink silk and black flowered net, her strong, supple hands quick and neat as machines. Her parlor was her workroom—there was a recent-model Singer sewing machine by the window where the light was best, and the silks draped over racks and hangers were as elegant as anything Dr. Patterson's ladies brought with them to Bellevue in their copious luggage. Beside the fireplace—which had been re-modeled to accommodate a little heating-stove—hung photographs of Abraham and Mary Lincoln, and of two little white boys whom John guessed were Willie and Tad. On the other side hung a larger one, of Frederick Douglass, the black runaway who had been abolitionism's spokesman for twenty years.

"I heard Mrs. Lincoln is at your sanitarium," said Mrs. Keckley, and her soft voice was sad. "Poor woman."

"Do you think she's insane?"

She regarded John in surprise over her reading-glasses. "You're the doctor, John. And you've seen her. I haven't seen nor spoken to her since 1868."

"Was she insane then? Or when you knew her first?"

She was silent, neatly whipping thread through the shank of the button, watching him from her beautiful dark eyes. "Why do you ask?"

"Is she insane?"

"Yes." And then, "No. Not really." She tied off her thread, snipped it with small gold scissors shaped like a crane. "Crazy," she said. "But not insane."

He smiled wryly at the distinction. "Did she get worse, after her son died?"

Lizabet Keckley sighed, and sat still, the needle and scissors motionless in her hands. "I think any woman goes crazy for a time when her child dies, John. I know I did. You keep thinking there was something you could have done, or done differently. And mostly there wasn't."

She brought the pink and black gown around in her lap, with a gentle rustling of silk taffeta, and threaded up her needle again. Her hair was graying at the temples, and the lines in her face were more pronounced than they'd been ten years ago: there were more shadows of weariness accumulated in her eyes. She positioned a flounce of black lace, and spoke as she sewed, neat and perfect.

"Willie's death struck her down like she'd been hit with a two-by-four. She was never the same after that. She told me that it was all her fault. That it was God's vengeance on her for holding such a splendid reception the week or two before."

"That's common," said John, thinking of all the hundreds of women he'd encountered—at Dr. Brainert's clinic, at Lake Forest and Jacksonville—who were convinced there was something they could have done. It no longer surprised him.

"From the day I met her," Lizabet said, "—the day before the Inauguration—she could be so sweet and genuinely thoughtful some days, and other days would fly into rages or take pets over anything. She'd make all kinds of threats and say anything that would hurt you, and later she'd come back apologizing in tears. And she'd be truly upset, truly sorry, not pretending just to use you. I think she genuinely couldn't help the things she said. That was how she was."

John nodded, remembering the woman who'd held his shoulders through paroxysms of sickness that first day, with the tender firmness of a mother—and like no mother John had ever had—and the next moment had been shrieking like a harpy at the ladies of the Freedmen's Relief Association for not keeping better order in the tents.

It crossed his mind to wonder whether Lizabet Keckley got along so well with Mary Lincoln because at some time in her life, Lizabet had learned to deal with someone even more abusively capricious, from whom she was not free to walk away.

"And she was inconsistent," Mrs. Keckley went on. "She had such lovely manners, the kind they teach in young ladies' deportment classes. Yet I've seen her—"

She laughed softly, ducking her head. "Oh, dear, I shouldn't tell this story on her. . . . One day Mrs. Taft, the mother of Tad and Willie's little friends, came calling wearing a new bonnet, straw trimmed with purple ribbon, embroidered in black. Mrs. Lincoln thought this was the prettiest thing she'd ever seen, and went to the same milliner—Willian's on Pennsylvania Avenue—and asked for another just like it. Mr. Willian told her that he had no more of the purple velvet ribbon with the black figures, so Mrs. Lincoln went to Mrs. Taft and asked her to give her the ribbon off *her* hat."

It was exactly the kind of thing John's mother did, when she'd had a drink or two, or a nip too many of "pain medicine." Not drunk enough to be noticeable, but not quite paying attention to what she should be doing.

"Mr. Lincoln knew there was something wrong." Lizabet returned to her sewing, and her eyes filled with tears at his name. "She'd always been temperamental, but this was different. He knew it. He knew there was something wrong, and he knew it was getting worse. He was frantic over it. But he didn't know what the problem was, and there wasn't even anyone he could talk to."

No, thought John. Not in the riven world of Washington politics, with every newspaper in the country watching and waiting for him to fail.

"The President didn't have clerks and aides and a staff the way he does now. Just his secretaries. They lived as part of the household, and all of them working together in that same big room like a shoemaker and his apprentices in the same shop. Every decision about the War had to come to him—nobody else could make it. Four years, I don't think the man had a full night's sleep. He could see there was something happening to her, but he didn't know what he could do and he couldn't spare a minute of his attention from taking care of the country and running the War. He was like a sentry on duty, that no one remembered to relieve."

She sewed in silence for a time, and in the little garden behind the house, two children ran back and forth among the laundry, screaming with laughter.

"So she was alone," went on Mrs. Keckley. "And when you're alone like that, in as much grief as she was, it's terribly easy for the unscrupulous to take advantage of you. You'll believe anything they tell you. She was never one who could endure the deaths of those she loved. She was a faithful church-goer, but her faith wasn't strong. And when the blows fell on her, there was nothing to ward them off."

She hesitated, looking up from her work, as if there were something else to be said that she was uncertain about trusting him with. Her eyes went to a corner of the room, where a framed daguerreotype hung, a young man who looked almost like he could have been white, but for a suggestion of fullness in the lips. He wore the uniform of the First Missouri Volunteers—not a colored regiment—but John was long used to the subtle signs identifying those who "passed."

A small vase stood on the table before the picture, with a fresh-picked rose.

"And in this world," finished the seamstress in her soft voice, "if you seek the solace that the dead offer to the living who reach out to them anyone will call you insane."

MARY HAD NO RECOLLECTION OF SUNLIGHT AT ALL, IN THE SPRING OF 1862. For a month after Willie's death she kept to her room, with the curtains tightly drawn. Sleep and waking blurred together in a long, confusing haze. She had memories of waking in darkness, head throbbing, eyes hurting—remembering, and weeping afresh.

Willie was gone.

Sometimes Elizabeth was there, or Lizzie or her nieces Young Bess and Julie Baker—blessed, blessed comfort of having women she knew around her, women she trusted, before whom she did not have to even think about keeping up the façade of politeness or restraint. For many nights Lizzie slept in bed beside her, so that when Mary woke from her suffocating nightmares she had someone to cling to, someone to hold.

Sometimes Lincoln was there, exhausted and haggard. She had a confused impression of shoving him away, of screaming at him things that her mind refused to bring back when she thought of it later . . . maybe the whole incident was a dream. Surely she would never, ever say to him, *He would not have died if we'd stayed at home. . . . You killed him, bringing him here so you could be President. . . .*

Surely *that* was a dream. And in any case it was *her* fault, *her* whose pride and vainglory God was punishing. If it wasn't a dream, would he have, in other fragments of recollection, cradled her in his arms as he did, rocked her on his knees like a child?

It was only later that Elizabeth told her how sick Tad was, during those days of mourning. Between the crushing demands of Cabinet meetings, conferences with Generals, and diplomatic consultations, Lincoln spent hours with his youngest son, who had emerged from his own fever to be told that the brother he cherished was dead.

Mary knew she should have gone to Tad, should have come out of her room to comfort her husband. But the thought of emerging even into the hallway filled her with dread. The thought of speaking to anyone was both frightening and confusing, as if for a time no one was real anymore.

She could not imagine living without Willie.

When, in moments of self-pity, she had in the past pictured her own deathbed, she had always imagined that it would be Willie beside her, clasping her hand as he'd held it against the terror of prairie thunder. It was Willie with whom she would spend her old age, after Mr. Lincoln—who was after all a decade older than herself—passed on.

Now Willie was gone.

The newspapers resounded with Union victories at Fort Donelson, Tennessee, and in Missouri: *15,000 Prisoners Taken. Missouri Cleared of Rebels in Arms. The People Disgusted with Secession.* But though Mary was as aware as Lincoln was of how critical those victories were, they felt unreal to her. She knew she should care, but couldn't.

Willie was gone.

It was Lizabet Keckley who first told her that those who had passed the veil of death could speak through it to the living who were willing to hear. Mary had sobbed, "He's gone . . . he's gone . . ." as she had sobbed for days—weeks, maybe—in the dim, stuffy room, while Lizabet held her, her scented cheek pressed to Mary's hair. "He's gone and I'll never see him again."

"But he's so happy where he is," Lizabet said gently. "Happy in the Summer Land. He wants you to be happy, here on earth."

She spoke with calm confidence, the first person, of all those who'd come to her in her bereavement, who seemed to have anything to say besides *I'm so sorry* and *You must be brave. . . .*

"They all want us to be happy, for the few seasons that we're on opposite sides of the Veil that divides this world from the next."

And Mary raised her head and looked at her, remembering things Lizabet had said, when in the course of fittings, or while the seamstress dressed her hair for parties, they'd spoken of griefs passed, and of the sons each of them had lost. Mary whispered, "Is it true? You told me once you'd . . . you'd spoken with George." George was the son who had died in battle in Missouri, at the age of twenty-one, having enlisted as a white man since men of color were permitted in the ranks only as ditchdiggers and teamsters.

Lizabet nodded mutely. Mary had listened with interest at the time that she had first spoken of the "Circles" that met in darkened parlors by candlelight, to hear the words of the dead through the lips of mediums, but it had been like hearing about the ceremonial customs in the court of the Tycoon of Japan. She recalled the giggling séance in the parlor at Rose Hill, the summer Lincoln was in Congress, and how she and the Wickliffe girls had all jumped a foot every time the old house creaked.

Remembered, too, Granny Parker's acrid opinions about the famous Fox sisters of New York that summer, and their spirit-rapping ghosts.

Indeed, it had been Meg Wickliffe Preston who had, on a recent visit to Washington, introduced Mary to a "trance-medium" named Cranston Laurie: "His control has revealed the most astonishing things about the future," Meg had assured her.

Like the clear metallic click of a key in a lock, Mary thought, *I can talk to Willie again. Hear his voice.*

I can ask him to forgive me. . . .

It was as if a paving-stone of granite laid over her heart cracked, revealing beneath the first green shoots of spring.

LIZABET KECKLEY WENT WITH HER TO CRANSTON LAURIE'S HOUSE IN Georgetown for that first séance. Mary told Lincoln she was going to spend the evening with old Jesse Newton, of the Department of the Interior, and his wife. Lincoln expressed only deep gratitude that she was feeling well enough to go out. Elizabeth, Lizzie, and the girls had returned to Illinois by that time, though Lincoln, Mary knew, had begged at least Lizzie to stay. Though chilly, the air was beginning to smell of warmth renewed.

Mary was obsessed with the thought of meeting someone who could possibly communicate with Willie, with the thought of speaking again to her son.

Of asking his forgiveness, for her vainglory and her pride.

She had dreamed of him, over and over, in the month of darkness in her room. Dreamed of being back in the house in Springfield, of hearing his footsteps running up the stairs ahead of her, of hearing his laughter, only to open the door of his room and find no one there. From these dreams she would wake weeping, her head throbbing and all her limbs seized with painful restlessness. She knew she was taking more of Dole's Cordial or Indian Bitters than Dr. Wallace would probably approve, but she knew too that they were the only solace she had. She would, she vowed, reduce her consumption of them when her sadness had passed and she was feeling better. Lizabet bought them for her, and brought them to her in her sewing basket . . . and Mrs. Cuthbert and Ruth Pomeroy, each ignorant of the other two, did the same.

But the thought of speaking to Willie swept away any need for oblivion, and she stepped down from the carriage in front of the small Georgetown house with her heart pounding in anticipation.

Cranston Laurie was a man of quiet, silver-haired dignity. He and his wife welcomed Mary with gentle goodwill, and the others gathered in the candlelit parlor—how sweet candle-light seemed, after the cold modern White House gaslight!—greeted her but kept their distance, respecting the grief that was as clear on her face as it was in the sable crape of her dress. The Lauries' daughter, Mrs. Belle Miller, spoke of her own experiences with the spirits: "My spirit control loves music, and will sometimes take me over when I'm playing. Everyone tells me that at such times my playing is completely different, strong and unearthly." She laughed a little and waved at the shiny black grand piano that filled a quarter of the parlor. "I wish I had been acquainted with the spirits when I was a girl and forced to have lessons!"

Her parents laughed as well.

"Just as well you weren't, Puss," smiled Laurie. "You'd have sent your music-teacher running. When Belle is seized by her spirit control—a French nobleman named Ramilles, who studied with Mozart and was later guillotined in the Revolution—the strength of the spirit music will sometimes lift the piano bodily from the floor!"

"What is it like?" asked Mary timidly. "When the spirits come?" She thought of Mammy Sally's ghost-tales, and of the stories Meg had heard from her mammy and whispered in their room at Rose Hill, of haunts that followed people back from cemeteries in the darkness, to pluck at the covers of their beds.

Young Mrs. Miller frowned. "I can't really say. Once Ramilles enters into my body, I remember nothing. Only a deep sense of well-being and peace." She smiled, her face lit with the memory of ecstasy. "Of course you understand that in forming a Circle, we pray and sing hymns, and surround ourselves with a shell of pure thoughts, so that no evil or angry spirit can enter. Please do not think that there is any danger in what we do!"

Mrs. Laurie exclaimed in denial of the very thought, but Mr. Laurie said gravely, "Please, Mrs. Lincoln—we would like to share with you the comfort that we partake of during our Circles, but if you have the smallest doubt or mental reservation, by all means withdraw. We would not for the world wish you to do anything you were not comfortable with."

"No," said Mary slowly, "no, what you say is . . . is familiar to me, in a way. As if I half-knew it already. I would like very much to see a medium in action."

Mr. Laurie beckoned. From the shadows near the fireplace a young lady rose, diminutive and childlike in her white schoolgirl dress and hair-ribbons. "Nettie, dearest," said Mrs. Laurie, "this is Mrs. Lincoln. Mrs. Lincoln, Miss Nettie Colburn. She's come to Washington to be closer to her father and her three brothers. All of them have enlisted in the Army. Nettie has been receiving visits from the spirits since she was quite a tiny girl."

Nettie curtseyed gravely, and regarded Mary with childishly wide-set blue eyes. "It's a gift God has given me," she said. "They want so badly to come, to comfort those who weep for them—and to bring messages from the Other World."

The half-dozen other people in the parlor assembled around the table in its center, Belle Miller going to the piano. There she played "Shall We Gather at the River," and Mary felt both self-conscious and uneasy as she sang, wondering what Dr. Smith back in Springfield would say—or her sister Elizabeth, for that matter. Yet the atmosphere was soothing, and the prayer Mr. Laurie invoked to "The Highest Lord of the Universe" unexceptionable. Glancing sideways, she saw Lizabet Keckley's face relaxed and serene, eyes closed, waiting in confident joy.

Nettie Colburn sat with bowed head for a few moments, then looked up suddenly and gasped, "She's coming . . . !" and her head dropped over sideways, exactly as if she had fallen asleep. In the candlelight her face seemed suddenly older. At her side, Mr. Laurie breathed to Mary, "It is her spirit control, an Indian spirit named Pinkie."

"Many spirit here tonight," said Nettie—Pinkie—opening her eyes, and her voice was different, a deep contralto instead of the girlish soprano in which she'd spoken before. "Many spirit cry out to be heard; cry out to welcome wife of Big Chief."

It's true, thought Mary, shocked, staring across the table at the girl's transformed face. *The spirits do come. . . .*

"Is my son one of them?" she demanded breathlessly, and Nettie—Pinkie—regarded her with an infinity of compassion.

"Big Chief lady lose two son," she said softly. "Both here—both so happy. Little boy, bigger boy . . . big boy say he came to take the little one's place. Two men, one short, one tall . . ."

"Father . . ."

"Two women," said Pinkie. "One old, old—she wears a shawl. And one young, so pretty. So sad. She hold out hand, she say *'My little girl. My little Mary Ann.'* " Then the medium shuddered, her head jerking, and her face altered again. She closed her eyes, and when she opened them, looked straight across the table at Mary and said, in what seemed to Mary to be exactly Willie's voice and expression, "Mama?"

Mary began to sob, barely conscious of Lizabet's comforting fingers squeezing her hand. She did not know exactly what had happened, there on the other side of the table, in Nettie Colburn's thin body. But she knew the terrible weight of loneliness eased and lifted, as if light had shone through the Veil from the Summer Land beyond.

Chapter Forty-eight

She went back, again and again, to the house in Georgetown.

She did other things in those weeks. She visited the wounded and the sick in the Washington Army hospitals.

A battle was fought at Shiloh Church on the Tennessee River, fought for two days, leaving almost 24,000 men wounded or dead on the blood-soaked field—a quarter of all the soldiers involved. Wounded poured into Washington, and Mary, like nearly every other woman in town, went to visit them, to write letters home for them, to fetch water for them in the heat of the hospital wards. To bring them fruit and keep their spirits alive in the face of exhaustion and pain.

With Lizabet Keckley's guidance she became involved in the work of the Freedmen's Relief Association. Upon occasion she rode out in the carriage with Lincoln to the Navy Yard to watch the testing of new guns, and even received a few private callers. But in truth she lived from séance to séance, and the days between were often a blur.

All of Willie's things she gave away, except his pony, Napoleon, which Tad refused to part with. She found herself unable to even look at the Taft boys, or Julia, and sent Julia a note asking her to stay away. Tad himself went into hysterics at the sight of the girl who had been his and Willie's friend. Tad's behavior worried and frightened Mary, for the boy missed his brother frantically, and his tears would trigger in her fits of uncontrollable weeping. Lincoln could deny the boy nothing, and let Tad sleep in bed with him, to still the child's nightmares. Many nights Lincoln stayed in his office until two or three in the morning, conferring with

Generals or debating in agony over the military pardons of which he was the final judge of life or death. Tiptoeing down the dark hall, Mary would see the skinny, pale-faced child asleep in Lincoln's bed, waiting for him, his black hair sticking up stiffly in all directions like his father's, surrounded by a half-dozen slumbering cats.

She felt paralyzed. She knew there was something she should do, for her husband and her son, but could not bring herself to face their pain as well as her own. The spring heat advanced, and she began to suffer again from chills and fever, and from agonizing recurrences of the female infections that had plagued her since Tad's birth. There were days now when she could not get out of bed without a spoonful or two of Indian Bitters, Braithewaite's Patent Nerve-Food, or Dole's Quaker Cordial.

Lonely and confused, without even the Taft boys for company, Tad refused to proceed with his lessons, and poor young Mr. Williamson was reduced to simply keeping the boy occupied and amused for a few hours a day. Even what little Tad had learned, he seemed to have forgotten in his distress. She could see the boy retreating daily into a world peopled by his father and by animals—a Philadelphia merchant had sent him a family of white rabbits, to which had been added Nanko and Nanny, a pair of enterprising goats. Always outgoing, Tad had a lot of friends, especially among the White House military guard, but there was no one, it seemed, to whom he now gave his heart.

And piled on top of all of the grief and worry, there was the continued nightmare of the bills. They poured in without cease. Though Mary dismissed more servants, and even appointed Johnny Watt's twenty-one-year-old wife, Jane, as White House steward in return for a portion of her salary, it did not seem to help. The newspapers were relentless, running articles about how the President's wife was buying cashmere shawls and carriages for her relatives out of taxpayers' money, while soldiers starved and shivered in their camps on the Potomac.

There was a poem someone had written, about the ball she'd given in February . . . the ball during which she'd been frantic with worry over Willie lying sick upstairs.

What matter that I, poor private,
Lie here on my narrow bed,
With fever gripping my vitals
And dazing my hapless head!
What matters that nurses are callous
And rations are megre and small,

So long as the beau monde revel
At the Lady-President's ball!

The condition of the soldiers, at least, was no exaggeration. Trainloads of wounded were pulling daily into Washington—wounded men, and men who had come down sick from the diseases of the camps: typhoid, pneumonia, measles. Houses and churches all over Washington were converted into hospitals, including that of Adele Douglas on Lafayette Square. Simon Cameron's system of favoritism, contracts, and bribery was having its inevitable result in mismanagement and shortages of which the ultimate victims were the men.

Men—and boys no older than Robert—lay tossing on those narrow bunks, waiting for someone to change crusted bandages or soiled sheets; delirious, sometimes dying before anyone ever saw them. As the spring advanced and the weather turned hot, flies tormented them, and such was the dirtiness of most hospitals that sickness spread among the men like fire in old straw.

Fighting now raged up and down the Shenandoah Valley of western Virginia, as Stonewall Jackson outflanked and outfought three Union armies at Cross Keys, at McDowell, at Strasburg. In addition to thousands of casualties, the rebel forces supplied themselves happily from captured Union depots.

Though Mary did no actual nursing, she was aware that merely the presence of the volunteers, and the members of the newly founded Sanitary Committee, cheered the wounded. Some of them laughed with her over Lincoln's brief foray as actual Commander-in-Chief, when he'd gone down to Fort Monroe in May. General McClellan had been "too busy" to see him, so Lincoln had looked around him and enquired if anyone had thought to take the rebel-held Navy yard at Norfolk—something that had evidently never occurred to McClellan. Lincoln had personally supervised the reconnaissance for landing-sites, and had the Navy start a bombardment. The rebels had cleared out in a matter of days.

"Service is the best cure for grief that there is," said Lizabet, one afternoon in the full heat of spring, as they carried water in from the big water-butts in the center of the hospital camp at Mount Pleasant among the trees on Fourteenth Street. In the tent wards they, and a woman from the Sanitary Committee, dipped up water from the pail in tin cups and carried it to the men who lay on the cots, moaning softly with pain or murmuring under the influence of the opium pills the surgeon had handed out.

There was no banter, no joking in this ward. Most of the men didn't even know who she was.

This was the ward of men newly brought in, where their field dressings would be cut off and from which they would be taken for surgery in their turn. Mary shivered at the smell of blood and dirt, at the smell of gangrene. Minié balls did savage damage, literally disintegrating the bone within the flesh; these men would return home minus an arm or a leg, if they returned at all.

Yet strangely, these days she did not often find herself thinking, *Not Robert . . .* as she moved from bed to bed with her dripping cup. In the bearded—or pitifully beardless—faces, she saw other women's husbands, brothers, sons, men who had thrown themselves into battle for those things that Lincoln himself would have fought for: for the Union, and the right of the government to say to the individual states, *I don't care if it's what the majority of your citizens find most profitable, some things are simply WRONG.*

When she visited the hospitals—and, more and more now in Lizabet's company, the growing number of contraband camps—she found sometimes even her dread and terror of the mounting bills in her secretaire didn't torment her. There were now days when she was even able to put her grief aside.

"You're right about that, Madame." The woman from the Sanitary Committee looked up from the letter she was writing for a scared-looking young soldier: a tall, stout, fair-haired woman with a hooked nose and a decided chin. She, too, wore the deep black of mourning, her sleeves turned back over stout forearms. She laid one broad, soft hand comfortingly on the wrist of the man in the bed, and said to Mary, "If we cannot ask why those we love were taken from us, at least we can demonstrate our trust in God's goodness by doing His work. And goodness knows," she added, with a quick flash of humor in her hazel-gray eyes, "with the amount there is to do around here, one is simply too tired to grieve."

She rose from her stool beside the cot: "We've met before, I think, haven't we, Mrs. Lincoln? In Chicago, during the convention? My name is Myra Bradwell. I'm one of the organizers of the Sanitary Committee."

Mary remembered her, a schoolteacher, she'd thought, and probably a proponent of women's rights. But the black of her clothing touched Mary's heart and she said, "Bless you for what you're doing—especially in the face of your own loss."

The look of briskness—of running her life and everyone else's with maximum efficiency—faltered for a moment in the taller woman's eyes. "Thank you," said Myra softly. "I was so sorry to read about your son.

Your brother, too, wasn't it?" And Mary nodded, surprised that the woman would have read newspapers so closely to have picked up that small an item.

"Sam was my half-brother," she said. "We weren't close. . . ." Her throat closed hard, thinking about the fair-haired child at the breakfast-table in Kentucky, all those years ago. Thinking about the other brothers who *were* close—Alec and David, and Emilie's husband Ben, all of them somewhere being shot at by these broken and bloodstained soldiers in blue. Angrily, she added, "I suppose that was one of those articles that said I was sending him—or one of my other brothers—secret papers that I'm stealing out of my husband's desk?"

"Considering the number of people in Washington who *are* sending information across the river to the Confederates," remarked Myra, "I can only wonder that they'd think you were sending anything General Lee didn't already know about. But from the time of Jezebel on, men will point fingers at a foreign woman married to their chief. It's a good way of proving how patriotic and vigilant you are without actually putting yourself in danger."

Mary laughed, surprised at the sound of her own laughter, and instantly guilty. She thought, *Willie* . . . she had not, she thought, laughed since he'd fallen ill.

She gave Myra Bradwell a card, and invited her to call. The Blue Room salons were less glamorous without the presence of the Chevalier, and Mary still felt humiliated over the way Lincoln had ejected him, without so much as an inquiry, and in the presence of all of her friends. Sometimes Watt—whom Mary had talked her fellow-Spiritualist Jesse Newton into giving a job as special agent in the Department of the Interior—would send her up a message that Wikoff wanted to meet her, and would let the Chevalier into the conservatory, to which he still kept a copy of the key. Both Wikoff and Watt lent Mary money, not once but several times, never asking a thing in return.

Wikoff may have been a bit of a rogue, thought Mary resentfully, but at least he treated her like a beautiful woman. At least he talked to her, instead of retreating into her husband's guarded silences. At least he asked her opinions, instead of—silently but firmly—relegating her to receptions, to ordering books for the White House library, to bearing gifts of flowers and fruit to the hospitals which they both visited.

It's because my health isn't good, Mary told herself, when he'd gently change the subject away from war plans or politics, when he'd put off her questions with a story that made her laugh. *He keeps me out of important decisions because I so often don't feel well.*

But in her heart, she suspected that this was not true, and the suspicion was like powdered glass in her clothing, inflaming her at every move.

All those things were her daylight life. Mostly, she lived for the darkness of Cranston Laurie's parlor, and the soft voices singing hymns in the candlelit gloom.

There was a medium named Colchester, the illegitimate son of an English Duke, through whom Willie spoke to her as well. Colchester's séances had a stronger emotional charge than Nettie Colburn's, for under his mental summons the dead would actually take ectoplasmic form. Often, in the darkness, she heard voices murmuring behind her and in the corners of the room, and felt the brush of unseen hands on her shoulders, hair, and face. When the blurred shapes of drifting light formed up in the darkness, Colchester described their faces and clothing. On several occasions the glowing shapes walked around the table, while the distant music of horns and tambourines breathed in the shadows.

It was at one of Colchester's séances that Mary, a little to her surprise, encountered Myra Bradwell. "I only want to know that my girl is happy," whispered Myra, startlingly different from the bustling woman she had encountered at the hospital camp. "She was only seven when she was taken away last year. It's cold comfort, being told by some minister that it's the Will of God. And why should we not speak to them, if God allows it?"

Mary couldn't speak, but hugged Myra like a sister, and in her dreams now she sometimes saw Willie and little Myra playing together in the Summer Land.

Predictably, Nicolay had nothing good to say about either Nettie Colburn or Lord Colchester. "The man's a fraud and a fake," the secretary stated, on one of those rare occasions on which he came to the Lincoln parlor—in general, these days she and Nicolay kept as far apart as possible. "He's certainly not the son of an English Duke, though he may be illegitimate for all I know. . . ."

"Oh, *Heaven* forfend that a man not of legal birth be able to speak to those on the Other Side," snapped Mary, throwing up her hands in mock dismay.

"Heaven forfend," countered Nicolay grimly, "that every Spiritualist and medium in the country take it upon themselves to advise the President on how he should conduct the War. Or ask him for government posts for their relatives and friends."

Mary colored hotly, because, in fact, both Nettie and Lord Colchester had at times received information from the spirit world about rebel troop movements and intentions, which she had naturally relayed at once to Lincoln. And of course, her gratitude for contact with Willie again was such that she couldn't let their friends and family go away empty-handed, when they needed jobs and money so much.

"Now, the spirits have as much right to tell me what to do as anyone else does," put in Lincoln mildly, looking up from the papers Nicolay had brought him. "May be God's way of tellin' me that even killin' some of those office-seekers won't get 'em off my back."

But a few weeks later, when Mary had invited Mrs. Laurie, her daughter Belle, and Nettie Colburn to a small "circle" in the Red Parlor, hardly had Belle gone under the influence of her control and begun to play the piano when the door opened quietly and Lincoln stood framed in the darkness of the hall.

The music faltered and stopped. The gaslights had been turned off—spirits having a far more difficult time materializing in the harsher blue emanations of such illumination—and only three candles cast their glow across the dark-crimson wallpaper. "So this is our little Nettie, is it?" Lincoln asked, looking down at the thin young lady in her schoolgirlish white dress. Nettie nodded.

"Do you mind if I join you? Mother?" He looked across at Mary. Beside her, General Sickles and Mr. Newton of the Department of the Interior had the air of schoolboys caught out in mischief.

Hesitantly, Belle Miller said, "You know the spirits don't often materialize in the presence of a skeptic," and glanced across at Mrs. Laurie, but Nettie Colburn said firmly, "No, that's quite all right, Mr. President."

They didn't make a circle that night: Lincoln sat silently on the sofa beside Mary, watching and listening as Nettie went under the influence of the spirit Pinkie. Willie did not materialize, though he was there, Nettie told them, and was happy to see his papa. Turning to Lincoln with her blank, enchanted eyes, she said, "The spirits call to you, beg you, to go through with what you are considering, about freeing all the slaves. God and the angels will support you in this, you will be doing His work. . . ."

Mary glanced quickly sidelong at Lincoln's face. It was something she'd heard rumor of, but since the Wikoff affair he'd spoken to her so little of any plans or thoughts. His face was impassive, as it was in court, but he smiled a little.

Chapter Forty-nine

By May the heat was nearly intolerable, the dust choking, and the stench of the camps a foul miasma that cloaked the city. Tad was ill again, which threw Mary into a panic of migraine and tears. In July she took him and went north, with Lizabet Keckley as a companion. Anything was better than staying on in a city rank with damp and sickness, and hideous with memories of her lost son.

New York, as always, cheered her, even in the agony of her grief. It was a real city, with bustle and activity, paved streets and beautiful stores, not like the provincial filth of Washington. Though there was no opera or theater at this time of year, merchants invited her to lovely parties and bowed to her when she came through the doors. She missed Lincoln desperately, but she felt on the whole less lonely than she did trapped in the dark parlor of the White House, knowing he was at the far end of the hall and she wouldn't see him until nearly eleven at night and maybe not then.

She slept better when she was away from Washington, though she still woke in tears and there were many days on which she simply could not get out of bed. It was good only to be away from the constant disapproving presence of Nicolay and Hay, away from servants who pried and told tales. It was so comfortable to be able to take medicine when she needed it, instead of worrying about whether the two secretaries would somehow find how many bottles she had hidden away.

Not that she needed medicine nearly as much, away from Washington. She had Lizabet to keep her company, the best of companions, and Tad, and Robert, who met them in New York. She even had John Watt, who had decided to try his luck outside of Washington—Mary had agreed to help him get settled in gratitude for his silence in the Wikoff affair. It was Watt who introduced her to Republican cronies of his, Simeon Draper—a real-estate developer—and Abram Wakeman, who promised "assistance" in paying some of her debts. "No, no, it's all for the good name of the President," purred Draper. "We're all good Republicans here. But if you could put in a good word for me, when your husband is seeking a good man to become customs collector for the port of New York. . . ."

For a time she had Myra Bradwell, too, in New York raising money for the Sanitary Committee.

Money was needed. After seven days of fighting around Richmond, General McClellan had limped back to Washington. Sixteen thousand of his men—almost a sixth of his force—were dead or lay wounded in the Washington hospitals. McClellan called for 100,000 more.

Leaving Tad with Lizabet at the hotel, the two women attended the séances of Lord Colchester—in New York also—at a neat brownstone on Fifty-second Street near the river, where the spirits warned Mary to beware the lies of slanderers, who would cast stones in their ignorance at men of the spirit.

"Meaning himself, I take it," said Myra, as they climbed back into the carriage which Lord Colchester had himself sent to bring Mary that evening. "Covering his back in case of scandal. My husband's a judge," she added, intercepting Mary's shocked, inquiring look. "I've studied a great deal of law in order to help him with his cases—when this War is over I'm thinking of seeing if I can pass the Bar. So I've learned to watch and listen, I think a lot more than some of these poor souls do, who come seeking anyone they think will help them with their grief. And Colchester doesn't ring true to me."

"You're not a feminist?" asked Mary, appalled at this revelation in her newfound friend. It was one thing for a woman to know about politics, and to utilize the power of patronage behind the scenes. Ladies did that, although of course no lady would ever let the gentlemen know. It was quite another to put on men's trousers and make men stay home and take care of the children, the way the newspapers said—not that it wouldn't have done Mr. Lincoln a great deal of good to know what Mary had to go through, in their early Springfield days.

Myra shot her a slantways glance, then laid a reassuring hand on her wrist. "That's a word men like to throw at any woman who won't do what they expect her to. The same way they'll tar every medium with the brush that a few crooked ones have mucked up. But just because some men lie," she added, "doesn't mean Truth doesn't exist."

Myra must have heard rumors—or been prescient herself—for shortly after that, before Mary returned to Washington in mid-July, a young California newspaper reporter named Noah Brooks attended one of Colchester's Washington séances under the guise of a seeker after truth, and seized one of the ghostly, glowing apparitions around the waist. The apparition was solid enough to struggle like a tiger and give Brooks a smart blow to the head, after which Colchester left the country rather precipitously.

Brooks, to Mary's grateful surprise, didn't use the incident to attack her credulity, as most reporters would have, but merely had a good laugh about fraudulent mediums in general. His name began to appear regularly in Lincoln's letters to her, and she gathered that the good-natured young journalist and the President were becoming fast friends.

When she returned to Washington, Congress had risen and the city was somnolent under a blanket of heat, filth, and dust. Elections were approaching, with men dying and money being spent on battles the Union did not win.

A few days before her return Lincoln moved out to the stone cottage on the grounds of the Soldiers' Home again, and it was there that Tad and Mary joined him. She slept better there, and felt better: the water of Rock Creek tasted cleaner, for one thing, than the murky Potomac liquid that issued from the White House pipes. She and Lizabet could walk in the wooded grounds without feeling spied upon. Tad still cried at night, and on most nights insisted on sleeping with his father. Mary had hoped to cure him of this, but Lincoln only shook his head and said, "He doesn't take up much room, Mother."

On nights when Lincoln worked late at the White House, to which he rode horseback in the pre-dawn cool of every morning, Tad slept with Nanko and Nanny instead.

The journey to New York had helped, and not being in the White House helped. But simply the return to Washington brought back recurrences of Mary's blinding grief. These would come on her suddenly, in debilitating waves, and there were days when it was as if Willie had died only the day before. Her grief lifted a little when she worked with Lizabet, at the hospitals or at the contraband camps that were springing up all around Washington, but her spells of grief were still so intense that Lincoln once took her to the window, and showed her the walls of the building where the mental cases were housed. "Try and control your grief," he begged, "or it will drive you mad. . . ."

Often after that she was aware of him watching her with worried eyes.

When the rumor circulated that Lincoln was going to proclaim an end to slavery—when the Northern Army refused to return Southern slaves who escaped across the frontier between the two enemy countries—runaways poured into Washington. They camped in sheds or under blankets, or simply beneath the stars. They surrounded every fort of the city's defensive line, clustered in trashy and disorderly zones around every military camp.

Nearly all of them were field hands, untrained for any other kind of labor, illiterate due to the nearly universal application of Black Codes throughout the slave states, and unaccustomed, most of them, to fending for themselves in any fashion. The Freedmen's Relief Association did what it could, to find them food, blankets, places to live, jobs, but the absorption rate was painfully slow. The Irish teamsters who worked for the Army—and for the civilian merchants who were making fortunes off the concentration of soldiers—hated them. Mary's newfound young friend John Wilamet was far from the only one who was beaten and left in a ditch.

"They understand what this war is about better than any of your husband's Generals, Madame," commented Frederick Douglass, the acknowledged leader of the freedmen, as he walked with Mary and Lizabet through the messy snaggles of shelters that spread around Camp Barker. Douglass, whom Mary first met through the Freedmen's Relief Association, was a tall, harsh-faced somber man who had not been content with merely escaping to freedom himself, but who had worked, for the twenty-four years since his flight, to free the whole of his people. "They know it's about their freedom, whether your husband will admit it or not."

She looked around her at the camp, at the ragged men and women clustered around the rough marquee where Mrs. Durham—a greengrocer who doubled as a midwife and who had taken a dozen fugitives into her own small house—was dishing out what meager rations of corn and beans had been passed along to the Association by the Army. Compared to the wise Nelson, the starchily well-mannered Pendleton, and the competent Chaney and Jane, most of these contrabands seemed to Mary hopelessly primitive and ignorant.

Yet Pendleton, Chaney, and Jane had all been sold, when her father had died, to pay his debts and satisfy those of her brothers who needed cash money quick. As had the tall man beside her, dressed in his immaculate dark suit and cravat. As had Lizabet, beautiful, understanding, strong Lizabet . . . Even young John, following behind them with another box of blankets, would have been sold before he was very much older, separated for all time from his mother and sisters.

Quietly, Mary replied, "I tell him that. He says if he proclaimed the Negro free he'd lose three states and half his Army."

"For every fool Irishman who quits in disgust," said Douglass, "there will be seven black men striding forward to fight for their brothers, their wives, their children whom they left behind in bondage. Would you not fight, John?" he asked, turning to the youth who'd become Mary's messenger in the camps.

"To be free?" The youth looked up at the tall man with his large near-sighted eyes. The scar he'd taken on his forehead from a gang of teamsters on the day of his arrival was still a raw welt. "To know they couldn't come after me, couldn't take me back because there's no place to take me back to?" He grinned, a shy sweet flash of a smile quickly put away. "In a minute."

"Your husband is a lawyer." Douglass looked down at Mary again. "He keeps his mouth shut, and waits. He's doing all he can to re-settle us elsewhere, to send us back to Africa or down to Central America—to offer money to the Southerners for our release. Anything to avoid unilateral abolition by proclamation. He can afford to do all that. He's white. White men have been arguing and bartering and delaying, trying not to offend other white men, for fourscore years and six, while the black man has waited in chains, and seen his children grow up and grow old in chains, and die. Tell him to put aside his fear. Tell him to take up the sword whose hilt God has been thrusting at his hands for all these months. He will not regret it."

Mary answered something—she didn't know what. In her mind she saw Saul come into her father's kitchen, and put his arms around Jane: saw the way Jane relaxed into him, stealing the preciousness of love from the realities of other men's property rights.

In her mind she saw Jane weeping in Mammy Sally's arms, hugging herself as if to keep her heart from tearing itself out of her body with grief, at the news that Saul had been sold.

And superimposed on them both, she saw the foul drawing, the letters written in blood. *Make your peace with God, nigger-lover. . . .*

If he frees them, she thought, *those who wrote that letter will have his life, whether the Union wins the war or not.*

And he knows it.

IT SEEMED, IN THE LATE SUMMER OF 1862, THAT THE RUMORS OF Lincoln's plan to emancipate the slaves gained strength and force. It was as if, as Douglass had said, everyone knew that slavery was the true issue, though Lincoln continued to speak only in terms of Union, and of not letting slavery spread to new territories. Lincoln continued to seek the alternatives of colonization and recompense, seeing the contraband camps and fearing the influx and dislocation that outright emancipation would bring.

And meanwhile the swaggering General John Pope led the Union Army of Virginia against Manassas Junction again in the hopes of taking that vital gateway to the rebel heartland.

He lost a fifth of his men—14,000 wounded or slain.

At a séance at the Soldiers' Home just before that battle the Indian spirit Pinkie spoke through Nettie Colburn, urging Lincoln to use the dictatorial powers he had already taken as a result of the War, and give the slaves their freedom.

Sitting in his rocking chair in a corner of the parlor, Lincoln made no reply, though afterwards, when the guests had departed, he commented to Mary that it seemed a little hard for the spirits to be taking a stand on the matter, too. "Though I don't see why they shouldn't, I suppose," he added resignedly. "Everyone else in the country tells me what I should do about it, from Governor Seward on down to the little old Quaker ladies who come to my office to tell me how God wants this War to be run."

He sounded tired, barely more than a tall shadow in the gloom of the vine-covered porch. Even here above the creek, the night was uncomfortably warm, almost too warm to sleep. General McClellan had been in the field—though not making the slightest effort to actually attack the rebel capital—and Lincoln and his new Secretary of War, the neurotic Edwin Stanton, had essentially been in command in Washington. Frustrated, Lincoln had telegraphed his chief General, *If you are not using your army, might I borrow it?*

It was obvious to Mary that McClellan was either a rebel sympathizer, or simply had his eye on the 1864 elections as a Democratic, Northern peace candidate—a curious goal for a General.

"But I can't issue any proclamation now, Mother. Not while we're being beaten all hollow in Kentucky. It would do the slaves no good, if we scream *'You're free!'* over our shoulders while we're high-tailin' it for cover in Washington—and it'll turn the whole issue into a joke. Maybe the spirits don't see that."

Now she said, hearing the defensiveness in her response, "And why shouldn't the spirits have a concern, for a matter so close to the true destiny of humankind? They have given you warnings before."

"Like the warnings that Seward, Chase, and Stanton are all traitors?"

Mary colored in the darkness, for she was the one who'd relayed the warnings to him. Even before Nettie Colburn had given her Pinkie's warning, she had hated and mistrusted the former New York and Ohio governors, as she mistrusted the new Secretary of War.

"I can't sack my Cabinet on the word of . . ." Lincoln paused, then went on, ". . . of spirits." He stroked the ears of the curly-haired brown puppy he'd brought back from the Army camp, picked up stray outside a mess tent; the little animal was already inseparable from him.

"You sound like you don't believe that the dead can speak." Mary tried hard to keep her annoyance out of her voice, that anyone, even he, would question that Willie—*his* son, too!—had spoken that night.

Sometimes she felt a great deal of sympathy for the chubby, long-departed Miss Owens back in Illinois, who had refused to marry this stubborn man.

"I never said that," answered Lincoln quietly. "I think the dead can speak, if they wish. But whether they speak through the likes of Nettie Colburn or Lord Colchester is another matter, Mother."

IN THAT SAME HOT AUGUST, REBEL FORCES INVADED KENTUCKY, AND raised the Stars and Bars over Frankfort. Mary shivered when she read of the fighting around the Kentucky city of Richmond, of the savage small-scale conflicts between neighbors, and the devastation of the countryside she had known. Was Rose Hill still standing? she wondered. Were Cousin Eliza and the sisters of Mary Jane Warfield Clay still all right? Shortly after Second Manassas word had reached her that her youngest brother, handsome little Alec, had been killed in battle outside of Baton Rouge.

France and Britain, Mary also knew, were both close to officially recognizing the rebelling states as a separate nation—a nation that would sell unlimited amounts of cotton to English mills, and wink at the French control of Mexico. And once that precedent was set, that states *could* resign from the Union, how long would it be before California got annoyed and pulled out, or some New England coalition that didn't approve of an election or a future President's policies?

They were only waiting, she knew, for a Southern victory.

In September, Robert E. Lee led his army across the Potomac into Maryland.

On the seventeenth, McClellan's army met Lee on the banks of Antietam Creek. After fourteen hours of fighting, a third of Lee's army was wounded or dead, and a third of McClellan's men who'd fought, almost 23,000 men, the population of a city. Whole regiments had ceased to exist. Whole generations of the young men of certain towns, certain families, who had enlisted together to fight side by side.

Unpursued by McClellan, Lee withdrew silently over the river.

Three days later, on the twenty-second of September, Lincoln signed a Proclamation that set aside the original intent of the United States Constitution. Unless the Southern states rejoined the Union, it said, by the first of January, 1863, all slaves in those states would be "then, thenceforward, and forever free."

Chapter Fifty

Letters of congratulation and praise poured in from abolitionists, writers, Quakers, ministers.

Letters of abuse poured in, too, from abolitionists who carped that slavery had only been ended in the rebel territories—that men and women in the border states, and in the conquered areas of Louisiana and Virginia, were still as unfree as ever. Just how they thought Lincoln would have kept the border states from joining the Confederacy if he liberated *their* slaves, they didn't say.

Workingmen who volunteered to fight for Union ceased volunteering in droves. They also ceased subscribing to government securities to support the skyrocketing expense of the war.

Southern Unionists felt betrayed. Slave-holders in Maryland, Kentucky, Missouri muttered, seeing the day coming, inevitably, when their human property, too, would be taken from them—tens of thousands of dollars' worth, shattering their ability to continue agricultural production as they had known it. Moreover, as Frederick Douglass had pointed out, the fact that free territory existed close by meant that more and more slaves would run, knowing that no one there would return them to their owners.

"It doesn't matter." Mary flung down the *New York World* and reached across the lunch-table to clasp Lincoln's hand. "In a hundred years—or a dozen—people will recognize this for what it is. Thousands and tens of thousands who live in slavery in the South already recognize it."

"If they know of it." Lincoln sounded tired; he'd been up most of the night dealing with plans for the raising of additional forces in rebellious eastern Kentucky and querulous letters from slaveholders in Maryland. Several columns of comments about his being *"adrift on a current of radical fanaticism"* and *"an act of Revolution"* that would render *"the restoration of the old Constitution and Union impossible,"* were not what he needed.

"They'll know." Mary remembered those shadowy forms slipping through the darkness of her father's yard, those cryptic signs written on the alley fence. "Davis and his government may forbid anyone to tell them, but they'll know."

MARY WENT BACK TO NEW YORK FOR THE SENATORIAL ELECTIONS. Between the numbing horror of casualty statistics, the workingman's outrage at Emancipation, and Lincoln's unilateral decision to suspend the right of *habeas corpus* in the interests of security, these were an unmitigated disaster for those who supported Lincoln, Union, and the war. She remained there or in Boston through most of November, unable to bear the thought of moving back into the White House with the coming of the Congressional and social winter season.

Her official year of mourning was up. Indeed, most women mourned only six months for a child. She knew she would have to resume entertaining, receiving visitors, acting as hostess at receptions and balls . . . which would still be planned by that supercilious cold-fish Nicolay. Returning Congressmen and their wives were already leaving cards at the White House, and there were very few of them Mary actually wanted to see. The hollow inside her ached, not only for Willie, but for Sam, for handsome little Alec who had played with Robert in her father's garden on Main Street. Through a Boston medium her youngest brother had said to her, "Tell your husband I forgive. . . ."

She returned to Washington in a state of soul-sick dread. Rumors were flying again, exacerbated by the wild undercurrent of excitement among the contraband and free colored communities as they watched the days count down to January the first, and the confusion and indignation among the slave-owning population of Washington City about the status of their bondsmen. A Union attempt to capture the rebel capital at Richmond resulted in a resounding defeat at Fredericksburg and yet more trainloads of shattered men poured into Washington early in December. Lincoln visited them whenever he could in the dozens of hospitals around the city; Mary resumed her quiet work among them, often with only Lizabet or John Wilamet for company.

One December evening, as she and her Spiritualist friends Mrs. Dixon and Jesse Newton were putting on their cloaks in the White House hall to leave for an evening at the Laurie home in Georgetown, Lincoln stepped quietly out of the half-hidden door of the servants' stair. "Where are you bound for, Mother?" He'd been in a Cabinet meeting since before supper—Mary had expected him to be closeted with them most of the night. She could hear Seward's extravagant voice upstairs still, as the men descended the main staircase: Lincoln had early acquired the habit of coming and going by the servants' dark and narrow stair.

"To Georgetown," she said guardedly. "To a Circle."

"Hold on a moment," said Lincoln, "and I'll go with you."

Her eyes widened, but she wasn't nearly as startled as Cranston Laurie and his wife were, twenty minutes later, to see the President's tall form unfold itself from out of the carriage in the wintry darkness. Lincoln shook hands with the Lauries, bowed to Belle Miller and Nettie Colburn, then retired to a rocking chair in the corner, still wrapped in his gray shawl with his big hands folded over his waist.

One of the things people forgot about Lincoln was that, for all his skill with words and sounds—he could imitate bird-calls, as well as every member of his Cabinet, with equal ease—he had the frontiersman's quality of silence. In the dim glow of the single candle that burned on the table, Mary was conscious of him watching. The others, she was almost sure, nearly forgot his existence, as one forgets the presence of a sleeping cat. The faces around the table gradually relaxed, as Belle Miller played the triangular grand piano—Mary could hear when the spirit control Ramilles took possession of the slight young woman's body. As the chords gained in strength and manliness, crashing like waves on the rocks, the piano itself began to rock and sway, lifting from the floor and moving to the music, like a ship at anchor in a heavy sea.

Nettie spoke, in the thick voice of one of her several spirit guides, this one old Dr. Bamford: "Well, I sees we got us a new guest here tonight. Troops a little low these days, Abe, on account of that spat out in Tennessee?"

Silently, Lincoln got to his feet and walked over to the moving piano. Mary had told him of how the spirit of Ramilles would enter the piano itself, lifting and rocking it with the force of his unearthly music. The piano at the Soldiers' Home had moved a little, when Belle had played it there, but it had stopped within moments. This instrument showed no signs of stopping. Even in the darkness she could see its back foot lifting far off the floor. Lincoln put his hand on the piano, then under the back of it, while Belle played on, her eyes blank, her face filled with the passion of the French musician's spirit, so that in the dense gloom it seemed in fact to be a different face entirely.

Mr. Laurie seemed about to protest, but the spirit Dr. Bamford called out jokingly, the words eerie in the mouth of the slender blonde girl, "Hey there, Abe, you want a good look at that-there pi-anny? Ramilles, old friend, why don't ya just step back an' let the man see?"

Face like an automaton's, Belle Miller rose, her hands still sweeping, crashing over the keys. Lincoln ran his hand thoughtfully beneath the keyboard, then placed a hand on one of Belle Miller's, while her other hand continued to play. Then, as the piano rose and fell again, he said, "Well, let's see if we can manage to hold that thing down," and with a light move, like a boy hopping up to sit on a fence, he swung up and perched on the piano's lid.

The piano rocked like a bucking horse, then rose and fell again. Even when Lincoln was joined by two other gentlemen of the Circle, the powers of the spirits were unaffected.

Mary didn't know whether to feel fascination, triumph, or mortification that her husband—the President of the United States!—would so make a fool of himself.

"I told you," she said, as Burke the coachman drove them back to the White House an hour later. "Now do you believe that the spirits of the dead come? That they are capable of crossing the boundaries of the world to speak to us?" Her voice trembled a little, with earnestness and desperation to believe. "Do you believe that that piano was raised and moved by invisible forces?"

The carriage was dark, the city around them sinking into slumber. Only the faintest gleam of the carriage-lamps, and the glow of sentry-fires near the Treasury Building, cast threads of gold on Lincoln's eyebrows and beard as he looked down at her. He drew in his breath to speak, then let it out, and put his arm around her. When he did speak, his voice was gentle. "I do allow that that piano was raised and moved by unseen forces," he said. "And I am sorry, Molly, that you were not able to speak to those you longed to hear from tonight."

Although Nettie had professed them present, neither Willie, nor Mary's father, nor Alec had spoken directly to Mary that night.

They never did, on those occasions when Lincoln was in the room.

AFTER THE DEBACLE AT FREDERICKSBURG, IN JANUARY LINCOLN REplaced the affable and inefficient General Burnside with General Hooker, hoping against hope that the change would do some good.

It didn't. In early May Hooker marched south in yet another attempt to take Richmond and was surprised one afternoon, while sitting on a farmhouse headquarters porch near Chancellorsville, by Stonewall Jackson's forces charging out of the near-by woods. The general had somehow entirely missed the fact that they were in the area.

Eighteen thousand perished or were wounded at Fredericksburg. Almost twice that, at Chancellorsville.

Every night after supper Lincoln would slip out by the servants' stair, and walk through the bitter-cold darkness of the President's Park to the War Department to read the dispatches as they came in. Many nights he'd fall asleep on the sofa in the telegraphers' room, to be waked by the clerks an hour before dawn so that he could return to the White House in time to wash, shave, change his clothes for another day.

Other nights, wakeful herself, Mary would hear the thump of boots in the downstairs vestibule, the hushed voices of Stackpole the doorkeeper and messengers—or more often the Generals themselves. Then the boards in the hall would creak and going to her door, Mary would see Nicolay and Hay, nightshirted and bedroom candles in hand, at Lincoln's half-open door. And Lincoln would go padding down the hall barefoot in his yellow nightshirt, with his long legs bare as a stork's and Jip trotting faithfully at his heels, to confer with Generals on the landing in the dark.

Mary tried to get him to eat, tried to make sure he slept. His dreams after Fredericksburg and Chancellorsville were fearful.

The Union held Kentucky and Tennessee with a sliding grip. The rebels, although they had lost New Orleans, still kept their hold on the middle of the great Mississippi River valley, laughing to scorn the Union forces that besieged Vicksburg. Across the country men muttered against the draft, and those who could afford to, hired other men to take their places in the ranks.

Every day brought hundreds of wounded into Washington's hospitals. After a few editors were summarily arrested, the newspapers were quiet, but Mary knew that privately printed fliers circulated the city about her rebel sympathies—some of them even handed around in Congress—and rumors continued to fly.

Late in June word came over the wires that rebel forces under Robert E. Lee had crossed the Potomac again. They were marching through Maryland, and on to strike into Pennsylvania.

Mary had taken Tad to Philadelphia the week before, to escape the pestilential stink of Washington in summer. Sally Orne was delighted to see her, and her undemanding friendship was a great comfort. Through the winter season and into the spring, Mary had presided over official receptions and her private salons in the Blue Room, though large gatherings of strangers filled her with dread. By the end of March, she had discontinued the receptions.

At the news that a rebel army had invaded the state, the city of Philadelphia went into a panic. Lincoln telegraphed Mary, "I do not think the raid into Pennsylvania amounts to anything at all," but she returned to Washington anyway, to the cooler precincts of the Soldiers' Home. There Tad could ride, accompanied by William Crook, a soldier specially appointed to guard him. Washington was still alive with rumor about plots to kill Lincoln, or to kidnap him, to ransom in exchange for the thousands of Confederate warriors languishing in prison camps. Mary was obsessed by the fear that some rebel sympathizer might take it into his head to kidnap Tad instead.

She saw as little of Lincoln as ever. He would leave before dawn, riding horseback with Nicolay and Hay to the White House through the cool twilight. Some nights he didn't return at all. He'd send messengers—and occasionally flowers from the White House gardens—but Mary guessed he was sleeping on the sofa in the telegraph office, Jip at his feet.

"God knows what Hooker's intelligence is up to," reported Charles Sumner, who called with flowers—Mary suspected it was Sumner who reminded Lincoln to send the bouquets she received. "Nobody seems to know whether Lee's still in Pennsylvania or not, or what he's doing there."

Days later word came that the enemy was only a few miles from Harrisburg, where the railroad ran down to Washington.

Lincoln dismissed Hooker, and put a man named Meade in command.

On the last day of June word came that Meade had met Lee's army, near the Pennsylvania town of Gettysburg.

For two days Mary saw nothing of her husband. Sumner and Ginny Fox came to the Soldiers' Home with snippets of news. "Your husband has barely stirred from the telegraph office," said the Massachusetts Senator, taking the plate of gingerbread that Mary handed him. "The clerks get him sandwiches, but I don't think he eats them, which is probably just as well, considering where the food has come from. He goes back and forth to his office, and that mob of imbecelic petitioners and office-seekers there makes me want to go up and down the hall with a whip, like Jesus in the Temple, and drive them out so the poor man can get some sleep. You know if Lee wins, it will mean we'll have to sue for peace."

Mary said, "I know." Sumner too looked haggard—it had taken him two years to convalesce from his caning by a Southern Senator and in some ways he'd never completely recovered. She guessed that he could see as well as anyone else, what would become of Emancipation, if the North could not put down the rebellion in the South.

All those young men dead, at Antietam, at Chancellorsville, at Shiloh. Ellsworth and Alec and Ed Baker. The Republican Party, fissured already among moderates and bloody-shirt radicals, would turn on Lincoln like wolves, to save their own votes in the North.

"Is he all right?" she asked after a time. "Mr. Lincoln? Would it help him if I at least visited and got him to eat?"

"I think that's a splendid idea, Mrs. Lincoln." Sumner smiled his beautiful smile. "At least they'd have to let him alone for an hour for that."

Mary returned it with a little sideways twist of her lips. "I think you underestimate the forbearance of the average office-seeker, sir. They would not let him alone if he was dying. We can but try. If nothing else," she added, "I can hear for myself what's going on, rather than get everything second-hand."

Not, she reflected, that she actually would. Lincoln seldom spoke to her of matters either political or military these days.

Nevertheless she sent the cook over to the White House the following morning to make a light lunch, and a little before noon had the carriage brought around, and drove down Pennsylvania Avenue through grilling heat and a choking fog of dust. Though opening the windows of the family dining-room let in the stinks of the camps, the river, and the stables, it was better than suffocating. She even visited the greenhouse for a small cluster of roses to put on the table.

Lincoln looked like ten miles of bad road, but smiled when he came into the dining-room—half an hour late—and saw lunch ready. "What's the news?" she asked him, and he shook his head.

"Nothing good. It can't go on much longer, they've been at it since Sunday. . . ." He passed a hand wearily over his face, as if trying to clear from his mind the darkness of the future. "We can only hope, and pray."

He spoke no more of the battle, but she knew he was thinking of it; he was preoccupied and silent, and excused himself early. "I must go," he said. "Word usually comes in about this time."

"Of course." She told herself that if she'd given him a glass of water when he was thirsty, he was no less grateful even though too tired to say, *Thank you*.

He walked her to the door, and handed her into the carriage. The dust, and the supply wagons and artillery moving through the streets, kept the carriage to a walk along Pennsylvania Avenue, but once they reached the road along the Rock Creek bluffs, Mr. Burke whipped up the horses.

The team sprang forward into a trot. . . .

Mary heard Burke yell in shock and surprise at the same instant that she saw the high driver's seat of the barouche jerk, sway, and drop at one end. Burke snatched at the railing for balance and Mary screamed, and at the same instant the horses, panicked at the unfamiliar noises, the jerk on the reins, leaped and bolted. The carriage-wheels jarred on the roadside. She thought, *The creek-bottom* . . . as the carriage reeled and teetered. . . .

Almost without thinking she caught up her skirts and flung herself over the door and out. . . .

SHE CAME TO IN THE DARK, THINKING, *CHOLERA. THERE'S CHOLERA IN the town and we'll all die.*

Her father and Nelson were getting down trunks from the attic, to give to old Solly to bury the dead.

Pain went through her skull like white-hot daggers, her whole body hurt as if she'd been wracked by the Inquisition. *I must have caught the cholera after all.* . . . She listened for baby David crying, but heard nothing.

David must have died. . . .

No. It's Willie who died.

Someone came over to her, when she started crying. "Mrs. Lincoln?"

Ruth Pomeroy, who had been Willie's nurse. Mary had the confused impression that there had been something else after Willie's death . . . a trip to New York? A battle? Why did the image come to mind of Lincoln sitting on a piano in a darkened room, with his long legs dangling over the edge?

Or had she only dreamed it?

"Mrs. Lincoln, how do you feel?"

She managed to whimper, "Hurts," and Mrs. Pomeroy gave her a glass of something that had the swoony bitterness of laudanum. She drank it gratefully, hoping it would forestall the preliminary lightning-flashes she could already see in the corners of her vision. Sometime later she heard Sumner's voice, muffled and distant, as if in the hallway.

"What happened?"

Through her shut eyelids, she saw them clearly, the tall Senator and the homey Quaker woman framed in the dim glow of the single oil-lamp in the hall.

"The carriage-seat came off," said Mrs. Pomeroy's voice. "They took her first to the military hospital nearby, and sent for Mr. Lincoln. . . ."

She tried to recall Lincoln being with her, and failed.

"An accident?" asked Sumner—in her dreamlike vision she saw Mrs. Pomeroy shake her head.

"The bolts that fastened the driver's seat were removed, and the seat fixed up with glue, that would hold just until the carriage picked up speed. The carriage was in the stable. According to Governor Seward, nearly anyone could have got at it. They must have thought Mr. Lincoln would be returning with her. She's lucky to be alive."

SHE FELT WELL ENOUGH THE FOLLOWING DAY TO CONFER WITH YOUNG Mr. Stoddard about the details of the White House Fourth of July reception, but remained in bed. The migraine retreated, but for months afterward she had the feeling that those burning jagged lines, those rains of fire wavering in her vision, were never far away, lurking behind the curves of her skull-bones. On the night of the Fourth she heard the fireworks at the White House, far off toward the center of the town. When she drifted off into half-sleep she would jerk awake, thinking they were gunfire and wondering if Lee had marched south from Gettysburg, to seize the capital. Would they fortify the Treasury Building again, were soldiers camping in the East Room on her new sea-green-and-rose carpet? In dreams she saw Lincoln lying dead on the White House steps in a pool of blood.

She woke to the sound of Lincoln's footsteps, and Tad's shrill cries of welcome.

The door of her room flew open, Lincoln's face radiant in the light of the branch of candles he held.

"Lee's retreated!" His voice shook with relief. "He's on the run. Meade should have him surrounded by the end of the week. Dear God, and then it will be over."

AT THE SAME TIME THAT NEWS REACHED MARY THAT HER FRIEND GENeral Dan Sickles had been severely wounded in the battle, a telegram came to Lincoln from General Meade: *We will drive the enemy from our soil.*

"We don't *want* to drive the enemy from our soil!" fumed Lincoln, when he came to visit her at the Soldiers' Home. "We want to *capture* the enemy and his whole army and then the war will be *over.* I've got a good mind to go up there and take over command of the Army myself."

"Ca' I gum?" asked Tad promptly, enthralled at the prospect.

Lincoln sighed, and shook his head, and laid a reassuring hand on Mary's wrist, for she had started up with panic in her eyes. "The office-seekers wouldn't let me get ten feet outside the city limits," he said regretfully. "Plus, if I led the Army, sure as check we'd come to a gate someplace and I still can't remember the order to file 'em through it."

Mary laughed shakily, and settled back among the pillows. Though at first she had thought she'd taken no more hurt from the carriage accident than sprains and bruises, the cut on her head had become infected, leading to great pain and fever. For days she lay tossing—and weeping with pain at every movement—in the grilling summer heat, between fever and laudanum only vaguely aware of where she was. Mrs. Pomeroy was kind and gentle, but in her fever Mary hated the sight of her, for it brought back to her the recollection of Willie's death.

When she came out of her delirium, it was to the news that General Sickles would recover, though he had lost a leg—

—and that the city of Vicksburg, that controlled the Mississippi River and with it the whole center of the Confederacy, had been taken, by a Western General named Ulysses S. Grant.

Lincoln's face fairly glowed in the light of the bedside lamp as he gave Mary this news. The stream of food supplies from Texas—and of European arms, textiles, ammunition, and machinery coming to the Confederacy through Mexico—was now cut. Grant was on his way to assume command over the Union forces fighting for Chattanooga, the major junction of the South's network of railroads whose heart lay in Atlanta.

"We got a wedge in the log," he told her. "We have the chance, now, to split 'em wide open.

"A delegation of Gospel ministers came callin' on me in my office today," he went on. "They said, 'You can't appoint General Grant to command at Chattanooga—he drinks.' I asked if they knew what his brand is—I wanted to buy a barrel apiece for my other Generals."

Chapter Fifty-one

As soon as she was well enough to travel, Mary left for New York with Tad and Mrs. Pomeroy. She tried not to complain to Lincoln, for she knew he had troubles enough for any man, but she felt that the carriage accident had injured her far more severely than the doctors knew. Her headaches had redoubled, not only in ferocity but in frequency. The fear of the pain prompted the habit of taking a few precautionary spoonfuls of Female Elixir to stave them off before they began.

She suffered, too, from agonies in her shoulder and back, so that on some days she felt unable to get out of bed at all without the assistance of a good deal of medicine. She disliked it—it made her sleepy sometimes, and at other times she heard herself saying things that she knew she shouldn't, but anything was better than the pain.

Her nightmares worsened, nightmares in which Robert ran away and enlisted, nightmares in which Mary walked down endless lines of cots, crying his name. Sometimes she found him on a bloodstained plank at the Navy Yard, where Ellsworth had lain, his face wax-yellow in death and flecked with blood. Sometimes she saw him sitting up, alive, in a chair, like General Sickles, but instead of having a single leg as a bandaged stump, it was both legs and both arms, and his blinded eyes wrapped with a bandage beneath which blood flowed down like tears.

From this she would waken screaming, and fumble for the bottle on her nightstand, to drown the image from her mind.

It was after such a nightmare—such a remedy—when she sank back dazed onto her pillows, that she first saw Willie step through the wall.

Later she wondered if it were a dream, for she felt very strange and detached from herself. She didn't think so. Wondering, trembling with joy, she saw her son come through the wall, not only Willie but little Eddie, shining faintly blue in the darkness. Both boys smiled joyfully and reached out to her. She woke weeping, though with joy or sorrow she didn't know.

ROBERT JOINED THE LITTLE PARTY IN NEW YORK, AND ESCORTED them to Mount Washington, one of the dozen quiet summer resorts in the White Mountains of New Hampshire. It was a relief to have Robert with her, for she knew Tad would be well looked after by his brother. For all his tendency to nag, Robert cared deeply for his brothers, and in his gentleness with Tad, she saw the memory of his own loss of Eddie. With this worry lifted from her, she was free to meet other women who sought, in the White Mountains, to escape the pressure and heat of the cities. Wealthy women, most of them. And many of them women who, like herself, had suffered crushing losses.

When her headaches, and the pains in her back, permitted, she took refuge in the comfort of séances with a medium who lived in Mount Washington, a hollow-eyed woman named Mrs. Guinan, whose controlling spirit could raise and lower the table in the center of her parlor while the music of harps and tambourines drifted bodiless through the dark.

"Poppycock," said Robert irritably. But it was Robert's disbelief, and not Mary's faith, she thought—and said—that was poppycock. Robert spoke to her again about enlisting: "The Army is desperate for men," he said, which was true. There had been riots in New York against the draft, a week before Mary's arrival there. "And I look about me at the men who are left at Harvard, and I'm ashamed."

But the thought of losing him threw Mary into hysterics: "If anything were to happen to you I should die!" she sobbed. Tad, frightened, began to hiccough and cry, and Robert took him away for a walk in the woods while Mary retreated to bed with a few spoonfuls of Indian Bitters.

The subject was not spoken of again.

She lingered in New Hampshire for almost two months, where the air was pure and the war far away. Only when the leaves turned red and gold, and Robert had to go back to Harvard, did she return to New York, terrified to the last that Robert would steal away secretly and enlist. Even in her days of pain, or of dreamy lassitude when she would not stir from the sofa, Mary had followed the progress of the war through newspapers. There had been horrific fighting all around Chattanooga in Tennessee, with tens of thousands wounded and dead. But she was in New York when Lincoln's letter reached her, two days before her return to Washington, that her sister Emilie's husband, Ben, had received a mortal wound, fighting against Grant's men on the banks of Chickamauga Creek.

EMILIE WAS PASSED THROUGH THE UNION LINES AT FORT MONROE, Virginia, early in December, with her two children. Betsey, thin and weary in home-dyed mourning, her fair hair nearly white, escorted her. All her sons by Robert Todd were dead by Yankee bullets. With the blue-coated soldiers standing around the freezing-cold depot in Fort Monroe, Mary held her frail stepmother in her arms and wept.

Betsey took Emilie's younger girl on to Lexington, which had been captured twice in rebel raids but was now back in Federal hands. Emilie and her dark-haired little daughter Katherine boarded the military train for Washington with Mary, and moved into the big bedroom at the northwest corner of the White House's second floor. At twenty-six, Emilie seemed like a shadow of the gay girl with the red-gold hair who'd sat beside Mary in the gallery of the Springfield State House, upon whom Robert had developed his first eleven-year-old case of calf-love. She was almost literally a shadow: food was no easy thing to come by, in a countryside ravaged by war. Though Mary was sick with grief at Ben's death and Emilie's sorrow—Emilie was with child, too, from Ben's last furlough—it was good beyond words to have her little sister there. Good to have someone to talk to who knew Lexington, who had visited Springfield.

If Mary could not return to those peaceful places, those joyful times, the next best thing was to know that Emilie remembered them, too. In a way, her memory made them that much more real.

Emilie refused, however, to swear allegiance of any kind to the Union—Tad and Katherine came close to blows one evening in the library, over who was the real President. And Emilie refused, with a stubbornness that irritated Mary in spite of her love for the girl, to come with her to the Circles at the Laurie house: "Ben will be able to speak to you, I know he will!" Mary cried, but Emilie only burst into tears and shook her head.

When Mary told her about the visits she received—almost nightly, some weeks—from Willie and Eddie, and sometimes her brother Alec, Emilie stared at her as if she heard the ravings of a madwoman.

Emilie remained at the White House for over a month. She received no visitors and refused to join in the rare family excursions to various Washington theaters. On the day of Kate Chase's wedding—to a wealthy

Rhode Island Senator and political General who promised to be of maximum assistance to her father's upcoming Presidential campaign—Mary and Emilie remained ensconced in the oval parlor, drinking tea and indulging themselves in recreational slander.

But word got out. The newspapers published that one of Mrs. Lincoln's Confederate relatives had been foisted onto honest Father Abraham at the White House—that there was a spy in place in the government's heart. In November, shortly after Lincoln's return from the dedication of a new cemetery on the Gettysburg battlefield, General Sickles arrived at the White House to visit while Mary and Emilie were having tea in the Blue Parlor with Cousin John Stuart, who was in Washington on business.

With Sickles was New York Senator Ira Harris, red-faced and belligerent with drink. Sickles, thin from privations in the Army hospital and limping on two canes, was resentful and bitter at the loss of his leg: Mary guessed almost at once that the men had only come to be able to say they'd seen Mrs. Lincoln's rebel guest. She supposed allowances could be made for Harris—his only son was in the Army—but the New York Senator seemed to think that rebel women merited nothing in terms of gentlemanly behavior: "I see the rebels are running like scared rabbits from Grant in Tennessee."

"I'm sure they were only following the example the Yankees set for them at Bull Run, and Manassas, and Chancellorsville, and Fredericksburg." Emilie dropped a lump of sugar into her tea and returned his hostile glare with a Southern belle's sweetly merciless calm. "Will you have bread-and-butter, Mary, dearest?"

"They could be mopped up in a week," went on the Senator, "if we had the men to pursue them. What about your son, Mrs. Lincoln? How is it that he isn't in uniform? He's old enough, and strong enough, to serve his country. . . ."

"Robert is . . . is making his preparations to enter the Army," Mary faltered, praying that this wasn't in fact the case. "He is not a shirker, as you seem to imply. If fault there be, it is mine. I have insisted that he should stay in college. . . ."

"I have only one son," thundered Harris, rising from his chair. And, returning his glare to Emilie, he added, "And if I had twenty sons, they should *all* be fighting rebels."

"And if *I* had twenty sons," retorted Emilie, coolly dabbing butter on her bread, "they would all be fighting yours, sir."

As gatherings went, reflected Mary, this one ranked right up there with the fatal first of January, 1841. Emilie rose from the sofa and glided from the room with no appearance of hurry, but Mary heard her break into a run the moment she was in the hall: "Excuse me, sirs," Mary said quickly, and hurried after her. She caught up with her in the stygian gloom of the upstairs hall, while Emilie was fumbling with the knob of the guest-room door. "Darling . . ."

Emilie stiffened like a ramrod, nearly invisible in the shadows in her black dress, but a sob broke in her voice. "It's all right, dearest. I know he's nothing but a damn Yankee."

Mary folded her sister in her arms, and for a time the two women clung together in the dark, refugees alike from a world that was no more.

The clump of crutches on the stairs. Sickles passed them without seeing their sable clothing in the gloom of the hall, turned in to the little corridor that led to Lincoln's room. "Oh, now that is too much!" whispered Mary furiously. Lincoln had come back from Gettysburg with a high fever and was still listless and exhausted. She started to go toward the bedroom but Emilie's arms tightened around her. "Probably thought of some really juicy lie to tell him . . ."

Sickles's voice rose to a trumpet, and there was an emphatic slap, as if he'd struck the table with his hand: ". . . and it is unwise of *you,* sir, to have that rebel in this house!"

"General Sickles . . ." Lincoln's voice was dangerously soft. "My wife and I are in the habit of choosing our own guests. We do not need from our friends either advice or assistance in the matter."

Beside her in the gloom, Emilie whispered, "Oh, Molly, I should not have come."

"Nonsense! We need you here, both Brother Lincoln and I. You are good for us. . . ."

"It was kind of you to ask me, and to take me in," her sister murmured. "But I see that I will have to go."

Chapter Fifty-two

Emilie left for Lexington in December. Mary was desolate. She pleaded with Lincoln to put in his word with her sister, and he said, "I have asked her already. She has made up her mind. Let us not make departure harder for her than it already is."

Mary went with Emilie as far as Philadelphia, where she stayed for a day or two with Sally Orne, yearning for the younger woman's friendship to ease the hurt of her isolation. She felt her loneliness more sharply now, for a few months previously she had had a falling-out with Elizabeth over Ninian's dismissal from the Army commissary post that Lincoln had arranged for him. Both Ninian and Ann's husband Clark Smith had been accused of corruption. Neither Elizabeth's letter, nor Ann's, had been forgivable.

The nation was tired of war. Tens of thousands of men had died—torn apart by minié balls, wasted by pneumonia, measles, and dysentery in the camps, eaten up by gangrene in the hospitals. There was no end in sight. In the darkened parlors of Cranston Laurie and the other Spiritualists, Mary met more and more black-clothed women, women who had lost their husbands or their sons, women who spoke with bitterness of the bloodshed that would surely resume again in spring. Across the Potomac, General Meade and Robert E. Lee maneuvered and skirmished in the thick woods of the wilderness that lay between Washington and Richmond. Meade was cautious: "Like an old lady trying to shoo a flock of geese across a stream," muttered Lincoln. Lee—with half the Union numbers, ill-fed, ill-armed, ill-supplied—eluded them.

Lincoln was facing re-election with almost no chance of winning it.

Salmon Chase electioneered tirelessly for the Republican nomination, backed by Sumner, who had decided that Lincoln was doing nothing for the slaves he'd promised to free. The various wings of the Republican Party scrambled to dissociate themselves from Lincoln's failure. McClellan was running for the Democrats on a promise of peace.

"Which doesn't surprise me," mused Lincoln, when he came into Mary's bedroom to bid her goodnight, the night of her return from Philadelphia. "When he was General of all the armies he purely did his best to avoid sheddin' anybody's blood."

"The tide has turned," insisted Mary, sitting up sharply in bed. She was glad to see him, though the sight of him filled her with guilt. She'd done some shopping in Philadelphia with Sally, and though many businessmen of the city—including the ex–Secretary of War Simon Cameron—had generously promised to help her out with her debts, she was still very much afraid of what Lincoln would say if he found out how much she'd spent. Even she wasn't clear what that sum was, but she knew it was bad.

"With the Proclamation of Emancipation there has been no more talk of Britain or France entering the War on the rebel side," she went on, not liking how beaten his face looked, in the glow of the gaslight. "Their people would not stand for it! Nor, with the victories we have won, will our people simply . . . simply whistle down the wind the men who have already died, the blood that has been shed."

"The blood that has been shed," repeated Lincoln softly, and turned his hand over, looking at the palm as he had that day in the Navy Yard, when he had seen the corpse of his young friend Ellsworth brought in from the first skirmish of the war. *"Will all great Neptune's ocean / Wash this blood clean from my hand? / No, this my hand will rather the multitudinous seas incarnadine / Making the green one red."*

He turned his head, and gazed for a time at the mirror over Mary's cluttered dressing-table, where his own reflection could be glimpsed, chalky blurs of face and shirt-front standing out from the dark of hair and beard and coat, and the darkness all around.

"You are right, Mother," he said, after a long time. "I shall run, and if General Grant wins another victory I may just win. And then, I suppose, we shall see."

He came over and kissed her, but she could see he was exhausted, and she told him to go to bed himself. She heard his footsteps on the floorboards of the hall, and heard them pass his own little bedroom and go on instead to the main corridor, that led to his office.

It was only many hours later that Mary, waking from inchoate and frightening dreams, remembered the vision he had had, before they left Springfield, of the doubled reflection in his mirror: his living self, and a ghostly afterimage that whispered of death in his second term.

ROBERT ARRIVED IN JANUARY, AND FORMALLY REQUESTED HIS father's permission to join the Army: "With McClellan seeking the Presidency, it looks worse than ever, for you to order every man in the nation to give up his son, and hold your own out of the fray."

Mary wailed, "No!" when Lincoln came into the parlor and told her of Robert's request—Robert, fearing a scene, had consulted his father in his bedroom. She sobbed, "Don't let him go!" and sank to her knees. "Please don't let him go!" Robert's dour glance at his father was full of a world of *I told you so.*

"I shall die if anything happens to him! Are you trying to take away all my boys?" It took Lincoln hours to comfort her, while the winter rain hammered on the parlor windows. She wept herself into a blinding headache, but when Robert returned to Harvard, it was with the understanding that he would enroll in law school there the following year.

A week or so after Robert's departure, she was reading to Tad in the parlor after supper when he looked up sharply and said, "W'at dat?"

Fire blazed red in the dark beyond the parlor windows. As she dropped her book and sprang up she heard running footsteps crash in the hall. She caught up her shawl, ran downstairs, hearing someone shout, "The stable's afire!" Hay and Nicolay passed her on the stairs. Stumbling out the kitchen door, Mary saw in the wild glare of the flames Lincoln dash for the stables, clear the boxwood hedge that lay between as if it hadn't been there. Servants were pelting after him; she could already hear the horses screaming inside. Beside her, Tad yelled desperately, "Teeda! 'Poleon!"

Lincoln yanked open the stable door. Flame billowed out to meet him and he fell back, shielding his face with his arm. Tad screamed the names of the two ponies and made a lunge down the steps—Mary snatched at him, and Stackpole the doorman grabbed the boy in his arms. Tad promptly bit him, drawing blood, but the big Irishman held on.

The men around the stable were falling back. Lincoln made two more tries to find a way inside—Nicolay took his arm, pulled him back toward the house. Mary put her shawl over her ears, to keep out the screams of the burning horses inside. When Lincoln reached the house again he was weeping. "It's 'cause a N'poleon," said Tad softly, calm now, to Mr. Brooks, one of the journalists who'd been in Lincoln's waiting-room when the fire started. "He wa' Willie's pony." Then Tad himself burst into tears, grieving the final link with his brother that was gone.

IN MARCH, WITH MUTTERINGS OF DISCONTENT SWEEPING THE COUNTRY, Lincoln called General Ulysses S. Grant from Chattanooga and offered him supreme command of the Union forces. "The man's a butcher," protested Mary, as she and Lincoln descended the Grand Staircase to the reception in Grant's honor. "As well as a drunkard." Thanks to the "vampire press" she felt that she knew most of the Generals as well as their own wives did, if they had wives. "The casualties among the men fighting for him have been appalling!"

She had spoken, too, to men who'd served under Grant, as she'd made the rounds of the hospitals. "He don't care how many men he kills," had said one soldier. "Just so he gits where he's goin'."

"I can't spare that man," said Lincoln quietly. "He fights. Him and his pal Billy Sherman, they're a team of fighters."

He laid his gloved hand over Mary's, which lay on his elbow. Below them, the murmur of diplomats, Congressmen, officers rose from the hallway outside the East Room like the soughing grumble of the sea.

"If we don't have victories by November—if the war doesn't look to be ending—McClellan will let the Southern states go. It will be for nothing: Emancipation, Gettysburg, deaths . . . all the suffering and the compromises and the wars we have fought so far, for the Union to survive. Then God knows what will happen. Once the principle of Union is breached, there is nothing to hold either the North or the South together, and we will destroy ourselves piecemeal, or be eaten up by the first aggressor strong enough to take us on one at a time."

As Lincoln shook hands with a seemingly endless stream of guests, someone near the doors shouted "There he is! The man who took Vicksburg! Let everyone have a look at you, General!"

There was a rowdy confusion, then several Western Congressmen half-lifted General Grant up to stand on the nearest sofa, to Mary's fulminating indignation—she knew exactly what that crimson brocatelle had cost. She and Lincoln were forgotten as people crowded around Grant, fighting to get a sight of him, to get near him, to touch him. Anger at the slight—and her own growing suspicion that Grant was probably eyeing the Presidential nomination himself—turned her heart to unforgiving flint.

Ulysses S. Grant turned out to be a medium-sized, scruffy, shy man in a rumpled dress-suit, his newly trimmed beard redder than his hair. Since the formal reception-line seemed to have disintegrated anyway, Lincoln breasted through the crowd to the sofa, leaving Mary and Nicolay to keep what order there remained. When Lincoln finally brought the General over to meet her, Mary inquired with cool politeness, "Ulysses—what an interesting name, General. And what does the *S.* stand for?"

Grant replied expressionlessly, "Hiram."

He looked like a man who craved a stiff drink.

His wife, Julia, who came to Washington later and called at the White House, was in Mary's opinion worse: buxom, common, cross-eyed, and, Mary suspected, ambitious.

But Grant got things done. He and General Sherman—Uncle Billy, the soldiers called him, and said quite seriously that he was not entirely sane—went after the rebel forces like war-dogs unchained. Grant proceeded to cross into Virginia and attack Robert E. Lee in the tangled nightmare of the wooded peninsula that guarded Richmond; Sherman went south through Tennessee, following the rails to the Confederacy's supply-depot and manufacturing heart: Atlanta.

And Lincoln turned to the agonizing task of fighting a war that after three years nobody wanted anymore, and getting himself re-elected in whatever spare time was left to him.

Receptions were held twice weekly at the White House: Congressmen, diplomats, Senators, Generals, and their wives. Mary put off her mourning to attend them, standing at Lincoln's side as he shook hands until his right hand was so swollen he needed Hay's help getting his glove off. But the crowds of petitioners grew gradually less, and several nights a week he was able to escape from the White House completely.

While the armies were in winter quarters he took Mary, and sometimes Tad, to the theater often. Lincoln loved the theater deeply, and in the carriage on the way home they would talk of what they had seen, *Faust* or *Der Freischutz* or the gorgeously romantic young John Wilkes Booth in *Marble Heart,* and Mary could pretend a bit to herself that they were courting in Springfield again.

But not entirely like Springfield. Lincoln no longer talked to her of politics, or the conduct of the War or the country, the things that illuminated his life and hers. On nights when he was tired, having very little in the way of small-talk anyway, he barely spoke to her at all. She sensed him walking on eggs around her, and it maddened her.

She knew her temper had grown not only short, but uncertain as well since the carriage accident. Things angered her, or terrified her, for no reason. She knew that those spells of disorientation—of feeling herself about to do or say something unthinkable—were more frequent, and that they had been joined, usually in the evenings, by episodes of dreaminess, as if she were about to disappear.

She knew, too, that she was taking more medicine than was probably good for her, but why not? The pains in her head and her back were almost constant. She could usually pull herself together for the receptions, but often she found herself looking at the faces of the men and women around her and wondering, *Who are these people? And why am I here?*

And almost worse than the pain, almost worse than her continuing grief at Willie's death, pervasive as darkness or summer dust, was her growing guilty terror about the bills.

Above all, she sought relief from that shame.

They never stopped coming in. Mary knew she couldn't *possibly* be spending as much as they said, but each individual bill could be checked. Every purchase she made was only after haggling down the original price. She simply didn't understand how it happened. Shopping itself, which filled her heart with restful delight, had become such a pleasure that she could not forgo it. It was one of the only joys she had. She would sort through her purchases as she'd once sorted through her father's presents, obscurely warmed by their beauty and by their reassurance that as the President's wife, she now owned the best. She sometimes found things in her luggage, returning from a trip, that she barely recalled purchasing at all.

But she knew that if Lincoln didn't win the election in November, all the bills would be presented—and he would no longer be so caught up in petitioners and testing new rifles and arguing over increased draft quotas that he did not notice.

Then he would suffer disgrace, as well as she: for who would believe, once the newspapers got hold of the matter, that he hadn't known?

Shame scorched her at the thought, shame and terror. He cherished his honor—his reputation for honesty—above all things. *He never wanted to marry me,* she thought in despair. *If all this comes out, he will turn from me . . . and then I will die.*

"He has to win," she said one afternoon to Lizabet Keckley, as the dressmaker was fitting the bodice on a glossy gown of eggplant satin. "He must, Lizabet!" Her voice shook—she had had a headache earlier in the day, and still felt strange, from its aftermath and from the extra Cordial she had taken. The words came tumbling out of her mouth as they so often did at her Blue Parlor receptions, things she had planned never to tell a soul.

But of course Lizabet could be trusted.

"Moreover, if McClellan and his lackeys get hold of my debts, they'll use them against my husband—use them to defeat him, and it will all be my fault! I have a good mind to go to those politicians who've been making a fortune off Mr. Lincoln's patronage. It is only fair that *they* should help me, Judd and Lamon and Mr. Weed in New York, and that fat toady Davis. *If* they could be trusted not to tell."

When she went to Philadelphia for a few days in spring to visit Sally, and again in the summer, she met with Cameron, and with the German bankers the Seligman brothers, promising to use her influence should Lincoln win. She had long become adept at political deal-making, and at least in the past Lincoln had taken her advice. Anything, anything to keep Lincoln from finding out! She reached home again only days before a rebel force struck up past Grant's army and bore like a band of devils straight for the capital.

In the sticky July heat the few servants at the Soldiers' Home packed what they could of the family's clothes, and Lincoln, Tad, and Mary moved back to the White House, its reception rooms under sheets, its mirrors swathed in gauze. "If Washington is taken, might it even have the effect of uniting the country, of stiffening resistance?" asked Mary, fighting panic as the carriage joggled through the early-morning streets of Washington. "It might even help your campaign. . . ."

"Washington won't be taken," said Lincoln. But he, like Mary, was listening. In the morning hush, she could heard the spatter of rifles.

Two days later they all went out to Fort Stevens, on the perimeter of Washington's ring of fortresses, where the rebel forces under Jubal Early were trying to break through. Fort Stevens, like most of the other forts in the defensive ring, was a square of rammed earth walls, surmounted by a parapet and occupied by rough plank buildings crowded together: sutler's store, artillery park, powder magazine. Beyond the wall, a trashy ruin of scrap lumber, filthy blankets, and trampled or burned spots in the ground showed that there'd been a contraband camp there, whose inhabitants had fled.

From the woods a hundred yards away, rifle-fire cracked out. Mary remained in the carriage in the middle of the enclosure, her hands locked around the protesting Tad's arm in a death-grip—there were two young boys barely a year older than her son, drummers, running along the wall fetching ammunition or water for the men crouched behind the parapet. Lincoln climbed the rough wooden steps to the parapet itself and walked along it, stopping now and then to speak to this man or that—a soldier close by him jerked back suddenly and fell.

Lincoln turned, startled, and a soldier crouching near yelled, "Get down, you imbecile!" and grabbed the skirts of his black coat. "You'll get your fool head shot off!" Lincoln sprang down from the parapet to the walkway behind it where the men crouched under cover. He was still head and shoulders over the parapet and, cursing, the soldier shoved him completely behind cover.

Already soldiers were carrying away the dead man, crouching as bullets whined overhead. Mary closed her eyes, feeling as if she were going to faint.

Any of her soldier brothers would have shot that tall black figure, killed him. . . .

Had any of her three soldier brothers been left alive.

By Sunday, two corps of Grant's men had filed into Washington's defensive ring, marched double-time from the siege camps before Petersburg and Richmond. General Early was forced to withdraw. The band of rebel horsemen went on to elude their pursuers and burn Harrisburg, Pennsylvania, increasing the cries for the war to be stopped.

Which, she supposed, was the point of the whole raid. The summer was one of agony. Grant returned to the siege-lines before Petersburg, unable to break through to capture Richmond. Lee, undermanned and starving, held him in a death-lock. Patiently, Lincoln negotiated with Republican politicians about what promises could be made for treatment of the seceded states once they were conquered, *if* they were conquered. And all the while, wounded men came back from the fronts by the trainload.

Through it all she visited hospitals, distributing fruit and flowers to the sick men and reporting on the conditions—still horrible despite all the Sanitary Committee could do—in the vain hopes that Lincoln might be able to have changes made. She met Myra Bradwell again, working indefatigably among the wounded, and had her and her English-born husband to supper one evening. Lincoln and Myra talked about law and women's suffrage until past midnight, and Mary was much taken with Myra's big, slow-moving, gentle husband: the Judge, she called him.

But the heat, and the stink, and the miasma of sickness hovering over Washington in the summer proved too much, and in August Mary took Tad and fled to the cool mountains of Vermont.

It was there that she read that Uncle Billy Sherman, Grant's fellow butcher, had taken Atlanta, dealing the Confederacy a crippling blow.

The bloody tide had turned.

Mary—and everyone else in the country—could see that victory was only a matter of time.

Chapter Fifty-three

The summer of 1864 was a strange time, frightening and dark. She remained in Vermont until late in the autumn. Sometimes she spent whole days lying on the sofa in a haze of migraine and paregoric, surrounded by newspapers. They were filled with editorials and letters about Lincoln's call for Negro regiments: jeers from white men in both North and South who scoffed that a servile race—a people who had submitted to slavery for generations—would be useless as soldiers.

They were swiftly proven wrong. Black men flocked to the Union standards with a kind of angry joy, and fought with courage and ferocity at Port Hudson, Louisiana, in South Carolina, and in the Crater before the fortifications at Petersburg. When they were captured by Confederates they were generally slaughtered out of hand, for violating the cardinal law of the slaveholding states: that no black man carry arms against a white. Reading accounts of the battles—or letters from Lizabet Keckley, or Frederick Douglass, or even from her young friend John Wilamet, now with the medical corps in Grant's camp before Richmond—Mary wondered if Lincoln's hesitation in using the black troops more frequently was because he feared to further alienate the population of the South.

The reactions of the Northern soldiers were bad enough. "I'd rather be a private in a white troop than the General of a nigger regiment" summed it up.

On days when she felt better she would write long letters, to Mercy Conkling, or Cousin Lizzie, or to Lincoln. She had tried to get Lizzie the job as postmaster for Springfield, for which Mary considered her cousin far better qualified than most men she knew, but did not succeed. She tried again to get Lincoln's permission for Emilie to sell her cotton without taking the loyalty oath, in order to avoid destitution, but Lincoln refused.

Mary didn't know whether she should feel anger at his wretched stubbornness about honor, or pity for the pain she knew he felt. Both Margaret and Mattie—Emilie's full sisters—made similar requests, and Mary's pity dissolved when it came to her ears that in the expectation of receiving the coveted permit, Margaret had purchased hundreds of bales of other people's cotton at dirt-cheap prices, with the understanding that the profits would be split.

To make matters worse, when Mattie visited the White House briefly that fall, she had obtained an exemption from Lincoln to having her luggage searched. She had immediately bought up enough medical supplies—mostly quinine and opium—to fill several trunks and had borne them back in triumph to the Confederacy, along with a new uniform for Robert E. Lee.

With Atlanta taken, and victory assured, Lincoln was easily re-elected in November. His Vice-President this time was Andrew Johnson, a dour and self-educated War Democrat from Tennessee. There was now little talk of making peace. When Mary returned to Washington late in November, she saw the ranks of the blue-clothed, dark-faced soldiers march past at military reviews, singing: "Mine eyes have seen the glory of the coming of the Lord. . . ."

And she wondered if somewhere, Saul, Nelson, and Pendleton were listening, and any of those men chained on the deck on the Ohio River steamboat who'd kept four-year-old Robert from falling into the paddlewheel, all those years ago.

She found her husband deeply withdrawn, exhausted, like a man running completely on nerves. Tad was wilder than ever, charging the flocks of petitioners on the office stairway a nickel apiece "for the benefit of the Sanitary Committee," or harnessing Nanko the goat to a laid-down kitchen chair and racing this improvised chariot up and down the White House halls. He still slept with Lincoln every night, and visited his father in his office a dozen times a day through the "secret passage" Lincoln had had built that fall, a short hallway cut out of one end of the office anteroom that led directly from his own office to the parlor. Tad had a special knock: Lincoln would even interrupt Cabinet meetings to let his son in.

"You're spoiling him rotten," snapped Mary, during one of those sharp-tongued squabbles that she'd initiate in the hopes of breaking through the wall of her husband's silences.

Lincoln didn't mention the weeks she'd take Tad to Philadelphia and the

White Mountains with her, and let him run wild, buying him anything he asked for. He said only, "He'll grow out of it," with a patience that made Mary, her nerves in shreds, itch to pull his hair out by the roots.

He wasn't well, either. On those rare occasions when she saw him in full daylight it was obvious to her that he'd lost nearly thirty pounds over the past four years, and his color was not good. But to her questions he merely replied, "I feel fine, Mother. Just tired."

And he looked at her with a gaze as probing, as questioning, as worried as her own. She sometimes wondered whether he knew about her debts, or about the deals she'd made with businessmen and politicians to cover them. She didn't think so. She knew him well enough to know that his devil-take-the-hindmost honesty would not have tolerated the situation, if he knew. But the fear that he might guess created still more silence between them, a silence she had no idea how to break.

With Atlanta taken, and the broken-down nexus of the South's railway system in Union hands, the end came rapidly. Without shipments of supplies, the Confederate troops were starving. They fought without boots and sometimes without guns or ammunition, running forward under fire to snatch the weapons from the hands of the enemy dead. Still they hung on, maneuvering with dwindling strength in the tree-clogged swampy country around Richmond.

Unable to sell their cotton, Confederate civilians were starving, too. Mary dreamed one night of Arabella Richardson Bodley, her girlhood nemesis, sitting alone in the echoing shadows of an empty house, weeping in a faded dress of home-dyed black. That fall Emilie wrote to them of her brother Levi's death, from the physical hardships of starvation on a constitution undermined—Mary strongly suspected—by drink. Still, Emilie's accusation hurt, that they had contributed to his death. "The last money I have in the world I used to make the unfruitful appeal to you . . . I request only the right which humanity and justice always gives to widows and orphans. I would also remind you that your minié bullets have made us what we are."

Lincoln did not afterwards mention his "Little Sister," but Mary could read the grief in his face.

Dozens of women now waited among the petitioners in Lincoln's office, to beg for the release and reprieve of brothers, husbands, sons imprisoned for military crimes, usually desertion or dereliction of duty. Mary always regarded these women with suspicion, as she regarded any woman who came close to Lincoln. In her more reasonable moments she knew perfectly well that she had not the slightest cause for mistrust—Lincoln would no more betray her than he would betray the Union.

But he had never lost his liking for women. And with his neglect of her—his maddening distance from her—her jealousy festered.

In January of 1865, against Mary's pleas and sobs, Lincoln finally asked General Grant if he might have room on his staff for Robert, who was commissioned as a Captain early the following month. The Army was still camped before Petersburg, twenty-five miles from Richmond on the Appomatox River. Mary lived in an agony of apprehension, expecting every morning that the day would bring her news of her eldest son's death.

When Lincoln told her, early in March, that he was making a trip to Grant's headquarters, she said at once, "You cannot leave me behind."

"Ca' I go doo?" demanded Tad in the next breath—Alexander Williamson, though he still couldn't entice the boy back to his studies, had at least worked with him on his speech, with the result that he was becoming slowly more intelligible. "I wanna see dem rebels—ca' I day my gun?"

So a party was organized: Mary and her maid Mrs. Cuthbert, Tad and his bodyguard Billy Crook, traveled downriver on the small steamboat *River Queen,* which was anchored below the bluff at City Point. Though Lincoln was quite clearly ill he asked to be taken to see the fighting. Mary wept again and pleaded, remembering the soldier who had fallen only feet from him on the parapet of Fort Stevens. "These men are shedding their blood—giving their lives—for my principles and my decisions," replied Lincoln quietly. "The least I can do is let them know how I value them."

She absolutely insisted that Tad remain with her on the *River Queen,* however, and even the boy's subsequent tantrum and tears would not move her. She posted Lieutenant Crook to keep an eye on him and keep him busy, and spent the day pacing, nervous, and endeavoring to be polite to Julia Grant. The train back from field headquarters was late and she sent a dozen messages to the telegrapher's tent, demanding to be told why. When the reply came that it was hauling several cars full of wounded, and thus forced to travel slowly, she was convinced that this was only a lie to calm her, and got into a quarrel with Julia Grant on the strength of it.

Lincoln got off the train silent and pale. "Did you see fighting?" demanded Tad, as he seized his father's hand.

"Only the field afterwards," Lincoln said, "and the burying of the dead." He went to his cabin and closed the door.

In the morning he looked a little better, and set out on horseback to watch General Phil Sheridan's men coming in across the river. The plan was that he would meet Mary and Mrs. Grant at General Ord's camp at Malvern Hill in the afternoon to review Ord's troops. Mary alternated between annoyance that she was relegated to following in a mere ambulance wagon, and agony that Lincoln's party would be overwhelmed by rebel cavalry, a situation which wasn't helped by Julia Grant's matter-of-fact "Nonsense, the rebels haven't either the horses or the men to take on a bodyguard."

"That's exactly the kind of lie I expect *your* husband *would* tell you," snapped Mary as Colonel Porter helped her into the wagon.

Julia Grant's square face reddened. "Just because your husband managed to get himself re-elected, you think you know everything about soldiering," the General's wife retorted. "But let me tell you, if it weren't for *my* husband's victories, McClellan would be in office now!"

Colonel Porter began hesitantly, "Ladies, now, it's a long ride. . . ."

But Mary ignored him, ignored everything but the rush of uncontrollable fury that filled her. "Oh, and you're just waiting until the next election, aren't you, for you to move into the White House!"

"Ladies . . ."

"Well, if we do I *certainly* wouldn't be able to come up to *your* standard of balls and receptions, even if it's *not* wartime. . . ."

"Of *that* I haven't the smallest doubt!" Mary shot back at her. "But what the diplomatic community might think of being served whiskey punch and cookies instead of more customary hors d'oeuvres I shudder to imagine, even if you *do* manage to get yourself a decent dress!"

Mrs. Grant stared at her in shocked fury, and then turned her face away, breathing hard. Mary whirled at once upon Colonel Porter and demanded, "Can't your driver go any faster? The review shall be over by the time we get there."

"The going is very difficult over corduroy roads like this one, ma'am," replied the officer nervously. He nodded out the front of the wagon, past the driver's rigid blue-clad back, to the band of felled trees laid side to side over which the ambulance wagon was cautiously bumping. "It's swampy country from here to Malvern Hill, ma'am. This's the only kind of road—"

"Don't you think I know about the kind of terrain that justifies a corduroy road?" shouted Mary. "Don't treat me like a child! And just because the road's bad doesn't mean your driver has to stop and make a separate decision at each log!"

Porter swallowed. "See if you can't speed 'em up a little, Tim," he said to the driver, and Julia Grant said icily, "I ought to warn you, Colonel, that I am an absolute martyr to seasickness in a swaying vehicle!"

"Well, in that case, I suggest that you stay here," retorted Mary, "and I shall *walk* to Malvern Hill. Stop this cart."

"Mrs. Lincoln, it's a sea of mud between here and there. . . ."

"I'm sure the mud will part for her, as the sea did for Moses," put in Mrs. Grant.

"I said stop this cart and let me out!" Mary shrieked at the Colonel. "Or else make your man move those horses a little!"

"Ma'am, I don't—"

Mary swung around on the driver. "Speed those horses up!"

"Ma'am—"

Her head gave an agonizing throb—really, Carrington's Nerve Elixir was nearly useless in keeping headaches at bay . . . "I said speed them up or stop them and let me walk!" she screamed, tears suddenly bursting from her eyes at the thought of missing the review—missing the chance to stand by her husband's side at a time when it really mattered—at the thought of having the moment spoiled by a headache.

"Do it, Tim," ordered Colonel Porter, and Tim laid on the whip, starting the ambulance forward with a brutal jolt that flung Mary against the back of the wooden seat and caused Julia Grant to cry, "Oh, my God!" The next jar flung both women up off the seat entirely, cracking Mary's head on the bow of the ambulance's roof.

But because Julia had already begun to moan and whine about the jolting motion, Mary only said, "Well, if *you're* not interested in seeing *your* husband—and I can certainly sympathize!—I am interested in seeing *mine.*" And clung grimly to the back of the seat, as those horribly familiar barbed lines of fire began to crawl across her vision, and the pain in her back and shoulder blended with the pain in her head into a jagged symphony of agony.

When, nearly two hours later, the ambulance finally rocked to a stop at the camp, the review was already in progress. She heard the music of the bands while they were still bouncing and hammering through the woods, and screamed at the driver for yet more speed. Julia Grant was sobbing and threatening to be sick, a ploy Mary herself had used far too many times to take seriously. She held out her hand peremptorily to Colonel Porter, and as he helped her down from the wagon, the first thing that met her eyes was Lincoln, mounted on a tall bay horse, leaning over to speak to a very pretty blonde woman riding beside him to review the troops.

Mary saw red. For a moment it was as if she'd finally surprised Lincoln courting Tilda Edwards, or lingering in the woods with his landlady's young sister, all those years ago. When he turned the horse her way, and started to dismount, she screamed, "How *dare* you . . . !" and lunged at him, so that he had to catch her wrists to keep her from physically striking him. "How *dare* you send me by that roundabout way, in that *heinous* vehicle, with only a few soldiers for guard, so that I could have been captured by the rebels at any moment, while you put up another woman to ride with you before the Army, as if she were your wife instead of *me*!"

The blonde woman, still in her sidesaddle, reined away, startled, as from a snarling dog. General Ord rode over quickly and put an arm protectively around her—his wife, thought Mary. Or his doxy—she looked like a designing slut . . . !

"Molly . . ."

"Don't you 'Molly' me! Don't you treat me as if I haven't eyes, as if I count for nothing! Without me you'd still be scratching out a living trying land disputes in the backwoods! The closest you'd have gotten to real politics would be arguing them around the cracker-barrel in Irwin's store!" His face and the faces of those around him appeared and disappeared behind floating slabs of yellow light. She lost track of what she was saying, until she turned away in fury. Someone took her arm—she didn't know who—and led her toward the tents. Looking back, she saw Lincoln still standing, one moment surrounded prosaically by half a dozen blue-clothed and embarrassed officers, and the next, it seemed, alone and wreathed in an aureole of incandescent flame.

Chapter Fifty-four

Mary didn't even know how she got back to the *River Queen,* or for how many days after that, on and off, her migraine lasted. She had dim recollections of Secretary Seward escorting her back to Washington—recollections of chattering to Illinois Congressman Carl Schurz, who accompanied them, about military dispositions and her opinion of Grant's armies. Between burning clouds of migraine agony and the blessed haze of Nervine, excruciating nightmares intruded. She hadn't *really* shrieked at Lincoln in front of the entire General Staff . . .

. . . had she?

Or demanded that he dismiss "that drunken butcher Grant"?

Or called Julia Grant a cross-eyed whore?

Dimmer still was the recurring image of her husband riding in review of troops at the side of a beautiful blonde woman, who sometimes had Mrs. Ord's face and sometimes that of Tilda Edwards. All the men saluted, salutes that should have belonged to her, Mary. . . .

Had he sent her in the ambulance because he hadn't wanted her at his side? Had Colonel Porter had orders to make her late? When she asked Mrs. Cuthbert, timidly, if Mr. Lincoln were back from the headquarters yet, her maid said he wasn't. The President had sent word he would be delayed another two days.

A lie?

He doesn't want to come home to me, thought Mary bleakly. *He doesn't want to see me. . . .* As soon as the maid had left she stumbled to her feet and found her bottle of Nervine. It wasn't a headache remedy—at least, it didn't say so on the label—but she'd found it worked as well as paregoric.

But the following day the shame and guilt and horror and pain were swept away like yesterday's tracked-in mud by voices in the corridor, by Mrs. Cuthbert bursting into the room: "Ma'am, it's true. The news is confirmed by dispatch, it'll be in the papers tonight. Jefferson Davis and his government have abandoned Richmond."

Mary blinked painfully in the curtained twilight. "Abandoned . . ." For a few moments the words had no meaning.

Then, "Abandoned *Richmond*? You mean, left it? For our troops?"

The maid nodded, her face flushed with nearly disbelieving joy. "They're marchin' into Richmond today, ma'am, and your husband with them. He's sent you a telegram. . . ."

Mary sat up with a jolt that made her head feel like it was coming off her shoulders, almost grabbed the yellow envelope from the maid's hand. "I should be there," she said. "I should be beside him, when he rides in!"

Was Mrs. Ord at his side?

ENTERING RICHMOND TODAY. MILITARY ESCORT WAITING TO BRING YOU IF YOU ARE FEELING WELL ENOUGH.

"What time is it? Draw me a bath, and have Peter get out my trunks. . . . Tell Mr. Hay I'll be going to Richmond tomorrow." She fumbled herself into the wrapper Mrs. Cuthbert held for her. "He should have waited for me!"

"I don't expect General Grant would have let him bring you when they all first went in," said the maid tactfully. "Not till they'd made sure all the rebel troops were really gone."

"I'll believe that when I hear Grant didn't have that cross-eyed cow of a wife with him." She shook back her hair and settled it into place with a pair of jeweled combs that had been a gift from the Seligman bankers. "Not that he'd care. He looks like the kind of man who takes more thought for his horses than he does for a mere *wife*. Especially that one. Put in the dark-green velvet, I'll need to look like the President's wife when I ride in. I should ask dear Senator Sumner to accompany me, and Secretary Harlan's sweet daughter. Robert is so fond of her. . . ."

She paused, as it crossed her mind who would most rejoice in the news. Who would most long to enter the ruined capital of the Confederacy, to see the chief city of the slaveholding states crushed in final defeat?

"And bring me my lap-desk, please," she added. "And tell Mr. Hay that I'm going to ask Mrs. Keckley to accompany me."

"IT WAS ONE OF THE KINDEST—AND ONE OF THE GREATEST—THINGS anyone ever did for me," said Lizabet Keckley softly, gazing out the window into the laundry-hung yard of the Lewis boardinghouse, as if she could see back across the ten years that separated that hot April from this sweltering July of 1875.

Ten years, thought John.

It was not so very long a time.

"I'd heard the day before, that Richmond had fallen. I gave all my girls all the day off." She laughed a little, at the memory of the time when her business had been large enough to support a little workshop of "girls."

"We took the *River Queen* down to City Point the next morning, and the military train on into Richmond. Mr. Lincoln met us there."

She shook her head wonderingly, and John knew exactly what she was recalling, for he had been there too. The burned buildings, the charred bricks of chimneys like the pillars of ancient Roman ruins—the fires lit by the rebel forces to destroy the bridges, the tobacco works, and the military warehouses had run wild, destroying nearly a third of the city. Some women watched them, silent and gaunt in home-dyed mourning. The slaves—ex-slaves—crowded the streets to watch the soldiers march in. . . .

"She was like a little girl," said Lizabet. "She was wild. She glowed. It was *his* triumph, *his* vindication. But I think it was more for her than that. She'd spoken to me many times about her father's slaves, people she grew up with, parts of her family. I know slavery in Kentucky—at least for the house-servants—wasn't what it was farther south, but she hated it. Hated that people she cared for could be taken away like that. I don't think she ever got over that."

"I know *I* never did," remarked John drily, and Lizabet glanced over at him, and laughed.

"Under it all she has a good heart, you know. She was so much a lady of the South, but she saw what slavery was, and what it did to us. One of the first things she did was take us into the Legislature, where all the desks and chairs were tumbled around from the Confederate Congress leaving so fast, and papers still scattered on the floor. She brought me up to the front of the room and had me sit in Mr. Davis's chair. I picked up some of the papers lying on the floor—one of them was the bill saying free people of color would not be permitted to enter Richmond. I still have it."

Her smile turned reminiscent and a little weary. As if she looked further back still from that high seat in the Confederate Legislature, backward down the long road she'd trodden, the road they'd all trodden. As if she saw straight back to her days in the unceiled cabin in Virginia, to the first time she was whipped at the age of four, and to her parents, weeping over the news that her father's master was moving West, and taking his human chattels with him. To the beatings of a mistress determined to "break her insolence" and the rape that had given her her only child.

For years, John knew, Lizabet had "worked out" so that her wages might support master, mistress, their family, and others. She had humiliated herself, begged, and negotiated with her circle of white customers in St. Louis to help her buy her freedom. When she'd begun working in Washington, she had paid them back every penny of what her freedom had cost.

"She gave a dinner that night in Mr. Davis's mansion," Lizabet said after a time. "And she had a lot to say about Varina Davis's taste in wallpapers and clothing, I remember, and none of it good, though it was so close to her own that you could barely have told them apart. I remember her friend Senator Sumner at that dinner, in his fancy vest, and Robert so handsome in his uniform, with Mary Harlan, whose father was a Congressman and in Mr. Lincoln's Cabinet—and both the young people more caught up with holding hands under the table than with the fact that the Union had broken the back, not only of the rebellion, but of slavery for all time. Which was as it should be." She smiled again, at that long-ago sight, of new love like the first blossoms on the black ruin of war.

"She must have apologized to Mr. Lincoln, and begged his pardon, as she always did. When she and I went out to Richmond in the train she was shivering and wound up like a clockspring, but at the dinner they were friends again.

"They were sweet together, you know?" Her eyes softened, rueful and kind. "Him so tall and grave, and all in black, for he never really came out of mourning for Willie. And her fussing around him in a circle with all her ribbons fluttering, making him bend down so she could slick his hair for him, and always watching him out of the corners of her eyes, worried whether he was all right. Which he wasn't," she added. "He was sick by then, and always tired. His hands and feet were always cold, he said, and his color was bad. But he'd go to the hospitals with her, and shake hands with thousands of men."

John nodded, remembering those two figures in the moonlight on the deck of the *River Queen*. Remembered how Mary had reached out her hand for her husband's; remembered Lincoln taking off his tall hat, and bending down to kiss the small, plump woman in her costly black silks.

Remembered the love and partnership in that kiss, and the unspoken knowledge that the other would always be there.

EIGHT DAYS AFTER THE FALL OF RICHMOND, ROBERT E. LEE, WEARING his last good uniform—probably the one Mattie had smuggled him from Washington—rode up to Appomattox Courthouse and handed his sword to Ulysses Grant.

And it was over.

Lincoln read a speech, to the thousands who assembled by night on the White House lawn. It became one of Mary's clearest memories of him, standing in the window, with Tad beside him holding a lamp. Lincoln's face was cruelly gouged with weariness but very calm, as he spoke of his plans for rehabilitating the secessionist states back into the Union. His strong tenor voice carried out into the sticky darkness against the roar of the cicadas in the trees.

She had a headache that day. Even Robert's return the following day—Thursday—to the White House from Appomattox, or the prospect of seeing *Our American Cousin* on Friday night, didn't cheer her. Only when she went on her carriage-ride Friday afternoon with Lincoln did her spirits lift, with the fresh air and sunlight, and the chance to be with her husband alone, if one discounted the presence of fourteen cavalrymen clattering their sabers all around.

It was the first time they'd been alone together since the disastrous review at Malvern Hill, which he did not mention at all. When he referred to the trip, he spoke of the tortoise he and Tad had found beside the railroad track, and she of Varina Davis's gowns which had still been in the house at Richmond—"Most of them could have stood a stitch or two," she sniffed, which made him laugh, as she hadn't heard him laugh since Springfield.

"The War is over," he said, leaning back on the carriage-seats in the dogwood dapple of slanted evening sunshine. "All but the shouting—of which there'll be plenty, when the Legislature hears that I don't plan to hang every Democrat politician in sight. But it's over, Mother. And you and I are free."

The carriage turned up the last stretch of Pennsylvania Avenue, still damp enough from winter and spring so as not to be dusty. The White House seemed to shine ahead of them through its sheltering trees. She closed her eyes briefly and took Lincoln's hand, then smiled up into his face as his immense grip returned her squeeze.

The last sunlight warmed her face, and made her feel alive again, after all those years of darkness and terror and unsurvivable grief.

Willie was gone. All her brothers—except the obnoxious George—were dead.

The world of peace and beauty that had been the South—the world of black and white in which she'd grown up—had vanished, its passage marked by blackened walls and the black clothes of widowed belles who, like her, would never forget what they had lost.

But she was here, and the spring evening was sweet. She and Lincoln had survived the War together. She felt as if they'd spent a long hideous night both clinging to opposite ends of a shipwreck spar adrift in a stormy ocean. Unable to speak to one another, unable to do anything but hang on and pray their strength would last till daylight.

Now they'd been cast up together on an unknown beach. What would lie in the land beyond she didn't know. But somehow, after four years of grief and confusion and separation, she had her husband back.

SLEEPING IN THE AFTERNOON, IN HER ROOM AT BELLEVUE PLACE, Mary dreamed that she was in the dream that Lincoln had had, a day or two after his return from Richmond.

She dreamed of the White House, its long upstairs hall utterly dark. The air felt stuffy and silent, as of a house long deserted. She saw Lincoln, asleep with the sleep of exhaustion in that small spartan bedroom. Saw his eyes snap open, saw him look around. It was dark in the room and cold, but she heard now—as he heard—the sound of someone weeping, somewhere in the house, weeping jaggedly . . . as if he or she had been crying for hours but could not stop.

He sat up, and ran his hand through his hair. He was dressed in shirtsleeves and trousers, barefoot as if he'd lain down too tired to even completely undress. For a time he listened, then got to his feet and went to the door, listening in the darkness. Mary watched him pad soundlessly through the empty halls, looking into the rooms, first upstairs and then down. Beds empty and stripped of their sheets, his office bare in the ghostly moonlight, no papers. No charts on the long battered pine tables, only a tattered map of the Union and Confederacy still pinned to the smoke-defaced paper of the walls and that stained old picture of Jackson above the fireplace. He looked into her room, and Tad's. Both were empty and cleared out. Even the cats had gone, and little curly-haired Jip.

Downstairs the East Room was a cavern of darkness, in which candles burned like constellations of fevered stars. A huge dim shape reared in its center, a black canopy shrouded with black curtains; every window was hung with black. Here alone were people—men, soldiers, standing around a black-draped coffin. Now and then one would shift his feet and the creak of boot-leather and the clink of a buckle were loud as cymbals in the deathly silence of the house.

Lincoln crossed the thick green carpet with its pink roses, from Carryl's of Philadelphia. Stood for a moment looking up at the sable canopy, the coffin that it sheltered. Distantly the sound of weeping began afresh. He stepped forward to one of the guards, the soldier tired, like a picket after a long night's watching.

"What is it?" asked Lincoln softly, and looked at the coffin in the shadows. "Who is dead in the White House?"

The guard answered, "The President. He was shot by an assassin. He's dead."

Chapter Fifty-five

Washington July 1875

"She gave away everything he owned," Lizabet Keckley said. "She told me she could not bear the memories they held."

Late-afternoon sunlight glared on the waters of the Potomac, glimpsed through the ragged screen of trees. Closer, pools and puddles that studded the Mall's unkempt grasses flashed like silver. At the far end of the long park, closer to the Capitol, some effort was being made to transform the open land into the sort of *tapis vert* that its designers had originally envisioned, but at the moment it was pretty much as John remembered it from a decade ago: a swampy strip of ground where people grazed their cows. The granite monument to George Washington didn't look any further along than it had been when the money to build it ran out in the late 1850s.

Beside him, Frederick Douglass nodded. Though his hair was whitening he still stood tall and regal, his hard, almost frightening features relaxing into a rare expression of personal grief. "She gave me a pair of his spectacles," he said, in his deep, beautiful voice. "And one of his canes—one that I think he actually used once or twice. People were forever presenting him with canes, and of course he had about as much use for a cane as I have for a pink silk petticoat. At fifty-five he had the body of a twenty-year-old. You have his coat, don't you, Lizabet?"

The seamstress shook her head. "I forget who she gave his coat to. She gave me his brush and his comb, because I'd often comb his hair, the last thing before they went down to a reception. I cut it, once or twice—he was always letting it get too long. I wish I had kept the cuttings."

"We don't think," said Douglass softly. "Not until it's too late." He paused in his long stride as three little boys dashed across the path with their hoops. "She gave the rest of the canes—and a number of his other things, like waistcoats and gloves—away to people who she thought might pay some of her debts."

"Was it true, that he left her in debt?" asked John.

"You know what they say, about how you find a cobbler in a village?" asked Lizabet wryly. "You look around and see which children have no shoes, and you follow them home. He'd gone bankrupt once, for trusting a feckless partner in that store he ran back in New Salem—I think he was twenty-three. The sheriff sold his surveying-tools and horse at auction. His friends clubbed together and bought them back for him, but I don't think he ever got over it. When he died his estate ran to something like eighty thousand dollars. . . . But he left no will."

John blinked, not understanding, and Lizabet smiled with a kind of reflective irony. Few who had been slaves had ever even thought of making wills, for what was there to leave? Legally, until January of 1863 neither John nor his mother, nor the kingly man who walked now at his side, had even owned their own bodies.

"When a man doesn't leave a will," Lizabet explained, "it means his wife and his children can't touch a penny of his money till the estate has been probated. Sometimes that takes years. Mr. Lincoln knew better. He was a lawyer—he'd spent twenty years cleaning up the affairs of men who hadn't left wills. And it wasn't that he didn't know his life was in danger, from the moment he was elected to office. People turn strange, when they think about death." Her eyes strayed toward the dazzling river again, and John saw in his mind the burned-down candles, the fresh flowers, before the picture of her nearly white son.

"I think it might have been a blind spot for him, the way money was for her," she said. "Or maybe he was just more frightened than he ever let on."

"So what happens," asked John—who had never encountered or much thought about this aspect of the lives of the white and rich, "—while the courts are probating a man's estate? What do his wife and children live on?"

Lizabet and Douglass exchanged a glance, then Douglass said, "Nothing. I don't know how the ancient Hebrews arranged such matters, but when Jesus of Nazareth urged charity to widows and orphans, he was *not* talking in generalities. Mostly they go live with their families . . . only Mrs. Lincoln had managed to have a fight with two of her sisters and wasn't speaking to them, and the rest had been on the wrong side of the War. When Lincoln died, Mrs. Lincoln had managed to personally insult most of *her* family and *his* Cabinet—I think at one point about two weeks after the assassination she called Secretary of War Stanton to the White House and accused Andrew Johnson of being part of Booth's gang. Then over the next few weeks she made a clean sweep of it and alienated everyone else she'd formerly missed."

John saw in his mind Cassy and Clarice haul Phoebe back from physically assaulting Lionel—Phoebe spitting at their big, good-natured housemate, screaming insults and threats and lashing out with her nails. . . . He lived in daily dread of hearing that the whole family had been evicted from their half of the broken-down dwelling because his mother had attacked the rent-collector again.

Mrs. Lincoln accusing her husband's successor of having compassed his murder—he could just picture her leaning forward in her creaking corset, could hear her high, sweet voice breathlessly gasping the words behind the crape screen of her veil—seemed laughably mild.

Through the whole of the afternoon, until late-falling summer darkness cloaked the park and mosquitoes drove the three former slaves back to the omnibus and Mrs. Keckley's stifling room at the Lewises' again, John listened to his friend's recollection of the black nightfall of Mary Lincoln's life. And while Lizabet would speak calmly of those weeks of sitting in the darkened guest-room in the White House—for Mary could not bear to enter even her own room there, much less sleep in the big carved bed in which she had on rare but treasured occasions lain with the husband she'd adored—he could feel the suffocating gloom of that curtained chamber, and hear the woman's keening, like an animal howling in a trap.

Mary had been brought back to the White House that wet morning of Holy Saturday by Secretary Welles's wife, Mary Jane, and by her fellow Spiritualist Elizabeth Dixon, the only friends who could be located at short notice. Throughout Easter Sunday, she had been forced to listen to workmen building the towering black catafalque in the East Room to enthrone his coffin. Lizabet had arrived late Saturday morning and sat beside her, holding her hands when Mary would let her.

"She wept until she was ill." Lizabet shook her head, as if across the dark river of years she could still look straight into that cramped little room with its closed curtains, could still hear the hammering downstairs. "I've never seen a woman in such grief. She said, many times, that she wanted to die, that she'd rather Booth had shot her as well. We were all of us worried—Dr. Henry who'd been in town from Oregon, Mrs. Welles, Mrs. Lee that was one of the Blair family and sister to Ginny Fox, Mr. French that had helped her out with her debts, Senator Sumner. . . . Those were the only ones she'd see. Mr. Stanton, the Secretary of War, was running the country, since the same night Mr. Lincoln was killed his

Secretary of State, Mr. Seward, was attacked by another of Booth's gang, and stabbed so badly that his life was despaired of. That's something almost no one seems to remember about the assassination."

"They would have got Johnson, too," said Douglass in his velvety bass. "Only Booth's man turned coward at the last minute and went and got drunk instead."

John reflected privately that it was astonishing the would-be killer hadn't encountered the Vice-President in the tavern to which he'd fled.

"Mrs. Lincoln never stirred from that room for six weeks," said Lizabet softly. "Sometimes sleeping—she slept a great deal. Sometimes only sitting and staring. Sometimes screaming and wailing, like a woman in an opera or a play. We all made sure she was never alone. I must have heard her recount that last evening, detail by detail, three hundred times in that month and a half, sometimes twice and three times in the space of a few hours, until I was ready to scream myself. Even Dr. Henry, who was the most patient of men, said to me once in the hall, 'Isn't she aware that the rest of us have lost a dear friend, too?' "

"You would be, and I would be . . . I hope," said John. "But Mrs. Lincoln isn't like that."

"No." A wry and reminiscent expression tugged the corner of Lizabet's mouth. "No, she isn't."

Certainly no one is like that, he added mentally, *who's had four or eight tablespoons of Battley's Cordial or Indian Bitters, three or four times a day for years.*

And who would deny a woman so bereft the comfort of medicine for her pain?

Lizabet went on, "She felt that it was somehow her fault, as she did when Willie died. She was always one to see misfortune as God punishing *her,* for something she had done. She kept trying to see what could have been done differently, as if she could go back and take another path, so that he could live. Poor Mr. Johnson stayed in his boardinghouse—with a pack of children and grandchildren and his poor sickly wife—and Secretary Stanton ran the country. I think Mrs. Lincoln couldn't face the thought of coming out of that room. Of emerging into a world that she wouldn't share with him."

In his mind he saw again that lanky silhouette against the evening sky of Virginia, taking off his hat and bending down to kiss the plump little figure at his side.

"Where did she go when she did come out?" he asked. "Back to Springfield?"

Lizabet shook her head. "It wasn't that easy."

And John thought, *No. Nothing was ever that easy with Mary Lincoln.*

Give her a difficult situation, and she was bound to make it worse.

In between paroxysms of grief, Mary had managed to quarrel with every single friend and neighbor in her adopted hometown of Springfield over the resting-place of her husband's body. (*What else?* thought John with an inner sigh.) She could not bring herself to attend the funeral, but when Robert returned from Springfield with the news that its town fathers had lovingly formed a Lincoln Monument Association, and spent $5,300 on property for a magnificent tomb at the center of town, she had flown into blind rage that the tomb would not include a family crypt.

"I don't know whether it was because she truly couldn't endure the thought of eternity not spent at his side," said Lizabet, "or because she wanted, once and for all, to be recognized as the wife of the martyred hero, the way she'd always wanted to have everyone know she was the President's wife. Probably both," she added, with a touch of sad affection for her friend. "Probably both."

"After all the mud that had been flung at her in the papers for four years," mused John, "who can blame her for wanting to claim her place?"

"She wrote back to Mr. Conkling—who was the husband of her best friend in the old days—that Mr. Lincoln had expressly wished to be buried in Oak Ridge Cemetery in Springfield, in a family vault," said Douglass. "I gather from something she said to me later that he'd only said once that he wanted to be buried in someplace 'green and quiet'—not a description of downtown Springfield, whichever way you look at it. For all that he became a lawyer, and a politician, and the servant of his intelligence and his destiny, I think he was always a bit of a backwoodsman in his heart."

When first he'd come to the cities of the East, wondered John, had Abraham Lincoln found them as confusing and noisy as he himself had found Washington, that first autumn of his freedom? Did he dream of the woods, as John dreamed of them, over and over in the stinking South Side slums?

"So of course she couldn't go back to Springfield."

Douglass raised his eyebrows. "Not after threatening to have her husband's body buried in Washington if the Monument Association didn't do things her way, she couldn't."

Lizabet chimed in, "She claimed also that Lincoln had intended to move the entire family to Chicago after the end of his second term, because, she said, he couldn't face returning to the house where his beloved Willie had lived."

"Hadn't they lost another child already in that house?" asked John, remembering Mary's rambling account of her life.

"Of course," said Lizabet. "And in my hearing he spoke a number of times, about when they would be able to go back to Springfield. It was she who couldn't face it. Her friend Myra Bradwell and her husband lived in Chicago—still live there, in fact—and Mrs. Bradwell was part of the community of Spiritualism there. I know Robert wanted to return to Springfield, where they owned the house at least and he could be apprenticed to practice law. But Mrs. Lincoln . . . had her way."

Of course she did, thought John, recalling his own mother's wild rages and arbitrary demands. *Of course she did.*

"It was nearly summer by the time they left the White House," said Mrs. Keckley softly. "The day they left was the day before the Army of the Potomac was to return to town, after the final surrender of the last Confederate troops, and the capture of Jefferson Davis. Carpenters were building a reviewing-stand in front of the White House for General Grant and President Johnson—hammering filled the halls, as it had when they were building the canopy for Mr. Lincoln's coffin. The place looked as bad as it did when Mr. Lincoln and Mary had first moved in, because after the funeral sightseers went through the lower floor and helped themselves to nearly everything. Silverware and dishes were showing up just weeks afterwards in pawnshops from Washington to Boston, and of course the papers all said she'd made off with them, in all these trunks.

"And after all that," she sighed, "it was just Robert and Tad and I, and the two White House guards Tom and Will, who loaded up the luggage. I know she'd angered some people with her hysterics, and turned others away with how she'd go on and on. But when it came to it, I nearly cried that there were so few, to see her on her way."

CHAPTER FIFTY-SIX

MARY, ROBERT, LIZABET KECKLEY, AND TAD RODE TWO DAYS AND two nights by train to Chicago, where they lived first in a downtown hotel, and then in a cheaper hotel in Hyde Park, at the end of the new streetcar line, seven miles south of the city on the shore of the lake. John Wilamet remembered Chicago in the Sixties, before the fire: wealthy neighborhoods of fine brick houses along Michigan Avenue and on the lakefront, surrounded by wide grounds and trees, interspersed with ragged shantytowns called "patches"—Conley's Patch, Goose Island, Little Hell, and Ogden's Island—where the Hungarians, Poles, Germans, and Irish lived in rickety sheds or minuscule rooms subdivided from the upper floors of commercial buildings.

There were few blacks in the town in those days. They lived in unbelievable squalor south of Maxwell Street. He remembered the trains that would roar through the crowded neighborhoods of the poor without slowing down; remembered the stench of the river that was an open sewer for the lumber, soap, and packing plants all along its banks. Remembered rats fed so fat on slaughterhouse offal that a trap wouldn't kill them. You had to listen for the noise of the bar slamming down, then go out and finish the job with a hammer.

Remembered the tangles of alleyways where the poor kept pigs, cows, chickens in tiny yards, along with fodder, stored hay, coal oil, and kindling for stoves. No wonder the place had gone up like tinder.

It had been Hell, waiting only for the touch of the Fire.

Lincoln's estate had been put in the hands of Judge David Davis, his old friend of his circuit-riding days. While all over the country Lincoln was being apotheosized from a shrewd jokester into a saintly martyr, Congress was refusing to vote so much as a dollar toward a pension for his wife and children. This was partly because Mary had managed to personally insult and offend nearly everyone in the government, and partly because, quite simply, no Presidential widow had demanded one before.

William Henry Harrison and Zachary Taylor—log cabins and hard cider notwithstanding—had both been wealthy planters. Congress had paid their elderly widows the remainder of their husbands' first-year salary, and they had retired to the family plantations in ladylike dignity, surrounded by adult children and hosts of grandchildren to care for them.

The Re-United States, moreover, had been facing the debts of four years of ruinously expensive warfare running to hundreds of millions of dollars. In the midst of dealing with martial law in a conquered rebel territory—and hundreds of thousands of former slaves who had no idea where to go or how to make their livings—Congress had not wanted to listen to a middle-aged, abrasive widow demanding at the top of her lungs and in every "Letters to the Editor" column in the East, to be paid at least the balance of her husband's salary for the year 1865, and a pension on top of it.

"She was entirely justified," remarked Douglass, as he, John, and Lizabet walked through the cobalt twilight past the red-brick towers of the Smithsonian Castle, toward the park's edge. "It was Lincoln's election that started the War, and Lincoln was its final casualty. She was owed at least the pension that any soldier's wife would have had, for giving a husband to an enemy bullet."

"Not that a soldier's pension was what she asked for," mused Lizabet. "But in her mind the principle was the same. And then of course in those days both the country as a whole and every wealthy Republican in sight were showering gifts on General Grant—including two houses, horses, carriages, and everything from ornamental swords to gold-rimmed dinner service for a hundred. They could all see that he was going to be the next President, and wanted him to remember them kindly. Mrs. Lincoln was furious that she had been 'forced' to live in a common boardinghouse. Judge Davis—and Robert, I'm sure—would point out that she had a perfectly livable house in Springfield, but she wouldn't hear of living in it . . . nor of selling it. Through all her letters to me during 1866 and '67, I don't think she ever once mentioned selling the Springfield house."

They crossed Constitution Avenue, walked along Seventeenth Street where it bordered the President's Park. Through the trees, lights could be seen, though John couldn't imagine President Grant and his family were still in residence at this grisly time of year. Without the War, and in the deeps of summertime, Washington had subsided into what it had been all along: a hot, sticky little Southern city floating on a marsh.

Was Mary Lincoln sitting this evening in her window back at Bellevue tonight, he wondered, as he so often saw her, looking out at the gathering dark? Was she keeping consumption of opium down in his absence? Or would they have to go through the whole heartbreaking process of illness, depression, restlessness, pain again?

His heart ached for her, as it ached in spite of himself when his mother would sit weeping on the rear porch of the house, rocking like a child for hours with her arms around her knees.

Give them shots of morphine every few hours. Why not?

He shook his head, his mind returning to Lizabet's words, and to Mary's account of her Washington years. "She was still in debt, wasn't she?" he asked. "The debt that she'd never told Lincoln about?"

Lizabet's lips drew tight.

"You have to understand," she said, after a time of silence, "that for Mrs. Lincoln, spending money was a sickness. Shopping was how she spent her days, how she got out of herself . . . how she rested. Many were the days she'd spend hours, showing me all she'd got. She hoarded up treasures like a drunkard drinks, almost without thinking. And she couldn't stop."

In March of 1867 (Lizabet said), she received a letter from Mary Lincoln, pleading—in her usual imperious fashion—with her to meet her in New York between August and September of that year, to assist her in selling up her wardrobe. *I cannot live on $1,700 a year,* she wrote, and would be forced to give up the house that she had so recently bought—the house that she had hoped to make her permanent home—and return to living in a boardinghouse.

December would see the opening of Congress and by October the local Washington hostesses would be putting in orders for new gowns . . . but Lizabet went.

"I'd heard from her twice, maybe three times after I left them in Chicago," said the seamstress, as they left the gaslights of Pennsylvania Avenue, entered the darker and shabbier precincts beyond. "I'd read in the newspapers about the subscriptions to raise money to pay her debts. She claimed Judge Davis was undermining these efforts by telling everyone she'd be perfectly able to pay her own debts once he got done probating Lincoln's estate. I don't know what the truth was, but Washington is worse than a girls' school, for gossip. But Mrs. Lincoln was my friend, and she needed me. So I went."

Mary's original plan was that Lizabet should go to New York first and procure rooms for them at the St. Denis Hotel, a plan conveyed in a letter written after Mary must have left Chicago, so there was no chance for Lizabet to write back suggesting any other scheme. Annoyed and filled with trepidation—Mary had a habit of proposing schemes that were abandoned at the last minute—Lizabet closed up her business.

She found Mary, however, at the shabby-genteel establishment near Union Square, as directed, and after an argument with the manager over the hotel's policy of not renting rooms to people of color—something Mary hadn't even thought of—they were given adjoining triangular chambers on the fifth floor, barely larger than cupboards.

"How provoking!" Mary sat down on Lizabet's bed, panting a little from the climb. "I declare, I never saw such unaccommodating people. I shall give them a good going-over in the morning."

The next morning, however, Mary knocked on Lizabet's door at six and urged her to come with her out to breakfast—since the St. Denis refused to serve persons of color in the dining-room, and it hadn't occurred to Mary to send for dinner in their rooms the night before—and to sit in the park and discuss the situation.

"That fat blackguard Judge Davis, who I daresay wants to keep the interest for himself, still hasn't made a distribution of my Sainted Husband's estate." Mary's face was pink with anger in the black frame of her turned-back veils. "I have written and written to those ungrateful Republican politicians whom my husband helped to positions of power, begging them—and *threatening*! For they are *all* scoundrels—to contribute *something* of what they owe to His memory, to my support. That young Mr. Williamson, that was Tad and Willie's tutor, has *supposedly* been acting for me in this, but he is a most *dilatory* young man!"

Lizabet couldn't imagine what influence a Scots schoolteacher would have on the gang of hard-line radical Republicans currently in control of Congress, but didn't get a chance to speak, which was probably just as well.

"I managed, by the most *terrible* sacrifices, to pay off some of my debts, with the niggardly *pittance* Congress gave me—only the first year's salary of my Dearest One's second term, after taking out six weeks' portion *and Federal taxes*! I was able to purchase a house in Chicago for Tad and myself, on the same street as my dearest Myra! But without money to keep it up, I have been forced to rent it out, and live once more at the Clifton House on the proceeds, a most *plebeian* atmosphere, when one considers the glory that once I knew."

Tears filled Mary's eyes, and Lizabet put her arms around those plump shoulders. For all her pretensions, her rages, and her blithe conviction of entitlement, Mary Lincoln had a sweetness to her, a genuinely good heart whose warmth drew Lizabet in spite of what she'd learned over the years of this strayed Southern belle. In the bright morning sunlight of the park, Mary looked somewhat better than she had that hot May day when she'd left Washington. She had noticeably put on weight over the past two and a half years, and she moved as if every gesture gave her pain, but there was, at least, a little of her old sparkle to her eyes.

But it was brutally clear to Lizabet that her friend had lost the mainspring of her life. This beaten quality closed Lizabet's mouth on any remark she might have made about those who at least *had* a house, who were able to get their debts paid by others instead of having to work with thread and needle themselves. When she spoke, it was only to ask, "What did you have in mind?"

"Say what you like about Mrs. Lincoln," sighed Lizabet, as she threw open the windows in a vain attempt to lessen the day's accumulated heat in her boardinghouse rooms, "she wasn't one to sit quietly on the sidelines waiting for events to take their course. Will you have coffee, Mr. Douglass, or tea?"

WILLIAM BRADY AND SAMUEL KEYES, DIAMOND MERCHANTS OF 609 Broadway, assured Mrs. Lincoln that the gowns she'd worn while the President's wife, the furs in which she'd wrapped herself and the jewelry that had glittered on her throat in the midst of those terrible days of war, would bring in somewhere in the neighborhood of a hundred thousand dollars. Lizabet had distrusted those two smooth-talking gentlemen, when they came to call at the St. Denis, but had held her peace. "The people will not permit the widow of Abraham Lincoln to suffer; they will come to her rescue when they know she is in want."

For several days Lizabet walked around New York City in quest of dealers in secondhand clothing, and drove with Mary to various stores on Seventh Avenue with the dresses worn during her four years as the Republican Queen. Afterwards, Lizabet tried to push the squalid bargaining, the polite dismissals, the barely concealed contempt, from her mind. Brady insisted that Mary write letters to him, purportedly from herself in Chicago, which he would then, he said, show to prominent politicians, forcing them to buy or be exposed as abandoning Lincoln's widow to her fate.

When these letters were roundly ignored, Mary threw up her hands, turned the whole business over to Brady and Keyes, and returned to

Chicago—with the request that Lizabet remain in New York as her agent, continuing the quest and overseeing Brady's exhibit and sale of the dresses, shawls, and jewels.

"I DON'T KNOW WHAT SHE THOUGHT I WOULD LIVE ON." LIZABET shifted the kettle onto the single burner of the iron heating-stove, knelt to puff the coals beneath it to flame. "She'd already borrowed six hundred dollars from Mr. Brady, not a penny of which she gave to me. I was angry—and the results of Mr. Brady's 'exhibit and sale' I think you already know."

The newspapers had been merciless in their criticism, both of the sale itself and of the dresses: . . . *they are jagged under the arms and at the bottom of the skirt, stains are on the lining . . . some of them are cut low-necked, a taste which some ladies attribute to Mrs. Lincoln's appreciation of her own bust. . . .*

As a rider, one or two journals brought up again the gossip of wartime Washington, the accusations of spying or bringing in relatives to spy in the White House, the tales of financial chicanery and cutting up the Presidential sheets for drawers. They spoke of her "good Republican" friend Simeon Draper, whom she'd recommended for the highly lucrative post of customs collector for the port of New York after he'd paid $20,000 of her debts.

One newspaper spoke of her as "a termagant with arms akimbo, shaking her clenched fist at the country, and . . . demanding gold as the price of silence and pay that is her due because she was the wife of a President." Another spoke of "conduct throughout the administration of her husband . . . mortifying to all who respected him . . ."

People had stared—people had whispered—but few bought.

"AT THE SAME TIME AS ALL THIS WAS GOING ON," SAID DOUGLASS, from the faded brocade sofa, "Lizabet was making the rounds among the free colored of New York like the hero she is, trying to get up a lecture series whose proceeds would go to Mrs. Lincoln. I agreed to lecture. So did the Reverend Henry Garnet, and other men of color who had led in the abolitionist movement before Emancipation. But Mrs. Lincoln declined . . . for reasons best known to herself."

It had been years ago, thought John, but the bitterness of the rebuff still tinged Douglass's voice.

"And all that time," the flame-glow of the lamp warmed Lizabet's features as she measured out tea from a slender stock, "she wrote me, urging me to keep after Brady and Keyes—as if a pair of white diamond-merchants would pay the slightest attention to anything a woman of color said—and to remain in New York to look after her interests. I had to go back to sewing just to pay my rent. Naturally I'd abandoned the Union Place Hotel the moment Mrs. Lincoln was gone, and was boarding with a private family. When a Mr. Carleton contacted me about writing a memoir, I should have suspected something. Maybe I was too angry to care."

From the street below, musical with distance, rose the voices of children playing, and the sing-song cry of the candy-seller making a final round.

"I'd just heard, through a mutual Spiritualist friend, that she'd finally got the distribution of Mr. Lincoln's estate, and was fairly well-off. She never offered to send me so much as a dollar. Mr. Carleton's people interviewed me, and published the book under my name. But they'd rewritten it, to make her look foolish—not that she wasn't completely capable of making herself look foolish when she tried. The chapter about the sale of the clothes was . . . nastier than it needed to be." She hesitated, then sighed again. "And I sold them the letters she'd sent to me. They promised they'd only use a few excerpts. I can't imagine why I was stupid enough to believe them. Of course they published them in full. She never forgave me for that."

"While you forgave *her,*" Douglass pointed out gently, "for stranding you in New York, for causing you to lose your very profitable business in Washington, for treating you like a servant, while she went back to where she had friends, a house on whose rental she could live, and a pile of government bonds?"

Lizabet shook her head. "It wasn't an easy time for her either," she said. "That was just after Mr. Lincoln's old law partner, Mr. Herndon, began lecturing about Mr. Lincoln's life—claiming that Mr. Lincoln had only married Mrs. Lincoln in the wake of losing the single, great, true, and *only* love of his life . . . a New Salem girl named Ann Rutledge."

"Was that true?" John had read Herndon's biography a few years before, and had found it a welcome relief from the mawkish torrent of hagiographical idealization of Lincoln that had deluged the country immediately after the assassination. He couldn't imagine what the real Mr. Lincoln would have said of those awful paintings of George Washington welcoming Lincoln to Heaven while Liberty herself held a halo of stars over the Emancipator's neatly brushed hair.

On the other hand, he reflected, Mary Todd Lincoln would have bought every print of those she could get her hands on.

"That he loved Ann Rutledge?" Lizabet gazed for a moment into her tea, as if the truth might be divined in its slow-settling leaves. "I think he did. That she was the only woman he ever loved with the whole of his heart? No. Did you ever see them together? Mr. and Mrs. Lincoln?"

John nodded, remembering again those two disparate figures, silhouetted in the twilight.

"I don't think anyone ever knew the whole of Mr. Lincoln's heart," said Lizabet slowly. "I never met Mr. Herndon, but Mrs. Lincoln loathed the man—in the whole time he was Lincoln's law partner she'd never have him in her house. It isn't surprising he couldn't imagine that his friend would or could really love her. But whatever Mr. Lincoln felt about Miss Rutledge when he was twenty-five, he loved Mary. For all her faults, he told a visitor once—I forget who—that 'my wife is as handsome as when she was a girl and I a poor nobody.' He fell in love with her then, he said, and had never fallen out."

"Did you ever see her again," asked John, "after that trip to New York? After your book came out?"

Lizabet set her tea down, and folded her hands. Older and grayer, thought John, but still with that rock-strong calm that had struck him first in the provision tent at Fort Barker, all those years ago. That same patient affection for her volatile friend. "After I read the book—my book, I mean—and saw what they'd done with my story, I wrote her asking forgiveness. I don't know if she ever got my letter. She may have been taken up with Robert's preparations for marriage—I'm pleased to say his young Miss Harlan, the daughter of the Senator from Iowa, stayed faithful to him even when he ceased to be the President's son and became just a law clerk in Chicago. And after that, of course, Mrs. Lincoln left the country. I never saw her again."

Chapter Fifty-seven

Bellevue July 1875

"We've been all over this before, Mother." Under his heavy fair mustache, Robert's mouth was starting to pinch up. "Dr. Patterson says that you need rest, and you certainly wouldn't get rest living with Aunt Elizabeth."

Mary immediately lowered her shoulders and cast down her eyes, an old trick of her belle days that she'd remembered. She couldn't think when she'd stopped doing it, but knew she hadn't done it in years. "Of course you're right, Robert," she made herself say, in a tone of contrition she was far from feeling. Betsey would have been proud of her. "It's been many years since your aunt and I have seen eye-to-eye, if we ever did. But Elizabeth still is my sister. And time heals many wounds. It would be a blessing and a comfort if I could at least write to her."

She tucked her chin and raised her eyes to his, hoping she looked as timid and hopeful as she had when she'd been trying to wheedle a new gown out of her father. Much as it scorched her with humiliation to realize it, she had to admit that John Wilamet was probably right about the medicine. Since she'd cut herself down to two watered spoonfuls a day—come headaches, hell, or high water—she'd found that in between feeling anxiety and depression, she was thinking much more clearly. The memories of her younger days were bringing not only pain and regret, but the awareness of how she'd manipulated gentlemen to get what she wanted.

Like permission to write letters.

She could just hear Mammy Sally's voice, *Now, child, you know you catch more flies with honey than you do with vinegar. . . .*

"Very well." Mollified, Robert reached across the space between her sofa and his chair, to take her hands. "I know what a comfort it is to you, to write to *responsible* friends who have your best interests at heart—who know not to excite you with trifles. I'll speak to Dr. Patterson before I leave."

But Mary made sure to follow Robert to the carriage, and, when he simply started out the door, ducked her head into Dr. Patterson's office to call out gaily, "Oh, Doctor, my dearest, *dearest* son has said that I might now write to my sister!" She threw all the gladness of which she was capable into her voice, and Robert, instead of looking annoyed, merely smiled indulgently. "Whoever had a more thoughtful and generous son?"

You treacherous, unnatural blackguard, I will thwart you if I can.

"My mother seems to be so well recovered, I don't see the harm in it for her to write to her sister Elizabeth Edwards in Springfield," said Robert. "And to . . . Who else would you like to write to, Mother? Perhaps Mrs. Conkling? Or Mrs. Wheelock?"

She nodded with an expression of joy, though she had had no contact with either of her former Springfield friends since the bitter quarrel over the Lincoln Monument and didn't want any. The things those wicked traitors had said! But one didn't waste possible opportunities that might be needed later.

After two months in Bellevue she knew better than to suggest permission to write to any of the Spiritualist friends who'd given her such understanding support.

After Robert got into the Patterson carriage to be taken to the train-station, Mary went to gather a handful of stationery, an inkwell, and an envelope from the desk in the parlor: "I want to write my sister a nice *long* letter," she explained, beaming at Mrs. Patterson as the doctor's wife came in from the garden. "We have so much to catch up on! It's true we've been estranged for many years, but Elizabeth raised me, you know, and in so many ways stood as a mother to me. I hope and pray that she will at least let bygones be bygones, and be my friend again."

Her heart was pounding as she sat in the gloomy parlor, conscious of every person passing through the room. When John Wilamet—just returned from his trip to New York—came in and asked if she were well, she nearly jumped out of her chair with guilt. But she folded her hands in a most natural way over the letter, and asked after his trip: "Did you speak to the nerve-doctor that you said you wished to consult there? Was the result as you hoped?"

The minute the young man's back was turned she slipped two more envelopes from the desk into her skirt pocket.

And, the next time the parlor was empty, two more.

She folded the five written sheets, in her jagged, closely crossed handwriting, sealed them in an envelope, and addressed it to Elizabeth. "Could you ride with me to the post-office?" she asked Mrs. Patterson, when that lady returned to the parlor. "It's such a lovely afternoon, now that it's growing cooler. Perhaps Blanche would like to bear us company?"

Gratified, Mrs. Patterson fetched Miss Blanche from her room. The simpleminded girl's face was bright with pleasure at the prospect of a drive into town. And indeed, though Mary's heart hammered as if she were back at Rose Hill hiding copies of *The Liberator* under her mattress again, she found the sultry evening air pleasantly sweet.

Mrs. Patterson—as Mary had hoped—remained in the carriage with Blanche. Mary tripped up the Post Office steps, and once inside that gloomy little lobby pulled the four stolen envelopes from her pocket and broke the seal on Elizabeth's letter.

She left only one sheet—the one actually to Elizabeth—in that envelope. Working fast, she addressed three others to the most politically prominent men whose addresses she could remember, and the fourth to Myra Bradwell. It took most of her little money to post them....

"Dear, they must test those postal clerks for slowness," she laughed, as she hurried, panting a little, down the steps to the carriage. *"What, she sold a single stamp in under five minutes?"* Her voice flexed to mock an imaginary inspector's outrage. *"No job for her!"*

And Blanche crowed with laughter.

In the carriage riding back to Bellevue, Mary was hard put to keep from trembling, had to fight the waves of agitation that welled almost sickeningly behind her sternum. *I'll never get to sleep tonight,* she thought. *Surely this justifies another little teaspoonful. . . .*

She thrust the thought from her mind, barricading the mental door with the image of the self-satisfied expression on Robert's face.

One of them has to come, she thought desperately. *One of them has to help me; has to bring a real doctor here to testify to my sanity.*

And when he, she, or they did, Mary realized, the game would be up, as the children would say. Patterson would be furious. This was "will to insanity" with a vengeance. He might lock her up in earnest—he would certainly consult with Robert. What legal rights, exactly, *did* Robert have over her? As a convicted lunatic, Mary knew that she no longer had any rights at all. *The madwoman's family may do with her as they think best. . . .*

And anger flooded her, almost swamping, for a moment, her terror. Rage at the Pattersons—despite her gay chuckles at Mrs. Patterson's tale of some petty victory over the laundress—blind fury at Robert.

At her father.

At God, for ripping Lincoln from her and leaving her to face all this alone.

She took a deep breath, and looked away, over the side of the carriage, at the pleasant white-painted shops, the blue shade of elm-trees, that made up Batavia's small downtown along Union Street. *I can't let her see me tremble. I can't let her see my tears.*

Tears of bitterness and rage.

One of them has to answer. The men—General Farnsworth and the others—she put no trust in. She never had known a man who hadn't betrayed her. She realized the next moment that that statement included Lincoln, but didn't change it in her mind. She knew it was illogical, but she could no longer pretend that she didn't feel it: deep anger at him, that he was gone.

But Myra would come.

Myra who had come to her in the most terrible hour—save only for the nightmare of Ford's Theater—in her life.

WHEN JUDGE DAVIS FINALLY DISTRIBUTED LINCOLN'S ESTATE IN November of 1868—and it still rankled with Mary that Lincoln had never bothered to make a will, for in that case instead of the legal one-third she'd probably have inherited everything, enough to keep house on—she began making arrangements to go to Europe. Robert came over to the Clifton House, where she and Tad were living, and put his foot down firmly. "You will not take my brother to live like a Gypsy in a succession of cheap German watering-places. He needs a proper education and he can get no better one than here in the United States."

"Tad is my son!" Mary put her arm around the skinny fifteen-year-old's shoulders, pulled him to her with a fierce grip. "He is all that I have left to me, since *you* have chosen to make your home apart from us!"

She almost spit the words at him, and Robert's lips tightened. The Clifton House, though respectable bordering on genteel, was, when you came right down to it, a boarding hotel, and the two rooms she had occupied there since the previous March were the cheapest and dreariest in the place. Like every boardinghouse room she had ever occupied, they were jammed with trunks, boxes, and chests of her possessions—with packages of newer purchases piled higgledy-piggledy on top—and this increased their stuffy gloom. When first they'd come to Chicago three years before, Robert, then twenty-two, had elected to get his own rooms rather than share crowded quarters with his mother and Tad.

She'd never quite forgiven him for that, either. Financially it would have made better sense for the three of them to remain together, instead of dividing the small income that Davis had paid them yearly from the estate.

"Don' worry about me, Bob." Tad's voice was just beginning to break. It would be light, as Lincoln's had been. "Last I heard, there were schools in Europe." And he grinned, bringing an answering smile from his older brother.

Three years in Chicago had altered Tad drastically from the restless hellion he'd been in Springfield and in Washington. At Robert's insistence, Tad had been sent to a number of elocution teachers, and as a result could speak and be understood by even those outside his immediate family. Perhaps because of this—or perhaps because of the terrible changes after his father's murder—much of Tad's wildness and anger had dissipated. He attended school regularly now, and had begun to catch up with the boys who were so far ahead of him. He had Lincoln's gray eyes, and coarse black hair. From beneath the softness of childhood, craggy familiar features were beginning to take shape.

Mary supposed that Tad would have learned more quickly still, had he been sent to boarding schools. But without her boy—without wondering when he'd be home that day, and what he'd been up to—her life was nearly unbearable, and she'd turned away from several that Robert had urged her to investigate.

Robert's mouth thinned to an ungiving line. "I forbid it."

Mary, her face beginning to pinken with anger, retorted, "Pooh! It's my money now, and I shall do with it as I please. You only want me to stay so you can borrow my money and get in on Judge Davis's real-estate schemes."

And Robert, stonily silent, made no reply.

The distribution of Lincoln's estate had freed Robert, too, from having to live solely on his earnings as a newly fledged attorney. That November he was making preparations of his own, to purchase a home on Wabash Avenue—in a considerably better neighborhood than Mary's now-rented house on West Washington, she reflected resentfully—and to marry Miss Harlan. In an atmosphere of chilly tension he took the train to Washington and formally proposed: the wedding was set to take place in Washington at the end of September. Mary and Tad would depart two weeks later on the *City of Baltimore.*

When Mary had left Washington, workmen were tearing down the last of the black draperies from the White House windows, left from Lincoln's funeral.

She and Tad stayed in Baltimore. She never ventured from her hotel room. She hated this city that had plotted Lincoln's murder before he'd ever arrived in Washington, but she did not think she could bear more than a necessary few hours in the capital itself. They took the train to Washington only on the morning of the wedding, Mary heavily veiled in black and fortified with Indian Bitters and Ma-Sol-Pa Herbal Infusion and leaning on Tad's arm. "Don't leave me, Taddie," she whispered, clinging to his elbow as they mounted the steps of James Harlan's rented town house, as she saw the moving host of beautifully dressed Cabinet members, Senators, family friends. "Stay right beside me every minute and don't leave me." Though almost six months had passed since Lizabet Keckley's infamous book had appeared, and over a year since Herndon's lectures on Ann Rutledge, she felt every glance, every whisper, as if they were burning coals being applied to her flesh.

Her veils were the only armor she had, her only means of keeping the curious at bay. Like a black opaque cloud amid the puffs and bows, satins and silks, fashionable pale pinks and blues, Mary spoke her briefest greetings to even her old friends like Ginny Fox, Jacob Seligman, and Charles Sumner. She wished only to be gone.

Robert's bride—also named Mary—was a fair, pretty, and ethereal-looking young lady in a gown of white satin, everything a well-bred young lady should be. She smiled sweetly as Mary took her hands.

"*How* I have always wished for a daughter! My dearest child, I have *so longed* to see this day!"

Other than that she recalled little of the reception, beyond an overwhelming sense of dread that she assuaged by a couple of surreptitious sips of Indian Bitters in the cloakroom. For nearly a year after Willie's death she had found herself unable to bear large groups of people, particularly strangers or semi-strangers. After Lincoln's death, the presence of anyone other than a few well-loved and well-known friends (which had included, alas, the *perfidious* Lizabet Keckley!) had filled her with a sense of nearly unendurable alienation from the whole race of humankind. She longed for comfort, yet when Charles Sumner came over to speak with her she found herself on the verge of tears.

Few others approached her. In three years, the cast of characters had changed in Washington, and people had heard enough about her battles with Congress over a pension.

She spent much of the ensuing three weeks in Baltimore in her room at Barnum's Hotel, emerging only for carriage-rides with Tad, or to visit a medium named Gibson, whom Cranston Laurie had recommended. Mr. Lincoln was present in the room, Gibson assured her, and disavowed any knowledge of any Ann or Nan Rutledge. There was no such person there with him in the Summer Land, nor had he known anyone of that name in his life.

But he did not materialize, nor speak to her. The night before the *City of Baltimore* was to depart she dreamed of him, in the dappled sunlight of the Land that lay beyond Death's Veil—dreamed of him walking hand in hand with the red-haired girl that Herndon had so eloquently described.

Chapter Fifty-eight

Tad and Mary were in Europe for three years.

And if she could not be happy—and she could never be happy, she reminded herself every morning when she woke, when her Beloved One had left her here alone—at least she felt at peace.

She took a room in the Hotel Angleterre in Frankfurt, intending to stay for a week. Jacob Seligman had highly recommended Dr. Hohagen's Institute on the nearby Kettenhofstrasse, and it was here that she enrolled Tad. But from the first night, the friendly and un-curious camaraderie of the English and American expatriates who lived at the Angleterre drew her in and made her welcome. These were people who had not been raised with the rending questions of abolition, who had not gone through the horror of war firsthand; people who had the distance to be objective, and the pleasant good manners that Mary craved.

She stayed another week, and then another. After all, she could not abandon Tad. On his single day off each week they would take a carriage along the zigzag paths of the park where the city ramparts had once stood, or cross the bridge to Sachsenhausen and so to the green and peaceful countryside beyond. Sometimes they would take the train to Weimar, to see Goethe's house, or take a little excursion steamer down to the Rhine at Mainz.

And when Tad was in school, to her surprise she found the days were not as long as she'd feared they'd be. The little group of Americans in the hotel called on her and invited her to visit their rooms, and her circle of acquaintance widened to their American and British friends in other parts of the little city. They were a lively group, the ladies always willing to get up excursions or day-trips to the spas of Wiesbaden or Marienbad, or to hold afternoon teas. Even after Mary removed to the less expensive Hotel Holland she retained a number of friendships, and would go to the Angleterre's reading-room to keep up on the American papers.

This was partly to follow how her old friends and enemies were doing—Charles Sumner was still in the Senate, and Mr. Seward, recovered from the wounds he'd received on the night of Lincoln's assassination, still ruled as Secretary of State. *(What a pity it was not he who had died that Terrible Night, if one must have died and the other be spared. . . !)*

And partly, to follow what was being done about her battle for her pension in Congress.

During her first summer in Frankfurt, she went for several weeks to Scotland, where she visited dear old Dr. Smith from Springfield, whom Lincoln had made a consul. On her return she encountered, of all people, Sally Orne from Philadelphia at one of Frankfurt's summer spas. It was good beyond words to talk American politics again with someone who truly knew Washington, who'd been through the War. The two women chattered non-stop for several nights—completely disturbing everyone in the hotel-rooms around them—and the upshot was that Sally, who'd been traveling in luxury with maid, valet, and daughter in tow, agreed to put pressure on all her political connections once again to have Mary's pension put through.

"It's a disgrace—an absolute disgrace!" Sally cried, looking around the dreary fifth-floor chamber of the Holland, carpetless and crammed nearly to the ceiling with trunks and packages. "Your husband gave his life for his country, as surely as any of those poor soldiers did! You deserve no less than they!"

In point of fact—as the American newspapers shortly pointed out in a succession of blistering satires on Mrs. Lincoln's requests for her pension bill to be passed by Congress—the average widow's pension was about twelve dollars a month, and Mary was asking for three thousand a year. "My case is entirely different!" she insisted to Sally, when that lady and her entourage were preparing to continue on their journey to Italy. "Those young men, though I say not a word in their disparagement, at least had respite and sleep at night—which my poor husband *never* had, in four years of war. And moreover I was very much his partner in his task of governing, for which I deserve at least some credit!"

Between shopping for Robert's Mary—Young Mary, she called her—and for Baby Mamie, who was born in the fall of 1869—and writing streams of letters to Congressmen, Mary felt herself revive.

The American consul, Mr. Murphy, called now and then with his son *(To keep an eye on me for that traitor Seward, I'll wager).* There were several American and British gentlemen—not to mention several more of the Seligman banking clan—who would squire her for Sunday drives. Her special friends from her days at the Angleterre, the Mason family, still included her in their circle as if she were an aunt. Two British ladies from the Angleterre—Mrs. Culver and Mrs. Blaine—were Spiritualists, and it was a relief to Mary to be able to talk of matters concerning those who had passed over the Veil. Twice they held séances, and though no spirits materialized or spoke on those occasions, she left them filled with a deep sense of calm.

More than anything else, she wished Lincoln could be here with her, to see the cathedral in its old-fashioned square, to pass the dark rocks where the Rhine maidens were said to guard their hidden gold.

"But he is here, don't you see?" asked Mrs. Culver, setting her teacup down—Mary had invited her up to her room at the Holland to take tea and look at the needlework vests, the blue- and white-silk wrapper, that she'd bought for Robert's bride. "When a soul passes to the Other Side, they can come and go here as they please, like the angels of God. When you walk down the Zeil looking into shop windows, be sure that he's there at your side. When you stand in the cathedral and look at the arches and tombs and stained glass, you are sharing that moment with him, as you would have in life had God so willed."

"Of course," responded Mary instantly, "of course. But knowing that somehow, sometimes . . . just isn't the same."

But it was close to that, when she was with Tad.

At Dr. Hohagen's, her son seemed to recover some of his old mischievousness, tempered now by European manners and the school's firm discipline. As the weeks and months floated by she was amazed and delighted at Tad's growth from boy to young man. He was beginning to read on his own, and talk to her like a man, and not a child, about the things he read. He took the lead in their excursions, escorting her to places his friends at school had said were *wunderbar*! From speaking only a few halting words in German—inculcated with enormous labor by his teachers in Chicago—Tad rapidly became far more fluent than Mary.

He was a comfort to her, too, when the American newspapers published indignant criticisms of her campaign for a pension. "They don't know you, Mama," he soothed, when she met him in front of the school brandishing the latest, a sarcastic account of how a fictitious German count was courting her in the hopes of getting hold of Old Abe's pension. "They're politicians. They'll say anything—they have to."

A later article pointed out that $27,000,000—nearly ten percent of the nation's budget—went to pensions already, and the widows of officers were content with $600 a year, not $3000: "poor needy widows who do not already have fifty or sixty thousand dollars." Another excoriated her for taking Lincoln's "brilliant boy" to be educated away from "American institutions." "They must have been talking to Robert," fumed Mary. As 1869 wore into 1870, the debates—duly sent on to her by Sally Orne—became more vicious, dredging up yet again the old rumors of her extravagance, her Confederate sympathies, and speculation of improper conduct with, of all people, the charming Commissioner Wood who had escorted her on her first buying-trip to New York.

Her headaches worsened. She wrote reams of angry letters to Sally, to her Spiritualist friend Ella Slapater in Pennsylvania, to Robert and his wife. Her neuralgia grew more frequent and painful as well, tightening the damaged muscles of neck and back and starting yet another round of sleepless nights, Godfrey's Cordial, Indian Bitters, and as many visits to spas as she could afford. Now fifty-two, she began to have night sweats, and her copious monthlies became erratic, until she never knew when they'd begin or how long they'd last. Sometimes it felt to her, looking back on those days, that she was angry all the time.

But in a curious way the anger made her feel alive. She was fighting, she told herself, for Tad's future—fighting, too, to be recognized for who she was: Abraham Lincoln's widow. The wife of the Great Emancipator. The woman who had stood by him through the terrible years of the War, the woman he had married—and loved, no matter what Billy Herndon said.

Just as she had been the legal keeper of his body, in the fight with the Monument Association, so now she was the keeper of his memory, and his son. She still lived for him, though he had gone on to the Summer Land; still managed his affairs in this world.

They could not deny her without denying him.

In July of 1870, President Grant signed the bill giving her a pension of $3,000 a year. This more than doubled her income, added to the $2,500 interest from the bonds Lincoln had left her and the rent from the Chicago and Springfield houses. She celebrated by buying pillowcases, a watch, and an evening dress for Young Mary, and several tiny bracelets for little Mamie, and by taking Tad, who was on summer holiday, to Austria.

In Austria, word reached them that France and Germany had gone to war. On their return to Frankfurt, the consul, Mr. Murphy, called on Mary at the Hotel Holland and warned her to leave—the French troops were advancing on Frankfurt, which controlled Germany's railroads as Atlanta had the South's. While she was still trying to organize her trunks and luggage—really, it was *astonishing* how much she'd accumulated in her travels!—one of the generals she'd met in Washington, little Phil Sheridan, who stood shorter even than she did—called to reiterate the warning.

"I didn't flee from Washington in the face of the rebels, sir, and I will not flee from here like a scared rabbit," she retorted. "The French were always America's allies. Surely they will offer us no harm." And she pulled Tad, who'd come that day to help her pack and label, closer to her side.

"No, ma'am," replied Sheridan, who Mary had always thought looked like a schoolboy dressed up in a false mustache. "But they may shell the town. And if there's a siege, I wouldn't like to see the pair of you caught up in it."

Tad's gray eyes brightened, and he said, "It wouldn't be our first." He was, Mary guessed, within an ace of asking Sheridan if he could go along with him and observe the upcoming battle, so she caught his hand and said crisply,

"We shall be quite all right, General. Thank you for your concern."

As it was, before she managed to arrange transport for all of her many trunks and crates, the battle was fought and over, and the German forces under Von Moltke—with Sheridan along as an advisor—were besieging Paris. Still, the pleasant little city of Frankfurt had become an army town, as Washington had been in the War. Too many soldiers, too many horses, skyrocketing prices of food and very few of her friends remaining. She would wake in the night hearing marching men in the street, and for an agonized moment she would be back in Washington, with torchlight flaring on the ceiling of her bedroom, and Lincoln's steps padding restlessly down the hall to confer in his nightshirt with Generals on the landing.

It was time to go home.

THEY LEFT FRANKFURT IN THE FALL OF 1870, FOR ENGLAND, INTENDING to remain there—as Mary had intended to stay at the Hotel Angleterre—only a few weeks. But the journey, and the tensions of travel, were hard on Mary. Her headaches multiplied and she broke her journey at Leamington, which like Marienbad and Baden-Baden was a hydrotherapy spa. The solicitousness of the doctors there, and the friendliness of the English, soothed her. Though Tad was wild to return to America, she lingered in Leamington until nearly Christmas, then moved up to London—again, for a short time only, she said—to visit her Hotel Angleterre friend Mrs. Culver.

She and Tad remained in London for another three months, at a boardinghouse in Woburn Square. With Mrs. Culver, she attended a number of séances among the Bloomsbury Spiritualists, but winter in London depressed her and brought on migraines and back pain again, accompanied now by the agonizing hot flushes of the change of life. The doctors—she could afford the best, these days—suggested a warmer climate for the remainder of the winter. Tad offered to take ship for America after Christmas, and she could follow after a few months of recuperation in Italy. But the idea of the young man facing the dangers of winter travel on the Atlantic brought her nightmares.

"I could not bear it, if anything were to happen to you, my darling!" she sobbed. "I could not bear it! Oh, do not do this to your mother!"

That said, she paid Tad's board in Woburn Square for the next few months, engaged a tutor for him, hired a nurse-companion for herself, and went to Italy. For two months she dreamed in the sun, marveled at the *David* in Florence and the multi-towered Cathedral in Milan. It was in many ways a dream come true. Growing up in that overcrowded house in Lexington, she had longed to see these things, to walk in the glittering Italian sunlight where Byron, Shelley, and Napoleon had walked.

Would she have chosen this path here, she wondered, had she been told through what griefs and pain it would lead?

She didn't know. But she got out more, and made a few friends. Her consumption of Female Elixir and Godfrey's Cordial declined as her health improved—it was in any case nearly as difficult to find them in Italy as it had been in Germany.

She and Tad returned to New York on the *Russia* in May. The weather was rainy and nearly as cold as winter. Tad caught a cold, and Mary nursed him assiduously in their tiny stateroom. In the dining-room, she had her own private table where she sat, heavily veiled in black; on the first evening of the voyage she was greeted by, of all people, little General Sheridan, on his way back from the German war.

She had never known the young commander well during the War, though since he was Grant's protégé she mistrusted him. But Sheridan was politely deferential to her, and on their arrival in New York he included her and Tad in his party that went ashore on the pilot's launch and avoided the three-day quarantine.

Thus, in contrast to their quiet leavetaking, she and Tad came ashore to bands playing "Hail to the Chief," and to reporters crowding around—mostly around General Sheridan, to be sure. But one at least came up to her, and asked—impertinently, she thought—how she liked to be home.

"I like it very much," replied Mary, and glanced back at the launch from which she had just stepped, bobbing in the dirty water at the dock. "So far."

Chapter Fifty-nine

It sometimes seemed to Mary, when she looked back on her return to America, that the *Russia* had taken a wrong turn somewhere and had deposited her and Tad on another planet, some world other than the one they had fled three years before.

Everything was different. While Europe had dreamed in its centuries-old walls of stone and forest, in three years America had barged ahead into an era of railroad barons, monumental industries, get-rich-quick schemes, patent stoves, patent vegetable-slicers, bustle dresses, and bicycles, a world inconceivably distant from the America of the War.

Still further off, like the landscape of a dream, lay the world she remembered so clearly, the world of Lexington in the Thirties, of shady alleys and Mammy Sally's kitchen, and flirting with young gentlemen under the locust-trees of Rose Hill. No one even talked about that vanished world anymore.

No one talked about slavery, either, or secession, or the rights of the states. It was as if it had all never happened. They spoke instead of money, of Progress, of new places to go and new things to see and buy: of railroads, homesteads in the West, and the foolishness of women who campaigned for the vote.

It was a Yankee world now, and Mary despised it.

New York—where she stayed for some weeks—had spread north on both sides of the Park, and its crowded Irish slums had been invaded by Jews and Italians following the demands of factory labor. There were more buildings, higher buildings, walling the narrow streets into grim canyons of red and gray. When she returned to Chicago the noise of the railroads and the stench of the stockyards and packing-plants hung over the brand-new mansions and the filthy "patches" like a pall.

The thought of surrendering the rent from the house on West Washington made her shudder. Her years of scrimping and saving, of the humiliation of seeing her Springfield friends ride by in their carriages, and later of fighting for the pension and for her inheritance, had left their mark. Everything cost so much more these days. She couldn't imagine running a household, even on $5,500 a year. With her ill-health and the migraine agonies of menopause, she calculated she would have to hire at least two servants, maybe three.

"That's quite sensible of you, Mother," Robert said, escorting her from the train to the rank of taxis and casting a resigned eye back at the army of black porters with the trunks. "You know there will always be a place for you in my home."

"Always" lasted all of about a month.

Robert's house on Wabash Avenue was modest, with three bedrooms, a neat double-parlor, and a tiny yard behind it. Tad—still suffering from fits of coughing that he could not seem to shake off—had a small room in the attic, Mary the guest room adjoining little Mamie's nursery. Young Mary, who in her letters had expressed such graceful gratitude for her mother-in-law's advice about child-rearing, pregnancy, fashion, and household economy, proved to be, in person and out of her white satin wedding-gown, nervous and, her mother-in-law judged, hypocritical. Mary recognized the embroidered pillowcases she had sent from Germany, but saw no trace of the several lovely plaid dresses she'd sent, nor of the needlework waistcoats she'd bought for Robert.

"Surely I thought you must have loved them," she commented over supper that first night. "They are all the fashion, you know."

She saw the glance between Robert and his wife: "They were so handsome, I thought I would save them for best," said Robert after a moment. "As a young lawyer just starting out, I've found it pays to dress more plainly."

"And that 'falling-leaf' color was the most elegant to be had." Mary heard the defensiveness in her tone, as she turned to Young Mary. "I spent quite fifty dollars on the silk, plus the cost of having Mr. Popp make it up. He sewed for the Princess of Prussia, you know, so the style must have been impeccable."

"It was," said her daughter-in-law quickly, setting down the soup tureen. The cook had laid out the dishes on the black walnut sideboard which badly cramped the inadequate dining-room—there didn't seem to be a maid to serve. "Only the dress didn't quite fit. . . ."

"And you haven't altered it in *three years*?" Mary recoiled a little from the soup: "Dear heavens, that isn't *beef,* is it? In weather like *this*? Beef makes me quite bilious. . . ."

Robert took the streetcar north into the city every morning, to the offices he shared with his law partner, Mr. Scammon. Tad, though he was still coughing and in Mary's opinion should have remained in his bed, went with him. The Lincolns kept no carriage, not even a buggy: "It's a ridiculous way of economizing, if that's what you're trying to do," protested Mary, after two days of being trapped on Wabash Avenue watching her daughter-in-law assist the maid-of-all-work in dusting knickknacks and sweeping floors. The thought of being stared at on the streetcars filled her with horror. "When Mr. Lincoln and I were first married, I assure you, we were *quite* poor, but we *always* had a buggy."

"I rejoice to hear it." An edge like glass glinted in Young Mary's voice. "As it happens, just now we do not."

"And it's equally ridiculous that you should be doing a servant's work," added Mary. "Surely for the money you're paying that cook, and that scullery-girl, you could get a couple of good parlormaids who know their way around the kitchen and can take care of Mamie as well. Why, times cannot have changed so much that you can't get a good girl for a dollar a week. . . ."

Robert's wife, Mary found in very short order, was also given to fits of tears. She suspected, and said to Robert after four days, that Young Mary drank as well. Within the first week they had two vicious arguments about the housekeeping money, steely-voiced on the younger woman's side, with Mary flying into rages which escalated into tears and migraines that laid her up for two days. Her daughter-in-law and Tad were forced to care for her with tisanes, quiet, drawn shades, and Nervine. Robert looked haggard when he came into her room to hear her side of it—through the closed door Mary had already heard Young Mary's twisted accounts of the quarrels the moment the young man walked into the house—and began to stay later and later at the office, as his father had before him.

As they all did, thought Mary in a fury of resentment. *Anytime any man doesn't want to deal with his women at home, he disappears into "business," and gives that shopworn excuse, "I'm the one who supports the household, I have the right to a little peace. . . ."*

At the end of a month came the worst quarrel of all, which ended in a screaming-match between the two women. In a way this gratified Mary, for generally Young Mary grew maddeningly quiet and spoke her unforgivable accusations in a calm voice that made her want to box her ears, as she had on many occasions done with her sister Ann when they were small.

When Robert came home—late—Mary was lying in her room with a pounding headache and the sick swoony dizziness that so often followed the taking of several tablespoons of Godfrey's Cordial. She'd heard Young Mary moving about her room for some time. It was full summer, breathlessly hot and unnaturally dry. The air felt electric, pressing her skull like a tightening iron band. Far off, thunder growled over the lake, only a few streets from Wabash Avenue on the other side of the small park. Her old sense of panic filled her, of the frightening approach of some crushing doom.

She heard Robert say, "Darling, what is this?" and Young Mary's voice, quiet as ice.

"It's a suitcase, Robert. And that smaller one is for Mamie. Your mother apparently doesn't consider me an adequate keeper of the household on your income. . . ."

I did not say that! thought Mary furiously. *Not in those words, anyway . . . And in any case, it's true!*

". . . though I can't imagine where she gets her advice from, having no experience herself in running a household within a budget. She saw fit to dismiss Mrs. Phelps today—for theft, she said, to her face. . ."

"Darling . . ."

"So I thought it best, if she thinks she can make a better home for you than I can, to get out of her way and let her do so."

"Darling!" Robert sounded desperate. *As well he should,* thought Mary resentfully, *if he's been married for three years to that whining little harpy.* "You must remember, my mother isn't quite right in her head."

It was the first time she had heard Robert say it out loud, though in the newspaper flurry that had surrounded what was now called the Old Clothes Scandal the awful word *insane* had been applied to her before—and reportedly, by Robert. Anger blazed up in her like matchwood and she staggered from her bed, catching her balance on the bedpost.

"She says things she doesn't mean. Since my father's death. . ."

"I have heard, every single, solitary day, about your father's death," replied Young Mary in a voice like over-wound violin-strings. "*And* how your mother has suffered since. And with all due respect to Mr. Booth, I would not at all be surprised if I heard that your father had *arranged* to have himself shot."

"That is *infamous*!" Mary shoved open the bedroom door and strode down the stairs. "How *dare* you say such things?"

Sitting among the pillows of the blue plush sofa, tiny Mamie—not quite two—began to wail, staring anxiously from face to face in the gaslit gloom. Tad, who'd retreated up the attic stairs at the beginning of the quarrel, came down looking as if he might start crying, too.

"I have a good mind to leave this house," cried Mary, "and to take that poor little child away with me, to get her out of the care of an ungrateful, whining, drunken—"

"Mother!" Robert thundered, as Young Mary's eyes overflowed with silent tears and she reached down for the handle of the small wicker suitcase at her feet.

The rest of the evening passed in a blur, first of shouted words that Mary barely remembered on waking the next morning, then of migraine agony and lurid dreams. It was nearly noon, and suffocatingly hot, when Tad came into her room and said gently, "If you meant what you said last night about finding a place to board, maybe I could take the streetcar into town and make some inquiries? Mr. Scammon and Mr. Trumbull both speak very highly of Clifton House these days."

She had no recollection whatsoever of saying she would look for a place to board, but felt too exhausted and sick to argue. She said, "Lyman Trumbull is a lying blackguard," forgetting entirely that Trumbull had been one of her chief supporters during the pension fight and at one time—many years ago in Springfield—her favored beau. She remembered only how he had refused to step aside during the Senate race in 1856, and had taken the office from Lincoln.

If he had not done so, she thought, tears flowing down at the memory of Lincoln—alive, breathing, present, caring for her—among that little band of supporters in the parlor of the Jackson Street house, *how much would have been different. . . .* "And his wife is a treacherous hussy. Any place that he would speak well of must be a den of infamy."

Two days later, she and Tad moved into the Clifton House.

They occupied two modest rooms on the second floor, and at Mary's insistence ate their meals in Tad's room rather than going down to join the other boarders in the dining-room. Tad's cold was worse, and she occupied herself in making poultices, steaming herbs, coaxing him to take a wide variety of patent medicines. When he was better, he said, he would begin clerking with Robert at Scammon's.

But he didn't get better.

Within two weeks he was so seriously ill that she sent for one of the best pediatricians in Chicago, though Tad was eighteen. "It isn't consumption, sir," she insisted, as Dr. Smith tapped the young man's thin chest. "It *cannot* be consumption, for I have taken very good care of his health. He is Abraham Lincoln's son!"

Tad, who like Robert had for the past ten years heard himself described in terms of his father, winced slightly and traded a sleepy glance with the doctor; Mary had found that Godfrey's Cordial not only eased her own neuralgia well, but was also a marvelous suppressant of coughs.

At Dr. Smith's suggestion, Tad was propped up to sleep, so that he could breathe better. First this was done with pillows on his bed, and then, as the suffocating dry heat of July deepened and his breathing labored harder against the edema in his lungs, in a specially made chair with a rod across the front, to prop him up when he fell asleep. Even a shaky stagger down the hall to the toilets exhausted him, and Mary carried chamber pots, made medicines, rubbed eucalyptus balm on her son's chest and back. Her world—so wide and pleasant only a few months ago in Italy—shrank to a single curtained room, a single other person, a young man whose face was so like Lincoln's that sometimes in her dreams she wasn't sure whether she was dreaming of one or the other.

Then the sound of his gasping would jolt her out of her catnap sleep, the thready weak voice—identical to Lincoln's in its lightness—would gasp, "Mama . . ."

Robert would come, after a day of writing briefs and taking depositions, and stay with Tad until long after dark, so that she could sleep. It was Robert who told her that Tad was dying, Robert who insisted that she face the fact and not exhaust his brother with selfish demands that he live on for her. "You know nothing about it!" she sobbed, "nothing . . . !"

And when Robert finally departed, at close to midnight when the final summer twilights had faded out of the burning sky, she would cling to Tad's hands and whisper frantically, "Don't leave me, Taddie. Don't leave your mother all alone! I shall die if you leave me, I shall die. . . ."

Towards the end she didn't even know whether he heard, though sometimes tears would flow down from his closed eyes.

Chapter Sixty

Tad died on the fifteenth of July, 1871. The anniversary of her father's death. A haggard Robert arranged the funeral at his home and afterwards took his brother's body down to Springfield. Tad was put to rest in the tomb in Oak Ridge Cemetery, with Willie, Eddie, and Lincoln himself. On his return Robert departed for one of the new resorts in the Western mountains, to seek rest of his own. He left his mother at his house: "Surely you will find it more comfortable than boarding, at this time." Young Mary and Mamie had gone back to Iowa, to care for Young Mary's ailing mother.

At any other time Mary would have responded to the news of Ann Harlan's illness with cynical suspicion that her daughter-in-law was simply fleeing from her, and thus deliberately depriving her of her only grandchild. At another time she might have queried why Robert didn't take refuge with his wife.

But she felt literally stunned, as she had in the days immediately following her carriage accident. Her memories of the days between July and October were little more than a blur of grief and cloudy dreams. Myra Bradwell came to the house daily, mercifully bustling and efficient, though she had, of all things, begun publication of a small legal newspaper and frequently brought long ink-smelling galley-sheets to read while Mary lay in numb silence on the sofa in her room.

Mary later was sure that it was Myra who made certain that one or the other of the Spiritualists came to sit with her, to make her meals that she did not eat, to sometimes brush her hair.

Mary did remember the heat, for like an obscene afterthought it exacerbated the tormenting itches of her female parts that had begun with Tad's birth. Twice or three times thunder tolled over the lake, but no rain fell. The river sank, and the stench of it crept over the city. The shacks and sheds filled with cow-fodder and firewood, the wooden sidewalks and the wood-block streets, all cracked and bleached in the slow-baking heat. The curtained guest-room at Robert's house was like a dark oven, where she would lie in silence, or talk in feverish broken sobs to whoever happened to be with her that day.

Ella Slapater, a woman she had met through the New York Spiritualists surrounding Lord Colchester, came from Pennsylvania to be with her for almost a month. Robert, when he returned from Colorado, got that tight, wooden expression in his face whenever Ella spoke of the comforts of speech with the dead, but forbore to argue the matter. On an evening when Robert was out—Young Mary still remaining in Iowa with her mother—Mary, Ella, and Myra formed a Circle in the parlor, sang a hymn, and asked the spirits to come for their comfort.

If any came, they did not speak, and Mary went to bed uncomforted.

Mostly, in those autumn days, she felt nothing but a sense of vast confusion.

Tad was gone. Robert had been stolen from her by that treacherous hussy of a wife.

She could not even imagine where she would live now, or how. The whole of her life stretched before her, a bleak process of going someplace and waiting to die. Elizabeth sent a letter inviting her to live with her in Springfield—Mary tore it up and threw the pieces on the floor.

Never would she go and live again as a pensioner in Ninian's house.

September turned to an October equally hot, equally dry. Desiccating winds breathed over the prairies from the southwest, like the exhalation of Hell.

ON SATURDAY, OCTOBER 8, A FIRE BROKE OUT ON THE WEST SIDE. The insurance men called that neighborhood "The Red Flash": a crowded maze of wooden shanties, lumberyards, saloons, and cheap frame houses. By morning the blaze had been put out, the stink of smoke adding to the city's multifarious stenches and the grit of it burning Mary's eyes when Myra came by, to have coffee with her on Sunday morning while Robert was at church. Mary spent the day in her room, while hot prairie winds rose and scoured the town.

"Will you come out with me for a walk in Lake Park?" asked Robert, when he brought her lunch.

The thought of the crowds in that small patch of greenery on a blistering Sunday like this one made her shudder. "Robert, how *can* you?"

"You cannot sit in a room for the rest of your life, Mother. You must come out sometime."

She merely covered her face with her hands, and turned away. "You don't understand! You cannot understand! If you did you would not demand that I . . . I *parade* myself for people to stare at . . . !"

When Robert said nothing she swung around to face him again, and noticed that he had left off wearing his black armband for Tad. His father, she recalled resentfully, had never worn anything but black, from the day of Willie's death to the day of his own.

Robert's mouth had a compressed look to it under his mustache, as if asking himself how he could put up with this woman. Mary lowered her head to her hands as a wave of heat swept over her, nauseating her. "Leave me alone. You want me out of here, so that little coward wife of yours will dare to come back!"

He did not reply. It was only later, after Mary heard the outer door of the house close, that it came to her that in fact he did understand—*as well as Robert could understand anything,* she thought. He had lost his last brother, as she had lost, now, all but one of her sons.

The howl of the wind and the smell of smoke followed her into her dreams. She dreamed of fire, of the smell of smoke—of the screaming of her sons' ponies as they burned to death in their stable—and waking, pulled her wrapper close around her and stumbled to the window. But she saw nothing, only the flat sleeping faces of the houses on the other side of Wabash Avenue.

Going downstairs she found Robert by the front door, still dressed, even to his jacket.

After his father's habit of walking around in his shirtsleeves—and barefoot half the time—Mary had worked all her life to inculcate proper dress and manners in her son, whom she had never seen half-dressed in all the years since he'd left Springfield for Exeter School in 1859. Looking out, she saw red staining the northern sky.

"It appears to be on the other side of the river." Robert's voice was calm. "The river should hold it." Far off, a dim clamor came to her, too indistinct to be clearly identified but terrifying, a whisper of primal chaos. "There's nothing to worry about, Mother. Go back to bed."

She obeyed, but lay awake. Even at this hour the heat was oppressive, parched wind screaming around the house-eaves. When at last she slept, her dreams were dreams of horror. The cities of the plain were burning, as they had in the Bible—she saw them, two of them, with flames a hundred feet high dyeing the lake-waters blood-red. Then she found herself in the streets of those burning cities, whose wooden sidewalks, crisped with the summer's heat, roared up into lines of fire. The streets themselves burned, for they'd been paved with blocks of wood, and wooden fences carried the blaze as wires carry an electrical charge. Men and women poured along the streets, dragging wheelbarrows or trunks, or clinging to the reins of terrified wagon-horses whose heads were wrapped in coats to keep them from running mad in the blaze.

But the fire roared up before them, blocking their way. There was nowhere to flee to.

She woke, trembling, to the sound of shouting, of wagons passing in the street. Running to the window she saw the fugitives from her dream: men and women, young girls or what looked like shoeshine boys and newsboys, pushing handcarts, dragging boxes, carrying sheets or tablecloths filled with papers or books or silverware. Dozens of them, hundreds of them, running and stumbling as they looked back over their shoulders up Wabash Avenue. She leaned out the window and shouted, "What is it? What's happening?" but no one paid her heed. She threw a shawl around her nightdress and ran downstairs with streaming hair, out the front door to the sidewalk. "What is it?"

She grabbed a man's arm, a fat laborer whose jowls were blue with beard. He yanked free of her grip and ran on, as if he feared the Devil would catch him if he halted for so much as a second.

And Mary, looking back, gasped in horror, for it was true.

The Devil was right behind them.

Flames poured skyward far up the street. Smoke made a pall over the city, so that it was impossible to tell what time it was, or whether dawn had come. Flame lay across Wabash Avenue, many blocks away yet but sweeping closer, driven by the wind, devouring the wooden houses, the wood-framed brick buildings, the woodpiles and coal-heaps and sheds full of fodder and kindling and lamp-oil and firewood. Flames rose above the buildings, licking in the rolling masses of smoke, a wall of flame stretching west and east, like the front of an advancing army. From that wall the wind threw showers of sparks, igniting everything they touched. The noise of it was a fearful bellowing, unlike anything she had heard in waking life—it dwarfed the roaring of the White House stable fire to a titter.

And above it rose the clamor of those who fled.

"It's jumped the river," gasped an older man, like Mary in his nightclothes and barefoot, his garment black with soot. "They're lootin' and robbin'—the firefighters can't stop it, it's got away from 'em, it's too big. . . ."

From the crowd a woman with streaming hair screamed, "Davey!" and the man ran to her, the two of them instantly swallowed up in the mob.

Mary turned back to the house, crying, "Bobby! Bobby!" and ran up the stairs to her son's room. She expected to find him dressing, putting his legal papers into a valise, readying himself in his usual methodical way to make an escape.

But he was gone. She stood in the doorway of the bedroom, shocked numb, staring at the neatly made bed—Myra used to joke that Robert made his bed *before* he got up—the empty clothes-stand.

He had left her. *He had left her!*

Mary's jaw dropped. Never in a lifetime had she thought that Robert would desert her.

In the street a woman screamed.

Mary shrieked, "Bobby!" and ran downstairs again, to the dining-room, the parlor, the study.

But he was indeed gone.

Panic gripped her.

She tore upstairs, breathless and gasping at the exertion, pulled on a skirt over her nightdress and buttoned the highest button she could without a corset, stuffed her feet without stockings into shoes. Clutching the shawl about her she fled down the stairs, ran into the street. People were shoving and thrusting, shouting and coughing in the smoke. The air was filled now with flying cinders; through the oily clouds she could see that it was daylight, early morning, grilling hot.

She thought she was fighting her way along Mitchell Street toward the lake but wasn't sure. The neighborhood was unfamiliar to her, and the street was jammed with carriages, struggling figures, horses, cows, and dogs running wild in panic.

A fat woman carrying a cage full of finches slammed into her, screamed as she struggled past. Two little girls in nightdresses darted by, barefoot and clinging to each other's hands. Smoke blinded her; she sprang out of the way of a man in a policeman's uniform who was riding a wild-eyed horse down the center of the street, then she turned and ran blindly. . . .

The fire was ahead of her. The fire was roaring toward her, vomiting sparks that lit on the wooden roofs of the buildings all around her, kindling them like touchwood. She had missed her way and was among the shops on State Street, near the Michigan & Southern depot. Mingled with the crowd of terrified fugitives were others shoving and struggling in the other direction, their barrows filled, not with household possessions, but with crates of liquor and bolts of gleaming silk.

Someone shoved her aside, throwing her down against the hot bricks of a wall. Three rough-looking young men smashed a shop window beside her, rushed in and emerged moments later with their hands full of necklaces and earrings that flashed in the light of the advancing flames. Across the street a man and a woman, roaring drunk and shrieking obscenities, dove into a deserted tavern and came out with bottles of whiskey in their hands. Others—they looked like laborers, men wielding clubs while their girlfriends hauled a barrow—stopped those who fled and wrested away from them whatever looked valuable, silver candlesticks, their jewelry boxes. The pavement glittered with shattered mirrors, trampled underfoot, with a smashed rummage of bedding, crockery, a broken guitar. Looking down, she saw the street was littered with paper money, trampled in with all the rest.

A spark caught her skirt, setting the black crape instantly ablaze. She screamed, struck at it with her hands, and ran on again with the scorched hole in the fabric still smoking. The mob carried her along, she could not struggle against it. She tripped, and found herself next to the corpse of a man sprawled in front of his looted store, his skull cracked open and bright blood leaking into the gutter.

The shattering roar of an explosion split the darkness; someone yelled, "They're blowin' up the buildin' for a firebreak!" Gunfire cracked; she couldn't tell from where or why. A girl ran past her shrieking, long blond hair blazing—one of the ruffians by a looted wine-store hurled a glass of liquor over her, and she ignited like a blue-burning torch.

Flame was all around them. She screamed "Abraham!" hoping against hope—against all logic and sense—that he'd come striding out of the smoke and the blaze of this hell, that he'd take care of her, lead her to safety. . . .

They reached the lake, hundreds, thousands crowding into Lake Park, running across the rails of the Illinois Central line to the water's edge. Fire towered in the blackened sky, north and west of them; ash and cinders rained down. Children screamed in terror and pain; women slapped wildly at their burning hair. The heat was infernal, as if the fire reached out to devour them, and Mary, stumbling with hundreds of others into the waters of the lake, thought desperately, *What if the fire comes to the lakeshore? What if the trees in the park, the grass that's been drying to tinder all these weeks, catch fire as well? What then? Will we all be driven deeper into the water, to drown?*

The world shook again with explosions. She saw fragments of masonry hurled high into the sooty maelstrom overhead.

Her wet skirt dragged on her, her wet nightgown sodden on her uncorseted breasts. Men and women shoved against her, pushing further into the water as they were pushed by terrified newcomers. The weeping voices, the frantic cries rose on all sides as women tried to find their husbands or children, as men shouted for their families. The sounds were like the lamentations of Hell.

Someone fell against her—a boy of nine or ten, carrying a baby. Mary caught him as he stumbled. Without her grasp, he and the sobbing infant would have simply slipped below the surface, for his soot-black face was blank with shock. The lake-water that came up to her hips came nearly to his shoulders and others were thrusting them both out deeper. She took the baby from his arms, cradled it against her breast with one arm, and steadied him with the other.

"Are you all right?" she asked, and the boy stared up at her with uncomprehending eyes. *"Bist du verletzen?"* she asked, guessing from his fair hair he might be one of the immigrant children from the filthy patches back of the stockyards, and he clung to her skirt and sobbed, *"Wo ist Mutti?"*

Where's Mama?

Mary tightened her arm around the boy, for it was a question she'd asked all her life, and had never gotten a satisfactory answer.

For hours they stood there in the water, the crowds pushing tighter and tighter around them. Mary felt that she would faint, but knew that to faint was to drown. No one would catch her, no one would hold her up. Through the jostling rank of shoulders between herself and the shore, she could catch glimpses now and then of the park and the trees in the sickly glow of daylight.

The trees were yellow and limp, but still unburned. The lawns swarmed with huddled shapes.

Beyond them, the first houses—the handsome houses of the lakeshore—stood deserted but intact. Now and then gangs of looters pulled carts up to them, helped themselves to rugs, clothing, jewelry in full view of the onlookers, and went unhurriedly on their way.

Gradually, the red wall of flame diminished. Smoke continued to pour skyward, but Mary heard—like the tramp of the New York regiment down Washington's silent streets—the voices of men, the clatter of fire-wagons. They, too, were soldiers. It wasn't just her memory. She saw flashes of Union blue coats. Northward the flames still scraped the sky.

Feeling she could stand no longer, she began slowly, stumblingly, to push her way ashore. The crowding in the water wasn't so bad now. Others were creeping out of the lake, falling to their knees on the wet cinders between the railroad and the park's edge. The baby in her arms began to cry again, weakly, and she felt a surge of joy—at least the poor little thing wasn't dead—and the boy beside her helped her to kneel on the land. She could still see nothing but a wilderness of knees, a sodden wilderness of slumped shapes under the hellish yellow glare of smoke-stained day, but someone said the fire was burning itself out at the Rock Island and Chicago tracks.

She held the whimpering infant in her arms and relayed the information to the child's brother in German. "My mother is lost," said the boy in the same language, and she said reassuringly,

"The Army will find her for you, once they get the fire out."

He put his head on her thigh and slept.

They remained there, through the whole of a hellish day. Exhausted, starving, and thirsty, Mary dozed sometimes, and in her dreams she wandered through the contraband camps around Washington during the War, where shattered men and women huddled, who had left their old lives behind. Now and then explosions sounded across the city, and the sullen clouds rained burning cinders.

Dark fell, and a few hours later real rain began. Those few who had remained—Mary couldn't imagine how—standing in the lake-water throughout the eternity of that hideous day finally waded ashore and collapsed on the mud and cinders. Someone took the baby from her arms—she didn't know who, or whether the little German boy ever found his Mutti. Men and women started coming through the darkness of the park bearing lanterns. Some of the men wore the blue uniforms of Union soldiers, and the women were of that indefatigable breed who had throughout the War made up the Sanitary Committees and the Volunteer Nurses associations.

By that time she was too shattered to be much aware of what was going on around her, staring before her in exhausted shock, numb with fatigue and the horror of the things she had seen. But she heard a familiar voice cry, "Mary!" and looking up, saw Myra Bradwell standing a few feet away, a lantern and a sack of blankets over her shoulder. By the shock in her eyes it was clear she'd barely recognized her, wet, disheveled, covered with mud and soot and ash. "Good God—*Mary*!"

And Mary held out her arms to her friend, and burst into tears like a child.

Chapter Sixty-one

Bellevue July 1875

Myra Bradwell.

Mary didn't think she'd ever been more grateful to see anyone in her life—not even Mr. Lincoln when he'd met her again after eighteen months in Bessie Francis's parlor—as she was to see that tall, sturdy figure stride to her through the smoke-black sodden limbo on Lake Michigan's edge.

Lincoln—though it was years since Mary had admitted this, even to herself—was just as likely to forget he was supposed to fetch the boys from school, or that he'd said he'd get fish from the market on his way home, or that Frances and Dr. Wallace were coming to supper (though, she had noticed, he never forgot appointments with his political cronies—that was just how his mind worked).

Myra, however, was like a rock.

From the window of her bedroom at Bellevue Mary watched the driveway under the sharp summer sunlight, praying that Myra would come.

Robert, Myra had told her, that rainy Monday night as she guided Mary back to the little house on Wabash Avenue, had heard at about daybreak Monday morning that the fire had jumped the river, and was moving south swiftly through downtown. Without waking his mother, he had set out on foot up Wabash Avenue for his office on Lake Street—no horse could be induced to go in the direction of the fire. The roof of the Crosby Opera House, in which he had his office, was already in flames when he reached the place. Opening his office safe, he'd piled his father's papers into a tablecloth, and with this tied up on his back had strode out of the burning building and through the inferno of looting, flames, and dynamited firebreaks for home.

Once out of the region of the fire he had encountered the dapper John Hay, who was also living in Chicago these days. The two men had stopped for breakfast at the Terrace Row house of Charles Scammon, Robert's law partner. Robert had advised Scammon's family against evacuating their home and clearing out its furniture and treasures. It might, he warned, affect later insurance claims, and in any case he thought the fire was slowing down.

After Robert and Hay left, the Scammons cleared out their possessions anyway and by noon the house was smoking rubble.

Robert was, of course, furious with Mary for leaving the house: "You were perfectly safe the whole time!" The fire had been stopped three blocks away by General Sheridan, Mary's erstwhile traveling companion on the *Russia,* who had ordered his men to blow up every building in its path. Every tree and bush in Robert's garden had been withered by the heat.

Later she learned that her dream had been accurate. Not only Chicago had burned that night. Baked tinder-dry by the same rainless autumn and fanned by the same scorching prairie winds, the town of Peshtigo, Wisconsin, across the lake—the depot for the whole of the Chicago timber trade that funneled building-wood from the northwest to the woodless Great Plains—had burned, too. Its destruction, unlike Chicago's, was complete.

LEANING HER ARM ON THE BARRED WINDOWSILL OF HER ASYLUM ROOM, Mary closed her eyes, saw again the red infinities of fire, the black curtains of smoke. Heard the noise it made—good God, that sound! Like the bellowing of an all-devouring monster. Saw a blonde girl run screaming past her with her flaming hair . . . saw the drunkard hurl his glass of liquor . . .

Nightly, for years, those scenes would replay against the lids of her shut eyes, and she would wake crying, thinking, *The city is on fire . . . !*

The city is on fire, and Bobby is gone, and I am alone. . . .

Mary opened her eyes just as Myra Bradwell and her tall husband climbed from a train-station hack and rang the bell at the iron gates at the end of the drive.

Her heart lurched, then triphammered with wild joy. *I knew it! I knew she'd come!*

Argus opened the gates, stood for a few moments talking to the pair. Myra hadn't changed much since the last time Mary had seen her—*good God, it can't be four years!* A little stouter, maybe, and she hadn't—*thank Heaven!*—started wearing "rational costume" of Turkish pantaloons and knee-length tunic as she'd been threatening then to do. Her neat dress of navy-blue chintz was perfectly plain, and being without a bustle—something Myra had steadfastly refused to wear—now put her, almost accidentally, into the very forefront of the mode.

Not, thought Mary, scrambling to her feet and calling for Gretchen, *that Myra would care.*

Myra's husband followed her up the walk, fair and bespectacled and still very English-looking in spite of half a lifetime spent in the United States. If she had not been married to Abraham Lincoln, Mary had frequently thought, she'd have liked to be married to Judge James Bradwell.

"Gretchen!" she called frantically. "Lace me up again . . . !" That morning General Farnsworth had come, making a lot of vague promises and telling her how much more rested she looked—*Of course I'm more rested, you imbecile, I've been locked up for two and a half months!* Returning to her room, she'd had Gretchen unlace her and had eaten a little lunch, meaning to remain indoors and rest. Though most of the physical pains of withdrawal from opium had abated, she still had bouts of queasiness, and without warning the darkness of depression would rise over her in smothering clouds.

"Get me dressed," she panted when her attendant entered, "at once, now. Someone has come to see me. . . ."

YOUNG DR. PATTERSON WAS STANDING AT THE HEAD OF THE STAIRS when Mary, trailed by Gretchen, came hurrying down the hall. She could hear Myra's strong, clear voice below: "Couldn't I see her, Doctor, in the presence of her attendant? My only object in coming here was to see her."

"Not without a paper from her son." Patterson senior's voice from the parlor had the air of one who has reiterated the statement several times. "She may be out in a few days, Madame. Then you can see her to your heart's content."

"Is it likely that she would be," responded Myra reasonably, "if you don't even consider her well enough to receive visitors?"

Mary attempted to step past Young Doc, who put a hand on her arm.

"I'm sorry, Mrs. Lincoln," he said softly. "No one is permitted to go down into the parlor this afternoon."

"That's ridiculous!" she gasped. Gretchen came up on her other side, quiet but tense. Ready for trouble. "You have no right to keep me from seeing my friends!"

"As your doctor," replied Young Doc thinly, "we have every right to keep you from doing things that will only worsen and exacerbate your condition—as you well know, Madam, in your saner moments."

Mary opened her mouth to lash out in protest, her face hot with anger. But his last sentence stopped her, as if she'd glimpsed Robert looking at her from around a corner—looking at her and waiting for yet another fragment of evidence that she was insane.

"I understood from your letters to the public that she is allowed to see her friends," Myra went on, in the voice of reasonable inquiry that Mary knew meant she had an unsheathed sword hidden behind her back.

"Well, Madame, she is no better"—Patterson's voice had an edge of impatience to it—"for meddlesome people come here to see her, calling themselves her friends, when in reality they come out of self-interest only, like that dreadful Mrs. Rayne from the *Chicago Post.*"

"Doctor, please don't attribute such a motive to me!" Myra sounded as if she'd never heard of a newspaper in all her life. "I assure you my visit is only out of pure kindness to Mrs. Lincoln. She is one of my oldest friends. As you are not willing to let me see her, will you allow me to leave a note for her?"

Pressing forward—Mrs. Patterson had joined Gretchen and Young Doc in the hall and there was now no chance whatsoever of getting past them without a fuss—Mary could see Dr. Patterson's back below. He glanced at his watch, a habit he shared with Robert's lawyer friend Swett, a way of signalling that his time was far more valuable than theirs. . . .

"There is no necessity for that, Madame. It would only disturb her mind. While she is under my care, I shall not permit her to be disturbed either by visitors or letters."

"If she is only permitted to see such persons as you choose, and is not permitted to receive letters except from such, she is virtually a prisoner, is she not?"

"No more so than other patients I have under my care." He glanced at his watch again, as if to say, *When will you take yourself out of here and stop wasting my precious instants, each more valuable than gold . . . ?*

"I quite understand," said Myra, in a cheerful voice that, Mary knew, presaged a serious skewering at some time in the future. "Doctor, it is some time until our train leaves—might my husband and I remain for a little time in your parlor, rather than sitting in the public depot?"

"Mrs. Lincoln," said Mrs. Patterson firmly, "Dr. Patterson has asked that no one be admitted to the parlor this afternoon. Now, you had one visitor this morning already, and I think we all agree that all he did was stir you up and make you uncomfortable. If your son thinks it's appropriate, you will be able to receive a visit from your friends on another occasion."

Mary made her face impassive, fighting not to burst into either tears or a tirade of abuse. *You smug hag, if you had a single friend in the entire world you would know what it means to be separated from them, when you have no one else!*

But as she had with Robert, she lowered her shoulders and her eyes and said, "Yes, of course. I quite understand."

And immediately Mrs. Patterson relaxed.

Down in the parlor, Myra was chatting with Dr. Patterson, inquiring about the difficulties of running a "rest home," as she called it, and pretending deepest fascination with the methods of "coaxing troubled minds back to sanity." All of which information, Mary was certain, was being mentally jotted down by the silent and self-effacing James. She heard Dr. Patterson say, "Mrs. Lincoln is quite a difficult case, very much troubled in her mind. As you know, she was sent here after an attempt to take her own life. . . ."

That isn't true!

Heart pounding, Mary walked back along the hall to her room. Did Myra actually believe her to be insane? Had she come only to learn how serious her aberration actually was?

No. No, she believes me. . . .

Does she?

Panic filled her, at the recollection of that expression of specious understanding in General Farnsworth's eyes that morning. What had that one-time abolitionist politician said to Patterson, after she had returned to her room? That she was insane but seemed sane most of the time, as Robert always said of her? That she "looked rested" as a result of her incarceration, so therefore her imprisonment ought to continue?

As Mrs. Patterson, young Doc, and Gretchen stood waiting for Mary to enter her room again, she saw John Wilamet turn the corner.

"Oh, Mr. Wilamet," purred Mary. "Perhaps before I lie down I could speak to you for a moment about . . ." *About what?* Her mind groped frantically for a convincing lie, ". . . about that poem your dear mother recommended that I read. Mr. Tennyson's 'Lady of Shalott,' was it not?"

John faltered slightly at the mere thought of his mother reading or recommending any sort of poem whatsoever, but Mary locked eyes with him, mutely pleading with him to understand. He nodded amiably, and replied, "It was indeed," and paused. In the face of a discussion of poetry, both Pattersons and Gretchen went on their ways.

"You must go after Judge and Mrs. Bradwell when they leave the house—they're down in the parlor now—and tell them that I am not insane!" Mary whispered desperately. "That I attempted to commit suicide *after* I was tried and condemned to perpetual imprisonment as a madwoman, not before! Please, please, John, let them know the truth as you have seen it! Mrs. Bradwell is a lawyer—her husband is a judge! They will know how to undo the law that has made me a prisoner here!"

John looked down at her gravely for a moment. *If he tells me that I'm too excitable or shouldn't be "stirred up," I shall kill myself indeed. . . .*

But he said, "And what will you do with your freedom, if they should undo the law?"

She almost cried, *I'd live!* But instead she said quietly, "That's no more your business, John, than it would have been my business to ask that of you, before my husband signed the Proclamation which set you free."

"Touché, Mrs. Lincoln. A palpable hit."

And turning with a smile, he hurried down the stairs.

JOHN WAS LOITERING WHEN DR. PATTERSON FINISHED HIS TEA—AND his lecture on Moral Treatment—and called for Zeus to harness the carriage, to take Judge and Mrs. Bradwell to the station. "I can drive them," he said, stepping into the parlor at precisely the right moment, as Mrs. Bradwell was shaking cake-crumbs from her skirts. "I need to stop in at Beck's Pharmacy. We're low on ipecac and salts."

"Thank you, Mr. Wilamet." Patterson smiled benignly. "Judge Bradwell—Madame—you have no objection to Mr. Wilamet driving you? Excellent . . . Mr. Wilamet is my assistant here. John, if you'd be so good as to ask at the receiving-office, we're also expecting a shipment of chloral hydrate—a very much more effective and modern inducer of sleep than laudanum," he added, addressing Myra. "We believe in a minimum of drugs here, only those that are necessary to restore the balance of the patient's mind. We have been working a great deal with sleep therapy, sleep being the greatest natural restorer that there is. . . ."

Even if you have to induce it with enough chloral hydrate to knock out a bear, thought John, as he led the way down the front steps to the carriage in the gravel drive. The previous September one of Dr. Patterson's patients, a Mrs. Harcourt, had died of "exhaustion" after an episode of mania, during which she'd been force-fed 110 grains of chloral hydrate over the course of a few hours. Patterson still sincerely believed it was the mania rather than the drug which had ended her life.

As they got in the carriage Mrs. Bradwell—whom John had met briefly during the War, though he doubted she remembered a mere member of General Ord's medical staff—said to her husband, "Well, what do you think, Judge?"

"Other than that the fellow's a self-important bore?"

Only when he'd driven through the gates and Argus had shut them behind the carriage did John draw rein, turn on the box, and say, "Please excuse me for interrupting, Judge, Mrs. Bradwell. . . ."

The older man regarded him with sharply raised brows—no Englishman of the upper classes ever quite got used to being addressed by a servant. It was as if, just for that first moment, one of the carriage-horses had spoken.

"Mrs. Lincoln begged me to speak to you—begged me to let you know that that suicide attempt of hers was after that . . . that farce of a trial. And she asked me to tell you anything you might wish to know about her condition." And, seeing—to his surprise—that Mrs. Bradwell was regarding him closely, he added, "We've met before, ma'am, briefly, during the War. . . ."

"You were with Ord, weren't you? At Crown Point?"

"I was, ma'am."

"And you've been caring for Mrs. Lincoln while she's been here?"

"Yes, I have, ma'am." He flapped the reins, guided the team over to the shade of an elm at the side of Union Street, and drew rein again. Far off the Illinois Central whistled, but none of them paid any attention. There would be, he knew, another train in two hours.

"And do you consider Mrs. Lincoln is insane?" Mrs. Bradwell's shrewd gaze remained on his face. He had never in his life heard of a woman lawyer, although he'd encountered a couple of women doctors in his time. But he could easily believe this stout, motherly-looking woman was one. There was something in her gaze that he wouldn't have wanted to try lying to.

"I consider Mrs. Lincoln is crazy," he replied, paraphrasing Lizabet Keckley's quite accurate summation. "I don't think anybody who knows her would argue that. But insane?"

"In the newspaper accounts of her trial the doctors say she was delusional." Judge Bradwell spoke for the first time. He had a big man's deep, mellow voice, with a trace of English accent in his vowels and r's.

"I suspect they were hallucinations rather than delusions, sir," answered John. "I believe that was the fault of some of the medicines she was taking, medicines that she has been weaned off of now. . . . She has certainly not had delusions of any kind since she's been at Bellevue. Dr. Patterson doesn't agree with my diagnosis. He says she needs rest . . . which I think she does. I think she's needed rest for a long time."

"Do you think she would be able to deal with life in the world?" asked Mrs. Bradwell quietly. "I'm very fond of Mary—Mrs. Lincoln—but I'm not blind to her faults. And I don't think anyone would argue that she was not doing a particularly good job of dealing with life in the world in the years between her son's death, and that last disastrous trip to Florida. I don't think there was one of her friends who did not fear for her sanity and her health."

Chapter Sixty-two

Four years.

Mary stood by her window, looking out at the iron palings, the elm-shaded fragment of Union Avenue, where the carriage had passed. Just the sight of Myra's sturdy blue-clad form—of James's reassuring bulk—brought back to her how long it had been since she'd seen them.

Brought back the makeshift Rock Island depot, a shelter of crude lumber hastily erected amid the scorched ruins of downtown Chicago, visible like a blackened battlefield through the building's open sides. Brought back the stench of ashes, and memories that she could not put out of her mind.

How long she'd remained at Robert's house after the Fire, she no longer recalled. She thought it was several weeks.

Conditions weren't good in Chicago that autumn. Ninety thousand had lost their homes, and every surviving house was jammed. Boxcar-loads of food were being shipped in from all over the country but prices were sky-high. The city fathers in charge of such things ruled that the wealthy who had been left homeless be given first priority in the assignment of shelter, since the poor were more used to hardship.

Winter winds blew cold across Lake Michigan.

With nowhere in Chicago left to move to—and with Robert not about to offer continued residence under the same roof with himself and his still-in-Iowa bride—Mary wrote to Spiritualist friends in St. Charles, not far from Batavia, asking for recommendations of good boarding hotels near the Spiritualist congregation that was forming in that town.

Anything was better than the nightmare stench of smoke and ashes that still hung over Chicago's ruins.

The community of Spiritualists in St. Charles had welcomed her. In the flickering candlelight of their darkened parlors she had sought, again and again, to hear Tad's voice, or Lincoln's, or to catch a glimpse of Willie's glimmering form coming toward her out of the gloom with outstretched hands. But it seemed to her she had lost all capacity or desire to make friends with the living.

Thus, the next three years were years of travel: Boston, the resort spas of Wisconsin, upstate New York, where Spiritualism and so many other odd movements had their birth. For a time she went to Canada, to another Spiritualist camp on the edge of Lake St. Catherine. Tad's inheritance, equally divided with Robert, made it possible for her to hire a nurse-companion. She found these women for the most part as grasping, irresponsible, and impossible to deal with as she'd long ago found the Portuguese and Irish girls of Springfield, and she went through them almost as quickly. Though she had hated slavery, she found herself longing for the good-natured reliability of Mammy Sally or Granny Parker's old Prudence. . . . Were there no such people left in the world anymore?

Even when she had a companion to look after her, she was alone.

"I DON'T KNOW IF YOU CAN UNDERSTAND," SAID MYRA BRADWELL softly, "the . . . *familial* quality of the Spiritualists. Not the charlatans, or the fakes like that absurd 'spirit photographer' in Boston—the one who 'miraculously' produced a photograph of her with the ghostly shape of Mr. Lincoln standing behind her. She went to him incognito, but of course he'd seen a dozen likenesses of Mrs. Lincoln and knew her the moment she walked in his door. She bored everyone to distraction with the story of how Lincoln had projected his image on the photographic plate without the photographer knowing. Poor Mary. She had the maddening quality of never letting anyone's grief be more important or deeper than her own. . . ."

She frowned a little, her sharp hazel eyes losing some of their focus, as if she looked again, from her seat in the Patterson carriage, into the dim recesses of a parlor lit only by candle-flame. As if she listened for spectral knocks, or saw a name being spelled out, letter by letter, by a planchette.

Then she glanced up at John again and her eyes were bright.

"Everyone who comes to Spiritualism does so because they're in grief—a grief that's too deep for them to endure with the 'holy resignation' that unimaginative preachers recommend. So whatever her faults—

or theirs—Mary sought other people of like experience. To her—as to me—it was a blessing beyond compare, to be able to talk to others who have passed over that same terrible road."

John recalled the sweetly reasonable Olivia Hill, whose steadfast Spiritualism was accompanied by an equally steadfast conviction that a squadron of demons was invisibly pursuing her and had to be destroyed at all costs. Remembered, too, the framed picture garlanded with flowers in Lizabet Keckley's sitting-room.

He asked, "Do you really speak to the dead?"

Would Lucy hear, if I called her name?

Myra smiled thinly. "I think the real question is, Do I really believe that the dead have spoken to me? Is it less reasonable to speak to the dead than it is to speak to an invisible Entity which created everything which is? At least we know who the dead were. We know they existed, once upon a time. Yet people—mostly men—present company excepted, Judge—claim every day that the theoretical Architect of the Universe takes time off from wars and famines to give them specific instructions about how people should behave, on whom they should love and how they should dress if they wish to please Him.

"Yes," she said firmly. "To answer your question, Mr. Wilamet, I believe that my daughter Myra has communicated with me, both through rappings, and through the movement of a pen held in a medium's hand. I do not believe that *all* communications purported to be from her were in fact from her. I certainly don't believe some of the ghostly white figures drifting around the parlors of such gentlemen as Lord Colchester were anything but Colchester's confederates draped in cheesecloth washed in a dilute phosphorus solution. But then my faith that little Myra lives on the Other Side, and loves me, is stronger than poor Mary's. She wants so desperately to believe. And she had—has—nothing else."

Two women strolled by, artificial flowers bobbing on their stylish bonnets. They glanced idly at the carriage, and John knew he would have to deposit the Bradwells at the station and return to Bellevue soon. He wasn't sure, but he thought Patterson was asking a little too frequently about his dealings with Mrs. Lincoln, and not because the doctor was interested in the progress of her case.

"Do you mean to help her?" he asked.

"I mean to see her, if I can." Grimness glinted in Myra Bradwell's voice. "If, as I suspect, she's been railroaded into that place, as so many women are railroaded for being Spiritualists if they happen also to be inconvenient to their menfolks—yes, I mean to help her. But an insanity verdict cannot be overturned for a year in this state. It will do her little good to be released from one asylum if she's only going to return to her son's house and her son's care . . . though it would serve him right," she added with a half-smile, "if it comes to that. Would you be willing to go down to Springfield with me tomorrow, to consult with Mrs. Lincoln's sister Mrs. Edwards? To see if we can convince her to open her house to her sister, as she offered to some years ago?"

"My day off is Wednesday. But nobody will question it if I trade it for Friday. I'll go down with you then."

"Excellent. Thank you. Could you meet me at the Galena Depot at noon, or as soon after noon as there is a train from Batavia? They must have shopper's trains in the morning."

"I'll be there. As to your getting in to see Mrs. Lincoln, that may be more difficult. Mr. Lincoln has said many times that his mother must be kept from Spiritualists, since they only feed her mania, as he puts it. As you found out, he's arranged with Dr. Patterson—"

"Robert knows perfectly well that I was a friend of his father's while Robert was still a schoolboy—or nearly so." A combative light flickered in Myra's eye. "As for Dr. Patterson, he'll find I'm not easily gotten rid of with two cups of tea, a lecture on Moral Treatment, and a piece of yesterday's cake."

Chapter Sixty-three

Springfield July 1875

John Wilamet took the first train into Chicago that Friday morning, and by two in the afternoon was stepping off, with Mrs. Bradwell, in the depot in Springfield within a stone's throw of the handsome sandstone State House with its graceful dome.

Though he'd lived in Chicago for almost six years, John had never visited the state capital. After the insane scramble of people rushing through the lakeside city's streets, the jackhammer noise of the trains, the jostle of wagons, drays, carriages, the overwhelming stench of the yards, Springfield seemed rustic under the crushing summer heat. As they walked along Second Street toward the Edwards residence, the hotels and boardinghouses around the State House—hushed and half-deserted during the summer's Legislative recess—quickly gave way to handsome frame residences surrounded by gardens, where cats blinked sleepily from under hedges of jessamine and yew.

"Did Mr. Lincoln live in one of these houses?" He tried to picture the man he'd seen riding through the burned streets of Richmond—the tall form silhouetted in the evening moonlight on the steamboat's deck—walking these board sidewalks and mud-wallow crossings, as Mrs. Lincoln had described, a marketing-basket in his hand.

Myra Bradwell shook her head. "They lived over on Eighth Street. In a place much less fine than any of these—just a simple frame house. No better than most, though Mary did furnish it up fine. I'll take you by there and show it to you. It's still rented out, and getting shabby these days. Most of their furniture—and Mr. Lincoln's books—were up in

Chicago, at a museum I think, or some Exhibit Hall, and burned in the Fire. Mary told me when they first lived here you could walk a block from their house and be on the prairie. But it's much the same as it was."

Mrs. Ninian Edwards was taller than her sister and didn't resemble her in the slightest. With her long jaw and firm mouth, she more closely resembled Mary's descriptions of her fearsome Granny Parker. But about her clung the old-fashioned formality, the steely strength, of a Southern lady. And John found that like many Southern ladies, she was far friendlier toward him as a black man than women like Mrs. Patterson. The doctor's wife seemed to regard him as an archetypal Representative of his Race rather than an individual man.

If she believed in her heart—and she probably did—that he couldn't be trusted with certain tasks and was of a species wholly foreign to herself, at least Elizabeth Edwards was friendly, and believed him capable of being a doctor.

"I'm glad to hear she's doing better," she said, bringing in tea—for the three of them, a tribute to her fine-graded evaluation of social niceties. Had Myra not been there, John guessed, there would have been no tea. "I was most distressed when Robert wrote to me saying Mary's mind had broken down at last under the griefs she had suffered. And God knows, the sorrows she's seen would be enough to drive anyone raving mad. Your Dr. Patterson must be a very wise soul."

"He is," agreed John. He had spoken to Myra of Mary's misuse of medicines because he knew from years on the South Side that it was plain stupid to lie to your lawyer and because, as a professional, he trusted Myra Bradwell's professional ethics. But it wasn't anything Mrs. Edwards had to know. Even had he not been bound by his position of trust, Mary's shame and humiliation about being a habitual opium-taker would have been enough to keep him silent.

There was gossip enough about her.

"The problem is that now that she is better, Robert still wishes her to remain at Bellevue," said Myra. "I think you'll agree with me, Mrs. Edwards, that even if she wished to remain there—which she emphatically does not—a lunatic asylum is scarcely an appropriate place for a lady, however eccentric, of good family."

Elizabeth's breath blew out in a sigh and she made a gesture that in anyone less well-bred would have been a dramatic up-flinging of hands. "Precisely what I told Robert! My sister is—and always has been—an eccentric, particularly since poor Mr. Lincoln's death. But my nephew has never had the patience—or, I am sorry to say, the sympathy—to deal with her. All his life she has been an embarrassment to him, and when I heard of her incarceration the first thing that went through my mind was to wonder whether she had in truth crossed over the line into insanity, or whether Robert had convinced himself she had because he didn't want her to be out running about the world in a position to embarrass him still further by her antics. Particularly if he aspires to go into politics. But then of course I read in the newspaper that she had attempted to take her own life. There is no further danger of that now, is there?"

"No," said John. "But she is . . . most unhappy at Bellevue, deprived as she is of her liberty. As any sane person would be."

"It is a pity," interposed Myra, "that she felt herself unable to come and live with you here four years ago, where she would have the quiet and regularity of life that she needs."

Elizabeth sighed again, and shook her head. "I thought it was, though I confess . . . Have you ever tried to live under the same roof as my sister, Mrs. Bradwell?" The affection in her crooked smile—suddenly extraordinarily like Mary's—was mixed with wry wisdom and a lifetime of exasperation.

She went on, "But a few years ago was . . . not a good time for Mary to come to Springfield. I would have preferred to see her do so, but 1872 was the year that oaf Billy Herndon chose to publish *his* biography of Mr. Lincoln—as if the world needed another one—and Mary was incensed. And since my sister is seldom incensed quietly, there was the usual shrieking-contest in the newspapers, with accusations of drunkenness on one side and insanity on the other, and everyone taking sides—mostly taking Mr. Herndon's side, because of that ridiculous quarrel over the Monument. All the wartime scandals were raked into the open again, and after all was said and done Mary felt that she could not come to the only family that she has."

"Did you read Mr. Herndon's book?" asked John curiously.

"Read it? I was in it. Billy came here—sober, for once—and asked a great many impertinent questions about my sister and Mr. Lincoln. And while I'm delighted that someone finally pointed out to the nation that Mr. Lincoln put his pants on one leg at a time like everyone else, Billy does tend to take straws and make trees of them simply because he likes the look of trees.

"The true problem was, I think," she continued, "that both Billy and my sister want to be the Keeper of the Flame, the True Authority on the National Martyr. The one that everyone else has to come to. The same way they both wanted to be first in his affection while he lived. But while Billy wanted to portray Mr. Lincoln as a man among men, Mary wanted to purge out all those unpleasant human details that showed him to be less than incomparably perfect—and that, incidentally, might reflect badly on her. And really, when it came to Billy claiming that Lincoln's mother was illegitimate—which true or false is taking realism a little far—or that Lincoln was an Unbeliever, I can understand Mary's point, though I do believe berating him like a fishwife in public print was not the best way to deal with the problem.

"The shouting seems to have died down now, though." She set her teacup down with a precise click. "I think that were Mary to come live in Springfield, she could do so without undue animosity."

"WHAT DO YOU THINK?" ASKED MYRA, AS SHE AND JOHN TOOK THEIR seats once again in the train for Chicago late that afternoon. At no time was train travel in summertime enjoyable, for smoke and cinders blew in through the windows every time anyone opened them in an effort to mitigate the stifling heat, and the Illinois Central, like other lines, tended to relegate its oldest rolling stock to duty as "colored" cars. The hard wooden seats and battered paneling gave off a smell of ground-in dirt, tobacco smoke, and the sweetish reek of tobacco expectorate; the window-sashes were either broken or loosened and rattled like castanets with every jolt of the wheels; and the floors were clearly not swept as frequently as elsewhere on the train.

In the other seats, mothers hushed sleepy children, and men talked of prospects for work, in Springfield and points west, in quiet, beaten voices. Some glanced curiously at the well-dressed white woman in her striped summer skirts and parasol, but no one commented, and the boy who came through selling peanuts and bottled lemonade gave her a friendly grin when she bought some of his wares.

"About Sister Elizabeth? Allow me." John gestured Myra to put away her coin-purse, and handed the boy a silver quarter. The boy dug in his pocket for the nickel change from two bags of peanuts and two bottles of lemonade, and John waved it aside. With another smile the boy opened the bottles for them in a great fizz of carbonation, and went on his way wiping his hands on his apron.

"About Mary." Myra settled back on the scarred old seat. "In your opinion, is she well enough to be released into her sister's home?"

"Yes. Although whether Dr. Patterson would agree with me—"

"You leave Dr. Patterson to me." She sounded like a very businesslike knight referring to a very old and toothless dragon. "I must see her myself to be sure, of course, before I commit myself to any course of action.

Or are you one of those who believe that such matters are best judged by physicians?"

John was silent for a time, cradling the lemonade bottle in his gloved hands. Thinking about Mary Lincoln. About the fragile and melancholic Mrs. Hill. About women he'd known in Jacksonville, women who'd been put there years before by husbands or fathers who found them troublesome, sowers of discord, constantly angry for no reason that those husbands and fathers thought justified . . .

Slowly he said, "No. Dr. Patterson doesn't agree with the law in this state that a jury trial is necessary—he's been working for years to have it overturned, to permit commitment on the signatures of two physicians. But in my years of working with the insane, I've met far more than two physicians I wouldn't want as judges of *my* sanity. The more I deal with the insane—the more I realize I just don't know. I don't think anyone knows."

He fell quiet again, gazing out the window at the green-gold wheatfields streaming past the windows, baking in the lengthening light of the evening sun. Birds flew up along the track, their calls drowned by the hammering of the wheels.

Peace and silence and stillness. The "rest" that Patterson kept advocating for the women under his charge, because their "systems" could not take the stress and noise of the cities . . . much as, before the War, John had heard it argued by his master's friends that to free black men and women from the joys of sixteen-hours-a-day agricultural labor would be no kindness.

He remembered that Abraham Lincoln hadn't liked agricultural labor sixteen hours a day, either, and had gotten out of that business as quickly as he could.

And for none of them—neither himself, nor Mary, nor Mr. Lincoln—had there been any going back.

"Do you know"—Myra Bradwell's voice broke into his thoughts—"how the law in Illinois came to be made, that a woman had to be tried by a jury to be committed insane, rather than simply locked up on the testimony of her husband?"

"Because of Mrs. Elizabeth Packard," John answered. "When I worked at the state asylum in Jacksonville I met guards who'd known her."

At the time that the Reverend Theophilus Packard had had his wife kidnapped and locked away for disagreeing with his doctrine of the total depravity of mankind, John had still been picking tobacco-leaves and wondering what would happen to his mother and sisters if his master sold him to one of the slave-dealers going down to New Orleans.

"At least four physicians," said Myra, nodding, "testified that Mrs. Packard was insane, on such grounds as claiming to be older than her actual age, being an abolitionist, and refusing to shake hands with one of those examining doctors when he left. I read the transcripts. She was also a Spiritualist, and had the temerity to argue, in public, with her husband's religious opinions. It doesn't take much for a woman to be adjudged insane. Most doctors believe that women are more or less permanently insane anyway."

He opened his mouth to protest at this generalization and then closed it, remembering Dr. Patterson's strictures on women's mental and emotional derangements due to "the cycles of the female system"—i.e., menarche, menstruation, pregnancy, lactation, periods of sexual abstinence, menopause, and post-menopausal "drying of the womb." He'd wondered frequently what Mrs. Patterson thought of her husband's convictions.

Did she simply accept her husband's word as law, like a good wife should?

"Before the War," Myra went on, "like Mrs. Packard, I was an abolitionist. I broke with the mainstream of abolitionists when they decided to concentrate all their energies on freedom for the slaves, rather than freedom for *all* those whose lives and liberty can be disposed of at the whim of others. Though I rejoiced when Mr. Lincoln got up the courage and resolution—and the political timing, I might add—to liberate the slaves, I think that a great opportunity was missed. In many ways we're still trying to save a people, soul by soul. And in the course of the battle, I hear many of the same arguments. Only in this case the whole nation is what the South was—and every man is a slaveholder who fears the loss of what he."

The train rocked as it slewed around a curve. At the front of the car in which they sat a child cried, fretful in the heat. Its mother murmured, "We be home soon, Sugarbelle, I get you some water then. We got no money for lemonade."

John got to his feet, and walked down the narrow aisle, catching his balance on the ends of the seats. He handed the mother the half-bottle of warm lemonade. She looked up at him, torn between the pride that spurns charity, and her child's thirst: John said gravely, "I didn't spit in it or nuthin'," and she laughed, her child laughing with her.

"You say thank you to the nice man, Sugarbelle."

Sugarbelle hid her face in her mother's skirts, giggling.

When John returned to his seat he told Myra, "Dr. Patterson spends Saturdays in town, seeing clients—he has an office on Washington Street. He leaves on Friday afternoons. If you came by the last train on Friday,

I'd let you in. You could speak to Mrs. Lincoln in her room, or out in the rose garden without him watching over your shoulder."

Myra was silent for a time, her face unreadable, save for the look of dispassionate calculation in her eyes. Like Cassy, John thought, when his sister was figuring out how to get money or food for the family when there simply wasn't any money or food to be got. Then her attention seemed to return to the here and now, and she said, "Thank you, Mr. Wilamet. That should do very nicely."

"From there . . ." He shook his head. "Even if Mrs. Edwards were to invite her sister to come live with her, we still have to contend with Mr. Lincoln. As Mrs. Lincoln's legal conservator, he has the right to dictate what Dr. Patterson does. And Dr. Patterson will obey him—he needs every patient he can get at Bellevue these days."

"Does he?" Myra raised her eyebrows. "How many women are there?"

"About twenty. More than a quarter of the rooms at Bellevue are empty. It's been that way since the banks crashed in '73. Of the families who are wealthy enough to afford Patterson's prices, many more would sooner hire an attendant for Granny or Auntie and send her to Europe, rather than admit to society that a family member is in an asylum."

"Hmn." Myra sniffed, and sipped her lemonade. "Rather than admit to the parents of potential sons- and daughters-in-law that there's insanity in the family, I daresay." She held the bottle away from her as the train rocked. "Yet he's supposed to give excellent care."

"He does," agreed John. "But it isn't cheap. And I know he's recommended incarceration to more than one of the gentlemen who bring their wives to him for treatment for their nerves. He isn't venal," he added earnestly, seeing the calculating look return. "He would never recommend a treatment that he thought was harmful. But he's like my master, back at Blue Hill Plantation in Halifax County, Virginia, where I was born. He honestly believes that what he's doing *is* best. I think Mr. Robert Lincoln is the same way. That's hard to fight."

"Robert is certainly the same way," murmured Myra. "He spent a part of his childhood in the Todd family in Lexington, while his father was in Congress. I suspect he was always a bit of a Southern gentleman in his heart, one of the old-style Southern gentlemen who *knew* they were the lords of creation. And growing up in a fishbowl the way he did—it absolutely *blistered* him to have the newspapers call him the 'Prince of Rails'—he's always been excruciatingly sensitive about his mother's newspaper donnybrooks. But it doesn't give him the moral right to have her locked up, whatever his legal rights might be.

"Yes," she said briskly, "we're going to have to deal with Robert. But as for Dr. Patterson . . ."

She set her lemonade aside, and withdrew a newspaper from her satchel.

It was the Bloomington, Illinois, *Courier,* folded open in the middle.

MRS. LINCOLN
IS THE WIDOW OF PRESIDENT LINCOLN A PRISONER?
NO ONE ALLOWED TO SEE HER EXCEPT BY ORDER OF HER SON
AN ACCOUNT OF A REMARKABLE INTERVIEW WITH
HER JAILER AND PHYSICIAN

"As I said, Mr. Wilamet, you leave Dr. Patterson to me."

Chapter Sixty-four

Bellevue Place August 1875

"Springfield, 30 July, 1875

My dearest sister,

This afternoon Mrs. Bradwell was kind enough to pay me a visit, at which the subject of your health and happiness was discussed. . . ."

Mary set the letter down and sat for a time looking out the window of her room, scarcely seeing the emerald of the lawn, the pale gravel of the drive glaring in the brilliant sun. Sunday stillness blanketed Bellevue, and the thick scent of cut grass. Like a jewel, the note of the church-bell in town touched the morning air.

If Robert is agreeable, Ninian and I would be more than happy if you would come and make your home with us."

She drew a deep breath, feeling as if she had stepped into a torrent, was being swept off her feet. Carried away by feelings she could not separate or name.

She should, she knew, feel relief and gladness. Myra was fighting for her, taking steps to free her.

Why did she feel disappointment and rage?

Why did she suddenly smell again the honeysuckle of summer twilight, and hear the retreating creak of Jimmy Shields's buggy-wheels along Second Street, and the quiet rustle of Merce's lavender muslin skirts? "They just want you to be happy," Merce said. "We can't stay forever in our fathers' houses."

Our fathers die. Handsome Robert Todd, and the lover, the husband, the friend I called Father. They abandon us. Can't we stay in our own houses?

Her eyes burned with tears as she thought of the brick-fronted house on West Washington Street, that she'd so briefly lived in but had not been able to keep up . . . *thanks to that lover, husband, friend being bone stupid enough not to make a proper will!*

I had the chance to live in my own house—my own place—for four years after Taddie's death, she thought.

And what did I do instead?

She squeezed her eyes tight, the tears sliding down her cheeks, and pressed her hand to her mouth as the final nightmare rose to her mind.

SHE RETURNED TO CHICAGO IN THE FALL OF 1873, NOT BECAUSE SHE wanted to, but because she could think of nowhere else to go.

In the first weeks after the Fire, businesses had reopened amid black mountains of charred brick in downtown Chicago while other areas of the town still smoldered. Within months of the fire, handsome structures of steel-reinforced stone went up along the great avenues. Houses were rebuilt on the lakeshore for the rich. Beyond the packing-yards, stock-pens, and railroad yards, miles of tiny cottages of wood and brick were built for the workingmen flooding into the city from the East. From a distance, in Waukesha and St. Charles and St. Catherine, she had read in the newspapers and in letters from Robert and Myra of how the city was leaping back from its ashes like a vulgar phoenix.

It was two years before she could bring herself to return.

Nightly, in her room in the new Grand Pacific Hotel, she would wake in panic, thinking she smelled smoke. Would rush to the window, heart hammering, fearing to see the wall of fire advancing, men and women fleeing before it like deer from a forest fire . . . A man on the sidewalk with his head bashed in. A drunkard hurling liquor on a young girl's flaming hair.

In her dreams she would be standing again in the black waters of Lake Michigan with the crowding, sobbing damned, watched the flames advance. In her dreams the waters rose over their heads, and burned like oil with the flame advancing across them, to destroy them all.

But Robert was in Chicago. Robert, her only living son, her only link now with the life that she'd lived. The only proof that she'd been loved.

Robert was Lincoln's son; Robert had played in the big garden of the house on Lexington's Main Street, with Alec and Emilie, with Sam and David. Robert was all that was left to her of those days.

She visited him when she felt well enough, though the sight of Lake Park and the streets around his house filled her with panic that was not lessened by her knowledge that it was unreasonable. Young Mary was "out with friends" when Mary called, more often than not. Robert refused to speak of her, or to answer the probing questions she asked about her daughter-in-law's housekeeping and child-raising habits.

But the servants, she guessed, looking around the neat, plain parlor, weren't being kept up properly at their work. And five-year-old Mamie, though perfectly dressed and exquisite as a tiny princess, seemed to her to be growing more timid by the day.

"She isn't treating that child rightly!" she stormed at Robert one Sunday afternoon, when his daughter burst into tears at spilling the sugar. "She's punishing her too harshly, isn't she? I daresay she slaps her for a trifling thing like that. Now, dearest, there's no need to cry, it's only a little sugar. . . ."

It was, in fact, about a half cup of sugar spilled into the blue-and-yellow Wilton carpet, and Mamie ground her small pink fists into her eyes and rushed from the room in confusion. Robert said, "It is not my habit to interfere in my wife's sphere, Mother, be the question one of servants or one concerning my daughter. Mary has shown herself to be a loving and willing helpmeet—"

"How would you know that?" demanded Mary, stung. "If you spend all your days in your precious law offices and the courts, how would you know the first thing about what happens under your roof? That poor child isn't getting enough to eat and clearly is being mistreated, and I have a good mind to come here some day when your precious Mary is 'out with friends' and take her away with me! I daresay your wife would scarcely miss the child until it came time to put her to bed and maybe not then!"

Mary spent that night—and the remainder of the week—so sick with migraine that Robert sent a doctor to see her. Throughout the wretched Chicago winter Mary was ill, lying in the darkness of her curtained room with her head feeling as if the mad Indian shaman who ruled her headaches were trying to twist the bones of her skull apart. Her back and shoulder throbbed where the long-ago carriage-accident on the day of Gettysburg had jammed and wrenched the nerves. Some days she would leave the room only to go to the pharmacy for medicine, or down the hallway to the toilets, a dozen times in the day and again and again in the night, peering furtively through a crack in the door until the hall was clear, then darting along in her wrapper and shawl, her long graying hair lying like a heavy cloak over her back.

Outside, the winds screamed across Lake Michigan in unbroken fury straight down from the wastes of Canada. In her room the stuffiness of the gas heater, the stink of the fishtail burners, made her head hurt worse. She spent her days dreaming on the sofa in wrapper and shawl, surrounded by newspapers and magazines, sending for her meals to be brought up to her and bribing the maids to get her medication for her pain. She tried dozens of patented cordials, balms, and elixirs that winter, sometimes individually and sometimes mixed. It didn't seem to matter. She was aware of long spells of dizziness but many days she had little sense of being in her body at all.

The winter was one long, sickening blur.

Sometime during the spring—and the days, by this time, were mostly the same—she was roused by some small sound in the night to find herself on the sofa where she'd drifted off in the midst of reading *The Moonstone.* It was late in the night, and the hotel deathly silent; only the hissing of the gas jet broke the stillness, and its cold small flame gave the room a frozen air, as if it could be anytime, day or night, outside the shut velvet curtains.

Lincoln stood in the room, ghostly and blue, shining as Tad and Willie shone when they would come to see her. His eyes had the bruised and sleepless look they'd had toward the last days of the War, but his face was the face of an old man, gouged with the lines of an age he had not lived to achieve. His beard, which flowed down over his chest now, was nearly white, as was his hair. He looked exhausted, and infinitely sad.

He looks as he would look today, thought Mary, shocked. *Like the husband I would have today.*

Dear God, I have aged too!

Their eyes met, and she thought, *It has been nearly ten years.*

I am fifty-six, and in February I will be the same age that he was, when he was killed.

How the years have crucified us both!

She tried to say, *My darling,* but her tongue felt thick as wet cotton. Lincoln smiled at her, that old familiar smile that lighted up the whole of his tired face, and said, *I look forward to being with you again on the sixth of September,* a sentence from one of his letters, written to her when she was at her father's in Lexington, getting ready to rejoin him in Washington for his speaking-tour of New England.

Waking, she thought, *Dear God, are those truly the length of my days? Will we truly be together, at last, in the Summer Land, on that date?*

Did he really come to me, to tell me, warn me?

In a way, it was as if the whole of the year, from that spring night until September, she was waiting. Waiting for him to come for her.

In her dreams, she would picture that scene, herself laid out on her bed in a darkened room. Once she'd imagined Willie kneeling by her bed. Now she saw Robert and Mamie there, weeping bitterly (Young Mary was "out with friends" and good riddance to her). The shining doors would open in the dark of the gaslit room, and Mr. Lincoln would come in, with Willie and Tad—Tad so tall, carrying little Eddie on his hip—trailed by all the others, her father and Ben Helm and Granny Parker and that glowing, radiant woman whose face she remembered in the tiniest detail, her mother, as lovely as she had been. . . .

Robert would look up and see them and sob, "I see them! I see them! Oh, Mother, I was so wrong. . . ."

(Or maybe Mamie would see them first, point and cry out, "Papa, shining angels!" And *then* Robert would look. . . .)

Mr. Lincoln would hold out his hand and smile. "Mother, I've come to take you home."

And she would sit up, young and pretty again as the girl in the pink ruffled dress, who'd perched in Ninian's carriage in the Globe Tavern yard, looking around her with wrinkled nose at the dusty pig-infested streets of Springfield.

As if her body were preparing, she was ill much of the year. There were wars with Indians who refused to give up their lands, and struggles in the Army-occupied South against the corrupt administrators that imbecile Grant had seen fit to put in charge, but it mattered almost nothing to her. She read of the events with a vast sense of detachment.

I look forward to being with you again. . . .

But she did not die in September. She couldn't understand what went wrong. Mr. Lincoln couldn't have been mistaken. She sat up all night on the fateful eve, with the gaslights flickering in her little room at the Grand Pacific, wondering what Robert would say when Mr. Turner the hotel manager contacted him in the morning, brought him to her chamber (she'd paid the maids specially to have it tidied that day) to see her lying cold and still on her bed. . . .

It was a windy night, not the great terrifying thunderstorms that sent her shuddering under the bedclothes, but a dry howling gale that filled her with the dread that she would smell smoke upon the wind.

At dawn she poured herself a glassful of medicine and drank herself to sleep.

Winter was coming on.

She had nothing to live for, not even, it appeared, death.

Throughout the year of waiting, dread, and illness she had gone out so seldom, and seen so few people. There was a lively circle of Spiritualists in Chicago, including Myra Bradwell, but they lived mostly in the northwest suburbs, and Mary did not feel herself able to deal with a streetcar, and grudged the expense of a cab. But she had kept up a correspondence with her friends, and Ella Slapater in Pennsylvania wrote warmly recommending that she journey to Florida, rather than endure another winter of Lake Michigan's brutal snows.

"There is a woman named Delia Crane in Jacksonville, of true spiritual power, in whose parlor I was at last able to speak face-to-face with my beloved mother once again. . . ."

So Mary packed her trunks, put more trunks into storage in the Grand Pacific's basement—after detailed instructions to Mr. Turner about their safety in case of another major fire—and took the train to Florida.

Robert did not see her off.

He had intended to, but when he'd come up to her room to help her pack, he'd discovered one of the special petticoats she'd made for herself, with pockets sewn in them so that she could carry money and bonds.

"Dearest, you know you cannot trust servants in these places these days," she'd explained, to his expression of horror. "The only safe place is to carry one's money about one's person."

"Safe?" Robert was aghast. "You refuse to invest your money—where it would actually *be* safe—and you carry it around with you, where any scoundrel could take it. . . ."

"They don't know I have it." Her anger rose at the disapproval tightening her son's brow. "Honestly, they haven't a pair of magic spectacles to see through a woman's petticoats—I *hope*! And as for investing it, or putting it in a bank, one has only to read a newspaper to see what comes of *that*! You only want me to do so because *you* want to collect the interest . . . *and* to borrow it to invest in land yourself!"

He turned bright red. "That's the most absurd thing I've ever heard! I want you to invest it so you won't spend it on idiotic silver-mining stock like you did during the War!"

"It was not idiotic! Mr. Wikoff's advice was always good—"

"Mr. Wikoff was a scoundrel and a spy and the stock he got you to buy was trash! You should invest in land because it's safe and profitable—"

"You want me to invest in land because you want to inherit it when I die!" stormed Mary, and Robert stalked in silence from the room.

Thus she and her nurse-companion Catherine Foy took a cab for the station and boarded the train alone.

It was the first time she'd trodden Southern soil since she'd been driven in the carriage through the burned-out streets of Richmond, to sit in Varina Davis's parlor and watch Lizabet Keckley walk about the shambles of the Confederate Senate chamber. From Mrs. Tucker—the owner of the Stephenson House, where she had stayed in St. Catherine—she had heard much of the outrages and injustices of the occupying Union troops after the war (Mrs. Tucker and most of her guests being expatriate Confederates), but she saw little of this in Jacksonville.

In many ways it was as if the bloodshed which had so nearly torn the country apart had not touched the small town on the St. Johns estuary. The servants at Mrs. Stockton's boardinghouse were colored, well-trained, quiet-footed, and respectful, the kind of domestic help Mary had longed for in vain for years. She and Mrs. Foy took the steamer upriver to Green Cove's sulphur springs, where her arthritis improved with heat and mineral baths. For the first spring in several years she did not suffer from devastating headaches.

But Jacksonville, though certainly more pleasant in December than Chicago, was just as hollow, like a better-heated room of the same empty, echoing house. She spent a desolate Christmas with Mrs. Stockton's family—three War-widowed daughters and their teenaged children, who treated Mary like a beloved and eccentric aunt—and passed many days thereafter in the dimness of laudanum, chloral hydrate, migraines, and cloudy dreams. Mrs. Stockton seemed to understand.

"The voices you hear in your spells are the voices of the spirits, speaking beyond the Veil," she assured Mary, one March afternoon on the gallery when the two ladies took tea together. "I hear them often myself." She took a bottle of Indian Bitters from her reticule and poured a hefty dollop into her tea, following it up with three spoonfuls of sugar: she had, Mary well knew, female complaints as severe and agonizing as Mary's own.

Her black-clothed eldest daughter—who actually ran the boardinghouse—paused on the way back to the kitchen to cast a glance of patient exasperation at her mother, then went through the side door. Her husband, like Emilie's Ben, had died at Chickamauga Creek. A balmy breeze drifted in off the estuary, bringing with it the perfumes of salt-water and orange-blossom.

"Do you hear music also?" Mary remembered the séances at St. Catherine and the Spiritualist camps along the Fox River.

"Oh, dear, yes. The Colonel—my husband—used to play the fiddle, and often I'll hear it, coming from the bedroom door as I go up the stairs."

She spoke cheerfully, but Mary shivered. The voices that seemed to exude from the walls or the floor when she was having one of her spells had been angry voices, voices of malice, whispering of evil and death.

Spy, they said. *Hellcat. Limb of Satan. Liar.*

Perhaps it was the little bit of extra Cordial she drank at tea with Mrs. Stockton that brought them back that night, because as she lay awake in her room, staring at the amber pool of the night-light's tiny gleam, she heard them again.

Sometimes it was a hissing whisper. Sometimes merely a low mutter that she could almost make out—this she feared with all her heart, for it sounded like the muttering of the men in the hallway of that awful little house across from Ford's Theater on that terrible spring night. *Get that woman out of here. Who gets to tell her he's dead? Can we find some woman to take her back to the White House without a scene?*

Ten years ago. In two weeks it would be ten years exactly.

Desperately she sat up in bed and cried, "Tad! Taddie, darling, where are you?" And then, hopefully, praying the next moment that she'd see her middle son, her sweet-faced boy, her little champion, with his hands full of flowers from the White House conservatory, she called: "Willie?"

Were those two glowing shapes taking form there by the wall her cherished boys?

She saw their faces, their eyes and their hands, appearing and disappearing in a shining cloud. Saw their mouths forming words, their hands reaching out of the light toward her . . .

"Bobby," Willie said, his voice echoing Mary's own. "Bobby is lost. Bobby is lost. Bobby will die. . . ."

And she saw, as if through a window, Robert crossing his own tidy parlor back in Chicago. Saw him stop, cough, soundless as a dumb show, clutch at his chest, knees slowly buckling as he collapsed to the floor. Saw Mamie run in, shaking her father frantically by the shoulder, sobbing in wild terror, her mouth moving mutely, *Papa! Papa!*

Where Young Mary was—where the servants were (if there were any that week)—Mary didn't know. But she heard Tad saying, "Bobby will die. Bobby will die."

Bobby will die.

She screamed, *"No!"* and the dream exploded like shattering glass.

Mary wired frantic messages from the telegraph office in Jacksonville the following afternoon: *My belief is my son is ill telegraph me at once without a moments delay,* she scrawled, addressing her wire to Robert's new partner, Edward Isham. *On receipt of this I start for Chicago once your message is received.*

And also to Isham, with instructions to deliver it to Robert on his sickbed: *My dearly beloved son Robert T. Lincoln rouse yourself and live for my sake All I have is yours from this hour. I am praying every moment for your life to be spared to your mother.*

She spent the night feverishly packing. Mrs. Foy tried to talk her out of returning—"Sure, you'll get to the station to find word that Mr. Robert is flourishing"—but Mary shook her head.

"He will lie to me," she snapped. Her hands trembled with agitation and she fumbled the cap from a bottle—she didn't care which bottle. They were all the same. "And that scoundrel Isham will lie. They don't want me near my son. Isham is thick as thieves with that mealy-mouthed hussy. She wants to keep me away from my son, away from my granddaughter. . . ."

Upon reaching the train station she tore up unread the telegram that was waiting for her. It would only be Isham's lies.

Start for Chicago this evening hope you are better today you will have money on my arrival.

Anything, anything to get him to live. To keep him at her side.

All the way to Chicago, three endless, nerve-shattering days on the train, she thought, *If he leaves me, too, I shall die.*

Three days in a bone-shaking train car, her arthritis and neuralgia racking her like the Inquisition's den of torments. Three days of tension and terror feverishly reading newspapers and magazines without the slightest awareness of the words. Three nights of lying on her narrow bunk, waiting for Catherine's breathing to deepen so that she could slip one of her bottles of Godfrey's Cordial or chloral hydrate out of her bag or her petticoat pockets, to take the few extra mouthfuls that would give her blessed sleep.

Three nights of sitting beside Tad's chair in the Clifton House, listening to the agonized gasping of his breath.

Of sitting beside that immense rosewood bed in the White House, with its ostentatious hangings of purple and gold, looking down at Willie's still face.

Of lying on that stiff horsehair sofa in Petersen's parlor, hearing men's voices muttering in the hall . . .

Dear God, let him live! she prayed as the train jolted and shook her aching bones. *Dear God, let him live until I get there! Preserve his life. . . .*

But she knew too well that God never answered such prayers.

The train reached Chicago on a leaden evening. After Jacksonville's balmy warmth, the chill of the half-constructed train-station cut her flesh like a knife. She stumbled from the train car, catching Catherine's arm, shaky as a drunken woman.

After the peace of Jacksonville, the noise of Chicago was like being beaten with a thousand iron hammers, the stench—of smoke, of soot, of packing-yards, of horse-dung, of unwashed humanity streaming along the platform all around her—was like one of the lower circles of Hell.

"You have to fetch a cab," she gasped to the nurse. "Put the luggage into storage here. I must get to Robert's immediately. I'll worry about a hotel later—after we get to Robert's, I'll send you to the Grand Pacific to make arrangements. I pray I'm not too late. . . ."

Catherine turned her head in the direction of the waiting-rooms, at the end of the long gloomy platform. The gas-lamps made splodges of yellow in the thickening twilight; the figures crowding and pushing toward the train cars and away from them were also hellish, a confusion of smelly tweeds and crowding shoulders, demon-faces leering from shadow.

The sturdy Irishwoman said, "I don't think you need worry about being too late, Mrs. Lincoln."

Jostling his way through the crowds on the platform, in obviously flourishing good health, his face flushed with annoyance, was Robert.

Chapter Sixty-five

Bellevue Place August 1875

"I think from the moment I returned to Chicago in March," said Mary softly, "Robert intended to have me incarcerated as insane."

She reached across the short distance that separated her chair from the one John had filched from the hallway for Myra, and clasped Myra's gloved hands. Even through the shut curtains of her room, the sunlight leaked in brilliant bars. The house was hushed, for dinner was served in the afternoon on Fridays, with only a small cold supper at night, so that Dr. Patterson could have a good meal before getting on the Chicago train at four. Myra had come walking up the drive at just after four, only a few minutes after Mary had taken her post at the window to watch for her: Mary's heart had pounded so hard with relief, with joy, with apprehension that even now her friend would be turned away, that she'd had to sit down to still her trembling.

She was still trying to get her breath when John had knocked on the door, and shown Myra in.

She hadn't heard what he'd said to Amanda, in the next room with the communicating barred window, but before she had even dried the tears of relief that streamed from her eyes at the sight of Myra she had heard the attendant's footfalls whisper away down the corridor carpet.

John brought in the chair from Amanda's room, and sat quietly in a corner while Myra and Mary talked.

"John has told you, about . . . about how I slid into . . . *misuse* . . . of my medicines." She could scarcely get the words out. She couldn't think of a soul besides Myra to whom she would even mention the possibility of such behavior, much less confess to what it had caused her to do. "I didn't think he could possibly be right, but since I have followed the regimen that he outlined for me, I have not had a 'spell,' nor any of the . . . the *delusions* that plagued me so."

She broke off, biting her lips and feeling tears sting, and Myra squeezed her hands encouragingly.

"Nevertheless, I did sometimes have dreams—*long* before I began taking medicine—that foretold disaster. Mr. Lincoln had them, too. So when I dreamed that Robert was dying, it seemed to me . . ."

She shook her head. It was impossible to rid her mind of the stony-eyed fury and suspicion in her son's face under the harsh gloom of the station gaslight.

"Well," she said, "he wasn't dying. Then I believed for a time that the dream had presaged some terrible accident, and of course he would not listen to me. And I admit that I acted like a crazy woman. Much of it I don't even remember, so I must have been taking . . . well, a great deal more Cordial than was good for me.

"I obtained rooms again at the Grand Pacific, and Robert took one next to mine. But as usual, we quarreled—over my money, which he wanted to borrow to invest, and over my going about the city by myself, and over my shopping. Yes, I know I spend too much money, but I *never* pay full price for things anymore. . . . I will *only* buy after I have argued the shopkeepers down. And what harm does it do, to me or to anyone? Except of course to Robert, who views every trinket I buy as that much less he will inherit."

She heard the anger in her voice, felt the familiar deadly heat of it flush her face, and bit back the several other animadversions that rose to her lips about her only living son's determination to control her and her money.

Far easier to berate Robert, she thought, than to talk about the weeks she had spent, living in Chicago alone.

"I had . . . such terrible dreams. Dreams that the city was burning again. Dreams that Robert was planning to kill me for my money. I remember dreaming that he'd cut a door between his room and mine, and was going to creep in at midnight and smother me with pillows—I ran from the room into the hall, where he seized me. . . . I must have been sleepwalking, or still dazed from the dream, for I *did* scream that he was going to kill me, or at least he claims that I did. I—I may have. I honestly don't remember.

"He sent Dr. Danforth to visit me, and I remember almost nothing of the visit. He said—Dr. Danforth said—that I claimed that someone had tried to poison me at a train-station in Georgia on my way up from Florida. Again, I have no recollection of saying anything of the kind, but I do remember reading a story in a magazine—the *Saturday Evening Gazette,* I think it was—that involved the heroine being given poisoned coffee, and drinking a second cup in order to make herself sick enough to purge her system."

Her fingers tightened around Myra's, as if the sensibly gloved hands were a lifeline that would draw her from this deceptively sunny, quiet maelstrom of helplessness.

"Then Robert had me followed. He claimed it was because of the money I carried around with me in my petticoats, which he said would make me a target for robbers. But he gave the men instructions to make note of who I talked to, and who came to see me at my hotel. That tells me that his intention was not entirely disinterested, and that he was planning this for some time."

"They certainly must have told him what time you could generally be found in your room," commented Myra thoughtfully. "They were right on the spot when you returned from your shopping that morning, you know. And the judge—a busy man with schedules to keep—and jury were *waiting,* already empanelled, in a courtroom that was held ready. The witnesses all have to have been contacted at least a day in advance. It was nicely planned."

"I suspect that was Mr. Swett." Mary almost spit the name. "He never approved of me, not even when my dearest husband and protector was alive! I told Robert that I was planning to leave Chicago again, to go to California. He was horrified, of course, and forbade me to go, as if I was his child rather than a grown woman! But after he left the Grand Pacific and went back to live in his home again—we quarreled over my poor little Mamie, too, and how that dreadful mother of hers treats her!—I saw no reason to go on staying in that horrid room, with nothing to do day after day but visit the shops. Mr. Lincoln had spoken of going to California, and Mrs. Stockton in Jacksonville set me thinking of it again, telling me that it is a marvelously healthful climate, and now that the railroad runs there even a poor widow like myself can travel and live there safely."

"When was this?" asked Myra, and Mary shook her head.

"I don't remember. It was sometime after the first of May, because I know I wrote to Ella Slapater's cousin in San Francisco on the first. Robert urged me to go back to Springfield and live with Elizabeth—where he could keep an eye on me, I daresay."

She closed her eyes. All those quarrels—in the Grand Pacific's red plush lobby, in Robert's painfully neat parlor, in the kitchen of the house on Eighth and Jackson Streets back in Springfield—blurred into a single nightmare, of Robert's voice growing colder and colder. . . .

Only it wasn't Robert's voice. And it wasn't Robert, who drew away from her, who walked out of the room.

"And within ten days," said Myra thoughtfully, "you were locked up."

WHEN JOHN ESCORTED MYRA DOWNSTAIRS AN HOUR LATER, TO CONfer with Young Doc, Mary sat for a long time in the dimming twilight of her room.

Thinking about living again in Elizabeth's house.

Thinking about Robert.

Thinking about Lincoln.

All those quarrels with Robert, the cold reasonableness of his voice . . . she knew now why they triggered in her such rage.

He sounded exactly like Lincoln. The Lincoln she had screamed at, during those years of loneliness during the War. The Lincoln she had tried again and again to hurt, when he would shut her out, when he would meet her attempts to play her old part in his political life with such impenetrable evasiveness. He would listen to her spitfire rages, then walk away down the hall to his office, to fulfill a destiny in which she had no more place.

It had all come down to that: that he'd left her behind.

In a way, she realized, she'd known it even then. It was as if he saw further than she did, some larger plan beyond the day-to-day trading of influence and jobs that had been politics for her father and for every other man she'd ever known. As if he'd been looking down from above on a maze in which she wandered, only able to see a few feet before her. He'd gone ahead of her to where she could not follow. Had slipped from their earlier partnership, and abandoned her to the consolations of shopping and the gossip of her Blue Room salons.

In some corner of his heart he had to have known it, too, she thought. He was kind, but in his indulgence and care, had there been some element of guilt as well? Guilt that he had left her out, that he had run on ahead to become what he must be, leaving her to be what she was?

But at least, she thought, *he was kind. He cared for me, made sure—in the best way that he could—that I was all right.*

Does Robert tell himself that's what he's doing?

And now she would return to Springfield. To live again in Elizabeth's house. To walk on those streets once more, to pass by the market where she and her beloved had shopped for fish—with Lincoln stopping every three paces to talk to some crony . . . To be perpetually waiting to see him round some corner, straining to hear, in any crowded room, that crowing silvery laugh . . .

I can't do it!

To meet those other ghosts on every muddy street, on every dusty pathway in the countryside . . . on Ninian's porch . . .

Dapper Stephen Douglas, bowing as he handed her up into his buggy.

Intelligent, gentle Dr. Henry, listening in that perfect peaceful quiet by the fireside to anything she had to say. Returning from Washington only weeks after Lincoln's death, Dr. Henry's ship had gone down off the California coast. News of it had reached her during that first hellish summer in Chicago.

Simeon Francis's bright blue eyes peering over the tops of his spectacles in that freezing, ink-smelling newspaper office.

Edward Baker's chiming laugh.

Eddie's quick pattering footfalls across a kitchen floor . . . Willie emerging from between the rows of the vegetable garden, covered with mud and his hands filled with wildflowers . . . the look on Tad's face as he sat in the parlor window, watching for his father coming up the street.

I can't do it.

Does that mean you'd rather Myra didn't try to get you out?

That you'd rather live here in the land of the lotos-eaters forever?

She laid her head down on her crossed wrists on the windowsill, too tired even to weep.

Myra Bradwell spent the night in the watch-room adjoining Mary's, where Gretchen and Amanda generally took turns sleeping. Mrs. Patterson even had the cook send them up supper on a tray. John, lingering in the parlor while Myra talked to Young Doc in the office, had to marvel at the way the woman maneuvered the younger doctor, agreeing with everything he said, nodding and regarding him with an expression of awed respect that John hadn't believed her square, pleasant features capable of assuming.

"Of course poor Mary is insane," he overheard—Young Doc seldom shut the office door. "Good heavens, Doctor, I've known her since Mr. Lincoln was President, and I saw this coming for years. The improvement you and your father have wrought in her is absolutely marvelous. . . ."

John could only shake his head in amused wonder.

"Of course, I'm not sure that a lunatic asylum is the proper place for her, when she does have family to stay with. . . ."

"I would agree with you, Mrs. Bradwell"—Young Doc always started out by agreeing with everyone—"if Bellevue Place were indeed a lunatic asylum. But it is not. It is merely a haven for those whose nerves are distraught, as Mrs. Lincoln's most certainly are. . . ."

And it was still Robert, thought John, who was calling the tune.

Something told him that it would take more than entreaties from family and doubts concerning propriety, to gain that tall young lawyer's permission for his mother to leave Dr. Patterson's care.

At about ten the following morning, when Young Doc was starting his rounds, Myra Bradwell came downstairs—having breakfasted with Mary in her room—and sought John out in the rose garden. "Would you keep an eye on the front of the house after noon or twelve-thirty," she asked softly, with a watchful glance at Zeus and Gretchen, who were helping Minnie Judd to a comfortable seat on a bench in the sunshine. Miss Judd had woken in a sobbing fit last night, screaming out that she had committed the Unpardonable Sin and must be punished—she was still visibly woozy from the chloral hydrate that had finally quietened her into sleep.

"There's a young gentleman coming to visit Mrs. Lincoln, with whom I'll be working to secure her release. I would appreciate it if he could come in to confer with us both in quiet."

Lawyer, thought John immediately. Though Myra Bradwell was barred from practice herself—no woman being legally able to enter into independent contracts—after their first meeting he had found and read copies of the *Chicago Review of Law,* which she edited and published. She undoubtedly had at her beck and call a score of hopeful newcomers to the profession.

If not a lawyer, a tame doctor.

"I'll be waiting," he promised her.

When she returned a few hours later—from the train-station, presumably—he guessed the brisk young man in the tobacco-colored suit who accompanied her was a lawyer, rather than a doctor. He was far too flashy to engender confidence in a patient. She introduced him as Mr. Wilkie, and John guided them around the house to the small door of the family wing, then checked to make certain Mrs. Patterson was nowhere in sight before letting them in with his key.

Wilkie and Myra left together at about four. After seeing them to the end of the drive, John returned to Mary's room, and found her still sitting by the window, the curtains half-open, as if she had watched them pass across the yellow-gold triangle of visible gravel.

"Do you feel all right?"

When she glanced up at him her face answered his question. It was calmer and more relaxed than he had seen it, he thought, since her arrival three months ago. Her eyes had a perpetually bruised look, from sleeplessness and weeping, but within the puffy flesh it pleased him to see that they were alert, as they usually were these days.

"I am," she said, in her small, sweet voice. "Thank you for asking, John. You seem to be the only one these days who's genuinely concerned about what my answer to that question might be. You and Myra, and Myra—well, once she sees a solution to a problem she goes at it like a bull at a gate, and doesn't ask what one feels about it, so long as it gets done."

On the corner of her dressing-table he saw the pages of Mrs. Edwards's letter from Springfield, and a half-dozen sheets, scribbled and crossed out, in Mary's erratic hand.

"You'd best not let Gretchen find those in your room and tell Mrs. Patterson that you have pen and ink," he warned. "I'll keep them in my room for you, if you'd like." And seeing her mouth pucker with weary anger at being always observed, always forbidden, like a schoolgirl, he added, "Or I'll help you pry up a floorboard under the bed, like prisoners do. You can wait till Amanda goes down the hall to the toilet, then whip out your pen and write a few lines. . . ."

And her puffy face broke into its sidelong smile. Leaning close, she whispered, "Amanda *never* goes to the toilet. Nights when I lie awake, I can hear every sound. . . . I believe the woman is made of iron. Or is solid all the way through, like a carrot. . . . Dear God, what it is, to laugh again!" she added, as John gathered up the scribbled sheets, corked the ink-bottle securely, and slipped it into his pocket. "I don't think I've had a laugh since . . . since my friend Sally Orne came to stay with me at that *dreadful* little hostelry in Germany, and we kept every other traveler on our floor awake all night with our giggling and carrying-on!"

"I take it the interview with Mr. Wilkie went well?"

Mary hesitated, the joy wiped from her face, her tired eyes filling with tears once more. "Do you know, I dare not even think about it? That *equal poise of hope and fear* that Milton speaks of . . . it all seems so . . . so hopeless. And yet I cannot give up hope. I *will* not give up hope. I will *banish squint suspicion*. . . ." She fished in her drawer for a clean handkerchief. Every one had black borders an inch deep.

"Will you walk with me a little in the garden, Mr. Wilamet? It has been a long and tiring day."

IT WAS ALMOST A WEEK BEFORE MARY WROTE BACK TO ELIZABETH. During the scorching, humid August days, as John assisted Dr. Patterson or Young Doc with Mrs. Wheeler's hydrotherapy or in force-feeding Miss Judd, he overheard the comments of Mrs. Patterson: comments that sounded less and less like the observation of symptoms and more and more like backstairs tale-telling.

Mrs. Lincoln ordered cornbread again for breakfast and then refused to eat it. Mrs. Lincoln asked for the carriage to be brought around and then delayed for three hours, ultimately deciding to spend the day in her room. Mrs. Lincoln had her room changed back to the first floor and then complained about having a different set of bedsprings, even though the new ones were of the same pattern as the old....

When he saw her during those days, to walk in the gardens or to talk in the parlor, he read the nervousness that lay behind her capriciousness, the tension that brought on headaches, the recurring waves of hope and fear.

She spoke to him many times about Springfield: about having been sent there by her stepmother, "in the hopes I'd land a husband and wouldn't be on her hands for the rest of my life, God forbid!" About what the town had been like in the 1830s and '40s, with muddy streets and a hog-wallow the size of a small lake occupying one corner of the State House grounds, and the green prairies blanketed with flowers, two blocks' walk from the little brown house on the corner of Eighth Street and Jackson. About buggy-rides in the countryside with one or another of her many beaux, and picnics in the shade along the Sangamon River; about political-speakings in the State House square and the crying of crickets in the long blue twilights, when she'd sit on the porch with Merce Levering or Julia Jayne and chat about friends or fashion or politics when politics was still a game....

"I never thought I would have to go back to living under Ninian's roof."

On Wednesday John took the train to Chicago, melting and stinking and scorching on the shores of the lake. Most of Cassy's customers had gone out of town, leaving the family broke but with a little breathing-room. By dint of burying small sums of money under the floor the way they used to as children in the quarters at Blue Hill, Cassy had saved enough for a family picnic on the lakeshore, and for once everything went well.

His mother was feeling well, and when washed and dressed and with her hair put up was still the wildly beautiful woman he had worshiped as a child. She talked and laughed and made jokes that had the children whooping with delight, and joined them in their hunt for fireflies in the bushes of Lincoln Park as the sun went down. He watched them from the bench where he sat with his arm around Clarice, loving the touch of his wife, the scent of her flesh and her hair, glad to be alive.

When times were bad they were bad, he reflected, smiling at Selina as she sat with baby Cora on her blanket, weaving a chain of daisies from the grass. But when times were good, there was nothing sweeter than these long summer twilights, other loving couples walking along the path in the park, the tall bronze shape of Lincoln's statue standing against the luminous cobalt sky.

Robert Lincoln came to Bellevue Friday morning, rigid with outrage. Though John was fully occupied with Mrs. Wheeler—who had spent the night screaming and pounding on the walls of her room, and had had to be sedated and, in the morning, forcibly gotten up and walked in the gardens to restore her "vital system"—he caught snatches of the lawyer's furious voice through the open windows:

". . . the woman is a pest and a nuisance, the queen of a gang of Spiritualists, whatever you might say! I've warned Aunt Elizabeth against her—and against whatever henchmen she may choose to employ in this self-serving campaign to give you back control of your money!"

And later, as John guided the still-groggy and weeping Mrs. Wheeler through the hall to her own room again,

"Mother, I've gone to considerable trouble to find you a place where you will be safe, happy, and well taken care of! Now, thanks to your table-tapping friend, Dr. Patterson is in a panic, terrified of what bad publicity will do to this entire establishment . . . !"

"Well, God forbid that the jail where I have been locked in by my own child—where other women are locked up as well!—should have *bad publicity*! Oh, get me my smelling salts lest I faint with chagrin!" Mary's voice was shrill with sarcasm.

And when John emerged from Mrs. Wheeler's room after turning her over to Gretchen, Zeus passed him in the hallway and whispered, "Mr. Lincoln's gone to talk to Dr. Patterson. He don't look like a happy man."

Robert Lincoln was just coming out of Patterson's office when John came down the stairs to the parlor—Mrs. Lincoln was nowhere in sight. Through clenched teeth, Robert said, "I quite understand your position, Dr. Patterson, but please consider mine. In spite of appearances my mother is *not* competent to live on her own, at my Aunt Elizabeth's house or anywhere else! You can have no idea how difficult it is, to deal with someone who is insane in one area and appears normal in other respects. . . ."

"I can," replied Patterson drily, "and believe me, Mr. Lincoln, I do. I have been in touch with the Bradwell woman this week, too—all these Spiritualist harpies are alike!—but I am in an extremely difficult position, both financially and, to be frank, legally. Laymen who have no understanding of the workings of the deranged mind and the feminine nervous system are more a nuisance than anything else, for all they see are the rights of the sane and the normal. But those, unfortunately, are the laws that bind us!"

"Please," begged Robert. "Please do not do anything until you hear from me. This matter will be straightened out—it *must* be straightened out. The thought of my mother rambling about at large with the whole of her fortune stuffed into pockets in her petticoats—going off to California or God knows where to get into God knows what kind of scandal . . . ! Though trying to convince any of the Bradwell woman's gang of Spiritualists of anything may well be beyond any *man's* abilities. But I will try."

Patterson saw him to the door and paused, turning back, as he glimpsed John passing through the parlor. "John," he said, "I want a word with you." And to Robert, holding the door, "If they threaten to publish, there is not much that I can do."

"What you can do," replied Robert, "is get anything—anything at all—to support a diagnosis of continued insanity in my mother. We both know she is insane. What more do we need? It is, after all, for her own good."

And he strode down the brick steps, to where his cab stood in the graveled circle of the drive.

Patterson turned back, and stood for a moment, regarding John with tired and angry eyes.

Without a word being spoken, John felt his heart sink and turn cold.

"Mrs. Patterson informs me, John, that you were the one who admitted Mrs. Bradwell's friend Mr. Wilkie to the house last week, in my absence, to visit Mrs. Lincoln."

"Yes, sir." He wondered who Mrs. Patterson had heard it from.

"Did you inquire who Mr. Wilkie was?"

"No, sir. Mrs. Bradwell said he was a friend of Mrs. Lincoln's."

"She was lying," said Patterson quietly. "Something she does rather readily." In his mind John heard Mary's voice: *Myra . . . Well, once she sees a solution to a problem she goes at it like a bull at a gate, and doesn't ask what one feels about it, so long as it gets done.*

And Myra's voice, as she handed him the newspaper on the train: *You leave Dr. Patterson to me.*

No, he thought, seeing what was coming.

No.

It was as if he stood in a burning house, looking up and watching the ceiling collapsing down upon him in an avalanche of flaming debris.

"Mr. Franc Wilkie is a reporter for the Chicago *Times,*" said Patterson. He drew a deep breath. "I know you and I haven't agreed on the diagnosis of Mrs. Lincoln, John. And I have made countless allowances for your lesser experience and for the flaws in your education, as well as, perhaps, your prejudice concerning the widow of the Great Emancipator. But I did trust that you would be professional enough to consult with me, rather than taking matters into your own hands. I am very sorry that I am going to have to dismiss you."

Chapter Sixty-six

Chicago August 1875

All the way back to Chicago, John kept thinking: *What am I doing going back so soon? I just rode this train. . . .*

He felt numb with shock, as if he'd offered his hand to help a child who'd fallen on the street, and the helpless tot had produced an ax and chopped off his arm.

Not just the pain of betrayal—the question of how he was going to get through life missing an arm.

He'd have to tell Clarice.

He'd have to tell Cassy.

He could just hear his sister's scathing voice: *You lost your job over helping a white woman? A crazy woman? If you gonna lose your job helping a crazy woman, how come you don't help Mama?*

The fact that Mary Todd Lincoln was Abraham Lincoln's widow wouldn't cut any ice with Cassy. And in fact, John had not helped Mrs. Lincoln with any thought in mind that assisting her toward liberty was in any sense a payment for his own freedom.

She was eccentric, and in need of help, which he had given her as far as he was able. But once she ceased being delusional—and had apparently learned to control the cause of her delusions, at least for the time being—she did not deserve to be locked up simply so that Robert Lincoln would not be embarrassed.

John leaned his head sideways against the jolting wooden wall of the "colored" car, and stared out at the yellow wheat-fields streaming by under black-floored mountains of gathering clouds.

Would he have helped Mary Lincoln if he'd known that assistance was going to cost him, not only the job that supported his family, but the career toward which he'd striven the whole of his adult life?

He didn't know.

Myra Bradwell.

He closed his eyes, and felt the anger rise through him, like pain coming on as the numbness passed away.

A reporter. The man she'd brought in was a Goddamned reporter. And it had never even occurred to her to ask John what the repercussions of that would be.

Even in his fury and despair, he had to admire the cleverness of the maneuver. It completely circumvented the issue of whether Robert Lincoln would give permission for his mother's release or not. Dr. Patterson couldn't afford bad publicity—he was in financial trouble already. When the "Mary Lincoln Is a Prisoner" article came out—and it would undoubtedly contain the words *habeas corpus* somewhere in its text—all those other families who were keeping their female relatives in Bellevue would begin to pull *them* out, too. Sooner than see that, Patterson would shove Mary Lincoln out the door, and at that point Robert would dare not put her elsewhere . . . not unless he wanted to learn the *real* meaning of public embarrassment.

Oh, oops, we happened to squish a Negro in the process, but at least Mrs. Lincoln is free! Hip hip hooray!

Sorry about your job, and your career, and all. . . .

Even a white attendant guilty of that kind of betrayal couldn't hope to find another position of trust, much less a patron willing to teach him. But a white man would at least have the option of seeking a post as a guard—if he really wanted to go on working with the insane—or of going west and looking for work in California or Oregon, far away from the close-knit circles of the Association of Medical Superintendents of American Institutions for the Insane.

A white man could usually get another white man to at least listen to him when he said, "I didn't know. I'll never do it again. . . ."

His salary of sixty dollars a month, joined to what Lionel made in the stockyards and the income from Cassy's laundry business, was barely enough to make the rent on the house, buy firewood and soap for the laundry, and feed the dozen-plus members of the household. He knew a white man would be paid far more—a railroad porter would make more—but he had looked on the work as the road to better things.

And now there was nothing.

He debarked from the local train at the Twelfth Street station and for a time simply stood on the platform, the hot reek of the city beating on him, crushing him. For two years now the knowledge that he could go back to the green quiet of Batavia had sustained him every time he walked east toward the hellhole streets between tracks and packing-yards.

Now he could not face the thought.

For the first time since he'd left the Army he thought, *I really need a drink.*

Walking into the wrong neighborhood grog-shop, of course, could get you killed, if you were Irish or black or Hungarian or whatever the local regulars were not. But he knew there were saloons all along State Street near the levee and the yards where they didn't care if you were black or white, male or female, human or a pig escaped from the stock-pens, provided you had money to pay for your liquor, and one of these was Flossie's.

Flossie's was a three-story brick building rammed in between two other three-story brick buildings in the block called Coon Hollow. Flossie herself, a blowzy harridan who'd run a parlor-house in New Orleans during the War and a string of brothels in Mobile immediately afterwards, kept a bordello on the upper floors and, according to Lionel, owned the panel-house next door where the customers were robbed systematically rather than intermittently. Flossie's barroom was long, dark, and nearly empty at this time of the day—four in the afternoon—furnished with rough tables and chairs at which gamblers plied their trade in the evenings.

He bought a whiskey from the slatternly waiter-girl behind the bar and then another, and retreated to the dimness to think about what he was going to say to Clarice.

What he was going to say to Cassy.

At this time of the day, it was mostly the sneak-thieves and pickpockets of the levee, the strong-arm men who made their living selling "protection" to local shopkeepers, the whores from upstairs jolting down preliminary drinks to get them through their first few johns of the evening. A man came in with two girls—the man dark-skinned but with the features of an Italian or a Spaniard, the girls white and barely pubescent—and the waiter-girl behind the bar said, "You better vamoose, Dago; you know better than to bring those little chickabiddies in here."

"You jealous they'll take your customers?" sneered the pimp. "Wouldn't be hard. Give us a couple toots of shock for the girls, and a whiskey for me, and I mean *all* whiskey, not that camphor shit you dole out to the niggers."

John settled back against the wall—after a preliminary check to make sure there wasn't anything walking up it just then—and cradled the faintly camphor-smelling whiskey between his palms. He knew what they cut liquor with in places like this and didn't much care. Griffe

Moissant's booze would be the same, closer to home, and there'd be the chance of walking into Lionel there or, God forbid, Phoebe.

He closed his eyes, listening to the voices. So many of them with the smoky inflection of the South: Missouri, Mississippi, Louisiana. So many men, like himself, like Lionel, who'd come north looking for something other than sharecropping the land they'd once worked on as slaves, and more coming in every day.

And finding nothing. Since the banks had collapsed two years ago a man was lucky to have a job sweeping blood off the killing-floors into drains. And those jobs, he knew, went to those who knew people in the yards already. As the voices drifted to him in the saloon's gloom he heard those of men coming in after hunting work, or laboring a few hours stacking lumber or slapping pork in cans amid clouds of steam and pounding machines that could take off a hand or a finger if you blinked. . . .

More men, who hadn't even found that.

"I hear Mushmouth lookin' for a couple boys to help him knock off a big place out by Douglas Park." John glanced up as the voices passed his table, a couple of laborers listening to a dapper weaselly man whom Cassy had pointed out to him once as an enforcer for one of the protection bosses. "You boys lookin' for a few dollars?"

And later—how much later he wasn't sure—he overheard someone say, "Three dollars a day, they askin'! Three dollars to stay on that corner, without them runnin' me off . . . Some days I don't shine three dollars' worth o' shoes!" The man who was speaking looked at least seventy years old. John wondered how much he had to pay for rent on top of that three dollars, and if he had a family to support.

Get used to it, he thought, his eyes going to the men crowding around the bar as their shift ended at the yards, or slumped morosely on the benches around the room. Three card-games were in progress, run by slick-looking men in flashy suits with diamonds on their stickpins and fingers. In the back room, the click of billiard-balls could be heard, and men's voices, loud with anger and drink.

This is your world now, the only world you're going to have. Luck gave you a single open door, and you let that chance slip away.

Because you pitied a woman who treated you like a human being when no one else did—and because you trusted her friend.

Despair brought the taste of bile to his mouth, and the metallic nastiness of whatever the waiter-girl had given him.

This place, and the house, with Cassy and Mama and all the children, and the stench at the back of the yards. These would be the limits of his experience. And of Cora's, too, when she grew up.

He knew he was getting very drunk, but couldn't remember why he should care. Like Mrs. Lincoln, he had nowhere that day to go. He could smell the stockyards from here, and hear the constant, clanging roar of the trains as they rolled through not three blocks away.

Already it seemed to him that everything he'd gone through and worked for since the War's end was dissolving like a coat of cheap whitewash in the pouring rain of reality.

This was the world into which he had been freed.

The world in which he'd believed that it was possible to make a life for himself.

I was the insane one, he thought.

Dago the Pimp was back, with another girl this time. She couldn't have been as old as Selina, and her round, scared, pretty face reminded him heartrendingly of his sister Lucy—before Lucy had taken to drinking and whoring. One of Flossie's strong-arm men went over to talk to Dago, shoving him. The girl clung close to him, staring around her in desperation, and one of the yard-men went over to her in his shirt and pants all gummed with dirt and dried blood, and pinched her shallow breasts as he talked to her.

It was as if John watched someone else lurch to his feet. One of Flossie's girls intercepted him: "Ain't seen you 'round here before, Handsome." She was "bright," as the white men said. Her hair had been straightened with lye and dyed vivid red and her dress was cut away nearly to the nipples. She was fleshy, like a light-brown satin pillow.

"Excuse me," he said politely, and stepped around her. He caught the blood-caked slaughterer by the wrist and heard himself say, "You old enough to be that poor little girl's daddy. You should be ashamed."

The man turned around, baring broken teeth at him. Dago broke off his argument with the house strong-arm and said, "Now, my friend, that little girl knows more about pleasin' a man than any ten other nymphs of the pavement, and she'll be more than happy to prove it to the both of you." He seized her arm so that his fingers dug into the tender skin. "Won't you, sugar?"

"You get the fuck out of here, Dago, and take your whore with you!" screamed the red-haired girl who'd followed John from his table. "Or I'll tell Flossie!"

"You can stick Flossie up your—"

The red-haired whore snatched a bottle off the bar, smashed it on the bar's edge, and slashed at Dago. Dago's little nymph screamed, and the next second, it seemed, the barroom erupted into violence. Someone—John was never sure who—grabbed him and hurled him back against the bar, the edge gouged his back. The young girl screamed again and John lunged to drag her out of the sudden morass of struggling limbs and slashing glass and steel that had churned into life in the cavelike semidarkness.

Something struck him and he fell, rolling, his old instincts kicking in. He tucked to protect his belly and face as a boot smashed into his ribs, and another caught him glancing on the side of the head. He smelled fresh blood and spilled beer and someone tripped over him, even in the corner against the bar into which he'd rolled. There was shouting and a man bellowed, "Oh my God, oh my God . . . !" the way he'd heard men shriek when they brought them into the hospital tents with their intestines dangling. Then shock caught up with him and he felt himself sinking, colder and colder, down into the earth, to come out chilled to the bone, and aching all over into sudden quiet, near-darkness, and the stink of blood.

John started to sit up and, as it had in the tent at Camp Barker years before, nausea seized him and he rolled over fast, choking as vomit spewed from his lips. A thick Irish voice said, "What d'we got here, Sleepin' Beauty?" and men laughed.

One of the dark shapes in the now nearly empty barroom reached him in two strides—blue-clothed, like the Union soldier all those years ago, with a nightstick instead of a rifle in his hands. John raised his hands to show them empty and the policeman struck him, casually and with full force, slamming him back to the floor and sending lancing agony through his right arm.

The next moment his hands were jerked behind him, and the pain blacked out his mind. When he came to, he was lying with his cheek in a puddle of beer-diluted vomit, handcuffed and looking at the three policemen gathered around the two bodies in the middle of the floor. A woman was talking, shrill and furious—

"—I pay my money to the stationhouse and this sure as hell isn't the kind of service I expect—"

It wasn't until one of the cops dragged the bodies closer to the single gaslight still burning near the bar that John recognized Dago the Pimp, with his throat cut from ear to ear and his whole flashy green suit a single black wash of gore.

The other body was that of his little whore.

HE WAS TAKEN TO THE TWENTY-SECOND PRECINCT HOUSE ON Maxwell Street, and in the morning—night had somehow fallen while he had mused in his camphorene-induced haze and the fight had taken place at close to eleven—was taken to the jail of the Cook County Courthouse on Clark Street, and indicted for murder.

And passed a week in Hell.

He'd had a little money in his pockets when he'd risen from his table at Flossie's, but there was none there when he was arrested. His watch, hat, and jacket had vanished, too. One of the men in the jail-cell with him was a thick-shouldered angry laborer named Klauswijz who knocked John's head against the brick wall and took the meager plate of food he was given—the other men simply moved aside and watched—and thereafter stole food from him whenever it was brought. Anyone with any connection to the protection gangs or gambling bosses had, naturally, been bailed out on the night of their arrest, so the cells were populated by the pettiest of independent criminals, smash-and-grab thieves or thugs for hire, too mentally deficient or too far gone in drink or drugs to be of use to anyone: angry, sullen, violent.

One of the men in the cell turned out to be a cousin of Dago the Pimp. John kept very, very quiet about why he was there.

It seemed to him that he never slept that first week. There were four bunks and eight men in the cell—two men slept on the floor in spite of the roaches and the rats. John sat in the corner near the latrine bucket with his arms folded around him and simply tried not to speak to or look at anyone; thirsty, nodding with exhaustion, legs and arms cramping from days of inactivity, his right wrist puffed up and hurting so that the pain sometimes made him faint.

"They won't even expect me at home till Wednesday," he whispered one night, half-delirious, to Bailey, one of the two other black men in the cell, a scared and rather simple-minded youth who divided his share of the water with him after Klauswijz snatched his away again. "I could be hanged by then."

"Don't break yourself into a dew of sweat about that, boy-o," remarked a wizened Irish drunkard who'd taken over one of the upper bunks. "They're not gonna get 'round to tryin' the likes of you for weeks. . . . You kill a nigger or a white?"

"I didn't kill anyone," whispered John.

The Irishman crowed with laughter. "Sure, and neither did I!" There was dried blood caked all over his shirt.

By the following Friday morning John would have been willing to be tried and convicted if only for the chance to get out of the cell and walk. When the guard came to the bars and said, "Wilamet? Somebody here to see you," he nearly fell, his legs and body were so cramped and his mind so hazy with exhaustion and hunger.

Cassy was waiting for him in that long room where prisoners were brought, always supposing there was anyone on earth who wanted to see them. John had been there more than once, when he and Cassy had gone to bail out their mother. There was a table and some broken-down benches. The Courthouse was barely four years old—rebuilt after the Fire like everything else in this part of town—but already the visiting-room had the soiled drabness of hard use and neglect, the smells of dirty clothing and dirty flesh, expectorated tobacco, and cigar-smoke.

Most of the visiting women matched the men who were in the cells. Nobody with any money or any connections had anything to do with the Cook County jail.

Even without his glasses—which had also disappeared at Flossie's—he could see the anger that stiffened his sister's body when he told her he'd been sacked. "God damn it, am I the only one . . . ?" she rasped, then stopped herself, breathing hard. He saw her big, knotted hands ball on the grimy table. Saw how she made herself relax. "Are you okay, brother?"

"I think I broke my wrist—broke it or sprained it. Cassy, they got me for murder, for killing a pimp and his girl. I didn't do it, I got caught in a brawl at Flossie's, when I come to they were dead already—"

Cassy whispered, "Jesus." For the first time in her life, she sounded hopeless, and scared.

Cassy, who would walk up and spit in the Devil's face.

That, as much as his own fear of what would happen when he was brought up before a court of white men, felt like the crushing weight of a tomb falling on his shoulders.

She straightened her back. He could almost see her gather up a mouthful of spit. "What're we gonna do?"

"Get in touch with Mrs. Myra Bradwell," said John, and realized, with another cold jolt of shock, that he had no idea where she lived. Panic flashed through him, then he thought a moment, and said, "She's the wife of Judge Bradwell. Somebody here will be able to tell you where to send her a letter, or somebody at the Chicago *Times,* or the *Chicago Review of Law.* They'll be in the City Directory."

Just being out of the cell, being able to move, to talk to his sister, revived something inside him, that had been numbed by days of shock and thirst and pain. One foot in front of the other . . .

I got away from Blue Hill Plantation, and got Mama all the way to Washington without being caught. Anybody who could do that should be able to get through damn near anything.

He drew a deep breath.

"You tell her that I got sacked—and I got into this trouble—because I helped out her and Mrs. Lincoln." He braced himself for Cassy's spitfire retort, but she said nothing. Squinting across the table at her, he saw that her fear for him had even swamped the anger of him losing his job.

She loved him, he realized. Loved him more than the thought of their home, their survival as a family. Those paled for her beside fear for his survival.

The understanding of the depth of her love—and of his love for her—was honey and sunlight, in the midst of Hell. It burned his eyes with tears.

"And you think that's gonna get this white woman to lift a hand?" Cassy's voice was bitter.

"I do, yes. Cassy, please." She'd dealt with too many wealthy white women who wanted their sheets and petticoats washed right away and not starched too much, to have any high opinion of the breed. "She'll help," he said.

Cassy sniffed.

"She's got to know lawyers. She's a lawyer herself. She owes me."

"I got lots of white ladies owe me," retorted Cassy, getting to her feet. Through the haze of myopia John saw she was wearing her Sunday-go-to-meeting dress, faded sage-green chintz, the neatest she had. Like armor against the dirt and poverty and scorn of the jail. "And if they didn't need me for somethin' else, not a one of them would pay me." She reached across the table, and took his left hand.

"You keep strong, John. We'll get you out. With or without your white lady lawyer friend."

When John got back to the cell, Klauswijz and the boy Bailey were both gone. Before evening their places were taken by a gambler—who was bailed out within hours—and a morphine addict who proceeded to vomit, purge, and howl for the remainder of the day and night, but at least John got his own share of water and food. The gambler brought a newspaper with him, and left it behind. It contained a letter to the editor from Judge James Bradwell, accusing Dr. Patterson of treatment "calculated to drive Mrs. Lincoln insane" and a threat to come knocking on the "prison-house" doors with a writ of *habeas corpus.*

That night he slept like a dead man, and dreamed of the tangled woodland battlefields of the Wilderness between Crown Point and Richmond. Dreamed of searching through the woods, and finding dying soldiers as they lay sobbing amid hackberry and weeds. Dreamed of carrying them back to the ambulance-carts, with their blood dripping down his back. He saw the dim shapes of the dead-carts above him, the piles of bodies heaped like cordwood. A tall man in shirtsleeves was working there alone, lifting the dead onto the cart, and as he came nearer John saw it was Mr. Lincoln, wearing a butcher's bloodied apron, his hands and arms crimson to the biceps. Every time he turned, John saw the gaping wound in the back of his head, where Booth's bullet had smashed through the skull.

John asked him, "Did you know this was going to happen?"

"I guessed it," said Lincoln. "Yes."

"Was it worth it?"

Lincoln bent to help John load a corpse onto the cart. It was the little whore who'd stared around her in such terror at Flossie's, the little girl who so resembled Lucy. The older man stood looking down at her for a moment, then sighed like a death-rattle. "I think so."

"Even for this?" The fog was thinning. The battlefield lay exposed, stretching as far as anyone could see, filling the world. Smoke drifted, with the stink of blood and sulfur. Flies roared in black clouds. This then was the glory of the coming of the Lord, John thought: bodies lying like the trampled skins of grapes, wrath hanging like a poison over the stricken field. Somehow he knew they'd be picking up the bodies of the slain for months, for years. His mother was out there dead somewhere, and Cassy and Lionel and Lizabet Keckley and Frederick Douglass, and men and women not yet born. "None of them asked to die. They asked only to live."

Lincoln said, "We all die, John." And with a self-conscious gesture fingered the wound in the back of his head, looked at the blood on his hand, then shrugged and wiped it on his trouser-leg. "Would you go back if you could?"

John grinned up at him. "Not a chance."

And Lincoln grinned back, suddenly young. "Neither would I."

Chapter Sixty-seven

"I do not know what I am going to do with you!" Robert slapped the newspaper down on the bench beside Mary, the strained violence of his movement speaking volumes for a lifetime of restricting what he felt and how he reacted. A lifetime of dealing with Mary. Of being pointed at as Abraham Lincoln's son.

He'd come on her in the rose garden, striding up the gravel drive—Mary had seen Argus let him in at the front gate, had seen by the way he walked that he was furious. She'd considered going into the house and making him ask Dr. Patterson to bring her to the parlor, where at least he couldn't shout and rail at her, but a kind of weary anger kept her in her seat.

Let him shout, she thought. Though Dr. Patterson had only told her that John Wilamet had "decided to quit us," she knew Robert must have had something to do with his dismissal a week ago. And her anger at the loss of her friend—at the loss of the only person in this place who truly had her good at heart—had fire-cured the hard knot of strength within her that had somehow gotten lost in the soft haze of her medicines. She found that even in cold blood, she no longer really cared whether Robert was angry at her or not.

She picked up the paper and glanced at the place to which Robert had folded it open.

"Why is it necessary that you do anything with me?" she asked quietly. "Because you can't endure the thought of having a mother who travels around the country without a male protector? Or a mother who is interested in politics and writes letters to newspapers? Or is it just that you don't like the sight of me spending money that you think of as yours?"

"We've been through this before, Mother." He spoke as if trying to conceal a painful carbuncle whose existence was beneath the dignity of Abraham Lincoln's son. "You think that by getting your friends to bring calumny down upon Dr. Patterson and his family—none of whom have ever done you the slightest harm..."

"Not done me *harm*? Not done me harm, to suggest to you that the best thing that you could do with an embarrassing female relation is to have her declared mad and locked up? In *his* private madhouse, at the rate of two hundred dollars a month . . . Or did you find Bellevue with a pin and a City Directory?"

Robert's blue eyes shifted, then returned to hers aflame with indignation. "It didn't happen like that at all. Dr. Patterson's brother examined you in Washington, when you had your carriage accident. Dr. Patterson was one of several doctors I consulted about your sanity."

"The only one who runs a private institution and was looking for patients to fill it up, I daresay. And on the subject of calumny, you have been calling me insane—in the public newspapers, no less—since the time I began fighting for Congress to give me the remainder of your father's salary so we could have something to live on while that dilatory hog Judge Davis collected the interest on your father's estate. You called me insane while I tried to get a pension to live on at a time when Congress and every wealthy businessman in the East were shoving handfuls of greenbacks and house-deeds into Sam Grant's pockets for doing less to save the Union than your father did, and at far less cost to himself. Don't think I don't know that you were calling me insane to your cronies at Harvard and in the Army as well."

"You *are* insane!" he shouted at her. "Good God, Mother, you should have seen yourself when you came off the train last March, raving that I was going to die! When you were wandering around the halls of the Grand Pacific in your nightdress, swearing that voices were speaking to you out of the walls!"

Tears filled Mary's eyes and with them, the blinding urge to turn on him her old weapons of sarcasm and hysterics, of guilt and shame. Instead she said, "Obviously, I was ill, and now am better. You can ask Dr. Patterson, or his son, if I have had any such delusions while I have been here. I reserve the right to remain eccentric—I never noticed anyone trying to lock up your Uncle Levi when he'd go on shouting rampages, or for heaven's sake Cash Clay...."

"The only reason no one has tried so far to lock up Cassius Clay is because they're afraid he'll shoot them in the process."

"The only reason no one has tried to lock up Cash," said Mary firmly, "is because he is a man. And a man can make as much of a jackass of himself as he pleases, writing letters to newspapers or switching political sides or speaking to mobs of freedmen urging rebellion against Reconstruction . . . or keeping a harem of Russian dancing-girls and driving his poor wife to distraction and divorce, for that matter. And half the members of Congress, over the years, haven't been much better."

She folded the newspaper with James Bradwell's letter in it and set it again on the bench at her side, and shaded her eyes as she looked up at her son. "But a woman is considered mad if she spends her own money to excess, or loses her temper too often and too loudly, or seeks communication with the souls of those she loved in life, in order to comfort her grief."

"If she hands all her money to charlatans who claim to be the 'media' of that communication, yes, I'd say that was insane," snapped Robert.

"But it is *my money.* If I were to hand it all to the Catholic Church, or to the Freedmen's Relief Association—or to the clerk at the jewelry counter at Marshall Field's, for that matter, like some women I could name—it is *my business,* and not yours."

And she saw him stiffen up with stubborn anger at the idea that any doings of his female belongings—whether mother, wife, or daughter—were not his business.

She went on, "My sister tells me that you wrote to her warning her that Myra Bradwell was the 'high priestess' of a 'gang of Spiritualists' who were trying to get their hands on my money. And that she is in perfectly good health, and not—as you specifically told me—that she was too ill to have me go and stay with her."

"I did not say *specifically* that she was too ill."

She promptly fished for the letter in her reticule, and with blotches of anger staining his cheekbones Robert raised his hand. After a moment he said, "I was only thinking of you, Mother. This place is good for you. You said yourself you have ceased having those delusions, and it is because you have been living quietly here, and not exciting your brain with the confusing distractions of travel and of those da—" He caught himself from swearing, and corrected, "—those wretched table-tappers who do nothing but raise the passions of women to such a degree that they result in derangement."

"You mean they raise the passions of women to such a degree that they result in disagreement with men," retorted Mary. And then, as Robert opened his mouth, she added, "As you just said yourself, we have been through this before, and we shall probably never agree. But there is a law of *habeas corpus* in this state—"

"You damned—wretched—women, quoting the law . . ."

"The law that you'd rather we didn't know about? As slaveholders preferred that their chattels not learn about it? I expected better of your father's son!"

Mary stood, and shook out her black skirts. The morning was growing hot. The scent of the roses swathed her like a veil, as if the sweetness were intended to mask the dim screams coming from the house. That would be Mrs. Hill, strapped in a hydrotherapy tank.

"There is a law of *habeas corpus* in Illinois, Robert. And I *am* going to get out of this place. As I'm sure that neither of us wishes me to come live with you and your *lovely* wife—" her voice twisted with scorn "—perhaps it would be best if you stopped lying to my sister, and Mrs. Bradwell, and Dr. Patterson, and accepted that fact. It is possible for me to be sane in places other than the one you sanction, and to get help from sources other than those of which you approve."

"I will not have you running about the world creating an embarrassment for the Lincoln family!"

"Your embarrassment is your own problem, Robert, not mine," she pointed out icily. "Please feel free to disown me. And if at any time in the future I start hearing voices coming out of the floor, or begin having delusions of men following me—that is, men other than those *you* have hired yourself—you may call in your mad-doctors to examine me again. But not until that time. May I take this?" She held up the newspaper.

Robert turned from her without a word, and walked stiffly away down the gravel drive to the gate. She watched him go, her heart aching. Not with the loss of the man, she realized. For years, she understood now, he had been a stranger to her. Maybe he always had. But she was losing the sturdy boy who'd run through the leafy aisles of the vegetable garden on Jackson Street, the boy the other children had called Cock-Eye, the boy who'd darted about the steamboat deck to look at the paddles, and the young man who'd written to her wild with excitement: *The other boys said how proud I must be, to have him for my father. . . .*

Her heart went back further, to the rainy November night and the silence of Simeon Francis's house; Lincoln's weight pressing her body into the worn sofa. The hoarse gasp of his breath, the brush of his lips on her face, the fire reflected in his gray eyes.

Life is short. We don't know what the future will bring. I don't want never to have done this. . . .

She realized that she still felt the same way. That if she could go back, and erase everything that had passed between that night, and the tall angry figure striding from her down the garden path, she would not. It was all precious to her, every moment, the painful along with the sweet. The lie that she had told had made Robert what he was, and what he would go on to be: the whole of their relationship implicit in those few impulsive words that she could not take back, once they'd been spoken.

Everything that had come of that lie seemed to settle into her heart, like wings folding. It was what was. For the first time in over thirty years, she felt no shame, only a profound sadness.

Robert was gone. With him he was taking Mamie, and the other children Young Mary would bear: Abraham Lincoln's grandchildren. *Her* grandchildren.

With him he was taking the past, and whatever future that she might have had, with Abraham Lincoln's only surviving son.

And though a tear crept down her face for that vanished future, she was still glad that she had done what she had done, and had what she had had.

CASSY AND CLARICE BOTH CAME TO THE COOK COUNTY JAIL ON SATurday to visit John, and again on Sunday with Selina and Phoebe and a box of apples and hard-boiled eggs. If there had been any repercussions or rage on Phoebe's part—or Cassy's, for that matter—about money and the future, they had taken place at home. Just the knowledge that his family knew where he was, that they cared about him enough to endure the streetcar ride and the walk in the brutal August sun, made the jail-cell bearable.

On Monday a young white gentleman named Leeland turned up. A lawyer, he said, and a friend of Mrs. Bradwell, he was willing to argue John's case. In the crowded visiting-room he listened to John's account of the evening at Flossie's, and took notes. This was more than was being done, John couldn't help noticing, by the sparse scattering of pro bono attorneys pulled from the court roster to help the more deserving or endangered of the other prisoners. One of these, a stout sleepy gentleman in an appalling checked suit, kept shaking his head at his client's impassioned protests of innocence and saying, "I'll do what I can, Mr.—uh—Mr. Belker—but you understand I mostly do probates, not murders. . . ."

He also couldn't keep from noticing what was obvious even without his spectacles: that he was the only black man in conversation with a member of the legal profession, probates or otherwise. He guessed—his guess a near certainty—that without Myra Bradwell pulling in a favor, he'd have been arguing his own not-very-convincing case in court.

"Oh, they haven't got a leg to stand on," said Leeland, when John had finished his account of what little he'd seen of the fight. "The police had a couple of bodies on their hands and wanted to make an arrest to impress their sergeant. I'd wager they don't even have any witnesses, other than the flatfoot who made the arrest."

"That'll be enough to get me hanged, if we don't have at least one witness that I was knocked out on the floor," pointed out John grimly. "And you're going to have your work cut out for you finding one. I surely don't advise you to try going into Flossie's alone and asking questions."

"Good God!" Leeland looked horrified at the thought. "I know better than to do that. But we'll be all right." The young lawyer gave John a cheerful slap on the shoulder. "Half the time, when the judge hears that there's going to be an attorney for the defense at all, he just drops the charges, especially if there's no witnesses. I'll see what I can do."

He stood—he'd talked to John for all of about five minutes, an eon in that room and those circumstances. The man at the next table seemed to be vainly trying to state his case in a language his attorney didn't understand. Leeland said, "Mrs. Bradwell told me to get you off, and she'll never speak to me again if I don't."

"You work for her?" John stood also—the bored-looking guard came forward, to take him back. When John moved, the manacles on his wrists jangled on the battered wooden table, rubbing older scars. He was surprised at how angry it made him, to wear chains again.

"In a manner of speaking." Leeland resumed his stylish new derby with a flourish. "She got me work in her husband's office when I first started out, and had no money, and let me earn extra writing articles for her newspaper. I owe her."

As he walked John back to the cell the guard muttered, "Lawyers for niggers, what'll they want next?"

Through the next nerve-wracking week he was keenly aware of how lucky he was, as he saw some of those who'd been in the holding cell before him taken away. He heard from others about the cursory trials that lasted barely twenty minutes, testimony from policemen, storekeepers, bartenders who merely shrugged off the questions put to them by the accused, or answered with wisecracks that drew grins from the jury.

The fact that he knew he wasn't going to have to get up and question a couple of white cops who wanted to impress their sergeant with their detective abilities eased his mind considerably, but did nothing to reduce the furnace of sour anger burning within him. He would—probably—walk out of here with his life, but there remained the question of where he would go when he did. And in the weeks in the cell, he saw what he had always been able to turn away from before: the sheer extent of what poverty did, to those whom no one regarded as quite human enough to employ.

To all intents and purposes, John understood that he was back at Camp Barker yet again, being told off by Washington ladies' yard-hands and beaten up by Irish teamsters.

All because he had tried to help the woman whose husband had freed him. The woman who had treated him kindly, on his first day in the Promised Land.

JOHN HAD FEARED THAT MR. LEELAND'S CASUAL REMARKS ABOUT THE charges being dropped were a mere justification for not putting himself to the danger of going out and looking for a witness, but it turned out that the lawyer had a clearer awareness of the courts' corruption than John did. On the eighth of September—almost a month after his arrest—he was taken out of his cell, informed that the charges against him had been dropped, and let loose onto the streets of Chicago. He was bearded, filthy, and shaky with lack of exercise. Through the two-mile-plus walk to the grid of dirty alleyways between train-tracks and stockyard near the levee, he had to stop repeatedly to regain his strength and his breath.

If the breezes hadn't been cool that day off Lake Michigan he wasn't sure he'd have made it.

At the house—where everyone had been living on oatmeal because Lionel was carrying the whole family on his slender wages—John had a bath in Cassy's used laundry-water, shaved, and slept for twenty-six hours. When he woke, the first thing he saw was Phoebe, sitting beside his cot with a fan of braided newspaper in her hands, keeping the flies off his face.

The following day he walked back uptown to Michigan Avenue, to pay a visit to Myra Bradwell.

The house was three stories, fronted with brown brick, reminding him a little of those he'd seen in New York. He had to squint to see the house number. Griffe Moissant had lent him a pair of glasses and they weren't nearly strong enough. A German servant answered the door, and she looked him up and down in horror. He wondered if a white man, clothed in the clean but shabby second-best suit that for a miracle Phoebe hadn't pawned for medicine-money, would have been asked over the threshold.

"Yes?"

"I'm here to see Mrs. Bradwell. Would you please tell her that Mr. John Wilamet from Bellevue Place is here?" A little awkwardly, because his arm was still in a sling, he put one of his cards on her tray.

Put that in your pipe and smoke it.

The woman's expression clearly indicated that only superhuman Christian charity prevented her from pointing out that she had knick-knacks to dust and could not afford the time to be announcing Negroes to Mrs. Bradwell. When she closed the door in his face John kept his temper by counting the seconds. It was six and a half minutes—far longer than it would take for a woman to climb a flight of stairs and grunt a visitor's name—before the door was opened again, and the maid said grudgingly, "Please come in." She took his hat with the delicacy of one who expected it to be lousy and put a piece of newspaper on the marble-topped rosewood hall table before setting it down, then followed him up the stairs like a detective trailing a prospective shoplifter.

John was sorely tempted to turn around and yell, "Boo!"

"Mr. Wilamet, I am delighted to see you!" Myra rose from her desk, strode to the door to meet him. The room—a bright little chamber above the kitchen that in any other house would have been a sewing-room—was clearly her fortress and sanctum, lined with shelves that bore law-books stacked neatly on their sides, long inky newspaper galleys, docketed folders of papers, and a dozen big commonplace-books of clippings. Wooden file cabinets and an old but spotless desk took up most of the room. There was one chair for a visitor and one at the desk, a bright rag rug, and pots of ivy on the sill of the windows that ran the length of the room and gave a view of a rather overgrown garden below.

On the wall, bordered in black, was a sepia ambrotype of a little girl in a white dress, with bunches of fresh asters in the vase in front of it.

Myra went on in her brisk voice, "Leeland told me Monday Judge Hertford was dropping the charges. Old Hertford's always ready to save himself trouble. I don't blame you for resting a few days before coming to see me."

Monday, he thought dourly. And yesterday—the day of his release—had been Wednesday. Two days, before they'd gotten around to actually letting him go. It figured. He was lucky they hadn't lost the papers until Christmas.

"You're so thin, my poor boy! And your arm... I'm afraid you've had a most dreadful time. But Leeland is truly a marvel. You're lucky to have caught me—I'm leaving this evening for Springfield, to be there tomorrow when Mary arrives at her sister's house."

"It's settled, then?" He wasn't really surprised. He'd followed the bitter interchange of letters in the papers, which Cassy and Clarice had brought him almost daily, including the quite masterful article by Franc Wilkie in the *Times.* Caught between Robert Lincoln and fear of public disgrace,

Dr. Patterson had put up as much of a fight as he could, but the conclusion, John had guessed, was foregone.

"There will be universal satisfaction to know that Mrs. Lincoln has been restored to her reason and to her friends," proclaimed one journal, and another, *"When a woman spends her own money lavishly and appears a little different from others she ought not to be placed behind iron bars. She has borne all and wronged no one."*

Dr. Patterson had written in a letter to the *Tribune, "I am willing to record the opinion that such is the character of her malady she will not be content to do this, and that the experiment, if made, will result only in giving her the coveted opportunity to make extended rambles, to renew the indulgence of her purchasing mania, and other morbid manifestations."*

"DR. PATTERSON," James Bradwell had responded in a final blistering letter to the *Chicago Post and Mail, "IS A VERY PECULIAR MAN. . . ."*

"Robert is frothing at the mouth." There was rich satisfaction in Myra's voice. "I've received some of the most frigidly polite letters in the English language from him, once he saw that he could not keep his mother under lock and key where she would be forced to stop spending the money that he's counting on, and behave the way he thinks a real woman ought to. I must say, he certainly doesn't have his father's way with words—or his mother's either, for that matter. It was Wilkie's article that did the trick, though!"

She turned back to her desk, where she laid hands on it at once, already neatly cut and tucked into a folder.

"That's what set off the round of support. You know there were ministers who made her the subject of sermons, demanding her release? Probably preached by the very same ministers who execrated her a few years ago for trying to sell off her old dresses. But there's nothing like a good newspaper campaign to force an issue. . . ."

"You might have told me."

At the hardness of his tone, her hazel eyes narrowed.

"I daresay I might have," she replied evenly. "Would you have helped, if you knew?"

"If I'd known that it would cost me my job? The sole support of my wife, my mother, and my child? I don't know."

He saw her face change, all the triumphant ebullience leaving it, and that lawyer mask with which he was so familiar emerging, like the skull through the skin. "Is that why you're here?" she inquired. A lawyer's voice, like the face, that gave away nothing: every word precisely graded so as to offer not the slightest handhold to an opponent.

He wondered if Lincoln had gotten like that in court, and then realized, *Of course he had.*

"If you mean, am I here to ask you for money, no." And to his complete surprise—because he hadn't had the slightest idea of what he was, in fact, going to say to her, he went on, "I'm here to thank you for sending Mr. Leeland to get me out. I probably owe him—and you—my life. Black men get very brief trials in this town."

She inclined her head, still watchful. "If you thought I would have abandoned you after the help you gave me and Mrs. Lincoln, you can't have formed a very complete picture of my character." She was still angry.

"To tell you the truth, Mrs. Bradwell, in the twelve years that I've been a free man—and the fifteen years I was a slave—I learned the hard way never to completely trust whites, because so many of the things that go into making up their characters are . . . not things that I—we—have experience with. It's sometimes hard for me to read whites. Mostly, on Maxwell Street, we just know what's done to us."

His eyes were on hers as he spoke—and it was still strange to him, to look into a white woman's eyes after half a lifetime's training not to—and it was her gaze that fell.

After a moment she said, "Won't you sit down, Mr. Wilamet?" She reached for and rang the silver bell on her desk. "Heidi . . . Please bring coffee for Mr. Wilamet and myself," she told the maid and took her seat at the desk, turning her chair to face him as he sat down. "I'm sorry," she said simply. "I was quite wrong not to trust you . . . not to consider the results of my action more carefully than I did. You must admit I was justified."

"I admit you were justified," replied John quietly, and adjusted Griffe's glasses, which were too narrow and gave him a headache. "But you were also wrong."

Myra's lips tightened, and John recalled her words on the train from Springfield, about how the feminists in the abolition movement had been betrayed by those men who thought they could win if they separated freedom for black men from freedom for all. Enough to make a woman carry a grudge, if she didn't know too much about how those black men got treated after their much-talked-about Freedom finally came through.

"Yes, I was wrong," she told him. "And even giving you back a future isn't sufficient payment, if I've damaged that future beyond repair. What can I do for you?"

"I don't know. What *can* you do for me? Besides colonizing me to Africa."

Myra laughed, just as Heidi came in with the coffee-tray. The maid's face was like stone as she set it down, but John guessed she'd have a few words to say to the cook about their mistress's eccentricities in welcoming a Negro as an equal. He wondered if the cup he drank from would be accidentally "broken" in the interests of "cleanliness," while Myra was in Springfield.

"How well do you write?" Myra asked. "How clearly? Most lawyers want clerks with some legal training, but I can certainly bully one of my husband's staff into taking you on as an assistant clerk. The pay won't be much. . . ."

"It's better than rolling cigars," said John.

Myra looked surprised.

"Or sweeping a saloon—which are just about the only jobs a black man can get in this town, unless he knows someone. And black men never know anyone, except other black men."

"Rather like being a woman," she replied drily. "A woman seeking employment—other than prostitution or sewing—encounters exactly the same thing. They take one look at *you* and say, 'Oh, you're black.' They take one look at *me* and say, 'Oh, you're a woman. You have a "nervous constitution" and can't be trusted not to—' "

She broke off. "Mr. Wilamet," she said, with a different emphasis on the words, "how well do you write? Because I need articles for my newspaper about laws concerning the treatment of the insane—particularly women. You worked at Bellevue—and as I recall you said you worked at the Jacksonville asylum as well. Do you think you could research in the law and medical journals to write about the abuses there, in the light of your own experience? Again, the pay won't be much."

"Again," said John, "it's better than rolling cigars."

He stepped out the door of Myra Bradwell's home into sunlight, and wind blowing across the spangled surface of the lake. Beyond the trees of Lake Park a train rolled by along the dark cindery line of track between water and land, noisy even in this fashionable neighborhood. A policeman walking his beat eyed him, but didn't cross the street. John wondered if, in between writing about madhouses, he might slip in a few articles about the Cook County jail as well.

He realized that for the next few years he'd be working with Myra Bradwell.

Not how he'd pictured the Promised Land.

But it was a start.

Feeling as if he'd found a dollar in the streets of wartime Washington to carry back to Camp Barker, he set off down Michigan Avenue for home.

Chapter Sixty-eight

"I trust everything is to your satisfaction, Mrs. Lincoln?"

Dr. Patterson's voice was stiff, as he stood in the doorway of her little room, an indistinct shape against the gaslights of the hall. For the past month—since he had learned from Robert the identity of the Mr. Wilkie whom Myra had brought to see her—Patterson had been hard put to be polite to Mary, lecturing her several times a day on her untruthfulness, as if it were a mark of insanity to mistrust one's jailers. Every time she turned around, she'd encountered Gretchen or Zeus or Mrs. Patterson, scribbling notes of her behavior.

Searching, she knew, for evidence that she was insane, and that Dr. Patterson and Robert were right.

Lately—since Mr. Wilkie's article had appeared—this had ceased. But she still felt anxious, as if everything she did would be used against her.

Patterson went on, "Your son will be here in the morning, to escort you to your sister's house. I have made arrangements for your trunks to be shipped at the end of the week. I hope you know what you're doing, in insisting on leaving Bellevue, Mrs. Lincoln. . . ."

It was a rhetorical opening to a lecture on the virtues of lotos-eating, but she responded sweetly, "That is the entire case at issue, Doctor, is it not?"

He pokered up exactly like young Mr. Presby used to, when Mary had pinked a hole in the tutor's Yankee self-righteousness. He said, "Good-night, Mrs. Lincoln," and stalked off down the hall.

She closed the door. She could hear Amanda moving around in the adjoining room. Packing, she supposed. Amanda had agreed to accompany her as a nurse to Springfield, for despite—or perhaps because of—or in addition to—her reduction in her medicines, Mary still felt far from well.

Her back, neck, and shoulder still hurt; her privates itched and she still had to use the toilet a dozen times a night (and wouldn't *that* be a pleasure with Elizabeth's room next to hers!). She still quarreled unreasonably with whoever crossed her path some days, still had those strange moments of feeling detached from her body, of feeling she was on the verge of losing herself.

And that was, she supposed, what her life would become. Amanda was one of the few who had agreed with John Wilamet's judgment that no more than two watered spoonfuls of medicine were to be taken on any one day, no matter what she said or felt. Mary knew this was best, but no day went by that she didn't think, at least once: *Just one more spoonful, because my back is extra bad today. . . .* She thought about the long years ahead and shivered.

It had been easier to put such thoughts away when she'd had John to talk to. Myra had told her that Patterson had dismissed the young black man assisting them, and that he'd later gotten into trouble—wrongfully—with the police: that she was getting one of Jamie's law cronies to help him. Once she got to Elizabeth's, she reflected, she'd ask Myra where to write to him, perhaps even see him. On the days when the cravings were so bad, it did her good to talk.

On the nights like tonight, the thought of seeing Myra, or John, or one of her other friends was the only thing she could hold on to, like lights glimpsed in a wilderness of dark.

If she went back to taking more medicine than she should, Robert would be able to lock her up again. This time forever.

The little warm stir of anger—of fight—helped. *I'll show him.*

In nine months, Myra had told her, they'd be able to go to court and have the judgment of insanity lifted from her.

In nine months she'd be truly free.

And then, I will return to Europe, where Robert will not be able to touch me. Where he'll never be "embarrassed" by me again.

She closed her eyes, recalling the warming sunlight of Italy, the tumbled bronze-purple hills of Scotland, London's rain-gray streets. The wooded hills above Frankfurt, its cobbled lanes and the bright-hued dresses of the ladies strolling along the Zeil in the chill sunshine.

Nine months of living with Elizabeth, whom she had not seen in ten years. Of living under the same roof as Ninian, as she had when she was twenty-one.

Nine months of coming downstairs every day to the double-parlor where Dr. Henry had sat by the fire: *He is a man whose heart is stronger than his body. . . .* Nine months of crossing the porch where Ninian had stood in the snow and told Lincoln to relinquish his sister-in-law's hand.

We cannot always be children under our fathers' roofs. . . .

Nine months of eating dinner in the dining-room where Lincoln had slipped on her finger the now-too-tight gold band that said, *A.L. to M.T. Nov. 4 1842 Love Is Eternal.* Of seeing his gray eyes looking out of every shadow at her.

Of knowing that Merce Conkling and Julia Trumbull and her perfidious sister Ann and all the other false friends of former days were whispering about her over their afternoon tea.

She did not know how she was going to endure it.

Nor could she even contemplate how she was going to live through the years to come.

THAT NIGHT SHE DREAMED ABOUT LINCOLN.

She was in the carriage with him again, under the dappled shade of the Washington dogwoods. She thought, *No! Not this again . . . !* unable to bear the thought of what was coming. To sit beside him in the theater, to hear the crack of Booth's pistol and feel her husband's arm jerk in her grip, then the weight of him slump down on her shoulder. "We must both try to be more cheerful," he was saying, and looking up, she saw again how worn his face was, how lined with four years of sleepless nights, four years of sorrow. "With our dear Willie's death, we have both been very miserable."

"I have been very miserable," said Mary firmly, and took his hand. "And not just because of Willie's death."

He looked surprised, because this had not actually happened, nor had she ever dreamed of stepping out of the actual past before. This memory of their last afternoon together had always been too precious to alter, even to evade the grief that followed. He put his arm around her then, and sighed. "I know," he said. "I am sorry, Molly."

She could feel the warmth of his fingers through the gloves they both wore.

"You did the best you could," she told him quietly, and rested her head on his shoulder, thankful that this dream didn't include the cavalry escort. "And you did a hero's work. But you abandoned me. You left me behind—left me out of your life. After all our years together. And then you left me alone."

It was the thing she had always longed to say to him, in all those darkened parlors, in all those ghostly rooms where the music of far-off violins had whispered across the Veil between the worlds. She never had, for it would not do, to let anyone know the truth about him: that like other men he was a man, capable of temper and thoughtlessness, and of ignoring or disappointing his wife.

It would never do to let anyone know the truth about her: that her wholehearted love had been mingled, all along, with anger, frustration, and the selfish, devouring need to have more of his love than he would give. More than he *could* give.

Maybe more than anyone could ever give.

She had never known how to break past this: first because he would be great, then because he was President, and finally because of the death that had raised him to martyrdom and herself to the thankless role of a martyr's wife.

And he had never appeared to her, as Tad and Willie and Eddie had, in those hazy, glowing spells that she now recognized as opium-dreams.

He asked gently, "Do you think I really wanted to leave you, Molly? In the end?"

In life she would have wept, but in her dream she seemed to have control of both her temper and her tears. "No. And I know I'm not an easy woman to live with. I could have done better. . . . But so could you. I know you didn't mean to hurt me, but you did. I wish I could say that I never meant to hurt you. . . . I am sorry that I *did* mean it, sometimes."

He smiled at her, as he had when she'd work herself into a fret about a fancied slight or some day-to-day crisis in their Springfield days, and squeezed her shoulder gently with one long arm. "It happens. I recovered."

The sun was sinking, and looking past him, she saw that they weren't in Washington at all, but driving along the Richmond road on the outskirts of Lexington. She saw Henry Clay's house, Ashland, among its beautiful gardens, and the low brick shape of Rose Hill on the other side of the road. But the countryside that lay beyond them was the Illinois prairie, as it had been when first she and her father had taken the stage up from St. Louis, empty, baked, and golden in the fading evening light.

She took a deep breath, and said, "I'm sorry I lied to you. About Robert, I mean."

"Bob's a good boy," said Lincoln. "And a fine man. He has his own path to walk. You did for him what you could."

"I just didn't want to be alone." And hearing her own words, she smiled her rueful sidelong smile. "And now after all that, here I am, alone anyway."

"We're all alone sometimes, Molly," said Lincoln gently. "Sometimes that's the way we need to be. We all do what we have to do about it. Like the old farmer said, some days you get the bear and some days the bear gets you. I am purely sorry that I made you unhappy—and glad that I could make you happy, when I did. Promise me you'll do what you need to do, to be as happy as you can."

She sighed, and answered, "I'll do what I can."

"That's my Molly."

They were coming into Springfield, passing the Globe Tavern, where she glimpsed an empty carriage standing waiting for her, and a gaggle of loungers listening to a storyteller in the darkness of the porch. In the flare of torchlight as they went by the tavern's doors she saw that it was John Wilamet driving the carriage in which they rode—Myra, she thought, must have gotten him that job after he'd been dismissed from Bellevue. His eyes met hers and he smiled.

Then Lincoln drew her to him, and kissed her in the sunset's amber glow, the strength of his arm so familiar, the taste of his mouth what it had always been. They held each other like adolescents in the first wild springtime of love.

The carriage turned down Second Street, and Mary saw Elizabeth waiting for her in the dim glow of the porch lamps, Ninian standing tall behind her. Myra was beside her, and Robert, looking like he'd been sucking a lemon. In the soft blue twilight with its thick scent of honeysuckle, she glimpsed other forms on the porch: Lizabet Keckley, she thought, and handsome young Elmer Ellsworth in his Zouave uniform, and Stephen Douglas like a dandified little bantam rooster, and Dr. Henry and Cash Clay.

The carriage drew to a halt, and Lincoln opened the door and swung lightly down, holding out his hand to her to steady her on the high step.

"You can't come in with me?" Mary asked, though she knew that wasn't allowed. "Even for a little?" He shook his head.

"I'll meet you a ways down the road."

Mary smiled at him, gathered up her petticoats, and stepped down. She was wearing, she noted, the pink faille that she'd had on that first evening in Springfield, when her father had gone looking for Ninian and drunken old Professor Kittridge had come over to lecture her on the evils of slavery.

She looked up at Lincoln and smiled. "I'll look forward to it."

"As will I."

He took off his hat and leaned down to kiss her, then sprang up into the carriage again. "You have a good time, Molly."

Not at all sure that she would, Mary walked up the path to her sister's house through the dream's blue twilight, trying not to look back.

Epilogue

On June 15, 1876, the Chicago court reversed its decision and declared Mary Todd Lincoln sane. She left Springfield in September, traveling to New York with her great-nephew Lewis Baker and thence to Europe, where she settled in Pau, a pleasant town at the foot of the French Pyrenees. For four years she lived there alone, alternating between profound self-pity and the comfortable solitude of an expatriate widow. Though always a recreational spender, she never again ran into serious debt and always kept meticulous track of her money through a financial manager. She traveled to Italy and through southern France, and even stayed out of politics (mostly).

When former President Grant and his wife stopped in Pau in December of 1879 on their round-the-world post-Administration trip, Julia Grant claimed that she had "not learned" of Mrs. Lincoln's presence in Pau until the night before they were leaving town, and it was "too late to make her a visit" or invite her to any of the receptions, parades, or banquets given the war hero by the city fathers.

In 1880, her health and eyesight failing, Mary returned to Springfield. There she lived as a semi-invalid in four rooms of Elizabeth's house: bedroom, sitting-room, and two rooms in which to store the sixty-four trunks whose weight nearly caved in the floor-boards. Her relatives describe her as living alone in the darkened rooms (kept dim because of corneas literally abraded from half a lifetime of tears), compulsively sorting through the contents of her trunks. But when President James Garfield was assassinated in 1881 and his widow was given a pension of

$5,000, Mary assembled helpers and rushed to Washington to demand parity. She got it, plus back payments, plus interest.

She collapsed on the eleventh anniversary of Tad's death—July 15, 1882—and died of a stroke the following day, which was the thirty-third anniversary of her father's. Robert came to the funeral, and inherited close to $58,000.

Mary was buried with Willie, Eddie, Tad, and Mr. Lincoln in Springfield.

Robert Todd Lincoln lived to be eighty-three, serving as President of the Pullman Company and dying a millionaire. He was Secretary of War, to James Garfield and Chester A. Arthur, and his objections and obstructions about sending support to the Greeley Polar Expedition of 1884 have been blamed for the disaster that overtook the explorers. From 1889 to 1893 he was the U.S. Minister to Great Britain.

In 1881, Robert Lincoln was among President Garfield's party at the train-station when Garfield was shot by a disappointed office-seeker, and was present at the President's deathbed. In 1901 he happened, purely by chance, to be in the crowd at the Pan-American Exposition in Buffalo when Leon Czolgosz shot President William McKinley, and thereafter refused all invitations to the White House or to any occasion on which he would be in the same room as the President of the United States.

He selectively pruned his father's papers, burning some and putting others under seal not to be opened until twenty-one years after his own death.

He died in July of 1926, and in keeping with his desire to be perceived as a man in his own right and not as Abraham Lincoln's son, lies buried in Arlington National Cemetery, on the hillside just below Robert E. Lee's house.

His estate threatened Myra Bradwell's granddaughter with a lawsuit until she sold them not only all of Mary Todd Lincoln's correspondence with Myra, but all of Myra's correspondence with Mary, and the article that she was writing about the events of July–September 1875. All of these were destroyed.

Author's Note

The Emancipator's Wife is a work of fiction. I've made surmises about the way things may have happened, and the possible reasons events took place, that cannot be substantiated, but I've tried not to portray anything contrary to documented events. As all historical novelists must, I have taken my best guess at those occurrences or motivations for which there are no records.

Nowhere have I found any biographer who came out and said that Mary Todd Lincoln had a substance abuse problem. Given the list of her known ailments—an unspecified "female problem" resulting from Tad's birth, migraines, menstrual problems, what sound like allergy-related sinus headaches, and injuries from her carriage accident in July of 1863—it would be astonishing if she didn't. Opium and alcohol figured prominently in most over-the-counter medicines in that era, and her biographers agree she took them in quantity: one friend described her as pouring dollops from five or six various bottles into a glass and chugging the result. Before the early twentieth century, no manufacturer of the various female cordials, soothing elixirs, and patented cure-alls was required to list anywhere the percentage of narcotics that these "medicines" contained. Many, many women of stronger will and character than Mrs. Lincoln ended up addicted.

It is also a fact that although she became seriously delusional during the period after Tad's death, when she was solitary and had little to occupy her time, nowhere have I found even a hint that she suffered delusions either while she was incarcerated in Bellevue Place, or following her release. In fact, after she emigrated to Europe in 1876 she also kept herself clear of major debt.

Did Mary Todd entrap Abraham Lincoln into marrying her? Looking at the manipulative chicanery she later indulged in with White House funds, and with promises dealt out to get her debts paid, I can only say that I wouldn't put it past her. She loved him deeply and possessively. She waited for him for twenty months after their breakup in January of 1841 while he tentatively pursued at least two other young ladies. Several of Lincoln's friends attested to the strong streak of physical passion that underlay his iron self-control. When they started spending time together again—unchaperoned and late in the evening at Simeon Francis's house—Mary was a month shy of twenty-four, approaching old-maid territory by almost anyone's standards. They were married on a half-day's notice and their son Robert was born nine months less four days later.

Was Mary Todd Lincoln really insane?

She was undoubtedly eccentric. It's generally held now that she was bipolar—even people who loved her describe her as being subject to wild and abrupt mood-swings, starting in childhood; friends and neighbors interviewed by Billy Herndon in Springfield, and Lincoln's two secretaries Hay and Nicolay, agree that she had a horrendous and perhaps hysterical temper. Recent biographers have suggested the effects of untreated diabetes as well. After the deaths of three of her children, and two separate incidents of major trauma—having her husband's brains blown out while he was sitting beside her and later having the Chicago Fire come within three blocks of her less than ninety days after the loss of her beloved son—she was, if nothing else, a candidate for serious therapy. Though I have been able to find no specific account of what Mary did during the Chicago Fire, her delusion, reported at her trial, that "the South Side of the city was on fire" sounds a great deal like a flashback of post-traumatic stress syndrome.

Descendants of the Todd family to whom I've spoken say that the family tradition is very clear that both Mary and her brother Levi were "crazy."

The Spider Incident is completely fictitious, but there was certainly friction between the second Mrs. Todd and her husband's children by her predecessor. There may be no more to Elizabeth's departure from the Todd home in Lexington before her marriage at the age of seventeen than overcrowding, but the departure of all four of the first Mrs. Todd's daughters seems more than coincidental. The fact that Mary was sent away to boarding school a mile and a half from her father's house sounds like a compromise to deal with some underlying problem.

John Wilamet and his family are completely fictitious, but I have tried to be as faithful as I could to the experience of post-Reconstruction blacks.

BARBARA HAMBLY
Los Angeles, 2003

About the Author

Barbara Hambly attended the University of California and spent a year at the University of Bordeaux obtaining a master's degree in medieval history. She has worked as both a teacher and a technical editor, but her first love has always been history. Barbara Hambly is the author of *A Free Man of Color, Fever Season, Graveyard Dust, Wet Grave, Sold Down the River, Die Upon a Kiss, Days of the Dead,* and *Dead Water.*